Dictionary
of
Politics

Dictionary of Politics

SELECTED AMERICAN AND FOREIGN POLITICAL AND LEGAL TERMS

7th Edition

by

Walter John Raymond, Ph.D., S.J.D.

Dictionary of Politics, Seventh Edition

Copyright © 1992, 1978, 1973 by Walter John Raymond

Second Printing, with corrections, 1980

This edition is a major revision of Dictionary of Politics, Selected American and Foreign Political and Legal Terms, copyright © 1978.

Library of Congress Cataloging-in-Publication Data

Raymond, Walter John, 1930-
     Dictionary of politics : selected American and foreign political
and legal terms / Walter John Raymond.—7th ed.
        p.   cm.
     ISBN 1-55618-008-X : $60.00
     1. Political science—Dictionaries.   I. Title.
JA61.R39   1992
320′ .03—dc20   92-14215
                                                             CIP

Printed on acid-free paper to satisfy the requirements of American National Standard for Information Sciences—Permanence of Paper for Printed Library Materials, ANSI Z39.48–1984.

Published in the United States of America
by
Brunswick Publishing Corporation
P.O. Box 555
Lawrenceville, Virginia 23868

For my wife,
Marianne,
and my sons,
John and William

Table of Contents

Preface

The listing of terms in this volume is not exhaustive, and due to the dynamics of the social sciences, meanings may change with time. The ever growing body of knowledge and terminology in politics and public law outpaces one's ability to capture and to record it with the desired accuracy and speed.

Acknowledgment are due to many persons who have contributed to the production of this work: Christopher Antonio Bracey, Heather Victoria Bracey, Sherry Lynn Floyd, Regina Dawn Gibson, Nannie Phipps Powell, and John Cornelius Raymond.

My words of gratitude go to Professor Dr. Robert J. Horgan for his research assistance and Georgia Hammack for valuable assistance with copy editing. The ultimate credit goes to the chief strategist of this project, my beloved wife, Marianne, whose attention to all details of language, facts, and format determined the outcome. For myself, I reserve blame for all errors and shortcomings.

W. J. R.

"Under a government which imprisons any unjustly, the true place for a just man is also in prison."

HENRY DAVID THOREAU, 1817-1862

A-95. An areawide comprehensive planning organization or State agency officially recognized by the U.S. Office of Management and Budget (OMB) to notify other affected local or State governmental units of proposed Federal aid or direct Federal projects before they are funded, and to perform reviews of such projects and comment upon them as to their consistency with areawide or State policies. See PLANNING.

A-95 Review. See A-95, PLANNING.

A Posteriori. See POLITICAL ANALYSIS.

A Priori. See POLITICAL ANALYSIS.

AAPSS. See AMERICAN ACADEMY OF POLITICAL AND SOCIAL SCIENCE.

ABA. See AMERICAN BAR ASSOCIATION.

Abacus Syndrome. See COORDINATING COMMITTEE FOR MULTILATERAL EXPORT CONTROLS (COCOM).

Abatement. Some relief that can be granted by a court of law, e.g., by alleviating payment of dues if there are insufficient funds; in law, a termination of legal proceedings, and in equity, a temporary suspension of court proceedings.

ABCD Conspiracy. See LOOKING EAST.

Abdication. Resignation of duties and privileges (e.g., monarch giving up his throne), or a change-over from one dynasty to another. See DETHRONIZATION.

Ability-to-Pay Principle. A doctrine which prevails in the American politico-economic-legal system which finds its application in, among others, the following situations: (1) all taxation is to be fixed on a sliding scale and must not arbitrarily exceed the taxpayer's income or wealth; considered an equitable taxation system; (2) one may not be deprived under bankruptcy laws of certain items incident to one's principal means of earning a living (e.g., certain essential tools); also, a householder is allowed exemption of certain household items; and (3) one shall not be subjected to imprisonment or punishment for one's inability to pay debts.

Abjuration. Renunciation of rights and privileges, usually under oath or affirmation (e.g., giving up citizenship). See CITIZENSHIP.

Abolitionist. One opposing the institution of slavery or any form of involuntary servitude.

Abortion Laws. See RIGHT TO PRIVACY.

Abrogation. An annulment of contractual agreement (e.g., treaty obligations), or a contract.

Absentee Ballot. Ballot cast in an election in absentia (e.g., while away in military service, school, or diplomatic service abroad).

Absentee Ownership. The owner(s) of a business enterprise or corporation, so named in the articles of incorporation, who does not participate in management and is often unknown to employees or management. Also common practice among businesses engaged in illicit operations as in the case of the Mafia or in the case of ownership by foreign nationals.

Absolute Equality. See EQUALITY OF OPPORTUNITY.

Absolute Law. A law that is clear, to the point, and unquestionably binding. See LIBERAL CONSTITUTION.

Absolute Majority. A number of votes cast in an election representing more than half of the registered voters. See SIMPLE MAJORITY, TYRANNY OF THE MAJORITY.

Absolute Monarchy. See MONARCHY.

Absolutism. A strict governmental rule with direct flow of power from the central authority down to the lowest unit of government and to the masses (e.g., dictatorship or absolute monarchy).See MONARCHY.

Abwehr. The Nazi Germany Military Intelligence Service under the leadership of Admiral Canaries, which also conducted world-wide intelligence operations. The Abwehr's full name was "Amt Ausland Abwehr," in the German language, "Foreign Office of the Armed Forces." It was anti-Nazi, but forced to collaborate during Adolf Hitler's government of terror (1933-1945). Abwehr was engaged in assassination attempts on Hitler and was also allegedly collaborating with western intelligence services, mainly the American Office of Strategic Services (OSS), in the eventual freeing of Germany of Nazi rule. See SCHWARZE KAPELLE.

ACA. See AMERICANS FOR CONSTITUTIONAL ACTION.

Academic Freedom. The freedom of educators and pupils to express their views (even unpopular ones) in an uncensored environment.

Academy of Political Science (APS). A learned society established in 1880 and affiliated with Columbia University in New York City for the purpose of studying and disseminating research results on new trends and developments in economics, politics, government, and public law. The Academy publishes the *Political Science Quarterly* and holds annual conventions.

ACAG. See ALLIED CONTROL AUTHORITY FOR GERMANY.

Acceleration Clause. A provision in a contract, agreement or an international treaty among states, stipulating that any violation of any provision by either party shall render the document null and void and/or may grant the suffering (grieved) party the right to seek reward for damages. In cases of loans, failure to make payment may require the borrower to pay the whole amount stipulated immediately and in full.

Access to Justice. See HUMAN RIGHTS: AMERICAN DEFINITION, JUSTICE, Appendices 8, 50, 51.

Accession. The act of joining international organizations, confederations, or the acceptance of terms of convention or treaty obligations by a state.

Acclamation. An overwhelming approval or acceptance of a candidate for public office by those entitled to vote and voting.

Accord. An understanding between representatives of foreign governments on policy reconciliation without having the force of a treaty.

Accountability. See DEMOCRACY, POLITICAL THEORY, TOOLS OF GOVERNMENT, Appendices 1, 3, 3-A, 51.

Accretion. A gradual transfer of territory of one state to another by forces of nature such as the rise of the surface of land, depositing of silt, or a change in the flow of waters.

ACEN. See ASSEMBLY OF CAPTIVE EUROPEAN NATIONS.

ACIR. See ADVISORY COMMISSION ON INTERGOVERNMENTAL RELATIONS.

ACLU. See AMERICAN CIVIL LIBERTIES UNION.

Acquisition. The gain of territory through discovery, occupation, treaty, or conquest.

Acquisitive Lobby. See LOBBY.

Acquittal. The dismissal of charges against an accused person by court decree or by a jury.

Act of War. According to accepted norms of international laws, an act of war must be duly declared by the government of the state and delivered through the proper channels (e.g., the diplomatic envoy, such as the ambassador), stating the reasons for the commencement of war. War could also commence through an undeclared (and often sneaky) act such as invasion, mistreatment of diplomatic representatives, hostile propaganda activity, refusal to give proper treatment to nationals of one state visiting or residing in the territory of another, seizing cargo, vessels, or other property of another state, or as a matter of preventing an adversary from consolidating its power and eventually launching a war (preventive war). See BLACK SUNDAY, DETERRENT, WAR.

Acting Royalty. See CIVIL LIST.

Acting to Excite a Disorganizing and Revolutionary Spirit in the Country. See IMPEACHMENT.

Action Policy. A policy that is meant to be implemented and enforced.

Actor. A sovereign entity—a state—in international relations, or its government which ordinarily speaks for and represents the state.

Ad Arbitrium. In the Latin language, "arbitrarily" or "at will."

Ad Hoc. In the Latin language, "for the purpose alone" or "for this reason only."

Ad Hoc Committee. See SPECIAL COMMITTEE.

Ad Interim. In the Latin language, "in the meanwhile" or "meantime."

Ad Rem. In the Latin language, "as the matter at hand stands."

Ad Valorem. In the Latin language, "in proportion to the value stated."

ADA. See AMERICANS FOR DEMOCRATIC ACTION.

Adhesion. Acceptance in part or acceptance in principle of a treaty obligation by a third party which originally was not a party to that treaty or agreement. See TREATY.

Adjournment Sine Die. The closing of business for the day without fixing the date of reconvening. (In the United States Congress neither house may adjourn for more than three days without the consent of the other. In case of disagreement the President is empowered to adjourn both Houses.) See CONGRESS OF THE UNITED STATES, Appendices 8, 10, 11.

Adjudication. The settlement of dispute by a judicial or administrative agency. See ARBITRATION.

Administration. A systematized process of implementing the policies of the government; a set of predetermined interactions among individuals directed toward the achievement of a specific goal, such as implementing a given policy; a governmental agency charged with a specific policy implementation (e.g., General Services Administration or the Veterans Administration); or the administrative apparatus (persons and policies) of a given President (e.g., the Carter Administration). Frank J. Goodnow defines administration as "the execution of this community will, as accomplished by the executive officers and the courts." See OAKS' LAWS, POLITICS.

Administration Bashing. See CONGRESS BASHING.

Administration-Oriented Congress. See CONGRESS-ORIENTED ADMINISTRATION.

Administrative Constituency. The notion that each administrative agency of the government, its bureaucracy, has a unique constituency of its own which it favors, and which in turn is supported, and protected by the bureaucracy (e.g., the Federal Communication Commission's constituency would be the radio, television, cable, and satellite manufacturers and users which the agency regulates); and that the regulating bureaucracy will be reluctant, in the final analysis, to regulate any of its clients out of business for fear that it may put itself out of business if that particular constituency shrinks, revolts, or ceases to exist. All bureaucracies, some claim, have the same objective regardless of the nature or form of government under which they serve; they want to preserve and sustain themselves, and always grow in order to justify their need for existence.

Administrative Discretion. In the United States, the right of the executive branch of government to exercise considerable latitude, or discretion, on how legislative acts should be implemented. The cabinets and specialized agencies write the particular rules and regulations on how a Congressional law will be implemented, often adding language which was not necessarily intended by Congress. Such discrepancies between the law and administrative interpretation may trigger Congressional hearings.

Administrative Law. The body of laws created by administrative agencies in the form of rules and regulations; also, that part of public law which deals with regulation of powers of administrative agencies and officials.

Administrative Lie. A law that may be passed by a legislative body to merely satisfy some demands of the public but lacking provisions for enforcement, or whose enforcement provisions are so ambiguous that no one understands them.

Administrative Oversight. See LEGISLATIVE OVERSIGHT.

Administrative State. A sovereign nation state which is administered by trained civil servants selected on the basis of merits rather than spoils; who are dedicated to the interpretation and the implementation of law according to the intent of these laws and not biases and predilections that may be demanded and/or imposed by special interests groups, lobbies, religions, political parties and pressure groups, any particular segment of the society characterized by some unique features (e.g., race, class, or national origin); and where administrative processes are not hindered by any single strong leader (e.g., a Führer in Nazi Germany who in reality established a "leader state"). Vatican City, though a religious state, maintains a temporal, non-clerical, civil service; civil services in Japan, Germany, England, the United States, France, Spain, Italy, the Scandinavian states, are very well organized in spite of efforts by political parties to meddle in administrative processes. France provides the best training for civil servants among the modern democracies, because it is almost totally insulated from politics and partisan interests. Partisan politics is confined to electoral and legislative endeavors. Many top professional administrators in America, end up either during mid-career service or upon retirement, as lobbyists and servants to vested interests, either domestic or foreign, rarely for the interest of the state or society, but rather for personal ambitions and enrichment. In France, for example, the pantouflage, are mid-career civil servants who decide to retire early and enter service in politics or parliament. Similarly, the Japanese bureaucrats, called the "amakudari," usually upon retirement rather than in mid-career, decide to actively become involved in electoral or parliamentary politics. As a rule, both in France and in Japan, the primary motive of the bureaucrats is to serve the state and the society in different capacity rather than serve foreign interests and to enrich themselves. Therefore, American firms operating abroad, particularly in Japan, France, and Germany, find it difficult to attract native and knowledgeable lobbyists, because of patriotic consideration. Most of them construe working for a foreign firm somewhat of a treasonous act. Many of those who are recruited, are usually agents of intelligence services who are to concentrate primarily on industrial espionage.

Admiralty Law. That body of law which pertains to ships, seagoing vessels and personnel on navigable waters. (In the U.S. all admiralty cases fall within the jurisdiction of federal courts.)

Admonition. A warning issued by an authority stipulating penalty for noncompliance. See WRIT OF COMMON USE.

Adversarial Culture. See NEW CLASS.

Adversary Relationship. That set of interactions among individuals of opposing views, different political parties, or governments, which allows them to maintain mutual cooperation and to conduct desired relationships in a spirit of cognizance of the differences that divide them otherwise. The opposing parties in a legal controversy (e.g., the prosecuting attorney, and the accused and his attorney), litigation, or arbitration.

Advice and Consent. See UNITED STATES SENATE.

Advisory Commission on Intergovernmental Relations (ACIR). A permanent bipartisan organization created by Congress (Public Law 86-380, first session of the 86th Congress and approved by the President on September 24, 1959) for the purpose of giving continuing attention . . . to the critical areas of friction in Federal-State, Federal-local, interstate and interlocal relations.

Advisory Opinion. See DECLARATORY JUDGMENT, MOOT CASE.

Advisory Primary. A primary election for local, state, and national officials (e.g., mayors, governors, or U.S. presidents) which is not binding (a straw-vote). See COMMISSION ON PRESIDENTIAL NOMINATION AND PARTY STRUCTURE, PRIMARY ELECTION, STRAW VOTE.

Advocacy Planning. Advocacy planning is activist in nature. The aim is more or less rapid social change to alter particular social conditions. Advocate planners may work outside rather than within a planning organization.

Aesthetic Pollution. See DECADENCE.

Affidavit. A written statement under oath or affirmation attesting a certain truth. See PERJURY.

Affirmation. A promise to carry out certain tasks under trust (e.g., to carry out faithfully the responsibility of an office) assumed without reference to God. See OATH.

Affirmative Action. A policy of the U.S. Federal Government aimed at implementing equality of opportunity (e.g., in employment or education) for certain categories of persons (e.g., racial minorities and women) who have been denied such opportunities in the past, in proportion to their percentage of total population (quotas). In the so-called "Philadelphia Plan" of 1967, the quota system was used for the first time (although the federal bureaucracy does not like to use the term "quota") when the U.S. Office of Federal Contract Compliance directed contracting firms bidding on federal projects to submit detailed plans (affirmative action programs), indicating what percentage of persons representing the minorities (mainly blacks) would be employed on each project. Affirmative action programs have been implemented under the authority of the Civil Rights Act of 1964 (mainly its Titles VI and VII), which prohibits discrimination in private employment and in federally aided programs. Although the Act does not call for quotas or goals, the general acceptance of its provisions has been very slow: therefore, the policy implementors in the Johnson Administration decided to shift from the traditional policy of equality of opportunity by nondiscriminatory practices to more specific goals or objectives, such as the affirmative action programs. Affirmative action programs were the result of the interpretation of the law by the Johnson Administration, drawing on the 1946 precedent when U.S. President Harry S. Truman desegregated the armed forces by an executive order, and they do not necessarily reflect congressional intent. See CIVIL RIGHTS ACTS, EQUALITY OF OPPORTUNITY, REVERSE DISCRIMINATION.

Afghanistan Doctrine. Following the Soviet intervention in Afghanistan (Dec. 27, 1979), the USSR asserted the right to intervene in any neighboring nation which threatened the interests of the USSR directly.

Afghanistan Khalg Party. The ruling political party in Afghanistan, whose pro-Soviet leanings and Soviet military support enabled them to hold power. Afghan President Hafizullah Amin was one of its leaders. The Soviet Union sent forces to Afghanistan in December 1979 to prevent the regime's downfall from attacks by the opposition forces of the various tribes, the Mujihadin. The Soviets lost about 15,000 killed and missing in action, billions in war materiel, and withdrew their forces from Afghanistan on February 15, 1989. The rebels overthrew the government in April 1992.

Afghanistan Syndrome. See VIETNAM SYNDROME.

Afghanistan War. When the pro-Soviet government took power through a coup in 1978, several nationalist Afghan groups, such as the Hezb-i-Islami and the Jamiat-i-Islami, under the leadership of Dr. Burhanuddin Rabbani, a science professor educated in the West, along with four other dedicated Islamic groups, commenced open military action against the imposed government. This provoked the Soviets to send thousands of soldiers to Afghanistan in December 1979. The guerrilla tactics of the Mujihadin proved to be effective, particularly after receiving a shipment of American missiles and other weapons. The Soviets, noting that this was a protracted war, withdrew in 1989, leaving behind about 15,000 killed and missing in action. The war is often referred to as the "Soviet Vietnam." See Appendix 101.

Afghans. The Muslim fundamentalists who are striving to gain political power in Algeria through a revolutionary means. The official election to be held in January 1992 was canceled because of the Muslims' desire to introduce government by the Koran. They call themselves "Afghans" because many of them participated in the Afghanistan War. See ALGERIAN MUSLIM FUNDA-MENTALISM.

AFL-CIO. See AMERICAN FEDERATION OF LABOR-CONGRESS OF INDUSTRIAL ORGANI-ZATIONS.

African National Congress (ANC). A political-military organization of black South Africans which for decades has struggled for the right to vote and for an equal share in the national government of South Africa, with implementation of the American electoral principle of "one man, one vote." The ANC, being declared subversive, terrorist, and illegal by the South African government, operated from neighboring Zimbabwe, Zambia, and Botswana, launching attacks on military targets. The ANC leaders were either in exile or, like Nelson Mandela, in prison. Mandela was released in 1990 after 27 years of imprisonment. South Africa's President, Frederik W. De Klerk, pledged to end apartheid and to refrain from supporting other native political forces, such as the Inkatha Freedom Party, which consists mainly of the Zulu tribe, led by Chief Buthelezi. The IFP is a bitter rival of the ANC and Mandela. The Western world imposed trade sanctions against South Africa, in 1986, called for by Bishop Desmond Tutu, a native black African and Nobel Prize winner. The military arm of the African National Congress is the Umkhonto we Sizwe. See APARTHEID, GORBACHEV OF SOUTH AFRICA.

African Socialism. See UJAAMA.

Afrikaaner Broederbond. See CONFERENCE FOR DEMOCRATIC SOUTH AFRICA (CODESA).

Afrikaaner Resistance Movement (ARM). A political and military organization of opponents of integration in South Africa, pro-apartheid and allegedly pro-fascist group of white South Africans, who oppose any form of accommodation with the black majority. Its leader, Eugene Terre Blanche, organized its armed group, known as "Iron Guards," and declared that if it comes to "one-man, one vote," in South Africa, there will be a revolution. Also, the overall resistance to the pro-integration and anti-apartheid policies of the South African government and President Frederick W. de Klerk. De Klerk advocates an introduction of democratic electoral process in order to include the black majority led by Nelson Mandela, the president and leader of the African National Congress (ANC), who was freed by President de Klerk on 11 February 1990 after 27 years of imprisonment. The white opponents of this accommodation with the blacks opposed de Klerk when he caused the repeal of the Separate Amenities Act, the statutory and legal basis for apartheid; and on 9 August 1991 the Resistance Movement clashed with the government and the police on a major scale for the first time. Also for the first time, the pro-apartheid Resistance Movement proclaimed the use of force, if necessary, to fight integration. Judging from all appearances on the South African political scene, if there will be any share of power among the force quadrangle in South Africa today: the government and President de Klerk's group; the anti-apartheid African National Congress (ANC); the Afrikaaner Resistance Movement; and the Zulu political group, the Inkhata Freedom Party, that power will be dispensed, to paraphrase Mao Tse-tung of China, "from the barrel of the gun." See APARTHEID.

Afro-American League of the United States. An organization founded in 1890 by T. Thomas Fortune, which was dedicated to the struggle against all forms of political and civil injustices, particularly against segregation.

Age of Great Events and Small Men. Winston Churchill (1874-1965) the world's most talented states-man and politician, the holder of many high posts including that of prime minister of England, and a Nobel prize laureate in literature, characterized the 19th century as "an age of great men and small events." To reverse that statement, one can venture to observe that in the twentieth century events are great, but there are no leaders to manage them to the betterment of mankind. Since the end of W.W.II, guns still are not silenced; since 1945, 247 wars have been fought in different parts of the globe, varied in size and degree of death and destruction. Enormous resources were spent to contain communism, but when communism collapsed, leaders of large adversary states panicked and offered only token solutions for the disarming of deadly forces everywhere, for helping people achieve peace and dignity, and for preventing future global problems. There are no leaders of the caliber of Ghandi, Nehru, F. D. Roosevelt, Churchill, Bismarck, Lenin, or Kennedy. Even the petty despots and the dictators and warmongers of today are of a caliber that would never match that of Hitler, Mussolini, Stalin, and Peron. Public service is more a search for monetary and material rewards than what it used to be—public service. Those few with great vision for the "New World Order" include: former U.S. President Richard M. Nixon (who allowed himself to be derailed by greedy apparatchicks); Helmut Kohl, Chancellor of Germany (who, because of his meager and long-range solution to the problems of Germany, Europe, and world, and his inability to deliver the sausage for today's meal, encountered problems and lack of appreciation); Francois Mitterand, president of France; Boris N. Yeltsin, president of Russia; Jacque Delors, leader of the European Community; Bishop Desmond Tutu of South Africa; and Pope John Paul II. These and a very few more, may, in some way, realize our hopes for a better world tomorrow.

Age of Great Men and Small Events. See AGE OF GREAT EVENTS AND SMALL MEN.

Agency Agreement. A campaign finance practice of the American National Republican Senatorial Committee which, through a special agreement with the Republican Party state organizations, acts as the surrogate for the state parties in senatorial elections, utilizing their combined funds as it becomes necessary, without obviously violating the federal spending limits for each. The legality of this practice was challenged before the Federal Election Commission by the Democratic Party leadership, but the U.S. Supreme Court and the Commission upheld the practice as fair and legal. See FEDERAL ELECTION COMMISSION (FEC).

Agency for International Development (AID). An agency of the Department of State of the U.S. established in 1961 to channel funds to foreign states that need assistance in developing their principal national resources through training of manpower, technical assistance, health services, population control, and other necessary services that would enable these states to become self-sufficient. These programs are financed by AID in cooperation with the World Bank. See MARSHALL PLAN, Appendices 36, 40.

Agency Law. That body of laws which deal with contracts between parties. See CONTRACT CLAUSE, LAW.

Agency Politics. The ways of interaction among employees of any one specific governmental agency characterized by personal and professional conflicts among individuals concerning policies, agency functions and limitations, etc.

Agenda. A list of items to be discussed during a meeting; issues to be considered by a legislative body. Also a particular set of issues or problems with implication as to public interest and concern, which may be presented for resolution by the legislature (e.g., the U.S. Congress), the executive (e.g., the U.S. President), citizen groups or individual persons (personal agenda). Agendas often contain preconceived notions on which, when and how certain issues should be resolved and what the outcomes ought to be. See CALENDAR.

Agent Identity Protection Act. Philip Agee, a former CIA undercover agent who operated in Latin America, became disenchanted with the agency and wrote a book revealing entire espionage networks in Latin America and elsewhere, endangering the safety of agents in many places throughout the world. Following the assassination of a CIA station chief in Greece, Congress passed the Agent Identity Protection Act which imposed a severe penalty for disclosing the name of a CIA agent. A similar law, the Foreign Agents Registration Act, requires that persons serving as agents of foreign governments register with the U.S. Justice Department as "foreign agents," regardless of whether they work for pay or whether they are political and military spies or simply ones representing foreign commercial interests. Failure to register constitutes a felonious crime. Persons suspected of espionage fall under the jurisdiction of Intelligence Division of the Federal Bureau of Investigation (FBI); the agency may obtain permission for surveillance and wiretapping of suspected persons from the special court known as the Foreign Intelligence Surveillance Court. The court, staffed by regular judges, operates round the clock. See FOREIGN AGENTS REGISTRATION ACT, INTELLIGENCE.

Agent of Influence. See INTELLIGENCE.

Agent Provocateur. An official of police, secret police, or an intelligence service whose task it is to entice one to reveal some secret information or to commit a crime, usually an offense against the state or the government. The term originated, in modern usage, during the French Revolution. Common practice among totalitarian political systems, particularly in Imperial Germany, Tsarist Russia, also in the former Soviet Union and, to some extent, in the United States. See CHAOS, COINTELPRO, ENTRAPMENT, FENCING, SEXPIONAGE, SEXPOLITICS.

Agents and Tools of Socialization. See POLITICS, SOCIALIZATION.

Agents of Democratic Government. See TOOLS OF GOVERNMENT.

Aggiornamento. In the Italian language, "updating." Also a term used by Roman Catholic Pope John XXIII to bishops assembled in St. Peter's Basilica on 11 October 1962, calling for modernization and reaching out to the world. This reorganization laid the foundation for the election of a non-Italian Pope, Karol Cardinal Wojtyla of Poland, who was then able to challenge the communist system and aid in its downfall. This also helped make the Solidarity movement in Poland possible, along with the liberation movement throughout the Soviet empire, since the Polish Pope understood the Soviet system better than anyone who held that position of leadership before him, and could cope with it and was dedicated enough to challenge it. The personal motto of the Pope was: "Entirely Yours," or, in Latin, "Totus Tuus."

Aggrandizement. See IMPERIALISM.

Aggravated Assault. Bodily harm inflicted with a deadly weapon, or some malicious act of a harmful nature which does not result in the loss of life.

Agipunkt. See PROPAGANDA CENTER.

Agnosticism. The notion that the human being is not capable of knowing whether or not God or gods really exist; or a state of suspended judgment pertaining to the existence or nonexistence of any spiritual being (e.g., a God). See THEISM.

Agonizing Reappraisal. John Foster Dulles, U.S. Secretary of State, 1953-1959, and one of America's most active cold warriors, in 1958, allegedly sent a highly secret memorandum to President Eisenhower calling for an "agonizing reappraisal" of American political and military strategy in its efforts to contain communism and to preserve the power and influence of the American state and the Western alliance. In formulating this perspective he drew on personal knowledge of the Soviet system, on information provided by his brother, Allen Dulles, Director of Central Intelligence and the Central Intelligence Agency, who was one of America's most experienced intelligence operatives during W.W.II in Europe where he serviced the so-called "Swiss Corridor;" and on intelligence information regularly delivered by trusted agents from inside the German General Staff in Berlin to his quarters in Switzerland. This intelligence was reliable because it was acknowledged by subsequent ULTRA intercepts. Among these agents was German General Reinhard Gehlen, Chief of the Nazi Foreign Armies East espionage apparatus in the Soviet Union, founder of the so-called "Gehlen Organization" (the "Firma"). The "Firma" furnished the Americans with a list of agents left behind in the Soviet Union; subsequently it was reorganized to serve as the German intelligence agency, the Bundesnachrichtendienst (BND). Since information came from a wide network of agents in the Soviet Union and Eastern Europe, Dulles advised that the United States reconcile itself to the fact that the Soviet state was a real power and that it would so remain for a long time. Since America could claim no clear victory in Korea, insurgency was on the rise and was encouraged everywhere by the Soviets, who proclaimed support for each and every liberation front and people's democracy in fighting capitalism and foreign domination. The Soviets also had the might—i.e., atomic and hydrogen weapons—at their disposal to back up their rhetoric. Such a shift in attitude of U.S. policy toward the Soviet Union, as advocated by Dulles, contributed to the concept of bipolarity, parity in armaments, and allowed the Soviet Union to remain the other dominant superpower in world politics. With time, the Soviet Bloc gained respectability among rulers and bureaucrats in America to the point that, aside from fellow travelers and members of Soviet front organizations, many bureaucrats in the executive branch of government, especially the State and Defense Departments as well as the intelligence community, viewed criticism of anything Soviet on a par with anti-Americanism. (A possible exception was FBI Director, J. Edgar Hoover [1895-1972] who never allowed his driver to make a left-hand turn in order to avoid being misconstrued as a "leftist.") See COORDINATING COMMITTEE FOR MULTILATERAL EXPORT CONTROLS (COCOM), GEHLEN ORGANIZATION.

Agrarian Democracy. A political system whose constituencies consist mainly of farmers rather than city dwellers and which favors an agricultural economy and mode of living over an industrial one. Thomas Jefferson, U.S. President (1801-1809), and his Antifederalist followers favored such a system, while the Federalists preferred an industrialized society with agriculture as a supplementary element in the economy.

Agricultural City. In the Russian language, "agrogorod," short for "agrikulturnyi gorod." As envisioned by former Premier Nikita S. Khrushchev of the Soviet Union, an agricultural compound for the exclusive purpose of producing agricultural commodities. The farm workers were to give up their private plots of land, move to newly erected housing projects, and commute to their jobs as industrial workers do. (The idea was abandoned with the removal of Khrushchev from power in 1964.)

Agricultural Production. See HUNGER WARS.

Agrocity. See AGRICULTURAL CITY.

Agrogorod. See AGRICULTURAL CITY.

AID. See AGENCY FOR INTERNATIONAL DEVELOPMENT.

AIPAC. See AMERICAN ISRAEL PUBLIC AFFAIRS COMMITTEE.

Air Force One. Official plane of U.S. President. See BARNSTORMING.

Air Force Two. Official plane of U.S. Vice President. See BARNSTORMING.

Air-Land Battle. See MILITARY REFORM MOVEMENT.

Aix-la-Chapelle Congress. See QUADRUPLE ALLIANCE.

AJC. See JEWISH LOBBY.

Al Fatah. See FATAH.

Alabama Syndrome. A term often used in the parlance of politics of planning whereby, as writer J. Sharkansky once stated, "The tendency to lump all the states with the worst."

Alaska Purchase. See SEWARD'S FOLLY.

Albany Plan of the Union. A plan of unification of the American Colonies under the single centralized leadership of a president-general appointed by the King of England and of representatives selected by the various colonies. Advanced by Benjamin Franklin during the Albany Convention of 1754.

Alderman. A member (elective) of a city council in some jurisdictions (e.g., in the city of Atlanta, Georgia).

Alfa Club. An exclusive, private, informal organization of the most influential men (men only) in the United States, who gather once a year in Washington, D.C. for a black-tie dinner where they exchange political jokes.

Alford Plea. A plea under which a defendant may choose to plead guilty, not because of an admission to the crime, but because the prosecutor has sufficient evidence to place a charge and to obtain conviction in court. The plea is commonly used in state and local courts in the United States.

Algerian Muslim Fundamentalism. When the Algerian Muslim Fundamentalists defeated the ruling National Liberation Front in legislative elections, the president of Algeria and leader since 1979 of the Front, resigned on 11 January 1992 in protest. The military was allowed to take over in order to prevent the Muslims from gaining power. A newly-constituted Constitutional Council, headed by Abdelmalek Benhabyles, was to serve as an interim executive and was to establish the date for a new election for president. The run-off election was canceled because the military and the National Liberation Front followers oppose the imposition of strict, Islamic laws in the country. The Muslim group threatens to resort to revolutionary means to gain power. See AFGHANS.

Algeria's National Liberation Front. See ALGERIAN MUSLIM FUNDAMENTALISM.

Al-Hizb ad-Dimuqraati al-Kurid. In the Arabic language, the name of the Democratic Party of Kurdistan. See BAATH SOCIALIST PARTY.

Al-Hizb es-Shyu'i al Iraqi. Arabic name of the Iraqi Communist Party. See BAATH SOCIALIST PARTY.

Alien. A national or citizen of one state residing within the jurisdiction of another. Such persons do not enjoy certain rights, such as voting or holding offices of trust. See IMMIGRATION, UNITED STATES PERSON.

Alien Act. See ALIEN AND SEDITION ACTS.

Alien and Sedition Acts. Four congressional acts that were passed in 1798 and which were subsequently declared void by the U.S. Supreme Court as unconstitutional in *Marbury v. Madison* (1803). They were: (1) the Naturalization Act which made fourteen years of residence a U.S. citizenship requirement; (2) the Alien Act under which the President had the power to deport any alien considered dangerous; (3) the Alien Enemy Act which empowered the U.S. President to expel enemy citizens residing in the U.S.; and (4) the Sedition Act providing for fines and imprisonment for anyone criticizing the government, the President, or the Congress. See also McCARTHYISM, RED MENACE, SCUM.

Alien-Enemy Act. See ALIEN AND SEDITION ACTS.

All Deliberate Speed. A phrase used by the U.S. Supreme Court in 1955 when it directed immediate implementation of its school desegregation decision made in *Brown v. Board of Education*. It gave U.S. Federal District Courts the power to require local school boards to commence a "a prompt and reasonable start toward full compliance" with the *Brown* decision and insisted that the law be implemented "with all deliberate speed." See JUDICIAL ACTIVISM, Appendix 48.

All-European Parliament. See COUNCIL OF EUROPE.

All German Bloc/Association of the Expelled and Disenfranchised (BG/BHE). In the German language, "Gesamtdeutscher Bund/Block der Heimat Vertriebenen und Entrechteten." A minor political party in West Germany composed mainly of refugees from territories previously of the German Reich which after World War II came under the administration of Czechoslovakia (Sudetenland), Poland (Silesia), and the Soviet Union (Prussia).

All Men are Equal, but Some are More Equal than Others. See VALUE THEORY.

All News is Bad News—if it is About Us! This was the motto of the British Secret Intelligence Service (SIS), divided into MI-5, domestic intelligence and security, and MI-6, foreign intelligence. To this day the director of the MI-6 is known only as "C," or "Chief," and, under the strict official Secrets Act, his name is never revealed to the public. The intelligence and the courts are authorized to impose gag rules on information which, if revealed to the public (e.g., by journalists), could be detrimental to the security of the country. The Latin motto "Sic Transit Gloria Intelligentsia" ("toward the glory of passing information") is deeply entrenched in the intelligence culture of the British system which elevated intelligence to the status of a supreme art. Secret service, claim the British, "is too dirty a game for anyone but a gentleman to play." General Reinhard Gehlen, the founder of the German Bundesnachrichtendienst (BND), paraphrasing this dictum, added, "This job is so dirty that only the cleanest of people should have the right to meddle in it." See INTELLIGENCE.

All Politics is Local. The notion that all political interests, activities, and needs originate with the individual person, the family and the community, then transcend to wider and larger political subdivisions, from state, to nation, to the international community of nations. See RETAIL POLITICS.

All-Russian Social-Democratic Labor Party. The official name between the years of 1898-1918 of the Communist Party of the Soviet Union (CPSU). See COMMUNIST PARTY OF THE SOVIET UNION (CPSU), RUSSIAN SOCIAL-DEMOCRATIC LABOR PARTY (RSDLP).

Allegiance. The obligation, based on moral and/or legal grounds, of service, loyalty, and fidelity of a citizen or national to his own country or nation.

Alliance for Progress. A policy initiated by President John F. Kennedy and subscribed to by many Latin American republics during a conference held at Punta del Este, Uruguay (August 1961), aiming at mutual economic cooperation between the U.S. and Latin America. The U.S. was to funnel funds through the Agency for International Development to any nation that needed them for economic development, mainly in the area of agriculture. The U.S. committed over $20 billion to this program between 1962-1972.

Alliance of Convenience. An understanding between two or more parties to pursue certain common objectives merely for the sake of convenience or expediency, and one that usually is not meant to be lasting. See SUMMIT CONFERENCE.

Allied Control Authority for Germany (ACAG). A joint authority established by England, France, the Soviet Union, and the United States in 1945 to supervise the conditions of capitulation of Nazi Germany.

Allied Debt. At the end of World War I, foreign nation-states (particularly the allies: France, England, and Italy) owed the United States the sum of approximately $10.4 billion (mainly for war materiel), most of which was never repaid. One exception has been Finland, a small Scandinavian state which repaid its debt to the United States in full. The exact figures for World War II debts are difficult to determine because most statistics and reports are contradictory and sketchy, but they come to about ten times the amount of W.W.I. See NATIONAL DEBT OF THE UNITED STATES, U.S. FOREIGN AID in Appendix 39.

Allied High Commission. A tripartite authority (England, France, and the U.S. after the USSR pulled out of the ACAG), established in 1949, to oversee the interests of the Allies after the new West German government was set up.

Allied Intervention in Russia. See WAR COMMUNISM.

Allocation of Powers. See TYPES OF GOVERNMENTS.

Alpha 66. See SOCIALISM OR DEATH!

Alpha Group. A highly-trained, all-purpose highly mobile commando force of the Russian Army and intelligence, formerly the Soviet KGB, similar in structure and purpose to the American Delta Force. See DELTA FORCE.

Alte. See DER ALTE.

Alternat. A procedure followed in diplomatic protocol whereby a state, signatory of an international agreement or treaty, will place its signature uppermost on the copy which it receives.

Alternate Delegate. A substitute delegate who may perform designated functions (sometimes even vote) for the regular delegate to a conference, convention, or any other gathering at which important decisions are made. See PARTY CONVENTION, VOTING.

Alternative Vote. An electoral system which enables a voter to cast a second preference vote in order to avoid a possible run-off election. See PRESIDENTIAL ELECTOR, PROPORTIONAL REPRESENTATION.

Ältestenrat. In the German language, "Council of Elders." See COUNCIL OF ELDERS.

Althing. See MOTHER OF PARLIAMENTS.

Am an-Nakba. In the Arabic language, "year of catastrophe." See ARAB NATIONALISM.

AMA. See AMERICAN MUNICIPAL ASSOCIATION.

Amakudari. In the Japanese language, "Descent from Heaven;" the practice of Japan's top bureaucrats to retire from government employment after twenty or twenty-five years of service to join private business enterprises in order to share government experience for the benefit of the business. The motivation for the retiring public servants to join private businesses is not necessarily personal enrichment, but rather a matter of satisfaction that one is of use after retirement; that one becomes a part of an organization with the view of helping it and the nation as a whole to accomplish better ends. The re-employed retirees are not viewed, and do not consider themselves to be lobbyists for their new employers. See ADMINISTRATIVE STATE.

Ambassador. A diplomatic officer (of the highest rank) who is designated (usually by the head of state) to represent the state (and its government) outside its jurisdiction, either before an international organization or before another state (and its government), by special accreditation (acceptance by the receiving state). Sir Henry Wotton (1568-1639), the personal envoy (ambassador) of England's Queen Elizabeth I to Venice (now Italy), remarked, "An ambassador is an honest man sent to lie abroad for the good of his country." The Queen found little humor in this remark and promptly called Wotton home where he became Provost of Eton College due to personal friendship with powerful and influential people, including the Earl of Essex. Some of his writings such as *On His Mistress, the Queen of Bohemia* ("You Meaner Beauties of the Night"), and *The Character of a Happy Life,* contain rich source materials on politics of his time. See DIPLOMATIC RANKS.

Ambassador is an Honest Man Sent to Lie Abroad for the Good of His Country. See AMBASSADOR, FLAGRANTLY IMPROPER ACTIVITY.

Amen Corner. (1) A section of pews, usually near the pulpit, reserved for church elders who lead the congregation responses, especially the "amens." Variantly, such a section of pews is regularly taken over by the vocally fervent. (2) NYC machine politics. In late nineteenth and early twentieth century, a suite in a New York City hotel, permanently reserved as a meeting place for politicians. (For putting their heads together as if in prayer? For allowing the ward healers to say "Amen" to whatever the bosses said?)

Amende Honorable. In the French language, "reparation" or "satisfactory apology."

Amendment. See CONSTITUTIONAL AMENDMENT.

Amendments, Proposal of. See CONSTITUTIONAL AMENDMENT.

Amendments, Ratification of. See RATIFICATION, Appendix 8.

America 2000 Opportunity. See WEED AND SEED PROGRAM.

America Bashing. Shintaro Ishihara, member of the Japanese Diet, leading member of the Liberal Democratic Party in Japan, and an author (*The Japan That Can Say No: Why Japan Will be First Among Equals,* New York: Simon & Schuster, 1991), opposes the "Japan Bashing" in America. He points out America's internal ills (using data from a study by MIT: "Made in America: Regaining the Productive Edge") as the source of its current standing as an uncompetitive economic power. They are: (1) quarter to quarter bean counting rather than long-term planning. (SONY's Corporation Chairman, Akio Morita, supports that notion; as he put it: "The United States looks ten minutes ahead while Japan looks ten years ahead."); (2) lack of cooperation between government and business in America; (3) great disparity in income between labor, management, and business leaders (Minimum wage for many, while the yearly salaries and bonuses for major industry leaders add up to millions of dollars. For example, the New York Times Service reported in a dispatch on 20 January 1992 the annual salaries and stock options of several top executives of large American corporations: Steven J. Ross and N. J. Nicholas, Jr., co-chief executives of Time Warner earned together in 1990 $99.6 million; Paul B. Fireman of Reebok Internationl, $33.3 million; Leon C. Hirsch of U.S. Surgical, $15 million; Rand V. Araskog of ITT, $11.5 million; and Michael D. Eisner of Walt Disney, $11.2 million. According to Professor Graef Crystal of the University of California, Berkeley, typical yearly salaries of top U.S. executives are, on the average, $3.2 million while comparable executives in England made $1.1 million, in Germany, $800,000, and in Japan, $525,000. Further, "executive pay is the real hot-button issue for institutional investors, according to James E. Heard, president of Institutional Shareholder Services, an advisor to big investors. "It's typical of what's wrong with American management and why the U.S. is not more competitive economically."); (4) shoddy products and poor service (The speaker of the Japanese House of Representatives stated bluntly on 20 January 1992, that the reasons for America's trade deficit with Japan include the fact that "U.S. workers won't work hard and a third are illiterate."); and (5) poor coordination and communication. "Under constant pressure from stockholders," adds Dr. Kenichi Ohmae (*The Borderless World; Power and Strategy in the Interlinked Economy*, New York: Harper Business, 1990), ". . . many American companies have lost vision. They have become traders of assets, not long-term builders of value," because "the legal system in the United States . . . is a wonderful mechanism for spoiling the soil for business." (Reference to the Sherman Act regulating competition and pricing to prevent monopoly practices.) A fragment of the "Japan Bashing"—"America Bashing" campaign is what author Michael Lewis ("Shame: The Exposed Self," Free Press, 1992) points out the difference in one's attitude toward work and responsibility. In the Japanese culture the worker views itself as a part of the whole social system of production and failure is not considered as a shame for self, but shame for letting down the group for disappointing the enterprise and its workers. No worker of an American enterprise will be ashamed if the employer makes no profit. During the 1992 Winter Olympics, young Japanese skater, Midori Ito, apologized to her people and the nation as a whole, for letting them down by being second, with a silver medal, instead of being first with a gold medal. See JAPAN BASHING, KYOIKU MAMA.

America-Firster. A super-patriot, one totally dedicated to the national interest of the U.S. over that of any other state. See CHAUVINIST, HARD HAT, JINGO.

America is One People. See WEED AND SEED PROGRAM.

America is the Eagle, not the Ostrich. U.S. President George Bush so characterized the posture and the resolve of the United States in both domestic policies and foreign relations, during his speech in Knoxville, Tennessee, on 19 February 1992. He called for decisive leadership, resolve and support by the American people to empower the eagle. By announcing a new program of National Technology Initiative, the president outlined plans to "transfer America from an arsenal of democracy to one also of science and technology," with emphasis on education, improved research, improving the infrastructure and clean air. The federal government is to be an equal partner with private business organizations in the realization of this plan. The president also stated that the federal government does not have an industrial policy, because this is the domain of private enterprise, but the federal government will lend a helping hand. See ARSENAL OF DEMOCRACY.

America's New Nationalism. Following the dissolution of the Soviet empire in 1991, and the American (and Allied) victory in the recent Persian Gulf War against Saddam Hussein of Iraq, the American economy, always subject to cycles, suffered a setback. The American people, faced with growing unemployment and declining living standards, placed greater demand on their leaders, particularly the president, to concentrate more on internal problems, to limit foreign aid and the stationing of American troops at foreign bases, and to assert that more American goods be accepted on foreign markets. Patrick Buchanan, the Republican challenger to President Bush in the 1992 presidential election, was a spokesman for, as well as a beneficiary of, the internal forces striving to divert America's attention from internationalist to nationalist tasks at hand. This nationalist trend does not necessarily embrace isolationism and protectionism, but advocates balanced growth at home and an equitable share for American products abroad.

American Academy of Political and Social Science (AAPSS). A society of professionals and laymen dedicated to the study and dissemination of information on trends and developments in government, politics, and the social sciences. The Academy awards research fellowships and publishes numerous research papers in addition to its bimonthly *Annals*.

American Agricultural Movement. See TRACTORCADE.

American Association of University Women. See WOMEN POLITICAL ACTION GROUPS.

American Bar Association (ABA). A professional organization of persons in the legal profession (e.g., attorneys-at-law and judges).

American Camelot. See CAMELOT.

American Century. A term epitomizing the sum total of America's achievements in the general improvement of the human condition at home and abroad through literature, film, political philosophy, pop culture, the shiny automobile and the defense of the oppressed through military means. In spite of the multiplicity of internal problems in the "land of the round door knob," there are ways and means to resolve any conflict, and millions around the world want to come and live in America. Through President Ronald W. Reagan, America condemned the "evil empire" of the Soviet Union and stood up against it, thus enabling the people in Eastern Europe and the Soviet Federation to gain freedom and brought about the dissolution of that "evil empire." With tactful and able diplomacy, the United States, through President George Bush, was even able to persuade the "evil empire" to condemn the aggression of Iraq against Kuwait, and to allow the Desert War Coalition to restore the independence of Kuwait. The "New World Order," proposed by President Bush and adhered to by Soviet President Mikhail S. Gorbachev, resulted from American resolve and the inspiration of the "Thousand Points of Light" envisioned by President Bush. Such slogans as "American Home," "Come Home, America!," and "The World Has Come Home to America," (just as "Four Freedoms," "New Deal," "Square Deal," "Save the World for Democracy," and "Fair Deal," before them) were effective mobilizers of American and global public opinion. They have strengthened the global constituency which the "uni-power," "the single superpower" today, the United States, and its allies everywhere, will need to sustain the "New World Order." A world without fear of a new war, of a nuclear war, or fear of, eventually, a war by hungry people.

American City Bureau. A private organization which trains civic workers for the chambers of commerce in the U.S. It also strongly advocates the city-manager plan of local government.

American Civil Liberties Union (ACLU). A libertarian organization founded in 1920 to assist individuals in protecting their constitutional rights. During recent years, the ACLU has been very active in defending the rights of national, ethnic, and racial minorities.

American Civil War. The war between the United States of America (USA) and the Confederate States of America (CSA), which began with the attack by Confederate forces on Fort Sumter in Charleston, South Carolina, on April 12, 1861, and ended with the surrender of the Confederate Trans-Mississippi forces under General Kirby Smith on May 26, 1865. (The Commander-in-Chief of the Confederate forces, General Robert E. Lee, had signed an official instrument of surrender with the Commander-in-Chief of the Federal forces, General Ulysses Simpson Grant, on April 9, 1865, in Appomattox Court House, Virginia.) The USA Army had consisted of approximately 1,500,000 men (including about 200,000 Negroes in the Army and 35,000 in the Navy) and its total casualties were approximately 640,000 men. The strength of the CSA Army had consisted of approximately 1,100,000 men and its casualties were approximately 360,000 men. Most of the casualties on both sides were due to untreated illnesses. The populations of the two belligerent states were: 9,000,000 (including 3,500,000 slaves) in the CSA, and 22,000,0000 in the USA. Among the major causes of the war were: (1) nullification (non-acceptance of federal legislation as binding); (2) secession (separation from the union by states); (3) states' rights (as guaranteed under the U.S. Constitution, Amendment X); (4) slavery (some persons in the North, the USA, were genuinely opposed to slavery on ethical grounds while others were simply jealous of the South's having an abundance of free or cheap labor); and (5) federal tariffs which tended to strangle the southern economy, and that ought to be in reality the major cause of the war. It was not the issue of slavery and bleeding hearts, but pure desire on the part of the Confederates to retain power and wealth. The ultimate cause of the war, therefore, was the attempt by the North to prevent the South from buying British manufactured products which were cheaper and better than those produced in the North. If such trade was tolerated, the North would never conquer the South. One should not overlook the fact that it is inherent in the nature of politically organized communities, just as it is in any single person, to escape from an imposed authority and to create one's own. The War of Secession appears probably under as many names as there were attempts to write its definitive history. It is known in different references and sources as the "Confederate War," "War Between the States," "American War of Secession," "War of Second Revolution in America," "Mr. Lincoln's War," "Mr. Davis's War," "War Against Slavery," and "Anti-Slavery War." See Appendix 87.

American Colonies. The British Empire held the following three types of colonies in North America: (1) royal colonies—owned and operated by or for the British monarch in every aspect of its life (e.g.,

New York, New Jersey, New Hampshire, Virginia—which had originally been a proprietary or charter colony, but once Virginia's tobacco became a marketable commodity, the British King claimed it as a royal colony—and North Carolina, South Carolina, Georgia, and, after 1691, Massachusetts); (2) corporate colonies—operated under a corporate charter whereby the land was held under a grant by the British crown which allowed the colony to maintain some degree of autonomy and self-rule. Corporate colonies were: Rhode Island, Connecticut, and Massachusetts (the status of Massachusetts was changed in 1691 to royal colony); and (3) proprietary colonies—based on a feudal charter and operated by a landlord under a grant by the crown (e.g., Pennsylvania, Maryland, and Delaware).

American Communism. See McCARTHYISM, RED SCARE.

American Conservatism. See CONSERVATISM.

American Conservative Union. An active political action and educational organization in the USA, under the leadership of David Keene, advocating small but effective government, with particularly strong and decisive leadership at the executive level of all echelons of American government, federal, state and local; also calling for a conservative fiscal policy and political discipline among citizens.

American Constitution. See CONSTITUTION OF THE UNITED STATES, SUPREME LAW OF THE LAND.

American Constitutional Government, Principles of. See PRINCIPLES OF AMERICAN CONSTITUTIONAL SYSTEM.

American Definition of Human Rights. See HUMAN RIGHTS: AMERICAN DEFINITION.

American Dream. See AMERICAN CENTURY.

American Economic Assistance to the Commonwealth of Independent States (CIS). Following the dissolution of the Soviet Union and the communist regime there in 1991, the United States, on the initiative of President George Bush, provided on 10 February 1992, an economic package to permit the newly-formed Commonwealth to survive the difficult transitory period from a communist to a market economy. The package known as "Operation Provide Hope," of $5 billion total consists of the following components: $645 million humanitarian-technical assistance; over $3.75 billion, food credit guarantees; $210 million, U.S. Department of Agriculture and Department of Defense surplus food; $400 million for nuclear disarmament; $100 million for Department of Defense emergency transportation services; $645 million from the Agency for International Development, for medical assistance, of which only $30 million was spent as of 31 December 1991. Of the total amount designated, only approximately $700 million requires congressional approval. In order to protect the storage and the distribution of aid items from possible theft and misallocation, the City of Moscow police chief set up a special police unit, called the "economic police," of 1,300 officers. See AMERICAN-SOVIET COLLUSION.

American Farm Movement. See TRACTORCADE.

American Federalism. See PRINCIPLES OF AMERICAN CONSTITUTIONAL SYSTEM.

American Federation of Labor–Congress of Industrial Organization (AFL-CIO). One of the largest associations of labor unions in the United States.

American Foreign Aid. According to data from the United States Congress, the United States has given to other countries, during the period of 1946-1992, over one-trillion dollars ($1,000,000,000,000.00) in the form of grants and loans (many loans, in time, are either written off, or are reduced in the amount to be paid back). Among the largest recipients of foreign aid in the form of grants are Israel, Egypt, the Philippines, and Pakistan. In some cases, only about 36¢ out of a dollar went to the cause for which the grant was awarded. During the Second World War, under the Lend-Lease program, first England, then the former Soviet Union, received considerable amounts of money, food, clothing, and war materiel, ranging from bread to aircraft, which was never repaid. Some countries repaid small portions of the loans, usually in a ratio of 5¢ or 10¢ on a dollar. Finland is the only country which repaid its loans in full. It is also estimated that an additional $500 billion was given to foreign nations by private persons and organizations in America. The data on grants and loans is very extensive and obviously too bulky for a more detailed presentation here, but one can say one thing about it with certainty, paraphrasing Winston Churchill, that never in the history of mankind have so few given so much to so many and received so little in return! See FOREIGN AID, Appendix 40.

American Foreign Policy. See KLINGBERG CYCLE.

American Friends of the Middle East. See ARAB LOBBY.

American-German Friendship Institute. See ATLANTIC PARTNERSHIP.

American Home. See AMERICAN CENTURY.

American Hostages in Iran. See IRAN'S REVOLUTION, OCTOBER SURPRISE.

American Ideology. See AMERICAN CENTURY.

American Independent Party. A third party—George Wallace was presidential candidate of that party in 1968. Received almost 10 million votes.

American Indian Movement (AIM). See WOUNDED KNEE REBELLION.

American Insurgency and Counterinsurgency. See COUNTERINSURGENCY IN AMERICA.

American Intervention in Russia. See WAR COMMUNISM.

American Israel Public Affairs Committee (AIRPAC). The only organization registered to lobby for Israel. See JEWISH LOBBY.

American Jewish Community (AJC). See JEWISH LOBBY.

American Judicature Society. A society of judges, attorneys-at-law and professors of law dedicated to the continuous process of clarification of existing laws as well as evaluation of new ones.

American Labor Party. A minor political party, founded in 1936, which opposed the Tammany Hall organization in New York City, but which otherwise supported the national Democratic Party.

American Legion. An organization of former members of the U.S. Armed Forces founded in 1919 in Paris, France. The Legion's purpose is to promote the interests of veterans in particular, and to foster American ideals in general.

American Legislators' Association. An organization composed of members of state legislatures in the U.S., founded in 1925 and merged with the Council of State Governments in 1933. The purpose of this organization is to conduct studies and to design methods for the improvement of state legislative systems and practices. See COUNCIL OF STATE GOVERNMENTS.

American Liberalism. See LIBERALISM.

American Liberty League. A private organization established during the 1930s and 1940s by opponents of President Franklin D. Roosevelt and his "New Deal" policies.

American Medical Political Action Committee (AMPAC). The political arm of the American Medical Association (AMA) which is involved in lobbying activities for the purpose of protecting the vested interests of the medical profession. See LOBBY.

American Municipal Association (AMA). An organization of municipalities set up for the purposes of protecting the autonomy of local governments from national interference and strictly observing the provisions contained in Amendment X to the U.S. Constitution. See NATIONAL LEAGUE OF CITIES (NLC).

American National Party. A minor political party founded in 1784 to oppose all secret societies and associations, to restrict the powers of monopolies and to initiate direct election of the U.S. President.

American Native Party. See AMERICAN PARTY.

American Near East Refugee Aid. See ARAB LOBBY.

American Party. A minor political party founded in the 1850s. It opposed socialist and anarchist elements in the nation and demanded that an alien should reside in the U.S. for a period of at least fourteen years before being eligible for U.S. citizenship by naturalization. This party was also known as the "Know-Nothing-Party." Also known as "American Native Party."

American Plan. See WELFARE CAPITALISM.

American Political Science Association (APSA). An organization comprised of teachers, government officials, writers (on civic matters) and others interested in government and politics. The Association sponsors research projects, seminars, conferences, and a Congressional Fellowship Program for persons interested in gaining firsthand experience by working as special congressional assistants.

American Proportional Representation League. A private organization advocating the implementation of the system of proportional representation in the U.S. See PROPORTIONAL REPRESENTATION.

American Protective Association. A secret political organization founded in Iowa in 1887, which was opposed to all influence by Catholics and foreigners, and combated any foreign cultural influence in the United States.

American Relief Administration (ARA). See NEW ECONOMIC POLICY (NEP).

American Revolution. The war of independence from England that was waged between 1775 and 1781 by the American colonies dissatisfied with oppressive and exploitative British practices. The British were defeated in the final battle of Yorktown, Virginia, when General Cornwallis surrendered to General George Washington in October 1781. England recognized the independence of the American colonies by the Treaty of Paris of 1783. On March 1, 1781, the colonies formed a confederation (see the ARTICLES OF CONFEDERATION in Appendix 6) and, subsequently, a federation on March 4, 1789, when the new U.S. Constitution was ratified. See U.S. CONSTITUTION, Appendix 8.

American Society for Public Administration (ASPA). A professional research organization concerned with the study of public administration, governmental policies, and urban studies in developing nations. Professional organization for administrational personnel in public service.

American-Soviet Collusion. While on his state visit to the United States (September 15-17, 1959) Nikita S. Khrushchev, Chairman of the Council of Ministers and General Secretary of the CPSU (1956-1964), suggested closer cooperation between the United States and the Soviet Union, to the extent of exchanging top executives (he asked Averill Harriman, former U.S. Ambassador to the USSR, an adviser to many U.S. Presidents, and a millionaire in his own right, to join Khrushchev's staff in Moscow) and exchanging information (suggesting to Allen Dulles, Director of the CIA, that the two states combine their intelligence services, the CIA and the KGB, because, as Khrushchev stated, many of the CIA agents were working for the KGB anyway and collecting two salaries for no reason at all). Those suggestions by Khrushchev were not taken seriously, but only added to the already deep suspicions of the real intentions of the Soviet leader. Relationships between America and Russia, beyond some trade and the usual diplomatic relations, have been hampered by a multiplicity of circumstances and events. The Russians, subjected to invasions and wars for over a thousand years, are always suspicious of foreign machinations and double-talk, double-think diplomacy. The principal sources of the antagonism are: (1) the Alaska Purchase is viewed by Russians as a result of manipulation by agents who were governing Alaska and who were not even Russians. The majority of Russians became aware of the transaction only many years after it was completed; (2) the treaty between England and Japan in 1902, which was designed to hold in check Russian influence in the Far East and which freed the Japanese to attack the Russian fleet and to defeat it at Port Arthur in 1904. The Russians suspected the Americans were partners with England, because of growing American expansion in Asia, the Philippines, and in China. Subsequent intervention by U.S. President Theodore Roosevelt who was instrumental in restoring peace among the warring partners (see TREATY OF PORTSMOUTH) dispelled that suspicion; (3) toward the end of W.W.I in 1918, when the Russian Bolsheviks ceased anti-German hostilities (see TREATY OF BREST-LITOVSK), the European Allies sent a contingent of troops, including about 5,000 American soldiers, to the northern part of Russia in Archangel to prevent Russian weapons from falling into German hands; in addition, about 10,000

American soldiers, the Expeditionary Force were dispatched by President Woodrow Wilson to Siberia to prevent the 75,000 Japanese troops stationed there from gaining control over Siberia. Trapped there were 45,000 Czechoslovakian troops; and the supply warehouses of the Bolshevik Red Army were located there; (4) the "Red Scare" campaign in America, the refusal to trade with Russia and to allow the Soviets to sell their products abroad on a large scale. This included the embargo on technologies and products, introduced in the West (and in America in particular) after the Bolshevik victory in Russia, and retained to the present; (5) when the Soviets were attacked by the German Nazi forces in June 1941, Josef Stalin begged the British and the Americans to open a second front from Europe in order to relieve the pressure on the Soviet forces. That request materialized only in "Lend-Lease," a massive war materiel shipment to the Soviet Union, but no second front. When the Soviets defeated the main Nazi forces in Stalingrad in 1943, forune turned in their favor; they were subsequently marching rapidly toward Poland and Germany, and, the Allies fearful that the Soviets would not stop until they reached Paris and London, decided on a massive offensive from England, "Operation Overlord," in the spring of 1944. By the time the Soviets reached Berlin they had lost over twenty million people; (6) the dropping of the atom bombs on Hiroshima and Nagasaki in 1945 was viewed by the Soviet leadership as a demonstration of a new force against them; therefore, they subsequently acquired their own nuclear capability; (7) the insurgency operations against the Soviet Union and the communist Soviet puppet governments in Poland, Albania, and others, organized by American intelligence, and taking various forms, from sending spies and saboteurs, to floating balloons with propaganda leaflets over Poland and the Ukraine. The Soviets knew of these insurgency operations in advance, because Kim Philby of the British Intelligence, the MI-6, in charge of Soviet Counterintelligence efforts, was, like many others, a Soviet spy for many years. Therefore, all the insurgency operations were compromised; (8) the "Berlin Tunnel," an operation conceived by the American and the British intelligence services in West Berlin designed to tap Soviet communications from a tunnel dug underground stretching well into East German territory. The project was revealed to the Russians by William Blake, Soviet agent and an officer of the British intelligence; (9) the U-2 overflight operation over Soviet territory for reconnaissance purposes which was revealed when the American plane was shot down on 1 May 1960 over Soviet territory and the captured pilot, Francis Gary Powers, revealed all the secrets to the Russians. President Dwight D. Eisenhower apologized to the Russians and cancelled the spy missions; (10) the Soviets firmly believed that the United States orchestrated the massive flights of people from East to the West, mainly in Germany, where the Wall had to be erected, in order to cause a brain drain that would be costly to the East German economy; they also believed the United States orchestrated anti-communist and anti-Soviet demonstrations and revolts in Poland, Hungary, and Czechoslovakia, to cause them to abandon the Soviet orbit, as had been done in 1948; and (11) the aid to the Afghanistan insurgents against the Soviet invaders was also construed as a hostile act. It was not until 1 February 1992 that for the first time in American-Soviet relations, the leaders of the two states, President George W. Bush of the United States and Boris N. Yeltsin of the Russian Federation, met (on Yeltsin's birthday) at Camp David where the two leaders agreed to forget the past and to commence new, friendly, and peaceful relations. See AMERICAN ECONOMIC ASSISTANCE TO THE COMMONWEALTH OF INDEPENDENT STATES (CIS), I WILL BURY YOU, Appendices 74, 103.

American War of Independence. See AMERICAN REVOLUTION.

American War of Secession. See AMERICAN CIVIL WAR.

Americanism. Knowledge of things American in the continental sense, such as culture, customs, folklore, anthropology, music, etc. Experts in these fields are usually called Americanists. Development of Americanism is growing due to the steadily awakening consciousness of various American nations regarding their heritage, traditions, customs and above all their distinct literary artistic achievements, frequently based on regional patriotism and pride. See AMERICAN CENTURY.

Americans for Constitutional Action (ACA). A private organization established in 1958 to promote the election of persons (whom it judges to be loyal to the Constitution and America's traditional values) to the U.S. Congress. See LOBBY.

Americans for Democratic Action (ADA). A political organization founded in 1947 of left-wing elements of the Democratic Party to promote liberal policies and legislation. The organization has actively supported liberal candidates for the U.S. Congress and has been opposed to America's military involvement abroad. Hubert H. Humphrey (1911-1978), former U.S. Senator (1948-1965 and 1970-1978), U.S. Vice President (1965-1969), and nominee of the Democratic Party for President in 1968, was one of its co-founders and a strong supporter.

Amicus Curiae. In the Latin language, "friend of the court." In practice, it is one who is not a party to a case but one who testifies in court for the sake of justice.

Amnesty. The return to freedom and restitution of legal disabilities, of persons convicted of crimes and serving terms in prisons or penitentiaries. Amnesty may cover certain categories of convictions such as petty larceny or political offenses. It usually excludes persons convicted of murder and/or kidnapping, or persons considered to be otherwise dangerous to society, unless a general amnesty is granted, in which case it covers all persons in confinement. In the U.S., amnesty may be proclaimed by the President upon prior authorization by Congress.

Amnesty International. An informal international organization of young intellectuals dedicated to the preservation of human rights everywhere. The London-based organization investigates all cases of mistreatment of human beings, particularly those prosecuted or imprisoned for political reasons (political prisoners). It compiles statistical information for the people of the world and their governments. The organization was instrumental in unmasking mistreatment of political prisoners in many modern states (e.g., the Soviet Union, East Germany, and in some Latin American states). It has also exerted considerable pressure on American leadership to grant amnesty to all deserters and draft dodgers of the Vietnam era.

AMPAC. See AMERICAN MEDICAL POLITICAL ACTION COMMITTEE.

Amt Ausland Abwehr. See ABWEHR.

Anarchism. See ANARCHIST, ROLE OF STATE.

Anarchist. One who by thought or action demonstrates disregard for the political organization of a state, the government and its institutions, or any authority, particularly political, or one who actively participates in acts that aim at disrupting normal political or governmental processes, usually by drastic action.

Anarchistic Theory. See ROLE OF STATE.

Anarcho-Tyranny. According to columnist Samuel Francis of *The Washington Post*, "a system that ignores such basic duties of government as protecting citizens against crime and dotes instead on criminalizing the innocent."

Anatomy of Power. See AUTHORITY, POWER, Appendix 3-A.

ANC. See AFRICAN NATIONAL CONGRESS.

Ancien Régime. In the French language, "old regime." Absolute rule (e.g., absolute monarchy) such as that under King Louis XIV of France, or any regime before the 1789 Revolution.

Ancient Order of Hibernians. A secret Irish organization consisting mainly of Catholic men, established ca. 1565, and dedicated to the total liberation of Ireland from British domination.

Andean Initiative. U.S. President George Bush initiated a plan in 1989 to aid governments of narco-trafficking areas of Latin America, mainly Colombia and Peru, designed to help their economies by introducing substitute crops to replace coca production. It also offered police-enforcement assistance in prosecuting drug producers and smugglers who undermine political stability in the region. The main target was the Medellin Cartel in Colombia. Subsequently, on 15 February 1990, George Bush met in Cartagena, Colombia, with the presidents of Bolivia, Colombia, and Peru for the purpose of designing effective anti-drug strategies, but the Latin American leaders demanded that the United States first limit imports and market demands for the illegal product at home. Most coca needed for the production of cocaine is grown in Peru and Bolivia, and about 80 percent of the global cocaine supply comes from Colombia. See Appendix 89.

Angary, the Right of. Under traditional rules of international law, the right of a belligerent state to seize and/or destroy a foreign merchant vessel or other property whenever military necessity warrants it, provided that such vessel or property, at the time of seizure or destruction, was within the jurisdiction of the belligerent state.

Angel. In American political folklore, one who donates cash to the campaign fund of a favorite politician. The supporter of a candidate who collects and distributes campaign funds on behalf of the candidate is called a "bag man."

Angka Loeu. See KHMER ROUGE.

Annapolis Convention. An informal gathering held in Annapolis, Maryland, in 1786, of twelve delegates from five states of the American Confederation to find some means acceptable to all on the regulation of interstate commerce. Upon the insistence of Alexander Hamilton, a recommendation was presented to the Continental Congress and the thirteen independent states to meet in Philadelphia, Pennsylvania, for further talks. This recommendation was adopted and in 1787 the Philadelphia Constitutional Convention met and drafted the Constitution for the United States of America.

Annexation. The act of transfer of a territory from one jurisdiction to another done usually for the purpose of improving governmental services to the inhabitants. The absorption or incorporation of a part or the whole of a territory of one jurisdiction by another. (In the State of Virginia annexation falls within the domain of judicial tribunals.)

Anschluss. In the German language, the act of "incorporation" or "absorption of the territory of one state by another" (e.g., Hitler incorporated the free state of Austria into the German Third Reich in 1938).

Anthropomorphism. The practice of viewing the spiritual being (e.g., a God) in terms of a human being (the *homo sapiens*). See THEISM.

Anti-Clericalism. See CLERICALISM.

Anti-Comintern Pact. See AXIS, COMMUNIST INTERNATIONAL.

Anti-Communist Offensive. See COUNTERINSURGENCY IN AMERICA, McCARTHYISM, PALMER RAIDS, RED MENACE.

Anti-Fascist Coalition. See GRAND ALLIANCE.

Antifederalist. An opponent of the policies of President John Adams and the Federal Constitution as originally drafted (without the Amendments), or a supporter of the policies of Thomas Jefferson and his Democratic-Republican Party. See FEDERALIST, JEFFERSON DOCTRINE, JEFFERSONIAN REPUBLICANISM.

Antigag Law. A rider attached to the Post Office Appropriation Act of 1912 granting federal employees the right to organize themselves for the purpose of petitioning Congress individually and collectively, and asserting that no federal employee shall be dismissed from his job without good cause. When dismissed, such an employee shall be informed in writing of the charges against him to which he may reply.

Anti-Israel Three-Nos Doctrine. See THREE-NOS DOCTRINE.

Anti-Masonic Party. A minor political party active during the 1820s and 1830s, mainly in New York, Pennsylvania and Vermont, founded for the purpose of combating the activities of the Masonic Order.

Antimonopoly Party. A minor party founded during the 1880s advocating, among other things, direct election of U.S. Senators, federal income tax, industrial arbitration and federal regulation of interstate commerce, all of which were realized in later years.

Anti-Narcotics Summit. See ANDEAN INITIATIVE.

Anti-Radical Division. See GENERAL INTELLIGENCE DIVISION.

Anti-Saloon League. See WOMAN'S CHRISTIAN TEMPERANCE UNION (WCTU).

Anti-Semitism. An attitude of hostility toward persons of the Jewish faith, Jewish ideas and Jews as a politically organized society, as in the state of Israel. Anti-Semitism dates back to ancient Rome when the Roman Empire officially adopted Christianity; Jews were expelled from England, France, and Germany during the 1100s and from Spain during the Inquisition in 1492. They were subjected to bloody pogroms and extreme discrimination in Eastern Europe, mainly in Poland and Russia; Chancellor Bismarck of Prussia blamed them for the ills of his economy. During the 1890s the French tried a young Jewish officer in the French Army, Captain Alfred Dreyfus, for alleged espionage activities for the Germans, in order to hide corrupt bureaucratic practices of the administration. Germany's Nazi leader, Adolf Hitler, was responsible for the death of about six million Jews during W.W.II. Jews were subjected to terrorist practices by the Ku Klux Klan in the United States, and since the establishment of the Jewish state of Israel have been subjected to discrimination in the Soviet Union and by terrorist Arabs in the Middle East.

Anti-Slavery War. See AMERICAN CIVIL WAR.

Anti-Statism. See GUIDED FREE ENTERPRISE, STATISM.

Antitrust Legislation. Laws in the United States, established for the purpose of preventing large businesses from consolidating into monopolies.

Anti-Vietnam War Protests. During the 1960s and 1970s, the great movement against the war in Vietnam (also referred to as the "consciousness movement") was reflected in mass protests, teach-ins on the evils of the war, and such slogans as: "Make war on poverty, not people"; "Make love, not war"; and "Hey, hey, LBJ, how many kids did you kill today?" "Hell no, we won't go" was the slogan of those facing the draft. Those opposing the war were called "Vietniks" or "Peaceniks." See COUNTER-INSURGENCY IN AMERICA, VIETNAM MORATORIUM DAY.

Anything that Does Not Need Fixing, Don't Fix it. See COORDINATING COMMITTEE FOR MULTILATERAL EXPORT CONTROLS (COCOM).

ANZUS. See AUSTRALIA–NEW ZEALAND–UNITED STATES TREATY, Appendix 29.

Aparatchik. Full-time party worker, member of the party bureaucracy, or a party propagandist in the former USSR.

Apartheid. The Afrikaans' policy of segregation in the Republic of South Africa. The terms, "parallel" or "separate development," are also used. See PARALLEL DEVELOPMENT DOCTRINE, WORLD APARTHEID MOVEMENT (WAM).

Apolitical System. See CENTRALISM.

Appeal Court. See COURT OF APPEALS, SUPREME COURT OF THE UNITED STATES.

Appeasement-Before-Country-Liberals. U.S. Senator Philip ("Phil") Gramm, Republican of Texas, so characterized opponents of U.S. involvement in the Persian Gulf War against Iraq in 1991.

Appeasement, Policy of. The practice of easy compromise (e.g., the granting of concessions by one state to another with the hope that this will prevent some future problem, such as war). See MUNICH AGREEMENT.

Appellant. One who appeals.

Appellate Jurisdiction. The authority of one court to review cases of another without conducting trial proceedings anew. (The U.S. Federal District Courts and the U.S. Supreme Court have both original and appellate jurisdiction, while Federal Courts of Appeal have appellate jurisdiction only.) See COURT OF APPEALS.

Appellee. One against whom an appeal is made from the decision of a lower court to a higher one. See COURT OF APPEALS, Appendices 44, 45, 50, 65, 66.

Apportionment. The manner of allocating representation to a constituency on the basis of population. See ONE MAN, ONE VOTE, UNITED STATES HOUSE OF REPRESENTATIVES.

Appropriation. An authorization for expenditure of funds. See BILL.

Appropriation Bill. See BILL.

April 19 Movement (or M-19 Movement). Anti-government Marxist-oriented guerrilla movement in Colombia.

April Theses. See LENIN'S APRIL THESES.

APS. See ACADEMY OF POLITICAL SCIENCE.

APSA. See AMERICAN POLITICAL SCIENCE ASSOCIATION.

Arab Boycott. Following the Arab Oil Embargo of 1973, the memberstates of the Arab League, mainly the oil producers (e.g., Libya, Saudi Arabia, and Kuwait), concluded a secret agreement among themselves to boycott any foreign business enterprise if the same enterprise is doing business with the state of Israel at the same time. The U.S. Government forbids U.S. business enterprises to boycott the state of Israel. See ARAB LOBBY.

Arab-Israeli War of 1967. See ISRAELI-ARAB WAR OF 1967.

Arab League. An organization of Arab states founded in 1945 for the purpose of a unified struggle for Arab causes, particularly against the possible emergence of the state of Israel, which was founded in 1948. The original members of the League were: Egypt, Iraq, Jordan, Lebanon, Saudi Arabia, Syria, and Yemen. In 1967 Kuwait, Morocco, Tunisia, Algeria, and Libya also joined the League.

Arab Lobby. An informal conglomeration of Arab and Arab-American organizations which are involved in lobbying activities for the cause of Arab nations. The most active lobbying group is the National Association of Arab-Americans which claims to speak for the 1.5 to 2 million Arabs residing in the United States, concentrated mostly in urban areas such as Detroit, Michigan (often called "the mother city for Arab Americans"), Los Angeles, California, Chicago, Illinois, Houston, Texas, and New York City. The other Arab organizations which comprise the so-called "Arab Lobby" are the Middle East Institute, the Association of Arab American University Graduates (of the American University in Lebanon), the American Friends of the Middle East and the American Near East Refugee Aid. One of the least effective lobbies in the United States. See HARDWARE DIPLOMACY, JEWISH LOBBY, SADAT-BEGIN SUMMITS.

Arab Nationalism. Among the first of the Arab leaders to raise the banner of Arab nationalism was Egyptian Jamal-ud-Din al-Afghani (1838-1897); subsequently, when the French and the British sought help from the Arabs against the Turks of the Ottoman Empire, British Agent T. E. Lawrence (1888-1935), known as "Lawrence of Arabia," made hints of independent Arab kingdoms once the Turks were defeated. The Turkish Empire fell apart after W.W.I, but so did the Arabs' dream of independent kingdoms, because in 1920 the French expelled the Arabs from Syria and Lebanon and took the lands as their protectorates. The Arabs refer to this period as the "year of the catastrophe," (or in the Arabic language, "am an-nakba"). The Arabs miscalculated the resolve of the French because at that time they were involved in rivalry with the British over possession of German colonies of the Cameroon, Tanganyika, and Togo, which the Germans lost after W.W.I. Following W.W.I, the Wafd organization, under the leadership of Saad Zaghlul Pasha (1860-1927), rose against the British, demanding complete independence for Egypt which, after years, was finally granted. Arab nationalism re-emerged again as a strong force after W.W.II, particularly under the leadership of Egypt's president Gamal Abdel Nasser (1954-1970).

Arabian Purchase. Saudi Arabia's King Khaled presented his plan for solving the Arab-Israeli dispute over territories conquered by Israel during the 1967 War (a major issue during the Sadat-Begin peace dialogue of 1977-1978). He presented an offer to U.S. President Jimmy Carter (during Carter's January 1978 trip to Saudi Arabia) to purchase from Israel (at a fair market value) the West Bank and the Gaza Strip where the proposed Palestinian state could be established. "You try to solve the Palestinian problem," King Khaled told President Carter, "and we are ready to give you all the oil you want."

Arbeit Macht Frei. See LABOR SHALL MAKE YOU FREE.

Arbitrary Government. A government which has little regard for the individual and treats him harshly (e.g., guarantees no due process of law or disregards civil and political rights and liberties). See TOTALITARIAN STATE.

Arbitration. A method of settling disputes by submitting the issues to a panel of experts for advisory opinion. Such opinion may be accepted or rejected by the parties to the dispute. In some instances, compulsory arbitration may be imposed by a governmental agency or court of law. See CONCILIATION, GOOD OFFICES, MEDIATION.

Arcana Imperii. In the Latin language, "secrets of the state" or "state secrets."

Archon. See COMPULSORY VOTING.

Are You Better Off Now than You Were Four Years Ago? See NEW BEGINNING.

Are You Now, or Have You Ever Been, a Member of the Communist Party? Such was the first question asked of witnesses appearing before the House (U.S. House of Representatives) Un-American Activities Committee in the 1950s. See McCARTHYISM, RED MENACE.

Areawide Government. Commonly, a government that is set up upon either consolidation of two or more jurisdictions (municipalities) or an annexation of the territory of one jurisdiction (municipality) by another (e.g., the UNIGOV created after the merger of Indianapolis and Marion County in Indiana, the consolidation of Miami and Dade County in Florida, and the unification of Davidson County with the City of Nashville in Tennessee). Also referred to as consolidated government or government consolidation.

Areawide Planning. Refers to the geographic territory which encompasses the whole area of influence of a program, or the whole area of impact of a problem to which planning is to be addressed, usually transcending the boundaries of any single unit of local government.

Argentina-Britain Falkland Islands War. See FALKLAND ISLANDS WAR.

Argot. A special language of political, professional, or social groups, which they develop for internal communication and which anyone outside the group will not understand. An internal vernacular (language).

Aristocracy. The possession and disposition of governmental powers by a small (elite) group of persons.

Arm Yourself, if You Want to Prevent War. See HARDWARE DIPLOMACY, SIVIS PACEM PARA BELLUM.

Armaments Race. Race between the two super powers, USA-USSR, for better and more military armaments prompted by fierce rivalry by each to be the unilaterally stronger.

Armistice. Suspension of hostile military activity during a war.

Arms and War Materiel Sales. During the period from August 1990 to February 1992, sales of weapons and war materiel by the United States were, according to the Arms Control Association, as follows: $14.8 billion to Saudi Arabia; $2.17 billion to Egypt; $37 million to Bahrain; and $467.9 million to Israel. (Israel, also a seller of weapons, especially the Uzi submachine gun, has purchased weapons from different countries in the past. Before the state of Israel was established in 1948, Czechoslovakia was the largest weapon seller to the Israelis; subsequently France, where nuclear technology was obtained; and then, the United States, where the Nuclear Materials and Equipment Corporation provided nuclear technology as well as uranium. Some of the uranium was allegedly stolen by Israeli agents from a plant in Pennsylvania.) Also, $350 million to Kuwait; $250 million to Morocco; and $150 million to Oman. The former Soviet Union was the largest seller of arms between 1985 and 1989. It sold during that period over $25 billion worth of arms and war materiel as follows: $13 billion to Iraq; $6.1 billion to Syria; $1.6 billion to North Yemen; $1.4 billion to South Yemen; and $1.2 billion to Jordan. Marshal Josef Stalin of the Soviet Union personally allowed his puppet government in Czechoslovakia to sell arms and war materiel to the Haganah warriors in Israel after 1948. The Israelis were purchasing weapons from Czechoslovakia before that time. Among the other major sellers of arms and war materiel are the following: the People's Republic of China, North Korea, (it was reported in February 1992 that North Korea was sending to Syria over $100 million worth of sophisticated missiles and other war materiel, including Scud-C missiles), Japan, Singapore, Argentina, Mexico, Brazil, France, Great Britain, Poland, Switzerland, Germany, and Austria.

Arms Control and Disarmament. See HARDWARE DIPLOMACY, STRATEGIC ARMS LIMITATION TALKS (SALT).

Arms Control and Export Act. See ARAB LOBBY.

Arm's-Length Doctrine. The prevalent view among America's foreign policy planners, developed at the end of World War II, that security arrangements for the North American continent should be designed in such a manner as to keep potential enemies, primarily the Soviet Union, as far from the North American continent as possible. See COEXISTENCE, CONTAINMENT, CUBAN MISSILE CRISIS, HARDWARE DIPLOMACY, MONROE DOCTRINE.

Army for Violent National Liberation. See FUERZAS ARMADAS DE LIBERACION NACIONAL.

Army Rangers. An elite force of about 2,000 U.S. soldiers of high selection, superior education and training; ready for deployment on a minute's notice by sea, air, or surface transport, anywhere in the world; particularly for night deployment. The rangers date back in tradition to pre-Revolutionary America when the New England settlers were engaged in guerrilla war against the Indians, the French, and the British. In modern times, the Rangers, particularly its 75th Regiment, have been deployed in combat ranging from gun-boat days to the Persian Gulf War. The other special combat units of the American armed forces are the Navy SEALS, the Green Berets, and the Delta Force. See STANDING ORDERS, ROGERS' RANGERS, Appendix 30.

Arraign. The act of requiring one to appear before a court of law upon indictment and to answer to the charges.

Arrondissements. Administrative divisions of the departments in France.

Arsenal of Democracy. A generalized term for states which adhere to and maintain governments on democratic principles (e.g., Athens in Greece during the fifth and fourth centuries BC); in modern times, the Western European states such as France, Germany, Italy, Switzerland, Great Britain, Norway, Sweden, Iceland, Holland, Denmark, Austria, Luxembourg, Belgium, and Spain; in the Americas, the United States, Canada, and Mexico; and in Asia, Japan, India, the Philippines, and Singapore. Iceland's parliament (the "Althing), established in 930 AD, is the oldest parliament in continuous existence, next to the Synod of Cardinals in the Vatican; the third oldest governing body is the British Parliament. More often than not, the term arsenal of democracy is applied chiefly to the United States, a country which from its very first day of existence, has striven to improve the lot of human beings regardless of race, religion, national origin, or political and cultural predilection, and has extended a helping hand—in money as well as in blood, to other nations in need, very often at great sacrifice. No other nation on earth has engaged more in endeavors of this type than the United States. See AMERICA IS THE EAGLE, NOT THE OSTRICH.

Arson. Felonious crime of destroying property by fire.

Artel. A type of cooperative enterprise organized for the purpose of producing certain commodities in the former USSR. Also, a name for a collective farm unit in the former Soviet Union (e.g., Sovkhoz or Kolghoz).

Articles of Confederation. The constitutional instrument of the thirteen American states drafted by a committee appointed by the Continental Congress on June 11, 1776, and approved on November 15, 1777. (It went into effect, upon ratification by the states, on March 1, 1781. It called for a weak congress and a weak chief executive with no power to collect taxes or any form of compulsion, and amendments could be adopted only upon consent of all constituent states. The ARTICLES were replaced with a new constitution in 1789.) See Appendix 6.

Articles of Incorporation. A written legal document creating a new legal person, e.g., private or public corporation, for service or for profit, specifying the name, officers, functions, special purpose, if any (e.g., charitable organizations that may seek tax-exempt status), and one that is fully recorded and overseen by some governmental authority such as a state in the American federation. As a legal person, a corporation can sue and be sued in a court of law.

Articles of War. All the regulations established by the U.S. Congress regarding duties of military officers and enlisted men, organization and procedures of military tribunals (court-martials), and the maintenance of discipline. See RULES OF LAND WARFARE.

Artificial Growth of Government. See POLITICAL DEVELOPMENT.

Artillery of the Heavens. Some of the political adversaries of Benjamin Franklin (1706-1790), among them the reputable theologian, Jonathan Edwards, accused Franklin of tampering not only with political power, but with that of God as well ("presuming on God") by his discovery of the lightning rod; they considered lightning as the "artillery of the Heavens," not for Franklin to tamper with. Franklin, referred to often as the "first civilized American," made a great impact on the shaping of America's political philosophy, culture, and standards of morality through his writings as well as his lifestyle. He wrote, printed, and distributed his own books (*Poor Richard's Almanac*, which he edited from 1732 to 1758, was one of the most popular). Dr. Franklin made a lasting imprint on many minds around the world with such catchy phrases as "Honesty is the best policy" and "Fish and visitors stink in three days."

Aryan Nation. A militant organization of Caucasians which advocates the purity of the white race, freedom to work and to live in segregated places of employment and housing, and on occasion celebrates such events as the birthday of Adolf Hitler, founder of the Nazi Party in Germany and the Chancellor of the German Third Reich (1933-1945). The organization, currently under the leadership of Richard Girnt Butler, collaborates closely with the groups of young skinheads. The Aryans maintain contacts with similar organizations in other states, particularly Canada, Australia, England, Germany, and Austria, where the Aryan movement is the most active. On occasion, the Aryans meet and exchange ideas with the Ku Klux Klan, the American Nazi Party, and the Posse Comitatus—all of which share views in the issue of maintaining the purity of the white race of people, the Caucasians.

Asamblea Legislativa. The unicameral legislature, or Legislative Assembly, of Costa Rica.

Asamblea Nacional. The legislative body, the National Assembly, of Nicaragua.

Asamblea Nacional del Poder Popular. The unicameral legislative body—the National Assembly of the People's Power—of Cuba.

Asia-Firster. See CHINA LOBBY, COMMITTEE FOR A FREE CHINA.

Asian Home. Echoing Gorbachev's statement on "European Home," Japanese business leader, Yotaro Kobayashi proposed that Japan "re-Asianize" itself by finding its home in Asia, obviously as an economic leader among the "Mini-Tigers" of the Pacific Rim. Subsequent suggestions were to include the Peoples Republic of China, which is currently seeking a permanent seat on the Security Council of the United Nations. Japan and the People's Republic of China may soon become members as well as be the "Maxi Tigers."

Asian Triangle of Power. See HIMALAYAN CRISIS.

Ask Not What Your Country Can Do for You: Ask What You Can Do for Your Country. A statement that was made by John F. Kennedy, U.S. President (1961-1963), during his inaugural address on January 20, 1961, which helped him solidify national public opinion during his short tenure as President. President Kennedy was assassinated by Lee Harvey Oswald in Dallas, Texas, on November 22, 1963. A similar statement was made once before by Roman statesman, Cicero, in 63 B.C., when he addressed the Roman Senate urging more dedicated public service at a time when the Roman Empire was falling apart.

ASPA. American Society for Public Administration.

Assassin. One who kills a human being due to differences, disagreements, or rivalry in matters political, ideological, or religious doctrine. An act of murder usually motivated by non-monetary regards. The term originated from the Farsi (Persian) language meaning "hashshashin," or a "hashish-eater," when the Shiite sector of the Islamic faith introduced the practice of physical elimination of all who opposed its faith by killing them off in a secretive and surprise manner. The assassins were originally situated mainly in "Eagle's Nest" (Alamut), in the Elburz Mountains. According to legend as transmitted by Marco Polo, the leader of the assassins, whom he referred to as "The Old Man of the Mountains," lured young men drugged with hashish to a secluded place full of sensuous young girls where they were also given wine. They were promised that once they carried out designated assassination missions they could again return to that paradise and remain there forever. The ruling Shiite Muslim sect in Iran advocates assassination as an instrument of policy and ordered many assassinations of its adversaries, including former prime ministers, presidents, and foreign writers.

Assault and Battery. An intentional violent act inflicting bodily harm upon a person.

Assembléa Fédérale. The bicameral legislature of Switzerland composed of Conseil d'états (upper house) and Conseil National (lower house).

Assembléa Regionale. Regional unicameral legislature in Italy.

Assemblee Nationale Populaire. The unicameral legislative body, the People's National Assembly, of Congo.

Assembly for the Republic. A new political party formed on December 5, 1976, by Jacques Chirac, former Prime Minister of France, who described it as a "movement of citizens, of free men who want to shape their history with their own hands and who refuse the fatality of all dictatorships, of fascism and of collectivism." The Gaullist Union for the New Republic (l'Union des Démocrates pour la République) has been officially dissolved and the bulk of its followers joined the Assembly.

Assembly of Captive European Nations (ACEN). A coalition of political organizations from East European states (e.g., Poland, Lithuania, Latvia, Estonia, Czechoslovakia, Rumania, Hungary, Bulgaria, and Ukraine) which was founded in London, England, after WWII, and which struggled for the liberation of these lands from the communist regimes which were supported there by the Soviet Union. All members of the Assembly maintained token governments in exile and cooperated through various programs (e.g., manifestos, protests, and lobbying with Western governments such as the United States for economic and spiritual support for their people).

Assembly, Right to. See HUMAN RIGHTS: AMERICAN DEFINITION, Appendices 8, 51.

Assertiveness. An act or activity which either the U.S. Congress, the U.S. President, or the U.S. Supreme Court may undertake. It is neither clearly within their specified powers nor clearly forbidden, but is a result of boldness and obvious necessity (e.g., the U.S. Congress may initiate legislation which it deems necessary although the President has not asked for it; the U.S. President may initiate an action by an executive order, just as U.S. President Harry Truman ordered desegregation of American armed forces after W.W.II; the U.S. Supreme Court, under the leadership of Chief Justice John Marshall, asserted the power of judicial review). Such assertiveness may often amount to an aggrandizement of powers of one branch at the expense of another (e.g., the U.S. Supreme Court may rule on an issue pertaining to interstate commerce although the Constitution, in Article I, reserves regulation of interstate and foreign commerce to the Congress). See POLITICAL STYLE, PRESIDENTIAL DECISIVENESS, Appendix 8.

Assessment for the United Nations. A system by which the United Nations Organization receives funds from member nations to finance its administrative apparatus and activities. On December 3, 1977, the General Assembly of the UNadopted a new assessment scale which has considerably raised the assessment for twenty-two highly industrialized nations and reduced it for eighty-five underdeveloped or developing countries. Under the new scale, the U.S. contributes 25 percent of the budget, or approximately 100 million dollars a year. The U.S. has protested this scale (which was approved by a vote of 101 to 1, Singapore being the lone dissenter, and with eleven other nations, including the U.S., abstaining). The United States pointed out that twenty-seven developed countries would pay 89.0 percent of the budget while 120 underdeveloped or developing nations would contribute only 10.96 percent (considering the fact that the underdeveloped and the developing nations gain most from the services rendered by the UN) See UNITED NATIONS ORGANIZATION, Appendices 75, 76, 77, 78, 79.

Assessor. One with expertise in evaluating the current market value of property for taxation purposes.

Asset. Items of certain, commonly recognized and accepted value. In intelligence, a source of information (e.g., an agent or an organization which provides useful information).

Assignee. In the language of law usually found in written wills and contracts, a certain right or benefit is transferred from one person, the assignor, to another, the assignee.

Assignor. See ASSIGNEE.

Association, Freedom of. See HUMAN RIGHTS: AMERICAN DEFINITION, Appendices 8, 51.

Association of Arab American University Graduates. See ARAB LOBBY.

Association of Elder Brothers. See SECRET SOCIETIES.

Aswan Statement. During his January 4, 1978, meeting in Aswan, Egypt with Egypt's President Anwar Sadat, U.S. President Jimmy Carter stated his position on the Arab-Israeli conflict: "We believe that there are certain principles, fundamentally, which must be observed before a just and a comprehensive peace can be achieved. First, true peace must be based on normal relations among the parties to the peace. Peace means more than just an end to belligerency. Second, there must be withdrawal by Israel from territories occupied in 1967 and agreement on secure and recognized borders for all parties in the context of normal and peaceful relations in accordance with U.S. Resolutions 242 and 338. And third, there must be a resolution of the Palestinian problem in all its aspects. The problem must recognize the legitimate rights of the Palestinian people and enable the Palestinians to participate in the determination of their own future." See SADAT-BEGIN SUMMIT.

Asylum, Political. Refuge granted to one who is under the threat of arrest for political reasons.

At Large. The representation of the entire electorate within a specified geographic area rather than just a part of it (e.g., a U.S. Senator representing the entire state rather than a district constituency). See ONE MAN ONE VOTE, REAPPORTIONMENT, Appendix 21.

Atheism. See THEISM.

Athenian Democracy. See COMPULSORY VOTING.

Atlantic Charter. Alarmed by Hitler's military success in Soviet Russia, which he had attacked on June 22, 1941, and cognizant of his *Lebensraum* policy design, England's Prime Minister Winston Churchill and U.S. President Franklin D. Roosevelt met on August 14, 1941, on a British battleship off the coast of Newfoundland to discuss measures against the spread of Nazi domination in Europe (England was under constant threat of attack by the Nazis). They agreed on a declaration of principles which contained eight points: (1) prevention of national aggrandizement; (2) the right of nations to self-determination; (3) encouragement of international trade without restrictions; (4) protection of basic freedoms of individual persons everywhere, including the right to select governments of their choice; (5) restoration of governments abolished by outside aggression (by Nazi Germany and Japan); (6) nonrecognition of territorial conquests; (7) disarmament; and (8) international peace and security under a permanent system of general security—the future United Nations Organization. The Axis powers' reply to this Charter was a Japanese assault on the U.S. Pacific Fleet at Pearl Harbor in Hawaii on December 7, 1941, and Fascist Italy and Nazi Germany declared war on the United States on December 11, 1941. The provisions of the Charter were implemented in large part into the working agenda of the August 21, 1944, Washington Conference on the United Nations. The Soviet Union reluctantly adopted the Charter a year later. See DUMBARTON OAKS CONFERENCE.

Atlantic Partnership. A series of events and documents which forged the partnership between democratic nations of Europe and those of North America, ranging from the VE-Day victory in Europe over the German Nazi forces on 8 May 1945, through the NATO arrangments, the GATT arrangements, and a series of bilateral and multilateral treaties. During the 21-22 March 1992 Camp David summit conference between German Chancellor Helmut Kohl and U.S. President George Bush, the partnership was reaffirmed by the creation of a special German-American Research Institute (also known as Friendship Institute) whose task will be to disseminate information about both nations, about American military presence in Europe, and about joint American-German efforts to maintain democracy in the former Soviet empire. See DEFENSE PLANNING GUIDANCE, EUROPEAN ENERGY CHARTER, WHO LOST CHINA?

Atlantic Wall. The system of fortifications erected by the armed forces of Nazi Germany during W.W.II, stretching from Spain to Denmark. The Wall was, however, broken by the invading Allies who went on to victory over Germany, culminating with Germany's capitulation on 8 May 1945.

Atman. The official title of an elected official among the Mongolian societies in Asia (e.g., the Cossacks).

Atom for Peace Program. U.S. President Dwight D. Eisenhower (1953-1961) introduced the "Atom for Peace Program" in 1954 in order to show the path toward non-proliferation of nuclear weapons that all nations with good intentions to maintain international peace and security could follow. Most of the Western nations signed the document agreeing to abide by its contents.

Atomic Family. A cohesive, tightly held together family group, which includes extended family members, especially the elderly; a family unit where the younger learn from the older and give due respect hierarchically. See DECADENCE.

Atomistic Society. A society in which persons join various organizations or associations for different reasons ("nation of joiners") with many overlapping allegiances and loyalties. See OPEN SOCIETY, SOCIAL MOBILITY.

Atrocious Crime. See TREASON.

Attaché. In the French language, "one assigned to" or "one a part of." Also, a diplomatic representative assigned to a diplomatic mission abroad (e.g., embassy) and charged with a specific responsibility (e.g., military, political, cultural, economic, or concerned with education, labor, or trade). See DIPLOMATIC RANKS.

Attachment. A legal document issued by a court which authorizes its holder to collect certain property or place a lien against it.

Attainder, Bill of. See BILL OF ATTAINDER.

Attentat Clause. A customary rule of international law expecting foreign governments to extradite any person involved in a harmful act against any chief of state or member of his party.

Attorney-at-Law. See ESQUIRE.

Attorney General List. A list of organizations, societies, and associations construed as being subversive, compiled by the U.S. Attorney General for public record. The President must issue a special order before the list can be revealed to the public. See MCCARTHYISM, RED MENACE, Appendix 27.

Attorney General of the United States. The director of the Department of Justice in the U.S., who also holds a seat in the president's cabinet; the head law enforcement officer of the U.S.

Attorney-in-Fact. A lawyer or legal expert, retained and authorized to speak and act as an agent of the retainee through special authorization known as power of attorney. See ATTORNEY OF RECORD.

Attorney of Record. A lawyer or legal expert retained just in case her/his services will be needed in the future or as a matter of prestige and "protection." See ATTORNEY-IN-FACT.

Attrition. The mode of reduction of personnel in business, government, or the military, through gradual processes such as retirement, deaths, resignations, or discharges for a cause, instead of a mass firing or a mass layoff. See WAR OF ATTRITION.

Attrition Warfare. See MILITARY REFORM MOVEMENT, WAR OF ATTRITION.

Auftragstaktik. In the German language, "task-oriented tactics." See COMMAND AND CONTROL.

August 13 Committee. See BERLIN WALL.

August Coup. See STATE COMMITTEE ON THE STATE OF EMERGENCY.

Aunt Thomasina. See UNCLE TOM.

Ausländerhass. See GERMAN UNIFICATION.

Australia-New Zealand-United States Treaty (ANZUS). A mutual defense treaty of 1951. See Appendix 29.

Australian Ballot. A secret ballot used in the election of public officials which is prepared and distributed at the expense of the state. The ballots of different colors contain names of the candidates seeking election and provide for write-in of names of persons not listed. Originated in Australia, the ballot was first used in the U.S. in 1888. Today it is being used in Indiana, where candidates are listed by party column, and in Massachusetts, where candidates are listed by office block.

Autarchy. A state enjoying unlimited sovereignty or that is ruled by one person accountable to no one. See AUTOCRACY.

Autarky. The condition of economic independence and self-sufficiency of a state, or a group of states; a state that has sufficient supply of raw materials and whose economy does not depend on either imports or exports.

Authoritarian. Emphasizing rigor in human interaction, strict efficiency and expediency above anything else and allowing no diversity, opinion, or feedback. Common practice under monarchies and dictatorships.

Authoritarianism. See AUTHORITARIAN.

Authority. In democratic theory, authority is legitimately granted power, exercised to protect the society and the state, or, now, an international order, a "new world order." Historically, authority was acquired by birth, granted by few, or simply taken, usurped; and the ring, the robe, or the seal became the symbol of that authority; likewise, the eagle, a coat of arms, the flag, or sacred objects in religious authority, e.g., the priest's attire, are symbols of authority. In a democratic society, the locus of authority and the means to transfer it to one or many, are described in a constitution, and that constitution, or additional electoral statutes, may build additional filters and obstacles (such as in federalism, confederalism, checks and balances, and separation of powers). The granting of authority thereby becomes a tedious and, by intentional design, a difficult task. This is why nations with short political temperaments have no lasting constitutions and no stable governments. Max Weber in *"Theory of Social and Economic Organization,"* (Oxford University Press) points out that there are three distinctive types of authority noted throughout history; (1) charismatic,—arising from and resting on the personal attributes of the holder; (2) rational-legal—granted by law; and (3) traditional—acquired through long, continuous usage, e.g., the institution of the Pope or that of a monarch. Prof. Burns suggests a third type: "heroic leadership, such as ". . . faith in the leaders' capacity to overcome obstacles and crises," or a belief in a leader because of the leaders' "personage alone." See POWER.

Autocracy. The disposition of sovereign powers by one person or a group without accountability. See AUTARCHY, Appendix 1.

Autonomation. See TOYOTA'S PRODUCTION SYSTEM.

Autonomous Authority and Control. See LIBERAL CONSTITUTION.

Autonomous Elite. A group of persons under a liberal system of government pursuing some common objectives which are not detrimental to the politically organized society at large (e.g., religious, educational, or economic enterprises). See LIBERAL CONSTITUTION, LIBERALISM.

Autonomous Region. A self-governing political subdivision of homogeneous peoples in the former USSR, smaller than an Autonomous Republic but larger than a National Area. There were eight such regions in the USSR. Each region elected its own local government and was entitled to five deputies in the House of Nationalities of the Supreme Soviet (Parliament) of the USSR.

Autonomous Republic. A self-governing republic of homogeneous peoples within a Union Republic in the former USSR. There were twenty such republics in the USSR. Each republic elected its own government and was entitled to eleven deputies in the House of Nationalities of the Supreme Soviet (Parliament) of the USSR. See Appendix 74.

Autonomy. Conditional or limited independence, based on law or custom, and subject to change by the authority which grants it (e.g., the local governments in relation to state governments in the United States).

Autosuccession. An electoral system under which one can succeed oneself to the same office for another term. The U.S. President, for example, is limited to two terms (U.S. Constitution, Amendment XXII), and most state governors in the United States may not succeed themselves. One may, however, wait out one term, then run again.

Axis. An alliance among two or more states. Also, the military, trade, and anti-communist Comintern alliance between Nazi Germany (under Adolf Hitler) and Fascist Italy (under Benito Mussolini). The alliance was extended in 1941 to include militaristic Japan (under Emperor Hirohito) and extended later again to other pro-Nazi and pro-Fascist states such as Croatia, Vichy France, Romania, and Slovakia. See LEBENSRAUM, TRIPARTITE PACT OF BERLIN.

Ayatollah. The highest rank among the priests (mullahs) of the Shiite Moslem faith, which prevails in Iran. See IRAN'S REVOLUTION, MOSSADEGH LEGACY, SHAH, SHIITE DISSIMULATION, WHITE REVOLUTION.

"I sit on a man's back, choking him and making him carry me, and yet assure myself and others that I am very sorry for him and wish to ease his lot by all possible means—except by getting off his back."

LEO TOLSTOY, 1828-1910

Baath Socialist Party. In the Arabic language, "Hizb al-Baath al-Arabi al-Ishtiraki"; the ruling party of contemporary Iraq under the leadership of President Saddam Hussein Takritti. The Baath party is an offshoot of the Arab nationalist movement in the Arab countries, particularly in Syria, which originated during the 1930s. To a limited degree, two other parties are allowed to exist in Iraq: the Iraqi Communist Party (in the Arabic language, "Al-Hizb es-Shyu'i al-Iraqi"), mainly because of close rapprochement with the former Soviet Union; and the Democratic Party of Kurdistan (in the Arabic language, "Al-Hizb ad-Dimuqraati al-Kurid"). In 1972, the leader of the Kurds, General Mulla Mustafa al-Barzani, established from the remnants of the DPK the Kurdistan Revolutionary party and moved in 1975 to Iran. See KURDISH UPRISINGS.

Baby Boom Power. See BOOMER POWER.

Back to Africa Movement. Marcus Garvey, a black leader, organized an intensive campaign in 1919-1921 in the United States, aiming at a mass emigration of black Americans back to Africa, where, in his opinion, blacks would have a better opportunity to enjoy their political and civil rights. Only several thousand actually left for Africa and many of them returned to the United States upon finding that politically organized African communities were not particularly anxious to accept them. The "Back to Africa" movement was patterned after the recolonization movement during the Administration of President James Monroe (1817-1825), when several thousand freedmen left the United States in 1822 and, on July 26, 1847, officially proclaimed the Republic of Liberia on the Southwest coast of West Africa. The Republic established a constitutional government very much like that of the United States and also established a capital city, Monrovia, named after President Monroe.

Back to the Land Movement. See HUNGER WARS, YEAR ZERO.

Backlash. A term commonly used to describe social, economic, cultural, or political actions which deny or limit the rights and privileges of a racial, religious, ethnic, or political minority within a society. Also the negative reaction to the assertion of such rights and privileges.

Backroom Crowd. Informal advisers and supporters of a politician or a political group or party who gather to help design strategy and organize support for election day. Also known as "kitchen cabinet." See KITCHEN CABINET.

Backyard Industrialization. Mao Tse-tung, Chairman of the Communist Party of the People's Republic of China and of the Chinese State, when deprived of foreign capital and technological know-how, decided to develop China's economy through "backyard industrialization" (e.g., by having peasants produce pig iron in their backyards) in what became known as the Great Leap Forward period. China, like the Soviet Union during its formative years (e.g., the period of the War Communism and the NEP), when it was isolated from the West and surrounded by hostile states, rebuilt its economy through internal domestic efforts without outside assistance. See ENCIRCLEMENT, GREAT LEAP FORWARD, MAOISM.

Bacon Rebellion. See CAVALIER.

Bacteriological Warfare. See CHEMICAL WARFARE.

Bad Tendency Test. In American judicial practice, a court of law may prohibit a certain activity (e.g., freedom to speak on a certain issue or at a given time and place, such as shouting "fire" in a crowded theatre) if, in the opinion of the court, that activity or practice may cause some harm to someone in the future, or might be generally detrimental to the society at large. See Appendix 48.

Badger Game. The practice in electoral politics of discovering some incriminating evidence against a political aspirant for public office and using it to discredit her/his character and reputation so as to cause voter apathy or resentment toward the candidate. Sex is the weapon commonly used. See CHARACTER ASSASSINATION, KISS AND TELL FOR SALE, SEXPIONAGE.

Bag Man. See ANGEL.

Baghdad Pact. See CENTRAL TREATY ORGANIZATION (CENTO), MIDDLE EAST TREATY ORGANIZATION (METO), Appendix 29.

Bail. Sum of money posted by persons accused of criminal acts as a condition to pre-trial release. The constitution specifies (Amendment 8) that bail shall not be excessive.

Bailiff. Minor official who executes writs, assists the court during its proceedings, and maintains order.

Baker Affair. Robert G. "Bobby" Baker, once a secretary to Lyndon Baines Johnson, when Johnson served as the Democratic leader in the U.S. Senate during the 1960s, and Johnson's protégé ever since he started as a page boy in the U.S. House of Representatives, was convicted in December 1970 and sentenced to a three-year prison term for grand larceny, fraud, conspiracy, and attempted tax evasion. This embarrassed Johnson, who had attempted to intercede with federal agencies on behalf of Baker. This intercession led the press to refer to the White House as a "Whitewash House." Baker had risen from poverty to wealth in a relatively short time with the aid of his mentor and protector, Lyndon B. Johnson. His holdings included several motels, one of them the exclusive Carousel Inn in the resort city of Ocean City, Maryland, as well as several townhouses in Washington, D.C., some of which were occupied by his "cousins," as he called his female companions.

Bakke Case. See REVERSE DISCRIMINATION.

Baladiyah. An administrative division, a municipality, in Bahrain.

Balance of Payments. The practice of period accounting for all purchases and sales (e.g., imports, exports, fees, loans, debts and grants) transacted between two states. A state which purchases more than it sells will have an unfavorable, deficit balance of payments and, vice versa, a state with more sales and less purchases has a favorable, or surplus balance of payments. Similar accounting applies to the balance of trade. If imports exceed exports, the importing economy will be weakened by such an unfavorable, deficit balance of trade. During the two terms of the Reagan administration (1981-1989) the deficit rose to $152.1 billion in 1987, and President George Bush inherited a deficit of $118.5 billion. This deficit was reduced by 1991 to $66.2 billion.

Balance of Power. A traditional concept of international relations which asserts that peace among nations rests upon a delicate international equilibrium, or international distribution of power, and that whenever one state (or group of states) becomes too strong and powerful (which could potentially upset that balance), other states are duty bound to diminish the power and the influence of that state (or states) by any means possible, including war. See BIPOLARITY.

Balance of Terror. A concept prevalent among some students of contemporary world (global or international) politics to the effect that the international balance of powers rested on the notion that the two major superpowers, the former Soviet Union and the United States, both had at their disposal sufficient arsenals of modern weapons capable of exterminating each other several times over (overkill) if either of them decided to upset the balance. See STRATEGIC ARMS REDUCTION TALKS (STAR).

Balance of Trade. See BALANCE OF PAYMENTS.

Balanced Budget Act. Per U.S. Congressional Budget Office, "Common shorthand for the Balanced Budget and Emergency Deficit Control Act of 1985, also known as Gramm-Rudman-Hollings. The act sets forth specific deficit targets and a sequestration procedure to reduce spending if the targets are exceeded. The Budget Enforcement Act of 1990 established a revised set of targets through fiscal year 1995, which excludes the Social Security trust funds. The President is required to adjust the deficit targets for revised economic and technical assumptions when submitting the budget for 1993, and has that option for the budgets of fiscal years 1994 and 1995."

Balanced Budget and Emergency Deficit Control Act of 1985. See ZIGZAG MAN.

Balanced Delegation. The National Committees of the Democratic and the Republican parties in the United States require their state committees to select delegates to national party conventions (every four years for the purpose of nominating candidates for the President and the Vice President) by many criteria. These include a balance in age (young and old), gender, (men and women), race and ethnic origin (Black, Hispanic, Asian, and others), vocation, and education, as well as geographic factors and religion.

Balanced Ticket. It is viewed as a democratic practice in electoral politics, to distribute representation as much as possible horizontally; that is, to represent on a ticket most if not all voters in a given constituency (e.g., a city, county, state, or nation). Geographic balancing of representation is commonly practiced in international and global organizations (e.g., the United Nations); it is believed that not all elected representatives, elected particularly from a single party, should be from certain clusters. It is also believed that a ticket should be balanced vertically; that is, it should reflect different ethnic groups, genders, professions, and political and social philosophies. In presidential politics in the United States, the running mate of the president, the vice president, is always selected from another geographic area; he also often has minor differences in political philosophy, religion, or professional background life. See ELECTABILITY.

Balfour Declaration. Arthur James Balfour, British Prime Minister (1902-1905) and Foreign Secretary, made a promise, on 2 November 1917, on behalf of the British government, to the Jews in Palestine (who were constantly attacked by the Arabs and had to be defended by the British) that Palestine would be their homeland under a British protectorate. In 1948, the British were expelled and the protectorate ended; the United States was the first foreign power to recognize Israel as a sovereign state, on the personal direction of U.S. President Harry S. Truman (1945-1951).

Balkanization. A state of persistent disunity, hostility, mutual mistrust and dislike between states, marked by hostile acts and activities by one state against another. The term originated during the lengthy and exhausting Balkan Wars between Serbia, Macedonia and the territories belonging to the Montenegrean Kingdom—all later constituting the Federal State of Yugoslavia. The Balkan states fought not only among themselves but also often joined together to challenge the ancient Ottoman Empire (also known as the "Sick Man of Europe" which was established in 1290 by Osman I, and which consisted of present-day Turkey, Yugoslavia, Bulgaria, Albania, Greece, parts of Austria and Rumania). The Ottoman Empire, which collapsed during W.W.I, and particularly the parts of present-day Yugoslavia and Bulgaria, which consisted of many small kingdoms, have been constantly involved in mutual aggression, acts of verbal abuse, chicanery, dissent, division, mistrust, and suspicion. Also applied to describe the situation in dissolved Yugoslav federation of 1991.

Ballot. An instrument used to record one's preference in voting. Ballots can be written; or mechanical (e.g., a voting machine); or, in the future, electronic—voting via computer. See AUSTRALIAN BALLOT, BALLOTA.

Ballot, Nonpartisan. See NONPARTISAN BALLOT.

Ballot, Short. See SHORT BALLOT.

Ballota. In the Italian language, a "little ball." A device once used to cast a vote, hence the term "ballot." See VOTING.

Bamboo Curtain. A term used to epitomize the iron-clad control over the movement of persons, goods, and ideas between the communist states of Asia (People's Republic of China, North Korea and, since 1975, Cambodia and Vietnam) and the West.

Banana Bunch. A term used by U.S. President Theodore Roosevelt (1901-1909) to describe Latin Americans, particularly Cubans, during and after the Cuban-American-Spanish War of 1898, especially during the years of 1906-1909 when Cuba was under U.S. occupation. See BIG STICK POLICY.

Banana Republics. A term for several small Latin American countries, whose economies are based on agriculture, especially bananas.

Bandwagon. The practice of giving support to one (usually a political candidate during an election) who seems to be winning, regardless of one's political philosophy. Also, a term used to characterize a pragmatic approach to practical politics. See POLITICS, POLITICAL PARTY.

Bantustan. A self-governing homogeneous district of non-white peoples within the apartheid system of the Republic of South Africa. Also known as "homeland." See APARTHEID, PARALLEL DEVELOPMENT DOCTRINE.

Barbarossa. The codename of Hitler's operational plan of attack on the Soviet Union during World War II.

Barbary Pirates. The gangs of pirates from Algiers, Morocco, Tripoli, and Tunis, under the leadership of Khair ud-Din, Berber chief and pirate, which were liquidated on orders of President Thomas Jefferson after they had harassed American vessels. President Jefferson requested, and on February 6, 1802, Congress passed a law authorizing the deployment of U.S. military forces (for the first time in U.S. history) in Tripoli "for the protection of commerce and seamen"; (it was not a declaration of war). The Barbary Pirates were defeated by the U.S. Navy and a peace treaty was signed in Tripoli on June 4, 1805.

Bargaining. A process of interaction whereby individuals or groups (e.g., states as agents in international relations) use certain techniques in order to influence each other and to achieve certain desired objectives. Some of the major techniques are: (1) persuasion, (2) offer of reward, (3) the actual granting of a reward, (4) threat of punishment (e.g., by ordering a mobilization or concentration of forces near a border), (5) the actual infliction of a mild punishment as a retaliatory measure (e.g., breaking off trade or diplomatic relations), and (6) the actual use of force (e.g., armed attack).

Barnhopping. See BARNSTORMING.

Barnstorming. A term commonly applied to politicians who travel extensively among constituencies seeking their support and/or vote, and particularly to presidential candidates during their campaigns or while in office. U.S. President Dwight D. Eisenhower (1953-1961) was the first U.S. President to barnstorm on an extensive scale, both at home and abroad. Taking advantage of technologically advanced aircraft (the U.S. President has at his disposal several aircraft and helicopters, but his official aircraft is "Air Force One," and the Vice President uses "Air Force Two"—both stationed at Andrews Air Force Base in Maryland just outside Washington, D.C.), President Eisenhower started his first major barnstorming trip in December 1959, when he visited eleven nations in seven days and covered 18,500 miles—a record. The term "barnhopping" is also used. See WHEN IN TROUBLE, TRAVEL; WHISTLE STOPPING.

Barrio. In Spanish speaking countries, a ghetto; or a ghetto of Spanish speaking people in large cities in the U.S.

Barrister. See ESQUIRE.

Barshchina. Compulsory labor rendered by a serf to his master in Tsarist Russia.

Baruch Plan. An early attempt to introduce international disarmament, with inspections and controls, which never materialized due to systematic opposition by the Soviet Union. The Plan was proposed by Bernard Baruch, American diplomat, after the Second World War.

Base Community. See LIBERATION THEOLOGY.

Base, Economic. See ECONOMIC BASE OF SOCIETY.

Base Force. See UNIPOLARITY.

Baseline. Per U.S. Congressional Budget Office, "A benchmark for measuring the budgetary effects of proposed changes in federal revenues or spending with the assumption that current budgetary policies are continued without change. As specified in the Budget Enforcement Act of 1990, the baseline for revenues and entitlement spending generally assumes that laws now on the statute books will continue. For discretionary spending, the projections for fiscal year 1993 are based on the appropriations for fiscal year 1992, adjusted for inflation. In this report, however, the discretionary spending projections for 1993 through 1995 are based on the discretionary spending caps set by the act and are adjusted for inflation thereafter."

Bashing Campaign. The practice of criticizing opponents, especially criticism of trade policies and practices by nations which suffer disproportionate trade deficits in trade with nations that achieve trade surplus. See AMERICA BASHING, JAPAN BASHING.

Basic Law. Under the American multiple system of laws (e.g., federal, state, and local), state law is the basic law for the states. Also, the name of the 1949 Constitution of the Federal Republic of Germany. See NEGATIVE REVOLUTION, SUPREME LAW OF THE LAND.

Basket Three. See DÉTENTE WITH A HUMAN FACE.

Basketball Diplomacy. See PING-PONG DIPLOMACY.

Bastion of Democracy. See ARSENAL OF DEMOCRACY.

Batakusai. In the Japanese language, "smelling like butter," a term used to describe persons of Japanese ancestry who have lost contact with Japan, or have abandoned or neglected Japanese culture and mores. The term is particularly applicable to one who has been assimilated into Western culture. It is not unusual for a Japanese who has spent some time in the West, particularly in America, and demonstrates Western influence while in Japan, to be ostracized by Japanese society.

Battleground States. As pertains to presidential politics in the United States, states which hold presidential preferential primary elections. Data from past elections indicates, that if a presidential candidate wins in that primary he will most likely win in the national election, or, at least, people will think that this will be the case and vote for him. No candidate enters such primaries unless he or she has some tangible advance intelligence (information, which is usually derived and generalized through a variety of pre-primary polls) that a victory is possible; otherwise, losing such a primary can be construed as meaning that a given candidate is not a vote-getter and his or her popularity will decline. Sometimes a popular Republican candidate will enter such a primary in a Democratic state where victory will enhance his or her popularity and Democratic candidates do the same by entering primaries in Republican states. Also, states with a large block of electoral votes which every presidential aspirant strives to win to his or her side in order to become elected. See Appendix 21.

Bay of Pigs. The abortive invasion of Castro's Cuba by Cuban exiles (April 17-21, 1961), code named "Mongoose," which failed due to lack of support from the U.S. Government although the U.S. Central Intelligence Agency (CIA) had sponsored the excursion in secrecy since 1959 when Fidel Castro took power, nationalized foreign interests, closed American-owned gambling casinos, eliminated prostitution, and declared himself "Marxist-Leninist." President Eisenhower approved of the preparations for the elimination of Castro, but his successor, John F. Kennedy (1961-1963) was reluctant. About 2,000 Cuban patriots perished in the attack. The actual attack on Cuba was code-named "Zapata Plan." See MONGOOSE.

Bazaar Economy. In 1978, approximately twenty percent of all the working capital in Iran's economy came from the "Bazaaris," the operators of the bazaars; they are the source of an easy credit; most of the bazaaris are Shiite Moslems from whom Ayatollah Khomeni drew strong support for his struggle against the Shah. The bazaars are also a center of politics, religion and education (some bazaars have libraries well stacked with Islamic literature) and are the operating base of the mullahs (most bazaars display the likeness of Ali, the saint of the Shiite Moslems). The Shah's attempt, through his White Revolution, to weaken the power of the bazaari, was one of the main sources of his troubles. See MOSSADEGH, WHITE REVOLUTION.

Bazaari. See BAAZAR ECONOMY.

Beachhead. A military stronghold established by hostile forces on the territory of a state (e.g., through approach from the sea or river) for invasion purposes.

Bean Counter. An accountant or a financial officer in an organization; one responsible for gathering and controlling financial assets or funds.

Bears and Bulls. In the language of high finance (e.g., trading on a stock market) the "bears" signify the cautious, while the "bulls", the brave and daring, the risk-takers.

Bedroom Community. A community of persons who work under one jurisdiction (e.g., in a city) but reside under another (e.g., in a suburban area) and pay their taxes to the government under whose jurisdiction they claim their domicile. See URBANIZATION.

Begin-Sadat Summit. See SADAT-BEGIN SUMMIT.

Behavior Control Program. According to press reports, the Central Intelligence Agency (CIA) experimented during the 1950s with several drugs, including LSD, in order to determine how they affect the human mind, especially if they can alter memory—causing one to forget knowledge stored in the brain; and how if the drugs could be used to extract information from spies. The "Experiments on Behavior Control" proved catastrophic to Dr. Frank Olson, a civilian scientist working for the Army's drug experimental center in Maryland, when on 19 November 1953, he took an overdose of LSD and ten days later, in a high stage of depression caused by the drug, plunged to his death from a hotel room in New York City. (His wife sued the Army and received $10 million compensation.) The "truth" drug was allegedly a serum which allowed information to be extracted subconsciously from persons. The behavior control program also called for the drug to be administered to all employees of the CIA who were retiring or resigning, in order to relieve them of knowledge, confidential and secret, stored in their minds.

Behaviorism. A doctrine which claims that observed behavior provides the only valid data of psychology and denies the usefulness of introspective psychology. The term "Behavior" includes all observable actions, ranging from violent physical activity to highly abstract speech.

Behaviorist Political Theory. See POLITICAL THEORY.

Behind-the-Scene Power. A term commonly used to denote persons who do not hold elective or appointive positions of power, either in public or in private life, but who nevertheless possess all the necessary attributes to exert political influence. These persons, due to wealth, friendship, or family ties with others who are in or have access to centers where power is generated and allocated, are able to influence private and public decision makers, and simply get things done. Such behind-the-scenes power is often attributed to wealthy and influential hostesses in high political circles (e.g., in Washington, D.C., Bonn, Paris, London, Tokyo, Peking, or Moscow) who can bring important people together and, through such informal interaction, influence policy decisions and outcomes. They are also known as "fixers," because they can often "fix" things which otherwise would not be fixable through ordinary processes. If the ancient dictum that most human concerns involve sex and money is correct, then the informal setting in a cozy environment at a reception or any social gathering certainly perpetuates that myth (or reality). One of the most influential, most powerful and popular hostesses in Washington, D.C., was Perle Mesta (known as the "hostess, with the mostest"). See SEXPIONAGE, SEXPOLITICS.

Beijing Spring. See TIANANMEN SQUARE MASSACRE.

Beirut of American Politics. The state of Michigan, situated within the rust-belt, smoke-stack region, has suffered political problems resulting from the losses sustained by its traditional heavy industries. Growing layoffs and unemployment impose burdens on local political subdivisions; they must provide the basic services to communities such as water, sewer systems, roads, fire protection, and schools, but the tax base from which the revenue is expected is shrinking because of economic disruption and dislocation.

Belgrade Conference. See DÉTENTE WITH A HUMAN FACE.

Belgrade Conference on Human Rights. See STRATEGIC ARMS LIMITATION TALKS (SALT).

Belgrade Document. Adopted by the Special Committee of 24 on the Decolonization of Zimbabwe and Namibia. It called on the Security Council for further sanctions against Southern Rhodesia and comprehensive sanctions against South Africa in view of continued illegal occupation and domination of those territories by the racist regimes of Salisbury and Pretoria.

Belligerent. A warring or hostile person or government of a state is described this way.

Bellum Justium. In the Latin language, "a just war." Also, a principle in international law allowing one state to initiate war against another as a punishment or a sanction for some violation of some norm of international law, or as a measure of self-help. The traditional notion was that any sovereign state, by virtue of being sovereign, could initiate war for any reason it chooses. Under the United Nations Charter, however, any kind of war, preventive, retaliatory, or preemptive, can be initiated only upon the consent of the United Nations Security Council. See OVERT ACT, WAR, Appendix 75.

Beltway Bandits. A derogatory term commonly applied to a large variety of business warriors, public relations firms, lobbyists, contracting firms, think-tanks, foundations, and all sorts of do-gooders— some searching for new enemies if there are none, especially after the dissolution of the Soviet Union. Creating enemies is often more profitable than creating friends! They are located in the suburbs surrounding Washington, D.C., in the northern part of Virginia along the Washington Beltway (I-495) which surrounds the American nation's capital. These groups lobby for lucrative government contracts and mobilize to influence the legislation of Congress and the policies of the President's large bureaucracy. The most lucrative contracts are those awarded for defense. Many represent private, non-government interests; some offer various services to foreign nations, especially to those in the former Soviet Empire, ranging from teaching democratic government systems and techniques, to market economy, to restructuring the entire societies on the only model they know, the American.

Beltway Warriors. See BELTWAY BANDITS.

Benelux. A customs union of 1944 between Belgium, the Netherlands (Holland), and Luxemburg.

Benevolent Dictator. See ENLIGHTENED DESPOT.

Benevolent Domination. See UNIPOLARITY.

Benign Neglect. Phrase coined by an English Parliamentarian, the Earl of Durham, in 1839, in a report on Canada to the British Parliament in which he stated that "through many years of benign neglect by Britain, Canada had become a nation much more prosperous than England itself," and recommended that the Dominion of Canada be granted full self-government. The phrase was used again by Daniel Patrick Moynihan, special counselor to U.S. President Richard M. Nixon (1969-1974) in 1970, in a memorandum on January 16, 1970, to the President on the "Negro situation in the United States" (during the height of the "Black Revolution"). In it, he stated that the Negroes have made "extraordinary progress" and hinted that "the time may have come when the issue of race could benefit from a period of "benign neglect" because of a "virulent form of anti-white feeling" throughout the "black lower classes" and portions of the "large and prospering black middle class," and suggested instead that more attention be given, not to "extremists of either race" (including the Black Panthers), but to the "silent black majority." The memorandum was considered by black leaders as a reflection of Nixon's philosophy of "Southern Strategy" which during the 1968 presidential election meant that no attempt was really made to seek support from black voters, especially in the South. See SOUTHERN MANIFESTO.

Bequest. That which is left to one through a will (e.g., real or personal property).

Berg Report. See LAGOS PLAN OF ACTION.

Berlin Airlift. See BERLIN BLOCKADE.

Berlin Blockade. The act of blocking off all land access to the Western Sectors (American, British, and French) of the city of Berlin by the Soviet Military Government at the height of the "Cold War" (between April 1, 1948, and September 30, 1949). In order to avoid military conflict with the Soviets, the Allies used their massive aircraft fleets to ship the necessary supplies to that city of over two million people. See BERLIN WALL, COLD WAR.

Berlin Conference. See WEST AFRICAN CONFERENCE OF BERLIN.

Berlin Solution. The plan to assassinate Adolf Hitler, Nazi leader of Germany (1933-1945) by anti-Nazi groups. See SCHWARZE KAPELLE.

Berlin Treaty. See RAPALLO TREATY.

Berlin Wall. On August 13-14, 1961, the government of the German Democratic Republic (East Germany), with the aid of its army and its Soviet ally, erected a high wall along the border dividing the Eastern sectors of Berlin from the Western sectors. (At the end of World War II, the city of Berlin had been divided into four sectors and the German state into four zones of occupation by the victorious allies: England, France, the United States, and the Soviet Union.) East Germany wanted to halt the mass exodus of persons from East Germany into West Germany via Berlin (e.g., by 1977 approximately 500,000 persons, mostly highly-skilled professionals badly needed in East Germany to rebuild the devastated economy, had fled to the West). The East Germans, assisted by the Soviets, succeeded in this project because the international situation caused some relaxation of tensions between the Soviets and the Americans: (1) Konrad Adenauer, the strong, anti-communist Chancellor (Kanzler) of the German Federal Republic (the West German state that was established within the British, French, and American zones of occupation) lost majority support in the 1961 election for the Bundestag (the West German lower house of parliament); (2) U.S. President John F. Kennedy shifted from the policy of massive retaliation (massive war against the Soviet Union in case of a provocation, a policy which had been held by the Eisenhower Administration and particularly by his Secretary of State, John F. Dulles) to the policy of flexible response (e.g., to prosecute aggression only where it really occurs, without massive attack on the Soviet Union and its satellite states in Eastern Europe), and sought accommodation rather than confrontation with the Soviet Bloc; (3) the abortive "Bay of Pigs" invasion of April 17, of the same year, 1961, made the East Germans and the Soviets believe that the United States was not anxious to go to an all-out war purely for ideological reasons (e.g., to contain the spread of communism); and (4) the much-talked about and highly-desired unification of both Germanys, East and West, appeared to be more remote and of lesser concern to the Western allies (including the Common Market states of Europe who feared a new economic competitor from the East if unification took place and that a united Germany would become the major power in Europe). The Wall appeared to be a successful measure for stopping the brain-drain from East Germany and allowed the communist state to consolidate its power in spite of protests from the West that the wall was illegal according to allied agreements. President Kennedy visited Berlin shortly after the wall was erected in order to encourage West Berliners to remain in the city, but, although he told them in 1962 that he, too, was a Berliner ("Ich bin ein Berliner"), many young West Berliners abandoned the city and moved West, fearing that the allied protection of the city would not last. The August 13 Committee, a civil rights group named for the date on which the Berlin Wall was erected, encouraged East Berliners to come to the West via any means possible, usually through third countries. (In 1977 only a little over 4,000 East Berliners and East Germans were able to flee to the West, usually through third countries.) The Wall was opened in November 1989. See BERLIN AIRLIFT, FLIGHT FROM THE REPUBLIC.

Besser Wessi. See GERMAN UNIFICATION.

Better Dead than Red. See RED OR DEAD.

Beyond the Shadow of a Doubt. See PRESUMED INNOCENT UNTIL PROVEN GUILTY.

Bezbozhnik. In the Russian language, "one not believing in God." In Tsarist Russia, non-believers were treated on par with enemies of the state while under Soviet rule the situation has been practically reversed. Article 124 of the Stalin Constitution stated that: "In order to ensure the citizens freedom of conscience, the Church in the U.S.S.R. is separated from the state, and the school from the church. Freedom of religious worship and freedom of antireligious propaganda is recognized for all citizens." Religious freedom was restored in December 1991 after the dissolution of the USSR.

Bezirk. In the German language, "district," or "region." Also, either a small political subdivision in a large city or a larger subdivision in rural areas. Often the entire state may be divided into such districts, e.g., the "Regierungsbezirke" ("government districts") in the Federal Republic of Germany (West Germany).

BFV. Bundesamt für Verfassungsschutz. See FEDERAL OFFICE FOR THE PROTECTION OF THE CONSTITUTION.

BG/BHE. See GERMAN BLOC/ASSOCIATION OF THE EXPELLED AND DISENFRANCHISED, SPECIAL INTEREST-TYPE POLITICAL PARTY.

Bharatya Janata Party. See HINDU BHARATYA JANATA PARTY.

Bible Belt. See SECTIONALISM.

Bicameral Legislature. A legislative body that is composed of two separate chambers or houses (e.g., all state legislative bodies in the United States, with the exception of Nebraska, which is the only state with unicameral legislature; the United States Congress which is composed of the House of Representatives and the Senate; the House of Commons and the House of Lords in England; the House of the Union and the House of Nationalities in the former Soviet Union; the House of Representatives and House of Councillors in Japan; and the Bundestag and the Bundesrat in the Federal Republic of Germany, to mention only a few).

Biennium. A period of two years (e.g., some state legislatures in the United States meet only once every two years; the United States Congress appropriates money for a two-year period only).

Bifurcated Session. A session of a state legislature in the United States which meets for two separate periods during a single session. The first period, lasting approximately one month, is devoted to procedural and housekeeping matters such as introduction and recording of bills and the passage of very urgent legislation, or committee assignments. The second period is devoted entirely to deliberations and voting upon legislation introduced during the first period. See BICAMERAL LEGISLATURE, BIENNIUM.

Big City Politics. See WARD.

Big Five. See BIG THREE.

Big Four. See BIG THREE.

Big Lie. A term commonly associated with the practice by sovereign states (particularly in the area of international politics and diplomacy) of purposely distorting or falsifying factual information or of simply inventing falsehoods and, by using the authority of the state, making them appear credible. Such practices are designed to achieve some desired objective (e.g., to justify certain acts or activities already committed or contemplated for the future, to mobilize domestic or foreign support, or simply to influence the writing of history). Some such major lies in history were: (1) the decision of Nazi Germany to attack Poland was not made, as "official" German documents indicate, upon the conclusion of the Nazi-Soviet pact of August 23, 1939, but in May of the same year, prior to the conclusion of this pact; (2) in order to justify his bid for power and to discredit the communists, Adolf Hitler accused the communists in Germany of burning his Reichstag (parliament); and (3) the extermination of the Jews by the Nazis was justified on the grounds that the Jews were communists and that they also controlled Josef Stalin, the leader of Soviet Russia, Winston Churchill, the leader of England, and Franklin Roosevelt, the leader of the United States, and therefore, war against these nations was also justifiable.

Big Mouth and Small Minds. According to Professor Thomas Sowell, one of America's accomplished economists and political and social commentators, many events on the local, national and international scene are often presented to the American public by some reporters and politicians in questionable accuracy and often with great distortion of the actual facts and exaggeration. For example, a riot becomes an uprising, an uprising a revolution, and a revolution a global war; violent acts by few of a certain race or ethnicity is ascribed to of the people falling into that category. There is lack of restraint on the part of such exaggerators due to poor education, limited knowledge of events on which they comment, or simply the result of one's ulterior agenda.

Big Stick Policy. A term often applied to the manner of conducting international relations whereby a state may sometimes find it necessary and expedient to resort to high-handed, authoritarian tactics (particularly with weaker states) in order to protect its own vital interests. The phrase, "speak softly and carry a big stick, you will go far," was taken from one of Roosevelt's speeches made in 1912 in which he characterized his relations with the New York Republican leaders, mainly Thomas Platt. Platt opposed him in his bid for the Presidency on the Bull Moose ticket, as well as in his unique political style in dealing with foreign nations. (Wallace Irwin characterized that policy, in his "Ballad of Grizzly Gulch," as follows: "The constitution rides behind/and the Big Stick rides before,/Which is the rule of precedent/In the reign of Theodore.") See AMERICA'S NEW NATIONALISM, NATIONAL PROGRESSIVE PARTY, NEW FREEDOM, PANAMA CANAL TREATIES, STEWARD OF THE PEOPLE, WHITE MAN'S BURDEN.

Big Three. The alliance among the three major powers during W.W.II (the United States, the Soviet Union, and the United Kingdom) which concentrated its efforts on the European theatre of war against Nazi Germany and its allies. The alliance also included China when issues of the Pacific theatre of war, particularly against militaristic Japan, were involved. Thus, the alliance was referred to as the "Big Four." The term "Big Five" was applied when France joined the alliance in 1944. See CAIRO CONFERENCE, DUMBARTON OAKS CONFERENCE, POTSDAM CONFERENCE.

Bigger Bang for the Dollar. Term used in the Committees on Appropriations of the United States Congress, particularly the Armed Services Committees, where the legislators bargain among themselves within a single party, or among the members of both parties (Democrats and Republicans) on the one hand, and the lobbies which represent the "death merchants," the producers of weapons and war materiel on the other, for getting the most firepower for the minimum of expenditure of the taxpayers' money. Obviously, this is not a favorite notion among the lobbyists and the armament producers—often called the "death merchants."

Bilateral. By or of two parties, or between two states or governments (e.g., bilateral treaty or conference). See TREATY.

Bill. The text of a proposed law before its enactment. According to the U.S. House of Representatives Manual of 1871 (as amended), bills (whether permanent—which subsequently become the law of the land; temporary—those that expire after the designated period of time; general—those that deal with broad national issues; special—those that deal with unique and very specific matters; private—those that pertain to specific problems of individuals or groups and public—those that are requested by and pertain to the policies of the government) may be introduced in either the House of Representatives or the Senate (except that bills pertaining to constitutional amendments, revenue and appropriations must originate in the House). House-originated bills will carry designation "H.R.", meaning House of Representatives; and Senate-originated bills will carry designation "S," meaning the Senate; then follows the number of the bill. A bill becomes the law of the land after: (1) both Houses agree on its text; (2) the U.S. President signs it; (3) the U.S. President fails within ten days while Congress is in session to return the bill with specific objections to the House in which the bill originated. The President may not veto any particular part of a bill (item veto), but must accept the entire bill or reject the entire bill, although there may be only a certain part in a bill that is not acceptable to him; (4) both Houses of Congress override a presidential veto by a two-thirds vote in each House. (If Congress is not in session, a bill opposed by the President simply dies—pocket veto.) A bill must be properly communicated (announced) to the people as "public law" ("P.L." and a number and the number of the Congress which adopted it), otherwise the enforcement of an unannounced law would make it an *ex post facto* law. Bills signed by the President are sent to the administrator of the General Services Administration for publication in the *Congressional Record,* while bills rejected by the President, but re-enacted over his objection (veto) are published in *United States Statutes at Large,* which contains bills of each session of Congress. The first publication of a bill is in the form of an unbound pamphlet; it subsequently will be included in its final form in the *United States Reports (U.S.).* See FEDERAL LEVEL in Appendix 48, 49, JOINT RESOLUTION, LEGISLATIVE PROCESS IN THE UNITED STATES.

Bill of Attainder. A statutory law or decree which provides for the punishment of persons accused of a crime without the benefit of a proper hearing and trial in an open court (or trial by an impartial jury). Such bills are prohibited in the United States under the provisions of Article I, Sections 9 and 10 of the U.S. Constitution. See Appendix 8.

Bill of Particulars. Those additional facts and information of a definite nature which may be required in judicial proceedings for the purpose of clarifying the issue at hand.

Bill of Rights. Commonly, a constitutional or statutory document containing certain enumerated rights of persons which are subject to protection by the authority of the state. (In the United States, the first ten amendments to the U.S. Constitution). The American Bill of Rights, though an integral part of the Constitution, was originally not a part of the text but was introduced later as a result of compromise between the Federalists (who favored the original text only) and the Anti-Federalists (who insisted on the Bill of Rights).

BINGO. See MULTINATIONAL CORPORATION.

Bipartisanship. A term implying close cooperation between the political parties under a two-party system whenever important national issues are involved.

Bipartyism. A political system in which two main political parties dominate the political life of a state, e.g., the Democratic and the Republican parties in the United States; the Labour and the Conservative parties in England; the Christian Democratic Union (CDU) and the Social-Democratic Party (SDP) in the Federal Republic of Germany; or the Liberal and the Progressive Conservative parties in Canada.

Bipolarity. A view prevalent among many students of politics (e.g., as a framework of analysis of international politics) to the effect that the contemporary world, ideologically and politically, is divided into two major spheres of influence (or blocs): the East, or the socialist bloc of nations, led by the Soviet Union, and the West, or the capitalist bloc, led by the United States, and that the international balance of power is, in reality, determined by the two major powers. The two leading powers of the bipolar world coexist and cooperate (e.g., through peaceful coexistence, according to the Soviet view) through a series of arrangements (e.g., détente, rapprochement, and proxy wars) in order to avoid direct confrontation (e.g., U.S.-USSR war). The validity of this concept is seriously questioned by those who believe in multipolarity (i.e., the notion that there are more than just two major centers of power). The multipolarists consider, for example, that the People's Republic of China and the Third World nations which are not aligned with any of these two major blocs are also centers of power of equal strength and importance in maintenance of the international balance of power and peace. With the dissolution of the Soviet empire officially with President Mikhail S. Gorbachev's resignation on December 25, 1991, the United States remained as the only superpower. See BIPOLYCENTRISM, DELIAN LEAGUE, INTERDEPENDENCE, INTERNATIONAL SYSTEM, POLYCENTRISM.

Bipolycentrism. A concept in contemporary world (global or international) politics whereby individual states within the bipolar system (one led by the Soviet Union and the other by the United States) pursue their independent objectives without abandoning the formal alliances—at least not ideologically—with either of the two super-powers (the USA and the USSR). (France, for example, pursues its policies independently from the United States but remains within the western alliance and while Yugoslavia acted independently from the Soviet Union, it supported the Soviet Union on many vital issues against the West.)

Birch Society. See JOHN BIRCH SOCIETY.

Birth Rate. The total number of persons born in a country during a year, divided by the total population at the midpoint of the year and multiplied by 1,000. The same formula is used to determine death rate. See Appendices 85, 86.

Bite the Bullet. An endurance remedy often recommended by politicians to Americans during times of recession, inflation, and other consumer hardships. President Gerald Ford, 1974-1977, used that phrase often during the 1974 oil shortage. According to author John Ciardi (in *A Browser's Dictionary*, Harper & Row, Publishers, 1980), the term is known to have been used by British soldiers during the 1850s who, before loading their rifles, had to bite off a piece of paper on the cartridge in order to expose the powder to the spark; the faster the action was completed the better their chances were of not being hit by an enemy bullet. Also, in the American West, surgery was often performed with a bullet placed between the patient's teeth as a substitute for an anesthetic.

Black Bag Job. An act of surreptitiously entering premises, e.g., an office or a home, by illegal means, e.g., breaking in, to obtain information, evidence, or to install listening devices (bugging). A practice common among intelligence services.

Black Budget Item. Federal money appropriated for a special, unnamed item, usually a clandestine intelligence operation or some other secret project, under a fictitious name and usually hidden within the defense budget.

Black Capitalism. A notion developed by leading black political and business leaders (including Floyd McKissick, the Director of the Congress of Racial Equality and founder of Soul City in North Carolina) during the Black Revolution days of the 1960s, that blacks would benefit more by turning from bullets to ballots (e.g., by voting and taking part in the political processes of the nation, rather than by shooting) and by active participation in economic activities, primarily through private ownership of business enterprises. The U.S. federal government established a series of incentive programs for blacks wishing to engage in private enterprise, such as the granting of low-interest loans through the Small Business Administration (SBA) and guaranteeing an equal opportunity to bid on government contracts.

Black Caucus. See CONGRESSIONAL BLACK CAUCUS (CBS).

Black Chamber. America's first code breaking and signal interception agency operated in the U.S. Department of State by the Signal Corps which was closed and disbanded in 1929. See GENTLEMEN DO NOT READ ONE ANOTHER'S MAIL, POLITICAL ETHICS.

Black Codes. Upon the introduction of the "Johnson Government" in the Southern Confederacy in 1865-1866, there was a great fear among Southern politicians that the former slaves (freed under Amendment XIII to the U.S. Constitution) would undermine the economic structure of the Southern states and, as a matter of revenge, turn against the whites and exterminate them. New laws were soon implemented (called "Black Codes") which aimed at curbing the activities of the Negroes as free people by such measures as: compulsory work on assigned jobs; arrest and detention of those who quit their jobs without permission (substantiated on the grounds of breach of contract); prohibition against testifying in courts of law in favor of (but not against) blacks; long-term imprisonment for possession of firearms; and fines for violation of curfews. The Black Codes bore a resemblance to the pre-Civil War Slave Codes, a body of rules and regulations aimed at maintaining blacks in a subservient position to whites and at sustaining and perpetuating the institution of slavery. The Slave Codes were enforced by special patrols, which later became the state militia (or state police forces). See JOHNSON PROCLAMATION, RECONSTRUCTION.

Black Consciousness. See BLACK POWER.

Black Hand. See MAFIA.

Black Insurgency. A group of black revolutionaries staged an insurgency in Cuba in 1912 demanding that: (1) the United States withdraw its military forces stationed in Cuba; (2) all American-owned and American-operated enterprises be Cubanized; and (3) that African culture and heritage be restored in Cuba, and all American influence be eradicated ("Africanization of Cuba"). The insurgency was squashed by Cuba's President José Miguel Gómez after receiving a note from Washington, D.C., warning him that if he were not able to "maintain republican government in Cuba," the U.S. would intervene with a large force. This "Cubanization of Cuba" insurgency became a part of Fidel Castro's revolutionary doctrine. See BIG STICK POLICY.

Black Legislators. See CONGRESSIONAL BLACK CAUCUS (CBC).

Black Manifesto. James Forman, leader of the Student Nonviolent Coordinating Committee (SNCC, or "Snake" as it was often referred to), declared during a rally held in Detroit, Michigan on April 18, 1969, that "White Christian Churches and the Jewish Synagogues in the United States and all racist Institutions" owe blacks the sum of $500 million in reparations for past injustices and exploitation, and demanded that sixty percent of all assets held by whites in America be turned over to his organization for distribution among blacks. The Black Panthers joined Forman in his demands and proclaimed plans to design ways and means of collecting the reparations over time; however these never materialized. See BLACK PANTHER PARTY FOR SELF-DEFENSE, STUDENT NONVIOLENT COORDINATING COMMITTEE (SNCC).

Black Muslims. An organization of militant blacks in the United States, formed during the early 1930s, which advocates, among other things, the establishment of a separate state for blacks within the United States, with complete independence and sovereignty, and the superiority of blacks over all other races. Its new leader, Wallace D. Muhammad (son of Elijah Muhammad who died in February 1975), proclaimed in March 1975 before a crowd of 40,000 followers in New York City the end of racist policies and allowed whites (whom his father called the "blue-eyed devils") "worthy of respect" to join the Nation of Islam. The Muslims maintain a close-knit, highly disciplined society, marked by an extreme respect for women and children and the rights of others, including whites. Their corporate enterprises (store outlets, farms and business enterprises) are worth approximately 50 million dollars. The Headquarters are located in Chicago, Illinois. The modern name of the organization is the "Nation of Islam." The rival organization of the Nation of Islam is the Hanafi Moslems led by Hamaas Abdul Khaalis, headquartered in Washington, D.C. The Hanafis are seeking revenge by sword, in what they term a "holy war," against the Nation of Islam whom (according to widely described accounts by the liberal Washington press, such as the *Washington Post* and *Star*) they blame for the slayings of seven Hanafi followers in 1973. The Hanafis became known when they occupied the Jewish B'nai B'rith Building in Washington, D.C., on March 9, 1977, when one reporter was killed and nineteen persons were injured. Khaalis and his followers were subsequently tried and convicted for terrorist activities.

Black Orchestra. See SCHWARZE KAPELLE.

Black Panther Party for Self-Defense. A revolutionary political and paramilitary organization formed in 1967 in California by Bobby Seale and Huey P. Newton and soon joined by Eldridge Cleaver who became official spokesman for its ideology (ideologue). The party (commonly known as the "Black Panthers") was strongly influenced by the events that took place at the Black Power Conference held in 1967 in Newark, New Jersey, which called for "partitioning of the United States into two separate independent nations, one to be homeland for white and the other to be a homeland for black Americans." It further advocated revolution as a means through which blacks could gain power ("black power"), it subscribed to the Black Manifesto and closely collaborated with the Students for Democratic Society (SDS) and the Student Nonviolent Coordinating Committee (SNCC, or "SNAKE" as it was commonly referred to). Cleaver called for "total liberty for black people or total destruction for America." The party rank-and-file became involved in several shootouts with the FBI and police forces throughout the United States during the late 1960s and early 1970s, and it became seriously decimated. The leadership split on ideological issues: Cleaver, charged with killing a policeman, fled the country but returned in 1975 as a "new man" who not only had abandoned revolution and black power, but embraced the capitalist system of the United States with religious zeal (in his book, *Soul on Ice*, Cleaver describes his raping of a white woman as a symbolic form of struggle against white society), Seale became involved in local politics in Oakland, California and Newton left for Cuba to continue his revolutionary struggle against the United States from abroad. The party ceased its operations in 1980. See BLACK CAPITALISM, BLACK MANIFESTO.

Black Power. A slogan calling for the awakening of black consciousness among the black peoples in the United States and elsewhere for the purpose of advancement as a homogeneous group. See BLACK MANIFESTO, BLACK PANTHER PARTY FOR SELF-DEFENSE.

Black Power Conference. See BLACK PANTHER PARTY FOR SELF-DEFENSE.

Black Propaganda. See PROPAGANDA.

Black Reconstruction. See RECONSTRUCTION.

Black Reparations. See BLACK MANIFESTO.

Black Revolution. See OMNIBUS CRIME CONTROL AND SAFE STREETS ACT OF 1968.

Black Sea Pact. An agreement for mutual peaceful collaboration in the area of the Black Sea that was signed in March 1992, by the Commonwealth of Independent States: Russia, Ukraine, Armenia, Azarbaijan, Georgia, Moldova, Bulgaria, Romania, and Turkey. The primary goal of the Pact is to revitalize the economic life in the area by enabling freer movement of persons and goods across national boundaries, as well as to explore the rich resources of the area. The Pact will also address political issues with time, primarily to eliminate the existing frictions between peoples of the area, mainly the Turks and the Kurds. See Appendix 96.

Black September. The confrontation between Jordanian authorities and the Arab guerrilla groups residing there, mainly the Popular Front for the Liberation of Palestine (PFLP) and its founder, Dr. George Habash) following a series of hijackings and bombings of airplanes in Jordan in 1970. Subsequently, the guerrillas moved to Tunisia to organize attacks against Israeli targets.

Black Shirts. Followers of Italy's Fascist dictator Benito Mussolini, during the 1920s, armed to fight communists and keep Mussolini in power. Elevated to the status of a militia of volunteers.

Black Sunday. The day of the Japanese attack on Pearl Harbor in Hawaii on Sunday, December 7, 1941, which was an undeclared, sneaky act of war. See ATLANTIC CHARTER.

Blanket Primary. A nominating election in which the voter may choose candidates for public offices from among many different political parties, but only one candidate for each position. See PRIMARY ELECTION.

Blanquism. A type (and theory) of insurrection by a small, dedicated group of conspirators. So named after its originator, Louis Auguste Blanqui (1805-1881), a French revolutionary. Karl Marx, who advocated a mass revolution, erupting not only within one state but around the world, involving the proletariat (the working class) as well as all the masses of people, distinguished the Blanqui method as one that is not adaptable for a socialist revolution. (In reality, however, all the Marxist as well as non-Marxist revolutionaries use the Blanqui method.) See MARXISM.

Blanquist. See ANARCHIST.

Blitzkrieg. In the German language, "lightning war." Also, a war in which the total might of the state, combined military forces, with tanks, aircraft, infantry, missiles, and naval units are deployed in a coordinated manner for a quick and speedy victory through psychology, manpower and hardware.

Bloc. A partnership among politicians from different parties uniting for a specific purpose; organization of states or governments agreeing to act in unison on a specific single issue; or a coalition of individuals, groups or public organizations (e.g., government or governmental agencies) based on either a common political philosophy (e.g., the communist bloc of nations) or a unity of purpose in achieving certain desired outcomes.

Bloc Voting. The practice of casting ballots for or against an issue or a policy not on the merits (or lack of them) of the issue at hand, but according to a group, party, or a bloc to which one belongs. This is a common practice in the United Nations Organization, where most issues are voted on by the groups or blocs (elites) formed on ideological, cultural, or racial grounds; e.g., the black nations of Africa often vote with Asian, or Latin American nations as a bloc against the white (Caucasian) nations, as simple demonstration of racial solidarity. Dr. Daniel Patrick Moynihan, Senator of New York and former U.S. Ambassador to the U.N. (1975-1976), introduced a resolution before the General Assembly of the U.N. in 1975 aimed at the elimination of bloc or group voting, but it was defeated by the African-Asian bloc—the dominant bloc in the U.N. today. (The United States decided to withdraw from one of the oldest international organizations, the International Labor Organization for this very reason.) See VOTING.

Block Grant. Matching grants for broad purposes, usually subject to general planning requirements and other flexible conditions which leave a good deal of discretion to the grantee with respect to how the funds are to be used within the broad category specified; also a general purpose grant made by federal agencies to states and localities as a means of implementing federal programs and policies.

Block Leader. See PRECINCT.

Bloody Sunday. Named after the incident that occurred on January 22, 1905, before the Winter Palace in the city of Saint Petersburg (the official residence of the Russian Tsar) when thousands of workers assembled to petition the Tsar for redress of their grievances and, instead of the Tsar, they were met by a large number of soldiers and were fired upon. This incident, which resulted in the death of several hundred innocent people, is generally considered as the beginning of the end of tsarist monarchical rule in Russia. It was followed in 1917 by a democratic revolution, the provisional government of Alexander F. Kerensky and the Bolshevik Revolution under Vladimir I. Lenin, who gained final control over the state. Kerensky spent the rest of his life at Stanford University in California where he was teaching Russian History until 1971.

Blue Book. See INTER-AMERICAN CONFERENCE ON PROBLEMS OF WAR AND PEACE, WHITE PAPER.

Blue Chip Stock. Stock of usually old and well established enterprises which are duly registered, traded on a stock exchange and, although they may command a low yield, are stable and usually held by stockholders who are concerned more with security, prestige, and stability than profit.

Blue-Collar Caucus. See CONGRESSIONAL CAUCUS.

Blue-Collar Proletariat. See NEW LEFT.

Blue-Eyed Devils. See BLACK MUSLIMS.

Blue Law. Usually a state law within the United States which forbids certain business activity (e.g., the sale of goods in stores) on Sundays and/or holidays.

Blue Light Operation. The attempt to rescue American hostages held in Iran after the 1979 Revolution and the occupation of the American Embassy in Teheran. The Delta Force was sent on 21 May 1980 to rescue the 53 U.S. hostages, but due to sand storms and poor logistics, eight American servicemen died in Desert One when the mission helicopters collided with an airplane and the mission was aborted. See HOSTAGES IN AMERICA, OCTOBER SURPRISE.

Blue-Ribbon Jury. A special jury that may be selected by the Commissioner of Jurors in the state of New York (in large counties with a population of one million or more) for the purpose of hearing important cases or conducting investigations. See JURY, Appendix 50.

Blue-Ribbon Panel. A body of selected persons (who are well known and generally respected) that may be called upon by either the President of the United States, a state governor, or a city mayor, to undertake a special task, such as an investigation of irregularities in governmental agencies; to study the rise of crime; or to study the ways and means of reorganizing the government, and to present its finding to the proper authority for action. See JURY.

Blue-Sky Law. One of the several federal statutory laws which aims to protect the general public in the United States from fraudulent sale of securities and stocks or bonds.

Blunt Message. TRIPARTITE ALLIANCE.

B'nai B'rith. See JEWISH LOBBY.

BND. See BUNDESNACHRICHTENDIENST.

Board of Education. See SEXPOLITICS.

Board of Zoning Appeals. See ZONING.

Boat People. See FREEDOM FLOAT.

Body Brokering. The practice of employing foreign labor at very low wages and poor working environment, involving collusion on the part of the employer, the agent or agency providing the labor, and the government of the state which allows the labor to emigrate for employment purposes—all these share in profit from the wages. It was a common practice in many communist states, especially the former Soviet Union, for the government to collect the major portion of the earning obtained abroad by its nationals, e.g., musicians, actors, persons competing in sports, or those invited abroad for work. Currently, the People's Republic of China and particularly some of its agencies abroad (e.g., the Lia Tong and the China Lianoning Corporation on Guam) are allowing labor to emigrate and are collecting a large portion of the wages earned abroad as fees for permission to emigrate. A new form of slavery and exploitation of man by man.

Body Politic. Commonly, the whole people organized and united under a single authority, or a politically organized society within a single state. See POLITICS, STATE.

Bodyguard of Lies. In the language of intelligence and counterintelligence, espionage and counterespionage, the necessity that may arise to resort to plain lying and distortion—in a "wilderness of mirrors"—in order to protect sources and methods of intelligence, as well as to obtain useful and needed information. The bulk of positive intelligence, however, roughly about 95 percent of it, is obtained from open, legal, overt sources (e.g., books, periodicals, news reports, professional publications, open and perfectly legal travel throughout a given country, and conversations); and about five percent of desired intelligence requires covert espionage activity, particularly as it pertains to intentions. One of the Soviet Union's most talented spies, Willie Fischer (also known as Fisher), alias Rudolf Ivanovich Abel, was able, because of his special training and talent, to derive useful intelligence from open sources. Abel, a general in the KGB, operated in New York City during the 1950s. His identity was disclosed to the FBI through an accidental turn of events: In a pocket of one of his slacks he had a hollow coin with a coded microdot message in it. His housekeeper, without Abel's knowledge and anxious to please her employer, took the slacks to a drycleaning establishment where the coin fell from the pocket, opened by itself, and revealed the message which the suspicious merchant delivered to the FBI. Abel was subsequently exchanged for Francis Gary Powers, the American pilot who flew the CIA's U-2 spy plane that was shot down over the city of Svierdlovsk on 1 May 1960. During W.W.II, the deception plan for Operation Overlord, the actual invasion of Europe by the Allies, was named "Bodyguard." The Allied intelligence services conceived a deception plan which was widely reported to the Nazi German forces by their intelligence agents operating in England. These agents were turned or double-exed (Double XX) by the Allies to deliver to their masters false information—that a First U.S. Army Group under the command of U.S. General George S. Patton, Jr. (a military genius whom the Germans feared because of his military talents and guts) was being mobilized in England for an invasion of Europe via assault on Pas de Calais instead of the actual site of Normandy. That information acknowledged previous intelligence of a false nature that was fed to the Germans by letting them discover the body of an Allied officer washed ashore in Spain; the body carried a briefcase of classified war plans that included invasion at places other than Normandy. One of the turned Allied agents, Juan Pujol Garcia, code-named Garbo, was able to deceive his masters with information furnished to him for transmittal by the Twenty Committee (XX Committee or Double-Cross Committee). He was simultaneously awarded the German Iron Cross by his Abwehr masters and the British M.B.E. for his service to the Allies. (Also, books by the same titles: *Bodyguard of Lies* by Anthony Brown and *Wilderness of Mirrors* by David C. Martin, respectively.) See COUNTERINTELLIGENCE, INTELLIGENCE.

Bog-Hopper. See MICK.

Bogota Hostages. See APRIL 19 MOVEMENT.

Boland Amendments. U.S. Representative Edward P. Boland, Democrat from Massachusetts and Chairman of the House Permanent Committee on Intelligence, introduced three amendments in the House, all of which were directed to limit the CIA involvements in support of the Contras in Nicaragua in their struggle against the pro-Soviet and pro-Cuban Sandanista Government in Nicaragua. They were: Boland I—an amendment to the defense appropriations bill for fiscal year 1983, which prohibits the CIA from using federal funds "for the purpose of overthrowing the government of Nicaragua," the Sandanistas; Boland II—an amendment to the omnibus appropriations bill of October 1984, which prohibited all U.S. intelligence agencies, including the CIA, from spending U.S. funds "for the purpose, (or which) would have the effect, of supporting, directly or indirectly, military or paramilitary operations in Nicaragua by any nation, group, organization, movement or individual." This amendment was passed in spite of the fact that William J. Casey, Director of CI and CIA, 1981-1987, apologized to Congress for not informing it about CIA activities and promised to do so from then on (known as *Casey Accords*); and Boland III—of December 1985 authorizing the CIA to provide the Contras only with communications equipment and to exchange intelligence, nothing else. See IRAN-CONTRA AFFAIR, SANDANISTA LIBERATION FRONT.

Bolshevik. In the Russian language, "majority," or "a member of a majority." Also, the official name of the political faction of communist revolutionaries led by Vladimir I. Lenin in Russia, which had emerged from the Russian Social-Democratic Labor Party (1870-1924). The Bolsheviks gained control of the Russian State in 1917 and renamed their faction the "All-Union Communist Party (of Bolsheviks)." The party was known as the Communist Party of the Soviet Union (CPSU). See MENSHEVIK.

Bona Fide. In the Latin language, "in good will," "in good faith," or "in all honesty." "Mala Fide," means bad faith, bad will.

Bonapartism. In Marxist revolutionary strategy, the transitory period between the time a capitalistic regime is abolished by the socialist revolutionary party assisted by a military force and the time the actual power is being transferred to the proletariat (e.g., the Soviets in Russia after the Bolshevik Revolution of 1917). The term was coined by Vladimir I. Lenin, the founder of the Soviet State and the method was taken from Napoleon I (Bonaparte, Emperor of France, 1804-1815), since such was his *modus operandi.*

Boomer Power. Following a major war, population in most situations increases rapidly. The baby boom serves as a good indicator of a large increase in demand for consumer goods. Also, once the young reach voting age, they make a considerable impact on political processes and institutions, and on the general direction and nature of government policies, national, state and local. In the United States, at the end of W.W.II, due to the increase in population and to educational attainment through the GI Bill of Rights, the political and economic milieu of the American nation changed considerably, both in its political outlook and in the improvement of the standard of living.

Bootstrapping. Refers to state governments in the United States taxing certain services reimbursable by the federal government (e.g., Medicaid payments to physicians and hospitals), in order to gain additional revenue. Currently 37 states have such laws in effect.

Borba. In the Russian language, "struggle," "war," or "conflict."

Bordaberization. A term coined after President Juan Maria Bordaberry of Uruguay, elected in 1973, soon dissolved the legislature and replaced it with an advisory council, inviting the military to help him rule the country as a matter of expediency and efficiency. Such military coups are not new in Latin America, but Bordaberry improved the system. A civilian-military coup appeared to the voters as an orderly expedient for governing the country, but in reality, coups are generally motivated by a personal greed for power, impatience with slow democratic processes, and desire for enrichment of the few. President Alberto Fujimori of Peru who also took absolute power with the assistance of the military in April 1992—an action called "Fujicoup"—dissolved the elected legislature and ruled by decree, allegedly to maintain law and order and to fight against corruption and drug traffickers. As a rule, in the Latin American type of Bordaberry coups, the civilian leader himself is with time removed by a military coup, as was the case with President Bordaberry, who was removed by the military in 1976.

Born Again. As a result of the bitter division of the American nation over U.S. involvement in the Vietnamese conflict, the Black Revolution during the 1960s and 1970s, and the unethical governmental practices by rulers of major democracies (e.g., the Watergate scandal in the United States which led to the resignation of U.S. President, Richard M. Nixon in 1974—an unprecedented occurrence in American political history), large segments of the population have shifted their trust from their political leaders to spiritual leaders and to Jesus Christ in whose teachings they've found a new life. Echoing the evangelical teachings of Billy Graham, distinguished leaders (e.g., U.S. President Jimmy Carter) and others, some of whom have themselves participated in unethical designs at one time (e.g., Charles Colson, former assistant to President Richard M. Nixon, who served time in prison for his involvement in the Watergate affair), have embraced Jesus Christ and joined the Jesus Movement and proclaimed "I have been born again." The Born Again or Jesus Movement received considerable support from the Moral Re-Armament groups which were very active (in the United States as well as in other Western Democracies, particularly in England and West Germany) during the late 1950s and early 1960s. While the Moral Re-Armament movement was oriented mainly toward anti-communism, the Jesus or Born Again movement appears to be directed against unethical and immoral practices and policies of government officials.

Borough. A self-governing political subdivision; a unit of local government or a small town in Great Britain. Also, a small political subdivision of the municipal government of New York City or a large town in Connecticut, Pennsylvania, Minnesota, or New Jersey. See COUNTY GOVERNMENT, ROTTEN BOROUGH, Appendix 67.

Borrowed Bag of Tools. A phrase coined by Charles Hampden-Turner (in his *Radical Man: The Process of Psycho-Social Development.* Cambridge, Massachusetts: Schenkman Publishing Company, 1970) and pertaining to social sciences which attempt to analyze society with tools borrowed from the physical sciences. See EPIRICISM, POLITICAL THEORY.

Boston Massacre. See TOWNSHEND REVENUE ACT.

Boston Tea Party. The culmination of a series of events aimed at extracting additional revenue from the American colonists by the British government by taxing tea imported from England by the East India Company (which held an exclusive monopoly on selling tea in the colonies and whose principal salesmen were Thomas Hutchinson, the loyalist governor of the colony, and his two sons). The colonists (led by Samuel Adams, the revolutionary leader) opposed the tea tax in accordance with the adopted principle of "no taxation without representation"; this led finally to the Revolutionary War between the colonists and England. On December 16, 1773, when the colonists refused to pay the 12 pence tax on each of the 342 chests of tea (worth approximately $18,000) and decided to return the tea to England, Governor Hutchinson, with the aid of the British Navy, detained the ship in the Boston Harbor until the tax would be paid (the deadline was December 17, 1773), or the tea would be confiscated. In response, the colonists went aboard the ship at night disguised in Indian garb and dumped the tea overboard. In retaliation, the British Parliament passed the Boston Port Act in 1774 which closed the Boston port and maintained a blockade until the cost of the tea and the tax were paid. This confrontation led in turn to the stationing of British troops in private homes and subsequently to broader revolutionary events; but neither the tea, nor the tax on it, were ever paid for by the colonists. See TOWNSHEND REVENUE ACT.

Boswash. See MEGALOPOLIS.

Boudoir Government. Traditionally, a derogatory term used to describe the role of women in public service, and particularly in executive positions of the government. Sometimes the term is used to describe the practice of mixing sex (sexpolitics) with government. During U.S. President Woodrow Wilson's illness in 1920, Mrs. Edith Wilson, the President's wife, was allegedly acting as President for several months, even signing legislation. The term was then very popular in Washington gossip circles. Russia, under Tsar Nicholas II (1894-1917), is said to have been ruled from the boudoir of his wife, Alexandra, unaware that strong revolutionary forces were preparing for a deadly attack which came in February 1917. The actual ruler of the Russian Empire was not the Tsar, but his wife, Empress Alexandra, and her friend and mentor, Rasputin. Georgi Efimovich Rasputin (1871-1916) was a fanatical monk who advocated debauchery as a way to repentance and salvation. When he supposedly healed Alexandra's son of hemophilia, the Empress was convinced of his unusual power, which she wanted to use to save the falling Empire. Rasputin and Alexandra (by way of her boudoir) were instrumental in the implementation of the repressive policies of the Tsar until the military commanders decided to eliminate him (by assassination) when they saw catastrophe coming to the ailing Empire. Rasputinism is generally considered as the major cause of the fall of the Russian Empire in 1917 and the emergence of the communist regime under V. I. Lenin.

Bourgeois Mentality. See EASTOXIFICATION.

Bourgeoisie. In the common parlance of Marxism, the wealthy exploiting class in a capitalistic society, who, as the enemy of the working class, the proletariat, must be overthrown and exterminated by the proletariat. The lower class of the bourgeoisie, called the "petite bourgeoisie," are those capitalists who work side-by-side with their employees, many of whom will sooner or later join the proletariat when they are forced into bankruptcy as a result of stiff competition with the rich capitalists. See MARXISM.

Bourse, Börse. See STOCK EXCHANGE.

Boxer Rebellion. An armed uprising that was staged by the anti-foreign, anti-Christian elements in China, the Celestial Kingdom, in 1900 (mainly in the City of Peking). Upon the death of the German ambassador to China, which was caused by the Boxers, the United States, together with other European powers, such as England, Russia and Germany, decided to intervene militarily in order to protect lives and property. The Boxers were defeated shortly and the Chinese government agreed to pay the United States the sum of $24,000,000 in reparations. (Out of this amount, $13,000,000 was later refunded to China for the purpose of establishing fellowship funds for Chinese students who desired to attend American colleges and universities.) The term "Boxer" was a nickname given by Europeans to a person of Chinese nationality, especially those who came to Europe with boxing teams and who were very muscular and strong. The term is an approximate translation of I-ho-ch'uan, which in the Chinese language means "righteous and well-trained fists" or "fists of righteous harmony." Since many of the leaders of the Chinese revolutionaries were boxers and others looked like boxers, they were given that name instead of the long Chinese translation. Following the successful "scramble for Africa," the European powers expected easy going in China, but they had forgotten the lessons of ancient Chinese philosophers who for thousands of years were reminding their neighbors (even by building the Wall), that uninvited nationals of one state settling in the territory of another will not be tolerated! The climax of the rebellion was reached when the Chinese were required to obey German laws and customs and conversion to Christianity by British missionaries became almost compulsory. "Sha! Sha!" ("kill! kill!") was the Boxer slogan, with the fists, because there were not enough weapons to go around. The atrocity of the day is epitomized by a decision to decapitate a victim instead of dismembering and slicing as a gesture of "mercy." The European diplomats held by the Boxers were the first hostages held in this century, in large numbers, and, unlike the American hostages in Iran in 1979, these were liberated by joint forces commanded by German Field Marshal Count Waldersee, who at age 72 supposedly spent more time with his new Chinese mistress than on the battlefield.

Bra in the Ring. See HAT IN THE RING.

Brain-Drain. Because of lack of freedom, liberty, or the ability to improve one's living conditions, or because of political prosecution, many talented persons throughout the world depart their native lands and seek fortunes, usually in the West and particularly in the United States of America, regardless of consequences. Many political systems around the world, especially those that have chosen to remain arbitrary, oppressive and confiscatory, have lost the best of their talented persons because they emigrated to other lands to live in freedom and better living conditions. Many modern states have collapsed because of lack of creative manpower. See CONFISCATORY POLICY, IMMIGRATION, QUOTA.

Brain Industries. See COMPARATIVE ADVANTAGE.

Brain Trust. A group of persons (selected on the basis of merit) who may be gathered for the purpose of rendering some useful service or advice. (Presidents Franklin D. Roosevelt, John F. Kennedy, Lyndon B. Johnson, and Richard M. Nixon are known to have relied heavily on the advice of persons with diversified backgrounds and experiences.)

Brainwashing. Also known as coercive persuasion, a term coined by Dr. Louis West (University of California at Los Angeles). The practice of manipulating another's sense of values for the purpose of either extracting useful military or intelligence information (in case of spies and military prisoners of war caught by the enemy) or converting one to a different political philosophy in general. The process of brainwashing is ordinarily pursued short of physical violence to the individual being subjected to the process. According to Erich Fromm, brainwashing entails "suggestive hypnoid techniques which produce thoughts and feelings in people without making them aware that 'their' thoughts are not their own." The practice of brainwashing was commonly inflicted upon American prisoners of war caught by the North Koreans and the Chinese communists during the Korean War (1950-1954), many of whom turned against their own country (the United States) and denounced it as "an imperialist aggressor" against the "innocent people of Korea." Scientific studies made have shown that the men who have made such shifts in their ideological outlook were either of a low intelligence quotient (IQ), or were simply semi-literate as far as the understanding of values of the society from which they had come was concerned.

Branches of Government. In the U.S., the three branches established by the Constitution are: (1) the Legislative consists of the U.S. House of Representatives, and the U.S. Senate; (2) the Judicial is composed of the Supreme Court and other lesser federal courts; and (3) the Executive or the president.

Brandeis Brief. Louis D. Brandeis, Associate Justice of the U.S. Supreme Court (1916-1939) originated the practice of relying on political, social, and economic information and legal arguments as well as on the examination of the points of law and the points of fact in the process of arriving at a judgment. This technique of multidisciplinary, crossdisciplinary, or interdisciplinary judicial interpretation of law and facts greatly broadened the degree and the scope of judicial activity for decades to come, particularly as applied to civil rights cases. His technique was first acknowledged and applied by the U.S. Supreme Court in the case of *Bunting v. Oregon*, 243 U.S. 426 (1917). See JUDICIAL BRIEF.

Breach of Contract. The refusal or failure to uphold the terms of an agreed upon contract; to receive restitution the damaged party may invoke a lawsuit.

Brennender Sorge. See ENCYCLICAL.

Brest-Litovsk Treaty. The peace treaty that was signed between the Central Powers (mainly Germany) and the newly-formed regime of Communist Russia on March 3, 1918. (This was the very first and the most humiliating treaty the Bolsheviks have ever signed. Communist Russia was forced to give up all her claims to Poland, Ukraine, Finland, the Baltic states, and the Caucasus, formerly within the Russian Empire) and to respect international treaty obligations entered into by the Tsarist regime. The treaty was abrogated by the Bolshevik government of Russia in November 1918 upon the defeat of Germany. Also known as "No Peace, No War" Treaty.

Bretton Woods Conference. One of the major conferences held during World War II and one that produced the International Monetary Fund and the International Bank for Reconstruction and Development. The conference was organized by the United Nations Monetary and Financial Conference and was held in Bretton Woods, New Hampshire in July 1944, to decide post-war economic policies aiming at the preservation of international peace and security. Italy, where the Fascist regime of Mussolini had already been overthrown, wanted to attend, but at the British request, was denied a seat. See COMPARATIVE ADVANTAGE, INTERNATIONAL MONETARY FUND, MORGENTHAU PLAN, PRODUCT CYCLE, UNILATERAL GLOBAL KEYNESIANISM.

Brezhneyev Doctrine. The official Soviet policy pronounced, in 1968, under the leadership of Leonid I. Brezhneyev, to the effect that any threat, military or otherwise, to either the Soviet Union or a socialist (satellite) state (within the Soviet sphere of influence), would bring about direct military action by the Soviet Union and her allies (the East European satellite states). This doctrine was proclaimed during, and as justification of, Soviet and its satellites' intervention in Czechoslovakia in 1968 when the regime of that state decided to liberalize slave-like conditions of the Czechoslovak peoples. See CHARTER 77.

Bricker Amendment. An amendment to the United States Constitution, proposed by U.S. Senator John Bricker of Ohio in 1954, designed to limit the scope of treaties, executive agreements, and presidential powers in foreign affairs in general. (The amendment failed in the U.S. Senate due to lack of the two-thirds plus one vote required for passage.)

Brief. See JUDICIAL BRIEF.

Bring the Boys Home for Christmas. See KOREAN WAR.

Bring the War Back to America. A powerful slogan, used by civil rights leaders and most of their black Afro-American followers, and by draft dodgers and war protesters in general during the Vietnam War era, particularly during the 1965 Watts disturbances in Los Angeles, California, and until the war ended in 1974. The slogan was repeated during the Persian Gulf War in 1991 but in a somewhat different context. This time there was no protest against the war itself, but rather, against the enormous amount of money and manpower that the United States deployed to liberate a dictatorial government in Kuwait while it was felt the money could have been better spent at home on a war against racism and poverty. The slogan was repeated again on 29 April 1992 when protests and looting spread in Los Angeles after the acquittal of four policemen charged with the brutal beating of a black motorist, Rodney King, on 3 March 1991. This time 51 people died as a result of the riots and looting in Los Angeles, and the property damage was estimated to be over $800 million. The riots subsided on 2 May 1991 when U.S. President George Bush made an official pronouncement that the four policemen would be tried under federal laws for violating King's civil rights. Because 1992 was a presidential election year, the president, fearful of negative political fallout, decided to act in order to pacify the antagonism and the fury. Black Americans hold decisive votes in presidential elections. See POLICE BRUTALITY, URBANIZATION.

Brinkmanship. The practice of conducting diplomacy by dangerous, risky means. Term associated with the "massive retaliation" notion advocated by U.S. Secretary of State under President Dwight D. Eisenhower, John Foster Dulles, 1958-1959, and seriously questioned by the opposing Democrats, particularly Adlai Stevenson, as risky, irresponsible and dangerous. See DIPLOMACY.

Britain-Argentina Falkland Islands War. See FALKLAND ISLANDS WAR.

British Commonwealth of Nations. All the possessions, colonies, former colonies, and territories, once a part of the British Empire, that have voluntarily decided to remain within the Commonwealth system. Reasons include: tradition; pride in being associated with a nation whose culture, political and legal traditions, and educational institutions are of a high caliber; the sharing of a common language; or other benefits ranging from need for protection from attack to desire for favorable trade relationships. Canada, for example, had been a self-governing dominion under England since 1931, but in 1982 Canada cut off links with England, amended the 1867 British North America Act, and became a fully sovereign state. This act is known as "taking the constitution home" (e.g., from England, to Canada).

British Labour Party. See LABOUR PARTY OF ENGLAND.

British Official Secrets Act. See ALL NEWS IS BAD NEWS—IF IT IS ABOUT US.

British Security Service. Branch MI5, British domestic security and intelligence force. Equivalent of the FBI in U.S. See SCOTLAND YARD, SECRET INTELLIGENCE SERVICE (SIS).

Broad-Gauge Political Theory. See POLITICAL THEORY.

Broad Interpretation of the Law. See JUDICIAL ACTIVISM, POSTURE OF MORAL ABSTENTION.

Broker State. See POLITICS OF SPECIAL INTERESTS.

Broker-Type Political Party. A political party that is primarily interested in winning elections rather than converting the electorate to any particular political philosophy. Its program is usually geared to the broad interests of the electorate and centered around popular leaders rather than specific party ideology. (The two major political parties in the United States, the Democratic and Republican, as well as those of Great Britain, the Labour and the Conservative, are of that kind.) See POLITICAL PARTY.

Brokered Convention. Aspirants for election to the American presidency run, as a rule, on either the Democratic or the Republican party tickets. Very rare are occasions when a third party makes a strong showing, and independent candidates have practically no chance, due to the difficulty of obtaining the required citizen petitions in all states, as requirements to be listed on a ballot differ from state to state. During the campaign, candidates for president campaign in primaries and caucuses in order to obtain pledged votes. If they do not receive a significant number of votes, the party convention, Democratic or Republican, will select a candidate for the president and one for the vice president. Once a candidate receives the required majority of votes, from committed votes plus the votes of the super delegates, he gets the nomination. During the 1992 presidential campaign, the Democratic party designated a total of 4,288 delegates; to be nominated, a candidate needed 2,145 votes. The Republican party designated 2,209 convention votes and 1,105 were required for nomination. Both the major candidates, Bill Clinton of the Democratic Party, and George Bush of the Republican Party, received a considerable number of pledged votes. For example, as of April 1992, Clinton had 1,267 pledged delegates and George Bush had received 963 delegate votes. See DEMOCRATIC AND REPUBLICAN

PARTY CONVENTIONS AND THEIR CANDIDATES in Appendix 18, PRIMARY ELECTION, SUPER TUESDAY.

Brook Farm. See UTOPIA.

Brush-Fire War. Light, sporadic war or police action. A war of harassment rather than one intended to defeat an adversary totally. See POLICE ACTION, WAR.

Brussels Treaty. See DUNKIRK PACT, NORTH ATLANTIC TREATY ORGANIZATION (NATO).

Brutum Fulmen. In the Latin language, "an ineffective, futile threat or display of force." See WAR.

Bryan Treaties. U.S. Secretary of State under President Woodrow Wilson, William Jennings Bryan, 1913-1915, reflecting President Wilson's idealism about world peace, negotiated about thirty international treaties with many states in order to enshrine the President's desire. Included among them was a treaty with Nicaragua which gave the United States the option to build a canal across Nicaragua. This treaty was mutually abrogated in 1970, because the Panama Canal provides adequate services.

Bubba. See PRIMARY ELECTION.

Bubbarette. See PRIMARY ELECTION.

Bubble. A period of active trading of a certain commodity or a stock, usually at high prices; once the demand is saturated, or some irregularity is discovered, prices fall radically at a great loss to the holders of such commodities or stocks.

Bubble Economy. Economic activity that is temporary, deceptive, and based and evaluated on faulty premises (e.g., lack of clear theory or statistical measurements). For example, the boom in housing and commercial real estate construction in America during the 1980s was purposely stimulated by dishonest financial and real estate manipulators, including many Savings and Loan institutions, and aimed to steal money. Many were deceived by a few crooked manipulators. See CREATIVE FINANCING.

Buck Stops Here, the. See IF YOU NEED A FRIEND IN WASHINGTON, GET YOURSELF A DOG; GIVE THEM HELL, HARRY!

Budget. A detailed plan of actual or anticipated revenues and expenditures for a given accounting period. See GOVERNMENT BUDGET.

Budget and Accounting Act of 1921. See GOVERNMENT BUDGET.

Budget Resolution. Per U.S. Congressional Budget Office, "A resolution, passed by both Houses of the Congress but not requiring the President's signature, that sets forth a Congressional budget plan for the next five years. The plan must be carried out through subsequent legislation, including appropriations and changes in tax and entitlement laws. The Congressional Budget Act of 1974 established a number of mechanisms that are designed to hold spending and revenues to the targets established in the budget resolution." See Appendix 35.

Buffer State. A state, usually politically neutral, dividing two or more states with hostile intentions, or one state artificially created for the purpose of keeping apart two or more hostile states. See STATE.

Buffer Zone. See BUFFER STATE.

Bugharinovyetz. In the Soviet official parlance, synonymous with a counter-revolutionary; an opportunist; one opposing the policies of the Soviet leadership or sympathizer of Nicole I. Bukharin (1888-1938), once one of the strongest opponents of Josef Stalin, in his bid for control of the party and state. Bukharin strongly opposed Stalin's bid for unlimited control over the party membership, the party apparatus in the entire party hierarchy, from the lowest cell to the Central Committee and often condemned Stalin's strong hand in handling peasants reluctant to join collective farms and workers to be exploited for the cause of socialism.

Bull Moose Party. See NATIONAL PROGRESSIVE PARTY.

Bullets and Ballots. See BLACK CAPITALISM.

Bund. In the German language, "union" or "organization."

Bundesamt für Verfassungsschutz (BFV). See FEDERAL OFFICE FOR THE PROTECTION OF THE CONSTITUTION.

Bundesarbeitsgericht. Federal Labor Court in the Federal Republic of Germany having jurisdiction over all labor disputes. See REGIERUNGSBEZIRK.

Bundesdisziplinarhof. Federal Court of Discipline in the German Federal Republic having jurisdiction over all disciplinary matters of federal officials. See BUNDESARBEITSGERICHT.

Bundesentschädigungsgesetz (BEG). In the German language, "Federal Law of Compensation." See BUNDESRÜCKERSTATTUNGSGESETZ (BRÜG).

Bundesfinanzhof. Federal Finance Court in the Federal Republic of Germany having jurisdiction over all fiscal and monetary matters on a regional level. See BUNDESARBEITSGERICHT, REGIERUNGSBEZIRK.

Bundeskanzler. The Federal Chancellor in the German Federal Republic, the real head of the government and leader of his (majority) party. See CHANCELLOR.

Bundesnachrichtendienst (BND). The intelligence collecting and evaluating agency of the German Federal Republic (West Germany), established on April 1, 1956, mainly by federalizing the Gehlen Organization which had been working for the United States. See GEHLEN ORGANIZATION.

Bundesrat. One of the two chambers of the federal parliament in the Federal Republic of Germany (West Germany). Its members are appointed by the several states (Länder). The Bundesrat performs duties similar to those of the U.S. Senate. See BUNDESTAG.

Bundesrückerstattungsgesetz (BRÜG). In the German language, "Federal Restitution Law," a statute passed by the newly-formed Federal Republic of Germany of 1949, on 19 July 1957, to pay claims for property lost as a result of Nazi Germany's predatory policies between 1933 and 1945. Under this law, the Federal Republic of Germany paid over DM4,250 billion; and under another law, the Federal Law of Compensation (in the German language, Bundesentschädigungsgesetz or BERG, an additional DM80,564 billion was paid and another DM22,089 billion was scheduled to be paid within the next several years as compensation to victims of Nazism. The largest settlements were paid to Jews. Other European victims of Nazism received additional compensation for damages as a result of global agreement by the Federal Republic of Germany. They were paid in millions of DM as follows: Luxembourg, 18; Norway, 60; Denmark, 16; Greece, 115; Holland, 125; France, 400; Belgium, 80; Italy, 40; Switzerland, 10; the United Kingdom, 11, and Sweden, 1. In dealing with the legacy of the Hitler regime, the Federal Republic of Germany has established a precedent, namely that of legislating and carrying out a comprehensive system of restitution for injustice. See FINAL SOLUTION.

Bundestag. One of the two chambers, the lower house, of the federal parliament in the Federal Republic of Germany. Its members are elected by single member constituencies. The Bundestag performs functions similar to those of the U.S. House of Representatives. See BUNDESRAT.

Bundesverfassungsgericht. Federal Constitutional Court in the Federal Republic of Germany having jurisdiction over constitutional matters, including judicial review. See BUNDESRAT, BUNDESARBEITSGERICHT.

Bundesverwaltungsgericht. Federal Administrative Court in the Federal Republic of Germany having jurisdiction over all administrative matters. See BUNDESARBEITSGERICHT, BUNDESRAT.

Bunge. The unicameral National Assembly of Tanzania.

BUPPIE. See YOUNG URBAN PROFESSIONAL.

Burden of Proof. According to the American system of jurisprudence, an individual accused of a crime is not considered guilty until proven so and the proving of guilt rests with the plaintiff and/or the prosecuting attorney. Proof usually must be material (*corpus delicti*), supported by tangible evidence, and may not be based on suspicion or probability alone, or on innuendoes (hints or intimations), or incomplete evidence or presumption of guilt (hindsight). Under most judicial systems of the world (e.g., France, the USSR) the reverse is the case: the burden of proof of innocence is shifted onto the accused, who, in order to be relieved of it, must prove himself innocent.

Bureau of the Budget. See OFFICE OF MANAGEMENT AND BUDGET (OMB).

Bureaucracy. Those persons who interact through specific organizations or bureaus for the purpose of carrying out (e.g., interpreting and implementing) the decision of the policy makers (e.g., those of the U.S. President and Congress); also, a large administrative apparatus charged with implementation and enforcement of policy decisions. See ADMINISTRATION, OAKS' LAWS.

Bureaucratic Insurgency. See ANTIGAG LAW.

Bürgermeister. A mayor of a city, town, village, or a commune in German-speaking states. See BUNDESRAT.

Burgess. An elective member of the colonial assembly in Williamsburg, Virginia; a member of a board governing a borough in the state of Connecticut; or the executive officer of a borough in the state of Pennsylvania.

Burma Road. See TRIPARTITE PACT OF BERLIN.

Burma's National League for Democracy. See NATIONAL LEAGUE FOR DEMOCRACY.

Burn Baby, Burn! See URBANIZATION.

Burr Conspiracy. Aaron Burr, U.S. Vice President (1081-1805) under Thomas Jefferson, was accused in 1806 of treason on the grounds that he had conspired to separate the western part of the United States, unite it with a territory west of the Louisiana Purchase which was to be conquered from Mexico, and form a separate state. He was brought to trial in Richmond, Virginia, but the case was dismissed by Chief Justice John Marshall when the prosecution failed to present two witnesses as required in all trials for treason under the U.S. Constitution, Art. III, Sec. 3. See TREASON, Appendix 8.

Bush Flu. After the temporary incapacity of U.S. President George Bush during his 1992 visit and dinner with Japanese politicians in Tokyo, when the main topic of discussion was American-Japanese trade relations, the Japanese coined the term "Bush Flu," in the Japanese language, "Busshu Kaze," as a malady that affects Japanese officials "while negotiating trade issues with the United States." See AMERICA BASHING, JAPAN BASHING.

Bush-Kohl Summit of 1992. See ATLANTIC PARTNERSHIP.

Bush-Yeltsin Summit. See PREVENTIVE DIPLOMACY.

Bushido Code. See SAMURAI.

Business Cycle. Per U.S. Congressional Budget Office, "Fluctuations in overall business activity accompanied by swings in the unemployment rate, interest rates, and profits." Over a business cycle, real activity rises to a peak (its highest level during the cycle), then falls until it reaches its trough (its lowest level following the peak), whereupon it starts to rise again, defining a new cycle. Business cycles are irregular, varying in frequency, amplitude, and duration.

Business International Nongovernmental Organization (BINGO). See MULTINATIONAL CORPORATION.

Business of America is Business. U.S. President Calvin Coolidge (1923-1929) stated on January 27, 1925, "The business of America is business," meaning that the prevailing psychology of the nation, as well as the government which it served, was to aid profit-oriented and profit-generating business enterprises, particularly in the private sector of the economy, rather than to generate and practice welfare and welfarism. President Coolidge, known for his decisive action in breaking up the Boston police strike in 1919 while he was Governor of Massachusetts, reiterated the belief that government should aid business activity, rather than curtail it through excessive government regulations. This was in contrast to the "trust busting" pronouncements of President Theodore Roosevelt (1901-1909). See TRUST BUSTING.

Business of Congress is Re-election Business. To paraphrase President Calvin Coolidge's statement that "America's business is business," a similar analogy can be applied to the U.S. Congress because a two-year tenure means, in practice, that the first year is spent learning the legislative process, and the second year, charting pathways for an easy march to victory the next election year. Therefore, it has been suggested many times that the tenure of members of the House of Representatives ought either to be extended to four years with eligibility to be re-elected for another term, or to six years, to conform with the staggered system of the Senate where by every two years one-third of the membership (100 Senators) is due for re-election. One of the founding fathers, Roger Sherman, pointed out that the House of Representatives should be composed of "citizen legislators" and they "ought to return home and mix with people. By remaining at the seat of government, they would acquire the habits of the place, which might differ from those of their constituents." Some voices suggest also that the tenure of all members of Congress should correspond to that of the President and that they all be limited to two terms of office. See ROOKIE LEGISLATOR, U.S. CONSTITUTION, AMENDMENT TWENTY-TWO, Appendix 8.

Busing. See EDUCRATS.

Busshu Kaze. See BUSH FLU.

Buy American! See AMERICAN CENTURY.

Buying-In. State financial contribution to non-Federal matching requirements in what previously had been largely Federal-local programs. The state is generally able to channel Federal funds as a consequence of "buying-in."

Buyuk Millet Meclisi. The unicameral legislative body, the Grand National Assembly, of Turkey.

By-Election. A special election held to fill a vacancy which occurs between regular elections or an election held between major national elections. Congressional elections in the U.S. are held every two years while presidential elections are held every four years, thus the election held between the presidential (or gubernatorial) elections is referred to as a by-election. See ELECTOR, VOTING.

By-Law. Rule or regulation governing a certain activity or one that constitutes the legal basis upon which an organization (public or private) operates.

By-Year Election. See UNITED STATES HOUSE OF REPRESENTATIVES.

Byrd Machine. See POLITICAL MACHINE.

C

"If you can't stand the heat, get out of the kitchen."
HARRY S. TRUMAN, 1884-1972

C. Official designation for the "Chief" of the British Secret Intelligence Services (SIS), or MI-6, an equivalent to the American CIA. Under the Official Secrets Act, one is expected to never reveal the actual name of the Chief of MI-6. That position, though a reality, is not listed anywhere in official documents of civil service or other government offices. The British traditionally subscribe to the notion that what is meant to be secret, ought to be secret. The traditional denial of the existence of such organizations as Secret Intelligence Service or MI-6, the external intelligence and espionage service, and MI-5, the internal security and counterintelligence service, was abandoned when the newly-elected government under Prime Minister John Major openly stated on 6 May 1992 that "The time has come to acknowledge publicly the continuing existence of the Secret Intelligence Service," and its present "C," or "chief," Sir Colin McColl. The counterintelligence and internal security MI-5 is headed by Lady Stella Rimington. Her identity and that of the agency she heads was made public for the first time in 1989.

C³I. See COMMAND, CONTROL, COMMUNICATIONS INTELLIGENCE (C³I).

Cabinet. The body of top governmental executives in charge of major departments and responsible to the head of government and/or head of state. See PARLIAMENTARY DEMOCRACY.

Cabinet Dictatorship. A term often applied to the cabinet of the ruling party (common under cabinet-parliamentary form of government, e.g., England or Canada) which, because of strong party discipline, may dictate legislation that best suits its general program and interest. See PARLIAMENTARY DEMOCRACY.

Cabinet-Parliamentary Government. A system of government whereby the cabinet and its leader (prime minister, premier or chancellor) are nominated to their position by the parliament (the legislature) and are directly responsible to it. This type of government can be dissolved at will by the parliament (legislature) by means of a vote of no confidence or the leader of the cabinet may dissolve the parliament whenever it cannot function any longer in harmony. The oldest working cabinet-parliamentary government is that of Great Britain. See PARLIAMENTARY DEMOCRACY.

Cabotage. The trade and navigation between various points of the same coast under the territorial jurisdiction of one state.

CACM. See CENTRAL AMERICAN COMMON MARKET.

Cactus Wall. Unable to cope with the massive illegal border crossings by Mexicans coming to the United States to seek a better life, the U.S. Immigration and Naturalization Service, short on manpower and equipment, has erected iron fences, mainly in desert areas where cacti grow. The fences have proved ineffective due to the overwhelming inflow stretching from Texas to California. The Immigration Service decided in February 1992 to add an additional 300 border patrol officers to the present force of 3,788 and 1,480 criminal investigation officers.

Caesar. See CAESARISM.

Caesarism. A form of rule over a politically organized society which is characterized by a style of capriciousness, brutality, totalitarianism and total disregard for basic human rights and liberties; a dictatorship exercised usually by a single person who is not restrained by any legal (e.g., constitutional), moral, or ethical laws. The term originated in ancient Rome where Gaius Julius Caesar (102-44 BC) exercised unlimited powers over the Roman Empire. In modern political history,

Caesar-like propensity to rule has been demonstrated by such dictators as *Il Duce* (in the Latin language, "leader") Benito Mussolini (1922-1945) of Italy; *Caudillo* (in the Spanish language, "leader") Francesco Franco Bahamonde (1936-1975) of Spain; *Voschch* (in the Russian language "leader") Josef Stalin (real name Josef Visaryonovitch Djugashvili), a communist leader (1922-1953) of the Soviet Union; *Führer* (in the German language "leader") Adolf Hitler (1933-1945) of Germany; Juan Domingo Perón (1946-1974) of Argentina and his wife Eva (Evita), who herself helped Perón introduce a series of reforms, known as "Perónismo" and who was declared a saint after her death in 1952 and Marshal Idi Amin Dada of Uganda. Also known as "praetorianism," after the Praetorian Guards of Ancient Rome, the elite force guarding the Caesar and the government officials as well as the offices and residences of officials. Similar to American "Federal Protective Service" and the Secret Service. See GARRISON STATE.

Caesaropapism. A type of rule by royal theocracy (clergy as kings and kings as clergy), common in Europe during the Middle Ages, dating particularly from the reign of Zeno (474-491), whereby kings exercised temporal or earthly (political and governmental) powers, as well as ecclesiastical powers (ruled over the clergy and the church and often decided matters of religious doctrine). See ECCLESIASTICAL AUTHORITY, TEMPORAL AUTHORITY, TWO SWORDS THEORY.

Cairo Conference. A summit conference held in Cairo, Egypt on November 20, 1943, between President Roosevelt of the U.S., Prime Minister W. Churchill of Great Britain, and Generalissimo Chiang Kai-shek of China, at which an agreement was reached to the effect that only unconditional surrender could be accepted from Imperial Japan. See CASABLANCA CONFERENCE.

Calendar. A roster used by legislatures to list bills and resolutions in the order in which they are to be considered. See CONGRESS OF THE UNITED STATES.

Calendar of Business. See PRIVATE BILL.

Calendar Wednesday. A practice in the U.S. House of Representatives whereby bills of a non-controversial, nonfiscal nature, that could not be passed without unanimous consent, suspension of the rules of the house, or special orders, can be brought on the floor for consideration. These bills usually concern regional or local problems. In order to give such bills a chance, each Wednesday, except two weeks before the end of each session or when suspended by a two-thirds vote, the various committees may be called upon (in the order in which they appear on the roster according to Rule X of the House Manual) to bring up such bills for debate (which may not exceed two hours on each bill). See CONSENT CALENDAR, HOUSE CALENDAR, PRIVATE BILL, UNION CALENDAR.

California Plan of Judicial Appointments. See JUDICIAL ELECTION.

Call of the Calendar. A procedure used in the U.S. Senate to bring up bills of a controversial nature for consideration. When the Calendar is called, these bills must be given consideration. See UNITED STATES SENATE.

Calumny. Under common law, an act of slander, defamation, or false accusation or prosecution.

Calvo Doctrine. A principle of international law whereby a state is legally relieved from responsibility and liability for the loss of lives or property of aliens which resulted from unforeseen civil war or insurrection, provided that the state has made *bona fide* attempts to protect them. (Named after Carlos Calvo, 1824-1906, Argentinean diplomat and international lawyer.) See FLAGRANTE BELLO.

Camara de Diputados. Lower chamber or chamber of Deputies in Mexico. See CAMARA DE SENADORES, CONGRESO DE LA UNION.

Camara de Representantes. The lower house, or Chamber of Representatives, in some Spanish-speaking countries.

Camara de Senadores. Upper chamber or Senate in Mexico. See CONGRESO DE LA UNION, CAMARA DE DIPUTADOS.

Cambodian Massacre. See KHMER ROUGE.

Cambodian Reconstruction. The effort to establish some degree of stability in Southeast Asia, particularly in Cambodia. After the departure of invading North Vietnamese forces in 1989, Cambodia fell into a total political disintegration, due to the struggle for power among several groups, mainly the discredited Khmer Rouge, which had ruled in Cambodia from 1975 to 1978, and the neutralist forces of the Cambodian Prince Norodom Sihanouk who had returned from exile in the People's Republic of China to stabilize the political life in the country. Unable to reach a peaceful solution, the Cambodian groups agreed that the United Nations step in and establish, at its discretion and in its own manner, some political order. It is an unprecedented act for a state in modern times to ask an external, neutral body, to step in and solve internal domestic problems. The United Nations established a special body in the winter of 1992, the United Nations Transitional Authority for Cambodia (UNTAC), which, under the leadership of Yashushi Akashi, is to introduce about 20,000 troops from an international peace-keeping force; at a cost of about $2 billion, the chaos is to be brought under control and stability maintained. See YEAR ZERO.

Camel is a Horse Created By a Committee. See VOTING.

Camelot. An affectionate comparison of U.S. President John F. Kennedy's time in office (1961-1963) to the reign of legendary King Arthur in Camelot.

Camera de Diputados. Chamber of Deputies in some Spanish-speaking countries.

Camera dei Deputati. Lower chamber or Chamber of Deputies in Italy. See SENATO.

Campaign. See POLITICAL CAMPAIGN.

Campaign Dirty Tricks. Wherever and whenever there is intensive politicking, as during presidential campaigns in the United States, there are partisan pranksters (some say one is germane to the other) whose sole aim is to disrupt and embarrass the opposition. During the 1960s and 1970s some of the major "dirty campaign tricks" were: (1) During the August 24-27, 1964, Democratic National Convention in Atlantic City, New Jersey, rumors were circulated that Lyndon B. Johnson, the President incumbent, refused to see some black delegations from the South which were denied their seats at the Convention. Large groups of blacks, mainly youths, stormed the Convention Hall in an attempt to disrupt it. The Republican presidential candidate, Barry M. Goldwater, and his followers denied any part in this scheme; (2) During the August 26-28, 1968, Democratic National Convention in Chicago, Illinois, presidential contender Hubert H. Humphrey suspected the opposition of instigating some of the disruptive acts that had taken place there; (3) During the August 21-23, 1968, Republican National Convention in Miami Beach Florida, a large reception (worth several thousand dollars in food and beverages) was "organized" in the name of the Republicans but the Democrats denied any knowledge; (4) The Republicans retaliated for this act in 1972 during the July 10-13, 1972, Democratic National Convention in Miami Beach, Florida, when thousands of letters (written on the official stationary of the Democratic National Committee) were circulated suggesting that U.S. Senator Hubert H. Humphrey and U.S. Senator Edmund S. Muskie, both potential choices of the Democrats for the presidency, were involved in extramarital sexual activity. The Republicans denied any involvement. It was soon revealed, however, that Donald Segretti was hired by the Republicans to plan and carry out such schemes and he was subsequently convicted and imprisoned; and (5) One of the better known pranksters of the Democrats was Dick Tuck. One of Tuck's greatest "achievements" was realized in 1968, when, dressed as a railroad trainman, he directed a train on which Richard M. Nixon was riding (and from the rear platform of which Nixon was to make a major speech to a crowd of followers) to a side track, thus making it impossible for Nixon to meet his audience. See WATERGATE AFFAIR.

Campaign Disclosure Law of 1972. See CAMPAIGN FINANCING.

Campaign Finance Act of 1974. See CAMPAIGN FINANCING.

Campaign Financing. Under the Corrupt Practices Act of 1925, Congress made some attempt to regulate campaign financing, such as prohibiting corporations from donating to political campaigns for federal offices (but not for state elections). In spite of these restrictions, Richard M. Nixon received $100,000 from the Gulf Oil Corporation and $55,000 from American Airlines, and Barry M. Goldwater received $40,000 from Goodyear Tire and Rubber Company. According to U.S. Representative Les Aspin (D-Wisconsin), as quoted in *The Washington Post,* December 10, 1973, before the disclosure law took effect on April 7, 1972, some of the contributions made by executives of large corporations doing business with the federal government to Nixon's campaign funds were as follows: $2.1 million from W. Clement Stone, a wealthy Chicago insurance executive; over $1 million from the family of Richard Mellon Scaife of Gulf Oil and other interests (excluding $100,000 of illegal corporate donations which were made after the law went into effect); International Business Machines (IBM) $326,545; $251,000 before the 1972 law and $56,287 after the 1972 law from Tenneco; $232,550 after the 1972 law from City Investing Company; $191,131 from Litton Industries; $105,000 from Northrop Aviation (makers of the F-5 military aircraft); $84,432 from McDonnell-Douglas (another aircraft and missile maker); and $76,718 before the 1972 Disclosure Act and $41,282 after, from Texas Instruments. Together, the Nixon Finance Committee to Re-Elect the President received over $3.2 million from one hundred top business executives (selling goods to the government) before the 1972 Disclosure law. The federal campaign law that took effect on April 17, 1972, limited campaign spending in federal elections to 10 cents per voter, and required the disclosure of all contributions of $100 or more. Under the October 15, 1974, Campaign Finance Act: presidential candidates are required to make disclosures of their personal finances; individual taxpayers may donate $1.00 of tax money each year to political campaigns to a party of one's choice or to the general campaign fund; public financing is allowed on a matching basis (e.g., if a candidate received $1,000 from one family, he or she would receive a matching contribution from the federal campaign fund in the amount of $250, but if the same family made four individual donations of $250 each, the candidate would get an extra $1,000 from the public fund); a limit was placed on campaign spending ($20 million for a presidential candidate and $25,000 for congressional candidates—for the U.S. Senate and the U.S. House of Representatives); individual contributions were limited to $5,000 per candidate, with no restrictions on total contributions; a six-member Federal Election Commission was established to administer the law (two members each are appointed by the President, the Speaker of the U.S. House of Representatives, and the President pro tempore of the U.S. Senate). Some of the largest contributions to political campaigns (that were made before the 1974 Act) were made in 1974; the American Federation of Labor-Congress of Industrial Organizations (AFL-CIO) donated $1.4 million; the American Medical Association donated $792,697; the National Association of Realtors donated $272,092; and the National Association of Manufacturers donated $275,996. The costs of some presidential campaigns in recent years were: 1964, $38 million (or 54 cents per voter); 1968, $62 million (or 85 cents per voter), and 1972, $94 million (or $1.20 per voter). Campaigns for members of the U.S. House of Representatives and the U.S. Senate were approximately $15,000 to $300,000 per candidate. According to data by U.S. News & World Report (24 February 1992) and the Federal Election Commission in Washington, D.C., since 1976 spending in presidential campaigns by both parties was as follows: in 1976, Gerald Ford (Republican), $13.6 and Jimmy Carter (Democrat), $12.04 million; 1980, Ronald Reagan (Republican), $19.8 million and Jimmy Carter (Democrat), $18.05 million; in 1984, Ronald Reagan (Republican), $26.2 million and Walter Mondale (Democrat), $27.0 million; in 1988, George Bush (Republican), $30.6 million and Michael Dukakis (Democrat), $28.2 million; and estimated spending for 1992: George Bush (Republican), $33 million and the Democrat $10-15 million. President Bush is expected to gather about $90 million and the total spending for all parties is expected to reach about $400 million by election day in November 1992. Under the "fairness doctrine" all major presidential candidates are entitled to equal time to present their views over radio and television networks (which are licensed by the Federal Communications Commission). Because of the restrictive nature of the campaign financing laws in recent years, most political party organizations resort to other forms of fund raising, such as parties, receptions, or dinners ranging from $10 to $1,000 per plate per person. During the 1992 presidential campaign, the Democratic and Republican candidates received each $55 million in federal money. A candidate of a new party is eligible for public money for campaign costs after the election according to the total votes the candidate received. Each presidential candidate, if he accepts public funds, is allowed to spend up to $50,000 out of his pocket. In order to circumvent the law, private individuals may donate as much as they want to state party organizations and party organizations may spend the money as they wish, provided it is an indirect aid to their presidential candidate and money is not dispensed in his name. Tax law allows American taxpayers to allocate $1.00 of their tax money to the presidential campaign fund. In 1992 only about 20 percent of taxpayers have done so. Because of lack of support, the funds is expected to be depleted by 1996. It is estimated that presidential hopefuls spend between fifty to seventy-five percent of their time raiding the wallets of supporters. Former Governor of Texas and a Republican contender for the presidency in 1980, John B. Connally, spent over $11 million of privately-collected funds, by-passing with pride the federal money, and, as a result, declared personal bankruptcy. Connally was Governor of Texas in 1963 and rode with President John F. Kennedy in the convertible when President Kennedy was assassinated, and Connally was wounded. See AGENCY AGREEMENT, FEDERAL ELECTION COMMISSION (FEC).

Campaign Rhetoric. See POLITICAL RHETORIC.

Campus. The modeling of the American intelligence establishment on the university campus where scholars gather and derive intelligence from overt and covert sources in order to aid the American leadership in shaping its domestic and foreign policies. Beginning with the Office of Strategic Services (OSS) to the recent Central Intelligence Agency (CIA) and other members of the American intelligence community, strict scientific methodology was applied to research, particularly in the research and analysis branches. See INTELLIGENCE.

Canada First Policy. See LIBERAL PARTY OF CANADA.

Canada's Distinct Society. See QUEBEC DISTINCT SOCIETY.

Canada's Pacific Partnership. See PACIFIC PARTNERSHIP.

Canadian Armed Forces Interoperability Concept. See INTEROPERABILITY.

Canadian Cession. After nine years of continuous warfare along the North American border, the French and Indian War ended on February 10, 1763, and France ceded all claims on Canada to Britain. This act of British consolidation in Canada was aimed at better control of revolutionary aspirations of the North Americans who were actively preparing for independence from England.

Canadian Home Rule. See BRITISH COMMONWEALTH OF NATIONS, TAKING THE CONSTITUTION HOME.

Cancer of the Pacific. General Hideki Tojo, Premier of Japan 1941-1944, declared that a "new order" must be implemented in the Pacific Rim. He felt that the United States' influence should be erased from Asia, particularly China and the Philippines, where Japan's sphere of influence was thought to extend. (Tojo was hanged as a war criminal in 1948.) The so-called "Greater East Asian Co-Prosperity Sphere" (GEACPS) was formed toward this end.

Cancer on the Presidency. See WATERGATE AFFAIR.

Candidate Who Can't Win Can Afford to Tell the Truth. According to Lynn Nofziger, an expert on American politics and once political aide to President Ronald Reagan, candidates for public office refrain from clearly identifying problems or needs as they see them so that they will not be associated with inept leadership in the past, or have brought into question their ability to deal with problems in the future; the belief that statements made during a campaign may harm candidates in the future.

Cannon Revolt. Joseph G. ("Uncle Joe") Cannon, as the Speaker of the U.S. House of Representatives (1903-1911), had the exclusive power to make committee appointments at his discretion. Insurgent Republicans, led by George W. Norris of Nebraska, revolted against that practice in 1910, first by taking away his power to appoint members to the Rules Committee (appointments became subject to election by the House membership) and then by excluding Cannon from that committee.

Canon Law. The body of laws of an ecclesiastical authority (e.g., church or religious order).

Canton. A political subdivision in the Swiss confederation, which consists of 23 cantons.

CAP. See COMMUNITY ACTION PROGRAM, COMMUNITY SERVICE ADMINISTRATION (CSA).

Capital Gain. The actual gain on an asset (e.g., real estate, stocks, or bonds) resulting from the difference between the purchase of the asset and its sale. Such gains are taxed now in the United States, and President George Bush proposed in his State of the Union message in January 1992, repeal of the tax as it hinders economic activity. The Democrats in the U.S. Congress favor the tax, because it allegedly affects only the rich with incomes over $200,000, about one-percent of the U.S. population. When President Bush announced a modification of the capital gains tax in his January 1992 State of the Union address, his Democratic critics were not satisfied with it, claiming that, as presented by the president, it still favors the one-percent of the very rich. Democratic Senator Tom Harkin commented in jest while campaigning for the presidency in the New Hampshire Primary, that the president's proposal will provide, "Caviar for the wealthy, but cheese dip for the middle class."

Capital Gains Tax. See CAPITAL GAIN.

Capital Levy. A tax on income in addition to regular income tax (e.g., a corporate tax).

Capital Offense. A crime considered so serious that death maybe considered an appropriate punishment (e.g., murder or treason).

Capital Punishment. The capital punishment—death by hanging, shooting (in the State of Wyoming one has a choice to be shot or to be hanged), gas, electrocution, or lethal injection—is not uniformly applied in the United States. The voices for and against death penalty, similarly as in the case of abortion, are about evenly divided. In recent times, the death penalty was restored in the U.S. in 1976 and since 156 persons have been executed in 16 states.

Capitalism. A system of economy based on free enterprise with minimum interference by government; an economic system in which the bulk of the means of production (e.g., the production facilities and the capital) and the means of distribution (marketing facilities and systems) of goods and services are privately owned and operated; or a system of economic activity whereby the individual uses his talents and/or capital for the purpose of earning a profit. To paraphrase one economist, it is a system of incentives and work for profit; a system of "two cows and one bull," and not the other way around.

Capitalist Malady of Contentment. A thesis advanced by Professor John Kenneth Galbraith (*The Culture of Contentment*, Houghton Mifflin), world famous economist, social theorist, and educator, to the effect that the U.S. is suffering from the "malady of capitalist contentment" and not devoting sufficient attention to the poor in America (who are growing in number). The "functional underclass," as he calls them, are not encouraged to participate in electoral processes, by which means they could influence public policy. Professor Galbraith considers the "underclass," which consists mainly of recent immigrants, as crucial to American economy. "Minority communities," writes Professor Galbraith, "once poor but benign and culturally engaging, are now centers of terror and despair; because of neglect.

Capitalist Mentality. See EASTOXIFICATION.

Capitalist Worker Partnership. "Pure" capitalism or industrial capitalism. It occurs when the workers purchase stock in the company for which they work, and thus become partners and capitalists.

Capitalistic Encirclement. See ENCIRCLEMENT.

Capitol Hill. The hill in Washington, D.C. on which the U.S. Capitol building rests. Also a general term for the U.S. Congress.

Capo Consigliere. See MAFIA.

Capo di Capi. See MAFIA.

Captive. In the language of business, an autonomous business enterprise set up by a major corporation in a different geographic area (most often in another state or in a foreign country), for the purpose of securing the assets from losses due to different wage scales, unions, product liability, kidnap, ransom, pollution liabilities, and property/casualty risks, and above all, as a tax shelter. This practice is common among insurance companies which in 1980 had over 1,000 such captives located in Bermuda alone where there is no income tax, no restriction on reserves, premium dollars, or investment, and where the sum of $120,000 is sufficient capital to operate an insurance company.

Carbon Paper. A chemically treated paper used for clandestine, "invisible" writing. A message can be written on such paper, usually between the lines of a very open and visible innocent letter, with onion juice, salt water, or chemicals. The recipient can retrieve the invisible message by treating the paper with special chemicals or by simply ironing the paper in order for the text to come out. See INTELLIGENCE.

Card-Carrying Communist. See CARD-CARRYING MEMBER, MCCARTHYISM.

Card-Carrying Member. An admitted member of an organization (party, club or an association); one who pays dues and is actively involved in its work. See MCCARTHYISM, RED MENACE.

Care-Taker Congressperson. See CARE-TAKER GOVERNMENT.

Care-Taker Government. A government of a temporary nature; one that governs in the interim between the outgoing and the incoming government. Also known as a "provisional government" The term "care-taker" may also be applied to a member of the U.S. Congress (the Senate and/or the House of Representatives) when, in case of vacancy due to death, resignation or removal, the governor of the state appoints a person to serve for the unexpired term (e.g., the appointment of Mrs. C. Boggs of Louisiana when her husband, Hale Boggs, was killed in an airplane accident; or Mrs. Muriel Humphrey, who was appointed on January 25, 1978, to serve part of the term (till November 1978) of her husband, Sen. Hubert Humphrey, who died on January 13, 1978). The practice of appointing spouses for such vacancies is becoming more popular with time. The same may occur in case of the death or resignation of a governor. Also, a popular governor who cannot succeed himself (auto-limitation) may help his wife to become elected for one term, and then run again (e.g., George Wallace, the governor of Alabama, let his wife Lurleen B. Wallace (1966-1970), "hold" the post for him for four years). In international relations, a state lacking diplomatic relations with another may have its interests represented by a third state, one which, as a "care-taker", will be compensated for its services (e.g., the Swiss Embassy in Havana, Cuba, represented the interests of the United States in Cuba, until special representatives were exchanged in 1976, while Cuban interests in the United States were represented by the Embassy of Czechoslovakia in Washington, D.C.) Under a monarchy, the "care-taker" may be a regent who is appointed to govern until a new king is elected, or until a prince or princess reaches the age of maturity. See COALITION, PROVISIONAL GOVERNMENT.

Care-Taker Governor. See CARE-TAKER GOVERNMENT.

Care-Taker Rules. See CARE-TAKER GOVERNMENT.

Care-Taker Senator. See CARE-TAKER GOVERNMENT.

Caribbean Black Belt. See TELLER AMENDMENT.

Caribbean Free Trade Association (CARIFTA). An information association created in 1968 for the purpose of mutual trade and collaboration among the poor regions of the Caribbean, mainly Barbados, Bahamas, Guyana, Jamaica, and Trinidad, and including also Antigua, Belize, Dominica, Grenada, Montserrat, St. Kitts, St. Lucia, and St. Vincent. The joint office of the organization is located in Georgetown, Guyana.

CARIFTA. See CARIBBEAN FREE TRADE ASSOCIATION.

Carpetbagger. A financial speculator before the Civil War in the United States, whose only possessions were wrapped in a carpet. Also, a speculator or an adventurer who migrated from the North to the South after the Civil War in order to obtain employment there, usually with the federal government, or to enter some profitable business. Those Southerners who aided the carpetbaggers were generally considered by the population in the South as traitors to the interests of that region and were derogatorily referred to as "scalawags" (a kind of small and not-too-handsome Shetland pony).

Cartagena Drug Summit. See ANDEAN INITIATIVE.

Cartel. A loose association of business enterprises organized for the purpose of better controlling the sources of raw materials, markets, and prices, and improving methods of operation and efficiency.

Carter Doctrine. In the main, it is the policy statement that President Jimmy Carter made in his State of the Union address to Congress, 23, January, 1980, stating that: "Any attempt by any outside force to gain control of the Persian Gulf region will be regarded as an assault on the vital interest of the United States. It will be repelled by any means necessary, including military force." This was the major tenet of the Doctrine. See ERA OF CREATIVITY, LAGOS DOCTRINE, NOTRE DAME DOCTRINE, WAKE FOREST DOCTRINE.

Carter-Ford Debate. See GREAT DEBATES.

Carterization. See HARMONY CONVENTION.

Casablanca Conference. A summit conference held in Casablanca, (French) Morocco, on January 14-24, 1943, between U.S. President Roosevelt and British Prime Minister Churchill, at which an agreement was reached to the effect that only unconditional surrender could be accepted from all the Axis powers (Germany, Japan, Italy, Vichy France, Croatia, Slovakia, and Rumania). Similar exploratory talks on the issue of unconditional surrender were held at the Cairo Conference. Because of the persistent demand by the allies for an unconditional surrender, the enemies decided to fight up to the last moment. See CAIRO CONFERENCE, SCHWARZE KAPELLE.

Casework. The individual cases (e.g., complaints or requests for assistance in solving problems related to government) which a member of Congress handles for his constituents. See CONGRESS OF THE UNITED STATES, UNITED STATES HOUSE OF REPRESENTATIVES, UNITED STATES SENATE.

Casey Accords. See BOLAND AMENDMENTS.

Cash for Trash. See KISS AND TELL FOR SALE.

Cassandra School. See URBANIZATION.

Cassandra Theory. See URBANIZATION.

Casual Theory in Political Science. See POLITICAL THEORY.

Casus Belli. In the Latin language, "event leading to or justifying war" or "provocative act leading to war." See CAUSUS POEDERIS, WAR.

Categorical Grant. Matching grants of the usual type, restricted to use in a single functional field for narrower purposes (categorical expenditure limits) than block grants. Categorical grants are usually subject to very specific planning requirements and other conditions on their use. Opposite of block grant.

Categorical Grants-in-Aid. Given by the federal government for specific purpose upon application by localities or states which match a fraction of a grant.

Category Killer. A supermarket which retails all sorts of goods, ranging from foodstuffs to medicines, set up by wealthy retailers focusing on consumer products sold at lower prices. The investment comes, as a rule, from groups with capital to invest who aim to eliminate smaller retailers. The employees are trained to perform like robots, with minimum wage pay plus about 5¢ an hour extra, most of them not even knowing who the owners of the business are. The superstores are not necessarily discount outlets, because once the competition from smaller retailers is eliminated, they monopolize the market and dictate the prices. The profits are derived from economy as a result of sale—from sales in large quantities, often at the expense of quality; the aim is profit rather than service to the community. See GROUP, MONOPOLY.

Caucus. A closed gathering of selected and trusted persons (usually leaders of a political party or organization), held for the purpose of choosing candidates for important elective and/or appointive positions. The caucus system was commonly used in the U.S. before the system of primaries or conventions was introduced (1824). Most early presidents, congressmen, and governors were selected in this manner. The caucus system is also extensively used during party conventions and in the U.S. Congress, mainly in the Senate.

Caudillo. See CAESARISM, FASCISM.

Causality. The manner in which causes and effects operate and are mutually interrelated.

Causes of War. See WAR.

Causus Foederis. In the Latin language, "the condition under which an agreement becomes operational and binding." Also, a doctrine applicable to relations among states when, by a mutual agreement, one state agrees to aid another (e.g., in cases of external aggression or an insurrection) automatically, without being reminded of such an obligation, any time a situation occurs that is described in the agreement. Article 5 of the NATO Treaty, for example, requires any one of its signatories to aid the others militarily in case of outside aggression, once it has been established that such aggression has actually taken place. See WAR.

Cavalier. One who supported the personal rule and was loyal to England's King Charles I in his imperial and colonial policies of dominating other geographic areas during the 1640s (e.g., the North American Colonies). The Cavaliers were opposed by the Parliamentarians, known as "Roundheads," under the leadership of Oliver Cromwell. The power-center of the Cavaliers was the Old Dominion, the Royal Colony of Virginia, which became known as the "Cavalier State" and a leading example of aristocratic rule in America. The aristocrats quickly gained power and influence (e.g., the Byrd family in Virginia acquired 179,000 acres of land and the largest library in the Colonies—consisting of 4,000 volumes—and continued to make an impact on the political life of Virginia, leading to the emergence of the "Byrd Political Machine" during the 1900s). Nathaniel Bacon rebelled against the aristocrats in Virginia in 1676, challenging their power and wealth. See POLITICAL MACHINE.

Cavalier State. See CAVALIER.

Cave Dweller. One of Washington's resident social elite of at least moderate wealth; member of the "right" clubs.

Caveat Emptor. In the Latin language, "buyer, beware!" In modern markets in open societies, to protect the buyer, there are often legal prohibitions against false advertising. These laws against fraud and defective products are known in the United States as "Truth in Lending" laws.

CBC. See CONGRESSIONAL BLACK CAUCUS.

CC. See CENTRAL COMMITTEE.

CDMR. See CHRISTIAN-DEMOCRATIC MOVEMENT OF RUSSIA.

CDU. See CHRISTIAN DEMOCRATIC UNION.

CEA. See COUNCIL OF ECONOMIC ADVISERS.

Cease and Desist. An order that may be issued by a judicial or semi-judicial agency of the government, requiring a sudden termination of a certain activity or a practice which is considered illegal or harmful. Such orders are commonly issued by the National Labor Relations Board to labor union organizations or to employers, commanding a stop to a certain unfair activity (e.g., a strike by a labor union or disrespect for employee's rights by an employer).

Celestial Kingdom. See BOXER REBELLION.

CEMA. See COUNCIL FOR ECONOMIC MUTUAL ASSISTANCE.

Censorship, Office of. A federal agency, established in 1941 by presidential order, to censor all communications between the U.S. and foreign states, particularly those at war with the U.S. The agency was abolished in 1945.

Censorship Program for the World. See DECLARATION ON FUNDAMENTAL PRINCIPLES GOVERNING THE USE OF THE MASS MEDIA IN STRENGTHENING PEACE AND INTERNATIONAL UNDERSTANDING AND IN COMBATING WAR PROPAGANDA RACISM.

Censure. A mode of accountability for checking upon and scrutinizing the activities and policies of the government, one of its agencies or officials or of private organizations and their officials. Censure is very common under the cabinet-parliamentary system of government (e.g., in England). In the U.S., the censure of the federal government can best be exemplified by occasional congressional hearings or investigations and by the refusal to confirm nominations or to appropriate funds.

Census. See UNITED STATES HOUSE OF REPRESENTATIVES.

Center. The middle faction within a political party, legislative body or any gathering where decisions are made. A faction that avoids extremes by choosing the middle-of-the-road course.

Center Alliance. The remnants of the once powerful and world-renowned Solidarity under the leadership of Polish President Lech Walesa. Solidarity was split in 1990 between the Center Alliance and the Civic Movement for Democratic Action (Polish acronym, ROAD), which emerged as an opposition to Walesa under the leadership of Poland's first premier of the Solidarity government, Tadeusz Mazowiecki. Once a loyal supporter and follower of Walesa, Mazowiecki was rewarded with the premiership, but he soon developed an appetite for political power and decided to challenge Walesa for the presidency in the 1990 election. Walesa was elected president, but his victory margin was too small and a run-off election had to be held in order to secure his position. See SOLIDARITY.

Centesimus Unnis. See ENCYCLICAL.

CENTO. See CENTRAL TREATY ORGANIZATION, Appendix 29.

Central American Common Market (CACM). An informal, unstructured understanding among the several Central American states on trade relations, exchange of marketing technologies, transport, and possible joint banking facilities. An underlying notion is to trade together as a unit with South American states and Mexico and North America, rather than follow the traditional bilateral mode. The member states are Panama, Costa Rica, Nicaragua, El Salvador, Guatemala, Honduras, and Mexico. Since dialogue began between Mexico and the United States, in 1990 and 1991, on mutual trade arrangements, the CACM has remained inactive, waiting for the outcome of the U.S.-Mexico dialogue.

Central Committee (CC). "Tzentralnoy Kommitet" in the Russian language. The policy-making and the ruling body of either the former Communist Party of the Soviet Union (CPSU), the Soviet Trade Unions, the Soviet Government or the Youth Organization (KOMSOMOL). It was dissolved in 1991.

Central Intelligence Agency (CIA). An agency of the federal government of the U.S. (established under the *National Security Act of 1947* and responsible to the President via the National Security Council), charged with the tasks of collecting and evaluating intelligence data and informing the President on security matters through daily reports, or "intelligence estimates." The Agency collaborates closely with the intelligence services of the Army, Navy, Air Force, the Bureau of Intelligence and Research of the U.S. Department of State, and the Federal Bureau of Investigation (FBI) on all matters pertaining to intelligence and counter-intelligence. In response to adverse publicity, U.S. President Gerald R. Ford (1974-1977) announced on January 4, 1975, that an intensive investigation would be made of all illegal activities of the CIA and the FBI and on January 5, 1975, named an eight-member commission with U.S. Vice President Nelson Rockefeller as its chairman. On January 27, 1975, the U.S. Senate also created a similar investigative body, a special committee, under the chairmanship of U.S. Senator Frank Church (D-Idaho). The House set up a similar panel on February 19, 1975. These panels found that the FBI and CIA have been involved in illegal activities, mainly the domestic surveillance of persons and organizations suspected of revolutionary activity or those who simply voiced their dissent (e.g., Dr. Martin Luther King, Jr., the black civil rights leader, was sent a letter by the FBI suggesting that he terminate his life.) The CIA has been involved in domestic spying (which is contrary to its mission), has attempted to unseat anti-American governments abroad, and has even planned the assassination of political leaders (including Fidel Castro of Cuba). In order to further curb all illegal activities by the CIA (which does not have police powers and whose jurisdiction is strictly limited to the conduct of intelligence activities outside the United States) as well as other intelligence and investigative agencies (e.g., the FBI), U.S. President Jimmy Carter (1977-1981) issued an Executive Order January 24, 1978 (superseding the Executive Order issued on February 7, 1976, by U.S. President Gerald R. Ford, (1974-1977), which stipulates that the supervision and coordination of all intelligence activity by the United States will rest with the "Special Coordinating Committee" (then directed by Dr. Zbigniew K. Brzezinski, Assistant to the President on National Security Affairs and head of the National Security Council, which includes the Central Intelligence Agency, The Federal Bureau of Investigation, the Drug Enforcement Agency of the U.S. Treasury Department, and the Defense Intelligence Agency of the U.S. Department of Defense). The National Security Agency (NSA), which was involved in photographic satellite reconnaissance and electronic communication interception (listening to radio, telephone, and telegraph conversations among leaders in foreign states and possibly foreign embassies in the United States) was included in this reorganization. These operations were supervised by a National Security Council panel (known as "N-skids"). The Order forbids all intelligence agencies from conducting covert surveillance of American citizens and resident aliens (termed "United States Persons") by any means, including the use of electronic devices, without the prior authorization of the President and the approval of the U.S. Attorney General. The Director of the Central Intelligence Agency (CIA) serves as Director of Intelligence (DI) with the authority to coordinate all intelligence products of the various agencies, prepare budgets, and supervise the assignment of personnel to the various intelligence tasks. He is responsible to the President through the Special Coordinating Committee. The activities of the intelligence apparatus are periodically reviewed by the "Policy Review Committee of the National Security Council," which "defines and establishes priorities for intelligence consumers" (the principal consumer is the U.S. President), under the direction of the Director of Intelligence. See BAY OF PIGS, COVERT ACTION, INTELLIGENCE CYCLE, POLITICAL ETHICS, PROPAGANDA ASSETS INVENTORY (PAI), WATERGATE AFFAIR, Appendix 32, 33.

Central Intelligence Authority. See PEOPLE'S COMMISSION FOR INTERNAL AFFAIRS (NKVK).

Central Planner Economy. See TYPES OF POLITICO-ECONOMIC SYSTEMS in Appendix 83, TYPES OF MARKET SYSTEMS in Appendix 84.

Central Powers. See VERSAILLES TREATY.

Central Treaty Organization (CENTO or CENTRO). A series of military and defense agreements of 1955 among Iran, Pakistan, Turkey, Iraq, the United Kingdom, and the U.S. (Iraq withdrew in 1959.) CENTO collapsed during the 1977 Islamic Revolution in Iran. Also known as the "Baghdad Pact." See MIDDLE EAST TREATY ORGANIZATION (METO), Appendix 29.

Centralism. A political system in which all decision-making, control and/or executive functions are exercised centrally by a single body (e.g., single dictator or a collective), with little or no autonomy given to other elites in the society. A system that rests on a rigid, authoritarian exercise of authority and control through command rather than political bargaining processes; an apolitical system which allows little or no political processes for policy inputs and outputs. See COMMUNIST PARTY OF THE SOVIET UNION (CPSU), DEMOCRATIC CENTRALISM.

Centralism, Democratic. See DEMOCRATIC CENTRALISM.

Centralized Authority and Control. See LIBERAL CONSTITUTION.

Centralized Federalism. See FEDERALISM.

Centrist. See CENTER AND MIDDLE-OF-THE-ROAD.

CENTRO. See CENTRAL TREATY ORGANIZATION.

Certificate of Convenience and Public Necessity. See PUBLIC INTEREST CONVENIENCE AND NECESSITY.

Certiorari. See WRIT OF COMMON USE.

Cession. Voluntary transfer of territory from one state to another, usually by a treaty. See TREATY.

Chancellor. The head of government and leader of his party (majority) in the Bundestag in the German Federal Republic or in the Republic of Austria. Also, the title of a judge presiding over a court of equity or a top administrative officer of an educational institution.

Chancellor of the Exchequer. See EXCHEQUER.

Chancery. Court of equity as distinguished from common law court; the office of an ambassador and his immediate staff; or a court of record under some jurisdictions. (In England, once the highest court of justice but, since 1873, a division of the High Court of Justice.)

Chancery Court. A court having jurisdiction in cases of equity.

Change of Venue. See VENUE.

Changing of the Guard. A phrase used in politics to signify the change of government (e.g., from one party to another or changes in the personnel in government, in a party or in an organization). See PALACE GUARD, PRESIDENTIAL TRANSITION.

Chaos. See COUNTERINSURGENCY IN AMERICA, HT/LINGUAL.

Chapultepec Act. See INTER-AMERICAN CONFERENCE ON PROBLEMS OF WAR AND PEACE.

Character Assassination. As applied to practical politics, an act damaging a person's reputation and dignity and minimizing his suitability for holding public office. Congressional Committee hearings in the United States revealed, for example, that former F.B.I. Director, Herbert Hoover, despised Dr. Martin Luther King, Jr., because he was black and outspoken. Hoover used every trick to discredit King, including bugging his hotel rooms, recording conversations, proposing that he commit suicide and similar acts. King remained unintimidated. See POLITICAL RHETORIC, SKELETON IN THE CLOSET.

Chargé d'Affaires. Diplomatic official, usually one in charge of the diplomatic mission in the absence of the ambassador or minister. See DIPLOMATIC RANK.

Charisma. As used in the language of politics, uncommon, extraordinary qualities or abilities (such as personal appearance, presentment, ability to speak effectively and to arouse general sympathy and admiration) to influence others, mainly to get them to behave (e.g., to vote) in a desirable manner. Term taken from a Greek word meaning "divine gift."

Charismatic Authority. See AUTHORITY.

Charismatic-Type Political Party. A political party that is primarily interested in demonstrating its support of some well-known public figure or its showmanship-like characteristics rather than bidding for the control of government (e.g., the Nazi party of Adolf Hitler, the Peronista party of Juan Perón or the Union for the New Republic (UNR) of France which supported Charles de Gaulle). See POLITICAL PARTY.

Charlie. See VIET-MINH.

Charter. An official document issued by an authorized agency of the state to a local political subdivision (city, town, township, or village) designating the area of its jurisdiction and describing the manner in which the powers granted are to be exercised. See DILLON'S RULE, MUNICIPAL CORPORATION.

Charter 77. A coalition of intellectuals, clergy, and young people, which was formed in 1977 in Czechoslovakia in response to U.S. President Jimmy Carter's call for protection and respect for human rights. The principal leader of the Charter 77 movement is former minister of foreign affairs, Jiri Hajeck, who has been living under house arrest in Prague since February 1977. Most of the 80 signers of the Charter lost their jobs soon after the document appeared in January 1977. In its Charter, the group appeals to all freedom-loving nations of the world to influence the behavior of communist rulers everywhere, particularly with respect to the observance of human rights in the spirit of the Helsinki agreement. The Charter was not signed, but it was endorsed by Aleksander Dubcek, the Secretary of the Communist Party of Czechoslovakia, who, between 1966-1968, attempted to restore democratic institutions and processes in his country (known as "Prague Spring"). But this displeased the Soviet Union and, in 1968, Warsaw Pact nations stepped in and removed Dubcek by force. Czechoslovakia has since returned to totalitarian rule. Dubcek was first assigned to minor posts in government and then lived in Slovakia as a "non-person" (a term used in the former Soviet Union and the East European socialist states for a demoted, disgraced government official whose political career has been ruined forever, one who lives under constant surveillance by state security forces and is forbidden to travel abroad or to keep contact with political leaders abroad or at home). Dubcek fought for human rights and political and economic freedoms in Czechoslovakia, for which he was charged with "counterrevolutionary disruption." In 1992, Dubcek renewed his political activities. See BREZHNEYEV DOCTRINE, HUMAN RIGHTS-AMERICAN DEFINITION, SIBERIA OF BUREAUCRACY, VELVET REVOLUTION.

Charter Colony. See AMERICAN COLONIES.

Charter of San Salvador. See ORGANIZATION OF CENTRAL AMERICAN STATES (ODECA).

Charter Project. See COUNTERINSURGENCY IN AMERICA.

Chauvinist. Fanatical patriot; one boastfully showing devotion to a cause. (Named after one Nicholas Chauvin, a soldier of Napoleon I, who was notorious for his bellicose attachment to the lost imperial cause.) See AMERICA-FIRSTER, HARD HAT, JINGO.

Checkbook Diplomacy. A pejorative term applied to states which are engaged in "supplementing diplomatic efforts with ready cash." Often applied to contemporary Japan due to its large cash reserves from global trade. See DOLLAR DIPLOMACY.

Checks and Balances. A mode of statecraft whereby one branch of government checks the powers of another for the purpose of maintaining a balance and preventing aggrandizement of power. In the U.S. the legislative branch, Congress, composed of the House of Representatives and the Senate, serves as a check upon the remaining branches of the government—the President and his Cabinet and the Judiciary (the Supreme Court and Federal Courts)—by means of appropriations and confirmation of appointments to the executive and judicial branches, by giving "advice and consent," (by the Senate) or by its ability to impeach the executive officers or the judges. The executive branch, on the other hand, may delay or refuse to enforce congressional laws or judicial decisions, or enter into agreements without the advice and consent of the Senate by means of "executive agreements" or pardon persons convicted by the judiciary. The judicial branch, too, may check upon the two remaining branches of the government by declaring their acts unconstitutional (judicial review).

Cheka. See EXTRAORDINARY COMMISSION FOR COMBATING COUNTERREVOLUTION, SABOTAGE AND THE DERELICTION OF DUTY.

Chemical Warfare. The use of chemicals (e.g., toxic, lethal, or nerve gases, or liquids, or other artificially manufactured chemical agents of mass destruction) to combat, incapacitate, or destroy an enemy. In case of bacteriological warfare, virulent bacterial agents causing illness and/or death are used against the enemy.

Cherezvytchayka. In the Russian language, "Czerezvytchaynaya Kommisya K'Borby Konterrevolutzyi, Sabotagzu, y Ofitzyalnygh Prostuplenyi," or CHEKA for short See EXTRAORDINARY COMMISSION FOR COMBATING COUNTERREVOLUTION, SABOTAGE AND THE DERELICTION OF DUTY.

Chicano. A person of Mexican, Puerto Rican, or other Latin-American descent; or one whose native language is either Spanish or Portuguese.

Chicken Hawk. See WAR HAWK.

Chicken in Every Pot ... Car in Every Garage. Such were the promises made to the American electorate by Herbert Hoover, presidential candidate of the Republican Party in 1928. Soon after he was installed in office, the stock market crashed and the nation's (and the world's) economic depression commenced.

Chicken Salad Syndrome. See POLITICAL SYSTEM, SYSTEMS ANALYSIS.

Chicken War. The term refers to the discriminatory tariffs that the member-states of the European Common Market imposed on the American export of fifty million dollars worth of poultry during the latter part of 1963. Since the poultry was shipped to Europe with the bulk of agricultural commodities which the European states agreed to purchase, U.S. President John F. Kennedy threatened to stop all shipments and also to impose retaliatory tariffs against European goods that were sold in the United States. The problem was resolved within the framework of the General Agreement on Tariffs and Trade (GATT) to the mutual satisfaction of all parties concerned. See KENNEDY ROUND.

Chief Justice of the United States. The chief executive officer of the collegially organized Supreme Court, nominated by the President (for a term of *good behavior*) and confirmed by the Senate (through the standing Committee on the Judiciary). The Chief Justice presides during the hearing of cases, assigns cases to individual justices for study (he himself takes turns on an equal basis), appoints members of the Court to housekeeping functions (e.g., revision of the rules of procedure), administers the oath of office to the President; and presides in Congress during impeachment proceedings against the President and/or Vice President.

Chief of Protocol. See DIPLOMATIC PROTOCOL.

Chief of Staff. Head of White House staff, especially under Eisenhower and Nixon. See HEAD OF STATE.

Chief of State. See HEAD OF STATE.

Chieu Hoi. See OPEN ARMS PROGRAM.

China Lobby. See COMMITTEE FOR A FREE CHINA.

China Spring. See TIANANMEN SQUARE MASSACRE.

Chinese Proletariat. See EIGHT POINTS OF ATTENTION.

Chinese Volunteers in Korea. See KOREAN WAR.

Chip Commission. It comprised the International Commission of military representatives from Canada, Hungary, Indonesia, and Poland, which was called upon by the parties to the Paris Peace Agreement of 1973 to oversee the cease-fire in Vietnam.

Chistka. In the Russian language, "clean house." A term associated with periodical "cleaning" of the party ranks of persons who have shown little dedication to the party cause or who have failed in their positions of responsibility, either in party or government service, and are thus not worthy to remain party members. This practice originated with the so-called "purges" that were common under Josef Stalin between the years of 1926-1953. He did not hesitate to liquidate anyone who opposed him. See PURGE.

Chivalry. The dominant political philosophy of the ruling classes in Medieval Europe, particularly among the French and Anglo-Saxons.

Christian-Democratic Movement of Russia (CDMR). An organization which originated in the Soviet Union during the 1980s, and is currently active in the Commonwealth of Independent States (CIS), particularly in the Russian Republic, which advocates democracy and a free-market economy of the Western (particularly the American) style. The organization draws on the historic experience and achievements of the traditional Russian Tsarist "Landed Councils." These councils ("Ziemsky Sober," in the Russian language) were under the leadership of locally elected leaders and had a Christian (Russian Orthodox) orientation. The leadership of the Sobor alleges that the revival of the Sobor system constitutes the continuity of a legitimate rule in Russia.

Christian Democratic Union (CDU). In the German language, "Christlich Demokratische Union." One of the two largest political parties in the Federal Republic of Germany. The party, which was organized after World War II under the leadership of Dr. Konrad Adenauer, Germany's first postwar Chancellor, commands considerable influence and was instrumental in restoring stability and prosperity in West Germany. Its southern faction, the Christian Social Union (CSU), is very strong in the State of Bavaria and it supports the CDU on all major issues.

Christian Social Union (CSU). In the German language, "Christlich Soziale Union." The southern (Bavarian) faction of the Christian Democratic Union (CDU). For purposes of national elections, the CSU and the CDU present a joint ticket. Franz Josef Strauss is one of its founders and now the principal leader. See CHRISTIAN DEMOCRATIC UNION (CDU).

Chrysanthemum Kissers. Americans who speak in defense of Japan, Japanese and their trade practices in light of the "Japan Bashing" campaign. Author Michael Crichton (in *Rising Sun*) equates those who speak up for Japan "chrysanthemum kissers" and such, with Nazi Germany collaborators. See AMERICA BASHING, JAPAN BASHING.

Chu-Goku. In the Chinese language, "center of the universe." A concept of great importance to Chinese society, which for centuries has cultivated the notion that China is the center of the universe, despite any harassment by external adversaries. This motivates and inspires its people to survive, function, retain equilibrium, and ultimately maintain a stable and happy society.

Church Committee. See HT/LINGUAL.

Church State. See ADMINISTRATIVE STATE.

CIA. See CENTRAL INTELLIGENCE AGENCY, Appendices 32, 33.

CIPA. See CLASSIFIED INFORMATION PROCEDURES ACT.

Cipher Pad. A pad of paper containing pre-printed nonrepetitive keys used by clandestine operators in sending coded messages to their superiors. Also known as "one-time pad." See INTELLIGENCE.

Circuit Court. Any court of record (in which all proceedings are duly recorded and maintained) at the state level in the United States; any of the eleven Federal Courts of Appeal or Federal Circuit Courts and, prior to 1911, the official designation of any of the Federal Courts of Appeal. See JUDICIAL SELECTION COMMISSION.

Circular A-95. See PROJECT NOTIFICATION AND REVIEW SYSTEM.

Citizen Advisory Board. See PUBLIC ADVISORY BOARDS.

Citizen Feedback. See POLITICAL SYSTEM.

Citizen Legislator. See BUSINESS OF CONGRESS IS RE-ELECTION BUSINESS.

Citizen Reform Groups. Voluntary organization of citizens' interest groups who work toward a common goal, (e.g., senior citizens for specific benefits for the aged or environmental groups for clean air, etc).

Citizen's Arrest. An arrest conducted by a private citizen instead of an officer of the law; citizens may make arrests if they have cause to believe that a crime has been committed.

Citizen's Lobby. See COMMON CAUSE.

Citizenship. A set of legally delineated relationships between an individual person and the authority of a sovereign state, creating mutual legal rights and obligations on the part of each party (e.g., the state guarantees protection of one's property, or the right to participate in political processes such as voting and the individual in turn agrees to obey the laws and to generally support the state by, for example, paying taxes and aiding in the defense of the state). The rights of U.S. citizens (and all resident aliens as of 1978) are protected by specific constitutional provisions and judicial decisions: (1) the writ of *habeas corpus* may not be suspended except in cases of rebellion or invasion (Art. I, Sec. 9); (2) the federal and state governments may not pass bills of attainder or *ex post facto laws* (Art. I, Sec. 9 and 10)—(See *Calder v. Bull*, 1798; and *United States v. Lovett*, 1946); (3) the accused is entitled to a trial by a jury, except in cases of impeachment (Art. III, Sec. 2 and 3); (4) the citizens of all states are equal; they are entitled to all immunities and privileges on an equal basis (Art. IV, Sec. 2);

(5) religious affiliation may not serve as a basis of qualification for public office under the authority of the United States (Art. IV, Sec 2); (6) freedom of speech, religion, press, and assembly may not be abridged (Amendment I); (7) one's private quarters may not be requisitioned for stationing troops (army) (Amendment II); (8) procedural rights of persons accused of crimes must be observed (Amendments IV through VII); (9) the Civil War Amendments forbid slavery (Amendment VIII), guarantee protection of rights of citizens (equal protection under the law) (Amendment XIV), and the right to vote (Amendment XV); (10) discrimination in the right to vote on account of sex is forbidden—women's suffrage (Amendment XIX); (11) the abridgment of voting rights by the federal government as well as by states through such devices as poll taxes is prohibited (Amendment XXIV). This prohibition has been extended to state elections by the case of *Harper v. Virginia State Board of Elections* of 1966; (12) racial discrimination in primary elections (white primary) was held unconstitutional in *Smith v. Allwright,* 1944; (13) separate education is not equal (it is inferior), held by the Court in the two cases of *Brown v. The Board of Education* in 1954; (14) the Civil Rights Acts of 1960 and 1964, as well as the Voting Rights Act of 1965, bring further remedies for segregation practices and broaden the rights of citizens. Since the infamous *Dred Scott* case of 1857, judicial interpretation of the right to citizenship well reflects the turbulent development of America's political history: (1) the *Wong Kim Ark* case of 1898 recognized citizenship through *jus soli* and *jus sanguinis;* (2) citizenship through naturalization could be denied under the cases of *United States v. Schwimmer* of 1929, when a pacifist woman refused to pledge to fight for the United States; *United States v. Macintosh* of 1931, when a man took the oath, but without stipulating his willingness to take up arms in the defense of the United States; and *United States v. Bland* of 1931, when a Canadian nurse had shown no interest in serving the United States in case of war. These three cases have subsequently been overruled in *Girouard v. United States* of 1946, when a Seventh Day Adventist agreed to substitute service in the U.S. Armed Forces for combat duty. (Similar to this was the Court's ruling in a *per curia* Decision in *Cohnstaedt v. Immigration and Naturalization Service* of 1946); (3) The Nationality act of 1940 stipulated that an American citizen may be deprived of citizenship for voting in a foreign election or for desertion from the armed forces in wartime. The Court declared these provisions unconstitutional in *Trop v. Dulles* in 1959, and in *Kennedy v. Mendoza-Martinez* in 1963. In 1964, the Court ruled in *Schneider v. Rusk* that a naturalized citizen may not be denaturalized for living abroad for three continuous years or more; and in *Afroyim v Rusk* of 1967, it held that voting in a foreign election alone, as was the case in *Perez v. Brownwell,* is not sufficient grounds for losing U.S. citizenship. In *Trop v. Dulles* the Court stated that U.S. "citizenship is not a license that expires, but a fundamental right." An Executive Order by U.S. President Jimmy Carter (1977-1981) on January 24, 1978, reiterated legal protection by the state to all "United States persons"—that is, those who are citizens of the United States as well as those who are nationals of another state, but who are legally admitted to residence in the United States. (Under the provisions of that Order, United States persons may not be subjected to "surveillance by television or other electronic devices" without the prior authorization by the U.S. President and the approval of the U.S. Attorney General.) Some juridical systems (e.g., France, the USSR, and most of the Socialist states) provide for either temporary (e.g., for a period of conviction for a crime) or permanent (e.g., in case of treason) deprivation of citizenship. Under many systems, including the United States, a person may give up citizenship of the native state and even remain a stateless person. Such persons are protected under the United Nations Charter. See JUS SANGUINIS, JUS SOLI, NATURALIZATION, POLITICAL SELF-ESTEEM, STATE UNTO ONESELF, SUBJECTS MIXTES, UNITED STATES PERSON, CIVIL RIGHTS ACTS, VOTING RIGHTS ACT OF 1965, OPINIONS OF THE U.S. SUPREME COURT IN SELECTED LANDMARK CASES in Appendix 48.

Citizenship Day. On February 29, 1952, U.S. President Harry S. Truman (1944-1953) designated September 17th of each year as Citizenship Day. This law replaced the "I Am an American Day" which was observed on the 3rd Sunday in May, and the "Constitution Day" which was formerly held on September 17th.

Citizenship is Not a License that Expires. See CITIZENSHIP, *TROP V. DULLES,* Appendix 44.

City. A municipal corporation, ordinarily chartered by the state (or the United States Congress as in the case of the city of Washington, District of Columbia) and one having its own autonomous government. In some states, political subdivisions must meet certain criteria before they can qualify for city charters. In the state of Virginia, for example, the primary requirement is a population of 5,000 or more. A municipal corporation may elect its own officers, issue its own ordinances, organize a separate school district and police force, and even impose certain local taxes on property (valuation tax).

City Council. The legislative (and sometimes the legislative and the executive) body of a city government which exercises powers granted to it under a charter. Its principal function is to enact ordinances and oversee the activities of the city government. See CITY, MUNICIPAL CORPORATION.

City-County Consolidation. The practice of combining the various functions of a city government with that of a county for the purpose of avoiding duplication of functions, and to provide better services to the community. Such consolidations are common when either the city or the county (the suburban area) is expanding.

City Manager. The executive officer (ordinarily appointed by the city council) who is responsible for the day-to-day operation of the administrative agencies (the government) of the city.

City-State. A small, sovereign, and ordinarily self-sufficient state like that of ancient Athens or Sparta, Vatican City or San MaFino today.

Civic Movement for Democratic Action (ROAD). See CENTER ALLIANCE.

Civil Conservation Corp. (CCC). Public work program was begun during the Depression of the early 1930s to provide work for some of the many unemployed.

Civil Disobedience. The practice of resisting and disregarding the lawful authority of a state (e.g., the refusal to obey the existing laws, such as paying taxes or serving in the armed forces). See SATYAGRAHA.

Civil Disorder Control Plan. See COUNTERINSURGENCY IN AMERICA.

Civil Liberty. See DEMOCRACY.

Civil List. The official register of all federal employees in the United States. Also, the amount of appropriation fixed for the upkeep of the royal family or civil servants (e.g., in England). In April 1978, for example, the annual royal tax-free allowance in England providing for the upkeep of the royal establishment was increased from $4.85 million to $5.29 million (or 9.2%) to compensate for inflation (which was running at 9.7% in England at that time). The Laborite government, which had approved this increase, warned through one of its members (William Hamilton, a Laborite member of the Parliament) that none of this allowance should go to Princess Margaret, the sister of Queen Elizabeth II, because she had been neglecting her royal responsibilities (e.g., not appearing in public on ceremonial occasions and generally not acting as royalty) and had instead been spending her time in exotic places outside England with a wealthy socialite, Roderic Llewellyn. Princess Margaret's personal allowance in 1977 was $101,750 per year.

Civil Religion. See MANDATE OF HEAVEN.

Civil Rights. See CITIZENSHIP, CIVIL RIGHTS ACTS.

Civil Rights Acts. (1) On February 6, 1866, the U.S. Congress passed a Civil Rights Act, which, for the first time in the history of American jurisprudence, defined citizens as all persons born in the United States, except non-taxed Indians. It stated that all citizens of every race and color should have equal legal and property rights. The Act became the Fourteenth Amendment to the Constitution, and was ratified on July 28, 1868. (2) The March 1, 1875, Civil Rights Act (a part of the Reconstruction policy in the South which had been defeated during the War of Secession—Civil War of 1861-1865) stipulated that all persons, regardless of race or color, were entitled to the "full enjoyment of the accommodations, advantages, facilities, and privileges of inns, public conveyances on land or water, theaters, and other places of public amusement." In 1883, however, with Reconstruction fading away, the U.S. Supreme Court voided the Act in *Civil Rights Cases* 109 U.S. 3; 3 Sup. Ct. 18; 27 L. Ed. 835 (1833), which were five separate cases brought before it on appeal, on the grounds that segregation on account of race is a social matter and that it is within the domain of Congress to protect political and legal rights but not social rights-meaning that white supremacy was outside the domain of federal laws. (3) *The Civil*

Rights Act of 1957 reasserted the right to vote of all citizens, regardless of color, race, creed, religion, or national origin and authorized the U.S. Attorney General to seek injunctions against public and private interferences with the right to vote on racial grounds. The Act was tested and sustained in the case of *United States v. Raines*, 362 U.S. 17 (1960). U.S. Senator Strom Thurmond (D-South Carolina, who soon became a Dixiecrat and then a Republican), established a filibuster record by holding the Senate floor for 24 hours and 18 minutes (August 28-29), thus beating by one hour and twelve minutes a previous record which was made in 1953 by Senator Wayne Morse (D-Oregon). Thurmond spoke against the Civil Rights Act. (4) The 1960 Civil Rights Act reinforced the 1957 Civil Rights Act as it pertains to voting. It permitted "the joinder of states as party defendants" and gave the U.S. Attorney General access to local voting records. It also authorized the courts to register voters in areas of systematic discrimination. (5) The 1964 Civil Rights Act expedited the hearing of voting cases before three-judge courts that were convened specifically for that purpose and outlawed all tactics aimed at preventing Negroes from voting. The portion of the act which deals with equal accommodations was contested and upheld by the U.S. Supreme Court in *Heart of Atlanta Motel v. United States,* 379 U.S. 241 (1964). It was further tested in *Katzenbach v. McClung,* 379 U.S. 294 (1964). The court stated that "the commerce clause power is as broad as the economic needs of the nation." (6) The Civil Rights Act signed by President Lyndon B. Johnson on April 11, 1968 (seven days after the assassination of Dr. Martin Luther King in Memphis Tennessee, April 4, 1968) called for protection of civil rights workers and forbade discrimination in housing. The so-called "open housing" provision of the Act was subsequently voided by the U.S. Supreme Court (in June 1968) under a century-old law (of April 9, 1866) and applied only to some housing. See U.S. Constitution, Art. I. Sec. 8, Clause 3 in Appendix 48.

Civil Rights Hustler. One who knowingly profits from acts or activities which allegedly are designed to eradicate poverty and protect the civil rights of the poor and the oppressed, mainly poor black Americans, and one who in reality knowingly and willfully engages in the perpetuation of these evils of society and sees them as a source of good personal income. One of America's ablest black economists, Professor Walter E. Williams, calls such people "civil rights hustlers" and "poverty pimps." Every year the American Congress allocates billions of taxpayers' money for thousands of programs designed to aid the poor and the underprivileged; and hundreds of thousands of bureaucrats at all levels of government—federal, state, regional, and local—are creating, designing, and administering these programs. Should poverty and discrimination suddenly disappear, many of them would be unemployed, and particularly the lawyers, the physicians, and the accountants, who are the main agents determining public policy outcomes, would be the first to rise up in protest. Poverty and discrimination are major industries that grow and prosper as long as citizens have no tangible real knowledge of the undergirding motives for sustaining them. The study of government and politics in general is discouraged; few schools require knowledge of these subjects, and many substitute courses in basket-weaving and belly dancing for the study of government and politics, both domestic and foreign.

Civil Service. The body of all employees of a government (national, state or local) who are selected on the basis of merit (by examinations) rather than spoils (appointed by politicians regardless of merit) and who perform certain specific functions for the government on a non-political basis. Civil servants are ordinarily placed under the jurisdiction of some agency (the Civil Service Commission in the United States) which selects them and also protects them from arbitrary dismissal without good cause. (The United States Civil Service was established under the Pendleton Act of 1883. The Act provides that no civil servant may be dismissed without good cause and that he/she is entitled to due process.) See CIVIL LIST, HATCH POLITICAL ACTIVITIES ACTS.

Civil Service Reform Act of 1978. Became effective January 11, 1979. The U.S. Civil Service Commission was replaced by two agencies: Office of Personnel Management (OPM) and the Merit System Protection Board (MSPB).

Civil War. A military conflict that may erupt between opposing political or military groups within a single state. See AMERICAN CIVIL WAR.

Civil War Amendments. Amendments to the U.S. Constitution that were adopted during the Civil War (War of Secession), 1861-1865: Amendment XIII (anti-slavery), XIV (equal protection under the laws) and XV (right of citizens to vote). See CITIZENSHIP, U.S. CONSTITUTION in Appendix 8.

Civil War in Russia. See WAR COMMUNISM.

Civilian Complaint Review Board. See OMBUDSMAN.

Civitas Maxima. In the Latin language, "international community" or "community of the highest order." See INTERNATIONAL LAW, STATE.

Class. See TOOLS OF ANALYSIS OF A POLITICALLY ORGANIZED SOCIETY.

Class Action. See CLASS ACTION SUIT.

Class Action Suit. The act of bringing before a court of law for adjudication a case which may affect other persons, not parties to the case, who fall in a similar category.

Class Consciousness. The notion that one should be aware of her or his status in society, or in a stratum within a society, and should remain loyal to others of her or his kind. (According to Karl Marx and Friedrich Engels, socialist revolution may be impossible as long as the workers, the proletariat, develop no class consciousness.) See COMMUNISM, MARXISM.

Class Power. See POWER.

Class Struggle. A concept, as developed by Karl Marx, pointing out that class struggle is one of the inherent contradictions of a capitalistic society between those who have (the capitalists, or bourgeoisie) and those who have not, (the workers, or the proletariat), and that the existence of classes in a society is only bound up with a particular historic phase in the development of production. Class struggle will necessarily lead to a proletarian revolution during which the proletariat will abolish the bourgeoisie and will establish a new social order involving a dictatorship by the proletariat. This dictatorship, however, will only be a transition to a classless society, one without a concept of private property, need for wars, or need for any type of political organization (state or government). See CLASS CONSCIOUSNESS, MAOISM, MARXISM.

Classified Information Procedures Act (CIPA). Congressional legislation of 1980 which allows judges of courts of law in the United States to hold trials in secrecy in order to protect secrets concerning national security. See FREEDOM OF INFORMATION ACT, GRAYMAIL, INTELLIGENCE.

Clausula Rebus Sic Stantibus. In the Latin language, "a formula that nothing remains stable." Also, a principle in international law according to which all international treaties and agreements are presumed to be valid and must be observed to the letter unless some important changes take place as to the parties of the treaties or agreements, or the subject matter (e.g., if an existing agreement is considered illegal or if any party to the treaty, a state, disintegrates or becomes conquered). See PACTA SUNT SERVANDA.

Clean Bill. Term used in the United States Congress to describe a bill which was cleared by committees and is ready for final voting, with or without amendments. See CONGRESS OF THE UNITED STATES.

Clear and Present Danger. A rule formulated by U.S. Supreme Court Justice Oliver W. Holmes in *Schenk v. U.S.*, 249 U.S. 47 (1919), which limits the right to free speech under the provisions of the First Amendment to the United States Constitution if such speech can be considered as causing "clear and present danger." Justice Holmes stated in part: *"The character of every act depends upon circumstances in which it is done . . . . The most stringent protection of free speech would not protect a man in falsely shouting 'fire' in a theatre and causing a panic . . . . The question in every case is whether the words are used in circumstances and are of such a nature as to create a clear and present danger that they will bring substantive evils that Congress has a right to prevent. It is a question of proximity and degree."*

Clearinghouse. See PROJECT NOTIFICATION AND REVIEW SYSTEM.

Clericalism. The practice of clergy of established religions directly engaging in political and governmental processes, usually as an effort to instill certain doctrinal principles, (e.g., the case of the Shiite Muslims in Iran, and also in many states in Europe where clergy, especially of the Catholic faith, were engaging in secular, political/governmental processes). At the beginning of the 1900s the strong influence of the clergy triggered anti-clerical reaction and resulted in many priests being killed, both by the government and by vigilantes. In some countries, where the basic laws (constitutions) made no provision for the separation of church and state, the influence of clergy was considerable. In many states, (e.g., pre-Soviet Russia, Poland, and France), clergymen were on a par with government employees, and were paid regular wages from the national treasury. In the United States, at the Vatican's direction, Roman Catholic priests and nuns were to give up their temporal posts. Accordingly, a member of the U.S. Congress from Massachusetts resigned his post.

Clerico-Fascists. A term derogatorily describing the philosophical outlook and membership of the Christian Social Party in Austria (as well as similar clerical fascist alliances in other European states during Hitler's rise to power in Germany, 1933-45). The principal aim of those groups was to oppose Marxist socialism in any form anywhere. The Austrian clerical fascists had even established their own private army known as the Heimwehr, which subsequently aided Hitler's take-over of Austria.

Clerk of Court. An official of the U.S. (elective or appointive) who records the proceedings and issues the processes of a court of record (and of the county government in cases when the office of the Clerk is combined with that of a County Clerk).

Clifford Memorandum. See SCARE THE HELL OUT OF THE COUNTRY.

Cloak. Term used commonly to describe covert intelligence and/or counter-intelligence gathering and evaluation, espionage and/or counter-espionage. See DAGGER.

Cloaking. The practice of concealing assets of one state in the territory of another by either investing in existing foreign enterprises, or creating new ones for the purpose of drawing benefits from international trade in case of war. Nazi Germany, under Adolf Hitler (1933-1945), originated that practice by setting up business enterprises (legitimate or phony corporations) in states which most likely would remain neutral in an expected or anticipated future war (e.g., the I. G. Farben concern), in order that they would be able to conduct legitimate international trade and aid the German war-oriented economy. In modern times private persons use such practices as a means of avoiding high taxes.

Closed Diplomacy. The practice of conducting diplomatic or international relations covertly (in secrecy). See COVERT ACTION, HARDWARE DIPLOMACY, SUMMIT CONFERENCE.

Closed District. See SAFE DISTRICT.

Closed Party System. A political system which either denies the rights of other political parties to exist and compete for power, or imposes strict regulations (constitutional or statutory) which discourage the proliferation or activities of political parties. See ONE-PARTY SYSTEM, PRIMARY ELECTION.

Closed Political System. A political system which is not susceptible to changes by either coincidence or design, a totalitarian system. One that hinders social mobility by creating some artificial obstacles (e.g., China Wall or Berlin Wall).

Closed Primary. A primary election during which only the registered members of a particular party may vote—those who declare themselves to be members of that particular party. See OPEN PRIMARY.

Closed Shop. A place of employment requiring membership in a labor union before one can be hired. See OPEN SHOP, WAGNER ACT.

Closed Society. See OPEN SOCIETY.

Closure. See CLOTURE.

Cloture. A procedural device used in the U.S. Congress and designed to prevent filibustering by imposing a time limit on debates of any issue and/or limiting the number of amendments to a bill or resolution before the vote is taken. In the U.S. Senate (under Rule 22) a debate can be limited by either unanimous consent or by a two-thirds majority. A motion for cloture, which can apply to any measure before the Senate, requires sixteen signatures of individual Senators for introduction and two-thirds of the Senators present and voting for it. The vote upon cloture, taken by a roll-call, can be taken one hour after the Senate meets the next day. If passed, each Senator is allowed one hour to speak on any one issue. See UNITED STATES SENATE.

Clout. See PANDIT.

Club. A secret, informal organization that was formed in Paris, France, in 1972, by the world's major producers of uranium, for the purpose of controlling the production, distribution, and price of this radioactive substance which is essential for the production of nuclear weapons. The formation of this cartel is in violation of American anti-trust laws. Major private corporations from the United States (e.g., the Gulf Oil Corporation) and Canada are dominating members of this club. See MULTINATIONAL CORPORATION.

Coalition. An alliance between persons, organizations, political parties, or governments, set up by combining forces and resources for the purpose of achieving desired objectives (e.g., a political party lacking the necessary majority to form a government under cabinet-parliamentary form of government may join ranks with another party and form a coalition government). See CABINET PARLIAMENTARY GOVERNMENT, PARLIAMENT.

Coalition for Rural America. A bipartisan informal organization composed of political, business, and educational leaders "to speak for the total rural community . . . in a way that the Urban Coalition and the U.S. Conference of Mayors speak for the large cities." One of its major objectives is to obtain a differential in favor of enterprises which locate in rural areas (investment tax credit). The bi-partisan groups' first recommendation called for amendment of the President's investment tax credit proposal to provide a differential in favor of enterprises that locate in rural areas. The President, through proclamation 4094 of 1971 designated the week of November 19 through November 25 as National Farm-City Week and requested the leaders of agricultural organizations, business and labor groups, and other interested organizations to focus their attention upon the interrelationship of urban and rural community development.

Coalition Government. See COALITION.

Coattail. A strategy commonly used by political parties in electoral politics, whereby the name of the well known, well respected, and popular candidate is listed on a single ballot among other less known and less popular persons running for different offices, with the hope that the popular candidate will help the others get elected as well. Very often, however, the case of reverse coattail may occur when, for example, a popular candidate running for a low-echelon state office will help a candidate running for a high-echelon office (e.g., the presidency of the United States, the governorship of a state or other office). Such practices are often considered a matter of loyalty to the party as well as to the candidate running for a high office.

COCOM. See COORDINATING COMMITTEE FOR MULTILATERAL EXPORT CONTROLS.

Cod War. For a number of years, England and Iceland disputed each other's rights to fish for cod in certain areas of the North Sea after Iceland started to enforce the 200-mile territorial waters rule. In 1975, England and Iceland exchanged gunfire from their naval units, which almost commenced a major war, but the NATO Council, of which both states are members, intervened, and war was averted. Similar incidents over fishing rights and the 200-miles of ocean claimed by some states as territorial waters, have occurred in Latin America, mainly Peru, which threatened military reprisal against any nation fishing for tuna in waters adjacent to its territory. Several American tuna vessels have been detained during recent years, and released after payment of heavy fines (ranging from $5,000 to $50,000 per boat). See TUNA WAR.

Code. A body of laws of a nation, state, city-state, or an international body, compiled and arranged systematically for easy reference and application by judicial officers. See DRACO CODE, HAMMURABI CODE, NAPOLEONIC CODE, UNITED STATES CODE.

Code Napoleon. See NAPOLEONIC CODE.

Code of Official Conduct of 1974. A code of conduct for the members of the U.S. House of Representatives which was adopted in 1974, and which called for non-discrimination against congressional employees on the grounds of race, sex, religion, or national origin. See LAST PLANTATION.

CODESA. See CONFERENCE FOR DEMOCRATIC SOUTH AFRICA.

Coercive Persuasion. See BRAINWASHING.

Coexistence. As applied to politics, the peaceful accommodation of two or more divergent political systems or blocs (e.g., capitalistic and socialistic states) short of an open, armed conflict. Also, one of the officially pronounced principles of Soviet foreign policy with non-socialist states. That concept was strongly emphasized by former Soviet Premier and Secretary of the Communist Party of the Soviet Union (CPSU), Nikita S. Khrushchev, particularly as applied to Soviet-American relations.

COG. See COUNCIL OF GOVERNMENT, NATIONAL ASSOCIATION OF REGIONAL COUNCILS (NARC).

COINTELPRO. Counterintelligence Program: A branch within the Federal Bureau of Investigation (FBI) which was charged with subversive activities against individuals and groups who were critical of the policies of the U.S. Government and were considered threats to the nation. The organization maintained extensive files and tried to undermine the careers of individuals through the planting of defamatory information in the press or through the grapevine (rumors). The program began in 1956 and ended in 1971. See COUNTERINSURGENCY IN AMERICA, COUNTERINTELLIGENCE PROGRAM, FEDERAL BUREAU OF INVESTIGATION (FBI).

Cold Feet. A condition which may be ascribed to an elective or appointive politician who fails to deliver on promises to constituents for fear of controversy which may affect her/his government and political career; also, a witness who at the last moment changes her/his mind about delivering testimony, for fear of reprisal. Other names in similar circumstances used in public life are "coward" or "liar." In legal slang, a witness failing to testify at the last minute.

Cold War. A concept epitomizing the ideological rivalry between the Soviet Union (socialism or communism) and the United States of America (capitalism), and the conduct of formal diplomatic relations in a hostile atmosphere but short of open war. (The "cold war" often takes the form of a "hot war" in regional conflicts (e.g., in the Middle East, Southeast Asia, or Latin America). The "cold war" ended with the introduction of the notions of "perestroika" and "glasnost"—openness and freedom of expression to include criticism—by Soviet President Mikhail S. Gorbachev. They were proclaimed in 1987 and accepted by the communist party. The "war" ended in 1989. When U.S. President George Bush made public pronouncements that the United States won the Cold War, former Soviet President turned journalist stated in 1992, that this was not the case. Mikhail S. Gorbachev stated that "... the long years we spent plunged in the Cold War made losers of us all," and "in our own time," he added, "the world's rejection of confrontation and hostility has made us all winners." See AMERICAN-SOVIET COLLUSION, CONTAINMENT.

Cold War is Over and Japan Won. A facetious slogan popular in 1991 throughout Europe, Asia, Latin America, and among anti-American elements within the United States, bashing America for being a pauper-power. Some anti-American press accounts indicate that the American victory over the Soviet Union in the Cold War was insignificant, because the Soviet empire decided to dissolve itself and was not conquered; further, it would never be conquered by a superpower which cannot produce commodities that can compete on a global market.

Cold War Orphan State. The term "orphan state" was coined by journalists Melinda Liu and Peter McKillop (*Newsweek*, May 11, 1992) and originally pertained to the Philippines, where, with the Cold War collapse and revival of nationalism, the U.S. had abandoned physical presence (e.g., naval bases) and extensive economic and military assistance. There are other Cold War orphan states throughout the globe, all within the former Eastern or Western military alliances (e.g., NATO and the Warsaw Pact). Some were able to assert their identity and march on their own into the family of sovereign nations with considerable economic and political stability (e.g., Turkey and Israel on the side of the Western Alliance, and Hungary, Czechoslovakia, and Poland on the Eastern side). States which could not cope with the Cold War syndrome and were thus unable to assert their identity and sustain themselves are: Romania, Yugoslavia, Bulgaria, Cuba, and Albania. Some of the major democracies (e.g., Germany, japan, and South Korea) took on the status of superpowers and are among the least affected. The greatest identity crisis affects former East Germany, which is additionally aggravated by West Germany's rejection of them. Germans reversed the "Drang Nach Osten" (drive to the East") with "Fluct vom Osten," ("flight from the East"). During his "Cold War Prologue" speech of 6 May 1992, in Fulton, Missouri, former Soviet President Mikhail S. Gorbachev called for a single global government in order to prevent conflicts among the many independent states, most of which are not able to govern without the support of other larger, richer states. This idea is not new, but is as unrealistic as ever. Single global government is only possible through force and the extermination of the non-compliant populations of the world.

Cold War Prologue. See COLD WAR ORPHAN STATE.

Cold War Syndrome. See COLD WAR ORPHAN STATE.

Collateral Damage. In the language of warfare, the loss of civilian life or damage to private property because of close proximity to a destroyed military target (e.g., destruction of civilian schools or hospitals accidentally destroyed during an attack on military targets). In modern warfare, military targets under attack (e.g., Iraqi soldiers during the 1991 Persian Gulf War) would seek sanctuary in children's hospitals, mosques, or schools with the hope that these targets would not be subjected to an attack.

Collateral Estoppel. A legal concept meaning that an issue already decided in a trial once cannot be decided again, pertaining to the same person, on the grounds that this would constitute double jeopardy. See DOUBLE JEOPARDY.

Collective Bargaining. A process by which the employer and the employees (who are unionized) mutually agree on the amount of work required in order to receive certain rewards (e.g., pay and other benefits).

Collective Leadership. The exercise of executive powers by more than one person, e.g., in the former Soviet Union top executives of both the party and the government voted, as a rule, on every major policy of party and government. In some cases such leadership may be referred to as "collegial leadership." See LEADERSHIP, NATIONAL SALVATION COMMITTEE.

Collective Security. A system of security arrangements that nation-states may set up for the purpose of maintaining their independence and territorial integrity on a regional basis, such as the North Atlantic Treaty Organization (NATO), or on an international or global basis, such as the arrangements under the Charter of the United Nations Organization. See COLLECTIVE VIOLENCE, HARDWARE DIPLOMACY, WAR, Appendices 29, 31.

Collective Violence. A term describing the contemporary system of collective security which is rather a system of collective violence, managed in the final analysis by only a few major powers, set up in a milieu of a global order that is characterized by great inequalities in income, power, and justice. See COLLECTIVE SECURITY, HARDWARE DIPLOMACY, WAR, Appendix 31.

Collectivism. A system of economic or political controls (e.g., of an economic enterprise, government, or state) implemented by more than one person with equal authority (e.g., a committee, a collective, or a college).

Collectivistic Theory. See ROLE OF STATE.

Collectivization. See KOLGHOZ.

College of Cardinals. A folkloric name for the chairmen of committees in the U.S. Congress when they gather in a conference, referring to their enormous powers, often unchecked by anyone except the voters on election day. The term is taken from the powerful and independent action the Cardinals hold in the hierarchy of the Roman Catholic Church.

Collegial Leadership. See COLLECTIVE LEADERSHIP, LEADERSHIP.

Colonial War. See AMERICAN REVOLUTION.

Colonialism. The practices of subjugating a community of persons, organized into some cohesive union such as a tribe, a state, or a group of the same, for an unspecified period of time, as opposed to a temporary control over people and land in case of occupation without intent to colonize. Colonization goes in hand with imperialism, because it subjugates peoples against their will, using force and compulsion when necessary to take control of their lives, well-being, property and infrastructure, although some degree of autonomy for internal governance may be granted depending on the type, notion, and modus operandi of the colonizer. The people of Africa have had their experience with colonialists, and they had their response to missionaries, whom they viewed as agents of the colonizers: "We have your Bibles—you have our land." The practice of colonization is as old as man; once greed for wealth and power arose, colonization was the method to achieve them. People, communities, and states on all continents were, at one time or another, under some form of colonial rule. The great colonial powers like England, France, Spain, the Netherlands, Belgium, Germany, Portugal, Turkey, and, on a smaller scale, Italy, Japan, Russia and the United States, were often in conflict with one another over spheres of influence and power. Today, only small remnants remain of the colonial past, such as, for example, Hong Kong, which will be released from British control to mainland China in 1997. The traditional colonizers, with imperialist objectives, were usually seeking physical possession and control of people and their land ("territorial imperialism"); a few civilians and many soldiers, were sent to conquer, to occupy and to explore human and material resources. The more sophisticated form of colonization and imperialism is of a non-military, intellectual nature ("horizontal imperialism"), where conquest is pursued and often achieved by neatly-dressed bureaucrats in flannel suits, carrying instead of guns, briefcases that contain contracts, patents, loans, or joint-venture (mutually owned enterprise) proposals. The main target of this type of colonialism (neo-colonialism; imperialism or neo-imperialism) is the consumer ("consumer imperialism"), rather than the people at large, the government, or the infrastructure of the state. See AMERICA BASHING, IMPERIALISM, JAPAN BASHING.

Color War. See RACE WAR.

Columbia Hostages. See APRIL 19 MOVEMENT.

Columbo Plan. A blueprint designed for the mutual cooperation (economic, political, cultural, or military) and development of Southeast Asian members of the British Commonwealth of Nations, agreed upon in 1950, in Columbo, Ceylon (renamed "Sri Lanka" in 1972), by the foreign ministers of Afghanistan, Australia, Burma, Bhutan, Cambodia, Ceylon (now Sri Lanka), Canada, Pakistan, India, Nepal, Indonesia, Malaysia, the Philippines, New Zealand, South Korea, Thailand, and the United Kingdom (England). The United States, though not a member of the British Commonwealth, also became a party to this plan.

Come Home, America. The campaign slogan of George McGovern, U.S. Senator from South Dakota and a nominee of the Democratic party for U.S. President in 1972, who was bitterly opposed to U.S. involvement in and further escalation of the War in Vietnam under President Richard M. Nixon. McGovern's anti-Vietnam War stand received considerable support from younger people (particularly males of draft age, who feared being drafted and sent to Vietnam), but had not been synchronized with the black revolutionary movement, and was totally ignored by a large segment of the electorate. As a result, McGovern carried only the electoral votes of the state of Massachusetts and the District of Columbia, while Richard Nixon was elected by a landslide. McGovern's predictions about the Vietnamese fiasco proved to be correct: the U. S. withdrew from Vietnam two years later and abandoned its ally, South Vietnam, who was soon conquered by North Vietnam. The slogan, "Come Home, America," was McGovern's appeal to the American public for unified demand to end the War in Vietnam, and, as the Senator explained, "I wanted nothing more for my country than to see it come home to the old-fashioned values of dignity and compassion which we associate with Jefferson and Lincoln, Norris and Roosevelt." See AMERICAN CENTURY, TRAGIC SITUATION.

Come, Let Us Reason Together. See LET US REASON.

Comeback Kid. A presidential contender in American politics, who lost in a primary election in one state and seeks a comeback in another.

COMECON. See COUNCIL FOR ECONOMIC MUTUAL ASSISTANCE (CEMA).

COMINFORM. See COMMUNIST INFORMATION BUREAU.

COMINT. See INTELLIGENCE.

Comintern. See COMMUNIST INTERNATIONAL, FIRST, SECOND, THIRD.

Comitas Inter Gentes. In the Latin language, "comity among nations" or "mutual respect among nations." A principle in international law, whereby sovereign states are expected to respect each other regardless of the size or the internal political system or the external image of a state.

Comity. A concept of mutual respect; a courtesy that customarily is extended to foreign officials, nationals, flags, vessels, or other possessions or acts of another sovereign state in the conduct of international relations. See COMITAS INTER GENTES.

Command and Control. The crux of modern leadership under the defense doctrines of the United States and its Allies, particularly the North Atlantic Treaty Organization (NATO) arrangement, whereby conventional tactical military forces operate under mission-oriented command and control. The concept was developed by the Germans within the NATO ranks, called "auftragstaktik," or "mission-oriented tactics." According to Commander Gerry T. Thomas, U.S. Navy (in *Control of Joint Forces: A New Perspective*, AFCEA International Press, 1989), it is "a command and control procedure within which the subordinate is given extensive latitude in carrying out a mission under the broad guidance of the commander's expressed intentions. Such tasking must be possible with forces, resources and authority availble to the subordinate and must only include those restraints which are indispensable. This style of command and control requires responsible action, sound judgment and initiative based on uniformity of thought as articulated by the central authority. Its major advantage is that it ensures that operational organizations will continue to function tactically, even when out of contact with higher headquarters." For a broader application of this style of command, communications and intelligence are necessary. See COMMAND, CONTROL, COMMUNICATIONS, INTELLIGENCE (C^3I), INTEROPERABILITY.

Command and Control Federalism. See FEDERALISM.

Command, Control, Communications, Intelligence (C^3I). The ultimate in military command of modern armies, coordinated supervision, management, flow of information exercised in a unified manner to achieve positive results on the battlefield, in the air, on sea, and in space. In the United States, C^3I commences with the U.S. president at the White House, or from his aircraft, "Air Force One," or any other location in case of an all-out war. Command and control over nuclear weapons remains constantly and exclusively under the president's control and supervision. See COMMAND AND CONTROL, INTEROPERABILITY, NORTH ATLANTIC TREATY ORGANIZATION (NATO), PENTOMIC ARMY.

Command Economy. See POLITICO-ECONOMIC SYSTEMS in Appendix 83, TYPES OF MARKET SYSTEMS in Appendix 84.

Commander in Chief. Title of the president, who is officially the highest ranking officer in the U.S. Armed Forces.

Commerce Clause. A stipulation contained in the United States Constitution which reserves for the U.S. Congress the sole authority in that sphere. (The provision states that the U. S. Congress has the sole power ". . . to regulate commerce with foreign Nations, and among the several States, and the Indian tribes."—Article I, Sec. 8, Clause 3.) See *Gibbons v. Ogden* in Appendix 48, Appendix 8.

Commission on Intergovernmental Relations. See PRESIDENTIAL COMMISSION ON INTERGOVERNMENTAL RELATIONS.

Commission on Interstate Cooperation. Facilitates national, state, and regional programs, formulates and promotes interstate compacts, and contributes to the enactment of uniform and reciprocal legislation and procedures.

Commission on Presidential Nomination and Party Structure. A Democratic policy group that was set up during the month of January, 1978, in the White House under the direction of Mark A. Siegel, Deputy Assistant to the President for Policy Analysis, to revise the rules of presidential nomination, and primarily to eliminate the early Iowa primary elections (Iowa caucuses) which are held in January of every presidential election year (the first series of primaries held). A critic of the program, U.S. Representative Donald M. Fraser (D-Minnesota), accused the Carter team of attempting to prevent the emergence of a challenger to President Carter in the election of 1980. (Historically, any presidential candidate who wins in those two early primaries usually wins the election by gaining the necessary amount of national exposure and publicity.) See COMMISSION ON PRESIDENTIAL NOMINATIONS, PRIMARY ELECTION.

Commission on Presidential Nominations. The national party organizations of the Democrats and the Republicans introduced a series of party reforms after the 1980 election, but those of the Republicans refrained from any major overhauls of their party. The National Democratic Party created the Commission on Presidential Nominations in 1980, headed by James B. Hunt, governor of North Carolina, hence also known as the "Hunt Commission." Its purpose was to streamline the delegate selection process to party conventions and to democratize the party itself, broadening the base of political participation by increasing input into the process of selecting presidential candidates; to strengthen accountability of public officials and to strengthen the party itself whose base was weakened by the vigorous activities of the Republican Party. Among some of the reforms introduced were: the substitution of proportional representation in party elections for "winner-takes-all," in selection of delegates to party conventions; binding delegates to the party candidate for president through connection balloting; adoption of affirmative action goals for representation of minorities and women; elimination of open primaries to voters registered in other parties; the use of primaries as the principle selection machinery with the party convention serving merely to ratify the outcome of the primary elections. The Hunt Commission called for: (1) larger participation in the work of the convention by political professionals who would not be required to declare their presidental preferences in advance and as a condition for sitting at the convention; (2) the House and Senate Democratic Caucuses would be allowed to designate up to 60 percent of their members as unpledged to the convention; (3) state party chairpersons and 250 additional delegates, mainly among the governors and city mayors, would participate as unpleged delegates to the convention; and (4) granting state party organizations the right to select delegates to the party convention according to several alternative methods. The Commission also recommended that the primary caucus system be shortened to five weeks. General criticism of previous party reforms had begun after the 1972 election, when in 1973 the McGovern-Frazer Commission of the Democratic Party broadened the democratic base of the party, as well as after the Charter of the National Democratic Party was adopted in 1974. The Charter introduced rather strict rules on how state party organizations were to be organized and how they were to function. The Charter allowed for a significant number of convention delegates to be chosen by congressional and senatorial caucuses rather than by primaries; this weakened state and local party organizations, and the nationalization of the party, and also weakened local initiative and even created resentment among state party leaders who had to follow strict directives of the national party organization (e.g., party leaders in Wisconsin were very unhappy about the directive to discontinue the tradition of open primaries in the State). The Republican Party, on the other hand, decided to maintain the confederate character of its party organization, and, instead of forcing national rules on state and local party organizations, it has chosen to render professional services to them through its local election divisions. These services include training through seminars, surveys, direct personal assistance, and financial aid. Instead of procedural reforms, favored by the Democrats, the Republicans chose administrative reforms considerably unifying efforts of the national, congressional, state, and local party organizations by placing the main emphasis on aiding party candidates for elective offices. This process of party unification was considerably advanced under the leadership of Party Chairman Bill Brock, 1977-1981.

Commission Plan. A form of local government used in several cities in the U.S. during the 19th century (e.g., in Sacramento, California, in 1863; in New Orleans, Louisiana, in 1870; in Memphis, Tennessee, in 1878; in Mobile, Alabama, in 1879; and in Washington, D.C., which was under congressional supervision), but which was most successful in Galveston, Texas, in 1900. A tidal wave destroyed the city in 1900, and the then-existing mayor-council type of government proved unable to cope with the disaster. A small group of prominent businessmen hastily organized a commission to put the city back on its feet and drew up a charter for the city which was approved by the Texas legislature in 1901. Each of the commissioners was in charge of a specific function of the government. The commission consisted of five members. Following the Galveston success more than 100 other cities throughout the United States adopted this plan of local government by 1910.

Commissioner-Manager Plan of Government. A system of government of some cities and/or counties in the U.S. in which the elective commissioners appoint a manager who serves as the real executive of the government. See Commission Plan.

Committee for a Free China. An informal, partisan organization formed in California during the 1970s by Dr. Walter Judd, which advocates strong ties with the Republic of China (Nationalist China) and Taiwan (Formosa), including the preservation of the Republic of China as a free and independent state and limited relations with the People's Republic of China (Communist, or mainland China). The Committee strongly opposed President Carter's (and before him President Ford's) policy of "normalization" of relations with the People's Republic of China and the so-called "one-China" policy. During the 1940s the "China-Lobby" urged an all-out support of Chiang Kai-shek and the Kuomintang against Mao Tse-tung (Mao was already emerging on the international political horizon as a strong leader, but his philosophy, aims, and objectives were little understood outside China) and the Communists. Its principal spokesmen were Dr. Judd, Alfred Kohlberg, Freda Utley, and William C. Bullitt. The group is also known as the "Committee of One Million," for claiming to have that many registered supporters.

Committee for an Open Convention. A political component of the new left which was concentrating on the August 1968, Democratic Party convention in Chicago, demanding that it be open to "peace" and "anti-Vietnam War" candidates. The bloody riots in Chicago contributed to the downfall of presidential aspirant Hubert H. Humphrey. See NEW LEFT.

Committee for State Security. In the Russian language, "Komitet Gosudarstviennoy Bezopachnosti" (KGB). One of the largest and most active intelligence agencies in the world, charged with internal security as well as foreign espionage throughout the world. In 1991, it was "Foreign Intelligence Service" and was divided among the republics of the Commonwealth of Independent States. The core of the organization, however, remains within the Russian Republic. See INTELLIGENCE, PEOPLE'S COMMISSION FOR INTERNAL AFFARIS (NKGB).

Committee of Correspondence. A body of men appointed by a colonial legislature (in the British colonies of North America) as a liaison body with the legislatures of other colonies. After 1773, such committees were widely organized on county levels and were very instrumental in channeling information (and intelligence) vital to the preparation of military insurrection against England.

Committee of Five. See LOYALTY LAW.

Committee of Forty-Eight. Special committees organized by liberal and socialist elements in all forty-eight states of the American Union in 1919, for the purpose of disseminating ideas of socialism. These groups joined ranks in 1920, and formed the Farmer Labor Party. See FARMER LABOR PARTY.

Committee of Independent Workers. See FASCISM.

Committee of Notables. See COUNCIL OF EUROPE.

Committee of One Million. See COMMITTEE FOR FREE CHINA.

Committee of the Whole House. A committee in the U. S. House of Representatives, "On the State of the Union," composed of any hundred or more members of the House present, with the speaker of the House acting as its chairman. It considers only such legislation which deals directly with appropriations, taxation, or any measure which would place a heavy burden upon the general public. (In practice, however, taking advantage of the small quorum required for the function of that committee, other, nonfiscal matters are often considered.) All bills, before they can be considered by that committee, must be properly cleared by the regular standing committees and be listed on the calendar of the Whole

House. Members of the House may demand a roll-call vote on any amendment to a bill adopted by the Committee of the Whole House. See UNITED STATES HOUSE OF REPRESENTATIVES.

Committee on Committees. A body of persons empowered to create other committees or make appointments to them. In the U.S. House of Representatives, the Democratic Committee on Committees consists of members of the Ways and Means Committee, the speaker (if of that party), and the floor leader (majority or minority as the case may be). The Committee on Committees of the Republican Party is composed of one member from each state having Republican representation in the House who has as many votes as there are Republican representatives from that state. In the U.S. Senate the Steering Committees of the two major political parties make committee assignments. The majority party leaders also exercise considerable influence over committee assignments. See CONGRESSIONAL COMMITTEES.

Committee on Political Education (COPE). The political arm of the American Federation of Labor-Congress of Industrial Organizations (AFL-CIO) and its principal lobbyist. It keeps the AFL-CIO leadership and membership constantly informed on all political, economical, and social developments in the nation, particularly on those that are of direct concern to labor. In addition, COPE keeps constant watch on Congress and its legislative activity and is extensively involved in political education of persons inside and outside the union ranks.

Committee on the Present Danger. An informal partisan organization, formed in 1972, mainly by intellectuals in the institutions of higher learning and in government, which keeps track of public policy inputs and outputs with the goal of keeping the United States out of foreign wars and preventing major internal catastrophes. Among other things, the Committee favored a "watch-out" attitude toward the communist states, particularly the former USSR and the People's Republic of China, whom it viewed as the principal adversaries of American interests. Dr. Eugene Rostow, former U.S. Under-Secretary of State and a Yale University professor, was one of the principal leaders of the coalition. See COMMITTEE FOR A FREE CHINA, MILITARY PREPONDERANCE.

Committee on the State of the Union. See COMMITTEE OF THE WHOLE HOUSE.

Committee to Reelect the President (CREEP). See WATERGATE AFFAIR.

Committeeman. See DEMOCRATIC NATIONAL COMMITTEE, REPUBLICAN NATIONAL COMMITTEE.

Committeewoman. See DEMOCRATIC NATIONAL COMMITTEE, REPUBLICAN NATIONAL COMMITTEE.

Commodity. Any article of value or utility which can be bought, sold or exchanged in barter.

Common Carrier. Any means of transport that is duly licensed, with designated rates and schedules of service, carrying persons and goods (e.g., railroads, buses, airlines, trucks, and pipelines). Such facilities constitute an important part of a state's infrastructure, because they will be used by the armed forces in case of an emergency or war.

Common Cause. A private Washington, D.C.-based organization, headed by former Secretary of the Department of Health, Education and Welfare, John Gardner, seeking to influence the policies of the government (legislative, executive, and judicial) on behalf of all the people as a lobby. Also known as "Citizen's Lobby." See LOBBY.

Common European Home, A concept of European unity expressed in 1989 by the former President and leader of the communist party in the Soviet Union, Mikhail S. Gorbachev and his desire for the former Soviet empire to become a part of it.

Common Law. A body of judicial decisions (precedents), customs, or scholarly writings serving as the source of other laws. Common law does not apply in U.S. federal courts.

Common Market. See EUROPEAN ECONOMIC COMMUNITY.

Common Pleas, Court of. The name of a civil court with original jurisdiction in some states in the United States.

Common Sense. A fiery pamphlet written by North American revolutionary Thomas Paine and published on January 10, 1776, denouncing the British tyranny over North American colonists and calling for complete independence from Britain. This piece of revolutionary literature is credited with enhancing and unifying revolutionary forces in America against British oppression.

Common Sense Agenda. See WEED AND SEED PROGRAM.

Common Site Picketing Bill. A measure aimed at granting the right of sympathy picketing to all labor unions working on a single project once one of the unions was on strike. This bill was defeated in the U. S. House of Representatives by a vote of 217 to 205, on March 23, 1977. A similar measure that passed in 1974, was vetoed by President Gerald R. Ford (1974-1977).

Common Situs. See COMMON SITE PICKETING BILL.

Commonwealth. An organization, usually a government, representing the common good; any self-governing political body (e.g., the British Commonwealth, the Commonwealth of Australia); also an independent or semi-independent state with some ties linking it with another. Some American states (e.g., Virginia or Pennsylvania) consider themselves of commonwealth status in relation to the American Union (usually a political campaign rhetoric), which they do not have. Only Puerto Rico and the Northern Mariana Islands are of the status of a commonwealth. Dr. Fidel Castro, President of Cuba, introduced a resolution in the United Nations on 25 October 1982, demanding that Puerto Rico receive complete independence from the United States. A very resourceful and assertive U.S. Ambassador to the United Nations, Dr. Jean Kirkpatrick saw to it that the resolution was defeated. On the same occasion, Castro also proposed that Israel be expelled from the UN. as a terrorist state.

Commonwealth Attorney. An elective or appointive prosecuting officer and legal advisor to a governmental body in many counties in the United States.

Communalism. A socio-political-economic system characterized by closely-knit relationships among the persons residing in a community; sharing, mutual cooperation, trust, and lack of greed to own and possess. Ceylon (Sri Lanka) made its national public policy to implement a communal system in its society. Common in African tribes and Latin America.

Commune. A small, self-governing political subdivision such as a village in France or Germany, or a settlement or business enterprise in the People's Republic of China.

Commune Bonum. In the Latin language, "common good." Also, a commonly accepted doctrine in public law that the state has as its primary function the protection of the "common good." See EMINENT DOMAIN.

Communi Consensu. In the Latin language, "common consent."

Communiqué. A written document issued by parties to an important conference stating their accomplishments or their views. Communiqués are commonly used by conferring heads of state and/or heads of government upon the conclusion of their talks. They may be issued separately or jointly (joint communiqué). See DIPLOMACY.

Communism. An economic, political, and social philosophy, usually associated with Marxism, which advocates a classless society, elimination of private ownership of the means of production and distribution of goods and services, and the eventual elimination of the state. It also negates the existence of God and considers all religions as "... the opiate of the masses." See MAOISM, MARXISM, PHONY COMMUNISM, SOCIALISM.

Communism with a Human Face. See EUROCOMMUNISM.

Communist Control Act of 1954. A measure that was introduced by Representative John Marshal Butler, a Republican, giving the Subversive Activities Control Board the authority to decide which public organizations were "communist-infiltrated" and thus required to register with the SACB. This law supplemented the McCarren Internal Security Act of 1950, which created the Subversive Activities Control Board (a semi-independent investigative agency dealing with matters related to the ideological: "purity" of Americans and communist infiltration), and required all organizations designated as "communist-action" or "communist-front" to register with the Board. U.S. Senator Hubert H. Humphrey (1911-1978), a liberal Democrat from Minnesota, proposed an amendment to the Act which declared the Communist Party of the United States (or, as the Party often calls itself, the "Communist Party of America") illegal as an "agency of hostile foreign power" and placed it outside the law. See MCCARTHYISM, RED MENACE.

Communist Hysteria. See RED MENACE.

Communist Information Bureau (COMINFORM). An agency established in 1947 by the Soviet Union and her East European satellite states (Czechoslovakia, Hungary, Rumania, Bulgaria, Yugoslavia, Poland, and representatives of Communist China as well as representatives of communist parties in non-communist states) for the purpose of coordinating the activities of all communist parties by means of dissemination of relevant information. It was dissolved in 1956 due to an ideological split within the communist bloc, mainly between the Soviet Union and the People's Republic of China. See COMMUNIST INTERNATIONAL, COMMUNIST ORGANIZATIONS, POLYCENTRISM.

Communist International, First (COMINTERN). Established in 1864, as the International Workingman's Association by exiles from various countries (including Karl Marx, who was expelled from his native Germany) for the purpose of advancing the cause of the workers. After the defeat of the Paris Commune in 1871, the International was dissolved. See COMMUNIST INFORMATION BUREAU (COMINFORM).

Communist International, Second (COMINTERN). Established in 1889 as a loose federation of individual socialist parties and associations to serve as a link between them. It ceased to operate during World War I. See COMMUNIST INFORMATION BUREAU (COMINFORM).

Communist International, Third (COMINTERN). Established in 1919, in Moscow, Russia, as an agency of the Russian communists under the leadership of Vladimir I. Lenin. Its primary function was, among other things, to sustain Lenin in power, to help stabilize communist power in Russia as well as to promote the cause of communism throughout the world. It was dissolved in 1943, by Josef Stalin as an act demonstrating good will towards the United States and her allies. The Internationals are also known as Cominterns. See COMMUNIST INFORMATION BUREAU (COMINFORM).

Communist League. See COMMUNIST ORGANIZATIONS.

Communist Manifesto. A pamphlet published by Karl Marx and Friedrich Engels in 1848, upon the request of the Communist League in London, England, which contains statements of principles, programs, and objectives of the communist movement.

Communist Mentality. See EASTOXIFICATION.

Communist Organizations. Communist League—(1847) Communist League organized under Marx's influence from the League of the Just. (1852) Communist League dissolved at Marx's proposal. First International—(1864) The First International, or International Workingmen's Association, founded in London. (1872) First International voted to move headquarters to New York on Engels' proposal. Split over the proposal caused eventual dissolution. (1876) July 15: First International dissolved at Congress in Philadelphia. Second International (Socialist)—(1889) July 14: The Second International formed at Paris. (1914-18) Effective work of Second International, to all intents and purposes, ended during World War I. Violently attacked by Lenin as "bourgeois." Third (Communist) International (also known as COMINTERN)—(1919) March 2-6: Formed in Moscow. (1920) July-August: Second Congress of COMINTERN in Moscow, which adopted the "twenty-one points" of admission. (1935) July 25-August 20: Seventh Congress of COMINTERN in Moscow, at which United Front program instituted. (1943) June 10: COMINTERN dissolved. Communist Information Bureau (also known as COMINFORM)—(1947) Formed in Poland, with headquarters to be in Belgrade, Yugoslavia. (1948) COMINFORM denounced Tito and threatened expulsion of Tito and his top aides for "hateful" policy toward Russia. Denunciation prepared at meeting of COMINFORM in Romania. Yugoslav Communist Party defied charges. (1948) July: Headquarters of

COMINFORM moved to Bucharest, Romania. (1956) April: COMINFORM dissolved. Young Communist International—(1919) Young Communist International formed in Berlin. (1943) Dissolved. International communist Publications—(1919) May: First issue of *The Communist International,* organ of the Executive committee of the Communist International. (1943) July 5: Last issue of *The Communist International,* after dissolution of COMINTERN. (1947) November 10: *For a Lasting Peace, for a People's Democracy!* published in Belgrade, characterizing itself as "Organ of the Information Bureau of the Communist Parties in Belgrade" (published in Bucharest, Romania after COMINFORM attacked Tito). (1956) April: *For a Lasting Peace, for a People's Democracy!* ceased publication.

Communist Party of the Soviet Union (CPSU). In the Russian language, "Kommunistitcheskaya Partya Sovyetzghogo Soyuza." The original name of the party was "Vsesoyuznaya Kommunisticheskaya Partya (Bolsheviks), VKP (b)," or "All-Soviet Communist Party (of bolsheviks). From 1917 to 1991, the ruling and only legal political party in the USSR (now dissolved). Some of its characteristic features were: selective membership, strict control within the party ranks, highly centralized leadership, dedication to secrecy, and closely knit discipline. It commanded obedience and respect of all governmental agencies, enterprises, societies, and associations. According to the official claims of the Soviet government, the party did not rule *per se,* but merely advised and gave general direction on policies to the government and other segments in the society. The party supervised all organizations, particularly the youth organizations, and only through the ranks of the youth organizations, mainly Komsomol, could one become a candidate member and possibly a full member. The guiding principle of the party was the so-called "intra-party democracy" or "democratic centralism." The origin of the party goes back to the 1880s when the All-Russian Social-Democratic Labor Party emerged in opposition to the Tsarist regime. The party was soon infiltrated by radical elements: the V. I. Lenin faction (calling itself the "Bolsheviks," or the majority) and the liberal democratic faction of Julius Martov (named by the Bolsheviks the "Mensheviks," or minority) soon split up, and the Lenin faction gained control over the state during the October Revolution in 1917, after the abolishment of the provisional government of Alexander Kerensky. In 1918, the party changed its name to the All-Russian Communist Party (Bolsheviks); in 1922, the name was changed again to the All-Union Communist Party (Bolsheviks); and again to its final name, CPSU, in 1952. The highest organ of the party was the Congress, which, in accordance with party statutes, met every four years. Between Congresses, the party leadership was exercised by the Central Committee, the Political Bureau (Politburo), and the Secretariat. (The Secretary-General of the party was considered to be the most powerful man in the USSR). The role of the party, according to Lenin, was to serve as a "transmission belt between the government and the masses." The party was suspended and subsequently dissolved after the failed Moscow coup of 1991. U.S. Democratic Senator from Iowa, Tom Harkin, commented on the achievements of the collapsed Soviet Communist Party while campaigning in New Hampshire in 1992, as a presidential hopeful: "What do you call members of a political party whose policies benefited only a very narrow few, who spent insane amounts of money on the military and whose policies bankrupted their nation? . . . . Well, they might try calling themselves Republicans!" The CPSU was suspended by the Supreme Soviet on 29 August 1991. See DEMOCRATIC CENTRALISM, MARXISM, STATE COMMITTEE ON THE STATE OF EMERGENCY, Appendix 74.

Communist Party of the United States. A minor political party, formed in 1919, at the insistence of the Third International and the Bolsheviks in Russia. The party claims to follow Marxist-Leninist lines and lists among its ultimate objectives the overthrow of the constitutional system of government in the United States. See COMMUNISM, NEW LEFT.

Communist Sympathizer. See FELLOW TRAVELER.

Communitarian Capitalism. See INDIVIDUALISTIC CAPITALISM, POLITICO-ECONOMIC SYSTEMS in Appendix 83, TYPES OF MARKET SYSTEMS in Appendix 84.

Community Action Program (CAP) See COMMUNITY SERVICE ADMINISTRATION (CSA).

Community Development Act. Designed to render financial assistance to needy communities for the financing of such programs as comprehensive community recreation facilities to be shared by more than a single jurisdiction, coordination of interjurisdictional social programs, development of comprehensive community planning programs, improvement of water supply and solid waste disposal facilities and similar projects.

Community Property. Under many state laws in the United States, both spouses own their possessions equally, both during and after termination of marriage, (e.g., divorce). Some states with community property laws do not honor pre-nuptial agreements, which are documents assigning ownership of possessions to the individual who brought them into the marriage.

Community Service. Those services in a politically organized community which are paid for from general revenue funds. Among these are: defense, major roadways (some highways may be paid for by the users and the traveling public by collecting tolls), parks, police and fire protection, libraries, public schools, museums, and galleries. The underlying assumption is that the entire population, directly or indirectly, benefits from these services and that it would not be feasible to have only the users pay for them. Some states even subsidize religious temples. (e.g., Moslem mosques in Pakistan and Catholic churches in Spain and Italy are subsidized by general revenue). See also EMINENT DOMAIN.

Community Service Administration (SCA). Supervises such programs as the Community Action Programs (CAPs), which were extended by Congress and approved by the President on January 4, 1975, to help the poor and homeless in depressed areas.

Community Standard. One of the many elusive concepts in daily usage in a politically organized society, referring to what a given community determines, through consensus, is good and bad; what it will allow and tolerate and what it will not. Also a set of certain standards and values that the community wishes to preserve and enjoy. Term applied often concerning objections to pornography, the showing of certain films, or certain stage productions and concerts, etc. Such imposed standards often conflict with the rights of individuals and groups to privacy and to freedom of expression and association under the First Amendment to the U.S. Constitution.

Community Value. See COMMUNITY STANDARD.

Commuting Citizen. See OVERSEAS CONSTITUENCY.

Compact. An agreement, arrived at voluntarily, among persons or states, pursuing common goals. See MAYFLOWER COMPACT.

Comparative Advantage. Concept developed by Professor Lester C. Thurow (*Head to Head: The Coming Economic Battle Among Japan, Europe, and America*) which explains the competitive edge great economic powers (e.g., Japan and Germany) now have over the United States, because they place emphasis on process technologies rather than re-inventing the wheel, and spend the bulk of the R & D (Research and Development) funds for that purpose. Few American executives have sufficient knowledge in process technologies (e.g., 30 percent in the United States and 70 percent in Japan). In simple terms, "Those who can make a product cheaper can take it away from the inventor." Professor Thurow names seven major industries which will dominate the next few decades. They are: "Microelectronics, biotechnology, the new materials industries, civilian aviation, telecommunications, robots plus machine tools, and computers plus software." He calls them all "brain industries," and maintains that in order to remain competitive in these industries, one must not only have the brains but must be able to manage the industry so that it can survive on the market of "newprocess technologies" rather than "newproduct technologies" (Reverse engineering will be the main skill of the "newprocess technologies.") In order to achieve an advantage over competition, labor and management must have a solid education rather than just some training. Training is temporary; education is forever. A better understanding of the adversary's politics and culture is as important as knowledge of tools, materials, and production and marketing processes and strategies. Today, few schools teach that. The traditional factors of production—land, labor, and capital—are not enough. An educated labor force is the paramount factor. See AMERICA BASHING, JAPAN BASHING.

Comparative Negligence. See CONTRIBUTORY NEGLIGENCE.

Compellent Threat. See DETERRENT.

Competence Impact Statement. A concept developed by Dr. Kenneth E. Boulding of the University of Colorado, pointing out that such statements ought to be required from those poor nations which seek outside help, but which refuse to help themselves. The author calls for a "competence statement on the impact of the modern world—through governments or corporations or international agencies or churches or traders—on the capacity of local societies to handle their own affairs . . . " where " . . . the very impact of the modern world in technology, trade, even aid, and still more in psychological and political remnants of imperialism, both capitalist and socialist, often impairs local competence and capacity."

Competitive Administration. A term associated with U.S. President Franklin D. Roosevelt (1933-1945) and his administrative *modus operandi* (way of running the administrative apparatus). Roosevelt, instead of firing an incompetent bureaucrat, would hire an additional one to do the same work, preferably in a different agency, in order to get the job done. President Roosevelt was an experienced administrator (he was once Governor of New York and Assistant Secretary of the Navy), but, as he himself admitted to U.S. Secretary of War, H. Stimson, he was a "softy" and hated to "fire" any incompetent bureaucrat; he would rather maintain a "joyous disorganization" than a totalitarian efficiency. Some students of Roosevelt's style (e.g., Dr. Clinton Rossiter of Cornell University) suggest that the President personally enjoyed the squabbling, backbiting, and bickering that permeated the Roosevelt Administration as a result of the "joyous disorganization." See POLITICAL STYLE.

Competitive Coexistence. A concept developed by Chairman Mao Tse-tung of the People's Republic of China envisioning coexistence between states with different political systems on a competitive basis. Mao envisioned long-range economic competition with the West while the forces of communism would unite the uncommitted nations of Asia, Africa, and later, other parts of the world into one communist bloc of nations under Chinese leadership. See COEXISTENCE.

Competitive Planning. A term applied mainly to regional, uncoordinated planning, characterized by lack of inter-regional allocation of resources and planning practices and objectives.

Competitive Theory of Administration. See COMPETITIVE ADMINISTRATION.

Components of State. See ELEMENTS OF STATE.

Comprehensive Planning. A process by which the general policies of a unit of government are interrelated over a period of time extending into the future. Such planning is done for the purpose of coordinating more detailed functional planning. This type of planning activity encompasses all aspects of societal life such as political, economic, social, and physical aspects. See PLANNING.

Comprehensive Urban County Plan. Metropolitan areas that are confined within the boundaries of a single county; an alternative to city-county consolidation is the comprehensive urban county plan. Such plans call for the reassignment of government functions rather than the merging of municipal and county governments. See POLITICAL INCREMENTALISM, REGIONALISM.

Compromise. One of the fundamental ingredients of the political process whereby, as in the market place, each bargaining agent (politician) strives to achieve the maximum by give-and-take, but is willing to settle for whatever is possible and achievable under given circumstances. When U.S. Senator Everett Dirksen was asked to state his major political principle, his answer was "to compromise." See POLITICAL COMPROMISE.

Compromise d'Arbitrage. In the French language, "special understanding between parties (states) to a treaty" or "a compromise reached by process of formal arbitration."

Compromise of 1877. See HAYES-TILDEN DISPUTE, RECONSTRUCTION.

Comptroller General. A federal officer heading the General Accounting Office. His primary function is to audit the accounts of all agencies of the federal government, to prevent the disbursement of public funds for measures not authorized by law, and to standardize the methods of account-keeping by federal agencies. The office was established by the Budget and Accounting Act of 1921.

Comptroller of the Currency. An official of the U.S. Department of the Treasury who is responsible for the examination of national banks and for the issuance and redemption of federal reserve notes and federal reserve bank notes.

Compulsory Voting. A notion about voting based on the assumption of Solon (638-558 BC) that "He shall be disfranchised who, in time of faction, takes neither side." Many contemporary states require, under penalty provided by law, that all citizens who are eligible to vote, do so. Such laws exist, for example, in the Soviet Union, all socialist states, and Australia. Solon, an Athenian lawmaker, political philosopher, and a government official, considered voting by citizens one of the most fundamental means of shaping the policies of the government and implemented that obligation in his constitution (the first constitution ever written) together with the obligations to pay taxes and conscription (also introduced for the first time ever). As one of the nine archons (a body of top temporal and ecclesiastical rulers in ancient Athens), Solon recognized that voting, paying taxes, and serving in the armed forces are a citizen's obligation in return for the enjoyment of rights and privileges by the individual person in a politically organized community. Persons who consistently failed to vote were reduced to a status of slaves and chattels.

Concentration Camp Amendment. See McCARRAN INTERNAL SECURITIES ACT OF 1950.

Concentration Camps without the Ovens. See JAPANESE INTERNMENT.

Concept. A human perception of some real or imagined phenomena, a product of some organized experience (e.g., an imagined state of reality or the real empirical reality), which allows one to identify, classify, relate (in time and space) and define attributes and functions of some entities, which in turn can be articulated and explained in some language. Concepts are the product of some theory, some method of explanation. The primary function of theory is to invent, modify, and clarify concepts in order to expedite communications and to transfer knowledge from one person to another. Also one or more words to which a specific meaning has been assigned (e.g., "democracy," "freedom," or "totalitarian state"). Among some of the formulated conceptualization methods are: (1) concept by imagination, which can also be divided as those of pluralistic nature and of monistic nature; (2) concept by intuition, which in the stage of research can be found in factors which can be recognized and apprehended without delay; and something that is obviously, easily identifiable. The positivists hold that there are only concepts by intuition; and (3) concept by perception, which also falls into two categories: (a) pluralistic, in which concepts designate many externally related factors and (b) monistic, where concepts designate a single, all-embracing factor. See EPISTEMOLOGY, FORECAST, KNOWLEDGE, POLITICAL THEORY, SCIENCE.

Concept by Imagination. See CONCEPT.

Concept by Intuition. See CONCEPT.

Concept by Perception. See CONCEPT.

Concepts by Postulation. See POLITICAL THEORY.

Concert of Europe. See CONCERT OF POWERS, GRAND DESIGN.

Concert of Powers. An agreement between two or more states on preserving or sustaining a certain *status quo*. In international politics, it also means the coordinated action by two or more states against one or more states (e.g., Concert of Europe). See GRAND DESIGN.

Concession Theory. A legal doctrine (prevalent mainly among English-speaking nations, including the U.S.) according to which a person or a group of persons can act as a corporation only upon authority expressly granted to this effect by an appropriate agency of the government. See DILLON'S RULE.

Conciliation. A third party's voluntary service offered to mediate a dispute between two or more parties for the purpose of achieving a compromise. See ARBITRATION, GOOD OFFICES, MEDIATION.

Conclave. A secret assembly of the Cardinals of the Roman Catholic Church convened for the purpose of electing a Pope from among themselves.

Concordat. An agreement or a treaty between the Papal State of the Roman Catholic Church (Rome) and a government of another state.

Concurrent Jurisdiction. The practice of sharing authority (e.g., between governmental agencies, between state government and local government, or between state government and national government). See METROPOLITAN FEDERATION.

Concurrent Majority. See TYRANNY OF THE MAJORITY.

Concurrent Powers. See CONCURRENT JURISDICTION.

Concurrent Resolution. A legislative act of a non-controversial nature which is agreed upon jointly by the House and the Senate of the U.S. Congress (carrying the designations of "H Con. Res." in the House and "S Con. Res." in the Senate), and one having the force of law but requiring no signature of the U.S. President. Concurrent resolutions may, among other things, concern rules applicable to both Houses, such as the fixing of the date of adjournment of Congress, condolences or congratulations to be sent to foreign governmental bodies, or granting of an honorary citizenship to a foreign national by by-passing all the channels required by law (e.g., Winston Churchill of England was granted U.S. citizenship by concurrent resolution and without presidential approval). Further, concurrent resolutions are not challenged by either the executive (the President) or the judiciary (the U.S. Supreme Court).

Conditional Discharge. A judge may order an early release of a prisoner under certain conditions (e.g., regular visits with the probation officer, restoration of damages, or the promise to refrain from criminal acts). See CRIMINAL LAW.

Conditions of a Democracy. It is generally recognized that the following conditions and essentials must be met in order for a democratic society to sustain itself and to function, in the order of importance as listed: (1) a relatively high literacy rate among the electorate, if not all of the people; (2) a widespread distribution of wealth among small elites; (3) the absence of widespread racial, religious, national, or class antagonisms; (4) the general prevailing belief, which is ordinarily nourished through a widespread political education, that any change within the states and/or the government should be made according to existing laws and not by men guided by greed at a given point in time; (5) the nourishment and respect for private overlapping loyalties instead of secretive societies and associations with self-serving interests, which as a rule, are pursued by one elite at the expense of another; and (6) the understanding of, and the will to resolve conflict by consensus. These conditions require such essential attitudes on the part of the populace, and especially the rulers, as well as institutions which allow: (1) the maintenance of an open society rather than a closed one; (2) the free exercise of rights and obligations; (3) respect for the individual person regardless of station in life—the dignity and the worth of each individual person must be recognized in degree and in time; (4) a prevailing notion that the government is the instrument of the state and a means, not an end; (5) the individual should fully understand the limits of dissent against prevailing orthodoxies; (6) a widespread utilization of suffrage rights; (7) each individual should work towards his or her goals with a view of the goals of the society as a whole, and with a minimum of friction between the individual and the societal goals; and (8) the electorate should periodically review the activities of the rulers through voluntary participation in political and governmental decisions and processes and to retain or remove persons from power without malice, but according to their actual output. Since there is no single formula on what a democratic system ought to look like, one can assume that, therefore, the success of a democracy increases in proportion to the intellectual capacity and capability of those who interpret and apply its basic precepts. Democracy, as an abstract concept, is the product of strong minds and its utility in application appears to require minds that are even stronger. Seymour M. Lipset (in *Political Man*, Garden City, New York: Doubleday, 1960) makes several observations pertaining to the conditions and essentials of democracy. He established, in his empirical examination of the hypothesis, that political development on the basis of a democracy is directly related to economic well being and education: "In each case," writes Lipset, "the average wealth, degree of industrialization and urbanization, and level of education are much higher for the more democratic countries"; that the coexistence of extreme poverty juxtaposed with an extreme wealth "results either in oligarchy . . . or tyranny"; that "The higher one's education, the more likely one is to believe in democratic values and support democratic practices." Lipset does not claim that "a 'high' level of education is a sufficient condition for democracy," but that "it comes close to being a necessary one." See DEMOCRACY, OPEN SOCIETY, APPENDICES 1, 51.

Condo Commando. See PRIMARY ELECTION.

Condominium. Joint rule over a territory or a state by two or more states (e.g., the Anglo-French condominium of the New Hebrides in the South Pacific).

Confederacy. See CONFEDERATE STATES OF AMERICA (CSA)

Confederate States of America (CSA). The real union of several Southern states which was established upon their secession from the United States during a special meeting held in Montgomery, Alabama (which for a time was the capital city of the Confederacy until it was moved to Richmond, Virginia, on July 20, 1861), and which subsequently found itself at war with the federal government and anti-secessionist (mostly Northern) states. The member-states of the Confederation were: Alabama, Arkansas, Florida, Georgia, Kentucky, Louisiana, Mississippi, Missouri, North Carolina, South Carolina, Texas, and Virginia. (Western counties of Virginia remained loyal to the Union, and subsequently established the state of West Virginia, the only state of the American Union to be born by "illegitimate means.") The Confederation established its own central government, with a president elected for a six-year term (Jefferson Davis, its first and only president) and the city of Richmond, Virginia, as its capital. The Confederation was dissolved in 1865, after the decisive victory of the Union armies and the signing of an instrument of surrender by Gen. Robert E. Lee to Gen. Ulysses S. Grant at Appomattox Court House in Virginia on April 9, 1865. See AMERICAN CIVIL WAR, CIVIL WAR, Appendix 87.

Confederate War. See AMERICAN CIVIL WAR.

Confederation. A loose association of distinct political governmental or business entities (e.g., states, political parties, or business or civic organizations) established for the purpose of a specific goal, and one in which the central authority is limited by and responsible to the units (the parties) of the confederation. Also, an organization set up for a specific purpose comprised of members who join it voluntarily. See CONFEDERATE STATES OF AMERICA (CSA), Appendices 80, 87.

Conference for Democratic South Africa (CODESA). An informal umbrella organization designed by South Africa's President F. W. de Klerk in early 1992, to continue dialogue with the African National Congress (ANC) and its president, Nelson Mandela, on the process of eliminating apartheid, introducing a new constitution and including the black majority in sharing power. When President de Klerk released Nelson Mandela from almost three-decades of imprisonment, it was his intention to include people of Mandela's moderate political temperament in the process of negotiations toward the final constitutional settlement and to "rid our country of suspicion and steer it away from domination and radicalism of any kind." The "radicalism" that President de Klerk had in mind was the revolutionary-military arm of the African National Congress (the Umkhonto we Sizwe, as it is known in the Zulu language). That guerrilla group had maintained arms caches throughout South Africa and was getting support from leftist elements from outside, including Cuba and, until 1990, the Soviet Committee for States Security (KGB), the intelligence agency of the Soviet Union. The Conservative Party (anti-de Klerk and anti-Mandela) and small black militant groups do not favor the de Klerk-Mandela plan for different reasons: the all-white Conservatives are against sharing power with blacks, and the black militants demand the one-man-one-vote electoral system which would remove white from power. Fearful of revolution from many directions, de Klerk and Mandela seek the support of other groups, including the white but liberal Democratic Party and the conservative segments of the National Party of President de Klerk. The conservative Afrikaaner Broederbond and the Dutch Reform Church both favor some sort of constitutional settlement rather than a national revolution among the many factions. The March 17, 1992, white referendum gave de Klerk the mandate, with almost 70 percent of the vote, to proceed with integration. See AFRIKAANER RESISTANCE MOVEMENT (ARM), APARTHEID.

Conference of Commissioners on Uniform State Laws. A national organization primarily composed of legislators and attorneys who are appointed by state governments to study and draft laws which could be enacted by state legislatures in the U.S. on a uniform basis. The organization was established in 1892. It drafts legislation for possible adoption by state legislatures without significant changes, (e.g., the Uniform Commercial Code). A maximum of five commissioners from each state are designated by governors.

Conference on Negro Problems. A series of yearly conferences that were held between 1896 and 1914, at Atlanta University under the direction of W.E.B. Du Bois, at which, among other things, various strategies were discussed on achieving political and civil liberty for all blacks in America.

Conference on Security and Cooperation in Europe (CSCE). On 1 August 1971, thirty-five nations, including the United States and the Soviet Union, gathered in Helsinki, Finland, where an agreement was reached, known as the Helsinki Agreement or Accord, concerning cooperation among states in many areas but particularly in human rights. All the traditional rights and liberties known to people were to be upheld by the signatories. The Soviet Union never accepted the "Western" definition of human rights until 1991, when the Soviet empire was dissolved. See HELSINKI ACCORD.

Confirmation Hearing. Hearings held by the United States Senate to decide upon appointments (e.g., to the cabinet or Supreme Court) proposed by the president.

Confiscatory Policy. A legislative or an executive act authorizing excessive collection of dues, (e.g., fines, fees, or taxes), from those who hold an excess of wealth, through, for example, excise taxes, taxes on luxury, or taxes as a penalty. Under Nazi rule in Germany, Jews were required to pay exorbitant taxes and fees simply as a measure to drain them of all wealth; under soviet-communist systems in the Soviet Union and the East European satellite states, large taxes were imposed on private enterprises and all sorts of private initiatives, particularly on individual farmers in order to force them into collectivization. Persons not able to pay such fees or taxes lost their holdings to the state treasury. Incompetent and unimaginative politicians and bureaucrats seek to find additional revenue, as a rule, among those who have an excess of wealth, instead of taxing trade transactions or other sources. Excessive confiscatory practices, all legitimate under law, stifle private and personal initiative, motivation, self-esteem, and the desire to contribute to the creation of the general wealth of a nation or an economy. Such practices are often referred to as "highway robbery," and very often cause the flight of labor or capital. For example, high confiscatory taxes in Britain prompted resourceful citizens to settle in the United States or Switzerland, or to establish official domiciles in these countries in order to avoid high taxes on earnings, sometimes as much as 80 percent. Former communist-socialist states in East Europe, as well as Cuba, North Korea, and China, often confiscated up to 90 percent of the earnings of artists, athletes, or inventors, paid in domestic currencies. Such practices contributed to brain-drain, that is, to talented persons voting with their feet—escaping to the West or seeking political asylum in the West. But only a few had such opportunities, either to travel to the West or to escape, and those who remained at home were stifled by internal incompetence, apathy, and terror, and were whipped into obedience without any opportunity to develop their talents and creative skills. In order to attract persons with talent and applicable skills, the U.S. government issued special visas, called "liberty visas," to such persons allowing them to settle in the U.S. and work, without having to go through the usual immigration prodecures and channels. See BRAIN-DRAIN.

Conflict of Interest. An inconsistency which may arise between the personal interest and public interest of a person called upon to serve in public capacity (e.g., one being appointed or elected to a position which requires the regulation of certain business enterprises while having vested interest or stocks in those enterprises). Under some federal and state laws in the U.S., public officials are required to divest themselves from holding financial interests in enterprises which they are to control, supervise or regulate. Under the State of Virginia conflict of interest law, material financial interest or monetary gain of $5,000 accruing to one individual must be proven in order to sustain the application of that law.

Conflict of Laws. See PRIVATE INTERNATIONAL LAW.

Conflict Resolution. The basic assumption of politics is that there is constant conflict in a human society among individuals and groups which clash and collide with each other over the allocation of values in a society; that is, about who gets what, when and how. The purpose of politics is to resolve that conflict with the aid of the government, which may use force if necessary to settle an issue and to minimize, if not eliminate, the conflict.

Conglomerate. A business enterprise composed of other enterprises manufacturing different products.

Co-Governor. See FIRST LADY.

Congreso. Congress in some Spanish-speaking countries.

Congreso de la Union. Bicameral National Congress of Mexico. See CAMARA DE SENADORES, CAMARA DE DIPUTADOS.

Congreso Nacional. National Congress of Paraguay.

Congress. A major gathering of individuals, public or private organizations, governments, or international bodies, for the purpose of setting up principal guidelines, or achieving other desired objectives. See CONGRESS OF THE UNITED STATES, QUADRUPLE ALLIANCE.

Congress Bashing. Criticism of the United States Congress (the Senate and the House of Representatives) as an institution, its processes, rules, and the personal and legislative behavior of its members. Very often the president of the United States will blame Congress for his misfortunes (e.g., in 1948, President Harry S. Truman bashed the Congress during his reelection campaign as the "do nothing 80th Congress"). President George Bush even issued deadlines to the legislators to pass needed legislation by a specific time, e.g., calling in his January 1992 inaugural address for specific legislation needed to heal the American economy to be passed by Congress by 20 March 1992. Since legislation passed by Congress was contributing little to the problems at hand, U.S. Senator Warren Rudman, Republican from New Hampshire, author (with Senator Phil Gramm) of the Gramm-Rudman Act which was aimed at balancing the budget and at controlling federal spending, announced in disgust that there was a "conspiracy of silence" between the administration, the Congress, and a large segment of the electorate corrupted by powerful lobbies, and that he would not seek reelection to the Senate when his term expired in 1993. Not less often, Congress chastises the president and the administration, usually along partisan lines, for poor results in the implementation of congressional laws. See ZIGZAG MAN.

Congress for Democracy. See INDIAN NATIONAL CONGRESS PARTY.

Congress of Europe. See COUNCIL OF EUROPE.

Congress of People's Deputies. See SUPREME SOVIET.

Congress of Racial Equality (CORE). An organization formed in 1942 as the offshoot of the Fellowship of Reconciliation, a socialist group which advocated the replacement of capitalism with collective ownership of the means of production and distribution of goods and services. CORE pursues the struggle for black Americans and their rightful place in the American society. See BLACK CAPITALISM.

Congress of the United States. The legislative branch of the federal government in the U.S., established by the Federal Constitution (Art. I of 1787) and composed of two Houses, the Senate and the House of Representatives. See CONGRESSIONAL CAUCUS, UNITED STATES HOUSE OF REPRESENTATIVES, UNITED STATES SENATE, Appendices 8-12.

Congress of Vienna. See QUADRUPLE ALLIANCE.

Congress-Oriented Administration. A generally unsupported notion that the U.S. Congress favors a President and his administration if the President served previously in the Congress and vice-versa, that a President who has previously served in either House of Congress tends to be less antagonistic, less suspicious, and more adept at cooperating with Congress.

Congress Party. See INDIAN NATIONAL CONGRESS PARTY.

Congress Watch. An organization concerned with lobbying on Capitol Hill.

Congressional Aggrandizement. See ASSERTIVENESS.

Congressional Assertiveness. See ASSERTIVENESS.

Congressional Authorization. See CONGRESSIONAL MANDATE.

Congressional Black Caucus (CBC). An informal organization of black members of the U.S. House of Representatives established in 1971, for the purpose of unified action in bringing about legislation favoring black people in the United States. When the caucus was organized in 1971, there were only thirteen black members of the House.

Congressional Budget Office (CBO). Created by the Congressional Budget and Impoundment Control Act of 1974. Staff provides budget analysis for Congress. Submits a report to the Congressional Budget Committees (House and Senate) on the President's budget, and suggests alternative budget options.

Congressional Campaign Committees. Loose organizations, composed of members of the U.S. Congress and sympathizers, engaged in the task of electing or re-electing members to that body. These committees work in cooperation with (or without) national, state, or local party committees, organizations, and clubs. The Republican Party Committee was first established in 1866, and the Democratic Party Committee in 1880. See CONGRESS OF THE UNITED STATES.

Congressional Caucus. During the past several years a number of congressional caucuses have evolved in both Houses of the U.S. Congress (the Senate and the House of Representatives), which strive to represent and favor certain specific interests of their constituencies or geographic areas. They are: (1) the *Black Caucus* (consisting of 16 members), which favors more spending on domestic programs (e.g., urban renewal and housing for blacks) at the expense of military spending; (2) the *Blue-Collar Caucus* which was formed in 1977, in the House of Representatives by persons who, prior to becoming members of Congress, were earning their living through physical labor (with their hands); their main concern is the protection of domestic jobs by curbing foreign imports; (3) the *Congressional Clearinghouse* which keeps tabs on and informs local constituencies, state and local governments as well as other members of Congress, on legislation which affects states and localities; (4) the *Congresswomen's Caucus* which looks after the interests of women, particularly in employment and social security benefits; (5) the *Democratic Study Group* which keeps tabs of pending legislation that favors liberal causes (e.g., civil rights, liberties of the individual, and equality in political and legal processes) and informs other members of Congress and their respective constituencies on progress; (6) the *Environmental Study Conference*, which favors legislation pertaining to the protection of the environment and energy resources; (7) the *Great Lakes Senators* who favor the restoration of the $6 billion dollars which had been appropriated for the protection and restoration of the Great Lakes area but which was slashed in the House in 1977; (8) the *Hispanic Caucus*, which strives to bring about legislation that would favor Hispanics, Chicanos, and other persons and communities with Hispanic background; (9) the *Members of Congress for Peace Through Law*, which strives to bring about the peaceful resolution of international conflicts through judicial processes rather than through war; (10) the *New England Congressional Caucus*, which aims to protect the constituencies of the New England states (which were the hardest hit during the Arab oil embargo in 1973) by opposing higher fees on imported oil and, generally, to control domestic oil prices; (11) the *Northeast-Midwest Economic Advancement Coalition*, which lobbies for retention of military installations in that area and against tax changes which would affect older cities; (12) the *Port Caucus* which favors legislation allowing federal financing of port construction, operation costs, and maintenance (e.g., dredging); (13) the *Solar Coalition*, which favors development of solar energy by federal as well as private enterprises; (14) the *Steel Caucus*, which lobbies for legislation and administrative measures aimed at limiting foreign imports of steel and steel products in order to protect domestic production; (15) the *Suburban Caucus*, which seeks legislation aimed at protecting suburban communities (See Bedroom Community); and (16) the *United States Military Security Lobby*, which favors strong military posture for the United States and high spending for the production of arms and other military material. See

BLACK CAUCUS, CONGRESS OF THE UNITED STATES, LOBBY, UNITED STATES HOUSE OF REPRESENTATIVES, UNITED STATES SENATE.

Congressional Clearinghouse. See CONGRESSIONAL CAUCUS.

Congressional Committees. Each of the two houses of the United States Congress, the Senate and the House of Representatives, operates through a committee structure whereby all legislative measures (bills, resolutions), judicial and investigative functions (presidential appointments and hearings aimed at scrutinizing the acts and activities of the remaining branches of the government), are first being closely examined and acted upon by a group of legislators before being submitted to the entire body for final action. According to established practice, unfavorable action by a committee disposes of a matter before it receives consideration by the entire body of the legislative chamber—"kills it." The standing or permanent committees in the U.S. Senate are: Agriculture, Nutrition, and Forestry; Appropriations; Armed Services; Banking, Housing and Urban Affairs; Budget; Commerce, Science, and Transportation; Energy and Natural Resources; Environment and Public Works; Finance; Foreign Relations; Governmental Affairs; Human Resources; Judiciary; Rules and Administration; and Veterans' Affairs. Standing or permanent committees in the U.S. House of Representatives: Agriculture; Appropriations; Armed Services; Banking, Finance, and Urban Affairs; Budget; District of Columbia; Education and Labor; Government Operations; House Administration; Interior and Insular Affairs; International Relations; Interstate and Foreign Commerce; Judiciary, Merchant Marine and Fisheries; Post Office and Civil Service; Public Works and Transportation; Rules; Science and Technology; Small Business; Standards of Official Conduct (established after Representative Adam Clayton Powell of New York was investigated for misconduct in office, and was denied his seat on January 9, 1967); Veterans' Affairs; and Ways and Means.

Congressional Digest. See CONGRESSIONAL RECORD.

Congressional Directory. A publication privately owned and operated, not affiliated with or subsidized by the federal government, containing up-to-date biographies of the members of Congress, the Executive branch and the Judiciary, in addition to maps of congressional districts in the U.S. and charts of the organizations of the three principal branches of the federal government.

Congressional District. An area from which one person may be elected to the U.S. House of Representatives every two years. The Federal Constitution stipulates (Art. I) that each state is entitled to at least one representative or more, according to its population. Every ten years a national census is taken and, following its results, state legislatures are to reapportion congressional districts accordingly, which may result in either gaining or losing representation. There are two additional representatives, one from the District of Columbia and one from Puerto Rico—the Resident-Commissioners—elected for a term of four years. They both serve on committees, but do not vote. Members of the U.S. Senate are elected by states at large, each state being entitled to two Senators, regardless of the size of the state or the number of its inhabitants. See Appendix 21.

Congressional Ethics. See CODE OF OFFICIAL CONDUCT OF 1974.

Congressional Law. See BILL.

Congressional Lobby. See CONGRESSIONAL CAUCUS.

Congressional Mandate. Those acts and activities which Congress may authorize by law or resolution (e.g., granting relief to an individual, a group, or a corporation from some hardship, allowing the U.S. President to deploy military forces abroad under the restrictions of the War Powers Act). See CONGRESS OF THE UNITED STATES, MANDATE.

Congressional Medal of Honor. Often called the Medal of Honor; acknowledges bravery or leadership above and beyond the call of duty, the highest military decoration awarded in the U.S.

Congressional Pay Amendment. On 7 May 1992, the state of Michigan became the 38th state to ratify this amendment to the U.S. Constitution which provides for the curbing of the pay of lawmakers. The amendment, written by James Madison, was introduced in the first Congress and sent together with eleven other amendments to the states for ratification on 25 September 1789. This amendment was intended as the second amendment to the Bill of Rights as it appears today, but was not acted upon. No time limit was imposed on the ratification of this amendment and 203 years passed before three quarters of the states ratified it, with Michigan being the decisive vote. There is some doubt that this amendment will survive the constitutional test due to the length of time it took to be ratified. There are many such amendments that were never acted upon which are now collecting dust in pigeonholes. The congressional pay amendment reads as follows: "No law, varying the compensation for the service of senators and representatives, shall take effect until an election or representatives have intervened." See REASONABLE CONTEMPORANEOUSNESS RULE.

Congressional Pay Legislation. See CONGRESSIONAL PAY AMENDMENT.

Congressional Record. An official daily publication which contains texts of proceedings in Congress such as debates, statements, speeches, and reports of committees of both houses of Congress. Each member of Congress is entitled to have his remarks or any materials he desires (e.g., a letter from a constituent) printed in the Appendix to the *Record*. The activities of the regular congressional committees are reported in the *Congressional Digest*, printed on the back pages of the *Congressional Record*. The first *Record* appeared on March 4, 1873, and the *Digest* on March 17, 1947.

Congressional Relief. See CONGRESSIONAL MANDATE.

Congressional Reorganization Acts. The first Act of 1946, reduced the number of standing committees from about 47 to 18, limited the private bills each legislator could submit, and required lobbyists to register (with the Secretary of the Senate and the Clerk of the House). The 1970 Act established a system for the public scrutiny of House members (charged with misconduct in office) and allowed for an August recess during non-election years. See CANNON REVOLT, UNITED STATES HOUSE OF REPRESENTATIVES.

Congressional Resolution. See RESOLUTION.

Congressional Select Committee on Intelligence. See CENTRAL INTELLIGENCE AGENCY (CIA), COVERT ACTION.

Congressional Session. See UNITED STATES HOUSE OF REPRESENTATIVES.

Congressional Term. See UNITED STATES HOUSE OF REPRESENTATIVES.

Congressman at Large. A member of the U.S. House of Representatives, elected before the completion of reapportionment, to represent the entire state rather than any single district constituency. See UNITED STATES CONGRESS, UNITED STATES HOUSE OF REPRESENTATIVES.

Congresswomen's Caucus. See CONGRESSIONAL CAUCUS.

Connally Amendment. See INTERNATIONAL COURT OF JUSTICE (ICJ).

Connecticut Compromise. See PLANS OF THE AMERICAN UNION.

Conoscenza. Italian term for the custom prevailing in Sicily, where a young suitor must ask the father of his prospective bride, through a sponsor, to see his daughter. See MAFIA.

Conquer and Rule. See DIVIDE ET IMPERA.

Conquest. The act of taking over the territory of one state by another, usually by means of war. See AGGRESSION, WAR.

Conquistador. See DIVIDE ET IMPERA.

Conscientious Objector. One who refuses to carry out a military obligation on moral or religious grounds; to receive such a deferment one must exhibit a sincere objection and usually perform noncombat service instead.

Consciousness Movement. See ANTI-VIETNAM WAR PROTESTS.

ry (based on and regulated by law) recruitment of manpower or ilitary purposes; the draft of manpower. Conscription ended in the of the Selective Service Act on January 27, 1973, and subsequently, the s. On May 6, 1980, Congress tabled a request by President Carter to es. See DRAFT.

anguage, "council of state." Also, an agency of the French Government ation and administrative reforms, but whose opinions are not binding the executive branch of the government. Also *consiglio de stato*-body nton-members vary from 5 to 11 members (Switzerland).

ional. The upper house or Economic and Regional Council of the African Republic.

ody in which are vested the executive powers of the Swiss government,

of Swiss legislature.

. The unicameral legislative body, National Consultative Council, of

OF DEMOCRACY.

of agenda items of a local government (city, town, county) meeting items (ordinances, resolutions) are then voted on "En Banc" rather an objection, an item may be removed to be voted on separately. Items placed on the consent agenda are usually procedural in nature, or unanimously agreed upon.

Consent Calendar. A calendar in the U.S. House of Representatives listing any non-controversial bills of the Union or House Calendars which are called to the floor normally on the first and third Mondays of each month. Consideration of a bill proposed through the Consent Calendar may be objected to by any member on the floor. When objection occurs for the second time by at least three members, the bill is stricken from the Consent Calendar and placed again on the Union or House Calendar. If there is no objection from the floor, the bill is given immediate consideration. See CALENDAR WEDNESDAY, HOUSE CALENDAR, PRIVATE BILL, UNION CALENDAR.

Consent Order. A directive which may be issued by a governmental regulatory agency (e.g., Federal Communication Commission or Federal Trade Commission) to a private enterprise to refrain from certain activity such as stifling free competition, and demanding consenting agreement to such effect. The Federal Trade Commission (FTC), for example, issued such a consent order and acquired a consent agreement from the Peoples Drug Stores in October, 1975, which was involved in anti-competitive shopping center leases, which gave the drug chain the right to prohibit other businesses from selling similar products in the same shopping center.

Consent Socialism. See PARLIAMENTARY SOCIALISM.

Conservatism. Resistance to change, adherence to old established order, customs, procedures, ideals, or institutions. Often accompanied by ethnocentrism or egocentrism.

Conservative. Persons, policies, and/or beliefs associated with or promoting conservatism.

Conservative Federalism. See NEW FEDERALISM.

Conservative Party, British. The older of the two major political parties in England (dating to 1679, and also known as the Tories) strongly advocating a free enterprise system of economy and as little governmental control as possible. See TORY.

Consigliere. See MAFIA.

Consiglio Comunale. Elective body of local governments in Italy.

Consiglio di Stato. See CONSEIL D'ÉTAT.

Consolato del Mare. The first known private code regulating maritime practices in 14th Century Venice (Italy). Also, an important source of international maritime and consular law. See MARITIME LAW.

Consolidated Government. See AREAWIDE GOVERNMENT.

Consolidation. In terms of school districts, the combining of many small-school districts into one large school district.

Conspiracy of Silence. See ZIGZAG MAN.

Constable. Peace officer (policeman) in a small town, mainly in New England states (e.g., Massachusetts), or England proper.

Constituency. The body of citizens qualified to vote within a certain geographic area (e.g., congressional district, judicial district, school district, etc.). Also, a self-contained political subdivision (e.g., town, city, or a state). See ELECTORATE, UNITED STATES CONGRESS.

Constituent. A voter who is represented by government officials.

Constituent Assembly. Usually, the legislature of a newly-formed state which has the task of implementing basic laws and determining the form of government. Such constituent assemblies may also be called when the state is undergoing a structural change of the political system (e.g., from a monarchy or dictatorship to a parliamentary or representative democracy; or due to a revolution, as was the case in Russia in 1917). See DUMA.

Constitution. Basic, fundamental, organic law which creates a state and its government; describes its form, character, and identity; delineates the powers and responsibilities of officials both elective and appointive; states the rights and obligations of citizens and aliens, and describes relationships with other states. All modern states have written constitutions, ranging from several pages to 460 pages (in the case of India). Most modern constitutions are, to a great extent, modeled after the American Constitution adopted in 1787, the first modern constitution still in continuous use. The second is that of Poland and the third, that of France. See CONSTITUTION OF THE UNITED STATES, SUPREME LAW OF THE LAND, Appendix 5.

Constitution Day. See CITIZENSHIP DAY.

Constitution of the United States. The fundamental law of the American Federation, composed of a Preamble (non-enforceable), seven Articles, and twenty-six Amendments, drafted by the Constitutional Convention in Philadelphia, Pennsylvania, in 1787, and ratified in 1791, together with the first ten Amendments (known as the *Bill Of Rights*). See SUPREME LAW OF THE LAND, Appendix 8.

Constitutional Amendment. An additional provision added to a constitution for the purpose of extending the scope of or limiting or adding additional provisions: a way modifying a constitution. The U.S. Constitution can be amended, not revised. Many constitutions (e.g., that of the former USSR), may be modified—amended or revised—by a majority vote of both houses of the legislature. The ERA amendment was defeated in 1980. Another amendment proposed, calling for a balanced budget, was defeated in the U.S. Senate on March 17, 1980.

Constitutional Bill. See BILL.

Constitutional Compromises. See PLANS OF THE AMERICAN UNION.

Constitutional Council of Algeria. See ALGERIAN MUSLIM FUNDAMENTALISM.

Constitutional Crisis. A deadlock or an impasse which may occur between two or more branches of a government on a policy resolution, either due to a lack of clear constitutional provisions or differences in its interpretation. In cases in which the government is based on clear constitutional provisions, a constitutional test can be made (provided the system allows for judicial review) through the courts which, in the final analysis, may resolve the constitutional dispute by adjudicating in the strict meaning of the constitution or in its general spirit. See Amendment XXV in Appendix 5, CRISIS, WATERGATE AFFAIR.

Constitutional Government. See SUPREME LAW OF THE LAND, Appendix 5.

Constitutional Law. A body of laws derived from or pertaining to the constitution; normative law on which other laws are based (e.g., statutes and judicial decisions in the United States). See CONSTITUTION, CONSTITUTIONAL CRISIS.

Constitutional Liberalism. See LIBERAL CONSTITUTION.

Constitutional Majority. See TYRANNY OF THE MAJORITY.

Constitutional Monarchy. See MONARCHY.

Constitutional Statutory Code. Most of the state constitutions of the fifty states in the American Federal Union contain not only the normative guidelines (like the federal constitution), but also include all statutes that are passed by the legislatures. Federal statutes are held separately.

Constitutional Union Party. A splinter, nationalistic, political party composed of the "Whig" and "Know-Nothing" elements in the Southern States of the United States during the 1860s. See AMERICAN PARTY, WHIG, WHIG PARTY.

Constitutionalism. An ancient notion, dating back to Aristotle (384-322 BC), a Greek political philosopher and scholar, that every politically organized society should have a single document to serve as the normative law upon which the government will be organized, and its powers, functions, and limitations defined. See CONSTITUTION.

Constitutionality Test. The practice of forwarding a state legislative act to the state's Supreme Court, asking it to determine whether the measure does or does not violate state and/or federal constitutions or statutes. See CONSTITUTIONAL CRISIS.

Constructionist. One who reads and interprets laws and regulations exactly to the letter. Term often applied to Justices of the U.S. Supreme Court who read and interpret the U.S. Constitution neither in the narrow nor in the broad sense, but strictly according to the commonly agreed meaning of the language. See JUDICIAL ACTIVISM.

Constructive Engagement. The official policy of U.S. President Ronald Reagan (1981-1989) toward the Republic of South Africa and apartheid, its practice of separation of races. This resulted in a vote for economic sanctions against South Africa by the U.S. Congress on 22 July 1985. The policy was implemented in response to emergency measures and repression of blacks in South Africa, mainly against the African National Congress (ANC) and its leadership, including Nelson Mandela who was subsequently released from imprisonment. The black South Africans demand a share in government based on the American principle of "one man, one vote." See Appendix 29.

Consul. An administrative, nonpolitical, nondiplomatic representative of one state performing designated functions in the territory of another. (For example, he issues visas to foreign nationals for travel to the country which the consul represents, renews passports for his nationals and assists them with arrangements when necessary, performs marriages and records vital statistics of his nationals abroad, keeps records of visiting ships and aircraft, settles disputes arising among their crews, and orders investigations of improper acts or even arrests and detains those violating laws.) Consuls are not covered by diplomatic immunity unless reciprocal agreements to this effect are in place between the sending and the receiving states. See DIPLOMATIC RANKS.

Consumer Democracy. See CONSUMER SOVEREIGNTY.

Consumer Durable Goods. Goods bought by households for their personal use that, on the average, last more than three years—for example, automobiles, furniture, or appliances.

Consumer Economics. See PRODUCER ECONOMICS.

Consumer Imperialism. See COLONIALISM.

Consumer Price Index. A written record (index, former name—"cost of living index") of the fluctuation of prices of approximately 400 goods and services purchased by customers in large quantities in selected large population areas throughout the United States. The Index is compiled by the Bureau of Labor Statistics.

Consumer Protection. One mode of extending political democracy to the market place. See CAVEAT EMPTOR, LEMON LAW.

Consumer Sovereignty. The freedom of choice that consumers in open societies enjoy by choosing between products and brands and by purchasing what they like regardless of whether the product is of domestic ("buy American") or foreign origin. Patriotism, say some, ends at the pocketbook! Countries restricting travel of their own citizens as well as citizens of other countries, restrict consumer choice. A notion to the effect that in polyarchic, democratic societies, the consumers determine production outcomes, and influence political-governmental policy outputs. See AMERICA BASHING, JAPAN BASHING, MULTINATIONAL CORPORATION.

Consumer Welfare. A government's protection of consumers against fraud, misrepresentation, false advertising, and mislabeling of products by providers of consumer goods and services. In another context, consumer welfare is understood to mean the efficient and widespread distribution of ways and means to maximize national resources for the benefit of society at large. Antitrust legislation in the United States, for example, has been upheld by the U.S. Supreme Court because it protects consumer welfare.

Consumerism. See CONSUMER SOVEREIGNTY.

Consummate Presumption. As applied to politics, particularly in the state of New York where the budgets are in reverse proportion to the magnitude of problems to be solved, this expression means a "distorted view of reality" held by a public figure who sincerely believes his view to be true. The term was used by New York Governor Mario M. Cuomo when commenting on President Bush's State of the Union message on 29 January 1992, when after having assured the American people for the past eighteen months that there was no inflation, the President admitted that there was inflation, but that it would go away very soon.

Containment. The official policy of the United States Government toward the Soviet Union and its Eastern European satellite states in the 1940s and 1950s, which rested on the assumption that the USSR was a totalitarian, imperialistic state, which sooner or later would initiate a war against the West, particularly the United States, for the purpose of destroying capitalism and introducing communism. The Administration of U.S. President Harry S. Truman (1945-1953) was alerted by U.S. Ambassador to the USSR, George F. Kennan (in his article printed in *Foreign Affairs* in 1947 and signed "X"), the first U.S. Ambassador to that country who spoke Russian, that the USSR was making serious preparations for an all-out attack against the United States. Kennan urged speedy preparations in order to meet the challenge. This was at a time when the Soviet Union firmly controlled its satellites, including Albania and the People's Republic of China (as a monolithic bloc); subsequently, however, the Soviets not only did not attack, but refused to become pawns for any satellite for the larger purpose of spreading communism. In spite of the prevailing dogma of Marxism-Leninism, which Soviet leaders recited for public consumption, their concerns were in reality more defensive and internal; they did not demonstrate a desire to conquer lands, although they continued to influence other nations through propaganda. See COLD WAR.

Contemporary Community Standards. The U.S. Supreme Court ruled, on October 31, 1977, that matters pertaining to obscenity cases (e.g., pornography through books, movies, and other displays) are to be judged on the opinion of a given community as to what it considers to be obscene and what it does not. Thus, the Court refrained from making a landmark decision that would serve as a norm for judging all obscenity matters.

Contempt Citation. See CONTEMPT OF CONGRESS.

Contempt of Congress. A premeditated, disorderly conduct or willful noncompliance with commands issued by any of the congressional committees or subcommittees of the United States Congress (e.g., refusal to answer questions under immunity, or cooperate otherwise). Congress may issue a contempt citation (an order of indictment and confinement) with which the judicial branch may not interfere.

Similar acts of disrespect for the authority of a court constitute "contempt of court" and are punishable under law. See EXECUTIVE PRIVILEGE.

Contempt of Court. See CONTEMPT OF CONGRESS.

Contiguous Zone. Land or territorial waters, located in close proximity to the territory of a state and considered to be under its jurisdiction.

Continental Congress. The body of representatives from the thirteen original colonies in North America, called in 1774 in Philadelphia, Pennsylvania, for the purpose of petitioning the British Government for the redress of grievances. In 1775, the Second Continental Congress adopted strong measures for organized resistance which led to the revolution against England.

Continental Shelf. The seabed and subsoil of underwater areas adjacent to the coast but outside the territorial waters of a state, to a depth of 200 meters or beyond that limit, where the nature of the superjacent waters allows the exploitation of natural resources of these areas; the seabed and subsoil of like underwater areas surrounding the coast of an island.

Contingency Planning. Contingency planning refers to the preparation of multiple plans, each of which may be appropriate for a particular set of conditions. In effect, the contingency plan answers the question, what would we do if . . . ?

Continuing Appropriation. See CONTINUING RESOLUTION.

Continuing Resolution. A resolution that may be passed by the U.S. Congress which authorizes disbursement of federal funds (e.g., for payroll) at the rate according to the criteria that were authorized by the latest appropriations. It simply lets the President continue business as usual until the new legislation (usually a new budget) is adopted, so as not to disrupt the normal administrative processes. Such measures are rarely taken; usually when, due to unforeseen circumstances, Congress was not able to approve the budget on time (e.g., the beginning of the fiscal year). See CONGRESS OF THE UNITED STATES.

Contract. A written (as a rule) or an oral (rarely, except under common law rules) agreement between two or more parties which is considered binding and can be upheld in a court of law.

Contract Clause. The provision in the U.S. Constitution (Art. I, Sec. 10) which forbids the state legislatures to enact laws impairing the obligations of contracts. With the decision in the case of Dartmouth College (*Dartmouth College v. Woodward, 1819*), the Supreme Court extended the meaning of the clause whereby public authorities may grant charters and franchises to individual persons and/or corporations. See Appendix 8.

Contract Theory. A body of theories attempting to explain the origins of the existing obligations of the individual who conforms to the social and political institutions in a state. See ORIGINS OF THE STATE THEORIES.

Contract Theory of Government. See ORIGINS OF THE STATE THEORIES.

Contractual Democracy. See TERRITORIAL DEMOCRACY.

Contractual Right. A right secured under or derived from a contract.

Contradictions of Capitalism. According to Marxists, it is the discrepancy between the social character of production (the social relations entered into by many workers in order to produce) and the individual retention of profit (by the capitalist); the value is created by many and the profit is retained by one or a small group of persons. See MARXISM.

Contras. See IRAN-CONTRA AFFAIR, SANDANISTA LIBERATION FRONT.

Contributory Negligence. A rule in common law whereby negligence on the part of an injured employee relieves the employer of liability for damages. (This rule was modified by statutory laws in most of the states in the U.S., known as "comparative negligence," under which the employer is relieved from responsibility in proportion to his negligence.)

Control from the Top. See DEMOCRATIC CENTRALISM.

Control through Command. See LIBERAL CONSTITUTION.

Controlled Escalation. A term which U.S. President Lyndon B. Johnson (1963-1969) used to describe the gradual escalation of America's involvement in the Vietnamese conflict (1954-1975) by deploying a sufficient amount of military power in order to control the spread of communist forces (e.g., the Viet Cong and the North Vietnamese) in South Vietnam, but refraining from the deployment of a larger force which could bring victory. This "controlled escalation" policy alienated the military establishment, which often complained that this was a "no-win war," conducted by politicians for political reasons, in which the military forces were used only as pawns. See VIETNAMIZATION.

CONUS. Continental United States.

Convenience and Public Necessity. See PUBLIC INTEREST CONVENIENCE AND NECESSITY.

Convergence of Power. An authority which originates from different sources, but which is used for the achievement of a single desired objective (e.g., the governments of opposing political systems may utilize their powers to achieve a desired common goal such as international peace and security, which is considered beneficial to all). Also, a notion which once prevailed among some politicians and statesmen of the capitalist (the United States) and the socialist (the former Soviet Union) politico-economic systems to the effect that, in the final analysis, there are no fundamental differences among the goals, aims, and objectives of these two systems. In the future, then, all ideological differences will disappear and these two powers will join forces for either closer cooperation or perhaps a merging into a global empire. With the dissolution of the Soviet Union on 25 December 1991, the chances are greater than ever that the present Commonwealth of Independent States (CIS), as well as the other free republics that were once part of the Soviet Union (e.g., Estonia, Latvia, Lithuania, and Georgia), may join the European Community with time.

Conversation with Oregon. Due to general increased suspicion of government, the state of Oregon in the United States, in order to regain citizens' confidence, initiated two programs in 1991: one program provides that the governor and other top government bureaucrats meet with constituents in small groups, in various locations, to listen to grievances and suggestions, and ask for input in policy formation. The second program, called "Oregon Benchmark," will allow citizens to participate in forming policies on specific issues. These programs were approved in 1989 by the state legislature at the request of Governor Neil Goldschmidt, and are now being continued in the administration of Governor Barbara Roberts. This modern-day experimentation with a mixture of elements—direct democracy, referendum, and local option—is unique to this particular state. Citizen input into policy formation, by referendum and initiative, originated in Oregon at the turn of this century. The governor, upon authorization by the state legislature, set up a special board to oversee the progress and the utility of these two programs. See DEMOCRACY, DEMOCRACY, DIRECT (or PURE DEMOCRACY), LOCAL OPTION, PARTICIPATORY DEMOCRACY.

Cook County Political Machine. See POLITICAL MACHINE.

Cookie Pusher. A term often applied to professional diplomats and top government executives of the United States who often spend more time attending parties and receptions (eating cookies) than performing their official duties or preparing (through study and research) for their tasks. Some U.S. Presidents (e.g., F. D. Roosevelt who often referred to his diplomats and cabinet members as "cookie pushers on the embassy circuit") preferred to be their own secretaries of state, ambassadors (negotiating directly with other heads of state and heads of government through summit diplomacy), or special envoys; or used special assistants for other important tasks. (For example, Colonel House was closer to President Woodrow Wilson than his Secretary of State and Harry Hopkins, rather than the Secretary of State, carried out important assignments for President Roosevelt.)

Cooley's Doctrine. A notion developed by Thomas M. Cooley, a jurist and authority on municipal law, which asserts that the right of local government in the U.S. to shape its own institutions and policies should not be taken away, as Dillon suggests (See Dillon's Rule), but preserved as a means of checking the power of the state government; and that states, as well as the federal government, must be balanced by countervailing power, namely the power of the local government.

Cooling-Off Period. A predetermined period of time during which parties to a dispute agree not to resort to any action, e.g., a period of time agreed upon by labor and management during which the parties will not resort to strike (labor) or lockout (management). See TAFT-HARTLEY ACT.

Cooling Off Treaties. See BRYAN TREATIES, TAFT-HARTLEY ACT.

Cooperative Federalism. See FEDERALISM.

Coopersmith Self-Esteem Inventory. See POLITICAL SELF-ESTEEM.

Coordinating Committee for Multilateral Export Controls (COCOM). An informal but effective organization, set up in 1950 in response to the Soviet and East European Council for Economic Mutual Assistance (CEMA) and the Berlin Blockade by American and Western intelligence services. It was designed to control transfer of technologies, critical raw materials and sophisticated products to the Eastern Bloc for military use. The legal framework of this organization was the American Export Control Act of 1949, amended several times since. The organization operates from its headquarters in Paris, France. In spite of these controls, Soviet intelligence apparatus was able to obtain western technologies which enabled the Soviets to produce advanced weapon systems. Due to a poor infrastructure and management and the lack of freedom to innovate and expand, they were not able to employ all of the technologies that they received. They were often given more credit than was due them; some of the technology was simply mismanaged or abandoned. Authors Linda Melvin, Nick Anning and David Hebditch point out (*Techno-Bandits*, Houghton Mifflin, Boston, 1984) that, while the prevailing attitude among Western technicians was that "if it works, it must be obsolete," Soviets thought, "if it works, leave it alone." The ancient Chinese "adding machine," the abacus, remains in popular use by Soviets to this day, while electronic gadgets performing more functions faster and at less of a production cost are not very commonly used. (The above authors call this the "abacus syndrome.") In many respects, the West often overestimated actual Soviet power and capability, the limits of which have been demonstrated by recent events. See AGONIZING REAPPRAISAL.

Coordinative Management Assistance. Financial assistance to support activities of a state, a political subdivision thereof, or a regional council, for purposes of consistent implementation of specified programs.

COPE. See COMMITTEE ON POLITICAL EDUCATION.

Copperhead. A term commonly applied to anyone (particularly a member of the Democratic Party in the Northern states of the United States) who opposed the policies of President Abraham Lincoln against the South and Southern Confederacy, prior to and during the Civil War.

Co-President. See FIRST LADY.

Coram Populo. In the Latin language, "publicly" or "in public."

Cordon Sanitaire. In the French language, "armed guard charged with preventing the spread of hostile acts" or "quarantine." See PEACE-KEEPING FORCE OF THE UNITED NATIONS.

CORE. See CONGRESS OF RACIAL EQUALITY.

CORE Value. See NATIONAL INTEREST.

Coroner. A government official, or one authorized to act for the government, to determine the causes of an unnatural death of a person. Coroners are often assisted by juries (Coroner's Jury). Under some jurisdictions in the U.S., coroners are known as "medical examiners" (e.g., in New York City).

Corporate Citizen. See GLOBAL LOCALIZATION.

Corporate Colony. See AMERICAN COLONIES.

Corporate Culture. The sum total of relationships among persons within large business enterprises and the way these relationships affect interpersonal collaboration, labor discipline, production, and marketing.

Corporate Dictatorship. See CATEGORY KILLER, GROUP, MONOPOLY, MONOPOLY CAPITALISM.

Corporate State. A system of integrated governmental machinery with built-in controls of the national economy designed by Benito Mussolini in Fascist Italy during the 1920s. The system provided for two parallel sets of institutions: one for employers and the other for employees. At the base of the organizational pyramid were the local syndicates, or unions of workers and of employers for each major occupational category. These syndicates were grouped into national federations for each major industry which, in turn, were organized into national confederations representing several closely related industries. At the top of the pyramid were the corporations (a total of twenty-two) which included the employees and employers appointed by the government upon recommendation of the various national confederations.

Corporate Statism. See DEMOCRATIC CAPITALISM.

Corporate Totalitarianism. See CATEGORY KILLER, GROUP, MONOPOLY, MONOPOLY CAPITALISM.

Corporation, Municipal. See MUNICIPAL CORPORATION.

Corps Diplomatique. In the French language, "diplomatic corps"; also, a body of accredited diplomatic representatives in one state who are covered by diplomatic immunity. See DIPLOMACY.

Corpus Delicti. In the Latin language, "material proof at hand" or "tangible evidence." See BURDEN OF PROOF.

Corpus Juris. In the Latin language, "a body of laws" (e.g., the constitutions and the statutes, federal and state, in the United States).

Corroborating Evidence. See CORROBORATION.

Corroborating Witness. See CORROBORATION.

Corroboration. The acknowledgement of the truth of certain facts; the confirmation, by testimony or by evidence, of previously ascertained facts; supporting evidence presented in court on the material facts in a dispute; additional substantial facts or circumstances which help in ascertaining some truth (e.g.,fingerprints, ballistics or, chemical analyses of matter).

Corruption of Blood. A legal doctrine that was originated during the feudal era in Europe (and much earlier among some Asian societies) whereby persons convicted of a major crime (e.g., murder or treason) were considered to have corrupt blood and, therefore, neither those persons nor their offspring could exercise political or legal rights, including property rights (e.g., the ability to inherit or to transfer property). The U.S. Constitution forbids this practice. See Appendix 8.

Cosa Nostra. See MAFIA.

Cosmology. The study of the origin and the nature of the human environment (i.e., the world as man perceives it).

Cosmopolitan. As used in politics, one owing allegiance to no single state or authority; a citizen of the world. See WORLD GOVERNMENT.

Cost of Living Index. See CONSUMER PRICE INDEX.

Cottage Industry. An ancient form of manufacturing on a small scale, usually from one's dwelling, apartment, or home. A popular form of economic enterprise, particularly in the service sector, all around the world, because it saves the owners costs on renting or purchasing separate facilities; it relieves traffic congestion and pollution, and it allows family flexitime for work, raising children, and recreation.

Cotton Belt. See SECTIONALISM.

Cottonocracy. A political system which rests on a single-crop economy, namely cotton, such as that of the Southern states of the United States prior to the War of Secession (Civil War). See SECTIONALISM.

Council for Economic Mutual Assistance (CEMA). A plan for economic cooperation between the Soviet Union and her East European satellite states, proposed by Vyacheslav M. Molotov, former Soviet Foreign Minister, and signed in January 1949, by the USSR, Bulgaria, Czechoslovakia, Hungary, Poland, and Rumania (later joined by Albania which withdrew from it again after the Sino-Soviet split). The plan had four major objectives: (1) to industrialize the USSR and the satellite states; (2) to solicit the cooperation of the satellite states in the rebuilding of the Soviet economy; (3) to coordinate the economies of the satellites that were forbidden to participate in the Marshall Plan; and (4) to create a Soviet-East European common market. Dissolved in 1990. See COORDINATING COMMITTEE FOR MULTILATERAL EXPORT CONTROLS (COCOM).

Council for Mutual Economic Assistance (COMECON). See COUNCIL FOR ECONOMIC MUTUAL ASSISTANCE (CEMA).

Council-Manager Form of Government. See FORMS OF LOCAL GOVERNMENT.

Council-Manager Plan. Under this plan of city government, all legislative functions are in the hands of a council of five to nine members who are usually elected by a community at large. The council hires and fires the chief executive known as the manager. The manager is expected to run the city in a non-political way according to the policies set by the council.

Council of Economic Advisers (CEA). One of the fifteen separate Bureaus within the Executive Offices of the President of the United States charged with the responsibility of studying and advising the President on all matters related to the national economy. See ECONOMIC MESSAGE.

Council of Elders. In the German language, "Ältestenrat." A group of elder (age-wise) members of the Bundestag (the elective chamber of the Parliament in the German Federal Republic) selected by the respective political parties represented in the Bundestag to serve as a steering committee (or a committee on committees) and as a kind of reconciliatory body for any differences arising among the political parties on legislative matters, or on the general conduct of affairs of that legislative chamber.

Council of Europe. Following the establishment of the North Atlantic Treaty Organization (NATO) on March 17, 1948 (by the Brussels Treaty), and successful economic recovery under the Marshall Plan a group of European unification organizations and movements (e.g., the International Committee of the Movements for European Unity, established during the Congress of Europe held in The Hague, the Netherlands on May 8-10, 1948; the Economic League for European Cooperation; the French Council for United Europe; the European Movement, headed by Winston Churchill of England; and the Committee of Notables consisting of principal leaders of Western European states) agreed on January 18, 1949, to establish the Council of Europe with the following aims: (1) to unite Europe which was rigidly divided by conflicts over sovereign rights and military threat from Soviet bloc nations, (2) to establish close cooperation in addition to military arrangements under the NATO system (e.g., cultural and economic cooperation); (3) to establish a European Court on Human Rights with states as well as individual persons as subjects; (4) to adopt a European Convention on Human Rights and Fundamental Freedoms; and (5) to establish new channels of political, economic, and cultural cooperation and exchange (e.g., a European University which currently functions in Florence, Italy; reciprocal recognition of credentials, library cards, diplomas, insurance liability coverage, and other benefits, including free movement of labor, known as "guest workers" and medical benefits and facilities). All non-communist European states are members of the Council, and most of them ratified the several conventions prepared by the Council (e.g., recognizing the jurisdiction of the European Court on Human Rights before which individual persons may sue their own government). The principal components, designed to bring about speedy integration of Europe; the Common Market (dealing with economic matters); NATO (charged with military matters such as defense of Europe); and the Council of Europe (the political component of the European arrangement), were further unified politically after the All-European election for the European Parliament was held. The All-European Parliament (elected by qualified voters from all member states on the basis of proportional representation) served as a coordinating agency for the European integration (political) movement. The establishment of an international legislative body such as the All-European Parliament was an unprecedented occurrence in the political history of mankind. See Appendices 73, 73-A, 73-B.

Council of Government (COG). See NATIONAL ASSOCIATION OF REGIONAL COUNCILS (NARC).

Council of National Salvation. See I AM THE STATE, NATIONAL SALVATION FRONT.

Council of Revision. See PLANS OF THE AMERICAN UNION.

Council of State Governments (CSG). An organization established in 1925 and supported by state governments in the U.S. for the purpose of conducting studies and research pertaining to state governments.

Councilor. An elected official of an administrative county in Great Britain; also an elective member of the House of Councilors in Japan (one of two chambers of the Japanese Diet, or parliament, under the Constitution of 1947).

Counselor. An attorney or legal adviser, also an adviser (usually legal) to an ambassador or minister in the diplomatic service. See DIPLOMATIC RANKS, ESQUIRE.

Counterculture. The disregard for and opposition to the existing culture (political culture, institutions, and processes) often as a sign of protest, political apathy, or as an attempt to replace one culture with another. The term was popular in the United States during the 1960s and 1970s when large groups opposed American policies and traditional institutions and practices (e.g., the Vietnam War and unequal distribution of wealth).

Counterespionage. See COUNTERINTELLIGENCE.

Counterinsurgency. See COUNTERINSURGENCY IN AMERICA, INSURGENCY.

Counterinsurgency in America. The emergence of the Soviet state as a global power at the end of W.W.II triggered the revival of the "red scare" and anti-communism crusades around the world and in America in particular. The American law enforcement-intelligence-military complex had a tradition of insurgency and counterinsurgency. This dated back to the times when the United States sent military expeditions to Latin America and the Philippines, and to such activities as the "Palmer Raids," the "Bonus Army March" on Washington, suppressed by General Douglas MacArthur, and the wartime rounding up of German spies and other pro-Nazi agitators with the aid and assistance of American and Italian Mafia organizations. Further, Americans, with fresh memories of victory in W.W.II, were disenchanted by the Korean War of 1950-1954. The "cold war" political and social atmosphere was permeated with suspicion and mistrust fueled by MCCARTHYism. Other factors included the largest ever Soviet spy network in the West, operated by recent fugitives to the USSR, Kim Philby, Guy Burgess, and Donald Maclean, and the revelation of the American-British "Berlin Tunnel," a systematic listening post of Soviet communications which closed down after British Intelligence agent and Soviet mole William Blake informed his Moscow master about it. Some lighter moments also well characterize the era, such as the raid by Canadian security police on an exhibition of Cubist paintings, considered an act of subversion perpetuated by Fidel Castro! Lastly, anti-Vietnam War opposition, together with the civil rights movement of the 1960s and '70s, posed new challenges, so new ways had to be found to cope with the situation. According to author Ford Rowan (*Technospies: The Secret Network That Spies on You—and You*, New York: G.P. Putnam's Sons, 1978), some of the known measures undertaken include the following: The "Charter Project" was organized in 1948 by the FBI and CIA, with the Army participating at the end, to find a drug that would make a person talk and reveal the truth against his will. Such truth serum was used throughout the years, in addition to the so-called lie detector, or the polygraph. Operation "Midnight-Climax," organized during the 1950s by the CIA, involved the giving of LSD to females and their male partners, then observation of their behavior by CIA psychologists through two-way mirrors, and the recording of their behavior. The CIA operation code-named CHAOS was a massive domestic surveillance of at least 300,000 persons known to oppose the War in Vietnam, recording their movements, behavior, and contacts; a similar program was conducted by the FBI, known as COINTELPRO, or Counter Intelligence Program, designed to detect any eventual contacts with persons from outside the United States. Programs known as DAME and DASE were conducted by Army Intelligence, in which soldiers were taught to conduct wiretaps and burglaries on Americans in the United States. The U.S. Military, through the Pentagon's Division of Military Support, was training soldiers in the suppression of domestic insurrection, or uprising, by Americans against their bureaucrats. Another plan, designed by the Pentagon and code-named Garden Plot, was concerned with disturbances caused by black Americans. Operation Harvest, originated by the National Security Agency (known as the Puzzle Palace), and situated in Ft. Meade, Maryland, was to conduct electronic eavesdropping operations and to correlate and store information on Americans. The CIA illegally gathered information on Americans and stored it in a computer system code-named Hydra. One young lawyer, a desperate bureaucrat and White House aide to President Richard Nixon, Tom Charles Huston, designed a plan for domestic surveillance and intelligence operations against Americans—an operation known, for obvious reasons, as the Huston Plan. The Internal Revenue Service ordered its tax agents to gather information on political activists. Their Gathering and Retrieval System compiled information on almost 500,000 Americans. The FBI maintained a list of black activists, called the Key Black Extremist Index, and introduced a message-switching system to coordinate its activities with those of state and local police organizations; illegal interception of long-distance telephone conversations was monitored by using then-new microwave technology. Operation Minaret was conducted by the NSA in collaboration with the FBI and CIA to spy on persons with overseas contacts. The FBI set up the so-called Rabble Rouser Index and the Security Index of thousands of political activists with whom FBI Director J. Edgar Hoover was not particularly friendly. The IRS's Special Services Staff was to keep track of and disrupt anti-war or race-motivated protests. At the local level, communities were regimented into so-called District Planning Commissions, whose task, in addition to infrastructure planning, was to set up such disorder control plans in collaboration with local, state, and federal law enforcement and investigative agencies, as well as with the regional commands of the armed forces. These plans outlined in detail means for identifying disorder and for arresting and detaining troublemakers, and included provision for detention and medical services. Lastly, there was "Mount Weather," a code name for an operation calling for a network of underground bunkers to serve as the last resort command post and safe haven for government bureaucrats in the event of a national emergency. Most of these counter-insurgency programs became known as the "Family Jewels" and were subjected to Congressional investigation. See AMERICAN-SOVIET COLLUSION, BODYGUARD OF LIES, COUNTER-ESPIONAGE, DIES COMMITTEE, MCCARTHYISM, RED SCARE.

Counterintelligence. According to Professor Robin W. Winks (*Cloak and Gown, 1939-1961*, William Morrow and Company, Inc.), America's most renowned authority on intelligence and counterintelligence, Professor Norman Holmes Pearson, defined counterintelligence as "all efforts to neutralize, repress, and eliminate the activity of enemy inimical or other persons or groups or governments or their representatives, to secure intelligence, the obtaining of which adversely affects the national security." As for counterespionage, Professor Pearson considers it as a subdivision of counterintelligence which "involves human agents" (HUMINT) and which includes "all efforts to neutralize, repress, or eliminate the practice of spying or employment of secret agents by enemy inimical or other persons or groups or governments or their representatives to secure intelligence, the obtaining of which adversely affects the interest of the United States." Very often these two aspects of intelligence, counterintelligence and counterespionage, are considered related and inseparable endeavors. V. I. Lenin, founder of the Soviet Union and also of the KGB, the largest and most effective global intelligence apparatus ever created, viewed the purpose of counterintelligence and counterespionage as finding out political (or military) objectives. America's (and the world's) most accomplished theoretician and practitioner of the art and science of intelligence, James Jesus Angleton, chief of U.S. counterintelligence and counterespionage with the CIA (1944-1974), emphasized that these endeavors require not only tremendous skills on the part of the agent but also a broad liberal education (e.g., in history, politics, literature and even poetry) because intelligence is basically an intellectual exercise. He referred to it as the "wilderness of mirrors," because of the entanglements and crisscrossing operations required, together with a great deal of deception and lies. (Also, a book by that title by David C. Martin). See BODYGUARD OF LIES, CHAOS, DECEPTION, ECOLOGIST OF DOUBLE AGENCY, HT/LINGUAL, INTELLIGENCE.

Counterintelligence is Like a Dog Returning to Its Vomit. A notion often held by those who were engaged in counterintelligence, but were soon fed up with it and gave up. See COUNTER-INTELLIGENCE.

Counterintelligence Program (COINTELPRO). A program designed and carried out by the Federal Bureau of Investigation (FBI) for the purpose of surveillance and investigation of all radical revolutionary groups, organizations, and individuals who were considered involved in activities construed to be detrimental to the interests of the United States. The program was conducted from the early 1960s to the early 1970s. Some of the target organizations of the COINTELPRO were the Socialist Workers Party and the Young Socialist Alliance. See COUNTERINSURGENCY IN AMERICA.

Countervailing Power. That power which is used to balance the interests of opposing parties or policies (e.g., a binding arbitration); or the governmental powers which settle a dispute between two individuals in search of justice and equity.

County. A political subdivision into which most American states are divided for administrative purposes or for the purpose of general governance (e.g., to maintain law and order, collect taxes, provide education, regulate construction and land use through zoning laws, and to generally serve the immediate needs of the citizens). Counties in the United States are similar in form and function to the "Kreis" in Germany, the "county" or "county borough" in England, the "Oblast" in the old Soviet Union, or the "borough" in New York City. In the state of Louisiana, counties are known as "parishes." In some states (e.g., Virginia), counties constitute jurisdictions separate from cities, while in others (e.g., in the state of Georgia) counties and cities overlap (e.g., the city of Atlanta, Georgia, is situated within the jurisdictions of four separate counties). In such situations, in the area of police powers, for example, the city police will serve in the entire jurisdiction, while the sheriffs confine themselves to serving the needs of the courts of law (e.g., delivering summons). All counties elect their government representatives (e.g., county commissioners or county supervisors, known as the "board of commissioners" or "board of supervisors," also known as "constitutional officers") because they are provided for by the state constitutions. Most modern counties are governed by elected county supervisors and appointive county managers—professionals in county administration. Counties are the creatures of the state legislatures (which grant and may also withhold charters), and each state determines for itself how many counties will be established (e.g., there are 3 counties in the state of Delaware and 254 counties in the state of Texas). There were approximately 3,103 counties in the U.S. as of 1978. See DILLON'S RULE, Appendix 67.

County Board of Commissioners. See COUNTY.

County Board of Supervisors. See COUNTY.

County Board of Supervisors-Manager Form of Government. See FORMS OF LOCAL GOVERNMENT.

County Clerk. See CLERK OF COURT.

County Commissioner. See COUNTY.

County District. An unincorporated geographic area within a county designed for administrative or electoral purposes.

County Home Rule. Similar to Municipal Home Rule, in that the local government seeks to have less interference by the state legislature in local matters. Although a county may adopt a "Home Rule" charter by vote of the citizens, it still needs approval by the state legislature, if not previously stipulated. See DILLON'S RULE.

County Judge. Operates outside of municipalities. Holds the title "Justice of the Peace (JP)." Elected from a specific district-township in the midwest. Usually these judges have no formal legal training. Consequently, their jurisdiction is severely limited.

County Manager. See COUNTY.

Coup. See COUP D'ÉTAT.

Coup d'État. In the French language, "decapitation of the state" or "the sudden overthrow of an established authority by extra-legal means." A term commonly applied to the act of overthrowing a government without causing revolution or civil war. According to Professor Sherman Kent, theoretician (*Strategic Intelligence for American World Policy*) and a practitioner (OSS and CIA), what became known as the "Kent's Law of Coups," "those coups that are known about in advance don't take place." Obviously, one may add, what most likely takes place is a mass execution or suicide (as was the case of the 18 August 1991 coup in Moscow) of the coup organizers.

Coup Flu. See STATE COMMITTEE ON THE STATE OF EMERGENCY.

Court Crier. A minor official of a court who announces the opening and the closing of the court sessions.

Court Martial. A military tribunal conducting trials for violation of military laws and regulations.

Court of Appeals. A court of law (and of record) which reviews cases decided by lower courts but are brought before it on appeal by a party to a suit which is not satisfied with the decision of the lower court. Under most juridical systems (including the United States), any higher court automatically serves as a court of appeals of decisions by lower courts. For instance, decisions by a one-judge town or city court may be appealed to a circuit court (which usually consists of three judges); the same case may (if one of the parties to the suit is not satisfied with the decision of that court) in turn be appealed to the court of appeals (which, as a rule, has no original jurisdiction; the state supreme court (after the court of appeals), and the U.S. Supreme Court for a final decision (provided the U.S. Supreme Court decides to hear the case. If not, the decision of the previous court, the state supreme court, will stand). Decisions by state courts may be taken to federal courts (e.g., U.S. District Court) if a federal statute or constitutional issue is involved; if not, the decision by the highest state court (i.e., the state supreme court) is final. On the federal level in the United States, there are 11 courts of appeal (one for each district or circuit). There are 10 judicial circuits and the District of Columbia. See ORIGINAL JURISDICTION, SUPREME COURT OF THE UNITED STATES, WRIT, WRITS OF COMMON USE, Appendices 41-47.

Court of Assize and Nisi Prius. A court of law in England, composed of at least two judges (often called "commissioners") who travel throughout the kingdom twice a year and try jury cases under their jurisdiction.

Court of Cassation. Adjudicates jurisdictional disputes between administrative and ordinary courts.

Court of Chancery. See CHANCERY.

Court of Claims. A court established by the U.S. Congress in 1855, with the responsibility "to bear and determine all claims founded upon any law of Congress, or upon any regulation of an executive department, or upon any contract, expressed or implied, with the Government of the United States, which may be suggested to it by a petition filed therein;" and also all claims which may be referred to said court by either House of Congress.

Court of Equity. A court of law with jurisdiction over cases where a plain and adequate remedy cannot be found at law. See EQUITY, JUSTICE, Appendices 48-51.

Court of King's (or Queen's) Bench. A court of law under monarchy (e.g., a kingdom or an empire) where the monarch is the ultimate sovereign in whose name justice (or the lack of it) is pronounced.

Court of Record. See CIRCUIT COURT.

Court Packing. An attempt by U.S. President Franklin D. Roosevelt to reorganize the U.S. Supreme Court in 1937, in order to create a better climate for his "New Deal" programs. He proposed that justices reaching the age of 65 retire, and that the membership of the Court be increased from nine to fifteen. The proposal failed to pass Congress. See NEW DEAL.

Court System in U.S. There are two parallel court systems in the U.S.—Federal and State. The federal system consists of the U.S. Supreme Court, U.S. Courts of Appeals, and U.S. District Courts. The state court system consists of a supreme court, intermediate appellate courts, and trial courts. The state court system also includes minor courts, such as municipal courts and justices of the peace. In both the federal and state court systems there are specialized courts created by the legislature. See Appendices 44-51, 63-66..

Courtney Affair. See SEXPIONAGE.

Covenant. An agreement between two or more states pertaining to important issues such as elimination of war (e.g., the Covenant of the League of Nations.) See LEAGUE OF NATIONS, TREATY.

Covenant of the League of Nations. See LEAGUE OF NATIONS.

Covert Action. An act plotted and committed in secrecy, or an activity performed through secretive and clandestine means (e.g., in conspiracy, subversion, espionage, or intelligence operations). Under the new charter of the American Central Intelligence Agency, all covert operations (including "dirty tricks"), particularly high-risk espionage (which could embarrass or discredit the government), must be authorized by the U.S. President and approved 60 days prior to their execution by the 28-member intelligence committee of Congress, and the results of such operations must also be reported to the Congressional Select Committee on Intelligence. Furthermore, any covert acts and activities by the intelligence apparatus of the United States must be "essential," and not merely "important," to the defense of the United States or its foreign policy. For the success of such covert operations, the CIA charter permits the use of "third country" intelligence services and nationals in cases where the United States intelligence apparatus is not capable of acting. Congressional law demands that all "covert operations" must be reported to Congress, and that the President provide a "finding," in writing, authorizing such an operation. See CENTRAL INTELLIGENCE AGENCY (CIA), HARDWARE DIPLOMACY, INTELLIGENCE, UNITED STATES INTELLIGENCE BOARDS (USIB), OVERT ACT, PEOPLE'S COMMISSION FOR INTERNAL AFFAIRS (NKVD), SEXPIONAGE, WATERGATE AFFAIR.

CPSU. See COMMUNIST PARTY OF THE SOVIET UNION.

CPUSA. See COMMUNIST PARTY OF THE UNITED STATES.

Cradle-to-Grave Welfarism. A political-economic system in which the government provides comprehensive benefits to its citizens, from the time one is born to the time one dies, as in Sweden and other social-democratic systems of Europe. Socialism and communism made promises to deliver such benefits to all their citizens, but failed to deliver. See MIDDLE-WAY SOCIALISM, WELFARE STATE.

Craft Union. A labor union in which membership is limited to persons in a particular craft, trade, or profession (e.g., electricians or farm workers). See OPEN SHOP, TAFT-HARTLEY LAW.

Crawford Act. See POLITICAL MACHINE.

Creative-Cooperative Federalism. See FEDERALISM.

Creative Federalism. See FEDERALISM.

Creative Financing. Term associated with financial speculators, particularly those in the United States who were engaged in junk bond transactions, corporate take-overs, leveraged buy-outs, land and real estate speculation in the case of the Savings and Loan scandal where, as a result, few became rich and many lost their life savings. In the end, the American taxpayer had to foot the bill of over half a billion dollars. Very few of the thieves, however, were prosecuted and convicted.

Credentials Committee. A body of persons responsible for the examination of credentials of delegates to a meeting or party convention, resolution of disputes over credentials, and reporting of findings to the ruling body of the organization. The primary function of the credentials committee during a political party convention is to see to it that properly elected or appointed delegates to the convention are seated, and that impostors (or persons with false credentials) are kept out. During the 1964 and the 1968 Democratic Party national conventions there were duplicate delegations from some states (e.g., Mississippi) which sought recognition by the convention; some were legitimate while others were not. See POLITICAL MACHINE, PRESIDENTIAL ELECTOR.

Credibility Gap. The disbelief and mistrust on the part of the general public of the official policies and the actions of the government; also a lack of mutual confidence that may occur between the various branches of a government.

Credit Crunch. A significant, temporary decline in the normal supply of credit, usually caused by tight monetary policy or a regulatory restriction facing lending institutions.

CREEP. See COMMITTEE TO RE-ELECT THE PRESIDENT, WATERGATE AFFAIR.

Creeping Socialism. A phrase often used to depict the gradual advance of a socialist (or communist) system of economy and government in the U.S., as judged by the growth of social welfare programs; governmental controls of economic activity; the involvement of government in staging and subsidizing cultural, social, and political activities; and the rapid growth of the "welfare state" system in general.

Crime by Analogy. A provision contained in the Soviet Criminal Code (Ugolovnyi Kodeks, p. 8) calling for prosecution and punishment for any . . . *socially dangerous act which is not directly foreseen by the present Code, and where the limits of responsibility for such an act are determined by analogy to these articles of the Code which foresee offenses of a similar type.* See NULLUM CRIMEN SINE LEGE.

Crime Perpetrator Family Protection. See CRIME VICTIM PROTECTION MOVEMENT.

Crime Victim Protection Movement. Special, community, grass-roots civic programs which are becoming popular in many societies around the world, and particularly in the United States, England, France, Japan, Germany, Italy, Mexico, Thailand, Singapore, and South Korea, designed to establish some practical means, public and private, which would compensate victims of crime for damages sustained, as well as provide moral and spiritual support, usually through counseling, to aid persons affected by crime to return to normalcy and regain life equilibrium. Some communities in America were able to persuade their legislators to implement laws that would financially compensate victims of crime from either a general revenue fund or property confiscated from the crime perpetrators. Another program also ought to be introduced, a sort of "crime perpetrator family protection" under which counseling and protection would be made available to the families of persons who have committed crime, the perpetrators. These families suffer guilt, shame, and stigma associated with crime (in spite of the fact that the American system of jurisprudence does not allow corruption of blood) and often are subjected to harassment.

Crimen Laesae Majestatis. In the Latin language "crime of the highest degree" (e.g., treason by an act of rebellion). See FELONY, TREASON.

Criminal Justice. The sum total of laws, institutions and practices designed to protect the state and the society on the one hand, and the individual and her/his rights on the other. The administrative setup commences with the Supreme Court in the United States, then follows the Department of Justice and its specialized agencies, (e.g., the FBI), the Bureau of Prisons, and the system of probation through the police and prosecutorial officers at all levels—federal, state, and local.

Criminal Law. That branch of jurisprudence which deals with wrongful acts (crimes) of high magnitude against the state (e.g., treason), the society, the individual, or an international community (e.g., genocide or war), and which calls for severe punishment.

Criminology. The body of knowledge that pertains to penology, crime, and criminals, and to the many social, psychological, psychiatric, and pathological aspects of crime and criminals.

Crisis. In the language of politics, a sudden disruption of governmental processes (e.g., through revolution, rebellion, the death, resignation, or removal of the persons governing), as well as the dissolution of a government (due to lack of confidence, or as a result of a dissolution of coalition), may constitute a governmental crisis. A disagreement over political strategy or electoral processes by the members (or the leadership alone) of a single political party could create a political crisis; a major disruption in normal relations among sovereign states (e.g., due to the inability to settle an international dispute, such as the Middle East crisis between the Arabs and the Israelis), may constitute an international crisis; and an act or activity which threatens the existence of a sovereign state or some of its vital interests, as well as a sudden resignation, death, or removal of a chief executive under lack of provisions for an orderly succession, may constitute a constitutional crisis. See CONSTITUTIONAL CRISIS, U.S. Constitution, Amendment XXV in Appendix 8.

Crisis Diplomacy. The practice of conducting diplomatic and/or international relations in an unsystematic manner, acting only when a crisis arises. See DIPLOMACY, HARDWARE DIPLOMACY.

Crisis Government. A government which pursues unsystematic policies or one that functions actively only when a crisis arises. Following the April-May 1992 Los Angeles, California riot, the Republicans were criticized for their policies of neglect of the poor, the minorities in the main, a neglect that commenced with the Ronald Reagan Administration in 1981 and continued under the George Bush Administration. Looking at some areas of concern, assistance declined since 1981 as follows: (1) low income housing (in billions), $55.2 in 1981 to $15.3 in 1992; (2) family planning, $.28 in 1981 to $.15 in 1992; and (3) training and employment services, $11.5 in 1981 to $4.2 in 1992.

Crisis Staff. In the Polish language, "sztab kryzysowy"; the secret group of high ranking officials of the former Soviet military, government, the party and the KGB was created in 1980, to deal with and to oversee the Solidarity movement in Poland. It was charged with designing plans for the elimination of Solidarity, by military terror if necessary. The members of the Staff included: Mikhail S. Gorbachev (Soviet President and General Secretary of the party since 1985); N. Suslov (the guardian of the purity of the Soviet ideology); A. Gromyko; Marshal Ustinov; Yuri V. Andropov, the boss of the KGB (the intelligence and secret police service of the Soviet Union); and Konstantin U. Czernenko. Leonid I. Brehznev presided during all important strategic sessions of the Crisis Staff. The group was also referred to as the "Polish Club" (Polski Klub). The intermediary between the Staff and the Polish regime (mainly the Secretary of the then ruling Polish United Workers' Party, PZPR, J. Kania) was the Soviet Ambassador in Warsaw, Aristow. Polish General Wojciech Jaruzelski was also questioned by the Soviet emissaries, mainly Gromyko, but he insisted on dealing with Solidarity the Polish and not the Russian way. Jaruzelski prevailed and probably saved the nation from bloody confrontation with the Soviets, because the Soviets had a plan in place to attack and to crash Solidartity. See SOLIDARITY.

Criteria Country List. The U.S. State Department and the Justice Department compile and maintain a list of states which are hostile to the United States. The list serves for counterintelligence purposes as well as for withholding free trade of certain commodities (e.g., those of a strategic utility such as high-tech computers, weapons systems technologies, and technology transfers). See CRY UNCLE.

Critical Raw Materials. Select primary raw materials, the availability of which is limited, and which are imperative to American industry. The federal government regulates their use and maintains stockpiles under the supervision of the Federal Preparedness Agency. See Appendix 42.

Cromwell's Republic. See GLORIOUS REVOLUTION.

Cronyism. See POWER ELITE.

Crossdisciplinary Interpretation of Law. See BRANDEIS BRIEF.

Cross-Filing. A procedure used in primary elections in some states of the U.S., whereby a person may become a candidate for elective office of more than one political party. (The system of cross-filing was commonly practiced in California between 1914-1958. It was repealed in 1959.) See PRIMARY ELECTION.

Cross-of-Gold Speech. See PRAIRIE POPULIST.

Crossover State. State in which the existing election laws allow voters registered for one party to vote in a primary election for the candidate of another party. The states of Michigan, Montana, and Wisconsin were the last three states to allow this practice, but the National Democratic Committee ruled on January 21, 1978, to eliminate this practice, and warned that states which permit such primaries will not be allowed to seat their delegations at the next National Nominating Convention of the Party. This move was inspired by a November 1977 U.S. Supreme Court decision which stated that "a national political party has the right to set the rules for selecting delegates to its national conventions and that these take precedent over state laws." The term "cross-voting" is also used. See POLITICAL MACHINE, PRESIDENTIAL ELECTOR.

Cross-Ownership Rule. Ordinarily, an administrative edict which forbids monopoly control of certain services or commodities under single ownership in order to prevent the stifling of competition and to protect the interest of the public (e.g., a ruling by the Interstate Communication Commission—ICC—in the United States, which forbids a single ownership of radio and television stations, or radio, television, and newspapers, which serve the same community). At the time the rule was adopted, existing companies with a combination of ownership were exempted from that rule (grandfathering), but once the ownership of such facilities is transferred, the grandfather rule no longer applies and the exemption is forfeited.

Cross-Voting. See CROSSOVER STATE.

Cruel and Unusual Punishment. The U.S. Constitution placed a prohibition against cruel and unusual punishment in Amendment VIII of the Bill of Rights, but the language provides no extensive definition of "cruel" and "unusual." A justice of the U.S. Supreme Court stated, however, that "Cruel and unusual punishment depends on current significance of the punishment." See U.S. CONSTITUTION, Appendix 5.

Crump Machine. See POLITICAL MACHINE.

Cry Uncle. Term associated with American diplomatic practices throughout the world when gunboat or dollar diplomacy is used to persuade other nations to be friendly and cooperative with American agents and to support American political and economic interests. Those who cooperated are rewarded (e.g., with foreign aid or assistance in gaining political power through revolution or coup d'état); those who refuse to "cry uncle," or "say uncle" (reference being made to Uncle Sam), are punished by any method appropriate (e.g., refusal of rights to visit the United States or access to American markets). See DOLLAR DIPLOMACY, GUNBOAT DIPLOMACY, IMPERIALISM.

Cryptonym. An agreed upon code word used to identify agents, organizations, targets, or activities in order to detect surveillance and discovery. Very often a real name is used, e.g., "John Doe," known as a "pseudonym," for similar purposes. Every leader (e.g., head of state and/or head of government), particularly during wartime, is assigned a secret name for intelligence communication purposes and for security. For example, U.S. President Franklin D. Roosevelt (1933-1945) was assigned the code-name of "naval person," and U.S. President John F. Kennedy (1961-1963) was "Camelot." See INTELLIGENCE.

Crystal Night. See KRISTALLNACHT.

CSA. See COMMUNITY SERVICE ADMINISTRATION, CONFEDERATE STATES OF AMERICA.

CSCE. See CONFERENCE ON SECURITY AND COOPERATION IN EUROPE.

CSG. See COUNCIL OF STATE GOVERNMENTS.

CSU. See CHRISTIAN SOCIAL UNION.

Cuban Connection. See PROPAGANDA ASSETS INVENTORY (PAI).

Cuban Embargo. The United States declared a total trade embargo against Cuba upon termination of diplomatic relations in 1960, when Dr. Fidel Castro announced that he was a Marxist-Leninist dedicated to the destruction of "Yankee imperialism" (meaning the United States), and refused to compensate American citizens for their property that was confiscated (expropriated) by the Cuban revolutionary (communist) regime. The embargo was lifted on August 21, 1975, but the American business community has shown little interest in trading with Cuba.

Cuban Missile Crisis. In 1962, upon learning of an offensive missile build-up in Cuba by the Soviet Union, U.S. President John F. Kennedy (acting on the principles of the Monroe Doctrine) ordered air and naval forces to quarantine (embargo) all shipments of offensive military equipment to Cuba and asked the USSR to remove all offensive weapons already present on Cuban soil. A final agreement was reached with Soviet Premier Nikita S. Khrushchev on November 2, 1962, and all offensive missiles installed in Cuba by the Soviet Union were removed. U.S. Government information, declassified in January 1992, and corroborated by former Soviet generals, revealed that the Soviet commander in Cuba had 42,000 Soviet troops at his disposal, not 10,000, as President Kennedy was informed at that time, and nine tactical nuclear weapons with the blank authority to launch them against the United States as he saw fit. An elementary school child asked what she thought of President Kennedy's move, she replied: "He made peace because he did not want war."

Cubanization of Cuba. See BLACK INSURGENCY.

Cuius Regio, Eius Religion. A Latin phrase meaning "the ruler determines the religion" or "the king determines the religion of the state." Also a term that may be applied to a political leader (or leaders) who attempts to impose his or her personal religion or political philosophy upon those whom he or she rules. See IMPERIALISM, POLITICAL CULTURE.

Cult of Personality. An unquestionable loyalty, devotion, and worship of one person during his lifetime. A term associated with the cult of Mao Tse-tung of China, and Stalin of the former USSR, whose successor, Nikita S. Khrushchev condemned Stalin and promised to "de-Stalinize his country, during his speech before the party in 1956, which caused a considerable relaxation of terror in the Soviet Union. Even Stalin's body was removed from the Lenin-Stalin tomb, a shrine and Soviet tourist attraction and leader-worship place in Moscow. Other leaders who fall under this category include: Nkrumah of Ghana, Sukarno of Indonesia, the Shah of Iran, Ferdinand Marcos in the Philippines, General Manuel Noriega in Panama, and, one who still survives, President Saddam Hussein of Iraq, who has, so far, outsmarted the smartest intelligence services and the strongest armies in the world! See CULTURAL REVOLUTION, DESTALINIZATION.

Cultism. See POLITICAL RHETORIC.

Cultural Imperialism. See IMPERIALISM.

Cultural Pluralism. See POLYCULTURE.

Cultural Revolution. A movement initiated by Mao Tse-tung in the People's Republic of China between 1964-1968, designed to purge his opponents from positions of power and influence with the aid of "Red Guards," bands of politicized and armed youths. Anyone, according to the official pronouncement during the Great Proletarian Cultural Revolution, suspected of not adhering to and following the "communist principles" and "teachings of Chairman Mao" was subjected to dismissal from employment, possible detention, or even execution. See HUNDRED FLOWERS.

Cum Privilegio. In the Latin language, "privilege of license granted by proper authority." See JURISDICTION, MANDATE.

Cunning Diplomacy. A mode of conducting diplomacy in a very clever, intelligent, or even deceitful manner. See COVERT ACTION, DIPLOMACY, HARDWARE DIPLOMACY.

Curie. See RÖNTGEN EQUIVALENT IN MAN (REM).

Curzon Line. A boundary line proposed in 1919 at the end of World War I by George Nathaniel Curzon (First Marquis Curzon of Kedleston [1859-1925] lord privy seal and British Foreign Secretary) at the Lausanne Conference, for the division of Poland and the Soviet Union. The boundary was designed so as to incorporate the White Russians (Belo-Russians) and the Ukrainians into the Soviet Union. The line was not accepted by Poland until, as a result of World War II, the Soviet Union implemented it by force. The Soviet Union even took some Polish territory, not foreseen by the Curzon plan, and recompensed Poland with lands taken from the capitulated German state (mainly from Prussia and Silesia). See ODER-NEISSE LINE, POLISH CORRIDOR, Appendix 91.

Customs, Bureau of. A semi-independent agency of the U.S. Department of the Treasury, which is mainly responsible for the assessment and collection of import duties, the supervision of export controls, prevention of smuggling, and overall enforcement of administrative and fiscal regulations affecting foreign shipping and imports.

Cutout. A person used as an intermediary, for diversion purposes, used in order to allow a personal contact between agents of foreign intelligence, and to avoid detection by surveillance by counter-intelligence. See INTELLIGENCE.

Cybernetics. The science dealing with the comparative study of complex electronic calculating machines and the human nervous system in an attempt to explain the functioning of the brain and how to better control and utilize it. Serious attempts were made (particularly in the USSR) to employ cybernetics in policy-making.

Cynicism. A political philosophy of escapism from the realities of societal life, developed during the 200s BC. in Greece by Antisthenes and his close collaborator, Diagnose, as a form of protest against the political institutions of the city-state, which they rejected. The Cynics advocated a lifestyle of poverty and became spokesmen for the poor who lived an ascetic life. In their view, social and political institutions of an organized society (e.g., a state) hinder the well being of the individual, because they deny freedom: happiness arises from virtue and virtue from freedom. EPICUREANISM, STOICISM.

Cyprus Dissolution. See WOMEN WALK HOME.

Czistka. See CHISTKA, PURGE.

"The business of America is business."
CALVIN COOLIDGE, 1872-1889

Da Party. A political party that was organized in the state of Israel in 1991, by immigrants from the former Soviet Union, with the aim of coping with unemployment, and with the lack of housing and medical care which the overburdened Israel economy is not able to provide. The name "Da" comes from the Russian language meaning "yes." The party political orientation fits somewhere between that of the rightist Likud Party, currently in power, and the centrist position of the Liberal Party.

Dacha. A country estate belonging to a high official of the former USSR.

Dagger. Term commonly used to describe covert intelligence and/or counterintelligence gathering and evaluating, espionage and/or counterespionage. See CLOAK.

Dago. See MAFIA.

Dail Eireann. Lower house of the Irish legislature. See OIREACHTAS, SEANAD EIREANN.

Daley Political Machine. See POLITICAL MACHINE.

DAME. See COUNTERINSURGENCY IN AMERICA.

Damned Cowboy. A term often applied to U.S. President Theodore Roosevelt (1901-1909), denoting his cowboy-like political style characterized by the use of unpolished language in dealing with adversaries, and the wearing of cowboy outfits on frequent hunting trips. See POLITICAL STYLE.

Damned Murder, Inc., in the Caribbean. A name given by U.S. President Lyndon B. Johnson (1963-1969) in 1963 to the activities of the Central Intelligence Agency (CIA) in the Caribbean, when he learned, upon becoming President, that the CIA had been involved in plots not only to overthrow governments which were not friendly toward the United States (e.g., Cuba), but to assassinate their leaders as well (e.g., Fidel Castro of Cuba). The President found those activities repugnant and contrary to what Americans believe in and stand for. The murder plots were organized with the knowledge of U.S. President John F. Kennedy (1961-1963), and had been ordered by his brother, Robert, who then served as the Attorney General of the United States.

Damnum Emergens. In the Latin language, "direct compensation awarded to an injured state" (e.g., reparation or indemnity). See INTERNATIONAL LAW, TREATY.

Dangler. An agent of one intelligence agency put out and coached in such a way so that it will be recruited by another, usually an adversary intelligence.

Darius Code. See DRACO CODE.

Dark Horse. Term coined by Benjamin Disraeli (1804-1881), British Prime Minister, referring to unknown matters. As applied to American politics, a relatively unknown person who is nominated for or becomes elected to high public office. This usually happens as a result of a deadlock at party nominating conventions. In the U.S., several "dark horse" candidates were nominated for the presidency and were elected: Abraham Lincoln, James Polk, Francis Pierce, James Garfield, Warren Harding, Wendell Wilkie, and Harry Truman. Those who were nominated but failed to be elected were: Horatio Seymour in 1868 and William J. Bryan in 1896, both Democrats. In similar context, the term "pothouse politician" is often used to denote a politician, little known to the electorate, who, through long loyalty to his party and/or a particular party machine, becomes subsequently elected to an important public office as a result of strong party or party–machine support. U.S. President Chester A. Arthur (1881-1885) was one of the first presidents to be referred to as a "pothouse politician"; when he became U.S. President, the popular slogan of the day was: "Good God! Chet Arthur—President of the United States." See POLITICAL MACHINE.

DASE. See COUNTERINSURGENCY IN AMERICA.

Dateline America. See PROJECT TRUTH.

Davis-Passman Confrontation. See LAST PLANTATION.

Day that Will Live in Infamy. See PEARL HARBOR.

Days of Rage. See STUDENTS FOR DEMOCRATIC SOCIETY (SDS).

D.C. District of Columbia, the capital city of the United States.

De Facto. In the Latin language, "according to fact" or "as the fact indicates." Also, something that actually exists in spite of legal indications otherwise (e.g., a new government as the actual government in control of the state, but not necessarily as a legal one). See DE JURE, LAW.

De-Imperialized Imperial Presidency. See IMPERIAL PRESIDENCY.

De Jure. In the Latin language, "according to law," "derived from or based on law or rule," or "by right"; for example, a government of one state may recognize the government of another as a *de jure* government—that is, one that was established according to the laws of the constitution of that state; but it also may grant such recognition for the purpose of boosting the prestige of that government, even though that government was not established according to existing laws. (In any case, recognition of one government or state by another is a matter left strictly to the discretion of the recognizing state.) See DE FACTO, LAW.

De Lege Ferenda. See LEX FERENDA.

De Lege Lata. See LEX LATA.

Dead Cat in a Gutter. See SOLEMN REFERENDUM OF 1920.

Dead Drop. A spot, usually inconspicuous (e.g., a hollow tree stump, or a rock by a roadway), where clandestine messages are exchanged between secret agents. Messages, money, or instructions are left for the recipient agent, and intelligence information gathered is left for retrieval by another agent. See INTELLIGENCE.

Dead Person Strategy. A strategy often deployed during an investigation or court testimony for the purpose of placing all blame on a deceased person. During the Iran-Contra Congressional hearings in the U.S., many material witnesses suddenly developed acute amnesia and suggested that only William Casey, deceased director of the Central Intelligence Agency (CIA), could furnish that information or take blame for any and all infractions or violations of the laws of the United States.

Dean of Diplomatic Corps. See DIPLOMATIC DEAN.

Death Rate. See BIRTH RATE.

Death Squad. See FARABUNDO MARTI NATIONAL LIBERATION FRONT (FMLN).

Debasing of Voting Power. The practice of minimizing the voting power of a community, either by unequal districting (population-wise), lack of reapportionment, or combining several communities into one district.

Debriefing. The practice of extracting information from one person by another. It is a common practice among intelligence services to seek information about people, governments, or events from persons who possess such information or who have witnessed certain events (e.g., travelers to foreign countries which the intelligence service is otherwise unable to penetrate).

Debt Ceiling. See NATIONAL DEBT OF THE UNITED STATES.

Debt Default Act of 1934. A piece of congressional legislation sponsored by U.S. Senator Kiram W. Johnson, also known as "Johnson's Debt Default Act." It denied delinquent nations (nations owing the United States money for the purchase of war materiel during W.W.I) further extension of credit for the purchase of weapons. This law seriously limited the defense capabilities of weaker nations of Europe and gave considerable advantage to Franco's Spain, Hitler's Germany, and Mussolini's Italy in terrorizing their people, and built grounds for the coming war, W.W.II. See NEUTRALITY LAWS.

Decadence. The process of decay, deterioration, and decline of a once advanced, well developed, and well organized community, society, or state. Among the noted characteristics of the process of decadence are the following: apathy, disorganization, abandonment of and disrespect for discipline, self-discipline, responsibility and accountability; poor work ethic (e.g., pulling oneself up by one's bootstraps is replaced by demands for social promotion); decline in mores and manners; and weakening of family bonds. In a declining society, opinions must be politically correct and voluntaryism must be paid for; equality in the marketplace and in the political arena gives way to elitism and factionalism. Weakened family bonds are shown when children refer to their parents not as "father" or "mother," "mom" or "pop," but as "hey, you!"; when spouses engage in open marriage practices; and when disrespect is shown elders (e.g., placing healthy elderly, retired persons in retirement homes for convenience rather than necessity, robbing the family of their accumulated wisdom). Other signs of decadence: conflicts because of gender; decline of religion and those beliefs which have proven valuable to self-esteem and the well-being of society at large; decline in education and language communication (often "you know" and "stuff" suffice for conversation); growing intolerance and lack of mutual respect; poor interpersonal relationships among and between ethnic, racial, and national groups; and declining care for personal appearance causing aesthetic pollution (e.g., the shabbiest garments possible). Further symptoms are: too much emphasis on training for an immediate job with disregard for education for life; material greed and want; and lack of long-range goals, objectives, aspirations, and the desire to do one's best. Evidence of decline can be seen when elaborate and fanciful structures built for recreation and worship are idle about two-thirds of the time, while people go homeless and the young seek recreation in drug and crime-infested back alleys. In the final analysis, decadence leads to disregard for life, liberty, and the pursuit of happiness; to criminal activity, juvenile delinquency, domestic violence, and war; to child and spouse abuse; to the spread of diseases, particularly social ones (e.g., venereal diseases and AIDS); to corruption, racketeering, organized crime, and to private and public misuse of power and money; and when the wealthy and the powerful, like Leona Helmsley, known as the "hotel queen," since she owns millions in hotel facilities, cheat on federal taxes because, as she stated, "only the little people pay taxes."

Decadent West. See UNHEALTHY TENDENCIES.

Decembrists. A coalition of revolutionaries in Tsarist Russia composed mainly of lower-ranking nobles and intellectuals, who made several attempts to undermine the Tsarist monarchy in Russia and introduce a republican form of government. The Decembrists staged their first uprising against Tsar (and Emperor) Nicholas I (1825-1855) on December 26, 1825 (hence the name "Decembrists"). Nicholas had succeeded the throne two weeks earlier when Prince Constantine, not very popular with the Russian peasants, and then serving as the commander-in-chief of the Polish Army in Warsaw, refused to accept the throne. When the Decembrists appealed to the soldiers (who were mostly peasants) for support, promising them a better life under a government based not on the will of the Tsar but on a constitution, they failed to respond. The disinformation planted among the peasants by the pro-Nicholas I forces had them believing that the term "constitution" meant the name of Prince Constantine's wife. (The word "constitution" was virtually unknown to the Russians of those days, and particularly to the illiterate masses of peasants who were kept in bondage by the nobility.) Neither Constantine nor his wife were particularly popular among the peasants, being harsh landlords, and the peasants did not think "constitution" would make a good ruler of Russia. The disinformation worked well and the Decembrists failed. The Decembrists favored a constitution that had been prepared by Tsarist Colonel Muraviev of the Northern Society of St. Petersburg (now Leningrad), then the capital city of Tsarist Russia. The Northern Society, which was a secret revolutionary organization that had been active during the early 1800s, advocated a federal form of government patterned after the system of the United States. The legacy of the Decembrists was continued until 1917 when the Bolsheviks, led by V.I. Lenin (who himself adopted the American form of federalism), overthrew the provisional government of Alexander Kerensky and established a federal state based on communist ideology. See DISINFORMATION.

Decennial Census. See UNITED STATES HOUSE OF REPRESENTATIVES.

Decentralized Authority and Control. See LIBERAL CONSTITUTION.

Decentralized Federalism. See FEDERALISM.

Deception. The practice of planting false information among sources who will most likely deliver it to the adversary, the target for whom the deception was intended. This practice is employed by foreign intelligence agents, especially those whose loyalties have been reversed by hostile counterintelligence, as was the case with the Double X or Twenty-Two Committee in England during W.W.II. Such bits and pieces of factual, truthful information, mixed with false, deceptive information, are known as "whispers" or "tibs." Foreign agents caught by the Allies during W.W.II were turned against their masters by their captors, the Double-X counterintelligence personnel. One such turned agent of the Nazis, Dusko Popov code-named "Tricycle," informed the American FBI and its director, J. Edgar Hoover, about the shopping list the Germans furnished him, asking him in August 1941 (about three months before Pearl Harbor) to collect detailed information on Pearl Harbor. Since Nazi Germany collaborated with Imperial Japan, it was obvious that this information was of primary interest to the Japanese rather than to the Germans. Hoover ignored Popov's warning and his Pearl Harbor questionnaire ("shopping list"), because Popov, a young handsome man, pursued anything that wore a skirt and moved, and Hoover considered such behavior "immoral." Hoover condemned any open affection between the sexes, and condemned homosexuality as a "subversive communist malady." He himself never married, but had a male companion by his side at all times, one named Clyde A. Tolson whom he appointed as his deputy and to whom passed his estate upon his death. Popov's escapades served also as the model for British intelligence officer and author, Ian Fleming, in his James Bond series. Popov, a Russian, may possibly have been in the service of the Russians as well as the Germans, making him a triple agent. According to author and intelligence expert Ewen Montague (*Beyond Top Secret Ultra*), Hoover most likely buried the Popov "shopping list" because it came not from his sources and he and his bureau would have received no credit for it. See ECOLOGIST OF DOUBLE AGENCY, INTELLIGENCE, TRUST.

Decision-Making. An intellectual process directed towards an identification and a definition of a recognized problem, selecting alternative courses for solving it, and applying one of those alternatives toward the final solution of that problem. In a democracy, as a rule, decision-making is the result of interaction among large numbers of individuals and elites, inside as well as outside the decision-making apparatus.

Decisive Leadership. See LEADERSHIP, NUTS!

Declaration of Constitutional Principles. See SOUTHERN MANIFESTO.

Declaration of Independence. A statement of philosophy and not a public document, but one of considerable significance for the shaping of the independence policies of the American colonies and for democratic theory in general. It was drafted by Thomas Jefferson, John Adams, Benjamin Franklin, Roger Sherman, and Robert Livingston, with Jefferson doing most of the writing and final editing, and was adopted on July 4, 1776, by the Second Continental Congress (which on July 2, 1776, had to struggle for total independence from England by a vote of 12 to 0). The document enumerates basic human rights (e.g., life, liberty, and the pursuit of happiness); denounces the tyrannical acts committed by the British Parliament against the colonies (e.g., the denial of representation); and stresses the right to self-determination, self-government, and total independence from England. The President of the Second Continental Congress, John Hancock, signed the document with unusually large letters (to make certain that the British were aware of the real identity of the signer), and proclaimed it among the thirteen colonies. See UTOPIA.

Declaration of Mental Liberty. See UTOPIA.

Declaration of Principles. Usually a written document which reflects some consensus that has been reached between two or more parties (usually states in the conduct of diplomatic relations) on certain issues or problems of mutual interest and concern, and defines the manner in which they are to be solved (e.g., the discussions between Egypt and Israel in 1978, or the Atlantic Charter of 1941). See ATLANTIC CHARTER, SADAT-BEGIN SUMMIT.

Declaration of Rights of the Peoples of Russia. One of the first documents issued by the Bolshevik government of Russia on November 15, 1917, proclaiming the following: (1) sovereignty and equality for all the peoples of Russia; (2) the right of the peoples of Russia to self-determination; (3) the right of the peoples of Russia to form separate, independent states; (4) the right of free development of all peoples of Russia, mainly the national minorities and ethnic groups; and (5) the abolition of any and all privileges, national and otherwise, and all legal, political, cultural, or social disabilities.

Declaration on Establishment of People's Power. The official title of the constitution of the Popular Socialist Libyan Arab State of the Masses, adopted on March 2, 1977, under the leadership of Colonel Mu'ammar al-Qadhafi, who worked towards the elimination of government, particularly the legislative branch, and rule by a free association of people through voluntary committees. According to Col. Qadhafi, "democracy means the authority of the people and not the authority of a body acting on the people's behalf."

Declaration on Fundamental Principles Governing the Use of the Mass Media in Strengthening Peace and International Understanding and in Combating War Propaganda, Racism, and Apartheid. This draft proposal—the longest ever recorded in the history of diplomacy—was adopted at the Nairobi (Kenya) Conference in 1976, where the Third World states, together with those of the Soviet Bloc, were seeking, among other restrictions on the dissemination of information, ". . . the right to determine what should or should not be published within their boundaries." Under American leadership, this censorship measure was postponed for two years, and subsequently ended up in a pigeonhole at the United Nations' archives.

Declaratory Judgment. A non-binding opinion, rendered by a court of law to an administrative agency of a government on matters of interpretation of constitutional or statutory provisions, particularly when the powers of that agency are not clearly stated, or if there is some doubt on a point of law. In the U.S., such judgments may be rendered by U.S. District Courts (or the U.S. District Court for the District of Columbia) whenever a dispute arises between the Federal Government and any state (or group of states). See MOOT CASE.

Declaratory Policy. A policy containing purposes, objectives, and a certain course of action; but it is merely declaratory and not meant to be enforced. See POLICY.

Declaratory Statute. A legislative act which clarifies and removes any doubts as to the meaning of some law. See LAW.

Declared War. See ACT OF WAR, WAR.

Deconcentration. A division or decentralization of powers (e.g., powers exercised by more than a single authority).

Decree. Court judgment; judicial decisions; or an order having the force of law (e.g., presidential decree). See LAW.

Deep Freeze Diplomacy. An act of diplomatic activity that is ineffective, non-workable, or unproductive. See DIPLOMACY.

Deep Throat. A secret or confidential source of reliable, accurate information, a source in the highest echelons of government which relays in confidence, authoritative, reliable, accurate, and timely information to the news media or to intelligence agents or officers. News media persons in the United States, who, under law, are not required to reveal confidential sources of information, call such a source a "reliable source."

Defector-in-Place. A practice common among intelligence services whereby real or potential refugees or diplomats from adversary states who are seeking, or are contemplating seeking asylum in another state, remain in their present positions, and earn merits (and pay) by supplying needed information about the adversary state, mainly about the intentions of political leaders and policy makers (a task in which no machine can replace human beings). Such turned-around defectors (spies) may supply valuable information against their own states, and if their positions become endangered, the state for whom they collect information will clandestinely remove them to safety and retire them with abundant provisions for life, usually under a new identity. See CENTRAL INTELLIGENCE AGENCY (CIA), INTELLIGENCE, SECRET INTELLIGENCE SERVICE.

Defendant. One against whom a suit is brought in a court of law.

Defense Intelligence Agency (DIA). See CENTRAL INTELLIGENCE AGENCY (CIA), INTELLIGENCE COMMUNITY.

Defense Planning Guidance. In order to deal with the rapid changes around the world due mainly to the dissolution of the Soviet empire in 1991, and in order to sustain the plans and desires of nations to achieve the "New World Order," the United States, being a unipower now, is in the process of designing plans and strategies, military doctrines and diplomatic programs to achieve that objective, to prevent military conflicts in the future, and to protect its vital "national interests." Some observers call this plan a new "Pan Americana," while others call it simply a new "imperialism." America's fears of isolation and loss of a dominant role in world affairs are justified if one considers the following scenario: the European Community is in place, and integration in every respect is proceeding as planned; the new European-Commonwealth of Independent States, particularly Russia, has agreed to implement a comprehensive energy policy to the point that Europe will be self-sufficient by 1997 if not before; next, the Commonwealth of Independent States is joining forces with the European Community to create a market of about 600 million people with sufficiency in energy, wood, food products, machinery, industrial diamonds, uranium, and other minerals necessary to sustain a megapower. The republics of the former Soviet Union, combined with Eastern Europe and Western Europe, have all the resources they need. The only commodities they lack are know-how and time. The Western Europe-Eastern Europe-Commonwealth of Independent States axle would have a market twice the size of the North American market of Canada, Mexico, and United States combined. Together with economic integration, and in order to protect the large market, military integration is possible to the point of keeping outsiders out, by force, if necessary. Only dreamers hope that the Russians, Ukrainians, and Kazakhstanis will dispose of nuclear weapons and capabilities forever. Furthermore, should Japan and the mini-tiger states in Asia join forces with the People's Republic of China, additional and more comprehensive defense planning will be in order in Canada and the United States. Only a lunatic would assume that the Europeans and the Russians will look toward the United States or Japan for aid in protecting their market. See NATIONAL INTEREST, UNIPOLARITY, WHO LOST CHINA.

Defensible (Secure) Borders. See SECURE (DEFENSIBLE) FRONTIERS.

Deficiency Bill. Legislative act authorizing additional appropriations for the purpose of carrying out the task or objective for which the original appropriations were made, allowing additional funds for government contracts to offset the rise of costs. See CONTINUING RESOLUTION.

Deficit in the Balance of Payments. See BALANCE OF PAYMENTS.

Deficit Spending or Financing. See KEYNESIAN ECONOMICS.

Defining the Opponent. The practice of rivalry among those who seek love, wealth, and power is as ancient as the history of mankind, dating back to Biblical times, but is more refined as a useful tool in modern electoral politics, particularly in the United States, where aspirants for public elective office (e.g., to the presidency, Congress, or a governorship) make every effort to define the opponent in a light (usually bad) that influences the perception of the voters and deprives the target opponent of chances of success at the polls on election day. As a rule, each candidate has a staff of experts, called "opposition research specialists," who specialize in collecting factual information (as well as innuendoes and rumors) about the opponents which will subsequently be packaged and disseminated to the public through the mass media (radio, television, and the press). For example, during the 1964 political campaign, Democratic candidate Lyndon Baines Johnson was able to "define" his opponent U. S. Senator Barry Goldwater as a "warmonger," one who, once elected, would lead America to war and even deploy nuclear weapons. In reality, Barry Goldwater was far from having such intentions; he merely advocated a strong military posture in order to counter the Soviet threat and to contain communism—a position that Lyndon Johnson, once elected, began to implement in the case of the Vietnam War. During the 1988 election, Republican candidate George Bush was able to define his opponent, Massachusetts Governor Michael Dukakis, as one "soft on crime and criminals," because Dukakis, as a good gesture, had released from prison a convicted criminal, one Willie Horton, who, once freed, committed murder again. The so-called "Willie Horton Syndrome" to a great extent contributed to Dukakis' defeat and Bush's election as president. During the 1992 campaign, the OPO's President George Bush made every effort to define the "political character" of Democratic candidate and Governor of Arkansas Bill Clinton, as a womanizer, one fearful of military draft, and one whose wife had a conflict-of-interest (Hillary Clinton, an attorney and professor of law at the University of Arkansas, was allegedly engaged in legal work for the state while her husband was governor). In American politics, charges of immoral conduct very often weigh more than grand theft like the Savings and Loan fraud, known as the "Keating Scandal," which cost the taxpayers almost a billion dollars, or the Michael Milken junk bond fraud, which stole millions of dollars from mostly low-income or retired families. The Bill Clinton OPO's, in turn, attempted to define President George Bush as one whose ideas on solving the nation's problems had been already spent, and as a president without any viable plans, particularly for unemployment and health care, and as one who favored the rich by opposing heavier taxation of the rich. Defining a candidate's political character, which, among other things, means ascertaining in advance how he views the ends of power and how, if elected, he would manage and dispense power, consumes considerable time and effort by the opponents and their OPO's. Projecting the opponent's political character in a negative light serves as an effective tool of politics in modern times. This is not an easy task because electorates are more sophisticated than ever, and simplistic methods will not do, but defining "political character," as journalist Jonathan Alter (*Newsweek,* 30 March 1992) points out, is "like eating soup with a fork," or, "It's like Justice Stewart's definition of pornography, 'you know it when you see it.'" On the international scene, for example, the Arabs and the Israelis have made every effort for the past several decades to define each other as "terrorists" in world public opinion. See OPPOSITION RESEARCH SPECIALIST (OPO), POLITICAL RHETORIC.

Delaware Corporation. The state of Delaware, with a population of approximately 650,000, in an area of 2,057 square miles, and ranking 49th in size among the fifty states, has approximately one-third of the top American business corporations registered under its laws of 1899, as revised in 1964. Approximately 800 corporations apply each day for a corporate charter, one-third of which are listed on the New York Stock Exchange; hence, Delaware is often referred to as "The Little Home of Big Business."

Delian League. A multilateral alliance in name but, in fact, a hegemony (domination) which ancient Athens exercised over a group of smaller city-states. The league was formed under Athens' domination during the fifth century BC. Cognizant of the continuous competition between Athens and Sparta, the smaller states sought protection from Athens against Spartan encroachment on their rights and sovereignty and, in return, made contributions to the treasury of the League (in reality the payments went to the Athenian treasury), let the Athenian state represent them in international relations, and assisted Athens in its external wars. States which refused to participate in the League were usually invaded and occupied by Athens as a "preventive" measure to deter aggression by other states (e.g., Sparta). The superior Athenian laws and institutions were commonly adopted by the members of the League. In order to counteract the Delian League, Athens's adversary, Sparta also established a system of alliances, the major one being the Peloponnesian League which was formed after the Persian Wars (492-477). The Peloponnesian League, with its elaborate collective security system, was primarily concerned with deterring further expansion of the Athenian empire through its Delian League (a close resemblance to the Western NATO and the Eastern Warsaw Pact today). The Athenian alliance was much more successful than that of the Spartans, because it emphasized trade and commerce as an integral part of its international policy and, therefore, was able to acquire more wealth, grant more freedoms and liberties to its people, and to maintain a fairly open society. This was the opposite with Sparta. Its political system was rigid and the daily life of the citizens was regimented. The Hellenic alliances constitute an early form of bipolar division. See BIPOLARITY.

Deliberate Speed. See ALL DELIBERATE SPEED.

Delicta Juris Gentium. In the Latin language, "crimes against the law of nations" (international law), e.g., piracy on the high seas (international waters). See HIGH SEAS, INTERNATIONAL LAW.

Délits Complexes. In the Latin language, "crime of a material rather than a political nature." A principle in international law which denies the political character of offenses that are generally recognized as ordinary crimes, such as piracy on the high seas, murder, arson, or theft. See ASYLUM, POLITICAL.

Delors Plan. Jacques Delors, president of the European Economic Community, devised a plan in December 1989 to achieve economic and monetary union of Europe in three stages. First, all obstacles to capital movement within the member states were removed on 1 January 1991, to which all members agreed except England. The next step was uniformity in insurance, banking, and securities; and, in stage three, by the year 1997, the European bank (Eurofed) would begin operations. The new European currency introduced among the member states is the ECU—European Currency Unit. See EUROPEAN ECONOMIC COMMUNITY.

Delta Force. A special commando force—highly selected, thoroughly trained in all aspects of counterterrorism and guerrilla warfare, established in the United States during the 1970s after the Vietnam War, mainly as an anti-terrorist force. Its commander was Colonel Charlie Beckwith, a hero of W.W.II, Korea, and Vietnam. The Force experienced a setback when its operation on 24 April 1980, to rescue the American hostages in Iran (Operation "Eagle Claw") failed due to several mechanical and leadership mishaps at Desert One station inside Iran's territory. This caused the cancellation of the mission. The U.S. Navy operates similar forces, the SEALS—Navy Sea, Air, and Land Teams. These forces collaborate closely with similar anti-terrorist units around the world, especially with the French (GIGN), the German (GSG-9), and the British Special Air Service Regiment (SAS). See GUERRILLA WARFARE, Appendix 30.

Demagogue. A politician who often uses exaggerations, lies, and distortions in order to appeal to mass prejudices as a means of gaining or holding office.

Demagogy. The practice of appealing to the bias and prejudices of the masses, usually by means of feeding them half-truths, or simple lies.

Demarcation Line. A marked boundary line dividing separate states. Like the DMZ in Korea, in Vietnam until 1975, and Germany until 1989.

Demilitarized Zone (DMZ). A strip of territory dividing warring partners where, on the basis of mutual agreement, neither troops shall be quartered nor any kind of military activity whatsoever shall be conducted in that zone by the parties so divided. See DEMARCATION LINE, WAR.

Democracy. In the Greek language, "power of the people" or "rule by the people." Also, as commonly understood, a system of government whereby the rights of the individual person—political, civil, economic (e.g., property rights)—are respected and protected by the force of the government; a political system whereby the citizens determine their mode of rule, directly through participation (e.g., "direct democracy"), or indirectly (e.g., "representative democracy") by selecting government officials to whom they grant a mandate to rule; a rule by majority with respect and due consideration to the interests and rights of the minority; a system and a mode of governance whereby the citizens have the right to scrutinize the activities of the government; whereby the rights and liberties of the individual are protected from arbitrary action by the executive, legislative, or judicial components of the government; whereby the rights, duties, and limitations—of the government and the individual—are clearly articulated (e.g., in the constitution, statutory laws, and code of laws); whereby the government is designed to serve the entire body politic (the people); whereby major changes in the political and social structure of the society are to be made according to certain adopted procedures (e.g., vote, referendum, or plebiscite); whereby the minority (the "outs") may strive to replace the majority (the "ins"); and whereby all sovereign powers rest with and are derived from the people. Some of these comments on democracy well epitomize the diversity of views, from ancient times to the present: Plato—"Democracy is a charming form of government, full of variety and disorder, and dispensing a sort of equality to equals and unequals alike." (See *Republic*, 342 BC); Aristotle—"If liberty and equality, as is thought by some, are chiefly to be found in democracy, they will be best attained when all persons alike share in the government to the utmost." (See *Politics*, 321 BC); Daniel Patrick Moynihan—"Liberal democracy on the American model increasingly tends to the condition of monarchy in the 19th century; a holdover form of government, one which persists in isolated or peculiar places here and there, and may even serve well enough for special circumstances, but which has simply no relevance to the future. It is where the world was, not where it is going." (See Daniel P. Moynihan. "The American Experiment," in *The Public Interest*, 1975); and Michael Crozier, Samuel Huntington, and Joji Watanuli—"The decline in government authority resulting from the 'democratic distemper' in America reduces the capacity of the government to deal with complex problems. While public expectations rise, problems become more intractable. Economic nationalism is encouraged. Foreign burdens are resisted. The decline in the governability of American democracy at home means a decline in the influence of America abroad." (See "The Governability of Democracies," in the *Trilateral Commission Report*, 1975.) In his empirical examination of the hypothesis that political development on democratic principles is directly related to the economic well-being of a society, Seymour Lipset (in his *Political Man*) observes that, in democratic societies as a rule, the level of education is higher than in non-democratic ones, and such is the case also in regard to average wealth, with which the degree of industrialization and urbanization is associated. "A society divided between a large impoverished mass and a small favorite elite," observes Lipset, "results either in oligarchy . . . or tyranny." Although Lipset could not say that a high level of education is the decisive factor in establishing and sustaining a democratic society (including its institutions), his evidence suggests that ". . . it comes close to being a necessary one." Surveys of some major studies of democracy as a political system indicate that democracy, as an abstract political concept, is the product of strong and highly-trained minds and that its utility and application require minds that are even stronger. The degree of success of a democracy, it appears, increases in proportion to the intellectual capacity and capability of those who are called upon to interpret and to apply its basic assumptions (e.g., free men are more creative than enslaved ones, and all men seek reward in one form or another, not necessarily material, for their labor). See DEMOCRACY, DIRECT, DEMOCRACY, REPRESENTATIVE, DEMOS, KRATIEN, POPULAR SOVEREIGNTY, TOOLS OF GOVERNMENT.

Democracy, Direct (or Pure Democracy). A form of government in which citizens gather periodically for the purpose of passing laws, settling disputes within the community (or state), giving general policy directions, or making appointments to positions in government or the military. Typical forms of government in some ancient Greek city-states, mainly Athens and Sparta, or the early European settlements in America. See DEMOCRACY.

Democracy, Guided. A system of government whereby some of the traditional features of democracy are implemented within a society not accustomed to democratic processes (e.g., campaigning, voting, electing, or petitioning the government). In practice, a mild dictatorship in transition to democracy. The concept was developed by Dr. Sukarno, President of Indonesia, 1949-1967.

Democracy is the Worst Form of Government Except All Others. Democracy as a form of government was so characterized by England's Prime Minister Winston Churchill, during a speech in the House of Commons on 11 November 1947. The full text of his comment is as follows: "Many forms of government have been tried, and will be tried in this world of sin and woe. No one pretends that democracy is perfect or all-wise. Indeed, it has been said that democracy is the worst form of government except all those other forms that have been tried from time to time."

Democracy, Representative. A form of government in which the citizens (or voters, the electorate) rule through their representatives whom they periodically elect and keep accountable for their actions. See DEMOCRACY; DEMOCRACY, DIRECT; DEMOCRACY, GUIDED.

Democratic Base of Society. See VOTING.

Democratic Capitalism. Those economic institutions, interactions, and activities in a democratic society which: (1) produce for profit according to the wishes of the consumers (consumer sovereignty); (2) are subjected to minimum interference by the government; (3) set their own goals and priorities rather than being centrally or regionally planned by the government; (4) operate so that individuals or associations rather than the government own and control the means of production and distribution. Democratic capitalism is thus generally the opposite of totalitarian capitalism, or corporate statism, in which the government usually owns and controls the means of production and distribution, production inputs and outputs, markets, prices, and usually absorbs the profits (for the national or the ruling clique treasury). Democratic capitalism is also characterized by the response of the producer to the needs of the consumer and not the central planner; it cultivates production culture which requires good education and skills; and employees have stock options in the enterprise.

Democratic Centralism. In the Russian language, "Demokratitcheskaya Centralizatzya." The basic ruling principle of the Communist Party of the Soviet Union (CPSU) and other socialist and communist parties subscribing to the philosophy of Marxism-Leninism, according to which the authority of a higher organ of the party is derived from a lower one, and whereby party members during party meetings are expected to criticize their peers who do not adhere to the official party line (as well as criticize themselves— self criticism). But once a policy is agreed upon the criticism must stop, and the directions for the implementation of that policy will be channeled from the higher organs of the party to the lower ones, a rule from the top. Soviet ideologues often refer to it as an "intra-party democracy." See CENTRALISM.

Democratic Conservatism. A term used primarily by conservatives who seek support from democratic elements, because, for reasons not yet well articulated, the term "democratic" carries a positive connotation, and implies good rather than bad. Also, many of the non-communist, non-socialist parties in Europe do officially subscribe to the traditional precepts of democracy (e.g., government elected by and responsible to the people, but which in reality opposes any progress in societal development, such as equal rights for women).

Democratic Ethics. See HATE CRIME.

Democratic Government. See TOOLS OF GOVERNMENT.

Democratic Movement for Change. See LABOR PARTY OF ISRAEL.

Democratic National Committee. The continuous, interim organization of the Democratic Party functioning between national conventions, composed of top leaders elected by the National Party Convention every four years. The top leaders of the party are: the Chairman, one Vice Chairman, one Secretary, and one Treasurer. The members of the Democratic National Committee are elected by state party organizations (including the District of Columbia) which are composed of at least two persons, one woman and one man, and as a rule, the chairman of the state party organization is among them. This committee is the governing body of the party until the next national convention. The committee members representing the various states are known as "Committeewomen" and "Committeemen."

Democratic National Convention. See DEMOCRATIC NATIONAL COMMITTEE, PARTY CONVENTION.

Democratic Party. One of the two major political parties in the U.S., tracing its origin to the Democratic-Republican Party of Thomas Jefferson, which for the first time openly supported Andrew Jackson for the presidency in 1824. During the 1800s the party split into Southern and Northern factions, and again in 1948 when the Southern Dixiecrats emerged in opposition to Harry Truman's civil rights stance. The party became known as the "white man's party," and in 1948 the strong Southern wing of the party, known as the "Dixiecrats," nominated its own presidential candidate, J. Strom Thurmond, in opposition to Harry Truman. The Southern faction was mainly opposed to civil rights legislation and the abridgment of states' rights by the expanding influence and power of the national government. See Appendices 18, 19.

Democratic Party Charter. See COMMISSION ON PRESIDENTIAL NOMINATIONS.

Democratic Party of Kurdistan. See BAATH SOCIALIST PARTY.

Democratic Party Reorganization. See COMMISSION ON PRESIDENTIAL NOMINATIONS.

Democratic Republican. See REPUBLICAN DEMOCRAT.

Democratic-Republican Party. One of America's oldest political parties, loosely organized, tracing its origins to Thomas Jefferson. The party, generally considered to be the predecessor of the modern

Democratic Party, actively supported Andrew Jackson in 1824. See ANTIFEDERALISTS, DEMO-CRATIC PARTY.

Democratic Socialism. A socio-political movement, advocated by the British Labour Party, the Norman Thomas socialist movement in the U.S., and many of the socialist parties in Western Europe and Japan, calling for socialization of many phases of production (e.g., government ownership of banks, railroads, mines, control of education), but rejecting the instrument of revolution. It is also opposed to any form of revolutionary socialism or communism.

Democratic Study Group. See CONGRESSIONAL CAUCUS.

Democratic Theory. See DEMOCRACY, STATE, TOOLS OF GOVERNMENT.

Democratic White House. See IMPERIAL PRESIDENCY.

Democratic Zone of Peace. See UNIPOLARITY.

Demonstration Effect. See JAPAN LOBBY.

Demonstration of Force. A common practice by states, usually those with strong military forces and extensive vested interests in foreign countries, to demonstrate their military might on a variety of occasions and for military reasons. For example, a state may hold a major military parade during which modern weapon systems may be displayed for real and potential adversaries to see; a strong naval force may be sent into an area of interest to demonstrate strength and readiness; or a partial or a major mobilization may be ordered as a direct warning to adversaries that the state is prepared to go to war if need arises. The purpose of such demonstration of force may be to deter possible aggression, to influence political events in a given area or in a particular state, simply to render ostensive support to revolutionary forces in a given state, or as a warning to insurgents who contemplate overthrowing a government which the demonstrating state favors and wants to remain in power. The Soviet Union, for example, constantly displayed its forces not only within the territories of its empire, the satellite states, but also outside it (e.g., in the Mediterranean area, where the United States is doing the same thing). The United States, too, has demonstrated its force in many areas of the world (e.g., in Western Europe in order to render support to the NATO nations, and in Latin America, Asia, and Africa).

Demos. In the Greek language, "people." Added to the term *Kratien,* to "rule" or "to govern," produces the term "democracy." See DEMOCRACY.

Denationalization. The act of depriving one of the citizenship of his native state. See CITIZENSHIP.

Denaturalization. The act of depriving a naturalized citizen of his citizenship (e.g., when there is evidence that citizenship has been acquired by fraud). See CITIZENSHIP.

Denazification. The process of screening former members and sympathizers of the Nazi party in defeated Germany by the four victorious powers: England, France, the Soviet Union, and the United States, for the purpose of separating war criminals from those who were merely innocent bystanders. Those found to be involved in war crimes were tried and convicted; those with lesser crimes were placed in rehabilitation (denazification) camps for reschooling and reorienting in democratic and humanitarian ideals. These rehabilitation centers for denazification were discontinued in 1949.

Denunciation. The official notice of termination of treaty obligations sent by the government of one state to another; or an official condemnation of one state by another for some wrongful act.

Department. A small political nonautonomous subdivision in France; also, a cabinet ministerial-level administrative agency of the Federal Government in the United States. Executive departments are headed by secretaries, except the Department of Justice which is headed by the Attorney General; heads of executive departments comprise the presidential cabinet and report directly to him. See Appendix 15.

Department for State Political Administration (OGPU). In the Russian language, "Oddyelyenye Gosudarstvyennogho Polititcheskogho Upravlyennya." A state political police and investigative agency established in the USSR in 1923. The agency was also in charge of all police forces and the administration of prisons. In 1934 the agency was reorganized and renamed to NKVD.

Dependency. A term commonly used in international politics and international law to describe the scope and the degree to which a state has compromised its sovereign right by being influenced by or by simply being dependent for its existence on the will of another state (e.g., as a satellite state). It is not uncommon for weak states to depend on the power of strong states to protect their existence as separate entities in exchange for favors or services (e.g., casting votes in international organizations in favor of the protector-state). See INTERDEPENDENCE, INTERNATIONAL LAW, PENETRATED POLITICAL SYSTEM, STATE.

Dependent Variables. A variable is any occurrence, condition, or phenomenon within which any change may also cause a change in another occurrence, condition, or phenomenon. As Professor K. J. Holsti explains it, (see *International Politics: A Framework for Analysis,* Prentice-Hall) "In the physical realm, for example, variations in temperature cause changes in the properties of water"; that is, if the temperature reaches zero degree of Celsius, the water will freeze, provided all other conditions remain constant. Therefore, there is a real functional relationship between the two variables: water and temperature. To recognize such a relationship between or among variables in the social sciences (e.g., economics, politics, law, or history) is much more difficult than in the physical (or pure) sciences because (1) "many variables including change may be involved simultaneously, and (2) it may be impossible to hold all other conditions constant while observation or experimentation is taking place. For example, we may wish to examine the condition associated with outbreak of war. We could see if there is some type of relationship between the incidence of war and spending on armaments. If through a perusal of historical data we found a high correlation between variations in expenditures on armaments (independent variable) and incidence of war (dependent variable), we could say that the two variables are somewhat associated. It would still remain for us to define the exact nature of the relationship and investigate other types of variables, such as perceptions of threat or degree of commitment to objectives, that may be involved in the outbreak of war." See POLITICAL THEORY.

Depletion Allowance. A tax deduction (allowed by congressional law in the U.S.) given to individuals or corporations owning and extracting such natural resources as gas, oil, metals, timber, and other minerals, the supply of which may one day be exhausted. The owners of such resources may deduct from their income the cost of their investments as the resource is becoming more scarce. (In the case of oil, from 1926 to 1969, the allowance was 27.5 per cent.) In 1969 Congress lowered the allowance (under pressure from other interest groups which enjoy no such benefits) to 22 per cent.

Depoliticizing Politics. Those pronouncements and designs, dating back to the time when politically organized communities first emerged, which aim at removing government from politics and politics from government (on a mode similar to the notion of separation of church and state) as two incompatible entities, which, when combined, harm rather than favor the output (e.g., public policy). Such notions are common among bureaucrats, particularly those who lack the cognitive abilities to solve problems presented to them by political processes (the politicians, such as the U.S. Congress), and who lack the rational basis for reaching a consensus (due to impatience with democratic processes or simply a lack of capacity for intellectual analysis). The task of depoliticizing politics would in itself be a political task (it would require some consensus among the decision-makers); and, therefore, there is an obvious lack of convincing evidence which would support the notion that the politicians will ever find a political solution for depoliticizing politics. Taking politicians out of politics, or politics away from politicians would be like taking the clergy out of religion, religion away from the clergy and the organized church. Any paradigmatic constructs may not meet the test of realities. Politics, it appears, is here to stay.

Deposition. A testimony in writing, taken under oath or affirmation, which can be used in a court of law as evidence. Lying under oath constitutes perjury, a felonious crime.

Depreciation. Decline in the value of a currency, financial asset, or capital good. When applied to a capital good, the term usually refers to loss of value because of obsolescence or wear.

Depression. A period of low business activity which is accompanied by unemployment, low prices, and reduced income.

Deputat. A deputy, elective member of parliament (either the House of Union or the House of Nationalities) or a member of a lower legislative body in the former Soviet Union.

Deputy. An elective member of parliament (e.g., in France) or one to whom certain powers or authority are delegated, e.g., deputy sheriff. See PARLIAMENT.

Der Alte. An affectionate nickname of Dr. Konrad Adenauer, creator of the Federal Republic of Germany (West Germany) after W.W.II, and Kanzler (Chancellor or prime minister or premier) of Germany (1949-1963). Adenauer was 78 years old when he resumed his office with vigor and energy unmatched by his contemporaries.

DERG. The official name of the committee consisting of military officers and non-commissioned officers which seized power in Ethiopia in 1974, and removed the Emperor Haile Selassie, who died in detention in 1975. One of the principal leaders of the movement was Mengistu Haile Mariam, who subsequently became the chairman of the DERG and ruler of the country, proclaiming it Marxist-Leninist.

Descending from Heaven. In the world of close relationships between government, politics, and business in Japan, the practice of retiring government officials joining private business enterprises once under their official supervision or regulation.

Descent from Heaven. See AMAKUDARI.

Desert One. See DELTA FORCE.

Desert Shield. See OPERATION DESERT STORM.

Desert Storm. See OPERATION DESERT STORM.

Despot. An unscrupulous or tyrannical ruler.

Despotism. Unlimited, unchecked and unrestricted totalitarian exercise of governmental powers; also, a system of rule whereby the rights and liberties of the individual are ignored, and the welfare of the ruled is neglected. During his March 1992 speech, former U.S. President Richard M. Nixon warned the nation and the world against the possible emergence of a "new despotism," particularly in the former Soviet Union, where the vacuum of power and the economic disruption may undermine democratic reforms if the west, mainly the United States does not come to the aid of the new leaders there, especially President of Russia, Boris N. Yeltsin. The former President called for a more active involvement and more vigorous leadership in order to maintain peace and stability, and to "Not simply to support what is popular but to make what is unpopular popular" if that serves America's interest. See AGE OF GREAT EVENTS AND SMALL MEN, ENLIGHTENED DESPOT, Appendix 1.

Despotism of Liberty. See ROUSSEAU'S COLLECTIVISM.

Destalinization. The process of minimizing the importance and influence of Joseph Stalin, Soviet Premier and Secretary of the CPSU until 1953, on Soviet life and the success of the state. (The process was triggered by the new party boss, Nikita S. Khrushchev, in his speech at the Twentieth Party Congress in February 1956, in which he accused Stalin of abuse of state powers and unethical practices.) See CULT OF PERSONALITY.

Détente. In the French language, "relaxation" or "easing of tension." A term often used in international politics and diplomacy to describe the cooling-off period between two hostile nations, followed by some understanding (rapprochement), which may lead to the establishment of normal relations.

Détente with a Human Face. U.S. Chief delegate to the 1977 Belgrade conference on the evaluation of progress made in the implementation of the Helsinki Accord of 1975 and former Associate Justice of the U.S Supreme Court, Arthur J. Goldberg, so described the American position on future relations with the USSR and other communist states. Goldberg insisted, however, that human rights, particularly the "basket three" contents on reunification of families on both sides of the Iron Curtain, be observed as a condition for faithful implementation of the Accord in human terms.

Determinism. See ECONOMIC DETERMINISM.

Deterrent. An attribute of some tangible capacity (e.g., advanced weapon system) which one state holds over another, and which may be construed by the adversary as an instrument of threat. America's capacity to deploy neutron weapons in case of an attack, for example, is construed as a deterrent to nation-states which may contemplate an attack upon the United States or its allies. State "X", for example, may threaten to use force against state "B", if state "B" changes its position or behavior on certain issues which may endanger the security of state "X". If on the other hand, state "X" threatens to harm state "B" in order to influence the change of behavior or position of state "B" on certain issues, this, according to Thomas Schelling, constitutes a "compellent threat." A serious critic of all contemporary systems of deterrence, Herbert Marcuse, observes that "The deterrent also serves to deter efforts to eliminate the need for the deterrent." In the words of General Robert T. Herres, USAF ("Control of Joint Forces," AFCEA International Press), deterrence is "... dissuading potential enemies by making it clear that their war aims are too costly and cannot be attained. Everything we do and ... buy must stand the litmus test of making the Combat Commander better able to deter war, or failing that, better prepare to fight again." There must be a will to fight and to win. "Everyone has the will to win. Not everyone has the will to prepare to win," said Bobby Knight, Indiana University basketball coach. See NUCLEAR DETERRENT.

Dethronization. An act of involuntary removal of a monarch from the throne (e.g., by revolution, coup d'état, or simple abandonment). (This was the case with the Shah of Iran, Pahlavi, who simply departed from the Iranian capital in December 1979 when the forces of Shiite Muslim fundamentalist Ayatolla Ruhollah Khomeini challenged him.) See ABDICATION.

Deuxième Bureau. See SERVICE FOR FOREIGN INFORMATION AND COUNTERESPIONAGE.

Developing Nation. A nation whose economy relies on primitive farming methods and a few export crops, and where the average income per capita is substantially lower than in industrialized nations.

Development Planning. Commonly used in reference to developing countries, who are undergoing economic development of their state or a part of any of their areas. See INNOVATIVE PLANNING.

Devil's Decade. Term commonly applied to the period between 1919 and 1939, the end of W.W.I and beginning of W.W.II, when man demonstrated the most sophisticated capacity ever to inflict destruction and indignity on his own kind.

Devolution. The practice or an act of delegating some or all powers to a smaller political subdivision within a state, or to a group of people who seek autonomy, by the national, central government, short of total separation. As a rule, in the case of a devolution, the national, central government usually retains the authority to deal with matters of defense and foreign affairs. Also, the act of gaining autonomy or independence by peaceful, orderly means, short of revolution. See AUTONOMY, FEDERALISM, SEPARATISM.

DIA. See DEFENSE INTELLIGENCE AGENCY.

Dialectic. In the Greek language, "an argument;" a concept developed by ancient Greek philosophers and pedagogues like Plato, followed by Kant, Hegel, and Marx; a mode of learning by discussion by stating the thesis, the anti-thesis, then synthesis (in the case of Plato) in search for the truth. See DIALECTICAL MATERIALISM.

Dialectical Materialism. One of the principal elements of Marxist philosophy, conceived by Karl Marx and Friedrich Engels, and developed by Vladimir I. Lenin, embracing the general laws of the development of matter and society, and the methods of their identification and interpretation. See MARXISM.

Diaper in the Ring. See HAT IN THE RING.

Dictator. A single ruler, who is not responsible to the people he governs.

Dictatorship. Government carried out by one person or a group, and not responsible to the people or to their representatives.

Dictatorship of the Proletariat. See CLASS STRUGGLE.

Diehard Politician. A nonflexible, stubborn, and impractical politician who never abandons his views or actions regardless of their validity or usefulness, often to his personal detriment.

Diehard-Type Political Party. A political party that is primarily interested in the continuous advocacy of some lost causes rather than in bidding for control of the government (e.g., a score of fascist and royalist parties such as the Bonapartist and the Bourbon groups in France, or the fascist parties in the United States, Germany, and Italy). See DIEHARD POLITICIAN.

Dies Committee. The U.S. House of Representatives Un-American Activities Committee which was formed during the 1950s in the United States and which aided U.S. Senator Joseph McCarthy in hunting for communists everywhere, beginning with the president of the United States (D. D. Eisenhower was suspected of being a Soviet mole) and including the U.S. Armed Forces, the state department, the movie industry, and other segments of the American population. The committee was headed by Rep. Martin Dies and Senator McCarthy. Professor Robin W. Winks (*Cloak & Gown: Scholars in the Secret War, 1939-1961*) characterizes these two witch-hunters as unsystematic ideologues and "intellectual butchers of free speech," who were also "opportunistic, small-minded, fundamentally unintelligent men with mean-spirited political goals of the most selfish nature," who "practiced a form of random violence." See COUNTERINSURGENCY IN AMERICA, MCCARTHYISM, RED SCARE.

Diet. A law-making body; parliament (e.g., the Parliament of Japan). See PARLIAMENT.

Diffused-Bloc International Political System. See INTERNATIONAL SYSTEM.

Diffused Political System. See INTERNATIONAL SYSTEM.

Diffusion of Power. See DECONCENTRATION.

Dilatory Motion. A motion introduced on the floor in a legislative chamber for the purpose of delaying the vote on a bill. See PARLIAMENT.

Dillon's Rule. A principle widely recognized by courts and state legislatures in the U.S., to the effect that the powers of municipal corporations (county or city governments or any of their agencies) shall be narrowly construed (e.g., local government may not dispose of land under its jurisdiction, or reorganize its judicial branch without the consent of state government, the legislative, or the executive branch). These rules are outlined in John F. Dillon's treatise: *Commentaries on the Law of Municipal Corporation,* published in 1911. Departures from Dillon's Rule are not uncommon, and they are usually based on the rule that: A municipal corporation possesses, and can exercise, the following powers, and no others: first, those granted in expressly written word; second, those necessarily or fairly implied in, or incident to the powers expressly granted; third, those essential to the accomplishment of the declared objects and purposes of the corporation—not simply convenient, but indispensable. Any fair, reasonable substantial doubt concerning the existence of a power is resolved by the courts against the corporations, and the power is denied.

Dilution of Voting Power. See DEBASING OF VOTING POWER.

Dino. A pejorative name for one of Mexican descent. The term "grease-ball" is also used for Latin Americans, referring to their curly, shiny, black hair; this term is also applied derogatorily to anyone with such hair, especially a foreigner.

Diplomacy. The art and/or science of conducting international relations in a most delicate and refined manner, free of antagonisms or armed conflicts. See HARDWARE DIPLOMACY, SUMMIT DIPLOMACY.

Diplomacy by Crisis. See CRISIS DIPLOMACY.

Diplomacy in the Woods. See WALK IN THE WOODS.

Diplomatic Corps. The whole body of foreign diplomatic agents accredited to the government within one state.

Diplomatic Dean (or Doyen). The official spokesman for diplomatic officers of all nations before the government of the receiving state. The ceremonial title is ordinarily granted to a foreign diplomat with the longest continuous service within a single diplomatic community, in the territory of the receiving state. The seniority system was agreed upon at the Aix-la-Chapelle Congress in 1818. See DIPLOMATIC IMMUNITY.

Diplomatic Feelers. A common practice among states to constantly seek information (by overt or covert means) about the plans, intentions, and attitudes of leaders of other states toward each other (e.g., a state in conflict with another may seek information to determine if the other party would be susceptible to ceasing hostilities and negotiating peace). The United States, for example, sent a ping-pong team to China in order to "feel" out the Chinese on whether or not they would be susceptible to normalization of political relations as well as participation in sporting events. See DIPLOMACY, PING-PONG DIPLOMACY.

Diplomatic Immunity. The practice of exempting a duly accredited foreign diplomat from certain obligations to the receiving state (e.g., paying taxes, serving in the armed forces, or appearing as a witness before domestic tribunals unless such a diplomat agrees to do so, or is required by his government to do so or when his government withdraws his diplomatic status). Diplomatic immunity protects the diplomat from civil and criminal suits, search and seizure. Similar protection applies to his residence, family, and entourage. Diplomatic immunity is among the oldest forms of peaceful international cooperation among states, and it is well observed. An ancient Indian chronicle, *Mahobhorata* (200 BC), explicitly cautions that "The King who slays an envoy, sinks into hell with all of his ministers." The United States grants diplomatic immunity to foreign diplomats (of whom about half perform non-diplomatic functions) under the very broad provisions of the Immunities Act of 1790, and subsequent legislation. The 1961 Vienna Convention on Diplomatic Immunities and Privileges, holds diplomats responsible for damages to life and property. The U.S. State Department also announced on February 7, 1978, that "No longer will a disproportionate degree of immunity be granted to persons who have little, if any, representational functions to perform in connection with their service at a foreign post." See INNOCENT PASSAGE, THE RIGHT TO, PERSONA NON GRATA.

Diplomatic List. A record of all foreign diplomatic officers (listing their names, ranks, and the nature of their functions) and employees of foreign governments legally residing within the territory of one state. See DIPLOMATIC CORPS.

Diplomatic Protocol. A record of the officials of the various branches of government and accredited foreign diplomats and officials, listed according to "rank." In the United States the U.S. President is listed on the protocol roster as "Number One." He is followed by the Vice President (who is also the presiding officer of the U.S. Senate), Chief Justice of the U.S. Supreme Court, the Speaker of the U.S. House of Representatives, and the Secretary of State, then the members of the Cabinet. Since there is some question as to whether the Chief Justice of the U.S. Supreme Court outranks the Dean of the Diplomatic Corps, the two usually are not invited to the same ceremonial function. Matters related to protocol are under the sole jurisdiction of the Chief of Protocol, an official of the U.S. Department of State. See DIPLOMATIC CORPS, VERY IMPORTANT PERSON (VIP).

Diplomatic Rank. A rank assigned to a diplomat by the authority of the sending state (according to his education, experience, length of service, or capacity), designating his functions and remuneration. Ranks, and criteria for awarding them, differ from state to state, but the most common are the following (in hierarchical order): ambassador extraordinary and plenipotentiary (one having the broadest authority); ambassador extraordinary (one having limited powers); ambassador plenipotentiary (one having authority of a specified nature); and ambassador ordinary (one assigned as chief of a diplomatic mission without specifications as to his authority). Ministers have designations similar to ambassadors. Ministers head legations while ambassadors head embassies. Other ranks below that of ambassador and ministers are: chargé d'affaires (one acting as the chief of a diplomatic mission during the absence of the ambassador or the minister); counselor (legal officer or a specialist in some area); secretary (large diplomatic missions may have several, such as First Secretary, Second, Third, etc.); political and economic officers (if they do not rank as counselors or attachés); attaché (for military, cultural, or labor matters); and assistant attaché. Among the nondiplomatic personnel, rank designations are: consul-general (one in charge of several consulates within a single state), consul, and vice-consul, or consular agent. (An agent is ordinarily one who represents some interests of a foreign government within his own state.)

Diplomatic Recognition. See RECOGNITION OF A STATE.

Diplomatic Tap-Dancing. The long series of hit-and-hide, seek-and-hide exercises by the Israeli and the Palestinian teams during peace settlement negotiations in 1991-1992, in Madrid, Spain, and Washington, D.C., U.S.A. During the 4 December 1991 meeting in Washington, D.C., the Israeli team of negotiators asked for delays of several days to the great consternation of the Palestinian team as well as to U.S. Secretary of State James Baker, III. Baker told the Israelis that their good will in these negotiations was essential for a possible loan guarantee of $10 billion which Israel had requested in order to build settlement housing for new Jewish immigrants from the former Soviet Union. Since these settlements were to be built on Arab lands, the tap-dancing commenced on how to resolve this contradictory issue. The Israelis want and need the land to accommodate new arrivals, and they also want peace with the Palestinians, but the Palestinians also want their land back plus complete independence as a sovereign state. These issues can only be resolved by war, possibly by a war of long duration, a war of attrition.

Direct Democracy. See DEMOCRACY, DIRECT.

Direct Legislation. The participation of voters (or citizens) in law-making processes or the testing of the desirability of laws by referendums.

Direct Nomination. The manner of nominating one for elective (or appointive) office through petition or direct primary election. See DIRECT LEGISLATION.

Direct Tax. A tax levy which the states in the American Union were paying (allocated on the basis of the population of each state) to the federal government under Article I of the U.S. Constitution. This was modified by Amendment XVI when income taxes were introduced in 1913.

Direction Générale des Etudes et Recherches. See SERVICE DE DOCUMENTATION EXTÉRIEURES ET CONTRE-ESPIONNAGE (SDECE).

Disarmament and Arms Control. See HARDWARE DIPLOMACY.

Discharge a Committee. The method of relieving a congressional committee from jurisdiction over a bill. This method was often used in the U.S. Congress in the past. Rarely used in recent times. See DISCHARGE CALENDAR, DISCHARGE PETITION.

Discharge Calendar. A calendar kept by the U.S. House of Representatives listing motions to discharge committees from jurisdiction over bills and to take the bills to the floor for action. (This action, though rare, is only taken when there is a general belief that a particular committee would "kill" a popular bill.) See UNITED STATES HOUSE OF REPRESENTATIVES.

Discharge Petition. A motion that can be introduced in the U.S. House of Representatives to discharge a committee from jurisdiction over a bill and require that committee to send the bill to the floor for debate and possible voting. Such a petition requires 218 signatures out of the total number of 435 members of Congress. See DISCHARGE CALENDAR.

Discharge Resolution. A motion to relieve a committee from jurisdiction over a bill in the U.S. Senate. Any senator may introduce such a motion on the floor. See UNITED STATES SENATE.

Discipline. See HOT-STOVE RULE.

Discovery Law. Under many systems of jurisprudence, including that of the United States, one in possession of information pertinent to a case on trial before a court of law, must, under penalty, reveal it (e.g., an attempt to bribe a witness, a juror, or a judge).

Discretionary Power. A power or authority which may or may not be exercised at will or discretion. See AUTHORITY, POWER.

Discrimination in Congress. See LAST PLANTATION.

Disease Theory. The idea that propaganda efforts which aim at branding a given political philosophy or system as contagious, are like a disease, transferable by one person to another and by one society to another (e.g., communism in the West and capitalism in the East).

Disenfranchisement. An act aiming to deprive a person of a certain right (e.g., the right to vote or be voted upon). See APPORTIONMENT, RIGHT.

Disengagement, Policy of. See POLICY OF DISENGAGEMENT.

Disillusionment with Government. Reaction to political scandals and policy failures; frustration over "big government's" inability to act decisively.

Disinformation. The practice common among adversary groups, organizations, and political systems (e.g., the United States and the Soviet Union) who are competing for power and dominance, to feed each other erroneous information disseminated by overt or covert means, in order to confuse the adversary and to cause him to make erratic or inaccurate decisions. This practice is particularly common in intelligence activity. For example, Edward J. Epstein alleges in his recent book that Lee Harvey Oswald, the alleged assassin of U.S. President John F. Kennedy in 1963, was a KGB agent, and in order to hide that fact from the American public, the KGB sent a "defector" to the West in 1964. This Yuri Nosenko, a high ranking KGB case officer, spread rumors that the KGB had never been interested in Oswald while he was in the USSR and that he had never been "debriefed," in spite of the fact that Oswald once worked as a radar technician in Astugi, Japan. It was from here that U-2 spy planes were flying over China and the Soviet Union until one of them (with pilot Francis Gary Powers) was shot down over the Soviet Union, at a time when Oswald was living in the Soviet Union. See CENTRAL INTELLIGENCE AGENCY (CIA), PENKOVSKY PAPERS, PROPAGANDA ASSETS INVENTORY (PAI).

Dispensing Power. The right of the President of the United States (derived from Article II of the U.S. Constitution) to perform certain acts (e.g., to appoint officers in the executive branch of the federal government). See Appendix 8.

Dissenter. One who disagrees with the opinion of the majority (e.g., a judge or justice of the U.S. Supreme Court who disagrees with the majority opinion in adjudication.) An Associate Justice of the U.S. Supreme Court, William Johnson, 1804-1834, was the first to initiate the practice of dissenting. See CONSTRUCTIONIST, JUDICIAL ACTIVISM.

Dissenting Opinion. The opinion that may be expressed by a judge or justice (e.g., of the U.S. Supreme Court) who disagrees with the majority on the disposition of a case at hand.

Dissident. One who refuses to conform to common or dominant political or social values.

Dissident Movement. See HOSTILE AND SLANDEROUS ACTS.

Distribution Battle. In the German language, "Verteilungskampf," a term coined in the spring of 1992 in Germany, where the government under Chancellor Helmut Kohl imposed a so-called "unification tax" in order to pay for the costs (about 120 billion dollars) associated with the unification of the two Germanys. The former west Germans were very unhappy and bitterly opposed to such a redistribution of wealth and in May 1992, the well organized public sector employee unions went on strike, asking for a 9,8 percent wage increase. The German and neighboring economies sustained tremendous losses and delayed Kohl's plan for integration of the split nation about a decade. The Chancellor pleaded with German labor, ". . . is it possible in one of the riches countries on earth to give up at least part of one's growth in income" in order to keep the Germans in the East? The May 1992 strike in Germany upset the delicate economic equilibrium in Europe and inflicted tremendous loss upon the Germans themselves.

Distribution of Power. See TYPES OF GOVERNMENTS.

Distribution of Sovereign Powers. See TYPES OF GOVERNMENTS.

District. A unit of political subdivision within a state, large city, or county, designed for numerous purposes, such as a voting (electoral) district or administrative district; town, village, borough, or any subdivision with designated boundaries. Territorially or population-wise, designed for purposes of electing and/or appointing officials of the government.

District Attorney (D.A.). An official who represents the government during criminal prosecutions and court cases. See PROSECUTING ATTORNEY.

Diversification. See CONGLOMERATE.

Divide and Rule. See DIVIDE ET IMPERA.

Divide et Impera. In the Latin language, "divide and rule." Also, a doctrine under which Papal authority has been spread over temporal matters of states, empires, and rules by: (1) crowning kings and emperors as a symbolic act of granting upon them the power to divide and to rule (and removing such powers through excommunication—expulsion from the Church and the faith—for any anti-Church, or anti-Papal activities or acts. Fidel Castro of Cuba was the last ruler within the realm of the Catholic faith to be excommunicated by the Pope, in 1961, for making official statements referring to himself as a "Marxist-Leninist"); and (2) by dividing the Christian world into spheres of influence by nations and rulers (e.g., during the 15th century, the Latin American continent was divided among the Portuguese, Spanish, and French by Pope Innocent VIII, 1484-1492, and this was reaffirmed by Pope Alexander VI, 1492-1503, under the slogan of "conquer and rule," or, "victoria et impera"). The Spanish conquistadors conquered and ruled South and Central America, and small portions of North America as well, following Columbus' voyages. See PAPAL INFALLIBILITY.

Divine Gift. See CHARISMA.

Divine Right. God-given right or one derived from the will of God. See ORIGINS OF THE STATE THEORIES.

Division of Powers. The constitutional allocation of governmental powers between the branches of government—legislative, executive, and judicial as outlined in the U.S. Constitution; also, the allocation of powers between the central and the state governments or other levels of government.

Dixiecrats. In 1945 a group of Southern Democrats initiated this splinter political party to protest Harry S. Truman's Fair Deal programs (particularly his call for racial desegregation in the United States) and to uphold states' rights. During the 1948 presidential election, the Dixiecrats ran their own candidate for President, S. Strom Thurmond of South Carolina, whose platform consisted of anti-desegregation and anti-civil rights measures. Thurmond has since changed parties and now serves in the U.S. Senate as a Republican. The term "Dixie" denotes anything related to the Southern Confederacy, the Confederate States of America (CSA), and any of the states which have been a part of the Confederacy. It is also the title of the CSA's national anthem "Dixie." The Dixiecrats were also referred to as States' Rights Democrats.

Dizzy with Success. A phrase used by Josef Stalin, Premier of the Soviet Government and Secretary of the CPSU (1922-1953), to describe party and/or government officials whom he decided to purge, on the grounds that they employed terroristic methods in forcing collectivization upon the peasants through excessive zeal in order to please the party. Several million peasants, especially the "kulaks" (rich peasants) perished during the period of forceful collectivization.

Djibouti Liberation Movement (DLM). See LIBERATION MOVEMENT DJIBOUTI (LMD).

DMZ. See DEMILITARIZED ZONE.

Do. An administrative division—a province—in Korea (North and South).

Do Justice, Sir, Do Justice! When Judge Learned Hand suggested such a course of action to Justice Oliver Wendell Holmes of the U.S. Supreme Court, Justice Holmes replied in his celebrated terms: "That is not my job. It is my job to apply the law." Judge Robert A Bork, who was rejected by the Senate in 1988 for nomination to the Supreme Court, added that the U.S. Supreme Court "administers justice according to law. Justice in a larger sense, justice according to morality, is for Congress and the President to administer, if they see fit, through creation of new law." Such an approach represents the "original understanding" of the law, the Constitution; and, in actuality, represents the American legal culture.

Do Nothing 80th Congress. See CONGRESS BASHING.

Doctors Plot. Josef Stalin's scheme designed to exterminate a group of physicians (mainly Jews) in the USSR who were allegedly conspiring to cause the deaths of many distinguished Soviet and foreign dignitaries and party officials during the 1940s and 1950s.

Doctrinaire. See DOCTRINE.

Doctrine. The perceptions of the phenomena of human life as they are transferred by one mind to another (e.g., by a parent to a child or by a teacher to a student) for the purpose of being accepted, believed in, and followed (e.g., the doctrine of communism which promises an ultimately peaceful and just society among those who are willing to struggle for it, or capitalism which promises reward and a better life only to those who make a constructive contribution to their welfare by working and producing the necessities of life). One who obediently follows certain teachings and directions—the doctrine—in spite of existing evidence (e.g., empirical proof) that that doctrine is not what it claimed to be, becomes known as a "dogmatist," or a "diehard." The doctrine of capitalism, for example, considered to be progressive (see CAPITALISM) by most, is viewed as doctrinaire by some who believe in welfarism (e.g., the state as the provider for the upkeep of the individual). The communist doctrine is also viewed by some as doctrinaire, because a good life and a just society can be achieved without bloody revolutions and regimentation of people into rigid classes. The term "doctrinaire" is often associated with that political group in post-Napoleonic France which advocated the restoration of monarchy and the introduction of a constitutional system patterned after that of England which the majority of Frenchmen viewed as impractical, undesirable, futile, and visionary. See DOGMA.

Doctrine of Executive Privilege. See EXECUTIVE PRIVILEGE.

Doctrine of Interposition. A concept first articulated in 1832 by William Harper, Chancellor of the Supreme Court of South Carolina and a political philosopher, denoting the inherent inequality of man and the subservience of one man to another. According to Harper, "Man is born to subjection . . . . The proclivity of natural man is to be subservient." This doctrine was further exemplified by South Carolina's Governor, James H. Hammond, and Professor Thomas Cooper of the University of South Carolina, and it became the crux of Southern separatism throughout the Civil War period and the period of massive opposition to civil rights legislation. Hammond observed that "in all social systems there must be a class to do the menial duties, to perform the drudgery of life . . . . Such a class you must have or you would not have that other class which leads progress, civilization, and refinement. It constitutes the very mudsill of society and of political government." To Professor Cooper "no human being ever was, now is, or ever will be born free." The doctrine views segregation not as something that is imposed upon certain people, but as something that is voluntary ("voluntary segregation") and normal in any society. See SOUTHERN MANIFESTO.

Doctrine of Nonpartisanism. See NATIONAL MUNICIPAL LEAGUE (NML).

Doctrine of Urgency of the Situation. See IMPEACHMENT.

Dogma. That in which one chooses to believe as certain and unquestionable truth, regardless of the possible existence of empirical evidence to the contrary; a certain set of beliefs that one holds as truthful, stubbornly rejecting any challenge aimed at the dismissal of that belief; the assertions of one's opinions about certain truths which may be transferred to others and may become a dogmatic doctrine. See DOCTRINE.

Dollar Devaluation. See SMITHSONIAN AGREEMENT.

Dollar Diplomacy. A phrase used to depict some of America's diplomatic practices, whereby the American dollar was used as an instrument of bargaining, persuasion, or even force; mainly during the W. H. Taft Administration (1909-1913). See CHECKBOOK DIPLOMACY.

Domestic Council. An agency established by presidential Executive Order in 1970 to advise the U.S. President on national priorities and to seek solutions to major national problems. The members of the

Council are: U.S. President and Vice President, members of the cabinet dealing with domestic issues (e.g., Treasury, Interior, etc.), and other persons whom the President wishes to invite. Composed of highly placed government officials advising the president on domestic matters.

Domestic Partners. Under the laws in some states in the United States, e.g., California, Maryland, and Washington, two persons of the same sex may legally obtain a license as "domestic partners" which gives them the same rights as a legally married couple under the law.

Domestic Policy. The sum total of actions taken by public elected or appointed officials, from the President to the dog catcher, based on existing law and plans for additional laws which will enable the government to realize and set goals and objectives. Such goals and objectives are set by the Constitution, federal, state, local laws, and ordinances and should be implemented in such a way as not to upset the rights and goals of private groups and individual persons. In a democratic society, government policy is implemented with the support of groups and individuals through the political process, and in cases of conflict, the judiciary system steps in to resolve it. A policy that is implemented is assumed to be good for the many rather than the few, but the rights of the few must also be considered and taken into account. Policies are temporary expedients subject to constant change and revision.

Domestic Relations Court. A court of law handling cases related to family and domestic life such as marriage, divorce, and custody of children.

Domicile. One's legal residence, with which certain rights and obligations are connected, such as the right to vote or the obligation to pay taxes.

Dominant Industries of the Twenty-First Century. See COMPARATIVE ADVANTAGE.

Dominion. A self-governing, independent member of a commonwealth which maintains some ties with the mother country (e.g., the Dominion of Canada, as a member of the British Commonwealth).

Domino Theory. A guiding principle of America's foreign policy during the first Eisenhower Administration (1953-1957), directed mainly to Asia, where the U.S. was to protect any state from falling under communist control. The underlying belief was that the loss of one state or region would automatically result in the loss of others.

Donkey. A political cartoon introduced during the 1874 elections by Thomas Nast, and now symbolic of the Democratic Party.

Don't Do Something, Just Stand There. A derogatory statement about President Carter after he announced his plan to fight inflation (March 17, 1980) which was causing decline in the standard of living. Yet, he gained support in primaries (e.g., Florida, S. Carolina, and Illinois).

Don't Tread on Me. See POWER.

Doomsayer. One who mistrusts government policies and predicts hard times, particularly in employment and consumer purchasing power; also, one who predicts a bleak future for any given government policy, plan of action, society, or even the world. See POLITICAL PREMONITION.

Double-Cross System. See DECEPTION, ECOLOGIST OF DOUBLE AGENCY, INTELLIGENCE.

Double-Digit Inflation. An annual rate of inflation in a given economy which runs into two numerical digits on a possible scale of 10 to 99.

Double Jeopardy. The subjection of an accused person to stand trial more than once for the same offense. (Forbidden in the U.S. by Amendment V to the Constitution.) See COLLATERAL ESTOPPEL, VENUE.

Double-Patriot. One with split allegiance and political loyalty to two different political systems or nation states. Term originated during the 1920s, mainly in Western Europe, where many socialist elements have shown great support for the new Soviet state, the USSR. Similarly, during W.W.II, when the Western powers (mainly England and the United States) were willing to provide the USSR with the necessary weapons (under the Lend-Lease program) for the Soviet Union to fight the Nazi armies rather then having their own die, anti-Soviet propaganda in the West was muted, if not eliminated. Until the beginning of the "Cold War," there were many sympathizers to the Soviet cause; persons of the Jewish faith and Zionists, and the Irish, for example, who supported the states of their original birth or residence, but who also supported the State of Israel or the Irish Republic. During W.W.II, Japanese-Americans were evacuated to concentration camps in Arizona and other areas, as some of the pro-Nazi Germans were for either overt or covert demonstration of double-patriotism. Double-patriots are particularly frowned upon because they serve as the best source for and links to intelligence operations.

Double-Talk. See DOUBLETHINK.

Double X. See INTELLIGENCE, SECRET INTELLIGENCE SERVICE.

Doublethink. The practice not uncommon among politicians and hard-core ideologues, of externalizing their philosophical and ideological convictions in language that is often incomprehensible to the ordinary person, particularly when "love" is explained as "hate," and "hate" as "love," or "justice" as "injustice," and *vice versa* (e.g., "peace" to Soviet ideologues had a different connotation than it did to U.S. President Ronald Reagan); and which is often construed as double-talk (which it often is). The term was coined by George Orwell, a political satirist during the 1950s.

Douglas-Lincoln Debate. See GREAT DEBATES.

Dove. See WAR HAWK.

Doyen. See DIPLOMATIC DEAN.

Draco Code. A systematic code of laws compiled by the Athenian jurist, Draco, in 625 BC., which provides for very severe and harsh penalties for the smallest infractions (e.g., death for petty larceny). These laws are often known as "Draconic Laws." Similarly severe (death) penalty was provided for lying and introduced by King Darius in Persia as early as 500 BC. ". . . the man who is a liar, destroy him utterly," read the royal edict.

Draconic Law. See DRACO CODE.

Draft. The placing of a person's name for nomination or writing his name on a ballot (if write-in is allowed) for public elective office with or without the knowledge of that person; also, conscription of manpower for military service. See CONSCRIPTION.

Draft Beer, Not Students. So demanded one of the anti-Vietnam war slogans of groups of students picketing the White House in Washington, D.C., in May 1967, when U.S. President Lyndon B. Johnson began drafting non-active students into the armed forces. The draft was ended on January 27, 1973. See CONSCRIPTION.

Draft Dodger. One who evades the draft illegally as opposed to legally (e.g., conscientious objector).

Drago Doctrine. A principle of international law denying a state the right to intervene in any manner in the domestic affairs of another, for the sole purpose of protecting the monetary interests of its citizens or nationals if they are deficient in the payment of public debts or owe taxes to the state in which they reside. (Named after Louis Maria Drago, 1859-1921, Argentinean jurist and diplomat who first conceived it.)

Drang Nach Osten. See LEBENSRAUM.

Drive to the East. See LEBENSRAUM.

Droit des Gens. In the French language, "the law of nations" or "international law."

Drop. See DEAD DROP.

Drug Enforcement Agency. See CENTRAL INTELLIGENCE AGENCY (CIA).

Dual Democracy. See TERRITORIAL DEMOCRACY.

Dual Federalism. See FEDERALISM.

Dual Oppression. See LIBERALISM.

Due Process of Law. A body of procedural laws or rules intended to protect the accused person from arbitrary treatment and entitling her or him to certain procedural rights, such as proper arrest, proper hearing, trial by jury, the right to present witnesses in one's favor, and the right to confront adversary witnesses, the right to a speedy trial by an impartial jury and protection from excessive bail or infliction of cruel and unusual punishment. (See Amendments V and XIV, U.S. Constitution, Appendix 8.) Also, the implied right of an individual to be informed of the causes and to have the opportunity to clear oneself in case of denial or abridgment of any right or privilege (e.g., dismissal from employment). There is another side to the due process principle, one which was not originally intended but which has evolved as a matter of experience through the application of that doctrine in real situations; namely, that this principle may also serve as an instrument of delay, and if applied for that purpose, it can weaken the intended utility. A procrastinator can be well served while due process is taking its course. This may delay judicial remedy to a point of detriment, and justice delayed may amount to justice denied. See PALMER RAIDS, Appendix 50.

Duma. In the Russian language, "a place of thinking" or "a place of thinkers." Also, a legislative body (elective) in pre-Revolutionary Russia, or the national parliament of the Ukrainian Soviet Socialist Republic.

Dumbarton Oaks Conference. On August 2, 1944, the heads of state and/or government of the United States, the Soviet Union, China, France, and England gathered to consider the post—World War II global political order. An agreement was reached to establish the United Nations Organization—outlined in a special document: *The Dumbarton Oaks Proposal for the General International Organization*—whereby the Soviet Union demanded fifteen (15) votes, one for each of its Soviet Republics (the Soviet Union revised its constitution in 1943, giving each of the fifteen republics sovereign status); but when the U.S. delegation asked for forty-eight (48) votes for the United States, the Soviets, after some arguments to the effect that the states in the American Union are not sovereign, settled for three votes: one for the Soviet Union, one each for the Belorussian (White Russian) and the Ukrainian Soviet Socialist Republics. See ATLANTIC CHARTER, GRAND DESIGN, UNITED NATIONS ORGANIZATION (UNO).

Dump the Hump. An anti-Hubert H. Humphrey slogan when he was campaigning for the presidency in 1968. Humphrey (1911-1978) was the Democratic nominee for President, and was defeated by Richard M. Nixon.

Dumping. A predatory strategy used in international marketing, whereby a manufacturer of a product in one country markets it in another country at a substantially lower price—lower than the sale price of the same product at home and sometimes even lower than the cost of production. This technique is applied in order to saturate the market and eventually gain the entire market share, stifling or eliminating domestic producers of similar products in the process. Under the U.S. law of January 1975, dumping is defined as "selling a product abroad at a price lower than that charged in its home market," and is illegal. The law requires that "a product sold abroad must be sold at the actual cost of producing it, plus a ten percent allowance for overhead and another eight percent for profit." During the past several years, the Japanese have been accused of these practices and an agreement was reached in 1978 between Japan and the United States that these practices would be terminated. See ECONOMIC SUMMITS.

Dunkirk Pact. On March 4, 1947, England and France signed a fifty-year alliance aimed at mutual cooperation and assistance in case of future aggression by the reviving German state, the Federal Republic of Germany, which was being formed in the West by Dr. Konrad Adenauer, a former mayor of the city of Cologne. The Dunkirk Pact has been extended to include the Benelux States—Belgium, Holland (The Netherlands), and Luxemburg—and was signed on March 17, 1948, in Brussels, Belgium (known as "Brussels Treaty"). This extended pact was directed against the "new" enemy that emerged on the European Theatre, the Soviet Union.

Düsseldorf Doctrine. See LEBENSRAUM.

Dynamic Flow Region. See FUNCTIONAL REGION.

"Many forms of government have been tried, and will be tried in this world of sin and woe. No one pretends that democracy is perfect or all-wise. Indeed, it has been said that democracy is the worst form of government except all those other forms that have been tried from time to time."

SIR WINSTON CHURCHILL, 1874-1965

E Pluribus Unum. In the Latin language, "one out of many." Also, the inscription on the Great Seal Of The United States which was adopted by the Second Continental Congress (in 1785) as suggested by Benjamin Franklin, Thomas Jefferson, and John Adams—all members of a special committee called upon to design the GREAT SEAL and the MOTTO of the United States. The present motto, IN GOD WE TRUST, was adopted by Congress in 1956.

Eagle Claw. See DELTA FORCE.

Earth Summit. See RIO DE JANEIRO EARTH SUMMIT.

East European Mutual Assistance Treaty. (Also known as the WARSAW PACT or WARSAW TREATY). A defense and friendship treaty, signed in Warsaw, Poland, in May 1955, by Albania, Bulgaria, Czechoslovakia, German Democratic Republic (East Germany), Hungary, Poland, Rumania, and the Soviet Union. This treaty was primarily designed as a counter-measure to the North Atlantic Treaty Organization (NATO) of the Western, non-communist powers, and in 1968 Soviet and East European forces (e.g., Poland, East Germany) participated in squashing the Czechoslovak uprising under the pro-Western Administration of Aleksander Dubcek. It was dissolved April 1, 1991, in Moscow. See BREZHNEYEV DOCTRINE.

Eastern Block. The eastern states of Europe under communist leadership.

Eastern Establishment. Those individuals from the Eastern part of the United States who, because of accumulated wealth and extensive education, exert an influence upon the policies of the federal government to a scope and degree that is disproportionate to those of other areas of the U.S. Most often they are also of liberal rather than conservative persuasion, and cosmopolitan in outlook. Strongly attacked as traitors and "pinkos" by McCarthy. See ESTABLISHMENT, MCCARTHYISM.

Eastoxification. The task of eliminating the particular elements that influence one ideology (or religion) by another; the effort to eradicate any foreign and/or hostile elements of alien culture, politics, religion, or mores—notions, conceptions, practices, and rituals. For example, the communists worked to eradicate all remnants of the so-called "bourgeois ideology," "bourgeois or capitalist mentality," notions and practices from socialist/communist life, particularly among the young. After the 1979 revolution in Iran, Ayatollah Khomeini ordered the eradication of anything that was considered alien to Islamic culture, religion, ethics, and aesthetics, and any non-Islamic influence was considered the "work of Satan." Among other things, Khomeini required women to be properly clad, to refrain from dating, dancing, holding hands with the opposite gender, using cosmetics, driving a car, and more—all behavior was to be "proper" and according to Islamic traditions, Islamic jurisprudence was restored, all non-Islamic music was forbidden, and strict separation of genders was maintained in all public establishments. In the West, and particularly in the United States, ideologues battled all sorts of foreign influences on the American culture from the very day new immigrants arrived from Europe (e.g., the Puritans) seeking liberty by imposing terror among those with whom they have not agreed. There were countless campaigns of one group against another—canceling each other out in the process and thus allowing sober-minded practices to prevail. Such "anti-something" ideologies were common, e.g., the Anti-Masonic Party, anti-Semitic ideologies of the KKK, for example. These were built on negative foundations, being against

139

something rather than standing for something. Many of them were simply hate campaigns. Such campaigns ranged from hating the Catholics, the Jews, the Italians, the Asians, the Slavs, the blacks, and were against their influences on American society, to communists and royalists, and even the organizers of labor unions themselves were viewed as "messengers of Satan." The "purification" process in America came to a climax point during Senator Joseph McCarthy's campaign against communists and communist influence during the 1950s. See KU KLUX KLAN (KKK), MCCARTHYISM.

Ecclesiastical Authority. Authority that is presumed to be granted by or derived from some supreme being such as God. See CAESAROPAPISM, PAPAL INFALLIBILITY, TEMPORAL AUTHORITY, TWO SWORDS THEORY.

Ecclesiastical Monarchy. A monarchy in which the king, queen, empress, emperor, caesar, tsar, tsarina, or chief, is also the spiritual or religious leader. For example, the Pope is the head of the state of Vatican as well as of the Catholic Church, and in England, the queen is the head of the Anglican church. Secular monarchs lay no particular claims to religious leadership of any established church. In the case of Iran, the shah, Reza Pahlavi (1953-1979), was a secular monarch, but the man who launched a successful revolution against the shah, Ayatollah Ruhollah Khomeini, though not claiming to be a monarch, was the de facto temporal and ecclesiastical leader of Iran and the Shiite Muslims.

Ecologist of Double Agency. A term used by Professor Norman Holmes Pearson, one of America's pioneers of modern intelligence and counterintelligence theory and practice, to characterize persons engaged in intelligence work. An officer of the OSS and the CIA after W.W.II, Professor Pearson wrote the overall blueprint of the Double-Cross System (known also under other names such as "XX" or "Double-X,") which was a counterintelligence operation designed to turn German intelligence officers operating on Allied territories, especially England, against their masters. The Germans were given deceptive information to broadcast and hand deliver, mixed with authentic facts of no strategic importance, so as to establish credibility with their chiefs at the German centers. Professor Pearson, who with John Masterman, a British intelligence expert, also served as chairman of the Double-X Committee, outlined its primary goals. They were: (1) to control the enemy system; (2) to catch spies; (3) to learn as much as possible about personalities and methods of the Abwehr and other German intelligence bodies; (4) to make the German codes and ciphers reveal their secrets; (5) to study the questions asked by Germans as evidence of their intentions; (6) to influence their plans by the answers sent back; and (7) to deceive the enemy about Allied plans. See ENIGMA, INTELLIGENCE, SECRET INTELLIGENCE SERVICE.

Ecology. See POLITICAL ECOLOGY.

Economic and Social Council. See UNITED NATIONS ORGANIZATION.

Economic Assistance to the Soviet Union. See AMERICAN ECONOMIC ASSISTANCE TO THE COMMONWEALTH OF INDEPENDENT STATES (CIS).

Economic Base of Society. A concept developed by Karl Marx and Friedrich Engels, according to which each society has its own unique economic base: a capitalistic society has a capitalistic economic base and a socialistic society has a socialistic economic base, which is the mode of production and distribution of goods and services and the production relations upon which the superstructure of the society is built (e.g., such institutions as government, laws, standards of morality, religion and the family). Any modification of that base will, necessarily modify the superstructure. See MARXISM, SOCIALISM.

Economic Buffer Zone. A geographic area located on the border between two or more states which is utilized for mutual economic activity. (For example, the Sinai Desert is a buffer zone between Israel and Egypt; the two states have a feasible basis for cooperation, with Egypt providing water from the Nile River, and Israel supplying the know-how for economic development; the city of Juares, located between Mexico and the United States in Texas, is a center of joint economic ventures by Mexico and the United States; and the Danube River in Europe, a major commercial waterway, makes economic and political cooperation possible among many neighboring states).

Economic Community of West African States (ECOWAS). An organization similar to the European Common Market agreed on 28 May 1975 by heads of states of the following member countries: Nigeria, Benin, Togo, Burkina Fasso, Ghana, Côte d'Ivoire, Liberia, Sierra Leone, Guinea, Guinea Bissau, Gambia, Senegal, Mauritania, Mali, and Niger. Cape Verde joined on 5 July 1975 upon gaining full independence. The aim of ECOWAS is "to promote cooperation and development in all fields of economic activity particularly in fields of industry, transport and telecommunications, energy, agriculture, natural resources, commerce, monetary and financial questions and in social and cultural matters. These are done for purpose of raising the standard of living of the peoples of this sub-region. In order to achieve this main objective, they agreed, in due course, to eradicate all barriers prohibiting the free flow of trade among member countries like custom duties and governmental restrictions on free movement of persons, services, and capital."

Economic Debate in the USSR. See GREAT ECONOMIC DEBATE IN THE USSR.

Economic Determinism. A concept formulated after the development of Karl Marx's theory, according to which economic relations shape and determine the history of society, and the prevailing mode of production and exchange (economic base) determines the social, political, as well as intellectual and moral institutions of that society. Marx makes no distinctions between the science of economics and the science of politics. See MARXISM.

Economic Development District (EDD). A multi-county organization serving areas of the country with unemployment that is substantially above the national average. These districts are designated concurrently by the Economic Development Administration (EDA) of the Department of Commerce and State government. EDDs have the primary responsibility for developing an Overall Economic Development Program (OEDP) which is a comprehensive plan designed to stimulate and sustain economic growth in these depressed areas. Their operations are funded from a variety of federal, state, and local sources, and their governing board is made up of locally elected officials and citizens within the district.

Economic Equity. A fair and just monetary reward for one's labor comparable to that of other professions which require similar skills based on education and experience, and also taking into consideration risks and hazards associated with the tasks performed. For example, there is extensive debate among many professional groups in the United States, particularly teachers, law enforcement officers, nursing personnel, and firefighters, on the great disparities in pay between these and other professions. Police officers and firefighters, for example, protect life and property, and risk their own safety but often earn a small fraction (sometimes less than five percent) of what surgeons and other medical professionals, though rarely endangered in person, earn. Such extensive disparities in income create conflicts in a society in which, as the 1992 federal statistics indicate, about one-percent of the population received over forty percent of the national income, and ninety-nine percent of the population shared in the remaining sixty percent of income. This disparity leads to the diminishing of the middle class.

Economic Imperialism. See IMPERIALISM.

Economic Interest Theory. See ORIGINS OF THE STATE THEORIES.

Economic League for European Cooperation. See COUNCIL OF EUROPE.

Economic Message. During the month of January of each year, the U.S. President is required (by the Employment Act of 1946) to deliver to the U.S. Congress a message on the state of the economy (which is prepared for him by the Council of Economic Advisers and the Office of Management and Budget). In it, the President outlines the state of the national economy at the time of its delivery, makes projections and presents his future plans for the nation's economy, and proposes fiscal and/or economic policies for immediate or future implementation in cooperation with Congress. See COUNCIL OF ECONOMIC ADVISERS.

Economic Nationalism. See LIBERAL PARTY OF CANADA.

Economic Opportunity Act of 1964. See WAR ON POVERTY.

Economic Planning. Designs for the utilization of economic structures in the development of societal well being and prosperity, expedited mainly through the market of goods and services mechanisms. See PLANNING.

Economic Power. See POWER.

Economic Refugee One who emigrates, legally or illegally, to another country under the pretext of political prosecution and seeks political asylum, but who in reality is merely seeking more rewarding employment and a better way of life. About 99 percent of the refugees seeking sanctuary in the United States are economic rather than political refugees. See ASYLUM, POLITICAL.

Economic Shock Therapy. See POLITICO-ECONOMIC SYSTEMS in Appendix 83, SHOCK THERAPY, TYPES OF MARKET SYSTEMS, Appendix 84.

Economic Strategies. Global interaction between economically developed states, i.e., France, Japan, Germany, Italy, Great Britain and the United States, involves deployment of six major strategies to maximize efforts and achieve objectives: (1) innovation and technology, (2) quality and utility, (3) reasonable pricing, (4) politics, (5) marketing and (6) reliable service.

Economic Summits. The first economic summit (among heads of state and/or government) in modern times was held in 1933, in London, England, where six nations made an attempt to design ways and means to cope with global depression through stabilization of local currencies. U.S. President Franklin D. Roosevelt (1933-1945) emphasized that domestic economies are interdependent, and that domestic problems must be solved as part of global solutions. Represented were England, France, Italy, Austria, Belgium, Holland, and the United States. Such summits are held almost every year.

Economy of Scale. The term denotes a decreasing average cost as output expands. The concept is used mainly in the private sector, but may also be used in the public sector. In the public sector, economies of scale may be achieved in such public services as water supply and sewage disposal. However, economies of scale would not be applicable for such services as education, police, fire, and street maintenance, to name a few.

ECOWAS. See ECONOMIC COMMUNITY OF WEST AFRICAN STATES.

ECSC. See EUROPEAN COAL AND STEEL COMMUNITY.

EDC. See NORTH AMERICAN TREATY ORGANIZATION (NATO).

Edict. See DECREE.

Educational Dictatorship. See NEW LEFT.

Educrat. An educator (e.g., a teacher), who is also performing administrative functions in a school system; a bureaucrat; particularly one favoring the busing of children for the purpose of achieving a racial balance; one in favor of busing. The term was coined by an opponent of busing, A. Polly Williams, a state representative in Wisconsin. Miss Williams advocates "parental choice in education," meaning that the parents should decide, in spite of the existing law which commands busing, to which school, public or private, a child would go. Forced busing of children, it is generally assumed, is very costly and very unproductive. In order to pay for education in schools that teach well, the parents, under Miss Williams' plan, would receive from the state so-called "tuition vouchers." The state of Wisconsin was the first in the American union to pass legislation to this effect, the so-called "Parental Empowerment Bill," which went in effect with the 1990-91 academic year. See STEP-BY-STEP MIXING PLAN.

Eduskunta. The unicameral legislative body—Parliament—of Finland.

EEC. See EUROPEAN ECONOMIC COMMUNITY.

EEI. See ESSENTIAL ELEMENTS OF INFORMATION.

EEOC. See EQUAL EMPLOYMENT OPPORTUNITY COMMISSION.

Eerste Kamer. Upper chamber or First Chamber of States General, the legislature of the Netherlands. See STATEN GENERAAL, TWEEDE KAMER.

EFTA. See EUROPEAN ECONOMIC COMMUNITY (EEC), EUROPEAN FREE TRADE ASSOCIATION.

Egalitarianism. The belief that all men are entitled to equal rights and that any class differences shall be eliminated or be kept to a minimum. See CAPITALISM, COMMUNISM.

Egghead. Intellectually active member of a society; also, one who thinks up and designs policies for the government.

Egyptian-Israeli Summit. See SADAT-BEGIN SUMMIT.

Eight-F Gang. A group of wealthy Texas "kingmakers," led by Walter Mischner, a wealthy political philanthropist, who have decided who gets what, when, how, and why in Texas politics. Mischner, who himself was publicity-shy, was instrumental in raising the funds necessary to place some Texans high in public life. These include John F. Connolly (governor of Texas, Secretary of the Navy, Treasury, and presidential candidate until after his defeat in the South Carolina primary in March 1980, when he withdrew from the race.); Lloyd Bentsen (U.S. Senator); Lyndon Johnson (U.S. Congressman, Senator, Vice President under John F. Kennedy, President and a kingmaker himself); Dolph Brisco (Governor of Texas); and Barbara Jordan (congresswoman from Texas and capable black lawyer)—to mention only a few. The name "8-F" was adopted after a room number in the Houston's Lamar Hotel where the kingmakers have held periodic meetings. Mischner is also a land developer and building contractor, and chairman of Allied Bankshares, the largest bank holding corporation in Texas. See POLITICAL MACHINE.

Eight Points of Attention. In order to solidify his power among the masses of the peasants (the Chinese "proletariat") on the one hand, and in turn improve rapport between the masses and the army, Mao Tse-tung (1894-1976) issued in 1928 (and again, with small changes, in 1947) the following points to his followers (mainly soldiers) urging their observance by way of their conduct: (1) speak politely; (2) pay fairly for whatever you buy; (3) always return everything that you borrow; (4) pay for all damages you have caused; (5) always refrain from verbal and physical abuse of others; (6) avoid damaging crops; (7) do not get involved with other women; and (8) always treat your captives well. These were Mao's prerequisites for transforming the army into the people's army.

Ein Brera. In the Hebrew language, "no alternative." A notion developed among Israelis, particularly those few who survived the Holocaust, that, as David Ben-Gurion himself often said, as long as the Arabs hold the belief that they can defeat Israel by any means, they will not recognize the Israeli state and, therefore, Israel must arm itself and maintain strong defense forces in order to survive. Also, because Israel is encircled by Arab states, very often a preemptive strike is necessary in order to avoid a surprise attack.

Ein Volk, Ein Reich, Ein Führer. See ONE PEOPLE, ONE COUNTRY, ONE LEADER.

Eisenhower Doctrine. A series of policy aims and objectives outlined by U.S. President Dwight D. Eisenhower in his message to Congress in 1957 proposing, among others, the following: (1) the deployment of U.S. Armed Forces anytime a sovereign nation is threatened by international communism, provided that such assistance is requested; (2) U.S. economic assistance to any nation which desires to develop its economy; (3) U.S. military assistance to any nation which desires it; and (4) direct military assistance to any Middle East nation that feels threatened by a communist takeover; basically to prevent the Soviet Union from gaining influence in the area, and to ". . . make certain that every weak country understands what can be in store for it once it falls under the domination of the Soviets." (In 1958 President Eisenhower dispatched American military forces to Lebanon to prevent a take-over by the communist elements there.) The "New Republicanism" doctrine proclaimed by Eisenhower—which aimed at maintaining domestic and international political and economic stability and minimum interference by the federal government with the rights of states— did not materialize, due to the Sherman Adams scandal, the severe 1957-58 recession with which the President was not able to cope effectively, as well as the U-2 affairs—all of which seriously undermined the credibility of his administration. See U-2 INCIDENT.

Eisenhower's Communism. See EXTREMISM.

Elastic Clause. The vague yet enabling provision in the U.S. Constitution (Art. I, Sec. 8, Clause 18) stating that "*. . . Congress shall have the power . . . to make all laws which shall be necessary and proper . . . .*" It is presumed, therefore, that Congress is in no way restricted in its legislative functions. Also, any vague or loosely stated provision in a law or regulation. See Appendix 8.

Electability. The ability of a candidate for political elective office to win, due to timely attributes which are decisive in vote-getting on election day. As a rule, the attributes that voters expect candidates to have are the right age, charisma, a clear and realistic political program, intrepidity, no big skeleton in the closet, and, above all, that "something special" that in a certain election certain groups of voters find attractive and acceptable above other possible choices. This might include a specific achievement in military service, industry, science (e.g., astronaut), or public service. President Ronald Reagan's strongest electability point was that while governor of California he was able to balance the budget of the state, a rare occurrence. Or, as *Newsweek* journalists Howard Fineman, et al. observed in January 1992, "In the end, the only way to prove your 'electability' is to win." In American electoral politics, candidates from the South may have problems attracting voters in the North and vice versa. See BALANCED TICKET.

Election District. A geographically designated area from which a specified number of persons may be elected for specific offices.

Election-Oriented Political Party. See PARTY DISCIPLINE.

Elector. One qualified to vote and to elect; also, a member of the Electoral College in the U.S. which elects the President and the Vice President of the United States. See ELECTORAL COLLEGE, PRESIDENTIAL ELECTOR.

Electoral Board. A number of persons (usually an uneven number, such as three, five, or seven) who are designated by a local judge to appoint officers to some sub-governmental positions (e.g., a school board or a water control board) within a local government jurisdiction. Such boards are diminishing in popularity (particularly in the Southern states of the United States) as well as in number because they are considered undemocratic and anachronistic.

Electoral College. An informal body of persons, elected by either the presidential candidate in the U.S. or his party, who pledges to cast their ballots for him following the general presidential election. Electors must have the same qualifications as the person whom they are to elect (age, citizenship, and residency requirements). Electors are selected by states, each being entitled to the number of electors equal to its representation in Congress, that is, the total number of Senators and Representatives. Following each general presidential election, the slate of electors of the candidate who received at least a plurality vote within the state will gather at the state capitol and cast their ballots. Their ballots, in turn, will be forwarded to the President of the Senate who, in a joint session of Congress, will present the results. A majority of electoral votes—currently 270 out of 538—is required for the election of the President and Vice President. See Sen. Doc. 243, 78th Congress, 2d Session, 1944. On three occasions, in 1824, 1876, and 1888, a candidate with more popular votes lost in the electoral college to one with less total popular votes. See Appendix 8.

Electoral Commissions. See JOHNSON PROCLAMATION, RECONSTRUCTION.

Electoral Count Act. See HAYES-TILDEN DISPUTE.

Electoral Vote. See ELECTORAL COLLEGE.

Electoral Vote-Buying. See HAYES-TILDEN DISPUTE.

Electoral Votes by States. See Appendix 21.

Electoralism. A term coined by the British media and applicable to the strong desire by Neil Kinnock, the leader of the British Labour Party, to be elected prime minister of England in the 1992 election, unseating the incumbent, John Major. Kinnock stated during a March 1992 interview, that he was "happy to plead guilty, happy to be convicted, and happy to serve a life sentence" for electoralism.

When accused of being hungry for power and of pursuing policies described by Prime Minister Major as "pale pink Tories," Kinnock replied that this was only the result of his desire to return the party to "the mainstream of British and European democratic socialism, with a strong emphasis on the mixed economy and higher standards of social justice," as quoted by *Newsweek* (30 March 1992). When accused of being ruthless in his political style, Kinnock replied that since there were people in his party who were "deliberately standing in the way, then it is necessary to marginalize them organizationally and intellectually." He also described the years of leadership by Prime Minister Margaret Thatcher as "Thatcherism" which brought unemployment to the British people and lack of confidence in the future. See DEFINING THE OPPONENT, LABOUR PARTY OF ENGLAND.

Electorate. A collective constituency; the whole body of persons who are legally qualified and who register to vote: a body of voters; those who elect.

Electronic Town Hall. See GRASS-ROOTS PEROT.

Elements of Government. See TOOLS OF GOVERNMENT.

Elements of State. See STATE.

Elephant. A political cartoon introduced during the 1874 elections by Thomas Nast, now symbolic of the Republican Party.

Elephant Diplomacy. See RECOGNITION OF A STATE.

Eleven-week Dictatorship. Reference to U.S. President Abraham Lincoln in the exercise of his war powers when he called the militia to war against the South in 1861. Then, eleven weeks later when the troops were already on the front-line, he called Congress in session to deal with this matter according to the constitution. Lincoln allegedly explained himself in a very conciliatory manner, stating that, because the nation's capital, Washington, D.C., was filled with Southern spies and possible assassins, he had refrained from calling Congress in session earlier so as not to expose it to possible harm. The press was not impressed with that explanation, but since Lincoln had also suspended habeas corpus—meaning critics of the war with the South could be locked up before they were asked questions, there was little public dialogue about it. Had Lincoln lost the war, he would, no doubt, have been tried for treason, but the spoils and benefit of the doubt belong to the victor.

Eleventh Amendment. When U.S. President George Bush was asked by news reporters to characterize the political chances of Patrick Buchanan, his opponent in the 1992 New Hampshire primary, Bush replied that the Republican party's unwritten "Eleventh Amendment" provides, "Do not speak ill of another Republican."

Elimination with Extreme Prejudice. In the language of intelligence services, to kill an opponent or to assassinate a hostile leader. Assassination of foreign leaders is forbidden under a Presidential Order of 1976, issued by President Gerald Ford and upheld by all U.S. Presidents since. Also known as "executive action."

ELINT. See INTELLIGENCE.

Elite. Those who influence or control the outcome of decisions.

Elitist Party. See BACKLASH, MASS PARTY.

Emancipation Proclamation. An order by U.S. President Abraham Lincoln to abolish slavery, first in the revolting states (Sept. 22, 1862), and later in the entire United States (Jan. 1, 1863).

Emergency Force of the United Nations. See PEACE-KEEPING FORCE OF THE UNITED NATIONS.

Emergency Peace-Keeping Force. See PEACE-KEEPING FORCE OF THE UNITED NATIONS.

Emergency Powers. Those powers which the chief executive of a nation-state (e.g., the U.S. President), a state (e.g., a governor), or a local jurisdiction (e.g., a mayor or the chairman of a county board of supervisors or commissioners) may exercise on extraordinary occasions such as in case of a major rebellion, epidemic, labor strike, or a natural disaster (e.g., flood or fire). The principal authorization of emergency powers of the U.S. President, for example, is Art. II, Sec. 3, of the U.S. Constitution, which states in part that "he shall take Care that the Laws be faithfully executed," and Sec. 2 which grants him powers as Commander-in-Chief of the armed forces. Combining these two directives, President A. Lincoln coined the term "war powers" which a President may rightfully exercise without declaring war, which would require congressional approval. See WAR POWERS ACT.

Emigration. See IMMIGRATION.

Eminent Domain. The inherent right of a government to take possession of private or personal property for public use upon just compensation. See EXPROPRIATION.

Emir. In the Arabic language, "to command." Title given to the descendants of Mohammed, founder of Islam, through the line of his daughter, Fatima. Also a ruler, a prince, head of government, head of state, or both in some Arabic countries, e.g., Kuwait.

Emperor Fujimori. A nickname for Peru's president, Alberto Fujimori, who is of Japanese descent and the first person of Japanese descent ever to attain high office in Latin America. He was elected by a nation with practically no Japanese population. President Fujimori is considered one of the ablest politicians, statesmen, and administrators in Latin America. His campaign slogan was: "Work, Honesty, and Technology."

Empirical Reference in Political Theory. See POLITICAL THEORY.

Empirical Theory in Political Science. See POLITICAL THEORY.

Empiricism. In politics, a concept emphasizing experience as the only source of knowledge; also, the search for knowledge through observation and experience. Also a notion that all knowledge of the universe is the result of experience and perception. Perceptions can be those of conceptualization and those of a direct perception. To be accepted as evidence, perceptions must be somehow verified, usually by close observation. In its final analysis, empiricism attempts to define facts and truth in a way similar to how a statutory law attempts to define and delineate justice and fairness. Empirical evidence in political science is not easily achievable. Therefore, to achieve scientific results one must engage in scientific activity through the use of analytic methods, through ethical neutrality (lack of biases and predilections), (generalizations, sound structure and order of inquiry, empirical base, and sound explanations.) Therefore, scientists seek some consensus and engage in continuous and systematic re-definition of theories, going back to Plato and Aristotle, who, among others, laid the foundations for the study of politics. However, as Professor J. Whitehead reminds us in his famous epigram, "A science that hesitates to forget its founders is lost." Philistinism also holds that all classical theories in the literature of politics have only normative ethical relevance. See CONCEPT, POLITICAL THEORY.

Employment Act. See ECONOMIC MESSAGE.

Employment Quota. See AFFIRMATIVE ACTION.

Enabling Act. A legislative act creating or granting certain authority; e.g., an act of the U.S. Congress authorizing the people of a territory to call a constitutional convention and to determine their political status. The U.S. Congress allowed Puerto Rico to hold a national referendum on July 23, 1967, to determine whether the voters wished to remain a commonwealth, become a state in the American Union, or become an independent, sovereign state. The final vote was as follows: for total independence, 4,205 votes; for statehood, 273,315 votes; and for commonwealth, 425,081 votes. Thus Puerto Rico chose to remain a commonwealth.

Encirclement. In international politics, the surrounding of one state by another or by a group of states with hostile intentions (e.g., the state of Israel among the Arab states, or the Soviet Union after the Bolshevik Revolution of 1917). The Founding Father of the Soviet state, Vladimir I. Lenin, coined this term in 1920, when he insisted on retaining a strong army and a strong state—contrary to the teachings of Karl Marx that under a socialist system the state ought to wither away—because the newly-formed Soviet state was encircled by hostile powers with an opposing, capitalist, bourgeois political philosophy and economic mode of production (private enterprise). As long as such hostile encirclement—a *cordon sanitaire*—does exist, the Soviet Republics may not secede from the union in spite of the fact that the Soviet constitution allows it. It was on those grounds—of minimizing the capitalistic encirclement—that Josef Stalin took the Baltic states of Estonia, Latvia, and Lithuania; signed the Molotov-Ribbentrop Pact which divided Poland between Nazi Germany and Soviet Russia; and established the People's Democracies after W.W.II in Eastern Europe. See BREZHNEYEV DOCTRINE, HITLER-STALIN PACT, PEOPLE'S DEMOCRACY, SOCIALISM IN ONE COUNTRY, Appendices 29, 91.

Encomienda. A form of feudal system that was imposed on the Indian population of South America upon the arrival of the Conquistadores from Spain in the 16th century. Trusted Spaniards were assigned groups of Indians; the Indians were to be fed, and given a portion of the profits from their labor; (the Spanish overseers retained a part for themselves, and forwarded a part to the landlord in Spain. The system, in time, evolved into the latifundium—large land estates owned by an absentee owner and cultivated by servants who, in return for food, shelter, and clothing, labored at least twelve hours per day. Many of the contemporary revolutionary movements in Latin America are against the power of the existing latifundia, some of which, as in El Salvador, Costa Rica, Peru, and Colombia, resort to "death squads"—organized bands of killers for hire who are to protect the large landowners from losing their holdings to the landless masses of peasants. Numerous attempts at land reforms—one of the paramount problems in Latin America—have failed throughout the years. In some areas, about one percent of the population owns ninety-percent of the land, or ninety percent of the population owns only about one-percent of the land. The revolutionary movements are basically about land, and ideology (particularly Marxist, communist or socialist) is only a tool of convenience; by claiming adherence to their ideology, the revolutionaries were very often supported, with advice, weapons, and money by the Soviet Union and other socialist/communist states. Communism to these groups is as alien as democracy. Their ideology is tribalism. See FEUDALISM, LATIFUNDIUM, TRIBALISM.

Encyclical. An official written policy statement issued by the Pope of the Roman Catholic Church (who is also head of the Papal State, the Vatican State—Cita del Vaticano) on religious or political matters concerning the Church or Papal State. Some examples are: an Encyclical issued by Pope Leo XIII, *Rerum Novarum,* condemning socialism as a doctrine and any socialist form of government in any state; *Quadragesimo Anno* and *Brennender Sorge,* both issued in the German language by Pope Pius XI, the former advocating a Christian corporate state, the latter condemning Nazism; *Mater Et Magistra,* revising *Rerum Novarum,* issued by Pope John XXIII, containing approval of certain social improvements within the society of men; *Pacem In Terris,* also issued by Pope John XXIII, calling for peace on earth and elimination of nuclear weapons; and *On Human Life,* presented in the English language, by Pope Paul VI, reaffirming the doctrine of the Church on the practice of birth control by all Catholics. Also *Redemptor Hominis,* "Redeemer of Man," by Pope John Paul II, March 15, 1979, and *Laborem Exercens* of 14 September 1981, on condemning forced labor. The latest Papal Encyclical of 1991 is "Centesimus Annus," on the teachings of the Church during the last century and the well-being of the human being in times of continuous wars and misery. Pope John Paul II, who issued the Encyclical, is very much concerned with social issues.

End Sometimes Justifies the Means. A concept epitomizing the political philosophy and governing style of dictators, who, impatient with cumbersome democratic processes, resort to force and violence in order to achieve desired goals regardless of cost. Contemporary dictatorships, such as those in Somalia and Myanmar, struggle to sustain their power even if all those opposed, be it the entire population, are killed off in the process. See MACHIAVELLIANISM.

Ends of Power. See DEFINING THE OPPONENT, POWER.

Enemies' List. See WATERGATE AFFAIR.

Enemy of the People. Denoting one who opposes the official policies of the government. A concept originated by Josef Stalin, General Secretary of the Communist Party of the Soviet Union and Premier of the Soviet Government, 1922-1953. According to Nikita S. Khrushchev who held the same two positions between 1956 and 1964, Stalin first used this concept in 1922, when he became General Secretary of the party, and decided that those who oppose the official policies of the government and the party (both of which were of his making) should be purged from society by any means possible, including death. Khrushchev made this revelation during his famous "destalinization" speech on February 25, 1956, during the Twentieth Congress of the CPSU held in Moscow, USSR. See CULT OF PERSONALITY, DESTALINIZATION.

Enfranchise. To grant the right to vote, elect, or be elected to a person or persons who did not have such a right before; or the right to form a sovereign state (e.g., Amendments XV, XIX, XXIV, and XVI to the U.S. Constitution pertaining to voting rights). See VOTING, VOTING RIGHTS ACT OF 1965, Appendix 8.

Engrossed Bill. The final text of a bill passed in the U.S. Congress and certified by either the Clerk of the House or the Secretary of the Senate.

Enigma. The most advanced ciphering machine for cryptic intelligence communications ever invented by Germany, which has been acquired by Polish intelligence service in Warsaw by Polish intelligence agents, Henryk Zygalski, Marian Rajewski, and Jerzy Rozycki prior to W.W.II, then transferred to England where it aided the Allies read German secret communications throughout the war. This was the only replica of Enigma in existence outside the German intelligence service, the ABWEHR. The British maintained the greatest secrecy about the possession of the ENIGMA replica, which was designated "Ultra Secret," or "Ultra Most Secret" by a stamp which was affixed on all information received with the aid of this precious machine. The "Ultra" generated information enabled many military and civilian leaders on the side of the Allies to become "heroes." There are persistent rumors that Winston Churchill, Britain's wartime Prime Minister, and one of the principal ULTRA traffic recipients, knew in advance of the German Luftwaffe's plans to bomb the City of Coventry, where several thousand persons perished, but did not wish to reveal the Allied ability to read German messages. According to authors Jozef Garlinski (*The Enigma War*), Richard A. Woytak (*On the Border of Peace: Polish Intelligence Diplomacy, 1938-1939 and the Origins of the Ultra Secret*), and Wladyslaw Kozaczuk (*Enigma: How the German Machine Cipher Was Broken, and How It Was Read by the Allies in World War II*). The Polish intelligence officers were able to copy the model of enigma while one of the machines was in transit by a German diplomatic courier at the Warsaw main railroad station. Soon, the Poles made a fully operational prototype, started breaking the German codes and when Nazi forces were invading Warsaw, the prototype was moved to France and then to England. The Poles also helped the British to design a functional computer, known as "bomba," or "bomb," in the English language, which allowed for a more efficient operation of the equipment. See MAGIC, ULTRA.

Enlightened Despot. A term commonly applied to a ruler of a state (absolute monarch, dictator, or a popularly elected national leader) who terrorizes his people for the purpose of improving their lot. (The term is particularly applied to such rulers as Frederick the Great of Prussia, Peter the Great of Russia, Maria Theresa of Austria, Catherine the Great of Russia, Ho Chi-minh of Vietnam, and Mao Tse-tung of China.) The term "benevolent dictator" carries a similar meaning. See DESPOTISM.

Enlightened Pragmatism. See LAMAR SOCIETY.

Ennationalization. An act of changing citizenship and/or loyalties from one state to another, usually as a result of some wrong done by the former state; or an act of disowning a state.

Enrolled Bill. The final copy of the text of a bill or joint resolution which was passed by the legislature and is ready for signatures. See BILL, PUBLIC LAW.

Entangling Alliance. An alliance or treaty obligation which may become detrimental to the interest of the signatory; also, a phrase used by America's first President, George Washington, (1789-1797) to signal a warning to the future leaders of America that they should refrain from such alliances with foreign nations. See FOREIGN POLICY, ISOLATIONISM.

Entente. A loose type of alliance; also, a general understanding between two or more states (or governments) on the conduct of diplomatic relations among themselves or regarding other states (or governments). See ENTENTE CORDIALE, TRIPLE ENTENTE.

Entente Cordiale. In the French language, "friendly mutual understanding between states." Also, the alliance between France and England of April 8, 1904. See ENTENTE, TRIPLE ENTENTE.

Enterprise Zone. A plan developed by conservative economists and leaders of the business community during the late 1970s and supported by U.S. President Ronald Reagan in 1981 as a measure of self-help for inner cities and large and poor urban neighborhoods; whereby, with some federal and private business aid, communities would develop privately owned and operated enterprises for their own needs, providing jobs as well as an opportunity to own and operate small businesses. The U.S. Congress is considering new legislation in order to give more support to the enterprise zone concept, by allowing special tax incentives to businesses which locate in poor, depressed areas, e.g., the Watts area in Los Angeles where riots occurred in 1964 and 1992. In 1992, there were about 2,200 such enterprises zones operating in large cities throughout the United States.

Entirely Yours. See AGGIORNAMENTO.

Entitlements. Per the U.S. Congressional Budget Office, programs that make payments to any person, business, or unit of government that seeks the payments and meets the criteria set in law. The Congress controls these programs indirectly by defining eligibility and setting the benefit or payment rules, rather than directly through the annual appropriation process. The best known entitlements are the major benefit programs, such as Social Security, Medicare, Medicaid. Other entitlements include farm price supports and interest on the federal debt. Under the provisions of the Budget Enforcement Act of 1990, mandatory programs funded through the annual appropriation process are treated for budgetary purposes like entitlements. The rapidly growing entitlements, most resulting from effective lobbying by interest groups without corresponding growth of the national economy, are weakening the entire economic structure of the American economic system, creating income inequity, and causing a general decline of the American society as a whole. See DECADENCE, FREEZING OF THE MIND.

Entrapment. An attempt to covertly or overtly induce one to commit any act, criminal or one of a moral turpitude, and to obtain evidence which subsequently can be used against that person for criminal prosecution, character assassination, or simply for "kiss-and-tell for sale." In politics, the common device is sex and a sex scandal is the best means to destroy a political aspirant to an appointive or elective position of trust, particularly in communities where puritanical hypocrisy is rampant. Since the days of Adam and Eve, the male's pragmatic instinct has been expressed often as an attempt to dominate, possess, and to exercise power over not only the female, but the male as well. It is the inborn natural propensity of the male to diligently and religiously pursue anything that wears a skirt and moves. There are, so far, no recorded cases of entrapment of females for political purposes. In many criminal justice agencies in the United States, including the FBI, the DEA, and others, entrapments are often set up to identify or to arrest criminals, such as in fencing operations—in order to catch thieves selling stolen goods. The practice of entrapment is not new. In 1775, William Penn was tried before the Royal Court in England for making a speech (it was illegal to make speeches. There was a place set up in London Hyde Park where, standing on an empty soap box, one could deliver a political speech, but never challenge the Crown), and he was ordered to put on his hat. Once he did that, he was immediately charged with wearing a hat in the Royal Court, then a serious offense. See AGENT PROVOCATEUR, CHARACTER ASSASSINATION, FENCING, SEXPIONAGE, SEXPOLITICS.

Enumerated Powers. The powers explicitly stated in a written document (constitution) and allocated to a certain branch of the government. (In the U.S. Constitution the powers are enumerated for the legislative, the executive, and the judicial branches of the government as are the powers reserved for the states.) See Appendix 8.

Envelope Ballot. A ballot mailed to a voter who marks it at home and then returns it in person to the polling place on election day. (In the United States, only the state of Delaware uses such ballots.)

Environment Protection Movement. When the Arab states placed an embargo on oil exported to the United States, because of military and economic assistance, including intelligence support, that the United States had extended to Israel in its war against the Arabs in 1974, oil, mining, and timber companies in the United States commenced a huge campaign aimed at using American resources to meet energy needs, concentrating mainly on national park lands, forests, and grazing lands. This created a backlash, and numerous environmental groups sprang up to arrest the trend. Remarks by President Ronald Reagan such as "Trees cause pollution," and "You can't conserve your way to economic growth," antagonized the environmentalists even more. As a result, the government was forced to slow down programs, public and private, which would in any way further undermine the ecosystem. This strong environmental movement, lasting from 1974 to 1982, is known as the "sagebrush rebellion." See HUNGER WARS, Appendices 85, 86.

Environmental Impact Statement. See GOVERNMENT BY LITIGATION, COMPETENCE IMPACT STATEMENT.

Environmental Protection Agency. See GOVERNMENT BY LITIGATION.

Environmental Racism. An allegation voiced periodically by civil rights and environmental protection groups that many hazardous industries (ones that pollute the environment and are dangerous to workers) are located in or near poor, non-white neighborhoods, and that politicians, government officials, and environmental protection agencies make little effort to rectify the situation.

Environmental Study Conference. See CONGRESSIONAL CAUCUS.

Environmental Terrorism. The acts of willful, intentional destruction of the environment which upsets the equilibrium in the ecosystem with harm to fauna and flora (e.g., the setting on fire of the Kuwaiti oil fields by the forces of Iraq's President Saddam Hussein during the Persian Gulf War, 1990-1991 and their intentional release of oil into the Persian Gulf). Also, an act of poisoning the environment as a means of warfare.

Envoy. A diplomatic representative or a special agent who is representing the government or some branch of it externally (e.g., presidential envoy). See DIPLOMATIC RANKS.

Epicureanism. A Hellenic (Greek) school of thought which held that the goal of man should be a life of pleasure regulated not by any government but "serenity," "peace of mind," and "temperance." Its principal proponent, Epicurus, 342-270 BC., after whom the school was named, holds that pleasure is the ultimate goal of life (e.g., anything that any human being does in her or his life is motivated by the search for personal satisfaction and pleasure), and should be sought by matching desires with possibilities (excluding the use of force in order to satisfy personal desires). This political philosophy was expounded by Epicurus' followers (e.g., Titus Lucretius Carus of Rome, 96-55 BC, and the thinkers of the Renaissance.) See HEDONISM.

Epistemology. The study of the genesis, developmental process, and validity of all knowledge; a theory of knowledge. See IDEATION, KNOWLEDGE.

Equal Employment Opportunity Commission (EEOC). A federal agency created by the Civil Rights Act of 1964; its purpose is "to eliminate discrimination based on race, color, religion, sex, national origin, or age in hiring, promotion, firing, setting wages, testing, training, apprenticeship, and all other terms and conditions of employment." The commission oversees compliance with the law and can initiate lawsuits against violators. See SEXUAL HARRASSMENT.

Equal Justice Under Law. An inscription that is permanently placed above the front gate of the U.S. Supreme Court in Washington, D.C. See Appendices 8,27,44-51.

Equal Opportunity, But Not Equal Outcomes. See LEVEL PLAYING FIELD.

Equal Pay Act of 1963. See RESOLUTION.

Equal Proportion Formula. See UNITED STATES HOUSE OF REPRESENTATIVES.

Equal Protection of the Laws Clause. A constitutional provision (contained in Amendment XIV to the U.S. Constitution) which requires states to provide equal protection of the laws to all persons within their jurisdiction (e.g., regardless of race, sex, religion, or national origin). This provision was extensively applied by the Warren Court to protect the rights of blacks and other minorities, including women (e.g., prohibiting malapportionments of state legislatures). The present law of equal protection, according to Judge Robert H. Bork (*The Tempting of America: The Political Seduction of the Law*, The Free Press, 1990), "is unsatisfactory, because there is no adequate explanation for its choice of groups entitled to equal protection or for the differing degrees of protection it affords to the various groups," e.g., the Court applies stricter scrutiny on issues such as race but less on "distinction between economic interests." See APPORTIONMENT, JUDICIAL ACTIVISM, ONE MAN, ONE VOTE, Appendix 8.

Equal Rights Amendment (ERA). See U.S. Constitution, Amendment XXVII in Appendix 8.

Equalitarian. One favoring broad equality of all members of society.

Equality of Opportunity. Under the laws of the United States, each individual is entitled to rewarding employment, to education, to the protection of one's person and property, and to live according to one's choosing, regardless of one's race, creed, religion, sex, nationality, and political or philosophical persuasions. Equality of opportunity does not imply absolute equality. It implies only an opportunity for equality by prohibiting discriminatory acts and activities by one person against another. Absolute equality implies a system or regimented code of behavior in personal interactions as well as a rigid distribution of necessities supporting human life (e.g., food, shelter, medical care, and personal protection from bodily harm)—none of which has ever been achieved anywhere to any degree worth mentioning here. See AFFIRMATIVE ACTION, UTOPIA.

Equilibrium. See BALANCE OF POWER.

Equitable Taxation System. See ABILITY-TO-PAY PRINCIPLE.

Equity. A formal system of legal and procedural rules according to which justice is administered within certain limits of jurisdiction; also, supplementary rules and procedures aiding statutory and common law; a right, fairness, or law made by a judge. Also known as "King's Conscience."

Equity Court. A court of law deciding cases mainly on the basis of equity. Also known as "Keeper of the King's Conscience." See EQUITY.

ERA. See EQUAL RIGHTS AMENDMENT, Appendix 8.

Era of Creativity. On January 8, 1978, Dr. Zbigniew K. Brzezinski, Special Assistant to U.S. President Jimmy Carter for National Security Affairs, referred to the era of the Carter Administration as the "era of creativity." If a settlement is achieved in the Middle East (among the Arabs and the Jews), and the campaign for human rights succeeds this will comprise the so-called "Carter Doctrine" in years to come.

Era of Good Feelings. This phrase epitomizes that period of American political and economic history (mainly under President James Monroe, 1817-1825) when the influence of the Federalist (now the Republican) Party declined; Florida became part of the U.S. (1819); the Missouri Compromise was reached (1820); the Monroe Doctrine was promulgated (1823); and the nation was developing, growing, and prospering in considerable peace and tranquillity.

Eritrean Liberation Front. A separatist political and guerrilla organization in Ethiopia seeking independence and self-government for Eritrea. The organization commenced its separatist activities in 1975 when the monarchy of emperor Haile Selassie was abolished.

Errors and Nonfacts. A favorite phrase used often by the Speaker of the U.S. House of Representatives, 1977-1986, Tip O'Neill, describing media reporters who spoke or wrote with few facts in hand, or those who disseminated wrong information.

Es Necessitate Rei. In the Latin language, "because of the necessity of the cause" or "because the situation warrants the act."

Escalation. An increasing intensity of a war or a confrontation.

Escrow. In the language of law, in the custody of a third party. An object of value (e.g., will, legal papers, stocks, securities, or money) is placed in the custody of an "escrow agent" with the intent of being delivered to the rightful party (the owner) once the conditions stipulated in the written agreement are met.

Esperanto. An artificial language based on the Latin alphabet and using strictly phonetic spelling and pronunciation, devised by Polish oculist and philologist, Ludwig Zamenhof (1859-1917). It was the desire of its inventor that Esperanto should be the official language of diplomacy which would expedite better understanding among nations and eventually help eliminate all future wars.

Espionage Act. A congressional law in the United States (passed on June 15, 1917) prohibiting espionage, sabotage, and other obstruction activities against the United States on behalf of other states, carrying a penalty of $10,000 and/or 20 years imprisonment (or the death penalty in time of war). This legislation was aimed particularly against the socialist elements which were very active in the United States during W.W.I, and which criticized U.S. involvement in foreign wars. Soon after, additional legislation was passed in order to strengthen the Espionage Act; namely, the Enemy Act of 1917, the Sabotage Act of 1918, and the Sedition Act of 1918. This legislation, for example, empowered the U.S. Postmaster General to ban from the mails anything which he himself considered seditious and anti-American, allowed the courts to test the First Amendment to the U.S. Constitution (in *Schenk v. United States*), and sent the leader of the Socialist Party, Eugene V. Debs, to prison for criticizing the American war effort in Europe. See CLEAR AND PRESENT DANGER, RED MENACE, Appendices 8, 48.

Esprit de Corps. In the French language, "morale within a group of men pursuing a common objective" or "high morale."

Esquire. A title of professional distinction designating that one is a licensed attorney and has been admitted to practice law (read and interpret the law and to render service to others as a lawyer or an attorney-at-law). In medieval England the term was used by landed gentry (rich landowners or feudal lords) and later, to designate judicial officers in England (e.g., judges, sergeants or court clerks, lawyers, counselors, or barristers).

Essential Elements of Information (EEI). A series of actual, truthful, and important facts needed in order to assess knowledge about an adversary (e.g., names, places, dates, truthful statements, and other accurate data on which the recipient intelligence service can make an assessment for their leaders). See INTELLIGENCE.

Essential Right. See *POLKA V. CONNECTICUT* in Appendix 48.

Essentialist. Realist.

Essentials of a Democracy. See CONDITIONS OF A DEMOCRACY.

Established Church. A governmentally subsidized (often exclusively) and supported religious organization or denomination.

Establishment. A term often used to identify and/or to describe either of the following: the ruling elite in a given state; the bloc of states in international organizations or gatherings whose will prevails over those of others; or those persons who interact through institutions which hold a dominant position in a given political system (e.g., the eastern establishment, the political and business leaders of the industrial Eastern states, such as New York, Pennsylvania, New Jersey, and Ohio or Michigan, as compared and contrasted with the predominantly rural South which, until recently, had less access to centers where important national policies were made). See EASTERN ESTABLISHMENT.

Establishment Clause. That portion of text in the First Amendment of the U.S. Constitution which forbids the national government to establish or to declare any official church or religion.

Estados. Political subdivisions—states—in Mexico.

Esthetics. The study of the essence and nature of beauty or human sensations (e.g., by Emmanuel Kant); the science of beauty.

Estoppel. In the rules of evidence, a party may not deny anything, written or spoken, which was knowingly acknowledged or accepted as a fact, or a truth.

Estover. In the language of law, certain essentials one is expected to furnish (e.g., the keys to a rented apartment or a house; child or spouse support in the case of a divorce).

L'État C'Est Moi. See I AM THE STATE.

Étatisme. In the French language, "statism." See SENSE OF THE STATE.

Eternal Vigilance is the Price of Liberty. The motto of the Supreme Allied Powers in Europe. See NORTH ATLANTIC TREATY ORGANIZATION (NATO).

Ethics. The study and practice of that which is right and that which is wrong in terms of human conduct and behavior as determined by the existing standards of morality set by a given society (in time and place). See LOBBY, POLITICAL ETHICS.

Ethics Code. See LAST PLANTATION.

Ethics in Politics. See POLITICAL ETHICS.

Ethics Reform Act. Legislation passed by the United States Congress in 1976 and amended since, to the effect that high-ranking federal employees, on leaving office, should refrain, for at least a year, from taking employment in a private industry which was contracting with, or was regulated by, the agency in which the executive was employed.

Ethiopian Revolution. See DERG.

Ethnic Purity. When presidential aspirant Jimmy Carter used this phrase in April 1976, it was considered a "flippant remark" or a "Blooper" by most political analysts, both black and white. He said he did not think the government should "arbitrarily promote intrusion into certain communities by black or alien groups for the purpose of achieving desegregation and equality among citizens." Confronted with a wave of criticism, from black groups as well as his political adversaries (mainly U.S. Senator Henry "Scoop" Jackson, D-Washington), Carter apologized publicly and explained that the statement was not meant to imply racial segregation.

Ethnicity. A group identification of certain people with some characteristics held in common—race, language, national origin, or culture being among the principal factors. In a pluralistic, multi-cultural, multi-ethnic society such as the United States and the former Soviet Union, ethnicity has led to serious frictions among ethnic groups and, in the political arena, to serious conflicts. In the United States, most societal frictions arise among the large black population and among the Chicano, Spanish-speaking population. Demands for use of dual languages in schools and in places of employment are increasingly made by the Spanish-speaking population, there being no policy or law on making American-English the official language of the nation. The old notion of the "melting pot" in America has been replaced with parallel ethnicity but, according to Professor Arthur M. Schlesinger, Jr., *The Disuniting of America,* Norton, 1972), "Using some language other than English dooms people to second-class citizenship." Extreme ethnicism leads to disunity, and weakens the growth of a single national culture. See TOOLS OF ANALYSIS OF A POLITICALLY ORGANIZED SOCIETY.

Ethnocentrism. An attitude of superiority over other groups, races, or cultures.

Ethnographical State. A nation state consisting of people of a single race. See NATIONAL STATE.

Ethological Theory. As pertaining to planning, the application of manners, morality, and ethical values in the development of groups or communities within a society.

EURATOM. See EUROPEAN ATOMIC ENERGY COMMUNITY (EURATOM).

Eureka. See TEHERAN CONFERENCE.

Eurocommunism. A concept coined by Enrico Berlinguer, the Secretary-General of the Italian Communist Party (PCI), which tends to demonstrate in theory and practice that modern communism in Western Europe is dedicated to the preservation, respect, and further advancement of traditional human rights and freedoms; that the interest of the state should not be placed above the interest of the people, and that Eurocommunism (European communism) is the ideology of the future because it addresses itself to the basic needs and aspirations of the human being. This view is contrary to the Soviet version of communism which holds that the interest of the socialist state supersedes that of the individual. Eurocommunism, often referred to as "communism with a human face," or "socialism with a human face" (some communist leaders use the terms "socialism" and "communism" interchangeably), opposes any totalitarian form of government, particularly the Soviet, Chinese, Cuban, and that of any other communist state in Eastern Europe. Expressing his fear that the Communist Party of Italy (PCI) would enter into a government coalition, U.S. President Jimmy Carter stated his view on January 12, 1978, on Eurocommunism and communist parties in Western Europe in general: Italy's Communist party, in his view, did not share democratic "values and interests," and he urged Italy and other Western European nations to do everything possible to reduce the influence of communist parties. The Christian Democratic party of Premier Giulio Andreotti in Italy is a minority party in government, and is seeking a coalition in order to remain in power. The Communists, backed by Socialist and Republican groups, were supporting the Communist party's entry into coalition with the Christian Democrats. This was a great doctrinal change on the part of the Communists—which they themselves called a "historic compromise"—because never before had the Communists in Europe (particularly in France, where the Communist party was the largest and strongest outside the Soviet Union, as well as in Portugal and Italy) been willing to share power with another party, especially one of a Christian orientation. The Communists always sought absolute control without any partnership (e.g., coalition). The major fear was the fact that Italy was a major partner in the European defense alliance under NATO, and that the presence of communist elements in the government of Italy would undermine that alliance. See BREZHNEYEV DOCTRINE.

Eurocracy. A term for the new type of European bureaucracy under the unified system of the European Community introduced in 1992; a bureaucracy, similar to that of the United Nations Organization, that is not particularly loyal to any single state but to the European Community as a whole.

Eurodollar. See EUROPEAN ECONOMIC COMMUNITY (EEC).

European Assembly. A loosely organized quasi-legislative agency of the European Atomic Energy Community, the European Coal and Steel Community, and the European Economic Community, established in Strasbourg, France, in 1958, for the purpose of better utilization of the economic resources of the member-states of the European Community.

European Atomic Energy Community (EURATOM). A West European organization established in 1958 for the purpose of expediting cooperation between member-states in the development and utilization of atomic energy. Its member-states are: the Benelux nations (Belgium, Holland, and Luxemburg), France, West Germany, and Italy.

European Coal and Steel Community (ECSC). A West European organization, first proposed by Robert Schuman, French Foreign Minister in 1950 (also known as the "Schuman Plan"), founded by a treaty signed in Paris on April 18, 1951, and ratified on August 10, 1952, by Belgium, France, West Germany, Italy, Luxemburg, and the Netherlands (Holland). The purpose of the Community is to coordinate among the member-states the production and distribution (fixing prices and abolishing custom duties) of coal and steel. In 1953 the Community established a common market of coal and steel and has undertaken considerable improvements of coal and steel plants. The executive powers of the Community are vested in a High Authority (composed of a president and eight other members) which is empowered to set prices on coal and steel. The decisions of the Authority can be challenged before a Court of Justice (the European Court of Justice) which serves the three European Communities: the Coal and Steel Community, the European Atomic Energy Community, and the European Economic Community. (Since January 1, 1958, the activities of these three communities are directed by the European Assembly, which is composed of representatives selected by the three Communities.)

European Common Market. See EUROPEAN ECONOMIC COMMUNITY (EEC).

European Communism. See EUROCOMMUNISM.

European Convention for the Protection of Human Rights and Fundamental Freedoms. See COUNCIL OF EUROPE, EUROPEAN COURT OF HUMAN RIGHTS.

European Court of Human Rights. A court of law set up by a protocol of the Council of Europe in 1950 and given jurisdiction over civil and criminal matters by conventions. The Court may adjudicate cases brought before it only with the consent of the states involved, or the states which have signed a convention to this effect. The most recent case submitted in January 1992, was that of the Polish minority in Lithuania, which experiences repression from the Lithuanian government, including denial to own property. See Appendices 73, 73-B.

European Court of Justice. A court of law, set up by the European Assembly in 1958, having jurisdiction over disputes arising among any members of the European Coal and Steel Community, the European Atomic Energy Community, and the European Economic Community. See COUNCIL OF EUROPE, EUROPEAN ASSEMBLY.

European Crime Axis. See U.S. INTELLIGENCE COMMUNITY, Appendix 32.

European Defense Community. See NORTH ATLANTIC TREATY ORGANIZATION (NATO).

European Democratic Group. See COUNCIL OF EUROPE, Appendix 73-A.

European Democratic Party. See COUNCIL OF EUROPE, Appendix 73-A.

European Economic Community (EEC) (or Common Market). A West European trade organization established by the Treaty of Rome of 1957, and formed in 1958 for the purpose of coordinating and expediting trade relations and production activities, such as exchange of information, patents, labor, and eventual elimination of all trade restrictions such as tariffs between its member-states. Uniform library cards, equivalency of school diplomas, and uniform driver's license for citizens of EEC countries went into effect in 1986. See Appendices 73, 73-B.

European Energy Charter. During the June 1990 European Economic Community summit conference in Dublin, Ireland, Dutch Prime Minister Ruud Lubbers proposed a modern and comprehensive energy policy for unified Europe, a policy that would provide Europe with sufficient gas and oil, without disruptions in delivery (like that caused by the Arab oil embargo in 1974, which considerably devastated European production and commerce). Subsequently, in July 1991, thirty-five nations commenced the final steps to implement the charter. The oil and gas will come from the former Soviet Union. Lev Voronine, ambassador of the Commonwealth of Independent States to the European Community, pointed out that this arrangement would contribute to peace and stability in Europe, Easter Europe, and the former Soviet Union, because it would bring benefits to all. "How many wars," pointed out Ambassador Voronine, "have there been that in the final reckoning had the smell of oil about them!" If is often said that wars are basically about love, hate, and money, and, since 1939, those who had a sufficient supply of fuel, were victorious; Japan and Nazi Germany lost primarily because of lack of fuel for their aircraft, tanks, and other military vehicles. See ATLANTIC PARTNERSHIP, Appendix 73.

European Free Trade Association (EFTA). An agreement, based on a convention signed on November 20, 1959, in Stockholm, Sweden, and ratified on May 3, 1960, calling for the reduction of tariffs up to fifty per cent on all products (except agricultural commodities) traded between member-states. The members are: Belgium, Britain, Denmark, France, Germany, Greece, Ireland, Italy, Luxembourg, Netherlands, Portugal, and Spain. Waiting in the wings for an admission now, in 1992, are: Czech and Slovak Federative Republic, Hungary, Poland, and Turkey. In 1991, the Community introduced new currency, called an "European Currency Unit," or "ECU," but, according to reports, the Germans, as voiced by Chancellor Helmut Kohl, do not like that name, because to them it sounds like a "cow,"—"Kuh" in the German language. Some Frenchmen proposed calling the currency simply "coo-coo." This currency will replace all others, including the Eurodollar, or European Dollar. Other European nations formed what are called "European Free Trade Associations," because they pursue the policy of neutrality, which precludes them from taking sides in political matters, but which shall trade among themselves just like the other nations under the European Community. They are:

Austria, Finland, Iceland, Sweden, and Switzerland. See EUROPEAN ECONOMIC COMMUNITY (EEC), Appendix 73.

European Home. Soviet President and General Secretary of the Soviet Communist Party (CPSU), Mikhail S. Gorbachev (1985-1991), declared in 1990 that the Soviet Union had no intention of remaining an isolated empire, but wanted to find its home in Europe where it belongs. See Appendix 73.

European Integration. See COUNCIL OF EUROPE.

European Liberal Party. See COUNCIL OF EUROPE, Appendix 73-A.

European Movement. See COUNCIL OF EUROPE.

European Parliament. See COUNCIL OF EUROPE.

European People's Party. See COUNCIL OF EUROPE, Appendix 73-A.

European Recovery Program. See MARSHALL PLAN.

European Reformers Group. See COUNCIL OF EUROPE, Appendix 73-A.

Eurovote. American citizens who reside abroad (e.g., business employees, students, researchers, or those who simply desire a change of lifestyle) and who take an active part in American electoral politics. A large concentration of Americans (and some of the most well informed about politics) who, through effective organization, select delegates to stateside political party conventions and vote through absentee ballot.

Evacuation Tax. A levy on income that may be imposed upon industries, particularly those that either heavily pollute the environment or contribute to the congestion of an area, in order to encourage them to relocate to underdeveloped rural areas. Such tax is being seriously considered by the Japanese Diet (Parliament) and other industrial nations, particularly in Western Europe.

Every President Needs an S.O.B. A statement that was made by Harry Robbins Haldeman, Special Assistant to President Richard M. Nixon (1969-1974), during a press conference in 1972, just before the Watergate scandal. He stated that his job, as special assistant to the President and chief-of-staff, was to create a "Berlin Wall" around the President in order to keep out "those who had no legitimate business . . . Every President needs an S.O.B., and I'm Nixon's."

Every Worker a Manager. See PARTICIPATORY MANAGEMENT.

Evil Empire. U.S. President Ronald Reagan so characterized the Soviet Union (established by V. I. Lenin in 1922, and formally dissolved under President Mikhail S. Gorbachev in 1991) during his March 1983 speech before the National Association of Evangelicals, because of its adversary and hostile policies toward the United States and its allies, its extensive military and intelligence activities against the Western democracies, and an all-out effort to destroy and to conquer the West. See GREAT COMMUNICATOR, WINDOW OF VULNERABILITY.

Evolution Theory. See ORIGIN OF THE STATE THEORIES.

Ex Aequo et Bono. In the Latin language, "according to what is good and just."

Ex Cathedra. In the Latin Language, "a pronouncement by a high authority" or "an offhand ruling."

Ex More. In the Latin language, "according to custom."

Ex Officio. In the Latin language, "by virtue of the office held," "because of the position held," or "as a result of the office held."

Ex Parte. In the Latin language, "one side only," "in the interest of one party," or "in the name of one party." Also, a legal term pertaining to court proceedings where there is no adverse party present, or in cases where the adverse party is unable to be present and give testimony.

Ex Post Facto Law. A law calling for punishment for an act committed before such act was made illegal. The U.S. Constitution, Art. I, Sec. 10, explicitly forbids the states to pass such legislation, pursuant to the legal principle based on Roman law; namely, the principle of *lex retro not agit* (in the Latin language, "a new rule of law does not apply retroactively") which broadly stipulates that: (1) no person can be punished for an act committed when at the time of the commission such act was not forbidden by law; (2) the rules of law and punishment cannot have retroactive application; (3) no rule of law can be altered to the disadvantage of the accused person; and (4) no protection under the law can be decreased.

Ex Rel. See EX RELATIONE.

Ex Relatione. In the Latin language, "by the relation" or "as related to."

Exchequer, Chancellor of. An official of the British Government in charge of the Treasury, and one who supervises the activities of the Auditor and the Comptroller General of Great Britain.

Excise Tax. A levy imposed by federal and/or state governments on certain imported or domestic goods or services.

Exclusionary One-Party System. A tightly-knit political organization whose primary objective is to maintain political power for the few by excluding the many on some grounds such as religion, political and philosophical outlook, or race (e.g., the CPSU in the USSR; the Black Muslim party in the USA., which until recently was not open to whites; or the National party in South Africa which admits neither blacks nor coloreds). Also known as "elitist party."

Exclusive Jurisdiction. Also known as "judicial franchise." Discretion exercised by court judges within existing legal limits, without outside interference being considered, except in the case of error, which can be revealed upon appeal to a higher tribunal.

Exculpatory Evidence. Evidence that can be presented in a court of law by either an eyewitness or by experts, pertaining to the commission of crime, such as in cases of obscenity. See CORPUS DELICTI.

Executive Action. See ELIMINATION WITH EXTREME PREJUDICE.

Executive Aggrandizement. See ASSERTIVENESS.

Executive Agreement. An agreement that the President of the U.S. may enter into, without congressional "advice and consent," with a foreign government within the limits of the Constitution. A newly elected President may (or may not) keep such an agreement made by his predecessor in force. Executive agreements do not constitute a part of the law of the land as the Constitution treaties and statutes do. See TREATY.

Executive Assertiveness. See ASSERTIVENESS.

Executive Branch. A branch of government (federal or state) responsible for the task of expediting, exacting, and supporting laws created by the Legislature and defined by the judicial branch; executives include the President, Vice President, their advisers, and certain departments and agencies at the federal level, governors and staff members at state level; some legislation is proposed by this branch of government; the power to guide both domestic and foreign policy and to make appointments are privileges of the executive branch, although these powers are restrained by the checks and balances system.

Executive Calendar. A nonlegislative calendar kept in the U.S. Senate in which items pertaining to ratification of treaties, nominations of persons to governmental posts, and other documents submitted by the President are kept, and which require the Senate's "advice and consent."

Executive Clemency. By right established either by custom (e.g., under monarchies), or by law (e.g., in the United States), the chief executive, as well as the governors of the several states in the American union, may exercise the right to spare the life of a person convicted to die, or to release a person from confinement. Also known as "presidential" or "gubernatorial" pardon.

Executive Immunity. See EXECUTIVE PRIVILEGE.

Executive Offices of the President of the United States. The noncabinet-status offices under personal supervision of the President of the U.S. They are: White House Office, Office of Management and Budget, Council of Economic Advisors, National Security Council, Federal Property Council, Office of Special Representative for Trade Negotiations, Council on International Economic Policy, Council on Environmental Quality, Domestic Council, Office of Telecommunications Policy, Council of Drug Abuse Policy, and Office of Science and Technology Policy. See Appendix 14.

Executive Order. An order issued by the President of the U.S. which is published in the *Federal Register* and can be enforced, but one which requires no congressional confirmation.

Executive Oversight of Intelligence. See INTELLIGENCE OVERSIGHT.

Executive Perquisites. See PERK MAN.

Executive Privilege. The practice, based on custom rather than on law, of not requiring the President of the U.S. or any officer within the executive branch of the federal government to appear before either House of Congress, any of its committees or subcommittees, to testify or to answer questions directed by the judicial branch of the government, without the consent of the President. This doctrine was shattered during the Watergate era (1972-1974) due to the following developments. On July 23, 1973, President Nixon refused to release certain tapes as requested by the federal prosecutor (the existence of which his former assistant, Butterfield, disclosed to the Watergate Committee on July 16, 1973) on the grounds of executive privilege and the separation of powers principle. The U.S. Supreme Court ruled on August 3, 1974 (in *United States v. Nixon*), denying Nixon the benefits of executive privilege, and ordering the President to turn over the tapes. The Court stated, "Neither the doctrine of separation of powers, nor the need for confidentiality of high-level communications . . . can sustain an absolute, unqualified, presidential privilege of immunity from judicial process under all circumstances." On August 4, 1974, the President released three tapes as ordered by the Court, which revealed that throughout the Watergate ordeal, numerous attempts had been made to deploy the FBI to stop the Watergate probe on the grounds of danger to national security. On August 8, 1974, President Nixon resigned. On September 12, 1975, the House Select Committee on Intelligence submitted a request to the White House for certain information, but President Ford ordered Dr. Henry A. Kissinger, the Secretary of State, not to comply. When Congress threatened him with a contempt citation, President Ford gave in and complied with the Committee's request. Congress rejected the doctrine of executive privilege in this case, because the White House intelligence investigation panel, under Vice President Nelson Rockefeller, did not furnish Congress with all its findings. The first subpoena ever served by a federal court on a U.S. President was in 1807, when Chief Justice John Marshall asked President Thomas Jefferson to testify in the case of Vice President Aaron Burr who was charged with treason. President Jefferson never answered the subpoena, and the matter was not pursued any further. In the case of *Nixon v. Sirica* of 1973, when Federal Judge John Sirica requested that the White House tapes be released, the precedent, that a subpoena can be served on a U.S. President effectively was established. The doctrine of executive privilege is as old as the notion of an "executive" itself. Under monarchies, kings, tsars, and emperors have often enjoyed unlimited privileges, and, more often than not, have used them to the fullest extent. In the Middle Ages, for example, feudal lords considered as part of their executive privileges such notorious practices as spending the first night with the bride of a newly-wed serf (known as the "right to the first night"). See CENTRAL INTELLIGENCE AGENCY, Appendix 48.

Executive Session. See SUB ROSA.

Existentialism. A philosophy (primarily of an ethical nature) which holds that there is no essential human nature common to all men, but that each individual creates his own essence of character throughout his lifetime by his choices; thus existence precedes essence, since the latter is not completed until life and its endless series of choices is terminated by death. Existentialism involves little respect for any form of governmental authority. The movement was originated by Soren Kierkegaard (1813-1855), a Danish philosopher; was further developed by two German philosophers, Martin Heidegger (1889-1976) and Karl Jaspers (1883-1955); and in France after W.W.II by Jean Paul Sartre (1905-1980) and Albert Camus (1913-1960).

Exit Polling. The practice in elections, particularly in the United States, of interviewing persons coming out from a voting booth in order to ascertain for whom they voted and why.

Exitus Acta Probat. In the Latin language, "the event justifies the act."

Expansionism. See IMPERIALISM.

Expatriation. Voluntary or involuntary departure of persons from one state to another usually upon resigning (voluntarily or involuntarily) the citizenship of the state from which they depart. See CITIZENSHIP, LOYALTY LAW.

Expeditious Transit. See PANAMA CANAL TREATIES.

Experiments on Behavior Control. See BEHAVIOR CONTROL PROGRAM.

Explanation. See FORECAST.

Expressed Powers. Authority that is clearly and precisely stated and expressly granted to the various levels or branches of government. See U.S. Constitution, Art. I, Appendix 8.

Expropriation. The act of forceful and involuntary transfer of ownership of property located on a foreign soil, with or without compensation (e.g., property of Americans which has been confiscated in Cuba under Fidel Castro, or some American holdings in Tsarist Russia). In the United States, involuntary transfer of ownership of property must be decided by an appropriate adjudicative agency (court of law or an administrative court). In case of transfer of property under the eminent domain principle, the owner must be paid a "fair market value." See INDEMNIFICATION OF FOREIGN-OWNED PROPERTY, INDEMNITY.

Extended Family. See ATOMIC FAMILY, NUCLEAR FAMILY.

External Transition. See PRESIDENTIAL TRANSITION.

Extinction of States. See MONTEVIDEO DECLARATION.

Extortion. To obtain funds or data by the use of intimidation; an unlawful use of power or rank to gain money.

Extraconstitutional. Outside or beyond the scope of constitutional provisions.

Extradition. The forceful detention and return of a fugitive from justice to the authority under whose jurisdiction that fugitive committed a crime. The term "rendition" is often used among the states in the United States.

Extralegal. Outside the law or beyond the scope of law; illegal or not provided for by law. See INFORMAL POWER.

Extraordinarily Brutal Right to Dominate Others. See LEBENSRAUM.

Extraordinary Commission for Combating Counterrevolution, Sabotage, and the Dereliction of Duty (CHEKA). In the Russian language, "Czerezvytchaynaya Kommisya k'Borby Konterrevolutzyi. Sabotadgzu, y Ofitzyalnych Prostuplenyi." Sometimes referred to as "All-Russian Extraordinary Commission for Combating Counterrevolution, Sabotage, and the Dereliction of Duty, (Czerezvytchayka)." An investigative and policing agency established in 1917, after the successful Bolshevik Revolution, for the purpose of combating all opposition to the newly-formed communist regime of Vladimir I. Lenin. The agency was established and headed by Feliks Dzierzynski, a Polish aristocrat and a loyal friend of Lenin. In 1922, the CHEKA was reorganized and renamed State Political Administration (GPU). (In the Russian language, "Gosudartsvyennoye Politiczeskoye Upravlyenye.") See COMMITTEE FOR STATE SECURITY (KGB).

Extraterritorial. Beyond one's territory. A principle of international law granting a sovereign state the right to supervise its citizens, nationals, and mainly diplomatic personnel located outside the jurisdiction of the state, as well as property, ships, vessels on high seas, or aircraft flying over the territory of another state. See DIPLOMATIC IMMUNITY, RIGHT TO INNOCENT PASSAGE.

Extraterritorial Crime. See EXTRATERRITORIAL, JURISDICTION.

Extraterritorial Right. See EXTRATERRITORIAL, INTERNATIONAL LAW, TREATY.

Extremism. The view that purports extreme change of an economic, political, or social system (or any part of it). In popular usage, extremism stands for political radicalism of any form or variety such as of the left or the right (e.g., communism, Nazism, anarchism, etc.). On the extreme left, the guerrilla communism of the Chinese, Vietnamese, and Cambodian kind (one that is characterized by an irregular, unconventional, insurgency-type of partisan military activity) proved to be an effective means of gaining state power. On the extreme right, particularly in the United States, the struggle for the preservation of the *status quo* is mainly ideological, and of a non-insurgency type. The leader of the John Birch Society, Robert Welch, went even as far as to suspect America's national leaders of being communist agents: "... put bluntly," Welch writes in *The Politician,* "I personally think that he (Eisenhower) has been sympathetic to ultimate Communist aims ... and consciously serving the Communist conspiracy, for all his adult life .... But my firm belief that Dwight Eisenhower is a dedicated, conscious agent of the Communist conspiracy is based on an accumulation of detailed evidence .... " See JOHN BIRCH SOCIETY.

Extroversion. See KLINGBERG CYCLE.

Eye for an Eye, a Tooth for a Tooth. See HAMMURABI CODE.

Eyes of the Law. See VICTIMLESS CRIME.

"There is no finer investment for any community than putting milk into babies."

SIR WINSTON CHURCHILL, 1874-1965

Fabian Socialism. See FABIAN SOCIETY.

Fabian Society. A socialist, non-Marxist organization founded in England in 1884, by a group of middle class intellectuals which advocated the confiscation of all land and capital and vesting them in the entire community for the benefit of all. The Society was named after Fabius Cuntactor, the Roman general who had distinguished himself in exhausting the forces of Hannibal by deploying various delaying tactics in warfare. (The famous playwright, George Bernard Shaw, was one of its strongest supporters and the first registered member of the society.)

Faction. A minor political party or a splinter group within one party; also, a group of persons having certain views in common regarding the government or its policies (e.g., the Federalists and the Anti-Federalists in early America).

Fair Deal. On September 6, 1945, U.S. President Harry S. Truman (1944-1953) sent a message to the U.S. Congress in which he outlined a twenty-one point program for domestic legislation. These points included: extensive benefits to the entire population, such as higher income, minimum wages, rural electrification, flood control, full employment, and an end to segregation in the armed forces and all agencies of the federal government. His call for desegregation eventually led to the split of the Democratic Party in 1948, the emergence of the strong Southern wing, the Dixiecrats, under the leadership of South Carolina's S. Strom Thurmond, and a move to impeach the President, which did not advance very far. See DIXIECRATS.

Fair Employment Practices Agreement. See LAST PLANTATION.

Fair Labor Standards Act. Essentially a wage-and-hour law. It classified jobs for children into three categories: a) completely exempt; b) nonpermissible for children 14-15 years old; c) too hazardous for children 16-18. The act also set minimum wages and hours allowances. The wages section of the law has increased over the years by acts of Congress.

Fairness Doctrine. The practice that allowed opposing political parties to express their views via public news media (e.g., radio or television) on an equal basis by allotting them equal time. In December, 1979, President Jimmy Carter requested the three major networks, ABC, CBS and NBC, to sell him 30 minutes of prime time. All three networks had refused Carter 30 minutes of time in November on the grounds that at that time "only local scattered contests" were occurring in the pre-primary period and promised to give the President time after January 1, 1980. On November 30, 1979, the FCC ruled that the networks ignored the particular needs of the candidates, which is contrary to the reasonable access law. Carter needed the air time in December to coincide with his announcement to run for re-election, which he made on December 4. The FCC condemned the "blanket approach" by the networks. The U.S. Court of Appeals ruled that under the FCC's "reasonable access" law, a blanket refusal of TV time to a qualified candidate for a public office was not fair. The Federal Court so ruled on March 14, 1980, which then made it more difficult for the major networks to refuse time arbitrarily. The doctrine was repealed in 1987, but U.S. Democratic Senator of South Carolina, Ernest F. Hollings, proposed in June 1991, that the doctrine be restored. See CAMPAIGN FINANCING.

Faithless Elector. See PRESIDENTIAL ELECTOR.

Falange. The Spanish Fascist organization created in 1933 by José Antonio Primo de Rivera (the son of the Spanish dictator, 1923-1931), and continued by Generalissimo Francisco Franco as the only legal and ruling political party in Spain until Franco's death in 1975. In modern times the party's official name was the "National Movement," and Franco was its president until 1975. See SACERDOTAL SOCIETY OF THE HOLY CROSS AND OPUS DEI.

Falkland Islands War. On 2 April 1982, an Argentine force of 2,000 soldiers defeated the 84-man Royal Marine force in South Georgia, and on 14 June 1982, the Argentine forces surrendered to the British and ended the conflict. The United States aided the British by providing satellite intelligence on the Argentine order of battle and on troop movements. The final losses were: for the British—225 lives, 34 aircraft, 2 destroyers, 3 frigates, and 7 other crafts; Argentina—714 lives, 102 aircraft, 1 cruiser, 2 submarines, and 11 other crafts. The Islands are called the "Malvinas" by the Argentines. Subsequently, the government of Argentine President Leopoldo Galtieri was removed from power.

Falk Laws. See KULTURKAMPF.

FALN. Puerto Rican revolutionary organization demanding total independence of Puerto Rico, which enjoys the status of a commonwealth under U.S. jurisdiction. See FUERZAS ARMADAS DE LIBERACION NACIONAL.

False-Flag. A practice common among intelligence officers, of attempting to recruit agents for espionage purposes by deceptive means (e.g., never revealing the state or agency which the recruiting agent represents and, instead, making the recruitees believe that the agent represents some other state or organization). The Soviet KGB, for example, often used that tactic, making recruitees believe they represented a peace-loving organization in the West rather than a Soviet intelligence service. See INTELLIGENCE.

Family[2]. See MAFIA.

Family Jewels. See COUNTERINSURGENCY IN AMERICA.

Family Planning. To limit the rate and number of offspring of a country through education and birth control.

Family Protection Party. See PROHIBITION PARTY.

Famous Virginians. See VIRGINIA: MOTHER OF PRESIDENTS.

Farabundo Marti National Liberation Front (FMLN). A revolutionary guerrilla-type organization which has struggled for power in El Salvador since the late 1970s. Their main objective was land reform, since large land estates were deploying private armies, so-called "death squads," to assassinate public and private reform leaders. In January 1992, the FMLN agreed to surrender, integrate itself into society and share power with President Alfred Cristiani and his ARENA political party. The total casualties for the 12-year war period, 1978-1990, were about 100,000 dead, with about 25 percent of that from the death squads. Killings by death squads also occurred in other Latin American states (e.g., Brazil, Argentina, Nicaragua, Peru, and Chile).

Farm Block. A group of congressmen, both Democratic and Republican, hailing from the midwest, whose purpose is to attempt to entice the government to approve policies beneficial to farmers.

Farm State. In 1978, the communist-controlled state of Cambodia implemented a national policy to eradicate forever all cities and urban areas and their accompanying life style, and to transfer the urban population into the rural areas to live as peasants on the land. The government also abolished the traditional currency as a medium of exchange and returned to the ancient barter system. All persons who for generations had lived in cities and towns, were forcibly removed to seek a means of survival, without government assistance of any kind, in rural areas by growing primary crops and tending domestic animals through informally organized communes. See KHMER ROUGE, YEAR ZERO.

Farmandehi. See SHAH.

Farmer-Labor Party. A minor political party in the United States with socialist leanings which advocated, among other things, relief for farmers, government ownership of all public utilities and basic natural resources, legislation favoring labor, and American noninterference in European affairs. In 1920, the party nominated Paul P. Christensen for president, and, upon his failure to become elected, the party disintegrated.

Farmer's Alliance. A secret political organization of Texas farmers which, in 1874, attempted to capture control of the Democratic Party in the South.

Fasces. See FASCISM.

Fascho. See FASCISM, NATIONAL SOCIALIST WORKERS' PARTY OF GERMANY.

Fasci di Combattimento. See FASCISM.

Fascism. The political organization founded in 1919 by Benito Mussolini which allowed him, in 1922, to gain power and to install himself as the dictator (Il Duce) of Italy. The term "fascism" comes from "fasces," a bundle of thin rods with an ax across the top which in ancient Rome was the symbol of temporal power. Roman officials carried that symbol which by itself commanded obedience to the authority it represented, as a police officer's badge does today. Some forms of fascism were adopted by Adolf Hitler in Germany, (1933-1945); in Spain by Francisco Franco (1892-1975), there being called "falangism," and in many states in Latin America. On a lesser scale, some small European states also followed some of the tenets of fascism. Some of the characteristics of fascism were: extreme nationalism versus internationalism; egocentrism; disregard for democratic ideals and institutions; cult leadership (e.g., the Führer in Germany, Il Duce in Italy, and Caudillo in Spain); stiff internal discipline and obedience from citizens; control of the economy; and, internally, collective leadership. Some communist leaders (e.g., Josef Stalin in the Soviet Union, (1924-1953)) also adopted some of the practices and rituals of fascism. Fascism in all varieties stood for law and order, with stiff penalties for offenders, both political and common; execution immediately after a brief trial was common. Strict discipline was strongly emphasized in the military, government service, and education, as was thrift, vigor, and hard work. U.S. President Franklin D. Roosevelt (1933-1945) was himself impressed with some of the achievements of Italian fascism as he wrote in a letter to his ambassador to Italy in 1933. He was, he wrote, "deeply impressed by what (Mussolini) has accomplished and by his evidenced honest purpose of restoring Italy." Mussolini, it was said, was fanatically concerned with having the Italian trains, like those in Germany, run on time! Mussolini was caught by the Italian partisans and was executed, together with his mistress and dedicated assistant, Clara Petacci, on 27 April 1945. Their bodies, hanging with heads down, were displayed in a public place for several days—retribution for having dragged Italy into a losing war.

Fast Track Authority. The delegation of authority, or special powers by one agency of the government to another for the sake of expediency to deal with a certain issue at hand (e.g., the U.S. Congress may grant the executive branch, the U.S. President, authority to deal with certain issues by a presidential policy, presidential directive, or presidential order or finding, rather than pass a statute to this effect and then let the executive branch enforce it).

Fatah (or Al Fatah). A guerrilla-type organization composed mainly of Palestinian Arabs dedicated to the cause of freeing Palestine from Israeli control. See PALESTINE LIBERATION ORGANIZATION (PLO), Appendices 95, 102.

Fatalism. A notion holding that nothing that the individual or the society does will, in the final analysis, affect its destined fate; a philosophy of life commonly held by oppressed and exploited societies, political systems, or ruling elites.

Father of Monetarism. See SINGLE-MINDED IDEALIST.

Fatigue of Compassion. It is the general consensus among contemporary leaders of states and national and international charitable agencies and organizations that natural disasters (e.g., drought, earthquakes, floods, rainstorms) and man-made disasters (e.g., pollution, destruction of the ecosystem, war, and hate crimes), may cause a general disrespect and disregard for the welfare and well-being of human beings. Greedy and incompetent leaders may abandon concern for people, including their own; terror may grow to the extent that the crimes of mass genocide (e.g., by Adolf Hitler of Germany (1933-1945), or Pol Pot of Cambodia (1972-1985), may look, in time, by comparison, as mercy by an angel. Human will and material resources no longer meet the needs for compassionate care for humans, many of whom engage in warfare due to persistent lack of food (e.g., as in contemporary Somalia). See HUNGER WARS, KHMER ROUGE, YEAR ZERO.

Favelas. Makeshift slums on the outskirts of Rio de Janeiro or São Paulo.

Favorite Son. The practice of casting votes for a person from within the state in a national election (mainly presidential) or national party convention who later, if not successful in getting elected, will at least be in a position to bargain and trade his votes for some favors.

FBI. See FEDERAL BUREAU OF INVESTIGATION.

FCC. See FEDERAL COMMUNICATION COMMISSION.

FDIC. See FEDERAL DEPOSIT INSURANCE CORPORATION.

Fear as an Instrument of Political and Social Control. See MACHIAVELLIANISM.

February Revolution. The overthrow of Tsar Nicholas II of Russia and his regime in February 1917, by the revolutionary forces led by Alexander Kerensky (later the head of the provisional government, which was overthrown again in October of the same year by the followers of Vladimir I. Lenin, the Bolsheviks, and their Red Army).

FEC. See FEDERAL ELECTION COMMISSION.

Federal Administrative Regions. Ten regions created in 1969, for the decentralization of federal decision making and coordination of federal programs and assistance to state and local governments in receiving federal aid. Composed of regional directors of major federal agencies. See Appendix 43.

Federal Budget. See GOVERNMENT BUDGET.

Federal Bureau of Investigation (FBI). A semi-independent branch of the U.S. Department of Justice, established in 1908, to investigate all violations of federal laws within the United States and to report its findings to the Department for possible prosecution. The Bureau also has jurisdiction over counter-espionage activities and cooperates closely with other federal investigative and intelligence agencies (e.g., the Central Intelligence Agency and the Secret Service), as well as state and local law enforcement organizations, particularly through the training of law enforcement officers in its Academy, and the sharing of investigative techniques (e.g., through its Crime Information Center). During the past several decades, especially under the strong leadership of its first Director, J. Edgar Hoover (1924-1972), the Bureau has been instrumental in unmasking many subversive (mainly espionage) activities as well as organized crime (e.g., the Mafia and the Cosa Nostra). During the 1960s the Bureau was extensively involved in surveillance activities against individuals (e.g., civil rights leader, Dr. Martin Luther King, Jr.) and organizations which challenged some of the policies of the government (e.g., its involvement in the war in Vietnam), and in intelligence-gathering outside of the United States, for which it was strongly criticized. On January 24, 1978, U.S. President Jimmy Carter (1977-1981), issued an Executive Order which forbids the FBI from maintaining intelligence activities abroad (this is the domain of the Central Intelligence Agency) and from practicing surveillance on U.S. citizens and resident aliens (called "United States Persons") through any means without authorization by the President and approval by the U.S. Attorney General. Unlike the CIA, the FBI has police powers (e.g., can arrest and detain persons suspected of a crime). See CENTRAL INTELLIGENCE AGENCY, RED MENACE, SCUM, Appendices 26, 27, 32.

Federal Campaign Financing Act of 1974. A congressional law designed "to cleanse the political process" in the United States by providing public financing of presidential campaigns by major political parties in the United States. See CAMPAIGN FINANCING.

Federal Circuit Court. See CIRCUIT COURT.

Federal Communication Commission (FCC). Quasi-judicial, quasi-legislative agency of the U.S. Government charged with the task of setting standards and generally regulating communications media, such as radio and television stations and other communication facilities.

Federal Court of Appeals. See CIRCUIT COURT.

Federal Debt. See NATIONAL DEBT OF THE UNITED STATES.

Federal Deposit Insurance Corporation (FDIC). Quasi-judicial quasi-legislative agency of the American Federal Government charged with underwriting the guarantee of bank savings and deposits (up to $100,000 of value per depositor).

Federal Digest. A federal publication in the U.S. listing all cases brought before federal courts, including brief statements on the issues involved in each case.

Federal Election Commission (FEC). A federal semi-independent agency created in 1975 to enforce federal laws on election campaign financing, as a result of the misuse of campaign funds revealed by the Watergate scandal. Under the "Federal Election Campaign Act" of 1974, which provided for federal financing of presidential primaries and general elections, Political Action Committees (PACs) could contribute no more than $1,000 to any presidential or congressional candidate, and were limited, in a one-year period, to no more than $25,000 in contributions. On 18 March 1985, the Supreme Court ruled (in *FEC v. National Conservative Political Action Committee*) that such limitations denied freedom of speech. Such limitation, said the Court, was ". . . like allowing a speaker in a public hall to express his views while denying him the use of an amplifying system." Federal financing was made available to candidates who raised some campaign money on their own in at least twenty states; and if presidential candidates accept the limits imposed on private contributions, almost all campaign expenses may be paid from the federal treasury. The law requires candidates to disclose their finances in writing and to make periodic reports of expenditures. Money, being the mother's milk of politics, is, and has been since political parties began elections, an important attribute. Every U.S. politician receives money from many sources through many ways and means. President Harry S. Truman (1945-1953), was not a wealthy man, and he was not much in favor of a Jewish state, but he voted in 1948 to recognize Israel, because he was told that there was no money for his campaign expenses, and there were people willing to rectify that situation. Two political operatives and Zionists, Ed Kaufman, a jewelry store operator, and Abe Feinberg, who made a fortune during W.W.II supplying the U.S. Government with needed war supplies, promptly filled Truman's campaign chest with $100,000 (the equivalent, in terms of political matters, of about $5 million dollars in 1992). For example, as of 31 January 1992, presidential hopefuls in the United States, who have collected contributions in at least twenty states, will receive federal funds to match individual contributions under $200, each in the following amounts. Republicans: George Bush (incumbent), $4.2 million; Patrick Buchanan (opposing Bush), $1.23 million. Democrats: Bill Clinton $2.06 million; Tom Harkin, $1.57 million; Bob Kerry, $1.27 million; A. Fullani, $891,038; Jerry Brown, $552,761; and Douglas Wilder, $289,027. During his February 1992 campaign in the New Hampshire presidential primary, when Senator Tom Harkin was asked how it felt to campaign for the same spot with so many other candidates, he replied jokingly: "It's like being Elizabeth Taylor's seventh husband. I know what I'm supposed to do. But I just don't know if I can make it interesting." See CAMPAIGN FINANCING, KISS AND TELL FOR SALE.

Federal Executive Boards. See Appendix 43.

Federal Government. See FEDERALISM.

Federal Grand Jury. See GRAND JURY.

Federal Income. The sources of federal revenue (income) in the United States are: (1) individual income taxes (taxes on wages and salaries which are deducted by employers and forwarded to the federal treasury); (2) custom duties (fees and fines collected on goods brought into the country from abroad in excess of the $200 allowable tax-free import of goods); (3) corporation income taxes (deducted from corporate income which may be as high as 50% of the total income); (4) social insurance taxes and contributions to the social insurance trust fund—Social Security and Medicare and Medicaid (mainly the payroll deductions on wages and salaries which are paid equally by the employer and the employee); (5) excise taxes (fees of approximately 10% of the value of certain goods that are considered nonessential or luxury, such as objects of art, automobiles and jewelry, and fees on certain services and activities, such as the use of federal facilities for private purposes); (6) estate and gift taxes (e.g., inheritance of buildings, land, real-estate, or other valuables that an individual acquires as a result of a will, for example); and (7) miscellaneous receipts (e.g., fines by federal courts upon conviction or a fee for obtaining a passport). Personal and corporate income taxes amount to approximately 52% of the federal income; social insurance taxes (e.g., Social Security or FICA) amount to approximately 31% of federal income, and excise taxes amount to approximately 12% of federal income. See BUDGET, GOVERNMENT BUDGET, Appendices 37, 38.

Federal Information Center. An agency of the U.S. Federal Government, established in 1976, which now serves as an information dissemination center on and about the federal government in Washington, D.C. It furnishes available information to anyone via the mails or the telephone on all matters pertaining to the organization and location of agencies, but not on political, policy, or personal matters.

Federal Mediation and Conciliation Service (FMCS). An agency of the Federal Government in the U.S., with no quasi-judicial or quasi-legislative powers, created by the *Labor-Management Relations Act of 1947,* for the purpose of settling disputes over wages, working hours, and other fringe benefits of labor. The director (appointed by the President and confirmed by the Senate) is assisted in his work by the National Labor-Management Panel (composed of six representatives from labor and six from management, appointed by the U.S. President) which advises him on the ways best suited to avoid controversies that could be detrimental to the national economy.

Federal Office for the Protection of the Constitution (Bundesamt für Verfassungsschutz.) A federal semi-independent agency of the German Federal Republic of Germany charged with combating all anti-German activities through counterintelligence. Performs tasks similar to the American Federal Bureau of Investigation (FBI). See FEDERAL BUREAU OF INVESTIGATION (FBI), INTELLIGENCE.

Federal Preemption Policy. A directive by the U.S. Secretary of the Interior of 1924, whose department oversees the welfare of the Indian tribes in the United States, that neither the U.S. Government nor any state may interfere in the internal affairs of any Indian tribe residing on a reservation. Indian tribes determine their own mode of self-government.

Federal Program (Piggybacking). The funding of an organization for purposes of a Federal program when that organization also serves the purposes of other federal, state, or local programs. Multiple piggybacking is possible and not unusual.

Federal Protection Service. See PRESIDENTIAL TRANSITION.

Federal Regional Council (FRC). A committee of the heads of the regional offices of certain specified federal domestic departments and agencies. One of the regional office heads is appointed by the President as chairman. The purpose of the FRC is to coordinate the related activities of the various federal members without involving their Washington headquarters whenever possible, and to facilitate relationships with state and local governments. They are not independently staffed. They provide assistance to states in promoting rural and regional development and their work is overseen by an Undersecretaries' Group on Regional Operations (created by Executive Order 11647 in February 1972).

Federal Register. An official publication of the U.S. Government (since 1936) in which all Executive Orders of the President as well as all rules and regulations of the executive departments are published as a prerequisite for their enforceability. The *Register* is compiled and published by the National Archives and Records Service.

Federal Regulatory Independent Agencies. Agencies of the U.S. Government with quasi-judicial and quasi-legislative powers, which are authorized to regulate private enterprises which produce certain goods and services for consumers. Among the major agencies are the following: Atomic Energy Commission, Civil Aeronautics Board, District of Columbia, Export-Import Bank Board, Federal Maritime Commission, Federal Mediation and Conciliation Service, Federal Power Commission, Board of Governors of the Federal Reserve System, Federal Trade Commission,

National Aeronautics and Space Administration, National Foundation for the Arts and the Humanities, National Labor Relations Board, National Mediation Board, National Science Foundation, Railroad Retirement Board, Securities and Exchange Commission, Selective Service System, Small Business Administration, Smithsonian Institution, Tax Court of the United States, Tennessee Valley Authority, U.S. Civil Service Commission, International Communication Agency, Tariff Commission, and the Veterans Administration.

Federal Reserve Board. Established in 1913, a seven member board of governors that oversees the Federal Reserve System. The members are appointed by the president for a fourteen-year term. From its headquarters in Washington, D.C., the board supervises the Federal Reserve Banks located in twelve districts throughout the United States. Major concerns of the Board are monetary and credit policies which are set by the Board.

Federal Rules of Evidence. See RULES OF EVIDENCE.

Federal System. See FEDERALISM, Appendix 81.

Federal Technology and Transfer Act. A statute that was passed by the U.S. Congress in 1986, authorizing the licensing of technologies developed by national laboratories and think-tanks to private enterprises, with preference to enterprises owned by Americans. When it came to technologies such as aircraft, in which America leads the world, nationalist sentiment arose and foreign companies, among them the Japanese, were discouraged from gaining that technology. These practices gave name to such terms as "techno-nationalism," simply meaning that there are other cherished values besides cold cash or quick profit. Another catch phrase, "techno-globalism" refers to situations where nations share technologies among themselves in the global arena without any nationalistic hang-ups.

Federal Trade Commission Improvement Act. See LEMON LAW.

Federalism. A system of horizontal (geographic) and vertical (as to degree and scope) distribution of certain sovereign powers among distinct political entities, based on a contractual agreement (e.g., a constitution) delineating the scope and the degree of the utilization of those powers, with the aim of achieving some mutually agreed objective (e.g., to establish a union while retaining the separate identity of each member of the federation). Professor Daniel J. Elazar (*American Federalism: A View from the States.* New York: Thomas Y. Crowell Company, 1966) defines "federalism" as "the mode of political organization that unites smaller polities within an overarching political system by distributing power among general and constituent governments in a manner designed to protect the existence and authority of both national and subnational political systems, enabling all to share in the overall system's decision-making and executing processes." Some federations allow for secession from the union, others do not. The Soviet Constitution, for example, allowed secession (Art. 72 of the USSR Constitution) but the American federation is considered an irreversible political partnership and there are no legal provisions for secession, as the War of Secession or Civil War of 1861 has proved, although there were many suggestions for maintaining federalism in America without Washington. There are several forms of federalism according to the degree and scope to which sovereign powers are shared by the central government and the units of the federation. Some of them may overlap in time: (1) decentralized federalism, as exists in Canada, for example, where the units of the federation enjoy far greater autonomy than is the case in the United States; (2) dual federalism, as exists in the United States, where the state governments and the central (federal) government perform most of the governmental functions within their jurisdiction and under their own body of laws (including constitutions), but they also share powers in certain areas (e.g., taxation); (3) cooperative or functional federalism, whereby the central government shares powers extensively with the units of the federation as well as with the local governments (e.g., the Federal Republic of Germany); (4) creative-cooperative federalism, whereby the states participate very actively in expenditures on programs that have national impact, as was the case in the United States between 1961-1969; and (5) the so-called "new federalism" that emerged in 1969 in the United States, when the central government decentralized many federal functions by granting federal funds to states under a new revenue sharing system, and thus gave the states more discretionary powers in such matters as construction of public utilities and social services, including aid to education. States that do not follow the commands of the federal government or do not allow verification of their compliance by the federal government, may be penalized by losing funds withheld for many programs, including funds for highway construction. This is also known as "command-and-control federalism." See UNITARY STATE, Appendix 81.

Federalism Without Washington. See FEDERALISM.

Federalist. A series of brief yet penetrating essays that were written between 1787 and 1788, and published in parts in New York papers. One of the writers was the distinguished spokesman for the Federalists, Alexander Hamilton, who favored a strong union with a strong central government. Once he even proposed that George Washington declare himself a monarch and be coronated as the King of the United States, a suggestion which Washington rejected outright. John Jay and James Madison were the other writers. The papers were first published under the pen-name of "A Citizen of New York" and later "Publius." The papers urged the citizens of New York to approve the U.S. Constitution as it was, without the first ten amendments, which were subsequently included (the U.S. Constitution can be revised only by amendments) as the "Bill of Rights." The first ten amendments were the price for ratification of the Constitution by the Anti-federalists, who sponsored the Bill of Rights (as insisted upon by Thomas Jefferson). The eighty-five separate Federalist papers deal with a broad variety of issues, such as the necessity for a strong central government in order to be able to deal with the fragile, weak, and "corruptible" nature of man; the reconciliation of democratic liberties with territorial expansion—entities joining the American Union were to be treated as equal and not as domains in a colonial status (thus laying the foundation for the principle of equality of states, regardless of the size of the territory or population). The framework for conceptualization of the state and its institutions was also laid, primarily as instruments of protection of liberty and property and without an end of their own, and the concept of political equilibrium based on checks and balances was articulated to the point that, to this day, *The Federalist* papers serve as the normative statements of the political philosophy of the American system of government. Even during the impeachment proceedings against U.S. President Richard M. Nixon in 1974, members of the Congressional committee often made references to *The Federalist* papers as a source of political philosophy rather than a source of law. See ANTIFEDERALIST.

Federalization of Local Problems in America. See WEED AND SEED PROGRAM.

Fédération de la Gauche Démocratique et Socialiste (FGDS). The Federation of the Democratic and Socialist Left, a major political coalition of leftist political parties and pressure groups in France, organized mainly to oppose governmental policies of former French President Charles DeGaulle (1958-1969).

Feelers. See DIPLOMATIC FEELERS.

Fellow Traveler. A term coined in 1923, by Leon Trotsky, one of the leaders of the Bolshevik Revolution in Russia in 1917, to describe both those individuals who came to Russia out of curiosity to observe the newly-created socialist state, and those who claimed to be communists themselves without any communist party affiliation. The term has also been applied to American and foreign writers, poets, university professors, bankers, supporters of the United Nations, scientists and other intellectuals, persons with an international outlook, including U.S. President D. D. Eisenhower, and journalists (e.g., John Reed, a journalist, who is the only American to be buried at the place of honor at the Kremlin; singer Paul Robeson, a recipient of medals and prizes in the Soviet Union; and Angela Davis, a black American revolutionary of the 1960s and 1970s, who was awarded an honorary doctorate by Moscow University when the University of California denied her one) who either came to Socialist Russia to write good things about it, or who wrote favorably about it in their respective countries. During the "red scare," the "great fear," or "McCarthyism" periods in America, the term was often applied to persons who were overtly sympathetic with and who subscribed to the ideas and ideals of a certain political philosophy or political system without rendering any particular tangible service to or being a part of that system (e.g., Cyrus Eaton, a multi-millionaire American industrialist). See HT/LINGUAL, MCCARTHYISM, PALMER RAIDS.

Felonious Homicide. The killing of one person by another without any justification. See FELONY.

Felony. A serious crime calling for severe punishment (e.g., theft, murder, or kidnapping). See CRIMEN LAESAE MAJESTATIS, MISDEMEANOR, TREASON.

Fencing. See AGENT PROVOCATEUR.

Fetiales. An early type of centralized foreign diplomatic service in ancient Rome.

Feudalism. A social-political-economic system, whereby large landowners shape and control all aspects of economy, government, and social institutions in their respective domains. See TYPES OF STATES.

FGDS. See FÉDÉRATION DE LA GAUCHE DÉMOCRATIQUE ET SOCIALISTE.

Fiat. In the Latin language, "let it be done." Also, a body of rules stipulating the manner in which some authority may be granted; a parliamentary body; or arbitrary use of power.

Fiat Justitia Ruat Caelum. In the Latin language, "let justice prevail even if the heavens fall." A motto of Roman lawmakers.

Fief. In the French language, "a feudal state."

Fiefdom. The domain or feudal state of a feudal lord.

Field-Grade President. An unflattering characterization of U.S. President Dwight D. Eisenhower (1953-1961), who was a General (five stars) in the Army, and whose political style was to work through a chain-of-command, rather than by being personally involved in detailed political processes.

Fifth Column. The secret deployment of local (native) military or paramilitary formations for the purpose of overthrowing the government; or a group of revolutionaries seeking to abolish the government in power with outside assistance (e.g., rendered by another state). A tactic often practiced by guerrilla fighters. (The term originated during the Civil War in Spain in 1936, when the leader of the Falanga party, Francisco Franco, attacked the city of Madrid frontally with four columns while his fifth column, operating in secrecy within the city among the opposing forces of the Republicans, attacked from within and gave Franco a decisive victory.) The term is also often applied to communist revolutionaries throughout the world.

Fifth French Republic. See FRENCH REPUBLICS.

Fifty-Four-Forty or Fight. A slogan coined in 1846 by expansionist Democrats who, inspired by Manifest Destiny, demanded reannexation of Texas and re-occupation of Oregon along 54˚ and 40˚ (latitude and longitude respectively), and who were prepared to go to war with Mexico if these demands were not met.

Fighting Bob. See POLITICAL PROGRESSIVISM.

Fighting Jew. One of Israel's modern founding fathers, Menachem Begin (1913-1992), born and educated in Poland, prime minister and leader of his party, during a speech on the grounds of a West Bank settlement in 1975, described a new and modern kind of human being: "The Fighting Jew." "The Fighting Jew," he said, "loves books, loves liberty, and hates war. But he is prepared to fight for liberty." Although Begin lost the premiership in 1977, his successor, Prime Minister Yitzak Shamir, took over and made promises to "continue the struggle." Begin wanted to be remembered "as the man who set the borders of the land of Israel for eternity." See EIN BRERA, SADAT-BEGIN SUMMIT, THREE-NOS DOCTRINE.

Filibuster. A technique used to prevent the passing of a legislative act by making long and irrelevant speeches in order to delay or to prevent voting. The practice was very common in the United States Congress but has been limited in recent years by means of cloture or closure. By a rule of March 7, 1975, a vote of three-fifths instead of the previously required two-thirds now suffices to invoke cloture and to end a filibuster. See CLOTURE.

Final Act of the Conference on Security and Cooperation in Europe. See HELSINKI ACCORD.

Final Solution. An all-out effort, a genocide, to exterminate Jews in Nazi Germany and occupied areas; proclaimed in 1941, by Adolf Hitler, the *Führer* (leader) of the German Third Reich (1933-1945).

His solution to the "Jewish Problem" was to exterminate approximately six million Jews by May 7, 1945, the end of W.W.II. See BUNDESRÜCKERSTATTUNGSGESETZ (BRÜG), CRYSTAL NIGHT.

Finalism. The notion that all events in human life, in the life of society, or the entire human environment on earth are caused by the purposes which they serve.

Finlandization. An agreement between a large and a strong state (the former Soviet Union), and a small neighbor state (Finland) to the effect that the smaller state shall not enter into any military alliances or allow the stationing of foreign forces in its territory. Finland was forced to enter such an agreement and became a buffer state, through a treaty with the Soviet Union signed in 1948. See BUFFER STATE, MANNERHEIM LINE.

Fireside Chats. A means used by U.S. President Franklin D. Roosevelt to communicate his views to the general public, and thus solicit support for his policies, through periodic conversations held with newsmen gathered around the fireplace in the White House. That practice has been continued by other Presidents after Roosevelt, particularly Jimmy Carter. See PANAMA CANAL TREATIES.

Firma. See AGONIZING REAPPRAISAL.

First Amendment Freedoms. The guarantee of free expression created under the First Amendment; these freedoms are: Freedom of Assembly, Freedom of Press, Freedom of Religion, and Freedom of Speech. See Appendices 8, 48, 51.

First Chief Directorate. An administrative component of the formerly centralized Soviet intelligence apparatus, the KGB, responsible for foreign intelligence operations (e.g., collecting information about other nations and events outside the Soviet Union) and espionage. See PEOPLE'S COMMISSION FOR INTERNAL AFFAIRS (NKGB).

First Civilized American. See ARTILLERY OF THE HEAVENS.

First Continental Congress. See CONTINENTAL CONGRESS, TOWNSHEND REVENUE ACT.

First Industrial Revolution. See INDUSTRIAL REVOLUTION.

First International. See COMMUNIST INTERNATIONAL.

First Lady. In the United States, the wife of the incumbent President of the United States, and at the state level, the wife of the incumbent governor. Also referred to as "Co-President" and "Co-Governor."

First Lord. The Prime Minister of Great Britain who also is in charge of the Treasury (First Lord of the Treasury) and the civil service.

First Party System. See JACKSONIANS.

First-Strike Capability. The ability to initiate a crippling surprise attack against an adversary in such a manner as to limit or destroy any retaliatory capacity.

First War Powers Act of 1941. See WAR POWERS ACTS.

First Women's Conference of Seneca Falls. See NATIONAL ORGANIZATION FOR WOMEN (NOW).

FISA. See FOREIGN INTELLIGENCE SURVEILLANCE ACT.

Fiscal Policy. As it pertains to government, the determination of income (e.g., from taxes and fees), expenditures (e.g., government spending), and the need to borrow funds in order to allow a healthy functioning of the state's (nation's) economy. Per U.S. Congressional Bureau Office, "The government's choice of tax and spending programs, which influences the amount and maturity of government debt, as well as the level, composition, and distribution of output and income. An 'easy' fiscal policy stimulates the growth of output and income, whereas a 'tight' fiscal policy restrains their growth. Movements in the standardized-employment budget deficit constitute one overall indicator of the tightness or ease of federal fiscal policy—an increase relative to potential GDP suggests fiscal ease, whereas a decrease suggests fiscal restriction. The President and the Congress jointly carry out federal fiscal policy." "Monetary policy" is "the strategy of influencing movements of the money supply and interest rates to affect output and inflation. An 'easy' monetary policy suggests faster money growth and initially lower short-term interest rates in an attempt to increase aggregate demand, but it may lead to a higher rate of inflation. A tight monetary policy suggests slower money growth and higher interest rates in the near term in an attempt to reduce inflationary pressure by reducing aggregate demand. The Federal Reserve System conducts monetary policy in the United States." A course of action agreed on by either the executive branch of the government, the legislature, or both, on the management of the national budget—money allocated for the purpose of sustaining the state and its government—from moneys derived from taxes, fees, fines, or borrowing with the greatest economy in mind. As a rule, the policy works to achieve and maintain economic growth and to stimulate it, if necessary by allocating funds to needy projects. The American, and most of the world's economic policies, are based on the economic theories of John M. Keynes. See KEYNESIAN ECONOMIC POLICY, MONETARY POLICY.

Fiscal Year. A twelve-month period designed for accounting purposes. In many private businesses, the fiscal year runs from 1 July to 30 June the following year, as do most governmental fiscal years. The federal fiscal year in the U.S. begins on 1 October of each year and ends 30 September the following year.

Fish and Visitors Stink in Three Days. See ARTILLERY OF THE HEAVENS.

Fish-Bowl Diplomacy. The practice of conducting diplomatic negotiations on the basis of responses to public opinion, internal or external; or the conducting of diplomatic relations or negotiations according to what the general public may or may not tolerate or accept.

Fists of Righteous Harmony. See BOXER REBELLION.

Five Minute Rule. A rule that may be applied in the Committee of the Whole House of the U.S. House of Representatives whereby any one Representative is allowed to speak for five minutes when he proposes an amendment to a bill, or five minutes if he opposes an amendment. See UNITED STATES HOUSE OF REPRESENTATIVES.

Five Percent Rule. A device used in the Federal Republic of Germany under the Electoral Law of 1953, to prevent small and regional political parties from acquiring seats in the Bundestag (the elective Chamber of the German Parliament). The rule stipulates that only those parties are eligible to representation which receive at least five percent (according to party lists) of the valid second votes (*Zweitstimme*) cast for the entire Federal Republic, or those which receive at least three seats from districts by proportional representation. See PROPORTIONAL REPRESENTATION.

Five Percenters. The term applied to persons who were involved in the scandal that was revealed by a Senate investigation in the late 1940s, in which non-elected officials, including Major General Harry Vaughan, participated in peddling government contracts for a fee of five percent of the total value of the contract. The general, like many others, had received only a food freezer, valued at $520, and a mink coat (hence often referred to as the "Mink Dynasty"), which he termed simply "an expression of friendship." Vaughan remained in the Harry S. Truman Administration. Some of the other "five percenters" (all Truman's cronies) were: Donald Dawson who, as Truman's assistant was helping business executives to obtain loans from the Reconstruction Finance Corporation without collateral (he was retained by Truman anyway); E. Merl Young, a loan examiner for the Reconstruction Finance Corporation. Young subsequently resigned and took a job with Lustron Corporation, the recipient of a $37.5 million "refund" from the Reconstruction Finance Corporation, but soon was convicted and served an 18-month prison term on a perjury conviction; Matthew J. Connelly, former appointment secretary to President Truman, and Theron Lamar Caudle, a former chief of the Tax Division of the U.S. Department of Justice, both of whom were convicted in 1956 and served prison terms on a tax-bribery charge involving a St. Louis shoe manufacturer, Irving Sachs; and William M. Boyle, Jr., the Vice Chairman of the Democratic National Committee, who subsequently resigned but was not charged with any crime.

Five-Sided-Puzzle Palace. See PENTAGON.

Five-Year Plan. An economic plan with a duration of five years (highly complex and comprehensive) that was set up in terms of goals by the planning agencies of the former Soviet Union. Once the plan was worked out, all segments of the Soviet economy were expected not only to fulfill them, but surpass them.

Fixers. See BEHIND-THE-SCENE POWER.

Flag of Convenience. A term applied to a national, a citizen, or a business enterprise which conducts business under the laws of another state (e.g., a seagoing vessel carrying the registry and the flag of another state for the purpose of avoiding payment of higher fees, or in order to trade with nations at war with the state of the registry-holder). A large portion of seagoing vessels today are, for example, registered with Panama or Liberia, because the registration and inspection fees are less than those of other states. Registering states collect fees for the "lending" of their flags.

Flagrante Bello. In the Latin language, "during the time of war" or "during war hostilities." Also, a principle of domestic or international law under some systems of jurisprudence, whereby no liability exists (private or public) due to damages caused by war. See CALVO DOCTRINE.

Flagrante Delicto. In the Latin language, "during the actual commission of crime."

Flagrantly Improper Activity. A phrase that is commonly used in the language of diplomacy between sovereign states, which serves as grounds for asking a diplomatic agent of one state stationed on the territory of another to cease functioning and to leave the country. Such improper activity usually includes interference with domestic political processes, policy formation and implementation processes, and, above all, espionage. It is a common practice that the state whose agent has been expelled on such grounds will reciprocate in kind and expel an agent of similar rank in return. It is estimated that about half of the diplomatic personnel exchanged between adversary states consists of intelligence officers whose primary function is not to attend receptions and lobby for the causes of their countries, but to collect tangible intelligence (knowledge selected through intellectual processes and critical judgment) through locally developed sources (informants), and to relay that information to their home-states. "An ambassador is an honest man sent to lie abroad for the good of his country," Sir Henry Wotton, a British diplomat, once stated, for which he was promptly recalled by his government, but this dictum remains valid. See INTELLIGENCE, PERSONA NON GRATA.

Flat Tax. A tax at a fixed percentage of income, regardless of the amount of income. During the 1992 presidential campaign, presidential hopeful Jerry Brown, a Democrat, proposed a 13 percent flat tax rate together with a value added tax, but his opponent, Bill Clinton, charged that such a tax rate would penalize the poor. See VALUE-ADDED TAX (CUAT).

FLEAS. See FAIR LABOR STANDARDS ACT, *NATIONAL LEAGUE OF CITIES V. BRENNAN* in Appendix 48.

Flexible Constitution. A constitutional instrument which is considerably brief and one which allows broad rather than narrow or strict interpretation of its provisions. Also, a constitution which can be easily amended. (The United States Constitution is brief and allows considerable room for interpretation, but it is difficult to amend.) See CONSTITUTION.

Flexible Response. A major policy principle referring to America's external involvements in coping with military aggressions, according to which the United States would deploy military forces only whenever or wherever aggression occurs, without massive retaliation against the aggressor's territory proper. The policy originated with the military planners of U.S. President John F. Kennedy (1961-1963) after the so-called "Cuban Missile Crisis" in 1962. Also known as "proportional response" or "graduated response." See CUBAN MISSILE CRISIS, MASSIVE RETALIATION.

Flight from the East. See COLD WAR ORPHAN STATE.

Flight from the Republic. A decree by the parliament of the German Democratic Republic (East Germany), which made it a crime for anyone to leave the country (usually by escaping to West Germany or to West Berlin) without permission. (Similar laws have been in force in most socialist states, including the former Soviet Union.) Persons caught escaping to the West were harshly punished by long-term imprisonment. By a mutual agreement concluded between the two states in 1972, West Germany agreed to pay ransom for prisoners, approximately $15,000 per person. When the East Germans learned, according to a West German newspaper, *Die Welt* (World), that the Federal government appropriated $30 million dollars for the purpose of "buying" prisoners from East Germany, "human trade" became a common practice. The more the West Germans were buying, the more "criminals" and "spies" were caught in East Germany. "Human trade" was terminated in 1976 when the matter was brought up before the General Assembly of the United Nations, charging the German Democratic Republic with "slave trade." Currently, the Federal Republic of Germany (united Germany) is a member of the UN. See BERLIN BLOCKADE, BERLIN WALL.

Floater. One elected from and representing a floterial district. See FLOTERIAL DISTRICT.

Floating Currency. Currency (money) of a state that changes in value (purchasing power) according to its supply and demand on the international money market as opposed to currency with artificially fixed parity. See INTERNATIONAL MONETARY FUND.

Floor Manager. A legislator (e.g., a member of either house of the U.S. Congress, or a state legislature) who manages a legislative measure during the legislative process, such as seeing that the legislative proposal is properly placed on the calendar, that it is submitted to the appropriate committee on time, and that all possible support is engaged to assure that the measure becomes a law. See CONGRESS OF THE UNITED STATES.

Floterial District. An alternative system of apportionment for purposes of representation whereby several single-member districts are combined into groups of districts from which representatives will be elected *at large* rather than by single-member constituencies (districts). See ONE MAN, ONE VOTE.

Flower Power. During the anti-Vietnam War movement in the 1960s, young people who opposed the war and also the traditional policies of the government, rebelled with non-violence, calling for equality among races, more equitable distribution of wealth, and confrontation with police and the military during the many riots in major U.S. cities. Their symbols were the sign of peace and a flower, which they often placed in the barrels of police and soldiers' guns. The term is sometimes limited to hippies, but, in reality, it involved a larger segment of the young population and contributed considerably to the withdrawal of the United States from the Vietnam conflict.

Flucht vom Osten. See COLD WAR ORPHAN STATE, DRANG NACH OSTEN.

FMCS. See FEDERAL MEDIATION AND CONCILIATION SERVICE (FMCS).

FMLN. See FARABUNDO MARTI NATIONAL LIBERATION FRONT.

Focus Group. In politics and public opinion molding, a group of persons engaged in achieving some common goal (e.g., a clean environment); the group can be mobilized for other purposes (e.g., to support or oppose oil exploration in a given area). Focus groups can trade off their support or opposition to other focus groups. In the case of the abortion issue (with the American electorate just about evenly divided for and against), the politics of the pill relies heavily on focus groups, including those which lobby for and against foreign drug companies. For example, several focus groups are involved in the political struggle concerning the RU-486 pill from France and Germany, which the Federal Drug Administration keeps off the American market. Focus groups are highly sought after by public opinion molders and by office holders needing votes.

Foggy Bottom. A nickname for the southwest area of the nation's capital, Washington, D.C., once a swamp and a low land, where the U.S. Department of State is located. Bitter critics of the State Department often equate its output and the general atmosphere that permeates the chambers of high diplomacy with the original characteristics of the land.

Folketing. The unicameral legislative body—Parliament—of Denmark.

Food for Peace Program. In 1958, the U.S. Congress authorized (under Public Law 480) the distribution of surplus food to needy nations (e.g., those that were stricken with famine, flood, or other emergencies) at a very low price, to be paid in local currency of the recipient state (since most underdeveloped states lack foreign currency to pay for goods imported from abroad). The funds received for the food are in turn loaned to the recipient government, and such transactions constitute a subsidy, loan, and grant all at once.

Food Wars. See HUNGER WARS.

Force de Frappe. In the French language, "striking military force" or "a very mobile and powerful offensive force."

Ford-Carter Debate. See GREAT DEBATES.

Ford Doctrine. See PACIFIC DOCTRINE.

Forecast. A prediction, hunch, prophecy, or plain speculation (possibly made with the aid of mathematical and statistical tools) about the future, without the suggestion of ways in which one may intervene in order to control events and to achieve desired outcomes. Once one gains sufficient knowledge and understanding of past events, one can use forecasts as the basis for suggesting ways in which future events may be influenced or controlled; or for demonstrating how one can in the empirical world, intervene in situations in order to alter or control the course of events. See CONCEPT, EPISTEMOLOGY, KNOWLEDGE.

Forecasting and Planning. A series of rigorous conceptual models, assumptions, techniques, and intellectual processes which groups of scholars pursue for the purpose of predicting the future and how to better prepare the society for meeting the possible problems encountered, using minimum resources and efforts and obtaining maximum desired results. Among the major techniques are: the Delphi, Simulation, Trend Extrapolation, Gaming, Morphological Models, Scenarios, Relevance Trees, Input-Output Tables, Contextual Mapping, Brainstorming, Dialectical Planning, Critical Path, Scientific Questionnaire, etc.

Foreign Agents Registration Act. A congressional law of 1938, which requires all agents acting for or on behalf of foreign governments to register as such with the U.S. Attorney General if they perform tasks as political consultants, advise foreign governments on lobbying activities, render publicity, or, in any other way, aid foreign interests. (Exempted from the law are foreign diplomatic personnel, attorneys, persons engaged in legitimate trade, official guests of the state, or persons engaged in academic, religious, or humanitarian activities.) All literature distributed in the United States by foreign agents must be approved by the Attorney General, and it must carry a label to this effect. Failure to comply with the law may result in a penalty of up to $10,000, deportation (if the foreign agent is not an American national), or imprisonment. Foreign agents are prohibited from engaging in espionage activities on behalf of other states. See LOBBY, Appendix 27.

Foreign Aid. See AMERICAN FOREIGN AID, Appendix 40.

Foreign Commerce Compromise. See PLANS OF THE AMERICAN UNION.

Foreign Intelligence Service. See COMMITTEE FOR STATE SECURITY (KGB), PEOPLE'S COMMISSION FOR INTERNAL AFFAIRS (NKGB).

Foreign Intelligence Surveillance Act. A congressional law passed on 25 October 1978 designed to control wiretaps by all law enforcement agencies in the United States, particularly the Federal Bureau of Investigaiton (FBI) and the Central Intelligence Agency (CIA), against any person within the United States proper. The law allows wiretaps only for purpose of legitimate intelligence and counterintelligence, but not for the purpose for private information. Also, wiretaps are allowed only if needed information cannot be obtained by any other means. Surveillance of persons was allowed only if "there is a cause to believe" that one was engaged as an agent of foreign power. These two main tools of police and intelligence, surveillance and wiretapping, are very rigidly controlled by the federal courts, the Congressional oversight committees, and numerous private citizen organizations, e.g., the American Civil Liberties Union (ACLU). See CHAOS, COINTELPRO, COUNTERINTELLIGENCE, UNITED STATES PERSON.

Foreign Intelligence Surveillance Court. See AGENT IDENTITY PROTECTION ACT.

Foreign Legion. See FRENCH FOREIGN LEGION.

Foreign Policy. The scope and method of engaging in relations with other states and proceeding according to existing practices, norms of international law, customs and conventions. The best policy involves striving to achieve desired objectives through the best means available and acceptable at a minimum cost of and risk to the lives and property of persons, as well as respecting the inviolability of sovereign states.

Foreign Relations Committee. A Senate committee responsible for the task of supervising the bearing of foreign policy.

Foreign Service Officer (FSO). A career officer (duly trained, examined, and commissioned by the U.S. President) of the American Foreign Service of either the "junior" or the "senior" grade. Diplomatic officers (e.g., ambassadors) may be appointed by the U.S. President for specific tasks from outside the ranks of the career personnel, in which case they are known as "political diplomats" or "non-career-diplomats" (or simply "political cronies" or "political hacks"). Since the establishment of the American republic, the foreign service has grown throughout the years as follows:

Year	1798	1938	1948	1968	1978	1988	1991
Personnel	27	5,692	20,327	25,495	34,000	41,760	46,800

See WRISTON COMMISSION.

Forest War. When Nazi Germany invaded Poland on 1 September 1939 and thus commenced the Second World War, the Soviet Union made preparations to invade the eastern parts of Poland and the Baltic republics of Estonia, Latvia, and Lithuania. After the 1941 Nazi invasion of the Soviet Union itself, the Soviets attacked, conquered, and incorporated into the Soviet orbit the Baltic republics. However, the brave and courageous Balts did not submit to the two aggressors, the Germans or the Soviets, and continued fighting them through partisan-guerrilla means throughout the war, until 1945, when the Soviets at last prevailed. Many of the Baltic warriors and their families were forced to live in the wilderness throughout the war. The Baltic states regained their independence after the collapse of the Soviet empire, on 2 September 1991, and U.S. President George Bush recognized each of them as a sovereign, independent, and free state. All of the three republics were subsequently admitted as full members of the United Nations Organization. See Appendix 74.

Formal Region. See NATURAL REGION.

Former Presidents Act. See PRESIDENTIAL TRANSITION.

Formosa Resolution. In January 1955, the U.S. Congress passed a special resolution authorizing the U.S. President to use military forces to defend Formosa (Taiwan—a province of the Republic of China) and the near-by Pescadores Islands from aggression by the People's Republic of China (Communist China). The resolution was requested by U.S. President Dwight D. Eisenhower (1953-1961), who considered a free Chinese government in Taiwan to be important to American interests in the area. See CONTAINMENT, DOMINO THEORY.

Forms of Local Government. (1) Mayor-Council: Weak and strong; (2) Council-Manager: The above two are most popular in the U.S.; (3) Mayor-Administrator: (First in San Francisco, later in New York, Philadelphia, and Chicago; (4) County Board of Supervisors-Administrator.

Forty Committee. See NATIONAL SECURITY COUNCIL (NSC).

Forward Defense. See MILITARY REFORM MOVEMENT.

Forward Mistakes by the Masses. See JACKSONIAN DEMOCRACY.

Foshida Incident. See SPLENDID ISOLATION.

Founding Fathers. An affectionate name for all American revolutionaries, the members of the Philadelphia Constitutional Convention of 1787, who drafted the present Constitution of the United States, and those who contributed to the creation of the United States as a sovereign and independent nation. See Appendices 5, 6, 8.

Four Freedoms. Concerned about declining human rights and liberties everywhere, U.S. President Franklin D. Roosevelt (1933-1944), in his message to Congress on the State of the Union in January 1941, named four principal human freedoms which he considered most endangered. He stated: "In the future days, which we seek to make sure, we look forward to a world founded upon four essential freedoms. The first is freedom of speech and expression—everywhere in the world. The second is freedom of every person to worship God in his own way—everywhere in the world. The third is freedom from want, which, translated into world terms, means economic understanding which will secure for every nation a healthy peacetime life for its inhabitants—everywhere in the world. The fourth is freedom from fear, which, translated into world terms, means a world-wide reduction of armaments to such a point and in such a thorough fashion that no nation will be in a position to commit an act of physical aggression against any neighbor—anywhere in the world."

Four-Modernizations Plan. The People's Republic of China designed in 1978, a long-range plan which calls for the expenditure of over $60 billion on modernization and development in the four basic areas: agriculture, defense (e.g., in 1992 the People's Army was equipped with the latest in weapons systems), industry and technology.

Four-Party System. An observation which Professor James MacGregor Burns makes in his book, *The Deadlock of Democracy*, about the party system in the United States. He claims that this is in reality a four-party system and not, as it is commonly assumed, a two-party system (e.g., with the Democratic and the Republican Parties sharing power at different times). Professor Burns considers the congressional branches of the two major parties and the national committees as two separate entities, represented by different leaders, and addressing themselves to different issues. For example, while the national branches of the Democratic or the Republican Parties consider national issues at large, the congressional groups of these parties have their own unique Congress and legislation-related issues to consider, and are less concerned with matters national in scope. See POLITICAL PARTY.

Four Tigers. See MINI DRAGONS.

Fourteen Points. A major foreign policy statement pronounced by U.S. President Woodrow Wilson in his speech before Congress on January 8, 1918, preceding the final settlement of World War I. These points dealt with such matters as reaffirmation of the freedom of the seas; the removal of trade barriers among nations; reduction of armaments; better care for peoples living under colonial rule; checks on territorial expansion of Germany; independence for Poland; respect for the rights of states (large and small alike); protection of independent and sovereign states; political autonomy for peoples of Austria (the Austro-Hungarian Empire was dissolved at the end of World War I), Hungary, and Turkey; and the readjustment of the frontiers of Italy. One of its strongest points was the advocacy of the right of nations to self-determination, that is, the right to determine their own internal orders and modes of international cooperation.

Fourth Branch of Government. A term commonly applied to organized lobbies which systematically influence political and governmental processes in a polyarchic society. See LOBBY.

Fourth Estate. The mass information and communication medias (e.g., press, television, radio, and books) in their role as a link between the government and the people, and vice versa.

Fourth-Termite. A derogatory term that was applied to Franklin D. Roosevelt when he was nominated by the Democrats for an unprecedented fourth term as a presidential candidate in 1944, and subsequently elected. His running mate, Harry S. Truman from Missouri, was selected as Vice President over Harry A. Wallace as a result of a compromise (the "new Missouri Compromise"), since conservative Democrats had lost their trust in Wallace due to his pro-leftist views. The 1944 presidential election triggered the forces of opposition to Franklin D. Roosevelt (calling him the "fourth-termite of '44") as President for the fourth time, and subsequently, Amendment XX to the U.S. Constitution (see Appendix 16) was passed in 1951 limiting a president to two consecutive terms in office.

Fox and a Lion. Venetian political philosopher and historian, Niccolo Machiavelli (1459-1517) asserted that a successful leader of a state (a prince), in order to be effective and successful, ought to possess these two attributes: to be as decisive and aggressive as a lion, and as conciliatory and accommodating as a fox, as the situation may require. See MACHIAVELLIANISM.

Fragging. Acts of terrorism involving low-ranking non-commissioned officers (NCO's) or enlisted men, who kill commissioned officers (CO's), usually as a prelude to a military coup d'état or a revolution (e.g., a palace revolution) within a state. Such acts are aimed at depriving the armed forces of trained and experienced military leaders, paralyzing the military leaders, paralyzing the military establishment, and taking over political control of the state. Such fragging practices were common, among other places, in Russia during the Bolshevik Revolution in 1917; in Nazi Germany, by Adolf Hitler's followers; in Brazil, by the communists during their attempt, in 1935, to stage a military coup d'état and gain political power; in Cuba, by a corporal of the Cuban Army, F. Batista; and in Vietnam, by American soldiers who no longer wanted to follow combat orders of their officers during the protracted Vietnamese War.

Fragmentation of Power. The absence of a single center in which political power or public policy making is held and can be easily identified. In a unitary form of government, or under a dictatorship, the locus of actual power is easily identifiable, because it is held and exercised by one person or a small group of persons. This is not the case under federal or confederate systems which employ a fragmentation of power. For example, in the United States, power and policy making is not only shared by the three levels of government—federal, state, and local (a territorial or horizontal distribution of power)—but also by the three branches of government, the executive, the judiciary, and the legislative (a vertical distribution of power). See CONFEDERATION, FEDERALISM, UNITARY STATE.

Fraktion. In the German language, "splinter political group," "political party," "minor political party," or "faction." (In the German Bundestag, the Parliament, the term is commonly applied to members of different political parties.)

Frame Society. According to author Chie Nakane (*Japanese Society*, University of California Press, 1970), the Japanese society, unlike the Western society of individualism, is group-centered: "The nail that sticks out, will be pounded down;" it is a frame society. The author defines "frame" by contrasting it with "attributes." What one does is an attribute, and the institution, the employer with whom one is associated, is the frame. Japanese are proud of their frames, because about 35 percent of the Japanese live with such frames for the duration of their employment, employment for life. (Known in Japanese as "nenko.") The society is divided into "seniors" (in the Japanese language, "sempai") and "juniors" (in the Japanese language, "kohai"). Such is the hierarchy of organizations and individuals within those organizations. Those who disregard the hierarchy are known as "raiking." Simply translated, this means "a pawn rampaging around the chessboard in the absence of a hierarchical right to do so." From the top management in an enterprise to the lowest floor sweeper, Japanese refer to themselves as "senior" and "junior." The "seniors" have arrived by promotion, better pay, and respect; and the "juniors" are in the apprentice process on their way to the top. Teams are rewarded rather than individuals, and togetherness rather than individuality is encouraged even the point that people arrange for their children to marry in groups and even have graves in common. Hierarchy is the means for an upper mobility "governed by rules of seniority; "and unlike the situation in the United States, "social status in Japan," according to Dr. William S. Dietrich (*In the Shadow of the Rising Sun: The Political Roots of American Economic Decline*, Pennsylvania State University Press), "is linked far more to occupation than to wealth and income." The great effort on the part of the individual to achieve is directed by a concern for the good of the society and the state of Japan rather than for individualistic, personal satisfaction. On the assembly line the product designer, the engineer, works closely with others so that the product will be good, and it will not be released to the consumer unless it is good. The Japanese call this, according to Robert H. Hayes ("Why Japanese Factories Work," *Harvard Business Review*, 59, July-August 1981), "Pursuing the last grain of rice in the corner of the lunch box." In order to produce a good product, "strategic engineering and tactical production" are merged into one. Any problem noted must be resolved to the satisfaction of the designer as well as the producer. See AMERICA BASHING, JAPAN BASHING.

Framework for Peace. See SADAT-BEGIN SUMMIT.

France-Firster Party. See FRENCH NATIONAL FRONT.

Franchise. The grant of privilege or authority by a governmental agency or a private corporation (e.g., the right to vote, to be lawfully involved in some activity, or to pursue a certain line of business, free from competition). See VOTING.

Franchise (Political). The right to vote (as opposed to disfranchisement or invalidation of the right to vote).

Franchise d'Hotel. In the French language, "immunity of domicile." Also, a principle in international law according to which a diplomatic agent (e.g., ambassador, minister, or consul) is entitled to immunity from search and seizure, and his residence (as well as the premises of the diplomatic mission itself) are exempt from entry and search. See DIPLOMATIC IMMUNITY.

Francophone. The French-speaking Commonwealth. Also, a plan once advanced by Leopold Sedar-Senghor, President of Senegal, and Habib Bourguiba, President of Tunisia, to the effect that all French-speaking states, including France proper, Lebanon and Indochina (e.g., Vietnam and Cambodia), should form a union for the purpose of exploring and utilizing resources and plans that may arise from their commonalty of language. The plan was adopted on June 26, 1966. See FRENCH UNION.

Franking Privileges in the United States Congress. See FRINGE BENEFITS IN THE UNITED STATES CONGRESS.

Free Agent. A person acting independently on his own behalf, or a sovereign state acting (in international relations or diplomacy) in its sovereign capacity. See INTERNATIONAL LAW.

Free at Last, Free at Last! Thank God Almighty, We are Free at Last! See WALK FOR FREEDOM.

Free Enterprise. The production and distribution of goods and services, with the means of production (e.g., production plants and factories) and distribution owned and operated by individuals or groups (e.g., single proprietorships, partnerships, and corporations), with little or no control or interference by the government. In a free enterprise system of economy, the free market economy, the price of a commodity or a service is determined by the interplay of supply and demand rather than by centralized planning and setting of prices as is the case in a planned, or socialist economy. See LAISSEZ-FAIRE, OAKS' LAWS.

Free Germany Committee. See SCHWARZE KAPELLE.

Free-Market Absolutism. See GUIDED FREE ENTERPRISE.

Free Market Economy. See FREE ENTERPRISE.

Free Russia Committee. See VLASOV ARMY.

Free Society. See FREE WORLD.

Free Soil Party. A minor political party in the U.S., active during the 1840s and 1850s, mainly in the West, which opposed slavery in the western lands of America.

Free State. A state or a territory in the American union which allowed no slavery. Under the 1850 Compromise, free states included all the eastern, northern, and western states, the territories of California, Oregon, Minnesota, and the Unrecognized Territory (which became the Nebraska Territory under the Kansas-Nebraska Act of 1854, and was opened to slavery). Under the Kansas-Nebraska Act of 1854, the territories of Utah, New Mexico, and Indiana were open to slavery, while the Washington Territory was not. All the southern states below the Mason-Dixon Line, including Texas, were slave states.

Free Trade. See GUIDED FREE ENTERPRISE.

Free Vote. A vote that may be taken upon a legislative measure in a law-making body (e.g., Congress or Parliament) contrary to the instructions of the party or the party leadership. (Under the cabinet-parliamentary systems of government, in which party discipline is strictly enforced, such votes are rare, but they are very common in the United States Congress, where party discipline is rarely enforced.) See CONGRESS OF THE UNITED STATES, PARLIAMENT, Appendices 6-13.

Free World. A term commonly applied to non-communist, non-totalitarian states and societies, usually in the western world, which remain open, and preserve and guarantee the protection of civil, political, economic, and religious liberties and freedoms. Term often applied to the liberal democratic states in contrast to the closed system of the ex-Soviet Union, the East European socialist states, People's Republic of China, Cuba, Albania, North Korea, Vietnam, Laos, Cambodia, and other states where human rights and freedoms are limited. The United States was generally recognized as the leader and the protector of the free world, and the Soviet Union as the leader of the socialist not-free world. See BIPOLARITY, SOCIALIST COMMONWEALTH OF NATIONS, Appendix 29.

Freedman's Bureau. A federal agency that was established in 1865, despite President Johnson's opposition, to help the federal government deal with the problems of reconstructing the defeated Southern Confederacy. Its principal proponent was a white member of the U.S. House of Representatives, Thaddeus Stevens of Pennsylvania, who was instrumental in having Congress appropriate money for its many programs such as medical aid and food for approximately one million black freedmen and poor whites, the establishment of schools (including Howard University in Washington, D.C., Fisk University in Nashville, and Morehouse College in Atlanta), and industrial training. The Bureau was also instrumental in bringing the North and South together but Southern hostility toward the successes of the Bureau caused it to close down in 1872. (The National Urban League, which emerged in 1910, is continuing some of the traditions of the Bureau, particularly in the areas of integration and the creation of better living conditions in the urban environment.) See BLACK CODES, JOHNSON PROCLAMATION, RECONSTRUCTION.

Freedom. In a politically organized society, freedom is what the state says it is. Freedom and its limitations are usually defined by law (e.g., the U.S. Constitution and statutes). Under the liberal democratic tradition, freedom constitutes one's right to life, liberty, and the pursuit of happiness, as the Declaration of Independence states, and one may enjoy these in any manner one chooses as long as in that process one does not infringe upon the rights of others. See MAHATMA.

Freedom Float. A term applied to refugees from Cuba where, since Castro's consolidation of power in 1959, and the subsequent failure of the Bay of Pigs invasion, a socialist economy was introduced. This brought such poverty and misery to the Cuban people that the only recourse they felt they had was to "vote with the feet," or leave the country on anything that floats on water. One such large exodus from Cuba took place in April and May of 1980, and continues to this day. Similarly, refugees from other oppressive regimes, such as Haiti and Vietnam, risk death on the high seas to escape the totalitarian regimes ruling their homelands. The influx of "boat people" to the United States numbers over two million. They have been coming to America since 1975 from Cambodia, Laos, and South Vietnam following the collapse of the South Vietnamese regime, which the United States abandoned because of its corruption and incompetence. The "boat people," as they were called because most of them set out in small crafts and floated from nation to nation, were begging for acceptance. America took in 170,000 of them at a cost of $455 million.

Freedom House. A non-profit, non-partisan organization devoted to the collection and dissemination of information to the general public on any and all abuses of human rights and liberties and personal freedoms of the individual person world-wide. The House, which was founded in 1969 and is located in New York City, publishes an annual report on gains and losses of freedom and liberty in the entire world, including the United States.

Freedom is a Gift of God and God's Gift Cannot be Kept Forever from His Children. See MAHATMA, SATYAGRAHA.

Freedom of Association. See HUMAN RIGHTS: AMERICAN DEFINITION, Appendices 8, 51.

Freedom of Choice. See CONSUMER SOVEREIGNTY.

Freedom of Consciousness. See HUMAN RIGHTS: AMERICAN DEFINITION, Appendices 8, 48, 51.

Freedom of Employment. See HUMAN RIGHTS: AMERICAN DEFINITION, Appendices 8, 51.

Freedom of Information Act. Congressional legislation from 1977, aimed at giving citizens more access to the records that are kept by the government and particularly records pertaining to individual persons (e.g., FBI files). Any citizen has the right to challenge the information contained in his or her record, demand to know the identity of the source or sources, and obtain a copy for personal use. This Act supersedes the Disclosure of Information Act of 1966, and it is often referred to as the "right to know law" or "sunshine law." The only information that cannot be released is that pertaining to sources and methods of the information gathering agency. The Classified Information Procedures Act also regulates discolsure of once classified, secret data. However, the U.S. federal bureaucracy, like all other bureaucracies around the world, maintains the practice of classifying anything they can, and particularly matters that may reveal any shortcoming or plain incompetence. No other state, however, has such laws in existence, as of 1992. The prevailing practice outside the traditional Western democracies is to keep everything secret unless decreed otherwise. See RIGHT TO PRIVACY.

Freedom of Movement. See HUMAN RIGHTS: AMERICAN DEFINITION, Appendices 8, 51.

Freedom of Religion. See HUMAN RIGHTS: AMERICAN DEFINITION, Appendices 8, 51.

Freedom of Speech. See HUMAN RIGHTS: AMERICAN DEFINITION, Appendices 8, 51.

Freedom to be Just Let Alone. See HUMAN RIGHTS: AMERICAN DEFINITION, Appendices 8, 48, 51.

Freedom Rides. Organized massive rides, mainly by means of public bus transport systems, directed in 1957 by the Congress for Racial Equality (CORE) for the purpose of testing federal court decisions outlawing segregation in interstate transport. These rides were often called "freedom rides." Also the Montgomery, Alabama, bus boycott, when a black passenger refused to ride in the back of the bus, was one form of retaliation against inequality and injustice.

Freedom Summer. The summer of 1968 was particularly noted for mass demonstrations throughout the United States and in other countries. These included: protests against the Vietnam War, mass demonstrations by black Americans against the draft and for extension of civil rights and liberties, and the bloody confrontation of demonstrators with police and federal agents during the National Democratic Party Convention in Chicago, Illinois.

Freeholder. An elective member of a local county government, the board of supervisors (e.g., in the state of New Jersey, U.S.A.).

Freezing of the Mind. This notion was widely discussed during the 1992 presidential campaign by the two Democratic presidential hopefuls, Bill Clinton and Jerry Brown, as well as by U.S. Senator Warren Rudman, Republican from New Hampshire. Clinton and Brown challenged the present leadership, presidential and congressional, and maintained that the present system was incapable of properly addressing America's pressing issues due to the fact that special interest groups, rather than individual voters, exert controlling influence over elected officials. Major problems seen facing America include: shrinking employment and a shrinking tax base; poor education; lack of discipline; the rapid spread of crime; and fraud in private life to the point of thievery. (Manipulators, such as Keatting who generously donated to the campaign coffers of five U.S. Senators in return for protection of his schemes, and Milken and Boskey, to name but a few, were able to steal billions from Americans, and then the American taxpayer had to pay for their crimes. In addition, members of the U.S. Congress were guilty of overdrawing their bank accounts.) Other major problems: one-fifth of Americans have no access to medical care; few can afford to purchase a house, and one-percent of the population (approximately two million millionaires) received in 1992 over 40% of the national income and the other 99% of Americans shared the remaining 60%. The tax system benefits the rich and puts burdens on the poor and the middle class (the middle class being in a rapid decline, because fewer are getting richer and the majority is sliding into substandard living). Government bureaucracies, at all levels, unlike those in Japan and Germany, often work against rather than for business, thus forcing large American companies to move their production facilities and places of employment for American labor abroad, or simply to sell to foreign investors. The educational system is falling behind the rest of the world, and discipline in the classroom has been replaced with chaos. Schools place emphasis on training rather than educating. The only rapidly growing industries are prisons, courts, and an enormous criminal justice system together with lawyering (the taxpayers pay legal fees for defendants who cannot afford to pay them themselves). Division and distrust between the sexes (e.g., the Hill-Thomas Senate hearings) receive more publicity than a family reunion, because the family, a basic institution of any society, is in rapid decline in importance and stature (there is no cabinet-level agency on the family in the U.S. government). Senator Rudman stated in March 1992 that he would not seek re-election to the U.S. Senate because that institution was no longer effective and could not serve the real interests of the majority of the American electorate because strong interest groups were getting disproportionate benefits over the rest of the American population. There appears to be a case of the freezing of the minds of those in government today who serve the interest of the few and who refuse to recognize and to tackle the real problems, and who hope that because America is strong and rich these problems will rectify themselves with time. See DECADENCE, ENTITLEMENTS, INCOME EQUITY.

FRELIMO. See FRENTE DA LIBERTACAO DE MOZAMBIQUE.

French Connection. See XYZ AFFAIR.

French Foreign Legion. A guard and expeditionary force composed mainly of non-Frenchmen, stationed mainly in Africa to protect the interest of the French Republic.

French National Front. An ultra-conservative, nationalistic (some allege, semi-fascist and racist) political party in contemporary France; a "France-First" party under the leadership of Jean-Marie Le Pen whose main issue during the 1990s has been strong legislation against foreign immigration, legal and illegal. During the 22 March 1992 regional elections in France, the Front received 14 percent of the vote, while the Socialists of President Mitterrand only 19 percent. See FRENCH SOCIALIST PARTY.

French Republics. The First French Republic, 1793-1804, under Napoleon before he became an Emperor; the Second Republic, 1848-1852; the Third Republic, 1870-1940; the Fourth Republic, 1940-1958 (with some interruptions while the pro-Nazi Vichy government was in power); and the Fifth Republic, 1958 to the present. In 1958, a new constitution was introduced (the so-called "DeGaulle Constitution"), and its most characteristic feature is the aim to replace the traditional cabinet-parliamentary system of government (whereby the parliament was all-powerful and caused considerable instability) with a presidential system (after the American pattern).

French Socialist Party. A major political party in the French Fifth Republic, under the leadership of Francois Mitterrand who was elected president in 1981 and re-elected to a second term in 1988. In 1986, the government under the strong and capable leadership of President Mitterrand's commenced an extensive and far-reaching privatization process of over eighty-one nationalized industries. The prime minister in President Mitterrand's government, Edith Cresson, has gained popularity in France as well as in other countries, particularly Germany, because both nations are faced with a serious problem of mass immigration of legal and illegal entrants who compete for jobs and housing with the native population and burden underfinanced school and medical care facilities. Cresson resigned 1 April 1992. See FRENCH NATIONAL FRONT, PRIVATIZATION.

French-Speaking Commonwealth. See FRANCOPHONE.

French Union. The French Republic, once a major global empire, diminished in size and influence after W.W.II, but has retained considerable territories and influence throughout the world, such as the Overseas Departments (e.g., French Guiana, Guadeloupe, Martinique, Mayotte, Reunion, St. Pierre, and Miquelon). In addition, France controls several Overseas Territories (e.g., French Polynesia, the Martinique Islands, New Caledonia, and several others). Within the French Union, also known as the "Francophone," many former French colonies maintain close political and economic relations with France due to its attractive culture and educational system. See FRANCOPHONE.

Frente da Libertacao de Mocambique (FRELIMO). A coalition of political parties and civic organizations which joined forces into a national front for the purpose of liberating Mozambique from Portuguese occupation. On September 20, 1974, Mozambique was allowed to form a provisional government, and on June 25, 1975, became independent with FRELIMO as the single ruling party.

Mozambique became a member of the United Nations Organization on September 16, 1975. Somora Machel is the co-founder of FRELIMO and president of Mozambique.

Frente da Libertacao Nacional de Angola (FLNA). A coalition of civic and political party organizations with pro-western and anti-socialist (communist) leanings, which lost to the MPLA in 1975, and again in another attempt in 1977, in its bid to gain control over Angola. See MOVIMENTO POPULAR DE LIBERTACAO DE ANGOLA (MPLA).

Freshman Legislator. See ROOKIE LEGISLATOR.

Friend of the Court. See AMICUS CURIAE.

Friendship Force. On March 1, 1977, U.S. President Jimmy Carter, as part of promoting peace and understanding between citizens of the United States and those of foreign states through mutual visits and written communications, organized the so-called Friendship Force, a people-to-people type of program. (A similar program was initiated by U.S. President D. D..Eisenhower, but it turned, to a large extent, into an intelligence gathering operation, particularly in Asia, Africa, and Latin America.) Anyone could apply to participate in the program and accepted applicants paid $250 in transportation costs. However, subsidies of up to $200 were available from corporate donations for those unable to pay the full cost. This was a reciprocal program, whereby for each American going abroad, a foreign person was brought to the United States. Mrs. Rosalyn Carter, the President's wife, was the honorary chairperson of the organization.

Friendship Gifts. Monetary or in kind favors freely given by private business to public officials in Japan which are not considered to be bribes.

Fringe Benefits in the United States Congress. The benefits that members of the United States Congress receive in order to allow them to perform their legislative and leadership duties in comfort and with minimum stress. In addition to generous salaries, retirement benefits, at least a three-room suite and more for the staff, and at least an 18 persons staff with salaries and benefits at the discretion of the legislator, legislators are entitled to: a minimum of 33 free trips to their home district; stationery; mailing and printing privileges; dining facilities; sport and gym facilities, and barbershops and beauty shops. (The first beauty shop on Capitol Hill for ladies, was established for a single Senator, Margaret Chase Smith of Maine.) A host of other benefits include parking, the use of limousines, and travel on military aircraft. At present (1992), the base salary of a senator is $125,100.00 per year, plus allowances for staff and other expenses. The administrative and clerical allowances are determined by the size of the population which the legislator represents. According to the Congress Research Service of the Library of Congress, as of 1992, these allowances are as follows: In the Senate: the amount granted to a senator ranges from $847,410 for a state with a population of less than one million, to $1,836,990 for a state with a population of 28,000,000 or more. There are 29 population categories. Each senator may set a salary range for her/his staff at a rate of at least $1,530.00 and not more than $120,559 per year per person. In addition, each senator can spend an additional sum of $280,887 for legislative assistants selected at her/his discretion. Members of the House receive a base salary of $122,500.00 per year and can hire employees at salaries ranging from $1,200.00 to $101,331.00 per person per year; part-time help may be hired at $1,270.00 to $15,240.00 per person per year; and interns may be hired for up to 120 days at a rate of $1,160.00 per month, or $13,920 total per year. Each member may hire not more than 18 permanent employees, and has for that purpose an allowance of $475,000.00. Some other benefits are: telephone allowance of about $6,200 per year and travel allowance of about $6,200 per year. Overall expenses amount to about $190,000.00 per year per member. Congressional officers and leaders receive the following salaries and allowances: (1) President of the Senate (Vice President of the United States serving ex officio): $160,000.00 salary; a non-taxable expense allowance of $10,000.00; $1,387,000.00 for clerks and other expenses; stationery expenses of $4,500.00; an allowance of $2,500.00 for airmail and special delivery mail (other mailing privileges are the same as for other members of Congress), and retirement benefits and Secret Service protection; (2) Speaker of the House of Representatives: $160,000.00 basic salary; salaries and expenses for offices and staff for fiscal year 1992, $1,477.00, and other benefits to which all members of the House are entitled. Other House of Representatives leaders and employees and their salaries are as follows: Majority and Minority Party leaders—$138,900.00; Clerk of the House, $115,092.00; Sergeant at Arms, $115,092.00; Doorkeeper, $115,091; Parliamentarian, $115,091.00; and Postmaster,

$15,092.00. Leaders and Officers of the Senate: Majority and Minority Party leaders, $138,900.00; Secretary of the Senate, $123,600.00; Sergeant at Arms and Doorkeeper, $123,600.00 each; and President pro-tempore, $138,900.00 and $160,600.00 in the absence of the Vice President. Compensation for employees of Standing Committees are: (1) in the House, $115,092.00; and (2) in the Senate, $122,415.00 per annum.

Fritzflop. U.S. President Ronald Reagan on 15 October 1984, criticized presidential hopeful Walter Fritz Mondale for his flip-flop on taxation; at the beginning of the campaign Mondale had proposed tax increases in order to cut the deficit, then he turned around and suggested tax cuts.

From Cold Warrior to Comrade. A slogan that was widely popularized in the Soviet Union (now, since 25 December 1991, the Commonwealth of Independent States) during the 29 July 1991 Summit Conference in Moscow between U.S. President George Bush and Soviet President Mikhail S. Gorbachev. The slogan, especially popular in the churches of Moscow, epitomized the transformation of outlook among many Russians from that of a totalitarian communist to a citizen enjoying friendly relations with other peoples under a democracy.

From Each According to His Ability, to Each According to His Needs. See SOCIALISM.

Front for the Liberation of Quebec. A radical coalition of individuals and organizations of French-speaking citizens of Canada, struggling for the total independence of the Province of Quebec from the Canadian Federation.

Front for the Liberation of the Coast of Somali (FLCS). A revolutionary movement organized in 1964 for the purpose of liberating the Somali Coast from French domination. (Often referred to as the National Front for the Liberation of the Somali Coast.) The Somali Coast is also referred to as Djibouti, and it was granted full independence on June 27, 1977.

Front-Line States. The Black controlled states surrounding South Africa ruled by a white minority, which are determined to aid anti-white forces in the overthrow of white domination in South Africa; they aid mainly the African National Congress (ANC) and other revolutionary organizations by granting sanctuaries to their guerrillas. The front-line states are: Angola, Botswana, Mozambique, Tanzania, Zambia, and Zimbabwe. See AFRICAN NATIONAL CONGRESS (ANC).

Front of National Liberation. See NATIONAL FRONT.

Front Organization. An organization explored or set up for purposes other than those claimed in either its charter or bylaws; an organization pursuing, under disguise, objectives or activities other than those officially claimed (e.g., a communist front organization in a capitalist society and a capitalist front organization in a socialist society). Among the numerous Soviet-sponsored front organizations were the peace movement, women, youth, and trade union organizations operating in the West, particularly in Europe. Among the many American, CIA-sponsored front organizations were, in addition to numerous newspapers and radio programs, particularly in Italy, France and Latin America, the Asia Foundation, the International Confederation of Free Trade Unions (ICFTU), the International Student Conference (ISU), the World Assembly of Youth, and the Congress of Cultural Freedom. Radio Free Europe and Radio Liberty (directed at Eastern Europe and the former Soviet Union) were also sponsored by the CIA. See PROPRIETARIES, SUBVERSIVE ORGANIZATIONS IN THE UNITED STATES, Appendix 27.

Front-Porch Campaign. Once a popular and common mode of political campaigning from the front of one's house, usually the front porch where interested listeners gathered to hear the candidate speak; (now declining due to the popularity of the electronic media. Allegedly, Calvin Coolidge, a very poor and shy orator, was once provoked to speak from the front of his porch, but instead of addressing the political issues facing the presidential campaign, he commented on the weather. When asked to speak on the issues, he stated that he had nothing to say, because there were no problems in America).

Frontier of Prosperity. A concept articulated in 1992 by Janusz Reiter, Polish diplomat and the ambassador to the Federal Republic of Germany, meaning that should such a frontier emerge between Western Europe (specifically Germany) and Poland, a new "iron curtain," an economic one this time, would also emerge, and such a division would weaken stability between East and West. Poland, in his assertion, "can bring stability to the East only under the condition of being strongly linked with the West as an integral part of Western Europe . . . Poland will be an even more attractive partner for the East, the more closely it will be integrated with the West."

FSO. See FOREIGN SERVICE OFFICER.

Fuehrer (Führer). In the German language, "a leader" or "chief of state and/or government." Title assumed by Adolf Hitler, head of state and government, as well as leader of the Nazi Party in Germany (1933-1945). See CAESARISM.

Fuerzas Armadas de Liberacion Nacional (FALN). In the Spanish language, "Army for Violent National Liberation." Also, the liberation army of the Puerto Rican Socialist party which wants to liberate Puerto Rico from the United States. (Puerto Rico voted in 1967 to remain a Commonwealth, an autonomous entity of the United States.) The leader of the Socialist party of Puerto Rico, Juan Mari Bras, cooperated closely with Cuba and the Soviet Union, who supplied the Army with war materiel and funds for propaganda and terrorist activities. The FALN claimed several successful sabotage missions in the United States, including the bombing of the historic Fraunces Tavern in New York City in which five people died. See WORLD PEACE COUNCIL.

Führerprinzip. In the German language, "principle of one leader." Also, the principle of a single, one-man dictatorship in Nazi Germany (1933-1934) as exercised by Adolf Hitler who exercised unlimited power over persons and the state (the Reich).

Fujicoup. See BORDABERIZATION.

Fuken. Political subdivisions—prefectures—in Japan.

Full Faith and Credit. A stipulation contained in the U.S. Constitution (Art. I, Sec. 1) calling upon the states within the Union to give full recognition (". . . *full faith and credit* . . . .") and respect to all legislative and judicial acts, executive decisions, public records, and customs, of each and every state on an equal basis. See FEDERALISM, Appendix 8.

Functional Federalism. See FEDERALISM.

Functional Planning. Development of a single purpose plan such as transportation, housing, open space, or water resources management.

Functional Region. A designated geographic area, under single or multiple political authority, which is fairly self-sufficient in inputs and outputs. One authority on regional planning, John Glasson, defines functional region as "a geographic area which displays a certain functional coherence, an interdependence of parts, when defined on the basis of certain criteria . . . composed of heterogeneous units, such as cities, towns and villages, which are functionally interrelated." Also known as "polarized region," "nodal region," or "dynamic flow region."

Functional Underclass. See CAPITALIST MALADY OF CONTENTMENT.

Functions of Government. According to ACIR, the function, as pertaining to local government in the main, is described as follows: Sustaining functions are the housekeeping, financial, and revenue-raising functions and are subsidiary to liberty, equality, and welfare functions. When local government functions are dominantly liberty-oriented, sustaining functions are minimal and naturally administered in a manner comparable to liberty functions. Sustaining activity has increased along with the volume of welfare activity and has inherited the brunt of the conflict surrounding welfare values. See CONFLICT RESOLUTION.

Fund. See INTERNATIONAL MONETARY FUND (IMF).

Fundamental Law. A law derived from or based on the constitution of a state. See BASIC LAW, CONSTITUTION.

Fundamental Orders of Connecticut. In 1636, a group of disenchanted Puritans moved from Eastern Massachusetts Bay to the Connecticut River Valley where, in 1639, they formed a community based on a constitution, embracing the towns of Hartford, Wetersfield, and Windsor. The constitution, known to be the first such document at that time, consisted of an introduction, or preamble, and eleven articles, and reads in part as follows: "Forasmuch as it hath pleased the Allmighty God by the wise disposition of his divine providence so to order and dispose of things that we the Inhabitants and Residents of Windsor, Harteford and Wethersfield are now cohabiting and dwelling in and upon the River of Conectecotte and the Lands thereunto adjoyneing . . . that to mayntayne the peace and union of such people there should be an orderly and decent Government . . . to order and dispose of the affayres of the people at all seasons; doe theefore associate and conjoyne our selves to be one Publike State or Commonwelth; 1. It is Ordered, sentenced and decreed, that there shall be two generall Assemblies or Courts, the one the second thursday in Aprill, the other the second thursday in September where . . . Magestrats and other publike Officers Chosen . . . one of them Governour . . . to administer justice, and doe cohabittee within the Jurisdiction . . . 2 . . . the Election . . . every person shall bring in one single paper with the name of him written in yet who he desires to have Governour; . . . that noe person be chosen Governour above once in two years (Art. 4). Furthermore, government officials to be elected from all three towns, while all local laws to be passed by all the citizens of each town." This confederation placed no property or religious qualifications for voting or holding public office. This document served as one of the models of constitution—made well before the Philadelphia Constitutional Convention of 1787.

Fundamentals of the Israeli-Arab Settlement. During his January 4, 1978, visit to Aswan, Egypt, U.S. President Jimmy Carter and Egyptian President Anwar Sadat both agreed that there are three fundamental issues upon which the Israeli-Arab settlement rests, and that in order to be lasting, any agreement between these two parties must be cognizant of these fundamentals. They are: (1) the Palestinian people's right to help determine their future (now the Palestinians live in diaspora, scattered throughout Egypt, Jordan, Syria, Lebanon, and Palestine proper under Israel's rule); (2) Israeli withdrawal from territories occupied since the 1967 war; and (3) the final peace settlement between the Arab States and Israel must be based on "normal relations" of lasting duration and not just on non-belligerency. (Non-belligerency, which is in reality a temporary truce among or between warring states, never served well as a basis for peaceful settlement, as was demonstrated in Vietnam, for example. Once the truce had ended, war commenced, and all grounds for peaceful settlement were lost.) Presidents Carter and Sadat favored autonomy for the Palestinians, short of being a sovereign state, preferably in union with Jordan, a sort of Palestinian-Jordanian confederation, before a sovereign Palestinian state is formed. The U.S.-USSR Joint Declaration of September 1977, recognized "Legitimate Rights" of the Palestinian people, while Israel referred only to "Palestinian Interests." President Jimmy Carter stated on January 4, 1978, in Aswan, Egypt: "There must be a resolution of the Palestinian problem in all its aspects . . . the problem must be legitimate rights of the Palestinian people and enable the Palestinians to participate in the determination of their own future." Israel was unwilling to issue any general declaration of principles but preferred to limit the central political questions to self-rule for the Palestinians on the West Bank of the Jordan River, the Gaza Strip, and further disengagement in the Sinai Peninsula. See SADAT-BEGIN SUMMIT.

Funny Thing Happened to Me on My Way to the White House. A phrase repeated often in jest by Adlai E. Stevenson, former Governor of Illinois and nominee of the Democratic Party for President (July 26, 1952, and July 11, 1956), who was twice defeated by his Republican opponent, Dwight D. Eisenhower. Stevenson retired from politics as U.S. Senator from Illinois and, according to unconfirmed legends, earned more income by speaking and writing about how he never got to be President than President Eisenhower, who became one.

Fusion of Powers. See UNITARY STATE, Appendix 82.

Futures. A commitment, once made orally, now made usually in a form of a written contract, indicating amounts, delivery dates, and prices, for the purchase or sale of certain commodities, such as coffee, sugar, grain, and other products.

Fylke. A political subdivision—province—in Norway.

G

"The good of the people is the chief law."
CICERO, 106-43 B.C.

G-5. See GROUP OF FIVE.

G-7. See GROUP OF FIVE.

Gadsden Purchase. A piece of territory adjacent to New Mexico that was purchased from Mexico's dictator, Santa Anna, for a sum of $10,000,000 in 1835, by U.S. Minister to Mexico James Gadsden (a wealthy railroad man from South Carolina), on the order of U.S. Secretary of War Jefferson Davis. The U.S. Senate approved the transaction very reluctantly. See Appendix 97.

Gag Rule. A parliamentary device designed to limit or prevent one from speaking upon an issue at hand or from starting a debate. The first gag resolution in the U.S. Congress was introduced in 1836, after the Nat Turner uprising in Virginia in 1831, to table all anti-slavery appeals without debate and to abridge free speech and the right to petition pertaining to slavery questions. Courts applied the gag rule in various degrees, due to lack of uniformity in the American judicial system, but the U.S. Supreme Court held in 1975, in *Nebraska Press Association v. Stuart,* that "prior restraint on speech and publication are the most serious and least tolerable infringements on First Amendment rights," thus voiding the gag rule order of a Nebraska judge who curbed the right of a journalist to publish reports about a sensational murder trial. Currently, a gag order preventing professionals to discuss abortion with patients in clinics receiving federal government moneys remains in effect, and in 1992 President Bush vetoed legislation to repeal this gag order. However, as of March 20, 1992, an administrative order allows physicians to discuss abortion with their patients and to refer them to clinics where such procedures are available. See ANTIGAG LAW.

Gaiatsu. A new concept developed in the Japanese language meaning "foreign pressure." Traditionally, Japanese political culture is very hostile and resistant to foreign pressure of any kind—political, cultural, economic, or social.

Galloping Communism v. Creeping Socialism. See SOCIALIZED ENTERPRISES IN THE UNITED STATES.

Game Theory. A technique used to study and interpret international politics or to predict policy. Developed for the training of military commanders, it is based on war games in which participating individuals are assigned definite roles to play; decision-making processes are simulated in such a way as to take account of a wide range of variables in the international process and, on the basis of these variables, policy decisions are made. Simply stated, in game theory one wants to ascertain possible moves by "x," undertaken independently or as influenced by moves undertaken by "y." Writer Kelly Tice cites (in *Newsweek,* October 1988) a paradoxical situation of a known Warsaw joke about two Russians in conversation: "Where are you going?" says one. "To Minsk," replies the other. "To Minsk, eh? What a nerve you have! I know that you are telling me that you are going to Minsk because you want me to believe that you are going to Pinsk. But it so happens that I know you really are going to Minsk. So why are you lying to me?"

Gandhi's Totalitarianism. See TASHKENT DECLARATION.

Gandiism. See INDIAN NATIONAL CONGRESS PARTY.

Gang of Eight. See COMMITTEE ON THE STATE OF EMERGENCY.

Gang of Four. After the death (September 9, 1976) of Chairman Mao Tse-tung, the leader of the People's Republic of China, his widow, Ching Ch'ing and three of her associates, Wan Hungwen, Chang Chunchiao, and Yao Wen-yuan, all calling themselves "students of the leader," attempted to take control of the government, but instead were arrested and removed from power by the new leader, Hua Kuo-feng. They have since been condemned for holding China back in its cultural, economic, political, and social development. In April 1978, the Central Committee of the party directed the People's Red Army to maintain strong discipline within its ranks, saying "those who violate discipline would be criticized and given instruction, or in serious cases be disciplined."

Garden Plot. See COUNTERINSURGENCY IN AMERICA.

Garrison State. A state in which major governmental functions and policy making are exercised by the military (e.g., contemporary Iraq where President Saddam Hussein and his cabinet wear military uniforms and exercise dictatorial powers) and where military justice is to justice as march music is to music. See CAESARISM.

Gathering and Retrieval System. See COUNTERINSURGENCY IN AMERICA.

GATT. See GENERAL AGREEMENT ON TARIFFS AND TRADE.

Gavel Rule. An arbitrary exercise of authority by the presiding officer of a gathering, who may terminate business if he wishes by merely rapping the gavel. (This method is often used during political party conventions and in the U.S. Congress.)

Gay Bashing. See HATE CRIME.

Gay Power. The struggle by homosexuals and lesbians to erase from the books all laws which make lesbianism and homosexuality (sodomy) a crime, and to gain equal status with heterosexuals.

Gdansk Understanding. The understanding reached on 31 August 1980 between the Polish Solidarity Union led by Lech Walesa and the communist regime of Poland, that Solidarity and the government were to share power in managing the shipbuilding industry where Walesa was employed as an electrical technician. The agreement was signed in the port city of Gdansk where Solidarity had originated. This agreement was subsequently broken by the government and martial law was declared; Solidarity was outlawed, only to return to power a decade later. See CRISIS STAFF, SOLIDARITY.

GEACPS. See GREATER EAST ASIAN CO-PROSPERITY SPHERE.

Gehlen Organization. An intelligence-gathering and evaluating organization, set up in July 1946 by a former Nazi general and a former prisoner of war of the United States, Reinhard Gehlen, in the U.S. occupation zone of Germany, under the supervision of the U.S. Central Intelligence Agency (CIA). Gehlen, as the former chief of the German intelligence (Foreign Armies East) for the USSR, held control over his espionage network personally and kept it intact. In April 1956, his organization became the official West German Intelligence Service, under his leadership. He retired in April 1968, cited as the most talented spy ever, and the West German magazine, *Der Spiegel*, cited him as the "Grand Old Man of Espionage."

Gemeinde. In the German language, "village." A small political subdivision, such as a village or a small town, in German-speaking nations.

Gender Gap. See DECADENCE.

General Act for the Settlement of International Disputes. A declaration on peaceful settlement of disputes among sovereign states which was drafted during the 1899 Hague Conference and amended in 1907, during the second Hague gathering, at which fifty sovereign states agreed to establish the Permanent Court of Arbitration. It was agreed in Article 38 of the General Act that the signatories should rely on international conventions in settling legal international disputes, except in matters related to "national honor" which each state was permitted to settle according to its own discretion. See HAGUE PEACE CONFERENCES.

General Agreement on Tariffs and Trade (GATT). A series of agreements entered into by the states of the Western world, designed to work toward gradual elimination of all restrictions on international trade (e.g., tariffs) and to intensify international exchange. Some of the first agreements were reached in 1948, mainly in Europe. See CHICKEN WAR, COMPARATIVE ADVANTAGE, KENNEDY ROUND, PRODUCT CYCLE, UNILATERAL GLOBAL KEYNESIANISM.

General Assembly. One of the major organs of the United Nations. Also, the name of legislative bodies in some states in the U.S. (e.g., Virginia). See UNITED NATIONS ORGANIZATION, Appendices 75-79.

General Bill. See BILL.

General Charter. An instrument by which the state legislature enacts a general law that serves as the basis for the formation and operation of municipal governments.

General Classification Charter. An instrument of incorporation which may be granted to municipalities that have similar characteristics (e.g., similar population size).

General Council of the Valleys. Unicameral legislative body of Andorra.

General Court. The official name of the legislatures in the states of Massachusetts and New Hampshire in the U.S.

General Declaration of Principles of the Israeli-Arab Settlement. See FUNDAMENTALS OF THE ISRAELI-ARAB SETTLEMENT.

General Intelligence Division (GID). See RED MENACE.

General People's Congress. The unicameral legislative body of Libya.

General Public Interest. See POLITICS OF SPECIAL INTERESTS.

General-Purpose Government. See COUNTY.

General Revenue Sharing. Formula distribution of money from one level of government to another without matching requirements, special conditions pertaining to its use, or planning requirements.

General Services Administration (GSA). An agency of the U.S. Government charged with controlling and maintaining federal property and rendering a variety of auxiliary services to governmental agencies. The agency services all public buildings, provides transportation services, and maintains the National Archives and Record Service of the United States.

General Strike. A refusal to work by all of the workers in an area or nation, usually share-lived and intended to exhibit a unity among workers.

General Ticket System. An electoral system under which the voters may elect a variety of officers (e.g., in the U.S. citizens vote on the same day and often on the same ballot for the President, Vice President, Senators, Congressmen, Governors, members to state legislative assemblies, and a variety of local government officials).

General Welfare Clause. The provision contained in the U.S. Constitution (Art. I, Sec. 8) which grants Congress the power to tax in order to "*. . . provide for the common defense and general welfare of the United States.*" See Appendix 8.

General Will. According to French political philosopher, J. J. Rousseau (1712-1778), only "general will" ("volonté général") expressed by citizens (e.g., through voting) can be implemented as a policy and a law, and is assumed to be sufficient to achieve legitimate consent. In a society with a large and diversified electorate, this is the only consent possible, because the "will of all" is not. The American industrialist W. Vanderbilt had little tolerance for the will of the public when he stated: "The public be damned."

Generalissimo. A superlative title for a general officer in a military service, ordinarily the commander-in-chief of the armed forces who, at the same time, serves as the real head of state or head of government (e.g., Josef Stalin of the Soviet Union, Chiang Kai-shek of the Republic of China's Taiwan, or Formosa, and Francisco Franco of Spain).

Geneva Accords (or Agreements) of 1954. A series of agreements reached in Geneva, Switzerland, in May 1954, among France, Cambodia, Laos, and Vietnam, on terms for ending the war in Indochina and for pulling out French forces. The U.S., England, and the Soviet Union also took part in the Conference, witnessing an agreement of cease-fire between North and South Vietnam. In order to supervise the cease-fire agreement, a special International Control Commission (composed of representatives from Canada, India, and Poland) was set up. England and the Soviet Union were to serve as the co-chairmen of the agreement and were to supervise the International Control Commission.

Geneva Conference on Laos. A multi-national conference that was held in Geneva, Switzerland, in 1962, during which the representatives of the People's Republic of China demanded that all Western powers, particularly the United States, withdraw from Indochina (e.g., Laos, Cambodia, and South Vietnam) and let the people of those states determine their destiny. These demands were rejected by the United States until 1975, when the area was finally abandoned, as had been suggested by the Chinese in 1962. See TRAGIC SITUATION, VIETNAMIZATION.

Geneva Conventions. A series of four agreements or international treaties on the humane treatment of prisoners of war and those wounded on a battlefield, entered into by most civilized nations on August 21, 1864, in Geneva, Switzerland. In order to carry out the provisions of the Convention, a new organization was established, the Red Cross (the emblem of which, the red cross, was taken from the flag of the Swiss state). The second convention was signed in 1906, the third in 1929, and the fourth in 1949. The 1949 convention addressed mainly the issue of treatment of prisoners of war, mainly the often inhumane treatment by Nazi Germany and Militarist Japan. It also provided for the humane treatment of the wounded, children, pregnant women, and the elderly; protection from torture, reprisal, collective punishment, and deployment of any type of mistreatment in forced labor; and discrimination on account of race, sex, nationality, religion, or political persuasion. The conventions were supplemented with the Hague Peace Conferences of 1899 and 1907, which extended these protections to men of war engaged in maritime warfare. Further, under its "International Rules of Engagement," a soldier may shoot and kill in combat only when shot upon. Probably the first international document outlawing all kinds of discrimination.

Geneva Protocol. Nation states, members of the League of Nations, agreed in 1924, during a conference held in Geneva, Switzerland, that international disputes among states, as suggested by the Kellogg-Briand Pact, ought to be settled by peaceful means, instead of by open war. See KELLOGG-BRIAND PACT, PACIFIC SETTLEMENT OF DISPUTES.

Genghis. In the Mongolian language, "heavenly emperor" or "heavenly ruler." Also, the official name of Temuchin, known as "Genghis Khan" or "Heavenly Emperor of the Mongolian Khanate," (1162-1227). Genghis Khan established the largest empire in the documented history of man stretching from China to Western Europe, including India and Russia; he established the largest and most disciplined army ever. Known as the "Golden Horde" it was regimented into groups of tens, hundreds, and thousands for the purpose of organization and combat efficiency. The Khan's personal elite shock troops, known as "brave fighters" or the "guard," helped not only in administering the vast armies, but in local government organizations as well. Many leaders since have patterned their elite forces after these troops, e.g., the SS or "Schutz Staffel" in Nazi Germany, which constituted the elite and most dedicated force of the Nazi despot, Adolf Hitler (1933-1945).

Genocide. The premeditated annihilation of an entire race or nation (e.g., the holocaust conducted by the Nazis in Germany). In some African states, selfish political groups struggle for political control, spend whatever resources there are for weapons instead for the needs of their citizens and deny the civilian population access to food. These are open barbaric crimes against humanity exceeding those perpetrated by Adolf Hitler and his Nazi thugs during W.W.II against the Jews and the Slavs. Although this criminal activity is widely known, no international organization, e.g., the United Nations or the Organization of African Unity, took steps to initiate the criminal prosecution against the leaders through the World Court (International Court of Justice). There are precedences for the prosecution of crimes against humanity and the leaders responsible for such crimes ought to be arrested by an international police force and brought to justice. Crimes against humanity should not be tolerated by the world community even if it is necessary to violate the sovereignty of a guilty state. See INFANTICIDE.

Genocide Convention. A Convention approved by the General Assembly of the United Nations Organization in 1948, and signed by many states (the U.S. ratified it on February 19, 1986; the Soviet Union did not sign it); it considers any act committed with the intent to destroy, in whole or in part, any national, ethnic, racial, or religious group, an international crime and a crime against humanity. See KHMER ROUGE, WAR CRIME.

Genro. Elder statesmen who acted as unofficial advisors to rulers of Japan.

Genscher Doctrine. Dr. Hans Dietrich Genscher, foreign minister of the Federal Republic of Germany (prior to the reunification of Germany), proclaimed in 1988 that there should be closer collaboration among the four major powers, Germany, France, United States, and the former Soviet Union. He called for the "Washington-Paris-Bonn-Moscow Axis," as stipulated by the 20-year treaty that was signed between Germany and the Soviet Union, with these four countries engaged in close collaboration as "unrestricted partnership." It was Genscher's desire to "bring the Soviet Union and Eastern Europe closer to the EC and NATO." This notion also encompasses the notion of "common European home" proclaimed by Soviet President Mikhail S. Gorbachev, and was a continuation of the spirit of the 1975 Helsinki Agreement at the Conference on Security and Cooperation in Europe. This rapprochement was considered a major and decisive step in the direction of East-West collaboration, and a guarantee of peace among the superpowers. Dr. Gensher resigned on 27 April 1992.

Gentleman's Boss. A nickname for Chester A. Arthur, U.S. President (1881-1885).

Gentlemen Do Not Read One Another's Mail. With these words U.S. Secretary of War, Henry L. Stimson (1929-1933), ordered the "black chamber," America's first code breaking and intelligence interception operation to be closed and disbanded in 1929.

Gentlemen's Agreement. An agreement based on good faith (usually verbal) between two or more heads of government. It is not subject to confirmation or ratification, nor does it have the force of law or of a treaty. Such agreements are, as a rule, of short duration and binding only on the parties to the agreement.

Geoeconomics. The relationship between geographic and economic factors in human endeavors, and how they affect each other (e.g., in matters of food production, forests, waters, minerals, and the general ecosystem).

Geopolitics. The application of geography to politics, or the study of the relationships of geography and political phenomena in international politics (e.g., the notion that acquisition of territory contributes to the power of the state acquiring it). Concept developed by Professor Rudolf Kjellen of Sweden in his book *The State as a Form of Life,* in which the state is viewed as a geographic organism in space.

Geotechnics. A term coined by Sir Patrick Geddes (*Cities in Revolution: An Introduction to the Town Planning Movement and to the Study of Civics),* pertaining to Benton MacKaye's description for remodeling and transforming the earth into a better place to live through the systematic planned use of resources. See PLANNING.

German Bloc/Association of the Expelled and Disenfranchised (BG/BHE). A political organization, very active during the 1950s and 1960s in then West Germany—the Federal Republic of Germany— which consisted of about two million German people who either voluntarily moved from Eastern Europe (e.g., Poland and Czechoslovakia) to Germany, or were expelled for various reasons, and who lobbied the German parliament to somehow restore their lands and possessions. The group was represented in the German Bundestag and the Bundesrat (the West German Parliament), and recently, with the old generation dying out, it merged with the various political parties. Recently, the governments of Poland and the Chech-Slovak Federative Republic introduced a series of legislative acts to let the expelled Germans restore their property or be reinbursed for it in the form of bonds. See SPECIAL INTEREST-TYPE POLITICAL PARTY.

German Economic Miracle. In the German language, "Wirtschaftswunder," the phenomenal revival of the German economy—as well as social and political life—in Germany so devastated during W.W.II. The nation that was to have been "bombed to the stone age, or pastoral age" by the Morgenthau Plan, revived in a relatively short period of time, 1945-1949. By 1949, the German Federal Government was installed in its own right (the East Germans established their pro-Soviet German

Democratic Republic), and although American cigarettes became the prime currency of the day, Germany under the able leadership of Dr. Konrad Adenauer, soon restored its productive capabilities, and by 1955 brought the standard of living to a par with France, England and Italy. Because of well-understood work ethic principles and rigid discipline, the German state, under Dr. Helmut Kohl, surpassed the United States and Japan in many areas of quality of life by 1990.

German Federal Law of Compensation. In the German language, Bundesentschädigungsgesetz (BEG). See BUNDESRÜCKERSTATTUNGSGESETZ (BRÜG).

German Federal Restitution Law. See BUNDESRÜCKERSTATTUNGSGESETZ (BRÜG).

German People's Union. A small but active and vocal extreme-right political party in Germany which advocates "Germany-first" policies, opposes settlement by foreign, non-German people in Germany, and advocates strict and centralized control over the destiny of the nation. The party is also anti-communist.

German Reich. See THIRD REICH.

German Reunification. See UNIFICATION OF GERMANY.

German Secret Police (GESTAPO). In the German language, "Geheime Staatspolizei." A highly centralized, selective and disciplined police force whose task it was to protect the interests of the Nazi party and its officials, the Nazi state in general, and to protect the Führer, Adolf Hitler, in particular.

German Unification. With the failure of socialist (communist) economies everywhere, Germany, divided since the end of W.W.II into the capitalist Federal Republic of Germany (FRG) and the socialist (communist) German Democratic Republic (GDR), took steps to unify the country. The initial meeting held in Ottawa, Canada, was attended by the Big Four: the United States, Soviet Union, France, and the United Kingdom, as well as by foreign ministers from GDR and FRG to outline the steps leading to unification. Agreement on monetary unity was reached in July 1990, with the FRG mark emerging as legal tender. The actual merger of the two separate states was announced on 3 October 1990, with the first all-German election held on 2 December of that year. The Berlin Wall was eliminated in 1989, but differences among East and West Germans remained. Antagonism arose between the so-called "Ossi," East Germans, and "Wessi," West Germans. The Ossis resented some of the Wessi's policies and practices and coined the term "Besserwessi," or "Westerner who knows everything better," (The Society of the German Language in Wiesbaden honored this as the "best word" of 1991.) Other new phrases include "Preussenfieber" or "Prussian fever," pertaining to the revival of some aspects of Prussian militarism, and "Ausländerhass," meaning "hatred of foreigners." Violence often occurred against the "Guest Arbeiter," the "guest workers," who were foreign labor imported to do menial chores which the Germans preferred not to do. "Kurzarbeit Null" or "pay without work" describes the fact that many state-owned enterprises in East Germany (and also in other states in Eastern Europe) paid meager wages to workers but had no work for them. This is a socialist brand of Marxist "surplus value" (see SURPLUS VALUE), where the workers think they are being paid and the state employers think that they are getting their money's worth! See I LOVE GERMANY SO MUCH THAT I PREFER TO HAVE TWO OF THEM, Appendix 105.

German Workers' Party. See FASCISM.

Germany, Unification of. See UNIFICATION OF GERMANY.

Germany's Reparations. See HOOVER MORATORIUM.

Germany's Reparations for Nazi Atrocities. See BUNDESRÜCKERSTATTUNGSGESETZ (BRÜG).

Gerontocracy. The rule by elders or mature persons.

Gerontology. The science of the aging processes and the needs of older people in a society.

Gerrymandering. The practice of tampering with the boundaries of an electoral district so as to give an advantage in elections to one party over another, to eliminate a certain category of persons from voting, or to diminish their voting strength by re-designing the boundaries of a voting district. The phrase was coined from the name of Elbridge Gerry, the Governor of the state of Massachusetts in 1812, who was instrumental in having the State Legislature divide Essex County into two separate electoral districts, drawing the boundaries in such a way as to give an advantage to the candidates of the Jeffersonian Republican Party over the Federalist Party.

Gestapo. Geheime Staats Polizei. See GERMAN SECRET POLICE.

Get in the Ring with Me and Stay There! See NO CANDIDATE CANDIDATE.

Get the Country Moving Again. One of the major slogans, often referred to as the "one-million-votes slogan," of the J. F. Kennedy-Richard M. Nixon debates in 1960. The nation was anxious to see a man in the White House who would be able to move the nation after years of stagnation and international embarrassment caused by: (1) acute economic problems at home; (2) Soviet technological superiority as demonstrated by the launching of the orbital satellite Sputnik in 1957; and (3) the U-2 affair, when, for the first time in U.S. history, the President of the United States admitted publicly that the USSR was spied upon. See GREAT DEBATES.

Gettysburg Address. A major commemorative address delivered by U.S. President Abraham Lincoln on November 19, 1863, (during dedication ceremonies on the battlefield in Gettysburg, Pennsylvania), in which he defined American democracy as one having a "... *government of the people, by the people, for the people."*

GGU. See GHANA-GUINEA UNION.

Ghana-Guinea Union (GGU). An informal union that was set up between Ghana and Guinea on November 23, 1958, and later joined by Mali on April 29, 1961. See WEST AFRICAN SUMMIT CONFERENCE (WASC).

Ghent, Treaty of. See WAR OF 1812.

Gheroy Sotzyalistitchesghogo Truda. See HERO OF SOCIALIST LABOR.

Gheroy Sovyetzghogo Soyuza. See HERO OF THE SOVIET UNION.

Ghetto. A part of medieval cities where Jews were required to reside, segregated from the general population. Today, a certain part of a city in which a concentration of persons with some common characteristics or objectives (e.g., national, ethnic, religious, or racial) resides. This term is also commonly applied to urban residential slums which are usually inhabited by blacks or other minorities living in utmost poverty. See URBAN GROWTH POLICY, URBANIZATION, WARSAW GHETTO.

Ghetto Uprising. See WARSAW GHETTO.

Ghost District. See ROTTEN BOROUGH.

Ghost Vote. The practice of casting ballots in elections using the names of persons no longer alive.

GI. See GOVERNMENT ISSUE.

GID. See RED MENACE.

Gin and Jazz Mentality. See ROARING TWENTIES.

Give and Take of Politics. See TYRANNY OF THE MAJORITY.

Give Me Liberty or Give Me Death! An impassioned outcry for independence from British oppression, by Virginia's patriot, Patrick Henry, spoken at the Virginia House of Burgesses on March 23, 1775. The next year, 1776, Virginia drafted a new constitution, including the progressive Virginia Bill of Rights, and Thomas Jefferson drafted the Declaration of Independence. Patrick Henry, a brave legislator for those times, proposed a very controversial bill in 1784, which stipulated that any white female or male who married a native American, will receive ten pounds immediately and an additional five pounds for each child born. Also, all male children born from such mixed marriages, were to receive free education and subsequent tax breaks up to age 21. The measure passed two readings, but failed its third and final reading in the Virginia Legislature, because its author and sponsor became governor and had no access to sponsor the bill in the legislature. See TOWNSHEND REVENUE ACT, VIRGINIA BILL OF RIGHTS.

Give Them Hell, Harry! U.S. President Harry S. Truman (1944-1953), an energetic and grasping leader, who suffered fools poorly, and who was usually very open and blunt in his political style, using language "that made even lumberjacks blush." To those who complained to him about the burden of politics or political office, he would suggest: "If you can't stand the heat, get out of the kitchen!" Instead of his name, the presidential name plate on his desk read: "The buck stops here!" The "Give them Hell . . . " slogan originated during Truman's 1948 presidential campaign when he was bashing opponents of civil rights legislation (Truman desegregated the Armed Forces by a Presidential Order), and was receiving encouragement to proceed in his effort to eliminate the segregation among races.

Glasnost. See COLD WAR.

Glassboro, Spirit of. See SPIRIT OF GLASSBORO.

Glavnoye Razvyedyvatelnoye Upravlytienye (GRU). See PEOPLE'S COMMISSION FOR INTERNAL AFFAIRS (NKVD).

Global Collective Security. See Appendix 31.

Global Independence. See INTERDEPENDENCE.

Global Localization. A concept developed (in *The Borderless World*) by Dr. Kenichi Ohmae, a Japanese scholar, and by Akio Morita, chairman of the Sony Corporation, asserting that successful global corporations are without any specific nationality because they are multinational or transnational, global in ownership, and in scope of operations. At the same time, they also prove to be good and loyal citizens to the constituency or community in which they reside and/or which they serve.

Global Population Growth. See POPULATION GROWTH PROJECTIONS, POPULATION GROWTH: BIRTH RATES AND DEATH RATES in Appendices 85, 86.

Global Village. See GLOBALISM.

Globalism. The way of viewing the international community of nations as a single nation, the global village; also, a state with a broad outlook on the conduct of its foreign relations and policies. The terms, "global village" or "mondialism," are often used in a similar context.

Globalist. See ONE-WORLDER.

Globalization. The divergent global community is more interdependent than ever, despite economic, political, and social systems being in constant conflict with one another. Such notions as "competition" and "diversification" become obsolete in time because, as author Ohmae points out the needs and preferences of customers worldwide are globalized. Therefore, any enterprise whose market strategy is based on delivering value instead of beating the competition, can be successful. The creation and forging of alliances, rather than just joint-ventures or long-term contracts, are considered to be essential to globalization strategy, as are horizontal rather than vertical network linkages. Globalized horizontal network linkages are based on value, not patriotism, nationalism, or individual personalities. See AMERICA BASHING, INTERDEPENDENCE.

Glorious Revolution. During the struggle for power between the English Monarch Charles I (1625-1649) and the British Parliament, a revolution erupted (1642-1649) which resulted in the establishment of a republican form of government under the leadership of Oliver Cromwell (1649-1660), a Puritan. In 1660, however, monarchy was restored (British Restoration) to Charles II (1660-1685) under whom the Parliament not only became recognized as the lawmaking body of England, but also in 1688, under King James II (1685-1688), a Bill of Rights was introduced which further curtailed the powers of the monarch. England remains to this day a parliamentary monarchy with the Parliament having the ultimate authority of the Kingdom (the state). See REIGNING.

GNP. See GROSS NATIONAL PRODUCT.

Go West, Young Man, Go West! Advice that Horace Greeley (1811-1872), American politician and pioneer-journalist, gave in 1858 to a young man, Josiah B. Grinnell, who had become frustrated when his vocal cords went bad making him unable to perform his task as a clergyman in New York City.

Grinnell took Greeley's advice, went West, to Iowa, became a lawyer, member of the U.S. Congress (the House of Representatives) in 1863, established the town of Grinnell, a liberal arts college, and acquired wealth. Grinnell's success in the West triggered mass migration by others; the West was eventually conquered (from the Indians) enabling America to become a large, powerful, and wealthy nation. Greeley meanwhile remained in politics in the East, and founded the *New York Tribune* (one of America's largest newspapers which boasts among its former correspondents such famous persons as Dr. Karl Marx, the founding-father of modern Communism, and which surrendered to the all competitive medium of television and folded in 1978). Greeley also undertook some not too successful projects (e.g., putting up bail for Jefferson Davis, President of the conquered Southern Confederacy, and running for the presidency in 1872, to be defeated by Ulysses S. Grant). See IMPERIALISM, LEBENSRAUM, Appendix 97.

God Bless Our Marxist Revolution and John Paul! See LIBERATION THEOLOGY.

God! What a Job! Remark made by U.S. President Warren G. Harding, (1921-1923) about the magnitude and complexity of the American presidency.

Godfather. See MAFIA.

Golan Heights. See SADAT-BEGIN SUMMIT, Appendix 95.

Golden Horde. See GENGHIS.

Golden Parachute. An agreement that may be entered into by an employee and employer stipulating that in case of layoff, dissolution of the enterprise, or a merger, the employee will receive certain benefits, such as severance pay for loss of wages arising from such situations not caused by the employee.

Good God! Chet Arthur President of the United States. See DARK HORSE.

Good Government Party. See PROHIBITION PARTY.

Good Neighbor Policy. A series of policy pronouncements made by U.S. President Franklin D. Roosevelt during his first two administrations (1933-1941), in which he expressed the need for improved diplomatic and trade relations with the Latin-American republics, rejected the practice of the takeover of one state by another, and called for close cooperation in economic and mutual defense matters. (The foundations for the "Good Neighbor Policy" were laid down by Roosevelt's predecessor, Herbert Hoover.)

Good Offices. An offer which may be extended by a neutral party to mediate and to bring about reconciliation between parties to a dispute. (U.S. President Theodore Roosevelt successfully extended his good offices and brought about peace between Russia and Japan after the 1905 war. He was awarded the Nobel Peace Prize for this achievement.) See ARBITRATION, CONCILIATION, DIPLOMACY, MEDIATION.

Good-Will Diplomacy. A visit by a head of state and/or head of government to another for the purpose of maintaining good rapport and relations rather than transacting serious business. Such good will tours are often a prelude to more serious business that may follow. States with traditional ties of friendship practice such diplomacy whenever a change of government or major shift in policy occurs.

Gook. See VIET-MINH.

GOP (Grand Old Party). See REPUBLICAN PARTY.

Gorbachev of South Africa. An affectionate name for South Africa's president, Frederick W. de Klerk, who, in a brave but risky move, decided to call for a referendum on ending the system of apartheid in South Africa and including the black majority in the government. In this, he was somewhat like Mikhail S. Gorbachev in the former Soviet Union who opened the "evil empire" to democracy. The referendum was held on 17 March 1992, in spite of threats to de Klerk by opponents of apartheid. Almost two-thirds of the white population voted in the white-only referendum, in favor of his plan for a new constitution and restoration of a democratic electoral process.

Gosplan. See STATE PLANNING COMMITTEE.

Govern from Below. Sandanistas' slogan April 25, 1990, when Mrs. Chamorro took over as president in Nicaragua, to rule from above.

Government. Throughout the centuries, people in different parts of the world have defined their government in many different ways; what it is and what it is not; what it does and what it should not do—where, when, how, and why? In the temporal theory of the origin of government, there are no empirically evaluated facts or specific dates, but, most probably, when two men came out of a cave, one clobbered the other into submission and, hence, we have the beginning of government. Government is often viewed as the highest form of a political organization set up to manage people and institutions, with or without their will, as an instrument of oppression and organized terror, or as an organization set up to protect the weak against the strong. Government can be defined as an organization set up to maintain peace and tranquillity among people living under a certain set of rules, regulations, or laws called a state; government can also be defined as the institutionalized will of a given society to promote its aspirations in an orderly manner and on a continuous basis. Nowhere can a society today function without some form of political organization which it calls government. Governments, unlike states, may change often, and the end of a government does not mean an end of the state. There is a great variety of descriptions of government involving such criteria as where it comes from, whom it represents, and how—be it a government of law, a government of men, or, as President Abraham Lincoln (1861-1865) characterized the United States: a government "of the people, by the people, for the people." A government can be democratic or totalitarian, one that is the servant, a steward of the people, or one that lords over the people, a government for its own sake; as well as having countless other characteristics. The oldest governments in continuous existence today are the Vatican state and the small nation on the Italian Coast in Europe, San Marino (ca. 338 or 668 AD). See STATE, TOOLS OF GOVERNMENT, TWO SWORDS THEORY, Appendices 1, 3, 67-71.

Government as a Committee. See ROUSSEAU'S COLLECTIVISM.

Government Budget. A document (prepared in the United States by the Office of Management and Budget with the Assistance of the Council of Economic Advisers and other federal agencies working for the U.S. President) which outlines the anticipated cost of operating the government on the basis of expected incoming revenue during a single fiscal year. Under the provisions of the Budget and Accounting Act of 1921 (prior to that law there was no uniform budgeting system because each department submitted its own budget directly to Congress), all agencies submit their budgets to the President, who in turn submits a consolidated budget to Congress for approval and appropriation. The federal budget includes estimated expenditures for all of its three branches: The Congress, the Executive, and the Judiciary, for a fiscal year that begins on October 1 of each year. In 1974, Congress established special budget committees in both Houses, the House of Representatives and the Senate, which will examine more closely federal priorities and requested federal funds. See ECONOMIC MESSAGE, Appendix 37.

Government by Assembly. A system of government whereby the legislative branch plays a dominant role in the execution of national policies (e.g., under cabinet-parliamentary government). See CABINET-PARLIAMENTARY GOVERNMENT.

Government by Crisis. See CRISIS GOVERNMENT.

Government by Litigation. The Chief Justice of the U.S. Supreme Court, Warren E. Burger, stated in September 1976 that Congress is producing an unusually large amount of legislation (legislation explosion), a large proportion of which is in turn being brought in before the federal courts for testing of its constitutionality (judicial review). This overburdens the courts and leads to adjudication upon extensive litigation (government by litigation) and broadens the powers of the courts (judicial imperialism) over issues that once had been solved by political processes alone. Burger suggested that Congress require each of its committees reporting on a bill to provide an impact statement analyzing the effect of the proposed bill on the work of the courts. (Similar to the "environmental impact statements" which are required by the Environmental Protection Agency from builders of physical facilities e.g., factories, production plants, or schools, which are subsidized by federal money, in order to determine the possible harm that the building of the projects may cause to the environment.) See COMPETENCE IMPACT STATEMENT.

Government Commissioner. A member of a planning district commission designated to represent the government as such and not the public in general.

Government Consolidation. See AREAWIDE GOVERNMENT.

Government Corporation. A business-type, autonomous agency of the government set up to regulate or perform necessary services for profit e.g., the Tennessee Valley Authority, Export-Import Bank, Atomic Energy Commission, Library of Congress, Government Printing Office, Postal Service, and a host of other areas which the corporations (also known as "Public Authorities") control ranging from prisons, to transportation, to economic development, and housing. There are, according to Professor Donald Axelrod (*Shadow Government*) about 35,000 such public authorities in America and they control about $1 trillion.

Government, Functions of. See CONFLICT RESOLUTION.

Government-in-Exile. A normal practice by states which are overrun and occupied by foreign aggressors to move the government—a symbol of the continuity of the state—to a location provided by a friendly state. Governments in exile continue to function on a limited scale with the hope that once their nation is liberated they will be able to return. Some never do, because, as in the case of many East European states, the governments in exile simply expire. In the states that freed themselves from communist regimes (e.g., Poland, Czechoslovakia, Rumania, Hungary, Bulgaria, and the Baltic states), new political forces emerged from within the population to take over political control (e.g., Solidarity in Poland).

Government in the Sunshine. See SUNSHINE LAW.

Government Issue (GI). Anything that is issued by or placed at the disposal of the American federal government.

Government of, by, and for the People. A definition of democracy by Abraham Lincoln, U.S. President (1861-1865).

Government of Laws, Not of Man. An ancient notion, re-articulated by French and British political philosophers during the 18th and 19th centuries, and well taken by the Founding Fathers of the American republic, that, in the liberal democratic tradition, a politically organized society, in order to remain viable and lasting, must rest on laws which are obeyed equally by the governed as well as those who govern, and that the best means to preserve that end is a written constitution. See LIBERALISM.

Government-of-the-Day. A notion pertaining to the government under a cabinet-parliamentary system (e.g., England) which, upon a vote of no confidence by the parliament or the decision of the premier, prime minister, or chancellor, may be dissolved at any time and replaced by a newly-formed government. See CABINET-PARLIAMENTARY GOVERNMENT, HOUSE OF COMMONS, PARLIAMENT, PARLIAMENTARY DEMOCRACY.

Government of the Masses. See JACKSONIAN DEMOCRACY.

Government of Wall Street, by Wall Street, and for Wall Street. See POPULIST.

Government Regulation. An authority that every government everywhere exercises over its citizens, institutions and processes that affect human beings well being the moment of inception and beyond one's death (e.g., the protection of gravesides). In the United States there are about fifty regulations for every law passed by Congress and executive order by either the President, the governor, the county board chairman, or the city or town mayor. During the George Bush Administration, for example (1989-1991 period), over 5,000 new federal regulations were introduced as compared with only 4,000 regulations during the Ronald Reagan Presidency (1981-1989). By comparison, while almost two million Americans lost their jobs during the Bush Administration, federal employment of regulators rose by 6.8%. The cost of regulation in America at the federal level is about $30.00 per year household, or about $20 billion. President Bush issued a moratorium on new regulations—particularly those that stifle American business and its global competitive advantage—for ninety days in April 1992. See COMPARATIVE ADVANTAGE, CIVIL RIGHTS HUSTLER.

Government, Tools of. See TOOLS OF GOVERNMENT.

Governmental Crisis. See CRISIS.

Governmental Subdivision. Separate jurisdictions, units of local government such as county, city, town, or township. Planning district commissions are also considered governmental or political subdivisions.

Governmentalism. A notion that the political government is capable of solving all human problems in a society. President Ronald Reagan spoke against the growth of government and reliance on government for solving all the nation's problems; and in a speech on 15 October 1984, warned of the threat big government poses to personal initiative and even to liberty.

Governor. In terms of politics and government, the chief executive officer of any one state of the American federation. In most states, governors are constitutional officers (provided for by the state constitution) elected directly by the voters, usually for a four-year term, and most are subject to autosuccession (may not succeed themselves for a second term). The usual constitutional duties of a governor are to enforce the laws as passed by the state legislature; veto or approve legislative bills; serve as a working chief administrator; represent the state internally and externally; command the state militia (the National Guard) and state police; prepare the budget; suggest legislation; appoint all officers to the government, subject to approval by the legislature (e.g., cabinet, boards, commissions, special committees); and appoint members of Congress, both the Senate and the House, in case a vacancy occurs (sometimes governors appoint themselves) for the remainder of the unexpired term. In some states, he appoints judges at all levels, from the lowest district court to the state supreme court; he may also declare emergencies and request federal aid when appropriate and necessary. A governor is, to some extent, a "mini-president." See Appendices 57-61.

Governor Moonbeam. See SMALL IS BEAUTIFUL, WE, THE PEOPLE, TAKE AMERICA BACK.

Governors' Conference. An informal annual gathering of all state governors in the U.S. (since 1908), for the purpose of exchanging views and experiences on the adoption of uniform policies.

Goyim. In the Hebrew language, a person residing outside the state of Israel, usually a Jew, who is supporting Israel, usually by raising funds for defense or by building the infrastructure and housing for newly-arriving Jewish immigrants who settle on former Arab lands. The military effort of Israel is costly and it is the pivotal instrument in the expansion of the State. As Israel's Foreign Minister David Levy stated in 1990: "We believe in two things, the Jewish God and the Israel Defense Forces."

GPU. See DEPARTMENT FOR STATE POLITICAL ADMINISTRATION.

Gracchi Reforms. A series of drastic political, social, and economic reforms that were proposed by the Gracchi brothers, Tiberius and Gaius (Roman Tribunes, 133-122 BC) in ancient Rome. Their aim was primarily to cure the corrupt system of Rome, and thus save the state from total collapse by the implementation of such reforms as the confiscation of land of large land-owners and its distribution among the landless peasants. These reforms were never implemented due to strong opposition by vested interests. (The Gracchi Reforms serve as a source of inspiration to revolutionaries and social reformers.)

Gradualism. The practice of solving domestic or international problems by relying on conciliatory methods, such as bargaining and legislative or administrative action, rather than resorting to war or an all-out revolution.

Graduated Response. See FLEXIBLE RESPONSE.

Gramm-Rudman-Hollings Deficit Reduction Act. See ZIGZAG MAN.

Grand Alliance. The military collaboration between the W.W.II Allies and Russia, the victim of a surprise attack by Nazi forces in June 1941. The Allies included: the United States, Great Britain, France (the General Charles de Gaulle government in exile), Canada, Australia, and the several governments in exile of the conquered states (e.g., Poland, Czechoslovakia, Norway, Belgium, the Netherlands, and others). The Alliance lasted until the German Nazi government and the Japanese imperial forces were defeated and the "cold war" commenced. This Alliance is also referred to as the "Anti-Fascist Coalition," the "Big Three," "Big Four."

Grand Coalition. A term commonly applied to the coalition government in the Federal Republic of Germany (West Germany) that was formed by the two major German parties: the Christian Democratic Union (CDU), with its leader, Kurt Kissinger, as Chancellor (Kanzler, or Prime Minister), and the Social Democratic Party (SPD), with Willy Brandt, its leader, serving as Vice Chancellor (Vize Kanzler, or Vice Prime Minister). The coalition lasted from 1966 to 1969, when Willy Brandt was elected Chancellor (on October 21, 1969) and his majority party, the SPD, joined in coalition with the Free Democrats (FDP) to form a government. The rather unusual coalition of the predominantly Catholic CDU and the Socialist SPD was instrumental in unifying West Germany in the face of strong Soviet influence in Eastern Europe (e.g., the Czechoslovak invasion in 1968). See BREZHNEYEV DOCTRINE.

Grand Conseil. Also grand consiglio, Grossrat, or Kantonsrat. Elected representative body, cantonal legislature in Switzerland.

Grand Corps. In the French language, "grands corps;" also top administrators in France—a highly trained, individually selected group of about 7,000 individuals who, upon completion of specialized training, join the various corps, of which there are about twenty (e.g., administrative lawyers, accountants, financial specialists, diplomats, etc.), and from there are hired by government agencies for top positions. See ADMINISTRATIVE STATE, AMAKUDARI.

Grand Design. French King Henry IV (1553-1610) proposed to English King James I (1603-1625) in 1610, that a structured federation of sovereign European states (mostly kingdoms) be established through which the states could work "in concert" to prevent wars among themselves. Several months after the discussion with King James I, King Henry IV was on his way to Germany to present this idea, but was assassinated by his adversaries who were not interested in any "European Concerts," unless the music was by the roar of cannons! The Grand Design has been studied by international federators, power balancers, and peace proponents, including Woodrow Wilson who strongly favored the League of Nations after W.W.I, and the Western allies (the Big Four) after W.W.II, who supported the United Nations Organization. See CONCERT OF POWERS, DUMBARTON OAKS CONFERENCE, LEAGUE OF NATIONS, UNITED NATIONS ORGANIZATION.

Grand Duchy. A sovereign state or a territory ruled by a grand duke or grand duchess (e.g., the Duchy of Luxembourg in Western Europe).

Grand Duke. A title of nobility, usually ranking below the king or prince.

Grand Jury. A panel of up to twenty-three persons which may be convened to determine, on the basis of available evidence, whether a defendant should be indicted for a crime. If the grand jury finds the evidence sufficient to justify a trial, it will return an indictment against the defendant. If it finds insufficient evidence, the grand jury will return "not a true bill" and the defendant will not be put on trial. Grand juries, which serve as the buffer between the accused, the judge and the prosecuting attorney, are usually called for special investigations of some issue of significance (e.g., abuse of power by government officials). Federal grand juries consist usually of five or seven persons selected by the court from among citizens within the jurisdiction of the court. Federal law does not, however, require grand jury indictments in criminal cases.

Grand Old Man of Espionage. See GEHLEN ORGANIZATION.

Grand Old Party (GOP). See REPUBLICAN PARTY.

Grandfather Clause. A stipulation contained in many state constitutions in the U.S., mainly in the Southern states, allowing black Americans to register to vote without taking a literacy test, provided that they or their predecessors have been registered and have voted prior to 1867. (These stipulations were declared unconstitutional in 1915 by the U.S. Supreme Court and are no longer in force.)

Grandfathering. See CROSS-OWNERSHIP RULE.

Grands Corps. See GRAND CORPS.

Grant Consolidation. The combining of two or more narrow categorical grant programs into a single program with broader purposes and with greater discretion vested in the grantee to decide the nature of specific projects. Commonly refers to combining "categorical" grants into "block" grants.

Grant-in-Aid. Financial aid that must be granted by a central government to lower echelons of government for the purpose of performing certain services. Such grants may be conditional; that is, the funds appropriated must be used for specifically designed purposes; or they may be general, without stipulating for what purpose the appropriated funds are to be used. It is an appropriation made by Congress to assist the states or made by a state legislature to give assistance to local government units. The aid provides for maintenance of schools, construction of public works, provision for relief, or other public purposes of general interest.

Grant Packaging. The process of combining grants from several sources into a single funding plan for an individual grantee (as in the Integrated Grant Administration Program); or the process of combining two or more projects into a single application for funds from a given grant program, where the application may encompass all of the projects for a given area or region during a considerable time span, such as a year or a full funding cycle.

Grass-Roots. The very bottom of the electorate; the rank and file of the electorate; or the ordinary voters who elect the government officials and give them the mandate to govern.

Grass-Roots Perot. One of many political action organizations set up throughout the United States in order to organize support for industrialist and civic leader H. Ross Perot so his name could be placed as an independent on the national ballot for the November 1992 election for president of the United States. Perot would need, for example, 135,000 signatures in California and 54,000 in Texas. The States of Arkansas and Louisiana require no petitions. In other states petition requirements are as follows: in Texas, a third-party candidate for president must collect one percent of the last vote for governor of the state while an independent candidate, one without a formal political party organization, must collect one percent of the last vote cast for president which, is as a rule, is greater, because more people take part in presidential than gubernatorial elections. Until 1976 Texas allowed no independent candidate to run for president until Eugene McCarthy took the issue to the U.S. Supreme Court and Justice Lewis F. Powell, Jr., ordered McCarthy's name to be put on the presidential ballot. Maryland requires 63,000 signatures for an independent and only 10,000 for a third-party candidate; North Carolina, 43,000 signatures for a third-party candidate or two percent of the last vote cast for governor, while 65,000 petitions or two percent of the total number of registered voters in the state are required for independents; Florida requires 63,312 signatures; Maine requires 4,000 to 6,000 signatures; Virginia 13,920 signatures; Oregon 37,000 signatures or have 1,000 people to attend a public meeting at one time. His name on the ballot might mean that neither of the two major candidates (Republican or Democratic) would receive a majority of the electoral votes. The election would then be determined by the U.S. House of Representatives (selecting a president from the three top contenders), and by the U.S. Senate (selecting a vice president from the two top contenders). Perot advanced very challenging and popular slogans which reflected considerable voter dissatisfaction with the present leadership: "Politicians are buying votes with our children's money," and "We're the owners of this country . . . the guys in Washington work for us." H. Ross Perot came to national and international prominence when he extended personal aid to American soldiers fighting in Vietnam during the early 1970s; each Christmas he would hire airplanes, load them with turkeys and other gifts, and dispatch them to Vietnam, all at his personal expense. In 1979, when two of his American employees, were imprisoned in Tehran by the Revolutionary Guards of the Shiites, he hired professional soldiers trained in guerrilla warfare, who went to Tehran and freed his two employees from Gasr Prison, along with all of the other political prisoners held there by Islamic fanatics. That act showed up the U.S. Government's unsuccessful efforts to rescue the American hostages held in the Embassy. The failure of the government's rescue mission was a major blow to President Jimmy Carter and his presidential career. Perot founded his computer company, Electronic Data Systems (EDS) in 1962 with a capital of $1,000 and sold it in 1984 to General Motors for $2.5 billion. His guiding motto is "risk failure," do not fear making a mistake, and one has the responsibility "to determine what he or she can do to make the world a better place—and then go out and do it." Perot was a generous contributor to political campaigns through the years. According to the Federal Election Commission data, Perot and his family donated over $150,000 to congressional candidates in 1979, to the Richard Nixon re-election campaign in 1972 Perot donated $229,000 and an additional $100,000 to Representative Wilbur Mills, an Arkansas Democrat and once powerful chairman of the ways and means committee in the U.S. House of Representatives. Mills died in April 1992. Perot also set up a political action committee (PAC) at his company where his employees donated an additional $260,000 to favorite candidates. Being a man of accumulated wealth, Perot decided to spend his own money (about 100 million dollars or more), to finance his campaign instead of asking for federal funds. Perot has information and information is knowledge. One of his rivals in Texas, Hilmar Moore stated in April 1992 that Perot "has better files on people than the FBI and the CIA. I had never seen such complete files on people." If elected, Perot proposed to work with the people closely through so-called "electronic town hall meetings," where the voters will give input on policy. See NON CANDIDATE CANDIDATE.

Grass–Roots Politician. A politician who is close to the mass of ordinary voters and is concerned with their well-being. During the 1992 presidential election, for example, billionaire H. Ross Perot decided that he had solutions to the nation's problems and decided to have his supporters seek petitions in 48 states so that his name could be placed on the ballots for the November election. Perot depends on a grass-roots action by the voters. See GRASS-ROOTS, GRASS-ROOTS PEROT.

Gravitas. A currency system or rank account system in colonial America, which lacked uniformity and which inspired colonial merchants and manufacturers to support the political unity of the colonies in order to expedite financial and commercial transactions. This led to the Annapolis and Mount Vernon Conventions in which discussion of economic matters led to dialogue on political unification.

Gray Power. The increasing political influence held by the retired and elderly, whose numbers are expected to grow to 30-50% of the total population of some states within the next two decades.

Graymail. A tactic often used by defense lawyers to see that as much classified information as possible is injected into a case so that government prosecutors drop charges rather then reveal state secrets. Such a tactic was widely applied during the Iran-Contra hearings when President Ronald Reagan refused to cooperate with an order to reveal state secrets on the grounds that it would be detrimental to national security. The attorneys for the principals accused in the Iran-Contra case explored this concept to the fullest in order to have charges against the accused dropped. See CLASSIFIED INFORMATION PROCEDURES ACT (CIPA), INTELLIGENCE.

Grease-Ball. See DINO.

Great Commoner. See PRAIRIE POPULIST.

Great Communicator. An affectionate nickname and attribute ascribed to U.S. President Ronald Wilson Reagan (1981-1989) because of his ability to communicate with all types of people, especially the domestic and foreign media. His past experience as a radio sports announcer and movie star served him well, as his style was marked by jest, humor (sometimes at his own expense), unpretentiousness, and open friendliness. He presented complicated political issues in an honest and simple manner, and his views were well understood by friend and foe alike. This contributed to the dissolution of the Soviet Union—the Evil Empire, as President Reagan often referred to it. The President was also characterized as having a "teflon" quality because of his ability to deflect harsh criticism and achieve his desired goals. See PRESIDENTS OF THE UNITED STATES, Appendix 16.

Great Compromise. Within the framework of the THREE-FIFTHS COMPROMISE, an agreement was reached (during the Philadelphia Constitutional Convention in 1787) to the effect that each state in the American Union would have equal representation in the Senate (two representatives, Senators), regardless of the size of the state or its population, and that representation in the House of Representatives would be apportioned on the basis of population.

Great Compromiser. See PRAIRIE POPULIST.

Great Crash Of 1929. See GREAT DEPRESSION OF 1929.

Great Debates. A series of political debates, mainly between presidential candidates, that have taken place in America's political history. The first national debate took place in 1858 between the aspirants for the U.S. Senate from Illinois—Abraham Lincoln (called "Honest Abe" or "old Abe"), a Republican nominee, and Stephen A. Douglas, the incumbent. Lincoln had served in the U.S. House of

Representatives in 1847-49, and during the 1856 Republican nominating convention in Philadelphia had received 110 votes for the Vice Presidency when John C. Fremont of California was nominated for President. There were seven meetings between Lincoln and Douglas, and the issue was mainly slavery (the DRED SCOTT case of 1854, in which the U.S. Supreme Court upheld slavery). This was a prelude to Lincoln's future presidential aspirations—debating for U.S. Senate nominations was not necessary at that time because, until the passage of the 17th Amendment to the U.S. Constitution, U.S. Senators were elected by state legislatures. Douglas was popular in Illinois because of his loyalty to popular sovereignty, and was re-elected by the legislature over Lincoln. The debates are often considered the preliminary battlefields of the War of Secession or Civil War between the South and the United States (1861-1865). Lincoln's famous statement during the first debate pertained to national unity: "A house divided against itself cannot stand." There were four debates held between Kennedy and Nixon: (1) September 26, 1960, in Chicago, Illinois, where Kennedy, echoing Lincoln, declared that the world could not endure being half-slave and half-free. "Can freedom be maintained under the most severe attack it has ever known?" asked Kennedy. "I think it can. And I think in the final analysis it depends upon what we do here. I think it's time America started moving again." Nixon replied: "Senator Kennedy has suggested in his speeches that we lack compassion for the poor, for the old, and for others that are unfortunate . . . I know what it means to be poor . . . I know that Senator Kennedy feels as deeply about these problems as I do, but our disagreement is not about the goals for America but only about the means to reach those goals"; (2) October 7, 1960, Washington, D.C., the issues debated were the Fidel Castro communism in Cuba, the U-2 affair, and the decline of America's prestige abroad; (3) October 13, 1960, Los Angeles, California, and New York City (a two way link-up debate—Nixon spoke from Los Angeles and Kennedy from New York); the issues were the Quemoy and Matsu Islands off the People's Republic of China, which were governed by the Republic of China from Taiwan (Formosa), and which were under occasional attack by the Communists from mainland China; and (4) October 21, 1960, New York City, where both debaters reassessed issues from the previous debates. During the last debate, which was broadcast in color for the first time, Nixon appeared dressed in a dark blue suit and brown shoes which, according to press accounts the next morning, viewers considered an unfortunate combination of colors for the attire of a President-to-be of this rich and best-dressed nation of the world. The Jimmy Carter-Gerald R. Ford debates in 1976 were held as follows: (1) September 23, 1976, in Philadelphia, Pennsylvania; (2) October 6, 1976, in San Francisco, California; and (3) October 22, 1976, in Williamsburg, Virginia. A variety of domestic and foreign issues were debated (e.g., the unemployment problem, the Middle East crisis, and relations with the USSR as they pertained to international peace). President Ford's popularity declined when he stated during the second debate that, in his opinion, the East European communist states were not dominated by the Soviet Union.

Great Depression of 1929. Following World War I, an artificially inflated economy could no longer dispose of its products, causing investors and speculators to sell their securities, which reached a peak on Tuesday ("Black Tuesday"), October 29, 1929, when a record number of shares (16,410,030) were sold at very low prices (e.g., General Electric shares sold at $396 1/4 in September, and $168 1/8 in November of 1929). Business activity declined, prices rose, employers were discharging employees *en masse,* employees were losing their possessions (e.g., mortgages were foreclosed on a mass scale) and started a mass move into shantytowns ("Hoovervilles," made of paper houses), and slept under newspapers ("Hoover Blankets"), on streets, and in parks. Wages and salaries of the more fortunate ones were slashed; lines for free soup and bread were long ("Brother, can you spare a dime?" was a commonly heard greeting). A song of the times was: "Mellon pulled the whistle, Hoover rang the bell, Wall Street gave the signal, and the country went to hell!" Small bank depositors and stockholders lost approximately 40 billion dollars. (5,000 banks collapsed with uninsured deposits and securities.) The federal government established the Reconstruction Finance Corporation (RFC) to cope with depression problems in 1932, but that was too little and too late.

Great Economic Debate in the USSR. Following the period of the New Economic Policy (NEP) and after the death of Vladimir I. Lenin in 1924, the Soviet leadership was divided on the course the party and the government should take in building the socialist state. The debate lasted until the late 1920s when, upon the insistence of Josef Stalin, then in a position of unlimited power, the decision was made in favor of rapid collectivization and industrialization.

Great Emancipator. An affectionate appellate ascribed to U.S. President Abraham Lincoln (1861-1865), who was elected on an anti-slavery Republican platform and freed the slaves in his Emancipation Proclamation of 1863. In most of his speeches, including his Gettysburg and Inaugural Addresses, he delivered a message of individual freedom and liberty for all persons, regardless of race, religion, national origin, or political philosophy. To this day, his views on personal freedom and liberty serve as an inspiration to oppressed peoples everywhere. See PRESIDENTS OF THE UNITED STATES, Appendix 16.

Great Fear. See FELLOW-TRAVELER, MCCARTHYISM.

Great Harmony. One of the principal characteristics of communist society, according to Mao Tse-tung, who wrote, "the realm of Great Harmony means communist society."

Great Lakes Senators. See CONGRESSIONAL CAUCUS.

Great Leap Forward. A slogan issued by the leadership of the People's Republic of China in 1958, praising the managers of the economy for fulfilling the goals of the first Five-Year-Plan and encouraging them to continue. The Chinese leadership claimed that at the 1958 rate of development China would, in the near future, surpass all the major industrial powers (such as England and the United States) in economic production, and would become a totally independent state economically. See PYRRHIC VICTORY.

Great Mole Hunt. See HT/LINGUAL.

Great Moral Threshold. Following the dissolution of the Soviet Union in 1991 into fifteen independent states (the Commonwealth of Independent States), considerable anxiety permeated the minds of western leaders, particularly U.S. President George Bush, regarding the disposition of the mighty arsenal of Soviet nuclear weapons. President of the Russian Republic, Boris N. Yeltsin, together with presidents of the other republics, agreed to confine the arsenal to the four main republics: Belarus, Ukraine, Russia, and Kazakhstan. They also agreed that their nuclear scientists, numbering in the hundreds and among the best in the world, would not seek employment in other countries interested in developing their own nuclear capabilities (e.g., Iran, Iraq, Libya, and others). The Russian scientists declared that it is their moral obligation not to contribute their knowledge and skill to the proliferation of nuclear weapons.

Great Pacificator. See PRAIRIE POPULIST.

Great Patriotic War. The part of W.W.II fought by the Soviet Union against Nazi German invaders, June 1941-January 1945. Soviet casualties amounted to almost 20,000,000.

Great Persuader. An affectionate appellate ascribed to U.S. President Lyndon Baines Johnson (1963-1969) because of his unique ability to bend others to accept his views through mediation, conciliation and arbitration of political disputes among his followers as well as his adversaries. President Johnson was particularly effective while serving in Congress, both as Congressman (1937-1948) and Senator (1948-1961). As Vice President (1961-1963) and President (1963-1969), he continued his efforts to improve the quality of life of many Americans, particularly ethnic minorities, through his sponsorship and support of legislation advocating civil rights, welfare, tax reduction, anti-poverty concerns, and education. His grand design for making America a GREAT SOCIETY did not materialize, due to extensive involvement in the no-win war in Vietnam. See PRESIDENTS OF THE UNITED STATES, Appendix 16.

Great Proletarian Cultural Revolution. See CULTURAL REVOLUTION.

Great Satan. See EASTOXIFICATION.

Great Society. A policy statement issued by U.S. President Lyndon B. Johnson (during his speech at the University of Michigan on May 22, 1964), to the effect that he would use all the wealth and all the human and material resources of the nation for the purpose of improving the living standard and environment of every American and bringing about a general uplifting of the standard of American civilization in general.

Great Soul. See MAHATMA, SATYAGRAHA.

Great War. World War I (1914-1918) was so referred to before the Second World War broke out because of the enormous number of casualties on all sides.

Greater East Asian Co-Prosperity Sphere (GEACPS). A major foreign policy design conceived by militaristic Japan during the 1930s and 1940s to build, in unified East Asia, a unified form of government and international trade system under Japanese domination and control, and to prevent any non-Asian powers from participating in it. The plan collapsed with the defeat of Japan at the end of W.W.II. This plan was similar to Adolf Hitler's "New Order" and the "Thousand Year Reich" in Europe, except that Hitler placed on his priority list the extermination of certain races (e.g., the Jews) instead of first building a strong international economic system. See CANCER OF THE PACIFIC.

Green Berets. See ARMY RANGERS.

Green Book. A collection of writings on the Arab Muslim form of socialism by the leader of Libya, Colonel Mu'ammar al-Qadhafi, chairman of the Revolutionary Command Council and head of state of the Popular Socialist Libyan Arab State of the Masses. The book was written in four different parts during the 1960s and 1970s and is bound in a light green cover. Hence the name "green book."

Green Revolution. See HUNGER WARS.

Greenback Party. One of many splinter groups that emerged in the U.S. after the Civil War, seeking, among other things, an eight-hour work day for labor, a graduated income tax, stricter enforcement of laws regulating interstate commerce, termination of land grants to the railroad companies, continuation of the fiat money (paper money), and better treatment of small farmers. The party was most active between 1876 and 1884.

Grenzschutzgruppe 9 (GSG9). See DELTA FORCE.

Gringo. See YANKEE.

Gross Domestic Product (GDP). The total market value of all goods and services produced domestically during a given period. The components of GDP are consumption, gross domestic investment, government purchases of goods and services, and net exports. See GROSS NATIONAL PRODUCT (GNP), GROSS WORLD PRODUCT (GWP).

Gross National Product (GNP). The total market value of all goods and services produced in a given period by labor and property supplied by residents of a country, regardless of where the labor and property are located. GNP differs from GDP primarily by including the excess of capital income that residents earn from investments abroad less capital income that nonresidents earn from domestic investment. See GROSS DOMESTIC PRODUCT (GDP), GROSS WORLD PRODUCT (GWP).

Gross World Product (GWP). Approximately $24.5 trillion as of 1992. See GROSS DOMESTIC PRODUCT (GDP), GROSS NATIONAL PRODUCT (GNP).

Ground Zero Movement. On 17 April 1982, Dr. Roger Molander initiated an appeal to all Americans as well as to leaders of the entire world to oppose production and storage of nuclear weapons anywhere on earth. The anti-nuclear movement, in various forms, continues to this day all over the world, including the area of the former Soviet empire.

Group. An advanced form of monopoly designed to gain maximum control of as many aspects of economic life as possible: raw materials, the processing of raw materials, production, distribution and marketing, and control of the financial resources of a large segment of corporations, national and multinational; also, a higher form of monopoly, imperial and imperialistic. One of the aims of a group is to stifle smaller, independent enterprises either by absorbing them or forcing them out of business, a practice contrary to democratic capitalism. See DEMOCRATIC CAPITALISM, MONOPOLY.

Group of Five (G-5). A group of the five most economically advanced countries—Canada, Germany, Great Britain, France, and the United States—whose central bankers and finance ministers meet periodically to exchange views and to improve trade relations. During the late 1980s, the circle grew to include Italy and Japan, and is now known as the "Group of 7" (G-7).

Group of Seven (G-7). See GROUP OF FIVE (G-5).

Group of '77. Representatives of Third World nations and economically advanced nations met in Geneva, Switzerland, October 16—November 30, 1977, to discuss ways and means to restructure economic relations among developed and developing nations in order to equalize the distribution of wealth. The conference collapsed when the developing nations demanded the establishment of a special international fund to prop up Third World earnings from exports of their raw materials. The developed nations were accused by the chairman of the conference, Ljubomir Sekulic of Yugoslavia, of "lack of political will." The North-South dialogue (that is, the dialogue between the rich Western nations, Japan, and developing nations) will be continued.

Group Voting. See BLOC VOTING.

Groupe d'Intervention de la Gendarmerie Nationale (GIGN). See DELTA FORCE.

Groupthink. A term often applied to groups with special skills (e.g., brain trusts or think-tanks) which advise executives on policy decisions (e.g., presidential assistants or a committee dealing with a particular issue).

GRU. See GLAVNOYE RAZVYEDYVATELNOYE UPRAVLYIENYE, PEOPLE'S COMMISSION FOR INTERNAL AFFAIRS (NKVD).

Guadalupe-Hidalgo Treaty of 1848. A bilateral treaty between the United States and Mexico, which confirmed U.S. claims to Texas and territories along the Pacific Coast of California stretching to Oregon. The U.S. paid Mexico $15,000,000 and assumed claims of $3,250,000 by U.S. citizens in Mexico. Expansionist advocates, still under the spell of the Manifest Destiny Doctrine, demanded that Mexico be incorporated into the United States as well.

Guam Doctrine. See NIXON DOCTRINE.

Guardians of a Graveyard Philosophy. In such words U.S. President Ronald Reagan characterized members of the U.S. Congress who opposed his tax cut proposal in 1984, proposing instead a 12 percent tax increase. The president prevailed.

Gubernator. In the Russian language (and most other Slavic languages), a "governor." In Tsarist Russia, the top executive (appointive) of a large political subdivision (e.g., Gubernya, a province).

Gubernya. In the Russian language (and most Slavic languages), "district" or "state." Also, a large political subdivision, headed by a governor (gubernator), within the unitary state of Tsarist Russia. See GUBERNATOR.

Guerre à Outrance. In the French language, "a total war" or an "all-out war."

Guerrilla Communism. See EXTREMISM.

Guerrilla Warfare. An irregular, highly mobile, and highly disciplined group of persons involved in warfare, usually against their own state by means of hit-and-run tactics. See Appendix 30.

Guided Democracy. See DEMOCRACY, GUIDED.

Guided Free Enterprise. Ezra F. Vogel ("Guided Free Enterprise in Japan," *Harvard Business Review,* 56, May-June 1978), so characterizes present Japanese trade practices, because private enterprise is assisted by government, mainly the Ministry of International Trade and Industry (MITA)—often characterized by the Japanese as an "overprotective" or "overconcerned" mother (in the Japanese language, "kyoiku mama"). The American business community, on the other hand, insists on free trade with no government intervention. Another American scholar, Chalmors Johnson (*The Industrial Policy Debate,* Institute of Contemporary Studies Press) calls guided free enterprise "developmentalism." The Japanese characterize their trade practices as "winner-driven industrial policy" (or the result of strategic and consistent thinking), and the practices of the West as "loser-driven industrial policy"—chaotic, sporadic, erratic, and responsive only in crisis situations, such as lobbying the U.S. Congress for protection when threatened with stiff competition or denial of markets. For example, Americans want the GATT to declare the business practices of Airbus Industries as illegal in order to establish a foothold for the American aircraft industry in Europe. The Americans lost about 30 percent of their business to the English-French-German-Spanish owned Airbus, which produces jet passenger aircraft for domestic and international flights. American efforts, ignited by the Europeans, to stop Airbus are too little and too late. Europeans proceed according to their industrial policies, while Americans have none. According to Dr. William S. Dietrich, President of Dietrich Industries and author of *In the Shadow of the Rising Sun: The Political Roots of American Economic Decline*, free-market absolutism, anti-statism, and hyper-individualism hinder America's efforts in shaping a coherent industrial policy, which he defines as "the state induced willful shifting of the industrial structure toward high technology, high-value-added industries." National wealth and international power are created and sustained by productivity, technology, good management, collaboration (business-government-academia) and dedicated performance. An abundance of talented and dedicated people and great natural resources (e.g., oil) are not enough without a cohesive and coherent blueprint. See DEMOCRACY, GUIDED, KOKUTAI, PAPER ENTREPRENEURIALISM.

Guild. An association of persons in the same trade or profession established for the purpose of upholding the standards of that trade or profession and protecting the general vested interest of the craftsmen.

Guild Socialism. A movement (once most popular in England) striving to restore syndicalism. Its proponents advocate public ownership of the means of production and distribution (e.g., factories, plants, land, transport, etc.), functional representation in legislative bodies (parliament or congress), and the control of all production by strong industrial (labor) unions.

Guilt by Association. A judgement of guilt attributed to an individual, based on an association with certain people or organizations, instead of actual proof that said individual committed a crime.

Guinea. See MAFIA.

Gulag. In the former USSR, a network of prisons for those convicted of political crimes; also an acronym in the Russian language for Chief Administration of Corrective Labor Camps; millions have died from mistreatment and starvation in these camps.

Gulf of Tonkin Resolution. An authorization, granted by the U.S. Senate to U.S. President Lyndon B. Johnson in 1964 by a joint resolution (passed by a vote of 414 to 0 in the House, and 88 to 2 in the Senate—with Ernest Gruening of Alaska and Wayne Morse of Oregon opposing it), to use American military forces for war action against the Democratic Republic of Vietnam (North Vietnam) as a means of retaliation for its attack upon American warships in the Gulf of Tonkin. The authorization was repealed when the War Powers Act became law on November 7, 1973, when President Nixon's veto was overridden by Congress. See VIETNAMIZATION.

Gulf War. See PERSIAN GULF WAR.

Gun Control. Persons who oppose gun control laws, especially a national law, are known as the "Second Amendment Crowd," due to reliance on the provisions of the Second Amendment to the U.S. Constitution, which guarantees the right to bear arms to the militia and the people.

Gunboat Diplomacy. Foreign policy that relies on the use of arms (or the threat thereof) to achieve necessary goals. See BIG STICK DIPLOMACY.

Gush Emunin. In Hebrew, "Block of the Faithful." Jewish settlers on the West Bank of the Jordan River refuse to let Arabs have the West Bank. See ISRAELI SETTLEMENTS.

"I had rather be right than be President."
HENRY CLAY, 1777-1852

Ha Mossad L'Tafkidim Meyuhadim. In the Hebrew language, "organization for special missions or Mossad." See ISRAEL'S INTELLIGENCE.

Habeas Corpus, Writ of. See WRIT OF COMMON USE.

Habit of the Place. See BUSINESS OF CONGRESS IS RE-ELECTION BUSINESS.

Habitat. See UNIPOLITICS.

Haganah. See BALFOUR DECLARATION, ISRAEL'S INTELLIGENCE.

Hague Court. See PERMANENT COURT OF ARBITRATION.

Hague Peace Conferences. Two major international conferences held in the city of Hague, the Netherlands (Holland), for the purpose of, among other things, bringing about disarmament among nations and maintaining international peace. The First Conference was held in 1899, with twenty-eight nations participating, and the Second in 1907, with forty-four nations participating. The 1899 Conference produced a covenant which required war-prone states to put forth a declaration of war prior to attack and to refrain from surprise attack. All the participating states signed this covenant, and Germany and Japan violated it by surprise attacks on Poland on 1 September 1939 (commencing W.W.II) and the United States (Pearl Harbor) respectively on 7 December 1941. See GENERAL ACT FOR THE SETTLEMENT OF INTERNATIONAL DISPUTES, GENEVA CONVENTION.

Haigemony. A term coined by author William Safire epitomizing the tough measures taken by U.S. Secretary of State Alexander Haig in the Reagan Administration in dealing with the Russians, and his advocacy of a "get-tough" style of diplomacy with America's adversaries in general.

Hail to the Chief. See IMPERIAL PRESIDENCY.

Hakatism. A term for the process of German nationalization of communities in Prussia. Unless Poles residing in Prussia accepted the German language and culture and renounced their own, they would be expelled by Prince Bismarck and their land given to Prussians and Germans.

Half-Breeds. See PLUMED KNIGHT.

Half of Your Daily Bread is Baked with Marshall Plan Help. See MARSHALL PLAN.

Half-Party Government. See ONE AND ONE-HALF PARTY GOVERNMENT.

Hallmark of Racism. Black South African militants so refer to the white-only primary that President F. W. de Klerk proposes in order to achieve some sort of constitutional settlement with the black majority in South Africa. The Treurnicht Conservatives also oppose the white-only primary; they do not wish to share power with blacks and threaten revolt should the primary give President de Klerk a mandate to continue the constitutional settlement with Nelson Mendela and the African National Congress. The most important issue is the guarantee for whites of some sort of reserved authority, such as a special representation allotment so that their power base will not be wiped out completely by the overwhelming numbers of the black majority. The militants demand the introduction of the American principle of one-man, one vote; but, if taken literally, that would threaten the security of the whites. See CONFERENCE FOR DEMOCRATIC SOUTH AFRICA (CODESA).

Hallstein Doctrine. An official policy of the government of the German Federal Republic (West Germany) which reserved for itself the right to terminate unilaterally (or not enter into) diplomatic relations with any state which extended diplomatic recognition to the German Democratic Republic (East Germany), with the exception of the former Soviet Union. (The Doctrine was named after Dr. Walter Hallstein, Germany's State Secretary in the Foreign Office [1951-1958].) The doctrine was not strictly enforced.

Hamiltonian Statism. See UNREPENTANT INDIVIDUALISM.

Hammurabi Code. A systematic collection of laws pertaining to real estate, personal property, the family, business relations, personal injuries, and labor. It provides for penalties based on the principle of "an eye for an eye, a tooth for a tooth." These laws were codified under the leadership of Hammurabi, the King of Mesopotamia (circa 1750 or 1700 BC). One of the provisions in the Code stipulates that if a newly-built house collapsed and caused death, the builder of that faulty house would also be put to death.

Hanafi Moslems. See BLACK MUSLIMS.

Hansard. The official record of all proceedings of the British Parliament similar to the *Record* and the *Digest* in the United States. Named after its publisher, Luke Hansard.

Hanseatic League. An organization of north German cities, an economic union, formed around 1263 for the protection and promotion of the towns' commercial and political interests. The leading towns in the League were Bremen, Danzig (now Gdansk, a Polish city), and Hamburg.

Happy Warrior. See MISTER DEMOCRAT.

Hard Hats. A term associated with a very patriotic point of view; also, construction workers in the United States who wear protective helmets, "hard hats," at construction sites. Anti-war protesters clashed with hard hats during the Vietnam War.

Hard Money. See LOCOFOCOS.

Hard Rock State. A term often used in international politics and diplomacy to denote a government (agent) which is uncompromising, ethnocentric, stubborn, and uncooperative during negotiations, or one that is unreasonably demanding.

Hard State. See SOFT STATE.

Hardenberg Revolution. See REVOLUTION FROM ABOVE.

Hardware Diplomacy. The practice common among the superpowers (e.g., the former Soviet Union and the United States) aimed at settling international disputes among states (e.g., the Arabs and the Israelis) not only at the conference table but on the battlefield as well. The United States, for example, in addition to active personal diplomacy by the U.S. President through conventional means (at the conference table), sells large quantities of advanced weapon systems to both parties of the dispute, the Arabs (e.g., Egypt, Jordan, and Saudi Arabia) and the Israelis. If all laws pertaining to human motivation and behavior hold any validity, it can be expected that these weapons will be used for the destruction of peace rather than for its restoration and preservation. Such practices not only contradict all declarations about arms control and disarmament, but openly support war as an instrument of policy. What could be done instead is the following: instead of selling weapons to war-prone nations, the superpowers should initiate the practice of purchasing all existing weapons, piece by piece, in order to render such nations incapable of launching a war. Each rifle delivered by Israel or Egypt to the United States could, for example, be exchanged for a plow or a map for the local school; each rocket launcher, for a tool-making machine; and each war aircraft, for a water irrigation system or an electricity-generating plant. Such replacement of implements of war with implements of peaceful production would lead to gradual reorientation toward peace rather than war. Furthermore, through a system of rewards and punishments (administered, for example, by a special body of the United

Nations), a state which graduates a cadre of engineers would be rewarded by having them provided with appropriate jobs, while a state which graduates a cadre of military officers would be penalized by some means, such as trade embargo. See INTERNATIONAL ARMS AND WAR IMPLEMENTS COLLECTION AND DISPOSAL BANK (IAAWICADB), NEUTRON BOMB, OAK'S LAWS, STRATEGIC ARMS LIMITATION TALKS (SALT).

Hare Electoral System. A system of single-transferable-votes, used in proportional representation, whereby candidates whose votes in an election equal a certain fixed quota are declared elected, while the surplus votes, not to be wasted, go according to the next choice expressed by the voters, to candidates who need them in order to become elected. Candidates with the lowest number of votes are eliminated and the votes they received are transferred to candidates who have good chances to become elected but are short on votes. See PROPORTIONAL REPRESENTATION.

Harmony Convention. A term applied to characterize the general atmosphere of unity among the various party factions and among the races that prevailed at the Democratic National Convention on July 13, 1976, in New York City. Some politicians challenged the harmony theory and with it, then presidential nominee, Jimmy Carter. U.S. Representative Ronald V. Dellums (D-California) a black member of the House, claimed that Carter was able to unify the factions and the races through his personal friendship with black leaders (mainly Dr. Martin Luther King, Sr., the father of the slain civil rights leader, Dr. Martin Luther King, Jr.), as well as by his personal attributes (e.g., charisma). Furthermore, Carter allegedly made so many promises to the leaders of various factions (mainly blacks), that, combined with his appeal for unity and populist style, he succeeded in "Carterizing" the Convention.

Hartford Convention. Twenty-six leaders from several New England States (Connecticut, Massachusetts, New Hampshire, Rhode Island, and Vermont) met in secrecy from December 15, 1814 to January 5, 1815, in Hartford, Connecticut, to call on Massachusetts to design plans for secession from the American Union and to enter into a separate peace treaty with England because of their dissatisfaction over the conduct of the war with England by the federal government. The states also considered as another argument the fact that the federal government was not giving them aid for coping with the British, who were harassing their shorelines.

Harvest. See COUNTERINSURGENCY IN AMERICA.

Hashish-Eater. See ASSASSIN.

Hashshashin. See ASSASSIN.

Hat in the Ring. A symbolic phrase meaning that one announces candidacy or availability for an elective public office; or the announcement that one is entering politics or a career in public life. If the candidate is very young, it is said "diaper in the ring;" in case of female candidates, "bra in the ring."

Hatch Act of 1887. Amended in 1955. Provision of basic support to agricultural experiment stations.

Hatch Political Activities Acts. A congressional legislation of 1939 and 1940, aiming to regulate political activities of federal and state employees (who are partly paid from federal funds), prohibiting active participation in political party work (partisan politics). It forbids the use of federal facilities and personal influence of employees for partisan politics and solicitations of funds in the civil service circles; limits individual contributions to $5,000 during a calendar year to any candidate for public elective office or any organization which works to this end; sets the ceiling of $5,000 on expenditures on behalf of a candidate for the U.S. House of Representatives; $25,000 for the U.S. Senate, and $3,000,000 maximum expenditures for a national party convention; requires record-keeping—which is now the function of the Federal Election Commission; forbids labor unions and private corporations to make any direct contributions (campaign money) to political candidates or causes. (The 1939 legislation aims to bar from federal employment anyone who belongs to an organization that advocates the overthrow of the American Government, and the FBI was empowered to investigate all violations under that law.) Major revisions of the Act proposed on 27 June 1990 were rejected by Congress. See LOYALTY LAW.

Hate Crime. Any act, verbal or physical, directed against another person or persons, intended to downgrade, demean, frighten, or terrorize because of any one of such characteristics as race, religion, ethnicity, national origin, gender, outlook, or political, sexual, and/or cultural preferences: The "Hate Crimes Statistics Act," was signed into law by President George Bush on 23 April 1990, according to which law enforcement agencies (mainly the FBI) are required to collect information and keep current statistical data on such crimes.

Havana Conference of 1940. Upon the fall of France and Denmark in 1940 (to the German Nazi forces), the United States and its Latin American allies feared that Nazi Germany might claim their possessions in the Americas as well. It was agreed that the Monroe Doctrine would be upheld by all Latin American states and that the French and Danish colonies would not be given to Nazi control. Hence the unilateral statement of policy, the Monroe Doctrine, gained multilateral recognition and acceptance by twenty-one Latin American states. See MONROE DOCTRINE.

Hawk. An advocate of forceful and aggressive foreign policy, backed by the threat of military force.

Hay-Pauncefote Treaty of 1901. See PANAMA CANAL TREATIES.

Hayes-Tilden Dispute. On Monday, Oct. 7, 1878, the *New York Tribune* published a number of ciphergrams after decoding them which revealed that Samuel Tilden's nephew, Col. William T. Pelton had attempted to buy electoral votes to insure Tilden's victory during the disputed presidential election of 1876. The popular vote gave Tilden, the Democratic candidate, a lead over his Republican opponent, Rutherford B. Hayes, by a margin of 250,000. But the states of Louisiana, South Carolina, and Florida sent two sets of electoral votes to Congress, and dispute arose as to whether the Democrat or the Republican returns should be counted. To break this deadlock Congress passed the Electoral Count Act and set up an electoral Commission of fifteen men—five each from the Senate and the House of Representatives and five Justices from the Supreme Court—as stipulated by this act. The commission, composed of eight Republicans and seven Democrats, gave all disputed votes to Hayes which brought the total of electoral votes to 185. This was one more vote than Tilden had. Hayes' presidency was officially settled only two days before inauguration day through the Compromise of 1877. In return for their cooperation, the Republicans promised the Democrats a large share of federal offices, federal aid for certain projects, mainly railroads, to the Southern states, and the withdrawal of federal troops from the South. Charges of electoral vote buying by Democrats against Republicans led to the appointment of a congressional committee to investigate these charges. Some of the pre-election political telegrams which had been subpoenaed by the committee were leaked to the *New York Tribune,* whose editors deciphered and published them. They revealed, among other things, that the Democrats had sought to buy a Republican elector for $10,000 and that Florida's electoral votes had been offered to Tilden for $200,000. Because of this electoral dispute, President Hayes was often referred to as "Rutherfraud," "His Fraudulency," or "Old 8 to 7."

Haymarket Riot. See NOBLE ORDER OF THE KNIGHTS OF LABOR.

He Doesn't Seem to Stand for Anything. A remark allegedly made by former U.S. President Ronald Reagan (1981-1989), characterizing U.S. President George Bush during the 1992 presidential campaign. President Reagan declined a photographic session with President and Mrs. Bush, and declined invitation to a fund raising reception in California, but he officially denied that he had made such a remark. White House aides responded that Ronald Reagan was "too senile to make an appearance."

He is the Only Fire Hydrant at a Dog Show. So Georgia's Governor, Zell Miller, characterized the many attacks on Governor Bill Clinton of Arkansas, one of the Democratic presidential hopefuls in the 1992 primary campaign, when he was accused of womanizing and of having manipulated his draft status during the Vietnam war. See CHARACTER ASSASSINATION, KISS AND TELL FOR SALE.

He Shall be Disenfranchised Who, in Time of Faction, Takes Neither Side. See COMPULSORY VOTING.

He Shall Take Care that the Laws be Faithfully Executed. A constitutional provision (contained in Art. II, Section 3 of the U.S. Constitution) which grants the U.S. President the discretionary power to act as the chief executive and to enforce the laws as he deems fit and necessary. This is one of the vaguest and the broadest sources of presidential power. See EXECUTIVE ORDER, PRESIDENTIAL GOVERNMENT, Appendix 8.

He Wants to be Jesus Christ. A statement assessing Jerry Brown, a presidential hopeful during the 1992 campaign, made by Peter Finnegan, a friend of Brown's who once attended a Jesuit seminary with Brown in California. According to the Associated Press (29 March 1992), Finnegan stated, "Jerry, ex-Jesuit. He doesn't want to be president. He wants to be Jesus Christ." See SMALL IS BEAUTIFUL; WE, THE PEOPLE, TAKE BACK AMERICA.

He Who Does Not Work, Neither Shall He Eat. See COMMUNISM, SOCIALISM.

Head-in-the-Sand Legislation. See NEUTRALITY LAWS.

Head of Government. An elected or appointed official of the state who is in charge of the government and its administrative apparatus (e.g., premier, prime minister, chancellor, or, in some states, president).

Head of State. A person or collective of persons (king, queen, emperor, tsar, president, dictator, or a group of persons) authorized to speak for the entire state and to represent the state internally and externally in all official ceremonies; one who does not necessarily speak for the government of the day (e.g., the Queen of England, or the President of France). The U.S. President serves in a dual capacity, as the head of state as well as the head of the government. He is both the titular (ceremonial) and the real working executive of the government. See HEAD OF GOVERNMENT.

Hearsay. Information based on reports of others; in a court of law, information about another passed by word of mouth and usually inadmissable as evidence, not being the personal knowledge of a witness.

Hedonism. A notion which holds that human beings act and behave in a manner which will provide them with the most pleasure, enjoyment and satisfaction. See EPICUREANISM.

Hegemonism. See HEGEMONY.

Hegemony. As applied to international politics, the practice of control of one state by another brought about (voluntarily or involuntarily) by means of diplomacy or war (e.g., the control of Eastern European states by the former Soviet Union). The term "hegemonism" is often used by the leadership of the People's Republic of China accusing the United States of global expansionism and Pax Americana around the world and particularly in Asia.

Heimwehr. See CLERICO-FASCIST.

Heinous Crime. A felonious crime of the highest magnitude (e.g., treason or murder, or a crime committed with hate and premeditation).

Heisei. In the Japanese language, "achievement of peace"; a new era in which Japanese civilization would play a significant role, proclaimed upon the death of Emperor Hirohito in 1989, and the beginning of the reign of his son, Akihito.

Hell Fighters. See HOUSTON RIOT.

Hell No, We Won't Go. One of the many anti-Vietnam war slogans.

Hellenic League. See DELIAN LEAGUE.

Helsinki Accord. An informal agreement, based on good faith, that was signed at the capital city of Finland, Helsinki, on August 1, 1975, by Austria, Belgium, Bulgaria, Canada, Cyprus, Czechoslovakia, Denmark, England, Federal Republic of Germany (West Germany), Finland, France, German Democratic Republic (East Germany), Greece, Hungary, Iceland, Ireland, Italy, Liechtenstein, Luxemburg, Malta, Monaco, the Netherlands, Norway, Poland, Portugal, Rumania, San Marino, Soviet Union, Spain, Sweden, Switzerland, Turkey, United States, Vatican City, and Yugoslavia. It aimed to (1) endorse the political status quo in Europe, the political boundaries among states as established at the end of W.W.II (and Soviet sphere of influence in East Europe); (2) support a possible reunification of both German states; (3) broaden the détente between the Soviet Union and the United States; (4) strengthen respect for human rights and freedoms; (5) renounce force as an instrument of policy and condemn aid to terrorist movements; (6) expedite reunification of families separated involuntarily; and (7) work in concert to settle the explosive tension in the Mediterranean area, mainly between the Arabs and the Israelis. It was also agreed that periodic conferences would be held (e.g., the 1977 post-Helsinki conference in Yugoslavia) in order to determine the scope and degree of implementation of the accord's provisions by the individual signatories. U.S. President Gerald R. Ford commented during the signing ceremony, "Peace is not a piece of paper." The final document is formally known as "The Final Act of the Conference on Security and Cooperation in Europe,: and the *New York Times* (August 1, 1976) characterized it as a "codified set of moral principles against which the West has been able to measure Soviet behavior, much to Moscow's chagrin." See HUMAN RIGHTS: AMERICAN DEFINITION.

Helsinki Agreement. See CONFERENCE ON SECURITY AND COOPERATION IN EUROPE (CSCE), HELSINKI ACCORD.

Helsinki Summit. See HELSINKI ACCORD.

Her Majesty's Loyal Opposition. See LOYAL OPPOSITION.

Hero of Socialist Labor. In the Russian language, "Gheroy Sotyalistitchesghogo Truda." A title of honor (including a medal and monetary award) granted since 1938 to anyone in the former USSR who distinguished himself in spectacular achievements (e.g., in agriculture, commerce, industry, or education).

Hero of the Soviet Union. In the Russian language, "Gheroy Spvyetsghogo Soyuza." A title of honor (including a medal and monetary prize) granted to anyone in the former USSR who distinguished himself in heroic service to the Soviet Union (e.g., a spectacular military act or invention). The title was established in 1934. See HERO OF SOCIALIST LABOR.

Heroic Authority. See AUTHORITY.

Herut Party. A moderate political party in Israel which opposed the speedy establishment of Jewish settlements on Arab territories conquered by Israel in 1967. One of its better known members, Ezer Weizman, a Defense Minister in the Begin government, resigned in protest on May 24, 1980. See ISRAELI SETTLEMENTS.

Hess Mission. After the defeat of France in 1940, Adolf Hitler issued an order in May 1940, to refrain from military action against England if the British government acknowledged the status quo and signed a peace agreement with Hitler. Allegedly Rudolf Hess parachuted into Scotland to deliver this message from Hitler. Among other proposals presented to the British by Hess was a design for joint action against the Soviet Union. Many British parliamentarians, including foreign secretary Lord Halifax, favored rapprochement with Hitler, but Winston Churchill opposed any such partnership, and Hess was booked as an ordinary war criminal rather than treated as an emissary. Hess was subsequently tried and sentenced by the Nuremberg Tribunal to life imprisonment for war crimes; he served his time in the Spandau, Berlin, prison from 1946 until he died in 1987. He was the only prisoner guarded by American, British, French, and Soviet guards. Request for an early release was agreed to by the three western Allies in 1967, but was vetoed by the Soviets. Hess became an object of retribution for Nazism by the Allies.

Heteronomy. A political subdivision (e.g., a city, county, region, or a state) which is governed according to the laws or by the government of another subdivision; a political entity of dependent status, as opposed to autonomy. See AUTONOMY.

Hey, Hey, LBJ, How Many Kids Did You Kill Today? An anti-U.S. President Lyndon Baines Johnson (1963-1969) chant by a group of protesters who demanded to see the President on June 12, 1967, in order to ask him that the war in Vietnam be ended at once. The protesters were dispersed by police on the grounds that they were interfering with the normal flow of traffic. See ANTI-VIETNAM WAR SLOGANS.

Hezb-i-Islami. See AFGHANISTAN ISSUE, AFGHANISTAN WAR.

Hide Behind the Flag and the Constitution. See LIBERTY LEAGUE.

Hierarchical International System. See INTERNATIONAL SYSTEM.

Hierarchical Rule. See POLITICAL EQUILIBRIUM.

High Commissioner. A representative of the state or the government equipped with special powers to supervise a newly acquired territory or a state (acquired by diplomatic or non-diplomatic means). (E.g., U.S. High Commissioners to the Philippines when the island was a Commonwealth under American jurisdiction, or Germany when the German state was defeated as a result of World War II, or England's Governor-Commissioner or Governor-General in Canada, acting as Canada's titular head of state in the name of the British Monarch.)

High Councils of Government. Usually the top leadership of a politically organized society, where important decisions are made.

High-Risk Espionage. See CENTRAL INTELLIGENCE AGENCY (CIA), COVERT ACTION.

High Seas. The body of international navigable waters (seas, oceans, and other navigable international waterways) which, under existing rules of international law, are open and free to all nations; navigable waters over which no nation may claim exclusive jurisdiction.

High Technology. Sophisticated and highly advanced equipment (e.g., computers) and other related items (e.g., laser), which enable technologically advanced nations (e.g., the USA), to more effectively provide for the needs of the society as well exert economic and political influence on other nations. President Carter banned the transfer through trade of such high technology to the USSR after their invasion of Afghanistan on December 24, 1979; and on March 18, included stops to transfer of all technology, including "process technology," data on how the high technology is achieved, in order to prevent the Soviets from getting the clues about U.S. technological advances. As a result, about 700 export licenses were disapproved, worth over one billion dollars and only items needed for humanitarian reasons, such as parts for medical equipment, were allowed to be transferred.

Hillsborough Agreement. Great Britain and the Republic of Ireland agreed in 1985 that the government of the Republic of Ireland would oversee certain aspects of life in troubled Northern Ireland, which remains under British rule but is striving for independence. This collaboration pertains to social and economic matters rather than political. The political wing of the Irish Republican Army (IRA), the Sinn Fein, opposes any such measures short of total independence. In 1982, the British introduced a plan of "rolling evolution," which provided for a gradual introduction of home rule for Ireland, but this plan was rejected by the IRA, the Sinn Fein, as well as by the Social Democratic and Labour Party (SDLP). Subsequently, the Official Unionist Party (OUP) also withdrew support in 1984, leaving the British-Irish question unresolved to this day.

Himalayan Crisis. The border wars between the People's Republic of China and the Republic of India of 1962, which can be characterized as nothing else but China's attempt to humiliate India in the eyes of world public opinion and to demonstrate to the world that in the Asian triangle of power (India-China-Japan), China is the superpower.

Hindi Volunteer League. Paramilitary organization of several million Hindus in contemporary India which advocates and strives to achieve: exclusive political control by those of the Hindu religion, reconversion of Indian Christians and Moslems to Hinduism, and an introduction of a political system according to the ancient Roman principle *cuius regio eius religio*. The League was established during the 1920s while India was still under British domination, but because of its extremist philosophy which tended to divide the multi-religious society of India, it was declared subversive and banned from open activity by the government of Premier J. Nehru and subsequently by the government of Nehru's daughter and Prime Minister of India, I. Gandhi. After the removal of Mrs. Gandhi from office in 1975, and the suspension of all emergency laws forbidding open political activity by organizations considered subversive, the League became active again with renewed strength.

Hindu Bharatya Janata Party. After the Indian National Congress Party, one of the strongest pro-Hindu political parties in India; it strongly supports any means, including war, to retain control over Kashmir, also claimed by Pakistani Islamic groups. See INDIAN NATIONAL CONGRESS PARTY, JAMATT-ISLAMI.

Hip-Pocket Congress. A term coined in 1965 by adversaries of U.S. President Lyndon Baines Johnson (1963-1969) who, after the tragic death of President John F. Kennedy in 1963, exploited his good rapport with Congress (Johnson is considered one of the most popular leaders in Congress during the 20th Century), and endorsed the most progressive legislation (especially the civil rights area) in the history of the U.S. Congress. As a Texan, he was allegedly handling Congress as a cowboy handles his gun (or a cow!).

Hiroshima. See V-J DAY.

His Accidency. A not-too-flattering nickname that was bestowed on four U.S. Vice Presidents who succeeded to the presidency upon the death of the incumbent Presidents: (1) John Tyler (1841-1845) succeeded William Henry Harrison, who died in 1841; (2) Millard Filmore (1850-1853) succeeded Zachary Taylor, who died in 1850; (3) Andrew Johnson (1865-1869) succeeded Abraham Lincoln, who was assassinated in 1865 (Johnson was the first U.S. President to be impeached by the House for violation of the Tenure of Office Act—he was tried by the Senate and acquitted); and (4) Chester Alan Arthur (1881-1885) succeeded James Abram Garfield, who was assassinated in 1881. See Appendix 17.

His Face Has Seen Several Masks. See POLITICAL RHETORIC.

His Fraudulency. See HAYES-TILDEN DISPUTE.

His Highness. See MISTER PRESIDENT.

His (Her) Majesty's Loyal Opposition. See LOYAL OPPOSITION.

His Mightiness. See MISTER PRESIDENT.

His Only Achievement is that of Being a Virgin Several Times. See POLITICAL RHETORIC.

His Rotundity. A not-too-flattering nickname for the corpulent and seemingly overweight U.S. President John Adams (1797-1801). "Rotundity" taken after the rotunda of the Capitol building in Washington, D.C., the Seat of the U.S. Congress.

Hispanic Caucus. See CONGRESSIONAL CAUCUS.

Historic Compromise. See EUROCOMMUNISM.

Historic Waters. Bodies of water (e.g., rivers, lakes, gulfs) which, under international law are claimed by states as territorial waters.

Historical Materialism. The application of dialectical materialism to the study of society. See DIALECTICAL MATERIALISM, MARXISM.

Hitler-Stalin Pact. On August 23, 1939, barely one week before Nazi armies of Adolf Hitler were to march on Poland and thus officially commence World War II, the foreign ministers, Viacheslav M. Molotov and Alfred von Ribbentrop of the USSR and Nazi Germany (the German Reich) respectively, concluded a treaty of "friendship and non-aggression." As a result, Hitler and Stalin divided Poland, the Baltic republics fell under Soviet control, and the era of conquest had begun for both powers. The alliance, also called the "unholy alliance," lasted until June 22, 1941, when Adolf Hitler attacked the Soviet Union without formal declaration of war.

Hitler Youth (HJ). In the German language, "Hitler Jugend." An organization established by the Nazis for young men who were dedicated to the Nazi state and the Führer, Adolf Hitler, and who were to render any services when called upon. There was also a separate organization for young girls, known as Organization of German Girls ("Bund Deutscher Mädchen").

Hitlerism. See LEBENSRAUM.

Hizb al-Baath al-Arabi al-Ishtiraki. See BAATH SOCIALIST PARTY, REGIONAL COMMAND OF THE ARAB SOCIALIST RENAISSANCE PARTY.

Hizbullah. In the Farsi language, "Party of God"; also a political militant Shiite organization active in Lebanon, dedicated to the containment of Israel's expansion in the Middle East which is at the expense of the Arabs, particularly the Palestinians. The party has been engaged in guerrilla activities in the area. It receives support from Iran. Its forces operate mainly in the southern part of Lebanon close to the so-called "Security zone" established by Israel in the part of Lebanon that borders Israel. The leader of the Hizbullah, Sheik Abbas Musawi, and his wife and six-year old son were assassinated by the Israelis in February 1992 in Lebanon. His successor, Sheik Hassan Nasrallah, ordered an immediate retaliation against the Israelis in their security zone in Lebanon, and the new leader stated that war is the only language between the Jews and the Hizbullah, "a language that both parties are very fluent in." The Hizbullah was allegedly engaged in many terrorist acts, including holding hostages and the suicide bombing of U.S. Marine Corps barracks in Beirut in 1983, where 241 servicemen were killed. The party also violently opposed the Israeli-Palestinian peace dialogue, because it does not recognize the "Zionist entity," as it calls Israel.

Ho, Ho, Ho! See VIET-MINH.

Hold-Up Bill. A legislative measure which proposes placing some burdens or exerting pressures upon private corporations or special interest groups.

Hole in a Law. See JUDICIAL PRECEDENT.

Holier than You. See MUGWUMP.

Holistic Argument in Political Theory. See CONCEPT, PARADIGM, POLITICAL THEORY, SCIENCE.

Holocaust. Term for the extermination of Jews by Adolf Hitler's Nazi Germans during W.W.II, mainly by cremation in concentration camps. About six million persons, one-third of the Jewish population in the world, perished—a genocide second in size to the Spanish extermination of about fifty-million South American Indians (or about 80 percent of the Indian population) by the Spanish Conquistadores, by murder and disease. After W.W.II, the German Federal Government (then West Germany) paid billions of dollars to surviving Holocaust victims as well as to many Gypsies, who were also subject to extermination by the Nazis.

Holocaust Mentality. The general fear of the Israelis, dating to the World War II experience when six million Jews were murdered by Nazi Germany, that their homeland, Israel, may again be subjected to destructive wars, now, from the Arabs. Dr. Geoffrey Wigoder of Hebrew University explains: "Every Israeli has at least a subconscious fear that what happened before could happen again. There is a general fear of the destruction of Israel, especially since the Yom Kippur war. This almost hysterical reaction ... is connected to the underlying feeling that any retreat on the part of America would once again bring back the sense of isolation that Jews knew at the time of Hitler, the same feelings they had in the late 1930s and 1940s when they were on their own."

Holy Alliance. An agreement (of 1815) among Russia, Prussia, and Austria to apply the principles and ethics of the Christian religion to the rule of their peoples and to the conduct of relations among themselves. See QUADRUPLE ALLIANCE.

Holy War. See BLACK MUSLIMS, JIHAD.

Home Rule. The grant of powers to form a separate autonomous, political subdivision; the grant of powers and authority to form a city, county, or a state, to adopt a charter on the basis of which a government will be formed and the political rights of the citizens will be determined; or the grant of authority to a political subdivision (county or city in the U.S.) to revise its charter and change the form of government without prior approval by the higher authority, provided that such changes will not conflict with existing laws.

Homeland. See BANTUSTAN.

Homeostasis. The ability of a political system to maintain reasonable stability and balance while in the process of extensive internal changes or adjustments; a self-regulating, dynamic political system, one not easily susceptible to eradication.

Homestead. The real estate of certain acreage and of certain value in the possession and use by an owner which may not be forcibly sold for the payment of debts; also, an Act of Congress of the U.S., the Homestead Act of 1862, authorizing the disposition of public land for settlement by private persons. (Under the provisions of the Act, one person or one family could receive up to one-hundred-sixty-acres of public land and receive a title to it at the end of five years, or at the end of six months upon the payment of $1.25 per acre. The Act was repealed in 1910 due to lack of availability of public land.)

Homicide. The killing of one human being by another.

Homogeneous Region. See NATURAL REGION.

D'Hondt Electoral System. A method of electing persons to public offices in single-member districts (or single-member constituencies) by proportional representation. In the Federal Republic of Germany, for example, where the system is being used, each voter casts two votes on the same ballot; the first vote (Erststimme) and the second vote (Zweitstimme). The first vote (Erststimme) is for a person of one's preference and the second vote (Zweitstimme) is for the candidate on the party list. Candidates receiving an absolute majority of the votes cast are elected. Candidates who received very few votes are eliminated and their votes are transferred to those candidates who have good chances to become elected, but lack the votes. Allocation of seats to the parties is determined by the proportion of votes each party receives on the party lists. As a rule, loyal and dedicated party members have their names placed at the top of the party lists and upon receiving the necessary proportion of votes (minimum of five per cent), they will be seated in the Bundestag (the elective chamber of the Parliament). The system was named after D'Hondt, the Belgian mathematician who invented it. See PROPORTIONAL REPRESENTATION.

Honest Abe. See GREAT DEBATES.

Honesty is the Best Policy. See ARTILLERY OF THE HEAVENS.

Honeymoon. In the language of practical (day-to-day) politics, a short period of time between installation and/or inauguration of elected officials in a government, and the time when they come to transact the real business through political processes; the time between the official inauguration of the U.S. President, for example, and the time the U.S. Congress begins to consider (approve or reject) his legislative bills, or a judicial challenge of constitutionality (by the U.S. Supreme Court) of a legislative bill or presidential order is usually a sign that the honeymoon has ended.

Honeymoon of the New Deal. See NEW DEAL.

Honne. In the Japanese language, "the actual truth." See INTELLIGENCE.

Honor thy Father. See MAFIA.

Honorary Aryans. The Italian people as viewed by Adolf Hitler, the leader of Nazi Germany (1933-1945). Hitler's racial policy was to initiate and to maintain a strict segregation of the races, with the white (Caucasian) Aryan race as the leading and dominant race. But since Benito Mussolini (1922-1945), the founder of Italian Fascism and the leader of Fascist Italy, was also the political mentor of Adolf Hitler, as a token of appreciation, Hitler promised Mussolini in 1943, that upon the victory of Nazism everywhere, the Italians (many of whom are of dark skin) would be granted the status of "Honorary Aryans." Other races were slated either for "racial purification" or for total extermination (e.g., the Jews). A similar system of "honorary citizenship" has been granted to Asians residing in the Republic of South Africa. See LEBENSRAUM, PARALLEL DEVELOPMENT DOCTRINE.

Hoodwink. A scheme conceived by the Federal Bureau of Investigation (FBI) during the 1940s and 1950s, to spark conflict between the American Mafia and the American Communist Party so they could exterminate each other, particularly on the organized (unionized) labor front. The project was not very successful, because FBI Director J. Edgar Hoover never acknowledged there was such a thing as the "Mafia." The "war" was to commence with FBI agents sending phony leaflets to Mafia bosses, supposedly by the Communist Party, criticizing unfair labor practices in businesses which the Mafia owned or operated.

Hoover Blanket. See GREAT DEPRESSION.

Hoover Commissions. Two task forces, authorized by the U.S. Congress and headed by former U.S. President Herbert Hoover, set up to study ways and means for reorganizing and improving the executive branch of the federal government (the First Commission of 1947) and to determine the degree of intrusion by administrative agencies into judicial functions (the Second Commission of 1954). Similar task forces known as "Little Hoover Commissions," were established by some state governments.

Hoover Holiday. See HOOVER MORATORIUM.

Hoover Moratorium. U.S. President Herbert Hoover (1929-1933) ordered in June 1931, a one-year suspension on payment of war debts by European powers to the United States as a measure to revive European economies, particularly that of Germany, whose debt, by the agreement reached in Lausanne, Switzerland, in 1932, was scaled down from $32,000,000,000 (imposed during the Paris Peace Treaty in 1919) to $714,000,000. (Many historians claim that this burden placed upon Germany allowed Adolf Hitler and his followers to gain power in Germany and that World War II in reality commenced then.)

Hoover-Stimson Doctrine of 1932. When Japan invaded China in 1931, U.S. President Herbert Hoover (1929-1933) and his Secretary of State, Henry Stimson, declared that the United States would not recognize any territorial gains acquired through naked aggression. See STIMSON DOCTRINE.

Hooverville. See GREAT DEPRESSION.

Horizontal Distribution of Power. See FRAGMENTATION OF POWER.

Horizontal Growth of Government. See POLITICAL DEVELOPMENT.

Horizontal Imperialism. See COLONIALISM, IMPERIALISM.

Horizontal Social Mobility. See SOCIAL MOBILITY.

Hostages in America. When Nazi Germany declared war against the United States in 1941 following the Japanese attack on Pearl Harbor, U.S. President Franklin Delano Roosevelt ordered the detention of over 2,000 German and Italian diplomats who were held by the FBI in Greenbriar, West Virginia. Shortly after that, the Nazi Secret Police, the Gestapo, arrested about 180 American diplomats in Berlin in retaliation. Both sides exchanged the hostage diplomats within six months. Neither side made any attempt to rescue its hostages or to harm the hostages held. See BLUE LIGHT OPERATION, OCTOBER SURPRISE.

Hostess with the Mostest. See BEHIND-THE-SCENE POWER.

Hostile and Slanderous Acts. According to Soviet Criminal Code, anyone engaged in criticizing the Soviet system of government was committing a "hostile and slanderous" act, and was subject to criminal prosecution. On January 25, 1977, the Soviet authorities sent such a warning to Dr. Andrei D. Sakharov, one of the principal leaders of the dissent movement (struggle for freedom of expression, movement, and worship), and a Nobel Peace prize recipient. Sakharov, in turn, sent a letter to U.S. President Jimmy Carter asking for support. The President replied (a gesture without precedent in the history of U.S. Presidency) by sending a strong note to the Government of the Soviet Union reminding it about the Helsinki Accord and the accepted "international standards of human rights," which the Soviets should respect and observe. Dr. Sakharov was not harassed after that, according to press accounts. See HELSINKI ACCORD, HUMAN RIGHTS: AMERICAN DEFINITION.

Hostis Humani Generis. In the Latin language, "enemies of all mankind"; also a principle by which persons who commit certain heinous crimes (e.g., piracy on the high seas or war crimes) are punished under international law, rather than under the law of their individual jurisdictions. See INTERNATIONAL PIRACY.

Hot Button Political Issue. A single complex issue of policy, usually controversial and of a national scope, which emerges around the time of an important election (e.g., the U.S. Presidency) and is not susceptible to simple solutions (e.g., the issues of police brutality, poverty, and race relations), such as blacks/white relations in the United States following the 1992 Rodney King incident in Los Angeles, California. See POLICE BRUTALITY.

Hot Buttons. See NATIONAL ORGANIZATION FOR WOMEN (NOW).

Hot Line. The communication link (e.g., telephone and teletype) connecting the U.S. President (the White House) with the leaders of the Soviet Union (the Kremlin), set up for instant communications whenever serious crises arose. See TELEPHONE DIPLOMACY.

Hot Pursuit. The right to pursue and to seize a foreign vessel which is involved in invasion and to prosecute the invaders provided that the pursuit begins on the territorial waters or on land of the invaded state and that it is uninterrupted. The right to pursue ceases when the party being pursued reaches the territorial waters (or land) of another state unless that state renders consent. (Similar practice may apply to speeding motorists or fugitives from justice, for example, in the United States.)

Hot-Stove Rule. A term coined by Douglas McGregor with reference to punishment or penalty that one ought to expect for non-compliance with certain prescribed rules (e.g., violation of the laws of the state, the society, or the rules of a hierarchical organization). McGregor draws an analogy between undergoing discipline and touching a hot stove. When one touches a hot stove, one knows the consequences: the punishment (the pain that one sustains from burning) is immediate; the heat that a hot stove emits is sufficient warning; the penalty is consistent, because each time one touches the hot stove one will be burned; and the penalty is impersonal because the stove does not burn some and not others, but anyone who touches it. Likewise, superiors inflict punishment upon their subordinates for certain wrongful acts, and in order to avoid such punishment or disciplinary action, one ought to refrain from violating the rule or the law. McGregor suggests that punishment or discipline (e.g., a fine or imprisonment that a judge imposes or dismissal of an employee for certain intolerable acts) should be immediate (i.e., it should be inflicted without delay); with warning (the subordinate to be disciplined should know in advance which acts or activities may constitute grounds for disciplinary action); consistent (the discipline or punishment should always follow the infraction); and impersonal (it should not be given as revenge, and it should be commensurate with the infraction).

Hot Summer in America. Phrase associated with urban rioting and protests in the summer, usually by minorities and in the main by black Americans, many of whom reside in urban ghettoes with limited income, without access to such comforts as air conditioning or swimming pools. Hot, long summers with temperatures reaching 100 or 115 degrees F. (38 to 45 degrees Celsius) often trigger rioting upon the smallest pretext. Some black political leaders in America cleverly use this phenomenon as their bargaining tool with city, state, or federal government, demanding measures to provide better environmental and living conditions. Many of the most capable black leaders in America learned their political strategy and tactics not in ivy league universities, but in their most venerable and lasting institution: the black church. During the 1960s a popular slogan accompanying urban rioting was, "Burn, Baby, Burn." See URBANIZATION.

Hôtel De Ville. In the French language, "the seat of local government" (e.g., town hall or city hall).

House Arrest. Forcible detention carried out in one's home instead of prison.

House Calendar. An internal record of the House, in which all bills presented are recorded, except those for raising revenue and general appropriations of money or property. See CALENDAR WEDNESDAY, CONGRESS OF THE UNITED STATES, CONSENT CALENDAR, PRIVATE BILL, UNION CALENDAR, UNITED STATES HOUSE OF REPRESENTATIVES.

House Divided Against Itself Cannot Stand. See GREAT DEBATES.

House Journal. An official record of the U.S. House of Representatives (authorized by the U.S. Constitution in Article I, Section 5, Clause 3) which contains briefs of daily proceedings and votes taken. See CONGRESS OF THE UNITED STATES, HOUSE CALENDAR, UNITED STATES HOUSE OF REPRESENTATIVES.

House of Burgesses of Virginia. The oldest legislative body in the British colonies in North America, established in 1619 in Williamsburg, Virginia. England's King James I, distrustful of Virginia's strong and sophisticated leaders, planned to abolish the House of Burgesses which he rightly suspected to be a "seminary of sedition." An intercolonial Committee of Correspondence was established in 1773 as a standing committee of the House of Burgesses, to be followed by other colonies. The function of the Intercolonial Committees was to collect and disseminate information on revolutionary preparation toward independence, and with time, they evolved into the first American Congress. See VIRGINIA: MOTHER OF PRESIDENTS.

House of Commons. The elective chamber of the British Parliament and one of the oldest elective chambers in the world, being in continuous existence since the 15th century. (The oldest is Iceland's Althing, meeting continuously since 930 AD.) The House is composed of deputies called Members of Parliament, or MPs, elected from single-member constituencies for a tenure of up to five years (eligible for re-election). The majority party in the House of Commons selects the government-of-the-day. Also, the name of similar legislative bodies of the member-states of the British Commonwealth (e.g., Canada or Australia). See HOUSE OF LORDS, PARLIAMENT.

House of Europe. Another name for the European Common Market, the European Community, which, following the 1992 leap in integration of the market and the gradual inclusion of the former Soviet Union and the East European states, is expected to become the greatest economic and political power in the world, possibly a major rival to Japan and the United States. See COMMON MARKET, EUROPEAN ECONOMIC COMMUNITY, Appendix 73.

House of Lords. The non-elective chamber of the British Parliament (since the 14th century) with little legislative power (the House of Lords may only suspend legislation proposed by the House of Commons for a certain period of time) and some judicial power; composed of the Lords Temporal, the Lords of Appeal, and the Lords Spiritual (the Archbishops of Canterbury and York and twenty-four diocesan bishops of the Church of England). See HOUSE OF COMMONS, PARLIAMENT.

House of Nationalities. See SUPREME SOVIET.

House of Representatives. See UNITED STATES HOUSE OF REPRESENTATIVES, Appendix 10.

House of the Union. See SUPREME SOVIET.

Houston Riot. During World War I (1917-1918), about 300,000 Negroes were drafted into the U.S. armed forces to help fight the war in Europe, or what President Woodrow Wilson called the war "to make the world safe for democracy" and "war to end wars." The majority of black soldiers were assigned to labor battalions instead of combat units. Riots occurred in 1917 in East St. Louis where about 40 blacks and 8 whites died in confrontations. In Houston, Texas, 13 black soldiers were hanged for rioting and killing 17 whites. A compromise was reached when blacks were sent to Europe in the 369th Regiment which distinguished itself, earning the name "Hell Fighters" from the Germans themselves.

HT/LINGUAL. A covert operation conducted by the U.S. Central Intelligence Agency (CIA) under the direction of its counterintelligence (CE) chief, James Jesus Angleton, in which all mail incoming and outgoing to and from the Soviet Union and other communist states was opened and photographed in order to detect espionage and counterespionage contacts and to gather intelligence information. The operation was conducted secretly, mainly in New York City, from about 1947 to 1973; about 220,000 pieces of mail were opened and a list of about two million individuals was compiled as possible suspects. Together with that operation, another secret operation, codenamed CHAO, was also directed by Angleton and its objective was to fulfill the request of the FBI by spying on Americans living abroad in order to determine espionage activity among and by them. During the riots by students and anti-Vietnam War protesters, particularly in the late 1960s and early 1970s, U.S. President Lyndon Johnson and, later, President Richard Nixon demanded such information because they suspected that these protests were financed and instigated from abroad. The CIA and the FIA (CIA can operate abroad only and the FBI stateside only) were not able to find any evidence to that effect. These two operations were conducted contrary to American laws. Following an official hearing before the Church Committee (the U.S. Senate Select Committee to Study Government Operations with Respect to

Intelligence Activities, 94th Congress, 21st Session, and its subsequent report, *Intelligence Activities and the Rights of Americans*, 1976) Angleton made a statement on 24 September 1975 to the effect that "it is inconceivable that a secret intelligence arm of the government had to comply with all overt orders of that government." This caused the downfall of Angleton and the end of the "great mole hunt" which had been instigated by Angleton's strong belief that the CIA had been penetrated by moles installed by the Soviet KGB.

Hubris. In the Greek language, "arrogance," or "abuse of power." A term coined in ancient Greece describing the arrogant abuse of power by a power elite remaining too long in governing. A term often applied to despotic regimes which were once progressive but which in time turned despotic against their own people (e.g., Imperial Germany, Austria, Prussia, Russia, or Cuba under Batista).

Human Freedom Index. Special statistical information that is compiled yearly by the United Nations Development Program, evaluating, state by state, and region by region, the status of existing personal freedoms and liberties; the degrees to which governments tolerate human idiosyncrasies; and the degree to which governments in power provide for the well-being of their citizens. The 1992 Human Development report indicates that one-fifth of the population on earth goes hungry, has no access to health care and clean water, and that about fourteen million children under five years of age die yearly, mostly from preventable diseases. The two principal regions that are more severely affected by these deficiencies are sub-Saharan Africa and South Asia. Most of these calamities, however, are created by rulers who engage in war, and have a greedy attitude toward the problems of the people they govern, desiring to dominate over them rather than solve their problems. They keep the people they govern in apathy, desperation, and illiteracy.

Human Life Amendment. Anti-abortion forces seek an amendment to the Constitution to protect life (also known as "Pro-Life Amendment") particularly after the Supreme Court struck in February 1980 the Hyde amendment which banned federal aid for almost all abortions on demand. Now Medicaid funds are again available for abortions but the Human-Life groups seek an amendment to stop this practice forever. See MARCH FOR LIFE.

Human Misery Index. See HUMAN FREEDOM INDEX.

Human Resources Planning. A deliberate attempt to develop consistent and coordinated programs in such areas as manpower training, education, health, welfare, or population in general, to be carried out in some organizational context. See PLANNING, RESOURCE WAR.

Human Rights: American Definition. The United States Government released its official definition of human rights and the means of enforcing them (see U.S. Department of State, "On Human Rights." January 1978). They are: "Freedom from arbitrary arrest and imprisonment, torture, unfair trial, cruel and unusual punishment, and invasion of privacy; Rights to food, shelter, health care, and education; and freedom of thought, speech, assembly, religion, press, movement, and participation in government." The executive branch has undertaken several initiatives and executive/legislative cooperative actions aimed at the protection of these rights. These are: removing travel restrictions for U.S. citizens and liberalizing visa policies; appointing an assistant Secretary for Human Rights and Humanitarian Affairs along with human rights officers in each bureau of the Department of State; creating an interagency committee to review human rights and foreign assistance issues; encouraging citizens and groups to speak out on human rights matters; passing legislation to expand asylum and refugee programs; cooperating on policies to enhance human and political rights in southern Africa; and urging Senate approval of important international human rights documents. The Carter Administration made active concern for human rights throughout the world a central part of U.S. foreign policy. Although human rights issues have been fundamental to American thought and action, they have not always been a systematic part of our policies toward other nations. As specific issues, human rights have been dealt with through the UN and the Organization of American States (OAS). Both the executive and legislative branches have responded to widespread public sentiment that U.S. foreign policy should be more sensitive to human rights concerns. A positive policy offers hope to those whose rights have been denied. It also serves the national interest by reasserting American ideals as the foundation of our foreign policy, encouraging respect among nations for the rule of law in international affairs, and rebuilding domestic consensus in support of

American foreign policy. See HELSINKI ACCORD, HOSTILE AND SLANDEROUS ACTS, Appendices 8, 51.

Human Rights Party. A minor political party, active mainly in the state of Michigan, which advocates, among other things, free and unrestricted use of such narcotics as marijuana, and a socialist system of economy in the United States.

Human Rights Struggle. See HELSINKI ACCORD, HOSTILE AND SLANDEROUS ACTS, HUMAN RIGHTS: AMERICAN DEFINITION.

Human Trade. See FLIGHT FROM THE REPUBLIC.

HUMINT. See INTELLIGENCE.

Humphrey Amendment. See COMMUNIST CONTROL ACT OF 1954.

Humphrey-Hawkins Full Employment Act. A major legislative act passed by the U.S. Congress on April 13, 1978, which was submitted in 1977, by U.S. Senator Hubert H. Humphrey (D-Minnesota; died January 13, 1978) and U.S. Representative Augustus F. "Gus" Hawkins (D-California). This act sets as a national goal the reduction of unemployment to four percent by 1983, mainly by artificial creation of jobs with federal funds. U.S. President Jimmy Carter endorsed this bill on November 14, 1977, as did the Congressional Black Caucus and the AFL-CIO. U.S. Senator Muriel Humphrey, wife of the deceased Senator who was appointed to continue on her husband's job until fall 1978, when a special election was held in Minnesota, was instrumental in clearing the final stages for passage of this controversial legislation which was strongly opposed by conservative elements in Congress. Many former opponents to the bill have cast affirmative votes (sympathy votes) for the passage of this bill partially from great respect and admiration for the former Senator, Hubert H. Humphrey. See PRAIRIE POPULIST.

Hundred Days of New Deal Legislation. See NEW DEAL.

Hundred Days Session. Between March 9 and June 16, 1933, the U.S. Congress enacted most of the New Deal legislation; the most legislation ever enacted during a single session, due to the strong insistence of President Franklin D. Roosevelt, who was referred to by an envious Congressman as "that man in the White House." See HONEYMOON, NEW DEAL.

Hundred Flowers. A statement of national policy issued by Mao Tse-tung of the People's Republic of China in 1956, for the purpose of reviving free national discussion and criticism of the policies of the government (but not of the Communist party). The slogan appeared under the title of: "Let All Flowers Bloom Together, Let the Hundred Schools Contend." This slogan was not originated by Mao, it was explored by him in order to mobilize the masses. This slogan was first popularized in ancient times, by the first followers of Confucius, ca. 551-479 BC.

Hung. See SECRET SOCIETIES.

Hung Jury. A jury unable to reach a guilty or not guilty verdict. In the event of a hung jury a mistrial results and the case must be brought to trial again.

Hungarian Goulash Capitalism. The Hungarians, like the Poles, were the least obedient to the Soviet line of building socialism/communism in their state. In spite of pressure from Moscow to collectivize farms and nationalize (socialize) enterprises (particularly under the leadership of the communist leader, Mátyás Rákosi [1949-1956]), Hungary was able to maintain most of its agriculture in private hands and was also able to maintain, on a small scale, private ownership of the means of production and distribution. Even after the 1956 Revolution, when the Soviets suppressed the freedom movement in Hungary, the Hungarians, in their ancient wisdom, were able to hold on to capitalist production and trade the Hungarian way—doing just enough to keep the Soviet troops out, against which they were helpless. See HUNGARIAN REVOLUTION.

Hungarian Revolution. When the Hungarian people rebelled against the oppressive regime of the communist leader and Moscow agent, Mátyás Rákosi, in October 1956, and installed Imre Nagy in a government coalition, the Soviet agents invited Soviet troops, a force of about 200,000, which crushed the

Revolution leaving devastation and over 20,000 dead. The pro-democratic regime was replaced by another Soviet agent, János Kádar, on 4 November 1956. See HUNGARIAN GOULASH CAPITALISM.

Hunger Migration. The process of speedy industrialization after W.W.II caused great migrations of people from agricultural areas to large cities. According to the proposed "Universal Declaration on Every Man's Right to Proper Nourishment" to be presented by a special international commission in 1992, the exodus of people from the countryside to cities, now being intensified throughout the world, is triggered by shortage of food, and it will become a serious problem in the coming years. The commission predicts, according to *Parade Magazine* (9 February 1992), that ". . . by the year 2020 there will be more than 50 cities which have at least 10 million inhabitants." In Latin America the population is expected to grow from the present 72% to 83%, and in Africa from 68% to 84%. See HUNGER WARS, POPULATION GROWTH PROJECTIONS, Appendices 85, 86.

Hunger Wars. An overwhelming amount of contemporary literature on human wars—international, regional, and local conflicts within, between, and among nations—indicates that the future wars will be hunger wars fought by hungry nations desiring food rather than political control over peoples and territories. These projections of hunger wars are based on T. R. Malthus's writings; namely, his treatise of 1798, *An Essay on the Principle of Population*, in which he forecasts the shortage of food and a rapid growth of population which may lead to hunger wars. Malthus suggested a birth control system in order to deter the rapid population growth. In modern times such distinguished scholars as Margaret Mead; economists Robert L. Heilbroner, J. Commoner, and John K. Galbraith; and the Hudson Institute of New York—all address themselves to the need for saving food resources and controlling population growth, or facing a catastrophe. Dr. Normal E. Borlaug, the 1970 Nobel Peace Prize winner for innovative food production, helped start the "green revolution" which allows for the increase of crops at four times the rate of the conventional method. Dr. Borlaug also suggests that, in spite of the "green revolution," the miracle rice (which was developed during W.W.II by American and Filipino scientists, and which allows rice to be grown at twice the rate of the old conventional method), and in spite of the exploration of sea resources, food production and the food supply will not keep up with the demands of a rapidly growing population around the world. In Dr. Borlaug's opinion, the principal nutrients are: (1) grain, (2) sea food, and (3) animal food (e.g., beef and poultry), in that order. Agricultural production is declining due to (1) a shrinking supply of fresh and clean water needed for irrigation; (2) deterioration of land under cultivation due to (a) overexploitation, and (b) the use of artificial (chemical) fertilizers: (3) expanded use of arable land for commercial development (e.g., building of highways, airports, shopping centers, manufacturing plants, and housing for the growing population); and (4) the "sinking" or absorption of landmass by water (e.g., due to the melting of the ice caps). Another important source of food supply is the sea, but this supply is also shrinking due to: (1) overexploitation by man (e.g., mass fishing without replenishing with new schools, resulting in certain species disappearing forever); (2) water pollution; and (3) lack of coordinated planning on a global scale aimed at the management of sea resources. Hunger will also force many people back to the land, to the farm. See HUNGER MIGRATION, YEAR ZERO, Appendices 85, 86.

Hunt Commission. See COMMISSION ON PRESIDENTIAL NOMINATIONS.

Hurrah Patriot. See CHAUVINIST.

Hush Money. Those financial contributions that are made to a politician during an election campaign which can be spent at her or his discretion. For example, Richard M. Nixon spent about $450,000 of $62 million he had received in 1972, to silence the Watergate burglars. Such money is usually donated by individuals, often taken from special corporate funds ("slush funds") which are illegal, but difficult to deal with under present laws. See CAMPAIGN FINANCING, LAUNDERED FUNDS.

Hustings Court. A one-judge court of law with original jurisdiction that maintains records of its proceedings; also, the name of local courts in some subdivisions of the state of Virginia in the United States. The name is adopted from the past practice when judges had "to hustle" from one place to another to hear and adjudicate cases. See Appendices 63, 64, 66.

Huston Plan. See COUNTERINSURGENCY IN AMERICA.

Hydra. See COUNTERINSURGENCY IN AMERICA.

Hyperindividualism. See GUIDED FREE ENTERPRISE, INDIVIDUALISM, RUGGED INDIVIDUALISM.

Hypothesis. A certain assumption that one makes when undertaking a scientific study that something was, is, or will be a truth, an actual fact, cause, or event; or an interaction between factors that one holds as valid and true, and all events, interactions, or causes are a consequence of the assumed truth. See POLITICAL THEORY.

I

"War is much too serious a thing to be left to the military."
GEORGES CLEMENCEAU, 1841-1929

I Am an American Day. See CITIZENSHIP DAY.

I Am Not a Crook! A statement made by U.S. President Richard M. Nixon (1969-1974) about himself when confronted with evidence in 1973 that he had cheated the U.S. Government by taking a federal income tax deduction of almost $480,000 for Vice Presidential papers which he had deposited in the National Archives. The deduction was subsequently disallowed, and Nixon repaid the tax money to the federal treasury. Nixon's honesty was questioned once before, less successfully. During the 1952 presidential campaign, Dwight D. Eisenhower described his running mate, Richard M. Nixon, as being as clean "as a hound's tooth" when allegations were raised that Nixon had accepted large contributions from wealthy persons in violation of existing laws. Nixon went on television and explained that the only gift he had accepted was a homeless dog, Checkers, and that allegations of dishonesty were nothing but communist propaganda. The speech on the homeless dog was well received, and the ticket, Eisenhower-Nixon, was elected. This became known as the famous "Checkers" speech. See WATERGATE AFFAIR.

I Am the State. In the French language, "l'état c'est moi;" also the famous remark made by the King of France, Louis XIV (1643-1715) personifying the state, and as long as he was in power he was cheered: "long live the king." However, once he died, the people cheered "the king is dead, long live the new king." Louis XIV, like many monarchs throughout history, held the conviction that they were the state and that once they leave the scene so will the state. Even in modern times, dictators and political demagogues, like Nicolae Ceausescu, who together with his wife and a partner-in-crime was convinced that the state of Romania was their personal domain and the Romanian people their serfs. They were removed from power on 22 December 1989 by the National Salvation Front (or Council of National Salvation). See CULT OF PERSONALITY.

I Did it My Way. See SINATRA DOCTRINE.

I Have a Dream. See WASHINGTON DEMONSTRATION.

I Have Been Born Again. See BORN AGAIN.

I Have Had Enough of War. U.S. President Dwight D. Eisenhower (1953-1961) so informed the Soviet (Russian) leaders gathered for a conference in Geneva, Switzerland, in 1955, because the President in all honesty believed that the Soviet system could become accommodating after the death of Stalin on 5 March 1953, and the Soviet Leader's, Nikita Sergeyevich Khrushchev's proclamation the same year that the cold war would be replaced, in time, with "peaceful coexistence" between the two opposing socio-economic-political systems: the Soviet East and the American West. But soon after Khrushchev placed new demands upon the Western Allies: abandon Berlin and declare it a "free city;" withdraw Allied forces from the eastern portion, mainly the City of Berlin, but U.S. Secretary of State, John Foster Dulles, stated categorically that, "We are most solemnly committed to hold West Berlin, if need be by military force." This decisive stand softened the Russians per Lenin's tactical teaching, "attack when strong, retreat when weak," or "two steps forward, one step back, if necessary." All that Khrushchev could do was talk big (e.g., "We shall bury you," meaning the West, especially the United States). What Khrushchev said was purposely mistranslated for western consumption; Khrushchev said, "We shall surpass you."

I-Ho-ch'uan. See BOXER REBELLION.

I Love Germany So Much that I Prefer to Have Two of Them. A remark by a British politician who was not very happy with the reunification of Germany, fearing the potential threat of that great power against smaller states. See GERMAN UNIFICATION, Appendix 105.

I Shall Return! See SWITZERLAND OF ASIA.

I Would Rather be Right Than be President. So spoke presidential candidate Henry Clay, who lost the 1844 election to his rival, James K. Polk. Clay bitterly opposed unrealistic, politically-motivated promises made by presidential candidates during a campaign. He considered that practice to be immoral and simply wrong.

I Would Rather Have Him Inside the Tent P...ing Out than Outside the Tent P...ing In. U.S. President Lyndon B. Johnson (1963-1969) so characterized the necessity of good relationships with J. Edgar Hoover, the Director of the Federal Bureau of Investigation (FBI), and the potent and lethal power of the FBI empire. Since the FBI collects information on individuals, including high government officials, most U.S. presidents have shown partiality and favoritism toward that agency. See POLITICAL STYLE.

IAAWICADB. See INTERNATIONAL ARMS AND WAR IMPLEMENTS COLLECTION AND DISPOSAL BANK.

IAEA. See INTERNATIONAL ATOMIC ENERGY AGENCY.

IAMO. See INTER-AFRICAN AND MALAGASY ORGANIZATION.

ICC. See GENEVA ACCORDS (OR AGREEMENT) OF 1954, PARIS PEACE AGREEMENT OF 1973.

ICCS. See CHIP COMMISSION, PARIS PEACE AGREEMENT OF 1973.

ICFTU. See INTERNATIONAL CONFEDERATION OF FREE TRADE UNIONS.

Ichiwari Kokka. See TEN-PERCENT NATION.

ICJ. See INTERNATIONAL COURT OF JUSTICE.

ICMA. See INTERNATIONAL CITY MANAGEMENT ASSOCIATION.

Ideal Human Condition. See MAFISH HAKUMA.

Ideal State. See UTOPIA.

Ideation. The process of thinking by a human being; the process and the structure of thought and formation of an idea. See EPISTEMOLOGY, INSTRUMENTALISM.

Ideological/Religious Purity. See EASTOXIFICATION.

Ideological Vagrants. Patrick Buchanan, journalist, former speech writer for U.S. President Richard M. Nixon, and a Republican challenger to President George Bush in the 1992 campaign, so characterizes the political philosophy of the "Neoconservatives." See EVOLUTION OF THE TWO-PARTY SYSTEM IN THE UNITED STATES, Appendix 16.

Ideology. A set of beliefs instilled through the process of political socialization pertaining to the mode of making a living and residing within a political community; a set of assumptions, biases, and predilections pertaining to the nature of social, economic, and political institutions of a society and its core values, and the political order. As defined by Aristotle (384-322 BC), one of the greatest political philosophers ever, characterizes ideology in one of his major works, *Politics,* as follows: Every . . . state is a species of association, and . . . all associations are instituted for the purpose of attaining some good . . . . We may therefore hold . . . that the particular association which is the most sovereign of all, and includes all the rest (the state) will pursue this aim most, and will thus be directed to the most sovereign of all goods. The term "idéologie" was restated in modern times by a French philosopher, Antoine Destutt de Tracy, during the French Revolution of 1793-1797; to him it meant the "science of ideas." Some contemporary scholars define ideology as follows: (1) Karl Marx viewed ideology as a set of ideas with which he wanted to justify the overthrow of capitalism and establish a rule by the proletariat; (2) Anthony Downs—"a verbal image of the good society and the chief means of constructing such a society" (3) Carl Friedrich—"a reasonably coherent body of ideas concerning practical means of how to change, reform (or maintain) a political order" (4) Zbigniew K. Brzezinski—a systematized set of ideas that "ceases to be an intellectual abstraction and becomes an active social agent . . . when it is applied to concrete situations and becomes a guide to action" (5) Laswell and Kaplan—ideology is felt because of the "feelings it arouses or action it incites and (6) Reo M. Christenson, *et al.*—"a belief system that explains and justifies a preferred political order for society, either existing or proposed, and offers a strategy (process, institutional arrangements, programs) for its attainment." Professor J. Northtrop ideology is formed by the ends of social actions as defined by social doctrines; ideology is a theory defining the end or the aim of social action. It is a theory which designates the kind of society that one wants to achieve. See MARXISM.

If In Trouble, Travel! See WAR ECONOMIC THEORY.

If It Takes the Entire Army and Navy of the United States to Deliver a Post Card to Chicago, That Card Will be Delivered. See PRESIDENTIAL DECISIVENESS.

If It Works, It Must be Obsolete. See COORDINATING COMMITTEE FOR MULTILATERAL EXPORT CONTROLS (COCOM).

If It Works, Leave It Alone. See COORDINATING COMMITTEE FOR MULTILATERAL EXPORT CONTROLS (COCOM).

If the Tree Dies, You Die. See WHITE REVOLUTION.

If You Can't Stand the Heat, Get Out of the Kitchen. Such was the friendly advice given by U.S. President Harry S. Truman (1944-1953) to politicians who had neither the inclination, training, and stamina, nor patience and understanding for politics and political processes. See IF YOU NEED A FRIEND IN WASHINGTON, GET YOURSELF A DOG; POLITICAL STYLE.

If You Need a Friend in Washington, Get Yourself a Dog. Such was the advice rendered by former U.S. Senator and President, Harry S. Truman, to anyone who functioned in the cosmopolitan, gossipy and secretive atmosphere of the Nations' Capital. To those who couldn't "stand the heat," he advised, "get out of the kitchen." In decision making, the President was firm and demonstrated his acceptance of responsibility for his bureaucracy by placing a sign on his desk which read: "The buck stops here."

If You Want to Prevent War, Arm Yourself. See SIVIS PACEM PARA BELLUM.

Ignorance of the Law. See IGNORANTIA JURIS, LEGIS NEMINEN EXCUSAT.

Ignorantia Juris. In the Latin language, "ignorance of the law." See LEGIS NEMINEM EXCUSAT.

Ike. An affectionate nickname of U.S. President Dwight D. Eisenhower (1953-1961).

Il Duce. See CAESARISM, FASCISM.

ILC. See INTERNATIONAL LAW COMMISSION.

Iller. The administrative divisions or provinces of Turkey.

Illustrative War Scenario. See WAR SCENARIO.

ILO. See UNITED NATIONS ORGANIZATION (UNO).

Image Maker. See MEDIA STEROIDS.

Imarah. Emirate—an administrative division in some Arab countries.

IMF. See INTERNATIONAL MONETARY FUND.

Immigrants. See URBANIZATION.

Immigration. The transfer of one's residence from the jurisdiction of one country to another, usually for a permanent stay (domicile). Immigration varies from country to country, but most have strict laws regulating the arrival of permanent residents as well as the departure of the other residents country (emigration). The United States and the Federal Republic of Germany have the most lenient immigration laws, and in spite of statutory laws, and statutory provisions regulating immigration matters, the American system is very highly politicized in the sense that persons, sometimes in large numbers, are allowed to immigrate into the United States regardless of the conditions of the labor market. (For example, boat people or political refugees from oppressive systems are allowed entry. On the other hand, the former Soviet Union regulated its immigrations and emigrations with great severity.) American immigration (there are no emigration policies) is supervised by the Immigration and Naturalization Service of the U.S. Department of Justice, founded in 1891, which maintains offices throughout the United States as well as in foreign countries, usually at American consulates, embassies, or legations abroad. Immigrants settling in the United States are not required to become U.S. citizens, unless they so desire, and they can maintain the status of permanent resident alien. See UNITED STATES PERSON, Appendix 23.

Immigration and Naturalization Service. See IMMIGRATION, UNITED STATES PERSON, Appendices 85, 86.

Immunity. See DIPLOMATIC IMMUNITY, JURE IMPERII.

Impact Statement. See GOVERNMENT BY LITIGATION.

Impacted Area. A community with a limited tax base due to a large concentration of federal, non-taxable property (e.g., military bases). See URBANIZATION.

Impasse. A seemingly insoluble situation (e.g., a deadlock in negotiations). See ARBITRATION, DIPLOMACY.

Impeachable Offense. See IMPEACHMENT.

Impeachment. The act of removal from office of a high government official (e.g., the U.S. President and the Vice President; judges and cabinet members; ambassadors and commissioners) upon a charge based on properly substantiated material facts attesting to the effect that a crime has been committed. The U.S. Constitution empowers the U.S. Congress to impeach and the U.S. Senate to convict (see U.S. Constitution, Art. II, Sec. 4, in Appendix 8). There have been twelve impeachments in American political history, seven of which ended in acquittal, four in conviction; and one, that of Richard M. Nixon in 1974, who resigned (on August 9, 1974), was not completed. The first (and the only) U.S. President to be impeached was Andrew Johnson, on February 24, 1868 (by a vote of 126 to 47), when a radical Republican, Thaddeus Stevens, brought up charges against Johnson for firing the U.S. Secretary of War, Edwin M. Stanton (who was suspected of conspiring to weaken the President's efforts in implementing reconstruction policies in the defeated Southern Confederacy), for violation of the Tenure of Office Act (which prohibited the President from removing from office any official who was appointed with the advice and consent of the Senate before his replacement was confirmed). The trial of Johnson began on May 16, 1868 (with U.S. Chief Justice Samuel P. Chase presiding). Johnson was acquitted on the same day when the Senate was not able to muster the necessary two-thirds majority. (The vote was 35 to 19, or one vote short of the number required by the Constitution.) The vote that saved Johnson was cast by a radical Republican Senator from Kansas, Edmund G. Ross. In the case of President Richard M. Nixon (1969-1974), the Judiciary Committee of the U.S. House of Representatives came up with three articles of impeachment. Charge 1: taking part in criminal conspiracy to obstruct justice in the Watergate cover-up, on July 27, 1974 (by vote of 27 to 11); Charge 2: failure to carry out constitutional oath by abusing power, on July 29, 1974 (by a vote of 28 to 10); and Charge 3: defiance of Committee subpoenas, on July 30, 1974 (by a vote of 27 to 17). On August 5, 1974, the U.S. Supreme Court (in *United States v. Nixon*) ruled that President Nixon must release three tapes containing his secret conversations with White House aides (pertaining to the Watergate affair) to the Special Prosecutor, which the President did. (The tapes revealed that he was trying to use the FBI to stop probes into the Watergate scandal on the grounds that it would be detrimental to national security.) On August 9, 1974, the President resigned from office. (Nixon was given an unconditional pardon by President Gerald R. Ford on September 8, 1974, and on August 20, 1974, the U.S. House of

Representatives accepted the articles of impeachment as presented by the Judiciary Committee, by a vote of 413 to 3). The first member of Congress to be impeached was a U.S. Senator from Tennessee, William Blount, in 1797, for conspiracy to invade Spanish Florida with the aid of Indians and England. The charges in the Senate were dismissed, but Blount was subsequently expelled from the Senate. In 1804, a federal judge from New Hampshire, John Pickering, was removed for rendering improper decisions, drunkenness, and blasphemy. In 1805, an Associate Justice of the U.S. Supreme Court, Samuel Chase, was charged with intemperate judicial conduct and violation of the Sedition Act of 1798, but he was acquitted. A federal judge, James H. Peck, was charged in 1830 with arbitrary conduct on the bench, but was acquitted. In 1862, a federal judge from Tennessee, West H. Humphreys, was charged with abandoning the bench and joining the Confederacy. In 1876, the U.S. Secretary of War under President Grant, William W. Belknap, was charged with misconduct in office, but he resigned and was acquitted. In 1926 another federal judge, George W. Englis, was impeached; he resigned and was acquitted. Since 1926, there have been four other federal judges impeached, two of them were removed, and two were acquitted. Throughout America's political history, there were countless petitions for impeachment of Presidents—including Thomas Jefferson for concluding the Louisiana Purchase; John Tyler, for "acting to excite a disorganizing and revolutionary spirit in the country"; Abraham Lincoln, for deploying troops against the South and spending federal revenues without prior authorization by Congress, which Lincoln admitted but defended on the grounds of "urgency of the situation" (a doctrine which implies that the chief executive, as the Commander-in-Chief of the Armed Forces, has the right to act in an emergency), and on the grounds of concern for the personal life and safety of the members of Congress who, if called by the President for a special session of Congress would have been exposed to dangers since the capital city (Washington, D.C.) was crowded with Southern spies and saboteurs; Franklin D. Roosevelt, for a series of "high crimes and misdemeanors" (e.g., his attempts to "pack the U.S. Supreme Court and giving away war materiel—boats—to England in violation of existing neutrality laws and without congressional appropriation); Harry S. Truman for his attempts to desegregate the U.S. Armed Forces (which he did by a special order, and which gave rise to the Dixiecrats in the South); and Lyndon B. Johnson, for his civil rights legislation and the War in Vietnam. During the active phase of the U.S. Supreme Court in the 1960s there was a nationwide campaign to impeach Earl Warren, the Chief Justice of the U.S. Supreme Court. In 1970, the House Republican (minority) leader (and President of the United States [1974-1977]), Gerald R. Ford, brought impeachment proceedings against Associate Justice of the U.S. Supreme Court William O. Douglas (1939-1975), and defined an impeachable offense as ". . . whatever a majority of the House of Representatives considers it to be at a given moment in history," and a conviction upon impeachment as whatever ". . . results from whatever offense or offenses two-thirds of the other body considers to be sufficiently serious to require removal of the accused from office." Former U.S. Attorney General Richard G. Kleindienst well characterized the political nature of impeachment and removal of high governmental officials when he stated before a Senate hearing, "You don't need evidence to impeach a President, only votes." See WATERGATE AFFAIR.

Imperial Capitalism. See MONOPOLY.

Imperial Federation. A concept of a federation of states within one empire and under the ultimate authority of one ruler, the monarch, whereby each state enjoys considerable autonomy in arranging its internal affairs (i.e., determining the form of its own government). (This model of federation is strongly advocated by the apologists for the British Empire.)

Imperial Power. See POWER.

Imperial Presidency. A term often used to describe the pomp and circumstance that surrounded the U.S. Presidency under Richard M. Nixon (1967-1974), when he ordered that the protective service be dressed up in gold-trimmed uniforms similar to those of imperial guards of despotic rulers. When Gerald R. Ford became President in 1974, he ordered that the conspicuously overdecorated uniforms of the "palace guard," the protective service, be simplified to look more "democratic," and he discontinued the tradition of having the Marine Corps band play "Hail to the Chief"—which had always been played whenever the President appeared in official capacity, such as during state visits by foreign dignitaries. President-elect Jimmy Carter stated on November 6, 1976, that the White House would be democratic "with a little 'd' " and once in the White House, he took several measures to further deimperialize the imperial presidency.

Imperialism. A term denoting the inherent propensity of politically organized human beings (e.g., organized into states) to constantly seek ways to influence and control other states, either through open aggression or other more subtle ways of aggrandizement and expansion. Means of control and influence include: (1) the subversion of another state's language, cultural habits, religious beliefs and institutions, or ethical values, and also its political culture and political values—this form of influence is known as cultural or vertical imperialism; (2) the exposure of another state to new and more rewarding modes of production and distribution of goods and services which render more and better material rewards at less cost—this form of influence is known as economic imperialism; and (3) the interference with sovereign and territorial rights, either gradually through such means as immigration which may lead to assimilation (e.g., the Germanic tribes becoming a part of Roman society, thus causing the disintegration of the Roman empire, culture, and economy), or through open aggression and control—this form of influence is known as territorial or horizontal imperialism. Modern forms of imperialism fall into the first and the second categories (cultural and economic imperialism) because territorial aggrandizement (territorial imperialism) is expressly forbidden by modern norms of international law (e.g., the United Nations Charter) and by regional security arrangements (e.g., the NATO or the Warsaw Pact arrangements). In the past, however, following the classical forms of imperialist practices, a state would first invade and conquer the territory of another state, and, then subject the people to "deculturation." Tsar Nicholas I of Russia openly pronounced Russian policy in this regard when he stated in 1854, "Where once the Russian flag has flown, it must not be lowered." In his critique of imperialism as the highest stage of capitalism, V. I. Lenin (in his monumental work *Imperialism: The Highest State of Capitalism)* noted that under the capitalist system imperialist alliances are formed and ". . . no matter what form they may assume, whether of one imperialist coalition against another, or of a general alliance embracing imperialist powers, are nothing more than 'truce' in periods between wars . . . . Peaceful alliances prepare the ground for wars, and in their turn grow out of wars . . . ." See COLONIALISM, RUSSIFICATION, Appendix 91.

Imperialist War. See WAR.

Imperium in Imperio. In the Latin language, "sovereignty within a sovereignty" or " a state within a state" (e.g., a member-state within a confederation or one or the member-states of the British Commonwealth of Nations). See IMPERIAL FEDERATION.

Implied Power. Power that is not expressly granted, but which may be exercised in order to implement laws made under expressed powers (e.g., a democratic state guarantees its citizens certain rights and immunities, but in case of a national emergency these rights may be curtailed or even suspended).

Impolitic. An act committed in disregard of political principles and/or processes. One that is politically harmful (e.g., in election) to a politician.

Impounded Appropriation. See IMPOUNDED LEGISLATION.

Impounded Legislation. A law which the executive branch of the government decides not to enforce because: in its opinion, it may eventually do more harm than good; the need for which it was passed does not exist any longer (e.g., when a war ends, appropriations of funds for it are no longer necessary); or if enforced, it would be of some detriment to the national economy, such as requiring the raising of taxes. U.S. President Richard M. Nixon (1969-1974) impounded approximately $9.9 billion which had been authorized by Congress for water pollution, and it took a Supreme Court action (*Train v. New York*) in 1973, before the funds were released. The Court ruled that the President lacked the power to withhold spending money for programs authorized by Congress, and the Impoundment Control Act of 1974 limited the President's powers in withholding appropriations allowed by Congress.

Impressment. The practice of drafting citizens of one state into the armed forces of another. This was a practice of the British (until the Treaty of Ghent of 1814) by which U.S. sailors were kidnapped into the Royal Navy. During Nazi rule in Germany, German nationals who had become U.S. citizens were drafted into the Nazi army while visiting their homeland.

In Curia. In the Latin language, "in the court of law."

In God We Trust. An inscription on U.S. currencies.

In Loco. In the Latin language, "in that particular place."

In Loco Parentis. In the Latin language, "in place of a parent."

In Party. See INS.

In Perpetuum. In the Latin language, "forever," "continuously," or "in perpetuity."

In Search of Enemies. See BELTWAY BANDITS, WHEN IN TROUBLE TRAVEL.

Inalienable Right. An inherent right that one is born with (such as the right to live and pursue one's objectives), or which one acquires and which cannot be transferred or taken away without cause (e.g., right to life, liberty, and the pursuit of happiness). See Appendices 5, 47.

Inaugural Address (or Message). In the United States, the speech delivered by the President of the United States, following his installation in that office, in which he may make an important policy statement.

Incapacitation. As commonly applied to politics, the inability, voluntary (in case of negligence) or involuntary (physical detention, sickness, or assassination), to act and carry out the functions of an office. See Amendment XXV in Appendix 5.

Incitement to Disaffection Act of 1934. A parliamentary law passed in England in 1934, which aimed at stamping out communist propaganda in the British Armed Forces. The basic objective of this law was to discourage support of the International Brigade which during the Spanish Civil War in 1936 was under communist control, and in which over 500 Englishmen have died for the Republican cause in Spain opposing the anti-communist forces of General Francisco Franco.

Income of the U.S. Federal Government. See FEDERAL INCOME.

Incorrigibility. See JUVENILE DELINQUENCY.

Incrementalism. See POLITICAL INCREMENTALISM.

Incrementalist Presidency. A style of presidential governing characterized by responding to events as they occur, a "steady as she goes" course, instead of introducing any new and bold issues; a course of a conciliatory rather than an adversary nature, particularly in relations with the U.S. Congress. According to *Newsweek* (10 February 1992), an incremental style will characterize the second term of President George Bush if he is re-elected.

Incumbent. One currently holding office or a position of trust (e.g., U.S. President, member of Congress, state legislature, or a mayor).

Indefeasible Law. A law (statutory or constitutional) which may not be voided or undone for any reason whatever. All temporal laws, in the final analysis, can be modified, undone, or voided if the sovereign power so determines (although this is not a common practice). The Soviet Constitution (Art. 123), for example, stipulated: "Equal rights of citizens of the USSR, irrespective of nationality or race, in all spheres of economic, government, cultural, political and other social activity, is an 'indefeasible law.' " See Appendix 5.

Indemnification of Foreign-Owned Property. The practice of confiscating foreign-owned property in a state when a break of diplomatic relations or war occurs between the state and the one owning the property. See EXPROPRIATION, INDEMNITY.

Indemnity. A compensation, usually monetary, that one state receives from another for damages. By "damage" we understand physical destruction of material things or bodily harm to a human being (including death). According to established norms of international law, indemnity is due a state *ex jure* (a legal right arising under law), but often when a dispute arises as to the validity of the claim, a procedure of arbitration by third parties or by an international tribunal (e.g., the International Court of Justice) may be implemented. Under traditional international law, states could rightly initiate war against the delinquent state. Under modern international law, the injured states must seek remedy through negotiation and arbitration by an international body (e.g., the United Nations), and a unilateral self-help action war against the delinquent state is no longer permissible. See EXPROPRIATION, INTERNATIONAL LAW.

Indentured Servant. One who signs away his civil rights and subjects himself to the will of a master for a specified period of time. (This practice was common among early immigrants to the North American continent, mainly from Europe, who wanted to immigrate but lacked the funds for passage. These persons were indentured by their North American masters for periods ranging ordinarily from four to eight years. They worked for them until they paid off their debts.)

Independence. See SOVEREIGNTY.

Independent Agencies. Component of federal bureaucracy—heads report directly to president—specialized in function (e.g., EPA).

Independent Party. See GREENBACK PARTY.

Independent Regulatory Commissions. Component of federal bureaucracy, Interstate Commerce, Federal Commerce Commission, Federal Tract, Securities and Exchange—headed by boards or commissioners. Commissioners are nominated by the President and confirmed by the Senate for staggered terms from 5-14 years.

Independent Variable. See DEPENDENT VARIABLES.

Indian Crisis. See TASHKENT DECLARATION.

Indian National Congress Party. The major ruling political party in India, Asia's largest democracy, which was instrumental in Mohandas Kamarchand Gandhi's struggle for independence from British rule. Through the deployment of non-violent tactics, India achieved independence on 15 August 1945. After the assassination of Gandhi in 1948, leadership fell to Jawahar Lal Nehru, then in 1966 to his daughter, Indira Gandhi, who was assassinated in 1984. Her son Sanjay succeeded her as prime minister until 1989. He was assassinated in 1991. The Congress party's main opposition is a coalition of small parties and factions untied and called the Janata Coalition.

Indiana Ballot. See PARTY COLUMN BALLOT.

Indianapolis Unigov. A unified form of local government in the city or suburbs of Indianapolis, Indiana.

Indices. A list which contains the names of individuals considered to be real or potential enemies of the United States (e.g., persons disloyal to the United States government) who, in case of war or national emergency, are to be detained for security reasons. The list is maintained by the Federal Bureau of Investigation (FBI).

Indictment. A decision by a sworn jury acknowledging the commission or non-commission of crime; or a decision to let the charges stand as presented.

Individualism. A philosophical notion that the individual human being is, by nature, selfish, egocentric, and likes himself first before liking others; that the human being has his personal biases, predilections, rights, and will, which very often conflict with the collective will of a family, tribe, community, or a nation. The notion of individualism was theoretically advanced in modern times by the political and social philosophers of the Age of Enlightenment, in the idealism of George Wilhelm Hegel (1770-1831), as opposed to those who viewed the primary role of the human being as a member of the whole, the society (e.g., in Marxism, and socialism). The contradiction between individualism and communalism, the community, as well as the "global village" concept, remains unresolved in many western societies, and particularly in the United States. See COMMUNISM, ROLE OF STATE, RUGGED INDIVIDUALISM, SOCIALISM.

Individualistic Capitalism. The Anglo-Saxon (American and British) type of capitalist market economy as opposed to those of Germany and Japan which Professor Lester C. Thurow (*Head to Head: The Economic Battle Among Japan, Europe, and America*, William Morrow and Company, Inc.)

characterizes as "communitarian capitalism." See POLITICO-ECONOMIC SYSTEMS, TYPES OF MARKET SYSTEMS, Appendices 83, 84.

Individualistic Theory. See ROLE OF STATE.

Indo-Chinese War. See HIMALAYAN CRISIS.

Industrial Espionage. The ancient practice of seeking information about innovations, scientific and technical discoveries, and improvements of implements used in the production of goods and services, through clandestine, covert means as in political espionage. The major objects of industrial espionage, which may be conducted between foreign countries as well as within a single nation by the nationals or residents of the same state, are clothing designs (e.g., by famous designers in Paris and New York); proposed body stylings of new automobile models and other technological improvements which may make them more attractive to buyers; new ways to process tobacco for cigarettes; and products of a similar nature. The recipient of advance information about those products may thereby save on basic and applied research, and put the product on the market ahead of others, or offer better quality. According to some allegations, a young physics teacher arrived in Chicago from Germany in the early 1900s to demonstrate to American aviation pioneers his model of an airplane. Within several days his blueprints and the miniature model of his airplane had mysteriously disappeared from his hotel room causing him to return empty-handed to his native Germany. Several months later, the Wright brothers made aviation history in America with an airplane which very much resembled the model of the German scientist. Having no American patent on his discovery and invention, the German had no case, and history gave the glory of aviation breakthrough to others. In recent decades, the greatest amount of industrial espionage activity has been noted in the electronics industry, particularly in computer gadgetry, and in food processing and preservatives, since food supply in the world lags behind population growth. Next to atom, neutron, and other weapons systems technologies, the Soviet Union and other nations, for example, were eager to obtain the formula for the syrup from which the popular Coca Cola and Pepsi Cola drinks are made. The syrup formula is well guarded; five separate persons who do not know each other each know only one part of the entire formula, and these people are coordinated through an Atlanta, Georgia, bank which is beyond the reach of industrial spies. Not being successful in obtaining the syrup formula, the Soviets agreed that Pepsi Cola would itself supply the Soviet market with this popular drink, while India refused such marketing rights to Coca Cola unless they shared with the Indians the secret of the formula. Coca Cola decided to abandon the Indian market in favor of keeping its formula secret. The media reported in 1991, that the personnel on Air France, the French airlines, was extremely friendly and outgoing, but it was learned that the underlying reason for that unusual courtesy was to lull important passengers into conversation while French intelligence agents were recording the discussions between traveling business executives. French intelligence even admitted that one of its computers is named after the agency because it was they who transferred the technology from abroad by clandestine, illegal means. See INTELLIGENCE.

Industrial Policy. See GUIDED FREE ENTERPRISE.

Industrial Revolution. The introduction of innovative methods of production through the development of machines, steam power, electric power, railways, and surface transport, beginning about 1750, first in England; then in other European states (e.g., Germany); then in North America, particularly in the United States; then in Asia, mainly in Japan. This period is often referred to as the "First Industrial Revolution." In the main, human labor was relieved of an undue burden and was allowed to produce more for less, with benefits to the largest number of persons ever. The Second Industrial Revolution is considered to have commenced with the deployment of computer chips and other innovations in electronics which allowed speedy communications and calculations. The Second Industrial Revolution is also referred to as the "Information Revolution."

Industrial Society. See POST-INDUSTRIAL SOCIETY.

Industrial Union. A labor union in which membership is open to more than one craft or trade.

Inevitability of Wars Among Capitalist Countries. Josef V. Stalin, General Secretary of the CPSU and Premier of the Soviet Government (1924-1953), in his last work published in 1952, *Economic*

Problems of Socialism in the USSR, advanced the theoretical proposition that wars are an inherent part of the capitalistic system and that wars will inevitably continue within the capitalist bloc. Stalin writes: "Some comrades affirm that, in consequence of the development of international conditions after the Second World War, wars among capitalist countries have ceased to be inevitable. They consider that the contradictions (sources of tensions) between the camp of socialism and the camp of capitalism are greater than the contradictions among capitalist countries, that the USA has made other capitalist countries sufficiently subservient to itself to prevent them from going to war with one another . . . . These comrades are mistaken. They see the external appearances which glitter on the surface but they fail to see those profound forces which, though at present operating imperceptibly, will nevertheless determine the course of events." The "comrades" to whom Stalin referred were those like Nikita S. Khrushchev who favored peaceful competition with the capitalist bloc, instead of war. See COEXISTENCE, SOCIALISM IN ONE COUNTRY, WAR.

Infallibility. A notion commonly prevalent among determined ideologues or ruling elites, whether under democratic or totalitarian systems of rule to the effect that the rulers are always right and incapable of doing wrong. In England, for example, the monarch, whether a king or queen, can do no wrong; in the Roman Catholic Church the Pope is the final authority on matters of faith and morals (as well as the papal state), and he, too, can do no wrong; many single-party governments in the third world claim to be the ultimate source of all truth. Infallibility requires an absolute observance of discipline (e.g., party discipline as well as self-discipline), and in turn strict discipline draws its reinforcement from belief in infallibility. George Kennan (AMERICAN DIPLOMACY, 1900-1950), speaking of the infallibility claimed by the Soviet leadership, commented that "This means that truth is not a constant but is actually created, for all intents and purposes, by the Soviet leaders themselves." See PAPAL INFALLIBILITY.

Infanticide The practice of killing infants and young children, either because they are not the desired gender or because it is felt that another child cannot be supported because of lack of resources. This practice is still common in modern times in spite of global advancement in human rights, particularly in societies where traditionally males are preferred over females or when abortions are not legal. The practice of killing female infants is widespread among segments of the population in China, India, Somalia, and Ethiopia, just to mention a few. See GENOCIDE.

Inflation. A rise in prices of goods and services (commodities) associated with the oversupply of money which causes the decline of the money's purchasing power. Inflation is generally associated with low productivity (e.g., the decline in work performed per man-hour, which increases the cost of a given item). Low productivity can be illustrated by the ratio between what one gets out in return for what one puts in, or input-output ratio. A worker, for example, who gets paid regardless of how much he produces or the quality of his production, will soon lose the incentive to produce more and better, thus lowering productivity. On the other hand, a worker whose job and pay depend upon how much and how well he produces will have the incentive to increase productivity, and this in turn will minimize inflation. According to figures by the U.S. Bureau of Labor Statistics, the output per man-hour had been rising at the rate of 3.2 percent a year for several years after World War II, but in recent years has declined to 1.5 percent per year). See JAWBONING, MORAL EQUIVALENT OF WAR.

Informal Power. An intangible power that a high government official (e.g., U.S. President or state governor) may exercise because of the office held, one that is not provided for by law (e.g., to command the attention of the press, be admitted and allowed to address the Congress or a state legislature which are traditional powers exercised by high government officials everywhere). See INHERENT POWER.

Information Policy. Policy that governs information that the U.S. Government disseminates abroad through the U.S. Information Agency (USIA). See Appendix 34.

Information Security Oversight Office. A federal agency within the Office of General Services Administration, the housekeeper of the U.S. federal government agencies, which determines which documents of the federal government, in all of its agencies, will be classified and in what category of classification (e.g., top secret, secret, or confidential); for how long; and which will be declassified and when. According to Daniel Patrick Moynihan, Democratic Senator from New York, there were 6,796,501 new secrets created by the federal government in 1989 alone, ranging from those concerning the FBI, CIA, DIA, President, Congress, the judiciary, the military, and the diplomatic establishment, to the secret location of the seat of the U.S. government in case of war or national emergency.

Infrastructure. That complex network of activities and actions by individuals, groups, or institutions which, through their activities, support and sustain a political system (government), without being an integral part of it (e.g., mass media, political parties, pressure groups, and lobbies); or those subsystems of a system which are supportive of that system. See POLITICAL SYSTEM.

Inherent Power. As commonly used in politics, a power which is not expressly granted to an officeholder, but which is implied by virtue of his having that authority, or as being necessary for a government to function. See INFORMAL POWER.

Inherent Right of State. A notion commonly held by students and practitioners of statecraft that the legitimate government of a sovereign state, being the organization of the highest order in a politically organized society, has the inherent right to employ any means possible, including the right of depriving persons under its jurisdiction of liberty, property, and life, whenever the very existence of that state (and its government) is threatened. The United Nations system, however, mentions only one right of states (under Article 5 of the Draft Declaration on the Rights and Duties of States); namely, "Every State has the right to equality in law with every other state." See INHERENT POWER, NATIONAL SECURITY.

Inherent Role. See ROLE.

Initiative. A means by which the electorate may propose legislation or seek to influence the policies of the government. States which allow initiative are: Maine, Massachusetts, Florida, Ohio, Arkansas, Oklahoma, North Dakota, South Dakota, Nebraska, Montana, Wyoming, Colorado, Idaho, Utah, Arizona, Nevada, Oregon, Washington, and California. Such practice is not allowed in regard to federal legislation, because the U.S. Constitution (Article I) forbids the U.S. Congress to delegate its legislative function. On November 7, 1977, however, congressional legislation was introduced by Representatives James P. Jones (Democrat of Oklahoma) and Harold S. Sawyer, Jr. (Republican of Michigan) proposing enactment of a measure called "initiative petition," which would allow citizens to propose and to enact laws independently of the legislature (Congress). This legislation aims at weakening the effects of organized interest groups and lobbies which seek to influence Congress. See LOCAL OPTION, PETITION FOR THE REDRESS OF GRIEVANCES, PLEBISCITE, RECALL PETITION, SUNSHINE LAW.

Initiative Petition. See INITIATIVE.

Injunction, Writ of. See WRITS.

Injunctive Penalty. The penalty that results from the violation of an injunction.

Inkatha Freedom Party. See AFRICAN NATIONAL CONGRESS (ANC).

Innocent Passage, the Right to. A rule of international law and international custom requiring individual states to extend the privileges of diplomatic immunity to foreign diplomatic personnel traveling in their official capacity and crossing the boundaries of a state (or states) to which they are not accredited. This rule also applies to civilian aircraft overflying the air space of other states and to vessels passing through territorial waters. See DIPLOMATIC IMMUNITY, INTERNATIONAL LAW.

Innocent Until Proven Guilty. See PRESUMED INNOCENT UNTIL PROVEN GUILTY.

Innovative Planning. Planning concerned with the improvement and further development of the over-all existing planning system in depth and in scope. Also known as development planning. See PLANNING.

Input-Output. See POLITICAL SYSTEM.

Inquest. The process and procedure that may be applied in establishing some question of fact; e.g., determining the causes of death of a person by a coroner (medical examiner) or a coroner's jury (a body of persons sworn to make decisions upon the investigation of facts, whether or not there are grounds for criminal action). See CORONER.

INS. A term used to denote those individuals or elites who are "IN" power (e.g., ruling a state) as opposed to those who are "OUT" and striving to get "IN," either through an elective process as in a democracy, or by means of force, as in totalitarian systems. In the United States, for example, the Democrats were "IN" after the 1976 election (in control of the presidency and the Congress where Democrats held majorities in both houses), and the Republicans were "OUT," but striving to get "IN."

Insider Trading. The practice of profiting from the sale or purchase of valuable stocks, bonds, or securities of enterprises which plan to merge or otherwise restructure their operations, thus affecting their value, based on inside information before that information is made public. Such practices are now outlawed in the United States.

Instinct Theory. See ORIGIN OF THE STATE THEORIES.

Institute for Intelligence and Special Assignments. The actual name of the Israeli's Mossad. See ISRAEL'S INTELLIGENCE.

Institution. The delivery system for the implementation of an idea, a will, or a certain desired end, consisting of people who are behaving and interacting according to preset patterns (e.g., discipline and loyalty), and who perform their designated functions according to preset goals and objectives.

Institutional Democracy. Among the several meanings of this concept are the following: the application of democratic principles of governance inside institutions (internal democracy), such as reliance on the due process principle or resolution of conflicts through voting; democratic principles and practices that are characteristic of certain institutions in a society, but not all (selective democracy); or democratic principles and practices evolving from institutions rather than institutions evolving from a given basic law (e.g., a constitution or a statute), to be guided by and rely on democratic principles. See DEMOCRACY.

Institutional Pluralism. See PARTICIPATORY BUREAUCRACY.

Institutionalized Will of Society. All laws of a state (e.g., constitution, statutes, and treaties) and the institutions which are called upon to implement them in the name of the society, and which are considered, at least by the majority, to be legitimate. See CONCURRENT MAJORITY, DEMOCRACY.

Instructed Delegation. See INSTRUCTED VOTE.

Instructed Vote. A vote that may be cast by an individual or a delegation according to instructions given by a higher authority (e.g., party leadership or an agency of government). See VOTING.

Instructions of Voters. See PRESIDENTIAL ELECTOR.

Instruments of Government. See TOOLS OF GOVERNMENT.

Instrumentalism. The notion that the ideas of man, truth, and that which is determined by their effectiveness, are nothing more than instruments of human responses and adaptation to life in a given society. See PRAGMATISM.

Insurgency. The act of rebelling against any lawful authority; or penetration by foreign agent. See COUNTERINSURGENCY IN AMERICA.

Insurrection. An armed rebellion staged against the established authority of the state. See INSURGENCY, REVOLUTION, REVOLUTIONIST.

Integral Office. See RUNNING MATE.

Integrated Grant Administration Program. A simplified administrative procedure for funding a unified work program from several different sources of Federal funds, using a single application from the prospective grantee.

Integration. People of different races, from different ethnic backgrounds, associating freely; civil rights leaders advocate a public policy of integration as a way to overcome segregation.

Intellectual Communication Policy. See INFORMATION POLICY.

Intellectual Imperialism. See COLONIALISM.

Intellectual Property Law. Another name for laws protecting copyrights, inventions, patents, and other creations of the mind or intellect.

Intelligence. Smart knowledge and foreknowledge, factual, empirically verifiable pure knowledge of facts as they really are, free of personal biases and predilections; pure knowledge; the sense separated from the nonsense; factual and realistic information about people, particularly one's enemies, their actions and intentions; knowledge of plans, desires, aspirations, likes, dislikes, dreams, and hates, particularly as these relate to oneself or to others. The Japanese distinguish two truths: the official truth, "tatemae," and the actual truthful truth, "honne." Intelligence is information that has been processed from raw facts, after the facts have been separated from the fiction; it can be used immediately for decision making, or it can be stored for future use. Intelligence can have a personal, political, economic, military, or industrial character, and it can range from an adversary's order of battle, to preparation for war, to a new bikini design for the forthcoming fashion season. Intelligence is knowledge not easily available, purposely withheld; it must be obtained through rigorous research, overtly or covertly. The bulk of intelligence is obtained through study, reading, and/or conversations with other persons who may be privy to certain information; through radio, television, satellites, crypto (coded), or by an open interception of communications (COMINT); through electronic means (ELINT); through signal intelligence (SIGINT); through technical means (TECHINT); through telemetry (TELINT); or, simply, by spies. Spies include: moles (foreign agents planted secretly to gather information); sleepers (agents planted for reactivation in the future); double-agents (one spying for both sides, but those can be turned back, called "Double X"), or agents of influence—persons with influence in one country secretly promoting the interests of another (HUMINT). Since guarded information is ordinarily classified as top secret, secret, or confidential, people only have access to parts of it, the parts which they need to perform their particular tasks (compartmentalized information). Few persons know the whole of any given information. Every intelligence agency's most guarded secret pertains to its methods and sources; that is, where and how it receives desired information. Experience indicates that only human intelligence (HUMINT) can discern the adversary's intentions. They are called "assets." Intelligence is an intellectual property and sometimes is protected by copyrights or patents. It is also a commodity which can be bought and sold on the market. See BODYGUARD OF LIES, CENTRAL INTELLIGENCE AGENCY (CIA), COUNTERESPIONAGE, INTELLIGENCE CYCLE, Appendices 32, 33.

Intelligence Board. See UNITED STATES INTELLIGENCE BOARD. (USIB).

Intelligence Community. An informal name for the various intelligence agencies of the United States which comprise the Intelligence Board and keep the U.S. President informed on current events and developments in the United States as well as abroad. The main intelligence agencies within the community are: the Central Intelligence Agency (CIA), whose director serves also as the Director of (all) Intelligence (DI); the U.S. Department of State Bureau of Intelligence and Research; the Defense Intelligence Agency (DIA); the Federal Bureau of Investigation (FBI); the Office of Naval Intelligence (ONI); the G-2 Department of Army Intelligence; and the National Security Agency. See CENTRAL INTELLIGENCE AGENCY (CIA), UNITED STATES INTELLIGENCE BOARD (USIB), Appendices 32, 33.

Intelligence Cycle. The process by which raw information is acquired, gathered, transmitted, evaluated, analyzed, and made available as finished intelligence for policy makers to use in decision-making and action. There are usually five steps which constitute the cycle, according to the CIA. They are: (1) Planning and Direction: involves the management of the entire effort, from the identification of the need for data to the final delivery of an intelligence product to a consumer. It can be seen as the beginning and the end of the cycle—the beginning because it involves drawing up specific collection requirements and the end because finished intelligence, which supports policy decisions, engenders new requirements. The whole process is dependent on guidance from public officials. It is initiated by requests for intelligence on certain subjects by the policy makers—the President, his aides, the National Security Council, and other major departments and agencies of government. (2) Collection: the gathering of the raw information from which finished intelligence will be produced. There are many sources for the collection of information, including open sources such as foreign broadcasts, newspapers, periodicals, and books. Open source reporting is integral to the CIA's analytical capabilities. There are also secret sources of information. CIA operations officers collect such information from agents abroad and from defectors who provide information obtainable in no other way. Technical collection—electronics and satellite photography—has come to play an indispensable part in modern intelligence, such as monitoring arms control agreements. (3) Processing: involves the conversion of the vast amount of information coming into the system to a form more suitable for producing finished intelligence, such as through decryption and language translations. The information that does not go directly to analysts is sorted and made available for rapid computer retrieval. Processing also refers to data reduction—interpretation of the information stored on film and tape through the use of highly refined photographic and electronic processes. (4) Analysis and Production: the conversion of basic information into finished intelligence. It includes the integration, evaluation, and analysis of all available data and the preparation of a variety of intelligence products. The intelligence collected is frequently fragmentary and at times contradictory. Analysts, who are subject-matter specialists, weigh the information in terms of reliability, validity, and relevance. They integrate various pieces of data into a coherent whole, put the evaluated information in context, and produce finished intelligence that includes assessments of events or developments and judgments about the implications of the information for the United States. The CIA devotes the bulk of its resources to providing strategic intelligence to policy makers. It performs this important function by monitoring events, warning decision-makers about threats to the United States, and forecasting developments. The subjects involved may concern different regions, problems, or personalities in various contexts—political, geographic, economic, military, scientific, or biographic. Current events, capabilities, and future trends are examined. The CIA produces numerous written reports, which may be brief—one page or less—or lengthy studies. They may involve current intelligence, which is of immediate importance, or long-range assessments. The Agency presents some finished intelligence in oral briefings. The CIA also participates in the drafting and production of National Intelligence Estimates, which reflect the collective judgments of the Intelligence Community; and (5) Dissemination: the distribution of finished intelligence to the consumers, the same policy makers whose needs initiated the intelligence requirements. Finished intelligence is hand-carried on a daily basis to the President and the key national security advisors he designates. Dissemination to policy makers is accomplished by means of various distribution lists, each designed on a "need to know" basis. The policy makers, the recipients of finished intelligence, then make decisions based on the information, and these decisions may lead to the levying of more requirements, thus triggering *The Intelligence Cycle* over again. Sound policy decisions must be based on sound knowledge. Intelligence aims to provide that knowledge. See ALL NEWS IS BAD NEWS—IF IT IS ABOUT US!, CENTRAL INTELLIGENCE AGENCY (CIA), INTELLIGENCE, INTELLIGENCE OVERSIGHT.

Intelligence Estimates. The practice of informing the U.S. President, on a daily basis, of major events and crises in the United States and abroad. The estimates are prepared and delivered daily by the Central Intelligence Agency (CIA) to the President. Also known as "National Intelligence Estimates." See CENTRAL INTELLIGENCE AGENCY (CIA).

Intelligence Oversight. The oversight functions over the American intelligence community are divided between the legislative branch, the Senate Select Committee on Intelligence and the House Permanent Committee on Intelligence; and the executive branch, under the direction of the President, exercised by the National Security Council, the President's Foreign Intelligence Advisory Board, and the President's Intelligence Oversight Board. The Board functions as follows: (1) The President's Foreign Intelligence Advisory Board: maintained within the Executive Office of the President. Its several members serve at the invitation of the President, and are appointed from among trustworthy and distinguished citizens outside of Government on the basis of achievement, experience, and independence. They serve without compensation. The Board continually reviews the performance of all government agencies engaged in the collection, evaluation, or production of intelligence or in the execution of intelligence policy. It also assesses the adequacy of management, personnel, and organization in intelligence agencies and advises the President concerning the objectives, conduct, and coordination of the activities of these agencies. The Advisory Board is specifically charged to make appropriate recommendations for actions to improve and enhance the performance of the intelligence efforts of the United States. This advice may be passed directly to the Director of Central Intelligence, the Central Intelligence Agency, or other agencies engaged in intelligence activities. (2) The President's Intelligence Oversight Board: functions within the White House. It consists of three members from outside the government who are appointed by the President. One of these, who serves as chairman, is also a member of the President's Foreign Intelligence Advisory Board. The Oversight Board is responsible for discovering and reporting to the President any intelligence activities that raise questions of propriety or legality in terms of the Constitution, the laws of the U.S., or Presidential Executive Order. The Board is also charged with reviewing internal guidelines and the direction of the Intelligence Community. The Oversight Board is a permanent, non-partisan body. Periodically, as needs dictate, the President issues a National Security Directive, which deals with specific targets for the intelligence community. Directive No. 29 issued by President Bush in November 1991, called for "... a top-to-bottom examination of the mission, role and priorities of the intelligence community." See CENTRAL INTELLIGENCE AGENCY (CIA), NATIONAL SECURITY COUNCIL (NSC).

Intelligence Test. See SCUM.

Intelligentsia. That group in a society which is highly educated, highly trained, or highly skilled.

Interaction. All those daily reciprocal activities of individuals and groups in bilateral and multilateral settings in which the actions of one serve as stimuli for responses of the other. All political and governmental activity, like any other activities in an organized society, require constant interaction between and among individuals and groups. See POLITICAL SOCIALIZATION, POLITICS.

Inter-African and Malagasy Organization (IAMO). An informal organization set up between African states and Malagasy during the Lagos (Nigeria) Conference in 1962. The Charter which formed this informal organization—whose principal objective was mutual aid and economic cooperation—became the model for the Charter of the Organization of African Unity (OAU) of 1963.

Inter Alia. In the Latin language, "among other things."

Inter Alios. In the Latin language, "among other persons."

Inter-Allied Maritime Transport Council. A system of mutual aid and assistance that was designed by the allies during W.W.I and was continued during W.W.II against Nazi Germany and militarist Japan, particularly in the area of maritime transport and aviation.

Inter-American Conference on Problems of War and Peace. A major international conference held in Mexico City, Mexico, between February 15 and March 8, 1945, at which all Latin American republics (except Argentina) and the United States agreed to cooperate and not to engage in any acts or threats of aggression against one another until the end of W.W.II, under penalty of invasion of the aggressor by the combined forces of the signatories. This became known as the "Chapultepec Act," and later it was elevated to a treaty agreement by the Rio Pact (see RIO PACT) of September 2, 1947. Argentina was absent during the conference because the United States had accused its government (strongman General Edelmiro J. Farrell) of close collaboration with Nazi Germany (and of harboring Nazi spies in Latin America who were penetrating the United States) and thus of being an enemy of the United States. As an act of retaliation, the United States (on the advice of U.S. Secretary of State James F. Byrnes, who was the sponsor of the "get tough" policy toward pro-Nazi Argentina) published a "Blue Book" in 1946, which accused Farrell of collusion with Nazi elements in Argentina, aiding Hitler against the United States and Latin American nations during W.W.II. The purpose of the "Book" was to influence the Argentinean electorate during an election in which Farrell was seeking the presidency of the republic. The effect of the book was to give a good appraisal of Farrell's former Secretary of War, Colonel Juan D. Perón. (The differences between the United States and Argentina were resolved by the time of the Rio Pact in 1947, by the replacement of Byrnes with George

C. Marshall as U.S. Secretary of State, and Farrell with Perón as the leader of Argentina.) See GOOD NEIGHBOR POLICY, RIO TREATY.

Inter-American Convention on the Rights and Duties of States. See MONTEVIDEO DECLARATION.

Inter-American Human Rights Commission. An agency of the Organization of American States (OAS) overseeing the observance of human rights among its members. See HUMAN RIGHTS: AMERICAN DEFINITION, ORGANIZATION OF AMERICAN STATES (OAS).

Inter-American Treaty of Reciprocal Assistance. See RIO TREATY.

Inter-Linked Economy (ILE). See TRIAD.

Inter-Maghrebian Conferences. A series of conferences that were held among several North African nations for the purpose of forming closer ties and possibly establishing a political union. These conferences were held among Algeria, Libya, Morocco, and Tunisia in Tunis (1964), Tangiers (1964), Tripoli (1965), and Algiers (1966). There was no real unification as a result of these gatherings, but some trade agreements were entered into.

Inter Vivos. In the Latin language, "between living persons" (e.g., in the case of a living trust as opposed to a testamentary trust by a written will).

Interdependence. A notion generally accepted by students of government, politics, and power that, due to advanced technology (e.g., speedy communications and the capacity of a small nation to decimate the population of the globe with nuclear weapons), no nation state today is really independent; that no nation is self sufficient in providing for its people without the aid of other nations (oil, for instance, must be imported by some countries as a source of energy needed to sustain the food supply); that the destructive capabilities of modern states require closer cooperation in order to avoid a cataclysm which, through a nuclear war, could eliminate the human species (*homo sapiens*) as well as other forms of life from the earth; that within the global village, one nation, in order to cope with complex problems, may need the technological "know-how" of another which, in turn, may need its goods or services (this exchange is also known as "export technology" or "transfer technology"); and that the well-being of man (and nation states) on this planet will be determined in the final analysis by how well the concept of interdependence of nations is materialized, whether within or outside the bipolar framework. It is also generally agreed that today's global interdependence is to a large extent, facilitated by the capitalistic economies. (The U.S. dollar still remains the global medium of exchange in spite of the Marxist challenge to capitalism, and it is often said that whenever the dollar sneezes, other currencies contract pneumonia; and if the dollar contracts pneumonia, other currencies will die!) A more equitable rearrangement of wealth and reward distribution, however, may become necessary in the near future. See BIPOLARITY, CRITICAL RAW MATERIALS.

Interdiction. A judicial order which restricts one in the exercise of certain rights for one's own protection (e.g., of a minor or one of unsound mind).

Interdisciplinary Interpretation of Law. See BRANDEIS BRIEF.

Interest Group. See PRESSURE GROUP.

Interest-Group Mediation. See POLITICS OF SPECIAL INTERESTS.

Interest-Group Pluralism. See POLITICS OF SPECIAL INTERESTS.

Interest of the Individual. See EUROCOMMUNISM.

Interest of the State. See EUROCOMMUNISM.

Interest-Type Political Party. See SPECIAL INTEREST-TYPE POLITICAL PARTY.

Intergovernmental Cooperation Act of 1968. To achieve the fullest cooperation and coordination of activities among the levels of government in order to improve the operation of our federal system in an increasingly complex society; to improve the administration of grants-in-aid to the states; to permit provision of reimbursable technical services in state and local governments; to establish coordinated intergovernmental policy and administration of development assistance programs; to provide for the acquisition, use, and disposition of land within urban areas by federal agencies in conformity with local government programs; to provide for periodic congressional review of Federal grants-in-aid; and for other purposes.

Intergovernmental Personnel Act of 1970. The act sought to increase the professionalism of government employees through the temporary exchange of public managers/staff between all levels of government (federal, state, local). It also sought to enhance the training and career development activities of state and local governments by providing grants for training programs.

Intergovernmentalism. The view that in matters of public policy affecting more than one jurisdiction, the respective government subdivisions ought to deal with them collectively instead of assigning responsibility to only one government or creating a special agency or task force for that purpose. Under a federal system of government, local jurisdictions deal with local problems. The state or the federal government may step in in extreme situations where there is either a lack of will or resources to deal with a matter on the local level. In the case of the riots in Los Angeles, California, April-May 1992, U.S. President George Bush decided to federalize the problems of the area where the riots occurred, because the City of Los Angeles as well as the State of California, does not have the necessary funds to deal with the extent of the problems. Local jurisdictions will work in cooperation without the federal government.

Interlocking Directorate. See INTERLOCKING LEADERSHIP.

Interlocking Leadership. The system of staffing different positions of power and influence with the same people (e.g., the U.S. Vice President, a member of the executive branch of the federal government, also presides over the Senate, a part of the legislative branch; the head of the executive branch of government of the Soviet Union was, as a rule, also a member of the Central Committee of the CPSU; or a Deputy to the Soviet Parliament, the Supreme Soviet, may also have been a member of the central organ of the Party, which was the top policy-making body). The system of interlocking leadership, often called "interlocking directorate," is commonly used in the private enterprise system of economy (e.g., one person may hold several positions of power and influence: be a president of one bank and a chairman of the board of directors of another enterprise).

Internal Democracy. See INSTITUTIONAL DEMOCRACY.

Internal Revenue Service. A section of the Department of Treasury in the United States, the purpose of which is to collect federal taxes, with the exception of customs duties.

Internal Security Act. See LOYALTY LAW.

Internal Security Emergency. See McCARRAN INTERNAL SECURITY ACT OF 1950.

Internal Transition. See PRESIDENTIAL TRANSITION.

Internal Vernacular. See ARGOT.

International Adjudication. See ADJUDICATION.

International Arms and War Implements Collection and Disposal Bank (IAAWICADB). An international agency that could be set up under the auspices of the United Nations for the purpose of collecting and disposing of all arms and war implements delivered voluntarily by the nation states of the world, for which they would be paid specified amounts of money according to an agreed price list. The funds of the bank would initially consist of voluntary donations by states (according to an agreed assessment) and, subsequently, they would be replenished with income from sale of scrap metals and other materiel of war. See HARDWARE DIPLOMACY.

International Atomic Energy Agency (IAEA). An international body, under the auspices of the United Nations, charged with the task of monitoring the spread of nuclear materials and weapons, and of conducting on-sight inspections throughout the world. The main task of the agency is to keep tabs on uranium and plutonium supplies in order to ascertain that these materials are not diverted to the production of deadly weapons. In recent months there was great concern in the international community that thousands of nuclear weapons in the former Soviet Union might fall into the wrong hands, but it was agreed that the weapons would be sent to the Russian Republic for storage, and eventual destruction was promised by President Boris N. Yeltsin. In March 1992, however, the president of the Ukraine, Leonid Kravchuk, withheld such transfers of weapons to Russia, expressing fear that the controls there are lax and the weapons might fall into the hands of other states. There is concern that North Korea and Pakistan are on the verge of building nuclear bombs. Iraq's nuclear weapons capability has been set back by the Persian Gulf War, but not eliminated. Israel, which has achieved its nuclear capability, is fearful of mini-nuclear powers in the area. In order to prevent former Soviet atomic scientists from sharing their skills and know-how with nations desiring to develop nuclear weapons, the United States, in February 1992, arranged to pay about 100 Russian scientists to continue their research on nuclear energy for peaceful uses.

International Bill of Rights for China. See NINE-POWER TREATY.

International Brigade. A military force composed of communist and pro-communist volunteers, including an American brigade known as the "Lincoln Brigade," which, during the Spanish Civil War in 1936, fought for a republican form of government (along socialist lines) against the forces of Francisco Franco and his falange organization. See FALANGE, FIFTH COLUMN, INCITEMENT TO DISAFFECTION ACT OF 1934.

International City Management Association (ICMA). Set up in order for city mayors and managers to share experiences and publish the *Municipal Year Book* annually.

International Civil Service. See JEALOUSY COMMITTEE.

International Collective Security. See COLLECTIVE SECURITY, Appendices 29, 31.

International Communist Organizations. See COMMUNIST ORGANIZATIONS.

International Confederation of Free Trade Unions. (ICFTU). An informal association of non-communist trade union organizations established during the 1950s for the purpose of combating communist infiltration of labor-ranks. (The ICFTU is very active, particularly in Western Europe.)

International Conference on Solidarity with Puerto Rico's Independence. See WORLD PEACE COUNCIL.

International Control Commission (ICC). See GENEVA ACCORDS (or AGREEMENT) OF 1954, PARIS PEACE AGREEMENT OF 1973).

International Convention on the Elimination of All Forms of Racial Discrimination. A resolution adopted by the General Assembly of the United Nations Organization on December 21, 1965, which states in part that racial discrimination is . . . *an obstacle to friendly and peaceful relations among nations and is capable of disturbing peace and security among peoples* . . . . It enjoins the signatories to take any means acceptable by the UN Charter to eradicate all the existing vestiges of racism, particularly through the revision of municipal laws, and through finding. . .*amicable solutions* . . . to existing problems. See UNITED NATIONS ORGANIZATION (UNO), Appendices 73-B, 76.

International Court of Justice (ICJ). An international tribunal established by the United Nations Organization in 1945, in San Francisco, California, for the purpose of settling disputes between states. This court replaced the Permanent Court of International Justice (PCIJ), which was established in 1920, by the League of Nations and performed similar functions. The court is composed of fifteen (15) justices elected from member-states of the United Nations and only upon expressed declaration do the states recognize the compulsory jurisdiction of that court. (The United States, under the Connolly Amendment, named after U.S. Senator Tom Connolly under the Truman Administration, reserves for itself the right to determine whether a case falls within the jurisdiction of the International Court of Justice or domestic courts.) In spite of the Connolly Amendment, the U.S. Government fully supported the Court in most cases, and on December 10, 1979, U.S. Attorney General Benjamin Civiletti was the first ever to plead for the release of American hostages held at the U.S. Embassy in Tehran. The Iranian government ignored the judgment of the Court.

International Covenant on Civil and Political Rights. An international covenant which copies many of the provisions of the American Declaration of Independence and the U.S. Constitution, adopted by the United Nations in 1966 and enacted in 1976. U.S. President Jimmy Carter submitted the document to the U.S. Senate for ratification in 1979, but it was not approved until April 1992. The covenant obligates national states to refrain from cruel and inhuman torture of prisoners; to prohibit slavery of any kind to reject advocacy of national, racial, or religious hatred; and to guarantee a fair trial, privacy, freedom of thought and religion, freedom of expression, right to vote, and equal protection under law. Violations will be adjudicated by the International Court of Justice. See Appendices 73-B, 76.

International Criminal Police Organization (INTERPOL). An international, non-political, investigative agency established in 1914 for the purpose of combating common (e.g., non-political) crimes and exchanging information among the member states. INTERPOL suspended its operations during World War I and was reactivated in 1923. About one hundred member states are represented in INTERPOL, and each member has one vote. The Secretariat of INTERPOL is located in Paris, France. (The United States joined INTERPOL, upon congressional authorization, in 1958.)

International Crisis. See CRISIS.

International Equilibrium. See BALANCE OF POWER.

International Injury. See INTERNATIONAL LAW, VULNUS IMMEDICABILE.

International Jurisdiction. A territory (e.g., international waters, the high seas, and the polar regions) or a facility (e.g., the United Nations headquarters in New York City and other locations) which is under joint jurisdiction of the international community of nations.

International Labor Organization (ILO). See UNITED NATIONS ORGANIZATION (UNO).

International Law. A body of rules derived from such sources as treaties, international agreements, conventions, customs, and writings by scholars, which sovereign states agree to observe for mutual benefits. International Law is divided into: (1) Public International Law, which deals with political matters of states; and (2) Private International Law (also known as Conflict of Laws), which deals with private persons (and their property) of different states. International Law may also be divided into: (1) Traditional International Law, the basic characteristic of which is the acceptance of war as an instrument of policy of an individual state (mainly when war is commenced for the purpose of preserving the international balance of power); and (2) Modern International Law, which denies individual states the right to use war as an instrument of policy except in the cases of self-defense, as stipulated in the Charter of the United Nations Organization. In reality, International Law attempts simply to clearly establish what states may or may not do in time of peace and/or in time of war in their external relations. Unlike treaties, international law applies to all states equally. See JUS INTER GENTES, Appendices 73-B, 75, 76.

International Law Commission (ILC). One of the specialized agencies of the United Nations charged with the responsibility of promoting a progressive development of international law and its codification. The Commission is concerned with public as well as private international law. Its membership is elected by the General Assembly of the United Nations from among member states.

International Legal Person. All sovereign states and the United Nations Organization are recognized as international legal persons, but discussions continue on whether to recognize all international organizations as well as individual persons as international legal persons. Currently subjects of international law are those entities which have the capacity to enter into binding obligations and enjoy rights.

International Liquidity. The quantity of gold reserves, the foreign exchange holdings of all countries of the world, and their distribution.

International Military Tribunal. In addition to the International Courts under the Convenant of the League of Nations and the United Nations Charter, there were two major military tribunals on the international scene in modern history: (1) one at Nuremberg, Germany, set up by the United States, the Soviet Union, England, and France, on November 14, 1945, before which twenty-two ex-leaders of

Nazi Germany were tried for war crimes, crimes against humanity, and crimes against peace. On October 1, 1946, 19 of the accused were convicted, including 12 who were hanged; and (2) the International Military Tribunal for the Far East, composed of the United States, the Soviet Union, England, and France, which on November 12, 1947, convicted all 25 Japanese leaders, seven of whom were executed by hanging. See WAR CRIME.

International Monetary Fund (IMF). An international financial agency established under the auspices of the United Nations Organization for the purpose of assisting member-states with their international monetary problems. Member-states contribute to the Fund certain amounts of their currency and gold (twenty-five per cent of their quota or ten per cent of their holdings of gold in U.S. dollars, or whichever is smaller) and may borrow money against their holdings and in proportion to them. Due to acute shortages of gold, a member-state may draw a certain amount of money under the so-called "Special Drawing Rights." The Commonwealth of Independent States (CCIS), was admitted to membership on 27 April 1992, with promise of an economic assistance of about $170 billion for reconstruction. See BRETTON WOODS CONFERENCE, SPECIAL DRAWING RIGHTS.

International Piracy. The act of illegally subduing the crews of vessels engaged in international transport (e.g., airplanes, passenger liners, and cargo ships), and dispossessing the owners of their property by theft. International piracy is one of the most heinous crimes, and pirates can be tried and punished under international law. During recent years, according to *Fortune* magazine of 15 July 1991, most acts of piracy occurred in the following areas: (1) in Latin America: Panama, Colon, Maracaibo, Santos, and Guayaquil; (2) in Africa: Dakar, Senegal, Liberia, Abidjan, and Lagos; (3) in Asia: the Strait of Malacca, Madras, Colombo, Manila, Anambas Island, Phillip Channel, Jakarta, and General Santos. See HOSTIS HUMANI GENERIS.

International Relations. Those relations which individual sovereign states establish among themselves (e.g., through diplomacy and bilateral or multilateral treaties) for the purpose of advancing their individual well-being (e.g., power and influence).

International Rules of Engagement. See GENEVA CONVENTION.

International Security Assistance Act of 1977. An act of the U.S. Congress, passed as an amendment to the Foreign Assistance Act of 1961, placing prohibitions on military assistance to countries that receive nuclear materials and technologies or manufacture or detonate nuclear explosive devices.

International Standards of Human Rights. See HOSTILE AND SLANDEROUS ACTS.

International Supervisory Commission (ISC). See GENEVA ACCORDS (or AGREEMENTS) OF 1954.

International System. A term to describe international power on planet earth according to the political orders of individual states, the nature of the issues which cause or may cause international conflict, and the type of structures into which individual nations fit in relation to others. In modern times there have been five different international systems through which states have conducted their international relations: (1) the bipolar system (e.g., the globe was divided politically between the former Soviet Union, the socialist bloc, and the United States, the capitalist bloc.); (2) the hierarchical system, in which the weaker states follow the stronger ones and are usually dependent upon them for survival; (3) the diffused system (e.g., one characterized by the lack of any single center of power or powers, as in bipolarity, which states, especially the weaker ones, may follow); (4) the diffused-bloc system (e.g., the Soviet Commonwealth of Socialist Nations, which spoke with unity on some issues but not on others; that is, the Soviet satellite states supported the Soviet Union in its struggle against capitalist states and all Soviet adversaries, but they did not follow the Soviet domestic, internal system to the point of implementing it within their own societies); and (5) the multipolar or polycentric system, with several centers of power, such as the Soviet bloc, the Capitalist bloc, the Chinese bloc, and, possibly, the Third World bloc of non-aligned states. See DEPENDENCE, BIPOLARITY, POLYCENTRISM, UNIPOLARITY, Appendices 29, 73, 73-A, 73-B, 77, 79.

International Trade Organization (ITO). The Bretton Woods Conference envisioned an international organization on the settlement of disputes arising out of trade among nations. Like a court, the agency was to decide on complaints submitted to it for adjudication. All of the major powers agreed but the United States rejected this idea and decided to remain itself a judge in such matters. Today, however, the major economic powers, especially Japan and Germany, are no longer interested. As the matter stands now, every major economic power is its own judge. The European Economic Community compiled information on states engaged in unfair trade practices (European Community, *Report on United States Trade Barriers and Unfair Practices 1991: Problems of Doing Business with the U.S.*, Washington, D.C.: The Community 1991) where after Japan and Korea, it lists the United States, which hinders trade by means other than tariffs on about 25 percent of all imports on the American internal market. Since there is no international machinery to deal with such practices, the law of the jungle intensifies.

International Waterways. See HIGH SEAS.

Internationalism. See COMMUNIST INTERNATIONAL, GLOBALISM.

Interoperability. A concept forged by the Canadian Armed Forces, pertaining to the mode of collaboration of the various military forces that comprise the NATO Defense System. Because of the different languages used, and the mentality and the tradition that each national group represents, there must be a single, efficient, and unified system of collaboration among these forces to make the North Atlantic Treaty Organization (NATO) system function properly. Under that concept, communications, intelligence, command, and control are organized in such a way that there is a minimum of conflict and maximum of efficiency, which makes the NATO defense system a global force today. See COMMAND CONTROL, COMMUNICATIONS, INTELLIGENCE (C^3I), NORTH ATLANTIC TREATY ORGANIZATION (NATO), PENTOMIC ARMY.

Interpellation. The practice under cabinet-parliamentary systems of government of having executives accountable to the legislature. Commonly, any member of the legislature may request an explanation of acts or policies from any executive in the government. That executive is required, by law, to provide such explanations (in writing or orally) within a specified period of time. See EXECUTIVE PRIVILEGE, VOTE OF CONFIDENCE, VOTE OF NON-CONFIDENCE.

Interpol. See INTERNATIONAL CRIMINAL POLICE ORGANIZATION.

Interposition. See DOCTRINE OF INTERPOSITION.

Interregnum. In the Latin language, "the absence of a king" or "the absence of a ruler." Also, the time-period during which a throne is vacant, or the time-period between the end of one chief executive's tenure and the beginning of a new one. (In the United States, this is the time between 12 o'clock noon, when the tenure of the president ends, and the time when the incoming president, or the same person re-elected to that office, is sworn in.) David Rice Atchison, president of the U.S. Senate, pro tempore, acted as U.S. President for 24 hours, on 4 March 1849—5 March 1849, when Zachary Taylor was sworn in. This was possible, because U.S. President James K. Polk, whose term ended at noon on 4 March, became ill and left Washington, and the Vice Presidency was vacant since George M. Dallas resigned as president of the Senate on 2 March 1849. See VICE PRESIDENT OF THE UNITED STATES, Appendix 17.

Interrogation. See *MIRANDA V. ARIZONA* in Appendix 48.

Intersenatorial Courtesy. See SENATORIAL COURTESY.

Interstate and Foreign Commerce Clause. One of the powers of the United States Congress, contained in Article I, Section 8, of the U.S. Constitution, to regulate interstate and foreign commerce.

Interstate Commerce Commission. An agency of the United States federal government, that oversees the operations of interstate business carriers (i.e., railroads, ships, trucks, buses, oil pipelines and their terminals) of products and persons.

Interstate Compact. A formal agreement between two or more states of the United States, which may be entered into with the consent of the United States Congress. Agreements between two or more states with force of treaties between nations; drawn up by states involved; submitted for congressional approval.

Interstate Compact Body. An organization set up to perform governmental functions for a specified geographic area including jurisdictions in two or more states. They are almost always created by parallel acts of state legislatures or an identical compact to which Congress gives its subsequent approval. See INTERSTATE COMPACT.

Interstitial Law. See INTERVENING LAW.

Intervening Law. A constitution, statute, or a body of laws, which is supplementary in purpose rather than all-embracing as a system of laws (e.g., all federal laws and the Constitution of the United States are designed to fill the gap in the laws, or to supplement the laws of the several states). Also known as interstitial law.

Intestate. In the legal language, a lack of a written will concerning the disposal of one's possessions upon death. In cases where a person dies intestate, his/her property will be disposed of by probate (intestate succession) according to existing state laws.

Intestate Succession. See INTESTATE.

Intifada. A general uprising of the Palestinians in the Gaza Strip and West Bank which is under military occupation by Israel, which started in 1980 and continues to this day. The protest is mainly against expulsion and confiscation of land and dwellings of the Palestinians, mistreatment, and the fact of occupation itself. The Palestinians demand recognition as a sovereign, independent state and accept no offers of autonomy under Israel's jurisdiction.

Intolerable Acts. See TOWNSHEND REVENUE ACT.

Intra-Party Democracy. See CENTRALISM, DEMOCRATIC CENTRALISM.

Intrastate Commerce. Commercial and trade relations within one state in the United States, subject to regulation only by the state government.

Introversion. See KLINGBERG CYCLE.

Investigative Reporting. See MUCKRAKER.

Inviolability of Law. A law (usually a constitutional provision rather than a decree) which may not be violated under any circumstances (e.g., under Article IV of the U.S. Constitution the states in the union may not be dissolved or divided, and under Article V the states may not be deprived of equal representation in the U.S. Senate—two senators from each state). See Appendix 5.

Invisible Government. Usually a public or private agency or organization which yields extensive power and influence over people (by nature of the service it renders or the commodity it produces) without the people realizing it. Authors David Wise and Thomas B. Ross, in a book titled *Invisible Government,* described the U.S. Central Intelligence Agency (CIA) as one such "invisible governments in the United States, spending large sums of public money without public accountability." The CIA first attempted to suppress the publication of *Invisible Government* and when that failed, it considered buying out the first printing of the book to prevent it from reaching the market and the general public. When that failed, a vigorous campaign was initiated to encourage reviews degrading the book as dangerous and inaccurate. The book was published, it became a bestseller, and the CIA considered this a "period of great crisis" for the organization, but in spite of such challenges the CIA is as strong as ever! See also PROPAGANDA ASSETS INVENTORY (PAI), SECRET SOCIETIES.

Involuntary Manslaughter. The death of one person caused by another as a result of an accident, failure to perform a certain duty required by law to protect life, or as a result of negligence.

Involuntary Servitude. See PEONAGE.

Iowa Caucuses. The first presidential primary elections that are held in congressional districts in the state of Iowa. The Iowa primary is followed by the New Hampshire primary. See COMMISSION ON PRESIDENTIAL NOMINATION AND PARTY STRUCTURE, PRIMARY ELECTION.

Ipso Facto. In the Latin language, "by the very fact" or "by the very nature of the case."

Ipso Jure. In the Latin language, "by the law itself" or "by the very nature of the law."

Iran-Contra Affair. When the anti-American, pro-Soviet Sandanistas came to power in Nicaragua on 19 July 1979, following the overthrow of dictator General Anastasio Samoza (1967-1979), relations with the United States became strained, because the Sandanistas were supporting leftist guerrillas in El Salvador and elsewhere, and working diligently to undermine U.S. influence in Latin America in general. In 1983, U.S.-supported contra-Sandanistas, known as "Contras," launched an offensive against the Sandanistas and when the Sandanistas imposed rule by decree in 1985, the U.S. Congress, upon the request of President Ronald Reagan, extended aid to the Contras. Subsequently, the Contras themselves were abusing the liberated Nicaraguans, and when it was revealed that the CIA assisted in the mining of Nicaraguan ports, Congress imposed restrictions and subsequently cut off aid to the Contras under the Boland Amendments. William Casey, director of the CIA, Lt. Col. Oliver North, (both from President Reagan's National Security staff), Admiral John Poindexter, and others kept on supporting the Contras in order to gather funds no longer legally available from the U.S. They entered into illegal trade with the Iranians, offering weapons for cash and release of U.S. hostages. These funds were in turn clandestinely diverted to support the Contras. The whole affair was exposed, a special prosecutor was called to investigate, and the principles were tried and convicted, but in 1990, managed to stay out of prison. See BOLAND AMENDMENTS, GRAYMAIL, OCTOBER SURPRISE, SANDANISTA LIBERATION FRONT (SLM).

Iran-Iraq War. Iran and Iraq entered into war officially on 22 September 1980, after the Iraqi Air Force bombed several Iranian airports, including the Teheran Airport, resulting in costly damage to oil fields and port facilities in Iran. The war ended in August 1988, when Iraq accepted the United Nations' Resolution. The United States played a balancing role in the conflict, aiding the Iraqis mainly with intelligence information on Iranian troop movements and order of battle. Because of Iran's holding 62 American hostages taken at the U.S. Embassy in Teheran on 4 November 1979, the United States had no diplomatic relations with Iran. The United States was fearful of the spread of Shiite Islamic fundamentalism to Arab oil producing states, such as Saudi Arabia, Syria, Egypt, Jordan, Kuwait, and the Emirates. According to the Carter Doctrine, this area was declared vital to American interests for two basic reasons: geography (strategic balance against Soviet expansion in the area) and oil. The Iraqis were the first to use poisonous gas against the Iranians; many of the victims were boys as young as ten. The young children volunteered when the Ayatollah told them that all who died on the battlefield in defense of the Islamic state of Iran would go directly to heaven. Both sides claimed casualties from one to two million dead. This was truly a first major conflict among third world nations. The United States was furnishing the Iraqis with intelligence reports on Iran's order of battle while the Israelis were assisting the Iranians by selling them weapons and war materiel, and even small keys made out of plastic which were manufactured by an Israeli kibbutz for the young Iranian "martyrs," which, once dead, they were to open the gates of an eternal paradise.

Iran's Revolution. The overthrow of the Shah of Iran on 4 November 1979, by Islamic fundamentalist forces was led by an Iman, Ayatollah Ruhollah Khomeini, with the overwhelming support of the Iranian people. Since the Shah was an ally of the United States, President Carter froze Iranian assets (about $12 billion dollars) in the U.S. and withheld delivery of weapons and war materiel purchased and paid for by the Shah. The Khomeini government subsequently broke diplomatic relations with the U.S., declaring it to be the "Great Satan." Further, on 14 December 1979 American diplomats and support personnel from the U.S. Embassy in Tehran were allowed to be taken hostage. The hostages were released in January 1981, on the inauguration day of the next President of the United States, Ronald Reagan. See HOSTAGES IN AMERICA, MOSSADEGH, OCTOBER SURPRISE, TWO RIVERS OF BLOOD.

Irangate. See IRAN-CONTRA AFFAIR.

Iranian Revolutionary Guards. See PASDARAN.

Iranian Students. See IRANIAN REVOLUTION, JAPANESE POLITICAL CULTURE, OCTOBER SURPRISE.

Iraq-Iran War. See IRAN-IRAQ WAR.

Iraq's Baath Socialist Party. See BAATH SOCIALIST PARTY.

Iraqi Communist Party. See BAATH SOCIALIST PARTY.

Ireland's Democratic Union Party. One of the largest pro-British, anti-Catholic, anti-independence parties in Northern Ireland. It is under the leadership of Rev. Ian Paisley, who alleges that the Pope and the Roman Catholic Church are working closely with the Irish Republic Army against the Unionist forces. The party opposes any dialogue with Catholics on the change of status for Northern Ireland. The Rev. Mr. Paisley has stated on several occasions that the Pope is an anti-Christ who advocates the killing of Irish Protestants.

Irgun Tzevai Leumi. See STERN GANG.

Irish Crisis. The turbulence in Ireland between nationalist and poor Catholics and pro-Britain well-to-do Protestants, during a single year, June to June 1978-1979, resulted in 697 shooting incidents, 418 explosions, 169 bombs defused before they went off, 35 civilians killed, and 556 injured.

Irish Republican Army (IRA). The militant military and political organization of Northern Ireland struggling for independence from England. The Army was established during the 1920s, and was outlawed by the British Parliament on November 19, 1973; however, it still operates through clandestine means. See HILLSBOROUGH AGREEMENT.

Iron and Blood. See ZOLLVEREIN.

Iron Chancellor. See ZOLLVEREIN.

Iron Curtain. As used in politics, the invisible ideological boundary dividing the former Soviet Union and her satellite-states in Eastern Europe from the rest of the world. (The phrase was first coined by Dr. Paul Goebbels, Hitler's Minister of Propaganda during W.W.II, and subsequently repeated by England's Prime Minister Winston Churchill in 1946. Both men used the phrase to describe the impenetrable, tightly sealed system of a closed society, the Soviet Union.) The curtain collapsed in 1989. See BAMBOO CURTAIN.

Iron Curtain of Protectionism. U.S. President George Bush made a statement on 13 January 1991, to the effect that the European Community, once established as a reality in 1992, will become a protectionist market and, like the iron curtain of the Cold War era between the West and the East, it will become an economic rival of magnitude similar to the political/military rival of the once almighty and now dissolved Soviet Union.

Iron Guards. See AFRIKAANER RESISTANCE MOVEMENT (ARM).

Iron Lady. An affectionate nickname for Mrs. Margaret Thatcher, Prime Minister of Great Britain (1979-1990), first expressed by Soviet President and leader of the CPSU (1964-1982) Leonid I. Brezhneyev, because of her unusual political talents, statesmanship, and ability for sound, accurate evaluation of domestic and global events. For example, during her first meeting with Soviet President and General Secretary of the Soviet Communist Party, Mikhail S. Gorbachev, who was rather unknown to Western political bureaucrats at the time, Mrs. Thatcher announced to the world that she found him able and trustworthy in dealing with people. This act boosted Gorbachev's prestige considerably and influenced U.S. President Ronald Reagan to collaborate more closely with him.

Iron Law of Oligarchy. A notion that was developed by political philosophers during the early 1900s in Europe stressing mainly the fact that the socialist parties in Europe, like oligarchies, are not really revolutionary in the Marxist sense, and that, by virtue of possessing and controlling the distribution of wealth in a politically organized society, they actually control and determine the distribution and allocation of political power. See SOCIALISM, SOCIALISM WITH A HUMAN FACE.

Irreconcilables. Those in the U.S. Senate (e.g., Henry C. Lodge of Massachusetts) who adamantly opposed America's participation in the League of Nations, or even the granting of recognition to that new international organization by the United States. See LEAGUE OF NATIONS, VERSAILLES TREATY.

Irreversible Political Partnership. See FEDERALISM.

ISC. See GENEVA ACCORDS (or AGREEMENTS) OF 1954.

Iskra. In the Russian language, "spark." Also, the name of the first official newspaper established in 1899, by V. I. Lenin (first published in exile, in Switzerland). The name of the party organ was changed to *Pravda* (in the Russian language, "truth") in 1912. See PRAVDA.

Islam. In the Arabic language, "submission;" also a faith founded by Mohammed upon receiving revelation from a divinity which he called "Allah" (God), and a body of laws (the Koran). It requires unquestionable submission to Allah alone; propagates equality of men (but not women); and rejects separation of church and state, melting the Koran, the prophet and Allah into a single theocracy. Its symbol is the crescent. Islam holds that life on earth is only a transitional phase to eternity.

Islamic Jihad. See JIHAD.

Islamic Salvation Front. A fundamentalist Muslim political and religious party in Algeria, declared "legal" in 1969, but prevented from participation in the first-ever free election of parliament out of fear that it would gain the majority and take power in Algeria. The two principal leaders of the party, Abassi Madani and Ali Belhadj have been under arrest since June 1991. In January 1992, the military introduced strict control over the Front, including a prohibition of meeting in large groups in and around mosques.

Island of Stability. On 31 December 1977, U.S. President Jimmy Carter attended a New Year's state dinner in Tehran, Iran, where he was entertained by the Shah, and in his toast Carter stated that the Shah was "an island of stability in a turbulent corner of the world." The president had relied on a special study made for him by the CIA in August 1977, titled "Iran in the 1980s," prophesizing that the Shah would be "an active participant in the Iranians life well into the 1980s." The Shah was overthrown exactly two years later with no chance of being reinstated again.

Ismalia Summit. See SADAT-BEGIN SUMMIT.

Isolation. A policy that a sovereign state may adopt in order to refrain from any alliances, particularly those of a military nature, with other states. See ISOLATIONISM.

Isolationism. The policy of isolation; lack of external relations. See NEUTRALITY LAWS.

Israel's Intelligence. After the American CIA for foreign intelligence and the FBI for domestic security and counterintelligence, the Mossad and the Shin Beth, respective Israeli counterparts, are the best organized and most effective research, espionage, and security agencies in the world today. As in the American system, almost every agent in the Mossad or the Shin Beth is highly motivated, disciplined, and totally dedicated to the causes of Israel. The modus operandi and complete character of the organization is totalitarian. The agents are highly educated in general and specialized sciences (e.g., languages, politics, economics, and the arts and sciences, as well as in their individual specialty); and almost each one of the them can perform professorial duties at any top university department anywhere. Israel's intelligence apparatus differs from others in one important respect: it virtually runs foreign and domestic politics; every diplomatic mission is, above all, an intelligence operation under diplomatic cover. The principle general-purpose foreign intelligence apparatus is the Mossad, or "Ha Mossad L'Tafkidim Meyuhadim," (in the Hebrew language, "Institute for Special Tasks.") The Shin Beth is the principal intelligence apparatus for internal secret tasks. These organizations emerged from many others that were operated for decades by different Jewish groups in Palestine as well as throughout the world. One of the best known was the Haganah which was very effective during W.W.II, collaborating with other organizations for the purpose of establishing the Jewish state. Other organizations included: the Jewish Agency; the Zionist Federation under the leadership of Dr. Chaim Weizmann; the Shai; the Lehi military organization which carried out murders, one of the leaders of which was Yitzhak Shamir; and the Irgun under the leadership of Menachem Begin, which, with the Lehi, blew up many British soldiers and facilities, including the King David Hotel, and assassinated the Swedish diplomat and United Nations peacemaker in Palestine, Count Folke Bernadotte, in 1948. Another agency, the LAKAM, is engaged in industrial espionage abroad through a network of foreign agents (e.g., Jonathan Pollard, an American Jew who spied for Israel while serving as an intelligence analyst with the U.S. Naval Intelligence, and who was convicted in 1985 and is now serving a life sentence in Marion, Illinois). This agency transfers technology from around the world, mainly the West, to Israel. The Israeli intelligence apparatus maintains good and close working relationships with all friendly intelligence services around the world, including the SAVAK of Iran, which was the major tool of oppression by the Shah, but particularly with the United States. James Jesus Angleton (1917-1987), Chief of Counterintelligence in the CIA and the man in charge of liaisons with foreign intelligence services around the world, was allegedly Israel's agent of influence in the United States, and through him the Israelis were allowed to penetrate many aspects of American life, and received many benefits in terms of aid, loans, weapons, and even nuclear weapons technology. Upon Angelton's death in 1987, the Israelis placed a memorial plaque on the road linking Jerusalem with Tel Aviv, reading (in Hebrew): "James Jesus Angleton. 1917-1987. In Memory of a Good Friend." Because of the highly sophisticated Jewish lobby in America, the Israelis found easy ground on which to operate. The Jewish lobby was so powerful in America, according to Andrew and Leslie Cockburn (*Dangerous Liaison: The Inside Story of the U.S.—Israeli Covert Relationship,* Harper-Collins Publishers, 1991), that U.S. Secretary of State John Foster Dulles stated in 1956, when the United States threatened the British, French, and Israeli invaders of Egypt after the Suez Canal takeover with the withholding of economic assistance to them, " . . . how almost impossible it is in this country to carry out a foreign policy not approved by the Jews." He added, however, that "I am going to try to have one." Dulles succeeded, because President Eisenhower stood firm on the secession of hostilities against Egypt. The invaders pulled back.

Israel's Land for Peace Policy. If there is any substance to this issue, in spite of the Israeli-Palestinian agenda in recent (1991-1993) conferences, the issue may be resolved in a final arrangement whereby the Palestinians will achieve peace only if they agree to forsake the lands that they have lost to Israel. The only viable alternative appears to be "peace without land."

Israel's Security Zone. See HIZBULLAH.

Israel's Third Temple. The present state of Israel is often referred to as the "Third Temple," similar to the way present-day France is referred to as the Fifth Republic, and Poland as the Third Republic. The first Temple of Israel was the Jewish states destroyed by Babylonia in 537 BC; the second Temple was destroyed by the Romans in 70 AD. The modern Zionist movement and resettlement commenced in the early 1880s in Palestine, and the origins of the present Israel may properly be dated as of 1917 when the Balfour Declaration promised "a national home for the Jewish people."

Israeli-Arab War of 1967. The state of Israel, as a retribution for Arab harassment of its people on border settlements, launched an all-out war (June 5-10, 1967), conquering the armies of Egypt, Jordan, and Syria, and territory four times the size of Israel. The Sinai area has been returned to Egypt since. See ISRAELI SETTLEMENTS, Appendix 95.

Israeli-Egyptian Summit. See SADAT-BEGIN SUMMIT.

Israeli Settlements. Settlements by Israeli nationals which were established on territories conquered by Israel during the 1967 War with the Arab states, situated on the West Bank of Jordan, the Gaza Strip, and the Sinai Peninsula, against the UN. Resolutions 242 and 338 which directed Israel to return these territories to the Arabs. The settlements were organized, without official sanction by the Israeli Government, by organizations like the Gush Emunin (particularly on the Golan Heights taken from Syria) and the Land of Israel Movement—both of which were founded after the 1967 War in the occupied areas. These organizations, together with the Likud faction in the Knesset (Israeli Parliament), gave strong support to Premier Begin in his quest for power in the May 1977 election, and they aim to obstruct the eventual return of these territories to the Arabs. On March 1, 1980, the UN. Security Council, including the U.S., voted, condemning Jewish settlements on the West Bank. See ISRAELI-ARAB WAR OF 1967.

It is You Who Made Good Business on the Polish Revolution. In these words, according to journalist Andrew Nagorski (*Newsweek*, 17 February 1992), Poland's President Lech Walesa addressed all the Western states, many of whom had promised him help, but had delivered little or nothing at all. "We need your help," he told the president of the European Council in Strasbourg. "The West was supposed to help us in getting organized on new principles. Polish shops have been inundated by waves of your goods. It is you who made good business on the Polish revolution." President Walesa allowed himself to be exiled into a relatively ceremonial, powerless presidency, leaving policy making and the substance of governance to bureaucrats in the government and the parliament (the Sejm and the Senat), to feed on chaos. Unschooled in western ways, the president had to rely on the advice of many, among whom were those who confused western entrepreneurs with missionaries, and capitalist investors with the Salvation Army. The ancient adage that under capitalism there is no such thing as a free lunch never penetrated the minds of some of his closest advisers. The prevailing notion among them was that, since they represented Solidarity, they could get anything from the West when they wanted and asked for it—a malady common among states which have recently gained freedom and independence. This is true among countries of the former Soviet bloc, whose leaders show ignorance or lack of knowledge of the political culture and modus operandi of the states whose assistance and aid they seek. Fortunately, the West just does not operate that way! President Walesa was surrounded, out of necessity rather than choice, by persons with little experience and many terminal degrees in such banalities as mythological nonsense and political economy of socialism, all with mega ideas and aspirations, but mini resources and capabilities. Few of them were schooled in the West and experienced in the West, and those who were had hardly ever seen, read, or understood a spreadsheet of a capitalist enterprise. At the same time, the foreign advisers who crowded the Warsaw hotel suites and night clubs, had neither knowledge nor interest in Polish political culture, particularly in such a transitory period for Poland, and many of them were concerned with Western rather than Polish interests, or were simply spies. Vital information which Polish intelligence could furnish the president was not forthcoming, basically because the service was disoriented by past loyalties to their Moscow masters and the fear that the service might itself soon be faced with a fate similar to that of the East German Stasis. In addition, Solidarity and its leader, the president, were not among their objects of worship. See CAPITALISM, SOLIDARITY.

Item Veto. The practice of vetoing a part or parts of legislation without rejecting the entire bill. (In the United States, some state governors exercise such rights, but the U.S. President may not use it. He either approves the whole bill or rejects it in its entirety.) See PRESIDENTIAL VETO.

Izviestia. In the Russian language, "news" or "information." Also, the name of the official newspaper (daily) of the former Soviet Government. Like *Pravda* (meaning "truth), the organ of the CPSU, *Izviestia* was subject to strict censorship, and, the Russian readers often commented that "in *Pravda* there is no izviestia, and in *Izviestia* there is no pravda." Since 1991, the paper has served the Russian armed forces. See PRAVDA.

J

"I do not know which makes a man more conservative—to know nothing but the present, or nothing but the past."

JOHN MAYNARD KEYNES, 1883-1946

Jackson Resolution. See SOLIDARITY SUNDAY RESOLUTION.

Jackson-Vanik Amendment. See SOLIDARITY SUNDAY RESOLUTION.

Jacksonian Democracy. During the administration of President Andrew Jackson (1829-1837), who was also known as "Old Hickory," several changes took place as a result of his political style. He was the first U.S. President elected upon the nomination by a party convention instead of a political caucus. The government became more responsive to the needs of the masses over special interest groups through the following means: (1) the removal of all restrictions on visits to the White House by ordinary people—a practice often referred to as "New Democracy"; (2) the elimination of property qualifications for voting and holding public office (Vermont was the first state to implement this practice) under the slogan "government by the masses," instead of government of the masses by the upper class; (3) the politicization of the masses who gained more direct participation in policy shaping and popular control; (4) the gathering of strength through voting—"nose counting" democracy—which enabled people to better protect their interests as a mass from oppressive interest groups and governmental bureaucracy; and (5) for the first time, members of the Electoral College (who elect the President and Vice President of the United States) were elected by the people rather than by the state legislatures. On numerous occasions, the President emphasized the fact that the masses should govern rather than be governed; that the masses represent wisdom of the community; that personal involvement in government and politics contributes toward the growth and development of the individual and increases his (women were excluded) responsibility and accountability to the society and to the state; and that mistakes of the masses, whenever they may occur in this process, are mistakes forward rather than backward, positive rather than negative. President Jackson, like other presidents before and after him, believed in a popular government which James Madison, the fourth U.S. President, perceived to rest on knowledge, or popular information. "A popular government," wrote Madison, "without popular information or the means of acquiring it, is but a prologue to a farce or a tragedy or perhaps both. Knowledge will forever govern ignorance, and a people who mean to be their own governors must arm themselves with the power which knowledge gives." See JACKSONIANS.

Jacksonians. That group of populist democrats, active from around 1820 until the Civil War, from which Andrew Jackson emerged as a leader. That group is also known as the "second party system." The "first party system" is that of the Jeffersonians and the Hamiltonians. See JACKSONIAN DEMOCRACY.

Jacobin Democracy. A rule by simple majority. See JACOBINS.

Jacobins. A coalition of revolutionary, democratic elements, characterized by political radicalism, during the French Revolution of 1798. The name was taken from the Jacobin friars' monastery where the revolutionaries were meeting in secrecy. See ROUSSEAU'S COLLECTIVISM.

Jamatt-Islami. The main political party in Pakistan, ultra-Islamic, strongly anti-Hindu and anti-Indian, which also favors the return of Kashmir into Islamic hands. See JAMUU KASHMIR LIBERATION FRONT.

Jamuu Kashmir Liberation Front. A Muslim guerrilla organization in Kashmir seeking total independence from India under the leadership of Amanullah Khan. India, mostly Hindu, and Pakistan, mostly Muslim, fought two wars in 1948 and 1965 over Kashmir, which was artificially divided by the departing British in 1947.

Janata Coalition. See INDIAN NATIONAL CONGRESS PARTY.

Japan Bashing. The criticism, mainly by Americans, of the overwhelming Japanese influence on global markets and national cultures. This is mainly due to the fact that the Japanese Government supports and aids private Japanese companies in their external expansion. According to author Pat Choate (*Agents of Influence*, New York: Alfred A. Knopf, 1990, pp. xv-xvi), Japanese investment in the American economy increased to over 1,000 percent between 1980 and 1988 to $285 billion in stock and other assets; over $329 billion of banking (14% of total U.S. market share); 25% of the assets of California banks and 30% of its loans; real estate holdings exceed those of all members of the European Community combined; 30-40% of United States Treasury securities; 25% daily volume on the New York Stock Exchange; 20% of the semiconductors produced by Japan are sold in the United States; over 30% of Japan's automobiles, about half of their machine tools and other products are sold to American consumers. Among the popular American landmarks sold to Japan are Columbia Pictures and the Rockefeller Center in New York City. See COMPARATIVE ADVANTAGE, KYOIKU MAMA, LEVEL PLAYING FIELD.

Japan Federation of Student Self-Governing Organizations. See ZENGAKUREN.

Japan Lobby. A series of informal groups and organizations composed of American citizens, mainly accomplished opinion molders, lawyers, accountants and former government and military officials in the employ of Japanese interests. Since the pay is good (as demonstrated by example: "the demonstration effect"), there is no shortage of applicants.

Japan-Russia Treaty of 1905. See TREATY OF PORTSMOUTH OF 1905.

Japan's Industrial Policy. See KOKUTAI.

Japanese-American Security Treaty. The United States and Japan signed a peace and defense treaty in 1970, under which the United States is responsible for aiding in the protection of the sovereign and territorial integrity of the Kingdom of Japan against any and all enemies, but Japan, in turn, is not required to come to the aid of the United States should it find itself in armed conflict with other nations.

Japanese Do Not Have to Conquer the World if They Can Buy it! See AMERICA BASHING, JAPAN BASHING.

Japanese Formula. The Japanese were among the first to establish economic and cultural relations with Taiwan (Formosa)—Republic of China—instead of political ties. The U.S. followed this formula by abrogating defense treaty with Formosa on December 15, 1978, as announced by U.S. President Jimmy Carter, and establishing diplomatic ties with the People's Republic of China. Instead of political ties, the U.S. chose to maintain economic and cultural ties through a special Institute rather than the embassy. See SHANGHAI COMMUNIQUÉ, Appendix 29.

Japanese Internment. Following the Japanese militarists' attack on the U.S. Pacific Fleet in Pearl Harbor, Hawaii (December 7, 1941), U.S. President, Franklin D. Roosevelt (1933-1944), ordered the suspension of *habeas corpus*, and the transfer of all civilian authority of state governors to local army commanders. The military commanders were, in turn, empowered to close down all civilian courts and to try all military and civilian persons before military tribunals. Under these powers, many Japanese-Americans residing in the United States (citizens as well as legal aliens), particularly in California, were re-located to special internment camps (unofficially called "concentration camps without the ovens"—in which to burn people) in the far West (e.g., Arizona). Most of these people lost their jobs and property. After W.W.II, some of them were compensated for their losses at an approximate ratio of 10¢ on the dollar. The mass transfer was made on the grounds that the loyalty of the Japanese was uncertain. The criticism of the military justice was great (often characterized as "military justice is to justice as march music is to music"), particularly in California, where the Attorney General (and the future liberal Chief Justice of the U.S. Supreme Court), Earl Warren, was very helpful in interning Japanese Americans. Similarly, some German-Americans who became organizers of the pro-Nazi "Bunds" (organizations) in the United States were also interned. See President's Commission on Civil Rights. See ALIEN AND SEDITION ACTS, CITIZENSHIP, LOYALTY LAW, McCARRAN INTERNAL SECURITY ACT OF 1950, SCUM.

Japanese Political Culture. Every political culture is unique in some respect, and lack of understanding of one another's culture is one of the main causes of friction and war among states. As a rule, nowhere on earth do educational institutions make that subject part of the curriculum for the young, and when they do, it is usually at the college/university level and most often at the graduate level. Lack of understanding of a state's political culture leads to hostility. A group of American workers, employed in construction projects in Iran under the Shah, drove their powerful motorcycles through a group of Shi'ite Muslims in prayer, because they considered their prayer ritual strange and wierd, dispersing the gathering in horror. The same Iranians held that particular incident against the United States as a whole during the takeover by so-called "students" of the American Embassy in Tehran on 4 November 1979, and when 52 Americans were taken hostage and held for 444 days in captivity. It was seen as evidence, particularly by the young, that America, the "great satan" that Ayatollah Ruhollah Khomeini widely spoke of, has always been an enemy of the Iranian people and their culture. One of the tenets of Zen Buddhism well epitomizes the Japanese political culture: "The master of the art of living makes little distinction between his work and his play, his labor and his leisure, his mind and his body, his education and his recreation, his love and his religion. He simply pursues his vision of excellence in whatever he does, leaving others to decide whether he is working or playing. To him he is always doing both." See JAPAN BASHING, POLITICAL CULTURE.

Japanese Red Army. See ZENGAKUREN.

Jatiya Sansad. The unicameral legislative body—Parliament—of Bangladesh.

Jawboning. A national campaign, initiated by President Richard M. Nixon, after the oil embargo in 1973, to save energy (mainly fuel) through the lowering of thermostats in homes and places of work, to develop new sources and forms of energy, and to increase productivity so as to combat the major causes of inflation. Also, the appeals to industry and labor to hold down wages and prices in an effort to halt inflation. This campaign was continued by Presidents Gerald R. Ford and Jimmy Carter. See INFLATION, MORAL EQUIVALENT OF WAR, MULTILATERAL TRADE NEGOTIATIONS (MTN).

Jay's Treaties. The first, the Treaty of 1794, was bilateral between the United States and England, whereby the U.S. achieved concessions from England to evacuate all British troops from U.S. soil and to pay damages for losses of U.S. property. Through the other treaty, also with England, the Treaty of Greenville of 1795, the U.S. gained territories north of the Ohio River for settlement by whites. The French, suspicious of the British-American treaty of 1794, viewed it as a violation of the French-American Treaty of 1778, and retaliated by seizing defenseless American vessels (about 300 of them) and refusing to receive the U.S. Envoy in Paris, threatening him with arrest and asking for bribe money. See XYZ AFFAIRS.

JCS. See JOINT CHIEFS OF STAFF.

JDL. JEWISH DEFENSE LEAGUE.

Jealousy Committee. A group of highly selected and trusted individuals maintained by nation-states whose task is to select persons, nationals, and citizens of the state, for appointment to responsible jobs in international organizations (e.g., the United Nations, NATO, OAS, OAU, etc.) These appointments often offer lucrative rewards, but are also important to the nation-states because such individuals will influence and shape policies of great importance in their application. These jobs are very competitive, and there is a great deal of jealousy among the aspirants. Once appointed to international civil service (e.g., the United Nations staff), one is expected to give allegiance to that organization rather than to the nation-state of origin, and employees enjoy immunity from domestic jurisdictions, travel on international passports, and receive retirement and other fringe benefits outside any nation state system.

Jedburgh. A code name for the teachers of American, British, and French civilian and military teams who parachuted into German-occupied territories. The teams mainly targeted France in order to help the partisans, resistance fighters against the Nazis.

Jefferson Doctrine. A series of policy statements issued by U.S President Thomas Jefferson (1801-1809), calling for recognition of any state (and its government) which was formed by the will of its people. The Jefferson Doctrine has since become an important part of international law.

Jeffersonian Individualism. See UNREPENTANT INDIVIDUALISM.

Jeffersonian Republicanism. In the broad sense, a reflection of the political philosophy of Thomas Jefferson, 1743-1826, and his followers which has reinforced three vital elements of American political thought: (1) confidence in majority rule and minority right; (2) theory of natural rights and its corollaries, the periodic review and revision of fundamental laws, and the right to revolution when the government loses sight of reason and realities, and oppresses people; and (3) constant guard against man's propensity toward combining things, putting them together, centralizing governments and their functions and powers, and above all, man's propensity to centralize the power within his own hands. Localism, local initiative, local option, widely distributed law-making and governing practices, and laissez-faire are essential to a democratic society, with monopolies, multinational corporations, and conglomerates kept to a minimum. Of the three branches of government—the executive, legislative, and judicial—the executive is not to play the dominant, but the leading role in a democratic society.

Jerry. See KRAUT.

Jerusalem Summit. See SADAT-BEGIN SUMMIT.

Jesus Movement. See BORN AGAIN.

Jewish Agency. See HAGANAH.

Jewish Communism. Refers to leftist, pro-Soviet, and communism-oriented Zionist Jews who supported an independent state of Israel, but with a socialist economy, having features such as the kibbutzim (collective farm) system, and who considered the USSR as their socialist motherland. They opposed the "Socialist Zionism" of Ben-Gurion who favored the western European style of socialism, with a free market economy and private ownership of the means of production and distribution with the state as an equal partner. The collective farm system in Israel, the kibbutzim, was modeled on the Soviet Kolghoz and Sovkhoz.

Jewish Defense League (JDL). A militant Jewish organization, international in its scope of operations, established to protect the interests of the Jewish State of Israel, and Jews everywhere, or Judaism in general. The JDL was established in 1968 in New York City by Rabbi Meir Kahane, originally to confront black militant organizations and to persuade American Jews to support the American involvement in Vietnam, because few did, which made President Lyndon B. Johnson complain. See JEWISH LOBBY.

Jewish Entity. See THREE-NOS DOCTRINE.

Jewish Ghetto Uprising. See WARSAW GHETTO.

Jewish Lobby. A conglomeration of approximately thirty-four Jewish political and civic organizations in the United States which make joint and separate efforts to lobby for their interests in the United States, as well as for the interests of the State of Israel. Among those organizations which are most actively involved in lobbying activities at federal, state, and local levels of political and governmental institutions are: the American Israel Public Affairs Committee (AIPAC), the American Jewish Community (AJC), which was once headed by Arthur Goldberg, the former Associate Justice of the U.S. Supreme Court and U.S. Ambassador to the United Nations, and the B'nai B'rith which claims a membership of over half a million worldwide. The Jewish lobby claims to speak for the six million Jews residing in the United States (with half of that number, or approximately three million, living in New York State and mid-Atlantic states—which exceeds the total number of Jews in the State of Israel), and it is known to be the most loyal and most generous donor to campaign expenses of public officials, regardless of nationality and religion. Political aspirants often find that Jewish constituencies are the first to embrace them and the last to abandon them, no matter how rough the going. See ARAB LOBBY, JEWISH DEFENSE LEAGUE, SADAT-BEGIN SUMMIT.

Jewish Social Democratic Bund. A political organization of Jews, established in 1897 in Vilna, Lithuania, which in 1917, in cooperation with the Bolshevik faction of Vladimir I. Lenin in Russia, became instrumental in bringing about the downfall of the Tsarist regime. The party was also known as the "Jewish Workers Union of Poland, Lithuania, and Russia."

Jewish Workers Union of Poland, Lithuania, and Russia. See JEWISH SOCIAL DEMOCRATIC BUND.

Jihad. In Farsi, Afghan, and other Eastern languages of the Islamic people, "holy war." Also, the slogan under which many Muslim groups in Iran, Palestine, Lebanon, and Afghanistan, have struggled against Israel, the Soviet forces in Afghanistan, as well as their Western adversaries. All of them are engaged in guerrilla-type warfare, and some were involved in terrorist activities. Some of these groups call themselves the "Islamic Jihad." The Mujihadin in Afghanistan coordinate their guerrilla activities against the communist government there through the "Grand Council" (the "Loya Jirga" in the Afghan language).

Jim Crow Laws. A series of legislative acts passed (mostly in the Southern states in the United States) after the Civil War, aimed at keeping minorities (mainly Negroes) from active participation in public life and from sharing public facilities with whites (e.g., the Tennessee law of 1875 required black Americans to use separate railroad and streetcars). These laws have been repealed. See CIVIL RIGHTS ACTS, SEPARATE BUT EQUAL.

Jim Crowism. See JIM CROW LAWS.

Jingo. One who for patriotic reasons unreservedly supports the policies of a government regardless of the effects they may have on others (e.g., an aggressive war); an excessive demonstration of loyalty to a certain political system. Term originated with a song by the same title during the Russian-Turkish War of 1877-78, in which England was urged (Turkey being in its sphere of influence) to support the cause of Turkey against Russia. Jingoism is, as practice indicates, strongly encouraged by totalitarian political systems. See AMERICA FIRSTER, CHAUVINIST.

Jingoism. See JINGO.

JMC. See JOINT MILITARY COMMISSION, PARIS PEACE AGREEMENT OF 1973.

Job Corps. Established under the Economic Opportunities Act of 1964; provides training for disadvantaged youths.

John Birch Society. A private organization in the U.S. established during the 1950s to combat all forms of communism and socialism through education and dissemination of information.

Johnson Doctrine. A series of legislative acts, mainly the Civil Rights Acts of the 1960s, which were proposed by U.S. President Lyndon B. Johnson (1963-1969) and subsequently passed by the United States Congress. These acts aimed primarily at the improvement of the lot of black Americans.

Johnson Governments. See BLACK CODES, JOHNSON PROCLAMATION.

Johnson Proclamation. In his effort to implement the federal policy of reconstruction of the Southern Confederacy, as was laid out by President Abraham Lincoln (1861-1865), who was assassinated in 1863, President Andrew Johnson (1865-1869)—first U.S. President to be impeached—proclaimed on May 14, 1865, that slavery must be abolished; that all war debts incurred by the Confederacy must be repudiated; that all acts and ordinances introduced by the Confederacy upon secession must be declared void; and that Confederate leaders and all Southerners with a net worth of $20,000 or more were to be politically disenfranchised. In order to revive political life in the Confederate states, President Johnson ordered the creation of provisional governments (under military oversight and often direct control) and state legislatures (based on white suffrage) whose primary task was to modify state constitutions and bring them in line with the federal constitution. See BLACK CODES, FREEDMAN'S BUREAU.

Johnson's Debt Default Act of 1934. See DEBT DEFAULT ACT OF 1934.

Join the Salvation Army. In 1990, during the dialogue for reunification of the former German Democratic Republic (DDR) with the Federal Republic of Germany (FRG), the East Germans revealed their expectation that the act of reunification would allow their armed forces and police, especially, the dreaded Secret Police, the Stasis, to join and to be integrated with their counterparts in the West, but they were told that the only army they could join was the Salvation Army. As a result, only a small portion of people in uniform from the East were, after certain verification procedures, included with their Western counterparts; the Stasis were not included.

Joinder. The case of two or more persons joining forces as plaintiffs or defendants (e.g., in a class action suit).

Joint Chiefs of Staff (JCS). A body composed of the Chiefs of Staff of the U.S. Army, Air Force, Navy, and the Commandant of the Marine Corps, all of whom serve in an advisory capacity to the United States President, the National Security Council, the National Security Agency, and the Secretary of Defense on all military security matters (e.g., military preparedness and defense).

Joint Communiqué. See COMMUNIQUÉ.

Joint Committees. Comprised of members of both houses of Congress.

Joint Funding. Funding a single grantee from several Federal grant sources by means of a single application and single contract, as in the Integrated Grant Administration Program.

Joint Meeting of Congress. The U.S. House of Representatives and the U.S. Senate meet in a joint session only on very special occasions, e.g., when the U.S. President addresses it once a year to deliver his State of the Union message or when he convinces Congress to deliver a special message. In addition, a joint meeting of Congress may be held when a foreign dignitary is invited to address it. This is a rare occasion. Lech Walesa, now president of Poland, was invited to address Congress when he was leader of Solidarity, the only private individual ever so honored. See Appendices 10, 11, 13.

Joint Military Commission (JMC). See PARIS PEACE AGREEMENT OF 1973.

Joint Resolution. An act approved by the U.S. Senate, the U.S. House of Representatives, and the President, and used to submit Constitutional amendments, introduce or approve foreign policy, or to grant an appropriations proposal.

Jones Act of 1917. Legislation that was sponsored in 1917, by U.S. Representative S. Jones (D-New York), which granted Puerto Rico political autonomy, and the Puerto Rican people American citizenship, but not the right to vote in American national elections, unless residence has been established within the United States proper.

Journey for Peace. See PEKING SUMMIT.

Journeys to Understanding. During the difficult years of the Cold War, U.S. President D. D. Eisenhower (1953-1961), realizing the difficult military position of the United States, and, as former General of the U.S. Army (a five-star general, the highest military rank in the U.S. Armed Forces), knowing that war between the Soviet Union and the United States could have been triggered by the smallest of incidents, decided to undertake extensive foreign travel. By visiting foreign nations he hoped to help "defuse" the tense political situation in the world. These trips, known as "journeys to understanding," had the ultimate purpose, as President Eisenhower stated, of achieving not just peace in the world, but "peace with justice for all." See EISENHOWER DOCTRINE.

Joyous Disorganization. See COMPETITIVE ADMINISTRATION.

Judge Advocate. A military officer, usually trained in law, who serves as the prosecuting attorney during court-martial proceedings.

Judicial Activism. The practice of some Justices of the U.S. Supreme Court (e.g., Chief Justice Earl Warren, 1953-1969; Associate Justices Hugo Black, 1937-1971; William O. Douglas, 1939-1975; and William J. Brennan, 1956-) to disregard established judicial precedents or even some principles of law (favoring statutory rather than constitutional law) in order to protect and to broaden individual rights and liberties as political, economic, and social conditions may require (e.g., with the intent to aid the struggle against poverty and race and sex discrimination in America). The judicial activists, under Warren's leadership, (referred to as "The Warren Court," 1953-1969) were instrumental in eradicating *de jure* race segregation and other forms of discrimination (e.g., due to sex, nationality, or religion) by their progressive judicial decisions. Justices who refrain from judicial activism, are referred to as "self-restrainers," or "constructionists" (e.g., Felix Frankfurter, 1939-1962; T. C. Clark, 1949-1967; John M. Harlan, 1953-1971; Charles E. Whittaker, 1957-1962; and Potter Stewart, 1958-1981). The self-restrainers prefer to read and to interpret the U.S. Constitution by its exact language (without deviating from the meaning of the words, that is, without much reading into it or out of it), and they view activism as an interference with governing processes (which belong to the executive branch, the U.S. President) and legislative processes (which belong to the Congress). See CONSTRUCTIONIST, DISSENTER, GOVERNMENT BY LITIGATION, POSTURE OF MORAL ABSTENTION, UNITED STATES SUPREME COURT, Appendices 46, 47.

Judicial Aggrandizement. See ASSERTIVENESS, GOVERNMENT BY LITIGATION, JUDICIAL ACTIVISM.

Judicial Branch. In the U.S. local, state, and federal court systems, accountable for the interpretation of laws exacted by the Executive Branch and passed by the Legislative Branch. Criminal and civil cases are tried in these courts. An impartial resolution is attempted in order to protect the Constitutional rights guaranteed to every individual, within justifiable boundaries. Some courts act as Courts of Appeals, such as the Supreme Court, while others try original cases only. A system of checks and balances empowers Congress, on the federal level, to form federal courts. Judges on this level are appointed by the President and confirmed by the U.S. Senate. Judicial Review and injunction are powers exercised by the courts. See Appendices 44, 45, 66.

Judicial Brief. An official opinion, short and to the point by a judge in a court of law in which the points of fact and the points of law on which a certain judgment was based are fully explained. The term "brief" comes from the old Saxon word "braf," which means "brief," "to the point on the law and the facts." While addressing the Colorado Bar Association on 16 September 1990, U.S. Supreme Court Justice Antonin Scalia pointed out in jest that briefs today are "a subject full of paradoxes, not the least of which is in the name 'briefs' . . . these things are 50 pages long . . . and they go on and on at great length until it makes you sick." See BRANDEIS BRIEF.

Judicial Council. A body of experts that may be assembled in any state in the United States, whose job is to assure that the state courts and their judges carry out their duties in accordance with state laws. The highest judicial policy-making body in the U.S. See JUDICIAL ELECTION.

Judicial Decisions. See UNITED STATES REPORTS (U.S.), OPINIONS BY THE U.S. SUPREME COURT IN SELECTED LANDMARK CASES in Appendix 44.

Judicial Election. The mode and manner in which judicial officers, especially judges, are appointed or elected in some states in the United States. In most states, state-level judges are nominated by the governor or a special commission (usually upon the recommendation of the local bar organization) and approved by the state legislature. Under the California plan, adopted in 1934, the state supreme court and district court of appeals judges are nominated by the governor for consideration by a special Commission on Qualifications (which is comprised of the chief justice of the supreme court, the presiding judges of the courts of appeals, and the attorney general). A person who is approved by the Commission serves for one year as a judge, and subsequently may run for election to a twelve-year term. Under the Missouri plan of 1940, there were several selection commissions throughout the years, but the most recent system is similar to the California plan, whereby a commission (composed of the chief justice of the state supreme court as the presiding officer of the commission, three attorneys named by the bar, and three lay persons appointed by the governor) appoints candidates to judicial posts.

Judicial Franchise. See EXCLUSIVE JURISDICTION.

Judicial Immunity. A traditional doctrine recognized in most modern systems of jurisprudence, including that of the United States, which exempts trial judges of courts of law from all liability which may result from their decisions (e.g., confining a chronically sick person to imprisonment who may suffer ill health as a result of such confinement). This immunity applies only to decisions made while sitting as a judge (in adjudication or judgment). The U.S. Supreme Court first affirmed the doctrine of judicial immunity in 1872 (in *Evans v. U.S.*), holding that ". . . the immunity prevails even if the judge's action was wrong, malicious or in excess of his authority"; but added that a judge would be subject to liability if he had acted "in clear absence of all jurisdiction." On March 28, 1978, the Court reaffirmed that doctrine (in *Sparkman v. U.S.*). See Appendix 48.

Judicial Impact Statement. See GOVERNMENT BY LITIGATION.

Judicial Impeachment. See IMPEACHMENT.

Judicial Imperialism. See ASSERTIVENESS, GOVERNMENT BY LITIGATION.

Judicial Legislation. The power of the national court (e.g., the Supreme Court), particularly under political systems where judicial review is allowed, to determine what is and what is not a law. See JUDICIAL REVIEW.

Judicial Misconduct. Most political systems provide for some form of control over its judges. Under the American system of jurisprudence, federal judges are subject to removal upon impeachment by the U.S. Congress. At the state level there are different methods of nominating and removing judges for misconduct. In most states in the American Union, state legislatures establish agencies to conduct inquiry into the misconduct of judges e.g., in the State of Virginia, the Virginia Judiciary Inquiry and Review Commission reviews complaints of judicial misconduct and then submits its finding to the Virginia State Supreme Court. The Court in turn may issue a letter of censure and force retirement or removal from the bench.

Judicial Notice. The situation when a judge (or judges) ascertains the truth of certain facts without evidence, i.e., without official documents or written matter which can be easily verified and authenticated.

Judicial Pragmatism. The view prevalent among some jurists and justices to the effect that every rule of law must be applied flexibly and according to the changes of social doctrines in a society. See JUDICIAL ACTIVISM.

Judicial Precedent. A decision on a point of law that is made by a judge in a court of law when there is no explicit statute, the statute is unclear on a certain point (a loophole in the law), or there is a lack of precedent (previous decision on similar point of law). Judicial precedents are found most in common law, where few laws are codified. The U.S. Supreme Court, through its decisions, establishes such precedents (and fills the holes in law), which in time may again be replaced with a new interpretation (e.g., *Plessy v. Ferguson* was upset by *Brown v. Board of Education*). Judicial precedent is also referred to as the "rule of reason." See JUDICIAL REVIEW, Appendix 44.

Judicial Process. See SUPREME COURT OF THE UNITED STATES.

Judicial Review. The power and authority of the Supreme Court of the United States to declare any law or act of the legislative (Congress) or the executive (President) branches of the government unconstitutional whenever, in the opinion of the Court, the law or act in any way violates the U.S. Constitution. This authority was established by a precedent in the case of *Marbury v. Madison (1803)*, under the leadership of Chief Justice John Marshall (1801-1835).

Judicial Selection Commission. On February 15, 1977, U.S. President Jimmy Carter (1977-1981) issued an Executive Order setting up an independent advisory panel to recommend nominees for judges of the eleven Federal Courts of Appeal (or Circuit Courts). He also urged U.S. Senators, who as a matter of custom (senatorial courtesy), recommend nominees for judicial posts, to set up their own selection panels in addition to the presidential one. See SUPREME COURT OF THE UNITED STATES.

Judicial Self-Restraint. See JUDICIAL ACTIVISM.

Judicial Writs. See WRITS OF COMMON USE.

Judiciary. That branch of the government (as in the United States, other popular democracies, and some federal systems) or agency of the government (as in most unitary and totalitarian systems) which is charged with the interpretation and the application (adjudication) of laws and decrees to facts. Under some legal systems (e.g., as in the United States), the judiciary, which is appointive rather than elective (See U.S. Constitution, Art. III, in Appendix 8), is an autonomous branch of the government and renders opinions on the actions, decisions, laws, and decrees by the other branches of government (e.g., the legislature and the executive, including the bureaucracy), as to their compliance with basic, normative law (the constitution). The judiciary, through its hierarchy, considers decisions by lower courts on appeal on all points of law and points of fact (e.g., the Circuit Courts of Appeal and the U.S. Supreme Court as the final arbiter in all matters of law and fact). This power of judicial review maintains a system of checks and balances among the branches of government, and the landmark decisions by the Supreme Court serve as a source of law by precedent (case law). See JURISPRUDENCE, SUPREME COURT OF THE UNITED STATES.

Judiciary Acts. The Judiciary Act of 1789 created federal courts which were authorized under the U.S. Constitution, Art. III. (The U.S. Supreme Court was provided for by the Constitution itself and is, therefore, referred to as the "Constitutional Court.") The Judiciary Act of 1801, passed by the outgoing Federalist Congress, created sixteen additional judgeships and other judicial posts (e.g., justices of the peace) which President John Adams signed on his last day in office (the "Midnight Judges" or "Midnight Appointments"). The newly elected Republican (pro-Jeffersonian) Congress repealed the Judiciary Act of 1801, thus voiding the new judgeships. In a landmark case of 1803, *Marbury v. Madison*, the U.S. Supreme Court, under Chief Justice John Marshall, also declared the Act unconstitutional. (The case of *Marbury v. Madison* established in the United States the doctrine of judicial review.) See *Marbury v. Madison* in Appendix 48.

Juge D'Instruction. A judge of the local court or an examining magistrate in France.

Junge Sozialisten (JUSO). The left-wing, pro-communist faction of the Social Democratic Party (SPD) in the Federal Republic of Germany. The faction is known for its advocacy of communism (since the Communist Party of Germany, KPD, may not legally function) and anti-American bias.

Jungle Primary. See OPEN PRIMARY.

Junk Bond. A bond considered by credit rating services to be a speculative financial investment because of its relatively high risk of default or delay in meeting scheduled obligations. Junk bonds offer relatively high yields to compensate investors for their exposure to risk.

Junker. Once a large landowner or government official in Prussia.

Junta. In the Spanish language, "to join." Also, a group of persons, civilian or military, conspiring to gain control of the government within a state by means not provided for by law (e.g., coup d'état or revolution); a political clique.

Jure Gestionis. See JURE IMPERII.

Jure Imperii. In the Latin language, "law of the ruler." Also, a generally recognized principle in international law that immunity from jurisdiction is granted to all activities of officials (e.g., diplomats) performing legitimate functions in the territory of another state. Such immunity does not apply to private commercial activity—*jure gestionis* (in the Latin language, "private commercial right.") See DIPLOMATIC IMMUNITY.

Jure Officii. In the Latin language, "the acquisition of citizenship following appointment to a public office. See CITIZENSHIP.

Juris Dictio. In the Latin language, "judicial authority." See JURISDICTION.

Juris Peritus. In the Latin language, "one who is trained in law" or "a lawyer."

Jurisdiction. In the Latin language, "administration of justice" or "implementation of justice." Also, a certain power, right, or authority, that may be granted by a competent authority for a specific purpose over certain subject matter (persons or things), exercised within given geographic limits or over a certain time span. See JURIS DICTIO.

Jurisprudence. The science of law, the system of laws, or a given judicial system (e.g., the American or the Soviet system of jurisprudence). See JUDICIAL ELECTION, JUDICIARY, SUPREME COURT OF THE UNITED STATES.

Jury. A group of citizens randomly selected (from voting records, tax records, telephone directory, or other source) who sit in judgment during a legal process in a court of law and who determine, upon hearing the evidence, the guilt (conviction) or innocence (acquittal) of the accused. Under the U.S. system of jurisprudence, jurors may often recommend the scope and the degree of punishment (sanction), but may not impose it. This is the function of the judge. Jurors must be convinced beyond a shadow of doubt before they may vote their opinion in a case, and are presumed to be impartial. Decisions by the jury are delivered by the jury foreman, who is selected by the jurors from among themselves to be their spokesman. The size of trial juries varies in the United States from five to twelve persons. The U.S. Supreme Court upheld in 1970 (in *Williams v. Florida*) a six-member jury, but on March 21, 1978, it ruled (in *Ballew v. Georgia*) that a five-member jury is no longer constitutional because of "significant doubts about the consistency and reliability of smaller juries." Associate Justice Harry Blackmun explained the reasons as follows: "We readily admit that we do not pretend to discern a clear line between six members and five. But the assembled data raise substantial doubt about the reliability and appropriate representation of panels smaller than six. Because of the fundamental importance of the jury trial to the American system of criminal justice, any further reduction that promotes inaccurate and possibly biased decision making, that causes untoward differences in verdicts, and that prevents juries from truly representing their communities, attains constitutional significance." Five-member juries have been used in the states of Georgia, Louisiana, and Virginia in all criminal cases, including petty misdemeanors (crimes for which the maximum sentence is up to six months), although the ruling in *Williams v. Florida* allowed trials in such cases without juries. Federal laws do not require states to provide jury trials in civil cases. See ACQUITTAL, BLUE-RIBBON JURY, GRAND JURY, PETIT JURY, Appendices 48, 50, 51.

Jus Civile. In the Latin language, "civil law."

Jus Cogens. In the Latin language, "preemptory law." See PREEMPTORY NORM.

Jus Dispositivum. In the Latin language, "yielding law" or "law of disposition." Also, a principle in international law by which the obligations of a state are based on particular treaty provisions. See TREATY.

Jus Divinum. In the Latin language, "divine law," "God-given law," or "God-given right." See DIVIDE ET IMPERA, TWO SWORDS THEORY.

Jus Evocandi. In the Latin language, "the right to recall" or "the law upon which recall can be made." Also, a principle in international law recognizing the right of a state to recall its citizens from abroad, and to order them to transfer their foreign holdings to the state which is recalling them. See CITIZENSHIP, INTERNATIONAL LAW, RECALL PETITION.

Jus Gentium. In the Latin language, "the law of nations." A body of laws used in ancient Rome to try cases arising from disputes between Roman citizens and foreign subjects. See INTERNATIONAL LAW, JURISDICTION, JURISPRUDENCE.

Jus Inter Gentes. In the Latin language, "law among nations" or "international law." The concept was coined by Francisco de Vitoria (1480-1546), a Dominican monk and professor at Salamanca University, and now is associated with international law. See INTERNATIONAL LAW, JUS GENTIUM.

Jus Repraesentationis Omnimodae. In the Latin language, "the right of the head of state to represent his state at will." Also, a principle in international law granting a head of state the right to act in that capacity and to speak on behalf of the state without restrictions. See HEAD OF GOVERNMENT, HEAD OF STATE, INHERENT POWER.

Jus Sanguinis. In the Latin language, "right by association." Also, a principle of international law stipulating that one may acquire the citizenship of his parents regardless of his own birthplace. (The U.S. system of jurisprudence subscribes to that principle.) This principle of determining one's nationality and/or citizenship (often used interchangeably) is derived from medieval Germanic laws in Europe, and it prevails today in most states, including Europe and the USSR. See CITIZENSHIP.

Jus Soli. In the Latin language, "right acquired by birth in native land." (The President of the United States must be, in order to be qualified for that office, according to the U.S. Constitution, a *jus soli* citizen, that is "... *natural born*" or native born.) Its ethnocentric origins are found in common law. See CITIZENSHIP.

JUSO. See JUNGE SOZIALISTEN.

Just Cause Operation. See PANAMA INCURSION.

Just War. See BELLUM JUSTIUM, SCHOLASTICISM, WAR.

Justice. That which is fair and equitable; in law, balancing the punishment with crime; granting one what is justly her/his; equality before the law. See JUSTICE DELAYED IS JUSTICE DENIED, Appendix 50.

Justice Delayed is Justice Denied. According to the Sixth Amendment to the Constitution of the United States, "in all criminal prosecutions, the accused shall enjoy the right to a speedy and public trial . . . . This provision was spelled out in the Bill of Rights, because during colonial times, when judges were subservient to the King of England, trials were often delayed for months or years, while the accused were held in confinement waiting their turn to travel by boat to England where trials were held for felonious offenses. Under the 1971 Speedy Trial Act, all criminal cases are to be tried before civil cases, and, so mandates the law, most criminal cases should be tried within ten weeks from the time the defendant was indicted. See DUE PROCESS, Appendix 5.

Justice of the Peace. A minor judicial officer, usually not trained in law, who may be empowered to hear and/or try minor civil infractions, fix bail for appearance in court, or perform marriages. (In the United States justices of the peace are, with some exceptions, elected and derive their income from fees collected.)

Justifiable Homicide. The killing of one person by another for reasons that may be justifiable under law (e.g., killing in self-defense). See HOMICIDE.

Justinian Code. A systematic collection of laws and constitutions of Rome, compiled in 529 AD. by order of Justinian, Emperor of Rome (483-565), affirming the ruler's authority over all religious matters.

Juvenile Court. A court of law having jurisdiction in cases of delinquent persons of minor age. See JUVENILE DELINQUENCY.

Juvenile Delinquency. Those acts that young persons of a certain age (e.g., below the age of eighteen) commit and are punished for, but which would not be construed as crimes under law if committed by adults (e.g., incorrigibility—difficulty in reforming; truancy—skipping school; or running away from home). Juvenile offenders are usually tried by special courts (juvenile or family and domestic relations court, depending on the state), and upon conviction are detained in special facilities designed especially for young offenders. The criminal procedure pertaining to juveniles for common crimes is the same as for adults, except that more attention is given to them by various social services agencies; they are usually detained in separate facilities during trial; and if committed to serve time, are usually assigned to special corrective facilities which in many cases are reminiscent of boarding schools or vocational training centers. See DECADENCE, Appendix 89.

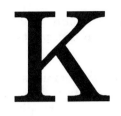

"A riot is at bottom the language of the unheard."

REV. DR. MARTIN LUTHER KING, JR., 1929-1968

K. K. Mountain Operation. The American Central Intelligence Agency (CIA) is the only intelligence agency known to farm out or subcontract intelligence work to other friendly intelligence organizations or to trusted individual persons, on a cost-plus basis (actual expenses plus a fee for services rendered). In order to draw on the knowledge that agencies in the area had of Middle Eastern cultures and languages, the CIA entered into numerous agreements and working arrangements with them during the period between the 1950s and 1980s, to prevent Soviet influence in the area. Agreements were entered with the following, each, of course applying its own definition of "danger to the area": the Turkish National Security Service (TNSS) which, in a "peaceful conflict" with the Russian Empire in the past and the Soviet now, used the arrangement mainly to suppress the national independence aspirations of the Kurds; the Iranian National Organization for Intelligence and Security (SAVAK) which interpreted the arrangement mainly as a license to suppress any opponents to the "Peacock Throne" of the Shah—killing in the process hundreds of thousands of Iranians who opposed his extravagant policies; (sent with the guidance of CIA operative Kermit Roosevelt) the Israeli intelligence, the Mossad, which believed in the Jewish God and the Israeli defense force, working diligently to sustain the existence and growth of the Jewish state (mainly in real estate purchased or taken from the Arabs); and the Jordanian intelligence and King Hussein himself in person (to whom about $20 million packed in elegant suitcases was delivered every month by the CIA resident agent in Amman as "petty cash" for the monarch). The Turks and the Iranians collaborated under the so-called "Trident Organization" agreement with the CIA. (This information was discovered among the secret files in the U.S. Embassy in Teheran by the "students" who took possession of them following the capture of the American hostages.) The entire operational arrangement was code-named "K. K. Mountain" by the CIA. In the European theater, the CIA farmed out work to the Gehlen (Nazi Germany General Reinhard Gehlen) Organization, known as the "Firma" or "Firm." The Gehlen Organization was reorganized into the present Bundesnachrichtendienst (BDN), the intelligence agency of the Federal Republic of Germany. This entire charade amused the Soviets, because they knew as everybody else knew, or should have known, but did not tell, that the Soviets had neither the desire nor the means (due to growing internal problems of incompetence in communist governance) to penetrate the area more than they did. It was good business for everyone involved and it appears to be a farce, the greatest international fraud of the century, courtesy of the American taxpayers. The letters "K. K." stand for CIA's internal digraph and/or designation for documents and dispatches dealing with and/or pertaining to the State of Israel and its intelligence service. See INTELLIGENCE, ISRAEL'S INTELLIGENCE.

Kadet. A member of the Constitutional party which had advocated constitutional and democratic government in Tsarist Russia; also, one who bitterly opposed any form of socialism or communism in Soviet Russia.

Kaiser. An early name for Roman Caesars. Also used as titles of the emperors of the Holy Roman Empire of the German Nation, 862-1806; Austria, 1804-1918; and Germany, 1871-1918. The last German Kaiser, Wilhelm II, went into exile after the capitulation of Germany at the end of W.W.I.

Kaizen. In the Japanese language, "persistence" or "obsession." Workers on the assembly line in Japan, particularly under the "Toyota system," constantly seek ways to improve production, eliminate waste, to help each other perform better as a matter of personal pride and satisfaction and not necessarily for extra recognition and reward (e.g., a bonus). It is not unusual under this system for assembly line workers to call a supplier and to complain about some delivered materials that were defective or arrived late (the "just-on-time production" method) without passing the matter to management to handle. See TOYOTA PRODUCTION SYSTEM.

Kanalarbeiter. In the German language, "sewer worker." Also, a term commonly used in German politics to describe one who obediently follows the directives of the leadership of a political party. A party crony. See CHRISTIAN DEMOCRATIC UNION (CDU).

Kangaroo Closure. A parliamentary device (commonly used in the House of Commons in England) whereby the leader of a debate may limit discussion to only one or several aspects of an issue, usually such aspects which are non-controversial and which will prevent division of opinion among legislators. See HOUSE OF COMMONS, PARLIAMENT.

Kangaroo Court. A self-proclaimed judicial process set up to try persons for some infraction outside the existing legal framework and procedure and in defiance of the existing system of jurisprudence of the state. Such courts are common among secretly operating groups such as insurgents, guerrillas, and prisoners in confinement. The term originated in the Australian penal colonies when Australia was a dumping ground for British prisoners, when unjust and often illegal trials were held in the open field with herds of friendly Kangaroos interestingly observing the "judicial" process as if they were a "jury." The term came to the United States with the arrival of many Australians during the 1849 gold rush days in California. Such kangaroo "trials" (often referred to as "mock courts") were held there with speed and brutal resolutions mostly by vigilante committees of miners over claims to parcels of land with possible gold deposits. See GUERRILLA WARFARE, INSURGENCY, Appendix 50.

Kansas Pythoness. See POPULIST.

Kanzler. See CHANCELLOR.

Kaplan Self-Derogation Scale. See POLITICAL SELF-ESTEEM.

Katyn Massacre. Following the Soviet-Nazi Germany alliance of 1939, Poland was divided between the two aggressor nations. After the German attack on Poland on 1 September 1939—commencing the Second World War—certain portions of the retreating Polish army that sought sanctuary in the Soviet Union were rounded up and the majority of them were executed in the Katyn Forest by the Soviet Security Police, the NKVD. See MEMORIAL.

KCIA. See KOREAN CENTRAL INTELLIGENCE AGENCY.

Keeper of the King's Conscience. See EQUITY COURT.

Keidanren. An organization of the 750 largest business concerns in Japan whose chief executives periodically gather together to design production and marketing plans and strategies for the present and the future, with the ultimate aim of providing what is good for the Japanese state and the Japanese society at large rather than just for individual businesses. The chairman of this voluntary organization is often referred to as the "prime minister of Japanese business." The organization works closely with the governmental bureaucracy and government-held information. As Professor Peter Drucker points out ("Behind Japan's Success: Defining Rules for Managing in a Pluralistic Society," *Harvard Business Review*, 59, January-February 1981): "A substantial portion of Japan's business leaders have traditionally subscribed to the rule that national interest comes first." See AMERICA BASHING, JAPAN BASHING.

Keiretsu. An informal organization of Japanese enterprise groups designed to keep external competitors out by maintaining close association and by doing business exclusively among themselves. In order to, what the Japanese call, "socialize the risk," each member business of the keiretsu is allowed to own about 10 percent of the stock in the other member companies; such interlocking ownership minimizes the risk of poor business results for any single company. An eventual loss will be spread among the members. See KEIDANREN.

Kellogg-Briand Pact. A treaty signed between the Republic of France and the United States of America renouncing war as an instrument of policy and calling for settlement of international disputes through pacific means. The treaty was signed in 1928 and has since become an important source of modern international law. Known also as the Treaty for the Renunciation of War. See PACIFIC SETTLEMENT OF DISPUTES.

Kenbei. A fairly new term coined in 1991 by Japanese novelist Yasuo Tanaka denoting contempt for America and an American person. In Japanese, the character "ken" stands for "hate," and "bei" stands for "America" as well as for "rice."

Kennedy-Nixon Debate. See GREAT DEBATES.

Kennedy Round. A series of trade negotiations between the United States and Western European states, held between 1964 and 1967 for the purpose of lowering tariffs on American goods sold in Europe. These negotiations were held mostly within the framework of the General Agreement on Tariffs and Trade (GATT) and were all preplanned by former U.S. President John F. Kennedy (1961-1963). See CHICKEN WAR, GENERAL AGREEMENT ON TARIFFS AND TRADE (GATT).

Kent's Law of Coups. See COUP D'ETAT.

Kentucky and Virginia Resolutions. Construing the Alien and Sedition Acts of 1798 by the Federalists—which aimed at the foreign elements in American life—as measures directed at the Jeffersonians and at Jefferson himself who was known to be friendly with foreign elements and those with liberal views Thomas Jefferson, then U.S. Vice President, drafted a set of resolutions which were introduced in the Kentucky legislature by John C. Breckenridge on November 8, 1798, and by John Taylor in the Virginia House of Burgesses on December 13, 1798. Although these humiliating laws (the Alien and Sedition Acts) were repealed, anti-foreign sentiments have not been fully eradicated from American life. See ALIEN AND SEDITION ACTS, NULLIFICATION, SCUM, SECESSION, STATES' RIGHTS DOCTRINE.

Kentucky Ten Commandments Law. The Kentucky legislature passed a law allowing the Ten Commandments to be displayed in schools throughout the state, and in an attempt to avoid any conflict it declared that the document constitutes a part of Western culture and civilization and that the framing was to be paid by private contributions. The U.S. Supreme Court, however, ruled in November 1980 although the document is sacred to the Jewish and the Christian faiths, posting it in public places such as schools, violated the First Amendment of the Constitution which prohibits official governmental bodies from taking a stand on religious matters.

Kerner Commission. During the wide-spread riots in America in the 1960s, the U.S. federal government created a special National Advisory Commission on Civil Disorders in order to investigate and to report on the causes of and possible remedies for these riots. The Commission concluded in its final report released on February 29, 1968, that (1) "Our nation is moving toward two societies, one black, one white—separate and unequal"; (2) the hopeless life in the ghettos where most poor blacks reside created an "underclass" people who are the wards of the government living an unproductive life on welfare in striking poverty; and (3) immediate attention by all levels of government, federal, state and local, was necessary in order to eradicate extreme poverty, unemployment, and racism as the principal causes of the disorders. The Commission was formed on July 27, 1967, by U.S. President Lyndon B. Johnson (1963-1969) after a series of race riots in Newark, Chicago, Detroit, Watts, Washington, D.C., and other major cities. The Commission was composed of distinguished government, community, and business leaders; among them Otto Kerner, Governor of Illinois (as chairman), John V. Lindsay, former Mayor of New York City (as vice chairman), Roy Wilkins, National Director of the NAACP; U.S. Senator Edward W. Brooke (R-Massachusetts), U.S. Senator Fred R. Harris (D-Oklahoma), U.S. Representatives James C. Corman (D-California), and William M. McCulloch (D-Ohio), I. W. Abel, President of the United Steelworkers of America, Charles B. Thornton, Chairman of Litton Industries, Katherine Graham Peden, Commissioner of Commerce of the state of Kentucky, and Herbert Jenkins, Chief of Police, Atlanta, Georgia. A survey conducted by the New York Times Company (publisher of *The New York Times*) and the Columbia Broadcasting System (producer of *CBS News*) ten years later, in January-February 1978, concluded that (1) racism has in part disappeared, but still remains in hidden forms (institutionalized); (2) working and living conditions of blacks have improved since the Kerner Report was published; and (3) lack of attention by whites to the problems of blacks is construed by most blacks as indifference, short of demonstrable racial overtones. See POLICE BRUTALITY.

Kestenbaum Commission. See PRESIDENTIAL COMMISSION ON INTER-GOVERNMENTAL RELATIONS.

Key Black Extremist Index. See COUNTERINSURGENCY IN AMERICA.

Keynesian Economics. Those concepts and schemes which were developed by John Maynard Keynes (Lord Keynes) in his book of 1936, *General Theory of Employment, Interest, and Money,* and which have been implemented in many economic systems, including that of the United States. In his book Keynes: (1) argues against *laissez-faire* practices; (2) argues for government intervention, in order to rectify economic problems (e.g., high unemployment or low productivity), including the use of the state's revenues and deficit spending; (3) argues for keeping interest rates low permanently in order to keep the flow of money supply high; (4) favors full employment at any cost (including public work programs subsidized by national revenues, a practice which was common during the New Deal era under U.S. President Franklin D. Roosevelt, 1933-1944, and which is still common today); and (5) favors subsidy of private enterprises which are vital to the national economy (e.g., Lockheed, Penn Central, and farm support programs in the United States). According to the Keynes multiplier factor, the larger the investment in equipment, machinery, and plants (capital investment) the larger will the return be, and after time, the return on the investment will exceed it several times. The same is true for exports. The multiplier is "the ratio between the total increase in national income and the increase in investment expenditure that stimulates it." See UNILATERAL GLOBAL KEYNESIANISM.

Keynote Speech. A speech that may be delivered by an important and well-known person which sets the tone for a major gathering and one which contains some important policy statements.

KGB. See PEOPLE'S COMMISSION FOR INTERNAL AFFAIRS (NKVD).

Khaki Election. The British Parliament election of 1900 when the Unionist party and the supporters of the Boer War in South Africa, emerged as victors. The Unionist party was opposed to the Liberal party which favored larger autonomy for Ireland as well as pro-labor legislation. Its victory at the polls diminished any chances for greater autonomy to Ireland. The election also favored England's alliance with Japan in order to restrain Russia's expansion into the Far East, an abandonment of the "splendid isolation" policy. Many veterans of the Boer War took part in the campaign (wearing khaki uniforms), expressing support of England's expansion abroad. Winston Churchill, the W.W.II Prime Minister and a strong ally of the United States, was elected to Parliament for the first time in this election.

Khan. In the Mongolian language, "a king," "a prince," or "a ruler" (elective) of a nation-state or an empire (e.g., a khanate). See GENGHIS.

Khmer Rouge. In the Khmer (Cambodian) language, "Red Khmer." Also, the communist revolutionary, guerrilla-type organization which, under the leadership of Khieu Samphan, gained total victory over Cambodia with the aid of the Viet Cong and the North Vietnamese on April 17, 1975. Soon after its victory, the Khmer Rogue government (known as "Angka Loeu"—in the Khmer language, "Organization on High") ordered a purge of all city dwellers into the countryside, a process in which allegedly about two million persons have died from starvation, lack of medical attention, and mass killings (by beating to death with wooden sticks), thus earning Cambodia the name of a "land of the walking dead." The government is determined to eliminate cities and return to rural-type living. Money, as a medium of exchange, has already been eliminated. Dr. Zbigniew K. Brzezinski, National Security Adviser to U.S. President Jimmy Carter, described the Angka Loeu as a "grotesque caricature of Marxism mixed with radical French leftist intellectualism and stirred up in the crucible of the jungle." See FARM STATE, VIETNAMIZATION.

Khnyaz. A prince, large land-owner, or country squire in Tsarist Russia.

Khrushchev's Concept of Power. See POWER.

Kibbutz. A collective farm unit or agricultural settlement in the state of Israel.

Killing Fields. See YEAR ZERO.

King Caucus. Until 1832, when the convention system of nominating candidates for the U.S. presidency was adopted, the party leaders in Congress selected candidates in secret caucuses. The American public began to question that mode of nomination and, in response to the criticism, the convention system was introduced allowing wider input by citizens. See EVOLUTION OF THE TWO-PARTY SYSTEM IN THE UNITED STATES, Appendix 19.

King of Kings. See SHAH.

King Who Slays an Envoy, Sinks into Hell with All of His Ministers. See DIPLOMATIC IMMUNITY.

King's Conscience. See EQUITY COURT.

Kingmaker. See EIGHT-F GANG.

Kingston Declaration. UN. Special Committee Against Apartheid met in Kingston, Jamaica, on May 25, 1979. Adopted a declaration calling for new strategies for decisive and effective action for the speedy elimination of apartheid in Southern Africa and mandatory sanctions against apartheid regime in South Africa.

Kinshasa Conference. The heads of state of Congo (now Zaire), Congo (Brazzaville), Burundi, Central African Republic, Kenya, Rwanda, Tanzania, Sudan, and Zambia met in February 1967 in Kinshasa, Congo, for the purpose of finding ways and means of working out and eliminating their differences in regard to the role and the function of the Organization of African Unity (OAU). In a Declaration drafted at the end of the Conference, the participants agreed to render unreserved support to the OAU in spite of any political differences that may exist among them. See ORGANIZATION OF AFRICAN UNITY.

Kiss and Tell for Sale. In some contemporary societies, particularly those that subscribe to strict puritanical values, the best way to assassinate another's character and to destroy the chances of a political aspirant is to advance a charge of moral turpitude (e.g., womanizing, excessive drinking). Quite often such charges are advanced for monetary reasons, because, while society frowns upon such behavior on the one hand, the consumer market for such information, or gossip, is great. Many media outlets in the United States, for example, pay very high stipends to those who deliver such first-hand information. Very often there is a double standard, however, when an attraction to the opposite sex is viewed as being more immoral than public corruption (e.g., the Savings and Loan scandal which cost American taxpayers over $520 billion, or the so-called "Rubbergate," where members of the U.S. Congress were writing rubber checks against non-existing deposits in their internal banking facility). If there is great noise about scandals for moral turpitude, as was the experience of one of the Democratic Party presidential hopefuls in 1992, Governor Bill Clinton from Arkansas, where the publicity was intended to assassinate his political and moral character, and which prompted Georgia's Zell Miller to quip that "Maybe they'll stop treating him like the only fire hydrant at a dog show." The magnitude of such moral turpitude scandal is in direct proportion to the demand for such information. The term "cash for trash" is also used. See CHARACTER ASSASSINATION, DEFINING THE OPPONENT, OPPOSITION RESEARCH SPECIALIST (OPO).

Kitchen Cabinet. In the language of politics, the practice of relying on the advice of persons outside the government rather than those within it. A practice (common to the chief executives of states and governments) of seeking advice on policy matters or assigning functions to persons outside the cabinet who ordinarily (and by law) are not charged with those tasks. U.S. President Andrew Jackson (1829-1837) was first in initiating this practice. See BACKROOM CROWD, CABINET, JACKSONIAN DEMOCRACY, SHADOW CABINET.

KKK. See KU KLUX KLAN.

Klingberg Cycle. Frank L. Klingberg characterizes American foreign policy as having two distinct modes of political behavior: introversion (period of withdrawal from active participation in global politics) and extroversion (periods of an active participation in foreign affairs):

Introversion	Extroversion
1776-1798	1798-1824
1824-1844	1844-1871
1871-1891	1891-1919
1919-1940	1940-1968
1968-1977	1977-1991 and on

Knesset. The official name of the Parliament of the state of Israel.

Knights of Labor. See NOBLE ORDER OF THE KNIGHTS OF LABOR.

Know-Nothing Party. See AMERICAN PARTY.

Know Thy Enemy. An ancient dictum followed by guerrilla warriors and intelligence gatherers throughout the world. See GUERRILLA WARFARE, INTELLIGENCE.

Knowledge. In general sense, the sum of organized human experiences; the mode of organizing these experiences (theory); the processes by which explanations are arrived at, formulated and re-explained (e.g., through education or learning) according to one's perception and cognitive adaptabilities and abilities (e.g., defining the limits of the possible and the impossible and the value and significance of the possible). The purpose of knowledge is to serve the principal needs of man: (1) to anticipate in so far as possible future events, so that man, a rational animal, can adapt himself properly; (2) to suggest ways of influencing future events (since past events cannot be recalled for modification); and (3) to develop new knowledge about the future in order to better influence or modify it. See CONCEPT, DEMOCRACY, EPISTEMOLOGY, FORECAST, JACKSONIAN DEMOCRACY, POLITICIZATION, SCIENCE.

Ko Lao Hui. In the Chinese language, "Association of Elder Brothers." See SECRET SOCIETIES.

Kohai. See FRAME SOCIETY.

Kohl-Bush Summit of 1992. See ATLANTIC PARTNERSHIP.

Kokkai. The bicameral legislative body, the Diet, in Japan. See SANGI-IN, SHUGI-IN.

Kokutai. In the Japanese language, "national polity;" the notion of the unity of the people, the emperor and the government all constituting a single cohesive entity. The 1947 constitution of Japan placed sovereignty in the people rather than the emperor, but the emperor remains the symbol of the unity of the nation. In Japanese political culture, the people act in unison together with their leaders, their government, and private institutions. Today, the Japanese Ministry of International Trade (MITI) is the guiding force in establishing and sustaining Japan's economic and political power, leading to Pax Nipponica throughout Asia and the world in deadly competition with other economic powers, mainly the United States. The Japanese refer to MITI as the "overconcerned mother" (in the Japanese language, "kyoiku mama"). MITI, pursuing a well defined and well executed industrial policy, is the main organizational and policy making force consisting of government officials, business leaders, and educators, which is determined to outbid the west in economic competition. One of Japan's influential business leaders, Konosuke Matsushita, stated openly: "We are going to win and the industrial West is going to lose out; there's not much you can do about it, because the reasons for failure are within yourself." See AMERICA BASHING, COMPARATIVE ADVANTAGE, JAPAN BASHING.

Kolghoz. A farm settlement in the Soviet Union, operated in common, with the land being owned by the former Soviet Government. (There was no privately owned or operated farms in the Soviet Union; all land belongs to the state.) Since 1991 the Russians started privatizing these farms. See SOVKHOZ.

Komintern. See COMMUNIST INTERNATIONAL, FIRST, SECOND, THIRD.

Kommandantura. A quadripartite body (England, France, the Soviet Union, and the United States) administering the city of Berlin since the surrender of Germany in 1945. See BERLIN AIRLIFT, BERLIN WALL.

Kommissar. In the Russian language, "commissioner" or "cabinet member." After World War II the designation is "minister."

Komsomol. See UNION OF SOVIET COMMUNIST YOUTH OF LENIN.

Komsomolskaya Pravda. In the Russian language, "the truth of Komsomol." Also, an official name of a daily newspaper, the organ of the Komsomol, in the Soviet Union.

Korea Connection. See KOREAGATE.

Koreagate. A series of activities (illegal, according to American law) in which a number of South Korean agents became involved in their attempts to buy favors for the Republic of Korea in the United States Congress. (Involved were the Ambassador of the Republic of South Korea to the United States, Korean businessman Tong Sun Park, and the agents of the South Korean Central Intelligence Agency stationed in the United States.) Two members of the U.S. House of Representatives, Otto Passman and Richard T. Hanna, were indicted on charges of accepting bribes. The bribes included free trips to Korea, expensive personal gifts, and honorary degrees bestowed by South Korean universities. Park, the principal witness in the bribe scandal, returned to the United States from Korea in early 1978 to testify before Congress. His testimony has implicated several other members of Congress who, like Hanna and Passman, had accepted bribes of several hundred thousand dollars or donations to their political campaigns. (During the Koreagate hearing in Congress, a humorous definition of morality in politics was circulated in Washington, which defined it as follows: "Morality is when you take influence money from a Korean lobbyist and give 10% to your church.") See HANNA AFFAIR, LOBBY, POLITICAL ETHICS.

Korean Central Intelligence Agency. (KCIA). See KOREAGATE.

Korean Lobby. See KOREAGATE.

Korean Police Action. See KOREAN WAR.

Korean Unification. See KOREAN WAR.

Korean War. During the Cairo Conference on 20 November 1943, Britain's Prime Minister Winston Churchill and China's Generalissimo Chiang Kai-shek agreed that once Korea was freed from Japanese occupation (which occurred in August 1945), Korea would remain a free and sovereign state. However, during the subsequent Potsdam Conference, 17 July-2 August 1945, U.S. President Harry S. Truman and Premier of the Soviet Union Generalissimo Josef Stalin agreed that Korea would remain in the sphere of American and Russian influence, with the country divided along the 38th parallel. Soviet troops entered the northern part of Korea on 10 August 1945, and American troops took positions in the southern part on 8 September 1945. Both Koreas installed governments, and on 25 June 1950, North Korean troops crossed the demarcation line and attacked South Korea. President Truman turned to the United Nations for a resolution to condemn the aggression. When the Soviet delegate, one of the five permanent members of the Security Council, walked out in protest, the UN voted a "United for Peace Resolution" condemning the aggression. The UN authorized an international military force, represented by sixteen nations, but with American forces predominant, to prosecute the war, or, as it was called, the "police action." US casualties in the war were: 54,000 dead; over 100,000 wounded; and over 3,700 taken by the North as prisoners of war. Many of these prisoners were brainwashed by the North Koreans to the point of committing treasonous acts against their country, the United States. The war cost the American taxpayers over $19 billion dollars. South Korea's losses were over 880,000 dead, including civilians. The losses to North Korea in Chinese "volunteers" were over a million. General Douglas MacArthur suggested that he be allowed to bomb not only the Chinese "volunteers" but to attack China proper, possibly with atomic weapons. This was not well-received, because the Soviets achieved their nuclear capability a year before, in 1949, and President Truman was against any extension of the war into China. Dissatisfied, General MacArthur, bypassing the President, sent a letter to the U.S. Congress, stating that "there is no substitute for victory," and when the President came to Asia to confer with him, the general was late to his meeting, and when he appeared with hat on and pipe in mouth, he never greeted his commander-in-chief by saluting him. President Truman relieved General MacArthur from command and appointed General Matthew B. Ridgeway. There was no clear-cut victor in the war, and an armistice was signed on 27 July 1953, with the demarcation line of ante bellum, but the negotiations to terminate the war continued on with conferences held in Geneva, Switzerland in 1954, which failed to resolve the conflict. President Dwight D. Eisenhower made a promise to the American public during his presidential campaign in 1952 (against his Democratic opponent, Adlai E. Stevenson, former governor of Illinois), that he will ". . . bring the boys home for Christmas," but failed to state which Christmas! The People's Republic of China withdrew its "volunteers" from Korea in 1958, and the United Nations Command was dissolved on 1 January 1976, but the United States stations there to this day about 38,000 soldiers. Since the armistice, the South Korean government made several overtures to the North for unification of these two states, but the North was reluctant, demanding that unification is only possible on their terms, that is if the South surrenders to the North. On 18 February 1992, the leaders of the two states, President Roh Tae-Woo of the South and President Il-Sung of the North, signed an accord on reconciliation, including banning nuclear weapons in the region and renounced hostilities in the future while the dialogue for a unification will continue. See BRAINWASHING, WAR.

Kornilov Rebellion. Former Tsarist General L. G. Kornilov was appointed Commander-in-Chief of the Russian Army on July 30, 1917, by the Premier of the Russian Provisional Government, A. F. Kerensky, because Kornilov knew how to implement strong discipline among the combat troops, already largely infiltrated by the pro-Lenin (communist) elements. By taking command, Kornilov was able to squash Lenin's (and the Bolsheviks') attempt to take power from the provisional government when, in July 1917, Lenin issued his famous decrees calling for immediate peace, land to the peasants (who were landless), factories to the workers (who were well exploited by their employers), and all political power to the Soviets (councils of government). In order to handle the tense political situation and to keep the provisional government from being deposed by the growing socialist forces of Lenin, Kornilov assumed dictatorial powers (known as "Kornilovshchina"—one-man rule by Kornilov) and, in order to exercise these powers, he asked the provisional government not to interfere with his plans to stop the Bolsheviks. Kornilov's actions clearly divided the nation into two hostile groups: (1) the Bolsheviks who supported the Soviets and (2) Kornilov and the provisional government (i.e., communism versus military dictatorship). The business community gave its support to Kornilov (e.g., during the National Political Conference which was held in Moscow on August 27, 1917), but the Premier of the provisional government, Kerensky, though by no means anti-communist, dismissed Kornilov from command of the armed forces on September 9, 1917, and in an alliance (of a very temporary duration) with the Bolsheviks, defeated Kornilov's forces in Petrograd (then the capital city of Russia). After Kornilov's arrest, the Bolsheviks, ending the alliance with Kerensky, moved against him and his government, and abolished it on November 7, 1917. Kerensky fled to the West and ended up teaching Russian History at Stanford University, California, while the communists consolidated their power.

Kornilovshchina. See KORNILOV REBELLION.

KPD. See COMMUNISM, COMMUNIST PARTY OF GERMANY.

Kratien. In the Greek language, "to rule" or "to govern." The term democracy is derived from a combination of *kratien* and *demos* (in the Greek language, "people"). See DEMOCRACY.

Kraut. Pejorative term for one of German nationality, or for German soldiers during W.W.I and W.W.II. The British soldiers used the term "Jerry" when referring to anyone of German extraction, or to a German soldier during W.W.I and W.W.II.

Kreis. In the German language, "district." Also, a small political subdivision that may be found in German-speaking nations. See COUNTY.

Kremlin. The official seat of the government of the former Soviet Union, located in an ancient fortress in Moscow. Term often used to express or describe the Soviet state, the power of the ruling party, the CPSU, or a distinct political system.

Kremlinologist. An authority on the behavior, policies, aims and objectives of the Soviet leadership; particularly during the Cold War years, 1945-1991; an expert in Soviet affairs who interprets them and advises others in dealing with Soviet leaders. (Kremlin, a centuries-old fortress in the city of Moscow, is the seat of the Soviet top leadership, namely the party and the government, in that order.)

Kristallnacht. Or Crystal Night. In the German language, "Night of the broken glass." After the 24 June 1922 execution of a prominent German Jew, Walter Rathenau, the foreign minister of Weimar Germany, by a gang of former Freikorps (pro-Nazi hooligans in Berlin) the anti-Jewish campaign, which was to bring "the final solution," commenced. It continued in various forms throughout Nazi rule, such as the 10 May 1933 public burning of books authored by Jews, Communists, etc., in Germany. "The future man of Germany," declared Dr. Goebbels, Minister of Propaganda, "will not only be of books but also of character." On the evening of 9 November 1938, Nazi troopers throughout Germany went on a wild spree of window breaking of Jewish homes and places of business. Thus began the campaign for the mass extermination of Jews. See FINAL SOLUTION.

Ku Klux Klan (KKK). A secret organization formed in Pulaski, Georgia, in 1865 for the purpose of terrorizing blacks as well as those who aided blacks in their struggle to gain full political and legal rights. When the U.S. Congress started an investigation of the terrorist practices of the Klan, its leader, Confederate General Nathan Bedford Forrest, disbanded it in 1869. The Klan was revived again in 1915 by a Methodist minister from Alabama, William Joseph Simmons, and by 1925 it had about five million registered members, among them such well known personalities as Hugo Black, the future liberal Justice of the U.S. Supreme Court. Black quit the Klan in 1925 when he decided to run for the U.S. Senate from Alabama. Added to the Klan's "enemies list" were Catholics, Jews, as well as all foreign, non-Anglo-Saxon elements. The Klan went out of existence in 1944 when the U.S. Internal Revenue Service demanded repayment of $685,000 in back taxes. The Imperial Wizard, James Colescott, declared the Klan dissolved. The Klan was revived for a third time in 1954 by Dr. Samuel Green, a dentist from Atlanta, Georgia, after the U.S. Supreme Court's decision to integrate schools (in *Brown v. Board of Education*). In 1961, under the leadership of Robert M. Shelton, Jr., it was expanded into a nationwide organization. Today there are two major organizations of the Klan: the United Klans of American Knights of the Ku Klux Klan, under the personal supervision of the Imperial Wizard, Shelton, and a confederation of scattered Klan organizations, some of which cooperate with Shelton and others which remain independent. See MISSISSIPPI WHITE KNIGHTS.

Kuhn's Paradigm. One of the modern and popular explanations of political phenomena and of conceptual frameworks in political theory is the paradigm concept introduced by Professor Thomas S. Kuhn ("The Structure of Scientific Revolution," University of Chicago Press). Paradigm is a common set of beliefs, constituting a kind of open-ended model that more or less explicitly defines the legitimate problems and methods of a research field, the working elements of what he calls "normal science." To Dr. Kuhn, social science, including political science, is now in the pre-or non-paradigmatic stage. See CONCEPT, POLITICAL THEORY, SCIENCE.

Kulak. In the Russian language, "rich farmer" or "large landowner." Also, an enemy of the former Soviet State in the jargon of the CPSU.

Kulturkampf. In the German language, "cultural war." Also, the doctrine of papal infallibility pronounced in 1870, which resulted in a cultural and religious struggle between 1872-1886 and in the formation of the so-called "Old Catholic Church by the German Government." In order to cope with the power and the influence of the Pope, the German Government sponsored several legislative acts (in 1873, 1874, and 1875) called the "Falk Laws" or "May Laws," which banned the Society of Jesus as a legal organization within the states, provided for education of the Catholic clergy in state-operated institutions, and introduced civil marriages as the only marriages legal and binding. These laws were partially repealed in 1879 after the reconciliation between Bismarck and Pope Leo XII. The part of the law on civil marriages remains in force to this day. The cultural imperialism doctrine of Kulturkampf was revived by Adolf Hitler and his Nazi followers, 1933-1945, but their methods were rather crude and barbaric, and the efforts failed. Following the reunification of Germany, there are again efforts on the part of some nationalist elements to impose the German language and culture on people who fell under the jurisdiction of the reunified state. See PAPAL INFALLIBILITY.

Kuomintang. The ruling Nationalist party in the Republic of China or Taiwan (Formosa) under the leadership of Generalissimo Chiang Kai-shek until his death in 1975. The party was established on mainland China in 1891 by Dr. Sun Yat-sen, the first republican president of China, and later its leadership was taken over by Chiang Kai-shek. During the 1920s Chiang Kai-shek, with the aid of the Soviet Union, attempted to absorb the communist elements into this party, but when that failed, he turned to mass extermination; and thus the Communist party of China, under the leadership of Mao Tse-tung, was established as a separate party. On October 10, 1945, the communist forces led by Mao Tse-tung and the Kuomintang forces led by Chiang Kai-shek signed an agreement (known as the "Ten/Ten Agreement") aiming at cooperation. But soon the Communists were able to repel the Nationalists and on October 1, 1949, the communist forces had taken complete control over the mainland and proclaimed the People's Republic of China while Chiang Kai-shek and the Nationalists retreated to Taiwan. The leadership of the party was taken over by Chiang Ching-kuo, the son of Chiang Kai-shek, in 1975. On May 20, 1978, Chiang Ching-kuo was sworn in as president of the Republic of China. See COMMITTEE FOR A FREE CHINA, WHO LOST CHINA.

Kurdish Uprisings. The Kurds, a non-Arab Muslim population about eight to twelve million strong, resided for centuries in the mountain regions spread through Iran, Iraq, the former Soviet Union, and Turkey. During the past century, the Kurds made numerous attempts to establish their own homeland, Kurdistan, or a Kurdish republic. In 1961 they revolted in Iraq, and again in 1975, but without success. The only time the Kurds experienced limited autonomy was in 1945-46, when the Soviet Army occupied portions of Iran in order to block Nazi Germany's supply of oil, but when the Soviets withdrew in 1946 their autonomy ended. According to John Stockwell (*In Search of Enemies: A CIA Story*, New York: W. E. Norton & Company) the Kurdish rebellion was inspired by the CIA. "In 1974 and 1975, the CIA, under orders from Kissinger, had mounted a program to arm and encourage the Kurdish people to revolt against the Iraqi government. This was done at the request of the Shah of Iran, who was contending with the Iraqis. When the Shah had reached a satisfactory understanding with the Iraqis, the CIA was called off and it abruptly abandoned the Kurds, leaving them helpless, unable to defend themselves against bloody reprisals from the Iraqi army." When Dr. Kissinger, then U.S. Secretary of State, was questioned about this incident by the Senator F. Church Committee (the U.S. Senate Committee investigating CIA activities) in 1975, his famous reply was: "One must not confuse the intelligence business with missionary work." During the Gulf War against Iraq in 1991 the Kurds again sided with the Coalition Forces left by the United States, were brutally suppressed by Iraq's Saddam Hussein, but the United States came to their aid by establishing a territorial sanctuary for them on the Iraqi-Turkish border. See BAATH SOCIALIST PARTY.

Kurzarbeit Null. See GERMAN UNIFICATION.

Kuwait Invasion. See PERSIAN GULF WAR.

Kyoiku Mama. See KOKUTAI.

"I have a dream that one day this nation will rise up, live out the true meaning of its creed: we hold these truths to be self-evident, that all men are created equal."

REV. DR. MARTIN LUTHER KING, JR., 1929-1968

La Cosa Nostra. See MAFIA.

La-ila-ha Il-lal-lah. Translated from the Arabic language, "There is no God but Allah." See ISLAM.

La Pasionaria. An affectionate battle-cry name for Dolores Ibarruri, one of the bravest politicians, war-and-guerrilla warfare strategists of the twentieth century, who during the Spanish Revolution, being on the Republican anti-Fascist side, caused more problems to General Francisco Franco, the leader of the Revolution, than the hundreds of thousands of Spanish and foreign volunteers. Franco made an offer to bounty hunters to deliver her dead or alive for a sum which exceeded that of equipping one division (of about 12,000 men) of soldiers at 1936 prices. She was never caught, because her followers guarded her well, and in her fiery oratory, she could inspire everyone; she was capable to speak extemporaneously during a single day in about fifteen different locations, and her audience was captivated by her charisma and zeal. Her popular slogan was "They [meaning the Franco Fascists who were aided by Benito Mussolini of Italy and Adolf Hitler of Nazi Germany] shall never pass," in the Spanish (Basque) language, "no pasaran." Hence, the name, "La Pasionaria," or, "one who does not allow things to pass." She inspired the Republican forces and the Basque people of Spain who seek independence, to look to her (she was a native of Basque) as her guide. After the defeat of the Republican forces among which was the American Lincoln Brigade of volunteers, she departed for the Soviet Union in 1939, returned to Spain after the death of Franco in 1977, and died at the age of 93 in 1989. Because the Soviet Union and socialist and communist groups throughout the world were interested in the struggle against Fascism in Spain, La Pasionaria accepted the aid but never the doctrine of Soviet (or any other) communism, and considered her collaboration with the communists only as a marriage of convenience for the good of her native country, Spain. Because of her great talent and charisma, the communists decided to claim her as one of their own. That she never was. Ibarruri is a symbol of unrelenting struggle against all forms of oppression, particularly among European and African societies. See FASCISM.

Labor-Management Act of 1947. See TAFT-HARTLEY LAW.

Labor Party of Israel. One of the major political parties in modern Israel which has governed that nation since its re-emergence in 1948. The LP was defeated, however, during the May 17, 1977, election by the Likud coalition, and its leader, Menachem Begin (a graduate of the Law School of the University of Warsaw, Poland), became the Prime Minister. Begin and his coalition captured forty-one seats in the 120-seat Knesset (the Parliament). The Likud coalition supported Prime Minister Begin in his strong intentions to hold on to the lands that were conquered during the 1967 Arab-Israeli War, and particularly the West Bank and the Gaza Strip which are rich in oil resources; these are also the areas where the Palestinians would like to set up their independent state, which Begin opposed as well. Another party that gained prominence during the 1977 election, is the Democratic Movement for Change led by a former Israeli Army General (and now an archeologist), Yigal Yadin. The Movement captured fourteen seats in the Knesset. See ISRAELI SETTLEMENTS in Appendix 95.

Labor Racketeering. See LANDRUM-GRIFFIN ACT OF 1959.

Labor Slavery. See BODY BROKERING.

Labor Will Make You Free. In the German language, "Arbeit Macht Frei;" also a motto ironically and cynically displayed above the main entrance gates of Nazi German concentration camps where, during the Nazi rule (1933-1945), millions perished by poison gas (cyclon) and were burned to ashes in high-temperature ovens. The first victims were Jews and opponents of the Nazi regime.

Laborem Exercens. See ENCYCLICAL.

Labour Party of England. One of two major political parties in England, established in 1900 under the name of "Labor Representation Committee" (renamed "Labour Party" in 1906 and also known as the "Whigs"). The purpose of the party is, according to its statutes, to ". . . establish a distinct Labour Group in Parliament, who shall have their whips and agree upon their own policy which must embrace a readiness to cooperate with any party which for the time being may be engaged in promoting legislation in the direct interest of labour." In its doctrine, the Labour Party advocates a democratic socialism—the maximum good for the largest number of persons to be achieved through parliamentary rather than revolutionary means. Under the leadership of Neil Kinnock, the Labour Party abandoned during the 1980s and 1990s, what Kinnock calls the "loony left," meaning the Party became more "capitalist" and less "socialist." See DEMOCRATIC SOCIALISM, LOYAL OPPOSITION.

Laffer Curve. A proposition conceived by Dr. Arthur B. Laffer of the University of Southern California which infers that a general tax cut will deprive the government of spending money and will stimulate the economy by putting money in the hands of the public. That notion was embraced by Ronald Reagan and served him well during his two terms in the White House. One of the 1992 presidential hopefuls, Governor Bill Clinton of Arkansas, has acknowledged that a tax cut is necessary to stimulate any stagnant economy; "You can't have consumer confidence restored until there's consumer cash," he stated. The so-called "peace dividends" (money saved on defense since the dissolution of the Soviet empire) could offset the eventual loss to government revenue. In his fiscal policy, President Reagan emphasized that a sufficient supply of money is pivotal to economic stability and prosperity, and his supply-side economics sloganeering, called "Reaganomics," helped him gain enough support to sustain considerable stability during his two administrations.

LAFTA. See LATIN AMERICAN FREE TRADE ASSOCIATION.

Lagos Charter. See INTER-AFRICAN AND MALAGASY ORGANIZATION (IAMO), MONROVIA GROUP.

Lagos Doctrine. During his five-nation, good will tour, March 28-April 3, 1978 (Venezuela, March 28-29; Brazil, March 29-30; Argentina, March 30-31; Nigeria, March 31-April 3; and Liberia, April 3), U.S. President Jimmy Carter delivered a major address on April 1, 1978, in Lagos, Nigeria, in which he: (1) stated America's commitment to racial equality in Africa and everywhere, so that the people of Africa can proclaim: "Free at last, free at Last! Thank God Almighty, we are free at last!"—a statement made by Dr. Martin Luther King, Jr., several years before in the President's native state, Georgia; (2) stated America's support for governments in Africa which are based on the principle of "one man, one vote"; (3) gave a promise to "hold our hands" with white minorities in African states (Rhodesia and the Republic of South Africa where blacks outnumber whites five to one) "if they decide to transform their society and to do away with the crippling burdens of past injustices"; (4) warned that international trade is a two-way street, meaning that when the United States purchased products from Africa (referring to Nigerian oil) it expected, in return, to sell American products to Africa. (Some African states sold to the U.S. for hard currency, but purchased commodities from the Soviet bloc.); and (5) pointed out that Soviet and Cuban military presence in Africa (e.g., approximately 17,000 Cuban troops and 1,000 Soviet advisors in Ethiopia) could have led to war: "We oppose such intervention by outside military forces. We must not allow great power rivalries to destroy our hopes for an Africa at peace." See WAKE FOREST DOCTRINE, WALK FOR FREEDOM.

Lagos Plan of Action. On 29 April 1980, fifty heads of state and heads of government of Africa signed the "Lagos Plan of Action" in Lagos, Nigeria. According to authors Robert S. Browne and Robert J. Cummings (*Lagos Plan of Action vs. the Berg Report,*" Brunswick Publishing Corporation), the plan constitutes the first "comprehensive continent-wide formulation and articulation of the preferred long-term economic and development objectives of African countries." The Lagos Plan met a challenge from the World Bank, in the so-called "Berg Report," prepared for the bank by Elliot Berg, which was somewhat critical of the Lagos Plan, indicating that expected progress to be realized by the plan would be difficult to achieve because of lack of measurable "growth in per capita income for Africa." The Berg Report was also critical of the manner in which the plan was to be realized.

Lagting. Upper chamber of Parliament in Norway. See ODELSTING, STORTING.

Laibach Congress. See QUADRUPLE ALLIANCE.

Laissez-Faire. In the French language, "free play." Also, a term often used to describe the government's limited ability to intervene in the economic activity of private enterprise, or a policy calling for unrestricted economic activity without governmental interference. See FREE ENTERPRISE.

Lamar Society. An organization, founded in 1969 in Durham, North Carolina, in memory of Lucius Quintus Cincinnatus Lamar (1825-1893), U.S. Senator from Mississippi (1867-1873) and Associate Justice of the U.S. Supreme Court (1888-1893), which advocates a political philosophy of "enlightened pragmatism," based on: systematic and continuous efforts to bridge the ideological gaps between the South and the North, wanting both to rise above petty ideological conflicts that are intellectually unsound and to eradicate remnants of racial segregation which are based on intellectually unsound prejudices and primitive reasoning. It calls for harmonious cooperation in all areas of public policy that will advance the entire society, and not just certain elements. The Society also sponsors the Lamar Foundation, located in Washington, D.C.

Lame Duck. An incumbent who is not eligible for re-election or re-appointment to the same office; or one who lost re-election or has not been re-appointed to the same office but is still exercising his authority for the remainder of his unexpired term. The Twentieth Amendment to the U.S. Constitution (see Appendix 8) moved the date of inauguration of the President from March 4 to January 20, and the commencement of the "new" session of Congress from March 4 to January 3 (thus shortening the term between the November election and the commencement of the "new" Congress to two months). See CONGRESS OF THE UNITED STATES, PRESIDENTIAL TRANSITION.

Lame Duck Amendment. See LAME DUCK.

Lame Duck Appointment. An appointment to an office that is made by an outgoing executive (e.g., an appointment made by the U.S. President shortly before the end of his tenure). See JUDICIAL REVIEW, *Marbury v. Madison* in Appendix 48.

Lame Duck President. A phrase that may be used to describe a United States President who either was not re-elected or is not eligible for re-election to that office, but is still exercising his authority for the remainder of his unexpired term. See LAME DUCK, LAME DUCK APPOINTMENT.

Land. In the German language, "state," "territory," or "province." Also, one of the states in the German federation (Federal Republic of Germany) which has its own autonomous government and appoints its representatives to the Bundesrat (the appointive chamber of the German Parliament).

Land Councils of Russia. See CHRISTIAN-DEMOCRATIC MOVEMENT OF RUSSIA (CDMR).

Land for Peace Issue in the Middle East. See ISRAEL'S LAND FOR PEACE POLICY.

Land of Israel Movement. See ISRAELI SETTLEMENTS.

Land of the Round Door Knob. See AMERICAN CENTURY.

Land of the Walking Dead. See KHMER ROUGE.

Land Use Policy. See ZONING.

Land Warfare, Rules of. See RULES OF LAND WARFARE.

Landesgericht. A court of law of any of the several states in the Federal Republic of Germany. Each state ("Land") in the German federation has its own independent court system whose decisions in some cases may be appealed to the Federal Supreme Court.

Landmark Case. A judicial decision that establishes some significant precedent, states or re-states certain principles of law, and one which becomes a source of law (e.g., *Marbury v. Madison* which established the doctrine of judicial review in the United States). See Appendix 48.

Landrum-Griffin Act of 1959. A congressional law which aims to eliminate all forms of labor racketeering, such as improper election practices, handling of union funds, and labor-management collusions. It was under this legislation that Jimmy Hoffa, President of the Teamsters Union, was jailed for eight years (1964-1972), for misuse of union pension funds. See TAFT-HARTLEY LAW.

Landsgemeinde. Cantonal legislature, composed of all male citizens, in some cantons of Switzerland .

Landslide. Term used when an overwhelming majority of votes are cast for one candidate in an election to a national public office (e.g., the presidency). See MINORITY PRESIDENT.

Landslide Lyndon. Nickname of U.S. President Lyndon B. Johnson (1963-1969), bestowed upon him by the mass media and his colleagues in Congress after his landslide (61% of the popular vote) victory in the presidential race of 1964.

Language of Politics. See POLITICAL SEMANTICS.

LaPalma Dialogue. U.S. President Ronald Reagan and newly-elected President of El Salvador, Christian Democrat Jose Napoleon Duarte, a moderate and an accommodating politician, conferred together at LaPalma in 1984 on the resolution of some of the major problems in this divided country. President Reagan insisted that the so-called "death squads"—extreme right executors at the service of the land-owners—cease their activities and, with American aid, the country assists in the stabilization of the region. The death squads acted allegedly in response to the provocation by the leftist elements from Cuba and Nicaragua.

Larceny. The theft of personal property.

Las Cortes Generales. The General Courts or National Assembly of Spain, consisting of an upper house or Senate and a lower house or Congress of Deputies.

Last Plantation. An unflattering nickname for the U.S. Congress which, though it passed a large number of civil rights laws during the 1960s and 1970s, has exempted itself from the provisions of most of them. As a result, it often handles its employees (particularly females and minorities) like the poorly-treated and poorly-rewarded working force of a feudalistic plantation. In response to the publicity that was generated by the Davis-Passman confrontation in 1974, the House adopted a Code of Official Conduct in 1974 (prohibiting sex discrimination), and a voluntary Fair Employment Practices Agreement in 1975 to which only 107 out of 438 members of the House have been subscribing as of 1977. The Senate passed a similar measure in 1977, the Ethics Code, which also forbids race and sex discrimination. See POLITICAL ETHICS.

Latifundium. A large estate usually owned by one person or a small group of persons and operated by servile or non-servile labor. The owner (or owners), as a common practice, do not reside on the estate. See MINIFUNDIUM.

Latin American Free Trade Association (LAFTA). An agreement signed in June 1961 by Argentina, Brazil, Chile, Colombia, Ecuador, Mexico, Paraguay, Peru, and Uruguay, to establish a free trade area, a type of common market between the signatory states. See LATIFUNDIUM.

Laundered Funds. Funds for political or business payoffs (bribes), or contributions to political campaigns by individuals or corporations which have been diverted through phony bank accounts set up for that purpose, or through foreign banks in defiance of existing laws. During the Koreagate scandal in 1977-78, it was revealed that Tong Sun Park, the Korean businessman who acted on the orders of the KCIA and the Korean government, channeled millions of dollars through Swiss banks, of which $500,000 allegedly went to former U.S. Representative Otto Passman in 1972. The Senate Ethics Committee has also learned that other members of Congress received various amounts of laundered money from the Korean operative. See CAMPAIGN FUNDS, KOREAGATE.

Lausanne Conference. See CURZON LINE.

Law. A rule or a set of rules ("dos" and "don'ts") carrying sanctions for non-compliance. Law creates rights, obligations, and institutions. The early American colonists, for example, subscribed to the traditional conservative notion that law should be an expression of right, not simply an act of will (such as the will of a capricious monarch), because rights do not change easily. A rule that is easily changed is known as a "decree." Although it often has the force of law, its scope and degree of application are lesser, and it is usually issued by the executive officers of the government upon approval by the legislature. Under the American system, the U.S. President has no decree power, because, under Art. I of the U.S. Constitution, Congress cannot delegate its legislative authority. Although by no means perfect, law is a result of compromise, of choice among alternatives, with the best prevailing. See JUSTICE, OAKS' LAWS.

Law Enforcement Assistance Administration (LEAA). An agency of the U.S. federal government established by the *Omnibus Crime Control and Safe Streets Act of 1968*, designed to render technical advice and financial assistance to state and local law enforcement agencies for the training of law enforcement officers in techniques of crime control and crime prevention, as well as in the purchase of modern equipment and facilities. On the substate level, the LEAA renders financial assistance to local jurisdictions through the regional planning agencies for updating their know-how and facilities, as well as financing so-called "civil disorder plans," whereby all law enforcement forces within a given region closely cooperate by mutual agreement in cases of civil disturbances.

Law of Blood. See JUS SANGUINIS.

Law of Heaven Americanized. A measure that was passed in the State of Maine ("Maine Law") in 1851 prohibiting the manufacture, distribution, sale, and consumption of intoxicating liquors. By 1857, about a dozen other states introduced such prohibitions, culminating with a constitutional amendment (Appendix 8) ratified January 16, 1919, but repealed on December 5, 1933. See PROHIBITION PARTY.

Law of Little Things. A term coined by journalist and writer Jonathan Alter in *Newsweek* magazine (23 March 1992); the law of little things determines that an issue is made out of anything that is small, e.g., the check-bouncing by members of the U.S. Congress (known as "Rubbergate") which cost little to the taxpayers, while larger issues receive less attention from the public, e.g., the Savings and Loan scandal for which taxpayers will have to pay over $500 million, and which the U.S. Government, including Congress, could have prevented. A small issue "resonates among the hoi polloi because it's so familiar, so easy to comprehend," writes the author. How much is there written, in plain language, about the theft by Michael Milken and his junk bond fraud? The people were really affected by such scandals and Congress could have legislated to close the loopholes in laws so that such things would not happen, but little is written or spoken about that. Cronyism and old-boy networking are ancient practices. To the unemployed in America, check kiting may be of interest but it is also of little consequence; on the other hand what Congress ought to do for the former Soviet Union and the new democracies in Eastern Europe may determine, for generations to come, how stable employment will be in America. See ATLANTIC PARTNERSHIP, DEFENSE PLANNING GUIDANDE, EUROPEAN ENERGY POLICY, WHO LOST CHINA?

Law of Neutrality. See NEUTRALITY.

Law of Place. See JUS SOLI.

Law of Soil. See JUS SOLI.

Law of Space. See SPACE LAW.

Law of Supply and Demand. An established reality in the economic activity of man to the effect that the cost of goods or services is lower when they are in ample supply, and that the cost of goods or services will rise if they are in short supply or become scarce.

Law of the High Seas. See HIGH SEAS, LAW OF THE SEA CONFERENCE, MARITIME LAW.

Law of the Jungle. See PREVENTIVE DIPLOMACY.

Law of the Land. See CONSTITUTION, SUPREME LAW OF THE LAND.

Law of the Ruler. See JUS IMPERII.

Law of the Sea Conference. A gathering of States called with the purpose of devising means for sharing more equitably the benefits derived from the exploration of deep-sea resources, which the United Nations Organization and especially the Third World bloc of nations consider a "common heritage of mankind." The 1978 Conference held in Geneva, Switzerland, was a follow-up of previous gatherings held in different parts of the world. The treaty was approved by 130 nations in 1982 with dissenting votes cast by the United States, Israel, Turkey and Venezuela. See HIGH SEAS.

Law's Business. See VICTIMLESS CRIME.

Laws of Humanity. All the norms of international law which, according to the UN. Charter, aim to preserve and sustain human life and well-being on earth through the preservation of peace, elimination of war as an instrument of policy, and international cooperation among states on an equitable basis.

Laws of War. See RULES OF LAND WARFARE.

Lawmaking Process. See LEGISLATIVE PROCESS IN THE UNITED STATES: THE FEDERAL LEVEL.

Le Sens de l'État. See SENSE OF THE STATE.

LEAA. See LAW ENFORCEMENT ASSISTANCE ADMINISTRATION.

Leader of the Free World. See FREE WORLD.

Leader of the Revolution. The official title of Colonel Mu'ammar al-Qadhafi of Libya, who is responsible to the elected Peoples Congress, the Parliament, but who, in reality, exercises power single-handedly with Parliament following his wishes.

Leader of the Socialist World. See FREE WORLD.

Leader State. See ADMINISTRATIVE STATE.

Leaders of the Soviet Union. See RULERS OF THE SOVIET UNION.

Leadership. One's ability to command obedience of others without the use (or threat) of naked force; one's ability to condition the behavior of others (or collective behavior of groups) according to one's wishes, values, biases, and predilections; or, to paraphrase U.S. President Harry S. Truman (1944-1953), one's ability to make others do things against their will, and then be loved for doing it, be decisive in decision-making. Also as one of America's most accomplished managers points out (*Up the Organization: How to Stop the Corporation from Stifling People and Strangling Profits*, Alfred A. Knopf), the most important skill of a capable manager is the ability to "eliminate his people's excuses for failure." A good manager ought to "get the available facts, marshal the allies, think through the opponents' defenses, and then go." See NUTS!, Appendix 3-A

Leadership Amendment. See PANAMA CANAL TREATIES.

Leadership by Pulling. A notion in leadership and management that it is easier and more productive and rewarding to motivate people to perform well; leading by example with the leader/manager showing the way. Opposite of this is "leadership by 'pushing,'" when the leader/manager demands obedience and/or action but is not showing the way. One style involves motivation, while the other implies command, compulsion or even threat. Leading by motivation and example is leadership, while pushing and threatening is tyranny. As Professor James MacGregor Burns points out (in *Leadership*, Harper & Row, Publishers), ". . . leadership is nothing if not linked to collective purpose." He identifies the following types of leadership style: (1) "transactional" leadership—

leaders engage in a tradeoff with followers, (e.g., jobs for votes, or good grades for studying hard); (2) "transforming" leadership—the leader seeks potential motives of prospective followers and tries to satisfy their needs. In this instance, the leader may transform followers into leaders and the leader himself becomes a "moral agent;" and (3) "moral" leadership—the leader is not interested merely in gaining power, but tries to fulfill the followers' aspirations, and inspires them to perform moral deeds. Moral leadership takes roots at home, within the family. To Prof. Burns, the "child's society" is the family and the "parental coalition gives unity of direction to the child." See Appendix 3-A.

Leadership Command. See SHAH.

Leadership Conference on Civil Rights. A major lobbying organization of black Americans, loosely associated with the National Association for the Advancement of Colored People (NAACP), which strives to influence Congress and the President on all matters that may be of benefit particularly to blacks (but it does not exclude other races). Roy Wilkins, the former leader of the NAACP, is the principal lobbyist for the organization. See LOBBY, NATIONAL ASSOCIATION FOR THE ADVANCEMENT OF COLORED PEOPLE (NAACP).

Leadership Resolve. See RESOLVE.

Leading Industry. Glasson's conceptualization indicates the following characteristics: (". . . a relatively new and 'dynamic' industry with an advanced level of technology injecting an atmosphere of 'growth-mindedness' into a region; it has high income elasticity of demand for its products which are usually sold to national markets; it has strong inter-industry linkages with other sectors"). Leading industry is also characterized according to Glasson—by propulsive firms, which are characterized by: being relatively large; generating significant growth impulses into its environment, possessing high ability to innovate.

League of Arab States. See ARAB LEAGUE.

League of Communists. The official name of the Communist party of Yugoslavia.

League of Nations. An international organization established in Paris, France, upon a Covenant agreed upon by the victors in World War I. Its first meeting was held at Geneva, Switzerland, on January 10, 1920. Once the present United Nations had undertaken its official functions, the League was formally dissolved on January 10, 1946. The League's primary aim and objective was to prevent the use of force (war) as an instrument of policy, and to maintain international peace and security. The United States did not ratify the Covenant due to strong opposition from the U.S. Senate, and, particularly, Senator Henry Cabot Lodge of Massachusetts, who felt personal animosity to U.S. President Woodrow Wilson, a strong proponent of the League. See UNITED NATIONS ORGANIZATION (UNO), VERSAILLES TREATY.

League of Three Emperors. An informal organization that was set up in 1872 between Austria, Germany, and Russia, which aimed at helping Russia's Tsar Alexander II strengthen his position in Central Europe. The League was revived in 1881 by Prussia's Chancellor Otto von Bismarck and dissolved in 1887, upon the breakup of relations between Austria and Russia. The formation of that League is considered as an early attempt to politically integrate Europe. See COUNCIL OF EUROPE.

League of Women Voters. See WOMEN POLITICAL ACTION GROUPS.

Lebanon Crisis. See EISENHOWER DOCTRINE.

Lebensraum. In the German language, "living space" or "elbow room." Also, the core of Adolf Hitler's philosophy of conquest of independent nations of Eastern Europe. Hitler (1933-1945) and his Nazi (National Socialism) Party undertook the conquest of these nations using the traditional slogan of *"Drang nach Osten"* ("Drive to the East"). This was the first step in Hitler's plan to expand the Third Reich of Germany and implement a "new order" in the world. The *"Drang nach Osten"* notion had been developed by a German geopolitician, Professor Carl Hanshofter (1869-1946), based on the geopolitical theories of Rudolf Kjellen. The events leading to the emergence and development of Hitlerism and Nazism were: (1) the Versailles Treaty of 1919 had imposed a heavy burden upon defeated Germany—it would take approximately fifty years, considering the growth of the German economy at that time, for Germany to pay war damages to the allies as imposed by the Treaty; (2) on November 8-9, 1923, Hitler and his followers (supported by General Erich F. W. Ludendorff) attempted to overthrow the Bavarian government and seize power, but failed; (3) on November 12, 1923, Hitler was convicted and confined to the Landsberg Prison to serve a five-year term, but was released eleven months later; (4) while in prison, Hitler outlined his blueprint for conquest—"Today Europe, tomorrow the entire world!"—in his book *Mein Kampf* ("My Struggle") which was not taken seriously by anyone on the outside; (5) during the presidential election of 1932, Hitler was defeated by a narrow margin by Paul von Hindenburg, a Marshal of the German army; (6) on December 12, 1932, Hitler delivered a speech to a group of German industrialists in Düsseldorf (which became known as the "Düsseldorf Doctrine") in which he outlined his concept of *Lebensraum*, or "conquest:" (a) Europe needs a "new order," new leadership, one based on Hitler's *Weltanschauung*; Europe would be divided into autonomous areas of self-governing peoples, but the center of power would be the Third Reich of Nazi Germany; this would constitute a "Monroe Doctrine of Europe"; (b) the Nazi German Reich would be a "power-state" (*Machtstaat*) in which government and business would work in partnership because they would be "mutually supporting": business would contribute toward the development and consolidation of power of the "power-state," and in turn the "power-state" would create the necessary conditions for business to develop and prosper, which would render even more support to the state and make it even stronger; and (c) since, according to Hitler, only the white race (the "master race") has been endowed with the capacity and the capability to effectively govern societies, that race had "an extraordinarily brutal right to dominate others"; imperialism by the white race would be pursued toward positive ends, because the "master race" would always strive toward perfection for itself and for others; such an outline sounded attractive to business people who were burdened with heavy taxes, suffered because of global depression, and saw a need for the rebuilding of the German society; (7) on January 30, 1933, President Hindenburg appointed Hitler Chancellor (*Kanzler*) of Germany; and (8) on August 2, 1934 (upon the death of Hindenburg), Hitler declared himself President and Chancellor of Germany (combining these two offices), and named himself the Leader (*Führer*) of Germany. On November 6, 1937, he announced the active phase of implementation of his *Lebensraum* doctrine, and by 8 May 1945, lost everything, including his life. See FLIGHT FROM THE EAST, GEOPOLITICS, NATIONAL SOCIALISM, PUTSCH, SCHWARZE KAPELLE, VERSAILLES TREATY, WELTANSCHAUUNG, Appendices 91, 105.

Lecompton Constitution. In 1857, Kansas applied for statehood to be formed on the basis of popular sovereignty. The pro-slavery forces, which were then in power in Kansas, proposed a new constitution for the state which would have allowed people to vote not for or against the entire instrument, but for or against legalization of slavery, since some provisions in this constitution contained protection for slave-owners. If the entire constitution were rejected, so would the protection for slave owners in that state. Seeing the deception in this constitution, the anti-slavery forces voted the entire constitution down, and Kansas was not admitted to the American Union until after the secessionists from the South left Congress and the War of Secession (Civil War) had commenced between the South and the North.

Lee's Resolution. Richard Henry Lee of Virginia submitted to the Second Continental Congress a resolution on June 7, 1776, stating that the colonies "are, and of right ought to be, free and independent states." This resolution led to the appointment of a committee to draft a Declaration of Independence which was headed by Thomas Jefferson. The resolution was adopted on July 2, 1776.

Legal Norm. A set of basic patterns of behavior of men in a politically organized society which are recognized and agreed upon as useful, practical, and applicable to all, as a means to expedite relations among peoples, governments, and nations in order to enhance their survival, development, and general well-being. Legal norms constitute the source of laws—both normative law, such as a political constitution of a state, and regulatory laws at all levels, municipal and domestic, as well as international. See LAW, NORMATIVE LAW.

Legal Positivism. Strict, to-the-letter interpretation of existing laws (e.g., the constitution) or the phenomena of politics; a legalistic attitude, one characterized by a lack of flexibility in the interpretation and comprehension of legal and political phenomena in the daily life of a politically organized community. See POSITIVIST VIEW OF LAW.

Legal Pragmatism. See JUDICIAL PRAGMATISM.

Legal Services Corporation. A semi-independent agency of the federal government in the United States, established in 1972 to furnish legal services to persons whose financial resources preclude their acquiring such legal assistance on their own. The scope of activities of that agency was considerably extended by amending legislation which U.S. President Jimmy Carter signed into law on December 28, 1977.

Legal Tender. The coins and paper money (currency) which by law must be accepted for payment of debts or commercial transactions within a single state.

Legend. A lie intelligently presented, such as a plausible account of one's identity or activities; information about persons or actions which sound true but which are in reality deceptive and false. See INTELLIGENCE.

Legis Neminem Excusat. In the Latin language, "the ignorance of law excuses no one" or "there is no excuse for ignoring the laws." See IGNORANTIA JURIS.

Legislation Explosion. See GOVERNMENT BY LITIGATION.

Legislative Agenda. See AGENDA.

Legislative Aggrandizement. See ASSERTIVENESS.

Legislative Assertiveness. See ASSERTIVENESS.

Legislative Bloc. A group of legislators who, regardless of party affiliation, usually vote together on legislation favoring certain interest groups. See VESTED INTEREST LOBBY.

Legislative Branch. In the U.S. a branch of government which creates the laws that are exacted by the executive branch and defined by the judicial branch. Congress and the fifty state legislatures compose the executive branch. Legislatures, both state and federal, consist of elected representatives who serve their constituents through the lawmaking process. Bills (or proposed laws) are sent to committees for modification and then debated in both houses. If passed, the law is modified even further before a final vote in both houses. The President can veto, or refuse to sign the bill into law, although the legislature can override that veto under the system of checks and balances. This system includes the power of impeachment, the power to confirm appointments and elect appropriations. See Appendices 8, 13.

Legislative Council. An informal body of state legislators (ranging in membership from five to the entire membership of the legislature) that is ordinarily charged with the task of searching for ways and means of improving legislative processes.

Legislative Court. A court of law other than the U.S. Supreme Court which may be established by an Act of Congress (under its judicial powers) in the United States (e.g., the U.S. Court of Military Appeals).

Legislative District. See CONGRESSIONAL DISTRICT.

Legislative Immunity. See LEGISLATIVE PRIVILEGE.

Legislative Oversight. The practice of overseeing the activities of the executive branch and the administrative bureaucracy by the legislature in order to determine if the laws passed are properly implemented and the funds appropriated are properly spent. In the United States, Congress maintains oversight over the executive administration through the confirmation process, congressional hearings, and its own Office of the Budget and the General Accounting Office. Frequently, the bureaucracy is reluctant to admit to an oversight. In many cabinet-parliamentary systems of government (e.g., Great Britain), the parliament exercises considerable oversight powers over the cabinet and prime minister and has the power to dissolve the power of the incumbent government with a "no confidence" vote. See CONGRESS OF THE UNITED STATES, IMPOUNDED LEGISLATION.

Legislative Oversight of Intelligence. See INTELLIGENCE OVERSIGHT.

Legislative Privilege. Also known as "legislative immunity." As a rule of custom or law (e.g., constitutional provision) legislators are exempt from prosecution for acts committed in the line of duty which otherwise would be subject to prosecution. The U.S. Supreme Court, however, ruled on 19 March 1980, in the case of Edgar H. Gillock, a legislator of the State of Tennessee, that such immunity, though fully recorded in the U.S. Federal Rules of Evidence, does not apply to state legislators charged with violation of federal law. The U.S. Supreme Court interpreted the speech and debate clause in the U.S. Constitution as a privilege applicable solely to federal legislators and the U.S. Congress (House and Senate). The Chief Justices decided that "In the absence of a constitutional limitation on the power of Congress to make state officials, like all other persons, subject to federal criminal sanctions."

Legislative Process. The manner in which a legislative body proceeds in passing (enacting) legislation (laws). See CONGRESS OF THE UNITED STATES, Appendices 8, 13.

Legislative Socialism. See PARLIAMENTARY SOCIALISM.

Legislative Veto. A device that allows the U.S. Congress to review and to check upon the execution of legislation by the President by attaching certain stipulations as to how the law is to be implemented (e.g., approving a foreign aid bill, but denying the right to sell certain commodities, such as computers or sophisticated aircraft and weapon systems).

Legislator. An individual elected or appointed to a legislative body. At the federal level such individuals are called "Senators" or "Congressmen." At the state level, most legislators are called "Senators" or "Delegates." At the local level, legislators go by a variety of names depending on the type of government (city, town, village, county). All legislators are required to reside (live) in the district they seek to represent. There are also age and citizenship requirements which vary with the levels of government.

Legitimacy. A notion applicable to statecraft whereby, as long as the electorate (or the people in general) obeys the government in power (provided that it is not a despotic dictatorship) and obeys the laws to the extent that the government can sustain itself, that government is considered legal and legitimate. Also, the basis on which the government-of-the-day may command obedience and use power with authority. See POLITICAL CULTURE, POLITICAL SOCIALIZATION, POLITICS.

Lemon Law. Under some congressional laws aimed at protecting the consumer from fraudulent business practices (e.g., the Federal Trade Commission Improvement Act of 1975), the consumer is entitled to a complete refund on any item purchased that costs five dollars or more, if the manufacturer is not able to repair that item within a reasonable time.

Lend-Lease. On March 11, 1941, the U.S. Congress authorized assistance to nations which were involved in combating the Axis powers, mainly Hitler's Germany and Hirohito's Japan, during World War II. The principal recipients of food-stuffs and war materiel (amounting to over fifty billion dollars) were the Soviet Union, England, and China. (In 1972-73, the Soviet Union agreed to repay the United States' part of the debt on the ratio of one cent per dollar.) The program was terminated on 17 August 1945, after the surrender of Japan.

Lenin's April Theses. A series of philosophical, policy, and tactical statements made by Vladimir I. Lenin prior to the 1917 Revolution in Russia which predicted the victory of the Bolsheviks. (Among the most powerful slogans of these was "Peace, Bread, and Land" for the people.)

Lenin's Testament. Vladimir I. Lenin, the founding father of the Communist Party of the Soviet Union (CPSU) and the Soviet State (after the Bolshevik Revolution of 1917), suffered a stroke on May 26, 1922, and on December 24, 1922, as an expression of his concern for a successor, wrote the party a memorandum known as the Testament, urging the leadership to select an appropriate replacement. In the memorandum he appraised the major leaders of the new Soviet State: Leon Trotsky—an excellent mind and capable, but with "too far-reaching self-confidence and a disposition to be too much attracted by the purely administrative side of affairs"; Piatakov—"distinguished in will and ability, but too much given over to administration and the administrative side of things to be relied on in a serious political question"; Bukharin he considered the most valuable as a theoretician, "but his theoretical views can only with the very greatest doubt be regarded as fully Marxist, for there is something scholastic in him (he never has learned, and I think never has fully understood the dialectic)"; and Josef Stalin, who in the end became the victor, Lenin considered as not always knowing "how to use that power with sufficient caution." On January 4, 1923, Lenin wrote a postscript to the Testament in which he further appraised Stalin: "After taking over the position of Secretary General, Comrade Stalin accumulated in his hands immeasurable power and I am not certain whether he will be able to use this power with the required care ... Stalin is excessively rude, and this defect, which can be freely tolerated in our midst and in contacts among us Communists, becomes a defect which cannot be tolerated in one holding the position of Secretary General. Because of this, I propose that the comrades consider the method by which Stalin would be removed from his position and by which another man would be selected for it, a man who, above all, would differ from Stalin in only one direction, namely, greater tolerance, greater loyalty, greater kindness and a more considerate attitude toward the comrades, a less capricious temper, etc. ..... " Lenin died on January 21, 1924. Stalin managed to purge his opponents, particularly Leon Trotsky (real name Leon Berstein), who would have been the most likely replacement for Lenin. Trotsky was first expelled from the party, then on November 14, 1927, deported to Alma Ata, then murdered in Mexico in 1940. Most statues of Lenin in the former USSR and Eastern Europe, were removed in 1991.

L'État C'Ést Moi. See I AM THE STATE.

Let Hundred Flowers Bloom Together, Let the Hundred Schools Contend. See HUNDRED FLOWERS.

Let Us Reason Together. A phrase often used by U.S. President Lyndon B. Johnson (1963-1969), whenever he saw a need to reconcile differences among the opposing views of individuals which could affect his policies. Johnson's political style is said to have been that of emphasizing the gains of the adversary achieved at his own expense.

Letter of Marque and Reprisal. A document that may be issued by a governmental agency to a private person authorizing him to seize or destroy enemy vessels for a fee.

Level Playing Field. According to Professor Lester C. Thurow (*Head to Head: The Coming Economic Battle Among Japan, Europe, and America*), partners (states) in international trade or diplomacy "must feel that they have an equal chance to win," as the Americans view it; the Germans call it "reciprocity," and the Japanese call it "equal opportunity, but not equal outcomes." According to press accounts, Edith Cresson, former prime minister of France, interpreted the Japanese position by stating simply, "Japan is an adversary that does not play by the rules and has an absolute desire to conquer the world. You have to be naive or blind not to recognize that," and "The Japanese have a strategy of world conquest. They have finished their job in the United States. Now they are about to devour Europe." See COMPARATIVE ADVANTAGE, PRODUCT CYCLE, UNILATERAL GLOBAL KEYNESIANISM.

Lex Ferenda. In the Latin language, "suggested legislation" or "new legislation to be considered." Also, "de lege ferenda" is used.

Lex Lata. In the Latin language, "the present law" or "the existing law." Also, "de lege lata" is used.

Lex Loci. In the Latin language, "the law of the place" or "law applicable within a certain jurisdiction only."

Lex non Scripta. In the Latin language, "unwritten law" or "common law."

Lex Posterior Derogat Priori. In the Latin language, "a new treaty supersedes an old one" or "a new treaty obligation repeals an old treaty obligation." See CLAUSULA, REBUS SIC STANTIBUS as it applies to international law.

Lex Rei Sitae. In the Latin language, "the law of domicile" or "the law of legal residence." See DOMICILE, JURISDICTION.

Lex Retro Non Agit. In the Latin language, "a new law does not apply retroactively." See EX POST FACTO LAW.

Lex Scripta. In the Latin language, "written law," "statutory law," or "codified law."

LFM. See LIBERATION FRONT OF MOZAMBIQUE.

Liaison Officer. An official within an agency or organization, private or public, who may be charged with the responsibility of maintaining close external contacts with specific persons, agencies, or organizations outside that agency (e.g., the President of the United States appoints a special assistant who is his legislative liaison, that is, one whose principal task is to keep in close contact with Congress and to advise individual members of Congress, congressional committees, or Congress at large on the wishes of the President; in return, he also reports to the President on the actions and activities of Congress). See PRESIDENT OF THE UNITED STATES.

Libel. An injury that may be sustained as a result of defamatory writing or circulation of any printed or photographic matter that may damage one's reputation, for which the injured party may bring damages. Similar injury inflicted by the spoken word constitutes slander.

Liberal. See LIBERALISM.

Liberal Constitution. A basic law of a nation which allocates power, authority, and control to the various components of a politically organized society with maximum power and authority being allocated to the electorate and a minimum of power, sufficient enough to sustain, maintain and to perpetuate the state of that community, to the hierarchies of government (e.g., federal, state and local). A system whereby certain elites (e.g., state and local governments and private economic enterprises) enjoy considerable autonomy which may not be easily withheld or withdrawn because it is protected by legal norms and institutions. The U.S. Constitution, for example, contains in its amendments the ultimate intellectual achievements of liberalism, which are protected further from abuses by governmental authority by such provisions as: "Congress shall have power to enforce this article by appropriate legislation" (Amendment XIII). Congress is the supreme lawmaking authority of the state, but it is also a political authority, subject to change through the influence of the electorate. Congressional law, therefore, is not an absolute but a relative law; that is, its enforcement depends on the circumstances of the day and on the wishes of the electorate at a given time. Under a liberal mode of governance there is a system of reciprocal controls—one elite exercising some degree of control over another, instead of unilateral control through command by a central authority in total disregard for the rights of other autonomous elites. See CENTRALISM, LIBERALISM.

Liberal Democracy. A politico-economic doctrine that originated in Europe during the post-Medieval period, aimed at liberating the individual from the dual oppression of the church and the despotic (absolute) monarchs. The notion was further developed by the French encyclopedists and the American political philosophers (e.g., Benjamin Franklin and Thomas Jefferson) who considered a liberal democracy possible only if a free market economy is sustained. In reality, liberal democracy rests on a free market for the exchange of ideas as well as goods and services. See DEMOCRACY.

Liberal Democratic Party of England. One of the three major political parties in England, under the leadership of Paddy Ashdown. Some British observers see little difference among the three political parties in England, the Labour, the Conservative, and the Liberal Democratic. Professor C. Butler of Oxford University commented once, "Because the parties are so close together, they're being bitchier than usual."

Liberal Ideological Restraints. According to some analyses of the basic assumptions of communism and liberalism, it is generally agreed that since the 19th century, particularly since the Age of Enlightenment, communist aspirations were directed towards economic equality, while those of liberalism were directed towards political rights and liberties of the individual. The Helsinki Agreement of August 1, 1975, and the conference held in Belgrade, Yugoslavia, in 1977, called to examine the Helsinki achievements, basically revolved around the issues of rights and liberties of the individual, an area in which the communist states have done little. See CAPITALISM, COMMUNISM, HELSINKI ACCORD, HUMAN RIGHTS: AMERICAN DEFINITION, LIBERALISM.

Liberal Law. See LIBERAL CONSTITUTION.

Liberal Party of Canada. Pierre Elliot Trudeau returned to power after the February 18, 1980 election, which unseated Tory Prime Minister Joe Clark, stated that the party would return again to the "Canada First" policy, strong central government, independence (from the United States) in world affairs, and economic nationalism—meaning an economy which favors Canada first, that benefits Canada above all. Trudeau stated that Canada stands between two superpowers and not within any particular camp—meaning the United States.

Liberal Republican Party of 1872. A coalition of splinter groups oriented against U. Grant's plans to run for the Presidency a second time in 1872. Under the slogan: "Turn the Rascals Out," meaning those from the South who were convicted and jailed as rebels for participating in the War of Secession (Civil War), the party demanded total and unconditional amnesty and a less zealous implementation of the post-war reconstruction program by the federal bureaucracy. Appendix 19.

Liberalism. A political philosophy which justifies, in the traditional sense, protest against an arbitrary government that is unresponsive to the needs of the vast majority. In the modern sense it means, more or less, deconcentration of economic and political powers and the widening of societal participation in policy formation and implementation.

Liberation Front of Mozambique (LFM). See FRENTE DE LIBERATACAO DE MOCAMBIQUE (FRELIMO).

Liberation Movement Djibouti (LMD). The coalition of political groups dedicated to the liberation of Djibouti, otherwise known as French Somalia, from foreign domination. Djibouti became independent in 1977, and the Movement was dissolved.

Liberation Theology. A religious-political movement widely spread, mainly in Latin America during the 1970s by Catholic clergy. According to author Malachi Martin (in his book *The Keys to This Blood*, New York: Simon and Schuster, 1990), ". . . basic Marxism was smartly decked out in traditional Christian vocabulary and retooled Christian concepts." About ninety percent of the population in Latin America, or some 380 million souls, live and dwell under the most incompetent and oppressive systems on earth, seeking salvation in Christian faith and Marxist economies. By the late 1980s, there were about 60,000 so called "base communities organized throughout Latin America, all pro-Soviet and violently opposed to the regimes in power as well as to traditional Roman Catholic practices. The Vatican was disturbed by these developments and the Pope made several trips to Latin America to regain dialogue and loyalty to the church's traditional doctrines and dogma. The missions by the Pope were well received and a new slogan was widely repeated: "God Bless Our Marxist Revolution and John Paul!" The major theoretical contribution to the concept of Liberation Theology, originated first with Las Scasas, who during the 1550s was voicing his resistance to the inhuman and predatory practices of the Conquistadores in South America, where they brutalized the Aztec's population, causing the death of about fifty million (50,000,000) persons due to killing and disease, all in the name of Christianity. As a clergyman himself, he appealed to reason, using the pulpit to try to end what has been called the first mass genocide in history, but to no avail. Also, the writings and teachings of Antonio Gramsci (1891-1937), a Marxist communist "revisionist," who is considered the founder of the Italian Communist Party and who contributed toward this movement.

Liberian Settlement. See BACK TO AFRICA MOVEMENT.

Liberman Incentives. In order to revive the Soviet economy, and to bring it to its maximum capacity of efficiency, Yevsei G. Liberman, Professor at Kharkov University, in 1964, proposed a series of capitalistic incentives: that payments be based upon one indicator, the rate of profit earned on total capital invested in an enterprise; that central planning be reduced to the coordination of regional planning, allowing for regional and local initiative; and that non-professional intervention of party operatives into technical economic processes be minimized. Most of these ideas were rejected as being departures from Marxism toward capitalism. See LVOV VARIANT.

Libertarian Party. One of the political parties in the United States using this designation. There are several such parties in the United States and most of them subscribe to these generalized views: (1) the U.S. federal government is too large, too strong, and influences the lives of Americans beyond constitutional authorization; (2) states' rights are being infringed upon by the federal government; (3) welfare and welfarism are bad, but free economic activity in private hands with minimum interference by the government is good; (4) all forms of socialism, communism, and internationalism are bad; (5) a tough foreign policy and no foreign aid is best; (6) high moral standards for the individual, the family, and the society as a whole are desirable (based on religion and patriotism); (7) greater value is to be found in sound fiscal policies for the nation, the states, and the local communities, than in federal support programs and deficit spending; (8) America's dominant role in international relations is to be retained. One of these parties nominated its own presidential candidate on August 30, 1975, for the 1976 presidential election, the producer of the popular television show "Little House on the Prairie," Roger Lea MacBride. His campaign slogan was: "Roll back big government." See CAPITALISM, LIBERTY LOBBY.

Liberté, Egalité, Fraternité. In the French language, "liberty, equality, fraternity;" slogan of the American (1776) and the French (1798) revolutions. See LIBERTY, EQUALITY, FRATERNITY.

Liberty Enlightening the World. See STATUE OF LIBERTY.

Liberty, Equality, Fraternity. A slogan of the American and French democratic revolutions, 1776 and 1798 respectively, whose goals were to enlarge the rights of men and citizens.

Liberty Function of Government. See FUNCTIONS OF GOVERNMENT.

Liberty League. A group of wealthy and conservative Republicans and Democrats gathered informally in 1934 in order to place a check upon "that man," "that man in the White House," meaning U.S. President Franklin D. Roosevelt (1933-1944). Their hatred of Roosevelt was compounded by Roosevelt's success in introducing a series of social programs (under the New Deal umbrella), many of which were considered "socialistic" if not "communistic." Roosevelt, learning of their hatred, stated that he welcomed it, because it came from people who "hide behind the flag and the Constitution when serious crises face the nation." The Liberty forces, out of fear that Roosevelt would choose to run for a fifth time as president, were instrumental in passing the 22nd Amendment to the U.S. Constitution (which, however, was not ratified until February 27, 1951).

Liberty Lobby. A private, Washington-based organization with conservative leanings seeking to influence the policies of the American national government. See LIBERTARIAN PARTY, LOBBY.

Liberty Party. An anti-slavery party active in the United States during the 1840s, particularly in New York State, where 16,000 of its votes helped James K. Polk get elected to the U.S. Presidency over his opponent, Henry Clay.

Liberty, Right to. See HUMAN RIGHTS: AMERICAN DEFINITION, Appendices 8, 51.

Liberty Visa. See BRAIN-DRAIN, CONFISCATORY POLICY.

Liberum Veto. In the Latin language, "free veto" or "unrestricted veto." As practiced in 16th century Poland, an objection to a bill by one deputy in the parliamentary body was sufficient to kill it. This practice eventually led to the downfall of the state. The American constitution-makers were aware of this evil and tried to avoid it in their document.

Library of Congress. Located in Washington, D.C., the largest library in the U.S., maintained by federal subsidies. It was originally intended as a research facility for Congress, but presently also serves the general public. The Library of Congress catalogues most all copyrighted publications and its classification method is used throughout the country.

Lifetime Learning. See POST-INDUSTRIAL SOCIETY.

Lifting as We Climb. See NATIONAL ASSOCIATION OF COLORED WOMEN.

Light at the End of the Tunnel. A phrase often used in diplomatic negotiations, when there has been a deadlock or an impasse on reaching an agreement or an understanding, signifying that an end is in sight. The term was used during the Vietnam War, particularly from 1965 to 1974, when President Lyndon Johnson, anxious to conclude the war either through victory or an otherwise honorable conclusion, was told that light could be seen in the tunnel, that is, that victory was soon to be his, but, as it appeared, there was hardly any light or even a tunnel. If there was tunnel it was the one in which the Viet Cong guerrillas were hiding, and if there was any light at the end of it, it was probably one that was managed by the Viet Cong. The phrase reappeared again, in Switzerland, when America was negotiating the ending of the war with the Viet Cong and the North Vietnamese; but the light was very small even at that time, and at last, the Americans solved the problem by pulling out of Vietnam and letting the North Vietnamese, with their corrupt (often anti-American) government, conquer the South Vietnamese. See VIETNAM WAR.

Light of the Aryans. See SHAH.

Likud Coalition. See ISRAELI SETTLEMENTS, LABOR PARTY OF ISRAEL.

Limited Democracy. See INSTITUTIONAL DEMOCRACY.

Limited Purpose Special District. See TEMPLE, MAKIELSKI IN SPECIAL DISTRICT GOVERNMENT IN VIRGINIA.

Limousine Liberal. A politician in America who advocates liberal causes (e.g., economic, political, and social equality) and looks at the state as the principal protector of the welfare of the individual, but who himself is wealthy and enjoys the ultimate comfort and luxury in his private life, including the practice of being chauffeured in an oversized limousine. See IMPERIAL PRESIDENCY.

Lincoln Brigade. See INTERNATIONAL BRIGADE.

Lincoln-Douglas Debate. See GREAT DEBATES.

Lincoln's Reconstruction Plan. Proceeding on the theory that the Southern states had not seceded from the American Union because legally there is no constitutional or statutory provision for such an act, but that they had rebelled, and that President Lincoln, as commander-in-chief of the armed forces must treat them as rebels, Lincoln issued a proclamation authorizing voters in the seceding states to form new governments with the consent of only 10 percent of the registered voters as of 1860. The new governments were to take oaths of allegiance to the Constitution, accept presidential and congressional decisions pertaining to slavery, and request readmission to the federal union. Arkansas and Louisiana formed such governments, but radical Republicans in Congress would not allow their congressional delegations to be seated in the U.S. Congress on the grounds that Lincoln was too lenient with the Southern politicians. They demanded vengeance against the South instead of reconciliation. West Virginia is the only state which was formed during the Civil War through a non-constitutional process. See RECONSTRUCTION.

Line Management. The decision-and policy-makers in an organization who also supervise the staff, the actual producers.

Linkage Diplomacy. A common practice in diplomatic relations among states, particularly during negotiations, to link one matter with another *quid pro quo* instead of considering each separately (e.g., in the SALT talks between the United States and the Soviet Union, matters considered were not only those of strategic arms limitation, but also peace in the Middle East, for example, and the role of each of the two partners in it). U.S. President Jimmy Carter stated on March 10, 1978, that America's contribution toward the Salt talks would be determined by what the Soviet Union did in Ethiopia and in Africa in general (heavy Soviet involvement in that area endangered America's interests). "The two are linked," stated President Carter, "because of actions by Soviets .... We don't initiate the linkage."

Linkage Function. Performed in Congress by aides and staff members who link legislators to other officials and persons outside the government structure.

Liquidity. That characteristic of "an asset which permits it to be sold at short notice with little or no loss in value. Ordinarily, a shorter term to maturity or a lower risk of default will enhance an asset's liquidity."

Literacy Test. See SCUM.

Little Home of Big Business. See DELAWARE CORPORATION.

Little Hoover Commissions. See HOOVER COMMISSIONS.

Little Ministry. A term often used to epitomize the power and the influence of some of the most powerful committees in the U.S. Congress (e.g. the Ways and Means and the Rules Committees in the House and Foreign Relations or Judiciary Committees in the Senate). See CONGRESS OF THE UNITED STATES, UNITED STATES HOUSE OF REPRESENTATIVES, UNITED STATES SENATE.

Little State Department. A nickname for the International Security Affairs Agency of the U.S. Department of Defense, which is responsible for the coordination of all international (mainly military) aspects of security in the United States and the Western democracies (e.g., the member states of the military alliances such as NATO). The agency, established by Robert McNamara, U.S. Secretary of Defense (1965-1972), often overlaps its activities with the U.S. Department of State—hence the name. See MILITARY-INDUSTRIAL COMPLEX.

Littoral Rights. See RIPARIAN RIGHTS.

Litvinov Plan. A grand design (by USSR's first foreign minister, Maxim Litvinov), to recruit disenchanted middle-class intellectuals, mainly university students, to work clandestinely against the capitalist system (mainly England, originally) in order to overthrow it and introduce socialism or communism of the Soviet kind. Famous Soviet spies include Kim Philby, Donald Maclean, and Guy Burgess (who, upon discovery by western intelligence services, sought refuge in Moscow), and Anthony Blunt, art curator for England's Queen Elizabeth II (who was granted pardon upon turning state's evidence). Litvinov first came to England after the armistice of 1918, as an unofficial representative of the new Russian state (socialist), married an English girl, Ivy Low, and through her extended his connection to British upper society, mainly the intellectuals in Cambridge and Oxford Universities. His main mission was to negotiate the exchange of prisoners of war with Winston Churchill, the pioneer of the undeclared war against Bolshevism.

Living Space. See LEBENSRAUM.

Living System. See RIO DE JANEIRO EARTH SUMMIT.

LMD. See LIBERATION MOVEMENT DJIBOUTI.

Load Line Convention. A multilateral agreement concluded in 1935 by thirty-six states, including the United States, for the purpose of promoting "... safety of life and property at sea by establishing ... uniform principles and rules with regard to the limits to which ships on international voyages may be loaded." The ultimate purpose of this agreement was to limit international competition in the loading of cargo vessels on international waters, and to keep the waterways free of congestion. See HIGH SEAS, INTERNATIONAL WATERS.

Loan-Sharking. See USURY.

Lobby. A person, group of persons, organization, group of organizations, foreign government or group of foreign governments joined in a coalition to influence the policies of a government, any one of its agencies or institutions or group of governments for some particular purpose. A lobby may have any one of the following aims, objectives or modus operandi: (1) single purpose (e.g., to prevent gun control legislation in which case it is characterized as "protective." If gun control passes, the gun ownership protection lobby, an "acquisitive" lobby, may seek to restore the original "rights" changed by such legislation). (2) multi-purpose, as in the case of a pro-gun-ownership lobby that may also aim at enhancing the interests of gun manufacturers or even the promotion of war. Any single lobby may therefore operate with different motives and try to influence different constituencies as its character and modus operandi changes.

Lobbying Act of 1946. A congressional law, which requires all lobbyists working for profit to register with either the Clerk of the U.S. House of Representatives or the Secretary of the U.S. Senate, depending on the chamber in which the lobbyist is planning to do the lobbying, and to report to them all financial transactions resulting from lobbying efforts (e.g., money paid for services to members of Congress or their staff, and/or money received—a rarity!). See LOBBY, Appendix 13.

Local and State Government Reorganization. See STATE AND LOCAL GOVERNMENT REORGANIZATION.

Local Government, Forms of. See FORMS OF LOCAL GOVERNMENT.

Local Option. An authority that may be granted by a state legislature in the United States to a local political subdivision (e.g., a county or a town) to hold a referendum (special vote) for the purpose of deciding some issue by the voters. See PERMISSIVE REFERENDUM.

Local Planning Commission. A local planning commission (for a county, city, or town) determines the details of how local needs are to be met within the framework of district and state planning processes. Members of local planning commissions also serve as Planning District Commissioners, completing the link between the agencies involved in the state development process. See PLANNING.

Local Politics. See WARD.

Local Redress, Rule of. See RULE OF LOCAL REDRESS.

Locarno Treaty. A contractual agreement that was entered into by Belgium, France, Germany, Italy, and the United Kingdom on 16 November 1925, whereby Belgium, France, and Germany were to maintain their existing borders and to abstain from the use of force against each other; Germany agreed to the demilitarized status of the Rhineland for perpetuity; and Italy and England were the guarantors that the treaty would be observed. The treaty was broken by Adolf Hitler of Nazi Germany in 1936 when Nazi troops occupied the Rhineland.

Locke's Contract Theory of Government. See ROUSSEAU'S COLLECTIVISM.

Locofocos. A nickname of the radical wing of the American Democratic Party in New York after 1835. This group came out in strong opposition to banks and paper money (soft money) after the credit and paper money collapse in 1819, favoring instead gold and silver (hard money) as a safe medium of exchange. The Locofocos, under the strong leadership of Thomas Hart Benton, viewed banking and paper money as the ultimate source of artificial wealth which had contributed to the emergence of an artificial inequality of wealth.

Locus of Sovereign Powers. See TYPE OF GOVERNMENT.

Lodge-Fish Resolution. U.S. Senator Henry Cabot Lodge, Republican of Massachusetts, and U.S. Congressman Hamilton Fish, Democrat of New York, introduced in 1922 a resolution in the U.S. Congress which repeated, word-for-word, the Balfour Declaration of 1917, calling for the creation of the State of Israel. The resolution was signed by U.S. President Warren Harding on 20 September 1922, and, later, served as the basis for the creation of Israel. See BALFOUR DECLARATION.

Lodge Reservation. Proceeding on the assumption that the entry of the United States into treaty obligations arising under the League of Nations Treaty of 1919 in Paris would involve the nation in an international alliance of uncertainty, U.S. Senator Henry C. Lodge of Massachusetts entered his opposition to that move on November 19, 1919, to the U.S. Senate, and again on March 19, 1920. As a result, the U.S. did not ratify that Treaty. See IRRECONCILABLES, LEAGUE OF NATIONS.

Log Rolling. The practice among legislators of granting mutual favors (e.g., trading votes or supporting each others' bills) as an "investment" for future favors—a quid pro quo. The term originated during America's pioneer days when timbermen would help each other roll logs. See POLITICS, SENATORIAL COURTESY.

Logic. A science of systematic reasoning which, according to Dr. Ernst Nagel, "seeks to evaluate the connecting links by whose means the flying movements of thought may become essential elements in the achievement of trustworthy beliefs"; it also "articulates the principles implicit in responsible critiques of cognitive claims", and "assesses the authority of such principles, and weighs the merits even of special postulates and intellectual tools that may be used in the quest for knowledge." The principal task of logic is "to make explicit the structures of methods and assumptions employed in the search for reliable knowledge."

Lok Sabha. See SANSAD.

London Agreement. Lancaster House agreement on Southern Rhodesia to ensure a free and fair election. Resolution 457 (1979), and 461 (1979).

London Club. An informal organization of the world's producers and exporters of nuclear energy and nuclear energy-related products, which meets periodically to discuss and design strategies for control of dissemination of nuclear materials. The member-states are: the United States, the Commonwealth of Independent States, England, France, the Federal Republic of Germany, Italy, Japan, India, Brazil, Argentina, Israel, Belgium, Sweden, and the Netherlands. During its 1977 meeting, the Club accepted a proposal submitted by the Soviet Union, that countries which use nuclear materials and devices accept the Club's safeguards and international inspections by the members of the Club, otherwise they will be denied these materials and facilities. See NUCLEAR TEST BAN TREATY.

London Economic Conferences. See ECONOMIC SUMMITS.

London Treaty of 1945. The W.W.II Allies—the United States, England, France, and the Soviet Union—agreed on August 8, 1945, during the London Conference of Foreign Ministers, to prosecute war criminals of Nazi Germany and militarist Japan. See WAR CRIMES.

Long, Hot Summer in America. See HOT SUMMER IN AMERICA.

Long March. The mass exodus of the Chinese Communist Party leaders and their People's Army under the leadership of Mao Tse-tung (1894-1976) and Chou En-lai (1898-1976) from the areas that were controlled by the Kuomintang Party of Chiang Kai-shek. The march commenced in November 1934, from Kiangsi, the center of Mao's operation, and ended in 1936, when the Communists settled in the territory of Shensi and in the northern portion of Kansu, with the capital in Yenan. It covered a total of 6,250 miles (approximately the round-trip distance between New York City and Los Angeles, California), and of the 100,000 men and women who had started the march in 1934, fewer than 20,000 survived. From Yenan, Mao's forces marched towards a final victory over the Kuomintang forces, which they defeated in 1949. They took over total control of mainland China on September 21, 1949. Chiang and his army fled to Formosa (Taiwan) and set up a republic there. See GREAT PROLETARIAN CULTURAL REVOLUTION, MAOISM.

Looking East. The Prime Minister of Malaysia, Mahathir bin Mohamad, urged his nation to "look East," towards Japan as a model to emulate and not to the United States or other Western states, particularly Canada and Australia. Another Asian leader, Singapore's former prime minister Lee Kuan Yew, also pointed out that the success of Tokyo has influenced the thinking of Asians to the point of readiness to abandon American ways of life and production, as well as the American political system which, in his opinion, has nothing to offer Asians. The Japanese are making every effort to influence the thinking of Asians so that they retain positive images of Japan not only as a leading political and economic power, but as an ally in the region. Japan obviously does not want to ever again experience isolation, as was the case in the so-called "ABCD Conspiracy," before and during W.W.II, when Japan felt isolated by the Western powers, mainly the United States and Britain. See AMERICA BASHING, JAPAN BASHING.

Loophole in Law. See JUDICIAL PRECEDENT.

Loophole Primary. See UNIT RULE.

Loser-Driven Industrial Policy. See GUIDED FREE ENTERPRISE.

Loss of Citizenship. See CITIZENSHIP.

Lot-Drawing Election. A manner in which a tie is broken between two candidates who receive an equal number of votes in a local election, in order to avoid a run-off election. In many local jurisdictions in the United States (e.g., towns, cities, and counties) which permit lot-drawing, the names of both candidates are placed in a box (usually supervised by the clerk of a circuit court) from which the election official (usually the chairperson of the local electoral board) will draw one name. The person whose name is so drawn, is declared legally elected for a given office. See VOTING.

Louisiana Purchase. The territory that was purchased from France in 1803 by the U.S. government under the administration of President Thomas Jefferson for the sum of 15,000,000 dollars (plus 7,000,000 dollars in interest) and embraced an area of approximately 830,000 square miles, stretching from the Gulf of Mexico, through the southwestern and midwestern states, to the borders of Canada. Before the transaction was concluded, Napoleon was informed that the land was really useless. "Nothing there, like Aca Nada" ("Canada" in the Spanish language), his informant told him, "few acres of snow." (That French informant never visited America in the summertime.) The land area embraced the present states of Colorado, Iowa, Kansas, Louisiana, Minnesota, Missouri, and parts of Montana, Nebraska, North Dakota, Oklahoma, South Dakota, and Wyoming.

Loya Jirga. See JIHAD.

Loyal Opposition. A term commonly applied to a political party (usually under a two-party system) which is out of office but which cooperates with the party in power without abandoning the desire to unseat it. (In England, for example, the party out of power may be referred to as "Her or His, as the case may be, Majesty's Loyal Opposition.") See POLITICAL PARTY.

Loyalist. One who is loyal and dedicated to a government and trusted by its leaders, regardless of the merits of the leadership and its policies. See CHAUVINIST, JINGO.

Loyalty Law. A series of presidential directives, executive orders, and legislative acts which demanded absolute loyalty from government employees. Along the lines of the Alien and Sedition Acts of 1798, and the "Red Menace Era" practices of the 1920s, U.S. President Franklin D. Roosevelt (1933-44) issued a directive which empowered the U.S. Civil Service to bar anyone from employment by the U.S. Government who was suspected of disloyalty. The first anti-sedition law in peacetime since 1798 was the Smith Act of 1940, or Alien Registration Act, which mandates that all aliens over 14 years of age register every January. On February 5, 1943, upon Roosevelt's Executive Order 9300, an interdepartmental committee of five was set up to recommend action on disloyalty cases of employees (except in the War and Navy Departments). On November 25, 1946, President Harry S. Truman (1944-1953), by Executive Order 9806, created a Temporary Commission on Employee Loyalty to recommend standards of procedure, legislation, and the removal of undesirable employees; to define standards of loyalty; and to provide standards for the protection of those accused of "pernicious political activity." In Executive Order 9835 of March 22, 1947, President Truman appointed the Loyalty Review Board which supervised the loyalty program. On August 20, 1950, when Executive Order 9835 expired after three years, the Summary Suspension Act was passed by Congress, which established penalties for violation of security rules. On September 23, 1950, Congress passed the Internal Security Act, the McCarran Act (U.S. Senator Pat McCarran), which gave department heads extensive powers to curtail free speech for national security reasons; then, in 1952, the McCarran-Walter Act (U.S. Senator Pat McCarran and U.S. Representative F. E. Walter) put extreme restrictions on immigration. On April 27, 1953, U.S. President Dwight D. Eisenhower (1953-1961) mandated the U.S. Civil Service Commission by an Executive Order to make sure that all employees of the federal government are "of complete and unswerving loyalty to the United States." With approximately 2.9 million employees, this is not an easy task to carry out, and, with the red scare gone, the Commission was allowed in 1977 to eliminate political loyalty questions from job applications. See ALIEN AND SEDITION ACTS, COMMUNIST CONTROL ACT OF 1954, HATCH POLITICAL ACTIVITIES ACT, JAPANESE INTERNMENT, KNOW-NOTHING, KU KLUX KLAN, McCARRAN INTERNAL SECURITY ACT OF 1950, SCUM, SUBVERSIVE ACTIVITIES CONTROL BOARD.

Lucrum Cessans. In the Latin language, "full or partial compensation awarded to an injured state." Also, a principle in international law, commonly recognized by civilized states, according to which an injured state may seek compensation for damages by either direct negotiations, an international tribunal of arbitration, or the use of good offices by a third party. See EXPROPRIATION, INTERNATIONAL LAW, NATIONALIZATION.

Lumpenproletariat. In Marxist parlance, the lowest echelon of the proletariat class (the workers who are illiterate, unskilled, and ignorant); those who do not possess any notion of proletarian consciousness or solidarity. See MARXISM.

Lvov Variant. In order to obtain hard foreign currency with which to buy Western technology and to pay off existing debts to the Western (capitalist) states, the Soviet Union gradually introduced capitalistic methods of production during the 1970s. (According to one Soviet production manager, "Marketplace demand must determine what we do in industry and how we do it," rather than the central planners and party ideologues.) Production was oriented toward quality rather than quantity, with the use of computerized quality control, consumer research, and assessment of market response—features virtually unknown to a socialist mode of production, though once suggested during the 1960s by Professor Liberman of Kharkov University, but then ignored. The main feature of the new drive for quality control to make Soviet products (virtually unavailable in the West) acceptable to consumers abroad was the system of capitalistic incentives which the Soviet rulers began to allow (e.g., better pay and housing to workers doing quality work). The main quality-production model (copied from a capitalistic model) was a shoe factory in the city of Lvov (hence the term, "Lvov Variant"). There, "barracks communism" (the use of communist ideology as an incentive to motivate workers to more and better work) was replaced with "income incentive" (better pay and housing for better production). The Lvov Variant brought good results and was duplicated in other industries throughout the Soviet Union. See LIBERMAN INCENTIVES, NEW ECONOMIC POLICY (NEP), TRANSFER TECHNOLOGY.

M

"Oh, East is East, and West is West, and never the twain shall meet."

RUDYARD KIPLING, 1865-1936

M-19 Movement. See APRIL 19 MOVEMENT.

Ma Fia. In the Italian language, "My daughter." See MAFIA.

Ma, Ma, Where's My Pa? .... Gone to the White House, Ha, Ha, Ha! Grover Cleveland (U.S. President 1885-1889 and 1893-1897) allegedly was the father of a child by a woman to whom he was not legally married; and, during the political campaign of 1884, his opponents, the Republicans, chanted a slogan designed to discredit Cleveland so that he would lose the election: "Ma, ma, where's my pa?" to which Cleveland's followers replied: "Gone to the White House, ha, ha, ha." The allegation of Cleveland being a father of an illegitimate child turned out to be true, but the presidential aspirant faced the fact courageously by explaining publicly that he and the mother of the child had mutually agreed long before the child was born, not to marry. His explanation was accepted and he went to the White House, not once, but twice. See PRESIDENTIAL DECISIVENESS, Appendix 16.

Maastricht Summit. The members of the twelve-nation European Community (EC) met in December 1991 in the city of Maastricht, the Netherlands (Holland), to streamline the procedure for transferring to a common, European market, to take effect in 1992. The major issues that were resolved were the political, economic, and monetary aspects of the union, which is viewed as being irreversible. The European Community, with about 345 million people, is the largest market in the world, and the free flow of goods and people will make the continent a major global power. The concept of a unified Europe—the United States of Europe—is becoming a reality. See COAL AND STEEL COMMUNITY, COMMON MARKET, EUROPEAN ECONOMIC COMMUNITY, Appendices 73, 73-B.

MAC. See MUNICIPAL ASSISTANCE CORPORATION.

MacArthur Constitution for Japan. Following the surrender of Japan to American (and Allied) forces at the conclusion of W.W.II, the Japanese military machine and some large monopoly enterprises were dismantled, but there was one almost invisible, hidden force that remained intact: it was the civilian bureaucracy. These were highly trained, experienced professionals in civilian government that proved pivotal to the revival of the greatness of contemporary Japan. That bureaucracy began rebuilding Japan and then passed on the legacy to the new generation which runs Japan today, and which established Japan in such a short period of time as a global power. Many students of contemporary Japan agree that the lack of such an able bureaucracy and strong central government would have prevented Japan from shaping a successful industrial policy. U.S. General Douglas MacArthur called upon Major General Courtney Whitney, head of the government section of the American forces, to prepare a guide for the Japanese. He produced one in six days and that became the Japanese Constitution. It was approved with minor changes by the Japanese on 22 February 1947 and was promulgated on 3 May 1947. The Japanese Constitution is not based on the American model, because the Americans and the Japanese knew that such model was not applicable to Japan. The Japanese constitution called a unitary and parliamentary typed of government and some of its provisions go beyond those to be found in the American Constitution, e.g., in addition to protection of all the rights and liberties of citizens, it includes the right to academic freedom, employment, and collective bargaining. Calling for a unitary rather than federal form of government, and a parliamentary rather than presidential system, it allowed for strong central government run by professional personnel selected on the basis of highly competitive examinations instead of appointments through the spoils methods, and allowed Japan to design an effective industrial policy.

Because Japan, geopolitically, was important to the protection of American interests in the area, since it is strategically situated in relation to America's principal Cold War adversary, the former Soviet Union, a strong Japan was highly desirable. America reversed its policy toward Japan from that of making it weak and insignificant, to that of allowing it to become a superpower. See COLD WAR ORPHAN STATE.

Machiavellian Leadership Style. A manner of managing people and events, in public or private life, characterized by deceitful, unethical, cold—blooded, selfish, and calculated methods, giving no moral consideration to other persons; a manner of management of leadership which holds that the end justifies the means. Named after Niccolo Machiavelli (1469-1527), political philosopher and author of *The Prince*, who lived in the state of Florence, now part of Italy. See Appendix 3-A.

Machiavellianism. Niccolo Machiavelli (1469-1527), Italian statesman and writer, author of *The Prince* (a treatise on the art and science of ruling a state), advocated the use of fear as an instrument of political and social control over the ruled, and justified the use of any means to achieve the desired end in ruling a political society. The ruler should be a fox and at the same time a lion; that is, flexible and humble when weak, decisive and ferocious when seeking to gain advantage over the adversary; and the ruler should be respected and obeyed rather than loved by his subjects. See POWER POLITICS.

Machine, Political. See POLITICAL MACHINE.

Machtstaat. In the German language, "power-state." See LEBENSRAUM.

Macro. On a large scale.

Macroeconomics. Approach to an analysis of the entire economy rather than any of its components; the economy considered on a large scale. Microeconomics, on the other hand, concerns itself only with some specific aspects that affect economy (e.g., marketing of products or behavior of consumers).

MacSharry's European Agriculture Plan. The European Economic Community introduced in 1992 many new laws, rules, and regulations. A European farm policy, of a more uniform nature than ever before attempted, was introduced by Ray MacSharry, the European Community Farm Commissioner. The plan calls for the lowering of subsidies paid to European farmers to avoid conflict with the European and international agreement under the General Agreement on Tariffs and Trade (GATT). The United States is a member of GATT; during 1990 and 1991, American agricultural products were largely kept off European markets because of unfavorable price arrangements. In the case of beef, Europeans refused to allow American beef to enter the European market on the grounds that chemicals used by Americans in raising beef posed a possible hazard to human life. See ATLANTIC PARTNERSHIP, EUROPEAN ECONOMIC COMMUNITY, EUROPEAN ENERGY CHARTER.

MAD. See MUTUALLY ASSURED DESTRUCTION, STRATEGIC ARMS REDUCTION TALKS (START).

Mafia. In tracing the origins and development of the secret organization, one must rely on some facts and more folklore. Allegedly a young girl in Sicily, when it was under French rule, was raped by a French soldier and the mother of the girl in desperation screamed: "My daughter, my daughter!" ("Ma fia, ma fia"). With the growing resentment of French presence, Guiseppe Garibaldi (1807-1882) came to Sicily in 1850 to recruit soldiers known as "the young ones" ("picciotti"); the more trusted among them, the "suitors" ("conoscenza"), were sponsored by their "godfathers." Soon the acronym for "Death to France, Italy cries out" ("Morte alla Francia, Italia anela") was created from the "My daughter, my daughter" phrase, and became a battle cry of the resistance movement. The insurgents took an oath of loyalty, "omertà," and, with time, the Social Union became a strong, highly centralized, father-oriented ("love thy father") organization of a number of families. In private and public life, the leaders of the families were known as "leaders of the leaders" ("capo di capi"); the lower echelon of advisers were the "capo consigliere" or "consigliere." (Among the many functions of the consigliere is to identify and to sponsor young men and a few women for university training as accountants, lawyers, managers, physicians, and other professions, who upon graduation will be employed in positions of trust in Mafia-owned or Mafia-operated legitimate and illegitimate enterprises.) The leaders, altogether, are commonly known as "mafiosos." With time, the organization spread outside Sicily, mainly to the United States where the immigrant population from Italy was facing rampant anti-Italian discrimination. (The pejorative name Italians are often called is "dago" or "wop.") The Mafia, once also known as the "Black Hand," dedicated itself to the protection of Italians. Then the Mafia engaged in all sorts of illegal practices ranging from loan sharking to racketeering, and illegal gambling. The term "Our Cause" (in the Italian language, "Cosa Nostra") was used. Information from the U.S. Justice Department, released in 1992, indicated that there are currently about twenty-two active Mafia "families" in America. Because the Mafia controlled the longshoremen unions in America during W.W.II, and because of its skill in eliminating undesirables by means of "extreme prejudice" (by contract or otherwise). Director of the FBI, J. Edgar Hoover (who never mentioned the name "Mafia" in public and never admitted that there was such an organization in America), deployed Mafia "soldiers" in catching Nazi, and after W.W.II, communist spies and saboteurs, in return for a fee or a favor or other kind of compensation. The Mafia organization was extensively used by the OSS and the U.S. Army intelligence in Italy during W.W.II, particularly in Sicily (the Mafia capital of the world), and some of its groups were on regular American intelligence payroll. According to author Rodney Campbell (*The Luciana Project: The Secret Wartime Collaboration of the Mafia and the U.S. Navy*), the Mafia was particularly skilled at helping Americans with agent penetration and order of battle of the Nazi German naval forces. The term "Our Cause" is used to characterize organizations with dubious aims, or that are rigidly controlled in great secrecy. A 1992 report by European law enforcement agencies indicated that the Mafia is actively engaged in an array of illegal enterprises, involving narcotics, extortion, and racketeering throughout Eastern Europe and the former Soviet Union, particularly on the "crime axis" of the Frankfurt-Berlin-Warsaw-Moscow line. Its 1992 profits are estimated to be around $18 billion.

Mafia Yuppies. See MUPPIES.

Mafioso. See MAFIA.

Mafish Hakuma. In the Arabic language, "ideal human condition." Also the prevailing philosophy and a desired way of daily life of the approximately eighteen different Bedouin tribes called "asilin." These Muslim nomadic herders of camels, goats, horses, and sheep, living in stone huts or tents, tolerate a bare minimum of government, but in recent years have rendered support to Arab and Muslim causes.

Magic. The code designation for the "Purple," a newer version of the Japanese "red machine," which allowed Americans to read Japanese diplomatic messages since 1935; and since 1940, provided good information on the Japanese order of battle, strategy, and tactics, as well as on war planes in the Pacific. The code was broken by America's most able cryptographer, William F. Friedman, once cryptanalyst on General Pershing's staff in France during W.W.I. MAGIC furnished advance information about Japanese plans for Midway, and on the flight of Admiral Yamamoto when he was shot down and killed. Speculations also persist that preparations for Pearl Harbor were known in advance to American military intelligence but that this information was either not taken seriously or was misrouted. Information not acted upon is useless. Like ULTRA, MAGIC also created many "heroes." Persons, civilian and military, who handled ULTRA and MAGIC decoded intelligence messages were required to sign secrecy documents. If information was revealed to an unauthorized person, that document also served as an order for liquidation "with extreme prejudice"—death, without judge or jury! See ENIGMA.

Maginot Line. A system of fortifications erected by France between France and Germany. The line, which extended along the French frontier from Luxembourg to Switzerland (about 450 miles long and costing approximately $450,000,000), was named after its originator, French Secretary of War André Maginot. The fortifications are currently for sale to the highest bidder, but to this day, they have not been sold.

Magistrate. A minor public official, elected or appointed, with judicial or executive powers (e.g., one authorized to try minor cases, pass arraignments, issue warrants, or exercise judicial control over police).

Magistrate Court. See MAGISTRATE.

Magna Carta. See MAGNA CHARTA.

Magna Carta Liberatum. When a group of party-controlled writers and journalists raised the demand in the early 1920s that all proletarian writing should have one aim—to serve—and that those who do not serve the cause of socialism and communism in Soviet Russia should be expelled from the society, the Central Committee of the Soviet Communist Party met in June 1925 specifically to consider this demand. The Central Committee decided that all writers are entitled to follow different literary forms and that they should not, as a result, be expelled from the socialist society (the Soviet Union). Hence, the name for that decision. This liberty, however, was withdrawn several years later; namely in 1927, when Josef Stalin, then the absolute ruler of the Soviet Union, decided to make all arts, written and performed, an instrument of the party and the state—an instrument of politics. Stalin then declared the era of "Socialist Realism" in all arts. See SOCIALIST REALISM.

Magna Carta of Civil Liberties. See PENDLETON ACT OF 1883.

Magna Charta. In the Latin language, "grand charter." Also the name of the document containing concessions granted by England's King John to his nobles (and large land owners), executed at Runnymeade on June 15, 1215. (The MAGNA CHARTA is considered one of the primary sources of modern constitutional law, for it contains provisions for the allocation of powers for the ruler and ruled alike.) See Appendix 4.

Mahan's Sea Power Theory. A geopolitical theory developed by U.S. Naval Officer Alfred Thayer Mahan (1840-1914), to the effect that a world power must also be a sea power. Mahan based his theory on the fact that Great Britain had achieved its global domination through the large navies and trading fleets which made her "Queen of the Seas." France, not a great sea power but rather a "land power," had difficulty countering British influence in Europe, as well as around the world. Napoleon Bonaparte once observed that if he could get control of the British Strait of Dover for only six hours, he would conquer the world. See GEOPOLITICS, Appendix 29.

Mahatma. In the Hindi language, "great soul." Also, the affectionate nickname of Karamchand Gandhi (1869-1948), which his followers bestowed upon him for his leadership in leading India to freedom from under the British yoke. Gandhi's most powerful slogan was: "Freedom is a gift of God and God's gift cannot be kept forever from his children." See SATYAGRAHA.

Maine Law of 1851. See LAW OF HEAVEN AMERICANIZED.

Majestas. In the Latin language, "sovereignty" or "independence." See SOVEREIGNTY.

Majlis. A form of welfare state democracy in the Kingdom of Saudi Arabia, whereby every day (except Thursdays and Fridays, the Muslim weekend holiday), the king and the members of his family meet with Saudi citizens to hear their wishes and complaints. Also, the Consultative Council of sixty trusted persons, created by King Fahd of Saudi Arabia, to advise him on important matters of state and politics.

Majlis al Nuwab. Chamber of Representatives, the legislative body, in Morocco (unicameral).

Majlis al-Sha'ab. People's Assembly, the legislative body, in Egypt, which is unicameral.

Majlis al Umma. The National Assembly, the legislative body, in Iraq, Jordan and several other Muslim countries.

Majlis ash Sha'ab. The unicameral People's Council, the legislative body, of Syria.

Majlis-e-Shura-e-Islami. The unicameral legislative body, the Islamic Consultative Assembly, of Iran.

Majlis Masyuarat Megeri. The unicameral legislative body—Legislative Council—of Brunei.

Major Capital Facility. Any structure or physical facility which has a pronounced areawide impact or intergovernmental effect on the implementation of policies for the development of a substate district. Areawide or regional significance might be defined to include projects which: (1) are located at or near the boundaries between local jurisdictions; (2) are part of an areawide system such as highways, rapid transit, or water and sewer facilities; (3) are of such magnitude as to establish new directions in the growth of the area or generate enough new activity to have a major impact on areawide systems of transportation or utilities; and (4) are related to the equitable or desired areawide distribution of such things as housing, employment, public services and public revenues.

Majority President. The President of the United States who receives the majority (fifty percent plus one vote) of the popular vote. Most presidents have been elected by a plurality vote and, therefore, they are often referred to as "minority presidents." See MINORITY PRESIDENTS, PLURALITY VOTE.

Majority Rule. See DEMOCRATIC THEORY.

Make Love, not War. See ANTI-VIETNAM WAR SLOGANS.

Make the World Safe for Democracy. See HOUSTON RIOT.

Make War on Poverty, not People. See ANTI-VIETNAM WAR SLOGANS.

Mala Fide. See BONA FIDE.

Maladministration. Poor and wasteful administrative procedures and practices.

Malapportionment. An unequal distribution of voters in electoral (congressional) districts. See APPORTIONMENT, ONE MAN, ONE VOTE.

Malayan Emergency. After decades of continuous guerrilla warfare, the leader of the Malay communists, Chin Peng, changed his heart and decided to surrender to the authorities together with his 10,000 man guerrilla army at the end of 1989. Since 1948, Chin had fought the British, the Fijians, the Gurhkas, the New Zealanders, and the Australians and, in spite of their superior forces, he was never defeated. In a gesture unprecedented for a communist guerrilla leader, Chin stated, "The peoples of the world are striving for peace and democracy"; he contributed to that cause by surrendering. Chin was also the leader of the Communist Party of Malaysia and his guerrillas operated throughout Thailand and Malaysia. Since 1948, about 15,000 persons had died in the struggle. Allegedly a very religious person, Chin Peng also demonstrated polite manners in dealing with his adversaries, and was often referred to as the "gentlemanly communist." Chin's about-face allegedly upset the communist leadership in China and in the former Soviet Union, which itself was on the verge of collapse.

Male Chauvinist Pig. Derogatory description of men who believe women to be inferior and not worthy of a position of equal status with men.

Malfeasance. An unlawful or improper administrative behavior of a government official. Misfeasance is an act that is performed in an improper manner, and which may be detrimental to another person. Nonfeasance constitutes the failure of a government official to perform the duties prescribed for the job, or as agreed upon.

Malinchismo. Word derived from Malinche, mistress of Hernán Cortés, conqueror of Mexico, also called Doña Marina. An intelligent native Indian girl who, knowing several native languages, was Cortés' interpreter with other Indian tribes in his Spanish conquest of various parts of Mexico. Contemporary Mexicans consider her a traitor. Today "malinchismo" signifies unfriendly feelings for foreigners who want to exploit Mexican riches with aid from untrustworthy Mexicans.

Malta Conference. See YALTA CONFERENCE.

Malthusian Law. See HUNGER WARS.

Malum in se. In the Latin language, "an offense in itself"; also, in law, any wrong action that is harmful (e.g., bodily injury, or theft). See MALUM PROHIBITUM.

Malum Prohibitum. In the Latin language, "prohibited offense;" also, in law, anything that is prohibited by law—by constitution, a statute, or common law—is legally wrong, although it may not be morally wrong. See MALUM IN SE.

Man's Mind, Once Stretched by a New Idea, Never Regains its Original Dimensions. See INTERNATIONAL COMMUNICATION AGENCY (ICA).

Man's Worst Crimes have Sprung from the Desire of being Masters, of Bending Others to Their Yoke. A statement by W. E. Channing (1780-1842), a Unitarian minister in New England, who considered all power, or the struggle for it, as the major source of all crime.

Managed Trade. Acknowledging the need for close collaboration between private business and government; Yasuchi Mieno, governor of the Bank of Japan, has pointed out, "Experience in Asia has shown that . . . the role of government cannot be forgotten." In Japan, the Ministry of International Trade and Industry assists private companies in reaching foreign markets. Japan can pride itself as an effective model of business-government cooperation for the benefit of the entire society. See GUIDED FREE ENTERPRISE.

Management. See LEADERSHIP, LEADERSHIP BY PULLING.

Management by Objectives. A joint decision by employee and employer (or a manager) to collaborate mutually in finding ways and means to perform certain tasks step-by-step in production or management—and to periodically discuss the progress for the purpose of improving the outcomes.

Management by Pushing. See MANAGEMENT BY PULLING.

Management of Things, Not of People. See MARXISM.

Mandamus, Writ of. See WRITS.

Mandate. The assumed granting of authority, by virtue of election, to an office holder to perform certain acts. Under the American political system, elected public officials are not necessarily bound to carry out in detail the divergent wishes of their constituents (recall petitions are, therefore, rare and difficult to accomplish), but may exercise their own judgment in policy formulation and implementation with the view of the overall interests of the constituents. U.S. Congressman Steven McGroarty of California expressed such independence of a legislator when he replied in 1934 to one of his persistent constituents: "One of the countless drawbacks of being in Congress is that I am compelled to receive impertinent letters from a jackass like you in which you say I promised to have the Sierra Madre mountains reforested and I have been in Congress two months and haven't done it. Will you please take two running jumps and go to hell."

Mandate of Heaven. In the secular civil religion and philosophy of Confucius of China (551-479 BC), one of the world's greatest social theoreticians and guides, the assertion is made that since every society has a hierarchical structure, rulers should be responsive to needs of the people; strive for harmony rather than division; reign, rather than rule, with secular piety—goodness and compassion in governing—because the mandate to reign comes from heaven, that is, from the people, and it should, therefore be exercised for the good of the people. A follower of Confucius, Mencius (371-289 BC), took the notion further, stating that once rulers adopt the way of virtue, people will spontaneously follow their lead without the need for brute force and compulsion. These notions permeate political philosophy, particularly leadership or statesmanship in many places around the world, but not always with great success due to the intensified competition among nations and within nations for naked powers; greed for wealth and need to subdue the ruled to the ruler's will. The teaching of Confucius and Mencius influenced the thinking of many European and American political philosophers and statesmen, especially Thomas Jefferson. His philosophy is also known as "Secular Piety."

Mandate Territory. See SOUTH-WEST AFRICA PEOPLE'S ORGANIZATION, TRUST TERRITORY.

Maneuver Warfare. See MILITARY REFORM MOVEMENT.

Manhattan Project. The code name given to the program in the United States that was developing and improving the atomic bomb eventually used on militarist Japan in Hiroshima and Nagasaki during W.W.II, bringing the war to an end. Proceeding on the basic data gathered by E. O. Lawrence (who built the cyclotron), scientists in the United States were able to develop the bomb in 1942. After over $2 billion had been spent, the bomb was tested on July 16, 1945, outside Albuquerque, New Mexico, and soon became a part of man's arsenal of destructive force, unprecedented in history. The bomb, which was developed in the strictest secrecy that America had ever experienced, enabled the United States to become an unquestionable world power and leader of the free world (which has altered the history of mankind). Ultimately America's problem will consist of not how and when to use this deadly weapon, but how and when to restrain itself from using it. An effort to undertake a research leading eventually to the release of atomic energy by fission had been undertaken in Nazi Germany during the early 1930s. It was intensified under Adolf Hitler, but due to persecution of Jewish scientists, many of them left Germany and settled in England or the United States where their talents were adequately deployed. Dr. Rudolf Peierls from Berlin, and Dr. Otto Frisch, from the Bohr Institute at Copenhagen, worked out a practical plan on the development and detonation of an atomic weapon. A letter prepared by Hungarian-born scientist, Dr. Leo Szilard and signed by Dr. Albert Einstein, was sent to U.S. President F. D. Roosevelt urging him to proceed with atomic research in order not to be overtaken by Hitler's scientists who were successful in splitting the uranium atom in 1938. Some other eminent scientists who were involved in the Manhattan project, were mostly refugees from Europe, including Dr. Kalus Fuchs from Germany (who later delivered atomic secrets to the Soviet Union in order not to give the United States a monopoly on the possession of this formidable weapon). See V-J DAY.

Manichean Doctrine. A Persian prophet (circa 216-276 AD), drawing on the teachings of Zoroaster, Buddha, and Christ, articulated the doctrine of eternal conflict between light and dark, good and evil. He laid early foundations for the equal right to worldly goods by anyone, including women, leading to major upheavals in Persia, Egypt, Greece and Rome where notions of equality and justice were either little known, understood or respected.

Manifest Destiny. A term commonly used after the annexation of Texas in 1845 to describe and justify America's westward territorial expansion and then later used to describe expansion in the Pacific Islands. This expansion was not looked upon as territorial conquest, but merely as a natural process associated with the growth of a modern state. The phrase was coined by John L. O'Sullivan, a journalist from New York City, who favored annexation of all lands surrounding the United States, including Cuba, Mexico, and Canada. See IMPERIALISM, LEBENSRAUM.

Manifesto. A formal proclamation of some objectives, principles, of philosophy, or of a program, and an appeal for its support (e.g., the *Communist Manifesto* by Karl Marx and Friedrich Engels issued in 1848 urging, "Workers of the World Unite!" You have nothing to lose but your chains!"). See MARXISM.

Mannerheim Line. A system of fortifications about 65 miles long, consisting of trenches and about 120 bunkers, on the Karelian Isthmus peninsula of Finland, designed by the commander-in-chief of the Finnish Army, Baron Carol Gustav Mannerheim (1867-1951), to deter Soviet aggression which commenced on 30 November 1939. Thousands of Soviet soldiers froze to death, delaying the Red Army's conquest of the eastern part of Poland which the USSR was to conquer and annex according to the Ribbentrop-Molotov Pact. The Line fell in 1940, but it had considerably weakened the Baltic forces of the Red Army.

Manslaughter. See INVOLUNTARY MANSLAUGHTER, VOLUNTARY MANSLAUGHTER.

Manslayer. A person who takes the life of another. See MANSLAUGHTER.

Maoism. The revolutionary doctrine of Mao Tse-tung (1894-1976), leader of the Communist Party of China and the People's Republic of China, 1949-1976, emphasizing reliance, for the purpose of socialist revolution, on the existing social forces (classes) in a society (peasants, in this case), instead of waiting for the emergence of the proletarian class which is created as a byproduct of industrial capitalism, as Marx has suggested. Mao claims that Marxism-Leninism does not provide all alternatives for a communist society, and that Marxism-Leninism "has in no way put an end to the discovery of truth." The struggle between that which is truth and that which is false, detrimental, and useless to a socialist society, constitutes the core of Mao's thinking and strategy. He realized that a correct paradigm for a socialist society has not been discovered as yet; that the task of communists is through analysis and expansion of man's cognitive abilities and skills to search for better ways of solving society's problems. Drawing on the rich heritage of ancient Chinese political culture, Mao does not claim to know, as the Soviet leaders seem to imply, for example, what the ultimate truth and the ultimate good are. He strongly believes that one should be constantly involved in searching for it, and that through proper utilization of one's intellectual processes, one will be able to recognize the truth when one sees it. In Mao's opinion, introspection, one's self-evaluation, and the desire to purge oneself from errors, will expedite the search for a good model of a just society. See EIGHT POINTS OF ATTENTION, CULTURAL REVOLUTION, HUNDRED FLOWERS, MARXISM, POWER COMES FROM THE BARREL OF A GUN, SINO-SOVIET SPLIT.

Maputo Summit on Rhodesia. See U.S.-BRITISH PLAN ON RHODESIA.

Maquiladora. Any one of the hundreds, and growing, manufacturing enterprises located on the Mexican side of the U.S./Mexican border, set up there due to cheap labor. Most are owned and managed by Americans. Their products are manufactured from raw materials and components shipped from the United States; ready products are shipped back to the United States, and the duty is paid only on the value that was added on the Mexican side. This arrangement is profitable to both the United States and Mexico: it provides employment for Mexicans in Mexico and slows the illegal influx of Mexicans to the United States where they not only compete with American labor, but put considerable strain on facilities, services, and entitlements, e.g., social benefits and schooling, which local political subdivisions must furnish. See CACTUS WALL.

March for Freedom. See WALK FOR FREEDOM.

March for Life. A coalition of individuals and groups, strongly supported by the Catholic Church, formed in 1972 for the purpose of battling all attempts to legalize abortion in the United States. The coalition proposes, among other things, an amendment to the U.S. Constitution (Human Life Amendment) which would forbid abortions on demand.

Mare Clausum. In the Latin language, "sea (or ocean) under the jurisdiction of one state" or "national waters."

Mare Liberum. In the Latin language, "open sea" or "international waters."

Maritime Law. A body of laws regulating navigation and shipping on navigable waters, including free access to navigable waters by all nations, according to the Paris Declaration of 1856. See CONSOLATO DEL MARE.

Market Economy. A system of economy (e.g., free enterprise system in a democratic society) whereby the consumer (the buyer and user of the product) determines the kind, quality, and price of the product. See POLITICO-ECONOMIC SYSTEMS, TYPES OF MARKET SYSTEMS, Appendices 83, 84.

Marshall Plan. A series of measures that were undertaken at the end of World War II to aid, militarily and economically, Greece and Turkey, who were threatened with takeover by communist forces aided by the Soviet Union. (The plan was first announced by U.S. Secretary of State George C. Marshall in 1947, and later was extended, within the framework of the "Truman Doctrine," to all nations of Europe which had participated in combating the Nazi forces. The Soviet Union and her East European satellite states refused to participate in the program on the grounds that they had no need for it supposedly due to "high prosperity" (the official explanation of the USSR and its satellite states). The $13 billion, four-year rebuilding program for nations devastated by the war (particularly those in Europe) was signed into law on April 3, 1948, and Ambassador A. Harriman became its administrator in Europe. Most European states have, thanks to the program, not only recovered, but have so strongly built up their economies that they have become serious competitors of the helper, the United States. During the implementation period of the program in Europe one could easily notice signs displayed in public places giving due credit to the United States for its assistance (e.g., a sign in a bakery window in Brussels, Belgium: "One-half of your daily bread is baked with Marshall aid!"). Once Europe had recovered, however, these signs were replaced in many places with new ones, such as "Yankee Go Home!" According to A. Harriman (see "Marshall Plan Is Recalled As Blocking Russian Move," *The Richmond Times Dispatch,* April 2, 1978), U.S. President Harry S. Truman (1944-1953), who in reality was the promoter of the Marshall Plan, decided to name it after the dedicated Secretary of State rather than call it the "Truman Plan," or claim it as a part of the Truman Doctrine. President Truman, according to Harriman, "decided it should be called the Marshall Plan because . . . he had almost a reverence for Gen. George Marshall." See Appendix 40.

Martial Law. The application of military laws and regulations to civilian populations, usually in a time of war or national emergency; or the control of a civilian population by military commanders.

Marxism. The teachings of Karl Marx (1818-1883), a German economic and political philosopher, author, and European correspondent for the *New York Tribune*, 1861-1864. He advocated, among other things, a communist society to be established by the working class (the proletariat) through violent and revolutionary means (socialist revolution); overthrow of the oppressive and exploiting capitalists (the bourgeoisie); and striving through class struggle toward a just, peaceful, stateless society of equals. As expressed in Marx's two major works, the *Communist Manifesto* and *Das Kapital* (Capital), capitalistic society is exploitative and, therefore, unjust. Capitalists feed on the labor of others, the workers, whom they exploit economically and politically by maintaining systems of social and political controls (namely, the apparatus of the state and its government) and by strict class division between the "have's" and the "have not's." Capitalists own capital and the means of production and distribution (e.g., factories and marketing outlets), and the workers own only their production skills (labor) which they exchange with the capitalists for wages that are designed in such a way that the worker never receives the full value of his productivity. He only receives a part, and the remaining part of the value which the worker's labor has produced (the surplus value) is the profit of the capitalist. As a result of such a system of exploitation, many become poor and a few get rich. The system cannot be rectified, Marx says, through legislation or parliamentary means, or even through bargaining among the employers and the employees, because the law of supply and demand regulates the labor market; therefore, a socialist revolution is necessary as the only means through which the capitalist economic base and the superstructure can be destroyed and a socialistic base be established, one that eliminates private ownership of the means of production and distribution. Marx justifies this on the basis of the study of stages of social development of society from the primitive communal society to feudalism, to capitalism, each of which is a superior and revolutionary stage; and so, he claims, is socialism or communism a superior and revolutionary stage that follows and challenges capitalism. Under socialism, according to Marx, people will manage things and not each other because the educational level and degree of consciousness will be so high that individuals will not be capable of exploiting each other. According to Marx's dialectical and historical analysis, world-wide socialist revolution is inevitable. Marx requires a large, class-conscious proletariat, an industrial proletariat for socialist revolution; in societies which lack such a proletariat because they lack the necessary industrial development, socialist revolution will not be possible. Lenin of Russia disagreed with Marx on this point, and a socialist revolution was accomplished with peasants and a small industrial proletariat; the same has happened in China where the poor peasants were the revolutionary force instead of an industrial proletariat. Intellectuals were viewed as the "head" while the workers as the "heart" of a socialist revolutionary movement. See CLASS CONSCIOUSNESS, CLASS STRUGGLE, COMMUNISM, MAOISM, SOCIAL SUPERSTRUCTURE.

Mashed Potato Circuit. The practice by public officials in the U.S. of going on speaking tours for the purpose of advancing their popularity among the electorate as well as earning additional income. (Some U.S. Senators and Congressmen were earning as much as $100,000 or more yearly from speaking engagements alone but a new legislation passed in 1991 does not allow that anymore.) Congress is considering legislation to put limitations on outside income by its members. The term was coined by Ronald R. Reagan (former movie star and former Governor of California) during his unsuccessful campaign to obtain the nomination of the Republican party for president in 1976. (The nomination went instead to Gerald R. Ford.)

Mason-Dixon Line. The boundary between free and slave states in colonial America as surveyed by Charles Mason and Jeremiah Dixon between 1763-1767. (The line followed the boundaries of Maryland and Pennsylvania.) See Appendix 107.

Mass Line. A claim by Mao Tse-tung and his followers, articulated mainly during the 1960's, that in order to maintain social and political control over the masses in the People's Republic of China, one must develop a two-way communication into a preceptoral system (persuasion on a person-to-person basis as means of control); develop a rule through education by which the communist "new man" is to rule himself rather than be ruled.

Mass Media. See FOURTH ESTATE.

Mass Party. A political party organization, the membership of which is open to anyone who in some way supports its causes, such as the Republican and the Democratic parties in the United States. Elitist parties, in which the memberships are restricted to persons who are deemed by the leadership to be worthy of membership (e.g., the Communist party of the former Soviet Union), maintain strict discipline and are selective in recruiting members. (For example, an agrarian party would prefer to have farmers instead of urban dwellers.)

Mass Society. Modern, industrial, urban society of the common man. The concept refers especially to a society marked by anonymity (loss of individuality), high mobility, and impersonal relationships.

Massachusetts Ballot. A type of ballot, similar to the Australian one, on which the names of the candidates are listed (in alphabetical order and with party designation) next to the offices which the candidates seek.

Massachusetts Plan. See URBANIZATION.

Massive Resistance. A term generally applied to mass opposition by a large number of Americans to forceful integration, especially to the policies of the federal government which aimed at integrating schools through busing of black children to predominantly white schools, and white children to predominantly black schools. See CIVIL RIGHTS ACTS, DIXIECRATS.

Massive Retaliation. A policy issued, following the Korean War (1950-1954), by John Foster Dulles, U.S. Secretary of State under the Eisenhower administration, to the effect that any act of aggression against the United States or any of its allies would provoke an all-out nuclear war against the aggressor, with massive deployment of American military forces. See FLEXIBLE RESPONSE.

Master Race. See LEBENSRAUM.

Mater Et Magistra. See ENCYCLICAL.

Material Fact. See CORPUS DELICTI.

Material Financial Interest. See CONFLICT OF INTEREST.

Material-Technical Base of Communism. According to the principal tenets of Soviet politico-economic philosophy, the USSR is currently in a transitory stage between socialism and communism, building a material-technical base for the arrival of communism. This is expected to emerge as soon as hostile, capitalistic encirclement and internal class struggle disappear through revolutionary wars among and within capitalistic societies and by the development of a high degree of communist consciousness, involving the changing of attitudes such as the still prevailing desire by individual persons to possess private property. See CAPITALISTIC ENCIRCLEMENT, CLASS CONSCIOUSNESS, CLASS STRUGGLE, MARXISM, SOVIET SOCIALISM.

Materialism. The practice of cherishing things of tangible, material value over those of spiritual nature. A desire to possess material goods as a basis of security, self-esteem, a feeling of power and importance. A materialist is one who subscribes to the notion that matter is the only tangible reality. In consumer (capitalistic) society easy credit, for example, encourages acquisition of material things. "Charge it—and feel like a king," proclaims an ad attempting to induce application for a credit card. The solons themselves have been accused of worshipping material goods over the well-being of the nation as a whole. U.S. Senator J. O. Eastland of Mississippi, for example, was a direct beneficiary of a law which he himself helped to legislate. He was paid $116,978 in 1968 by the federal government not to raise cotton, or simply to let the land be idle, while another federal program demanded millions from Congress for feeding the hungry under the War on Poverty program. Materialism is also the doctrine of Marxist communism, Marxism itself being economic determinism, claiming that all aspects of societal life are in the final analysis determined by material and not spiritual things. See MARXISM.

Materiel. All the implements that may be necessary to conduct a war, other than the manpower (e.g., weapons, tools, and other military supplies).

Mau Mau. A militant and terrorist organization, a secret society formed by the Kikuyu, Meru, and Embu tribes in Kenya between 1951 and 1960. Their main objective was to eliminate the influence of whites (Caucasians) on the political and economic life of Kenya through race war. This was the first open race war of blacks against whites in Africa in modern times.

Maverick Politician. One who is flamboyant in his political style, unorthodox, unusual, different from most; also, one who never follows a party line, but proceeds on his own; one who is doing things his/her way

May Laws. See KULTURKAMPF.

Mayaguez Incident. On May 12, 1975, the American Freighter *Mayaguez* was detained by Cambodian armed forces on international waters. Construing the incident as an act of piracy on the high seas, President Gerald R. Ford ordered her rescue, which was accomplished on May 15, 1975, at the cost of 31 killed and 50 wounded.

Mayflower Compact. Named for the ship which brought the Pilgrims to Cape Cod, Massachusetts, the Mayflower Compact (1620) instituted what is known as the civil body politic aimed at securing the common good by common consent. This consent, which, included the party of forty-one adult males of the Plymouth Colony, was one of the first foundations of direct popular government in America. Being a totalitarian model of government, it was not seriously considered elsewhere for adoption. The Mayflower document reads as follows: "In ye name of God Amen. We whose names are underwritten, the loyal subjects of our dread soveraign Lord King James, by ye grace of God, of Great Britaine, France & Ireland king, defender of ye faith &c. Haveling undertaken, for ye glorie of God, and advancemente of ye Christian faith and Honour of our king & countrie, a voyage to plant ye first colonie in ye Northerne parts of Virginia, doe by these presents a solemnly & mutually in ye presence of God, and one of another, covenant, & combine ourselves together into a Civil body politick; for our better ordering, & preservation & furtherance of ye ends aforesaid; and by vertue hereof to enacte, constitute, and frame such just & equall Lawes, ordinances, Acts, constitutions, & offices, from time to time, as shall be thought most meete & convenient for ye generall good of ye colonie: unto which we promise all due submission and obedience. In witness whereof we have hereunder subscribed our names at Cape-Codd ye-11-of November, in ye year of ye raigne of our soveraigne Lord King James of England, France & Ireland ye eighteenth, and of Scotland ye fiftie fourth. Ano Dom. 1620."

Mayor-Administrator Form of Government. See FORMS OF LOCAL GOVERNMENT.

Mayor-Council Form of Government. See FORMS OF LOCAL GOVERNMENT.

Mayor-Manager Form of Government. A type of local government, common in the United States, with an elected mayor (with limited executive powers) and an appointed administrative executive (with broad executive powers) who is responsible to the mayor.

MBFR. Mutual and Balanced Force Reduction.

McCarran Internal Security Act of 1950. A law that was passed by the U.S. Congress of September 23, 1950 (sponsored by U.S. Senator Pat McCarran), aimed at the curtailment of subversive activities in the United States, particularly by members of the Communist party of the United States, by such means as detaining persons suspected of subversive (communist-inspired) acts (including criticism of the United States government and its policies) without the benefits of *habeas corpus*. A substitute to the McCarran bill, proposed by liberal Democrats U.S. Senator Paul H. Douglas of Illinois and Harley M. Kilgore of West Virginia, called for an emergency detention plan and internment of persons suspected of subversion upon declaration by the U.S. President of an "internal security emergency." The substitute bill (labeled by the White House staff of President Harry S. Truman as "concentration camp" amendment) was not adopted. See COMMUNIST CONTROL ACT OF 1954, LOYALTY LAW, MCCARTHYISM, RED MENACE.

McCarran-Walter Act. See LOYALTY LAW.

McCarthyism. The practice of mass investigations and dismissals from employment of persons suspected of being communists or communist sympathizers. That practice, prevalent in the United

States during the 1950s, was initiated by a Republican Senator from Wisconsin, Joseph R. McCarthy, who accused the United States Department of State and the Department of the Army of harboring known communists, and the Democratic party of the United States, of "twenty years of treason." McCarthy promised to "sweep the communists out of government," but the manner in which he proceeded to achieve that objective offended many people, and Congress decided to censor him even though he was Chairman of the Senate permanent investigation subcommittee. See COINTELPRO, DIES COMMITTEE, LOYALTY LAW, RED MENACE.

McGovern-Frazer Commission. See COMMISSION ON PRESIDENTIAL NOMINATIONS.

McNamara Wall. A plan that was designed in 1965 under the leadership of U.S. Secretary of Defense Robert McNamara (1961-1969), to stop the spread of communism (particularly to stop the North Vietnamese and the Vietcong during the Vietnam War in Asia, 1954-1975) and to build a strong defense line across Asia which would be impenetrable by any force, at any time (a Maginot-type of defense line of permanent duration). The United States and its Asian allies were to man and to finance the "wall," which subsequently collapsed when it was attacked by the North Vietnamese and the Vietcong wearing rubber sandals and riding bicycles without tires.

Me Judice. In the Latin language, "in my opinion" or "in my judgment."

Me-Tooism. A term coined by U.S. Senator Barry M. Goldwater (R-Arizona) during the 1964 campaign when he ran for President on the Republican ticket, meaning that the nominee of each of the two political parties should clearly state his political philosophy and future programs so that the voters would be able to make a choice and be able to distinguish "between a liberal and a conservative philosophy," and so that each candidate would be a clear "choice, not an echo," and each individual voter could say, "Count me, too." Goldwater was defeated at the polls by Democrat Lyndon Baines Johnson, the incumbent President, when his forces succeeded in labeling Goldwater as a "war hawk." The irony was that it was Johnson and not Goldwater who was the hawk.

Media Steroids. Term used by former U.S. President Richard M. Nixon, who stated in 1992 that controversial, unpopular, and/or weak political candidates rely on exposure through the media to increase their importance and to gain voter attention. Continuous media exposure—for which candidates are coached and trained by their advisers and public relations specialists, so-called "image makers"—"beefs up" their stature and projects them to the voters as valuable candidates for whom they ought to vote.

Mediation. The manner by which a conflict or disagreement between two (or more) parties to a dispute may be settled, usually by a neutral third party. See ARBITRATION, CONCILIATION, GOOD OFFICES.

Medicaid. See MEDICARE.

Medicare. A program in which the U.S. Government participates by financing health care with hospitalization benefits for persons sixty-five or older who are eligible for such assistance under the social security insurance. This program was authorized by the Social Security Act of 1965 as a supplement to the original Social Security Act of 1935. Medicaid is a separate federal-state health assistance program designed for low-income persons and/or those who are receiving public assistance (e.g., the unemployed).

Medicine Ball Cabinet. In addition to his regular cabinet, U.S. President Herbert Hoover (1929-1933) surrounded himself with a circle of men, composed mainly of conservative businessmen (e.g., Andrew W. Mellon), who were to advise him on business matters in order to "cure" the American economy in the midst of the Depression and to restore confidence in his administration and the business community. This was a kitchen-type cabinet that many Presidents organize in order to get additional input and advice on policy matters.

Mediocracy. An unflattering term often applied to civil servants who no longer perform up to the expected standards of efficiency, but who may not be easily dismissed from employment because of protection by civil service laws or a seniority system. See MERIT SYSTEM.

Meech Lake Accord of 1987. An agreement between Canada's central government and the Province of Quebec, reached in 1987, whereby Quebec, as a reward for not withdrawing from the confederation and establishing itself as a sovereign, independent state, would be granted special status as a "distinct society," primarily due to the fact that Quebecans speak French rather than English. The special status of Quebec would be guaranteed constitutionally. Three of Canada's ten provinces, Manitoba, New Brunswick, and Newfoundland, opposed granting Quebec any special treatment on the grounds that such special status would give Quebec too much power. A referendum in 1990 rejected by a 60 percent vote the separation of Quebec from the confederation, as advocated by the Parti Quebecois. See PARTI QUÉBÉCOIS.

Meet the People Trip. U.S. President Jimmy Carter initiated the program of "meeting the people" by first appearing in Clinton, Massachusetts, on March 5, 1977, speaking to traditional town meetings. "I want the American people," said President Carter, "in three or four years, not to look at the federal government as an enemy, but as a friend." In addition, he also initiated the practice of "Presidential call-ins" conducted with the aid of a radio system. The first such call-in was held on March 3, 1977, in the White House, and was moderated by Walter Cronkite, anchorman from CBS TV. During the call-in, the President took 42 questions from persons in 26 states, on a variety of topics. This populist practice was well received by the public. See PERK MAN.

Megalopolis. In the Greek language, "large city." Also, the notion, based on the rapid urbanization of America, that if the trend of growth continues, one day there will be one large city along the East Coast of the United States, stretching from Maine to Florida, and another one on the West Coast, stretching from the state of Washington to the borders of Mexico. Boswash, for example, would constitute a single community under one jurisdiction, stretching from Boston, Massachusetts, to Washington, D.C.; Pitsnor—Pittsburgh, Pennsylvania, to Norfolk, Virginia; and Sansea—San Francisco, California, to Seattle, Washington.

Meiji Constitution. A law instituted in 1889, under which an elective lawmaking body (the diet or parliament) was set up in Japan under the leadership of the Japanese Emperor. (That law was replaced in 1947 with a modern constitution.) Following the collapse of the Tokugawa Shogunate and the restoration of Emperor Meiji in 1868, commenced the new era in the life of that great nation. One of the principal founding fathers of modern Japan, a statesman and future prime minister, was Ito Hirobumi. In 1870, he went on a voyage in search of a good constitution, and after studying the American model with the assistance of U.S. Secretary of State. Hamilton Fish, Ito was not impressed. The American model provided little for the formation and maintenance of stable government, allowing for diversity and free play by the strong at the expense of the weak. The model to copy was found in Berlin, and Otto von Bismarck was a generous host to Ito. Ito was impressed with the Lorenz von Stein concept of a "social monarchy," free of unchecked individualism and responsive to the need of the masses. As a result, the Meiji Constitution that was at last adopted in Japan in 1881, took almost verbatim forty-six provisions of the seventy-one in the German Constitution. In 1886, Ito outlined his model of government in his "Five Chapters on Governmental Reorganization" in which he placed emphasis on official responsibility of the bureaucracy, discipline, and economy and efficiency. The civil service system of examination adopted in 1888 was also based on the Prussian model.

Members of Congress for Peace Through Law. See CONGRESSIONAL CAUCUS.

Memorial. A grass-roots movement in the former Soviet Union, particularly in the Russian and the Ukraine republics, organized by people of good will in 1990 to reveal all crimes of the Soviet regime since the time of Joseph Stalin (1924-1953), and to honor those who lost their lives under that terror. This includes about 6,000 Polish officers, killed in a mass execution in 1940. The officers fled to the Soviet Union for protection during the advance of the Nazi German forces after the conquest of Poland in 1939. In the wooded lands of Katyn, the Russians erected a monument to memorialize the massacre of the Polish officers. See KATYN MASSACRE.

Memory. See PAMYAT.

Mending Fences. A term often used in practical American politics to describe the activities of a politician who is, first and above all, looking after the interests of the constituency (or a district) from which he was elected and which he represents. In the case of the U.S. President, whose constituency is the entire electorate of the nation, he is said to barnstorm or to barnhop from one community to another, including foreign countries (where the power elites are also his constituency), in order to gather and to sustain the necessary support for his policies. See BARNSTORMING, POLITICAL CAMPAIGN, PRESIDENTIAL ELECTORS.

Mens Legis. In the Latin language, "the spirit of the law."

Menshevik. In the Russian language, "member of a minority." Also, a member of the Russian Social-Democratic Workers party who opposed the revolutionary faction of Vladimir I. Lenin known as the Bolsheviks (in the Russian language, "majority"). See BOLSHEVIK.

Mercantilism. Between the 16th and the 18th centuries the main European powers (e.g., France, England, and Spain) sought to strengthen their economies in order to achieve autarky, through such measures as strict regulation of wages, prices, and conditions of labor, and by controls over imports and exports to retain more wealth at home. See EUROPEAN ECONOMIC COMMUNITY, ECONOMIC SUMMITS, Appendices 73, 73-B.

Merchants of Death. See ARMS SALES AND HARDWARE DIPLOMACY.

Merit System. The practice of selecting persons for employment in the government on the basis of qualifications and ability as determined by examination rather than other criteria such as personal friendship, party affiliation, or as a reward for support given a politician in an election—known as the spoils system. See PENDLETON ACT OF 1883.

Meritocracy. A political system under which the government is run by persons of merit. See MEDIOCRACY, MERIT SYSTEM.

Message of the State of the Economy. See PRESIDENT'S MESSAGE ON THE STATE OF THE ECONOMY.

Message on the State of the State. See STATE OF THE STATE MESSAGE.

Messenger of the Satan. See EASTOXIFICATION.

Messianic Determinism. A term often applied to the Marxist-Leninist model of a classless society. See ECONOMIC DETERMINISM.

METO. See MIDDLE EAST TREATY ORGANIZATION.

Metropolitan Area. The aggregate of a large city and its surrounding communities, such as smaller cities, towns, boroughs, villages.

Metropolitan Federation. A type of special government set up for the purpose of rendering some specific service to several units of local government which these governments, separately, would not be able to provide for themselves (e.g., air and water pollution control, sanitation, or fire prevention). This type of government performs only functions specifically assigned to it and in no way interferes with other local governmental functions.

Metropolitan Government. A form of centralized government embracing several smaller jurisdictions, usually a core city and adjacent suburbs. (Dade County and Miami, Davidson County and Nashville, and Marion County and Indianapolis, are places where such form of government has been the most successful.) There are about 480 such metropolitan governments in the United States today. Traditionally, jurisdictional division does prevail in most of the United States except where the so-called councils of government were introduced (e.g., the Metropolitan Washington Council of Governments composed of the core city, Washington, D.C. and neighboring jurisdictions, such as Montgomery County, Maryland). While a metropolitan government is unified and centralized, metropolitan councils work jointly only on issues of common interest (e.g., transportation matters— in which the Washington experience was the most successful) but retain their own governmental structures, jurisdictional rights and powers. Metropolitan government is centralized and unitary, while metropolitan councils of governments are decentralized and confederate. The argument against metropolitan government is that it tends to weaken the right of people to self-government, a cornerstone of American democracy.

Metropology. The study of metropolitan areas.

Mexican Cession. Refers to lands ceded to the U.S. by Mexico in 1848, embracing the present state of Nevada and parts of Utah and California. See GUADALUPE-HIDALGO TREATY OF 1848.

Mexico City Declaration. See INTER-AMERICAN CONFERENCE ON PROBLEMS OF WAR AND PEACE.

MFS. See MINISTERIUM FÜR STAATSSICHERHEIT.

MGB. See MINISTRY FOR STATE SECURITY.

MI-5. See SECRET INTELLIGENCE SERVICE.

MI-6. See SECRET INTELLIGENCE SERVICE.

Mick. A pejorative term for one of Irish descent, particularly a Catholic. Also called "bog-hopper."

Micro. On a small scale.

Microeconomics. See MACROECONOMICS.

Microstate. A sovereign state of small territory which usually depends for its survival (political and economic) on the good will of its neighbors (e.g., Gambia, Luxembourg, or Lesotho).

Mid-Term Election. See UNITED STATES HOUSE OF REPRESENTATIVES.

Middle America. See SILENT MAJORITY.

Middle-Class. See ECONOMIC EQUITY.

Middle East Institute. See ARAB LOBBY.

Middle East Treaty Organization (METO). An informal mutual defense alliance that was formed by the United States (personally by the U.S Secretary of State, John Foster Dulles) in 1956 as a deterrent to communist aggression in the Arab states. Also known as the "Baghdad Pact"; its members were: England, Iran, Iraq, Pakistan and Turkey. The U.S. was not a member, but Dulles justified the need for it as follows: "Many of the Arab League countries are so engrossed with their quarrels with Israel or with Great Britain or Greece that they pay little heed to the menace of Soviet Communism." The alliance remains virtually inactive.

Middle Eastern Settlement. See SADAT-BEGIN SUMMIT.

Middle-of-the-Road. A term often used in practical politics to describe the position or stand that one may take on important issues by avoiding extremes; or a philosophy that is neither too radical nor too conservative. See CENTER.

Middle Peasant. A small farmer who produces enough to sustain himself and his family, and one who neither hires labor nor is available for hiring.

Middle-Range Theory in Political Science. See POLITICAL THEORY.

Middle-Way Socialism. Term applied to countries with a mixed socialist—capitalist economy, e.g., Sweden, Denmark, and Holland, where employees pay high taxes so that the state in turn can furnish them with social benefits, e.g., education, medical care, and other benefits not provided to that degree anywhere else on earth. Also a term for welfare state, or cradle-to-grave welfarism.

Midnight-Climax. See COUNTERINSURGENCY IN AMERICA.

Midnight Judges. As an act of political payoff, U.S. President John Adams (1797-1801), a Federalist, appointed about 80 new judges during his last hours in office in 1801. The incoming administration of

Thomas Jefferson (1801-1809), an anti-Federalist, refused to honor these commitments and to deliver the instruments of appointment (commissions) to the appointees. The matter was taken to the U.S. Supreme Court which ruled in *Marbury v. Madison* (1803) that the acts of an outgoing administration do not have to be honored by the incoming administration. Further, John Marshall, the Chief Justice, established in this case the doctrine of judicial review; that is, that the Supreme Court of the United States has the right to review the constitutionality of laws and executive decisions. Appointments made late in the term by a lame duck president are known as "midnight appointments." See Appendix 48.

Midnight Pardon. See TREASON.

Mighty Dollar Era. See ROARING TWENTIES.

Mijlis-e-Shoora. The bicameral Federal Legislature of Pakistan.

Militarism. The practice of worshipping military virtues, ideals, or traditions; the subordination of civilian activities (including the control of the government) to those of the military establishment; and/or a state in which the military establishment is dominant and one that is involved in constant aggressive activities. See MILITARY-INDUSTRIAL COMPLEX.

Militaristic State. A state in which the institutions and policies of the government are dominated by the military establishment and one which usually pursues aggressive aims. In ancient times Sparta and Rome were typical militaristic states, as well as Nazi Germany and Japan during the 20th century until their demise in World War II.

Military Commission. See SADAT-BEGIN SUMMIT.

Military Doctrine. See ORDER OF BATTLE.

Military Government. See JAPANESE INTERNMENT, JOHNSON PROCLAMATION.

Military-Industrial Complex. A term used by U.S. President Dwight D. Eisenhower in his farewell address (January 1961) to describe the close inter-relationship between the industrial power and the military establishment in the United States, two forces which were, in his opinion, working closely together—often to the detriment of the overall interests of the nation. The President warned the American public by saying: "Only an alert and knowledgeable citizenry can compel the proper meshing of the huge industrial and military machinery of defense with our peaceful methods and goals, so that security and liberty may prosper together." The collusion between the military establishment in the United States and the industrial complex is often referred to as "military socialism" or "Pentagon capitalism," depending on who makes the characterization. See AMERICAN SECURITY COUNCIL, ARMS AND WAR MATERIEL SALES, HARDWARE DIPLOMACY.

Military Junta. See JUNTA.

Military Justice is to Justice as March Music is to Music. See JAPANESE INTERNMENT.

Military Oversight. See JOHNSON PROCLAMATION.

Military Preponderance. An official doctrine of the CPSU and the Soviet Government according to which a socialist state, like the USSR, will survive and become stronger only if it maintains a strong military posture. According to the Soviet newspaper *Pravda* (the Truth), such military preponderance must be made visible to the outside world which "will permit the USSR to transform the conditions of world politics and determine direction of its development." In the United States an organization emerged several years ago, the Committee on the Present Danger, which works on mobilizing public opinion and influencing the federal government toward a joint effort for combating the Soviet military superiority, mainly through the development of modern weapon systems. See COMMITTEE ON THE PRESENT DANGER.

Military Reform Movement. Selected members of the U.S. Congress gathered at the U.S. Military Academy at West Point, New York, on 2 June 1982, in order to reappraise the military doctrines of the United States and the NATO countries. The assertion, by one group, was that the concept of "attrition warfare" is outdated and should be substituted with "maneuver warfare," and the "forward defense" concept, widely popular among the NATO members of Europe, should be abandoned. Following the gathering, the U.S. Army modified its doctrine in favor of the "Air-Land Battle" concept, a concerted effort by various strategies and weapon systems deployed on the battle field. The strategy was deployed during the 1991 Persian Gulf War and, is said to have been effective. The gathering is also known as the "Reform Caucus."

Military Socialism. See PENTAGON CAPITALISM.

Military Strategy and Force Posture Review. A 117-page study released by the U.S. Government January 5, 1978, that was prepared for U.S. President Jimmy Carter with his input, which reassesses the world's military balance of power and contains some directives for strengthening U.S. defense posture. The study asserted, among other things, that: (1) the Soviet Union was strong in conventional forces (e.g., infantry, conventional artillery, tanks, airplanes, and battleships); in case of conventional warfare it would probably gain advantage over the United States and its allies on land, particularly in Western Europe and the Far East, but it could not win a final victory due to superiority of American and allied forces in strategic warfare (e.g., nuclear weapons, airpower and sea-power equipped with weapons with advanced guidance systems); (2) in assessing the possible impact of a major nuclear war between the two superpowers (USA and USSR), the United States could suffer 140 million casualties and the Soviet Union 113 million, allowing for smaller population density in the Soviet Union; (3) three-fourths of the economies of both nations could be destroyed; and (4) in the end, there would be no victor (Pyrrhic victory). The United States is, therefore, shifting emphasis to conventional forces, which were strengthened in Europe in 1978 by an additional 7,000 combat troops in order to discourage possible conventional war there. See PENTOMIC ARMY.

Millions for Defense, But Not One Cent for Tribute. See XYZ AFFAIR.

Minaret. See COUNTERINSURGENCY IN AMERICA.

Mini Convention. See PARTY CONVENTION.

Mini Dragons. Also known as the "four tigers;" the newly-emerged powerful economies of the once impoverished states of Hong Kong, South Korea, Singapore, and Taiwan (Formosa). These are the Newly Industrialized Economies (NIEs) of the Pacific Rim once controlled by Japan.

Minifundium. A medium sized farm (e.g., 10-40 acres) that is owned by an absentee landlord but cultivated by a tenant-farmer who pays for use of the farm and very often also votes according to the wishes of the landlord. Common in Latin America as one medium of social control. See LATIFUNDIUM.

Minination. A small (in area and population), sovereign, independent state.

Mini-President. See GOVERNOR.

Ministate. See MININATION.

Minister. A cabinet-rank government official (e.g., one heading a ministry or a department); also a diplomatic officer heading a legation. See CABINET GOVERNMENT, DIPLOMATIC RANK.

Minister President. An official designation of either the prime minister or the premier under some political systems, or the chief executive officer of a regional government within a federal state (e.g., the chief executives of the Länder governments in the Federal Republic of Germany).

Minister Without Portfolio. A government official of cabinet rank (e.g., minister or secretary) who is heading no particular department or ministry. See MINISTER.

Ministerium für Staatssicherheit. The Ministry for State Security of the German Democratic Republic (East Germany), which also conducted external intelligence activities and worked closely with all communist parties and front organizations (at home and abroad) that worked toward the advancement of communist societies. Similar ministries existed in all the socialist (communist) states. The officials of the ministry had almost unlimited powers at their disposal to deal with anti-state, anti-communist elements, including the right to arrest and detain in disregard of due process and *habeas corpus*.

Ministry for State Security. See MINISTERIUM FÜR STAATSSICHERHEIT.

Ministry of Internal Security (MVD). In the Russian language, "Ministerstvo Vnutrnygh Dyel." A cabinet-level agency charged with control of the police forces and internal security of the state in the USSR. (The agency was also involved in collection and evaluation of intelligence data on all internal security matters.) It was divided in 1991 into separate agencies among the Commonwealth of Independent States. See MINISTRY OF STATE SECURITY (MGB), PEOPLE'S COMMISSION FOR INTERNAL AFFAIRS (NKVD).

Ministry of International Trade and Industry (MITI). See GUIDED FREE ENTERPRISE, KYOIKU MAMA.

Ministry of State Security (MGB). In the Russian language, "Ministerstvo Gosudarstvyennoy Bezopatchnosty." A cabinet-level agency of the former USSR, charged mainly with the external security of the state (the collection and evaluation of foreign intelligence) through overt and covert means. See PEOPLE'S COMMISSION FOR INTERNAL AFFAIRS (NKVD).

Mink Dynasty. See FIVE PERCENTERS.

Minority President. A President of the United States who is elected without majority of the popular vote. Minority Presidents were:

President	Election Year	Percent of Popular Vote	Party
John Quincy Adams	1824	30.6	Dem.-Rep.
James Knox Polk	1844	49.7	Dem.
Zachary Taylor	1848	47.4	Whig.
James Buchanan	1856	45.6	Dem.
Abraham Lincoln	1860	39.8	Rep.
Rutherford Birchard Hayes	1876	48.4	Rep.
James Abraham Garfield	1880	48.3	Rep.
Grover Cleveland	1884	48.6	Dem.
Benjamin Harrison	1888	47.9	Rep.
Grover Cleveland	1892	46.4	Dem.
Woodrow Wilson	1912	41.9	Dem.
Woodrow Wilson	1916	49.3	Dem.
Harry S. Truman	1948	49.5	Dem.
John Fitzgerald Kennedy	1960	49.5	Dem.
Richard Milhous Nixon	1968	43.4	Rep.
James Earl (Jimmy) Carter	1976	48.1	Dem.

All other presidents received the majority of popular vote. See ELECTORAL COLLEGE, MAJORITY PRESIDENT, Appendix 16.

Miracle on the Vistula. When the Red Army of the Soviet Union attacked the newly-restored Polish republic in 1919, the outnumbered Polish Army was able to take the city of Vilna in Lithuania on 19 April 1919, and Kiev, the capital of the Ukraine, on 8 May 1920. The Soviet Army was defeated by the Poles around the city of Warsaw, the capital of Poland, on 26 June 1921, and the Soviets agreed to peace negotiations and to a treaty which was signed subsequently in Riga. The Polish Army under the command of Marshal Josef Pilsudski (1867-1935), who was nominated in November 1918 by the Polish Regency Council to be the leader of Poland, was small but well organized; two of its other commanders, General Josef Haller (1869-1934) and General Wladyslaw Sikorski (1881-1943), had had international combat experience. This was the first and only time in the history of the Soviet Red

Army that it was defeated by a smaller army; the Red Army had a superiority of ten Soviet soldiers to one Polish soldier.

Miracle Rice. See HUNGER WARS.

Miranda Card. In 1966 the U.S. Supreme Court ruled (in *Miranda v. Arizona*) that before a person is interrogated as a suspect of a crime, he must be informed of his legal rights. These rights are: (1) the right to remain silent; (2) the right to an attorney of one's choice (persons unable to pay fees will have one appointed for them by the court), and (3) the right to know that any statement one makes during such an interrogation may be used as evidence in court. All officers of the law with arresting powers (e.g., police officers and sheriffs) carry cards from which they read to the person to be arrested the statement of these rights. See Appendices 48-51.

MIRV. See MULTIPLE INDEPENDENTLY TARGETED RE-ENTRY VEHICLE.

Miscegenation Law. A law forbidding interracial marriages. (In the United States such laws were declared unconstitutional by the U.S. Supreme Court in 1967.)

Misdemeanor. A crime for which capital punishment may not be inflicted; or an infraction calling for a fine or short term imprisonment.

Misery Index. See HUMAN FREEDOM INDEX.

Misfeasance. See MALFEASANCE.

Missile Technology Control Regime (MTRC). Under the arrangements of the Nuclear Non-Proliferation Treaty, the major global powers which possess nuclear weapons and nuclear capabilities, agreed to control the distribution of that technology and to limit the sale of missiles and other related weapons to non-nuclear powers, thus maintaining control over the proliferation of destructive weapons. Most of the major powers have signed the Nuclear Non-Proliferation Treaty, including the former Soviet Union, the United States, and the People's Republic of China. Because of fear that nuclear scientists in the former Soviet Union might seek employment elsewhere, the United States and the Russian Republic signed an agreement on 5 March 1992, whereby over 100 Soviet nuclear scientists will be employed by American firms working on peaceful uses of nuclear energy. This includes nanotechnology (design and production of miniaturized, atom-size engines and other mechanical devices). The scientists will stay and work in their own facilities in Russia and in the other states of the Commonwealth of Independent States. Their starting salaries were set at $65.00 per month.

Missionary-Type Political Party. A political party that is more interested in converting the electorate to a particular political philosophy than in winning elections (e.g., the American Socialist, Communist, and Prohibition parties in the United States).

Mississippi White Knights. A coalition of individuals and organizations of the Caucasian race who were dedicated to white supremacy, and were struggling against civil rights legislation, participation by non-whites in politics and government, and federal interference with states' rights. It was established in 1960 in Jackson, Mississippi, and spread throughout the Southern states of the United States. Its main target was the Black Panther Party, a black-nationalist movement. See KU KLUX KLAN.

Missouri Plan. An elaborate plan according to which judges have been selected to a state court in the state of Missouri since 1940. First, a commission (of lawyers and laymen) compiles a list of persons suitable for judgeships and forwards it to the Governor of the state, who in turn selects from the list persons he wishes to appoint. Second, the persons so appointed by the governor serve in their judicial capacity for a short period of time (usually six months, or until the next election held in the state), and if confirmed by the voters, they are retained in their positions. This manner of electing judges was first proposed by the American Judicature Society in 1913, and has since been introduced in Alaska, Kansas, and Nebraska. Many other states (e.g., California) introduced this plan, with some variations. See JUDICIAL ELECTION.

Mistake Forward. See JACKSONIAN DEMOCRACY.

Mister Attorney General. See MISTER PRESIDENT.

Mister Chief Justice. See MISTER PRESIDENT.

Mister Democrat. A distinguished leader of the Democratic party in the United States who, after decades of continuous and dedicated service to the party as well as to the nation, comes to be referred to as "Mister Democrat." U.S. President Franklin D. Roosevelt (1933-1944) was referred to as "Mister Democrat" and also as the "Happy Warrior." He wrote a book under the same title—*The Happy Warrior.* During the past several decades, that honorable designation was given to the U.S. Senator of Minnesota, Hubert Horatio Humphrey (1948-1978), once a pharmacist, a political science professor, Mayor of Minneapolis, Minnesota (1945-1948), Vice President of the United States (1965-1969), and a nominee of the Democratic party for the presidency (1968). Humphrey was instrumental in materializing the following programs and legislation: the Peace Corps, the U.S. Arms Control and Disarmament Agency, Medicare, Medicaid, the Civil Rights Act of 1964, and the Humphrey-Hawkins Full Employment proposal of 1977, which was passed by Congress in April 1978. Of politics he said: "Politics isn't a matter of making love. It's making choices." Senator Humphrey, like President Roosevelt before him, had also been referred to as a "happy warrior." Among the younger Democrats nowadays, the young, energetic, and intelligent U.S. Senator of West Virginia and Democratic Majority Leader in the Senate, Robert C. Byrd, will most likely acquire the honorable designation in the near future. See MISTER REPUBLICAN.

Mister Justice. See MISTER PRESIDENT.

Mister President. A term established by practice and not by law, by which the President of the United States, the presiding officer of the U.S. Senate (the U.S. Vice President), and the President-Pro-Tempore of the U.S. Senate are addressed. The Chief Justice of the U.S. Supreme Court is addressed as "Mister Justice." The Speaker of the U.S. House of Representatives is addressed as "Mister Speaker." All cabinet officers or Secretaries are addressed as "Mister Secretary" and the U.S. Attorney General, as "Mister Attorney General." President Thomas Jefferson (1801-1809) originated the "Mister President" address of the chief executive in 1801. The two previous Presidents, George Washington (1789-1797) and John Adams (1797-1801) preferred, respectively, "His Mightiness," and "His Highness." See Appendix 16.

Mister Republican. A distinguished leader of the Republican party in the United States who, after decades of continuous and dedicated service to the party as well as to the nation, comes to be referred to as "Mister Republican." For a number of decades that distinguished designation was assigned to the U.S. Senator of Ohio, Robert A. Taft (1893-1953), a son of former U.S. President William Howard Taft (1909-1913), who earned the affectionate title from his Republican colleagues in the Senate. As the leader of the conservative wing of the Republican party, Taft opposed the New Deal policies of F. D. Roosevelt (1938-1944), was the co-sponsor of the Taft-Hartley Labor Act of 1947 which repealed the pro-labor Wagner Act of 1935, and ran for the presidency in 1940, 1948, and 1952. Between 1947 and 1949 he was the Chairman of the Republican Party Committee, and in 1953 became the Senate (Republican) Majority Leader. Ronald Reagan, former Governor of California and U.S. President (1981-1989), could probably be considered the current "Mister Republican" as well as the standard-bearer (spiritual leader and spokesman) for Republicans and Republicanism (at least the conservative wing of the party). Among the younger Republicans, the energetic and intelligent U.S. Senator of Tennessee, Howard H. Baker, Jr., will most likely acquire that designation in the near future. See MISTER DEMOCRAT.

Mister Secretary. See MISTER PRESIDENT.

Mister Speaker. See MISTER PRESIDENT.

Mixed Economy. A term often applied to describe the coexistence of state, cooperative, and private ownership of the means of production (e.g., production plants) and distribution (e.g., marketing outlets) in a given economy. See SOCIALIZED ENTERPRISES IN THE UNITED STATES, Appendices 83, 84.

Mixed Government. See POLITICAL EQUILIBRIUM.

MNF. See MULTILATERAL NUCLEAR FORCE.

Mob Rule. A type of mass democracy, or direct democracy, as envisioned by Plato and his followers, which sooner or later may lead to a tyranny by the majority; also, a government by a large number of incompetent persons. See Appendix 1.

Model Act. An effort by scholars and administrators in the United States to design and implement constitution and statutory laws which best fit the needs of the people throughout all of the states in as uniform a manner as possible. Such model statutes are the result of extensive study and practical experience. See Appendices 55, 56.

Model City Charter. See NATIONAL MUNICIPAL LEAGUE (NML).

Model State Constitution. A model design of a state constitution prepared by the Committee on State Government of the National Municipal League from which states in the American Union may draw the best features for adoption. Now in the sixth updated edition, the Constitution provides for a unicameral legislature (which thus far has been adopted only in the state of Nebraska); it contains a bill of rights and provisions for legislative referendum and initiative. See Appendices 55, 56.

Modern Democracy. See NEW FRENCH PHILOSOPHERS.

Modern Political System. See POLITICAL SYSTEM.

Modern Politics is Civil War Carried by Other Means! So legal scholar Alasdair MacIntyre characterizes modern politics, particularly as it pertains to the modern interpretation of the U.S. Constitution, specifically to the actual meaning of its provisions as written and the contemporary perception and understanding of that meaning—also known as "The Politics of Original Intention" (as presented in 1989 by legal scholar and writer G. McDowell in an article by the same title).

Modern Revisionism. See SOCIAL IMPERIALISM.

Modus Operandi. In the Latin language, "way of living" or "a way in which one arranges his affairs." Also, in international relations, an understanding between two or more states on a temporary solution to the problem, to be followed by final settlement.

Mogul. In the Hindi language, "Mongol"; an "autocrat" or a "politically powerful and influential person." A term originally applied to Mongolian invaders of India and now commonly used in the language of politics to describe powerful and influential persons (e.g., dictators, party bosses, and other persons with political clout). See PUNDIT, POLITICAL MACHINE.

Mohobhorata. See DIPLOMATIC IMMUNITY.

Mokrye Dyela. See WET AFFAIR.

Mole Hunt. See HT/LINGUAL.

MOLINACO. See MOVEMENT FOR THE LIBERATION OF COMORO ISLANDS (MOUVEMENT DE LIBERATION NATIONAL COMORO).

Molotov Plan. See COUNCIL FOR MUTUAL ECONOMIC ASSISTANCE (CMEA).

Molotov-Ribbentrop Pact. See HITLER-STALIN PACT.

Momentum. See POLITICAL MOMENTUM.

Monarchy. The rule by a king, queen, ceasar, kaiser, tsar, tsarina, regent (one who is ruling in the name of a monarch who has not yet reached the necessary age, e.g., a minor), emperor, or in tribal societies, a chief. With rare exceptions (e.g., in Poland where during almost a thousand years of monarchy some of the kings were elected by nobles and clergy) monarchies are hereditary, with the oldest child becoming the ruling monarch, as in England. Monarchs were, as a rule, laws upon themselves, responsible for their acts and actions only before God and history. Some modern monarchs (e.g., in Japan and England) do not rule but reign; they serve more as symbols of the unity of the nation, and exercise ceremonial powers; in some cases (e.g., in England) the monarch is the head of the state but not head of the government, which is headed by a prime minister and a cabinet. Some monarchs throughout history were very despotic and absolute, e.g., the tsars of Russia, and the kings of France. In modern times most monarchs are guided by a constitution (e.g., constitutional monarchies like that of England) whereby rights, duties, and responsibilities of the monarch are spelled out in written law or by custom. Some monarchs were called "enlightened despots," e.g., Catherine II, called the Great, of Russia (1729-1796). Of German descent, she became Tsarina of Russia through her marriage to the Russian tsar. She abolished serfdom and the bondage of persons to their feudal lords, often using heavy-handed tactics or plain police force, then, with the same force and vigor, insisted that the freed serfs be educated, against their will if necessary. See ENLIGHTENED DESPOT, DESPOTISM, POTEMKIN VILLAGE, Appendix 1.

Mondialism. See GLOBALISM.

Mondialist. See ONE WORLDER.

Monetarism. See MONETARY POLICY.

Monetary Policy. The ways and means of controlling the national economy by the manipulation of the money supply and credit. In the United States the Federal Reserve System is the maker of monetary policy, based on the monetarist notion designed by economic theorist and Nobel Prize laureate, Dr. Milton Friedman. He holds the view that a nation's economic health is determined by its supply of money. See FISCAL POLICY, SINGLE-MINDED IDEALIST.

Money Has No Conscience. Such is the rationalization of bankers who engage in guarding the identity of those who deposit "illegal" money, e.g., narcodollars (dollars earned from the sales of narcotics), or who otherwise engage in laundering.

Money is the Mother's Milk of Politics. An expression signifying that money is a medium without which candidates for public office, in America as well as around the world, will have no chance to become exposed to the electorate and receive the decisive votes on election day. Campaign costs for members of the U.S. Congress and governors in the United States run into tens of millions of dollars and for the U.S. presidency, into hundreds of millions of dollars.

Mongoose. The code-name of a series of operations—all covert—which were organized and/or supported by the U.S. Central Intelligence Agency (CIA), aimed at the overthrow of the communist regime of Dr. Fidel Castro in Cuba (including the elimination of Castro by any means), dating back to 1960, when Castro took over and declared himself to be a Marxist-Leninist. The so-called "Bay of Pigs Invasion" was a part of this operation. See BAY OF PIGS.

Monistic Characteristics of Concepts. See CONCEPT.

Monitoring Team. See PEACE-KEEPING FORCE OF THE UNITED NATIONS.

Monkey Business. See MONKEY TRIAL.

Monkey Trial. A young biology teacher in Dayton, Tennessee, John T. Scopes, taught his students Darwin's "theory of evolution" for which he was charged on July 24, 1925, with "corruption of mind" and "indecency," and was prosecuted by a Presbyterian fundamentalist, William Jennings Bryan (Democratic candidate for President in 1896, 1900, and 1908; U.S. Secretary of State, 1913-1915). Scopes was fined $100 and lost his job. His defense attorney, Clarence Darrow, appealed the decision to the Tennessee Supreme Court which upheld the conviction and established an official religion based on Genesis, but struck the fine. The "monkey law"—a law prohibiting the teaching of Darwin's theory of evolution—was repealed in Tennessee in 1968. The last "monkey law" in the United States was declared unconstitutional by the Mississippi Supreme Court on December 2, 1970.

Monocentrism. See POLYCENTRISM.

Monocracy. In the Greek language, "a rule by a single person" or "a rule by a monarch."

Monocrat. A term applied to those who support a single ruler (e.g., a monarch), pursue a specified objective in unison, or act in harmony in matters political. Thomas Jefferson, U.S. President 1801-

1809, often used this term to describe those Federalists who were pro-British, particularly during the war between France and England. See ANTIFEDERALIST, FEDERALIST, MONOCRACY.

Monopoly. A renown British classical economist, Adam Smith, wrote in 1776 about monopolies and their conspiracy against the public, society, and the state at large. "People of the same trade seldom meet together, even for merriment and diversion, but the conversation ends in a conspiracy against the public, or in some contrivance to raise prices." Monopolies are creatures of persons motivated by an insatiable greed for wealth and power. In a democratic society, if unchecked, they undermine the very fabric of democratic institutions, processes, democratic values, and morality. They are poisonous islands in the sea of fairness and free competition. At the end, as in the unrestricted practices of the Savings and Loan industry, which cost U.S. taxpayers over $500 billion, they lead to the reduction of many to the level of poverty, and the elevation of the few to an excessive accumulation of wealth. There are many monopolies in the United States in spite of legislation to protect the economic fabric of the nation from such practices. *U.S. News and World Report* (3 February 1992) mentions a small portion of them and their practices of stifling free competition and keeping retail prices artificially high on commodities in high demand by consumers. They are: (1) the milk monopoly which requires consumers to pay about 24 percent more for milk, because of federal price restrictions; (2) the sugar monopoly, (3) the health care monopoly, (4) the cable TV monopoly and (5) the airline reservations monopoly. Consumers pay more for these services and commodities because the industries monopolized their markets. Such practices are possible because the political committees of these industries make large contributions to politicians who in turn legislate for their protection. The PACs of dairy and tobacco companies alone, according to the publication, contributed in 1990 about $1.9 million to politicians so they could be re-elected to Congress and keep on guarding their interests. This destructive, anti-American practice of monopolies can only be broken by the voters who decide to better scrutinize the persons they elect to positions of power and trust. Economic power, like political power, highly concentrated in the hands of the few, will, with time, create an appetite for more power, absolute power; and absolute power corrupts absolutely. The monopoly system is sometimes referred to as "monopoly capitalism," but for what it does, it should rather more properly be referred to as "monopoly communism." See CAPITALISM, DEMOCRATIC CAPITALISM, GROUP.

Monopoly Capitalism. In the language of Marxist economics, the merging of privately-owned and privately-operated means of production and distribution into larger units (monopolies) in order to control production and prices, as well as to avoid competition (to be the sole producer and distributor). A monopsony in reverse.

Monopoly Communism. See MONOPOLY CAPITALISM.

Monopsony. A situation where there is only one buyer of a certain commodity in the market place. See MONOPOLY CAPITALISM.

Monotheism. See POLYTHEISM.

Monroe Doctrine. A policy statement (issued by U.S. President James Monroe in his message to the U.S. Congress on December 2, 1823) warning European powers against attempts to colonize or to intervene in the Western Hemisphere (North America, Central America, and South America), making clear that any such intervention would be considered a threat to the security of the United States. This policy has been reaffirmed several times throughout American diplomatic history. See CUBAN MISSILE CRISIS, HAVANA CONFERENCE, LEBENSRAUM, NIAGARA FALLS CONFERENCE.

Monroe Doctrine of Europe. See LEBENSRAUM.

Monrovia Bloc. See MONROVIA GROUP.

Monrovia Conference. See WEST AFRICAN SUMMIT CONFERENCE (WACS), MONROVIA GROUP.

Monrovia Declaration. See MONROVIA GROUP.

Monrovia Group. During May 8-12, 1961, a group of heads of states of African nations met in Monrovia, Liberia, where a Declaration was signed calling for extended mutual cooperation in political and economic matters in order to bring a closer unity of African states. The following states signed the Charter: Cameroon, Central African Republic, Chad, Congo (Brazzaville), Dahomey, Ethiopia, Gabon, Ivory Coast, Liberia, Libya, Malagasy, Niger, Senegal, Togo, and Upper Volta. The signatories of the Monrovia Charter—which, almost in its entirety, became the Charter of the Organization of African Unity (OAU)—later became parties to the Lagos Charter and are associated with the European Economic Community (EEC), the Common Market.

Monteneros. A Marxist-oriented political revolutionary organization in Argentina (with branches throughout Latin America), which believes that socialism must be introduced in Latin America by force. The Monteneros (the name was taken from bush fighters who battled regular armies in Latin American states during the 19th century) strongly supported Juan D. Perón, the former dictator of Argentina, but abandoned Perón in 1973 in favor of open warfare with the dictatorial governments (military juntas) in Latin America, and particularly in Argentina.

Montevideo Declaration. During the Inter-American Convention on the Rights and Duties of States which was held in 1933 in Montevideo, Uruguay, a declaration was signed by the participants (which included all the Latin American states, the United States, and the Western European powers) specifying the conditions for peaceful international cooperation and respect. They are: (1) the sovereignty of all states must be respected (sovereignty being defined as the supreme authority to make laws concerning the state regardless of the internal political system, that is, whether the state is democratic or totalitarian); (2) flowing from the rule of sovereignty, no state shall make laws applicable to the territory of another, and may not intervene, under any conditions, into the domestic affairs of another state; and (3) all states are equal before the law (i.e., international law), with equal rights and obligations, regardless of the size of the territory, population, or military capability, and in case of war, no state shall be dismembered, removed from existence, or extinguished. (According to Professor K. J. Holsti, the rule of not dismembering or extinguishing a conquered state has been fairly well followed throughout modern history, with these exceptions: the division of Poland among Austria, Prussia, and Russia in 1772, 1792, and 1795; the division of Poland between Nazi Germany and Soviet Russia in 1939; the incorporation into the Soviet state of several Asian and European republics, such as the Caucasian Republic in 1918 and Latvia, Lithuania, and Estonia during W.W.II; the establishment of the puppet state of Manchukuo by Japan, and the German "Anschluss" of Austria into the German Reich in 1938.) See INHERENT RIGHT OF STATE, INTERNATIONAL LAW, SOVEREIGNTY.

Montgomery Bus Boycott. See FREEDOM RIDES.

Montgomery Protest. See WALK FOR FREEDOM.

Montreux Convention. An international agreement entered into by the major powers of the world on the use of the Dardanelles waterway in Turkey which connects the Black and the Mediterranean Seas. The waterway, according to the agreement, is to be open to all nations for free navigation during times of peace (excluding warships over 10,000 tons, submarines, and aircraft carriers, except if directed by the United Nations or upon consent of the Turkish Government). The Turkish Government, however, retained the right to close the waterway to any belligerent at war with Turkey or to a neutral state giving aid to belligerents who are at war with Turkey. (The Convention was originally signed in 1936 and subsequently reaffirmed by the UN.)

Moon Treaty. An international treaty sponsored by the United Nations Organization pertaining to the exploration of the moon and other resources to the benefit of all mankind rather than to those who have either discovered or conquered them. The discovering or conquering nations, however, as well as nations lacking such means (e.g., the poor third and fourth world nations), will receive their appropriate share.

Moot Case. A case of a dead issue; one without practical significance due to some changes in law, in facts, or the parties to a suit (e.g., due to death or a settlement out of court). Also, a dress rehearsal as preparation for real judicial or arbitration proceedings; or a declaratory judgment of an advisory opinion—most of which are moot decisions or opinions because they are not binding.

Moral Equivalent of Our Founding Fathers. When the remnants of the Nicaraguan National Guard, the special forces of dictator Anastasio Samoza who was overthrown by the Sandanistas in 1972, renamed itself the "Nicaraguan Democratic Forces (FDN)," it promptly offered its services to the Americans as an anti-communist, anti-Sandanista force. In November 1981 President Reagan issued a finding stating that the United States would "support the opposition front through formation and training of action teams to collect intelligence and to engage in paramilitary and political operations in Nicaragua and elsewhere," because he considered the Contras to be the moral equivalent of the American founding fathers. The FDN became the nucleus force of the Contras and was instrumental in weakening the influence of the Sandanistas and in causing their eventual removal from at least the presidential office in Nicaragua. See IRAN-CONTRA AFFAIR.

Moral Equivalent of War. U.S. President Jimmy Carter stated in his inaugural address in January 1977, that one of the major problems facing the American nation is the acute shortage of energy and that his administration's main task will be to launch a campaign, the "moral equivalent of war," against that problem. Subsequently the President submitted to Congress his energy program and established a cabinet level agency, the Energy Department, to deal with the problem.

Moral Leadership. See LEADERSHIP BY PULLING.

Moral Majority. An informal organization established during the 1970s in Lynchburg, Virginia, by the Reverend Dr. Jerry Falwell, based on religious evangelism, politics, and the conservative, moral and philosophical values of many Americans. The organization stressed spiritual values, a strong family as the basic unit of society, the hard work ethic, and good will; and was instrumental in influencing many Americans to vote for Ronald W. Reagan and George H. W. Bush. The founder, Dr. Falwell, disbanded the organization in 1989 because, as he stated, its mission was accomplished with the fall of communism.

Moral Re-Armament. See BORN AGAIN.

Moral Turpitude. As pertaining to government and politics, immoral, dishonest, and anti-social behavior and conduct of public officials; disregard of the rules of law, customs, traditional institutions and processes and showing lack of respect for the individual citizen. See DECADENCE, ENTRAPMENT.

Morality in Government. See POLITICAL ETHICS.

Moratorium. An order that may be issued by one with authority, such as the President of the United States, calling for a delay in the execution of some acts. (e.g., raising prices or wages).

Morgenthau Plan. A plan designed by the Allies for the total destruction of German industry during World War II, through saturation bombings and other means to be worked out after the surrender of Germany, so that Germany would never have the capacity to launch another war. This plan was formulated by Henry Morgenthau, Jr. (1891-1967), and signed by U.S. President Franklin Delano Roosevelt and British Prime Minister Winston Churchill during their conference in Quebec, Canada, on September 16, 1944. The plan never materialized. An alternate plan, suggested by U.S. Congressman S. Elliott Rankin, was to retain the German war machine, mainly its productive capacity, for a possible future war with the Soviet Union. The Soviets were not informed of this plan, although it was approved by U.S. President Franklin D. Roosevelt at Winston Churchill's suggestion. Here also the Anglo-American rift was deepened when the United States, assured of victory over militarist Japan because of the approaching success of the atom bomb, no longer felt obligated to inform England of all of its future military plans. While the United States had nominally promised to inform England about the eventual use of atomic weapons, that promise was broken by President Harry S. Truman when, during the Potsdam Conference, he decided to deploy atomic weapons against Japan. Another blow to the British was Truman's sudden and unhinted at termination of the Lend-Lease program on August 17, 1945, on Victory Day. It was generally thought that this decision was primarily aimed at the Soviet Union rather than the Western allies. See TEHERAN CONFERENCE.

Moro National Liberation Front (MNLF). See PEOPLE POWER.

Morte alla Francia, Italia anela. In the Italian language, "Death to France, Italy cries out." See MAFIA.

Mosaic Society. A community under the jurisdiction of one state or government, voluntarily subdivided into distinguishable sub-communities along ethnic, religious, or racial lines. See TYPES OF STATES.

Moscow Coup. See STATE COMMITTEE ON THE STATE OF EMERGENCY.

Moscow Manifesto. An appeal issued by the leadership of the Communist Party of the Soviet Union (CPSU) in 1961 to all communist parties, to communist front organizations, and to friends and sympathizers of communism and the Soviet Union to undertake an active struggle against any and all anti-communist (and anti-Soviet) propaganda, particularly against that which the John Birch Society disseminated in the United States. See COMMUNIST PARTY OF THE SOVIET UNION (CPSU).

Moscow Summit. See NIXON-BREZHNEYEV SUMMIT.

Moscow Summit of 1991. See FROM COLD WARRIOR TO COMRADE.

Mossad. See ISRAEL'S INTELLIGENCE.

Mossadegh. In the Farsi (Iranian) language, "tested and true." A title once given to a 15-year old clerk at the finance ministry for his dedication to his work, Iran, and the Shah. But Mohammed Mossadegh subsequently turned against the Shah, whom he correctly accused of being a crony of foreign interests; went to France to study political science, earned a law degree in Switzerland and returned to Iran to run for parliament to struggle against Iran becoming a protectorate of England under provision of a British-Iranian Treaty of 1919. This of course would also mean complete control of oil fields, and when riots broke out against the British proposal, which now Mossadegh was instigating from his safe sanctuary in the Iranian Parliament, the Shah named him a prime minister; Mossadegh proclaimed that "the oil is ours," and "a million dollars a day" profit ought to go to Iran rather than foreign interests. Mossadegh nationalized British oil companies, but when they moved to other lands (e.g., Saudi Arabia) for oil the "million dollars a day" was not forthcoming, dissatisfaction grew in Iran, and Mossadegh's anti-Western attitude caused his removal into house arrest (he died in 1957) and a restoration of Shah Reza Pahlavi to power in 1953 (with America's CIA assistance) and introduced royal dictatorship. Mossadegh's philosophy of "negative nationalism"—meaning, to him, rendering Iran free of foreign influence and domination—was construed in America as a communist conspiracy, and McCarthyists in America accused him of liking the Iranian people better than the Americans. Mossadegh was the fourth wealthiest land-owner in Iran, valued at $100 million. The Shah accused him of governing during his two-years premiership with "much verve but little order," and proposed instead governance with "much order but little verve." The Shah paid General Zahedi $600,000 for keeping Mossadegh in house arrest where he died a prisoner in 1957. The Shah soon gained control and influence, proclaimed himself an elected rather than a hereditary king, and warned that "once you win power, you must exercise it to retain it." Mossadegh's desire to retain Iran's national identity was based on the old Persian saying, "to foreign culture open both the windows of thy house—then let foreign culture seep in through one window and leave from the other."

Most Favored-Nation. The practice of granting a preferential treatment to products of one state sold in the territory of another; an agreement of specific favorable trade arrangements (e.g., granting of credit or lowering import tariffs) designed to boost the economy of a weaker state. The United States has extended such preferential treatment to Poland and Romania, in April 1978. "Most favored-nation" trade status was also extended to Hungary and other states in 1990.

Mother of Parliaments. An affectionate name for the Icelandic Althing (Parliament), the oldest parliament in continuous existence (since 930 AD.).

Mother of Presidents. See VIRGINIA: MOTHER OF PRESIDENTS.

Mother's Milk of Politics. See MONEY IS THE MOTHER'S MILK OF POLITICS.

Motherland Party. One of the major political parties in Turkey, under the leadership of President Turgut Ozal. The party is strongly opposed to any autonomy of the Kurds, who represent about 20 percent of the Turkish population. Its rival for power is the Social Democratic Party with Suleiman Demirel, prime minister, being one of its leaders.

Motu Proprio. In the Latin language, "by one's own impulse" or "by one's own motion."

Mount Weather. See COUNTERINSURGENCY IN AMERICA.

Movement. See FALANGE.

Movement for the Liberation of Comoro Islands (MOLINACO). A coalition of political groups dedicated to the liberation of the Comoro Islands from South African domination.

Movimento Popular de Libertacao de Angola (MPLA). A coalition of civic and political parties with a pro-Soviet, pro-communist leaning, established in 1964. One of its co-founders, Agostinho Neto, became president when Angola gained independence from Portugal on November 11, 1975.

Moving Back the Clock. A practice in some state legislatures in the United States to move back the clock in order to allow additional time for clearing legislative matters. Under these rules, legislatures must complete their business before midnight on the day the legislative session is required to close.

Moynihan Memorandum. See BENIGN NEGLECT.

MP. Member of Parliament (e.g., a member of the House of Commons in England, Canada, or Australia).

MPLA. See MOVIMENTO POPULAR DE LIBERTACAO DE ANGOLA.

MPLA-CIA War. See WAR POWERS ACTS.

Mr. Davis's War. See AMERICAN CIVIL WAR.

Mr. Lincoln's War. See AMERICAN CIVIL WAR.

Mr. Madison's War. These were the words with which Federalist opponents of U.S. President James Madison (1809-1817) referred to the 1812 War with England. The war was difficult for Madison to carry on because of poor economic conditions and lack of support by New England states. Madison was forced to collaborate more closely with the Federalists in order to engage their support for the establishment of a national bank, protective tariffs, and funding of the national debt—all favored at one time by the Federalists and opposed by Madison, an anti-Federalist.

MRP. See POPULAR REPUBLICAN MOVEMENT.

MTCR. See MISSILE TECHNOLOGY CONTROL REGIME.

MTN. See MULTILATERAL TRADE NEGOTIATIONS.

Muckraker. One who writes and publishes critical statements about government officials, revealing their weaknesses, incompetencies, malfeasances, misfeasances, and other shortcomings. The term was first applied by U.S. President Theodore Roosevelt (1901-1909) on March 17, 1906, to Ida M. Tarbell, and on April 14, 1906, to Lincoln Steffens, the two most outspoken investigative reporters of that era. The muckrakers addressed themselves to social ills in addition to criticizing incompetent public officials. Some of their favorite targets were the growing slums in the ghettos of large cities, poverty, prostitution, and crime. In modern times, investigative reporting has become an important tool of the electorate in a democratic society (e.g., the Watergate investigation). See NATIONAL PROGRESSIVE PARTY.

Mud Bath. See MUD SLINGING.

Mudslinging. See POLITICAL RHETORIC.

Mudsville. See POOR PEOPLE'S MARCH OF 1969.

Mugwump. In the language of the Algonquin Indians, "a leader," "chief," "self-proclaimed chief," or "holier than you." A term often used in American politics to describe one who considers himself good enough to be a leader rather than a follower. (This epithet was commonly applied to those Republicans who, during the 1884 election, refused to support the Republican candidate for the presidency, James G. Blaine, and supported instead Grover Cleveland, a Democrat. The Mugwumps also insisted on some reforms to be introduced in the nation, such as better sanitary standards in city ghettos, and more rights for American Indians, Negroes, and women. They were also instrumental in exposing many corrupt practices in local governments.)

Muhafazat. Administrative subdivisions—provinces or governorates—in several Muslim/Arab countries (e.g., Egypt, Kuwait, Iraq).

Mujihadins. "Holy Warriors." Freedom Fighters, Rebel Moslem tribesmen fighting "godless" communist rule and Soviet invaders (in Afghanistan), defending the sanctity of religion and national independence. See AFGHANISTAN WAR.

Multidisciplinary Interpretation of Law. See BRANDEIS BRIEF.

Multi-Jurisdictional Organization. An organization whose area encompasses the jurisdiction of any two or more governmental units, but whose responsibilities are limited to certain functional planning and programs and do not include comprehensive planning or coordinated policy control of a general nature over functional programs, as is the case in an *umbrella* multi-jurisdictional organization. See PLANNING, POLITICAL INCREMENTALISM.

Multilateral. By, or of many parties or nations, or among or between parties or nations. See BILATERAL.

Multilateral Nuclear Force (MNF). The striking force of the NATO members (except France) equipped with nuclear weapons.

Multilateral Summit of 1977-1978. U.S. President Jimmy Carter traveled to seven nations between December 29, 1977, and January 6, 1978, on a good-will tour. Among the countries visited (in order of visit) were: Poland, Iran, India, Saudi Arabia, Egypt, France, and Belgium.

Multilateral Trade Negotiations (MTN). Alarmed by the rapid growth of a trade deficit (from $9 billion in 1976 to $31 billion in 1977, with imports of foreign goods rising to $28 billion and exports to less than $6 billion in the same period), the United States government undertook, in 1978, a vigorous campaign to rectify this unfavorable balance by intensifying exports to other nations within the system of the General Agreement on Tariffs and Trade (GATT). Through the GATT arrangement in Europe (with the Common Market countries) and through special negotiations with Japan conducted without much success since 1973, and known as "Tokyo Rounds," the United States hoped to establish better world markets for its products and thus improve or at least sustain the standard of living of Americans. An economic warfare (struggle for markets) between friendly states (e.g., the United States and Europe) is a reality with which the United States must cope since the United States is gradually losing its competitive edge. The success of foreign products among American consumers is attributed to two factors: (1) the products are often superior in quality to similar products manufactured domestically and (2) the products sell at lower prices. Both of these, again, are attributed to the better productivity of foreign manufacturers (e.g., producers who produce more goods of better quality), while the productivity of American workers is declining, which directly contributes to inflation of the national economy. See DUMPING, ECONOMIC SUMMITS, KENNEDY ROUND.

Multi-Member District. An electoral district from which more than one representative may be elected at-large. See VOTING.

Multinational Corporation. A corporate business enterprise, the assets of which are owned by the citizens of three or more distinct nations; one which operates under different jurisdictions (including corporate registration), and transfers its products (goods or services) across national boundaries (e.g., International Business Machines, Gulf Oil Company, Exxon, etc.). Multinational corporations are often referred to as "Business International Nongovernmental Organizations" (BINGO). According to author Theodore Levitt ("The Globalization of Markets," *Harvard Business Review* 61, May-June 1983), the multinational corporation is now being replaced with a global corporation, which produces high quality goods at a low price due to economy of scale, and which is shaping the market often ignoring the wishes of the consumer and acting just as Henry Ford did at one time when he had no competition in the automobile business, that the customers "can have any color they want so long as it's black." See CONSUMER SOVEREIGNTY, TRANSNATIONAL CORPORATION.

Multinational State. A state in which the population is composed of many different national and racial groups under a common political authority (e.g., the USA and the former USSR). See MOSAIC SOCIETY.

Multi-Party System. See TYRANNY OF THE MAJORITY, OPEN PARTY SYSTEM.

Multipolarity. See BIPOLARITY, POLYCENTRISM.

Multi-Purpose Lobby. See LOBBY.

Multiple Independently Targeted Re-Entry Vehicle (MIRV). One of the most advanced weapon systems in the U.S. arsenal—also called the "space bus"—designed to counter possible attacks with ICBM's. MIRVs can carry multiple warheads that can separate in flight and change trajectory, and can then fly independently to designated (pre-programmed) targets. The two other varieties of the MIRV, the Minuteman III and the Poseidon, each carrying three and ten warheads respectively, are capable of penetrating any ABM defense system. The Soviet Union has developed its own prototype of MIRV, the SS-9. See MULTILATERAL NUCLEAR FORCE (MNF).

Multiple System of Laws. See BASIC LAW.

Multiplier in Keynes Economic Theory. See KEYNESIAN ECONOMICS.

Munich Agreement. An agreement that was signed in Munich, Germany, on September 30, 1938, by Adolf Hitler (Nazi Germany), Neville Chamberlain (England), Edouard Daladier (France), and Benito Mussolini (Italy), allowing Hitler to incorporate into the German Reich part of Czechoslovakia (the Sudetenland) solely on the grounds that he demanded it. This agreement is often referred to as a classic example of the politics of appeasement because the signers hoped that, by giving Hitler this piece of territory, he would be satisfied and not move into any additional territories. Had the British and the French stood up firmly to Hitler in Munich, World War II might have been prevented, or at least delayed. After W.W.II, when asked if the Germans would have attacked Czechoslovakia (and later Poland) if England and France had kept their promises to defend them, Hitler's top military adviser and Chief of Staff, Marshall Keitel replied: "Certainly not. We were not strong enough militarily"; he added that the object of the Munich settlement was "to get Russia out of Europe, to gain time, and to complete the German armaments." See APPEASEMENT.

Munich Massacre. See PALESTINE LIBERATION ORGANIZATION (PLO).

Munich Putsch. See FASCISM, PUTSCH.

Municipal Assistance Corporation (MAC). A finance management control instrumentality created by the state of New York on June 10, 1975, to refinance 3 billion dollars worth of loans for New York City and to prevent the city from defaulting on notes and going bankrupt.

Municipal Corporation. Any duly constituted, incorporated, and chartered political subdivision and its government in the United States (e.g., a city or a county). Municipal corporations may own property, enter into contracts, sue and be sued, and exist in perpetuity. The powers of a municipal corporation may be altered or revoked by a state legislature within the limits of the corporate document (e.g., the charter) of the constitution of the state. See CITY, CITY COUNCIL, DILLON'S RULE.

Municipal Law. The law of a municipal corporation; also, in international relations, the domestic law of any state as distinguished from international law. See INTERNATIONAL LAW.

Municipality. A self-governing political subdivision (e.g., city, town, township, or village). The term is used synonymously with "municipal corporation." See MUNICIPAL CORPORATION.

Muppies. In America, a term applied to the young generation of mob-related financial manipulators, short for "Mafia-Yuppies;" operators who differ from the old mobsters by their advanced training, which is narrowly confined to modern, intelligent methods of theft and racketeering, and driven by personal greed, with a lack of attachment to any political doctrine or standard of public morality. Many of them are trained as attorneys, accountants (beancounters), business managers, stockbrokers, and other related professions.

Muri, Muda, Mura. See TOYOTA'S PRODUCTION SYSTEM.

Murphy's Law. A fatalistic notion often repeated by doomsday-prophets holding that if anything can logically go wrong, it will!

Mutato Nomina. In the Latin language, "the name being changed."

Mutually Assured Destruction (MAD). The notion that both the former Soviet Union (dissolved in 1991) and the United States had in their arsenals enough nuclear weapons to destroy each other (and the rest of the world) several times; also, that in case of nuclear war, there will be no winners but only losers.

Mutuus Consensus. In the Latin language, "mutual consent" or "by mutual consent."

MVD. See MINISTRY FOR INTERNAL SECURITY.

My Country, Right or Wrong, is Always Right. See OUR SONS OF BITCHES.

Myanmar National League for Democracy. See NATIONAL LEAGUE FOR DEMOCRACY.

Mystify, Mislead, and Surprise. A famous strategic and tactical dictum of Confederate General Thomas Jonathan "Stonewall" Jackson (1824-1863), which supplemented with the advice of U.S. Army General William T. Sherman (1820-1891) to "put the enemy on the horns of a dilemma," often applies today in guerrilla warfare, in international diplomacy, and in domestic and foreign marketing and management practices. Today, the general would, no doubt, add "Deceive."

Mythopoeia. See POLITICAL MYTH.

N

"A man with God is always in the majority."

JOHN KNOX, 1505-1572

N-Skids. See CENTRAL INTELLIGENCE AGENCY (CIA), Appendices 32, 33.

NAACP. See NATIONAL ASSOCIATION FOR THE ADVANCEMENT OF COLORED PEOPLE.

NAAWP. See NATIONAL ASSOCIATION FOR THE ADVANCEMENT OF WHITE PEOPLE.

NAC. See NONAUTONOMOUS CHANGE, NATIONAL ASSOCIATION OF COUNTIES.

Nagasaki. See V-J DAY.

Nairobi Declaration. See DECLARATION ON FUNDAMENTAL PRINCIPLES GOVERNING THE USE OF THE MASS MEDIA IN STRENGTHENING PEACE AND INTERNATIONAL UNDERSTANDING AND IN COMBATING WAR, PROPAGANDA, RACISM AND APARTHEID.

Naked Power. See POWER.

Nanotechnology. See MISSILE TECHNOLOGY CONTROL REGIME (MTCR).

Napoleonic Code. Systematized collection of the civil laws of France compiled in 1804 by order of Napoleon I (Napoleon Bonaparte, Emperor of France). This code served subsequently as a model of modern codified laws throughout the world, with the exception of Islamic laws and common law systems. (In the United States the state of Louisiana bases its laws on the Napoleonic Code.)

NARC. See NATIONAL ASSOCIATION OF REGIONAL COUNCILS.

Narcodollar. See MONEY HAS NO CONSCIENCE.

Narodnaya Volya. In the Russian language, "people's will" or "will of the people." A terrorist, anti-Tsarist organization in pre-Soviet Russia.

Narodnik. In the Russian language, "nationalist" or "populist." Also, one who was a member of the NARODNAYA VOLYA.

Narrow-Gauge Political Theory. See POLITICAL THEORY.

Narrow Interpretation of the Law. See JUDICIAL ACTIVISM, POSTURE OF MORAL ABSTENTION.

Nation of Islam. See BLACK MUSLIMS.

Nation of Joiners. See ATOMISTIC SOCIETY.

Nation of Peasants. See FARM STATE.

Nation-State. See NATIONAL STATE.

National. See CITIZENSHIP.

National Advisory Commission on Civil Defense. See KERNER COMMISSION.

National Anti-Slavery Society of 1833. A society established by W. L. Garrison which held slavery to be illegal on the following grounds: that no man has the right to enslave another as merchandise, a chattel, and to stifle his intellectual, natural, and social faculties; that the right to enjoy liberty is inalienable; that every man has the right to govern over his own body, enjoy the fruits of his labor, and have protection of law and privacy. Anything else was held to be alien and contrary to Judeo-Christian ethics, and slavery was against these ethics. See ABOLITIONIST.

National Area. A self-governing political subdivision of homogeneous peoples within a union republic in the former Soviet Federation. Each National Area elected one deputy (deputat) to the National House of Nationalities of the Supreme Soviet of the USSR. These areas were: Arginsky Buriat Mongolian, Chuckchi, Evenk, Khantimansi, Komi-Permyak, Koryak, Nenetz, Taymyr, Ustordynski Buryat Mongolian, and Yamalo-Nenetz.

National Association for the Advancement of Colored People (NAACP). The oldest civil rights organization in the United States, founded on February 12, 1909, in New York City by a black leader and intellectual, W. E. B. Du Bois, and a group of his white friends, for the purpose of advancing, through non-violent means, the lot of all peoples (mainly blacks) in the United States.

National Association for the Advancement of White People. (NAAWP). An informal organization that was established in 1954, in Washington, D.C., by white segregationists from the South in response to the *Brown v. Board of Education* decision. The NAAWP aimed at countering the civil rights activities of the NAACP, and during the 1960s, some of its aims and objectives were taken up by the White Citizen's Council. See SOUTHERN MANIFESTO, WHITE CITIZEN'S COUNCIL.

National Association of Arab Americans. See ARAB LOBBY.

National Association of Colored Women. An organization founded in 1895, by black women for the purpose of providing social services (e.g., schools, homes, and guidance) to women. "Lifting as we climb" became the motto of the organization. See NATIONAL ASSOCIATION FOR THE ADVANCEMENT OF COLORED PEOPLE (NAACP), NATIONAL ORGANIZATION FOR WOMEN (NOW).

National Association of Counties (NAC). Organization of county officials that lobbies for greater federal aid.

National Association of Regional Councils (NARC). An informal organization established in 1954 for the purpose of the dissemination of information and the exchange of experiences on the working of regional voluntary councils of government among separate jurisdictions. The number of regional councils in the U.S. grew rapidly, from 11 in 1954 to approximately 1,800 in 1978, to over 3,050 in 1992. See POLITICAL INCREMENTALISM.

National Black Political Convention. A coalition of black groups met March 10-12, 1972, in Gary, Indiana, to decide on political strategy during the 1972 national election. The convention did not endorse any particular candidate for the U.S. Presidency from the two major political parties (Democratic or Republican), and failed to nominate a candidate of its own, due to an internal split between proponents of a separate black party and those favoring accommodation within the existing party system. Out of the approximately 5,000 persons present, about 3,000 voted against forceful busing of children for the purpose of expediting integration, on the grounds that busing deprives black communities of the power to control their schools (e.g., educational programs and development of facilities).

National Census. See UNITED STATES HOUSE OF REPRESENTATIVES.

National Center for State Courts. A semi-independent agency of the federal government established in 1971 for the purpose of assisting state and local courts in the improvement of their procedures, systems, and efficiency. The Center is located at the College of William and Mary in Williamsburg, Virginia.

National Committee for an Effective Congress (NCEC). A private, Washington-based organization (active during the early 1970s) with liberal leanings, seeking to influence the U.S. Congress on liberal (e.g., civil rights) legislation. See LOBBY.

National Committeeman. See DEMOCRATIC NATIONAL COMMITTEE, REPUBLICAN NATIONAL COMMITTEE.

National Committeewoman. See DEMOCRATIC NATIONAL COMMITTEE, REPUBLICAN NATIONAL COMMITTEE.

National Communism. See SUMMIT OF COMMUNIST PARTIES.

National Debt of the United States. The amount of money which the U.S. Federal Government has borrowed in order to remain functional and solvent. The national debt in 1978 was $742 billion and was raised to $958 billion by President Reagan on January 29, 1981 and in 1982 reached $3.8 trillion. Numerous groups in America, including the National Taxpayers' Association, call for a constitutional amendment which would require Congress to balance the U.S. budget. See Appendices 38, 39.

National Democratic Party (NDP). In the German language, "National Demokratische Partei." In the German Federal Republic, one of several political parties pursuing traditional policies.

National Democratic Party Charter. See COMMISSION ON PRESIDENTIAL NOMINATIONS.

National Development. The composite of policies and systems that a nation-state develops for the purpose of advancing its growth and development through more and better planning and utilization of human and material resources.

National Disaster Area. Any given area that becomes adversely affected by some unforeseen catastrophe (e.g., earthquake, flood, or tornado) and is declared as such by the U.S. President or a state governor in order to become eligible for federal financial assistance.

National Emergency. See EMERGENCY POWERS.

National Farm-City Week. Presidential Proclamation 4094 of 1971 designated the week of November 19 through November 25 as National Farm-City Week in order to focus attention on the inter-relationship of urban and rural community development, and the cooperation between urban and rural communities. See TRACTORCADE.

National Front. A coalition of two or more political parties or organizations mobilized for the purpose of achieving some desired goal, such as gaining control over the government. After W.W.II such fronts were commonly organized by pro-Marxist revolutionary forces (e.g., the National Liberation Front in South Vietnam which helped North Vietnam to unify the country in 1975) as instruments of gaining power under the pretext of getting rid of the imperialists and the capitalists. See PEOPLE'S DEMOCRACY, VIETNAMIZATION.

National Front for the Liberation of the Comoro Islands. See MOLINACO.

National Front for the Liberation of the Palestine (NFLP). See PALESTINE LIBERATION ORGANIZATION (PLO).

National Front for the Liberation of the Somali Coast (NFLSC). A revolutionary movement organized in 1964 for the purpose of liberating the Somali Coast from French domination.

National Front Party. A small political party formed in London, England, in 1967 by former Labor Party organizer Derek Day, which opposes any form of coexistence between whites and non-whites. The party strongly objects to the immigration of non-whites and any attempts to racially integrate the British population.

National Front Ticket. See NATIONAL FRONT.

National Guard. See STATE MILITIA.

National Home. In 1917 England declared, in the Balfour Declaration, that there should be established a "national home" for the Jews in Palestine without violating the rights of the Arabs, but the state of Israel was not established until 1948.

National Industrial Policy. See AMERICA IS THE EAGLE, NOT THE OSTRICH.

National Intelligence Estimate. See INTELLIGENCE ESTIMATE.

National Interest. Those basic core values which a nation-state cherishes and strives to preserve at any cost (e.g., religious, culture, racial, ethnic, or economic tenets of a philosophical and practical nature). Ancient Greek political philosopher Thucydides (460-400 B. C.) noted that "identity of interest is the surest of bonds whether between states or individuals." U.S. President George Washington (1789-1797), echoing Lord Salisbury's notion that "the only bond of union that endures is the absence of all clashing interests," stated: "A small knowledge of human nature will convince us, that, with the far greater part of mankind, interest is the governing principle, and that almost every man is more or less under its influence. Motives of public virtue may for a time . . . actuate men to the observance of a conduct purely disinterested; but they are not of themselves sufficient to produce a persevering conformity to the refined dictates and obligations of social duty . . . . No institution, not built on the presumptive truth of these maxims can succeed." Max Weber perceives national interest as a sum of private individual interests which are "material and ideal" and "not ideas" that "dominate directly the actions of men. Yet the 'images of the world' created by these ideas have very often served as switches determining the tracks on which the dynamism of interests keep actions moving." To some contemporary students of national interests, particularly to Hans J. Morgenthau, national interest is simply what the nation says it is, making "a sharp distinction between the desirable and the possible— between what is desirable everywhere and at all times and what is possible under the concrete circumstances of time and place." See VITAL INTEREST.

National Islamic Front (NIF). An Islamic fundamentalist, militant political force in contemporary Sudan, which, under the leadership of Hassan al-Turabi, controls the ruling Revolutionary Command Council, and exerts considerable influence among other fundamentalist groups in the area, particularly in Egypt and Algeria. The organization, which supported Iraq during the Persian Gulf War in 1990-1991, maintains close ties with Iran and receives money and weapons from there. During his recent visit to Khartoum, Iran's President Ali Akbar Hashemi Rafsanjani praised it for its "revolutionary adherence to Islam." The NIF was instrumental in the return of Islamic law in Sudan and collaborates with other Islamic organizations around the world, to restore Islamic law and politics in all Islamic states.

National Labor Union. See NOBLE ORDER OF THE KNIGHTS OF LABOR.

National League for Democracy. A democratic political front organization struggling to deprive the military dictatorship of power and to restore in Myanmar (formerly Burma) democratic, representative government. One of the leaders of the League is a young woman, Mrs. Aung San Suu Kyi, an outspoken critic of the military regime for which she has been held under house arrest since July 1989. She was charged with a crime of "endangering the state" by calling for free democratic election. Mrs. Suu Kyi received the Nobel Peace Prize in 1991 for her non-violent political activity. In April 1992, under international pressure, the military regime allowed Mrs. Suu Kyi's family to visit her for the first time since 1989.

National League of Cities (NLC). Formerly the American Municipal Association (AMA).

National Liberation Front (NLF). See NATIONAL FRONT.

National Movement. See FALANGE.

National Municipal League (NML). A nonpartisan, nonprofit, civic and educational coalition of persons and organizations concerned with the advancement of knowledge about municipal (city, town) life, problems, and institutions, seeking models to advance the well-being of municipalities. The League, which also advocates the doctrine of non-partisanism (taking government out of politics and politics out of government), has prepared, and occasionally updates, a model city charter and a model state constitution. The Constitution of the State of Nebraska (the only state in the American union with a unicameral legislature) has been fashioned after the model constitution of the League. It distributes literature from its main office in New York City to anyone wishing to learn more about a municipal government.

National Organization for Women (NOW). A women's liberation movement organization founded by Betty Friedan in 1966. Its principal aim is to achieve equal rights for women with men in every aspect of societal life (e.g., in pay, in work, in the management of the family, business, and public affairs). In November 1977, the first National Women's Conference was held in Houston, Texas (financed by a congressional grant of five million dollars), during which a National Plan of Action was drawn up calling for more intensified efforts to advance the well-being of women. Some of the resolutions, called the "hot buttons," demanded legalization of abortions (called "reproductive freedoms") federal subsidy for abortions, and legalization of lesbianism. The principal anti-NOW movement is organized by Phyllis Schlafly of Chicago, in alliance, to some degree, with the John Birch Society and Catholic organizations, particularly on the issue of abortion. The NOW program of action was outlined in 1969 in a special document known as the "Red Stocking Manifesto."

National Party Chairperson. In the United States for both the Republican and Democrat Parties this individual is usually selected for this office by the Party's presidential nominee. The Party National Committee then formally elects the person. The party chairperson heads the National Headquarters staff, and is the party campaign manager during the presidential election campaign. Between presidential elections, he directs the activities of the central office in such activities as fund raising, research, and publicity.

National People's Coalition. See PEOPLE POWER.

National Plan of Action. See NATIONAL ORGANIZATION FOR WOMEN (NOW).

National Policy of Isolation. See SAMURAI.

National Political Conference. See KORNILOV REBELLION.

National Political Party Convention. See PARTY CONVENTION.

National Preemption. See SUPREMACY CLAUSE.

National Priority. See PRIORITY.

National Prohibition Act. Legislation passed by the U.S. Congress in 1919, also known as the Volstead Act which introduced the 18th Amendment of the U.S. Constitution prohibiting the manufacture, distribution, and transportation of alcoholic beverages containing more than five percent of alcohol. This was America's only amendment which had to be subsequently repealed by Amendment XXI in 1933. This is, in American history, the only law that most of the people refused to obey. See PROHIBITION PARTY, Appendix 8.

National Progressive Party. A splinter group of the American Republican Party formed and led by former U.S. President Theodore Roosevelt, who was seeking another term in 1911. (That party was also known as the "Bull Moose" party, so named after Roosevelt who once referred to himself as physically fit and strong as a "bull moose"—strong enough to again undertake the difficult task of the presidential office.)

National Republican Party. A political party that was formed in 1824 by followers of John Quincy Adams. In 1832 the party joined Henry Clay's emerging Whig Party to oppose re-election of Andrew Jackson. See WHIG PARTY, Appendix 19.

National Salvation Committee. A self-proclaimed group of Soviet hard-liners who organized under that name in order to seek ways and means to retain the status quo of the disintegrating Soviet empire and to maintain the Communist Party as the controlling agent of all political and military power. The group under the leadership of party apparatchik Vladimir Voronin, attempted to persuade former Soviet President Mikhail S. Gorbachev, in 1990, to admit failure of his leadership, to resign with dignity, and to let the hard-liners take over and exercise collective leadership. Gorbachev allegedly rejected that proposition, and that subsequently led to the Moscow Coup. The group was strongly supported by another pro-traditionalist Soviet rightist organization of several hundred persons, mainly within the Soviet parliament, called the Soyuz (or "Union"). This group was under the leadership of Army Colonel Viktor Alksnis. Soviet Foreign Minister Eduard A. Shevardnadze, a liberal bureaucrat of the Gorbachev group, openly resigned from the Soviet Parliament in December 1990, stating that he did not want to be any part of the dictatorship which the hard-liners were advocating. The warning about the forthcoming dictatorship by the hard-liners, and the firm opposition toward it by the foreign minister, can rightly be construed as the turning point in the history of the declining Soviet power and the emergence of the democratic forces of President Boris N. Yeltsin. See COLLECTIVE LEADERSHIP, STATE COMMITTEE ON THE STATE OF EMERGENCY.

National Salvation Front. A grass-roots revolutionary movement of anti-communists in Romania which deposed the communist dictator President Nicolae Ceausescu; he was captured and executed by the revolutionaries on 23 December 1989, following the 16 December 1989 massacre by Romania's troops in the city of Timisoara. Also known as "Council of National Salvation."

National Security. The composite of systematized acts and institutions which the top leaders of a nation-state initiate and employ for the purpose of protecting its people, institutions, processes, and ideology from harmful acts by adversaries (e.g., hostile foreign states). In order to preserve the security of the American state, for example, the U.S. President has the power by virtue of his office to order warrantless searches, electronic surveillance, and the breaking-and-entering into of the private premises of persons (e.g. foreign agents) suspected (by the FBI) of being engaged in acts harmful to the state (e.g., espionage). Especially susceptible to such actions are foreign agents not registered with the U.S. Department of Justice according to the Foreign Agents Registration Act. Warrantless break-ins, searches, and surveillance are done by the exclusive authority of the U.S. President, according to the Executive Order issued on January 24, 1977, by U.S. President Jimmy Carter. This order supersedes the Executive Order issued by U.S. President Gerald R. Ford in 1975 authorizing such practices not only against foreign agents, but also against terrorists and organized crime activities. See CENTRAL INTELLIGENCE AGENCY, FEDERAL BUREAU OF INVESTIGATION, NATIONAL SECURITY AGENCY, NATIONAL SECURITY COUNCIL.

National Security Agency (NSA). An agency of the United States Department of Defense charged with the task of gathering and evaluating intelligence for purposes of national security. Also known as the "Puzzle Palace," because few know what is going on inside of it. See CENTRAL INTELLIGENCE AGENCY.

National Security and Information Organization. In the Farsi language, "Sazeman Ettelaat va Amniyat Kashvar (SAVAK)"; an internal security and secret police and external intelligence organization of the Iranian government under Shah Mohammad Reza Pahlavi (1953-1979), whose primary job was to keep the Shah in power through collaboration with the American CIA and Israel's Mossad. SAVAK became famous for the most sophisticated and imaginative methods of torture and oppression of its own people, and particularly those who favored total nationalization of Iran's greatest wealth—oil. The Shah was installed in 1953 with the personal assistance of a CIA operative, Kermit Roosevelt. See "Roosevelt Erection" in PROPRIETARIES, IRAN'S REVOLUTION, MOSSADEGH, PEACOCK THRONE.

National Security Council (NSC). An agency within the Executive Offices of the United States President, established in 1947 (under the National Security Act) for the purpose of advising the President on domestic and foreign security matters, consisting of the President, Vice-President secretaries of defense and state, the DI and CIA and the Chairman of the Joint Chiefs of Staff. Other persons can be invited at the discretion of the President. The office and its activities are managed and coordinated by the President's Special Assistant for National Security (held currently by retired Air Force General Brent Scowcroft) and a highly selective staff of experts. All proceedings and decisions are kept in the strictest secrecy. No participant may take notes and no records are kept of the proceedings or the decisions made by the Council, particularly those by the Operations Advisory Group, known previously as the "forty committee," the panel of experts that debates long-range national security policy. See CENTRAL INTELLIGENCE AGENCY, UNDERSECRETARIES COMMITTEE OF THE NATIONAL SECURITY COUNCIL, Appendices 14, 15, 29.

National Security Directive. See INTELLIGENCE OVERSIGHT.

National Silver Party. A splinter group of the Republican Party in the United States which endorsed William Jennings Bryan for the U.S. Presidency and advocated more free silver in circulation to ease the scarce supply of money. The party was active during the last part of the 19th century.

National Socialism. The philosophy and political programs of the Nazi party of Germany under Adolf Hitler (1933-1945). See FASCISM, LEBENSRAUM, NATIONAL SOCIALIST WORKER'S PARTY OF GERMANY.

National Socialist Party of America. Another name for the American Nazi party in the United States (i.e., the one that was permitted by the court to have a mass march in Skokie, Illinois, in 1978).

National Socialist Women's Organization (of Germany). See NATIONALSOZIALISTISCHE FRAUENSCHAFT.

National Socialist Worker's Party of Germany. In the German language, "National-Sozialistische Deutsche Arbeits Partei" (NSDAP). The single ruling party in the German Reich (German lands, or Empire) from 1933 to 1945 which was led by Adolf Hitler. The party was referred to as Nazi," short for "Nazional Sozialismus." When the Soviet Red Army approached the main building of the Chancellery in Berlin (the headquarters of Hitler and his staff), Hitler arranged a special reception on April 30, 1945, attended by his closest associates, during which he was formally wed to his long-time mistress, Eva Braun. After the wedding ceremony, Hitler appointed Admiral Karl Doenitz as his successor, then committed suicide with his wife, his dog, and with Dr. Goebbels and his family. See FASCISM.

National Sozialismus. In the German language, "National Socialism" or "Nazism." See NATIONAL SOCIALISM.

National State. A sovereign state in which the people share many ideals in common, which makes its existence and perpetuation possible. Also, a political community. (Most of the states in the world today are national states, and not necessarily based on ethnographical principles.) See ETHNOGRAPHICAL STATE, MOSAIC SOCIETY, MULTINATIONAL STATE.

National Statesman Party. See PROHIBITION PARTY.

National Supremacy. A doctrine based on three theoretical and empirical precepts to the effect that the U.S. Federal Government, as the principal agent of the American nation, is superior over the states in all controversies arising from concurrent jurisdiction. Those precepts are: (1) Articles I and IV of the U.S. Constitution (See Appendix 8); (2) the judicial determination in *McCulloch v. Maryland, Gibbons v. Olden,* and *Missouri v. Holland* (see Appendix 48); and (3) the Civil War (War of Secession), which discouraged secession and established the fact that the Union is permanent, as determined by the national government. See AMERICAN CIVIL WAR.

National Union for Total Independence of Angola (UNITA). A political and guerrilla force in Angola, under the leadership of a pro-Western educator, Dr. Jonas Savimbi, which struggles to unseat the once Soviet-backed regime of the National Front. The UNITA has been supported by the United States as well as by South Africa, and it currently occupies about one/third of the state's territory. The former Soviet Union no longer provides military, economic, and ideological assistance to the pro-communist regime, which is sustaining itself in power with the help of a Cuban contingent of forces dispatched by Fidel Castro, president of Cuba.

National Union for Total Liberation of Angola (NUTLA). See UNION FOR THE TOTAL LIBERATION OF ANGOLA (UNITA).

National Unity Campaign. See NEW REALISM.

National Voter Registration. See UNIVERSAL REGISTRATION.

National Women Conference of 1977. See NATIONAL ORGANIZATION FOR WOMEN.

National Women's Political Caucus. The political and intellectual (intelligentsia) group of the Women's Movement, organized in 1971 by Jane McMichael, dedicated to the cause of advancing women to more active participation in government, politics, and decision making in the nation. See NATIONAL ORGANIZATION FOR WOMEN (NOW), WOMEN POLITICAL ACTION GROUPS.

Nationalism. As a concept of national consciousness, the feeling of belonging to a certain homogeneous group or community; the practice of worshipping anything that belongs to a certain nation. A feeling common among peoples whose existence or interests are threatened by an outside force, or a feeling among peoples during their struggle for national independence and national identity. Extreme nationalism leads, as history shows, to division and conflict, and is the major cause of wars.

Nationality Act of 1940. See CITIZENSHIP, *TROP V. DULLES* in Appendix 48.

Nationalization. The act of taking over private property (e.g., industry vital to national security such as steel mills or coal mines) for public use (e.g., for the welfare of the entire state) during an emergency (e.g., an extensive labor strike, rebellion, natural disaster, or war) by the proper authority of the state (e.g., the U.S. President or the governor of a state in the United States). Also, a term often applied to the confiscation of property of one state located on the territory of another and to the act of the U.S. President in federalizing (e.g., impressing into federal service and under federal authority) the state militia (e.g., state National Guard military forces). See EXPROPRIATION, PRIVATIZATION.

Nationalsozialistische Frauenschaft. In the German language, "National Socialist Women's Organization of Germany." A totalitarian organization, auxiliary of the Nazi Party, for women (1933-1945) charged with the responsibility of gathering support for the Nazi cause.

Native American Party. An anti-foreign, anti-non-white, anti-foreign-born, anti-non-Anglo-Saxon, anti-non-Protestant, splinter group active in the United States during the 1840s. See SCUM.

Nativism. See SCUM.

NATO. See NORTH ATLANTIC TREATY ORGANIZATION.

Natural Justice. The issue of the doctrine of "natural law," meaning that all human rights are based on moral principles universally recognized, arose during U.S. Senate confirmation hearings of Judge Clarence Thomas for the U.S. Supreme Court in 1991. Judge Thomas was as reluctant to state his notion of natural law as he was to reveal his stand on abortion and *Roe v. Wade.* However, Thomas made it clear that the natural rights that he understands are the fundamental principles of liberty and equality proclaimed in the American Declaration of Independence (not an official document of the U.S. Government). During the debate of the U.S. Supreme Court in 1798, in *Calder v. Bull,* U.S. Chief Justice John Jay held that the legislature lacked power to force laws that were "against all reason and justice," and Justice James Iredell maintained that "the idea of natural justice is too indefinite a basis for legal decisions." Because Judge Thomas frequently referred in his writings to natural law, some of his opponents (e.g., Professor Laurence Tribe) believed that Thomas, in his judicial decisions, might upset the balance of power of the U.S. Congress and of every state and local legislature. A discrepancy arose when Prof. Tribe criticized Thomas for holding the Bill of Rights was to preserve natural rights, while another Supreme Court nominee, Judge Robert Bork, rejected in 1987, criticized him for his notion that "rights are based only on the letter of the Constitution." Judge Thomas never invoked natural law in his judicial opinions in the past and he has stated that "interpreting the Constitution I would apply the approaches which the Supreme Court has used and I would be governed by Supreme Court precedents on those matters that come before me as a judge." Justice Thurgood Marshall invoked natural law in *Brown v. Board of Education* in 1954. According to Prof. Michael W. McConnel, "belief in natural law cuts across ideological categories of left and right." Conservatives like Justice Rehnquist and Judge Bork favor positivism, but so does Justice Hugo Black, otherwise a liberal. See NATURAL LAW, Appendices 6, 8, 48, 51.

Natural Law. The law that is derived from and directed by the forces of nature rather than made or directed by man. A notion that any right (natural right) derived from natural law is superior to any man-made law, or man-given right, and that it cannot be taken away by anyone at will (e.g., the right to life, or the right to liberty). The notion of natural law was first introduced by the Stoics, and Cicero considered it to be the foundation of the state. To Cicero (106-43 BC), natural law was a "right reason in agreement with nature . . . it is of universal application, unchanging and everlasting; it summons to duty by its commands, and averts from wrongdoing by its prohibitions." Thomas Aquinas (1225-1274) further developed the notion of natural law by adding to it a divine or eternal law, the law of God, which is superior to any law; and natural law is a way of man's utilization of the eternal law. See NATURAL JUSTICE, Appendices 6, 8, 51.

Natural Region. A geographic area which has some uniform and homogeneous characteristics (e.g., geography, climate, vegetation, types of industry or agriculture, government, culture, and social institutions). Also, often referred to as a formal, homogeneous, statistically uniform, or static region. See REGIONALISM, STATE.

Natural Right. See NATURAL LAW.

Natural Slavery. The ancient political philosopher Aristotle (384-322 BC) advanced the notion that slavery is a natural order of stratification in a society; that all persons are born to serve God and a few others, their leaders; and that only the few from among them will be chosen, by virtue of certain skills or talents, to be free as leaders whom the rest will have to obey for the good of all.

Naturalization. An act of granting citizenship to an alien person, or an act of taking the citizenship of another state. Under the Immigration and Naturalization laws of the United States, an alien (or stateless person) may receive United States citizenship upon: fulfilling a legal residence requirement—minimum of five years, unless in some service of the United States (e.g., serving in the armed forces), or upon the extension of U.S. jurisdiction over another territory, (e.g., Puerto Rico or the Virgin Islands), in which case U.S. citizenship is granted *en masse* and without individual application. See CITIZENSHIP.

Naturalization Act. See ALIEN AND SEDITION ACTS.

Nature of the Executive Organization. See TYPES OF GOVERNMENTS.

Navy Sea, Air, and Land Teams (SEALS). See DELTA FORCE.

Naxalites. See INDIAN NATIONAL CONGRESS PARTY.

Nays and Yeas. See VIVA VOCE VOTE.

Nazi Internment. See JAPANESE INTERNMENT.

Nazi Putsch. In 1923, Adolf Hitler and his followers staged, from a Munich beer hall, an attack on the police and the military in an effort to gain control of the German government. The Putsch failed; 18 of Hitler's followers were killed and the Nazi leader himself was imprisoned. While in prison, Hitler wrote his book, *Mein Kampf*, a blueprint for his conquest of Europe and the world. Rudolf Hess, Hitler's deputy, assisted Hitler with his book by taking notes and typing the manuscript.

Nazism. See LEBENSRAUM, NATIONAL SOCIALIST WORKERS' PARTY OF GERMANY, FASCISM.

NDP. See NATIONAL DEMOCRATIC PARTY.

Necessary and Proper. A provision contained in Art. I, Sec. 8, of the U.S. Constitution, under which most of the implied powers of the U.S. Congress are hidden. Exactly as to what those powers are and how and when they are utilized depends on the "sense" of Congress as to the times and problems which need solutions. Education, for example, is not in the federal domain but is in that of the states, according to Amendment X; however, Congress has decided to usurp powers over this area during the past several decades because states failed to do, in the opinion of Congress, what was necessary and proper—educating all the people and not just some of them. See ELASTIC CLAUSE, Appendix 8.

Need to Know. See INTELLIGENCE.

Negative Growth. See ROME CLUB.

Negative Income Tax. A system of taxation that may subsidize the taxpayer from general revenue in order to help him to survive or to bring about a more equitable distribution of wealth in a society. Also known as reverse income tax. Progressive tax, on the other hand, is one in which the rate of tax, in percent, increases together with the increase of the tax base. If the tax base increases but the tax remains the same, this is a proportional tax. If the income base increases but tax decreases, this is a regressive tax.

Negative Power. See TYRANNY OF THE MAJORITY.

Negative Revolution. America's most distinguished political scientist, Professor Carl Friedrich, so characterized the new 1949 constitution of the Federal Republic of Germany, called the "Basic Law," because it was "backward-looking," and rejected all the democratic revolution and the counterrevolution of the Weimar era. It took away the voters' right to directly elect the nation's president and the chancellor (Kanzler), and the upper house of the parliament, the Bundesrat. These officials are elected by the lower house of the Parliament. The Bundestag, and the upper house consists of representatives of the various states (10), the Länder. See BASIC LAW, WEIMAR REPUBLIC.

Negritude. A concept associated with the innate emotional qualities that bind Negroes together culturally, socially, and politically. (This concept is credited to Leopold Sanghor, a pioneer in Negroid studies.) See PAN-NEGROISM.

Nemine Contradicente. In the Latin language, "by unanimous vote," or "by acclamation without dissenting vote."

Nenko. See FRAME SOCIETY.

Neo-Colonialism. A term applied to former colonial powers (e.g., France, England, Belgium, Portugal, the Netherlands, etc.) which have given up political and administrative control over their former colonies but which have retained (open or subtle) control over economic and military matters, and are exerting a strong cultural influence. This term is also applied to states which create a dependency status for the economically weaker nations through unique military power or economic wealth, thus conveying the appearance of colonial practice.

Neo-Fascism. See FASCISM.

Neo-Isolationism. Recurring isolationist practices. See ISOLATIONISM.

Neo-Nazism. See LEBENSRAUM, NATIONAL SOCIALIST WORKERS' PARTY OF GERMANY.

NEP. See NEW ECONOMIC POLICY.

Nepotism. The practice of employing relatives in public service at the expense of the public, regardless of the merits of their ability to carry out the tasks assigned.

Net National Product (NNP). The market value of all goods and services produced by the national economy during a given fiscal year minus depreciation (capital allowance). See GROSS NATIONAL PRODUCT (GNP).

Networking. The practice of establishing contacts and relationships, vertically and horizontally, often globally as in the case of multinational and transnational enterprises, in order to expedite information for material or political gain. See POWER ELITE.

Neutrality. The practice of refraining from political or military alliances in relation with other states. Neutrality may be self-proclaimed (and in such case it may or may not be recognized by other states), or it may be recognized by other states if proclaimed and observed traditionally for an extended period of time. In order for a state to sustain the status of neutrality, it must refrain from aiding one belligerent state against another in case of war, or, if the neutral state decides to provide such aid, it must do so to all belligerents on an equal, impartial basis. Belgian neutrality was recognized from 1831 until Germany violated it by invading Belgium in 1914; the Belgian Congo (now the state of Zaire in Africa) has been recognized as a neutral territory since 1885; Luxembourg, since 1867; Laos, since 1962 (until 1975 when the communists took over); Austria's neutrality is recognized by the four major powers: the United States, Great Britain, France, and the Soviet Union; Switzerland's neutrality (one of the oldest and most durable ones) has remained intact since 1815 (the time of the Congress of Vienna); and Finland's neutrality rested on a bilateral treaty with the Soviet Union. The laws of neutrality (a matter of cooperation among states based on good will) are regulated by the experiences of the Genocide Convention, the Nuremberg Nazi War Criminals' Trials, the United Nations Charter, and bilateral agreements among states made specifically to this effect. The Swiss government raised the possibility of modifying its neutrality status once it becomes integrated into the European Community in 1992. Swiss President Rene Felber sought the opinion of U.S. President Bush on that matter in February 1992. Finland and Austria face similar redefining of their neutrality status. See NONALIGNMENT, Appendix 106.

Neutrality Laws. A series of four congressional laws which aimed at preventing United States involvement in foreign wars, particularly in Europe, but which inadvertently helped Adolf Hitler in Germany, Francisco Franco in Spain, and Benito Mussolini in Italy to consolidate their powers and to pursue external aggression, culminating in W.W.II in 1939. The first three acts of 1935, 1936 and 1937 stipulated that when the President of the United States proclaims the existence of a foreign war, certain curtailments of citizens' rights would go automatically into effect (e.g., no travel on foreign vessels, no shipping via belligerent carriers). These acts authorized operationalization of any policy which would prevent the United States from becoming involved in a foreign war. The 1939 law softened the Debt Default Act of 1934, by allowing foreign nations to purchase war materiel from the United States on a "cash and carry" basis only, so that there would be no war debt to collect, and American shipping would not be used, so as not to become a target for hostile (German) forces. In this case, the United States practically abandoned its right to freely use the high seas as international waters, and enhanced aggressive intentions of the totalitarian regimes in Europe, mainly those of Nazi Germany and Fascist Italy. These laws are often referred to as "head-in-the-sand" legislation. See ISOLATIONISM, KLINGBERG CYCLE, NEUTRALITY, NONALIGNMENT.

Neutralization. In the American defense vernacular, "assassination." Assassinations of foreign leaders by American officials or nationals was forbidden by an Executive Order issued by President Gerald Ford in 1976 and subsequently upheld in the executive orders of all presidents who followed him. See ASSASSINATION.

Neutron Bomb. A nuclear assault weapon system which, when deployed, destroys and kills living organisms (e.g., fauna and flora), but leaves inorganic matter (e.g., buildings) intact. As a gesture of good will and subtle diplomacy, in view of the SALT II agreement to be signed with the USSR, U.S. President Jimmy Carter announced on April 7, 1978, that the United States would refrain from mass production of this highly destructive tactical weapon. President Carter pointed out, however, that this decision to halt further production of the neutron bomb " . . . will be influenced by the degree to which the Soviet Union shows restraint in its conventional and nuclear arms programs and force deployment affecting the security of the United States and Western Europe." Following the President's announcement, the Soviet Union responded on April 9, 1978, with statements accusing the U.S. President of deceptive tactics. A dispatch by TASS (in the Russian language, "Telegrafitcheskaya Agentsya Sovyetskghogo Soyuza"—Telegraphic Agency of the Soviet Union), the official international telegraphic news agency of the former USSR, stated that while President Carter had ordered a halt on mass production of the neutron bomb, he had not precluded smaller versions being used by ground delivery devices (e.g., artillery or rocket launchers) for tactical purposes. On the other hand, Hsinhua News Agency, of the Peoples Republic of China, accused the Soviets of attempting to "intimidate" and to "blackmail" the United States with possible failure of the upcoming SALT treaty if the U.S. did not abandon the neutron bomb in any form or shape altogether. The Chinese favor America's neutron bomb arsenal as a means of maintaining military superiority over the Soviets, whom the Chinese fear the most. See ARMS AND WAR MATERIEL SALES, HARDWARE DIPLOMACY, STRATEGIC ARMS LIMITATION TALKS (SALT).

Never Told a Lie. A popular opinion about first U.S. President, George Washington (1789-1797), attesting to his honesty and integrity as national leader. See POLITICAL ETHICS.

New Africa. See REPUBLIC OF NEW AFRICA.

New Alliance Party. One of about five-hundred minor political parties and factions which presented candidates for election for president and vice-president of the United States during the 1992 presidential election. Its presidential candidate was Lenora Fulani.

New Beginning. One of the more popular slogans of presidential candidate Ronald Reagan, widely popularized in 1980. His slogan in 1984 was, "Are you better off now than you were four years ago?" The nation prospered and many were better off.

New Class. This label is applied to two different situations, and on two separate continents: (1) Milovan Djilas, Yugoslav author and former vice president of Yugoslavia under Broz Tito (subsequently imprisoned by Tito for his "free" thinking), characterized the "new class" (also the title of his book) to be the governing elite in communist states, including the USSR, who were oppressive, selfish, and self centered; (2) the new generation of American voters after W.W.II, well educated (under the GI Bill) and with broader understanding of the world and its problems, who are shaping the destiny of America and influencing world events.

New Communist Man. See MASS LINE, NEW LEFT.

New Congress Party. See INDIAN NATIONAL CONGRESS PARTY.

New Deal. A phrase used to describe the policies and the sweeping administrative reforms (which sought to restore the national economy after the depression years of the 1920s and 1930s) of U.S. President Franklin D. Roosevelt (1933-1945). The President used this phrase in his acceptance speech at the National Democratic Convention in Chicago in 1932. The New Deal Legislation (Acts), can be divided into three distinct categories: (1) recovery, (2) relief, and (3) reform. The (1) Recovery measures were as follows: closing of the banks on order of President Franklin D. Roosevelt, on 6 March 1933; Emergency Banking Relief Act of 9 March 1933; on 5 April 1933, the President ordered the surrender of gold; 19 April 1933, the President ordered the abandon of the gold standard; on 5 June 1933, the Gold-Payments Clause repealed; the National Industrial Recovery Act of 16 June 1933, created the National Recovery Administration (NRA) and the Public Works Administration (PWA). Under (2) Relief: Congress passed the Unemployment Relief Act on 12 May 1933, and created the Federal Emergency Administration (FERA) and the Agricultural Adjustment Act (AAA); on 13 June 1933, Congress passed the Home Owners' Refinancing Act and created the Home Owners' Loan Corporation (HOLC); and (3) Reform measures: Beer and Wine Revenue Act passed on 22 March 1933; the Tennessee Valley Authority (TVA) passed on 18 May 1933; the Federal Securities Act, passed on 27 May 1933, and the Glass-Steagall Banking Reform Act passed on 16 June 1933, creating the Federal Deposit Insurance Corporation.

New Dealocrat. A derogatory term for U.S. President Franklin D. Roosevelt (1933-1945) because of his New Deal programs and policies. See NEW DEAL.

New Democracy. See JACKSONIAN DEMOCRACY.

New Despotism. See DESPOTISM.

New Diplomacy. A call during the 1918 Paris Peace Conference for a radical shift from the past policies of tensions, conflicts, and wars among nations, and for the creation of a supranational organization, the League of Nations, which would oversee relations between and among states, guaranteeing that they were conducted according to norms and rules of international law and not individual ambitious interests. The leader of the "new diplomacy" group was U.S. President Woodrow Wilson—being the first U.S. President to travel abroad while in office—who was strongly supported in his efforts by another non-European statesman, General Jan Christian Smuts of South Africa. See PARIS PEACE CONFERENCE.

New Economic Policy (NEP). In the Russian language, "Novaya Ekonomitcheskaya Polytika." A series of economic reforms aimed at reviving and stimulating the national economy of the newly formed socialist state in Russia (1921-1923) under the leadership of Vladimir I. Lenin following the period of the so-called "War on Communism." The principal feature of this policy was a temporary return to a free (capitalistic) market economy in which private ownership of small enterprises was allowed, enhancing private (domestic and foreign) investments. Because of mass starvation in

Russia, the United States via the American Relief Administration under the leadership of Herbert Hoover, distributed about $50 million of aid to the people in Russia and Eastern Europe. After Lenin's death in 1924, the NEP practices were terminated by Josef Stalin with a sharp turn to massive and forceful collectivization of the land, confiscation of private property, and nationalization of all foreign property and investments. See GREAT ECONOMIC DEBATE.

New Economy. See NIXON'S ECONOMIC POLICY.

New England Dynasty. Like Virginia, New England produced a number of distinguished politicians and statesmen who were instrumental in shaping the destiny of the American nation. Some of them were: (1) Benjamin Franklin (1706-1790), writer, publisher, printer, scientist, philosopher; (2) John Adams, U.S. President (1797-1801); (3) John Quincy Adams, U.S. President (1825-1829); (4) Franklin Pierce, U.S. President (1853-1857); (5) Chester Alan Arthur, U.S. President (1881-1885); (6) Oliver Ellsworth, Chief Justice of the U.S. Supreme Court (1796-1800); (7) Roger Williams (1603-1683), founder of Providence, Rhode Island; (8) Thomas Hooker, co-author of the Fundamental Orders of Connecticut (1639); and (9) James Otis, a leader of the Massachusetts legislature (1761-1769). See VIRGINIA: MOTHER OF PRESIDENTS, Appendices 7, 16.

New Federalism. A notion pertaining to federal-state relationships in the United States, to the effect that the divergence and complexity of problems that each unit of the American federation faces today can only be coped with effectively by the governments of these units, rather than by the national federal government; that the federal government would render better service by sharing its revenues with these units instead of trying to solve their problems on a federal level. Also referred to as "cooperative" or "conservative" federalism. See FEDERALISM.

New Freedom. A core issue of Woodrow Wilson's presidential campaign in 1912 (also the title of one of his books) which emphasized the need for more economic freedoms from large corporations and monopolies which had practically gained control of the economy. Wilson called for reforms aimed at regulation of big business, particularly monopolies, and federal aid to small business enterprises. On the other hand, one of his opponents, Theodore Roosevelt, who ran on the "Bull Moose" ticket (the Republican candidate was William H. Taft), proclaimed his own "New Nationalism" doctrine in his campaign speech in Osawatomie, Kansas. He proclaimed that the national government must increase its power just as the leader of the Federalists, Alexander Hamilton, had urged many decades before, in order to be able to deal with existing abuses of power that caused social and political ills in the nation, meaning the large corporations and the monopolies which had operated almost uncontrolled and unregulated. To maintain better control over unscrupulous businesses, national power, urged Roosevelt, must be more centralized in order to be more effective.

New French Philosophers. A coalition of young intellectuals in contemporary France, composed of radical leftist elements, which seeks a modern alternative to governance of the contemporary state by means of large citizen participation in decision making in political and economic matters of the state. It rejects, however all existing models of governance, both by the socialist and the capitalist states, considering them inadequate for and incapable of a modern democracy in which, for example, the workers would decide the production plans in factories and the manner of disposition of inventories; production and trade would be market oriented and would not rely on centralized planning; and profits would be shared accordingly, with taxes being paid to the state.

New Form of Anarchy. See ANARCHIST.

New Frontier. A term used to describe the pioneer-like spirit which characterized some of the reforms advocated by U.S. President John F. Kennedy (1961-1963), mainly those that aimed at reviving the economic, political, and social life of the American nation.

New Hampshire Presidential Primary. Among the American states that hold primary elections for the presidency, New Hampshire is the first, usually in February. It is claimed by politicians that this primary sets the tone of the presidential primaries in other states, as well as the presidential election in November. See PRIMARY ELECTION.

New Harmony. See UTOPIA.

New Haven School. See POSITIVIST VIEW OF LAW.

New Jersey Plan. See PLANS OF THE AMERICAN UNION.

New Leadership Fund. See RIPON SOCIETY.

New Left. A conglomeration of political reformist groups, active in the United States during the 1960s and 1970s, advocating, among other things, the replacement of the present political, social, and economic system in the United States with a new one, preferably with that of socialism or communism. Organizations known to be subscribing to the philosophy of the New Left are: the De Bois Clubs, the Student Non-Violent Coordinating Committee, the Students for Democratic Society, the Mao-oriented Progressive Labor Party, and a score of others. Some of the major groups were the "counterculture" groups, the Youth International Party (Yippies); the Committee for an Open Convention (concentrated on the 1968 Democratic Party Convention in Chicago and caused serious disruptions and riots); and the National Mobilization Committee to End the War in Vietnam. Some of its former activists, like Tom Hayden (who was seeking followers among the rioters in large urban areas, using the tactics of the Russian revolutionaries of pre-Soviet Russia) and the intellectual Professor of Philosophy at the University of California, Herbert Marcuse (who advocated government through an "intellectual dictatorship"), went out in search of the "new proletariat" among the poor, the black, the unemployed, the war resisters, the ignorant, or whoever could be found. They went out to organize, although the act of organizing involved the establishment of authority, a basic concept against which the New Left had originally mobilized. Soon they both found that the "new proletariat" was simply not there. The blue-collar class, which they thought would be susceptible to revolutionary activity because of boredom of the assembly line and mortgage payments, was obviously satisfied with that status and has shown little revolutionary zeal. Marcuse had to conclude (in his study of *One Dimensional Man*) that the capitalist system is very successful in competing with Marxism by providing a high standard of living and relative civil liberties (including "sexual license"), all of which buy off the proletariat, and drain them "of any revolutionary propensities . . . ." Disappointed in their search for the "new proletariat," Marcuse turned his attention toward the discovery of a "new man" (described in *An Essay on Liberation*), one that will be "biologically" resistant to capitalistic incentives (the "good life") and the construction of a society governed by an "educational dictatorship," while Hayden went to work—dressed in suit and tie—for a "capitalistic employer." See STUDENTS FOR DEMOCRATIC SOCIETY (SDS), WEATHER UNDERGROUND.

New Look Army. See PENTOMIC ARMY.

New Missouri Compromise. See FOURTH TERMITE.

New Nationalism. See AMERICA'S NEW NATIONALISM, NEW FREEDOM.

New Order. See CANCER IN THE PACIFIC, LEBENSRAUM.

New Philosophers. See NEW FRENCH PHILOSOPHERS.

New Populism. A term commonly applied to U.S. President Jimmy Carter's way of communication with the common people and his political style, sometimes referred to by critics as "peanut populism," after the fact that President Carter was at one time a peanut farmer in Georgia. See POPULISM.

New Proletariat. See NEW LEFT.

New Realism. A campaign slogan of John Anderson, candidate for U.S. president in 1980, calling for a new look at domestic and foreign problems. Anderson, who called his campaign "The National Unity Campaign," advocated searching for realistic rather than "wishful-thinking" solutions. He maintained that the USSR, because of lack of resources, never intended to attack the United States directly, but has pursued instead an aggressive rhetoric with the hope that the capitalist system (and the United States) would fall apart due to internal contradictions, and the socialist, communist Soviet system would prevail by way of the Sun Tzu dictum: winning a war without fighting.

New Republicanism. See EISENHOWER DOCTRINE.

New Scotland Yard. See SCOTLAND YARD, SECRET INTELLIGENCE SERVICE (SIS).

New Spirit. See CARTER DOCTRINE AND STATE OF THE UNION MESSAGE.

New World. See URBANIZATION.

New World Order. See AMERICAN CENTURY.

Newprocess Technologies. See COMPARATIVE ADVANTAGE.

Newproduct Technologies. See COMPARATIVE ADVANTAGE.

NFLP. See NATIONAL FRONT FOR THE LIBERATION OF PALESTINE.

NFLSC. See NATIONAL FRONT FOR THE LIBERATION OF THE SOMALI COAST.

Niagara Falls Conference. The ABC powers (Argentina, Brazil, and Chile) met with the United States and Mexico in Niagara Falls, New York, in June, 1914, for the purpose of discussing problems which could have led to war between Mexico and the United States. U.S. Navy ships had taken control of the harbor of Vera Cruz, Mexico, for the purpose of intercepting German submarines. Mexico construed this move as an hostile act and, in return, detained American sailors in Tampico. The United States demanded from Victoriano Huerta of Mexico not only release of the sailors, but also an apology, a salute to the U.S. flag, and a twenty-one gun salute. Huerta complied with all demands and war was avoided. See GOOD NEIGHBOR POLICY.

Nicaraguan Democratic Forces (NDF). See MORAL EQUIVALENT OF OUR FOUNDING FATHERS.

Night of Broken Glass. See KRISTALLNACHT.

Night Watchman State. A state whose laws, institutions, and policies are solely devoted to the protection of public interests against the vested interests. See CAPITALISM, NATIONAL INTEREST, SOCIALISM.

Nihilism. A philosophy rejecting organized and institutionalized life of society. Literally, nihilism is a belief in nothing.

Nine-Power Treaty. A treaty signed during the Washington (U.S.A) Conference (November 12, 1921-February 6, 1922), by England, Japan, France, China, Italy, Belgium, the Netherlands (Holland), Portugal, and the United States, calling for mutual respect of sovereignty and territorial integrity of China; extension of aid to China for the purpose of maintaining effective and stable government; respect for commercial and trade relations with China by all nations; and the refraining of individual nations from seeking any special rights or privileges in China. This Treaty is also known as the "International Bill of Rights for China."

Nixon-Brezhneyev Summit. Soviet Communist Party General-Secretary (and President of the Soviet Union [1977-1982]), Leonid I. Brezhneyev, visited the United States on an official state visit (June 16-25, 1973), during which he conferred with President Richard M. Nixon and signed nine separate agreements pertaining to Soviet-American relations. One of the major agreements pertained to mutual consultations should a nuclear war seem possible.

Nixon Court. The four Associate Justices of the U.S. Supreme Court who were nominated to the nation's highest tribunal by U.S. President Richard M. Nixon (1969-1974). They are: Chief Justice Warren E. Burger, Justices Harry A. Blackmun, Lewis F. Powell, Jr., and William H. Rehnquist. See SUPREME COURT OF THE UNITED STATES, Appendices 46, 47.

Nixon Doctrine. In the main, the policy statement issued by U.S. President Richard M. Nixon during his trip to Southeast Asia in 1969, and which pertains to Asian nations. (This became also known as the "Guam Doctrine," since it was proclaimed while the President visited Guam.) The President stated that, in the future, free Asian nations which become threatened by (international or external) forces of communism would have to bear the responsibility for their own defense, and that direct American military assistance (combat troops and war materiel) would be provided only if that nation were directly threatened by a major foreign power, one with superior military capability. Nixon's so-called "Southern Strategy," no doubt, will with time be recognized as a part of his doctrine. The chief architect of the "Southern Strategy" was U.S. Senator Strom Thurmond (R-South Carolina) who advised Nixon during the 1968 election not to count on the black vote of the South. See I AM NOT A CROOK, SOUTHERN STRATEGY, WATERGATE AFFAIR.

Nixon-Kennedy Debate. See GREAT DEBATES.

Nixon-Mao Summit. See PEKING SUMMIT.

Nixon Round. The continuation of negotiations on the reduction of tariffs on commodities exchanged between the United States and Western European states, originated by President John F. Kennedy and continued under the administration of President Richard M. Nixon. See KENNEDY ROUND, NIXON'S ECONOMIC POLICY.

Nixon Tapes. See WATERGATE AFFAIR.

Nixon's Economic Policy. In the main, a series of economic measures undertaken by the President of the United States, Richard M. Nixon, during his two administrations, and aimed mostly at stabilizing the American economy overburdened by the involvement in Southeast Asia and external economic competition. On the domestic front, the following major measures were undertaken: the so-called "Phase One," introduced by an Executive Order of August 15, 1971, froze all wages and prices for a period of ninety days; "Phase Two" (November, 1971-January, 1973) established guidelines through the Wage Board and Price Commission (new agencies established to oversee these programs), allowing yearly wage increases up to five-and-one-half (5 1/2) percent and price increases up to two-and-one-half (2 1/2) percent per year; "Phase Three" (from January 1973 on) called for voluntary wage and price controls in line with the guidelines set up in Phase Two; and the President refused to spend money, appropriated already by Congress, for projects which the President deemed unnecessary at this time. (These funds were impounded in February 1973.) On the international front, the President freed the U.S. dollar for devaluation against the currencies of other countries (by loosening its ties with gold) and considerably halted the conversion of the dollar held by foreign banks into gold. On January 12, 1973, he devalued the U.S. dollar ten percent in order to stabilize the international balance of payment deficit. ("Phase Four" was planned, but was never undertaken.)

NKGB. See PEOPLE'S COMMISSION FOR INTERNAL AFFAIRS.

NKVD. See PEOPLE'S COMMISSION FOR INTERNAL AFFAIRS.

NLC. See NATIONAL LEAGUE OF CITIES.

NLF. See NATIONAL LIBERATION FRONT.

NML. See NATIONAL MUNICIPAL LEAGUE.

NNP. See NET NATIONAL PRODUCT.

No Compromise. See MARCH FOR LIFE.

No Contest. See NOLO CONTENDERE

No Deposit, No Return. See POLITICAL SYSTEM, Appendix 3.

No-Fault Legislation. National or state legislation aimed at eliminating expensive and costly litigation in lawsuits resulting from automobile or divorce cases, providing for the settlement of such cases without holding either party at fault. Several states in the United States have adopted such legislation, and the Senate Commerce Committee of the U.S. Senate, urged by consumer groups, has also approved a bill on no-fault automobile insurance that is national in scope. However, the House of Representatives is reluctant to approve it on the grounds that a formula must be found before the bill is approved to prevent insurance companies from amassing sudden windfall profits.

No-Growth Policy. See ROME CLUB.

No-Knock Provision. See OMNIBUS CRIME CONTROL AND SAFE STREETS ACT OF 1968.

No Left Turn. See AGONIZING REAPPRAISAL.

No More Cubas! When all attempts to remove Dr. Fidel Castro from power in Cuba failed, the United States government/military/intelligence complex unofficially declared: "No more Cubas" in the Western Hemisphere. Therefore, all efforts were made to oppose the Sandanistas in Nicaragua; and military intervention was taken in Grenada, and in Panama in order to stop the spread of Soviet and Cuban influence in the area.

No Pasaran. See LA PASIONARIA.

No-Win War. The war in Vietnam which was ended by the combatants in 1975 after the U.S. decided to terminate hostilities. See TRAGIC SITUATION, VIETNAMIZATION.

No-Wing. See WINGER.

Noble Order of the Knights of Labor. An informal organization launched in 1869 as a secret society to struggle for better working conditions by workers (an eight-hour workday and better pay). It organized producer cooperatives for black and white workers, for men and women alike; proposed codes of safety, health standards, and sanitary conditions at work. It excluded from its ranks liquor dealers, bankers, professional gamblers, stockholders, and lawyers. Its membership grew very rapidly under the leadership of Terrence V. Powderly, from 90,000 in 1870, to a million in 1886. Although it was successful in gaining some benefits for workers through a series of successful strikes, anti-labor forces were prepared to destroy the movement. On May 4, 1886, a bloody confrontation took place on Haymarket Square in Chicago, where, during a strike, police attacked and a bomb planted by a provocateur exploded, killing several persons, including a police officer. After that, the Order was under constant attack as an anarchist organization. It became less active, but passed its legacy to the newly formed American Federation of Labor (AFL), and by 1900 had merged with the new organization. In 1892, a German-born governor of Illinois, John P. Altgeld, sided with the labor organization and soon an eight-hour work day was secured. This standard was one of labor's most significant achievements, which was readily adopted throughout the United States, and other industrialized countries.

NOC. See NONOFFICIAL COVER.

Nodal Region. See FUNCTIONAL REGION.

NOFORN. Any document of a governmental agency in the United States, federal, state or local, which though it may be unclassified and available to Americans and alien residents in the United States, may be stamped "noforn," meaning it will not be revealed to foreigners.

Nolle Prosequi. In the Latin language, "not to prosecute" or "refrain from prosecution." A decision not to prosecute a case before a court of law made upon the request of either the prosecuting attorney or the plaintiff and regardless of the merits of the case (e.g., regardless of whether the party is guilty or innocent).

Nolo Contendere. In the Latin language, "no contest." In practice, when one charged with a crime pleads "nolo contendere" (no contest), it means that one neither admits nor denies the charges; but before the law, this plea equals admission of guilt. (Former Vice President Spiro T. Agnew pleaded "nolo contendere" on October 10, 1973, to charges of tax evasion in the state of Maryland, and he was sentenced by the court to three years probation and a $10,000 fine.)

Nolpro. See NOLLE PROSEQUI.

Nom De Guerre. In the French language, "name in war" or "alias in war." It is an ancient practice by military and political leaders, particularly those who must operate in secrecy (e.g., revolutionary and guerrilla leaders), to adopt such names in order to conceal their real identity. During the Bolshevik Revolution in Russia (1917), for example, Joseph Visaryanovitch Djugashvili changed his name to "Josef Stalin," and the leader of the Revolution itself, V. I. Ulyanov, changed his name to "V. I. Lenin." Mustafa Kemal of Turkey took the name of "Atatürk." During W.W.II, U.S. President Franklin D. Roosevelt was known in secret allied communications as POTUS, and Winston Churchill, the Prime Minister of England, as "Naval Person" (Churchill was appointed as First Lord of Admiralty in 1911). Even Patricia Hearst, when she decided to join the Symbionese Liberation

Army (SLA), took the name of "Tania," after a heroine who was fighting capitalism with Cuba's revolutionary, Ernesto "Che" Guevara, in the Bolivian mountains.

Nomos. An administrative division, a department, in Greece.

Non-Amendable Constitutional Provisions. See INDEFEASIBLE LAW.

Non-Candidate Candidate. A practice common in American electoral politics whereby aspirants for public office, uncertain of success, make hints that they may be interested; or those who are interested, deny it. Such candidates wait to the last moment hoping for certain contingencies: that they may be drafted by a political party; that their names may be put on ballot as a write-in during a primary election or that some candidates in the race might become victims of misfortune (e.g., some skeletons in the candidate's closet are revealed) causing them to withdraw, thus improving the hopeful's position. The governor of New York announced his non-candidacy, but allowed voters in New Hampshire to write-in his name during the February 1992 primary election there. On 20 February 1992, one of America's most intelligent business leaders, Ross Perot, was the first one ever to announce his non-candidacy-candidacy for the American presidency on live television ("Larry King Live," CNN), declaring that if a grass-roots movement in fifty states registers him as an independent candidate he will accept. "Get in the ring with me," he said, "and stay there!"—meaning that he will accept the challenge, but only with mass support. Before and after the election, he rejected the traditional lobbies, pressure or interest groups, and political parties, as vehicles useful in the delivery of his program for governance. See GRASS-ROOTS PEROT, HAT IN THE RING, PRIMARY ELECTION.

Non-Career Diplomat. See FOREIGN SERVICE OFFICER (FSO).

Non-Delegability of Powers, Doctrine of. It refers primarily to the United States Congress which, according to Article I of the U.S. Constitution, may not delegate its legislative powers. See CONGRESS OF THE UNITED STATES, Appendix 8.

Non-Person. See CHAPTER 77.

Non-Placet. In the Latin language, "dissenting vote."

Non-Vetoable Legislation. A bill which has overwhelming majority support in the U.S. Congress, and the passage of which is urgent (e.g., payroll, federal employees, or military appropriation in case of war or national emergency) and which has chances of an easy re-passage in case of presidential veto. Presidents, knowing that, do not veto such legislation. It is this kind of bill to which riders, additions that are not necessarily related and that ordinarily would not be easily accepted by the President, are usually attached for easy passage (easy ride). See CONGRESS OF THE UNITED STATES, RIDER, UNITED STATES HOUSE OF REPRESENTATIVES, UNITES STATES SENATE.

Nonalignment. The state of not being affiliated with, connected with, or not taking part in any association, agreement, or military alliance. The term "positive neutrality" is also used. See NEUTRALITY, THIRD WORLD.

Nonautonomous Change (NAC). See POWER.

Nonbelligerency. See BELLIGERENCY.

Noncentralization Principle. See FEDERALISM.

Nonessential Right. See *POLKO V. CONNECTICUT* in Appendix 48.

Nonfeasance. See MALFEASANCE.

Nongermane Amendment. See RIDER.

Nonofficial Cover (NOC). The practice of planting intelligence agents in professions or positions of employment which will not reveal their true identity and their association with an intelligence agency.

Nonpartisan. Beyond party lines; one showing no bias because of party loyalty; or one voting regardless of party affiliation. See PARTISAN.

Nonpartisan Ballot. A voting ballot indicating no party affiliation of candidates. See NONPARTISAN.

NORAD. See UNITED STATES-CANADIAN NORTH AMERICAN AIR DEFENSE SYSTEM.

Nordic Council. An agreement signed in 1952 by Denmark, Finland, Iceland, Norway, and Sweden on economic, legal, and social cooperation between the signatory states.

Normal Science. See KUHN'S PARADIGM.

Normalcy. U.S. Senator Warren G. Harding remarked in 1920 on the traumatic experience of W.W.I and the involvement in European affairs while economic problems at home were mounting: "America's present need is not heroics, but healing; not nostrums but normalcy; not revolution but restoration . . . not surgery but serenity." Harding served as U.S. President 1921-1923.

Normative Law. See ORGANIC LAW, LEGAL NORM.

Norris-LaGuardia Anti-Injunction Act of 1932. See GREAT DEPRESSION.

North-African Entente. See INTER-MAGHREBIAN CONFERENCES.

North American Accord. In order to mend his fences, presidential candidate Ronald Reagan called for a conference in November 1979 with the American neighbors: Canada and Mexico. The official pronounced objective was to establish good rapport since countries lack the luxury of choosing their neighbors. Once elected Ronald Reagan wanted Canada and Mexico to support his economic and military policies in the Western Hemisphere, and also, especially his policies with the Soviet (evil) Empire. In retrospect, his plans proved very successful; frictions with Canada diminished, and trade relations improved (the United States was purchasing more oil from Mexico than ever before, and also allowed a large influx of Mexican labor into the United States. Mexico's President José López Portillo met with the President-elect on 5 January 1981, in Mexico City and it was agreed that Mexico would not obstruct American policies in other parts of Latin America, particularly concerning leftist political movements and guerrilla action challenging American interests in the Hemisphere. See Appendices 29, 107.

North Atlantic Treaty Organization (NATO). A military defense organization of Western Europe and the United States which was created by a treaty signed in Washington, D.C., on April 4, 1949, as a measure to deter possible Soviet aggression against the Western European democracies. The agreement became effective on August 24, 1949, when it was ratified by: Belgium, Canada, Denmark, France (which withdrew its participation in 1966 without abrogating the treaty, causing the headquarters of NATO to be moved from Paris to Brussels, Belgium), Iceland, Italy, Luxembourg, the Netherlands, Norway, Portugal, the United Kingdom, and the United States. Germany (the Federal Republic of), Turkey, and Greece also joined later. In 1974 Greece ceased to participate in NATO activities after the Turkish invasion of Cyprus. The member-states of the alliance have agreed to settle all disputes among themselves through pacific means, to establish a system of collective security against attack (e.g., by the former Soviet bloc), and to regard an attack on one as an attack on all. NATO maintains several international commands (e.g., in Europe, the United States, and Canada). The first commander of NATO was U.S. General D. D. Eisenhower (subsequently U.S. President (1953-1961)). After the opening of the Berlin Wall on 9 November 1989, the East German regime, the German Democratic Republic (DDR) sought out some accommodations with the West German (German Federal Republic) government of Chancellor Helmut Kohl by having some East German officials appointed to the administrative corps of NATO, but such overtures were rejected. On 23 August 1990, the two Germanys united, which was accepted by the West German Bundestag and Bundesrat on 3 October 1990, and the communist state of East Germany ceased to exist. The military of East Germany, however, also sought the possibility of joining the West German Bundeswehr, the armed forces, but they were told openly that the only army they could join is the "Salvation Army." Subsequently, the army and the Stasi, secret police, were disbanded in East Germany. See INTER-OPERABILITY, PACIFIC SETTLEMENT OF DISPUTES, WARSAW PACT, Appendices 29, 105.

North-South Dialogue. See GROUP OF 77.

Northeast-Midwest Economic Advancement Coalition. See CONGRESSIONAL CAUCUS.

Northern Society of St. Petersburg. See DECEMBRISTS.

Nose-Counting Democracy. See JACKSONIAN DEMOCRACY.

Not to Look on the Federal Government as an Enemy, but as a Friend. See MEET THE PEOPLE TRIP.

Notary Public. A person authorized by the government (state or federal in the United States) to authenticate and certify documents and signatures of persons upon payment of a fee.

Notre Dame Doctrine. A policy statement made by U.S. President Jimmy Carter during his speech at Notre Dame University in Indiana on May 22, 1977, to the effect that opposition to communism as a threat to the United States is no longer one of the main objectives of United States foreign policy.

Noumenalism. From Kant's "noumenon"—ultimate reality as it is in itself.

Novus Ordo Seclorum. "New order of the Ages." Latin motto of the Great Seal of the U.S.

NOW. See NATIONAL ORGANIZATION FOR WOMEN.

NPD. See NATIONAL DEMOCRATIC PARTY OF GERMANY.

NPN. NATIONAL PARTY OF NIGERIA.

NPP. NIGERIA PEOPLES PARTY.

NSA. See NATIONAL SECURITY AGENCY.

NSC. See NATIONAL SECURITY COUNCIL.

NSDAP. See NATIONAL SOCIALIST WORKERS' PARTY OF GERMANY.

NSWPG. See NATIONAL SOCIALIST WORKERS' PARTY OF GERMANY.

Nuclear Club. The once exclusive membership in the nuclear club (e.g., the United States, England, France, and the former Soviet Union) grew in membership to about twenty nations in recent times following the dissolution of the Soviet Union in 1991. In the former Soviet Union, once a single nuclear power, there are several: Russia, Ukraine, Kazakhstan, Belarus, and possibly others. All efforts to have these nations surrender their arsenals are politically unrealistic and naïve. In addition, other nations such as Israel and North Korea have nuclear weapons capabilities and others are getting closer everyday. There is an increasing danger that one of these countries may use their nuclear forces to destroy the globe if politically cornered by adversaries.

Nuclear Deterrent. A weapon system of highly destructive capability (e.g., missiles with hydrogen or atomic warheads), which serves as a means to discourage aggression. See LONDON CLUB, NUCLEAR UMBRELLA.

Nuclear Family. A family consisting of parents and children. See ATOMIC FAMILY.

Nuclear Non-Proliferation Treaty. See MISSILE TECHNOLOGY CONTROL REGIME (MTCR).

Nuclear Test Ban Treaty. An agreement by Great Britain, the Soviet Union, and the United States, concluded in Moscow, U.S.S.R., in 1963, not to conduct nuclear tests in the atmosphere, under water, on the high seas or territorial waters, or at any place where such tests would create uncontrollable radioactive fallout. See LONDON CLUB, STRATEGIC ARMS LIMITATION TALKS (SALT).

Nuclear Umbrella. A notion pertaining to nuclear weapon capability whereby smaller states, because of lack of nuclear technology or unwillingness to develop it (e.g., saving national revenue for other purposes), rely on other states for their protection (e.g., the United States extends its nuclear umbrella to most of the Western states while the Soviet Union did the same with regard to the socialist states until

25 December 1991 when the USSR officially dissolved. Currently, there are four nuclear powers in the former USSR: Russia [with the largest stockpile of nuclear weapons], Belarus [with very few weapons], Kazakhstan and Ukraine. There are no indications, in spite of wishful thinking, that they will surrender their nuclear might to anyone in the near future). See LONDON CLUB.

Nuclear Weapons. See MANHATTAN PROJECT.

Nudum Pactum. In the Latin language, "a loose contract," "open contract," or "contract without specific restrictions."

Nullem Crimen Sine Lege. In the Latin language, "there is no crime against which there is no law" or "for every crime there is a law." See CRIME BY ANALOGY.

Nullification. The act of making a law non-applicable and void by making another law in its place; also, the right claimed by the states in the American Union to declare any act of Congress null, void, and not a law, and thus not binding upon any state, its officers, or its citizens, on the grounds that the state can act in a sovereign capacity through the convention of its people. See KENTUCKY AND VIRGINIA RESOLUTIONS, SECESSION, STATES' RIGHTS DOCTRINE, Appendix 8.

Numerical Majority. See TYRANNY OF THE MAJORITY.

Nuncio. A diplomatic representative of the Vatican State of Rome (and the Pope) accredited to a foreign government.

Nuremberg Laws. A series of legislative acts passed in Nazi Germany in 1935 which deprived Jewish people of citizenship and the right to practice certain professions (e.g., the practice of law) and prohibited marriages between Jews and non-Jews. See FINAL SOLUTION, LEBENSRAUM, NAZISM.

Nuremberg Trial. See WAR CRIMES.

Nuts! An American slang word meaning "crazy" or "ridiculous." This was the reply of Anthony C. McAuliffe, a young officer of the U.S. Army's elite 101st Airborne Division, to German forces during the Battle of the Bulge on 22 December 1944. German Nazi troops had surrounded a large number of American soldiers at Bastogne, and a German officer demanded that the Americans "honorably surrender" or face total "annihilation." McAuliffe, who subsequently became a general, sat for a moment in silence, then wrote a response: "To the German Commander: Nuts! The American Commander." The Germans were puzzled by the meaning of the word "nuts," and suspected some intelligence jargon. For cryptographic purposes the Americans used the language of the American Cherokees which is spoken and not written, and the Germans were never able to decipher the open communications. Subsequently, the Germans themselves were forced by the Americans to surrender. See LEADERSHIP, SELF-ESTEEM, WAR.

O

Oaks' Laws. Dr. Dallin H. Oaks, President of Brigham Young University and President of the American Association of Independent Colleges and Universities, delineates two "laws" which govern a modern society, such as the United States: (1) "Law expands in proportion to the resources available for its enforcement" and (2) "A bad law is more likely to be supplemented than repealed." Dr. Oaks explains the basis of his laws: "A government's bureaucratic army is never demobilized. If a government agency is created or a government worker is employed to accomplish a task that is later accomplished, experience teaches that the public employment rolls will not be reduced. The bureaucratic army will be transferred to another front, and if there are insufficient conflicts to justify their continued mobilization, they will start some. When this happens, we realize that the agency's formal goal of giving the service desired by taxpayers and citizens has been displaced by the controlling goal of providing continued employment for the workers and a secure power base for the leaders . . . . One law (e.g., minimum wage), puts the marginal employee out of work and other laws (e.g., welfare legislation) 'support him in idleness'." Dr. Oaks' laws also reflect and supplement the famous "laws" by C. Northcote Parkinson (in *Parkinson's Law*, 1978) which state that: (1) work expands to fill the time available for its completion and (2) expenditures rise to meet income. "Oaks' Laws" are possible in a society (like the United States) which is entering the post-industrial stage of its development when emphasis shifts from the production of tangible goods and services to the production of intangibles in the form of newly generated knowledge (information and skill—the "know-how"), the use of such knowledge, and related (quarternary) services. Some of that knowledge is of great utility to man (e.g., as it pertains to the extension of life through better medical technology and facilities, and the liberation of man from physical exertion by machines); and some is not (e.g., the manipulation of some genetic aspects of life or the study of sexual behavior of frogs somewhere in Europe). Since the major portion of the newly generated knowledge and its use are accomplished through public finance (subsidized by the taxpayer), the political system and its bureaucratic components constantly seek legislation which will enable them to accomplish these objectives. This leads to political incrementalism (the quantitative though not always qualitative, increase in institutions and services, and larger taxation and public spending). See BUREAUCRACY, POLITICAL INCREMENTALISM, QUARTERNARY SERVICES.

OAS. See ORGANIZATION OF AMERICAN STATES.

Oath. A promise to carry out certain functions or tasks faithfully (as upon election or appointment to a position of trust), made in the name of God or some other non-earthly supreme being. When there is no reference made to God, it constitutes an affirmation. The U.S. President, as the top national executive officer, may not execute an oath or affirmation of office. See AFFIRMATION.

Oath of Allegiance. An expressed declaration of loyalty or fidelity. See AFFIRMATION.

OAU. See ORGANIZATION OF AFRICAN UNITY.

Oberlandesgericht. Superior Regional Court of Appeals in the Federal Republic of Germany (West Germany). There are eighteen such courts today.

Oberstes Bundesgericht. The Federal Supreme Court in the Federal Republic of Germany (West Germany).

Obiter Dictum. In the Latin language, "an incidental remark by a judge." Also, under the American system of jurisprudence, remarks made by a justice which are not relevant to the decision at hand but which may provide an insight into the personal views of the justice or may reveal certain judicial trends and development. *Obiter Dicta* do not, as a rule, establish principles of law, and are ordinarily made by the Justices of the U.S. Supreme Court.

Oblast. Any large political subdivision, (e.g., a province or district) in the former Soviet Union.

Obstruction of Justice. The act of withholding evidence or failing to reveal knowledge of a criminal act or activity to the proper authorities of a state. Under most systems of jurisprudence, obstruction of justice—prevention of justice to take its course—is a felonious crime.

OCA. See OFFICE OF CONSUMER AFFAIRS.

OCAM. See L'ORGANISATION COMMUNE AFRICAINE ET MALAGACHE.

October Revolution. The overthrow of the provisional government of Alexander Kerensky (October 17, 1917) by the Bolsheviks of Vladimir Lenin and the Red Army, thus establishing a socialist regime in Russia.

October Surprise. The allegation, to be investigated by the U.S. Congress, that during the 1980 presidential campaign, the staff of candidate Ronald Reagan suspected President Jimmy Carter of having some surprise plan to liberate U.S. Embassy personnel held hostage in Iran in October 1980, just weeks before the election. In order to upset that surprise, Reagan's staff allegedly collaborated with the hostage takers, making a secret deal involving the promise of the supply of weapons and war materiel to Iran for use in their war with Iraq in exchange for not releasing the hostages until the moment Reagan was sworn in as President in January of the next year.

Octobrist. Member of the communist coup d'état during the October Revolution (October 17, 1917) which overthrew the provisional government and introduced a socialist form of government in Russia. Also, a member of the pre-school youth organization in the former Soviet Union. See OCTOBER REVOLUTION.

ODECA. See ORGANIZATION OF CENTRAL AMERICAN STATES.

Odelsting. Lower chamber of Parliament in Norway. See LAGTING, STORTING.

Oder-Neisse Line. The boundary line between the Polish People's Republic and the German Democratic Republic (East Germany) which was agreed upon temporarily by the participants of the Potsdam Conference in 1945 (England, France, the United States, and the Soviet Union), subject to ratification by a future peace treaty with Germany. The boundary has been recognized by the Federal Republic of Germany (West Germany) as the *de facto* border line between Poland and East Germany and was ratified by the West German Bundesrat (the upper house of the German Federal Parliament) on May 11, 1973. The Helsinki Accord of 1975 (including recognition by the United States) and the special declaration by Polish President Lech Walesa and German Chancellor Helmut Kohl in 1990 reaffirmed the boundary as permanent. See HELSINKI ACCORD, Appendices 91, 105.

OECD. See ORGANIZATION FOR ECONOMIC COOPERATION AND DEVELOPMENT.

OEEC. Organization for European Economic Cooperation. See ORGANIZATION FOR ECONOMIC COOPERATION AND DEVELOPMENT.

OEO. See OFFICE OF ECONOMIC OPPORTUNITY.

OFE. See OFFICE OF FEDERAL ELECTIONS.

Off-Year Election. See BY-ELECTION, UNITED STATES HOUSE OF REPRESENTATIVES.

Office-Bloc Ballot. See MASSACHUSETTS BALLOT.

Office of Consumer Affairs (OCA). One of the offices among the Executive Offices of the President of the United States, established in 1971, for the purpose of advising the President of the interests of consumers and representing him before consumer groups. The Office continues the task of the former Committee on Consumer Interests.

Office of Economic Opportunity (OEO). One of the offices among the Executive Offices of the President of the United States, established by Congress in 1964, in response to President Lyndon B. Johnson's declared war on poverty in America. (The Office was to be dismantled in 1973, but the federal courts denied President Richard M. Nixon the power to do so). See Appendix 12.

Office of Federal Elections (OFE). A semi-autonomous office, within the General Accounting Office (GAO), concerned with monitoring political campaign financing for federal offices and reporting any and all irregularities to the U.S. Congress or appropriate agencies for legal action.

Office of Management and Budget (OMB). One of the fifteen separate bureaus within the Executive Offices of the President of the United States charged with the responsibility of preparing the budget for the Executive Offices, scrutinizing the budgets proposed by all agencies of the Federal Government, and analyzing management practices for the President. (Until June 1970 all budgetary matters were handled by the Bureau of the Budget which since has been absorbed by the Office of Management and Budget). See Appendices 14, 15.

Office of Special Investigations (OSI). An investigative and intelligence-gathering arm of the United States Air Force.

Office of Strategic Services (OSS). An intelligence-gathering and evaluating agency of the American Federal Government, established in 1942 (under the leadership of William J. Donovan and Allen W. Dulles) for the purpose of advising the U.S. President on security matters. In 1949, the OSS was abolished and replaced with the Central Intelligence Agency (CIA), which was established by the National Security Act of 1947.

Official Secrets Act. A parliamentary law in England which empowers the prime minister to withhold any information it determines classified from the general public. Any governmental authority in England may censor any information to be transmitted by the press or electronic media at any time for any reason it deems necessary; may detain any person in spite of proclaimed rights of individuals, hold in arrest and deprive liberty.

Official Unionist Party (OUP). See HILLSBOROUGH AGREEMENT.

Ogharna. In the Russian language, "protection." Also, an agency of the Imperial Government in Tsarist Russia charged with the protection of the Tsar, his family, high-ranking government officials, and the state in general. See CHEKA.

OGPU. See DEPARTMENT FOR STATE POLITICAL ADMINISTRATION.

Oil Depletion Allowance. See DEPLETION ALLOWANCE.

Oil Embargo. See ORGANIZATION OF PETROLEUM EXPORTING COUNTRIES (OPEC), SEVEN SISTERS.

The Oil is Ours! See MOSSADEGH.

Oireachtas. The bicameral parliament of Ireland. See SEANAD EIREANN, DAIL EIREANN.

Old 8 to 7. See HAYES-TILDEN DISPUTE.

Old Abe. See GREAT DEBATES.

Old-Boy Network. See POWER ELITE.

Old Hickory. See JACKSONIAN DEMOCRACY.

Old Man of the Mountains. See ASSASSIN.

Old Tippecanoe. A nickname of U.S. President Benjamin Harrison (1889-1893). See TIPPECANOE AND TYLER TOO.

Oldest Parliament in the World. See MOTHER OF PARLIAMENTS.

Oligarchy. In the Greek language, "rule of the few," or "government by the few." A form of government in which only the few wealthy participate; or a government, according to Aristotle, by "perverted aristocracy." (If one may paraphrase Lincoln, a government by the few, of the few, for the few). See Appendix 1.

Oligopolitics. See OLIGOPOLY.

Oligopoly. A business enterprise or corporation which extends its activities into areas for which it was not originally designed and which as such considerably influences the policies of the government. Also, a conglomerate (a multi-purpose business enterprise).

OMB. See OFFICE OF MANAGEMENT AND BUDGET.

Ombudsman. In the Swedish language, "representative." An official, usually under the jurisdiction of the legislative branch of the government, who handles complaints and grievances of the people against the executive branch of the government and attempts to redress them. This office is most common among the Scandinavian states, e.g., Sweden, Norway, or Finland. Very popular in Northern Europe (part of the Constitution of Sweden since 1809, Finland 1919, Denmark 1955, Norway and New Zealand 1962—to mention only a few). An individual—responsible to the legislative rather than the executive body of government, on any level—who serves as a guardian of individual rights of citizens against any abuse of administrative functions or power. In 1966, Mayor Lindsay of NYC proposed the Civilian Complaint Review board which was to have a similar function; however, it was rejected by voters. In the U.S., in reality, the minority party performs the function of the ombudsman. See PEOPLE'S CONTROL COMMITTEE.

Omertà. See MAFIA.

Omnibus Bill. In American practice, a single congressional law covering a variety of issues which ordinarily would require separate legislative acts. The issues covered by such a single law, however, must be related (e.g., Omnibus Crime Control and Safe Streets Act of 1968).

Omnibus Crime Control and Safe Streets Act of 1968. A major anti-crime legislation allowing, among other things, the judge to determine if a voluntary confession by the accused can be admitted as evidence; allows the use of wiretaps (which was banned in 1934) and listening devices to obtain evidence with judicial consent; regulates the purchase and possession of firearms (a limited arms control law); allows the U.S. Attorney General to judge which evidence illegally obtained can be used in court as evidence; allows law enforcement officers to enter and search premises strongly suspected to contain evidence of crime through the so-called "no-knock" provision; and it established the Law Enforcement Assistance Administration (LEAA). The 1968 law has subsequently been broadened by the Omnibus Crime Control Act of 1970 which makes the following acts federal crimes: assassination of members of Congress; interference with the activities of the personnel of the U.S. President; and trespassing of the premises which the President may visit. The strict legislation was in response to the rapid rise of crime during the 1960's, particularly due to the "Black Revolution," the protest and riots by blacks in their struggle for equal rights and has been amended several times since. See Appendix 46, 47.

On Human Life. See ENCYCLICAL.

Once You Win Power, You Must Exercise it to Retain it. Such was the view on political power of the Shah of Iran Mohammed Reza Pahlavi (1953-1979). See POWER.

One and One-Half Party Government. A name commonly applied to a coalition government in a parliamentary democracy, where a party has plurality but lacks majority necessary to form a government; it enters into a coalition with another party so as to achieve the necessary majority. Practice indicates that such governments are not stable because once the coalition party (the half-party) pulls out from the coalition, the government falls, unless it immediately forms a coalition with another party. Such coalitions are common, among others, in Italy, France, the Scandinavian States, and sometimes in England, but are rare in two-party systems (e.g., in the United States, where the winner takes all, usually under the plurality rule). See CABINET-PARLIAMENTARY GOVERNMENT.

One-Child Policy. The People's Republic of China introduced the policy of one child per married couple in 1980 in order to control the exploding population (over one-billion). There were reported cases of forced abortion of women who violated that policy. Violators also are punished with financial disincentives. Many societies in Asia, including China, traditionally favor males over females, because males were potential laborers as well as providers for the family and/or the elderly parents. One result of the one-child policy is that many infants are killed, so that the family can try for male offspring, without suffering penalties imposed with the birth of a second child.

One-China Policy. See SHANGHAI COMMUNIQUÉ, PEKING SUMMIT.

One-Dimensional Man. See NEW LEFT.

One-Eight-Hundred Candidate. See WE, THE PEOPLE, TAKE BACK AMERICA.

One Man, One Vote. A principle pronounced by the United States Supreme Court in *Baker v. Carr* (1962) to the effect that each and every vote cast during an election should carry equal weight, and thus apportionment among counties and districts for purposes of elections should be made—as closely as it is practicable—according to the number of qualified voters in each. The doctrine was reinforced by *Reynolds v. Sims* (1964), when the Court ruled that popular approval of state apportionment schemes in a referendum did not validate unequal or discriminatory voting districts. See Appendices 48, 49.

One Must Not Confuse the Intelligence Business with Missionary Work! See KURDISH UPRISING.

One-Party System. A political system within a state that allows only one political party, usually the party in power, and tolerates no opposition or coalition government. Some of the states with one-party systems are: Cuba, the Democratic Republic of Vietnam, Laos, Cambodia, and the People's Democratic Republic of Korea (North Korea). See OPEN PARTY SYSTEM.

One People, One Country, One Leader. In the German language, "Ein Volk, Ein Reich, Ein Führer"; the motto of the Nazi party of Germany under the leadership of Adolf Hitler, 1933-1945. It also served as a mobilizing slogan.

One-Time Pad. See CIPHER PAD.

One-Thousand-Percent. See SKELETON IN THE CLOSET, PRESIDENTIAL QUALIFICATIONS.

One World. A concept epitomizing the notion that this world with all its divisions by regional interests, small and large states, military and economic blocs and alliances, races and religions, is, in reality one world, and the community of nations is a "global village"; and that the inhabitants of the world are bound together for survival in providing for food, shelter, clothing, and the maintenance of clean air and water and lasting peace. The "one-world" notion rejects all alliances that divide the world into spheres of interests (e.g., bipolarity, multipolarity, or polycentrism). See BIPOLARITY, MULTIPOLARITY, POLYCENTRISM, UNICENTRISM, UNIPOLARITY.

One-Worlder. One who advocates a world government instead of the present multiplicity of conflicting national states; also one who advocates the so-called "World Federalism" or "World Federal State." Also the term "mondialist" or "globalist" is often used.

Only the Little People Pay Taxes. See DECADENCE.

Ontology. The study of the inner and ultimate nature of things.

Onus Probandi. In the Latin language, "a burden of proof."

Open Arms Program. Between 1969-1974, this program (known in the Vietnamese language as "Chieu hoi," "open arms") was conducted by the South Vietnamese government with the assistance of the U.S. Central Intelligence Agency to induce North Vietnamese and Viet Cong to defect or surrender. The program was very successful at the beginning but with time, the South Vietnamese became more interested in the accumulation of personal wealth rather than saving their government.

Open City. A city within a war zone that may be exempt from exclusive occupation or bombardment by the warring parties because of its historical landmarks (e.g., the Cities of Rome, Italy, and Paris, France: both were declared "open cities" during World War II by the Allies and the German Forces, and neither was subjected to destruction).

Open Diplomacy. The practice of conducting diplomatic (international) relations openly and without secrecy or dishonesty. See DIPLOMACY, OPEN SOCIETY.

Open District. See SAFE DISTRICT.

Open Door Policy. A policy advocating equal participation of all states in trade and diplomatic relations among themselves without any single state attempting to create any spheres of influence or seek special privileges over the interest of other states. Such policy, for example, was pronounced by former U.S. Secretary of State John Hay in regard to China in 1899 and was reaffirmed by President Richard M. Nixon during his trip to the People's Republic of China in 1972.

Open Government. See SUNSHINE LAW.

Open Justice. The basic assumption of judicial systems, including that of the United States, is that the rendering of justice should be in public, open to the public as a public business unless some good reasons (usually to protect the innocent) require that a trial or hearing will be held *in camera* (or *sub rosa*).

Open Marriage. See DECADENCE.

Open Party System. A political system which places no restrictions on the number of political parties which may exist and be freely and actively involved in party politics. This system is also known as "multiparty system."

Open Political System. A system susceptible to environmental changes which interacts with the environment in receiving inputs and producing outputs, and one that changes its internal structure and processes according to the changes of the internal as well as the external environment. See OPEN SOCIETY, Appendices 1, 3.

Open Primary. A primary election in which any qualified voter, regardless of party affiliation, may cast his ballot. The confusion that arises under that system gave them the name of "jungle" primaries. The states that permit such primaries are: Alaska, Michigan, Minnesota, Montana, North Dakota, Utah, Vermont, Washington, and Wisconsin. The opposition to open primaries is based on the fact that they tend to distort the real strength of a political party although they may allow individual candidates to gain popularity. See CLOSED PRIMARY.

Open Shop. A place of work where membership in a labor union is not required. See CLOSED SHOP, TAFT-HARTLEY LAW.

Open Shoppism. During the 1920s, America's large corporations joined forces in order to combat the strongly emerging labor movement which was attempting to organize labor unions as a means for improving the working conditions and wages of workers. The businesses strove to maintain an open shop (where employees are not required to join unions as a condition for employment) under the slogan of the "American Plan" and blamed organized labor for all of the economic ills during the time of the Great Depression that was building up to explode in 1929 (see BLACK TUESDAY). American business claimed to be capable of providing welfare programs (welfare capitalism) to workers who needed help, thereby denying that function to labor. Very often, police and terrorist tactics were used to discourage labor groups from organizing. As a result of this anti-organized labor campaign by organized business, the membership of the American Federation of Labor declined from almost 4,500,000 in 1921 to about 2,500,000 in 1927. See CLOSED SHOP, OPEN SHOP, RIGHT TO WORK LAW, WELFARE CAPITALISM, YELLOW DOG CONTRACT.

Open Skies. A proposal, advanced in 1955 by U.S. President Dwight D. Eisenhower and directed to the Soviet Union, to initiate a bilateral agreement on the unrestricted, mutual inspection of aerial security zones for the purpose of avoiding surprise attack by either power. The proposal was then rejected by the

USSR, but its spirit continued to undergird the Strategic Arms Limitation Talks (SALT) with the USSR.

Open Society. A society which allows, among other things, unrestricted movement of persons and exchange of ideas internally and externally, and one in which all persons—citizens or not—enjoy equal protection under the laws, are free to pursue their objectives within the limits of the laws, and are allowed unlimited social mobility. The opposite of an open society is referred to as closed society. See OPEN POLITICAL SYSTEM, Appendix 51.

Operation Bulldozer. See YAKUZA.

Operation Desert Storm. See PERSIAN GULF WAR.

Operation Independence. U.S. President Richard M. Nixon (1969-1974) declared in February 1974, during the height of the Arab oil embargo (the energy crisis), that the United States must develop new sources of energy as well as trim its uses of imported energy in order to be self-sufficient and independent from foreign suppliers.

Operation Just Cause. See PANAMA INCURSION.

Operation Yellow-Bird. An effort by the United States diplomatic service in the People's Republic of China to rescue from arrest and oppression the Chinese pro-democracy leaders during the 1989 protest against the oppressive policies of the government, following the Tiananmen Square Massacre. Some of the leaders sought and were granted sanctuary and political asylum in the American Embassy in Beijing. Many others came to the United States and, on humanitarian grounds, were allowed to remain without being subject to the regular immigration procedures.

Operational Reasons. The practice, common among governments and their intelligence services, including the CIA, of planting and disseminating deceptive and misleading information in news media (e.g., radio, TV, press, books, and films) for the purpose of concealing the real and actual operations and activities of an agency or the government. This may be done for two reasons: (1) operational reasons, to mislead the adversary; (2) to boost the prestige of the agency doing the misleading, in order to gain better evaluation of effectiveness and efficiency (e.g., for purpose of higher appropriations from U.S. Congress). See DECEPTION, PENKOVSKY PAPERS, PROPAGANDA ASSETS INVENTORY (PAI), REPLAY.

Operations Advisory Group. See NATIONAL SECURITY COUNCIL (NSC).

Opiate of the Masses. A concept that was coined by Karl Marx (1818-1883), German political philosopher, who considered religion as one of the most serious impediments to socialist revolution and as a system of social control in a society which is the most difficult to overcome in order to bring about political changes by revolutionary means. See MARXISM.

Opinio Juris. In the Latin language, "judicial opinion," "judicial decision," or "opinion by a judge."

Opinion Leaders. Those individuals who influence others on public policy issues because of their positions held (e.g., employment), education, or popularity among certain elites.

OPO. See OPPOSITION RESEARCH SPECIALIST.

Opportunist. One who seeks to advance his personal interest by virtue of association; one who disregards moral or ethical consideration in favor of his own interest or advancement.

Opportunity Test. See SCUM.

Opposition Party. A political party organization, commonly found in polyarchic societies, which seeks political control through the unseating of the party in power in an election. The main function of the opposition party is to criticize the programs and policies of the party in power and to offer the electorate a choice of candidates during an election. There are no opposition political parties permitted in totalitarian and dictatorial systems. Some totalitarian political systems permit "loyal" oppositions to function, usually as a diversionary measure designed to mislead international public opinion. See LOYAL OPPOSITION.

Opposition Research Specialist (OPO). Persons well educated in politics, government, economics, and any other discipline that allows one to better understand political processes and institutions, who are highly sought after by people in government and politics. These highly trained specialists are capable of retrieving vital information, gathering new information and knowledge, and translating it into definite and acceptable policy models. Presidential candidates in the United States, candidates for governor, and candidates for the United States Congress, in particular, employ large staffs consisting of such experts. President George Bush had on his campaign research staff in 1988, 35 OPOs, and 52 in 1992. The increase of OPOs in 1992 was necessitated by the new complexity of international and domestic problems. Some among the OPOs specialize in one unique area of research which the political candidate may explore, e.g., "dirty tricks," or material that falls into the category of "kiss and tell for sale." See DEFINING THE OPPONENT, KISS AND TELL FOR SALE, POLITICAL CAMPAIGN, POLITICAL RHETORIC.

Optimal Ignorance. A notion advanced by two distinguished social scientists, Warren Ilcham and Norman Uphoff (*The Political Economy of Change*), suggesting that the oversupply of information (research data) available to decision-makers (policy-makers) in government may hinder their choices, because, as Peter Berger puts it, "if a plenitude of information increases awareness of all possible choices in a given situation, then there may well be a point of diminishing returns, after which any new input of information will simply paralyze those who have made the political decision." As a rule, decision-makers lack the necessary amount of timely information upon which to make policy choices and decisions, because adequate research is very time consuming and expensive, and decision-makers are faced with crisis situations upon which they must act regardless of whether there is research data available or not.

Opus Dei. In the Latin language, "work of God," or "God's work." The founder of this secretive organization, Monsignore Josemaria Excriva de Balaguer, native of Spain, was beautified by Pope John Paul II in a special ceremony in St. Peter's Square in Rome in May 1992, as was Josephine Bakkita, once an African slave, who was a holy nun. See SACERDOTAL SOCIETY OF THE HOLY CROSS.

Order of Battle. The actual number of soldiers, weapons and weapon systems and their locations, of interest to military leaders for security reasons. Military doctrine and the scope and method of conducting a war, including ascertaining the need for manpower, materiel and the deployment of strategies in order to maximize effort and achieve desired objectives, depend on an updated and systematic knowledge about the order of battle of at least the most adversary, hostile states. The primary function of military intelligence is to keep this information current, timely and complete for use by leaders.

Ordinance. A rule or regulation allowing a certain activity or restricting it (limited in scope and degree), which may be issued by a municipal corporation (local government) under authority derived from its charter (articles of incorporation) and in conformity with state and national laws. Some unusual local ordinances are: Crocodiles may not be hitched to fire hydrants in Detroit, Michigan. If you're planning to take an animal out onto the streets of Berea, Ohio, after dark, you'll be breaking the law unless the animal is wearing a taillight. A Denver, Colorado, law says that you must not step out of an airplane while the plane is in the air except in an emergency. Should a wife in Kentucky wish to move the furniture around the house, she must first have her husband's permission to do so. In Pine Island, Minnesota, a man must remove his hat if he meets a cow. Give this warning to any hunters you know who might be planning to go on a hunting expedition in the state of Arizona: It's against the law to hunt and shoot any camels there. A Maryland law says that it's illegal to knock a freight train off the tracks. In North Carolina, it's unlawful to use elephants to plow cotton fields. Are you taking a trip to Alaska? If you intend to take photos in Fairbanks, beware! In that Alaskan city it's against the law to disturb a grizzly bear in order to take its picture. In Atlanta, Georgia, it's unlawful for anyone to make faces at school children while they are studying in their classrooms. Fishermen have to be wary of the law in several states. In Ohio, it's illegal to fish for whales in any lake, river, or stream on Sunday. In the District of Columbia, it's against the law to catch a fish while on horseback. If you're going to a show in Baltimore, Maryland, remember that it's illegal to bring lions to a theater. In Trout Creek, Utah, druggists are prohibited from selling gunpowder as a cure for headaches. In Georgia, it's unlawful to open an umbrella in front of a mule.

Ordinance Power. The authority (of local government) to issue binding ordinances or regulations (local laws).

Ordinary Law. A statutory law which, as a rule, is not included in the constitution of a state and which can be repealed by a subsequent law. (Ordinary laws are also known as the "rules of the passing hour.")

Oregon Benchmark. See CONVERSATION WITH OREGON.

Organic Act. A legislative act by a central legislative body of a state allowing the formation of an autonomous government in a territory under its jurisdiction. Such an act was passed by the U.S. Congress in 1917 granting Puerto Rico the status of a Commonwealth.

Organic Law. A basic, fundamental law (e.g., the U.S. Constitution, Biblical laws) upon which a given society builds its nation-state and its political system. A law which serves as a norm, that is, one from which the other laws can be derived. See LEGAL NORM, WRITTEN CONSTITUTION.

L'Organisation Commune Africaine et Malagache (OCAM). On February 13, 1965, the heads of state of Cameroon, Central African Republic, Chad, Congo (Brazzaville), Dahomey, Gabon, Niger, Senegal, Togo and Upper Volta—all French-speaking—met for the purpose of discussing common problems and to improve cooperation among themselves, mainly between Malagasy and Africa proper in the spirit of the Charter of the OAU. This informal organization replaced the short-lived UAMCE. Considerable attention was given to the need for closer cooperation with the European Community, the EEC (Common Market) and other trade associations.

Organization for Economic Cooperation and Development (OECD). A regional international body formed in 1961 by the Western European States (and including the United States) to expedite world trade (by gradual reduction or elimination of tariff restrictions) and to work towards raising the general standard of living of Europeans and Americans. The OECD replaced the Organization for European Economic Cooperation (OEEC), which was founded in 1948 in conjunction with the European Recovery Program, the Marshall Plan, See Appendices 73, 73-B.

Organization of African Unity (OAU). A regional international organization set up at Addis Ababa, Ethiopia, in 1963 to promote cooperation among African States, particularly the newly emerged or emerging ones, which are in the process of eradicating the remains of colonialism; to promote continuous unity and solidarity; to provide for economic, cultural, and military exchange; and if necessary, to provide for common defense.

Organization of American States (OAS). A regional organization set up by the Ninth International Conference of American States at Bogota, Colombia, in April 1948, to coordinate programs for improving inter-American relations, for promoting cultural and economic exchange, and for establishing military cooperation. All Latin-American states are members of the organization, as is the United States. (The Republic of Cuba was excluded, on January 31, 1962, from its activities but not from membership).

Organization of Central American States (ODECA). A regional international organization formed by Costa Rica, El Salvador, Guatemala, Honduras, and Nicaragua on October 14, 1951, for the purpose of mutual cooperation. The Charter of San Salvador emphasizes the mutual heritage of these five republics (e.g., language, religion, and history of struggle for independence) as a basis for close cooperation.

Organization of Petroleum Exporting Countries (OPEC). An international cartel of oil producers and oil exporters set up for the purpose of coordinating supplies of oil reserves and prices. OPEC was founded by Juan Pablo Pérez Alfonso of Venezuela in 1960. Its members are: Algeria, Ecuador, Gabon, Indonesia, Iran, Iraq, Kuwait, Libya, Qatar, Nigeria, Saudi Arabia, the United Arab Emirates, and Venezuela. Since the cartel is overwhelmingly controlled by Arab states, it voted on October 19, 1973, to impose a total embargo on the export of crude oil to any states which support the State of Israel (the United States included). The embargo was lifted on March 18, 1974.

Organization of the Highest Order. See INHERENT RIGHT OF STATE.

Organization on High. See KHMER ROUGE.

Organizational Bureau (ORGBURO). One of the central administrative components of the Central Committee of the Communist Party of the former Soviet Union (CC CPSU), charged with the task of organizing and coordinating non-political activities of the party (internally), and assisting other communist parties (externally) in all administrative matters.

Organized Crime Control Act of 1970. See RACKETEERING.

Organized Free Trade. See PROTECTIONISM.

ORGBURO. See ORGANIZATIONAL BUREAU.

Original Jurisdiction. As applied to the administration of justice, litigation in a given category of cases may originate only before courts that are authorized and empowered in a certain geographic area to hear them (e.g., litigation in the case of a family dispute may originate before a Federal District Court, but must be taken before a local court that has jurisdiction over such cases).

Original Package Doctrine. An opinion delivered by the United States Supreme Court in *Brown v. Maryland*, 25 U.S. (12 Wheat.) 419, 6 L.Ed. 678 (1827) to the effect that a commodity is removed from the channel of trade and interstate shipment terminates when it is delivered to the point of destination and is removed from the package or container in which it was delivered.

Original Understanding of the Law. See DO JUSTICE, SIR, DO JUSTICE!, MODERN POLITICS IS CIVIL WAR CARRIED BY OTHER MEANS.

Origins of the State Theories. Among the many theories pertaining to the emergence of the states are: (1) the Divine Rights theory—it holds that it was not any single individual or any group of persons, but that the supernatural, that God has brought upon man the notion of a political organization known as "state" for the purpose of governing people on earth; (2) the Economic Instinct, or Economic Interest theory—claims that, in his struggle for survival, the inborn instinct of man—the political and social animal—led him to organize into groups which soon became a state; (3) the Force theory—claims that the organization of the state emerged as a result of force (physical force, the ability to inflict pain on people), by men organizing in groups and conquering other individuals and groups and forcing them into submission and obedience (a favorite with dictators and totalitarians); (4) Social Contract theory—a notion derived from the mode of life of tribal groups which have evolved into larger societies (e.g., in Africa and Eastern Europe). This theory was subsequently redeveloped during the 17th and 18th century in Europe by John Locke (1632-1704), an English political philosopher (see *The Second Treaties of Civil Government*), and Jean-Jacques Rousseau (1712-1778), a Swiss political philosopher (see *The Social Contract*). Locke held that the source of all political power is in the consent of the governed; and, in order to organize a political society, the individuals must agree to grant their consent by contract; while Rousseau emphasized that the state emerges where individuals reach a consensus, a general will (volonté générale) to be governed, and that a popular government is the expression of the general will of the people. These ideas were carried into North America by the first pilgrims, and later had a profound influence upon the thinking of the Founding Fathers of the American State; and (5) the Evolution theory—holds that the state has actually evolved through continuous association and common practices, when men gathered together and formed communities which became nation-states or multinational states (e.g., the United States today). See MAYFLOWER COMPACT, MOSAIC SOCIETY, PLURALISTIC SOCIETY, STATE, TWO SWORDS THEORY.

Orphan State. See COLD WAR ORPHAN STATE.

OSA. See ORGANIZATION OF AMERICAN STATES.

OSI. See OFFICE OF SPECIAL INVESTIGATIONS.

OSS. See OFFICE OF STRATEGIC SERVICES.

Ossi. See GERMAN UNIFICATION.

Ost Politik. In the German language, "eastern policy." A term used to describe traditional and contemporary German policies toward Eastern Europe, mainly Poland, Tsarist Russia, and the Soviet Union. In modern times, the term applies to the efforts by Willie Brandt, former Chancellor of the German Federal Republic, to defuse the "Cold War" rhetoric and to commence peaceful East-West dialogue and cooperation. See DRANG NACH OSTEN, ODER-NEISSE LINE.

Ottomanization. Term taken after the dissolution of the once powerful empire, the Ottoman empire following W.W.I., and applicable to a sudden dissolution of strong central authority followed by the dissolution of the state itself, e.g., the Soviet Union which dissolved due to internal contradiction rather than external attack, in 1991.

Our Sons of Bitches. When U.S. President Franklin D. Roosevelt was criticized in 1944 for having a double-standard in international diplomacy by fighting Fascists in Europe but allowing similar fascist governments to stay in power in Latin America, he replied that the Latin American dictators were "sons of bitches," but "they are our sons of bitches." Many had been put in power with American aid, to protect American interests there and they had done a fairly good job for America. Furthermore, President Roosevelt invoked the ancient dictum favored by all nationalists that "my country, right or wrong, is always right."

Out Party. See INS.

Outer Seven. See EUROPEAN FREE TRADE ASSOCIATION (EFTA).

Outer Space Treaty of 1966. An international agreement on peaceful exploration of outer space, including the moon and other celestial bodies, for the benefit of mankind. Under this treaty, astronauts landing on foreign soil or international waters are entitled to all aid and assistance that they may require, and they are not subject to detention by any state.

Output-Input. See POLITICAL SYSTEM.

Outs. See INS.

Overkill. A general estimation of wide acceptance that the two major powers today, the Commonwealth of Independent States (CIS) and the United States, possess enough sophisticated weapons in their arsenals to kill the entire population of the global village, the planet earth (approximately five billion human beings), several times over.

Overlord. The code-name of the World War II Allied cross-Channel invasion of Nazi-occupied Europe which was launched from England to Normandy, France, in June 1944. The invasion took place after the Soviet Union, with American aid under the Lend-Lease program, had developed the capacity to launch a major offensive against the Nazi forces. The Nazi resistance was stronger against the Russians than the Allied forces: there were 181 divisions of German troops and 40 divisions of Axis forces facing the Russians and only 27 divisions were facing the Allies. The Russians scored unexpected victories in ground attack (mainly with tanks and infantry) by saturated mortar shelling (there were 230 heavy guns per kilometer of the entire front line) of the German and the Axis forces. By the time the German forces capitulated in May 1945, the Soviet Union had suffered 7 million casualties of military personnel and 13 million civilians; the United States had suffered 405,000 casualties, and the British 375,000 (including civilian population killed by German attacks against British cities with V-1 and V-2 rockets).

Overseas Constituency. Those American Democrats who reside abroad in foreign states, but who, as of 1976, may send delegates and alternates to the Democratic National Conventions and vote for candidates for U.S. President and Vice President. The Republican Party does not provide for such overseas representation. The constitution of the People's Republic of China (Communist China) allows overseas Chinese to participate not only in party activity, but also to elect in *absentia* deputies to the Chinese People's Congress (parliament) representing Chinese nationals residing abroad. The law does not make a distinction between a "national" and a "citizen." Every national is *ex jure* a citizen. Similar is the practice of the State of Israel where any Jew, regardless of residence, may claim Israeli nationality and citizenship. Puerto Ricans, for example, are only part-time U.S. Citizens. They may vote in American national elections, provided they register and reside in the United States proper, but not while residing in Puerto Rico. Many Puerto Ricans of means, travel to the United States before election time, register, and upon voting, return to Puerto Rico. They are often referred to as "commuting citizens."

Overseas Department. See FRENCH UNION.

Overseas Territory. See FRENCH UNION.

Overt Act. An act of hostility or one demonstrating unfriendly disposition (e.g., an abrupt termination of a treaty obligation, interference by one state into the domestic affairs of another, or the practice of spying of one state on another) of one state against another which is done openly and without secrecy as in case of a covert act. Under traditional international law an overt act of hostility constituted sufficient reasons for a declaration of war, which, like open oppression, constitutes casus belli (cause of war) on just grounds. See BELLUM JUSTUM.

P

"Man is by nature a political animal."
ARISTOTLE, 384-322 B.C.

PAC. See PAN AFRICANIST CONGRESS, POLITICAL ACTION COMMITTEE.

Pacific Doctrine. On December 7, 1976, U.S. President Gerald R. Ford (1974-1977) announced the "Pacific Doctrine" in Hawaii—on the thirty-fifth anniversary of the Japanese attack on Pearl Harbor—stating as the desired goal for the area, "Peace with all—and hostility toward none. Our policy toward the new regimes," stated President Ford with reference to Indochina, "will be determined by their conduct toward us. We are prepared to reciprocate good will—particularly the return of the remains of Americans killed or missing in action or information about them. If they exhibit restraint toward their neighbors and constructive approaches to international problems, we will look to the future rather than to the past." The five tenets of the Pacific Doctrine are: (1) "Partnership with Japan is a pillar of our strategy"; (2) "Normalization of relations with the People's Republic of China"; (3) A "continuing stake in the stability and security of Southeast Asia"; (4) "Peace in Asia depends upon a resolution of outstanding political conflicts," with the United States being "ready to consider constructive ways of easing tensions" between the two Koreas; and (5) "Peace in Asia requires a structure of economic cooperation reflecting the aspirations of all the people of the region."

Pacific Partnership. The governments of Canada and Hong Kong in 1990 entered into several bilateral agreements ranging from trade to cultural collaboration. Canada's Prime Minister, Brian Mulroney, as an outgoing statesman and international ambassador, favors a wide range of involvements in global affairs. Thus far, Canada has had limited trade arrangements with Asian states, but with the growing Asian immigrant population in Canada, a Pacific partnership is timely and beneficial to all. See ATLANTIC PARTNERSHIP, EUROPEAN ENERGY CHARTER, Appendix 29.

Pacific Settlement of Disputes. A generally recognized norm of modern international law, expressed mainly in the Kellogg-Briand Pact and the UN Charter, among others, requiring states—parties to a dispute—to settle their differences through peaceful means (e.g., arbitration, conciliation, negotiations, and good offices). See HAGUE PEACE CONFERENCES, KELLOGG-BRIAND PACT, RIO TREATY, Appendices 29, 75.

Pacification. The process of rebuilding a war-torn country and bringing it to a state of normalcy. See VIETNAMIZATION.

Pacifism. The opposition to any war or the use of force in settling international disputes or engagement in international bilateral or multilateral agreements which may entangle a nation. Many neutral states, such as Switzerland for example, refuse to join the North Atlantic Treaty Organization (NATO) for fear of entanglement. See HAGUE CONFERENCES, KELLOGG-BRIAND PACT, MONTEVIDEO DECLARATION.

Pacifist. One who is opposed to the use of military force as an instrument of policy or as a resolution of an international conflict (war).

Package Legislation. Under the French legislative system, the executive branch exercises decisive control of the legislative process pertaining to public bills by determining: the kind of legislation to be considered by the parliament; the order in which the legislation will be considered; which amendments to bills will and will not be debated and voted on by the parliament and when; and which items in the legislation (e.g., in appropriation bills) will and will not be debated and voted on (e.g., item legislation). This practice enables the government to satisfy its needs by having its legislation approved as a package. See ITEM VETO.

PACSA. See PAN-AFRICANIST CONGRESS OF SOUTH AFRICA.

Pact of Paris. See KELLOGG-BRIAND PACT.

Pact with Satan to Drive Out the Devil. So Adolf Hitler, Chancellor of the Third Reich, and leader (Führer) of the state and his Nazi party so characterized the Molotov-Ribbentrop Pact (also known as "Hitler-Stalin Pact"). See HITLER-STALIN PACT.

Pacta Sunt Servanda. In the Latin language, "treaties must be observed." One of the fundamental rules of international law, particularly in treaty-making and treaty-obligations, that treaties must be observed by those who agree to abide by them. See REBUS SIC STANTIBUS.

Pactum Illicitu. In the Latin language, "an illegal agreement," or engagement in international bilateral or multilateral agreements which may entangle a nation. Many neutral states, such as Switzerland, for example, refulse to join the North Atlantic Treaty Organization (NATO), for fear of entanglement.

PAFMECSA. See PAN-AFRICAN FREEDOM MOVEMENT OF EAST, CENTRAL AND SOUTHERN AFRICA.

Pairing. In practical politics, an advance agreement among two or more legislators with opposing views or opinions, to refrain from voting upon any one issue, thus avoiding the cancellation of each other's vote. See VOTING.

Palace Guard. A ruling junta; or loyal followers; those who actually hold power in a state.

Palace Revolution. See DETHRONIZATION.

Pale Pink Tory. See ELECTORALISM.

Palestine Liberation Organization (PLO). A coalition of Palestinian Arab groups which are struggling for the recognition of Palestine as a separate, independent, and sovereign state. The organization emerged as a unified force during the first Palestinian National Congress, held in Jerusalem on May 28 and June 2, 1964, when the Congress resolved that "the Palestinian Liberation Organization shall alone possess the right to represent the Palestinians and to speak on their behalf" (Resolution 5). The Palestine National Covenant, which was adopted by that Congress, declared, "The people of Palestine shall, after liberation of their homeland, decide their own destiny in accordance with their desire, will, and choice." The Palestinians claimed the following population and territories: 963,000 in the territory of the East Bank of Jordan; 717,000 in the West Bank; 389,000 in the Gaza Strip; 364,000 in territories occupied by Israel (before the 1967 War); 257,000 in Lebanon; 174,000 in Syria; 150,000 in Kuwait; and 124,000 in Egypt, Iraq, Libya, Saudi Arabia, and other Arab states—a total population of 3,138,000. The PLO and its leader, Yasir Arafat, have been recognized by the United Nations General Assembly (controlled by the Arab-African-Socialist states bloc) and were invited to sit in the UN on November 13, 1975. The UN supports the PLO's claims to statehood, but Israel opposes it. There are several factions within the PLO; some of them, like the National Front for the Liberation of Palestine (NFLP), conduct their activities separately, and some have been (and are) involved in terrorist activity (e.g., the killing of Israeli athletes during the 1972 Olympics in Munich, Germany-known as the "Munich Massacre"). The dialogue with Israel since 1991, brought little progress to the solution of the Palestinian issue. See ISRAELI-ARAB WAR OF 1967, ISRAELI SETTLEMENTS, POPULAR FRONT FOR THE LIBERATION OF PALESTINE (PFLP), SADAT—BEGIN SUMMIT, UN RESOLUTIONS 242 AND 338, Appendices 95, 102.

Palestine Mandate. See ISRAEL'S INTELLIGENCE, ZIONISM.

Palestine National Covenant. See PALESTINE LIBERATION ORGANIZATION (PLO).

Palestinian Autonomy. One of the reasons for the Palestinians living in tents and shantytowns instead of being absorbed by their Arab brethren is that they do demand a Palestinian state of their own, and reject any offers of autonomy either under Israel or as part of another state (e.g., Jordan). The several meetings held by the Palestinian representatives and the Israelis, all held at the insistence of U.S. President George Bush and U.S. Secretary James Baker, are about real estate which both sides demand.

Palestinian Intifada. See INTIFADA.

Palestinian-Jordanian Confederation. See FUNDAMENTALS OF THE ISRAELI-ARAB SETTLEMENT.

Palestinian National Congress. See PALESTINE LIBERATION ORGANIZATION (PLO).

Palestinian Question. See ISRAELI-ARAB WAR OF 1967, ISRAELI SETTLEMENTS, PALESTINE LIBERATION ORGANIZATION (PLO), SADAT-BEGIN SUMMIT.

Palmer Raids. Following the Russian Revolution of 1917 and the subsequent takeover of power by N. Lenin and his Bolshevik Party, the echoes of political, anti-capitalist agitation and propaganda spread throughout the industrial world. In the United States, the Justice Department under the direction of Attorney General Mitchell A. Palmer, in response to the so-called "red scare," ordered mass arrests and prosecution of agitators of all persuasions, but mainly socialists and communists. In 1919 about 250 socialists and communists were deported to Russia without due process.

Pamyat. In the Russian language, "memory: also a political organization which emerged in the Russian republic during the 1990 debate over the process of the dissolution of the Soviet empire. The group first originated in 1987 under the leadership of Dmitri Vasilyev, with headquarters in Moscow and Leningrad, and has about 30,000 registered supporters. The Pamyat advocates racist and nationalistic traditional Russian policies, and is anti-Semitic and radically chauvinistic. See CHRISTIAN-DEMOCRATIC MOVEMENT OF RUSSIA (CDMR), NATIONAL SALVATION COMMITTEE, SOYUZ.

Pan-African Conference. In December 1900, a young black attorney from the West Indies, Henry Sylvester Williams, called a conference in London, England, for the purpose of outlining the need for closer cooperation among divergent black organizations everywhere in their struggle for the improvement of the lot of black peoples everywhere. There, the term "Pan" was used for the first time in reference to Pan-Africanism. This term was coined by Dr. W. E. B. Du Bois while he was attending the University of Berlin, Germany, between 1892-1894.

Pan-African Congress of South Africa (PACSA). An informal organization established in 1959 in the Union of South Africa by Robert Magnaliso Sobukwe for the purpose of liberating the black South African majority from the apartheid policies of the white minority. See PAN-AFRICANISM.

Pan-African Congresses. Inspired by the success of the London Conference in 1900, Dr. W. E. B. Du Bois called a Pan-African Congress to meet in Paris, France, in 1919. The Second Congress was held in 1921 in London, England; Paris, France; and Brussels, Belgium—the principal colonial powers. The Third Congress was held in 1923 in London, England, and Lisbon, Portugal; the Fourth Congress in 1927 in New York, U.S.A.; and the Fifth Congress in 1945 in Manchester, England, where, in addition to Du Bois, Kwame Nkrumah, George Padmore, Jomo Kenyatta, and Rayford W. Logan were also present. The participants in the Fifth Congress drafted a resolution for absolute independence and self-government of all African nations. See PAN-AFRICANISM.

Pan-African Freedom Movement of East and Central Africa.(PAFMECA). An informal organization established on September 17, 1958 (and renamed PAFMECSA in 1962), for the purpose of fighting all forms of colonialism and to serve as a vanguard of African unity. Its first chairman was Kenneth Kaunda of Zambia. See PAN-AFRICANISM.

Pan-American Conferences. See RIO CONFERENCE OF 1941-1942, WASHINGTON CONFERENCE OF 1889.

Pan-American Organization. See ORGANIZATION OF AMERICAN STATES (OAS).

Pan-American Union. An informal, regional, international organization of the Latin-American republics created in 1890 for the purpose of maintaining cooperation among the member-states. The United States is one of its members. See PAN-AMERICANISM.

Pan-Americanism. The movement to foster political, cultural, and economic cooperation among nations of the Western Hemisphere (North and South America) as pursued by the Inter-American Institute and the Pan-American Union. See NINE-POWER TREATY, WASHINGTON CONFERENCE OF 1889.

Pan-Arabism. A term often used in connection with some Arab leaders, mainly former President Gamal Nasser of Egypt, who were primarily interested in promoting Arab unity rather than African unity, or to some Arab leaders who have attempted to gain control of the Pan-African movement.

Pan-Islamism. A movement seeking the unification, through better cooperation, mutual assistance, and exchange of ideas, of all Islamic states to advance their interests and well-being.

Pan-Negroism. A concept that emphasizes the commitment of the people of the black race to their heritage, derived from their place or origin, Africa; the call for the development of black consciousness and unity of black peoples everywhere. The movement of Negroism (or Negritude), from which Pan-Africanism was derived, developed as an ideology among the English-speaking Africans and as an intellectual and cultural trend by French-speaking Africans in Africa and the West Indies. Its most effective proponents were George Padmore and Kwame Nkrumah. See NEGRITUDE.

Pan Nipponism. The vertical and horizontal spread and influence of economic and political influence of Japan as the leading economic power. With time, Japan shall acquire stronger political influence particularly among the smaller Asian powers, the mini-tigers, or mini-dragons, e.g., Hong Kong, Taiwan, Singapore, and Korea among others under the doctrine of Japanese Order (or Peace) Pax Nipponica. See AMERICA BASHING, UNILATERAL GLOBAL KEYNESIANISM, UNREPENTANT INDIVIDUALISM.

Pan-Slavism. A movement (strong during the 19th century) to unify, culturally, politically, and economically, all Slavic peoples in Eastern and Southern Europe (e.g., the Czechs, Slovaks, Bulgars, Sloventz, Poles, Ukrainians, Belorussians, Russians, Yugoslavs, Latvians, Lithuanians, and Estonians). Adam Mickiewicz (1798-1855), the Polish national poet, was one of its leaders.

Pan-Somalism. A term applied (by Kenya) to the Somalis, who have attempted to reorganize African states along tribal lines. Their views are often referred to as "tribalistic doctrine." See PAN-AFRICANISM.

Panama Canal Treaties. A series of diplomatic events and policy revisions throughout the history of the Panama Canal have preceded the latest U.S.-Panama Canal Treaty. In 1850, the U.S. and England, through the Clayton-Bulwer Treaty of 1850, agreed that the U.S. would not attempt to colonize any area in the Americas. That treaty was modified, however, by the Hay-Pauncefote Treaty of 1901, which freed the U.S. to sign the November 8, 1903, pact with Panama and build the Canal. The French builder of the Canal, who also built the Suez Canal, bankrupted the project in 1889, after 20,000 lives and an undetermined amount of money were lost. American railroad builder John Stevens directed the construction of the Canal after the treaty was signed by Hay and Phillipe Bunau-Varilla, a Frenchman acting for Panama. The Canal Zone was extended from six to ten miles, and the French Company received $40,000,000 in compensation for their assets. (The area once was part of Colombia, from which Panama seceded on November 3, 1903, and was recognized by the United States on November 6, 1903.) The United States agreed to maintain the Canal and "perfect neutrality" of the entire Isthmus as well. On September 7, 1977, in the presence of leaders from twenty-five other Latin American republics representing the Organization of American States (OAS), U.S. President Jimmy Carter and Panama's Chief of State (dictator) Omar Torrijos (killed in a plane crash August 1, 1981) signed two separate documents: one, the Treaty proper, which calls for transfer of ownership of the Panama Canal from the United States to Panama by the year 2000; and the other, a Treaty concerning the Permanent Neutrality and Operation of the Panama Canal. The treaty was subject to ratification by the U.S. Senate; while in Panama it was ratified by a plebiscite on Sunday, September 18, 1977, which revealed that out of 765,659 registered voters, 506,927 voted for the Treaty, and 245,112 voted against it. A poll of the American public conducted by George Gallup of the Gallup Poll indicated that those who favored turning the Canal over to Panama based their arguments on the belief that the transfer would break America's past with colonialism and improves public relations; that the Canal is no longer strategically important and is expensive to maintain; that it prevents conflict and that in case of war, the U.S. would take over the Canal anyway; and that it rightly belongs to Panama. Arguments against giving up the Canal were based on the belief that the U.S. owns it and should keep it, that communists might gain control of this important waterway which is vital to America's national security; that Panama's government cannot be trusted to live up to the treaty obligations; and that no financial aid should accompany the transfer of the Canal. (Currently, the U.S. pays Panama an annuity of 2.3 million dollars.) On February 1, 1978, President Jimmy Carter made his final appeal to the American people (during a "fireside chat" that was televised nationally) and to the U.S. Senate (which started a debate on the Treaty on February 8, 1978—the first Senate debate ever to be open to simultaneous transmission over radio networks), urging both to support and to approve the Treaty because, contrary to circulated rumors, American rights are well protected (e.g., by the so-called "expeditious transit" provision—giving U.S. vessels, in times of emergency which the U.S. will determine, the right to pass through the Canal ahead of other vessels without waiting their turn—a provision also known as the "Leadership Amendment"). The first Treaty, pertaining to the neutrality of the Canal, was approved by the U.S. Senate on March 16, 1978, (by a vote of 68 for and 32 against), and the second treaty, pertaining to the actual transfer of and operation of the Canal by Panama, was approved on April 18, 1978 (by a vote of 68 for and 32 against). In the main, the two Treaties specify these provisions: (1) perpetual neutrality of the Canal, even after Panama takes full control of the facility on December 31, 1999; (2) the facility is to be open in peace as well as in war to ships of all nations (including belligerents), and no vessel may commit any hostility in the waterway area; (3) Panama promises to operate the Canal efficiently and to refrain from charging excessive tolls for its use; (4) Panama and the United States are to mutually defend the Canal from hostile acts, but the United States may not interfere in the domestic affairs of Panama; (5) in times of crisis, the actual existence of which is to be determined by the states of Panama and the United States, American and Panamanian vessels (under the "leadership amendment") may use the facility ahead of other nations (i.e., "go to the head of the line"), and (6) until the Canal is transferred to Panama in 1999, the United States will continue to grant Colombia (which originally owned the territory on which the Canal was built) toll-free transit, and when Panama takes over, Costa Rica and Colombia may be extended the same privilege by Panama. In the final hours of debate the Senate added a reservation to the treaty. This reservation allows the U.S. to use its military forces if necessary to keep the canal open after Panama takes control. See Appendix 92.

Panama Incursion. Also known as "Operation Just Cause," its code-name; the American invasion of Panama on 20 December 1989 for the purpose of the deposition of General Manuel Antonio Noriega, dictator and head of the Panama defense forces. Noriega, also called "pineapple face," because of facial scars, had been an agent of the American CIA since 1978; he facilitated American interests in the area until it was learned that he also aided Cuba's Castro and the Sandinistas in Nicaragua, and engaged in drug trafficking and money laundering. The usefulness of Noriega as an American agent of influence declined; he spoke very unfavorably about President Ronald Reagan and the President George Bush; and it was perceived that it was time to remove him from power. Noriega was indicted on drug trafficking charges in Florida, and when he refused to appear in Florida for court hearings the U.S. imposed economic sanctions against Panama. Following the American invasion, Noriega sought asylum in the Vatican Embassy in Panama, but decided to surrender to American federal marshals on 3 January 1990, and was imprisoned in the United States to await trial. Noriega demanded of the American authorities that he be treated as a prisoner of war—a status that was granted him in a somewhat modified manner. He was provided in prison with an executive suite of quarters that included telecommunications equipment such as radio, telephone, and fax; secretarial and maid services were at his disposal, but he simply refused to say "uncle"—to submit to his captors and collaborate with the American federal prosecutors. He maintained a strong, hostile, anti-American posture while in captivity.

Pandit. In the Hindi language, a "learned person," a "leader," or an "adviser." The "pandit" or "pundit" in Indian politics is one who is close to the top leadership and who renders advice as well as favors to loyal party followers and supporters. The term is often used to characterize persons with extensive political power in American politics (e.g., party bosses or power brokers), as "pundits with political clout." See MOGUL, POLITICAL MACHINE, POWER, Appendix 3-A.

Panmunjon Armistice. See KOREAN WAR.

Pantouflage. See ADMINISTRATIVE STATE.

Papal Encyclical. See ENCYCLICAL.

Papal Infallibility. The accepted doctrine that the Pope, leader of the Roman Catholic Church and head of government in the Vatican state, is incapable of an error in matters of faith and morals. There is no known claim that this doctrine extends to politics. Pope John XXIII, who spoke fluently in several languages including Bulgarian, French, Latin, Italian, and Turkish, but experienced difficulties with the American-English language, admitted in jest, "the more I study English, the more I understand that papal infallibility does not extend to its pronunciations." The Pope, like many monarchs and other leaders throughout the world, is in reality responsible for his actions "only to God and history." The present Pope, John Paul II, who has command of about sixty foreign languages, has made no comment on the validity of that doctrine.

Papal Line of Demarcation. See DIVIDE ET IMPERA.

Paper Entrepreneurialism. So Professor Robert Reich, a political economist from Harvard University (*The Next American Frontier*), characterizes the contemporary younger generation of managers of America's major business enterprises who are preoccupied with paper work on such matters as financial management, mergers, acquisitions, litigation, tax loopholes, and accounting, rather than on technological innovations and the development of new and better products for domestic and foreign markets, which would make America strong, competitive, and prosperous. See COMPARATIVE ADVANTAGE.

Paper Gold. See SPECIAL DRAWING RIGHTS.

Paper Tiger. A derogatory term applied to the United States by Chairman Mao Tse-tung of the People's Republic of China describing the weakness and vulnerability of the United States in coping with international and domestic problems.

Paper Trail. Writing recorded on a paper, or a voice recorded on a tape, if preserved and retrieved when need arises, becomes a document. Preserved documents are the best means of searching past events, and they often project future events. A paper trail works to the detriment of lawbreakers (e.g., money launderers and falsifiers of documents).

Paradigm. In the language of politics, the total ecology in which problems of a political nature are studied, and which includes a set of normative assumptions of a world view or global outlook (*Weltanschauung*); perceptions and beliefs about the political phenomena and data that one deals with; degree and scope of the consensus on the legitimacy of questions posed; agreement on techniques for implementing public policy; and a frame of reference. Also, a model of a political system that is considered to include the most scientific and most advanced features.

Parallel Development Doctrine. Once the British government's legal colonial policy of separate development for whites and blacks in South Africa and former Rhodesia. Also known as the "two pyramids policy." Some serious steps toward racial integration have taken place in South Africa in an effort to share power with blacks. See APARTHEID.

Paramilitary Organization. A private or public organization which performs functions of a military nature, or one which serves as an auxiliary organization of the military establishment of a state.

Parasite Law. The Soviet Constitution (Art. 12) stated: "Work in the USSR is a duty and a matter of honor for every able-bodied citizen, in accordance with the principle: 'He who does not work, neither shall he eat.' The principle applied in the former USSR was that of socialism: 'From each according to his ability, to each according to his work.'" This constitutional provision was also strengthened by the Soviet Criminal Code which provided a penalty for anyone (e.g., under the parasite law) who did not have employment as a source of income (unless in school, of minor age supported by parents, or incapacitated) or who was living on the income of another. The post-Soviet system is under revision.

PARC. See POLITICAL AFFAIRS RESEARCH COUNCIL.

Parental Empowerment Law. See EDUCRAT.

Paris Commune. The communal-type of government that was established by dissatisfied members of the French National Guard, which had staged a successful rebellion against the republican government of France in 1871 after taking over the city of Paris. (Some Marxists, among them, Vladimir I. Lenin of Russia, claim that the Paris Commune was the first modern socialist government established in recent history anywhere.)

Paris Declaration on Human Rights. The United Nations held a special conference in Paris, France, in 1955, during which the member nations present—excluding the Soviet Union and the East European allies of the USSR, who refused to participate—adopted a declaration condemning all violations of human rights and liberties by states. The UN was empowered to study such violations and to report its findings to the General Assembly during regular sessions. Since the Third World and the Socialist states took control of the General Assembly of the UN as a bloc, this activity of the UN has become almost obsolete. See THE UNITED NATIONS.

Paris Economic Conference. See ECONOMIC SUMMITS.

Paris Maritime Declaration. See MARITIME LAW.

Paris Peace Agreement of 1973. A quadripartite agreement signed in Paris, France, in January, 1973, by the governments of the Republic of Vietnam (South Vietnam), the Democratic Republic of Vietnam (North Vietnam), the Provisional Revolutionary Government of the National Liberation Front (Vietcong), and the United States of America on the ending of hostilities (cease-fire) in North and South Vietnam. The agreement called for, among other things, total withdrawal of all foreign troops from both Vietnams within sixty (60) days from the time of the signing of the agreement and the exchange of prisoners-of-war. The cease-fire and the exchange of prisoners-of-war were to be supervised by the four parties to the agreement as well as by an International Commission for Control and Supervision (ICCP) composed of military representatives from Canada, Hungary, Indonesia, and Poland (also known as the "CHIP" Commission). The agreement also called for a cease-fire in Cambodia and Laos. The American forces left Vietnam by March 29, 1973, and the U.S. Embassy closed on April 29, 1975. On April 30, 1975, Vietnam's President Duong Van Minh announced the unconditional surrender of South Vietnam to the Vietcong and the North Vietnamese forces.

Paris Peace Conference of 1919. At the conclusion of W.W.I, the major Allies met to restore peace; Woodrow Wilson of the United States, David Lloyd George of Great Britain, Georges Clemenceau of France, Vittorio Orlando of Italy, and delegations from thirty-two other states, some of them asking for the restoration of the independence of their states, such as Ignacy Padarewski (1860-1941) of Poland, Edvard Benes (1884-1948) speaking for the Czechs, and Nikola Pasic (1845-1926), representing Serbian interests. They were not directly participating in the main discussion, and were not present when the Treaty of Versailles was concluded. The Conference was held from 12 January 1919 until 28 June 1919. Agreement was also reached on the establishment of the League of Nations, but the United States Senate never approved America's active membership. See FOURTEEN POINTS, LEAGUE OF NATIONS, NEW DIPLOMACY, VERSAILLES TREATY.

Paris Peace Conference of 1946. This was the continuation of the Moscow Conference of 1945, called to write peace treaties with minor European powers defeated during W.W.II whose regimes collaborated with the German Nazi occupiers. They were: Bulgaria, Finland, Hungary, Italy, and Romania. In a subsequent meeting in New York City in 1946, the Council of Foreign Ministers of the four major powers, Britain, France, the United States, and the Soviet Union, laid foundations for the resolution of the Italian-Yugoslav dispute over the City of Trieste, both states demanded exclusive control over that city, war reparations from Italy and restoration of navigation rights on the Danube River to all nations.

Parish. A unit of local government in the state of Louisiana corresponding to that of a county; also, an administrative unit of some religious denominations.

Parity. Equality of strength. See STRATEGIC ARMS LIMITATION TALKS (SALT).

Parity Gap. A notion prevalent among some students of politics and power to the effect that international peace and security may be preserved not because nations so desire, but because the major superpowers (the former Soviet Union and the United States) were reluctant to commence any global conflict themselves, or allow others to do so, for fear that their weapon systems may not be sufficient to conquer the adversary. The program of dismantling ex-Soviet arsenals began in 1991. See STRATEGIC ARMS LIMITATION TALKS (SALT).

Parity Law. See TRACTORCADE.

Parity Policy. A concept developed under U.S. President John F. Kennedy (1961-1963), whereby superiority in arms and nuclear weapons over the Soviet Union was substituted with parity, or balance of forces.

Parkinson's Laws. See OAKS' LAWS.

Parley. A conference held usually for the purpose of settling a dispute. See PACIFIC SETTLEMENT OF DISPUTES.

Parliament. A central or national legislative body of a nation state charged with the responsibility of passing legislation (laws) and, under cabinet-parliamentary systems, selecting the government-of-the-day (e.g., the premier, prime minister, or chancellor as well as the cabinet of ministers). Under democratic systems, the parliament also oversees the overall policies aiming to preserve the well-being of the nation state (e.g., in England, Japan, and the German Federal Republic). See BUNDESTAG, CABINET-PARLIAMENTARY GOVERNMENT, GOVERNMENT-OF-THE-DAY, HOUSE OF COMMONS, MOTHER OF PARLIAMENTS, PARLIAMENTARY DEMOCRACY.

Parliamentarian. One specializing in the deliberative procedures of a legislative body and the proper preparation of legislative bills; an expert on parliamentary procedures. See PARLIAMENT.

Parliamentary Commissioner for Administration. An officer appointed by the British Parliament to report on all abuses of administrative powers and general maladministration by government officials as presented to him in the form of grievances by or through the Members of Parliament (MPs). See OMBUDSMAN, PARLIAMENT.

Parliamentary Council. The constituent assembly which drafted the *Basic Law* (Constitution) for the German Federal Republic (West Germany) in 1948. See BUNDESRAT, BUNDESTAG, PARLIAMENT.

Parliamentary Democracy. A political system, in which the legislature (the parliament) selects the government-of-the-day—the premier, prime minister, or chancellor, and the ministers (the cabinet)—according to party strength as demonstrated in elections. In this system, the government has a dual responsibility—to the people as well as to the parliament. Such practices are normal in political systems which rest on the common democratic principles of governance. They do not occur in dictatorial or totalitarian systems (most of which are single-party systems). See CABINET PARLIAMENTARY GOVERNMENT, DEMOCRACY, ONE AND ONE-HALF PARTY GOVERNMENT.

Parliamentary Government. See CABINET-PARLIAMENTARY GOVERNMENT.

Parliamentary Monarchy. See REIGNING.

Parliamentary Socialism. A phrase describing the gradual implementation of socialist reforms through legislative processes rather than by abrupt, non-Marxist revolutionary means (e.g., Germany, Japan, England, and the Scandinavian States). See MARXISM.

Parliamentary Supremacy. See GLORIOUS REVOLUTION.

Part-Time Citizen. See OVERSEAS CONSTITUENCY.

Parti Africaine Pour Independent Guinea-Bissao et Cape Verde (PIAGC). A coalition of political groups which struggled for the independence of Guinea-Bissao and Cape Verde from Portuguese domination. Guinea-Bissao's independence was officially recognized on September 10, 1974, and Cape Verde was granted independence on July 5, 1975. See PAN-AFRICANISM.

Parti Québécois. A radical political party of French-speaking people in Quebec, Canada, struggling for political independence for the Province of Quebec from the Canadian federation. During the 1976 election, the Party came to power with the aid of labor unions. On December 31, 1977, Canada's Prime Minister, Elliot P. Trudeau, issued a nation-wide warning to the effect that he would order the armed forces to deal with the liberation movement. See SEPARATISM.

Participatory Bureaucracy. The bureaucracies of party, youth organizations, and the military, which through routine administrative processes not necessarily ideologically motivated, render support, legitimacy, and perpetuation to the existence of a given political system. Institutional pluralism is encouraged in order to portray the large dimensions and massiveness of the support that every political system needs. See BUREAUCRACY, OAKS' LAWS.

Participatory Democracy. A political system which allows a large number of persons to take a direct and active part in government or the formulation of public policy. Also known as "participatory politics." See CONVERSATION WITH OREGON, DEMOCRACY.

Participatory Management. A mode of managing people and institutions where most or many employees, workers, are also engaged in management either independently or in collaboration with middle and top management. Widely practiced in Japan and Germany, but not in the United States where, according to Bill Saporito ("The Revolt Against 'Working Smarter,'" *Fortune*, 21 July 1986), American middle management fears that sharing management functions with workers may undermine its existence. They prefer the traditional management systems where, "I, the boss," and "you, the worker;" "you work, and I boss." Every employee, every worker, ought to be to some degree a manager as well.

Participatory Planning. A planning of the processes which all segments of a society and all of its institutions are directly and actively involved in one form or another. See PLANNING.

Participatory Politics. See PARTICIPATORY DEMOCRACY.

Partisan. One who is partial (e.g., pursuing the philosophy and policies of one political party as distinct from another); an expression of partiality or bias. Also, a guerrilla fighter (e.g., against the occupation of one's territory by hostile forces of another state).

Partisan Primary. A primary election by and for a single party (e.g., a closed primary). See CLOSED PRIMARY, OPEN PRIMARY, PRIMARY ELECTION.

Partition. The absorption of a portion of the territory of one state by another state or group of states, either as a result of conquest or of dissolution of the state (e.g., the partition of Poland, Palestine, or the Ottoman Empire). See Appendix 91.

Partition of Poland. See PARTITION, Appendix 91.

Partito Dell'Amore. In the Italian language, "Party of Love"; also, a political party in Italy under the leadership of Illona ("La Cicciolina," in the Italian language, "little fleshy one") Staller, once wife of American artist Jeff Koons, a porno star, and a member of the Italian parliament until she resigned in the spring of 1991 to head the party.

Partner Leadership. Phrase coined by U.S. President Jimmy Carter (1977-1981) during his press conference on February 2, 1977, referring to the need for the President and the Congress to work together, on a bipartisan basis, toward achieving major national goals, such as pursuing an energy policy and full employment.

Partocracy. The rule by bureaucrats and political activists of a single political party (e.g., the now dissolved but once omnipotent Communist Party of the Soviet Union, (CPSU). The CPSU, as established by V. I. Lenin at the beginning of this century, was a cohesive force of professional and dedicated revolutionaries; but once educated ideologues were replaced with illiterate apparatchiks, the party and the government it controlled, became a farce and traitor to millions of trusting citizens.

Party Activist. See POLITICAL HACK.

Party Column Ballot. A type of voting ballot (known also as an INDIANA BALLOT or STRAIGHT TICKET VOTE) on which candidates for elective offices are listed in columns by party.

Party Conference. See PARTY SENATE CONFERENCE.

Party Control Commission. Once an organ of the Central Committee of the Communist Party of the Soviet Union (CPSU) which was charged with the responsibility of investigating all acts by party officials considered in violation of the statutes of the party and to bring charges against them. It also reviewed cases of individual party members. The CPSU was suspended after the 1991 coup attempt. See COMMUNIST PARTY OF THE SOVIET UNION (CPSU).

Party Convention. Since the Anti-Mason party convention which was held in New York City in 1931, nominating William Wirt for president, practically all political parties have followed suit, holding such conventions once every four years. In the United States both the Republican and Democratic parties assemble in convention. A major function of the convention delegates is to select the party's presidential and vice presidential candidates. The convention also adopts its platform—policy statements designed to attract voters, and to be implemented if the party's candidate is elected to the office of president. Other functions of the convention include the adoption of rules and the selection of a national committee to govern the party for the next four years. See DEMOCRATIC AND REPUBLICAN NATIONAL COMMITTEES AND THEIR CANDIDATES, EVOLUTION OF THE TWO-PARTY SYSTEM IN THE UNITED STATES, Appendices 18, 19.

Party Discipline. A term applied to the individual behavior that party members must demonstrate in order to remain members, such as attending party meetings, paying dues, and supporting the party on all matters, inside and outside the party ranks. Such strict rules of behavior are known to exist in socialist and communist parties where any deviation from the party line (e.g., demonstration of independent opinions or views) may bring penalties in the form of reprimand, warning, or, the highest penalty, expulsion. Under one-party systems, where a single party is in power, this may amount to the loss of lucrative employment or even imprisonment. In the United States, where political parties are built around elections, strong party discipline as well as a highly institutionalized party machinery are considered undesirable and unnecessary. Some of the political parties known to maintain strong discipline among their members are those of the communist-type such as the Communist Party of the ex-Soviet Union (CPSU), the People's Republic of China, and, in the West, the political parties in England and the Federal Republic of Germany.

Party Labeling. The practice of having candidates for elective public offices identified on the official ballots by party affiliation (e.g., as Democrat, Republican, Socialist or Independent). In some states in the United States (e.g., in Virginia), such party labeling is required by law (passed in March 1978). See HIZBULLAH, PARTY OF GOD, POLITICAL MACHINE, VOTING.

Party of God. See HIZBULLAH.

Party of Love. See PARTITO DELL'AMORE.

Party of Slovak Unity. A small, nationalistic, extremist political organization in Slovakia under the leadership of Stanislav Panis which advocates separation from the federation with the Czechs and the formation of an independent state. The party's legacy dates to 1939 when Josef Tison established a separate Slovak state, but was accused of collaboration with Nazi Germany. Slovakia constitutes about one-third of the what is now called "the Czech and Slovak Federated Republic." Until 1918 Slovakia had been dominated by Hungary, while the Czechs were dominated by Austria.

Party Organizations. Precinct, ward, city, county, congressional district, state, and national components of a party.

Party Platform. A document containing statements of philosophy to which a party subscribes or claims to subscribe, and also long and short term objectives and plans, or specific items which the party supports or opposes (known as "planks"), such as new tax laws, revision of the draft laws, or civil rights legislation. (The platform is presented at a party convention for approval, with or without revisions or amendments.) The party platform is the overall program by which the party and its candidates will be judged by the voters on election day. A written platform was produced in America for the first time by the Democratic Party in 1840, and very often a platform written by the leaders of a party was not necessarily acceptable to the presidential candidate of that party, as was the case in 1859, when Abraham Lincoln openly stated that he was "not wedded to the formal written platform system." According to Lincoln, the candidate's past record ought to suffice. One saying in the folklore of American politics is that platform is something to run on and not to stand on, and another saying proposes that "a platform is what you start by running on and end by running from" after the election. During his campaign for governor of the State of New York in 1928, Franklin D. Roosevelt made jokes about political platforms, criticizing promises made by the Republicans who kept record of promises made but no record of promises kept. The length of the platform document varies from election to election and from party to party. The 1840 democratic platform contained about 500 words, according to Professor Arthur Schlesinger, Jr., an expert in the field, while the Whig platform of 1844 consisted of only 350 words. A decade later, the Republicans produced a platform of 108 pages in a format of a printed book. The 1988 Republican platform, which presidential candidate George Bush supported, consisted of a little over 30,000 words. "The first party to produce a sensible and readable platform," concludes Professor Schlesinger, "may yet be astonished by the result."

Party Politics. The practice of using the party organization and party apparatus to achieve desired ends. In modern times, voters concentrate on personalities and issues rather than parties.

Party Reform. See COMMISSION ON PRESIDENTIAL NOMINATIONS.

Party Senate Conference. The policy and decision-making body of a political party in the United States Senate composed of the majority or the minority party leaders (as the case may be), the Whips, and all the Senators of the particular party. The Conference, among other things, selects members for committee assignments. See UNITED STATES SENATE.

Party State. See ADMINISTRATIVE STATE.

Party Whip. A high-ranking party official and a member of a legislative body (e.g., the Parliament in England or Congress in the United States), whom the party leadership selects to serve as a link between the top leadership and the remaining members of the party. The Whip, among his other duties, keeps the other legislators of his party informed on party strategy, records whether they are present and vote (or are absent and do not vote) on issues that the leadership favors (or opposes), and maintains general discipline among the members of the party. See CONGRESS OF THE UNITED STATES.

Pasdaran. The Iranian Revolutionary Guards, a conglomeration of military and civilian groups, all loyal to Ayatollah Khomeini and the Iranian Revolution and violently anti-American. The Pasdaran served as the main police force in Iran during and after the Revolution of 1979; their duties included maintaining control over the American hostages held for 444 days in the American Embassy in Iran. See OCTOBER SURPRISE.

Passive Resistance. The non-violent disobedience by citizens of official acts and policies of established authority. See CIVIL DISOBEDIENCE.

Passman-Davis Confrontation. See LAST PLANTATION.

Paternal Choice in Education. See EDUCRAT.

Paternalism. In act of protecting one from the consequences of his own ignorance (e.g., an individual's or governmental agency's intervening into affairs which are ordinarily outside their scope of activity for the purpose of rendering some useful assistance). Also, one person protecting another, or a stronger state protecting a weaker one, from harm by adversaries.

Pathet Lao. The communist and pro-communist forces led by Prince Souphanouvong which took control of Laos in 1975, following the collapse of Vietnam and Cambodia. The communist Prince once referred to the Laotian struggle as a "revolution with the gentle face," but, once he gained power, approximately one million out of the 3.4 million total population were detained in concentration camps, called "re-education camps," for "re-adjustments" to the new socialist life. See CAMBODIAN MASSACRE.

Patres Conscripti. In the Latin language, "founding fathers." Also, it was once the official name of Roman Senators.

Patrician. A term commonly applied to one who is wealthy, one who enjoys full political rights and utilizes them or takes advantage of them, or one who is generally influential among policy and decision-making persons. The term is derived from the Patrician class in ancient Rome which owned property, enjoyed full political rights, and was able to exert considerable influence in the shaping of public policies. See PLEBEIAN.

Patriotic Catholic Church of China. The Chinese leadership does not recognize the Vatican and in order to discourage contacts between Catholics in China and the Holy See, the government established the Patriotic Catholic Church. The membership is small as most Catholics silently observe the rituals of Rome. The Pope in a December 1991 address, urged Chinese Catholics to serve their country while at the same time "to continue to live their faith in fidelity to the Gospels and the church of Christ."

Patriotic Front. See ZIMBABWE CRISIS.

Patriotism Ends at the Pocketbook. See CONSUMER SOVEREIGNTY.

Patronage. As applied to practical politics, the practice of rewarding persons for past services rendered to the grantor by appointing them to positions of power, influence, prestige, or high income (e.g., the U.S. President may reward one who contributed generously to his campaign fund with an appointment to a position in government).

Patton Plan. U.S. Army General George Smith Patton, Jr. (1895-1945) devised a plan in 1938 for the retention of Japanese and Americans of Japanese descent residing in Hawaii and other Pacific islands in case of war with Japan, because there were persons among them who were intelligence officers and agents working for the Japanese government, and they were also capable of sabotaging American civilian and military targets. The plan, in a somewhat revised form, was implemented by U.S. President Franklin Delano Roosevelt (1933-1945) after the Japanese invasion of Pearl Harbor on 7 December 1941. The U.S. military had some advance knowledge of Japanese intelligence operations against the United States from intelligence received through decoded (crypto) messages intercepted in Washington, D.C. See PEARL HARBOR.

Pauper Law. See ABILITY-TO-PAY PRINCIPLE.

Pax Africana. See PAN-AFRICANISM.

Pax Americana. See PAN-AMERICANISM.

Pax Arabica. See PAN-ISLAMISM.

Pax Atomica. In the Latin language, "atomic peace." Also, an attempt by nation-states (e.g., the United States) and international organizations (e.g., the United Nations) to outlaw, or at least to limit deployment of atomic weapons as instruments of warfare (e.g., in a manner similar to that of outlawing the use of poisonous gasses).

Pax Britannica. Term commonly used to describe Britain's efforts in the past to dominate the world.

Pax Islamica. See PAN-ISLAMISM.

Pax Nipponica. See PAN-NIPPONISM.

Pax Slavica. See PAN-SLAVISM.

Pax Romana. In the Latin language, "Roman Peace." The term also describes the conditions of peace imposed in any territory or possession which was conquered by ancient Rome, or the relationship of Rome with other states.

Pay-as-You-Go Policy. A kind of fiscal management policy which calls for capital expenditure to be made from current incoming revenues rather than through the borrowing of funds. The "pay-as-you-go" system was originated by President Franklin D. Roosevelt (1933-1945) on January 10, 1943, when he signed a bill that authorized salary and wage tax deductions (effective July 1, 1943) to cover expenditures of the government. U.S. Senator Harry F. Byrd, Sr. (D-VA), was one of the strongest supporters of this legislation while Governor of Virginia and later as Virginia's Senator. His son, U.S. Senator Harry F. Byrd, Jr. (Ind-VA), continued that tradition of being a "watchdog" against government deficit spending. Such a policy has also prevailed in several states until recent years, with Virginia leading the way. The 1985 Balanced Budget and Emergency Deficit Control Act, a product of Republican Senators Phil Gramm, economics professor, and Warren Rudman, a lawyer, aimed to achieve the pay-as-you-go standard. See GOVERNMENT BUDGET, ZIGZAG MAN.

Pay Board. See NIXON'S ECONOMIC POLICIES.

Payoff. See MERIT SYSTEM, POLITICAL HACK.

PCIJ. See PERMANENT COURT OF INTERNATIONAL JUSTICE.

PDC. See PLANNING DISTRICT COMMISSION.

Peace, Bread, and Land. See LENIN'S APRIL THESES.

Peace Constitution. In the Japanese Constitution, adopted on 3 May 1947, the Emperor Hirohito renounced claim to divinity, made parliament the sole law-making body, and renounced war as an instrument of policy forever. The United States was charged with the defense of Japan. The prevailing opinion is that this allowed the Japanese to spend money on trade and commerce instead of on armaments and armies.

Peace Corps. A federal agency that was created by an executive order on March 1, 1961, by U.S. President John F. Kennedy (1961-1963), and voted into permanence by the U.S. Congress in April of the same year. The Peace Corps renders assistance to underdeveloped and developing nations by sending volunteer workers and technicians from the United States for a period of one to two years to assist in cultural and economic development. The program is paid for entirely by the American taxpayers.

Peace Dividends. See LAFFER CURVE.

Peace Feelers. See DIPLOMATIC FEELERS.

Peace in Our Time. Famous words spoken by British Prime Minister Neville Chamberlain upon his return in September 1938 from the Munich Conference with Hitler, who at the same time was making preparations for W.W.II, which started exactly one year later, September 1, 1939, with the attack on Poland. Following Chamberlain's statement, Hitler allegedly called Chamberlain a "little worm without a spine." See APPEASEMENT, MUNICH AGREEMENT.

Peace-Keeping Force of the United Nations. A team of combat-ready military units assigned by member-states of the United Nations Organization to the Command of the United Nations, appointed by the Secretary-General of the United Nations for the purpose of overseeing cease-fire violations among warring belligerents. The primary function of the Peace-Keeping Force is to maintain peace and security in a given area as directed by the United Nations. The Peace-Keeping Force has been used eight times by the United Nations since the inception of this international organization: (1) KOREA (1950)—military units of sixteen nations (including the United States) under an integrated UN Command were authorized by the "Uniting for Peace Resolution" of the United Nations to repress North Korea's aggression against South Korea. Although an armistice was signed in 1953, the UN force remains in Korea to this day, and the state of war still exists legally (during the Korean conflict of 1950-53, 33,629 Americans and 3,143 allied soldiers were killed in combat); (2) MIDDLE EAST (1956-1967)—a ten-nation, 6,000 man force was assigned to maintain and keep peace between Egyptian and Israeli forces. In 1967 the force was withdrawn at the request of Egypt's President, General Gamal Abdel Nasser; (3) CONGO (1961-1964)—a fifteen-nation force of 20,000 combat troops were deployed to maintain stability and prevent civil war among the competing factions in this former Belgian colony; (4) WEST IRIAN (1962-1963)—a nine-nation force of 1,600 men succeeded in pacifying Dutch New Guinea, where the voters, through a plebiscite, decided to join Indonesia; (5) CYPRUS (1964)—a nine-nation force of 6,500 soldiers prevented Greek Cypriots and Turkish Cypriots from engaging in open hostility until 1974 when the Greek Cypriots revolted against the dominating Turkish Cypriots. The force is maintained there to this day; (6) SINAI PENINSULA (1973)—a twelve nation, 6,000 man combat force was deployed to discourage Egyptian and Israeli forces from engaging in open combat by separating them through a buffer zone. The force is still there, but since 1977 it has been assisted by a monitoring team of civilian observers from the United States who observe military movements of both belligerents and report their findings to the United Nations; (7) GOLAN HEIGHTS (1974)—a four-nation, 1,200 man force maintains a buffer zone between Israeli and Syrian forces. The force is still there; and (8) LEBANON (1978)—a four-nation, 4,000 man force maintains a buffer zone between Israel and the Palestinian Liberation Organization (PLO) in the Litani river area in Lebanon conquered by Israel in March 1978, as a retaliatory measure against the PLO which had invaded Israel and had killed several innocent persons. The force is to remain there until Israel pulls out of Lebanon. A cease-fire was declared in the area on March 21, 1978, and the UN Peace-Keeping Force maintains a six-mile buffer zone. In addition to these peace-keeping forces, the United nations has deployed a variety of other peace-observing teams around the world wherever international peace and security are threatened. Trouble spots to which UN observer teams have been sent are: (1) MIDDLE EAST (1948)—a seventeen nation team of 500 soldiers was dispatched in a non-combat capacity to observe armistice violations between Israel and Palestinian Arabs after the 1948 Israel-Palestinian Arab War. The team is there to this day; (2) KASHMIR (1948)—a thirteen nation, 89 man force went to observe the Indian-Pakistani armistice line in Kashmir. The conflict between India and Pakistan (until the end of W.W.II, one nation under British rule) evolved over a small strip of arid land called Kashmir. The UN observer team is still there to this day; (3) LEBANON (1948)—a seven nation, 600 man military team assisted in maintaining peace among the Christian (pro-capitalist) and Moslem (pro-socialist) factions for six months following the withdrawal of U.S. Marines dispatched by President D. D. Eisenhower to prevent takeover by the Moslems; (4) YEMEN (1963-1964)—a ten nation, 200 man force was dispatched to assist in the pacification of the warring factions of Yemenis after the Egyptian forces, sent there previously for the same purpose, withdrew in frustration, and (5) INDIA-PAKISTAN (1965-1966)—a ten nation, 93 man team of observers was sent to report on cease-fire violations between the two belligerents. The peace-keeping operations and observer team deployment have cost the United Nations approximately $4 billion in all, with the major share falling on the shoulders of the American taxpayer. With the exception of Korea, the UN forces never engaged in combat, and they fired only when fired upon, which was rather rare. In Korea, the UN forces served as regular combat forces and were engaged in a war. In March 1992, a Peace Keeping Force of 14,000 was dispatched to Yugoslavia in order to separate the Croats and the Serbs. See UNITING FOR PEACE RESOLUTION, Appendices 75-79.

Peace-Observer Team. See PEACE-KEEPING FORCE OF THE UNITED NATIONS.

Peace of Portsmouth. See TREATY OF PORTSMOUTH OF 1905.

Peace Through Strength. See WINDOW OF VULNERABILITY.

Peace With All—and Hostility Toward None. See PACIFIC DOCTRINE.

Peace With Justice. See JOURNEYS TO UNDERSTANDING.

Peaceful Coexistence. See COEXISTENCE.

Peaceful Revolution. See REVOLUTION FROM ABOVE.

Peacenik. See ANTI-VIETNAM WAR SLOGANS.

Peacock Throne. A common reference to the splendor of the royal or imperial household and surroundings, including the throne (seating place) of the monarch, but particularly to the throne of Shah Reza Pahlavi of Iran (1953-1979), which was richly decorated with colorful jewels and metals. According to W. H. Forbis (*The Fall Of The Peacock Throne . . .*) and Lord Curzon (*Persia and The Persian Question*), the first peacock throne was that which Iranian conqueror Nadir Shah seized in Delhi, India, in 1739. Subsequently, Fath Ali Shah (1797-1834) ordered Isfahan craftsmen to make him a throne of the sun with the likeness of his new bride, Tavus (or Peacock). Pahlavi's "peacock throne" consisted of 26,733 jewels; the royal crown contained 3,348 diamonds, including a 191-carat Daria-i-Noor, one of the largest cut stones in the world, a Topkapi, tiaras, necklaces, etc. See IRAN'S REVOLUTION, SAVAK, SHAH.

Peanut Brigade. During the 1976 Presidential election campaign, Jimmy Carter's campaign manager, Jody Powell, organized groups of Carter supporters who would travel around the country in an effort to help Jimmy Carter's bid for the presidency. They became known as "peanut brigades" because of Carter's background in the peanut business. Jody Powell became President Carter's press secretary, and a number of former brigade participants joined the Carter Administration in Washington. See NEW POPULISM.

Peanut Populism. See NEW POPULISM, PEANUT BRIGADE.

Pearl Harbor. The U.S. Naval base in Hawaii, leased by the U.S. in 1889, was attacked by surprise on 7 December 1941 by 363 Japanese airplanes (known as "Zero" models) launched from aircraft carriers in two waves, each lasting less than one hour, destroying seven battleships, five other craft, and over 150 planes on the ground. Three U.S. aircraft carriers (the Enterprise, Lexington, and Saratoga) were spared by being outside the attack area. American casualties: over 2,400 dead and 961 missing, and 1294 wounded. The Japanese lost 29 aircraft and 5 midget submarines. Because of Japanese failure to destroy the U.S. aircraft carriers and also about 4.5 million barrels of oil in storage tanks, as well as repair facilities, the Pacific Fleet was able to subsequently defeat the Japanese Navy. (As Admiral Husband E. Kimmel, then commander of the Pacific Fleet, stated later the materiel not destroyed by the Japanese would, in the end, win the war in the Pacific.) The Japanese commander of the invasion was Admiral Isoruku Yamamoto (1884-1943), who was shot down by a U.S. P-38 spotter plane while on an inspection tour in the Solomon Islands. The Americans learned about Yamamoto's flight by reading radio traffic after breaking the Japanese code. U.S. President Franklin D. Roosevelt (1933-1945) asked Congress for a declaration of war and called December 7 "a day which will live in infamy." Ironically, U.S. Secretary of the Navy, Frank Knox, called for vigilance, stating on 4 December 1941: "Whatever happens, the U.S. Navy is not going to be caught napping." See DECEPTION.

Peasant Revolution in Russia. See KOLGHOZ.

Peeping Thomasina. See PEEPING TOM.

Peeping Tom. A man guilty of viewing and observing the activities of others in the seclusion of their privacy through covert or surreptitious means. For a female committing the same offense, the term is "peeping Thomasina." Peeping is a criminal offense under U.S. laws. The city of Mountain Brook, Alabama, was the first to amend its ordinance on January 9, 1978, providing for the prosecution of a "peeping Thomasina."

Peer. One of the same rank, an equal; or a nobleman (e.g., in England).

Peer of the Realm. A nobleman in England who has the right to a seat in the House of Lords (one of the two chambers of the British Parliament). The term "peer of the United Kingdom" is also often used. See HOUSE OF LORDS, PEER.

Peer of the United Kingdom. See PEER OF THE REALM.

Peking Manifesto. See PEKING SUMMIT.

Peking Summit. U.S. President Richard M. Nixon (1969-1974) visited Peking, the People's Republic of China, February 21-28, 1972, at the invitation of Chairman Mao Tse-tung, and two manifestoes resulted: one on "normalization" of relations between these two powers and the other on mutual respect in international relations and mutual consultations. In the departing statement, the Communiqué of Shanghai, Mao Tse-tung stated that U.S.-Chinese relations must be pursued in the spirit of the fact that "there is only one China," thus ignoring the existence of the Republic of China on Taiwan (Formosa). President Nixon made no move toward the "one-China" notion in his further relations with China and did not abandon Taiwan. See SHANGHAI COMMUNIQUÉ, TWO-CHINA POLICY, WHO LOST CHINA?

Peloponnesian League. See DELIAN LEAGUE.

Peloponnesian Tactics. See WAR OF ATTRITION.

Pendente Lite. In the Latin language, "pending suit" or "suit pending."

Pendergast Political Machine. See POLITICAL MACHINE.

Pendleton Act of 1883. In order to depoliticize (and to prevent from being politicized) the federal bureaucracy, the Act established a system of selection of government employees on the basis of merit (ability to do the work) instead of spoils (as a reward for services rendered to politicians). In order to eliminate or at least minimize cronyism, the Act forbids assessment of civil servants for political purposes. The Civil Service Commission was set up to oversee the provisions of the Act and to select and train federal bureaucrats. However the three branches of the federal government—the Congress, the U.S. Supreme Court, and the Executive Offices of the President—are exempt from the provisions of this Act. They remain within the spoils system.

Penetrated Political System. A system that is strongly influenced or even directed by another political system (e.g., the ex-Soviet satellite states of Eastern Europe). Professor J. Rosenau defines it as "one in which nonmembers of a national society participate directly and authoritatively, through actions taken jointly with the society's members, in either the allocation of its values or the mobilization of support on behalf of its goals."

Penkovsky Papers. An alleged personal journal kept by an American spy in the Soviet Union, one Colonel Oleg Penkovsky of the Soviet Army, which was published in the United States in 1965 at the request of the Central Intelligence Agency (CIA) for operational reasons. By showing the CIA's capability—in having a spy so well placed in the Soviet Union and in having penetrated the Soviet military establishment—the book was intended to boost the CIA's prestige, according to the U.S. Senate Intelligence Committee. This deception scheme was uncovered, and it turned out that the book was not a journal kept by Penkovsky ("Spies don't keep diaries," remarked one congressional aide), but was compiled from CIA records by Frank Gibney, an employee of the *Chicago Daily News* and a low-ranking KGB defector who was employed by the CIA. See CENTRAL INTELLIGENCE AGENCY (CIA), OPERATIONAL REASONS, PROPAGANDA ASSETS INVENTORY (PAI), REPLAY.

Pentagon. One of the largest office buildings in the world, employing about 24,000 persons and housing the bulk of the American military establishment, including the Department of Defense, the Joint Chiefs of Staff, and other components. Situated on almost 3,800,000 square feet of land in Arlington, Virginia, it is arranged in five concentric circles marked from "A" to "E." The building accommodates all kinds of facilities for the use of employees, ranging from a bakery and restaurants, to gymnasiums, shopping centers and water, sewer, and electric generating plants. The facility is designed to sustain itself as a self-sufficient island in case of a national emergency. Because of the secrecy that surrounds its operations, it is often called the "Five-Sided Puzzle Palace." See Appendix 28.

Pentagon Capitalism. See FREE ENTERPRISE, HARDWARE DIPLOMACY, MILITARY-INDUSTRIAL COMPLEX, SOCIALIZED ENTERPRISES IN THE UNITED STATES.

Pentagon Papers. A series of secret documents on the U.S. involvement in the Vietnam conflict which were revealed by a former Pentagon researcher, Dr. Daniel Ellsberg, in the *New York Times* and the *Washington Post*, on June 13, 1971. On June 15, 1971, the U.S. Federal District Court granted an injunction requested by the U.S. Department of Justice against the further publication of the highly classified papers, but on June 30, 1971, the U.S. Supreme Court allowed publication under the provisions of the First Amendment to the U.S. Constitution. Dr. Ellsberg was arraigned for the "leaking" of these 47 volumes of state secrets and charged with espionage, but the case was dismissed on the grounds of prejudice when it was learned that convicted Watergate defendants, E. Howard Hunt, Jr., and G. Gordon Liddy, had attempted to steal Ellsberg's medical records by breaking into the office of his psychiatrist.

Pentagonale. Another popular name for the union of states in Europe, the European Community. See EUROPEAN ECONOMIC COMMUNITY, PENTAGON.

Pentomic Army. A term associated with the major reorganization of the U.S. Armed Forces necessitated by the emergence of nuclear weapons and the experience, or lack of it, in guerrilla-type warfare in Vietnam. Under this "New Look" system of reorganization directed by Army Chief of Staff General Maxwell D. Taylor, the old system of regiments was replaced during the 1960s with battle groups; the "outpost line" became the "combat outpost line," and the "front line" became the "forward edge of the battle area." In addition, old uniforms were replaced with new ones, brown shoes with black, and "steel pot" helmets took on the look of Nazi Germany Wehrmacht; personnel was required to display name tags on uniforms; and the weapon systems were modified and updated. Strong emphasis was placed on the scholastic achievement of soldiers, such as higher education and knowledge of foreign languages and of modern management techniques. This system was subsequently replaced, within a year after the Pentomic army reorganization, with the so-called "Reorganization Objectives Army Division" (ROAD), to address the switch from "massive retaliation" during the 1950s to "flexible response" under President John F. Kennedy. The battle group format was replaced with the battalion, and streamlined to cope with conventional and nuclear warfare, counterinsurgency, and guerrilla warfare; the nukes with nuclear warheads, and helicopters and Special Forces were used (e.g., the Green Berets). The ROAD reorganization was directed by the Chairman of the Joint Chief of Staff, General Maxwell D. Taylor.

Penumbra. See PRIVACY LAW.

Peonage. Involuntary servitude of a person bound to serve for a debt.

People Must be Heard. See JACKSONIAN DEMOCRACY.

People Power. The overwhelming support of the Philippine people for the presidential candidate Corazon Aquino, widow of Senator Benigno S. Aquino, Jr., who had been assassinated by agents of President Ferdinand Marcos on 21 August 1983. Mrs. Aquino was able to bring about the downfall of Marcos and, with the support of the people, became president of the Philippines in 1986 when Marcos fled into exile. Mrs. Aquino was able to consolidate her power, but two revolutionary, pro-communist groups, the New People's Army in Luzon and Mindanao and the Moro National Liberation Front (MNLF), continue their struggle against the government and demand autonomy for their people and the removal of Christians from their area. During the May 1992 presidential election in the Philippines, from among the several candidates for the presidency such as Ramon Mitra of the Struggle of Democratic Filipino Party, Fidel Ramos from the present government ranks, and Eduardo Cojuangco, the leading candidate proposing to shake up the present bureaucracy, corruption and graft, is one of the Philippines brightest political stars, Miss Miriam Defensor Santiago, who was running under the People's Reform Party.

People's Commission for Internal Affairs (NKVD). In the Russian language, "Narodnoy Kommisaryat Vnutrnygh Dyel." A security agency established in 1934 upon reorganization of the Department for State Political Administration (OGPU) for the purpose of combating all anti-Soviet, anti-party activities. In 1964 an additional ministry was formed, the People's Commission for State Security (NKGB), which was mainly an intelligence-gathering agency. In 1954 all security matters were taken over by a newly-formed ministry, the All-Union Ministry for Security (in the Russian language, "Kommitet Gosudarstvyennoy Bezopatchnosty," KGB). In 1962 the Russian Republic Ministry of Internal Affairs—for the Russian Soviet Federated Socialist Republic, RSFSR—was renamed the Ministry for the Protection of Social Order (in the Russian language, "Ministerstvo Oghrany Obshchestvyennogho Poryadka"). Political and military intelligence, world-wide, is also conducted by the Glavnoye Razvyedyvatelnoye Upravlyienye (GRU), or the Foreign Intelligence Service. The KGB was divided among the Commonwealth of Independent States in 1991. See Appendices 74, 103.

People's Commission for State Security (NKGB). See PEOPLE'S COMMISSION FOR INTERNAL AFFAIRS (NKVD).

People's Control Committee. A group of persons, selected by their peers in any place of employment in the ex-Soviet Union, which is responsible for observing, investigating, and reporting to the press and the office of the procurator (prosecuting public attorney) any and all improprieties by the management (e.g., negligence, misuse of power and resources, bribes, theft, mistreatment of employees, and unethical personal conduct). These committees, whose members were protected by the state from harassment by employers, aided the Soviet authorities in combating mismanagement of national resources, theft of socialist property (in reality, state property), poor production practices, and other practices which tended to weaken the Soviet society and the state. See OMBUDSMAN.

People's Democracy. A form of state in which the government is controlled by a single political party (the communist party), with the possible insignificant participation of other (harmless) political parties in the form of coalition, and one that pursued policies, domestic and foreign, in accordance with directives provided by the Soviet Government and the Communist Party of the Soviet Union (CPSU). This form of state was designed by former Premier of the Soviet Government and the Secretary of the Communist Party of the Soviet Union (CPSU), Joseph Stalin, for use by states that had fallen under Soviet control at the end of the Second World War, namely, Bulgaria, Czechoslovakia, Hungary, Poland, and Rumania. The form of "people's democracy" was, according to Stalin, a transitory one, from capitalism to socialism, short of socialist revolution.

People's Movement for the Liberation of Angola. See MOVIMENTO POPULAR DE LIBERTACAO DE ANGOLA (MPLA).

People's Party. A minor political party in the United States which on August 31, 1975, nominated Margaret Wright, a black civil rights activist from Los Angeles, California, for President, subject to the 1976 presidential election in the United States. See POPULIST.

People's Power. A campaign slogan of Mrs. Corazon Aquino during her efforts between 1984 and 1986 to unseat President Ferdinand Marcos whom she held responsible for the assassination of her husband, Benigno Aquino (Philippine's political and possible presidential contender), on 21 August 1983. Mrs. Aquino mobilized the people and challenged the corrupt Marcos. After the 1986 election both claimed to be the properly and duly elected president of the Philippines. The Marcos forces fraudulently obtained votes and, in spite of the fact that Marcos was declared the winner by his supporters, declared a state of emergency on 24 February 1986 in order to intimidate the Aquino forces. On 25 February 1986 there were two separate presidential inaugurations held—one of Marcos and the other of Aquino. Viewing the political situation in the Philippines as a possible prelude to a bloody revolution, U.S. President Ronald Reagan sided with Mrs. Aquino and the Philippine people and made Marcos and his wife, Imelda, an offer of political asylum in Hawaii or the forfeit of all American support. Marcos compromised, took the offer of asylum, and left for Hawaii on 26 February 1986. His wife had to abandon her collection of 2000 pairs of shoes, however.

People's Principles. See THREE PEOPLE'S PRINCIPLES.

People's Reform Party. See PEOPLE POWER.

Per Capita. In the Latin language, "for each head" or "for each person."

Per Curiam. In the Latin language, "by the court of law."

Per Diem. In the Latin language, "by the day" or "per day."

Per Interim. In the Latin language, "in the meantime" or "meanwhile."

Per Se. In the Latin language, "in itself" or "essentially."

Peremptory Norm. A generally accepted norm of international law according to which a given norm stands as valid unless modified by a subsequent norm of general international law of the same character, a modification which must be recognized and accepted by states. Article 53 of the Vienna

Convention (of 1951) states that a treaty "... is void if, at the time of its conclusion, it conflicts with a peremptory norm of general international law." See INTERNATIONAL LAW.

Perestroika. Together with "glasnost," or openness and larger freedom through expressions of criticisms of the Soviet Regime, "perestroika," a national revival of political, economic, and social life in the Soviet Union was pronounced in 1987 and accepted by the Soviet Communist Party (CPS). It allowed the Soviet satellite states in Eastern Europe, (e.g., Poland and Hungary), to seek full independence; the Soviets decided to withdraw from Afghanistan in December 1987; they reduced military spending in 1988—all these acts led in 1989 to the end of the "cold war" and the subsequent dissolution of the Soviet Empire. Gorbachev resigned as Soviet president on 25 December 1991; Boris Yeltsin, president of the Russian Republic led the other republics, mainly Ukraine and Belorus, to form a Commonwealth of Independent States. See COLD WAR.

Perjury. A felonious crime which a person commits by not telling the truth (or telling a lie) while giving testimony under oath (or affirmation) before a jury, judicial officer, or a legislative committee (e.g., of the U.S. Congress). See SUBORDINATION OF PERJURY.

Perk Man. A nickname earned by U.S. President Jimmy Carter (1977-1981) (allegedly no individual on the White House staff wanted to reveal the identity of the originator of the term) when he introduced several money-saving plans to limit the various benefits (known as "perquisites" or "perks") that White House staffs have been used to in the past, such as free limousine service, radios and television sets in their offices, and free meals with room service. In 1978, following President Carter's limitation of "perks," the U.S. Congress suggested such limitations on perquisites or "perks" for business executives in the private sector, including the following benefits to top executives: medical examinations, special parking privileges, executive company cars, spouses traveling on company business, luncheon-club memberships, country club memberships, extended vacations, company airplanes, company apartments and hotel suites, executive dining rooms, financial counseling, medical-expense reimbursement, and sabbatical leaves. Following the Spring 1992 revelations of check bouncing and overdrafts by members of the U.S. Congress, where some Representatives admitted hundreds of overdrafts in the House of Representatives bank, and abuse of mailing privileges at the House post office, a perk war commenced. To divert the attention from Congress, Democratic Party Representatives zeroed in on the White House accusing the President and his staff of waste of public money on such extravagant items, as, among other, the following: expensive receptions for visitors to the White House; the large cost of operating the President's Air Force One, a 747 jumbo jet, which costs about $26,000 an hour to operate, and that during the past three years the American taxpayers had to pay about $25 million for 300,000 miles of flight; that the President's staff spent an additional $63 million for travel alone in the same period; and that the White House hides its costs in the budgets of other federal agencies: the U.S. Air Force maintains the aircraft; the U.S. Navy operates and maintains the dining facilities; the National Park Service maintains the White House grounds; and the U.S. Treasury Department provides protection through the Secret Service. See IMPERIAL PRESIDENCY.

Perk Wars. See PERK MAN.

Permanent Bill. See BILL.

Permanent Court of International Justice (PCIJ). An international tribunal established by the League of Nations in 1920 (in The Hague, the Netherlands) for the purpose of peaceful (pacific) settlement of international disputes among states. The Tribunal could issue only advisory opinions and exercise its jurisdiction only upon expressed consent of the parties to a dispute. In 1945 it was replaced by the United Nation's International Court of Justice (ICJ). See GENERAL ACT FOR THE SETTLEMENT OF INTERNATIONAL DISPUTES, HAGUE PEACE CONFERENCES.

Permanent Revolution. The slogan that was expounded by Leon Trotsky, the one-time close collaborator of Vladimir I. Lenin and Joseph Stalin, and one of the first and most influential Soviet leaders. He insisted that the revolution, in order to be successful and lasting as Marx predicted, must continue on a permanent basis until all capitalistic states are destroyed. This slogan had little appeal, for in the late 1920s Stalin was already in firm control of the Soviet state, and with the limited resources at hand, he was more interested in building socialism in his own country than in exporting revolutions abroad. (This issue contributed considerably to the deepening of differences between Stalin and Trotsky to the point that Trotsky was expelled from the party and the Soviet Union and finally was assassinated in Mexico City, Mexico, in 1940.)

Permanent Terror. See ANARCHIST.

Permissive Powers. Powers that are granted by a state legislature in the United States to a local political subdivision which may exercise them at its discretion. See DILLON'S RULE.

Permissive Referendum. The practice among some states in the United States (e.g., Virginia) to let the voters in local jurisdictions decide on any issue by a simple majority vote (e.g., "blue laws," bond issues, lotteries, etc.). See LOCAL OPTION.

Pernicious Political Activity. See LOYALTY LAW.

Peronismo. See CAESARISM.

Peroration. In political oratory, the end of the speech is considered one of the most important components because the orator usually sums up the speech with new and powerful words which may become a lasting slogan. Some examples: "I have a Dream . . .," Dr. Martin Luther King; "Ask not what your country can do for you . . .," President John F. Kennedy; "I pledge you . . . to a new deal . . .," President Franklin D. Roosevelt; "I shall return . . .," General Douglas MacArthur; "With malice toward none . . .," President Abraham Lincoln; and "Workers of the world, unite . . . you have nothing to lose but your chains," Karl Marx. As a rule, political speeches do not end with additional promises but rather with a catchy phrase which may inspire the listeners or insure lasting remembrance of the speaker.

Perot Rangers. See GRASS-ROOTS PEROT.

Perpetual Union. The merger of two or more independent and sovereign states into a confederation or federation for an indefinite period of time, or forever. (Under the Articles of Confederation, the American Union was formed for perpetuity.) See Appendix 8.

Perquisites. See PERK MAN.

Persian Gulf War. On 1 August 1990, the armed forces of Iraq under the leadership of President Saddam Hussein, attacked the kingdom of Kuwait under the pretext that Kuwait had in the past belonged to Iraq. Numerous appeals by many nations to Iraq to withdraw were ignored, and on 29 November 1990, the United Nations passed a resolution resulting in an ultimatum for Iraq to withdraw by 15 January 1991. Meanwhile, on 7 August 1990, the United States had dispatched troops to Saudi Arabia, and on 12 January 1991, the U.S. Congress approved President George Bush's plan to deploy U.S. Forces in Iraq, by a vote of 52 to 47 in the Senate and 250 to 183 in the House; subsequently, a 28-nation coalition force of about 700,000 troops, of which about 430,000 were Americans, opposed Iraq. The only allies of Iraq were the Palestinian Liberation Organization (PLO) and the kingdom of Jordan. During the preparations for attack, the Iraqis took foreign workers in Iraq as hostages, called the "human shield," as a protection against attack by the Coalition Forces. Among the hostages were 900 Americans, 200 Japanese, 1,200 Britons, and several Poles and Germans. The attack against Iraqi forces commenced on 17 January 1991, and the Iraqis were removed from Kuwait. The American casualties were: 148 dead, 25 of whom were killed by friendly fire; 467 wounded, 72, by friendly fire. Iraqi casualties were estimated at over 100,000 dead, and 180,000 surrendered voluntarily to the Coalition Forces. The Allies suffered about 200 dead and wounded. The casualties in manpower and materiel strength, among the Coalition-Iraqis were as follows: troops, 600,000 to 547,000 Iraqi; tanks, 3,370 to 4,240 Iraqi; artillery, 3,650 to 3,200 Iraqi; vehicles 2,900 to 2,000; helicopters, 2,000 to 163; aircraft, 2,750 to 775. Most of the Iraq aircraft were flown to Iran for protection from damage by the Coalition Forces. In his State of the Union message on 29 January 1991, President Bush stated that the purpose of the action against Iraq was to liberate Kuwait and not "the destruction of Iraq, its culture, or its people." The American Commander, General H. Norman Schwarzkopf hinted that the war should have continued for at least another two days, but this was denied by his civilian superiors and, no doubt, this may keep him from ever getting a fifth star. There was wide criticism of the president's decision not to pursue the leaders of Iraq, and especially President Saddam Hussein, who turned against and suppressed the Kurdish people fleeing from his rule, and also kept chemical and nuclear weapon components hidden for possible use in the future. The United States left a force of 25,000 soldiers and about 200 aircraft in the area for possible future use. Along with crimes against persons and property, the Iraqi leadership is charged with the heinous crime against humanity and against ecology, unprecedented in human history, of setting fire to the oil wells in Kuwait which subsequently burned for about six months. According to information released by the Pentagon, the total cost was $61.1 billion with $53.7 paid by other nations and $7.4 by American taxpayers. The main objective of the war was the liberation of Kuwait from Iraq's (Saddam Hussein's) aggression. The April-May 1992 riots in Los Angeles, California, following the acquittal of four policemen charged with brutality, cost almost one billion dollars. See Appendices 29, 102.

Persona Non Grata. In the Latin language, "undesirable person" or "person that is not desired." Commonly, a diplomatic officer whose presence is no longer desired by the host country and who is expected to be recalled by the government of the sending state or be faced with forcible deportation within a specified period of time (usually within 48 hours). See DIPLOMATIC IMMUNITY, INNOCENT PASSAGE.

Personal Agenda. See AGENDA.

Personal Diplomacy. See SUMMIT CONFERENCE.

Personal Union. The practice whereby two or more sovereign states may share the same person as their head of state or head of government. This practice was common under monarchies whereby, through marriage, the sovereign (king, prince, emperor, or tsar) of one state could also serve at the same time as the sovereign of another.

Petit Jury. Literally, a "small jury" of several qualified citizens sitting to hear a case in a court of law in order to determine guilt or innocence on the basis of the evidence at hand. See JURY.

Petition. In politics, a request, oral or written, by one person or more, presented to a governmental authority seeking a certain benefit, action, or a redress or relief; the act of gathering signatures of registered voters in order to enter the name of a candidate on an election ballot as a grass-roots action outside the regular statutory provisions, if any, regulating such matters. In law, an appeal or a plea, usually written, addressed to a court of law for a specific reason or purpose (e.g., an appeal for clemency or a request to a higher court for review [on appeal] of the petitioner's request). See GRASS-ROOTS, GRASS-ROOTS PEROT, PETITIONER.

Petition for the Redress of Grievances. One of the rights that is guaranteed to the citizens of the United States (contained in Amendment I to the U.S. Constitution)—to bring their complaints to the government or any of its agencies and to seek satisfaction or redress for any wrong-doing. See INITIATIVE, LOCAL OPTION, RECALL, REFERENDUM.

Petitioner. One who petitions (or appeals) the decision of a lower court to a higher one (mainly in cases of appeal to the United States Supreme Court by writ of certiorari); or one who petitions the government for redress of grievances.

PFLP. See POPULAR FRONT FOR THE LIBERATION OF PALESTINE.

PFP. Popular Front Party, a political party in Ghana; successor to the Progress Party (PP).

Philadelphia Plan. See AFFIRMATIVE ACTION.

Philippines April Six Liberation Movement. A movement opposed to Ferdinand Marcos, president of the Philippines (1966-1986), which led to the downfall of Marcos and his departure from the Philippines into exile on 26 February 1986. One of the principal leaders of that movement was Senator Benigno S. Aquino, Jr., who was assassinated by pro-Marcos soldiers on 21 August 1983, and whose widow, Corazon Aquino, became president after Marcos' departure into exile.

Philippines Modernization Plan. See SWITZERLAND OF ASIA.

Philippines New People's Army. See PEOPLE POWER.

Philistinism. See EMPIRICISM.

Philosopher Till Election Day. A series of assumptions about the attitudes of people of a polyarchic (democratic) society which prevail before, during, and after major elections: voters and non-voters, rich and poor, all become involved to varying degrees in dialogues concerning the political candidates and their philosophies; the political system itself and where and how it can be improved; who should be elected and why; what the priorities of the society should and should not be; what fundamental changes affecting the system should or should not be made (e.g., the electoral college in the United States debates for about six months every four years—at presidential election time). Once the election is over, the philosophizing subsides and those who have found their wishes materialized (in terms of elected officials whom they favored), as well as most of those whose wishes have not materialized (their favorite candidates have not been elected), return to their daily tasks, accepting the verdict of the electorate. The winners hope to advance their causes, the losers hope that things will somehow work out, and they look toward the next election, when they will have another opportunity to renew their struggle for change. Meanwhile the legitimacy of the government is recognized by all and the necessary support is given to it. Now the philosophizing shifts from candidates to the issues, tangible policies which are to be converted into laws, or programs. All these processes occur without violence and recrimination.

Philosophical Foundations of the Anti-Slavery Movement in America. Anti-slavery sentiments were advanced primarily by these three distinct movements: (1) W. L. Garrison and his belief in the lack of humanitarianism on the part of man and his propensity for immoral behavior; (2) the Free-Soil movement in the West pointing to political, social, and economic exploitations by man; (3) the New England movement whose intellectuals reasoned that the practice and perpetuation of slavery is contrary to all historical aspirations of man and the purpose of man in society, as propagated by Judeo-Christian ethics, and that slavery is immoral and destructive to society.

Phony Communism. In June 1956, industrial workers in Poland rose in protest against the government, accusing it of pursuing "phony communism," a "dictatorship over the proletariat," instead of "dictatorship by the proletariat," as Marxism-Leninism commands. Demanding better living and working conditions, abolition of dictatorship by the party (Polish United Workers Party, the party in power), and democracy, the workers were instrumental in bringing about a new government (under Wladyslaw Gomulka), more freedom, and a better life. However, similar attempts by the Hungarians (October 1956) were squashed by Soviet military forces (the Red Army).

Phony War. The period between the Paris Peace Treaty after W.W.I in 1920 and the commencement of W.W.II on September 1, 1939 (Hitler's attack on Poland), when all major powers were making preparations for a war, but without public admission; a period of time when war is imminent at any time.

Physical Planning. Designs for the utilization of such resources of the physical structure as communications, land use, roads and utilities of primary necessity. See PLANNING.

Picciotti. In the Italian language, "the young ones." See MAFIA.

Pigasus-the-Pig. A group of students, disenchanted with the American system of presidential elections in general, and with American involvement in the Vietnamese conflict in particular, submitted to the Democratic National Convention in Chicago, Illinois, in 1968 (during which U.S. Senator Hubert H. Humphrey received the nomination for the presidency), the name of their own candidate, namely, Pigasus-the-Pig, which turned out to be a real six-month old pig. The Democratic leadership of the Convention refused to register and to consider that candidate, and the nominators were arrested and charged with several infractions of the law (e.g., disturbing the peace and trespassing).

Pigeonholing. The practice of putting away (in a "pigeonhole") legislative proposals which are not favored or are considered undesirable by a legislative committee. In both Houses of the United States Congress (the Senate and the House of Representatives) such a bill may be forced out of a committee for floor action by a simple majority vote. See DISCHARGE PETITION.

Piggybacking. In connection with federal programs this term means the funding of an organization for purposes of a federal program when that organization also serves the purposes of other federal, state, or local programs. Multiple piggybacking is possible and not unusual. See FEDERALISM.

Ping-Pong Diplomacy. A phrase used to describe the newly-established relationships between the People's Republic of China and the United States, which first began with a visit by an American ping-pong (table tennis) team to China in 1971 and subsequently was followed by an official state visit by President Richard M. Nixon, his wife, and members of his staff in 1972 to mainland China. Similarly, the sport of basketball ("basketball diplomacy") was used as a means of rapprochement between Cuba and the United States in 1975, which subsequently led to political talks and an exchange of diplomatic agents (however, without full diplomatic recognition).

Pinko. A pejorative term mainly used in the 1950s-1960s for one who opposed the capitalistic system of society and its political institutions and policies in favor of a socialistic-communistic system. The term was often applied to labor organizers and fellow travelers. See FELLOW TRAVELER, RED SCARE.

Pitsnor. See MEGALOPOLIS.

PL. See PUBLIC LAW.

Plain Living and High Thinking. See UTOPIA.

Plaintiff. The party that commences a suit in a court of law, or the party that brings complaints before a court of law to seek a judicial settlement (adjudication).

Plank. See PARTY PLATFORM.

Planned Economy. See FREE ENTERPRISE.

Planning. An intellectual strategy designed to better utilize inputs and outputs in a politically and economically organized society (e.g., the design of a system of market control and the production of goods and services in an economy), through making rational choices among alternatives in order to achieve the maximum at the minimum expenditure of human and material resources; a system of forecasting future needs of a society and providing for their realization within the realm of existing and future possibilities; or an intellectual interaction of individuals, aiming at a cohesive and orderly advancement of the well-being of a given society with the minimum of harm to man and his ecology. The planning process can be unitary or decentralized, highly concentrated within a single institution, or one that is pursued by each political subdivision separately and independently. If all segments of the society and its institutions are involved, it may take the form of "participatory planning." If, on the other hand, this process concerns only certain areas (e.g., education), it may take the form of "interest-based planning." Some of the existing forms of planning are: (1) Physical planning (most common)—providing for anticipated needs of physical structures (e.g., highways, utilities, and schools); (2) program planning or strategic planning—the forecasting of needs in certain areas (e.g., development of specific technologies), without considering the concerted needs of the entire politico-economic system; (3) social planning—anticipating needs for social services and facilities (e.g., medical care and medical technology); (4) political planning—forecasting the kind of political processes and institutions which will be best adaptable to meet societal needs in the future; and (5) economic planning—providing for production of goods and services and their allocation. Professor Charles E. Lindblom recognizes two methods of planning: (1) synoptic, or all-embracing, long-range planning, one involving all components of the politico-economic system; a comprehensive planning, as opposed to (2) strategic planning, which is the most common form of planning, whereby one deals only with the problems at hand, by trial-and-error; an incoherent planning, unsystematic, and from one crisis to another. All planning involves three forms of analysis, according to Lindblom whereby the planner must determine: (1) how he can play his interactive role better to get what he wants; (2) how to enter into existing interactions most successfully to achieve some public purpose which one, as a public official, has a responsibility to pursue; and (3) "the basic analysis of possible changes in the basic structure of the interaction processes themselves." In recent years, comprehensive planning became an integral part of many political systems, including that of the United States, where all levels of government are involved in planning, and where planning commissions have been established for that purpose. At the substate level, planning is coordinated by state agencies. The federal government provides for comprehensive planning which is evaluated under the A-95 review system for its utility and applicability. Some states have established or are planning "service districts" which are autonomous governmental bodies responsible for planning and providing services to several small political subdivisions similar to those that each jurisdiction does for itself (e.g., governing, schooling, and social services). A mental process concentrated on designing, devising and projecting a set of alternative methods or courses of action aiming to achieve a goal through a set of objectives; a dynamic and deliberate process aimed at satisfying certain needs, and to meet qualitative and quantitative goals. There is considerable friction and rivalry between regional planners in America and those who oppose traditional political subdivisions, who consider regional planning an infringement upon their traditional institutions and practices.

Plans of the American Union. On May 17, 1787, a group of fifty-five delegates from twelve former British colonies (Rhode Island did not participate) assembled at Independence Hall in Philadelphia, Pennsylvania, under the direction of General George Washington, to consider a new constitution for the independent states to replace the inadequate Articles of Confederation. During the debates that lasted until September 25, 1787, two principal plans for the American Union emerged: the Virginia plan, favored by the large states, and the New Jersey plan, favored by the small states. The three branches of the new federal government were envisioned by the two major separate plans as follows:

Virginia Plan	New Jersey Plan

The Legislature:

Virginia Plan	New Jersey Plan
1. Bicameral.	1. Unicameral.
2. The upper house was to be chosen by the lower house from among persons suggested by state legislatures, while the lower house was to be elected by the voters. Representation in the national legislature was to be apportioned on the basis of free inhabitants in the state, or the state's monetary contribution to the national treasury, or both.	2. The national legislature was to be chosen indirectly by the state legislatures of each state and was to have one vote in Congress regardless of the number of representatives so elected.
3. The national legislature was to be given extensive powers.	3. The functions of the national legislatures were to be limited to the regulation of national commerce and collection of taxes if states failed to perform these functions adequately.

The Executive:

Virginia Plan	New Jersey Plan
1. The nation's chief executive was to be elected by Congress for a term of one year.	1. A plural national executive (of several persons) was to be elected by Congress for a one year term.
2. The chief executive was to possess only suspensive veto power over legislative acts, which was to be shared with the national judiciary assembled especially for that purpose and known as the "Council of Revision."	2. The plural executive could veto legislation and even employ force against states not complying with federal laws.

The Judiciary:

Virginia Plan	New Jersey Plan
1. The national judiciary was to be composed of judges appointed by Congress for life, and the lower courts were to be subservient to it.	1. The national judiciary was to consist of judges appointed by the plural executive for life, with lower courts subservient to state courts.

Before the final draft of the Constitution was agreed upon, several were reached, which have been credited to Benjamin Franklin and Alexander Hamilton.

Platform. See PARTY PLATFORM.

Platonic State. See UTOPIA, Appendix 1.

Platt Amendment. A rider attached to the appropriations bill of 1901 (and later incorporated in the treaty with Cuba of May 22, 1903) stipulating, among other things, that the United Sates should have the right to: guard the sovereignty and territorial integrity of Cuba; intervene whenever American interests were threatened or when law and order were to be maintained; and to establish military installations on the territory of Cuba, among them the naval installation at Guantánamo Bay. (The amendment was abrogated by the United States in 1934 and replaced with another treaty, but the Guantánamo Bay naval installation was retained by the United States, and is held to this day.) The amendment had been proposed by U.S. Senator Orville H. Platt of Connecticut.

Platt Political Machine. See POLITICAL MACHINE.

Plea. A lawsuit or an action brought before a court of law for settlement (adjudication); or a statement made before a court of law admitting or denying guilt. Under some systems, a person charged with several crimes may enter into plea bargaining with the prosecuting attorney, and, in return for pleading guilty to a lesser offense, testifying for the prosecution (and thus helping to resolve the issue), or turning in evidence, may have charges dropped for the major offense or for all offenses. See ALFORD PLEA.

Plea Bargaining. A situation whereby a person guilty of several crimes will plead guilty to a single felony in exchange for testimony against others. See PLEA.

Plea of Insanity. The request that a person accused of a crime can present in a court of law asking that no penalty be imposed because the crime was committed while in a state of mental incapacity.

Pleading. See PLEA.

Pleb. See PLEBEIAN.

Plebeian. A term commonly applied to one who is poor, uneducated, or ignorant; or one who has limited political rights or one who does not exercise them. (The term is taken from the Plebeian class in ancient Rome which owned no property and had no political rights, such as the right to vote or to be voted upon.) See PATRICIAN.

Plebiscite. The act of presenting an important issue to the whole people of a state for the making of a final decision by vote. (It usually concerns a change in the constitution or some revision of sovereignty status.) See ENABLING ACT.

Pledged Elector. See PRESIDENTIAL ELECTOR.

Plein Pouvoirs. In the French language, "full powers." Also, the credentials of a diplomatic agent sent abroad on a special, temporary mission (e.g., an ambassador at large or special emissary.) See DIPLOMATIC RANK.

Plenary Session. A conference or session of an executive or legislative assembly or the ruling body of a political body deliberating on important issues, usually with all members present.

Plenipotentiary. One person authorized to represent and to exercise full powers on behalf of another (e.g., a presidential envoy). See DIPLOMATIC RANK.

Pleno Jure. In the Latin language, "with full rights" or "with full powers."

Plenum. Once the periodic meetings that were held by either the Central Committee of the Communist Party of the former Soviet Union (CPSU) or by the party and the representatives of the Soviet Government for the purpose of deliberating on some important issues, usually with all members present. The Party was suspended following the 18 August 1991 failed coup. See PLENARY SESSION, Appendices 74, 103.

PLO. See PALESTINE LIBERATION ORGANIZATION.

Plumbers. See WATERGATE.

Plumed Knight. A nickname for James G. Blaine of Maine, who was the Republican candidate for U.S. President in 1884 and the leader of the "half-breeds," the liberal Republicans. The conservative Republicans, who were led by the U.S. Senator from New York, Roscoe Conkling, were called the "stalwarts," and supported James A. Garfield of Ohio for President in 1889.

Pluralism. A notion commonly applicable to democratic societies in which all governmental authority is presumed to be distributed among various groups rather than being centralized in a single source. (The opposite of monism or monolithism.) Political parties with divergent views are allowed and tolerated; and people of different races, cultures, traditions, and views tolerate each other.

Pluralistic Characteristics of Concepts. See CONCEPT.

Pluralistic Society. A democratic society in which political powers are channeled through many divergent groups. See PLURALISM.

Plurality Vote. In an election with a field of at least three candidates; the candidate who receives the highest number of votes is the winner by a plurality vote. This is possible under a system which allows at least three candidates to run for the same office. If, for example, (with three or more people running for the same elective office), candidate "A" received 33 per cent of the popular vote, candidate "B," 33 per cent, and candidate "C," 34 per cent, candidate "C" becomes elected by plurality. In the case of presidential elections in the United States, plurality will suffice in the case of the popular vote; that is, a presidential candidate receiving the plurality vote (not the majority, which constitutes 50 per cent of the vote plus at least one vote) may claim all of the electoral votes in the state from which he receives plurality (under the unit system, in which the winner takes all). Hypothetically, it is possible under the plurality system for one candidate out of an infinite number, to become elected with only two votes, provided that all the other voters but one were qualified for the same office and all but one of the voters were running for the same office and cast their ballots for themselves in the election.

Pluto. The underwater pipeline from England to the coast of France, set up to deliver fuel for the Allied invasion against German Nazi forces in 1944. Germans were never able to disrupt the flow of fuel to the Allies because, due to a lack of fuel on their part, their Luftwaffe planes were unable to fly.

Plutocracy. A government of, for, or by the rich and wealthy.

PNP. Peoples National Party. A political party of Ghana, successor to the Convention Peoples Party (CPP).

Pocket Borough. A term used in England to describe a "political machine" that controls the government of a borough or a county.

Pocket Veto. The power of the United States President to disapprove of a legislative bill by not signing it within ten (10) days from the time of receipt (weekends excluded), particularly when Congress in the meanwhile has adjourned. In this case the legislative act will die, having no chance to be re-passed, because Congress is not in session to over-ride the veto. See PRESIDENTIAL VETO.

Pocketbook Issue. See POCKETBOOK POLITICS.

Pocketbook Politics. The notion that within the realm of rational behavior, voters everywhere and at all times, will support candidates and issues which cost them (from their own pockets) the least and will benefit them the most. Therefore, the notion prevails among politicians in America that all politics is local. See ALL POLITICS IS LOCAL.

Pogrom. The practice of harassing Jewish people in Tsarist Russia and in territories occupied by it (e.g., Poland).

Point Four Program. A plan of financial and economic assistance initiated by United States President Harry S. Truman in 1949, to aid economically underdeveloped nations, particularly those that were susceptible to an easy takeover by communist-controlled forces. See MARSHALL PLAN.

Polarized Region. See FUNCTIONAL REGION.

Police Action. A term that was applied to the Korean War in 1950 when, under the Uniting for Peace Resolution by the United Nations, allied forces were dispatched. The Police Action lasted four years and took the lives of 157,530 Americans.

Police Action in Korea. See KOREAN WAR, POLICE ACTION.

Police Brutality. The application of excessive, unreasonable force and physical or verbal abuse, usually during an arrest; a common, worldwide, phenomenon occurring regardless of the political system or culture of a state. The 3 March 1991 beating of black motorist Rodney King in Los Angeles, California, by four white policemen, who used excessive force in arresting King for speeding, is an example that was videotaped by a opposing motorist. Four Los Angeles policemen were charged with the beating of King, the brutality of which shames Hitler's Nazi Germany Gestapo and Stalin's NKVD (KGB) in the former Soviet Union. The accused policemen are: Laurence Powell, Stacey Koon, Timothy Wind, and Theodore Briseno. They were tried, not in Lost Angeles, but, through change of venue, in Simi Valley—home to many California police officers, a well-to-do white suburb, where the Ronald Reagan Library is located. Twelve white jurors were drawn from that affluent white community (whose impressions of the videotape differed from that of over one billion TV viewers throughout the world, who had witnessed the beating on CNN) and acquitted the officers on 29 April 1992. This sparked a wave of protest by people of all races and political persuasions and led to a two day/three night spree of rioting and looting. The end results were approximately 60 deaths, about one billion dollars in property loss, and finally the deployment of 6,000 federal troops. With 1992 being a presidential election year, President George Bush, under criticism from civil rights leaders, decided to have the U.S. Department of Justice look into the matter of a possible new trial under federal civil rights protection laws. The abused Rodney King openly appealed to people everywhere to forget the incident and restore peace and harmony. The area most affected by rioting was known as Watts during the hot summer "Burn, Baby, Burn" days of 1965, when rioting and deaths occurred as a protest against neglect, lack of jobs, housing, and medical care. Members of police forces, particularly in multi-ethnic, multi-cultural, multi-racial societies, ought to be educated rather than trained (training should be confined to animals, e.g., K-9 dogs), with solid knowledge, understanding, and sensitivity to different cultural, ethnic, political, religious, racial makeup of the community they serve, the nation, and the world at large. A police officer ought to know the governmental, economic, and political milieu of the community or nation, the political institutions and processes, and ought to be rewarded not less than other professionals. In a modern, advanced society, a police officer's task consists of a combination of the following: teacher, guide, diplomat, ambassador, information officer, public relations specialist, social worker, substitute parent, combat soldier, attorney, accountant, preacher, facilitator, conciliator, mediator, arbitrators and sometimes even physician and midwife. Broad general knowledge is required because of the scope of police work today and the sophistication of a large segment of white-collar criminals (e.g., computer crimes). See WE ARE ALL STUCK HERE FOR AWHILE.

Police Power. The authority to command obedience, by force if necessary (e.g., arresting power of a police officer); the authority to maintain certain desired conditions in human relationships (e.g., by intervening in a war or a fight to restore peace); the constitutional power of all state legislatures and city councils to legislate (by passing laws or ordinances) on behalf of the public in such matters as health, safety, welfare, education, or standards of morality ("community standards")—all are known as "police powers."

Policies Plan. A single document which contains the description of the general goals, programs, and projects of a given government, together with specific plans which have been designed to bring about some specific changes and accommodate certain desired growth. The purpose of such a policies plan is to provide a certain degree of coordination between physical planning and financial planning and to designate the specific roles and functions of the agencies which are to carry out planned programs.

Policy. A way and a means of doing things; a modus operandi. See DOMESTIC POLICY, FOREIGN POLICY.

Policy Committee. A body of senators of either the Republican or the Democratic Party selected by the Party Conference in the United States Senate and charged with responsibility for the party's over-all legislative program. The Democratic Party committee members are appointed by the Majority or the

Minority Leaders (whichever the case may be) and confirmed for an indefinite period by the Democratic Senate Conference. The Republican Party elects its committee members for a tenure of two years. Senate Policy Committees, unlike those in the House of Representatives, are provided for by law and receive special appropriations for their staff and facilities. See UNITED STATES SENATE.

Policy Matrix. The effects which one policy may have on a broad variety of areas for which it was not necessarily intended (e.g., a tax reduction on inflation and a far-reaching disarmament on domestic employment), or the scope and degree that a policy pertaining to one issue may affect other issues. See POLICIES PLAN.

Policy Monotheism. According to journalist Leslie Gelb, who coined the term, some columnists in the American press "draw big lessons—called "theologies"—from a single experience and then wield them like clubs to destroy political adversaries."

Policy of Accommodation. Once a series of West (the United States and its allies) and East (the Soviet Union and its allies) understandings (e.g., the Strategic Arms Limitations Talks, the Helsinki Accord, International Limitation of the Sale of Arms) aimed at the preservation of the existing balance of power on a global scale (e.g., peaceful coexistence), international peace and security, and avoidance of war in spite of existing ideological conflicts among the superpowers. See BIPOLARITY, DÉTENTE, HARDWARE DIPLOMACY, UNIPOLARITY.

Policy of Containment. See CONTAINMENT.

Policy of Disengagement. A decision that a government of one state may make to refrain from any active interaction with another, short of breaking diplomatic relations and abrogating existing treaty agreements (e.g., ceasing trade, cultural and athletic exchange). See DIPLOMACY.

Policy Review Committee of the National Security Council. See CENTRAL INTELLIGENCE AGENCY (CIA), Appendices 32, 33.

Policy Science. See POLICY MATRIX, POLICIES PLAN.

Polisario Front. A political and a guerrilla organization in the western part of Morocco, striving for independence as a sovereign state known as the "Saharan Arab Democratic Republic." The Polisarios have been engaged in guerrilla warfare against the state of Morocco since 1976, and have been actively supported in their quest for independence by Algeria and Libya. The Polisarios were admitted to full membership in the Organization of African Unity (OAU) in 1981. See Appendix 100.

Polisario Uprising. See POLISARIO FRONT, SPANISH SAHARA.

Polish Club. See CRISIS STAFF

Polish Constitution of 1791. The basic law of the Polish state, also known as the "Governmental Statute," of 3 May 1791, was the first systematic constitution on the European continent and the second in the world after the American Constitution of 1787. The second European constitution was that of France, proclaimed on 3 September 1791. See Appendix 91.

Polish Corridor. A strip of land demanded by Germany from Poland between 1933-1939, to serve as a connecting link between East Prussia and the German Reich proper. Poland never compromised, in order to keep German influence from the East, the Baltic States, and the ex-Soviet Union. According to author David Irving (*Göring: A Biography*), when Herman Göring, chief of the German Luftwaffe (air force) was going to Poland to hunt wolves with the Polish leader, Marshal Jósef Pilsudski, Hitler gave him the following message to deliver to Pilsudski: "We are willing to recognize by treaty that the (Polish) Corridor question was not a bone of contention between our two countries . . . Germany can expand, in collusion with Poland, to the east: Poland would have the Ukraine as its sphere of interest, and Germany the northeast." Pilsudski allegedly rejected this preposterous proposition, because Poland was interested in rebuilding its devastated state rather than engage in aggressive machinations. According to renowned Polish historian Oskar Halecki (*History of Poland*), "the so-called 'Corridor' was by no means an artificial invention of the Treaty of Versailles, departing from Wilson's points, but—as before the Partitions—the natural result of the fact that since the time of the Knights of the Cross, East Prussia had formed but a German enclave on the east of Pomerania."

Polish Governmental Statute. See POLISH CONSTITUTION OF 1791.

Polish Officers' Massacre. See KATYN MASSACRE.

Politburo. See POLITICAL BUREAU.

Political Action. The practice of manipulating information and individual persons or groups, for the purpose of achieving a desired outcome; also, action to bring about a change of public policy or to achieve certain benefits through the political (e.g., elective officials) rather than governmental (e.g., appointive executives) channels of power. See POLITICS.

Political Action Committee (PAC). An organizational device through which private corporate interests (e.g., business enterprises operating for profit but chartered and regulated by governmental agencies) influence political outcomes in the United States within the limits of existing laws. Such committees donate money and support candidates for public elective offices (e.g., local, state, and federal), thus influencing the outcome of elections. Under the 1974 federal election law, a single PAC may contribute $5,000 to a presidential candidate before a nominating convention (after being nominated by a convention, a candidate who accepts public financing may no longer receive PAC money); a candidate for a congressional seat (either the Senate or the House of Representatives) may accept $5,000 before, and another $5,000 after, nomination. Individual PAC's may also donate $15,000 to a national party organization of their choice. Such PAC's are particularly designed for middle and upper-level management and the administrative personnel of business corporations (particularly those that do interstate business such as the Chesapeake and Potomac Electric Company) that are subject to systematic regulation by governmental agencies (e.g., regulation of the rates they charge consumers for their products). See COMMITTEE ON POLITICAL EDUCATION (COPE), FEDERAL ELECTION COMMISSION (FEC).

Political Activism. See POLITICAL APATHY.

Political Activities Regulations. See HATCH ACT.

Political Actor. See ACTOR.

Political Acumen. The ability to understand politics and its nature; political perception. See POLITICS.

Political Adaptability. See POLITICAL APATHY.

Political Affairs Research Council (PARC). One of the most influential committees which advises the Liberal Democratic Party in the Japanese Diet on political and policy matters. See ZOKU GIIN.

Political Alienation. See POLITICAL APATHY.

Political Analysis. The method by which political phenomena are read and understood, are being perceived and accepted for the purpose of better understanding. The most useful tools of modern political analysis are the concepts of class and race. Interactions among individuals, for the purpose of government and politics, are conditioned by who and what one is; what one has, and in what one believes; also, those tools (e.g., concepts, theories, theorems, or conceptual frameworks) which enable one to understand a political system (e.g., the systems approach). Political phenomena can be analyzed *a posteriori,* that is, through empirical reasoning in order to ascertain the truth by actual observation and experience; and *a priori,* through logical reasoning as a way of validating a proposition as the ultimate and valid truth, a theoretical truth or validity. See DEPENDENT VARIABLE, POLITICAL THEORY, Appendices 1, 3-A.

Political Apathy. One's disinterest in the political aspects of society's life due to disappointment or lack of understanding of political processes and systems, of the purpose of government and politics, and/or of the relationship between the individual and the government. Apathy may also be self-inflicted due to low self-esteem or a feeling of unimportance because of one's race (self-inflicted racism), one's nationality, religion, lack of social mobility, or by reasons of class association (e.g., extreme poverty), or lack of perception of political reality (e.g., what is and what is not possible politically). Such negative attitudes are also known as: political negativism, lack of perception of political reality, political defeatism, political alienation, or even anarchism. Persons free of these attitudes may be considered "politically normal," and those who become extensively involved in political processes may be referred to as political activists. See ANARCHIST, DECADENCE, POLITICAL SELF-ESTEEM.

Political Aptitude. See POLITICAL APATHY.

Political Assassinations. See PRESIDENTIAL ASSASSINATIONS.

Political Asylum. See ASYLUM, POLITICAL.

Political Awakening. See POLITICIZATION.

Political Beauty Contest. A term often applied to political party conventions in the United States at which the aspirants for public elective offices, particularly for the U.S. Presidency, present their views and personalities in order to attract votes on election day. The term also applies to primary elections. It is a common practice among aspirants for public elective offices to seek professional advice from academicians and other professionals (e.g., beauty and physical fitness experts) on the amelioration of speech patterns, public speaking, speed-reading, acting, memory, photogenic appeal, and even on such matters as table manners, walking, hand-shaking, and greeting people. Such beauty treatments are provided by a growing number of public relation firms specializing in this service.

Political Beauty Parlor. See POLITICAL BEAUTY CONTEST.

Political Belts. In the folklore of American politics, the country is divided into so-called "belts," with certain human, geographic, religious, or professional characteristics. Some of these "belts" may overlap. They are: the "Bible Belt"—the Southern states where the Baptist denominations are numerous; this belt also corresponds to the "Black Belt" and the "Cotton Belt," because of the large black population and former agricultural practices there; the "Rust Belt" or "Smokestack Belt,"—the old industrial areas of Pennsylvania, Michigan, Ohio, Indiana, which also correspond more or less, with the prevalence of cold weather, thus referred to as the "Ice Belt;" the "Cactus Belt"—stretching from Texas to California where cacti grow, also corresponding with the "Chicano Belt," because of the large Spanish-speaking population; the "Wheat" or "Corn Belt"—the agricultural plains states like Iowa, Nebraska, Kansas, and Missouri; the "Germanic Belt"—Pennsylvania, Minnesota, and the Northeast where the German-speaking population settled in large numbers; the "Slavic Belt"— basically the city of Chicago, and the states of Michigan, Pennsylvania, and New York where many Slavic peoples settled. Some political sociologists propose that persons within those "belts" share many political views in common and affect political policies and processes. See POLITICAL CULTURE, Appendix 22.

Political Biology. Nazism and other racist systems, advocate superiority of one race over another, selection of species, and survival of the fittest.

Political Bureau. In the Russian language, "Polityccheskoye Byuro;" until 25 December 1991, one of the most powerful organs of the Central Committee of the Communist Party of the Soviet Union (CPSU), which directly established all policies for the entire party, the government and the administration of the USSR, and the satellite communist parties and governments, all dissolved in 1991. See COMMUNIST PARTY OF THE SOVIET UNION (CPSU).

Political Campaign. The concerted effort that one desiring election to public office undertakes, requiring will, human and material resources, a good organization, and endorsements by important and influential individuals, groups, or political parties; the will and determination to speak as persuasively as possible to as many people as possible, mingling with crowds (known as "pressing the flesh"); kissing babies (but, after the Anita Hill-Clarence Thomas confrontation, avoiding women); inquiring among voters about the well-being of their spouses, families, and pets, and making promises to help them with their problems by vague statements such as "we shall take a look into that matter;" also being exposed to extensive travel, poor quarters, poor nutritional habits, and often abuses, verbal or physical, by the disenchanted. A campaigner for a public office is a missionary at work with very little time for the work! See BARNSTORMING, CAMPAIGN DIRTY TRICKS, CAMPAIGN FINANCING, HATCH ACTS, PRIMARY ELECTION, WHISTLE STOP.

Political Campaign Financing. See FEDERAL ELECTION COMMISSION (FEC).

Political Charlatan. See BOUDOIR GOVERNMENT.

Political Circus. See POLITICAL STYLE.

Political Clout. See PANDIT.

Political Commission. See SADAT-BEGIN SUMMIT.

Political Communication. See POLITICAL SEMANTICS.

Political Community. A geographically designated group of individuals living and working under a single political system, performing political roles, enjoying political and civil rights, meeting expected or prescribed obligations in the milieu of the prevailing political culture. See STATE.

Political Compromise. It is assumed, under democratic theory, that in a free society, with divergent and often conflicting interests and views, consensus, and laws, political decisions are reached as the result of a compromise. The description best epitomizing this process is a statement by Sam Rayburn, Speaker of the U.S. House of Representatives (1949-1953): "There's no limit to the amount of good you can accomplish if you're willing to let somebody else take the credit." Other practical advice that came from Speaker Rayburn: "Any jackass can kick down the barn door, but it takes a carpenter to build one." His advice to newly-elected members of the House was: "Learn your job. Don't open your mouth until you know what you're talking about;" and "No one has a finer command of language than the person who keeps his mouth shut." (Those who ignored this advice include, John McCormack, Speaker of the House (1962-1970), "in minimal high regard.")

Political Conflict Resolution. See CONDITIONS OF DEMOCRACY.

Political Consensus. See CONDITIONS OF DEMOCRACY.

Political Convention. See POLITICAL MACHINE, PRESIDENTIAL ELECTOR.

Political Correctness. A semi-fascist political-ideological movement during the 1980s and 1990s in the United States, propagated mainly by liberal groups striving to impose strict adherence to neutral language with regard to gender, age, sex, race, and civil rights legislation, and to curtail free expression or dialogue on these issues. The State of Iowa in the United States, for example, passed a series of laws since 1988 which mandate multicultural, non-sexist education (MCNSE) required of all students in public as well as in private and religious schools. Schools which refuse to provide such politically-correct-education are denied accreditation and financial assistance.

Political Credo. The belief in some ultimate political goal or objective; political creed, or political conviction.

Political Crime. The former Soviet Criminal Code (in the Russian language, "Ugolovnyi Kodeks") defined such a crime (in Article 58) as follows: "The active attitude or active struggle against the working class and the revolutionary movement..." and the "...non-denunciation of the reliably known preparation or commission of a counter-revolutionary crime, punishable by the deprivation of liberty for not less than six months." Non-denunciation arises when a person is fully aware of the preparation or the commission of crime and does not inform the competent public authority. Some legislators in the U.S. Congress, for example, favoring political correctness, suggested that some language in American legislation (e.g., the McCarren-Walter Act) be modified in order to remove that language which commands that immigrants with certain held views (e.g., communists) be denied visas.

Political Crisis. See CRISIS.

Political Culture. The conglomeration of belief systems (e.g., one's religion, ethical values, or political philosophy); political values (e.g., attitudes and preferences regarding matters of specific policies, such as law enforcement, electoral processes, systems of justice, or party politics); conceptions of authority (e.g., who governs, how, and why?); conceptions of purpose (e.g., what are the ends of government, does it or does it not advance the interests and the welfare of the individual persons or the interests of society as a whole?); emotional attitudes of the individual (e.g., does the individual feel a part of the system, does the individual feel an important member of the system or not?); and symbols (e.g., the flag, the eagle, the national anthem, or even a marching band—all instruments of support and sustenance of a political culture). Political culture also includes one's perception of what is good and what is bad in the government and politics of a given political system, and what one should or should not support. Each political culture is a generalized and approximate reflection of the various subcultures (e.g., the views, attitudes, beliefs, and patterns and degrees of supports and demands that the various elites in a society hold and demonstrate). See JAPANESE POLITICAL CULTURE, POLITICAL BELTS, Appendix 22.

Political Defeatism. See POLITICAL APATHY.

Political Development. The quantitative or horizontal growth of political and governmental institutions and programs, or a qualitative or vertical growth in terms of quality of the newly-emerged institutions or policies of the political society. Growth can often be artificially stimulated in order to justify the growth of bureaucracy and spending of public moneys for additional services and facilities. The term is often used interchangeably with "political modernization."

Political Diplomat. See FOREIGN SERVICE OFFICER (FSO).

Political Dissident. See POOR UNDERSTANDING OF REALITY.

Political Ecology. A term coined by author Peter Drucker, meaning the environment of man (the human being), such as society, polity, and economy, all of which are the creation of man, "are 'nature' to man, who cannot be understood apart and outside of them." The three elements constitute the system "in which everything relates to everything else and in which men, ideas, institutions, and actions must always be seen together" in order to be observable and to be understood. See ZOON POLITIKON.

Political Economy. The practice of interpreting economics in terms of political theories, practices, and processes.

Political Ego. See POLITICAL ETHOS.

Political Elite. Those in a political society who have access to, who determine, and who derive the most benefits from the system.

Political Entrapment. See CHARACTER ASSASSINATION, ENTRAPMENT, SEXPIONAGE, SEXPOLITICS.

Political Equilibrium. A concept formed by Aristotle (384-322 BC), one of the greatest political and social philosophers and writers of all times, in his monumental work, *Politics*. In it he studied and analyzed 158 polities and constitutions and concluded that the best government is one which is based on political equilibrium, that is, an equal relationship of the executive, legislative, and judicial functions—a mixed kind of government, as he called it. Distrusting democracy as mob rule, he favored a government by philosopher-kings, the best educated and the wisest men in a society who are preoccupied full time with study and policy-making, while the daily chores are taken care of by the middle class, the auxiliaries (e.g., soldiers, bureaucrats, craftsmen, and implementors of the policies conceived by the philosopher-kings). The lowest chores are performed by the populace, which is under the rule of the auxiliaries. He allowed for easy social and political mobility from one class to another, but the main criteria was intelligence and education. In Aristotle's opinion, this politico-economic system was best for avoiding revolution and maintaining peace and tranquillity. He praised the median golden rule without excesses, and rated the three classes as corresponding in virtue to gold, silver, and bronze respectively. See ARISTOTLE'S CLASSIFICATION OF GOVERNMENT in Appendix 1, BALANCE OF POWER.

Political Ethics. A generally accepted notion that persons performing public tasks, whether elective or appointive, supported by public funds (taxes), and holding the trust of their constituencies, are expected to behave, while in office, according to the moral and ethical standards set by the community. Public officials are expected to be shining examples of patriotism and high morality and ethics. Considering the unusually large demands on public officials and the limited support which they receive from their constituencies, high standards of morality are not always attainable. George Washington, one of America's founding fathers and the first president of the new state, is generally recognized as a shining example of an honest public servant, because it is said that he "never told a lie." Certainly few presidents after him can honestly claim to have maintained such virtue in this high office. Constituencies often demand from their officials not what is ethical and moral, but rather what is expedient and good for them. Certain, unique requirements of political systems may also lead public officials to dishonest and unethical practices. Lord Acton, an honest statesman in England, described himself in his role as ambassador to a foreign nation as "an honest man who was sent abroad to lie for his country." This honest statement caused his immediate recall into rustication. U.S. Secretary of War. Henry L. Stimson, considering clandestine operation in and by an open society as unethical, immoral, and a debasing business, ordered the abolition of the small cryptographic unit in the War Department (called the "Black Chamber") on the grounds that "Gentlemen don't read each other's mail." The "Black Chamber," which was the predecessor of the OSS and the CIA, was spying on Americans and others in time of peace. It is not unusual for many nations to decorate their national (or international) heroes with citations or medals; some for saving, extending, and preserving life (in case of medical technology), and others, for taking it away (in case of war). Ethics in politics is, therefore, the ethics of the society at large as externalized by those in public life who are, more than anybody else, exposed to public scrutiny by the very nature of their active and involving lifestyles and work. See LAST PLANTATION.

Political Ethos. The practice of avoiding certain political behavior which is either offensive to one's personal standards of morality, one's ego, or which may tend to be construed as offensive by others, short of legal sanctions; also, the value of political practices of proven acceptability by the society; a political morality or tradition. See ETHICS, ESTHETICS.

Political Fallout. See BRING THE WAR BACK TO AMERICA.

Political Favor. See POLITICAL HACK.

Political Fratricide. The practice of members of the same political group or a political party competing for power and influence, regardless of how that affects their commonly held views or the well-being of the party.

Political Freedom Versus Economic Want. See LIBERAL IDEOLOGICAL RESTRAINTS.

Political Hack. One who is used, or allows himself or herself to be used for political, partisan causes (e.g., endorsing certain individuals and/or their policies); one who can be hired (drafted) to run for a public office by a political party, or one blindly supporting certain political causes, policies, or individuals (cronyism), usually for anticipated future favors (political favors). See MERIT SYSTEM, PATRONAGE.

Political Hangover. See POST-ELECTION BLUES.

Political Honeymoon. In American politics, the period, lasting about three months, between the time when a new president is sworn in and the time when political haggling with the U.S. Congress over legislation begins.

Political Immolation. The act of taking one's own life in some public manner as a protest against some policies of the government (e.g., South Vietnamese Buddhist monks publicly set fire to themselves to protest that government's supposed religious discrimination). See ANTI-VIETNAM WAR SLOGANS, VIETNAMIZATION.

Political Incrementalism. A term that refers to the increasing number of governmental organizations by regions, particularly those in large metropolitan areas, and the problems that are associated with determining their structures and modes of decision-making. See OAKS' LAWS, PLANNING, REGIONAL PLANNING.

Political Institution. A goal-centered interaction of individuals designated through political processes, within certain jurisdictional limits. Professor Clyde D. McKee, Jr., in *Modernizing American Government*, defines a political institution as "a process constructed around a function, service, or problem deemed by society to be too vital to entrust to private discretion." That process requires certain tools which are: "appropriations and expenditures of public funds, definitions and descriptions of public interest, designation of authority, areas of jurisdiction, and sometimes the application of sanctions for the enforcement of its will."

Political Integration. The broadening and extending of the political base to a larger number of persons or jurisdictions; the act or process of politicizing persons once excluded from that process; or the practice of merging once separate political subdivisions for the purpose of unified governance and thus broadening the base for political participation.

Political Intelligence Test. See SCUM.

Political Irredentism. Separatist tendencies or activities by a homogeneous group living under the authority of one state and wanting to separate itself for the purpose of joining another state, without desiring to become a separate sovereign state (e.g., the Irish Catholics in Northern Ireland). See REGIONALISM, SEPARATISM.

Political Kicker. An issue which may affect the way voters perceive a candidate for public elective office and which may determine their vote. During the 1992 primary elections in Michigan and Illinois, voters turned against incumbent members of the U.S. Congress who were involved in the scandal of writing checks against empty accounts; the scandal was known as "Rubbergate." See KISS AND TELL FOR SALE, MUDSLINGING.

Political Kommissar. See POLITICAL WORKER.

Political License. That which a politician is allowed to do by virtue of being a politician or that which one is allowed to do when authorized by a politician or a political organization, either private or public (e.g., elected public officials may campaign for re-election without losing pay for absence from work). See EXECUTIVE PRIVILEGE, POLITICS.

Political Lieutenant. A trusted and dedicated member of a politician's staff, usually one with the authority to make binding decisions in the name of the candidate for a public elective office. The "commissioning" of such lieutenants usually takes place upon the completion of an extensive period of dedicated, good, and responsible work, often at minimum pay or no pay at all. Political lieutenants are apprentices in the art of politics and the craft of governance. The tasks of political apprentices vary, but, as a rule, the training begins with running errands, like fixing coffee, shuffling papers, licking envelopes, and sweeping the floor.

Political Loyalty. See CHAOS, HT/LINGUAL, LOYALTY LAW.

Political Machine. An informal organization, either built by or around a single politician or a group of politicians who is (or are) capable of commanding loyalty and obedience of followers, either due to its unique political philosophy or kind of policies, or simply due to its ability to grant and/or withhold rewards (e.g., appointments to well-paying jobs in government). One of the first and most effective political machines established in American politics was that of William H. Crawford, U.S. Secretary of Treasury under U.S. President James Monroe (1817-1825), U.S. Senator from Georgia (1807-1813), U.S. Minister to France (1814-1816), and political mentor of U.S. Senator and later U.S. President Martin Van Buren (1837-1841). The effectiveness of Crawford's machine created resentment in Congress, which in 1820 passed the Crawford Act, aimed at limiting appointments of minor federal employees to four years. Among the most effective modern political machines were; the Thomas C. Platt political machine in New York during the 1900s (which once supported T. Roosevelt); the Tammany Hall organization in New York City; the Byrd Machine in Virginia (strong and influential under U.S. Senator Harry F. Byrd, Sr., but declined under his son, U.S. Senator Harry F. Byrd, Jr.); the Pendergast organization in Missouri (established by Jim and Mike Pendergast before W.W.I) which was instrumental in coaching Harry S. Truman, U.S. Senator and President (1944-1953) in his political career; the Daley machine in the Cook County section of the city of Chicago (established by Mayor Richard J. Daley, a Democrat, during the 1930s); the Ed Crump machine in Memphis, Tennessee; and the "Boss" Tweed machine in New York City. The influence of political machines has declined in recent years with the broadening of the electoral base in America (e.g., by the Voting Rights Act of 1965). See CAVALIER, TAMMANY HALL.

Political Marginalization. Rendering a person (e.g., a political opponent, a group, or a party), insignificant and lacking influence on political events or policy making. See DEFINING THE OPPONENT, ELECTORALISM.

Political Messianism. See SHIITE DISSIMULATION.

Political Modernization. See POLITICAL DEVELOPMENT.

Political Momentum. A term commonly used when referring to the increasing strength of a political candidate who before or during an election appears to be a likely winner over others. See KOREAGATE, POLITICAL ETHICS, POLITICAL MORALITY, VOTING, WATERGATE AFFAIR.

Political Myth. Any set of beliefs held by individuals, groups, or societies, which are not susceptible to empirical scientific analysis, held strongly as truths regardless of degree or an obvious irrationality; beliefs that are held as dear and sacred, based on written history or oral history transmitted from generation to generation; beliefs often associated with and expressed through certain rituals. According to an expert in the area, author J. Malinowki, politics itself is one such myth, and "myth not only underpins ideas of legitimacy, but is necessary for that end." Political leaders throughout history have engaged in creating myths (a practice called "mythopoeia") when they saw them as necessary to maintain control over their people—subjects. Symbols are very often associated with myths (e.g., a flag, national anthem, coat of arms, or an eagle, star, cross, or a sword). Deliberate creation of such myths is also known as "remythology." The act of transferring from one political or economic system to another will require the rewriting of history and the substitution of new myths for old ones. The use of myths in politics is a common practice, and myths are powerful mobilizers. Myths are often supported with empirical evidence in order to be accepted as credible and good. Socialism and communism required decades of effort in human and material costs and sacrifices to make people believe these systems were superior to capitalism and liberal democracy, and vice versa. Strong adoration of myths has often led nations to war against one another. Myths constitute about fifty percent of the causes of any conflict, ranging from domestic disputes to international or global war.

Political Non-Existence of Women. See WOMEN'S POLITICAL RIGHTS.

Political Order. As a rule, totalitarian, dictatorial, authoritarian governments have a propensity for maintaining a highly disciplined society, either for the purpose of discouraging possible challenge to the rulers (the ruling elite) or in order to advance the society economically and militarily (and to prepare for possible future conquests). Adolf Hitler, the leader of Nazi Germany (1933-1945), had such political order in mind when he was referring to the "New Order" for Europe and the world. Polyarchies (democracies) often appear to persons accustomed to living under a totalitarian system to be disorderly, wasteful, and undisciplined. See LEBENSRAUM.

Political Party. An organization designed to gain and control political power for the purpose of regulating the activities of persons through government. A political party is the instrument of the recruitment of followers, voters, and candidates for public office; representation of certain policies in government through its members in power or as an opposition; and accountability for its actions. As it pertains to the United States, defined by E. E. Schattschneider (*Party Government.* New York: Holt, Rinehart & Winston, Inc., 1942, p. 61) is a "process," and accordingly, "the Party becomes, therefore, a process formed about the elections." See DEMOCRATIC PARTY, POLITCAL MACHINE, REPUBLICAN PARTY.

Political Party Convention. See PARTY CONVENTION.

Political Payoff. See POLITICAL HACK.

Political Perception. See POLITICAL APATHY.

Political Philanthropy. The support, financial or otherwise, of a certain political philosophy, cause, or a program regardless of one's personal attachment, often as a measure to counter-balance other philosophies or programs (e.g., Friedrich Engels' father supported the cause of socialism and communism of not only his son, but that of Karl Marx as well in spite of the fact that Engels was a wealthy millionaire and Marx advocated extermination, by force, of that particular class). See EIGHT-F GANG, LOBBY.

Political Philosophy. See POLITICAL THEORY.

Political Planning. See PLANNING.

Political Pluralism. See PLURALISM.

Political Posturing. A mode of presenting the personal traits or views of a candidate for public office; the practice of testing one's ideas on others; sending out feelers in order to receive feedback; testing the political "marketplace."

Political Power. See PANDIT, POWER.

Political Pragmatism. Flexible, practical, or realistic politics. See PRAGMATISM.

Political Premonition. The ability to foresee or predict political events; gut feelings.

Political Principle. A set of notions (opinions) that one holds about people, things, and processes, which guide and condition one's behavior on matters political. Former U.S. Senator from Illinois, Everett M. Dirksen, said once that one of his main political principles was "to compromise." See POLITICS.

Political Priority. See PRIORITY.

Political Process. See PROCESS.

Political Progressivism. A legacy of the muckrakers, the era between 1898-1914 was characterized by attempts to bring government closer to the people (e.g., through a system of initiatives, local options, and referenda), and to make governments more responsive to the needs of the people (as the result of more and better educational opportunities and the politicization processes that alerted a larger number of people than ever before as to what government is supposed to do). Legislation was introduced by state legislative bodies to fight corruption and to restrict donations to political parties and candidates by labor unions; the secret (Australian) ballot was introduced in elections on a larger scale than ever before; state and local presidential preferential primaries were introduced in many states. The principal leader and driving force behind the progressivism movement was Governor Robert M. (Fighting Bob") LaFollette of Wisconsin.

Political Question in Law. See JURISDICTION, SUPREME COURT OF THE UNITED STATES.

Political Reaction. The response to sudden political governmental changes for which one was not prepared, or which one had not expected; acts or activities to counter sudden moves (e.g., policy, strategy, or tactics) or maneuvers of a political adversary; or holding or disposing of extremely conservative views which may be considered detrimental to progress and/or innovation. See REACTIONARY.

Political Reality. See POLITICAL APATHY.

Political Refusnik. See POOR UNDERSTANDING OF REALITY.

Political Resolve. See RESOLVE.

Political Retrogression. Usually, an act of ostensive withdrawal by a state from an international conference, a treaty negotiation, or an international organization as a sign of protest. The United States, for example, withdrew from the International Labor Organization in 1977 as a protest against that organization's being controlled by the solid bloc of Third World and Socialist states. In the opinion of President Gerald R. Ford (1974-1977), who expedited the withdrawal, and President Jimmy Carter (1977-1981) who concluded it, the United States received little benefit from the work of that organization in return for its yearly contribution of $20 million to its budget, or one-fourth of the ILO's total budget.

Political Rhetoric. Unrealistic and unfulfillable promises made by a politician (e.g., during a political campaign), in order to attract a following and gain popularity, without his having the intention of keeping those promises. Due to the growing political sophistication of electorates everywhere (particularly in polyarchic societies), such practices are no longer rewarding. Political rhetoric may also be directed against persons whose names one wants to popularize (cultism), or against persons, such as political opponents, by minimizing their personal and professional attributes, or even calling them demeaning names or making derogatory statements (mud-slinging), such as: "His face has seen many masks," or, "His only achievement is that of being a virgin several times"—as the Democratic adversaries characterized the Republican Presidential candidate in 1968, Richard M. Nixon. During the 1992 presidential campaign, Patrick Buchanan, the conservative Republican attacked President Bush on many issues including hiring quotas, abortion, and lack of direction, and he declined to attack Vice President Dan Quayle, noting that he "didn't want to be accused of child abuse."

Political Right. Any (conditional) right that can be exercised by an individual person in a politically organized society (e.g., the right to vote or be voted upon). See CITIZENSHIP.

Political Science. As commonly understood, the organized study of the state and its components, such as government, laws, politics, and political processes.

Political Self-Esteem. The notion that the lack of self-respect for oneself (disliking oneself, feeling that one is of no importance in a society) leads to disrespect for the law, political institutions, and processes, and to low participation in voting and voicing opinions on public issues. The Coopersmith Self-Esteem Inventory and the Kaplan Self-Derogation Scale are often used by psychometricians to determine the degree and causes of lack of self-esteem. Obviously there are instances of high self-esteem: world boxing champion Muhammad Ali said, "When you're as great as I am, it's hard to be humble"; King Louis XIV of France (1638-1715) even asserted, "L'état, c'est moi" (in the French language, "I am the state"). His personification proved inaccurate, because when the king died, the state did not! The Rev. Jesse Jackson introduced a powerful and popular slogan which exemplifies his philosophy of self-esteem: "I am Somebody." Educator Jacqueline Oonder of Atlanta's East Lake Elementary School introduced among her male students the slogan: "I am a Noble African-American Boy!" Lack of self-esteem, particularly as it pertains to politics, is considered to be a global phenomenon which hinders the peaceful resolution of conflicts, at home and in the workplace, and in national and international relationships among states and societies. Some luminaries throughout history viewed self-esteem as follows: Mark Twain, "Deep down in his heart no man much respects himself;" Leo Tolstoy, "I am always with myself, and it is I who am my tormentor;" Oscar Wilde, "To love oneself is the beginning of a lifelong romance;" Margaret Thatcher, "I'm certain we will win . . . Not that I am ever overconfident;" Johann Wolfgang von Goethe, "I do not know myself and God forbid that I should;" and, H. L. Mencken, "Self-respect—the secure feeling that no one, as yet, is suspicious."

Political Semantics. Those written or spoken communications which one perceives as intentionally or unintentionally misrepresenting the truth or a given reality, due to misuse of words or erroneous definition of concepts; a disagreement with one's perception or understanding of articulated concepts, or simply linguistic differences pertaining to described political phenomena. Because of the very interdisciplinary nature of politics, precise communication—the language of politics—is not easily achievable. The politician's attempt to translate political thought into audible or visible communications may often be perceived as semantics, mainly because of a lack of clear-cut definition of a given concept, or the use of definitions of one discipline (e.g., the pure sciences) to describe those of another (e.g., the social sciences). Politicians rarely design conceptual frameworks or tools of analysis and communication. They just use them, and by using them in public before larger audiences than, for example, poets who read their poetry (considering also the possible controversial nature of the communication), are subjected to more misperception and misrepresentation. See DOUBLE-THINK.

Political Sickness. See POTOMAC FEVER.

Political Socialization. The process of acquiring information about a given political system or a political culture, transmitted in original or modified version from one person to another, from generation to generation; also the attitudes, views, biases, and predilections about a community and its political system that are transmitted from one person to another (beginning at the cradle and ending at the grave) in time and space. The paramount agent is the family (an institution in rapid decline around the world)—the church, school, and public and private organizations and associations are the principal agents—and the press, newspapers, books, radio, and television, are the principal tools. See DECADENCE, KNOWLEDGE, POLITICIZATION, POLITICS.

Political Sociology. The practice of interpreting sociology in terms of political theories, practices, and processes.

Political Stereotype. The practice of drawing definite conclusions about a given political system through the analysis of one or some of its variables (e.g., a single institution or a policy), without considering the complex totality of the system.

Political Style. The manner in which a politician projects the image pertaining to her or his likes and dislikes for people, policies, ideas, and implementation of decisions; and the manner of conducting and behaving in political communications and processes. In order to demonstrate his unique political style (a shoe-pounding diplomacy) as well as his ostensive disapproval of anti-Soviet speeches that were given at the United Nations, Nikita S. Khrushchev, the General Secretary of the CPSU and the Premier of the Government of the USSR, waved his clenched fists at anyone who spoke critically of the Soviet Union. He once interrupted a speech of England's Prime Minister Harold MacMillan, and, on October 12, 1960, when the president of the General Assembly of the United Nations, Frederick H. Boland, refused to recognize Khrushchev to address the gathering, Khrushchev, angered, took off his right shoe, waved it at Boland, and occasionally banged it loudly on his desk. The U.S. Delegates became so amused by this unusual display of a political style that the president adjourned the body until the following day because he was not able to call the membership to order. See COMPETITIVE ADMINISTRATION, DAMNED COWBOY, DAMNED MURDER, INC., GIVE THEM HELL, HARRY!, I AM NOT A CROOK!, IF YOU CAN'T STAND THE HEAT . . ., I WOULD RATHER HAVE HIM INSIDE THE TENT . . ., JOYOUS DISORGANIZATION, LET US REASON TOGETHER, THE BUCK STOPS HERE.

Political Subdivision. See GOVERNMENTAL SUBDIVISION.

Political Sugar Bowl. Every governor of a state in the American union, like any executive in a private enterprise, has at his disposal a certain amount of money which he/she can spend for state projects, at his/her exclusive personal discretion. Some of those funds are known as "special funds," "discretionary funds," "contingency funds," or simply "reserve funds." The amounts vary from state to state, but the average amount is from $20 to $150 million. The governor of Kentucky is the least restricted on how the funds, called the "State's Capital Construction Fund," may be spent.

Political Suicide. A term used in practical politics to describe any act that may cause one to forfeit one's chances for advancement in public life (e.g., by supporting the wrong policies at the wrong time, or by being associated with persons or causes of which the electorate does not approve.)

Political System. The total sum of components or subsystems (e.g., population, government, political philosophy, culture, and organizations) which together constitute a certain functional entity that is distinguishable from another entity; one which is in some way unique. Professor Robert Dahl (in *Modern Political Analysis*) defines a political system as " . . . any persistent pattern of human relationships that involves, to a significant extent, power, rule, or authority." According to Professor D. Easton, political system is an analytical tool designed to "identify those integrally related aspects of concrete social activity that can be called political." The system functions by inputs which are converted into outputs; there will be no output if there is no input, or, as the common language in politics has it, "no deposit, no return," or, "you can't make chicken salad out of chicken s..t." See Appendices 1, 3, 3-A.

Political Teleology. A notion, derived from the philosophical concept of teleology, which denotes a political society or a political philosophy that is characterized by a lack of innovation in government and politics, justified on the grounds that the political aspects of human life are pre-destined and not the result of deliberate and calculated efforts of man derived from empirical and theoretical notions;

that the fact of a political society cannot be successfully modified by man; and that one should, contrary to such political philosophers as Plato and Aristotle, accept life as it is, without attempting to modify or to redirect it. Such a notion of a political community prevails among traditional tribal societies and persons who are either disinterested in or disappointed with political systems and processes. See ANARCHISM, POLITICAL APATHY, TELEOLOGY.

Political Temperament. The manner in which the members of a certain political community react to political events in crisis situations (e.g., national mobilization, preparation for war, a major turnover in government, sudden policy changes, or the conduct of a war), or the manner in which certain elites (usually the dominant ones) in a political society perceive and in turn externalize their inner feelings in case of unexpected events which may appear to be leading toward undermining their *status quo*. Both Mao Tse-tung, Chairman of the People's Republic of China (1949-1976), and Ho Chi Minh, the President of the Democratic Republic of Vietnam—North Vietnam—(1950-1969), always viewed (and both emphasized this to their revolutionary followers) the American people, for example, as being very impatient and high-tempered politically—very impatient in a prolonged conflict when a clear victory was not in sight, and willing to take extensive steps in such situations to either win or give up. This was the crux of Ho Chi Minh's and General Giap's tactics during the Vietnam War. Ho Chi Minh, like Mao before him, expected to win in Vietnam, as he did, not because of a strong military machine and the unusual fighting spirit of his guerrillas, but because he prevailed in outwaiting his adversary. Where did Ho learn this strategy? Was it from spies? Of course not. He learned it through the American news media, which almost daily carried large headlines telling everybody (including Ho) that the American people were fed up with the war! "Either win or get out of Vietnam" characterized the general mood of the nation; or: "Simply declare that the war has been won, victory achieved, and pull out!" This disclosure of political temper helped realize Ho's dream. See DEMOCRACY, POLITICAL CULTURE.

Political Terrorism. See TERRORISM.

Political Theology. See LIBERATION THEOLOGY, THEOCRACY.

Political Theory. A broad set of generalizations which are either simple postulates or theorems about matters political. Once the postulates are harnessed, the theorems can be proven, or as Professor David Easton proposes, any kind of proposition about the relation between two or more variables can be demonstrated. Any generalization can be considered a theory because it is a statement of relationship which is only probably (not certainly and finally) true. Theory is necessary not only for practical application but also for conceptual and analytical purposes. A body of propositions is a set of concepts which aid in explaining political phenomena. Concepts by postulation help in observing facts and in understanding their meaning. A conceptual framework helps in selecting, sorting out, and accepting or rejecting certain observed facts; it serves as an instrument showing the direction in which research may go; it is a gauge which indicates the stage of development of a certain science at a given time; it serves as system of working hypotheses as long as it expedites empirical research; it serves as a test in understanding phenomena, and helps in selecting specific variables. Professor Easton favors the so-called "broad-gauge theory" in political science because it is more systematic than others; it is deductive, because it begins with a few postulates of empirical reference and from these deduces a series of narrower generalizations from which, in turn, stem singular generalizations capable of empirical proof. The so-called "narrow-gauge theory," also known as "synthetic theory," consists of a set of interrelated propositions that are designed to synthesize the data contained in an organized body of singular generalizations. The narrow-gauge theory is not necessarily deductive. Professor Easton favors "systematic theory," because: it renders research more reliable, facilitates comparison in research, shows need for new research, and is not hit-or-miss. Professor R. Meehan favors what is called the "middle-range theory" because no one knows how theories are produced, and "systematic inquiry depends upon and has as one of its goals as accurate, precise and unambiguous classification structure—the higher the standards of precision that classification can achieve, the greater the power of the generalizations derived from it." But, as a matter of precaution, Professor Easton advances what he calls "ancillary theory," which is a part of the general theory that may serve in cases when systematic, general theory fails. Easton's causal theory (also known as "empirical" or "systematic") seeks to show relations among political facts; serves to improve the dependability of our knowledge; applies to all generalizations; serves as an index of the stage of development of any science toward attainment of reliable knowledge; (and every description of uniformity is an attempt to state in a prepositional form the assumed relation between two or more variables). Value theory in political science concerns itself with the philosophy of politics such as to what ends are discoveries in political science used (value judgments). Philosophy can be defined as an explanation and clarification of propositions, the type of activity that political philosophers engage in to find answers and, in the final analysis, to show distinctions between sense and nonsense. The methodology in such inquiry usually comes from classical philosophy itself and above all from mathematics and natural sciences. The philosopher or researcher uses many tools such as logic, which according to Professor Ernst Nagel allows one to make explicit structures of methods and assumptions which are employed in the search for reliable knowledge; logic seeks to demonstrate the connecting links by whose means the flying movements of thought may become essential elements in the achievement of trustworthy beliefs; and it articulates the principles implicit in a responsible critique of cognitive claims; logic also assesses the authority of such principles and weighs the merits even of special postulates and intellectual tools that may be used in quests for knowledge. Political philosophy in the discipline of politics, is, as Professor D. Truman points out, "known by the questions it asks rather than by the answers that it provides." Many of the theoretical notions of politics are rather new to the field because, as Professor G. Almost points out, traditional political theory was "more a political sociology and psychology, and a normative political theory rather than a theory of the political process." Professor Truman suggests that until recently, political theory in the United States had six basic features: (1) concern with political system as such; (2) unexamined and implicit conception of political change and development that was optimistic and reformist; (3) neglect of theory; (4) enthusiasm for a conception of "science" which was often more than pure or raw empiricism; (5) preoccupation with things American which hindered comparative method; and (6) establishment of confining commitment to concrete description. Some contemporary political theoreticians, such as Professor Easton, suggest the term "science" may be in doubt because of a lack of a conceptual framework for the entire field of political theory; that there is a need, in his opinion, for orienting concepts, that is, where does the "political" begin and where does it end; and neither the concept "state" nor the concept "power" define political science as to what the science is all about?" Many theoreticians of the behaviorist persuasion have emphasized the need for a search for unity in political science in such main areas as history, general theory, standards of evaluations, empirical political sciences (specifically what is, what is not, and what ought to be) and speculation. There is a great need for general speculation in the field because speculation advances scientific theory. the behavioral approach to political science was first used during the 1920s when a journalist, Frank Kent, published a book in 1928 titled: *Political Behavior, the Heretofore Unwritten Laws, Customs, and Principles of Politics as Practiced in the United States.* That approach, as Professor R. Dahl points out, was basically European and principally German and was dealing with the "behavioral mood" rather than the "scientific outlook." Modern political theory (e.g., that of Professor E. Meehan) emphasizes the scientific method; it tends to be future oriented and, as many theoreticians demand, relevant and action-oriented; political theory must look for a new methodology, like that in the physical sciences; it must deal with abstractions; it must not avoid dealing with current problems; it must compare policy outputs with policy goals; it must anticipate crisis; it must avoid concern with notions based on value assumptions. Black political scientists and theoreticians in America (e.g., Professor Mack Henry Jones of Atlanta) hold the opinion that blacks are preoccupied with civil rights issues and with retaining their distinct identity. Because the whites "were the custodians of the black experience in America," desegregation rather than black nationalism were viewed as the legitimate means of integration. Any notions of black nationalism are viewed by the whites as separatism or even terrorism. The theory of politics is an ever-evolving process of analysis to examine, understand, and predict the actions of individuals, groups, and nations in the exercise of power. It can involve the study of "what is" in the current political spectrum. There is also an element of probability as to "what ought to be." Political theory essentially deals with the interrelationships between man and the state. Such a study involves making value judgments about man and about the state. It is a study of a statecraft. Political theory also involves the study of role relations of power in the society and the allocation of power among the members of society. Political theory may include a study of the institutions, and the systems of governance designed to afford a means of governance based on value systems espoused to be worthy of an established social organization. Political theory also involves systems of information gathering, information sorting, the weighting of information, and assigning values to the various types of information (data). Each of these systems involves choices as to which are most adequate for developing a knowledge of the meaning of statecraft. From the analysis of empirical information it is possible to develop theories of: (a) future conditions of what will happen; (b) future conditions as to what changes are needed to better man's condition: (c) why the conditions of man and his society are as they are: Political theory can encompass the studies of law, religion, morals, economics, ethics, and government. Each of these studies may lead theorists to a set of theses which are relevant at the moment and over time for the understanding of origins and processes of man in society. In each of these studies there are no absolutes, only relative value judgments as to what is the better condition for man and under what circumstances can certain values be achieved. A particular political theory is neither right nor wrong. Rather the rightness or wrongness are both debatable and subject to verification over time and may well be conditioned by the desired value ends of a people in the course of their history. Over time, writers (political theorists) have postulated theories of statecraft ranging from the rule of one (authoritarian), to the rule of many (democracy), to man in a state of nature (before the development of societies). Political theory as a particular statement of a theorist is ultimately based on the individual value placed on collected information. It is then further judged by the whole society according to the value it holds or aspires toward. As tools for scientific investigation are developed and refined, their use in the study of statecraft can certainly direct the study of political theory into new areas of analysis. From this there may come new or re-understood roles and relationships between man and the governance of man in a collective society. See BLACK POWER, CONCEPT, IDEOLOGY, PARADIGM, REPUBLIC OF NEW AFRICA, VALUE THEORY.

Political Tradition. See POLITICAL CULTURE, POLITICAL SOCIALIZATION, POLITICAL ETHOS, TRADITION.

Political Value. See VALUE.

Political Variables. See DEPENDENT VARIABLES, POLITICAL SYSTEM.

Political Warfare. See WARFARE, POLITICAL.

Political Worker. In the Russian language, "Polititcheskoy Trudhovnik." Until 1991, a full-time, dedicated party worker and a member of the Communist Party of the Soviet Union (CPSU), who was assigned to some governmental agency, school, factory, youth organization, diplomatic mission abroad, or the military to criticize, coordinate, and oversee its activities and to report all improprieties to the proper authorities of the party. Political workers were also charged with the dissemination of communist propaganda. They were often referred to as "Political Kommissars" or, in short, "Politruks."

Politicalization. See POLITICIZATION.

Politician. One who is actively involved in the art and science of politics as a result of politicization. See POLITICIZATION, POLITICS.

Politician-for-Hire. See POLITICAL HACK.

Politicians are Buying Votes With Our Children's Money. See GRASS-ROOTS PEROT.

Politicization. The process through which one becomes responsive to matters political; becomes aware and knowledgeable of matters political and/or of methods of political analysis in the interpretation of political data and phenomena; and becomes aware of the political character of society (e.g., who gets what, where, when, how, and why); or the process by which persons are brought into the mainstream of politics. Dr. Zbigniew K. Brzezinski, National Security Adviser to U.S. President Jimmy Carter, stated (December 31, 1977) that we live in a world "that has suddenly become politically awakened and socially restless." See DEPOLITICIZING POLITICS, POLITICS.

Politico-Economic Systems. See Appendices 83, 84.

Politics. Generally, those interactions among individuals and institutions which are employed to design and to implement ways and means of governing an organized society. The term originated with the ancient Greek city-states (Polis—meaning city; and Politikos—meaning a citizen, a wise person, some good of a public nature or some positive good). Among the many definitions, some articulate the concept of "politics" as the art and the science of man; as "talk" between and among people (see *The Language of Modern Politics* by Mark Roelofs): and as "who gets what, when, how" (see *Politics: Who Gets What, When, How* by Harold D. Lasswell). Politics is often looked upon as those interactions among individuals which, through allocation (and withdrawal) of power and benefits, expedite and bring about the processes of government through conflict resolution, always short of deployment of naked force. Politics is construed as an unavoidable activity of man, a political and social animal, without which government is impossible. Government, an agent of politics, will implement that which the politicians have decided. Frank J. Goodnow (*Politics and Administration.* New York: Macmillan, 1900), distinguishing between politics and administration, describes the former as ". . . the formulation of the will of the community and includes besides the activities of political parties, all elective and legislative processes, whether performed by conventions, legislatures, or courts," and the latter, administration, as ". . . the execution of this community will, as accomplished by the executive officers and the courts." To Charles E. Merriam, a one-time member of the City Council of Chicago, co-founder of the Special Research Council and vice-chairman of President Hoover's Research Committee on Social Trends (1929-1932), politics was "a process of readjustment, a constant re-adaptation to changing conditions," and, "perhaps its greatest task" was to reduce the shock of change. Politics must sit "around the table with psychology and statistics and biology and geography" in order to assimilate new scientific data and gain insights. Political institutions "are action patterns reaching into psychology, biology, geography, science and technology, always in terms of reason, reflection, experiment." Quincy Wright (in *Political Science: A Philosophical Analysis*) gives a definition of politics which can be applied to both foreign and domestic politics, as "the art of influencing, manipulating, or controlling major groups in the world so as to advance the purpose of some against the opposition of others with conflicting desires." To David Easton, politics is values which are authoritatively allocated in a society. Professors Winters and Bellows (in *People and Politics: An Introduction to Political Science*) provide a comprehensive definition of politics, using some of the elements from Easton and Van Dyke, which is: "a struggle between actors pursuing conflicting desires on issues that may result in an authoritative allocation of values." Peter Merkle (in *Political Continuity and Change*) defines politics pragmatically as "a noble quest for good order and justice; at its worst, a selfish grab for power, glory and riches." Some of the practitioners of the art and science of politics view it as "the gentle art of getting votes from the poor and campaign money from the rich, by promising to protect each from the other," Oscar Ameringer; "Politics isn't a matter of making love. It's making choices," U.S. Senator Hubert H. Humphrey (1949-1965 and 1971-1978); and Adolf Hitler, the *Führer* (Leader) of Nazi Germany (1933-1945), true to his totalitarian style, defined politics simply as the deadly battle between "views of life." Frustrated with the lack of unity in the social sciences and the lack of order in political science, and the lack of tools that economics, as a social science can, to some extent claim to have, he reconciled himself that this is actually the nature of that discipline. ". . . I think one of the beauties of the field, as I became more patient, is simply that it is unruly in that way, and you pick up a piece that can be segmentally powerful and know that you haven't said everything that there is to say, but you've said very well what there is to say within the limits. There's protean quality about political life as such that makes reducing to a—down to a simpler set of propositions just very difficult" (*News of the APSA*, No. 28, Winter, 1981). See DEPOLITICIZING POLITICS, POLITICIZATION, POWER POLITICS.

Politics is Local. See ALL POLITICS IS LOCAL.

Politics is the Gentle Art of Getting Votes from the Poor and Campaign Funds from the Rich, by Promising to Protect Each from the Other. See POLITICS.

Politics isn't a Matter of Making Love. It's Making Choices. See MISTER DEMOCRAT, POLITICS.

Politics of Contentment. See CAPITALIST MALADY OF CONTENTMENT.

Politics of Original Intent, The. See MODERN POLITICS IS CIVIL WAR CARRIED BY OTHER MEANS.

Politics of Special Interests. According to Dr. William S. Dietrich (*In the Shadow of the Rising Sun: The Political Roots of American Economic Decline*, Pennsylvania State University Press), America is losing its competitive edge in international trade and in global markets mainly because the American state became a "broker state," serving special interests rather than the general public; a system where once the political process was characterized by interest-group mediation and interest-group pluralism; now "parochial interests predominate over the national and the universal" interest of the nation as a whole. Through lobbying, special interest groups exert disproportionate influence over the legislative and the executive processes of the American nation. Such practices will lead, with time, to a situation where very few become rich, and very many become poor. See COMPARATIVE ADVANTAGE, GUIDED FREE ENTERPRISE, KOKUTAI, PAPER ENTREPRENEURIALISM.

Politics of the Pill. See FOCUS GROUP.

Politikos. See POLITICS.

Politiques. A political, philosophical doctrine which advocates that a truly free and sovereign state is one that is ruled by a single person, usually a monarch in whom the sovereignty is vested. The doctrine was originated by a group of political philosophers in France, under the guidance of King Henry IV (1589-1610), and its remnants survived in states like Vatican City (the Papal State) and Iran (under Shah Reza Pahlavi, until his downfall in 1979). See CONCERT OF EUROPE.

Politruk. See POLITICAL WORKER.

Polity. A community organized under any single, effective authority (e.g., a state).

Poll Tax. A tax levy imposed upon persons who wished to vote during elections. It was commonly found in many Southern states in the United States and used as a means to disenfranchise Negroes. The tax was rendered unconstitutional by the Twenty-fourth Amendment to the U.S. Constitution in 1964. See CIVIL RIGHTS ACTS, Appendices 8, 48.

Pollyanna School. See URBANIZATION.

Pollyanna Theory. See URBANIZATION.

Polski Klub. See CRISIS STAFF.

Polyarchy. A democratic, free, politically organized society which is characterized by: (1) high literacy of the electorate and high political participation (e.g., voting and participation in party activities); (2) political control over the distribution of wealth by forces from the grassroots, from the rank-and-file (the common people); (3) lack of centralized political controls, and little subtle control because of overlapping loyalties (through membership in divergent organizations and associations); (4) the ability by the ruling elite(s) to project the image of equality, a folkish quality; (5) broadly articulated civil and political liberties, religious tolerance, horizontal and vertical political and social mobility (ability to hold or to strive to hold high positions in society, private or public); (6) the feeling of each member as a power broker in the system, in private or public endeavor; (7) orientation toward a market economy. A higher stage of democracy, polyarchy is tolerant, but vigilant. See TYPES OF MARKET SYSTEMS, POLITICO-ECONOMIC SYSTEMS, Appendices 83, 84.

Polycentrism. Literally, many centers of political power. A term coined by former leader of the Italian Communist Party, Palimiro Togliatti (in 1956), to describe the once monolithic, monocentral, or unicentral communist bloc of nations led by the Soviet Union, which, after the death of Stalin, became divided into many centers (as exemplified by the Sino-Soviet rift and the various "roads to socialism" advocated by the leaders of the communist states (e.g., Poland and Hungary). See BIPOLARITY, THREE WORLDS.

Polyculture. A multicultural society; a society characterized by cultural pluralism, e.g., the United States, where different cultures, often conflicting ones (e.g., division due to race, wealth, ethnicity), are guaranteed, under law, equal protection, and which, in the final analysis, subscribe to some single good (e.g., Americanism).

Polytheism. The notion that there are many gods, as opposed to monotheism, which holds that there is only one god.

Pontifical Commission. Unicameral legislative body of Vatican City.

Poor Laws. Legislation passed in England in 1601, known as the "Poor Relief Act," which provided for taxing local political subdivisions for the purpose of creating jobs, not welfare, for the unemployed.

Under the subsequent Act of 1834, social welfare became the responsibility of the national government rather than local communities; the Act provided so-called "workhouses" for the unemployed, and unemployment benefits to those not able to work. This welfare system is considered one of the most advanced and well organized; it has survived to this day with some modification. It has served as a model followed by many countries around the world.

Poor People's March of 1969. On April 4, 1969, a group of black and white civil rights leaders and followers, under the direction of Dr. Ralph Abernathy of the Southern Christian Leadership Conference, led a march from Memphis, Tennessee, where Dr. Martin Luther King, Jr. had been assassinated on April 4, 1968, to the nation's capital, Washington, D.C. The marchers, about 12,000 strong, were joined by another group of 10,000 in Washington and settled in a shanty town ("Resurrection City"), which after heavy rains became muddy and was called "Mudsville." After petitioning the government, the marchers were driven out from the city by police who used tear gas. Soon riots erupted in Washington during which a major part of 14th Street in the Northwest part of the city was burned. The incident is also known as "the second burning of Washington" (the first being that of 1812 by the British).

Poor Richard's Almanack. See ARTILLERY OF THE HEAVENS.

Poor Understanding of Reality. The Soviet secret police, the KGB, took control in 1967 of severe mental institutions where political prisoners were held under the official pretext of having "poor understanding of reality" in the Soviet Union. In actuality, they were people who had criticized government policies (dissidents) or who had refused to serve in the armed forces, or had disobeyed the laws (refusniks).

Popocrat. See POPULIST.

Popular Consent. See ORIGINS OF THE STATE THEORIES, SOCIAL CONTRACT THEORY.

Popular Democracy. See MOB RULE.

Popular Election. See PRESIDENTIAL ELECTOR, POPULAR VOTE.

Popular Front for the Liberation of Palestine (PFLP). The second largest (after the AL-FATAH led by Yasir Arafat) Palestinian revolutionary and commando organization dedicated to the establishment of a separate Palestinian state and the destruction of the state of Israel. The PFLP, which emerged as a splinter group from Al-Fatah during the late 1960s under the leadership of Dr. George Habash, has been responsible for organizing many terrorist acts, and like other Palestinian and Arab revolutionary organizations, it refused to meet and to negotiate with Egypt and Israel during their encounters in December 1977. In January 1992, Dr. Habash came to France for medical treatment, under the auspices of the French Red Cross, and was detained by the French government when the news of his presence was revealed by the press, for further clarification. See PALESTINE LIBERATION ORGANIZATION (PLO), Appendix 95.

Popular Government. See JACKSONIAN DEMOCRACY.

Popular Republican Movement (PRM). In the French language, "Mouvement Populaire Republicain." A political party in post W.W.II France, with pro-business, pro-Christian orientation.

Popular Review. See POPULAR SOVEREIGNTY, PRINCIPLES OF AMERICAN CONSTITUTIONAL SYSTEM.

Popular Sovereignty. A political concept according to which the voters in a sovereign state are the ultimate and supreme source of all authority and may alter at will the form, structure, or political philosophy of their government.

Popular Vote. All the votes cast by registered voters during an election.

Population Explosion. See HUNGER WARS, POPULATION GROWTH PROJECTIONS, Appendices 85, 86, 89.

Population Growth Projections. According to available data, the estimated global population in round numbers, in the past and as projected into the future, is: 1,000,000 BC—2 million persons; 6,000 BC—5 million; 1600 AD—500 million; 1830—1 billion; 1930—2 billion; 1950—3 billion; 1977—4 billion; 2000—6 billion; and 2200—9 billion. See HUNGER MIGRATION, HUNGER WAR, POPULATION GROWTH, Appendices 85, 86, 89.

Populist. One who sees the most wisdom, virtue, and good in the masses of the people and not in some privileged or chosen groups. The Populist party or Populists, a small coalition group that emerged in the United States during the 1890s and was cynically referred to as "popocrats," was composed of and for farmers, toilers, and small merchants, both black and white, who criticized the government for being the agent of big business with such slogans as "government of Wall Street, by Wall Street, and for Wall Street." (Wall Street is the street in New York City where the major financial institutions in America, including the Stock Exchange, are located.) Some of the Populist leaders in America were Ignatious Donnelly, a three-time member of the U.S. Congress from Minnesota, and Mary Elizabeth ("Mary Yelling") Lease from Kansas (also referred to by her adversaries as the "Kansas Pythoness"). Mary Lease called on the people of Kansas to raise "less corn and more hell" in order to make the federal government more responsive to the interests and will of the people. When the admission of Montana and North and South Dakotas as new states came before Congress, she was quoted in New York's *Evening Post* as remarking, "We don't want any more states until we can civilize Kansas." Many of those slogans have been revived during the 1977-1978 Farmers' protest in America. See TRACTORCADE, TRUST BUSTING.

Populist Internationalism. According to writer Robert J. Samuelson, the cold war inspired solidarity among the people of America, Europe, and Asia (mainly Japan, South Korea, Taiwan, Hong Kong, and the Philippines) due to the Soviet and communist threat in general. With the end of the cold war, that threat has diminished. And each nation is now focusing more on solving its own problems, with international cooperation and solidarity eroded. This change in solidarity will weaken all joint efforts to address global problems. Solving local problems takes precedence over solving international and global problems. See ALL POLITICS IS LOCAL.

Porgan. Special Iranian assassination group under the Shah. See IRAN'S REVOLUTION, MOSSEDEGH, SAVAK.

Pork Barrel Legislation. Any legislation that favors the constituency which a particular lawmaker represents. The term originated during the 1830s when the U.S. Congress voted, for the first time in a uniform manner, to allocate funds for the improvement of harbors and rivers. The myth has it, that once the flow of rivers was improved and streamlined, more pork, stored then in barrels and immersed in deep and cool water as a means of refrigeration, could come to the lawmakers.

Porkopolis. See URBANIZATION.

Port Caucus. See CONGRESSIONAL CAUCUS.

Portfolio. A cabinet-level office (e.g., department or a ministry).

Positive Discrimination. The British version of an affirmative action program aimed at granting preference in employment to racial minorities (usually blacks and Asians) over whites. The program was first implemented on February 3, 1978, in the Borough of Camden, one of the political subdivisions of the city of London and, according to official literature, the program favors "coloured applicants for jobs . . . if two people of equal ability but of different colour apply for a job, . . . the coloured person will get it," because of large and disproportionate unemployment among non-whites. See AFFIRMATIVE ACTION PROGRAM, REVERSE DISCRIMINATION.

Positive Endeavors. See QUARANTINE SPEECH.

Positive Imperialism. See LEBENSRAUM.

Positive Law. According to some political scientists, laws which consist of definite rules of human conduct with appropriate sanctions provided for their enforcement, both of which are prescribed by the proper authority. See POSITIVE VIEW OF LAW.

Positive Neutrality. See NONALIGNMENT.

Positive View of Law. Pertaining particularly to international law, the positivists claim that any norm of international law which for any reason cannot be enforced is not a law, and a rule, properly called a "law," is that which is enforceable and can be enforced. Such a rule ordinarily carries a sanction and anything that does not is therefore not a law. Laws, for this reason, are properly the rules of states which have the power to enforce them. Today, this school of thought is represented mainly by Yale University and is also known as the "Yale" or the "New Haven" school.

Positivist Notion of Concepts. See CONCEPT.

Posse. See POSSE COMITATUS.

Posse Comitatus. In the Latin language, "the use of force upon authorization" or "the authorized use of force." Also, a group of armed persons which may be deputized by a sheriff to assist him in his police duties (e.g., the posse of the Old West). See ARYAN NATION.

Post-Cold War Syndrome. See COLD WAR ORPHAN STATE.

Post-Election Blues. A term associated with the disappointment of a political candidate and his staff on losing an election in which they had invested time, knowledge, and energy hoping to improve their lot; the general discontent that follows a lost election, with bills to be paid, funds in short supply, and the necessity for the candidate and the volunteer staffers to seek new ways to make a living. Also known as a "political hangover."

Post-Imperial Presidency. See IMPERIAL PRESIDENCY.

Post-Industrial Planning. See QUARTERNARY SERVICE.

Post-Industrial Society. A concept of a society which is characterized by: advanced knowledge and technology (acquired through well developed and highly advanced basic and applied research); advanced and highly sophisticated automation and production of knowledge (e.g., with the aid of computers); decline of manual exertion; high literacy rate; generation of knowledge in exchange for basic commodities; and is limited, by and large, to the production of basic services (quarternary services) necessary to sustain and to maintain its members (e.g., housing, transportation, education, recreation, etc.). The post-industrial economy draws on commodities produced by pre-industrial and industrial economies in exchange for its know-how. (In its preparation for the post-industrial era, the United States is placing strong emphasis, among other things, on mass education. An example is legislation—known as the "Womb to the Tomb Law" of "Lifetime Learning"—introduced in the U.S. Senate in 1976 by U.S. Senators Jacob K. Javits and Walter F. Mondale, then Vice President of the United States.) Under this Aid to Education legislation, needy persons as well as institutions, including libraries and museums (which the law considers learning centers), receive assistance through a variety of approximately four hundred different programs, designed for the very young as well as the elderly. The program was continued by Presidents Reagan and Bush.

Postindustrial Education. See COMPARATIVE ADVANTAGE.

Postulation in Political Theory. See POLITICAL THEORY.

Posture of Moral Abstention. According to Judge Robert H. Bork (*The Tempting of America: The Political Seduction of the Law*), "where the Constitution does not apply, the judge, while in his robes, must adopt a posture of moral abstention . . ., but he and the rest of us need not and should not adopt such a posture when entering the voting booth. It is there, asserts Judge Bork, "that our differences about moral choices are to be decided, if not resolved, until the next election." The debate over a narrow v. broad interpretation of the U.S. Constitution is eternal and has never been resolved. Should the judge read new meaning into, or rather out of, the Constitution, it is only through language as written in the Constitution. Regarding broad interpretation, Judge Bork adds, "The truth is that the judge who looks outside the historic Constitution always looks inside himself and nowhere else. And when he looks inside himself he sees an intellectual . . . some measure of intellectual class attitudes."

Potemkin Village. When Catherine II, also called "the Great," Tzarina of Russia and Empress of the Russian Empire (1729-1796) freed the serfs, she ordered the bureaucracy to see to it that the people had fairly decent housing and their children had schools. However, the incompetent bureaucracy, which consisted mainly of the wealthy gentry class, was not interested in such endeavors, fearing that once the lives of the serfs improved they would then ask for political power. When the Empress wanted to travel through villages to see the housing she had ordered built for the peasants, one of her aides, Field Marshal and Prince, Grigori Aleksandrovich Potemkin (1739-1791), ordered rural government agencies to put up elegant fronts of houses, painted and decorated, but uninhabited. The Empress took the tour and returned impressed with the elegant "housing" which, however, was promptly dismantled after her speedy tour by horse-drawn carriage. Imitations of that nature were also found in New York City in 1976, when U.S. President Jimmy Carter went to inspect supposed new housing for the poor. Shabby houses, unoccupied for years, had rapidly refurbished facades, but President Carter, trained as an engineer, could not be easily duped; the farce was discovered at once to the embarrassment of local housing officials.

Potentate. A person who possesses and disposes supreme powers or authority because of his position or office held, such as a king or emperor, or because of wealth.

Pothouse Politician. See DARK HORSE.

Potomac Fever. Term characterizing persons who come to Washington, D.C., America's capital city, either as elected or appointed officials and who soon develop a liking for the lifestyle and the pay and benefits, and do anything they can to remain there as long as possible. Potomac is the name of the river flowing through the city of Washington dividing the District of Columbia and the State of Virginia.

Potsdam Conference. A major summit conference held by the "Big Three": President Harry Truman of the United States; Prime Minister Winston Churchill of Great Britain (who toward the end of the conference was replaced by Clement Atlee, who defeated him in the 1945 election); and Joseph Stalin, Premier of the Soviet Union. The Conference was held in Potsdam, Germany, from 17 July to 2 August in 1945, during which time agreements were reached on: the unconditional surrender of Japan; the division of defeated Germany into four Power Zones of occupation; denazification; trial of war criminals; demilitarization, disarmament, and democratization of the German political, judicial, and educational systems; decentralization of political institutions; and deindustrialization of Germany. The Big Three agreed that should Japan refuse to obey the Potsdam Declaration and surrender unconditionally, the United States would use atomic weapons to be dropped on Hiroshima and Kokura. Hiroshima was first and, due to bad weather, the naval base City of Nagasaki, instead of Kokura, became the second target, August 6 and 9, 1945, respectively. On 15 August 1945 Emperor Hirohito announced surrender of Japan. Over 180,000 were killed and wounded in Hiroshima and 80,000 in Nagasaki. See MORGENTHAU PLAN.

Potsdam Declaration. See POTSDAM CONFERENCE.

Poverty Pimp. See CIVIL RIGHTS HUSTLER.

Poverty Won! A frequent quip by U.S. President Ronald Reagan (1981-1989) referring to the "War on Poverty" program that was initiated during the early 1960s by U.S. President Lyndon B. Johnson, but was never carried out due to the involvement in the Vietnam War. President Reagan claimed that the war has been won! See WAR ON POVERTY.

Power. In political usage: one's capacity to command obedience of other persons with or without their consent, and to determine the allocation of material things; a capacity to grant and to withhold rewards; or, using the concept of naked power as used by Mao Tse-tung, something that comes from the barrel of a gun. Power breeds authority and authority generates more power. In another context, power is information which has been realized and materialized at the right time. One of America's leading students of power, Adolf A. Berle (in *Power*), identified five major natural laws of power which, according to him, "are applicable wherever, and at whatever level, power appears." They are: (1) "Power invariably fills any vacuum in human organization." This notion rests on two propositions: (a) that human beings need organization in order to survive, and (b) some persons seek power over others. If one power structure breaks down, another one will emerge and fill the vacuum; (2) "Power is invariably personal," meaning that power can be held and exercised only by individuals or groups and that it can be passed on to individuals; (3) "Power is invariably based on a system of ideas or philosophy"; (4) "Power is exercised through, and depends on, institutions," meaning that for power to be effective, upon utilization, it must be institutionalized, the institution serving as vehicle for the distribution of power; and (5) "Power is invariably confronted with, and acts in the presence of a field of responsibility," meaning that the utilizer of power must pay attention to the scope and degree of effectiveness the power has on those over whom it is exercised. Berle also recognizes that a certain class, whether social or economic, may hold power in a society. Nikita S. Khrushchev, General Secretary of the CPSU and Premier of the Soviet Government (1956-1964), explained his meaning of power when asked why he had banished Georgi M. Malenkov, once a leader of the party and Premier of the government, to a minor post in Siberia in 1957. Khrushchev facetiously replied that Malenkov was not deprived of any power. He was, as a matter of fact, given all the power a man can have—he was appointed to manage a large electricity-generative complex! Professors Winter and Bellows (in *People Politics: An Introduction to Political Science*) define power: "one person or group exercises power over another when it is intentional and done in such a way as to affect in a predictable way the action(s) of another or others." Power "usually involves sanctions and rewards," but may also involve "rational persuasion or appeals to the emotions." The three important aspects of power in the definition of Professors Winter and Bellows are "relationship," "intention," and "predictability," all of which render power "relational" and "reciprocal," meaning that power affects those who exercise it as well as those upon whom the power is being exercised. The externalization of the relational aspect of power is explained through the concept of a "nonautonomous change" (NAC), which they define as that aspect of a policy decision which "refers to the effort or amount of change that the exerciser must spend if power is to be exercised." The desire to possess and to utilize power is not confined to any single sex; both men and women seek it and use it. "Wherever I found the living, there I found the will to power," observed Frederick Nietzsche (in *Thus Spake Zarathustra*). United States Secretary of State Henry A. Kissinger referred to power as "the ultimate aphrodisiac" (*The New York Times Magazine,* October 28, 1973). The motto of the urbanite has always been "Don't tread on me!" and man's greatest desire is to establish a territorial imperative, his exclusive domain. Heinrich von Treitschke, a German philosopher, observed: "Your neighbor, even though he may look upon you as his natural ally against another power which is feared by you both, is always ready, at the first opportunity, as soon as it can be done with safety, to better himself at your expense ... Whoever fails to increase his power, must decrease it, if others increase theirs." (quoted in Frederick Meinecke, *Machiavellianism, The Doctrine of Raison D'État and Its Place in Modern History*); United States President Lyndon B. Johnson (1963-1969), a dedicated student of power himself and a master of its application, made power part of his daily life, but the enormous power of the presidency made him admit (when urged to win the Vietnam War by the deployment of the mighty military machine of the United States) that the problem of the U.S. President, due to the enormity and vastness of power of the American state, is not how to use it, but how to refrain from using that power. Power is "the ability to bring about our desires" (Silvano Arieti, *The Will to Be Human*). Sir J. E. E. Dalberg (also known as First Baron or Lord Acton), English historian, is known for his assertion, "Power tends to corrupt and absolute power corrupts absolutely" (as quoted in Louis Kronenberger's *Animal, Vegetable, Mineral*). Although psychoanalysts may disagree on many things, they agree that "the will to power" is an essential part of humanity. Observes Alfred Adler, "Achieve! Arise! Conquer! Whatever name we give it, we shall always find in human beings the great line of activity— this struggle to rise from an inferior to superior position, from defeat to victory, from below to above." "Between Satan and Jesus," observes Malachi Martin (in *The Final Conclave*), "it has always been a dispute about power." Radical power-seekers are warned by Francis Bacon that "It is a strange desire to seek power and lose liberty." To paraphrase Tip O'Neill, Speaker of the U.S. House of Representatives (1977-1986), "power is ... something that is ... never given—it is only taken." See AUTHORITY, DEFINING THE OPPONENT, Appendix 3-A.

Power Broker. See POWER.

Power Comes from the Barrel of a Gun. See POWER.

Power Elite. A group of persons with the unique means and capability to influence or shape internal and external policies of a sovereign state. Elites, present in every society whether democratic or totalitarian, are active and influential in different degrees at different times, under different circumstances, but their ultimate goal is to maintain for themselves and those whose support they need (e.g., the masses of ordinary people, slaves, or feudal tenants) conditions favorable to their existence and, if possible, prosperity. Elites are formed by money (old money—inherited; or new money—earned), wealth and possessions, race, origins and birth, language, culture, philosophy, religion, schools, clubs, political parties, and other formal or informal organizations, even secret organizations and societies. Elites often engage in cronyism and old-boy networking. A pluralistic society tolerates elites become wisdom in a democracy arises from the mutual cancellation of opposing elites engaged in extremes, allowing a more rational view to prevail.

Power of the Purse. Students of politics with tendencies toward economic determinism claim that the ultimate power in a politically organized society is that which controls wealth and money, their sources and distribution. Under the U.S. Constitution (Art. I, Sec 7), that power belongs to the U.S. House of Representatives of the U.S. Congress: "All bills for raising revenue shall originate in the House of Representatives." See U.S. Constitution in Appendix 8.

Power Politics. The conduct of international relations by means of a constant demonstration of force, or by the actual use of force. Although the concept is as old as man himself, it is often associated in modern times with Machiavelli. See MACHIAVELLIANISM, POWER, POLITICS, REALPOLITIK.

Power State. See LEBENSRAUM.

PR. See PROPORTIONAL REPRESENTATION.

Practical Politics. See HONEYMOON.

Praetor Peregrinus. A high government official in ancient Rome, a magistrate, one charged with the development and administration of legal rules for the conduct of relations between the citizens of Rome and foreigners. See PONTIFEX MAXIMUS.

Praetorianism. See CAESARISM, GARRISON STATE.

Pragmatism. An approach to life or to problems which values anything that brings good results as attested by experience rather than theory. William James (1842-1910), in his work, "The Pragmatic Method," *Journal of Philosophy,* 1 (December 8, 1904, pp. 673-687), considers experience a way of verifying ideas: personal verification of perceptual experiences. American political and governmental practices are recognized and characterized as the most pragmatic ones anywhere. One may view the American way as the belief that, whenever there is a problem, one finds a solution, or makes one! See INSTRUMENTALISM.

Prague Spring. See CHARTER 77, VELVET REVOLUTION.

Prairie Populist. A term commonly applied to politicians who either were born or have been living in, or have demonstrated favoritism to, political communities of the Middle West and the West of the United States, communities which are characterized by informal personal interactions and a considerably slower-paced tempo of life as compared with other areas (e.g., the hustling East). This term has been affectionately applied to: Earl of Chatham, William Pitt (1708-1778); Henry Clay (1777-1852) who was also known as "The President Maker," because of his support of John Quincy Adams for the presidency in 1824, "The Great Compromiser," for his efforts in the nullification crisis in 1833, and "The Great Pacificator," for his efforts in prevention of a civil war in 1850; William Jennings Bryan (1860-1925), who was also known as "The Great Commoner" and edited a paper under the same name, became identified with the forces that favored silver money, and after the "Cross-of-Gold" speech was nominated for President by the Democratic Party in 1896. He served as prosecuting attorney in the "Monkey Trial" of J. T. Scopes who was tried and convicted for teaching Darwin's evolution theory; Adlai Ewing Stevenson (1900-1965), Governor of Illinois (1949-1953), U.S. Ambassador to the UN (1961-1965), and Democratic Party nominee for president in 1956; and Hubert Horatio Humphrey (1911-1978), Mayor of the City of Minneapolis, Minnesota (1945-1949), U.S. Senator (1949-1965), U.S. Vice President (1965-1969), nominee of the Democratic Party for president (1968), U.S. Senator (1971-1978), and Deputy President Pro-Tempore of the U.S. Senate, a job created especially for him in 1976. He was also affectionately called "Mr. Democrat" and "the Happy Warrior." See MONKEY TRIAL.

Praise the Lord and Keep Your Powder Dry. See SIVIS PACEM PARA BELLUM.

Praise the Lord and Pass the Ammunition. See SIVIS PACEM PARA BELLUM.

Pravda. In the Russian language, "truth." Also the name of a daily newspaper in the Soviet Union which was the organ of the former Communist Party of the Soviet Union (CPSU). It folded in March 1992. See ISKRA, IZVIESTIA.

Pre-election Campaign. In the American electoral system, the presidential election year is the pivotal point in political activity, because of the tremendous effort on the part of the political aspirants to gather sufficient support not only to sustain their availability, but to win in the primary elections and then to achieve the nomination of the in party. (Independent candidates do not participate in these party activities.) Candidates then must meet the hurdle of the November presidential election. In this election, in addition to the president, one-third of the membership of the U.S. Senate is elected, and the entire membership of the U.S. House of Representatives, all 435 of them; also, a number of governors, state legislators, and judges (in many states judges are elected rather than appointed, e.g., U.S. President Harry S. Truman (1945-1953) had been elected as a local judge in Missouri). Approximately another ten thousand or more other government officials, on all levels, are elected. There is one common and paramount slogan for all of them: "Show 'em You're a Winner!"

Pre-Industrial Society. See POST-INDUSTRIAL SOCIETY.

Pre-Nuptial Agreement. See COMMUNITY PROPERTY.

Pre-Sentencing Report. See PRESENTENCE REPORT.

Preamble. A statement of purpose that may be prefixed to a constitution or to a statute. Although a preamble is not considered a part of the law itself, it may be referred to by courts of law, in order to ascertain the intentions of the framers of a document whenever there is some ambiguity in the text of the constitution or statute. See U.S. Constitution in Appendix 8.

Precedent. A legislative, executive, or judicial decision upon which future decisions or courses of action may be based. See STARE DECISIS.

Preceptoral System or Rule. See MASS LINE.

Precinct. An electoral or administrative unit of a political subdivision, designed for the purpose of administration of elections. In the United States, precincts, sometimes called "wards," are designed usually for election purposes and are headed by a "precinct leader" or a "precinct captain" (or, in case of "wards," by "ward leaders," "ward captains," or "block leaders"). See POLITICAL MACHINE, POLITICAL PARTY.

Precinct Captain. See PRECINCT.

Precinct Leader. See PRECINCT.

Precinct Worker. A person engaged in voluntary election day activities, raising funds, recruiting candidates, or attempting to influence voters' choices.

Predatory Capitalism. See AMERICA BASHING, JAPAN BASHING, MONOPOLY, PREDATORY DEMOCRACY.

Predatory Democracy. A notion which holds that some democratic systems, while providing for extensive rights and liberties for the individual, do in reality accomplish this at a great expense to the majority (who barely survive) for the benefit of the minority (e.g., those who exploit these freedoms and liberties in order to accumulate wealth and power).

Predicting the Past. See CHISTKA, PURGE.

Predictive War Scenario. See WAR SCENARIO.

Preemption. According to accepted norms of international law, a state at war—a belligerent—has the right to acquire goods needed for the conduct of war from a neutral state upon compensation. See DETERRENT, WAR.

Preemptive Strike. A surprise massive attack against the military force of an adversary in order to minimize or to eliminate his capacity for aggression. The term "protective reaction" is also used. See WAR.

Prefect. See PREFET, PREFECTURE.

Prefecture. A unit of local government and administration headed by a prefet (e.g., in France).

Preferential Voting. A system of voting whereby the voter indicates on the ballot his first, second, or third preference by marking his choices opposite the names of candidates. See PRIMARY ELECTION, VOTING.

Prefet. In the French language, "prefect." An official appointed by the central government of France to represent its interests in a local government in a capacity similar to a state governor in the United States. See PREFECTURE.

Prejudice of Court. Grounds on which charges against an accused may be dropped if the jury or the judge sitting in judgment shows unfavorable disposition or attitude toward the defendant or toward the case itself. See VENUE.

Prejudice of Jury. See PREJUDICE OF COURT.

Preliminary Injunction. See WRITS OF COMMON USE.

Preliminary Society. See UTOPIA.

Premier. The head of the government under a parliamentary system of government, one usually elected by the parliament. See PRIME MINISTER.

Prerogative. A right or privilege which is derived from holding a certain office, or a position of power, influence, or trust. See EXECUTIVE PRIVILEGE, PRIVILEGE.

Presentence Report. A written document describing personal characteristics and/or history of the accused which is presented to a judge in a court of law before a final sentence is announced. Such reports are prepared by some party neutral to the case (e.g., the police or the welfare department).

Presentment. A basis for an indictment which may be presented by a grand jury to a court of law which is to decide a case.

President. An elective or appointive top executive officer of a private (e.g., a business enterprise) or public enterprise (e.g., a political government) who serves as a symbolic or real executive leader. See HEAD OF GOVERNMENT, HEAD OF STATE, PRESIDENTIAL ELECTOR, PRESIDENT-ELECT, Appendices 7-9, 14-16.

President Bashing. See CONGRESS BASHING.

President-Elect. In the United States, a person who receives the plurality of the popular vote during a presidential election and who, subject to a vote by the Electoral College (where a majority vote is required), will be installed on January 20 of the next year as President. The President-elect spends the time between his election and inauguration in presidential transitionary preparations, and for all practical purposes enjoys the privileges of the office (e.g., protection by the Federal Protective Service) and such other privileges as described by *The Richmond Times-Dispatch* in its November 1976 issue: "Most importantly the President-elect is happy because (1) he can be portrayed as soberly cautious and deliberate in making his decisions, (2) he can pay off a great many debts by just "considering" someone publicly, and (3) he can show himself to be at the center of real power in Washington without having to take up any of the reins of power, gaining the appearance of authority without the concomitant responsibility."

President-in-Waiting. A term applicable to the U.S. Vice President, who is next in line of succession to the presidency. Also referred to as "Stand-by-President." See PRESIDENTIAL SUCCESSION, U.S. Constitution, Amendment XXV in Appendices 8, 17.

President Maker. See PRAIRIE POPULIST.

President of the United States. See PRESIDENT, PRESIDENTIAL GOVERNMENT.

President Pro Tempore. A member of the United States Senate who is chosen to preside over that body during the absence of the Vice President of the United States, who by law, is the presiding officer of the Senate. Until 1890, Presidents Pro Tempore were chosen "for the occasion only," and since 1890 they have served "until the Senate otherwise ordered." In 1977 the Senate also established the office of the Deputy President Pro Tempore primarily as a reward to Hubert H. Humphrey, who was the first Deputy, and served until his death on January 13, 1978. See MISTER PRESIDENT, UNITED STATES SENATE.

President's Average Day in Office. Taken from the appointment calendar of Jimmy Carter, U.S. President 1977-1981, date unspecified, as presented by the "Junior Scholastic" 25 January 1977: 6:00 a.m.—The Signal Corps calls the President, as he requested, giving him the time, date, temperature, and weather report. The President dresses, takes the elevator to the Oval Office (his official office); 6:30 a.m.—the President reads summaries prepared by his staff and newspapers gathering material for his forthcoming speech on human rights; 7:00 a.m.—goes through his memoranda trying to decide whom to appoint to the post of Assistant Attorney General; 8:00 a.m.—meeting with National Security Advisor, Dr. Zbigniew Brzezinski, who passes intelligence reports for the day to him; reviews issues on Afghanistan, rioting in Iran, rumors of an attack on U.S. Embassy in Teheran, Iran; 8:15 a.m.— meeting with advisers on such issues as cutting hospital costs and sharing of ideas on legislative proposals and strategies, mainly which legislators may be for or against the President's legislative proposals; 8:45 a.m.—paperwork; 10:30 a.m.—Meeting with Press Secretary Jody Powell and exchange of strategies for the upcoming press conference; 10:45 a.m.—paperwork; Noon—luncheon with members of National Security Council to discuss current trends and developments in Africa, the Soviet Union and the United States: 1:15 p.m.—paperwork; 1:32 p.m.—meeting with high school students in the Oval Office and a photograph session; 1:45 p.m.—meeting with arriving Vice President, Walter Mondale; 2:20 p.m.—meeting with one of the speech writers who helps the President prepare a speech for a $100-a-plate fundraising dinner in Chicago to help the Democratic Party; 3:00 p.m.—meeting with Dr. Harold Brown, Secretary of Defense to discuss the development of a new jet fighter plane, ask questions about Soviet air force capabilities as well as about new aircraft; 3:40 p.m.—paperwork; 4:30 p.m.—back in the Oval Office, facing TV cameras and signing bills passed by Congress, often exchanging brief remarks with members of Congress invited for that occasion; 5:00 p.m.—more paperwork; 6:00 p.m.—the president goes upstairs for a family dinner; 8:30—back to the Oval Office to study latest data on unemployment and how to cut spending without laying off people; 10:28 p.m.—clears his desk, goes upstairs to read a favorite book then call the Army Signal Corps with tomorrow's wake up instructions.

President's Cabinet. In the United States the cabinet consists of the Vice President, heads of the Departments, Secretaries, the Attorney General, the U.S. Ambassador to the United Nations, and any other person whom the President may wish to include.

President's Commission on the Assassination of President Kennedy. See WARREN COMMISSION.

Presidents Defeated in Elections for Second Term. So far, they were: John Adams, John Quincy Adams, Martin Van Buren, Grover Cleveland (lost a second term attempt in 1888, but was elected again in 1892), Benjamin Harrison, William H. Taft, Herbert Hoover, Gerald Ford and Jimmy Carter. See Appendix 16.

President's Domestic Council. An informal gathering of persons charged with the task of advising the U.S. President on domestic policies and the best solutions to domestic problems. The Council, which was established in 1970 by presidential order, is composed of—in addition to the President and the Vice President—cabinet members dealing with domestic problems and persons from outside governmental service who are particularly well qualified to render constructive advice. See Appendices 14, 15.

President's Foreign Intelligence Advisory Board. See INTELLIGENCE OVERSIGHT.

President's Intelligence Oversight Board. See INTELLIGENCE OVERSIGHT.

President's Message on the State of the Economy. See ECONOMIC MESSAGE, STATE OF THE UNION MESSAGE.

Presidential Agenda. See AGENDA.

Presidential Assassinations. In the history of the American presidency there have been four successful assassinations of U.S. Presidents; five other presidents were the objects of unsuccessful assassination attempts.

Abraham Lincoln (U.S. President 1861-1865) was shot on April 14, 1865, while attending a theater performance (Ford Theatre) in Washington, D.C., by John Wilkes Booth, an actor and disgruntled Southern confederate. Lincoln died on April 15, 1865, and was succeeded by Vice President Andrew Johnson.

James A. Garfield (U.S. President 1881-1881) was shot on July 2, 1881, while entering the Baltimore and Potomac railroad station in Washington, D.C. by a dissatisfied office seeker, Charles J. Huiteau. He died September 19, 1881, at Elberton, New Jersey. Vice President Chester Arthur succeeded to the presidency and the assassin was hanged on June 30, 1882.

William McKinley (U.S. President 1897-1901) was shot on September 6, 1901, by a dissatisfied immigrant and anarchist, Leon Czolgosz, while he was addressing a gathering of citizens at the Pan-American Exposition in Buffalo, New York. McKinley's last words were: "It is God's way. His will, not ours, be done." McKinley was succeeded by Theodore Roosevelt; the assassin was shot by police.

John F. Kennedy (U.S. President 1961-1963) was shot on November 22, 1963, in Dallas, Texas, while riding in a motorcade from Dallas to Fort Worth in an effort to help Dallas Democrats score a victory in an upcoming election and to strengthen their ranks. The assassin was Lee Harvey Oswald, a confused revolutionary without a revolutionary cause. Oswald was in turn assassinated, while being transferred from a Texas jail to another facility, by one Jack Ruby in retaliation for killing the president. Soon a commission headed by U.S. Chief Justice Earl Warren investigated the assassination and the possible conspiracy, but produced little evidence to the effect that a conspiracy was involved. Kennedy was succeeded by Vice President Lyndon Baines Johnson.

Unsuccessful Assassination Attempts:

Theodore Roosevelt (U.S. President 1901-1909), who on September 9, 1901, succeeded to the office after the assassination of William McKinley, was shot and seriously wounded on October 14, 1912, in Milwaukee, Wisconsin, by a greedy partisan.

Franklin D. Roosevelt (U.S. President 1933-1945) had two separate attempts made on his life: first, on February 15, 1933, when (as President-elect) he visited Miami, Florida, by an anarchist, Joseph Zangara. An alert bystander saved Roosevelt from the attempt, but the bullet hit and killed Roosevelt's companion, Mayor Anton J. Cermak of Chicago, instead. Zangara was electrocuted on March 20, 1933. A second attempt was organized by Nazi commando forces under the leadership of soldier-of-fortune Colonel Otto Skorzenny, who planned to kidnap and assassinate Roosevelt. The plan failed when the U.S. Intelligence Service obtained advance knowledge of this scheme.

Harry S. Truman (U.S. President 1944-1953) was attacked by two members of the Puerto Rican Nationalist movement, Griselio Torresola and Oscar Collazo, who on November 1, 1950, broke into Blair House (the temporary residence of the President while the White House was being refurbished) across the street from the White house and killed one guard, Pvt. Leslie Colleft, during the attempt. One of the would-be assassins, Torresola, was killed, while the other, Collazo, was convicted on March 3, 1951, for the murder of Pvt. Colleft. On June 24, 1952, President Truman commuted his death sentence to life imprisonment.

Gerald R. Ford (U.S. President 1974-1977), who succeeded Richard M. Nixon, who had resigned during the height of the Watergate controversy, had two separate attempts made on his life. First, in Sacramento, California, on September 5, 1975, by a revolutionary, Lynette Alice (Squeaky) Fromme; second, in San Francisco, California, on September 22, 1975, by a revolutionary activist, Sara Jane Moore. In this incident, the President was spared when an alert bystander, Oliver Sipple, moved him from the range of fire. Both would-be assassins are now serving prison terms.

Ronald W. Reagan (U.S. President 1981-1989), was shot at and wounded in the chest on a street in Washington, D.C., on 30 March 1981, while walking with his aides and Secret Service escort to his limousines after giving an address. He recovered shortly. When visited in the hospital by his wife and adviser, Nancy, he was well enough to crack a joke from his movie days when he played cowboys: "Sorry, honey, I forgot to duck." There was another incident involving former President Reagan when a protester tried to get hold of the microphone as Reagan was speaking during a ceremony in April 1992. In the course of this attack, the two-feet tall crystal trophy awarded to Reagan was smashed, but Reagan was not harmed. After order was restored, the former President stated with his usual dry wit: ". . . the man was probably a Democrat."

Legislation which makes the killing of a President, Vice-President, or any high government official a federal crime was not passed until after the assassination of President Kennedy in 1963. See Appendix 16.

Presidential Beauty Contest. See PRESIDENTIAL PRIMARY.

Presidential Commission on Intergovernmental Relations. Also known as the "Kestenbaum Commission", appointed by President Dwight D. Eisenhower in 1950 to undertake a thorough study of American federalism. Its report and the accompanying task force of studies comprise an important basis for much of the contemporary research in the field of American federalism. In 1955 the Commission on Intergovernmental relations issued a major report of 16 vols. titled—*A Report to the President.* The body subsequently appointed by President Eisenhower in 1958, was the Joint Committee on Intergovernmental Relations which was to study federalism exclusively, determine how to turn functions back to the states, and which should be turned back. Its two reports, in 1958 and 1959, made limited recommendations and explain why these recommendations are limited. The Commission concluded, however, on the basis of its findings that: "*. . . many State constitutions restrict the scope, effectiveness, and adaptability of state and local action. These self-imposed constitutional limitations make it difficult for many states to perform all of the services citizens require, and consequently have been the underlying cause of state and municipal pleas for Federal assistance.*" See ADVISORY COMMISSION ON INTERGOVERNMENTAL RELATIONS, JOINT COMMITTEE ON INTERGOVERNMENTAL RELATIONS, 1958 and 1959.

Presidential Decisiveness. One of the attributes of effective leadership that the American people like to see in their presidents, is decisiveness and willingness to fight for what is right. Most U.S. presidents have possessed that attribute and demonstrated it on occasion. As an example, during the Pullman strike in Chicago in 1894, when the delivery of mail (a federal responsibility) was threatened, President Grover Cleveland (1885-1889, 1893-1897) announced, "If it takes the entire army and navy of the United States to deliver a post card in Chicago, that card will be delivered." This political style is often referred to as "you do your damnedest." See PRESIDENTIAL REVIEW MEMORANDUM (PRM).

Presidential Elector. A person who is duly selected (by the presidential candidate, the party, or the voters in a primary or during a general election) to cast a ballot for the U.S. President and Vice President in the Electoral College following a general election. Electors must be qualified voters (see U.S. Constitution, Art. I, in Appendix 8) and are bound (morally and not legally) to vote in the Electoral College for the candidate who receives the plurality vote in their state during the national general election. (Majority vote in the College is required to elect the President and the Vice President.) But there have been "faithless electors" who have voted otherwise. Of the 17,692 electors who have cast votes between 1789 and 1968, only six disregarded the "instructions" of the voters, and five of these did so during a single election in 1948 when the Democratic Party was split into two major factions. (The Dixiecrats had emerged against Harry S. Truman.) During the 1972 election there were two faithless voters in the College: Roger L. MacBride of Charlottesville, Virginia (a Republican himself), cast his ballot for John Hospers of Oregon, a Libertarian party candidate, instead of for Richard M. Nixon; and Dr. Lloyd W. Bailey of Rocky Mount, North Carolina, cast his vote for George Wallace, the Governor of Alabama, instead of for Richard M. Nixon. See DISTRIBUTION OF ELECTORAL VOTES IN THE UNITED STATES in Appendix 21, DIXIECRATS, ELECTORAL COLLEGE, HAYES-TILDEN DISPUTE, UNPLEDGED ELECTOR.

Presidential Finding. See COVERT ACTION.

Presidential Government. A type of representative government in which the president serves as the real head of the state and of the government, and is independently elected for that specific office. As a rule, he also serves as the chief administrator, the chief executive, the chief policy-maker, the chief diplomat, the commander-in-chief of the armed forces, the chief proposer of legislation, and the leader of his party. An additional feature of the presidential system is that the president may not dissolve the legislature, nor can the legislature remove him from office upon a vote of non-confidence. He may serve his tenure undisturbed unless removed by impeachment. (The oldest presidential systems in continuous existence are those of the United States and Mexico.) See PRESIDENTIAL REVIEW MEMORANDUM (PRM).

Presidential Hopeful. In American electoral politics, one who seeks the presidency by entering a primary election, hoping for a party nomination. Once the two major parties, the Republicans and the Democrats, nominate their candidates, the "hopefuls" fade away, because, traditionally, minor party nominees (there are about 20-30 of them, some nominated by their wives or just themselves) have no chance, neither do independent candidates.

Presidential Impeachment. See IMPEACHMENT.

Presidential Order. See EXECUTIVE ORDER.

Presidential Pardon. Under the authority of the U.S. Constitution, Article II., the U.S. president may pardon anyone for the wrongful commission or neglectful omission of acts. Gerald R. Ford was the first U.S. president to grant pardon to a former U.S. president; he pardoned Richard M. Nixon for his Watergate cover-up and improprieties while in office. Full and unconditional pardon was granted and signed by President Ford on September 8, 1974. On September 16, 1974, President Ford proposed conditional amnesty (upon completion of two years public service work) for all draft evaders of the Vietnam War period, but made no decision on deserters (about 100,000). President Jimmy Carter made no move, however, to pardon his nephew who was serving a long prison term (in the Soledad Prison in California) for two armed robbery convictions. Granting pardons has varied from president to president. The percentage of pardons granted out of the total applied for is as follows: F. D. Roosevelt, 22%; Harry S. Truman, 40%; D. D. Eisenhower, 26%; J. F. Kennedy, 36%; L B. Johnson, 25%; R. M. Nixon, 37%; G. Ford, 47%; J. Carter, 34%; R. Reagan, 22%; and G. Bush, 21%. As for state offenders, governors in 23 states can grant full and unconditional pardon; in 20 states they share that power with other state officials; and in 7 states they have no such powers. Pardons differ in degree and scope: an unconditional pardon exonerates the offender without any reservations or conditions; a conditional pardon may be confined to a certain period of time or be contingent on certain acts by the grantee; a general pardon, also called amnesty, covers all parties to a given offense. A commutation of sentence shortens the grantees time of confinement. All pardons do not necessarily erase criminal records, or restore political and civil rights (e.g., the right to vote, to be elected, to serve on a jury), and they are, as a rule, considered on a case-by-case basis. Pardons are ordinarily acts of mercy, except in cases where offenders were wrongly accused, and they allow recipients to enter restricted professions, such law, medicine, or other regulated trade. When President Ford granted a "full, free, and absolute" pardon on 8 September 1974 to former President Nixon following the Watergate scandal, this was rather unusual, because President Nixon had resigned, he was never tried and convicted of any crime, and his crime was considered purely political. See PRESIDENTIAL REVIEW MEMORANDUM (PRM).

Presidential Preeminence. The notion prevalent in American political philosophy as it pertains to the U.S. President whereby, since the President determines his administration's policy, after that policy is approved by his staff, he is entitled to active and tacit support by all members of his team. Those who are unable to agree with the President's policy, are expected either to resign or to remain silent. The President may also ask such critics to resign (e.g., the McClellan-Lincoln, Roosevelt-Wallace, and Truman-MacArthur disputes). Also by courtesy if not by law, presidential policies are expected to be supported by his administrative apparatus. See DEMOCRATIC CENTRALISM.

Presidential Preferential Primary. See PRIMARY ELECTION.

Presidential Radio Call-In. See MEET THE PEOPLE TRIP.

Presidential Review Memorandum (PRM). The opinions and comments submitted to the President of the United States by his assistants, pertaining to important issues, which may contain suggestions on policy actions and alternatives.

Presidential Style. See POLITICAL STYLE.

Presidential Succession. There are four major documents which pertain to presidential succession: (1) The Presidential Succession Act of 1792 established an order of succession after the Vice President; the President Pro Tempore of the U.S. Senate, followed by the Speaker of the U.S. House of Representatives, to serve until a new election; (2) The Presidential Succession Act of 1886 turned the order of succession after the Vice President to the members of the cabinet, according to the date the cabinet department had been established, beginning with the Secretary of State; (3) the Presidential Succession Act of 1947 returned the order of succession again to the Speaker of the House of Representatives followed by the President Pro Tempore of the U.S. Senate; and (4) Amendment XXV allows the U.S. President to nominate a Vice President, subject to confirmation by the Congress. U.S. President Gerald R. Ford (1974-1977) was the first U.S. Vice President selected under the provisions of Amendment XXV, and in 1974 succeeded to the presidency upon the resignation of Richard M. Nixon. Amendment XXV also provides for the vacating of the office of President through disability. (See U.S. Constitution in Appendix 8.) The law on succession to the Presidency of July 18, 1947, amended September 9, 1965, and October 15, 1966, reads as follows: "If by reason of death, resignation, removal from office, inability, or failure to qualify there is neither a President nor Vice President to discharge the powers and duties of the office of President, then the Speaker of the House of Representatives shall upon his resignation as Speaker and as Representative, act as President. The same rule shall apply in the case of the death, resignation, removal from office, or inability of an individual acting as President. If at the time when a Speaker is to begin the discharge of the powers and duties of the office of President there is no Speaker, or the Speaker fails to qualify as Acting President, then the President pro tempore of the Senate, upon his resignation as President pro tempore and as Senator, shall act as President. An individual acting as President shall continue to act until the expiration of the then current Presidential term, except that (1) if his discharge of the powers and duties of the office is founded in whole or in part on the failure of both the President-elect and the Vice President-elect to quality, then he shall act only until a President or Vice President qualifies, and (2) if his discharge of the powers and duties of the office is founded in whole or in part on the disability of the President or Vice President, then he shall act only until the removal of the disability of one of such individuals. If, by reason of death, resignation, removal from office, or failure to qualify, there is no President pro tempore to act as President, then the officer of the United States who is highest on the following list, and who is not under disability to discharge the powers and duties of president, shall act as President: Secy. of State, Secy. of the Treasury, Secy. of Defense, Attorney General, Secy. of the Interior, Secy. of Agriculture, Secy. of Commerce, Secy. of Labor, Secy. of Health, Education and Welfare, Secy. of Housing and Urban Development and Secy. of Transportation."

Presidential Tenure. See FOURTH-TERMITE.

Presidential Term of Office. Four-year tenure; until 1937, it commenced on March 4, at noon, and since 1937 it commences on January 20 at noon.

Presidential Transition. A time span of several months, beginning with the election of a new president, continuing through the actual changeover in January 20 and lasting approximately two months thereafter until all the offices have been filled and the staffs of the new President have taken over. Under the Transition Act of 1973, the President-elect receives the same information and briefings on policy matters as the President. Under the Secret Service Act of 1964, the President-elect and his family, as well as his immediate staff, receive full protection by the Federal Protection Service; and under the former Presidents Act of 1966, the outgoing President and his staff receive certain benefits which allow them to continue their often very active status. Presidential transition can be of two kinds: (1) external transition, decided at the ballot boxes; and (2) internal transition, in case of an assassination, death, or resignation (e.g., in the case of Richard M. Nixon in 1974).

Presidential Veto. According to U.S. Senate Library sources, the following U.S. Presidents exercised the veto power, both regular and pocket veto, as follows:

Presidential Vetoes 1789-1991 (as of February 1992)

Presidents	Regular Vetoes	Pocket Vetoes	Total Vetoes	Vetoes Overridden
George Washington	2	-	2	-
John Adams	-	-	-	-
Thomas Jefferson	-	-	-	-
James Madison	5	2	7	-
James Monroe	1	-	1	-
John Q. Adams	-	-	-	-
Andrew Jackson	5	7	12	-
Martin Van Buren	-	1	1	-
William Harrison	-	-	-	-
John Tyler	6	4	10	1
James Polk	2	1	3	-
Zachary Taylor	-	-	-	-
Millard Fillmore	-	-	-	-
Franklin Pierce	9	-	9	5
James Buchanan	4	3	7	-
Abraham Lincoln	2	5	7	-
Andrew Johnson	21	8	29	15
Ulysses S. Grant	45	48	93	4
Rutherford B. Hayes	12	1	13	1
James A. Garfield	-	-	-	-
Chester Arthur	4	8	12	1
Grover Cleveland	304	110	414	2
Benjamin Harrison	19	25	44	1
Grover Cleveland	42	128	170	5
William McKinley	6	36	42	-
Theodore Roosevelt	42	40	82	1
William H. Taft	30	9	39	1
Woodrow Wilson	33	11	44	6
Warren Harding	5	1	6	-
Calvin Coolidge	20	30	50	4
Herbert Hoover	21	16	37	3
Franklin Roosevelt	372	263	635	9
Harry S. Truman	180	70	250	12
Dwight Eisenhower	73	108	181	2
John F. Kennedy	12	9	21	-
Lyndon B. Johnson	16	14	30	-
Richard M. Nixon	26	17	43	7
Gerald R. Ford	48	18	66	12
Jimmy Carter	13	18	31	2
Ronald Reagan	39	39	78	9
George Bush	17	8	25	-
Total	1,455	1,059	2,491	103

See POCKET VETO, PRESIDENTIAL REVIEW MEMORANDUM (PRM), VETO.

Presidential War Powers Act of 1973. See WAR POWERS ACT, VIETNAMIZATION.

Presiding Officer of the United States Senate. See MISTER PRESIDENT.

Press Secretary to the President. Usually a skillful and knowledgeable image-maker for a given administration, one of the closest assistants to the President, and his official external spokesman. See PRESIDENTIAL REVIEW MEMORANDUM (PRM).

Pressure Group. A group of persons involved in influencing the policies of the government for the purpose of achieving certain goals desired by particular organizations or interest groups. Pressure groups are usually non-permanent and directed toward the achievement of a single goal at a time.

Presumed Innocent Until Proven Guilty. An ancient principle of administration of justice which considers one innocent of crime unless proven otherwise (e.g., in a court of law, through confession, or by a trial by jury). In some cases (e.g., in the United States) guilt must be established beyond the shadow of a doubt. See BURDEN OF PROOF, U.S. CONSTITUTION.

Preussenfieber. See GERMAN UNIFICATION.

Preventive Diplomacy. An agenda slogan introduced at the Security Council of the United Nations on 31 January 1992, calling upon countries, mainly the United States and Russia, which had agreed to cut their nuclear arsenals roughly in half, to work closely with the United Nations, through "preventive diplomacy" to retain peace and security everywhere. While addressing the Council (where, among others, U.S. President George Bush, Russian President Boris Yeltsin, and British Prime Minister John Major were present), French President François Mitterand stated that "the law of the jungle" had come to an end and it was now time, through "preventive diplomacy," to intensify the building of a "New World Order." Following the Council meeting, Russian President Boris Nikolayevitch Yeltsin conferred on 1 February 1992, with President Bush at Camp David mainly on reduction of armaments, both nuclear and conventional, and on issues of peace among the members of the Commonwealth.

Preventive War. See ACT OF WAR, PREEMPTION.

Price Commission. See NIXON'S ECONOMIC POLICIES.

Pricetag Politics. See POCKETBOOK POLITICS.

Prima Facie. In the Latin language, "as it appears on the face," "first impression," or "as it appears from the first impression."

Primary Election. Ever since the State of Oregon introduced the first presidential primary election in 1910, many states now hold such primaries, usually between January and July of an election year, during which voters of one or all parties (depending on whether a closed or an open primary is held) vote for their preference for the President (and the Vice President in New Hampshire) to determine the strengths and the weaknesses of the candidates. Primaries help to eliminate weak candidates or parties. Some states use this occasion for the election of other state officials and delegates to national party conventions. During the 1992 primaries, for example, Californians, in addition to a candidate for the President, selected 348 Democratic and 201 Republican pledged delegates to national conventions; Ohio selected 151 pledged Democratic delegates; Michigan and Illinois 295 pledged Democratic delegates; Florida, Massachusetts, Missouri and Texas. The "Super Tuesday" states selected a total of 783 pledged Democratic delegates and the Republican 500 delegates. (The "Super Tuesday" states are: Hawaii, Louisiana, Mississippi, Oklahoma, Rhode Island, Tennessee, Texas, Delaware, Florida and Missouri). The states where primary elections are authorized (but some states choose not to hold such primaries during a given election year or like Hawaii hold caucuses), are: Alaska, Arkansas, California, Colorado, Connecticut, Delaware, Florida, Hawaii, Illinois, Indiana, Iowa, Kentucky, Maine, Maryland, Massachusetts, Michigan, Minnesota, Missouri, Nebraska, Nevada, New Hampshire, New Jersey, New Mexico, North Carolina, Ohio, Oregon, Pennsylvania, Utah, Virginia, Washington, West Virginia, and Wisconsin. Under the Republican rules, "winner takes all, and in order to earn delegates, a Republican challenger must win in a particular congressional district. Under the Democrat's rules, a candidate who gets at least 15 percent of the vote in a congressional district earns delegates. According to authors Earl and Merle Black (*The Vital*

South), during the Super Tuesday primaries in the south, there are, among others, two important groups on whom the candidates concentrate: the so-called "Bubbas," the men, and the "bubbarettes," women, who are transplants from the North, holding lower-level jobs in the South and the "yellow-dog" Democrats, living mainly in large cities with large student and university faculty populations. In Florida, there are the so-called "condo commandos," the retired people, many of them wealthy Jews, who live in large condominium communities. There are proposals for a single, national primary, but states can't agree on the date it should be held. See COMMISSION ON PRESIDENTIAL NOMINATION AND PARTY STRUCTURE, WHITE PRIMARY.

Primary Party Organization. The smallest unit or cell (of at least three members) of the Communist Party of the former Soviet Union (CPSU), that had been set up in factories, schools, the armed forces, or even aboard vessels on the high seas. See COMMUNIST PARTY OF THE SOVIET UNION (CPSU).

Prime Lending Rate. See PRIME RATE.

Prime Minister. The "first minister," serving as the head of the government under parliamentary systems of government (e.g., in England, Canada, Australia, and New Zealand). His functions are similar to those of the Chancellor of the German Federal Republic (West Germany) and of the Premier of the Soviet Union. See PREMIER.

Prime Minister of Japanese Business. See KEIDANREN.

Prime Rate. A designated rate of interest, regulated by the Federal Reserve System (the Fed), which commercial banks charge for loans to their best customers, often for short-term loans. Normally, when inflation goes up, the Fed raises the prime rate to offset it. Also known as the Prime Lending Rate.

Primus Inter Pares. In the Latin language, "first among equals."

Prince, the. See MACHIAVELLIANISM.

Principality. A state or territory ruled by one with the title of a prince or princess (e.g., Monaco, a semi-sovereign state under the jurisdiction of the Republic of France.)

Principles of American Constitutional System. The American constitutional system rests on nine principal doctrines all incorporated into the U.S. Constitution (see Appendix 8); (1) Popular Sovereignty—all governmental authority is derived from the consent of the governed, the voters, who periodically review the policies of the government and those who govern through elections as well as through voluntary participation in political and governmental processes (a popular review); (2) Federalism—governmental powers are not exclusively concentrated within a single level of government, but are territorially distributed among the units of the federation (the states), which in turn share ruling powers (according to the principle of an autonomy) with units of local government; (3) Republicanism—the people being the locus of all sovereign powers (popular sovereignty) but not being able to rule directly themselves (e.g., under a direct democracy), they "lease" or "grant" some of these powers (e.g., to make laws and to execute them) to worthy and trusted individuals (either elective or appointive) for a period prescribed by law (e.g., four years for the U.S. President, two years for the members of the U.S. House of Representatives, six years for U.S. Senators, and usually four years for state governors, mayors, and sheriffs). If those powers are misused, the voters may take their powers back by recalling (or impeaching) public officials or replacing them on election day. Under the doctrine of republicanism, no individual may hold public office indefinitely (see Amendment XXII to the U.S. Constitution, Appendix 8), nor can power be transferred hereditarily as in a monarchy, which the Constitution forbids (including the use or acceptance of titles of nobility); (4) Limitation of Powers—the two principal levels of government: the federal (or national) and those of the states possess certain exclusive powers and share others among themselves (see U.S. Constitution, Art. I, Sec. 8 and Amendment X in Appendix 8) on a contractual basis (federalism). The U.S. Supreme Court serves as the final arbiter in matters of controversy or any doubt; (5) Separation of Powers—governmental powers are also distributed functionally between three separate branches of government: the legislative (Congress), the executive (the President and the administration), and judicial (the U.S. Supreme Court and the inferior federal courts), each branch being granted a limited control over the others; (6) Checks and Balances—by virtue of having limited authority to check upon each other, the three branches of government may modify each other's actions and activities (e.g., congressional law may be vetoed by the President; the U.S. Supreme Court may declare a congressional law or presidential order unconstitutional; the Congress may impeach judicial officers or refuse to increase their remuneration—salaries; the U.S. President, by virtue of his power of appointment of judicial officers, may influence the behavior of judges); (7) Judicial Review—the judicature (the U.S. Supreme Court, see *Marbury v. Madison*) is empowered to decide on the constitutionality of laws and executive acts as well as to serve as the final judge in matters of applicability of law to facts (usually upon appeal); (8) the Bill of Rights—the "price" that was "paid" by the Federalists (Hamiltonians) to the Anti-federalists (Jeffersonians) for the acceptance of the Constitution, and which enumerates certain basic rights of persons (whether citizens or not), without clearly stated corresponding obligations; and (9) Civilian Supremacy—only civilian persons (non-military) may utilize the sovereign powers of the people in governing them, including war powers (vested in Congress) and military command (vested in the President). See AUTONOMY, DILLON'S RULE, POPULAR SOVEREIGNTY.

Principles of Understanding. A set of rules, usually agreed upon by parties to a conference, that are observed in diplomatic or military negotiations among states and armed forces; The rules set parameters, determining the scope, method, and topics of an agenda. Also, as a rule, they include an understanding on a course of action in the case of inability to proceed, and an agreement on revealing the outcome through a public announcement. Also known as "rules of understanding." During the Vietnam-United States negotiations to end the war in Vietnam, many conferences were held, mostly in Switzerland, between North Vietnamese Vice Premier Li Doc Tho and the U.S. envoy, Dr. Henry Kissinger. Most of the meetings were never announced; Dr. Kissinger was shuttling back and forth between various meeting places in the world and Washington—a period known as "shuttle diplomacy." The most difficult and disagreeable issue to resolve in these negotiations was the size and shape of the conference table. The North Vietnamese and the Viet Cong demanded that only the United States and themselves be placed at the main table, while the South Vietnamese were to be at an adjacent, kitchen-type table. Since this was not acceptable to the South Vietnamese, the debate over the table extended over a year; meanwhile about 20,000 Americans and almost 185,000 Vietnamese, most of them regular soldiers and guerrilla Viet Cong, died in the jungle fighting each other. The issue of the table was never resolved; all conferences were held bilaterally rather than multilaterally, usually on couches with small side tables.

Prior Restraint. The principle that one's behavior can be modified in one of two ways: (1) by preventing one from committing a certain act, or (2) by inflicting punishment after that act is committed. Under a totalitarian system, everything is forbidden unless clearly allowed by the authority of the state; in a democracy, everything is allowed, unless forbidden by law. In the case of the Pentagon Papers, the U.S. Supreme Court ruled that the government could not (as the U.S. Justice Department wished) prevent the *New York Times* from publishing secret government documents, but it could prosecute the paper for doing so after the papers were published, e.g., on the grounds of illegal possession of classified information. (In this case, the secret was mainly the incompetence of bureaucrats in handling major policy matters.) See GAG RULE, *FREEDMAN V. MARYLAND* in Appendix 48, PENTAGON PAPERS.

Priority. An authoritative decision about the allocation of human and material resources on the basis of recognized needs (e.g., acute unemployment), as determined by persons with power and authority to implement certain policies or initiate certain programs now while deferring others ("first things first"); a determination to pursue policies or programs and to deploy human and material resources according to recognized urgency and necessity. In his "State of the Union Message" on January 19, 1978, U.S. President Jimmy Carter outlined U.S. national priorities as follows: ENERGY—"Almost five years after the oil embargo dramatized the problem, we still do not have a national energy program. (This) undermines our national interest both at home and abroad." TAXES—"We can make our tax laws fairer; ... we can—and we will—reduce the tax burden on American citizens by $25 billion." JOBS—"I am asking for a substantial increase in funds for public jobs for our young people, and I am also recommending that the Congress continue the public sector employment programs at more than twice the level of a year ago." BUDGET—"Next year the budget deficit will be only slightly less than this fiscal year—but one-third of the deficit is due to the necessary tax cuts I have proposed." INFLATION—"I am ... asking a voluntary program holding wage and price increases during 1978 below the average increases of the last two years." CIVIL SERVICE—"I consider civil service reform to be absolutely vital. (This reorganization plan) will provide greater management flexibility and better rewards for better performance without compromising job security." MIDDLE EAST—"We are contributing our good offices to maintaining the momentum of the current negotiations . . . ." PANAMA CANAL—"The treaties are to the clear advantage of ourselves, the Panamanians and the other users of the canal."

Privacy. See RIGHT TO PRIVACY.

Privacy Act of 1974. In order to rectify some administrative abuses from the past, Congress passed a freedom of information law, the Privacy Act, which was signed by President Gerald R. Ford on December 31, 1974, and took effect on September 27, 1975. It requires federal agencies to allow individual persons to examine investigation records that may be kept about them and, in case of discrepancies and inaccuracies found, to request that proper corrections be made. (There are approximately 6,000 different record systems kept about individual persons in the United States.) See FREEDOM OF INFORMATION LAW, RIGHT TO PRIVACY.

Private Bill. A legislative measure which may be brought up by a single legislator but is not sponsored by the government or a political party, nor is it national in scope. Private bills in the United States House of Representatives are placed on the Private Calendar and in the Senate on the Calendar of Business. See JURE GESTIONIS.

Private Calendar. See PRIVATE BILL.

Private Diplomacy. The practice of informally exchanging views, opinions, or information between foreign diplomats (with or without authorization by the governments they represent), which may lead to or become instrumental in solving some international crisis. See DIPLOMACY, PUBLIC DIPLOMACY.

Private International Law. The body of laws which regulate matters of a personal nature between a citizen of one state and a foreign government. The term "Conflict of Laws" is often used to distinguish Private International Law from Public International Law.

Private Law. See JURE GESTIONIS, PRIVATE BILL.

Privatization. The practice, opposite of nationalization, of selling public property or enterprises, which were nationalized in the past for reasons of national security (e.g., banking, power plants, mining, transport, or steel production), to be operated by private persons on a market supply/demand principle instead of by an inefficient government bureaucracy. Also, the practice of contracting certain public functions to private enterprises (e.g., road construction, refuse removal and waste disposal), and even the management of prisons and private courts. During and after W.W.II, many industrialized states nationalized major industries and public services, but the trend was reversed during the 1980s particularly in countries like Great Britain (especially under Prime Minister Margaret Thatcher, 1979-1990), the United States, France, Germany, Japan, Mexico, Italy, and even in socialist-Marxist economies such as the former Soviet Union, the Peoples Republic of China, and the East European states. See FRENCH SOCIALIST PARTY, NATIONALIZATION.

Privatization Through Restructuring. A concept developed in 1991, by the new managers of the state enterprises in Poland whereby unproductive state-owned establishments would no longer be sold out, but would receive assistance. According to the Polish International Development Agency, the government will "hire Western managers to reform the companies with the lure of fees now and equity later for managers who succeed." Following the dissolution of the communist government and the rush to privatization, many valuable assets had been sold, often to foreign and hostile owners, at a very low cost.

Privilege. A personalized capacity to do or to refrain from doing something; the capacity to enjoy certain benefits because of past services, inheritance, birth, or conquest; a capacity to receive, grant, or withdraw benefits which is not commonly shared by others; the capacity to act inside or outside a legal framework; or one's ability to hold certain positions of trust or benefit conditionally, not as a right derived from a situation defined by law. See RIGHTS, RIGHT TO PRIVACY.

Privileged Bill. Any legislative proposal in the U.S. House of Representatives which is sent directly to a particular committee, bypassing, as most often is the case, the Rules Committee (Committee on the Rules).

Privileges and Immunities Clause. A provision in the U.S. Constitution (Article 4) which guarantees U.S. citizens of one state the privileges and immunities of every other state in the union. See Appendix 8.

Privy Council. A body of advisers selected by the British Monarch to inform and advise him (or her) on political, administrative, and judicial matters.

PRM. See POPULAR REPUBLICAN MOVEMENT, PRESIDENTIAL REVIEW MEMORANDUM.

Pro Bono Publico. In the Latin language, "in the public interest" or "for the good of the public."

Pro Forma. In the Latin language, "for the sake of," "as a matter of procedure," or "as a matter of formality."

Pro-Life Movement. See MARCH FOR LIFE.

Pro Tempore. In the Latin language, "for the time being."

Probable Cause. In law and criminal justice, a person can be detained in spite of the lack of some tangible, prima facie material evidence, merely on the presumption that a crime or an offense has been committed. Since every duly sworn officer of the law is also an officer of the court, the benefit of the doubt rests with the arresting officer by virtue of authority, and by the presumption that the officer acts in good faith in the performance of her/his duty.

Probate Court. A court with original jurisdiction which considers the validity of wills and the disposal of property of deceased persons, assigns executors and administrators to carry out the provisions of a will, and provides for administration and disposition of property left by persons who had executed no will (intestate).

Procedural Question. See UNITED NATIONS ORGANIZATION: SECURITY COUNCIL, Appendix 75.

Procedural Right. The right of an individual to have his case determined before a judicial or administrative tribunal or to have a grievance heard by a proper authority as provided for by statutory or constitutional laws. See BILL OF RIGHTS in Appendix 8, MIRANDA CARD, PRIVILEGE, Appendix 48-53.

Process. As applied to politics, a certain interaction of variables in time and space, or a change within a single variable; also, a certain sequence of logical events or actions which are somehow related and which may generate desired outcomes.

Process Technology. See HIGH TECHNOLOGY.

Proclamation. An official pronouncement made by the chief of state or of government which may have general application and may be binding upon a state or upon a given community.

Procurator. Prosecuting attorney (e.g., in the former USSR), Poland, and other Napoleonic code systems.

Procurator-General. The prosecuting attorney or attorney-general of the former USSR, of any Union Republic or of an autonomous Republic in the former Soviet Union, Poland, and other Napoleonic code systems. See PROCURATOR.

Producer Economics. According to Professor Lester C. Thurow (*Head to Head: The Coming Economic Battle Among Japan, Europe, and America*), the Japanese economy can be characterized as a "producer economy," where emphasis is placed on producing more and consuming less; where a higher standard of living "at work may even be more important than a higher standard of living at home;" where esteem is not bought" but earned; where "consumption and leisure are not substitutes for power;" and where the desire to build, to win as a group or as a team rather than as an individual outranks the desire for personal leisure and consumption. Professor Thurow calls the American economy a "consumer economy," where "more consumption and more leisure are the sole economic elements of human satisfaction. Economic activity in Japan is a team effort and the profits are shared in various forms, but mainly on more team efforts to build even more, even better, and to win. While American enterprises are primarily profit-maximizers, Japanese enterprises are empire-builders. One of the rewards for a Japanese employee is lifetime employment and the employers' (or managers') effort to see that the employee succeeds in every endeavor of human life, at work as well as in private life. It is not unusual for a Japanese employer to serve as a match-maker in intra-company marriages and even to assist a new employee with living accommodations, insurance, and other benefits, from cradle to grave. See COMPARATIVE ADVANTAGE, JAPANESE POLITICAL CULTURE, PRODUCT CYCLE, UNILATERAL GLOBAL KEYNESIANISM.

Product Cycle. Refers to the way control of a newly developed product may move from the inventor and original manufacturer to another manufacturer who is able to produce it more cheaply. (Inventors are always individuals or a small group of individuals; rarely is anything worthwhile invented by a committee, with the possible exception of the camel, which was intended by the committee to be a horse.) If the original inventor and manufacturer is not alert, if he rests on his laurels and becomes dizzy with success, another manufacturer will improve the product and produce it more cheaply. The manufacturer may do this by moving to another location or country to seek cheaper labor, less restrictive zoning laws, and favorable tax incentives. Areas that are depressed welcome anyone who proposes to improve their well-being. Today's high-tech, becomes less-tech tomorrow, and low-tech the next day; the product is produced in a cheaper and better manner, and the original inventor and manufacturer may lose the competitive advantage forever. Very often the labor force producing the original product becomes complacent, hoping that the relatively high income will last forever, and neglects constant retraining for better and cheaper production; in time, that labor will be deprived employment and income. "Those who can make a product cheaper can take it away from the inventor," points out Professor Thurow. Constant retraining and reeducation is essential in high-tech economy—it becomes a continuous and never ending process. However, if prison buildings and facilities grow faster than schools and educational facilities, some will turn to jingoistic sloganeering instead, assuming that a once strong economy will remain so forever. That obviously is not the case. See AMERICA BASHING, COMPARATIVE ADVANTAGE, JAPAN BASHING, UNILATERAL GLOBAL KEYNESIANISM.

Productivity. As per U.S. Congressional Budget Office, "average real output per unit of input. Labor productivity is average real output per hour of labor. The growth of labor productivity is defined as growth of real output that is not explained by growth of labor input alone. Total factor productivity is average real output per unit of combined labor and capital inputs. The growth of total factor productivity is defined as the growth of real output that is not explained by growth of labor and capital. Labor productivity and total factor productivity differ in that increases in capital per worker would raise labor productivity, but not total factor productivity." See QUALITY CIRCLE.

Professional Teaching Engineers for the United States (PROTEUS). Recognizing the downsizing of the American Armed Forces and the surplus of highly-trained, highly-disciplined, and highly-motivated and dedicated personnel, particularly in the sciences, and recognizing also the shortage of teachers of mathematics and science in American schools, Norman R. Augustine, chairman of the board and chief executive officer of Martin Marietta Corporation of Bethesda, Maryland, has advanced a very realistic and easily realizable program of transferring surplus military personnel to school faculties. The Greek god Proteus was capable of changing into the shape of anything by merely applying his strong and creative will; similar benefits can be brought to young Americans who seem to encounter problems in their mastery of mathematics and science.

Profumo Affair. See SEXPIONAGE.

Program Planning. According to author J. Davis (*Program Planning*), a mode of planning which "refers to work within an organizational context aimed at forecasting future conditions (e.g., changes in workload, demand for services, available revenue, possible future developments in technology,) and designing the appropriate response." The process "begins with an assessment and evaluation of the status quo—that is, where are we now? What are we doing, or delivering to whom? With what effects, or, with the present resources and organizational structure, what is being accomplished?" See PLANNING.

Progressive Citizens of America. A group of left-wing organizations which together supported Henry A. Wallace for the U.S. Presidency in 1948.

Progressive Orthodoxy. See SECOND BILL OF RIGHTS.

Progressive Party. A conglomeration of Republican factions which supported Robert M. LaFollette for the U.S. Presidency in 1911.

Progressive Tax. See NEGATIVE INCOME TAX.

Progressivism. See POLITICAL PROGRESSIVISM.

Prohibited Powers. Powers which a national, state, or local government may not exercise because of statutory or constitutional prohibitions. See U.S. Constitution in Appendix 8.

Prohibition Party. The third oldest political party in continuous existence in the United States (after the Democratic and the Republican parties). It was established in 1869 primarily to implement prohibition of the manufacturing, distribution, and consumption of alcoholic beverages, which it succeeded in doing by 1919, when Amendment XVIII to the U.S. Constitution was ratified. This law was subsequently repealed in 1933 (Amendment XXI) because it was too impractical and difficult to implement. Its 1976 platform contained such issues of interest to the party as abortion, socialized medicine, forced busing, and communism—all of which it opposed; it favored constitutional limits on taxes and loans, and foreign aid to friendly countries only; the party polled 15,900 votes. (In the same year, the Democratic party polled 40,825,839 votes, and the Republican party, 39,147,770 votes). On October 23, 1977, the party announced that after 108 years it had decided to change its name (and its image) to National Statesman party, hoping that this could improve its vote-getting capability. (The other names proposed for the re-naming of the party were "Good Government party" and "Family Protection party.") Its monthly publication is *The National Statesman*. See WOMAN'S CHRISTIAN TEMPERANCE UNION (WCTU).

Project Notification and Review System. Refers to the procedure to be followed in the application for federal grants as outlined in Circular A-95 issued by the Office of Management and Budget in July 1969. Under this system, applicants for federal grants must notify the local planning commission and the state planning agency and secure their approval of the grant project. Prepared by the Office of Management and Budget at the office of the U.S. President which issued the so-called "Project Notification and Review System." Circular A-95 which established the procedure to be following in application for Federal grants. The applicant for grant, must, among other things, notify the local planning commission and the state planning agency about the intent for the application which serves as a means their input and whose approval is necessary in order to avoid detrimental impact which the financed project could have on the local environment. The circular was issued in July 1969. The Project Notification and Review System is an early warning system designed to facilitate coordination of state, local and regional planning, and the regional planning commission serve as clearinghouses. See PLANNING.

Project Truth. In order to counter Soviet and other hostile, anti-American disinformation and propaganda during the Cold War period, the United States set up an Advisory Committee on Public Diplomacy to oversee such countermeasures as "Soviet Propaganda Alert," a monthly analysis of Soviet propaganda and misinformation themes and targets; to prepare and disseminate information refuting hostile propaganda, and to maintain a news feature service, called "Dateline America," in cooperation with the United States Information Agency (USIA) and other federal agencies. The program was particularly intensive during the Reagan administrations (1981-1989).

Proletariat. As defined by Karl Marx, the working class in capitalistic systems of economy. In a broad sense, a transnational class bound together by proletarian solidarity. See MARXISM.

Promulgate. To announce publicly or to publish some important information—such as a new law, a judicial decision, an executive order, or an international treaty—which is meant to become official and binding. See CONGRESSIONAL RECORD.

Propaganda. The practice of disseminating factual information, usually about the government and its policies, for the purpose of educating and informing; a mass dissemination (e.g., through radio, print, and the spoken word) of information about public matters; also, a pack of lies disseminated for the purpose of influencing the opinions of the public. "White" Propaganda denotes information slightly slanted but based on actual truthful facts whereas "Black" propaganda consists of falsehoods. See PROPAGANDA ASSETS INVENTORY.

Propaganda and Agitation Bureau. In the Russian language, "Byuro Prapagandy y Agitatsyi," or, short, PROPAGIT. One of the organs of the Central Committee of the Communist Party of the former Soviet Union (CC CPSU) that was charged with the dissemination of party policies and of communism in general. See COMMUNIST PARTY OF THE SOVIET UNION (CPSU).

Propaganda Assets Inventory (PAI). A pro-American propaganda organization owned and operated by the U.S. Central Intelligence Agency (CIA), under the supervision of Frank G. Wisner, a CIA operative, and referred to as "Wisner's Wurlitzer." PAI was set up during the 1950's to combat communist propaganda around the world with the aid of about 800 different public information individuals and organizations, including college and university professors, journalists, writers, traveling business people, and Radio Free Europe (RFE). One of its publications intended for the dissemination of misinformation abroad, the *Quest*, which employed American and foreign journalists and intelligence officers, was closed down in 1961 on orders from the U.S. Ambassador to India, Professor John Kenneth Galbraith, but a network of similar journals and operations continued, as was disclosed in 1967 and in more recent publications. "Almost at the push of a button," according to press accounts, "the 'Wurlitzer' became the means of orchestrating, in almost any language of the world, whatever tune the CIA was in a mood to hear." The CIA was also involved in the practice of bribing heads of state and/or government, according to *The Washington Post* February 18, 23, 25, and 27, 1977; the CIA made payments of millions of dollars to Jordan's King Hussein and Zaire's Sese Seko Mobuto, for their support of America's aims and objectives in the respective areas. A Senate investigation (by the Church Committee) has also revealed that the CIA planned assassination of leaders who pursued policies and supported causes that were anti-American, such as Fidel Castro of Cuba. (Castro was to have been assassinated by a young woman who was to befriend him, feed him with a chemical that would cause him to lose his hair, and then assassinate him. The young woman changed her mind and refused to carry out the plan. Also known as the "Cuban Connection." PAI's mission was to prepare the ground for that event.) See CENTRAL INTELLIGENCE AGENCY (CIA), SEXPIONAGE, SEXPOLITICS, Appendices 32-33.

Propaganda Center. In the Russian language, "punkt agitatsyi," or simply, AGITPUNKT. Centers set up by the Committees of the Communist Party of the former Soviet Union (CPSU) throughout the country for the purpose of disseminating information on the policies and the activities of the party. Such centers are activated mainly before national elections, before and after party congresses or plenary sessions of the Central Committee of the party when important decisions are made. The main objective of such centers is to solicit broad support of the masses for the policies of the party and of the government. See COMMUNIST PARTY OF THE SOVIET UNION (CPSU).

Propagit. See PROPAGANDA AND AGITATION BUREAU.

Property as Authority. See WEALTH AS AUTHORITY.

Proponent. One in favor of any one issue.

Proportional Representation (PR). An electoral system under which the elective body (parliament or congress) represents the strength of divergent interests, opinions, and party affiliations. There are several forms of proportional representation. The one more commonly found (e.g., in the Federal Republic of Germany—West Germany) is the one in which the country is divided into several constituencies (or districts), each being entitled to elect several persons as determined by law. Under the "list system," the voters may express their preference for an entire slate of candidates listed, and the representatives are apportioned among the various lists according to the votes each list receives. Of different variety is the "single transferable vote system" (also known as the Hare system). Under this system, each voter may express his first choice for a candidate, second choice, or as many choices for as many candidates as there are seats to be filled. Under this system the weak candidates are eliminated and the votes that they received, in order not to be wasted, are transferred across district boundaries, or nationwide.

Proportional Response. See FLEXIBLE RESPONSE.

Proportional Tax. See NEGATIVE INCOME TAX.

Proposal of Amendments. See CONSTITUTIONAL AMENDMENT.

Proposition Thirteen. See TAX REVOLT.

Propositions in Political Theory. See POLITICAL THEORY.

Proprietaries. Business front organizations organized and maintained by the CIA to conduct legitimate operations but whose original purpose is to conduct intelligence operations. The front organizations include: airlines (e.g., Air America, Southern Air) book and newspaper publishing companies; and retail trade in certain commodities including weapons and other war materiel. The true identity of the CIA agents is hidden as they operate as employees of an ordinary enterprise. Most large intelligence services engage in such practices and some of the enterprises have proved to be very profitable. The Israeli Mossad, for example, maintained in 1975 aircraft dealerships specializing in selling jet aircraft to many world leaders including Idi Amin of Uganda and Colonel Mu'ammar al-Quadhafi of Libya. Of course, all these aircraft were equipped with a very sophisticated bugging system which transmitted conversations to the Israeli interception stations. In 1975, the CIA was ordered to turn over all profits from such proprietaries, and the eventual liquidation receipts, to the U.S. Treasury. In the past the CIA had retained the profits for its internal use, for such projects as covert and paramilitary operations and, very often, simply to bribe foreign leaders. It was from such funds that the CIA operative in the Middle East, Kermit Roosevelt (the same Roosevelt who engineered the restoration of the Shah in Iran in 1953), took a suitcase packed with three million U.S. dollars as a bribe to Gamal Abdel Nasser, president of Egypt and an outspoken leader of the Arab world during the 1950s. The purpose of the bribe was to influence Nasser in helping America keep Soviet influence out of the area. Although the act obviously offended Nasser's Arab pride, he accepted the cash, and subsequently gave it to a construction company in Cairo to erect an ugly structure which he called the "Roosevelt Erection."

Proprietary Colony. See AMERICAN COLONIES.

Propulsive Firm. See LEADING INDUSTRY.

Prosecuting Attorney. A person trained in law and authorized by the state, upon election or appointment, to prosecute cases before the courts of law in the name of that state.

Protection of Commerce and Seamen. See BARBARY PIRATES.

Protection of the Accused. See Appendices 8, 48, 50, 51.

Protectionism. Measures taken by a state (usually in the form of tariffs on foreign imports) in order to preserve its internal markets for domestic suppliers of goods and services, and to avoid deficit in the balance of payments. The practice of "dumping" (selling commodities on foreign markets for less than on domestic markets), so commonly used by modern industrial nations during the last decade is the major reason for protectionist tariffs. See SHIELD LAW.

Protectionist Wall. See PROTECTIONISM.

Protective Lobby. See LOBBY.

Protective Reaction. See PREEMPTIVE STRIKE.

Protectorate. A nation or a state placed under the supervision and protection of another state. See INTERNATIONAL LAW.

Protest Candidate. See PROTEST VOTE.

Protest Vote. A vote cast usually against the party or the incumbent in power, or against one's own party, as a demonstration of dissent. A political aspirant who campaigns for and receives such votes, is referred to as "protest candidate." See VOTING.

PROTEUS. See PROFESSIONAL TEACHING ENGINEERS FOR THE UNITED STATES.

Protocol. See DIPLOMATIC PROTOCOL.

Protracted Warfare. A term used in practical international politics to describe the continuous struggle for supremacy between two or more adversary states or blocs of states (e.g., the socialist states versus the capitalist states) by means other than open confrontation on the battlefield (e.g., an economic, cultural, or political struggle, or sporadic brush-wars of peripheral nature). See PROXY WAR, WAR, WAR OF ATTRITION.

Provide Hope, Operation. See AMERICAN ECONOMIC ASSISTANCE TO THE COMMON-WEALTH OF INDEPENDENT STATES (CIS).

Provincial Congress. Each of the thirteen original colonies in North America had such congresses (some of them were dissolved by the Governors for revolutionary activity, as was the case with the House of Burgesses in Virginia), and these became the state legislatures after the American Revolution of 1776.

Provisional Government. A government that is set up on a temporary basis, usually by appointment, within a state that has just gained its independence, generally changed its form of government, or undergone a revolution. See JOHNSON PROCLAMATION.

Provost. An official with specific duties and powers (e.g., one acting as a chief magistrate in a Scottish borough), one in charge of a police force, or an official in an institution of higher learning.

Provost Marshal. An officer in charge of military police, military prisons, and prisoners, and one who serves notices to witnesses for their appearance before military courts.

Proxy Vote. The practice of casting a vote in the name of one person by another upon proper authorization. See VOTING.

Proxy War. A term often applied to a war between states that is being fought on behalf of another state (e.g., Cuban forces fighting in Angola, Africa, in 1977, on behalf of the Soviet Union) or through confrontation of their agents or satellite states. According to Dr. Zbigniew K. Brzezinski, National Security Adviser to U.S. President Jimmy Carter, the war of December 1977 between Cambodia and Vietnam (both socialist states, Cambodia following the Chinese line of communism and Vietnam the Soviet one) was, in reality, a proxy war between China and the Soviet Union. Indications are that future wars will be predominantly proxy wars, rather than major confrontations between superpowers. See PROTRACTED WARFARE, WAR.

PRP. People's Redemption Party, Nigeria.

Prussian Revolution. See REVOLUTION FROM ABOVE.

Pseudonym. See CRYPTONYM.

Psychological Environment. In the language of international politics, the actor's (the state or those who speak for it) image of reality in the international situation.

Psychological Warfare. Those hostile acts that aim at undermining the credibility, reputation, or security of an adversary, pursued by means short of open warfare (e.g., written and spoken words). See PROTRACTED WARFARE, WAR.

Psychopatholitics. A political system which: lacks identifiable roots in some past traditions or unique values; does not appear to be secure and sure of its goals and objectives; but functions from day-to-day by merely satisfying the bare minimum of the needs of its people, and usually commands obedience by force. Ronald Hingley (*The Russian Mind,* New York: Charles Scribner's Sons, 1978) considered the Soviet political system as being psychopatholitical.

Public Advisory Boards. May be chosen by a governor, mayor, or established by a legislative body. They are charged with making or advising on policy for administrative agencies. Membership may include individuals from specific interest groups—industry or trade. After the riots in the United States in the late 1960s, citizen advisory boards were created to investigate charges of police brutality and to oversee police procedures. During the War on Poverty national legislation mandated that citizen advisory boards be created to assist local officials in setting priorities for expending program funds.

Public Agenda. See AGENDA.

Public Authority. An individual or an institution empowered, by virtue of occupying a state-related position, to issue binding rules and regulations, make authoritative decisions and/or enforce them, or one who allocates powers to others. See GOVERNMENT CORPORATION.

The Public be Damned. See GENERAL WILL.

Public Bill. See BILL, PUBLIC LAW.

Public Business. See OPEN JUSTICE.

Public Citizen Litigation. Attorney Ralph Nader, through his organization, is America's most recognized and appreciated protector of the personal interest of the individual person as a consumer. The Nader Organization, and Ralph Nader in person, are often engaged in litigation on behalf of consumers, individually or in class action suits, who did not receive what they paid for, and/or the products they purchased were unsafe or defective.

Public Commissioner. A member of a planning district commission designated to represent the public at large and not the government of any single member jurisdiction. See PLANNING.

Public Diplomacy. The practice of conducting diplomatic relations by overt (modern) instead of covert (traditional and secret) means. See DIPLOMACY, PRIVATE DIPLOMACY.

Public Domain. That which belongs to the public or must be known to the public (e.g., public records, court proceedings, laws in force, and acts and actions of public officials). See EMINENT DOMAIN.

Public Employment. See OAKS' LAWS.

Public Interest. See POLITICS OF SPECIAL INTERESTS.

Public Interest, Convenience, and Necessity. Most public utilities in the United States (e.g., telephone, electric companies, radio and television stations) operate under special authorization by either federal or state governmental agencies (e.g., the Federal Communications Commission), which give them the right to protect their interests (e.g., from unfair competition) and to pursue such a line of business for the need, interest, and benefit of the community *at large* rather than small segments of the population.

Public International Law. See INTERNATIONAL LAW.

Public Knowledge. A doctrine generally recognized in democratic societies (states) that the public has the right to know what its government is doing at any given time. See NATIONAL INTEREST, SUNSHINE LAW.

Public Law. The body of laws of a state that regulates the organization of government, the powers and the duties of public officers, and the relationships between the government and individual persons. All congressional acts in the United States are designated as Public Laws (PL). See LAW.

Public Opinion. The generalized popular response of a nation, state, or community to any current issue. See PUBLIC OPINION POLL.

Public Opinion Poll. A process by which the opinions of individuals (individuals as members of certain groups or elites, organizations, or clusters) can be ascertained pertaining to certain particular issues at a given time and place, and then evaluated according to certain criteria (e.g., the degree of honesty, bias, or deception), and presented as a "public opinion." Most commonly the universe or the population (the people to be polled) are selected by random numbers, and their opinions then molded into a single opinion, representing, for example, an attitude toward certain public policies or politicians at a given time (political temperature). Polls often serve as "feelers" for individuals, corporations, or governments, and are designed to determine how a given public would react (e.g., a kind of straw-vote by the public). To a government, this may give an early warning that a certain policy would not meet with support as a final product, and may give it a chance to make improvements. Very often, polls are designed to accomplish what the user of the information wants them to accomplish (e.g., if a politician wants to demonstrate to his constituents that he is ahead of his opponents, the poll can be arranged in such a way that this objective will be accomplished.) The major professional polling organizations in the United States, the ones which have a proven record of success because of their objectivity, scientific methods, and dedication to the task, are the Gallup, Harris and Jankelovich polling organizations. See PUBLIC OPINION.

Public Policy. In a broad sense, the reflection or approximation of the public will; the conversion of the will of the public into laws which will govern it; or the official policies of the government which in a democracy are based on the will of the majority.

Public Record. See PUBLIC DOMAIN.

Public Role. See ROLE.

Publius. See FEDERALIST.

Pueblo Affair. The seizure of the *U.S.S. Pueblo*, a United States intelligence ship which was caught collecting intelligence data off the shores of Korea for the National Security Agency (NSA) and the Central Intelligence Agency (CIA), on January 23, 1968, by the People's Republic of Korea (Communist North Korea). The crew of the ship, under the leadership of its captain, Lloyd M. Bucher, was released on December 22, 1968, after months of torture and humiliation, but the vessel was retained by the Koreans. The United States Government was required to extend its apology for the acts of "espionage" against Korea and it did so in order to have the crew released from captivity. See INTELLIGENCE.

Puerto Rican Socialist Party. See WORLD PEACE COUNCIL.

Pundit. See PANDIT.

Punjab Separatism. See SIKH SEPARATISM.

Pure Democracy. See DEMOCRACY, DIRECT.

Purge. The elimination of persons whose views or actions are no longer tolerable to those in power, from a party, government, or position of trust. In the Soviet Union, for example, Joseph Stalin, 1924-1953, eliminated about one million peasants and farmers, including any kind of opponents to his regime and his collectivization campaign, and, during a reception for foreign visiting dignitaries was asked by Lady Astor in 1932 when he will stop the killing, Stalin replied, "When it is no longer necessary." There was a popular saying in the former Soviet Union and other communist/socialist states where such purges were common that the biggest problem of living under communism was predicting the past. See CHISTKA, SIBERIA OF BUREAUCRACY, UNHEALTHY TENDENCIES.

Purple. See MAGIC.

Pursuing the Last Grain of Rice in the Corner of the Lunchbox. See FRAME SOCIETY.

Put America on a Diet. Because of the ratio of population to consumption of important raw materials per capita, America surpasses every nation (e.g., in timber, energy just to mention only two commodities). Many Americans voice the demand that America trim its appetite by going on a diet and trying to live with the notion that small may be beautiful. See SMALL IS BEAUTIFUL, Appendix 41.

Putsch. In the German language, "armed rebellion," "uprising," or "revolution." A term often associated with Adolf Hitler, the Chancellor of the Third German Reich and leader of the Nazi Party of Germany (1933-1945), who on November 8, 1923, persuaded the nationalist leaders of Bavaria to stage a revolution and to march on Berlin in order to overthrow the government of the Weimar Republic. He was, however, unsuccessful in his attempt and was subsequently arrested, tried, and imprisoned.

Putting the Enemy on the Horns of a Dilemma. See MYSTIFY, MISLEAD, SURPRISE.

Puzzle Inside, a Riddle Wrapped in an Enigma. Words with which England's Prime Minister, Winston Churchill, described the mysterious Soviet state and particularly the political style of its leaders (e.g., Josef Stalin) with whom the Western allies (e.g., Winston Churchill and U.S. Presidents F. D. Roosevelt and H. S. Truman) could not find common ground for negotiations on the solutions to post-W.W.II problems. See Appendix 74.

Pyrrhic Victory. A term commonly used to describe a victory obtained by extreme sacrifice; or a victory that is so costly that, finally, it may not be a victory at all. Pyrrhus, Greek King of Epirus, conquered the Romans at Asculm in 279 BC, but lost his entire army and his arm in the process. During the Great Leap Forward period in the People's Republic of China, the leadership initiated a policy to save on food by demanding that animals such as dogs, cats, and sparrows be exterminated. Rodents and insects subsequently destroyed most of the crops. In turn, the Chinese leaders gave secret orders to their diplomats abroad to purchase as many cats as possible and ship them to China to control the rodent (mice and rats) population. See GREAT LEAP FORWARD.

"God grant, that not only the love of liberty but thorough knowledge of the rights of man pervade all the nations of the earth, so that a philosopher may set his foot anywhere on its surface and say, 'THIS IS MY COUNTRY.' "

BENJAMIN FRANKLIN, 1706-1790

Quadragesimo Anno. See ENCYCLICAL.

Quadrennial Madhouses. A phrase coined during the progressive era of the early 1900s to describe the national nominating party conventions, particularly those of the two major political parties in the United States, the Democrats and Republicans. See DEMOCRATIC PARTY, PARTY MACHINE, REPUBLICAN PARTY.

Quadruple Alliance. During the Congress of Vienna in 1815, when Europe was rearranged after the defeat of Napoleonic France, a new alliance was formed by: Tsar Alexander I (1801-1825) of Russia; King George III (1760-1820) of England (who did not sign the final documents solidifying the Alliance); Prince Klemens von Metternich (1809-1848), Chancellor of Austria (who signed in the name of Emperor Francis II [1792-1835]); and Freiherr von Hardenberg (1810-1822), Chancellor of Prussia. Its purpose was to prevent France from re-emerging as an empire and experimenter with "revolutionary principles," as well as to work together on matters "most salutary for the repose and prosperity of Nations and for the maintenance of the Peace of Europe." The members of the Alliance held four congresses: (1) Aix-la-Chapelle in 1818, (2) Troppau in 1820, (3) Laibach in 1821, and (4) Verona in 1822. The Troppau Congress adopted a measure (the "Troppau Protocol") sanctioning the use of joint military forces in any country that is threatened by revolution if such aid is requested. This protocol was signed in England's absence and it soon became the instrument of destruction of the Alliance since England opposed such measures as "internal intervention" into the domestic affairs of a state. The Alliance was signed by all the states of Europe except the Papal State, Turkey, and England. The United States was also invited to join, but President James Madison (1809-1817) politely declined. See HOLY ALLIANCE.

Quai d'Orsay. The official seat of the French Foreign Office, the Ministry for Foreign Affairs.

Qualifications for U.S. President. The constitutional requirements (Art. II of the U.S. Constitution) are: (1) natural born (native born) citizen, *jus soli*; (2) 35 years of age; (3) residency for fourteen years within the United States before the election. The constitution does not require prior experience or educational attainment. Professor Herman Finer, one of the more astute students of the American presidency, suggests that anyone considered for that office should have the following qualities: consciousness, conviction, command, creativity, courage, conciliation, cleverness, coherence, constancy, constitution, conscientiousness, and charm or captivation. See QUASI-LEGAL QUALIFICATIONS FOR U.S. PRESIDENT, Appendix 8.

Qualified Law. A law that contains some stipulation as a condition for its enforcement. See LAW, SUPREME COURT OF THE UNITED STATES.

Qualitative Growth of Government. See POLITICAL DEVELOPMENT.

Quanguo Renmin Daibiao Dahui. The unicameral legislative body, the National People's Congress, of China.

Quantitative Growth of Government. See POLITICAL DEVELOPMENT.

Quarantine. As applied to international politics, the practice of curtailing the activities of an adversary state for the purpose of diminishing its power or as a reprisal against an aggressor.

Quarantine Speech. U.S. President Franklin D. Roosevelt (1933-1944), alarmed and disturbed by the growing number of totalitarian dictatorships in Europe and Asia, warned them in his speech made in Chicago, Illinois, on October 5, 1937, that "positive endeavors" must be made in order to "quarantine" the aggressors, commencing with economic embargoes. "The epidemic of world lawlessness is spreading," said the President. "When an epidemic of physical disease starts to spread, the community approves and joins in a quarantine of the patients in order to protect the health of the community against the spread of the disease . . . there must be positive endeavors to preserve peace." President Roosevelt was making reference to three main instances of naked aggression and brutal subjugation of one society by another, which had proceeded with little notice because America and other democratic states were preoccupied with their recovery from the Great Depression of 1929: (1) In 1931, the Japanese militarists occupied Manchuria, set up a puppet government, and in 1932 ended parliamentary government; (2) Benito Mussolini, the *Il Duce* of the Italian Fascists, attacked Ethiopia in 1933, and (3) Adolf Hitler, *Der Führer* of German National Socialists (Nazis) and Chancellor and Leader (Führer) of the German Third Reich, was making preparations to conquer the world. (Mussolini was Hitler's mentor.) The aggressors, having at their command modern and advanced weapon systems, had no problems crushing weak nations because: (1) the Johnson Debt Default Act of 1934 prevented nations late with payment for previous purchases from the United States, to purchase more on credit; (2) when Ethiopia's Emperor, Haile Selassie, appealed for help to the free nations as well as to the League of Nations, the response was (a) Neutrality Acts of 1934, 1936, and 1937, from the U.S. Congress, and (b) refusal by the League of Nations to enforce embargoes against the aggressors; and (3) Francisco Franco was crushing the Spanish Republicans (1936-1939) with the aid of Adolf Hitler of Germany and Benito Mussolini of Italy. It was in Spain that German and Italian armies received their "basic training" for W.W.II. See DEBT DEFAULT ACT OF 1934, NEUTRALITY ACTS.

Quarantine the Enemy. See QUARANTINE SPEECH.

Quarter-to-Quarter Mentality. Term often applied to some Western business establishments as well as some government agencies, particularly those in the United States, where success or positive progress is measured in terms of a three-month, or quarter-of-a-year period of time. If during that period positive results are not achieved, the whole undertaking is viewed as unsuccessful, wrong, unproductive, and unfortunate. Many investment institutions compound dividends or other benefits on a quarterly basis and often compare a current quarter with the corresponding quarter of the previous year to ascertain success, or lack of it. In Japan, by contrast, decades and quarters of a century are not uncommon as measures of success. See COMPARATIVE GLOBAL ADVANTAGE.

Quarternary Services. A phrase coined by Jean Gottmann (*Megalopolis: The Urbanized Northeastern Seaboard of the United States*, New York: The Twentieth Century Fund) to characterize those planned services of communities in a post industrial society which arise from applied research, communications, and professional skills, and which in such a society constitute the bulk of the services. See OAKS LAWS, POST-INDUSTRIAL SOCIETY.

Quasi-Judicial. The authority granted to regulatory agencies in the United States (e.g., the Interstate Commerce Commission or the Federal Power Commission) to issue orders affecting organizations or individual persons and to impose penalties for breach of these orders. Decisions of regulatory agencies can be appealed to Federal District Courts. (The term "semi-judicial" is also often used.) See QUASI-LEGISLATIVE.

Quasi-Legal Qualifications for U.S. President. Among the many existing stereotypes, the following appear to be the most often mentioned as the quasi-legal, or extra-legal qualifications for the U.S. Presidency: The candidate should: (1) be of Anglo-Saxon stock and preferably subscribe to the best of Anglo-Saxon traditions; (2) subscribe to some Protestant religious denomination (Al Smith, former Governor of New York, a Catholic, attempted to break the no-Catholic-for-President tradition in 1932, running against former Governor of New York and Protestant, Franklin D. Roosevelt; the second such attempt was made by a young U.S. Senator from Massachusetts, John F. Kennedy in 1960, who was successful because of his charismatic personal characteristics. He was the only Catholic ever to hold that high office.); (3) be not too rich, but not too poor; (4) be well educated, but not "overeducated"; (5) be a self-starter in his endeavors, whether in business, profession, or politics; (6) have experience in public affairs such as (in this order): (a) U.S. Senator, (b) governor of a state, (c) U.S. Representative, (d) U.S. Vice President, (e) high ranking general and hero; (7) be an active member of one of the two major political parties (Democratic or Republican), not any other; (8) be willing to serve and to work hard; (9) have a good, charismatic personality, good manners, good taste in dressing and grooming, and good health; (10) have a liking for sports and be sportsmanlike; (11) have a good family experience (no divorce or extra-marital affairs); and (12) have no skeletons hidden in the closet—his past must be clear and in the open. See MA WHERE IS MY PA?, ONE THOUSAND PERCENT, QUALIFICATIONS FOR U.S. PRESIDENT.

Quasi-Legislative. The authority granted to regulatory agencies in the United States to issue regulations and to require compliance. The term "semi-legislative" is also often used. See QUASI-JUDICIAL.

Quebec Conference. See MORGENTHAU PLAN, RANKIN PLAN.

Quebec Distinct Society. One of Canada's provinces, Quebec, is populated predominantly by French-speaking Canadians who, since W.W.II will have striven to achieve complete independence as a separate state. The central government and the other provinces would like to prevent that move by Quebec, and Quebec may receive a special status in the Canadian confederation by its recognition in the language of the constitution, as a "distinct society" with far-reaching autonomy. See SEPARATISM.

Quebec Liberation. See PARTI QUÉBÉCOIS.

Queen of the Seas. See MAHAN'S SEA POWER THEORY.

Quemoy and Matsu Incident. Two islands situated close to the coast of China were claimed by the People's Republic of China as well as by the Kuomintang government on the Island of Formosa (Taiwan). In 1954 and 1958, the Chinese People's Army shelled the islands as a prelude to an invasion, but the United States government issued a warning that if hostilities continued, the U.S. would proceed with a "massive retaliatory act." Since the concept of "massive retaliation" provided for the deployment of nuclear weapons, if necessary, the shelling ceased. See MASSIVE RETALIATION, Appendix 29.

Quest. See PROPAGANDA ASSETS INVENTORY (PAI).

Question of Fact. An act that is permissible and not restricted by law (e.g., in traditional international law, war is considered as a matter of fact and not of law); also, the fact to which a rule of law can be applied in adjudication as opposed to a question of law which, in adjudication, may disregard facts if a rule of law is being violated.

Question of Law. See QUESTION OF FACT.

Quid Pro Quo. In the Latin language, "something for something" (e.g., an exchange of favors). See LINKAGE DIPLOMACY, LOG ROLLING.

Quietus. Freeing one from debt obligation, discharging from office or obligation.

Quisling. One who is sympathetic to the policies or philosophy of another state and who in case of war goes against his own state by joining the aggressor and collaborating with him. The term was coined from the name of Major Vidkun Quisling, once a head of the Fascist party of Norway, who, upon the invasion of that country by Hitler's armies during World War II, established a government which served the German cause.

Quo Warranto. See WRITS.

Quoc Hoi. The legislative body, the unicameral National Assembly, of Vietnam.

Quorum. A stipulation that may be applied to a deliberating body (e.g., a conference, parliament, or congress) requiring the presence of a given number of persons before business can be transacted or a vote can be taken. Under the United States Constitution, the majority of members elected to each House (the Senate or the House of Representatives) constitutes a quorum.

Quota. As once applied to United States immigration laws, the specified number of persons that could be officially admitted to the United States for permanent residence during a single year. The quota system is no longer used. Also, a specified minimum of production output that is expected from an individual worker in the Soviet economy in order to receive the minimum of specified pay. Production goals are set in the USSR by the planning agencies at the national, regional, or local levels, and a worker who produces over and above the set norm, or quota, receives additional pay as an incentive. See BRAIN-DRAIN.

R

"Live with yourself: get to know how poorly furnished you are."

PERSIUS, 34-62 A.D.

Rabble Rouser Index. See COUNTERINSURGENCY IN AMERICA.

Race. See TOOLS OF ANALYSIS OF A POLITICALLY ORGANIZED SOCIETY.

Race Congress. A major gathering called in London, England, in 1911 for the purpose of studying and appraising the current state of race relations and what conclusions might be drawn from it for the black peoples. The Congress was called upon the inspiration of Dr. W. E. B. Du Bois and agreed that black peoples must unite in order to intensify their struggle for equality in the society of man.

Race Riot. The protest of people of one race who are persecuted or otherwise downgraded by another, a dominant race in a given society, is as ancient as mankind. In modern times race riots occurred mainly in multi-racial societies (e.g., the United States and the former Soviet Union). In the former Soviet Union following V. I. Lenin's legacy, Josef Stalin, being himself from an ethnic minority of Gruzians (Georgians), designated a compartmental state and national areas where people of different races and nationalities could reside and maintain their identity. That effort was accomplished by force rather than legislative policy and concensus. In the U.S. riots by black Americans raged from colonial times until the April-May 1992 riot in Los Angeles, California. The 1919 "Red Summer" riots that occurred in some major U.S. cities were the most extensive and over 80 black Americans were lynched as a result. The April-May 1992 riot in Los Angeles, California, following the acquittal of four white policemen charged with the criminal beating of black motorist Rodney King, was the most destructive of this decade, leaving 58 dead and about a billion dollars in property damage, not counting the backlash in American race relations. See Appendix 74.

Race War. A state of hostility between peoples of different races (e.g., Caucasian, Mongoloid, or Negroid) struggling for a dominant position (political power) in a politically organized society and unified on the basis of the race factor. The degree of that hostility can range from covert or overt segregation practices to a shooting war. Race wars occur most often in multiracial societies (where different races coexist together under a single authority) and evolve as a process of growing awareness (consciousness) of deprivation or an outright persecution of one race by another. Race identification (race consciousness), like nationalism (identification with a certain nation) becomes a dynamic political force as a result of deliberate politicization efforts. During the twentieth century racial wars occurred in China between the Chinese and the white Europeans (the Boxer Rebellion); between the Turks and the Armenians; between white Europeans and black Africans (in South Africa and Rhodesia); between the Indians and the Pakistanis; between the Israelis and the Arabs; between the Asians (especially those in Georgia—Josef Stalin's homeland) and the white Russians in the Soviet Union; between the Afro-Americans and Euro-Americans in the United States; between the Indians, mestizoes, mulattoes and Creoles, often as a coalition, and the white Europeans in Latin America; and between the Cambodians and the Vietnamese. Currently, inter-race antagonism is rising among the traditional power-holders and power-brokers, the whites (who now constitute approximately 12 percent of the world's population and who are declining in growth), and the other races, particularly the Negroid, Mongoloid, and the Mestizo-Mulatto-Creole bloc, which are growing. Shrinking sources of food supply coupled with intensive politicization efforts on the part of the poor nations, will intensify war propensities. See KERNER COMMISSION, POPULATION GROWTH in Appendices 85, 86, 90.

Racial Pollution. See NUREMBERG LAWS.

Racial Purification. See HONORARY ARYANS.

Racial Quota. See AFFIRMATIVE ACTION.

Racism Equals Zionism. See ZIONISM EQUALS RACISM.

Racketeer-Influenced and Corrupt Organizations Act (RICO). See RACKETEERING.

Racketeering. A felonious crime under American laws; acts of systematic fraud, extortion, and/or bribery, usually with force or violence, committed according to some pattern and frequency, usually in conspiracy with other persons, or organizations (e.g., organized crime). The "Racketeer-Influenced and Corrupt Organizations Act" (RICO), passed in 1970 by Congress as part of the Organized Crime Control Act of 1970, empowers federal prosecutors to prosecute persons involved in crimes showing patterns of corruption; convictions carry very stiff sentences.

Rada. The legislative assembly of the Ukrainian Republic of the former USSR.

Radical. One who advocates drastic changes of the laws, the structure of government, economic policies, or the overall character of the state or society.

Radical Right. See EXTREMISM.

Radio Liberation. See INTERNATIONAL COMMUNICATION AGENCY (ICA), UNITED STATES INFORMATION AGENCY (USIA).

Radio Marti. See RADIO WAR.

Radio War. In order to counter Soviet-inspired communist propaganda beamed over the radio of Havana, Cuba, the United States in retaliation launched the Radio and TV Marti program in February 1990, beaming from Florida to Cuba, thus provoking Fidel Castro's protest that this was an additional example of "Yankee imperialism."

Rainbow Coalition. A concept of coalition politics developed by the Rev. Jesse Jackson during his political campaign at various levels during the 1980s and 1990s, including his presidential campaign where he called upon all political groups, races, and nationalities in the American society to organize for the purpose of enhancing harmony among races and reducing poverty and crime in America.

Raison d'État. In the French language, "the reason of the state." Also, a political concept emphasizing the existence of the state as an end in itself which, in the final analysis, has the right to employ any means it chooses for the protection of its continued existence.

Raison d'Être. In the French language, "reason for being" or "justification for existence."

Raj. In the Hindi language, "state," "small dominion," one under the rule of a Raja.

Raja. In the Hindi language, "ruler," "king," or "head of state."

Rajya Sabha. See SANSAD.

Rally of the French People (RFP). In the French language, "Rassemblement du Peuple Française," a major and leading party in France after W.W.II under the leadership of General Charles de Gaulle, President of the French Government in exile during the Nazi German occupation of France, premier of France under the Fourth Republic (1946-1958), and the first President of the Fifth Republic (1958-). De Gaulle resigned in April 1969, but, under him, France had regained its dignity and honor as a superpower, as a leading democracy, and as a nation of great culture and civilization.

RAM. See REVOLUTIONARY ACTION MOVEMENT.

Rangers. See ARMY RANGERS.

Rank-and-File. See POLYARCHY.

Rankin Plan. Code name for contingency plans designed by the Allies (in reality by the British and the Americans) during W.W.II in the event of an early collapse of Germany (e.g., in the event the Rote Kapelle was successful in eliminating Hitler). Also a plan to revitalize Germany against the USSR. See MORGENTHAU PLAN, ROTE KAPELLE.

Ranking Member of Congress. In the U.S. Congress, Representative or Senator with longest service (seniority), or one with long service on a committee representing one of the two political parties, Democrat or Republican.

Rapacki Plan. A proposal once advanced by Polish Foreign Minister Adam Rapacki (before the United Nations in 1957) calling for the establishment of a zone between East and West Europe (i.e., the capitalistic and the socialist states) to be free of nuclear weapons. The plan was rejected by the Western powers on the grounds that it favored the Eastern bloc, mainly the Soviet Union, and contained no provisions for inspections.

Rapallo Treaty. A secret agreement signed by Germany and the Soviet Union in 1922 which provided for mutual collaboration of the two states both of which felt isolated to discriminated against by the European powers. Following W.W.I Germany was burdened with heavy war reparations and the Soviet Union was isolated and boycotted by the Western powers because of its communist ideology and strong anti-capitalist propaganda (emanating from Moscow and its agencies abroad, the COMINTERN). One major stipulation of the agreement entered into in Rapallo and subsequently presented in a more detailed form by the Treaty of Berlin of 1936, was the elimination of the Republic of Poland, which separated these two competitors and which refused to enter into any bilateral agreements with and against either of its neighbors. Both Russia and Germany had Machiavellian-type grand designs to outsmart and eventually conquer each other and eliminate Poland. Since Germany was restrained by the Treaty of Versailles from having a standing war navy and air force, and since the Soviet Union was isolated and boycotted by the West, Hitler proposed and Stalin agreed to allow the Germans to build their Luftwaffe (Air Force) and the Kriegsmarine (War Navy) on Soviet territory in great secrecy. Hitler's plan was to not only establish his war machine, but also to learn more about the Russians and their infrastructure and war capabilities, and never suspected that the "inferior" Slavs would learn anything about Hitler's war machine and plans. The Russians had similar notions and allowed Hitler to proceed so that they could learn about Hitler's war machine, technology, and military doctrine. At last, an agreement was signed in 1939 (the Molotov-Ribbentrop or Hitler-Stalin Pact). Poland was dismembered and the time came for the final kill, which was initiated by Hitler, but was well known by Stalin. The Russians outsmarted Hitler and destroyed his forces on Soviet and Polish territory and, together with the Allies, destroyed the German Third Reich. Soviet foreign intelligence and one of their top agents in Tokyo, Richard Sorge, and even Winston Churchill of England, alarmed Moscow about the German plan of attack, Operation Barbarossa. All were distressed that Stalin was not moved by such important intelligence, failing to realize that Stalin had known about it for several years, and his main concern was outwitting Hitler and catching him in his own trap.

Rapprochement. An understanding that may be reached by two or more formerly hostile states on the establishment of friendly relations. See DIPLOMACY.

Rasputinism. See BOUDOIR GOVERNMENT.

Rassemblement du Peuple Française (RPF). See RALLY OF THE FRENCH PEOPLE.

Ratha Satha. The bicameral legislature, National Assembly, of Thailand, consisting of an upper house or Senate, Woothi Satha, and a lower house or House of Representatives, Satha Poothan.

Rathaus. In the German language, "city hall," "town hall," or "a seat of local government."

Ratification. The formal acceptance and confirmation of terms and conditions arising out of an agreement. (In the United States all treaties with foreign nations must be ratified by the U.S. Senate.) See TREATY.

Ratification of Amendments. See U.S. Constitution, Appendix 8.

Rational-Legal Authority. See AUTHORITY.

Rationalism. The principle of accepting reason as the only authority in determining one's opinions or courses of action. Also, the theory that reason, or intellect, rather than the senses, is the true source of knowledge.

Ray Guns. U.S. President Ronald Reagan spoke on 23 March 1983 in favor of developing any weapon system, including "ray guns," which would deter the Soviets from their plan to gain control of the globe.

Rayon. A large political subdivision (e.g., a territory or province) in the former Soviet Union.

Reactionary. One who disapproves of any changes, and acts disruptively or disobediently; an extreme conservative.

Read My Lips—No New Taxes! A promise made by presidential candidate George Bush during his campaign in 1988, but, when the need for new taxation arose to revive the stagnated economy, he proposed taxes; the U.S. House voted down his proposal 422 to 1 on 25 February 1992.

Reading Into the Law. See JUDICIAL ACTIVISM, POSTURE OF MORAL ABSTENTION.

Reading Out of the Law. See JUDICIAL ACTIVISM, POSTURE OF MORAL ABSTENTION.

Reagan Democrat. See REPUBLICAN DEMOCRAT.

Reaganomics. See LAFFER CURVE.

Real Union. The voluntary merger of two or more states under a single authority. See PERSONAL UNION.

Realm. A geographic area under the exclusive authority of a certain government; or an area where a government can rightly exercise its powers (or a state can exercise its sovereign powers). Until the American Revolution, the thirteen American colonies, for example, were a realm of the King of England.

Realpolitik. In the German language, "power politics" or "politics based on realities." See POWER POLITICS.

Reapportionment. See ONE MAN, ONE VOTE, UNITED STATES HOUSE OF REPRESENTATIVES, Appendices, 8, 21,48.

Reason of State. Justifiable basis on which all acts and activities of government officials are based; officials' acts are based on authority derived from the very existence of the state. For example, when Queen Soraya, wife of the Shah of Iran Reza Pahlavi (1953-1979), was not able to bear children, she was divorced in 1958 as the Shah explained, "for reasons of state, I found it necessary to divorce Queen Soraya."

Reasonable Access Law. See FAIRNESS DOCTRINE.

Reasonable Contemporaneousness Rule. A rule in the American system of jurisprudence (also observed by many systems of jurisprudence worldwide) whereby statutes or otherwise authoritative orders, including court subpoenas, passed or issued but never properly ratified in accordance with the practices of the day, are considered over time to be void and expired. Presently at issue in America is the final ratification of the XXVII Amendment to the U.S. Constitution, which would eliminate the power of members of Congress to increase their salaries while in office (a benefit of which Congress has taken advantage). This Amendment was proposed 203 years ago by James Madison and was originally intended as Amendment II of the Bill of Rights (i.e., the first ten Amendments). The Michigan State Legislature ratified this Amendment on 7 May 1992, becoming the 38th state to do so and the decisive vote in its adoption. Because of the time lapse, the issue will be decided as follows: The Chief of the National Archives of the U.S. (Don W. Wilson, as of 1992) may issue a certificate of ratification, thus including the Amendment as part of the supreme law of the land (i.e., the U.S. Constitution). However, he may pass it on to Congress, which, in that case, would have the final say in the matter. Due to lack of precedence in such matters, and because the question is a political one and outside the scope and jurisdiction of the judiciary (i.e., the Supreme Court), the judiciary should not intervene. Should the National Archivist decide to certify the ratification, the present Congress may be reluctant to challenge him, because it is already under fire for several reasons: (1) Congress gave itself a salary increase in 1991 during late evening hours, without prior announcement (and after prime time news for the information media had concluded), thus ignoring the American electorate, and (2) the subsequent check bouncing and postal privilege abuse scandal committed by some members of Congress, many of whom were elected during the Ronald Reagan "good feelings" and relative prosperity era (1981-1989), when shady characters motivated by personal greed rather than service to their constituents and to the American state, escaped close citizen scrutiny and were elected to Congress. Should the Amendment be properly certified, members of Congress (retroactivity of law aside) ought to be deprived the 1991 pay increase short of a specific amendment to the effect that the tenure of members of the House (there is nothing wrong with that of the Senate), ought to be limited to one four-year term and eventually allow re-election for an additional four-year term, but on a one-four year skip basis, similar to the election of governors in some states (e.g., Alabama, Virginia). The House membership ought to be divided in four classes: the first class to be elected for a one year term; the second class for a two-year term, the third-class for a three-year term, and the fourth-class for a four-year term. This would allow for new blood in the House of a little over one-fourth of the membership every year. See CONGRESSIONAL PAY AMENDMENT, Appendix 8.

Rebellion. See INSURGENCY.

Rebus Sic Stantibus. See CLAUSULA REBUS SIC STANTIBUS.

Recall Petition. The recall of a public official (elected or appointed) by his constituents through petition.

Receiver. A person appointed by a court of law to manage the affairs of one who declares bankruptcy. See LAW.

Recess Appointment. An appointment that the President of the United States can make upon his sole authority while the Senate is not in session. Such appointments expire, as a rule, on the last day of the succeeding session of the Senate, unless the President decides to reappoint and seek confirmation by the Senate.

Recession. A phase of the business cycle extending from a peak to the next trough—usually lasting six months to a year—and characterized by widespread declines in output, income, employment, and trade in many sectors of the economy. Real Gross National Product (GNP) usually falls throughout the recession.

Reciprocal Legislation. Legislation that may be enacted separately in two or more states in order to establish a common policy or insure a mutually beneficial exchange of rights, privileges, or prerogatives (e.g., reciprocal agreements between the states in the United States on traffic violations or recognition of credentials of professionals such as lawyers, teachers, or physicians).

Reciprocal Political Control. See LIBERAL CONSTITUTION.

Reciprocal Power. See POWER.

Reciprocity. As applied to government and politics, the practice of recognition and respect of the laws, customs, or practices of one state by another on a mutual basis; the practice of granting special privileges and prerogatives to foreign nationals or diplomatic agents in return for similar treatment; or reciprocal trade agreements or tariff fees. See LEVEL PLAYING FIELD.

Recognition of a State. The act of acknowledging the actual existence (de facto recognition) or legal existence (de jure recognition) of a sovereign state as a legal entity, one capable of entering into legal obligations (e.g., capable of conducting international relations and living up to the traditional norms of international relations law). Recognition of states is voluntary and can be withdrawn at any time upon termination of diplomatic relations or dissolution of the state (e.g., through joining another state in a union). In the strict practice of international diplomacy, any act, such as contracts made by one state with representatives of another, may be construed as recognition (explicit or implicit) although such may not be the intention of the actor. For example, Egypt's President Anwar Sadat explicitly recognized the state of Israel by a personal visit to Jerusalem and by conferring with the Israeli leaders on November 19, 1977. France's General Charles de Gaulle (1891-1970) for example, was seeking recognition of his government in exile during W.W.II by the allies (e.g., England and the United States) who were reluctant to grant it, due partially to the animosity that existed between

England's Winston Churchill and de Gaulle. When in 1943, General de Gaulle shipped a live baby elephant as a gift to U.S. President Franklin D. Roosevelt (1933-1944), the U.S. State Department sought every means possible to prevent the animal's arrival in the United States because such a gift could not be rejected from the leader of a friendly nation, but its acceptance could also be construed as diplomatic recognition (de facto) of de Gaulle and his government in exile. Fortunately for all concerned, the elephant died during the turbulent voyage on the Atlantic Ocean, and de Gaulle's government was not recognized until two years later in 1945. See DE FACTO, DE JURE.

Recommittal. The return of a legislative bill to a committee for further study or consideration with or without instructions or amendments.

Reconcilable Neglect. Those practices in a political system, usually common at the local level of government, which, for fear of upsetting the order of traditional values and institutions (the status quo), reflect a tendency to disregard anything that is new and modern; even if it has value and utility, with the hope that, with time, mistakes and inadequacies will rectify themselves through reconciliation.

Reconciliation. Per the U.S. Congressional Budget Office, a process Congress uses to make its tax and spending legislation conform with the targets established in the budget resolution. The budget resolution may contain reconciliation instructions directing certain Congressional committees to achieve savings in tax or spending programs under their jurisdiction. Legislation to implement the reconciliation instructions is usually combined in one comprehensive bill. The reconciliation process primarily affects taxes, entitlement spending, and offsetting receipts. As a general rule, decisions on defense and non-defense discretionary programs are determined separately through the appropriation process, which is also governed by allocations in the budget resolution.

Reconstruction. Dissatisfied with the progress of reconstruction in the defeated Confederacy, the U.S. Congress passed the Reconstruction Act of March 2, 1867, which divided the South (with the exception of the state of Tennessee where reconstruction was progressing satisfactorily) into five military districts with martial law prevailing; a convention in each state (based on universal suffrage) was to draw up a new constitution for congressional approval, and states which had ratified the Fourteenth Amendment to the U.S. Constitution could reapply for admission to the Union. U.S. President Andrew Johnson vetoed the congressional action on the grounds that it was too harsh, and that the Negroes had not asked for the benefits that Congress was granting them, but the veto was overridden by Congress. When the states refused to call the conventions, Congress passed another Reconstruction Act on March 23, 1867, giving the military commanders of the five districts the power to call such conventions. The third Reconstruction Act of July 19, 1867, authorized the removal of all opponents to the reconstruction measures from government positions and the disenfranchisement of those who took the oath of office but who refused to and procrastinated in carrying out their duties. The official federal involvement in Reconstruction gradually diminished by 1877, when a compromise was reached and U.S. troops were withdrawn from the South. Also known as "Black Reconstruction." See BLACK CODES, CIVIL RIGHTS ACTS, FREEDMEN'S BUREAU, JOHNSON PROCLAMATION.

Reconstruction Acts. See RECONSTRUCTION.

Reconstruction Finance Corporation (RFC). See GREAT DEPRESSION.

Record Vote. The system of recording the votes by "yeas" and "nays" opposite the names of the persons voting. A record vote can be taken on expressed demand of one-fifth of the members present in either house of the United States Congress, and it is always used when voting on the overriding of a presidential veto. See CONGRESS OF THE UNITED STATES, RECORDED VOTE.

Recorded Vote. Either house of the U.S. Congress may require that, on a vote taken on any one bill, the names of those who vote for and against the bill be recorded.

Red Cat Theory. A notion pertaining to the policy of modernization of the People's Republic of China (e.g., the application of modern, advanced, and proven effective technology of the United States to develop China); supposedly once expressed by Teng Hsiao-ping, the Vice Chairman of the Chinese Communist Party, that it is irrelevant if the cat is red or not, as long as it catches the mice! Meaning: it is irrelevant if the know-how comes from a socialist or a capitalist state (society) as long as it benefits the Chinese society (state).

Red Eyebrows. See SECRET SOCIETIES.

Red Fox. A nickname for Anatoly F. Dobrynin, Soviet Ambassador to the United States (1961-1985), who was considered in diplomatic circles in Washington as one of the most shrewd, tactful, and sly communist diplomats stationed in the Western world; a fan of American fast food. He was instrumental in persuading President Mikhail Gorbachev and the Soviet leadership that America will not compromise in Soviet influence around the world, and that Washington's resolve is real and as such it would be costly to the Soviets to continue the arms race. He, better that any Soviet diplomat, understood America realistically.

Red Guard. See CULTURAL REVOLUTION.

Red Khmer. See KHMER ROUGE.

Red Menace. During the time-period 1919 to 1921, there was a "red scare" panic in the United States, where rumor had it that many alien organizations and many labor unions had been infiltrated by communist propaganda and that a serious anti-American conspiracy was working toward the abolishment of the American government by force. As a result, the Federal Bureau of Investigation (FBI) was allowed to establish a new division, the Anti-Radical Division. The newly-appointed head of that division, J. Edgar Hoover (August 1, 1919), preferred to call it the General Intelligence Division (GID), whose task it was to go after those "red radicals," or "Bolsheviks." In January 1920, Hoover's agents raided labor union and alien organization meeting places in thirty-three major cities in the United States, arresting over 4,000 persons suspected of radicalism. These events were triggered by two main factors: (1) there had been a Bolshevik Revolution in Russia which was victorious, and whose leadership, mainly V. I. Lenin, appealed to workers in the world to support it by any means possible; and (2) with the war in Europe ended, there was no longer a need for production of war materiel nor for a large standing army. Thousands of soldiers who had returned home had no jobs waiting for them. Some of them learned about the new "worker's paradise" in Russia, and raised their demands to anyone who was willing to listen to them, and Hoover's agents were the best listeners. By 1921, the GID succeeded in stifling any political debate in the United States, and is said to have collected card files on about 500,000 individuals who might be suspected of radicalism, and the world's best library of radical and subversive literature, most of which was taken during raids on publishing houses and personal libraries. See CHAOS, HT/LINGUAL, LOYALTY LAWS, MCCARTHYISM.

Red or Dead. A notion applicable to two distinct views pertaining to the future of communism: those who oppose communism suggest strong action under the slogan: "better dead than red," while those who either favor communism, or consider communism as the inevitable doctrine of the future, subscribe to the "better red than dead" slogan. During the McCarthy era the slogan of the day was "better dead than red." See MCCARTHYISM, RED MENACE.

Red Orchestra. In the German language, "Rote Kapelle;" one of the largest intelligence networks ever maintained; set up by the Soviet Union throughout the world, with particular emphasis on Western Europe and the fascist states (e.g. Nazi Germany, Spain, and Italy). It was organized and operated by Leopold Trepper (1904-), a Polish Jew from Nowy Targ. Trepper was recruited by the Soviet Military Intelligence, the GRU, in 1929, and during W.W.II, he was most effective in countries occupied by Nazi Germany, such as France, Belgium, Holland, and Germany proper. Among his many associates were Sandor Rodo, and Snia Kuczynski was in charge of the Red Orchestra's branch in England. Through that network the Soviet government in Moscow received valuable information on German troop movements as well as plans for conquest; Trepper, a communist himself, was able to deploy communist cell organizations in the various countries throughout Europe, and these in turn engaged all segments of the population in gathering intelligence. The German Gestapo caught and executed many of the best agents, but was not able to destroy the organization. See BLACK ORCHESTRA INTELLIGENCE.

Red Scare. See RED MENACE, RED OR DEAD.

Red Sox/Red Cap. The codename of an insurgency operation (1947-1956), conducted by the American Central Intelligence Agency (CIA) against the communist regimes in Czechoslovakia, Hungary, Poland, and Rumania. The CIA, and particularly its chief of counterintelligence, James Jesus

Angleton, Jr. (1944-1974), and Frank G. Wisner, director of the Office of Policy Coordination (OPC) of the CIA since 1948 and an OSS operative during W.W.II, were recruiting nationals from these nations; they trained them in paramilitary and guerrilla operations, and in "wet affairs" (killing, or eliminating/"terminating with extreme prejudice" communist leaders in Eastern Europe). According to authors Stephen Ambrose and Richard H. Immerman (*Ikes' Spies. Eisenhower and the Espionage Establishment*), some leaders were also to be kidnapped "... if they were not in sympathy with the regime, and could be spirited out of the country by our people for their own safety...." Kidnapping of people "whose interests were inimical to ours was also sanctioned." A special unity, named "PB/7," was to carry out assassinations on Wisner's and Angleton's orders. Hundreds of the insurgents that were smuggled into these countries perished, because the communist security forces there had prior knowledge of their arrival, mainly from Kim Philby, the chief of British counterintelligence who was also a Soviet agent in England and in America. See INSURGENCY, INTELLIGENCE, PROPAGANDA ASSETS INVENTORY (PAI).

Red Spears. See SECRET SOCIETIES.

Red Stocking Manifesto. See NATIONAL ORGANIZATION FOR WOMEN (NOW).

Red Summer. See RACE RIOT.

Redacted Information. Any information that is blacked out and rendered illegible on documents released under the Freedom of Information Act (FIA), which the government considers privileged information (e.g., on sources and methods by which this information was originally obtained, or names of governmental agents or informants).

Reeducation Camps. See YEAR ZERO.

Referendum. See PLEBISCITE.

Reform Caucus. See MILITARY REFORM MOVEMENT.

Refusnik. A term commonly used in the former Soviet Union to designate a person who refused to toe the official Soviet line, and who challenged the lack of personal freedoms as they pertained mainly to open criticism of the official Soviet policies and government officials. Term taken from English word "refuse."

Regency Council. A body of trusted persons charged by decree of a legislature or a monarch, or created ad hoc, which serves as the repository of the sovereign powers of the state until a new leader or ruler is elected or appointed. In monarchies, a regent was of the royal family, ruling until a young monarch reached an age, usually 16, when he was able to assume his duties as sovereign ruler. See MIRACLE ON THE VISTULA, Appendix 91.

Regent. A person who may be designated to assume the duties and functions of a monarch when the ruler is either too young to govern, is absent, incapacitated, or otherwise unable to perform his duties.

Regents of the University of California v. Bakke. See REVERSE DISCRIMINATION, Appendix 48.

Regierung. In the German language, "a government." The administrative apparatus of the state.

Regierungsbezirk. In the German language, "administrative area." Also the administrative divisions of the states (Länder) of the German Federation which are headed by appointed presidents who are responsible to the state (Land) legislatures.

Régime. In the French language, "government" or "the ruling element within a state."

Regime of Privacy. A notion that the *Roe v. Wade* ruling by the U.S. Supreme Court on 22 January 1973, that no state may prevent a woman from having an abortion during the first three months of pregnancy, fell under what Professor Bernard Schwartz called the "regime of privacy" (*The Ascent of Pragmatism: The Burger Court in Action*, Addison-Wesley Publishing Company, Inc., 1990). Including abortion in the right to privacy was, as Chief Justice Warren E. Burger himself acknowledged, " ... as sensitive and difficult an issue as any in this Court in my time." *Roe v. Wade* voided the anti-abortion laws in effect, in one degree or another, in 44 states. See RIGHT TO PRIVACY.

Regimen. See REGIME.

Regina. In the Latin language, "a queen" or a "female monarch."

Regional Arrangements. The regional international organizations (e.g., NATO, CENTO, SEATO, or the WARSAW PACT) established for the purpose of handling problems germane or unique to a specific geographic area or region without relying on major international organizations such as the United Nations which, being world-wide in the scope of its operations, may not be able to cope with regional problems.

Regional Citizen. A new type of resident who, according to Dr. Robert J. Horgan (*Regional Citizen*, Lawrenceville; Brunswick Publishing Corporation, 1992), uses the whole of the metropolitan area, including the city, town, and suburbs for living, working, shopping, and leisure activities, and rarely demonstrates loyalty to any particular political subdivision. Regional citizens are comprised of former distinctly rural or urban dwellers.

Regional Command of the Arab Socialist Renaissance Party. In the Arabic language, "Hizb al-Baath al-Arabi al-Ishtiraki," referred to as the "Baath Party." In contemporary Syria and Iraq the Baath Parties are the offshoot of the Arab international political movement of the 1930s aimed at the unification of Arab peoples everywhere, and at the protection of their political institutions and culture. See BAATH SOCIALIST PARTY.

Regional Council. An organization of local governments established to foster cooperative approaches to matters of area-wide concern. Its activities involve more than one policy or program area and its membership generally consists predominantly of elected officials or appointed representatives of constituent local governments.

Regional Planning. See PLANNING.

Regional Planning District Commission (RPDC). See COUNTERINSURGENCY IN AMERICA.

Regionalism. A system under which governmental powers are distributed among political subdivisions rather than being held by a single central authority (e.g., the autonomous powers granted to the states and local governments in the United States).

Regnal Populus. In the Latin language, "the rule by the people."

Regnum. In the Latin language, "kingdom," "monarchy," or "the domain of the ruler." See REIGNING.

Regressive Tax. See NEGATIVE INCOME TAX.

Regulatory Agencies. These determine application of legislation in specific situations, protect the interests of consumers or the general public from health and safety hazards and fraud, and include the Environmental Protection Agency, Food and Drug Administration, etc. See Appendices 9, 15.

Rehabilitative Justice. See RETRIBUTIVE JUSTICE.

Reichsrat. The upper house of the German Parliament under the Weimar Republic (1919-1933). See REICHSTAG, WEIMAR REPUBLIC.

Reichstag. The lower house of the German Parliament under the Weimar Republic (1919-1933). See REICHSRAT.

Reigning. Ruling a state or an empire under a monarchy by virtue of being a king or an emperor, but without being actively involved in policy formation and implementation; the exercise of sovereign powers by a monarch in a ceremonial capacity (e.g., in England, under a parliamentary monarchy, the monarch is said to "reign" and not to "rule," and, if reference is made to the monarch as a ruler, then it is said that the monarch "rules through the Parliament" or "rules in Parliament"; otherwise the monarch "reigns.") See REGNUM.

Relational Power. See POWER.

Relative Right. Any right that can be abridged, modified, or taken away. (Actually, there are no absolute rights. All rights, in the final analysis, are relative.)

Reliable Source. See DEEP THROAT.

Religious Police. A special force with police powers, common in Islamic states (e.g., Egypt, Saudi Arabia, and Iran), whose principal task is to police streets and other places to enforce Islamic laws and customs. It is illegal, for example, for a man and a woman to hold hands, or kiss or hug in public; to play Western music or to dance; and to drink alcoholic beverages. In some Islamic states women must wear certain attire to cover their legs and faces, and must refrain from driving automobiles.

Religious State. See ADMINISTRATIVE STATE.

REM. See RÖNTGEN EQUIVALENT IN MAN.

Remonstrance. An act of protest against the policies of governments or public officials, and the demand for reform or restitution for damages.

Remythology. See POLITICAL MYTH.

Rendition. See EXTRADITION.

Renegade. A turncoat, traitor, or deserter.

Renticare. A provision contained in the Housing Act of 1965 which authorizes rent subsidy to be given to poor people by the U.S. Government. (The Congress, however, failed to appropriate the necessary funds.)

Reorganization Objectives Army Division (ROAD). See PENTOMIC ARMY.

Reparation. A compensation, monetary or otherwise, rendered for damages inflicted by one state upon another.

Replay. The practice of planting deceptive misleading information in foreign news media (e.g., radio, TV, press, books, and films) with the expectation that the domestic news media will pick up that information and distribute it for domestic consumption, as it was originally meant. This is a common practice by governments and their intelligence services in their war of wits, including the Central Intelligence Agency (CIA). See also INVISIBLE GOVERNMENT, PENKOVSKY PAPERS, PROPAGANDA ASSETS INVENTORY (PAI).

Reports. See UNITED STATES REPORTS (U.S.).

Representative Action. See CLASS ACTION SUIT.

Representative Democracy. See DEMOCRACY, REPRESENTATIVE.

Representative Government. A form of government in which the supreme sovereign powers rest with the electorate, which in turn delegates them by a mandate to its duly elected representatives. Also known as "representative democracy."

Reprieve. A temporary delay in the carrying out of a sentence.

Reprisal. A retaliatory act by one state against another for some injury.

Reproductive Freedom. See NATIONAL ORGANIZATION FOR WOMEN (NOW).

Republic. A state in which sovereign powers rest with the voters rather than with a monarch, hereditary or constitutional. See Article IV of the U.S. Constitution, Appendices 1, 8.

Republic of New Africa. A black-nationalist and separatist organization (set up in 1968) struggling for the creation of a separate black state out of the following U.S. states: Alabama, Florida, Georgia, Mississippi, and South Carolina. The idea has been abandoned since. See BLACK PANTHERS PARTY FOR SELF-DEFENSE, BLACK POWER.

Republican Democrat. During his two presidential campaigns (and elections), U.S. President Ronald Reagan (1981-1989) received landslide support from voters, many of whom were registered Democrats but voted for a Republican president. Such crossover is not uncommon in American electoral practice, because party discipline is non-existent and many voters vote for the persons or the issues regardless of party affiliation. President John F. Kennedy (1961-1963) and President Franklin Delano Roosevelt (1933-1945) before him received decisive support from Republican voters.

Republican Earthquake. Term for the landslide election of Ronald Reagan as President of the United States on 4 November 1980, which strengthened the turn to conservatism and the rejection of the liberal policies of the Democratic Party and President Jimmy Carter. The American voters were obviously frustrated with President Carter's inability to bring about the release of the American hostages held in Iran for 444 days. Ronald Reagan had promised during his campaign to accomplish this. He did; the hostages were released immediately after Ronald Reagan was sworn in. See BLUE LIGHT OPERATION, OCTOBER SURPRISE.

Republican Form of Government. See REPUBLIC.

Republican Guard. The allegedly elite troops of Iraq under the command of President Saddam Hussein, about one-million men strong, which dissolved during the Persian Gulf War in 1991 without much effort on the part of the invading American and Allied forces. See PERSIAN GULF WAR.

Republican National Committee. The interim organization of the Republican Party functioning between national conventions and composed of leaders elected every four years by the National Party Convention. The top leaders of the Party are: a Chairman and several Vice Chairmen (usually four); one Secretary; and one Treasurer. The other members of the Republican National Committee are elected by state party organizations (including the District of Columbia) with the ration of one woman and one man plus the chairmen of the state party organizations. This committee is the governing body of the party until the next national convention. The committee members representing the various states are known as "Committeewomen" and "Committeemen."

Republican National Convention. See PARTY CONVENTION.

Republican Party. One of two major political parties in the United States, formed about 1854 of elements dissatisfied with the Kansas-Nebraska Act, former Whigs and Democrats, mainly from the Northern states. Among the traditional policies of the party were the abolition of slavery, the maintaining of strong protective tariffs, and the development of a strong economy based on a free enterprise system. Following the Civil War (1861-1865), the party implemented vigorous programs of reconstruction, but after World War I opposed the United States' entry into the League of Nations. The Republican Party was successful in electing the following U.S. Presidents: Abraham Lincoln (1861-1865), Andrew Johnson (1865-1869), Ulysses S. Grant (1869-1877), Rutherford B. Hayes (1877-1881), James A. Garfield (1881), Chester A. Arthur (1881-1885), Benjamin Harrison (1889-1893), William McKinley (1897-1901), Theodore Roosevelt (1901-1909), William H. Taft (1909-1913), Warren G. Harding (1921-1923), Calvin Coolidge (1923-1929), Herbert C. Hoover (1929-1933), Dwight D. Eisenhower (1953-1961), Richard M. Nixon (1969-1974), Gerald R. Ford (1974-1977), Ronald Reagan (1981-1989), and George Bush (1989-).

Republocrat. A term coined by Ray McAllister, columnist for the *Richmond Times-Dispatch*; a proper and simplified description for an ideal U.S. president who is good in foreign affairs, like the Republicans, and good in domestic affairs, like the Democrats.

Repudiation. The rejection of unjust accusations or the refusal to honor certain obligations (e.g., treaty obligations). See PACTA SUNT SERVANDA, REBUS SIC STANTIBUS.

Rerum Novarum. See ENCYCLICAL.

Res Adjudicata. In the Latin language, "a matter closed" or "a case stands as adjudicated." Also a common practice among courts of law to refuse to reopen cases once adjudicated unless there is strong new evidence presented which will justify the opening of a case and a retrial. See RES JUDICATA.

Res Judicata. In the Latin language, "a case to be settled" or "a suit to be adjudicated." See RES ADJUDICATA.

Res Publica. In the Latin language, "public matter," or "republic." Also, a state whose government derives its powers from the will of the governed and is presumed to serve the many rather than the few.

Rescission. An agreement to dissolve a treaty in force by the parties to the treaty. See PACTA SUNT SERVANDA, REBUS SIC STANTIBUS.

Residency. This term refers to the situation in which an agent or agents are assigned to a particular area or country for intelligence purposes, and are responsible for operational tasks only in that particular area or country. The Russians call it, "residentura." See INTELLIGENCE.

Resident Alien. See IMMIGRATION, UNITED STATES PERSON.

Resident Commissioner. The representative of Puerto Rico, who is elected by the Puerto Rican people for a four year term to the United States House of Representatives. The Commissioner enjoys all the benefits and privileges of any member of the House, but may not vote.

Residentura. See RESIDENCY.

Residual Powers. See RESIDUARY POWERS.

Residual Right. A right that may be acquired by one state over the territory of another as a result of war or treaty (e.g., the right of a victor to station military forces on the territory of the vanquished, or to occupy a territory for an indefinite period of time, or forever, as the spoils of war).

Residuary Powers. The powers that are left to the states and do not conflict with those of the federal government under the U.S. Constitution as a result of the separation of power principle. See U.S. Constitution Art. I Sec. 8, in Appendix 8.

Residue. That part of a testator's estate which remains after payment of debts and taxes.

Resolution. A statement of principles, or a decision to affect some persons or their acts or activities, which either house of the U.S. Congress may pass without the consent of the other house or the U.S. President; or both houses may pass a joint resolution. As a rule, resolutions and joint resolutions deal with non-controversial matters, and do not involve expenditures from the federal treasury. A resolution is not a law in the ordinary sense of a legislative act, but is a statement of philosophy, or a statement of position expressing the "sense of the Senate" or the "sense of the House." On September 9, 1977, the U.S. Senate passed a resolution forbidding discriminatory practices in congressional hiring, pay, and promotion on account of the sex, religion, or national origin of the employee although Congress, as the political law-making body of the nation, is not compelled by law to provide its employees the protection against discrimination that is required under the Equal Pay Act of 1963 and the Civil Rights Act of 1964. The Congress responded in this manner due to criticism that it discriminates against employees while it enacts laws for others against discrimination. See BILL, CONGRESS OF THE U.S.

Resolution on Palestinian Self-Determination. See PALESTINE LIBERATION ORGANIZATION (PLO).

Resolution Trust Corporation (RTC). An agency created by the Financial Institutions Reform, Recovery, and Enforcement Act of 1989 (FIRREA) to close, merge, or otherwise resolve insolvent savings and loan institutions whose deposits are insured by the federal government.

Resolutions 242, 338. See SADAT-BEGIN SUMMIT.

Resolutions of Interposition. See SOUTHERN MANIFESTO.

Resolve. A concept of decisive design of strategies and planning, with desired outcomes expected as a result of decisive leadership in business, the military, family, and politics, both domestic and foreign. Also, the ability, based on knowledge and experience, to make decisive and binding decisions regardless of consequences. The notion among leaders of all persuasions is that a bad decision is better than no decision at all. The ancient Chinese political and military strategist Sun Tzu proposed that a good resolve is when the enemy is subdued without fighting. That, he claimed, "is the acme of skill" and resolve. He also noted, "If your adversary is not winning in the battle, he is losing, and if you are not losing, you are winning." He also said, "the tools of resolve are stealth, deception, surprise, and decisiveness." The North Vietnamese and the Viet Cong took these teachings as a part of their daily military diet during the 1945-1975 Vietnamese War; the leadership of North Vietnam (with assistance from the Chinese) used the tactic of discouraging foreign soldiers from fighting by supplying them with free drugs. See GUERRILLA WAR.

Resource War. A term coined by U.S. Representative Robert K. Dornan (R-California) and his expert adviser on economics, Dr. Miles Costick, denoting the ongoing competitive struggle for control of the world's supply of raw materials by the former Soviet Union and the United States, particularly in mineral-rich Middle Eastern and African regions—a struggle which is dual in nature: military as well as economic, with ideology being only a one third consideration. Representative Dornan suggested (in a special study for the U.S. Congress) that, in the face of such a "resource war," détente with the USSR would have been beneficial only to the USSR and not to the USA, because the Soviet Union benefited not only from trade with the USA (most of it on a long-term credit extended by American banks) gaining mainly in technology which it imports from the USA and other western states, but the USSR also was gaining influence (e.g., by proxy wars in Angola, Ethiopia, and Somalia) in areas with a rich supply of raw materials.

Resources for the Future. A black organization in Washington, D.C., established in 1974 for the purpose of informing blacks on problems pertaining to regional planning and economic development in predominantly black neighborhoods.

Respondent. One against whom a petition is made on appeal from the decision of a lower court to a higher one. (This term applies mainly to petitions addressed to the United States Supreme Court by writ of certiorari.)

Responsible to God and History. Constitutions of some states limit the responsibility and accountability of the head of state (e.g., a president or monarch), only to "God and History." Absolute monarchs were also unrestrained in their actions. See STATE, TOOLS OF GOVERNMENT.

Ressemblement du Peuple Française (RPF). See RALLY OF THE FRENCH PEOPLE.

Resulting Powers. Powers which are not clearly enumerated or provided for by either statute or constitution but which, once exercised anywhere, may be used as a precedent to enforce a law (e.g., no state may secede from the American Union without the expressed consent of the U.S Congress).

Resurrection City. See POOR PEOPLE'S MARCH OF 1969.

Retail Politics. A mode of campaigning for public elective office by reaching important individuals in person on the local level rather than through the media. Although exposure through the media-radio, television, and the press—is important in any effort to reach the voters, all politics is considered local, therefore there is no substitute for a personal encounter. Grass-roots issues are more important than national or international problems according to this theory.

Retributive Justice. In law, punishment for the commission (doing it) or omission (failing to prevent it) of a wrongful act (act that is forbidden by law) that is commensurate with the crime (e.g., an eye for an eye). The opposite is rehabilitative justice, which constitutes a punishment for a wrongful act imposed for the purpose of re-educating the offender, so that he or she will refrain from similar acts in the future. Most penal systems apply punishment as a sanction for wrongful acts.

Retroactive Application of Law. See EX POST FACTO LAW, LEX RETRO NON AGIT.

Return to Normalcy. One of the most popular slogans of the conservative Republicans during the 1920 presidential election.

Reunification Express. See UNIFICATION OF GERMANY.

Revenue Bill. See BILL, UNITED STATES HOUSE OF REPRESENTATIVES.

Revenue Legislation. See UNITED STATES HOUSE OF REPRESENTATIVES.

Revenue Sharing. See NEW FEDERALISM.

Reverse Course Policy. See MACARTHUR CONSTITUTION FOR JAPAN.

Reverse Discrimination. Discrimination in reverse; a practice which may be externalized through words or action aimed at depriving a person of certain rights, privileges, or liberties, made by those who have in the past themselves been subjected to such practices; discriminatory practices aimed at former discriminators. The Allan Bakke case (ruled on by the U.S. Supreme Court on June 28, 1978) is generally considered an example of reverse discrimination sanctioned by state institutions. The Court held that although affirmative action in itself is permissible, any classification of applicants by race (Bakke was denied admission to the Medical School of the University of California in spite of his excellent grades so that a minority student could be admitted) is illegal.

Reverse Engineering. See COMPARATIVE ADVANTAGE.

Reverse Income Tax. See NEGATIVE INCOME TAX.

Review Board of the National Security Council. A six-member body of the U.S. National Security Council which prepares the agenda and sets priorities of issues to be considered by the full membership of the Council.

Revisionist. One who favors drastic revisions of a political program or of the general philosophy of the ruling elite in a state. This term was commonly used in the Soviet Union to denote anyone who disagreed with the interpretation of Marxism-Leninism by the CPSU.

Revolt. See REVOLUTION.

Revolution. A means by which individuals or elites seek to gain political power in a state through extralegal and usually violent methods, with the active support of some segments of the population of the state. Revolutions lacking popular support are often referred to as rebellions, revolts, or insurrections. The purpose of a revolution may be to replace the existing government, to alter some governmental institutions or processes, or to replace the existing politico-economic system with a new one (e.g., the socialist revolution in Russia in 1917 by the Bolsheviks). See PERMANENT REVOLUTION, REVOLUTION FROM ABOVE, REVOLUTION OF RISING EXPECTATIONS.

Revolution from Above. A term often applied to a peaceful change in the political system of a state (e.g., from a monarchy to a republic); the transfer of powers from one ruler to another within the same system (e.g., a palace revolution), without major disruption of political processes and institutions; or an implementation of major reforms which modify a given political system in some respects. In modern times, such a revolution from the top took place in Prussia under Chief Minister Karl Freiherr vom und zum Stein (1807-1808) and Chancellor Karl August Freiherr von Hardenberg (1810-1822), who had introduced a number of important and modern reforms while the Emperor Frederick William, was idling on the side. In order to "train the nation to manage its own affairs, and to grow out of this condition of childhood in which ever-restless and officious government wishes to keep the people," as Hardenberg stated in 1794, serfdom was abolished and former serfs were rewarded with grants of land. A civil service was established in 1808 on merit (through examinations) and open to anyone. ("From now on," stated Stein, "a claim to officer rank shall in peacetime be warranted only by knowledge and education, in time of war by exceptional bravery and quickness of perception.") Attempts were made to eradicate the "barracks mentality" (thinking in military terms) so much cherished by the past rulers of Prussia. Chancellor Hardenberg defined revolution from the top as one in which the "guiding principle must be a revolution in the better sense, a revolution leading directly to the great goal, the elevation of humanity through the wisdom of those in authority and not through a violent impulsion from within or without. Under democratic rules of conduct in a monarchical administration, such is the formula." The term "supraversion" is also used to describe revolutions from the top. See REVOLUTIONIST.

Revolution of Rising Expectations. A term commonly used after W.W.II by leaders of newly-emerged African states to describe their hopes for prosperity once independence from the colonial powers was achieved. However, many of these states had no skilled labor or technology to develop the natural resources available, and, as a result, many have found themselves still depending on their former masters (sometimes referred to as "new-colonialism").

Revolution with the Gentle Face. See PATHET LAO.

Revolutionary Action Movement (RAM). A highly secret, Marxist-Leninist, pro-Chinese Communist political revolutionary organization composed exclusively of blacks, which was organized in 1962 in Havana, Cuba, by Maxwell Stanford, and which was dedicated to the overthrow of the "white racist" government "of imperialist capitalists" in the United States. The organization closely cooperated with the Black Panthers, the SDS, the Weatherman, and other groups of the so-called "new left." As most leader-centered organizations it dissolved itself once Stanford lost interest in further revolutionary activity. See BLACK PANTHER PARTY, CORE, NEW LEFT, REVOLUTIONIST, SDS, WEATHERMAN.

Revolutionary Democracy. A political-economic system which is transforming from one form to another (e.g., from socialism to capitalist democracy), or one that has already been transformed from one system to another, but maintains radical reformation of its institutions and processes in order to achieve the desired stage of development. The so-called "shock therapy" applies to radical economic measures undertaken in post-communist Poland in order to rapidly change from a planner-oriented economy to a consumer/market oriented capitalist economy.

Revolutionary Sectarianism. An approximate characterization of religious sects which seek to gain political power with ecclesiastical philosophy (e.g., the various Muslim sects, such as the Sunnis and the Shiites, and the numerous national splinters throughout Africa, the Middle East, and Asia). The Iranian Muslim fundamentalists support many Muslim groups throughout the world, but particularly in the Asian part of the former Soviet empire where Islamic groups are seeking some sort of autonomy or total independence from their old masters. The division among these Muslim sects is particularly noticeable in Afghanistan, Kazakhstan, Kirgizstan, Azerbaijan, Tajikistan, Turkmenistan, Turkish Kurdistan, Nagorno-Kabarakhain, and among the Chechen-Ingushetians, Abhazians, South Ossetians, Trans-Dnieprians, and Gagauzans. See DEVOLUTION, SEPARATISM, UNILATERAL DECLARATION OF INDEPENDENCE.

Revolutionary Violence. A type of guerrilla warfare conducted through fragmented revolutionary uprisings against the established order, the legitimate government of a state, in order to give the appearance of a legitimate revolution. This type of warfare was commonly conducted by Marxist revolutionary movements in Africa and Asia, and particularly by the North Vietnamese and the Vietcong. See REVOLUTIONIST.

Revolutionist. One who advocates or actively participates in a revolution. See REVOLUTION.

Rex. In the Latin language, "king," "monarch," or "ruler."

RFC. See GREAT DEPRESSION, RECONSTRUCTION FINANCE CORPORATION.

RFP. See RALLIEMENT FRANÇAIS POPULAIRE.

Rhode Island v. Innis. See *MIRANDA V. ARIZONA*.

Rhodesian Crisis. See ZIMBABWE CRISIS.

Rhodesian Solution. See U.S.-BRITISH PLAN ON RHODESIA, ZANU, ZAPU.

Ribbentrop-Molotov Pact. See HITLER-STALIN PACT, MOLOTOV-RIBBENTROP PACT.

RICO Statute. See RACKETEERING.

Rider. An amendment, usually of a controversial nature, which ordinarily would not be passed on its own merits; but when attached to another bill, may "ride" with it through the passing process. Riders are ordinarily the product of last-minute decisions. Also called "nongermane amendments."

Right. As distinguished from privilege, a right is a personalized grant of the ability (by birth, or existing laws) to enjoy certain benefits, which either are described and regulated by law, and which cannot be easily revoked. See PRIVILEGE.

Right of State. See RAISON D'ÉTAT.

Right of Tyranny. See ROUSSEAU'S COLLECTIVISM.

Right to Abortion. See RIGHT TO PRIVACY.

Right to Accountable and Responsible Government. See HUMAN RIGHTS: AMERICAN DEFINITION, Appendices 8, 20, 21, 48, 51.

Right to be Let Alone. See RIGHT TO PRIVACY.

Right to Education. See HUMAN RIGHTS: AMERICAN DEFINITION, Appendices 8, 51.

Right to Family. See HUMAN RIGHTS: AMERICAN DEFINITION, Appendices 8, 51.

Right to Government: Election and Representation. See HUMAN RIGHTS: AMERICAN DEFINITION, Appendices 8, 51.

Right to Inheritance. See HUMAN RIGHTS: AMERICAN DEFINITION, Appendices 8, 48, 51.

Right to Know Law. See FREEDOM OF INFORMATION ACT.

Right to Liberty. See HUMAN RIGHTS: AMERICAN DEFINITION, Appendices 8, 51.

Right to Life Party. Anti-abortion coalition organized and supported by conservative elements and most religious faiths.

Right to Petition. See HUMAN RIGHTS: AMERICAN DEFINITION, Appendices 8, 51.

Right to Privacy. A constitutional doctrine in the United States, derived in part from the right to privacy as prescribed in the U.S Constitution and by common law, on the strength of which the United States Supreme Court, for example, did not allow states to interfere with the matter of abortion considering this practice protected by the very personal right to privacy. On January 11, 1973, the U.S. Supreme Court declared null and void all state laws which limited a woman's right to abortion during the first three months of pregnancy in the landmark decision of *Roe v. Wade*. On January 20, 1977, the Supreme Court allowed states to use their discretion in refusing aid for abortions under the Medicaid program, and on November 8, 1977, it refused to stay a Brooklyn Federal District Court ruling barring the federal government from withholding federal funds for elective abortions upon demand. On January 26, 1978, however, the U.S. Secretary of Health, Education and Welfare, Joseph Califano, ruled that federal funds may be used for abortions in cases of rape and incest for women who are poor and who report such cases to either police authorities or welfare agencies within sixty days from the time of the incident. Since there are approximately 6,000 different record systems in the United States which store information about individual persons, the Privacy Act of 1974 allows individuals to examine these records and to ask that, in cases of inaccuracies, proper corrections be made. Various aspects of the right to privacy have been tested in the courts in recent times. For example, in 1943, the U.S. Supreme Court ruled, while upsetting a prohibition on ringing private door bells because it interfered with the religious freedom of Jehovah Witnesses (in *Martin v. Struthers*), that the dweller may protect his privacy by posting a "no trespassing" sign; in *Saia v. New York* of 1948, the Court struck down a city ordinance against noise pollution by trucks, but a year later upheld such a prohibition in *Kovacs v. Cooper* of 1949; the right not to listen to a speech one does not want to hear has been protected in *Public Utilities Commission v. Pollack* of 1952; in *Griswold v. Connecticut* of 1965, the Court upheld one's right to be "let alone" as one of the basic rights "to privacy," although a year before in 1964, the Court ruled in *New York Times v. Sullivan* that the right to privacy may infringe upon the right of the press to know and freedom of the press, especially if there is no obvious intent of distortion on the part of the press (e.g., which was the essence in *Times, Inc. v. Hill* of 1967). See FREEDOM OF INFORMATION ACT, PRIVACY ACT OF 1974, REGIME OF PRIVACY, UNSOCIAL LIBERTY, U.S. Constitution, Appendix 48.

Right to Property. See HUMAN RIGHTS: AMERICAN DEFINITION, Appendices 8, 48, 51.

Right to the First Night. See EXECUTIVE PRIVILEGE.

Right to Work Law. The popular designation of Section 14 (b) of the Taft-Hartley Act; it allows states to prohibit closed or union shops as a condition for employment. Some state constitutions contain such provisions. See TAFT-HARTLEY LAW.

Rights to Protection. See HUMAN RIGHTS: AMERICAN DEFINITION, Appendices 8, 51.

Righteous and Well-Trained Fists. See BOXER REBELLION.

Rigid Constitution. A constitution that allows very limited interpretation of its provisions and is difficult to amend. (The U.S. Constitution is considered very flexible in interpretation but very rigid in its amending process).

Riksdag. The Parliament of Sweden (unicameral).

Rio Conference of 1941-1942. In June 1941, British intelligence intercepted a message from Major Elias Belmonte, the Bolivian military attaché to Berlin, addressed to Dr. Ernest Wendler, the German Nazi Minister to Bolivia, in which Belmonte revealed his plan to stage a coup d'état in Bolivia and to introduce a pro-Nazi military dictatorship there. The plot was revealed, the conspirators were arrested, and a major Pan-American conference was called for December 1941–January 1942 to Rio de Janeiro, Brazil. All Latin American republics with the exception of pro-Nazi Argentina, Chile, and Mexico conferred and, jointly with the United States, agreed to work together toward the defeat of Nazi Germany and Fascist Italy. (It was also during the Rio Conference that once pro-Nazi Brazil, under the leadership of President Getulio Vargas, decided to break relations with Germany and declare neutrality.) See VARGAS' NEUTRALITY.

Rio de Janeiro Earth Summit. A global gathering organized by the United Nations Organization, to be convened in the city of Rio de Janeiro, Brazil, on 1 June 1992, for the purpose of informing the attending heads of states and governments, and other persons concerned with ecology, about the catastrophic consequences facing the planet earth as a result of excessive carbon dioxide emissions. These emissions are the leading pollutant of the air and affect forests and water sources; in turn, the fauna and flora are affected. They are also believed to cause the greenhouse effect (i.e., global warming). The treaty, expected to be signed there, aims to bind world leaders toward greater efforts in protecting the planet.

Rio Pact. See RIO TREATY.

Rio Treaty. A regional security agreement (signed in Rio de Janeiro, Brazil, in 1947) between the Latin American republics and the United States binding all signatories to collectively aid any state which is party to the Treaty in case of an armed attack. The signatories of the Treaty are: Argentina, Bolivia, Brazil, Chile, Columbia, Costa Rica, Cuba, Dominican Republic, El Salvador, Equator, Guatemala, Haiti, Honduras, Mexico, Nicaragua, Panama, Paraguay, Peru, the United States of America, Uruguay, and Venezuela. Cuba withdrew in 1960. Also known as "Anti-War Treaty" or "Treaty of Reciprocal Assistance."

Riparian Right. An owner of property situated adjacent to a river, lake, or pond, has the right to a part of that body of water as well. Known also as "littoral rights."

Ripon Society. A partisan coalition in the United States which favors Republican causes, and which helps "progressive" Republicans get elected to all levels of government through its New Leadership Fund. According to U.S. Senator Mark O. Hatfield, (R-Ore.), the purpose of the fund is "to recruit and help elect fresh, new candidates for office—who are scrupulous, public spirited and tough." The principal aim of the Society is to inject new leadership into the Republican Party in order to make it adequately competitive with the Democrats.

Rising Sun. An affectionate name for the state of Japan, a society of great culture, traditions, and cohesiveness. The rising sun is also depicted on the Japanese flag. See CHRYSANTHEMUM KISSER.

Risk Failure. See GRASS-ROOTS PEROT.

Rites of Passage. The rituals associated with the transfer of the individual or a community from one social stage to another (e.g., the ceremonies and rituals accompanying birth, maturity, puberty, marriage, and death); also, the transformation from one form of political system to another; for example, the recent transformation of the Soviet and East European economies from socialist to market economies. Such rituals follow three main stages: (1) separation, (2) transition, and (3) incorporation or settlement. The term was coined by French anthropologist Arnold van Gennep in 1909.

Rivers of Blood. TWO RIVERS OF BLOOD.

ROAD. See REORGANIZATION OBJECTIVES ARMY DIVISION, PENTOMIC ARMY.

Roaring Twenties. A era between the end of W.W.I and the Great Depression of 1929 during the administrations of U.S. Presidents Warren G. Harding (1921-1923), and Calvin Coolidge (1923-1929), which was characterized in national politics by a lack of emphasis on the values of patriotism and hard work. It was a time of personal enjoyment (gin and jazz) and the worship of the "mighty dollar" while an economic crisis was creeping in. Also known as the "Era of Wonderful Nonsense" or "Gin and Jazz Mentality." The impact of the productivity decline during this time would be felt for decades to come.

Robert's Rules of Order. A system of parliamentary procedures and rules designed for the conduct of business by deliberating bodies and prepared by Major Henry M. Robert of the United States Army in 1876.

Robespierre's Radicalism. See ROUSSEAU'S COLLECTIVISM.

Roe v. Wade. See REGIME OF PRIVACY, RIGHT TO PRIVACY, Appendix 48.

Rogue Elephant. So characterized the U.S. Senate Intelligence Oversight Committee the Central Intelligence Agency (CIA) after the agency revealed its so-called "Family Jewels," and other rogue behavior by the agency. See CHAOS, COUNTERINTELLIGENCE IN AMERICA, HT/LINGUAL.

Role. That function which an individual in a politically organized society is expected to perform by virtue of being a citizen or a resident alien (inherent role), or the function which he chooses to perform by being elected to a public office (public role). In either case a penalty is provided for the failure to perform that role (e.g., not paying taxes or obeying other laws; or, in a case of a public official, failing to carry out the functions of a given office). See ACTOR, WRIT OF MANDAMUS.

Role of State. The state, being a creature of the political man, is viewed differently by different men as to its primary role in the life of a society. The following broad views prevail: (1) The Anarchistic Theory—views the state as a nuisance, an instrument of oppression of man because it restricts certain liberties; man should live through some sort of voluntary association, free of systematized rules and bureaucracies; (2) The Collectivistic Theory—views the state as an organization that is necessary to protect persons living in groups, and it ranges in scope and degree of organization from maternalism to paternalism; from welfarism to socialism and communism; (3) The Totalitarian Theory—views the state as an end in itself, and human beings as transitory agents who are expected to sustain and to preserve the state at all possible sacrifice (including human life, which is expendable while the life of the state is not). Totalitarian states, as most existing evidence suggests, usually serve as instruments for protecting and perpetuating the existence of the ruling elite; and (4) The Individualistic Theory—views the state as a necessary evil needed to protect individuals in the enjoyment of their rights, and if that instrument is diverted by any single individual or group for the attainment of their selfish interests at the expense of others, that state is considered oppressive and internal changes will be sought (e.g., through election or revolution).

Roll Back Big Government. See LIBERATION PARTY.

Roll-Call. The method of calling by name individual members at a party convention or in the United States Congress for the purpose of ascertaining the presence of a quorum. This method is always used in the U.S. Congress when a quorum is needed for a record vote on legislation of a controversial nature, the overriding of presidential veto, or at any other time upon the request of one-fifth of the members present.

Roll-Call Vote. See ROLL-CALL.

Rolling Devolution. See HILLSBOROUGH AGREEMENT, IRISH REPUBLICAN ARMY (IRA).

Romania's Council of National Salvation. See NATIONAL SALVATION FRONT.

Rome Club. An informal group of 85 business and government persons representing the major industrial nations of the world, which meets periodically to discuss major economic trends in the world and to seek solutions for critical developments, formed in Rome in 1975. During its 1977 conference in Rome, the club decided to retreat from a no-growth philosophy, particularly in economic and social matters, in order to meet the needs of the world, particularly the need for food by Third World countries. This reversal of the "no-growth" philosophy was triggered by a U.S. study, *The Limits of Growth*, presented to the Club in 1977, and subsequent studies, indicating that the trend in the present rate of growth will soon lead to starvation and disaster as expanding populations, particularly in the Third World countries, are using up the finite resources of the world; that growth must be expanded if there is to be more food for the hungry; that there must be new factories and more fertilizer plants, and, above all, a revival of profit for those who are willing to invest in those enterprises. "No-growth," "zero-growth," or "negative growth" ideas have been advanced on the national level in the United States (and in other industrial nations). Advocates insist that we must stop being wasteful, spend less, produce less, do with less, in order to save our resources, mainly energy and clean water. This movement triggered a variety of planning arrangements at all levels, national, state, and substate, for the purpose of better utilization of scarce resources. See PLANNING.

Röntgen Equivalent in Man (REM). Internationally recognized as a standard unit for measuring the amount or quantity of radiation that has been absorbed by a given mass, (e.g., a human being). The amount of radiation is generally measured by a *curie* (named after Dr. Maria Sklodowska-Curie, a Polish scientist and Nobel prize recipient), which is a measure of radioactivity with one curie being equivalent to 3.70×10^{10} disintegrations per second. According to recent estimates, 1.5 microcurie (one microcurie equals one-millionth of a curie) may cause the reduction of an average life expectancy by one half.

Rookie Legislator. One serving his/her first term in a legislative body (e.g., in the U.S. House of Representatives or the U.S. Senate); also applies to members of state legislatures and to office holders in local subdivisions (e.g., a city council or a county board of supervisors or commissioners). The term "freshman" is also used. See BUSINESS OF CONGRESS IS RE-ELECTION BUSINESS.

Roosevelt Corollary. United States military policy, evolved during U.S. President Theodore Roosevelt's administrations (1901-1909), according to which the United States was not to hesitate to deploy its military forces against any power intervening into the domestic affairs of any state in the Western Hemisphere (mainly Latin America). The purpose of this policy pronouncement was to uphold the Monroe Doctrine.

Roosevelt Erection. See PROPRIETARIES.

Roosevelt's Economic Recovery Slogan. In order to dispel the prevailing fear among Americans caused by the Great Depression and to launch his new policies of the New Deal to rectify the situation, U.S. President Franklin Delano Roosevelt (1933-1945), made several statements of lasting importance: during the Chicago Democratic Party Convention, 2 July 1932, "I pledge you—I pledge myself—to a new deal for the American people"; first inaugural address on 4 January 1933, "Let me assert my firm belief that the only thing we have to fear is fear itself"; second inaugural address, 20 January 1937, "I would dedicate this nation to the policy of the good neighbor," and "I see one-third of a nation ill-housed, ill-clad, ill-nourished"; pertaining to foreign affairs, 29 December 1940, "We must be the great arsenal of democracy"; and in an address to Congress on 6 January 1941, "In the future days, which we seek to make secure, we look forward to a world founded upon four essential human freedoms. The first is freedom of speech and expression—everywhere in the world. The second is freedom of every person to worship God in his own way—everywhere in the world. The third is freedom from want . . . the fourth is freedom from fear."

Roosevelt's Four Freedoms. See FOUR FREEDOMS, ROOSEVELT'S ECONOMIC RECOVERY SLOGAN.

Roosevelt's Second Bill of Rights. See SECOND BILL OF RIGHTS.

Rose Garden. A nickname for the White House on Pennsylvania Avenue, Northwest, in Washington, District of Columbia, where the U.S. President resides and officiates. Named after the handsome rose garden on the grounds in which presidents often stroll for meditation or to relieve pressure of the burdened office. See WHITE HOUSE.

Rose Garden Campaign. An incumbent president campaigning from the White House, without extensive travel.

Rote Kapelle. See RED ORCHESTRA.

Rotten Borough. An electoral district (e.g., a Congressional district in the United States designed for the purpose of electing one representative to the U.S. House of Representatives) with a small population which, as a result of either political machinations or lack of apportionment, has representation in the national legislature equal to that of a district with a larger population. (This is no longer possible in the United States under the ONE MAN, ONE VOTE formula). In England and Scotland, a borough is a constituency which elects a member to Parliament. A rotten borough was one that had lost most of its population, but still had representation in Parliament.

Roundhead. See CAVALIER.

Rousseau's Collectivism. Jean Jacques Rousseau (1712-1778), Swiss political philosopher and author, viewed government as a committee, in which sovereignty, under the general will, belongs to the people as a corporate body; government is merely an agent utilizing powers which are granted to it by the people, and which can be withdrawn at their will. The best government is that of direct democracy rather than a representative one, because people hold sovereignty, and sovereignty is something that cannot be represented. The right to exercise power may become the right to tyranny. He differed from John Locke (1632-1704), the English philosopher, who believed that government gains unique powers to govern by contract with the people. The general will of the people stands for social good, which is the standard of rights. Maximilian Robespierre, one of the Jacobin leaders during the French Revolution of 1798, stated that the will of the Jacobins "is the general will. The government of the Revolution is the despotism of liberty against tyranny." Robespierre commented further on the use of terrorism: "They say that terrorism is the resort of despotic government. Is our government then like despotism? Yes, as the sword that flashes in the hand of the hero of liberty is like that with which the satellites of tyranny are armed. The government of the Revolution is the despotism of liberty against tyranny." See Appendix 1.

Roving Ambassador. An individual with special skills and trust who is used for special state missions, trade or diplomatic tasks, usually on a single issue, who the chief executive of a state of government (e.g., the President of the United States) may use from time to time. Such persons are assigned diplomatic ranks (e.g., that of "special envoy," "minister," or simply "ambassador") for reasons of prestige, pay, and retirement benefits. Roving envoys deal, as a rule, with emergency matters, sending "feelers," testing the political and diplomatic grounds, or simply conveying confidential messages to heads of states and/or heads of government. In American diplomatic history, George Washington was the first U.S. President to deploy such envoys, and President Franklin Delano Roosevelt (1933-1945) made an art of it. Roosevelt's most trusted roving ambassador was millionaire and former governor of New York State, W. Averell Harriman (1891-1983).

Royal Colony. See AMERICAN COLONIES.

Royal Dictatorship. See MOSSADEGH.

Royal Theocracy. See CAESAROPAPISM.

Royalist. One who is loyal and dedicated to a monarch (king, tsar, emperor, or a queen), or one who favors the rule by a monarch, and opposes a republican form of government.

RPDC. Regional Planning District Commission. See COUNTERINSURGENCY IN AMERICA.

RPF. See RALLY OF THE FRENCH PEOPLE.

RS-DLP. See RUSSIAN SOCIAL-DEMOCRATIC LABOR PARTY.

RU-486 Politics. See FOCUS GROUP.

Rubbergate. See KISS AND TELL FOR SALE, LAW OF LITTLE THINGS.

Rugged Individualism. Term applied to persons supporting laissez-faire economic policies and resisting any form of submission to the will of others (e.g., community, society, or governmental control of private enterprises in the United States). See INDIVIDUALISM.

Rukh. A very active, contemporary, political movement in the Ukraine, formed in 1989; it was instrumental in restoring the nation's independence from the Soviet Union, and advocates evincing strong national characteristics in Ukrainian politics and culture. Its leader is poet Ivan Drach.

Rule. Those directives or prescriptions which stipulate certain conduct or actions, and which come from a legitimate authority.

Rule of Four. As a matter of tradition, the U.S. Supreme Court decides, usually by a vote of four justices, whether or not to issue a writ of certiorari and to hear a case presented to it on appeal. Once such a writ is issued, the case is placed on the Court's docket. See Appendices 44-49.

Rule of Law. See DEMOCRATIC THEORY.

Rule of Reason. See JUDICIAL PRECEDENT.

Rule Through Education. See MASS LINE.

Rule Twenty-Two. See CLOTURE, FILIBUSTER

Rulemonger. One obediently and unreservedly subscribing to and/or following certain rules, demanding their strict observance, or favoring exercise of leadership role through written rules rather than personal interactions. Common practice under totalitarian political systems.

Ruler Should be Respected and Obeyed Instead of Being Loved by His Subjects. See MACHIAVELLIANISM.

Rulers of the Soviet Union. After the abdication in 1919 of the last Russian Tzar, Nicholas II (forced by heavy losses to Germany during W.W.I and the approaching February Revolution in 1917), the Tzar, the Empress, his son and Crown Prince, the Tzarevich, and the Tzar's four daughters were murdered by Lenin's Bolsheviks on 16 July 1918 in the city of Ekaterinburg. (In 1992, President Boris N. Yeltsin directed the former Soviet KGB to declassify and make available to the public related files.) After the abdication of Nicholas, a provisional government was formed under the leadership of Prince Georgi Lvov and attorney Alexander Kerensky. The 17 October (old calendar 7 November) 1917 Revolution, known as the "Bolshevik Revolution," replaced the provisional government of Kerensky with a Council of People's Commissars under the leadership of a lawyer and the leader of the Bolsheviks, Vladimir Ilyich Ulyanov, who took the nom de guerre of "Lenin." Lenin died on 21 January 1924 leaving a testament, known as the "Lenin Testament," warning against Stalin. Lenin's temporary successor was Vyacheslav M. Molotov, but Josef Visaryanovich Djugashvili, nom de guerre "Stalin" (a "man of steel"), was the actual ruler since he was the secretary of the Bolshevik party. Stalin officially became president of the Council of Ministers of the USSR and de facto premier and commander-in-chief of the armed forces (with the rank of "marshal," or "generalissimo" as he preferred to be called. Stalin died on 5 March 1953 and was succeeded by party apparatchik Georgi M. Malenkov as premier, and by W.W.II Red Army Politruk, General Nikita Sergeyevich Khrushchev, as the first secretary of the party. Malenkov resigned on 8 February 1955 (due to disputes with the ethnocentric Khrushchev); he became deputy premier but was removed from power on 27 March 1957, and was succeeded as premier by Marshal of the Red Army Nikolai A. Bulganin on 8 February 1955. Bulganin was demoted and Khrushchev became premier on 27 March 1958. After the Cuban missile crisis, Khrushchev was removed from power and humiliated, but, unlike all other deposed Soviet rulers, was allowed to die of natural causes. He was succeeded on 15 October 1964 by Marshal of the Red Army Leonid I. Brezhneyev as the first secretary of the Party, and Aleksei N. Kosygin as the premier. Brezhneyev was elevated to the presidency on 16 June 1977; he died on 10 November 1982, and was succeeded by the former Director of the Soviet Intelligence and Secret Police (the KGB), Yuri V. Andropov. Andropov died on 9 February 1984 and was succeeded by party apparatchik Konstantin U. Chernenko as the secretary of the party. When Chernenko died on 10 March 1985, he was succeeded as general secretary of the party by a new breed of apparatchik, Mikhail Sergeyevich Gorbachev, who on 1 October 1988 also took the office of president. Since Brezhneyev's death this office had been held by the former Soviet Foreign Minister, Andrei Gromyko. Gorbachev resigned as president of the USSR on 25 December 1991. The presidency of Russia proper then went to Boris Nikolayevich Yeltsin who, since 1990, has been president of the Russian Federal Republic. See Appendix 74.

Rules Committee. A legislative committee in the U.S. House of Representatives charged with the task of developing and administering rules of procedure which determine if, when, and under what conditions bills approved by the other standing committees (except the Appropriations and Ways and Means Committee) will reach the floor of the House for final voting. See Appendices 10, 11, 13.

Rules for the Passing Hour. See ORDINARY LAW.

Rules of Engagement. Certain prescribed codes of behavior which soldiers, particularly those engaged in combat, are expected to follow as dictated by the military command. For example, in an ordinary engagement soldiers are not to fire unless fired upon, but this does not apply to a surprise attack during a war in progress or to guerrilla warfare. Guerrilla tactics call for attacking the enemy at any time by surprise and with a decisive force, and withdrawing if strong resistance is encountered. American soldiers in Vietnam were to observe the rule of firing upon an enemy only when returning fire, and to refrain from offensive warfare. When the North Vietnamese or Vietcong attacked Americans in Vietnam, and then promptly withdrew across the border to Cambodia, the Americans were not allowed to follow the enemy in hot pursuit. Such rules demoralized the combatants, and many preferred to either refrain from engagement or to frag (kill) their commanders who gave them orders to remain in combat. Such restrictive rules destroyed morale and resolve among the troops and favored the enemy, inspiring them to pursue the war to final victory. See Appendices 29, 30.

Rules of Evidence. A set of established rules of procedure that courts of law follow in admitting evidence in the trial of cases.

Rules of Land Warfare. U.S. rules regulating warfare both on land and sea rely on the following principles, according to the *Basic Field Manual 27-10 (1940)* of the Pentagon: (1) principle of military necessity—a belligerent state is justified, subject to the principles of humanity and chivalry, in applying any kind and amount of force in order to subdue its adversary with the minimum of expenditure of time, life, and material resources; (2) principle of humanity—forbids the use of any kind, amount, or degree of violence which is excessive and not necessary for the purpose of the war; and (3) principle of chivalry—forbids the use of means which are dishonest and dishonorable, no matter how expedient.

Rules of Parliamentary Procedure. See ROBERT'S RULES OF ORDER.

Rules of Understanding. See PRINCIPLES OF UNDERSTANDING.

Rules of War. See RULES OF LAND WARFARE.

Rum, Romanism, and Rebellion. See SCUM.

Rump State. A state that is in the process of disintegration, of losing its legitimate right to exist and to claim any sovereign powers (e.g., the decline of the Roman Empire, the Austria-Hungarian Empire, or the Ottoman Empire).

Run-Away Shop. A business enterprise of one state producing goods and/or services on the territory of another in order to benefit from cheaper labor. See MULTINATIONAL CORPORATION.

Run-Off Election. When no single candidate receives the necessary majority vote, a subsequent "run-off" election may be held in which only the two candidates who received the highest number of votes in the previous election will participate. This system does not apply where a plurality vote is allowed.

Run the Trains on Time! See FASCISM.

Running Dog of Imperialism. A term often used by the leaders of the People's Republic of China (Communist China) to depict any state (and its leaders) that closely collaborates with the United States and its government.

Running Dog of Wall Street. A derogatory term used by the Chinese Communist leadership applicable to anyone, American or otherwise, who supports and/or serves the interests of a capitalistic system, particularly that of the United States where the New York Stock Exchange and major investment bankers maintain offices on Wall Street in New York City.

Running Mate. One person joining another for a lower position of an integral office (e.g., the U.S. President and Vice President running on a single ticket for the central executive office of the nation). Running mates are, as a rule, selected by the principal candidate (e.g., the presidential candidate).

Rush-Bagot Agreement. The oldest treaty on the North American Continent, largely still in force though obsolete, and a symbol of peaceful accommodation of Canada, Great Britain and the United States. However, frictions between Canada and the United States arise from time to time, due mainly to the American expansionist economy (e.g., flooding Canadian markets with U.S. products, beaming TV programs, and otherwise invading Canadian culture). Being a neighbor of such giant as America is, like "sleeping with an elephant," once observed Pierre Trudeau, Canada's Prime Minister (1968-1979). The treaty pertains to navigational rights on the Great Lakes and, as revised during World War II, the construction of naval facilities in the interest of Canada and the United States. The original treaty was signed on 28-29 April 1817, by Sir Charles Bagot, Britain's Ambassador to the United States, and Richard Rush, America's acting Secretary of State. See TREATY.

Russian-American Antagonism. See AMERICAN-SOVIET COLLUSION, COUNTERINSURGENCY IN AMERICA.

Russian Revolution of 1905. See BLOODY SUNDAY.

Russian Social-Democratic Labor Party (RS-DLP). A major political party in pre-revolutionary Russia which had operated in secrecy due to constant persecution of its members and leaders by the Tsarist secret police. In 1903 the party split into two major factions, the moderate group led by Martov (and later renamed the "Mensheviks" or "minority" by Lenin), and the revolutionary group led by Lenin (and named by him the "Bolsheviks" or "majority"). The majority (Bolsheviks) gained control of the party during the October Revolution in 1917. The Communist Party of the Soviet Union (CPSU) claimed its heritage from the revolutionary group of the RS-DLP.

Russian Socialist Federated Soviet Republic (RSFSR). In the Russian language, "Rossyiskaya Sotzyalistitcheskaya Federatzyina Sovyetzkaya Respublika." The original and the largest (in population and territory) Union Republic (out of fifteen Union Republics) of the former Soviet Federation, and the dominant one. See Appendix 103.

Russification. The practice of requiring all persons in government service, in the military, or in the schools to study and to know the Russian language and to cherish the cultural heritage of Russia or the Soviet Union. This applied to all states or areas under direct Russian and Soviet jurisdiction or under indirect jurisdiction (e.g., the East European satellite states), until the Soviet empire dissolved in 1991. See IMPERIALISM.

Rutherfraud. See HAYES-TILDEN DISPUTE.

SACB. See SUBVERSIVE ACTIVITIES CONTROL BOARD.

Sacerdotal Society of the Holy Cross and Opus Dei. A political organization with religious orientation founded in 1928 by a group of Spanish priests, which attempts, like a lobby, to influence the policies of the government, but does not present its own candidates for election. The Opus Dei, as it is often referred to, encourages its members to actively participate in political and governmental processes, education, and business, and its principal tenet is sanctification through one's daily work and one's excellence in a chosen career. The organization closely collaborated with Francisco Franco and his National Movement (former Falange) Party and has world-wide membership. The Pope has recognized the organization as a secular association despite its strong Christian teaching and the discipline that it maintains among its members. See OPUS DEI.

Sacred Mission. See SADAT-BEGIN SUMMIT.

Sadat-Begin Summit. On November 19, 1977, Egypt's President Anwar Sadat (1921-1981) visited the state of Israel on what he referred to as a "Sacred Mission," to confer with Israel's Prime Minister Menachem Begin (1913-1992) on normalization of relations between these two states. Prime Minister Begin encountered little opposition to his participation in the Summit. President Sadat, was supported by right-wing Social Liberal Party, but was opposed by the National Progressive Union Party, as well as by most of the Arab leaders. President Sadat was extended an invitation by Prime Minister Begin, which was authorized by the Knesset (Israeli Parliament). The summit had been arranged by television newscaster, Walter Cronkite of the New York-based Columbia Broadcasting System (CBS), who on November 14, 1977, broadcast taped interviews with both leaders. It was then that President Sadat expressed willingness to go to Israel, and Israel through Premier Begin, extended him an invitation. During December 1-4, 1977, President Sadat visited Tripoli, Libya, to explain his plans, but the Tripoli Summit brought little unity to the Arab world. On December 5, 1977, the Palestine Liberation Organization (PLO), Iraq, Syria, Algeria, and Southern Yemen broke off diplomatic relations with Egypt; and Ismail Fahmy, Egypt's Foreign Minister, resigned in protest to Sadat's trip to Jerusalem. On December 25, 1977, Israeli Prime Minister Menachem Begin flew from Ben-Gurion International Airport to Tel Aviv to Abu Suweir Air Base in Ismailia, Egypt, to meet with President Sadat. This was the first time that an Israeli head of government (or anyone in an official capacity from Israel) had visited an Arab state. It is particularly notable that it was Begin, as he was considered by most Arabs to be a "fanatical hawk." During the Ismailia Summit, the two parties failed to reach agreement on two important issues: (1) the creation of a separate Palestinian state (Israel would like such a state to be an autonomous entity with political control by Israel), and (2) Israel's withdrawal from the Sinai Peninsula, Gaza Strip, and the West Bank of Jordan. Egypt wants a sovereign state of Palestine on the West Bank and in Gaza, and Israel wants the establishment of secure and recognized borders with the Arab states, in line with Resolutions 242 (of 1974) and 338 (of 1976) by the Security Council of the United Nations Organization, which called upon Israel to return these lands to the Arabs. Two separate commissions have been established: the Military Commission (to consider military matters), and the Political Commission (to consider political matters). The summit ended on December 26, 1977. During the many meetings that were held in January 1978, no progress was made, and President Sadat, in frustration, recalled his ambassador from negotiations in Jerusalem on January 18, 1978. Shortly thereafter, U.S. President Jimmy Carter called President Sadat, and urged him to keep the talks going, but Sadat replied, "Israel does not want peace, it wants

Egypt's land." Israeli Premier Menachem Begin denied publicly (during a press conference which was held at the National Press Club in Washington, D.C., on March 23, 1978) that Israel seeks Arab land, but upon his return to Israel on March 24, 1978, Begin was quoted (by *The New York Times Service*) as saying that the occupied West Bank and the Gaza Strip would be retained by Israel because they "are properly part of Israel because of their Biblical associations with the ancient Jews," a policy adhered to to this day. After Israel's excursion into Lebanon in March 1978, in retaliation for Palestinian terrorist attacks on Israel, the Egypt-Israeli dialogue came to a complete halt and upon Sadat's assassination on 6 October 1981, the rapprochement became history. See EIN BRERA, ISRAELI SETTLEMENTS, Appendix 95.

Safe Conduct. See INNOCENT PASSAGE.

Safe District. An electoral district in the United States (e.g., congressional or a state election district), which is dominated either by a single political party, party machine, or an individual; where the election results are usually predictable, and the prospective candidate feels well assured of a victory on election day.

Safe House. A place of residence for a safe meeting between clandestine agents; a place that is well secured from surveillance and easy discovery by counterintelligence. See INTELLIGENCE.

Sagebrush Rebellion. See ENVIRONMENT PROTECTION MOVEMENT.

Saharan Arab Democratic Republic. See POLISARIO FRONT.

Salic Law. A code of laws of the Germanic tribes and the Salian Franks; it pertains mainly to the exclusion of women from the right to inherit property or succeed to the throne under the French and the Spanish monarchies. Term often used to describe any law or political and legal system which discriminates against women. See NATIONAL ORGANIZATION OF WOMEN.

Saloning. A social movement in the United States, based on a tradition dating back to past centuries when European salons were famous as informal meeting places for debating issues, without any specific agenda or timetable. Some call this movement a "renewal of American democracy through participatory debate." Throughout the world, there have been informal meetings of persons, usually the young, artists, philosophers, poets, musicians, those happy with the times as well as those who were bored and sought change. Great ideas have been conceived in small gatherings, often spontaneously (e.g., by the philosophers of the Enlightenment; by socialists and communists and fascists, and by advocates of matters more noble); all commenced as a debate between two or more persons which casually and with time evolved into major doctrines of forces that have shaped our history. It is truism that once two strangers meet face to face, even without the exchange of a single word between them, they will never be the same once they part. In social change, there is no substitute for a personal encounter.

Saloon Must Go. See WOMAN'S CHRISTIAN TEMPERANCE UNION (WCTU).

SALT. See STRATEGIC ARMS LIMITATION TALKS.

Salutary Impact. As applied to international politics (or diplomacy), an act or incident (designed or accidental) which may bring about a solution to an existing international problem (e.g., the death of a leader or dissolution of government in a state which instigates international conflict). See DIPLOMACY.

Salvo Jure. In the Latin language, "protection of one's right" or "acting without prejudice to one's right."

Samokritika. In the Russian language, "self-criticism." It was once one of the fundamental principles of communist intraparty democracy and was based on the Leninist principle (including the CPSU in the former USSR) that a party member or candidate member was expected to admit before his peers during party meetings any deviations from the party line (actually committed or thought of), and to promise to refrain from such acts (or thoughts) in the future. Failure to do so constituted sufficient grounds for summary dismissal from the party ranks and employment. See COMMUNIST PARTY OF THE SOVIET UNION (CPSU).

Samurai. The ruling class in Japan's pre-industrial society—the warriors, who enjoyed privileged status opposite the three other classes into which the society was divided: the merchants, the artisans, and the peasants. Those class distinctions were strictly enforced, particularly after the adoption of a national policy of isolation from other nations and societies following the death in 1616 of Ieyasui, the warrior who had unified Japan in 1601. The Samurais were the war-lords in charge of shogunates (military and civilian governments) which ruled Japan for the Emperor. They lived by the Bushido Code which calls for loyalty, courage, simple living, and death by suicide (hara-kiri) rather than life with dishonor.

San Francisco Conference. Representatives of 51 nations met in the city of San Francisco, California, between April 25-June 26, 1945, to draw up a charter for the United Nations Organization on the basis of foundations laid during the August 21-September 28, 1944, Dumbarton Oaks Conference in Washington, D.C., between the United States, England, and the Soviet Union, and the September 29-October 7, 1944, conference between the United States, England, and China. The charter became effective upon ratification by the five permanent members of the Security Council (the United States, England, the Soviet Union, France, and China) on October 24, 1945. See UNITED NATIONS ORGANIZATION (UNO), Appendices 75-79.

San Ho Hui. In the Chinese language, "triad society." See MAFIA, SECRET SOCIETIES.

Sanction. The steps that may be taken to enforce a law. Also, as applied to international politics, the general approval by states of measures taken against an aggressor-nation by the imposition of such retaliatory measures as embargo, blockade, breaking off diplomatic or trade relations, or even the use of force.

Sanctuary Movement. See WETBACK.

Sandanista Liberation Front. With the overthrow of the dictator and president of Nicaragua, General Anastasio Somoza (1967-1979), the leftist-oriented Sandanista, under the leadership of Daniel Ortega as the new president, ruled by decree until 1990, when Violeta Barrios de Chamorro was democratically elected president. The Sandanistas, however, retained considerable control over the police and the army, and a complete stability has not been restored as of yet. The Reagan Administration extended considerable financial and military assistance to the so-called "Contras," but that aid was terminated by the U.S. Congress in 1985. Democratic sloganeering itself, provided little relief to the plight of the landless masses of Nicaraguans and, since the beginning of 1992, the Sandanistas together with the former Contras, once bitter enemies, joined forces against the impotent and penniless government of Mrs. Chamorro, and, if the land distribution issue is not solved within a reasonable time, a new revolution shall commence. The landless, semi-literate masses, exhausted during the many years of political conflict, demand land, jobs, food and shelter—the basic necessities of every human being anytime, anywhere. According to the democratic theory of capitalism, by giving people land, one has by and large solved their needs (and government's concerns) for jobs, housing, food, and shelter. Having land, they will provide for themselves, not needing government (or foreign aid) handouts. See DEMOCRATIC CAPITALISM ENCOMIENDA, FEUDALISM, IRAN-CONTRA AFFAIR, LATIFUNDIUM.

Sangi-In. Upper house of the legislature, the House of Councillors, in Japan. See KOKKAI, SHUGI-IN.

Sansad. The bicameral Parliament of India, consisting of an upper house, the Government Assembly or Rajya Sabha, and a lower house, the People's Assembly or Lok Sabha.

Sansea. See MEGALOPOLIS.

Santa Claus Politics. A policy of government, a legislative program of a law making body, or promises made by a candidate for public elective office, designed to attract voter support by dispensing benefits. Benefits might include increased Social Security payments, reduction of taxes, or some other type of tangible benefit that voters and citizens would like to receive. Term taken from the Santa Claus figure (St. Nicholas, in some parts of the world) who dispenses gifts at Christmas time. See PORK BARREL LEGISLATION.

SAS. See DELTA FORCE, SPECIAL AIR SERVICE REGIMENT.

Satellite State. See DEPENDENCY.

Satha Poothan. See RATHA SATHA.

Satrap. Once a title of the governor of a province or regional autonomous political subdivision, known as "satrapy," under the Persian monarchy. Also, a petty tyrant or despotic ruler or government official in charge of an agency of government. Once common among the Arab states and in other Middle-Eastern communities under the Ottoman rule.

Satrapy. See SATRAP.

Saturday Night Massacre. On Saturday, October 20, 1973, President Richard M. Nixon ordered the U.S. Attorney General to fire the Watergate Special Prosecutor, Harvard Professor Archibald Cox, after Cox had bluntly refused to drop a court order that President Nixon release his White House tapes containing information on Nixon's cover-up in the Watergate scandal. The Attorney General, Elliot Richardson, as well as his deputy, Richard Ruckelshaus, resigned instead. Acting Attorney General, Robert H. Bork, dismissed Cox on Nixon's orders, an action which the Court declared illegal, and this in turn triggered impeachment proceedings by the U.S. House of Representatives of Congress. President Richard M. Nixon fired U.S. Special Prosecutor Archibald Cox, who was to investigate and seek indictments against those involved in the Watergate incident. Elliot Richardson and his Deputy Attorney General also resigned in order to avoid firing Cox. In this case, the President had to do the firing himself. See SPECIAL PROSECUTOR, WATERGATE.

Satyagraha. In the Hindu language, "faithful obstinacy" or "non-violent disobedience." A term coined by India's spiritual and political leader Mahandas Karamchand Gandhi (1869-1948), called by his followers "Mahatma"—(in the Hindu language, "Great Soul"), and practiced by him and his followers against the British domination of India and the Portuguese domination of Gôa which India claimed and later regained as its territory. This concept was advocated and practiced by Dr. Martin Luther King and his followers in their struggle for the rightful place of blacks and the poor within the American society.

Saudi Arabian Consultative Council. See MAJLIS.

SAVAK. See NATIONAL SECURITY AND INFORMATION ORGANIZATION.

Sawdust Trail. In a democracy, one's success in electoral politics is determined by the number of votes, and in order to get them, one must endeavor during an election campaign to reach as many voters as possible, regardless of weather conditions and other obstacles.

Say Uncle. See CRY UNCLE.

Sazeman Ettelaat va Amniyat Kashvar (SAVAK). See NATIONAL SECURITY AND INFORMATION ORGANIZATION.

Scalawag. See CARPETBAGGER.

Scare the Hell out of the Country. U.S. Senator Arthur Vandenberg approached U.S. President Harry S. Truman in January 1946 suggesting that the president appear before the U.S. Congress and inform it about the Clifford Memorandum to the effect that the Soviet threat to the United States was real; that the Soviet Union had a standing army twice the size of that of the United States; that the Soviet Union already controlled the armed forces of the East European satellites in Eastern Europe, and the forces of Mao Tse-tung of China; and that it was capable, willing, and able to seriously·challenge the United States militarily. Clark Clifford (a young lawyer and an adviser to the President) stated that the Soviets had plans in place to militarily challenge the United States, particularly in Western Europe (e.g., in Germany), which Soviet Marshal Josef Stalin wanted under Soviet influence. Senator Vandenberg believed that Truman's presentation to the U.S. Congress was the only means "to scare the hell out of the country." Truman did speak to Congress, and soon America halted demobilization of its forces, stood fast in Europe and in Asia, and the next year the Marshall Plan was put in effect to protect Turkey and Greece from Soviet infiltration. The Soviet forces occupied a large part of Iran at the end of W.W.II and America and England feared that the Soviets would move on to Turkey and Greece. Greece was particularly vulnerable due to an internal struggle of strong communist forces against the republican and pro-monarchy forces (which the British were supporting). The Marshall Plan saved these two nations, and subsequently Western Europe, from Soviet penetration. See MARSHALL PLAN.

Schedule C Appointments. The stipulated number of high positions in the American federal government which a newly-elected president can fill from outside civil service channels. They are also known as "political appointments."

Scholasticism. An intellectual inquiry into the nature of things (e.g., phenomena of government, politics, and society in general) through observation and research instead of reliance on pure speculation. This method of scientific inquiry was developed and used by such medieval philosophers (also known as the "Schoolmen") as St. Augustine (354-430), St. Thomas Aquinas (1224-1274), and later philosophers such as Francis de Victoria (1486-1546), Dominic Soto (1496-1560) and Francis Suarez (1548-1617). The Scholastics, through an extensive examination of such dynamic political issues as nominalism versus realism and faith versus reason, laid the ground work for the modern science of politics and public law, both national and international, and especially the notion of a just war (*bellum justum*). See WAR.

Schoolmen. See SCHOLASTICISM.

Schuman Plan. See EUROPEAN COAL AND STEEL COMMUNITY (ECSC).

Schwarze Kapelle. In the German language, "black orchestra." The name given the effort to assassinate Hitler, when towards the end of 1942, the military and the intelligence decided to dispose of him. The principal architect of the plan was Colonel Hans Oster (1888-1945), the deputy to Admiral Wilhelm F. Canaris, the Chief of Abwehr, or German Intelligence, under Hitler. The other co-conspirators were General Erich Fellgiebel, Ewald von Kleist-Schmenzin, Field Marshal Erwin J. Rommel, and Marshal Gerd von Rundstedt. The plan was to execute Hitler after his planned arrest and trial for treason and to restore a parliamentary democracy similar to the Weimar Republic. Other German notables, in time, gave their approval to the plan. They were: former Chief of the German General Staff, General Ludwig Beck, General Karl-Heinrich Stülpnagel, General Friedrich Olbricht, General Erwin von Witzleben, General von Brockdorf-Ahlefeld, and Colonel Paul von Hase. Also, several civilian leaders such as Carl Goerdeler, once the mayor of Leipzig; Ulrich von Hassell, the German ambassador to Italy; Karl Friedrich von Weizsäcker from the foreign ministry; Erich Kordt also from the ministry; Hans von Dohnanyi, a court counsel and chief of the Berlin police; Wolf Heinrich von Helldorf, and his deputy, Count von Schulenburg. The chief of the criminal police, Arthur Nebe, also supported the conspiracy and expedited contact with Catholic and Protestant clergy and with other military and civilian groups. At last, in late 1944, Colonel Claus von Staffenberg placed a bomb in Hitler's headquarters in East Prussia, but Hitler was spared, with only minor injuries; subsequently most of the conspirators were executed by the Gestapo. The conspiracy actually dated back to 1938, following Hitler's Anschluss of Austria into the German Reich. One of the conspirators, Carl Goerdeler, went to France twice and also to England seeking collaboration against Hitler and the Nazis. He received little response; the greatest disappointment was in England where the government spokesman bluntly told Goerdler that his mission sounded like treason to his country, Germany. During the war, the conspirators were not successful in contacts with the Allies who demanded unconditional surrender from Germany, somewhat confusing the conspirators in their undertakings against Hitler. The Allies, and particularly England, were interested in victory and not compromise. When the anti-Nazi Free Germany Committee, under the leadership of General Walter von Seydlitz, who was taken prisoner of war in 1943, made an appeal to the Western Allies to free Germany from Hitler, Allen Dulles, the OSS representatives in Switzerland, stated, "The attempt on Hitler's life was dismissed as of no consequence. Churchill suggested that it was merely a case of dog-eat-dog." The anti-Nazi Germans became suspicious of Hitler's intent following his secret speech to a small group of his most trusted associates on 5 November 1937, in a small Cabinet Room of the Reichskanzlei (Chancery) in Wilhelmstrasse in Berlin. There Hitler informed them that he would proceed with his "Lebensraum policy," as outlined in his book "Mein Kampf" ("My Struggle") and in his 1932 speech in Düsseldorf. Few, however, took Hitler seriously at that time. See RED ORCHESTRA.

Science. A continuous and systematic search for knowledge of the universe and its contents as perceived by man, and how best the natural phenomena of the universe can be explained. Such explanations are sought primarily for reasons of utility for human purposes and needs. There are too many theories of science to mention here. Some of them, like epistemology, are concerned with the origins, the nature, the method, and the limits of knowledge. In political science the epistemological requirements are of concern in regard to methodology in dealing with the physical versus the social. In short, epistemology is concerned with how one gets to know and to understand phenomena. Ontology, on the other hand, is concerned with what one can know. Solipsism is a theory holding that the self can know nothing but its own modifications and that the self is the only existing thing. According to Professor E. Nagel, "Science seeks to discover and to formulate in general terms the conditions under which events of various sorts occur, the statements of such determining conditions being the explanations of the corresponding happenings." Nagel points out the need for scientific method, because "science requires hypothetic-deductive procedures and the integrated form of systematic explanation exemplified by the science of mathematics. It necessitates the use of a particular set of techniques regardless of type of inquiry." And, "the practice of scientific method is the persistent critique of arguments in the light of tried canons for judging the reliability of the procedures by which evidential data are obtained, and for assessing the probative forces of the evidence on which the conclusions are based." It is assumed that by such reasoning one arrives at knowledge, and knowledge becomes reliable, according to Professor D. Easton, "as it increases in generality and internally consistent organization." See CONCEPT, PARADIGM, POLITICAL THEORY.

Scientific Method in Political Theory. See POLITICAL THEORY.

Scientific Socialism. See MARXISM, SOCIALISM.

SCLC. See SOUTHERN CHRISTIAN LEADERSHIP CONFERENCE.

Scotland Yard. The special criminal investigation department of the London Metropolitan Police that was once housed in the Scotland Yard, a place that had served as residence for visiting kings and ambassadors.

Scramble for Africa. See WEST AFRICAN CONFERENCE ON BERLIN.

Scramble for China. See BOXER REBELLION.

Screw the Opposition. See WATERGATE.

Screwy Year. See ZIGZAG MAN.

Scrutin de Liste. In the French language, "voting for the entire slate of candidates on a ballot." See VOTING.

Scum. A derogatory term commonly used in the United States up to the end of World War I referring to a poor uneducated immigrant from Europe. The Federalists (and their principal leader, Alexander Hamilton, himself an immigrant from the Caribbean Islands and an illegitimate child) disliked foreign immigration. The Antifederalists favored it since this was the only means to broaden the democratic base, enlarge the electorate, and remove the Federalists from power. In 1798 the Federalists increased the residency requirement for U.S. citizenship from five to fourteen years. This was changed again by the Jeffersonians in 1802, when Thomas Jefferson became President (1801-1809), from fourteen years to five. Other anti-immigrant elements in the nation were the American Native party, the Know-Nothing party, and the Ku Klux Klan. In 1880 Chinese immigration was restricted, and in 1882 totally forbidden. Those who came after 1882 were either close relatives of legal residents or "wetbacks," "illegals," full of "rum, Romanism, and rebellion," coming without authorization. Under the 1882 restriction, paupers, convicts, and criminals were excluded; and in 1885, insane persons, polygamists, prostitutes, alcoholics, and anarchists were added to the restricted list. Other obstacles for citizenship were literacy tests or intelligence tests. Connecticut introduced such literacy tests in 1855, and Massachusetts, in 1857. In other areas literacy tests were introduced with time, and these tests appeared on the national level in 1901, 1913, and 1915 as criteria for naturalization and voting. President T. Roosevelt (who called the tests "opportunity tests" and not "intelligence tests"), Taft, and Wilson vetoed federal legislation on the literacy test. In spite of this, the test became law in 1917, and New York, where immigration was also the heaviest, was the first state to implement it in 1923. Other states followed suit. The Louisiana Constitution, for example, stipulates (Art. VII, Section 1d) that the registrant (particularly when black or poor white) be able to "understand and give a reasonable interpretation of any section of the state or federal constitution." A suit was brought under the provisions of the CIVIL RIGHTS ACT OF 1960, and the U.S. Supreme Court ruled unanimously in 1965—in *Louisiana v. United States*, 380 U.S. 145,151,153 (1965)—that such tests are unconstitutional. Justice Hugo Black observed: "There can be no doubt . . . that Louisiana's interpretation test, as written and as applied, was part of a successful plan to deprive Louisiana Negroes of their right to vote . . . . This is not a test but a trap, sufficient to stop even the most brilliant man on his way to the voting booth." See AMERICAN PARTY, KNOW-NOTHING PARTY, KU KLUX KLAN, MAFIA.

SDECE. See SERVICE DE DOCUMENTATION EXTÉRIEURES ET CONTRE-ESPIONNAGE.

SDI. See STRATEGIC DEFENSE INITIATIVE, WINDOW OF VULNERABILITY.

SDS. See SPECIAL DRAWING RIGHTS, STUDENTS FOR DEMOCRATIC SOCIETY.

Sea Food Production. See HUNGER WARS.

Sea Power. See GEOPOLITICS.

SEALS. See DELTA FORCE, NAVY SEA, AIR, AND LAND TEAMS.

Seanad Eireann. Upper house or Senate in Ireland. See OIREACHTAS, DAIL EIREANN.

SEATO. See SOUTHEAST ASIA TREATY ORGANIZATION.

Second Amendment Crowd. See GUN CONTROL.

Second American Revolution, the. The period between 1954—when the Supreme Court ruled in *Brown v. the Board of Education*—and the 1960s and 1970s, referring to the civil rights movement.

Second Bill of Rights. With his ever-expanding concern for human rights, U.S. President Franklin D. Roosevelt (1933-1944), upon viewing the human misery brought upon people abroad, particularly the suffering of Europeans during World War II, stated, "We have come to a clear realization of the fact that true individual freedom cannot exist without economic security and independence," and then outlined his "Second Bill of Rights" as: "The right to a useful and remunerative job in the industries or shops or farms or mines of the Nation; the right to earn enough to provide adequate shelter, food, clothing and recreation; the right of every farmer to raise and sell his products at a return which will give him and his family a decent living; the right of every businessman, large and small, to trade in an atmosphere of freedom from unfair competition and domination by monopolies at home and abroad; the right of every family to a decent home; the right to adequate medical care and the opportunity to achieve and enjoy good health; the right to adequate protection from the economic fears of old age, sickness, accident, and unemployment; the right to a good education." This "social management" concern—provision for human needs—as opposed to his "progressive orthodoxy"—cold-blooded concern for running government and developing programs in a business fashion based on cost accounting consistent with American business tradition and practice—developed in Roosevelt's political thinking during World War II, when he became aware that the United States, with its vast power and resources, could do more for mankind than had ever before been possible. In the construction of those programs, President Roosevelt was assisted by his brain trust, which consisted mainly of three professors from Columbia University: Adolf A. Berle and Raymond Moley (students and practitioners of national international politics); and Rexford G. Tugwell, an economist. The Second Bill of Rights was proclaimed in the President's State of the Union Message to Congress in January 1943.

Second Burning of Washington. See POOR PEOPLE'S MARCH OF 1969.

Second Class Man with First Class Brain. A not too flattering characterization of U.S. President Martin Van Buren (1837-1841), by his adversaries.

Second Continental Congress. Representatives of the colonies met in Philadelphia on May 10, 1775, urging the colonies to prepare their militias for revolution against England and appointed George Washington as the commander of the Continental troops. See CONTINENTAL CONGRESS.

Second Department. Many military intelligence agencies around the world, particularly military intelligence carry that designation, adopted from the French Deuxième Bureau, one of the best and oldest military intelligence agencies. See SERVICE FOR FOREIGN INFORMATION AND COUNTERESPIONAGE.

Second Industrial Revolution. See INDUSTRIAL REVOLUTION.

Second International. See COMMUNIST ORGANIZATIONS, COMMUNIST INTERNATIONAL, SECOND.

Second Oldest Profession. So is viewed the business of intelligence gathering, e.g., political, economic, military, and/or industrial espionage; the ancient quest for knowledge, possibly an advanced knowledge, in order to gain some advantage through deception and surprise, to gain power and/or wealth. Also a book by this title written by Phillip Knightly. Prostitution is considered to be the oldest profession.

Second Party System. See JACKSONIAN DEMOCRACY.

Second War Powers Act of 1945. See WAR POWERS ACTS.

Secrecy in Government. See INFORMATION SECURITY OVERSIGHT OFFICE.

Secret Intelligence Service (SIS). The British intelligence gathering, intelligence evaluating, and counterintelligence system of Great Britain. MI-5 is the division charged with counterespionage; MI-6 is charged with the collection and evaluation of foreign intelligence, and "Double X" or the "Twenty Committee" (double X meaning "double-cross") is responsible for turning foreign agents into spies for the SIS against their own systems. The SIS operates in strict secrecy. Its chief is never known to the general public; its budget is hidden in other appropriations; its headquarters outside London are unmarked, and the service will disavow any knowledge of any of its agents caught by the adversary. MI-5 was set up in 1887 as a Special Branch of the Scotland Yard, charged with the responsibility for all anti-government elements, mainly Fabians and their sympathizers. In 1905 military intelligence was transferred to the War Office and during W.W.II, M1-6, nominally under the Foreign Office, took over all intelligence and counter-intelligence activities. The SECURITY COORDINATION, which was set up as a part of the MI-6 during W.W.II, under the direction of Sir William Stephenson, (pseudonym "Intrepid.") a wealthy Canadian, served as a coordinating intelligence agency of the allies, mainly USA and England, and closely collaborated with the FBI and other US intelligence Services. See ENIGMA, INTELLIGENCE, ZIMMERMANN AFFAIR.

Secret Service Act. See PRESIDENTIAL TRANSITION.

Secret Societies. Throughout its five-thousand-year history, Chinese society was subjected to politico-economic-social controls by a variety of secret societies until the emergence of the Communist party during the 1920s. Some of the major societies which have been effective instruments of societal control were: the Red Eyebrows; the Yellow Turbans; the Ko Lao Hui, or Association of Elder Brothers (known for its revolutionary activities and terrorist violence); the Red Spears (a protective association of farmers); the Triad (or San Ho Hui) Society, also known as the Hung Society, and the Society of Heaven and Earth, both known for maintaining control over rural areas for centuries; and the White Lily and the White Cloud Societies (both dating from the twelfth century, they were organized by Buddhist monks but have been involved in revolutionary activities in China.) Most of these societies aimed at preventing exposure of the Chinese society to other cultures and political systems, particularly those of the West (Occident). Since these societies maintained a very strict discipline within their ranks, it was, therefore, considerably easy for Mao Tse-tung and his Communist party to use them and their tactics and strategy in forging the new state and gaining power in 1949, as well as in maintaining an effective control over the largest nation on earth population-wise (approximately 900 million persons), without offering much in return. See BOXER REBELLION, MAFIA, TRIADS.

Secretariat of the United Nations. See UNITED NATIONS ORGANIZATION.

Secretary-General of the United Nations. See UNITED NATIONS ORGANIZATION.

Sectionalism. One's externalized inner attitudes and personal feelings about a certain geographic area (e.g., a town, a city, a county, state, province, or a nation-state) which one favors (by word and actions) over any others. In the United States, sectionalism dates to colonial days and is expressed, for instance, by comparing the New England areas versus the rural South; slave states versus anti-slave states; industrial versus agricultural; the "Bible belt"—parts of the southern United States where the Baptist religious denomination is strong—versus the "wheat belt"—the wheat growing areas (e.g., the state of Kansas); the "cotton belt"—the Southern states where cotton was an important crop—versus the "steel belt"—the steel-producing areas (e.g., Indiana and Pennsylvania). The concept of sectionalism includes the variables of religious, ethnic, and racial composition of the area, principal economic characteristics, and cultural characteristics. The culminating point of the clash of sectional interests was the War of Secession (Civil War) between the North and the South, between the industrial democracy of the North, based on manufacturing, and the South's "cottonocracy" (democracy based on predominantly single-crop agriculture, cotton) or "slavocracy" (based on slave labor).

Secular Monarchy. See ECCLESIASTICAL MONARCHY.

Secular Piety. See MANDATE OF HEAVEN.

Secular State. A state that is founded on or subscribes to the principle that any religion, religious doctrine, or religious ceremony has no place whatsoever in the affairs of a state, in education, or in a political society in general; that all ecclesiasticism is a private and not a public matter.

Secularism. See SECULAR STATE.

Secured (Defensible) Frontiers. The central issue of the Arab-Israeli conflict during the past three decades. The state of Israel is surrounded by hostile Arab states (Syria, Egypt, Jordan, as well as the Palestinian Arabs scattered throughout the four states) and, as a measure of security, Israel holds on to Arab territories conquered during the 1973 war. The Arabs want their land back, and the Israelis want their security; this was the central issue of the Arab-Israeli rapprochement, the Sadat visit to Israel on November 19, 1977, and Begin's visit to Cairo December 25, 1977. The present Israeli-Palestinian negotiations proceed without settlement in sight. See ISRAELI SETTLEMENTS in Appendix 95, SADAT-BEGIN SUMMIT.

Security Classification. See SECURITY CLEARANCE.

Security Clearance. Under the American system, there are basically three security classifications (top secret; secret; and confidential),and potential employees in sensitive areas involved with any one of these, must be cleared (investigated and found reliable and trustworthy). "Secrecy," said Cardinal de Richelieu (1585-1642), chief minister to French King Louis XIII, "is the first essential in affairs of the state."

Security Council of the United Nations. See UNITED NATIONS ORGANIZATION.

Security Index. See COUNTERINSURGENCY IN AMERICA.

Sedition. Any hostile or harmful activity, short of treasonous acts, against the established authority of a state.

Segregation. Segregation, in general, is the policy or practice of compelling racial groups to live apart from each other, go to separate schools, use separate social/physical facilities such as hospitals, drinking facilities, toilet facilities, public transportation (streetcars, buses), parks, etc. In the United States in 1896 the Supreme Court upheld this concept in the case of *Plessy v. Ferguson* which established the doctrine of separate-but-equal facilities for different races (white and black). In 1954, this doctrine was challenged and overturned by the Supreme Court in the case of *Brown v. the Board of Education of*

Topeka, Kansas. This case set in motion the integration of U.S. public schools. In most instances, local school systems were ordered to bus both white and black children to schools within a system to achieve racial equality. See APARTHEID, Appendix 44.

Select Committee. See SPECIAL COMMITTEE.

Selective Democracy. See INSTITUTIONAL DEMOCRACY.

Selective Operations Unit. An informal name of experts and top policy makers within the U.S. Department of Justice and its Federal Bureau of Investigation (FBI), which reviews all undercover operations of the FBI in the field (e.g., ABSCAM: illegal granting of immigration visas to foreigners and BRILAB: bribery of public officials respectively) before they can be carried out by field offices. The U.S. Attorney General and the Director of the FBI monitor these proceedings.

Selective Service System. An agency of the U.S. Federal government charged with the registration and drafting of males for the U.S. Armed Forces. The agency was established in 1948, and has been revised by the Military Selective Service Act of 1967. The U.S. Supreme Court ruled in 1918—in the case of *U.S. v. Joseph S. Arver,* 245 U.S. 365 (1918)—that military service is not involuntary servitude, but an obligation to a state. The draft ended on January 27, 1973, and the armed forces are currently relying on volunteers. The term "Selective Service" comes from the Selective Service and Training Act adopted in 1940. This was intended to prepare the United States for the military activities going on in Europe and the Far East that may have been a threat. The Act established a means for registering, classifying, selecting and inducting, according to age, young males into various military units (Army, Navy, Marines). The system was commonly referred to as the Draft.

Self-Criticism. See SAMOKRITIKA.

Self-Determination of Nations. A principle of international law recognizing the right of any nation to determine its own political system, adopt its own philosophy, and set up a system of law and government free of external pressure or interference. See FOURTEEN POINTS.

Self-Esteem. See POLITICAL SELF-ESTEEM.

Self-Evident Truths. See DECLARATION OF INDEPENDENCE, Appendix 5.

Self-Governing Area. See AUTONOMY.

Self-Government. An autonomy that may be granted to a political subdivision to form its own government and to pass laws necessary for its governance.

Self-Help. One taking the law into his own hands; adjudication of a case outside the prescribed law or procedure; in international law and politics, a harmed state seeking remedy for a wrongful act outside the prescription of the UN Charter, which considers self-help illegal unless sought through the UN.

Self-Immolation. See VICTIMLESS CRIME.

Self-Inflicted Racism. See POLITICAL APATHY.

Selma to Montgomery Civil Rights March. See VOTING RIGHTS ACT OF 1965.

Semi-Judicial. See QUASI-JUDICIAL.

Semi-Legislative. See QUASI-LEGISLATIVE.

Seminary of Sedition. See HOUSE OF BURGESSES OF VIRGINIA.

Sempai. See FRAME SOCIETY.

Senado. The Senate in some Spanish-speaking countries.

Senate. See UNITED STATES SENATE.

Senate Calendar. See PRIVATE BILL.

Senato. The upper chamber or Senate of the Italian legislature. See CAMERA DEI DEPUTATI.

Senatorial Courtesy. A customary and unwritten rule whereby the President of the United States is expected to seek, in advance, approval of an appointee to a high federal post (e.g., judge, ambassador, or commissioner) by the senator or senators of the state in which the appointee claims his domicile (legal residence). If the President fails to do so, his nominee may be rejected in the process of confirmation by the Senate. The objection to such a nominee by one senator may, through intersenatorial courtesy, get the backing of the entire Senate membership. (This custom also serves as a check upon presidential powers and enables senators to share in the distribution of patronage appointments.) Also, the mutual respect that one senator extends to another in spite of political differences.

Senatus Consultum. In the Latin language, "a decree (or law) of the Senate."

Sendero Luminoso. See SHINING PATH.

Seniority Rule. Awarding of chairs by rule of seniority, i.e., the member of the majority party with the longest continuous service, no longer enforced.

Sense of the House. See RESOLUTION.

Sense of the Senate. See RESOLUTION.

Sense of the State. (Or "interest of the state.") In the French language, "le sens de l'état"; also a deeply ingrained notion in French political philosophy and political culture, dating back centuries to the time when France was a monarchy, that the state as represented by government is important to the political community, because the state guards the interest of the political community through its government and is therefore highly respected by all citizens. In modern times and especially after the Constitution of the Fifth Republic of 1958, the state, through its government machinery, does what is necessary to preserve democracy and the basic freedom of citizens. It is the state's role to maintain the balance between individuals, groups, and the society as a whole and the interests of the state and its government.

Sensitive Agency. Any governmental agency in the United States that handles classified information (e.g., top secret, secret, or confidential) pertaining to the policies and operational methods of the government (e.g., the State Department, the Central Intelligence Agency, the National Security Agency, and several dozen others).

Sensitive Information. State secrets of the highest order. Under a ruling by the U.S. Supreme Court in February 1980 (in the case of *Snepp v. United States* [444 U.S. 507 (1980)]), former and current agents of the CIA may be required to obtain advance clearance on anything that the employee writes for outside the Agency's use. Frank Snepp was required to turn over all profits from his unauthorized book, *Decent Interval.* See Appendix 44.

Sentence Bargaining. See PLEA BARGAINING.

Separate Amenities Act. See AFRICAN RESISTANCE MOVEMENT.

Separate but Equal. A series of state legislative acts introduced after the Civil War in the United States calling for separate but equal facilities (e.g., in railroad cars or restaurants) for blacks. This doctrine was upheld by the U.S. Supreme Court in the case of *Plessy v. Ferguson,* 163, U.S. 537; 16 Sup. Ct. 1138; 41 L.Ed. 256 (1896); but subsequent judicial decisions, mainly the case of *Brown v. Board of Education of Topeka,* 347 U.S. 483 (1954), declared it no longer valid and applicable. See KERNER COMMISSION.

Separate Development. See APARTHEID, PARALLEL DEVELOPMENT DOCTRINE.

Separation of Powers. A principle of dividing and separating the powers of a government (e.g., into executive, legislative, and judicial branches) in order to avoid collusion and to give each branch the capacity to modify the acts and the activities of the other. For example, the executive branch appoints major officers of the government who are subject to approval by the legislative branch; the judicial branch reviews the constitutionality of laws and executive acts; and the legislative branch appropriates funds for the operations of the two remaining branches of the government, the executive and the judicial. See FEDERALISM, SECTIONALISM, U.S. Constitution in Appendices 5-14.

Separatism. The propensity of some homogeneous peoples, motivated by nationalistic desires and aspirations to exist as a separate, sovereign, and distinct state rather than be a part of a larger, pluralistic state. Such a separatist step was taken in 1860 by the southern states of the United States (which caused the War of Secession between the Union and the Confederacy); and during the 1960s a black revolutionary group, the Republic of New Africa, advocated the creation of a separate black state in the territory of the United States. The French-Canadians in the Province of Quebec, Canada, advocate a separation from the English-speaking parts of Canada; after W.W.II the Palestinian Arabs (e.g., through the advocacy of the Palestine Liberation Organization) demand a separate and sovereign state of their own rejecting accommodation with any one of the Arab states (e.g., assimilation) or the state of Israel. See AMERICAN CIVIL WAR, PALESTINE LIBERATION ORGANIZATION (PLO), PARTI QUÉBÉCOIS, REPUBLIC OF NEW AFRICA, REVOLUTIONARY SECTARIANISM, UNILATERAL DECLARATION OF INDEPENDENCE.

Sequestration. Per U.S. Congressional Budget Office, "the cancellation of budgetary resources to enforce the Budget Enforcement Act of 1990. Sequestration is triggered if the Office of Management and Budget determines that discretionary appropriations breach the discretionary spending caps, that direct spending and receipt legislation increase the deficit, or that the deficit exceeds, by more than a specified margin, the maximum deficit amount set by law. Failure to meet the maximum deficit amount would trigger across-the-board spending reductions. Changes in direct spending and receipt legislation that increase the deficit would result in reductions in funding from entitlements not otherwise exempted by law. Discretionary spending in excess of the caps would cause the cancellation of budgetary resources within the appropriate discretionary spending category."

Serednik. Middle-farmer; a self-supporting farmer in pre-Revolutionary Russia.

Serf. A semi-free person attached to an estate and enjoying limited freedoms and privileges. (Most common in Europe and Russia until the late nineteenth century.)

Serocracy. A term popular among Russian historians during Tzarist times, when the government bureaucracy was staffed with faceless, dreary, stagnant, and corrupt persons, most of them related to some high government official or to the Tzar himself. Also, a corrupt, impotent, oppressive, unproductive bureaucracy or government institution.

Service at Pleasure. As a matter of tradition, rather than law, non-contractual employees serve as long as the employer wishes them to serve, and resign if the employer wishes them to do so. All political appointees serving governors and presidents, except judicial officers, are expected to turn in their resignations at the end of the chief executive's tenure, unless the incoming governor or president wishes them to remain.

Service de Documentation Extérieures et de Contre-Espionnage (SDECE). See SERVICE FOR FOREIGN INFORMATION AND COUNTERESPIONAGE.

Service District. See PLANNING, PLANNING DISTRICT COMMISSION.

Service District Commission. See PLANNING DISTRICT.

Service for Foreign Information and Counterespionage. (Service de Documentacion Extérieures et de Contre-Espionnage.) The intelligence gathering, intelligence evaluating, and counterespionage agency of the Republic of France. The agency set up in 1945, reorganized in 1958. Its previous name was Direction Générale des Etudes et recherches. Military intelligence is conducted by the Deuxième Bureau (Second Bureau). In recent times, the SDECE was allegedly extensively engaged in industrial espionage to the point of manufacturing a powerful computer with know-how and technology acquired clandistinely, and even naming it after the agency.

Seven Sisters. In the language of oil politics, the seven major oil companies, which together exerted influence on American and global politics, ranging from controlling markets to removing kings and other rulers of sovereign states, including the deposed Shah of Iran. They are: BP, British Petroleum (British); Exxon (formerly Esso, American); Gulf (American); Mobil (American); Shell (Dutch and British); and Texaco (American). Due to large windfall profits during the Arab Oil Embargo in 1974, the companies diversified into other areas by becoming owners and/or operators of the following businesses: British Petroleum owns Standard Oil of Ohio (Sohio), Union Carbide and Monsanto in Europe, and Veba A.G. in Germany; Exxon owns office systems, data processing, electronics, and mining (copper) interests; Gulf owns Corning Glass, Tenneco, and Guinness Beer; Mobil owns Montgomery Ward and Container Corporation of America, (ocean shipping); Shell owns about fifteen different subsidiaries, including Dutch Oil, Shell Italiana, Shell Senegal, and many others; Texaco owns Deutsche Erdol, Caltex Europe, and other interests. The unprecedented windfall profits when oil prices skyrocketed from below $1 before 1974 to between $15 and $80 per gallon after, were possible because of loopholes in oil import regulations. The regulations specified that the price of "old oil" was to be just about the pre-1974 level, and that applied to oil in storage tanks in the United States; the so-called "new oil," was to be brought in at new, exorbitant prices, but the fact is that most of the "new oil" was simply kept on oil tankers in ports and off shore, permitting the oil companies to market it as "new oil." The resulting cash flow to Exxon, for example, was so large, that, according to press accounts at the time, the company was unable to count the money fast enough! See Appendix 41.

Seven Years' War. The war between Austria and Prussia, 1756-1763, over control of Silesia that gradually expanded into a global war between France and England over control of North America and India. It ended with the emergence of England as a SEA POWER in control of major global sea routes and international commerce, a power England retained until the end of World War II when the British Empire disintegrated. See WARS WITH GLOBAL IMPLICATIONS, Appendix 88.

Severance Tax. Tax on the sale of certain minerals (e.g., oil, gas, or coal), which many states in the American union impose as an additional source of revenue.

Seward's Folly. A term used by the adversaries of U.S. Secretary of State, William H. Seward (1861-1865), who concluded the purchase of Alaska from the Russian Imperial Government for a price of $7,200,000 (or approximately 2 cents per acre). The other pejorative was "Seward's Icebox," and the property itself was referred to as an "Arctic Wasteland." See AMERICAN-SOVIET COLLUSION.

Sex Discrimination. See HATE CRIME, SEXUAL HARASSMENT.

Sexpionage. The ancient practice of using sex as a means of influencing the policies of government (e.g., by the extending of sexual services to male by a female, known as a "swallow"; or a female or a homosexual male by a male, known as a "raven"). Sexpionage is often used to blackmail compromised officials into cooperating with the adversary . Cleopatra, Queen of Egypt (69-30 BC), contrived with Julius Caesar, the Roman emperor, to eliminate her brother, Ptolemy Dionysus, with whom she was to share the throne. Then she formed a boudoir alliance (alliance through the bedroom) with Mark Anthony, and when their adversary, Actium, eliminated Mark Anthony, she joined with Actium. In modern times, Mata Hari, an actress, used seduction of influential politicians and soldiers of France during World War I in order to aid Germany. A British model, Christine Keeler, was set up by a Soviet intelligence officer and diplomat, Eugene Ivanov, to obtain information from John Profumo, Britain's secretary of state for war. This brought about the downfall of the government of Prime Minister Harold Macmillan in 1963. During his 1963 state visit to the USSR, Indonesia's President Achmed Sukarno was photographed with several "swallows" of the KGB in the "privacy" of his hotel room. When confronted the next day with blackmail, he asked the Soviet operatives to supply him with several copies of the long-footage film, because he told them, he would like to have them shown to his people at home who would be proud to see that their president had other abilities in addition to being president. The blackmail attempt was dropped. Anthony Courtney, a member of the British Parliament, was involved once with a "raven" while on a personal visit to the USSR in 1958. When, in 1963, he advanced legislation in the British House of Commons aimed at trimming the immunity of Soviet diplomats stationed in England, photographs of his 1958 escapades in Moscow were quickly circulated to the Prime Minster, the Parliament, and the press, and Courtney lost his election. Walter Jenkins, assistant to U.S. President Lyndon B. Johnson (1964-1969) and father of a large family, was compromised by his enemies for his homosexual escapades, and lost his job in the White House. See AGENT PROVOCATEUR, DECEPTION, ENTRAPMENT, INTELLIGENCE, SEXPOLITICS.

Sexpolitics. The use of sex as way and means to influence or learn political policy, to receive personal favors, or simply for the purpose of entrapment. Some of the major revelations in modern times were the following: (1) U.S. Congressman Wayne L. Hays hired a young and elegant (and no doubt willing) female for the positions of typist (she could not type) and filing clerk (she was allegedly a poor reader). Upon admission of his "error of judgment," the congressman resigned; (2) in the case of U.S. President John F. Kennedy (1961-1963), one Judith Exner was allegedly "furnished" to him by the Mafia in order to extract information and he was allegedly involved with movie star Marilyn Monroe. In 1977, the American press carried reports of private quarters on Capitol Hill assigned for the personal use of Speaker of the U.S. House of Representatives, Karl Albert (1971-1977), for political caucusing, which were also allegedly used for sex parties. Subsequently, this facility was referred to as the "the board of education"; and (3) a more recent case, in January 1992, concerned the alleged marital infidelity of Bill Clinton, governor of Arkansas and presidential hopeful; he denied the allegation. Allegations have been made that this was simply a case of "kiss-and-tell for sale." In cases of entrapment, the CIA allegedly used females to meet and to extract information from Fidel Castro, president of Cuba, and when that produced no results, Castro was to be killed or poisoned; when this failed, one female was furnished pills to be implanted into Castro's drink, which would cause his hair to fall out. The latter scheme was designed to at least cause this charismatic communist some embarrassment among his followers since his beard was symbolic of a Latin American macho revolutionary. When that failed, there were allegedly some suicides among the CIA cadres responsible for the failed mission. Finally, in the case of sex for patriotic purposes, such as protecting an invaded country from destruction: when France was invaded by the German Nazis in 1940, the French government under Paul Reynaud, Premier and Foreign Minister (1940-1942) was rather paralyzed and irresponsible to the invader's brutalities. In order to revive the vigor of the prime minister and to have him stand up to the invaders (allegedly saving Paris from destruction), a young lady was sent to him to boost his political standing by widely spreading rumors of his unusual masculine prowess (which, in reality, was not the case). See AGENT PROVOCATEUR, CHARACTER ASSASSINATION, ENTRAPMENT, SEXPIONAGE.

Sexual Harassment. Unsolicited, unwanted, unexpected, undesired sexual advances demonstrated or expressed explicitly, implicitly, or implied, in either a verbal or a physical manner by one person toward another. Obviously a common practice since the beginning of Homo Sapiens, but only recently recognized first as a social crime and finally as a criminal offense. The issue entered the spotlight in the United States during the U.S. Senate confirmation hearings for the nomination of Judge Clarence Thomas to the Supreme Court of the United States. The Senate hearings were to commence on 15 October 1991, and on 14 October 1991 one Anita Hill, a former co-worker of Judge Thomas, brought up charges of sexual harassment which allegedly took place about ten years previously. After an extensive investigation and corroboration of witnesses of both parties lasting several days, Thomas was confirmed. Guidelines by the Federal Equal Employment Opportunity Commission (EEOC) define "illegal sexual harassment" if "Either explicitly or implicitly, one individual makes another person's submission to such conduct a term or condition of employment or advancement: "Sleep with me, or you'll be fired (or not hired, or not promoted); conduct that "creates an intimidating, hostile or offensive working environment." Following the televised Senate confirmation hearings of Judge Clarence Thomas and the encounter with Professor Anita Hill, the Washington bureau of *Parade* magazine, under the direction of renown columnist and investigative reporter, Jack Anderson, conducted a poll in 1991 among men and women asking their opinions on this issue. The results acknowledged the difference of opinion on this issue. "While most of the women responding complained about being harassed, many of the men held that this is the man's role to be the sexual aggressor and to pursue women by asking them out." The issue of sexual harassment achieved statutory standing in the European Community four months before the American debate. On 3 July 1991, the European Community adopted a code of practice aimed at "protecting the dignity of women and men at work." According to the European document, sexual harassment in defined as "unwanted conduct of a sexual nature, or other conduct based on sex affecting the dignity of women and men at work, including unwelcome physical, verbal, or nonverbal conduct." The Republic of France, in addition, made it illegal "to solicit by order, constraint, or pressure favors of a sexual nature" from subordinates in a working environment. The penalty upon conviction is a minimum of one year in prison and/or a fine of up to $16,000.

Shadow Cabinet. A term applied, mainly under a two-party system in a cabinet-parliamentary democracy as in England, to a major political party which is out of power (the "outs"), but which is ready to step in any moment should the government-of-the day be voted out either through a non-confidence vote or a general election. Being prepared for any contingency, the party out of power will silently designate cabinet officers (e.g., ministers or secretaries) who will be observing the policies and activities of the cabinet in power and preparing themselves to step in at the most opportune moment. The term is sometimes applied to the loyal opposition as well. See LOYAL OPPOSITION, PARLIAMENTARY DEMOCRACY.

Shah. A king or a monarch in Iran, like Shah Reza Pahlavi (1953-1979), although in reality Pahlavi referred to himself as "king of kings," or "Shahanshah," and "Light of the Aryans," "Aryamehr," titles once used by Persian Emperor Cyrus (559-530 BC). All public documents were signed by the Shah as "We Pahlavi Shahanshah of Iran." Commonly the Shah was addressed as "His Imperial Majesty." In informal conversations with Westerners, the Shah referred to himself as "Ralph" or "George," and his wife, Empress Farah as "Martha." His governing style was based on a principle called "farmandehi," or "leadership command," which stressed "hard work, self-sacrifice and greater effort." Under his economic and cultural development program, which the Shah called the "white revolution" and was subsidized with money from oil sales, one farmer complained to him that the newly constructed housing for farmers lacked shower facilities, the Shah asked him to be self-reliable "Who clips your nails for you?" asked the Shah. The Shah was restored to the Iranian throne in 1953 with the aid of Kermit Roosevelt of the CIA, but was overthrown in 1979 by the Shiite Muslims of the Ayatollah Khomeini. See IRAN'S REVOLUTION, MOSSADEGH, ROOSEVELT ERECTION, SAVAK, WHITE REVOLUTION.

Shahanshah. See SHAH.

Shanghai Communiqué. A joint Sino-American statement that was issued in Shanghai, China (People's Republic of China) in February 1972, by visiting U.S. President Richard M. Nixon and China's Premier Chou En-lai. This communiqué implies that future normalization of relations between these two states will require termination of America's relations with the Republic of China on Taiwan (Formosa) and that the United States will abandon its two-China policy for a one-China policy. See PEKING SUMMIT.

SHAPE. See SUPREME HEADQUARTERS ALLIED POWERS IN EUROPE, NATO, Appendix 29.

Sharia. Moslem behavior code based on the Koran. In many Moslem countries laws are made in accordance with this code.

Shays' Rebellion. A group of farmers in Massachusetts, under the leadership of Revolutionary War veteran Daniel Shays, rebelled against the government under the Articles of Confederation in 1786-1787, when their demands to lower taxes, issue paper money, and postpone the collection of debts were not met. After the city of Springfield was taken by force, Governor James Bodoin dispatched a state militia force of 4,000 and defeated the rebels in 1787 in Springfield. The Rebellion triggered a nationwide call for a stronger federal union in order to manage economic matters more efficiently and to avoid future rebellions of this kind. See TRACTORCADE.

Sheik. An elderly person heading a tribe or one exercising political powers of a kingdom (sheikdom) in some Arab states.

Sheikdom. See SHEIK.

Sheng. An administrative subdivision, a province, in China.

Sherman Act. See ANTI-TRUST LAW.

Shield. See SOLDIERS FOR DEMOCRACY.

Shield Law. A legislative measure to protect domestic markets from competition with foreign imported goods, usually through tariffs or inspection laws. The U.S. Congress considered such legislation in the 1970s, directed primarily against Japan, which had refused to trim its exports to the U.S. at dumping prices. As a result, Japan achieved a seventeen billion dollar surplus in international balance of payments as of 1977, while the United States had about a six billion dollar deficit. In 1965, there was a "fabric war" between the United States and Japan when Japanese textiles flooded the American market to the point that many plants in the U.S. closed down. This is due to the fact that tariffs on Japanese products to the U.S. are very low, but import duties on U.S. products imported into Japan are very high. Protectionism is another term for shield laws. See AMERICA BASHING, JAPAN BASHING.

Shiite Dissimulation. The practice of subverting the precepts of one religion using another in order to convert and to gain control over its followers. Term associated with the "taqiyah," or "dissimulation" in the Persian language, where for centuries (until the Shiite victory in 1979, the dominant Sunni Moslems required the Shiite Moslems, the dominated minority in Persia, to make pilgrimages to Shiite shrines where they would be exposed and possibly influenced by the presence of Sunnis passing as Shiites. This act of religious subversion was considered a matter of great honor, and successful "missionaries" were generously rewarded for their achievements. This practice was in reality political rather than religious messianism. See SHAH.

Shining Path. In the Spanish language, "Sendero Luminoso," a guerrilla movement in Peru since the early 1970s. It is pro-communist and aided by Cuba in its struggle against the government of Peru as well as neighboring states, mainly Bolivia, where it has gained considerable influence among the poverty-stricken population of the campesino, the poor peasants. Their main demand is land reform. See TUPAC AMARU.

Shirtless Ones. The principal followers and supporters of the neo-fascist, populist movement of Juan Domingo Perón, president of Argentina (1946-1955); he was exiled for 18 years, then resumed the presidency in 1973-1974. He was succeeded by his wife and vice president, Maria Estela Martinez de Perón. Perón implemented favorable labor reforms, and it was the workers who supported him, marching without shirts. See CAESARISM.

Shock Therapy. In economics, a radical, sudden transition from a centrally planned economy to one that is consumer-oriented. This has happened recently in most of the East European states and in the Commonwealth of Independent States (CIS), the former Soviet Union. See TYPES OF MARKET SYSTEMS, TYPES OF POLITICO-ECONOMIC SYSTEMS. Appendices 83, 84.

Shoe-Pounding Diplomacy. See POLITICAL STYLE.

Shogunate. See SAMURAI.

Shopkeeper Politics. Prince Otto von Bismarck (1815-1898), Prussia's chancellor and statesman, so characterized the English imperial political system. The superior British navy and governmental policy of intervention in economic affairs not only influenced world events, but enhanced trade and industry, allowing British subjects to enjoy a better standard of living. In recent times, the so-called "Japan Bashers," critics of Japan's economic expansion into global markets, have characterized that country's policies the same way. The Ministry of International Trade and Industry (MITI) is in partnership with private business interests, effectively collaborating on the goal of advancing the power of the Japanese state, society, and individual, in that order.

Short Ballot. A ballot that is used in many states in the United States to elect top government officials only (e.g., the President and Vice President, Senators, and Congressmen). In some states top state officials may also be elected on the short ballot (e.g., governors, lieutenant governors, or state legislators). See VOTING.

Short Speeches, Long Sausages. A term coined by Father Johannes Fink, a Catholic priest in the city of Ludwigshafen, on the Rhine in Germany, where Chancellor of Germany Dr. Helmut Kohl was born in 1930, characterizing Kohl's political style of making short speeches that nevertheless delivered long range benefits (e.g., bringing down the Berlin Wall and the unification of Germany).

Shot Heard Around the World. A statement credited to Thomas Jefferson who stated that the release of the American *Declaration of Independence* of July 4, 1776 (of which Jefferson was the author), accompanied by the opening battles of the American Revolution at Lexington and Concord, would not only be heard at home but around the world as well. The revolutionary document, enumerating the noblest aspirations of man (which in the main justifies revolution against a regime that is oppressive) had a profound effect upon revolutionary movements everywhere (including communist movements such as those of Karl Marx, Mao Tse-tung, and Ho Chi Minh) and remains to this day the most sophisticated statement on the right of man to struggle for the preservation of his fundamental rights: the right to life, liberty and the pursuit of happiness, particularly in areas where democracy and dignity of the individual have not been realized. See Appendix 5, 46, 47.

Show 'em You're a Winner! See PRE-ELECTION CAMPAIGN.

Showing the Flag. The practice, common among powerful states of demonstrating power by sending ships or military aircraft to a region that is a source of international concern, often provoking protest from those in the affected region.

Shugi-In. The lower house of the legislature, the House of Representatives, in Japan. See KOKKAI, SHANGI-IN.

Shuttle Diplomacy. A term applied to the diplomatic efforts of U.S. Secretary of State, Henry A. Kissinger, to resolve the Arab-Israeli conflict in the Middle East through his extensive travels between Washington, Cairo, and Jerusalem—1975-1976. See SUMMIT CONFERENCE.

Sib. See DECEPTION.

Siberia of Bureaucracy. A phrase often used in the United States to describe the demotion of a once highly placed government official who for political reasons was stripped of his authority and transferred to an agency of lesser prestige. (The vast wastelands of Siberia were used for centuries, by the Tsars and later by the communist rulers, as the dumping ground for persons with unorthodox and non-conformist political views, where they would await their possible return to civilization or die forgotten.) See SATURDAY NIGHT MASSACRE.

Sic Transit Gloria Intelligentsia. See ALL NEWS IS BAD NEWS—IF IT IS ABOUT US!

Sic Utere Tuo Ut Alienum Non Laedas. In the Latin language, "conduct yourself in such a way that you will not injure others." One of the principal canons in Roman law, both private and public.

Siegfried Line. A system of fortifications erected by Nazi Germany between 1938-1945 as a defense line between Germany and other Western states, mainly France. The line, which extended for about 300 miles along the borders of Holland, Belgium, Luxembourg, France, and Switzerland, was designed mainly to protect Germany from an attack on its western flank while Hitler was preparing to open a front in the East, mainly against Poland and the Soviet Union. Also known as the West Wall, it was referred to in British music halls, "We're going to hang out the washing on the Siegfried Line." See MAGINOT LINE.

SIGINT. See INTELLIGENCE.

SII. See STRUCTURAL IMPEDIMENTS INITIATIVE.

Sikh Separatism. The people of the Sikh faith who resides in the state of Punjab seek independence as a sovereign state. Sikhs were responsible for the assassination of India's premier, Indira Ghandi, on 31 October 1984. This act was in retaliation for the Indian Army's attack on the Golden Temple, the holiest of Sikh shrines. About 4,000 Sikhs died during that attack, about 70,000 were left homeless, and the struggle continues to this day. In 1987, the Indian Government brought the state of Punjab under direct control of India's central government in New Delhi. There are about 19 million Sikhs among the 850,000,000 people in India.

Silent Black Majority. See BENIGN NEGLECT.

Silent Cal. One of the less flattering characterizations of U.S. President Calvin Coolidge (1923-1929), because he was withdrawn, publicity-shy, and hardly cared to attend any official ceremonial or social functions. While governor of Massachusetts, he was asked what he planned to do about the large accumulation of snow on state highways after heavy storms. He allegedly replied that "God put it there, and God will take it away." When informed that President Coolidge was dead, young starlet Dorothy Parker allegedly replied, "How can you tell?" See Appendix 16.

Silent Majority. A term that originated in American national politics during the 1960s which denotes the overwhelming majority of Americans who, unlike the vocal radical minorities on the left and on the right, sustain and perpetuate the American society in silence, not by outrageous and unrealistic political demands, but by hard work and support of policies and programs that aim at benefiting the society as a whole, not just certain elites. President Richard Nixon made frequent appeals for the support of his Vietnam policy. This concept was variously articulated during the 1968 and 1972 presidential elections. The term "middle America" has also a similar meaning. See BENIGN NEGLECT, SILENT BLACK MAJORITY.

Simple Majority. The minimum in an election of one-half of the votes cast plus one single vote (i.e., fifty percent of the votes plus one vote). See VOTING.

Simple Resolution. See RESOLUTION.

Simulation. See GAME THEORY.

Sin Tax. See TAX ON SIN.

Sinai Accords. See SADAT-BEGIN SUMMIT.

Sinatra Doctrine. Former Soviet President Mikhail S. Gorbachev (1985-1991) cited one of the songs sung by Frank Sinatra, "I Did it My Way," to epitomize his Glasnost and Perestroika policies and other reforms in the Soviet Union which, in the end, resulted in the dissolution of the Soviet "evil" empire and the resignation of Gorbachev on 25 December 1991.

Sine Die. In the Latin language, "for the day." Also, a term often used to designate the adjournment of the United States Congress at the end of a session without specifically setting the date for a new session. See U.S. SENATE.

Single-Choice Ballot. A voting ballot on which the names of the candidates are arranged according to party affiliation so that the voter, by marking one candidate, votes for the entire slate of the party. See VOTING.

Single Language. See ESPERANTO.

Single-Member Constituency. An electoral district with specific geographical boundaries from which only one person can be elected to a legislative body. See CONGRESSIONAL DISTRICT.

Single-Minded Idealism. A notion expressed by Professor Friedrich A. von Hayek (1899-1992), one of the world's most prestigious economists, political theorists, and teachers; a Nobel Prize laureate in 1974; and participant in famous economic debates during the 1930s with Professor Oskar Lange, a Polish educator and theoretician of socialist economy. Professor Hayek advanced the notion that the doctrines of socialism and communism are simply a fraud perpetuated by intellectuals seeking totalitarian control over the masses of people; that they are anti-democratic, anti-intellectual, and destructive to any society anytime, anywhere, in any form. The socialist/communist theoreticians allowed no leeway in the interpretation of their oppressive, collectivist doctrines, and Professor Hayek battled them alone until another young economist came on the scene, Professor Milton Friedman from the University of Chicago, who also received a Nobel Prize. In his theoretical reasoning, Professor Hayek demonstrated that the doctrines of socialism and communism as advocated by bureaucrats in the former Soviet Union, the East European satellites of the Soviet Empire, and other economy-by-command systems, were ideally suited for the eternal perpetuation of poverty, human misery, and suffering. See COMMUNISM, LENINISM, MARXISM, SOCIALISM.

Single-Party System. See ONE-PARTY SYSTEM.

Single Power. See TYRANNY OF THE MAJORITY.

Single-Purpose Lobby. See LOBBY.

Single Tax. A proposal advanced at the turn of the 20th century by American theoretical economist, Henry George, to the effect that there should be only one single tax, a tax on land, and no tax on the income derived from any other source.

Sinhalese-Tamil Antagonism. See TAMIL SEPARATISM IN SRI LANKA.

Sinn Fein. See HILLSBOROUGH AGREEMENT, IRISH REPUBLICAN ARMY (IRA).

Sino-Indian War. See HIMALAYAN CRISIS.

Sino-Soviet Rift. See SINO-SOVIET SPLIT.

Sino-Soviet Schism. See SINO-SOVIET SPLIT.

Sino-Soviet Split. The term refers to the ideological, political, and military differences that occurred from the 1950s to the 1980s between the leadership of the People's Republic of China (Red China) and that of the Soviet Union. Some of the major issues on which these two socialist states differed were the following: (1) Struggle for the leadership of the socialist states after the death of Josef Stalin (in 1953); (2) China disapproved of the accommodation of the Soviet Union with the United States; (3) Differences on the internal movements within the satellite states over which the Soviet Union claimed almost complete sovereignty and excluded China; (4) The Soviet refusal to support China's attack upon India (in 1959 and 1962) in order to regain territories once belonging to China; (5) The Soviet participation in settling the India-Pakistan War (in 1964) for which the Chinese retaliated by claiming territories which once belonged to China. As a result, throughout the years numerous armed conflicts erupted between China and the Soviet Union; and (6) The Indian-Soviet nonaggression pact of 1971 which China construed as a hostile act. The major areas of dispute along the 4,150-mile Sino-Soviet border, stretching from the Urals to the Pacific Ocean, are territories which the Russians took from China under the Treaty of Nerchinsk of 1689, the Treaty of Aigun of 1858 and the Treaty of Peking of 1860. After the dissolution of the Soviet empire in 1991, relations with Russia are stable.

Sinology. The study through reading, observation, and personal interaction with individuals in an effort to gain inside knowledge about the people, institutions, leadership, aims, and objectives of the People's Republic of China. Many political systems are involved in this kind of study by designating special groups of experts, known as "China Watchers" to such places as Hong Kong, in order to obtain the desired knowledge. All secretive systems attract such attention. See KREMLINOLOGIST, SINO-SOVIET SPLIT.

SIS. See SECRET INTELLIGENCE SERVICE.

Sitting. The annual term of the U.S. Supreme Court which begins on the first Monday in October and ends in June of the following year, is divided into two separate activities: (1) sittings—when the Court hears oral arguments on cases, announces its opinions, and rules on motions to admit attorneys to represent their clients before the Court, and (2) recesses—which alternate at two-week intervals with sittings, during which the Court, the individual Justices, do their routine work. See SUPREME COURT OF THE UNITED STATES.

Sitting on the Fence. Voters who are undecided or reluctant to reveal their preferences for issues and/or political candidates through public opinion polls. Such voters very often make up their minds while inside the voting booth. Such voters often swing the election results (e.g., for an issue, a candidate, or a party) at the last moment.

Sitting War. See SITZKRIEG.

Sitzkrieg. In the German language, "sitting war"; also a "phony war," such as that following the conquest of Poland by Nazi Germany in 1939, and the attack on Norway in the spring of 1940; there was a lack of any war activity and yet the world was at war. That period of time was referred to as "phony war." Although France and England signed treaties with Poland obliging themselves to help that state in case of attack, they broke the treaty and never came to the rescue of Poland. Britain's Neville Chamberlain and France's Paul Reynaud, sitting in inactive silence, allowed Adolf Hitler the time to prepare his war machine to soon fight them both, conquering France within weeks, demolishing England with heavy bombing, and having reserves to attack the Soviet Union in June

1941. The success of the Nazis and the inaction of the Allies promoted the Japanese militarists to attack the Unites States beginning with Pearl Harbor on 7 December 1941. In modern times, a "sitting war," or "phony war" was the period from the attack on Kuwait by President Saddam Hussein of Iraq with his elite Republican Guards on 2 August 1990, until 15 January the following year when the Coalition Forces (the United States and 14 other countries) responded military to the aggression. See PHONY WAR.

Sivis Pacem, Para Bellum. In the Latin language, "one should be armed in order to avoid war" or "one seeking to preserve peace, ought to arm himself." An ancient Roman proverb which in modern times has been supplemented with such phrases as "Praise the Lord and keep your powder dry," or "Praise the Lord and pass the ammunition," which to a large extent are subscribed to by modern nation-states in order to justify large standing armies and arsenals of modern weapon systems. See DETERRENT, WAR.

Six Ds of Guerrilla Warfare. Primary tasks for successful guerrilla operation cycle: delay, deceive, disorganize, damage, defeat, depart. See GUERRILLA WARFARE, ROGERS RANGERS STANDING ORDERS in Appendix 30.

Six-Day War. See ISRAELI-ARAB WAR OF 1967.

Skeleton in the Closet. In the language of politics, the practice of hiding in secrecy (from public disclosure) certain acts or activities from one's past, which, if revealed, may hinder one's chances for a public career (e.g., being elected to a public office). During the 1972 presidential election, for example, it was revealed that the Vice-Presidential nominee of the Democratic party (and the running mate of Presidential candidate George McGovern), U.S. Senator Thomas F. Eagleton (D-Missouri), had been treated for depression, and this revelation by the press caused his withdrawal from the race. The Presidential candidate, U.S. Senator George McGovern (D-South Dakota), stated officially that this disclosure was not important to him and that he was behind his running mate "one-thousand-percent," but made no attempt to persuade Senator Eagleton to stay on once the "skeleton" became a subject of national debate. In order to avoid public embarrassment, all major political parties (as well as all high-government officials at all levels of government) thoroughly investigate the background of persons whom they support in order to assure that there are no "skeletons" hidden. Illustrative is the case of a Republican Congressman from New Jersey, J. Parnell Thomas, who was a member of the House un-American Activities Committee and a predatory "red-witch-hunter." When Robert Taylor, the celebrated movie star, was called before the Committee as a suspected communist, he took a defense counsel with him and Thomas not only interrogated Taylor, but his lawyer as well. When Taylor protested that his rights were violated, Thomas replied: "The rights you have are the rights given you by this Committee." When Drew Pearson, a renowned journalist during the 1940s and 1950s, learned of this incident, he decided to look for skeletons in Thomas' closet and soon he found them. Thomas was a crook for many years; he was taking kickbacks from his Congressional employees, pleaded "no contest" when taken to court, was found guilty, and sentenced to 18 months imprisonment and a $10,000 fine. This incident considerably discredited the Committee as well as Senator Joseph McCarthy's smear campaign. See PRESIDENTIAL QUALIFICATIONS.

Skinheads. See ARYAN NATION.

SLA. See SYMBIONESE LIBERATION ARMY.

Slander. See LIBEL.

Slate of Candidates. A list of candidates for an election that may be informally agreed upon by a political party leadership or by a coalition of parties. See PRESIDENTIAL ELECTOR.

Slate of Electors. See ELECTORAL COLLEGE.

Slave Codes. See BLACK CODES.

Slave-Trade Compromise. See PLANS OF THE AMERICAN UNION.

Slavery. The practice or institution of owning or keeping of another human being under one's absolute control. In Article I, Section 2 of the U.S. Constitution it was understood that "all other

Persons" were slaves, and for the purpose of determining representation in the House of Representatives such "Persons" would be counted in such a manner (3/5) so that five (5) slaves would be necessary to equal three (3) free persons. In 1865, the 13th Amendment to the U.S. Constitution essentially banned "slavery" and "involuntary servitude."

Slavocracy. An economic-political system that rests on the system of slavery (e.g., the politico-economic systems in the southern states of the United States before the Civil War). U.S. Representative David Wilmot introduced a provision in 1846 which would have prohibited slavery in territories taken from Mexico. That provision intensified the debate on slavery which was not resolved until the War of Secession or Civil War (1861-1865) between the anti-slavery North and the pro-slavery South, when the southern states seceded, forming the Confederate States of America (CSA). See SECTIONALISM.

Slavophile. One who advocates the superiority of Slavic culture and societal values over others. The Slavophile Movement was particularly strong under Tsar Nicolas I (1825-1855) during whose reign such subjects as the history of philosophy, constitutional law, logic, metaphysics, and any teaching about the Western cultures were suspended in the Russian universities under the slogan of "Autocracy, Orthodoxy, and Nationality." To the Slavophiles the West was "decadent," everything Russian was superior, and the national minorities within the Russian Empire were subjected to intensive Russification. Among the more active Slavophiles were the following: Ivan V. Kireevsky (1806-1856), Peter V. Kireevsky (1808-1856), Ivan S. Aksakov (1823-1886), Constantine S. Aksakov (1817-1861), Aleksei S. Khomianov (1804-1860), Yuri F. Samarin (1819-1876), and Prince Vladimir A. Cherkassky (1824-1878). See PAN-SLAVISM.

Sleeper. See INTELLIGENCE.

Sleeping with an Elephant. See RUSH-BAGOT AGREEMENT.

Slum. Generally, a heavily populated area of a city characterized by poverty, poor housing, improper sanitation, and poor health conditions. During the waves of immigration to the United States new arrivals settled in cities. Lacking political or economic power, they were forced to endure the lowest of living conditions. Throughout the world, cities generally have an area known as a "slum" where those in the lowest socio-economic level found.

Slush Funds. See HUSH MONEY.

Small Claims Court. Courts of law originated in the United States during the 1920s, adjudicating cases in civil disputes ranging from $150 in Texas to $3,000 in the State of Indiana. The procedure in these courts is less cumbersome and more personalized and responsive.

Small is Beautiful. A slogan popular in America since the 1974 oil crisis, and one particularly propagated by California's Democratic Governor Edmund G. ("Jerry") Brown (1975-1983). After his service as governor, Brown ran for the U.S. Senate in 1982 and lost; he ran three time for the U.S. Presidency, in 1976, 1980, and 1992. As governor, he refused to be chauffeured in an elegant limousine and instead drove his own 1974 model Plymouth; he refused to reside in the governor's mansion and instead, rented a one-room apartment and slept on a mattress on the floor; as governor, he balanced the budget of California and cut government spending on non-essential projects. During his spring break from Yale University Law School in 1964, he drove his car to Mississippi, made an appointment with its anti-segregationist governor, Ross Burnett, and informed him that he came to campaign for the rights of blacks. Burnett immediately called Brown's father, Pat Brown, later defeated in 1966 for his third term as governor of California by Ronald Reagan, and told him to recall his son from Mississippi or he would be arrested. Brown, and others, support the small versus the large, including smaller cars to save gas, and a halt on spending by states and the federal government for non-essential projects, usually those demanded by strong vested interests with strong lobbies. In 1967 Brown campaigned against the Vietnam War; he assisted Senator Eugene McCarthy in his presidential campaign; he supported the activities of labor leader Cesar Chavez; in 1969 he defeated 132 candidates for the Los Angeles Community College Board (his first elective office). After his service as governor, Brown decided to take time off from politics and to seek reconciliation and better understanding of the relationship between politics, public service, and morality. In order to pursue that endeavor, he went to India to help Mother Theresa take care of the poor, then to Japan's Zen

Buddhist centers for meditation. Brown is considered an unorthodox maverick, and also one of the most intelligent and dedicated politicians of this century in America. See PUT AMERICA ON A DIET; WE, THE PEOPLE, TAKE BACK AMERICA.

Smelling Like Butter. See BATAKUSAI.

Smith Act. See LOYALTY LAWS.

Smithsonian Agreement. An agreement that was reached between the United States and other powers (among them England, France, the Federal Republic of Germany, Italy, and Japan) on the establishment of parities for the major currencies of the world, including the United States dollar, by fixing their exchange rates for the purpose of maintaining international monetary stability. The conference was held at the Smithsonian Institution in Washington, D.C., in 1971. (The U.S. dollar was since devalued in order to offset the deficit in America's international balance of payments and to make American goods more competitive abroad.)

Smithsonian Parity. See SMITHSONIAN AGREEMENT.

Smoking Gun Tapes. See WATERGATE.

SMSA. See STANDARD METROPOLITAN STATISTICAL AREA.

Snake. See BLACK PANTHER PARTY FOR SELF-DEFENSE.

SNCC. See STUDENT NONVIOLENT COORDINATING COMMITTEE.

Sneaky War. See ACT OF WAR.

Social Adjudication. See BRANDEIS BRIEF.

Social Contract Theory. See ORIGINS OF THE STATE THEORIES.

Social Control. An undetermined set of rules and institutions, short of the employment of naked force, which help to manage people; laws and institutions which encourage and protect interaction of individuals, and evolvement of overlapping loyalties by association in public and private organizations, with the ultimate aim of increasing the input of support for the existing political system.

Social Crime. See HATE CRIME, SEXUAL HARASSMENT.

Social Credit. An economic doctrine that evolved during the 1930s which held that all income that is generated from any economic activity (e.g., use of capital or production) is social in nature and, therefore, ought to be paid to the members of the community rather than go to individuals who claim the ownership of the means of production and distribution. The notion was first advanced by a Canadian, Army Major C. H. Douglas, and it did not claim association or any relation to socialism or communism. See MARXISM, SINGLE TAX.

Social Democratic and Labour Party (SDLP). See HILLSBOROUGH AGREEMENT.

Social Democratic Party (SPD). See JUNGE SOZIALISTEN (JUSO).

Social Engineer. According to Josef Stalin, former Premier of the Soviet Government and Secretary of the Communist Party of the Soviet Union (CPSU), 1924-1953, any intellectual who is actively involved in creative writing, teaching, the performing and creative arts, journalism, or any other vocation that directly influences and shapes the minds of people and gives direction to their views and attitudes is a social engineer.

Social Imperialism. A term often used by the leaders of the People's Republic of China (Communist China) to describe the aggressive policies, acts, and activities of the Soviet leaders and the Soviet State. The term "modern revisionism" is also used. See SINO-SOVIET SPLIT.

Social Management. See SECOND BILL OF RIGHTS.

Social Mobility. The conditions within a given society (of social, economic, or political nature) which allow the individual person to advance himself, horizontally and vertically, solely on the merits of his ability, and without any artificial restrictions (e.g., restrictions placed by the government or any of its agencies). Also, a free society which allows the individual person to develop himself freely and without any restrictions. See CLOSED POLITICAL SYSTEM.

Social Monarchy. See MEIJI CONSTITUTION.

Social Movement Party. A political party in contemporary Italy, small but gaining in strength and popularity. It advocates the revival of some of the policies of fascism and of Benito Mussolini. One of its leaders is Alesandra Mussolini, the granddaughter of Mussolini, who, in her campaign for the Italian Parliament, called for orderly economic reforms and work discipline. See FASCISM.

Social Planning. See PLANNING.

Social Security. A system of insurance benefits (e.g., retirement, medical care, dental benefits, disability benefits, and other old-age and survivor benefits) that is administered by the Social Security Administration, an autonomous agency of the U.S. Department of Health, Education and Welfare. The agency also administers federal grants-in-aid to state governments for similar purposes. The system was set up in 1935, as one of the "New Deal" programs, and was modeled after that of East Prussia, where in 1871 Prince Otto von Bismarck introduced such a system for the first time anywhere. The tax and benefits were modified by Congress and were signed by the President on December 7, 1977, and the Republican Whip in the House of Representatives, Robert H. Michael, commented, "This is the biggest tax bill we've ever passed." The legislation increased Social Security taxes by 227 billion dollars over the next ten years. In fiscal year 1977, there was a deficit in the Social Security fund of 5.6 billion dollars, and since benefits exceed the income to the fund), the fund was expected to go bankrupt by year 2000.

Social Superstructure. The concept, as advanced by Karl Marx and his collaborators, that every society in a certain stage of its development (e.g., communal, feudal, capitalistic, or socialistic) has its own economic base which reflects the modes of production and distribution, and that all human institutions (e.g., government, laws, morality, religion, or customs) in any society rest on, and are the reflection of, the economic base on which they were erected. Any change in the economic base will automatically cause a change in the superstructure, for the base modifies the superstructure according to the mode of production and distribution which Marx called "production relations." This base, therefore, may not be changed merely by the modification of any of the elements within the superstructure (e.g., changing the laws or the form of government). Decisive and just change, according to Marx, can only be brought about by the total destruction of the old economic base, and only by drastic, revolutionary means (and not parliamentary or legislative means), and a new economic base (socialist) established, on which a new superstructure can be built (socialist superstructure). See MARXISM.

Social Welfare. Social security, Medicare, unemployment, welfare, etc.

Social Will. Similar to Jean Jacques Rousseau's "volonté générale" ("general will"), the "social will" is described by Lest F. Ward (in *The Psychic Factors of Civilization*, Boston: Ginn, 1893) as that will which societies, as collections of separate individuals, like to have realized by their governments, where "Every government, even the most despotic, is to a certain extent representative of the state of society" over which it governs. The important facts to be noted in connection with the manifestation of social will are that: (1) all existing governments, regardless of form, are perpetually trying to satisfy the demands of individuals and groups, at least to a degree that allows the system to sustain itself (avoid a revolution); (2) the fact that a government remains in power for a prolonged time, even if the government is considered totalitarian or otherwise "bad," indicates that it has accomplished something (it has been effective in maintaining control), otherwise it would fall, or would cause the state to disintegrate; and (3) every government that remains in power for an extended period of time, no matter how oppressive and totalitarian it may be in its mode of ruling, the very fact of its survival indicates that there was sufficient social support (legitimacy), which allowed it to sustain itself. (E.g., it appears to be rational to assume that such totalitarian systems as those of the former Soviet Union, the Socialist states, the People's Republic of China, Cuba, and Uganda, for example, receive the necessary support which allows them to survive. It is inconceivable to assume that, for example, a small group of ruling party dignitaries in the former Soviet Union, could have terrorized 240 million people into blind obedience!)

Socialism. In the main, the philosophy which advocates (as the main prerequisite for a just society) common ownership of the means of production (e.g., factories, mines, banks, or public utilities—to mention only a few) and distribution (e.g., retail of goods and services); the elimination of a capitalistic system of economy by revolutionary means and the institution of a socialistic system of economy; and the elimination of classes by class struggle. (Karl Marx and his followers divided socialism into two categories: the "scientific" one, as advocated by Marx himself; and the "utopian," non-revolutionary and non-scientific, as advocated by such classical philosophers as Robert Owen, St. Simon, Fourier, or Blanc.)

Socialism in one Country. A concept developed by Joseph Stalin in 1924 to the effect that socialism under the existing circumstances (when capitalism entered its higher stage of development, the stage of imperialism which Marx could not foresee) can only be successful in one country at a time; and that state must pursue the implementation of socialism regardless of lack of industrial development and the capital necessary for such development. (This concept was contrary to the notion pursued by Leon Trotsky and his followers who insisted on "permanent revolution"; that is, that the Soviet state must continuously inspire and support revolutions outside in order to bring about a worldwide socialist revolution as envisioned by Marx. Stalin's notion prevailed and soon his opponents were eliminated.)

Socialism or Death! So remarked Cuba's President Fidel Castro in March 1992, when asked if he planned to abandon his demoralizing socialist policies in Cuba. Cuba, according to President Castro, is ready to defend itself against any foreign attack, including that by Cuban exiles in Florida who form the "Alpha 66" commando, which plans to return to Cuba, remove Castro, and establish democratic government.

Socialism with a Human Face. See EUROCOMMUNISM.

Socialist Camp. See SOCIALIST COMMONWEALTH OF NATIONS.

Socialist Capitalism. See WORKERS' COUNCILS.

Socialist Commonwealth of Nations. Those states which subscribe to the Soviet branch of socialism and which, as a rule, are situated in the Soviet sphere of influence (e.g., Czechoslovakia, Hungary, Rumania, Bulgaria, East Germany, Cuba, Angola, and Poland). See PEOPLE'S DEMOCRACY.

Socialist Competition. A system of capitalistic incentives (e.g., extra pay in the form of bonuses) that were given to Soviet collective farm workers in 1966 in order to spur food production and reduce Soviet dependence on the import of foodstuffs (mainly grain) from abroad (mainly the United States). Farm workers were organized in brigades for the purpose of the "socialist competition." The program was stifled by bureaucracy in the Central Planning Agency.

Socialist Democracy. A democracy which, according to contemporary Soviet ideologues (e.g., Mikhail A. Suslov, Kremlin's number one ideologue when), is only possible under socialism like that in the Soviet Union and other socialist states following the Soviet line, such as the East European satellites and Cuba; it was to be characterized by mutual respect based on socialist solidarity and proletarian brotherhood. This was, of course, the theory. In reality, it was master-vassal relationship.

Socialist Economy. See FREE ENTERPRISE.

Socialist International. An informal international association of socialist parties, particularly those that oppose any forms of communism. Willy Brandt, former Chancellor of the German Federal Republic, is one of its leaders and also its president.

Socialist Labor Party of the United States. A Marxist-oriented political faction which has been active in the United States since 1876 and which, among other things, advocates collective ownership of the means of production and distribution to be achieved by legislative (non-revolutionary) means. See SOCIALISM, SOCIALIST PARTY.

Socialist Mentality. See EASTOXIFICATION.

Socialist Misery Index. See SINGLE-MINDED IDEALISM.

Socialist New Born Things. During the period of the Great Cultural Proletarian Revolution in the People's Republic of China (1964-1968), the leader of China, Mao Tse-tung, ordered the removal of some remnants of capitalism (e.g., bonuses and salary increments for workers) and allowed the growth of socialism, which he called the "socialist new born things." See CULTURAL REVOLUTION, RED CAT THEORY.

Socialist Party. A political faction in the U.S., founded in 1898, as the Socialist-Democratic party and renamed in 1901 as the Socialist party, composed of elements which withdrew from the Socialist Labor party. The party opposed America's involvement in foreign wars and advocated, among other things, introduction of socialism by legislative means. Its presidential candidate for the 1976 general election was Frank P. Zeidler, former mayor of Milwaukee, who was nominated on September 1, 1975. See SOCIAL LABOR PARTY, SOCIALISM.

Socialist Party of Japan. The main opposition of the ruling Liberal Democratic Party.

Socialist Pluralism. A term applied to the different forms of socialism as it was practiced in the USSR, the People's Republic of China, the East European socialist states, in Africa, and in Europe. Although most of the socialist systems did subscribe generally to the teachings of Karl Marx and Engels, they did differ on the priorities in national policies and the relationships between the individual and the states, but what they all shared was misery and poverty.

Socialist Realism. The official Soviet policy, initiated under Josef Stalin during the late 1920s and early 1930s which demanded that creative artists depict the Soviet system not as it really was, but as it ought to have been, or as it would have been upon further advance into the higher stages of communism. Also, the demand that creative artists emphasize in their works the aspirations of the socialist state and its people, and did not merely record the facts or draw upon the experiences of the "decadent" West.

Socialist Revolutionary. One who favored social and political reforms in pre-communist Russia without necessarily subscribing to the doctrine of revolutionary socialism as advocated by Karl Marx and his followers. (This group in Russia soon became the biggest foe of Vladimir Lenin and his revolutionary movement.)

Socialist Solidarity. See SOCIALIST DEMOCRACY.

Socialist Workers Party of the United States. A splinter group of the Communist Party of the United States formed in 1938 of pro-Trotsky elements. The party advocates, among other things, the abolition of capitalism in America, legalization of abortion, abolition of all "right to work" laws, non-involvement in anti-communist wars abroad, and full equality of national, racial, and ethnic minorities. See SOCIALIST PARTY.

Socialist Zionism. See JEWISH COMMUNISM.

Socialized Enterprises in the United States. An economic enterprise which produces goods or services and which is fully or partially owned and/or operated by the government for the benefit of the people. Some of the socialized or partially socialized enterprises in the United States are: (1) electric power (the TVA); (2) water supply and purification; (3) railroad (AMTRAK); (4) urban and suburban transit; (5) insurance (old-age, unemployment, health—Medicare, Medicaid); (6) housing; (7) liquor (in some states, e.g., Virginia); (8) water irrigation; (9) highways and airport facilities and services; (10) parks; (11) conveyors and grain elevators; (12) printing (U.S. Government Printing Office); (13) postal service; (14) docks; (15) warehouses; (16) commissaries (PX, government cafeterias, including congressional sport and beauty-treatment facilities); (17) botanical gardens; (18) nuclear energy; and (19) education, including the academies (e.g., Army, Navy, Air Force, Marine Corps, and Merchant Marine). Some say that the United States is entering the era of creeping socialism, while others see it as galloping communism. Excluding the military and publicly owned enterprises, approximately 14 percent of America's civilian labor force is gainfully employed by government agencies and producing services. (As of 1992, there were approximately 14,000 socialized enterprises in the United States). See CAPITALISM, FREE ENTERPRISE, OAKS' LAWS, SOCIALISM.

Socialized Medicine. Generally, socialized medicine is an area of society controlled by a government which espouses a somewhat socialist theory. This theory focuses on government control of the major economic goods and services of a society. Through legislation and extensive regulation, a system is established whereby most areas of medical care are provided or controlled by a central authority. Because the government provides medical care, citizens have only to pay a minimal fee or the care is provided free. In addition, medical providers (doctors, nurses, etc.) are employed (and therefore somewhat controlled) by the government. Medical facilities (hospitals, nursing homes, etc.) are controlled in terms of what services they provide, cost, and to whom such services will be made available. The aim of socialized medicine is to assure citizens of the availability of medical health services, regardless of economic or social status. All citizens are treated equally and have the same level of medical care available to them. In the U.S., the concept of social medicine has been hotly debated over the years. As part of his Great Society program, President Lyndon Johnson sent a proposal to Congress (now known as Medicare) to provide medical care for the elderly in the U.S. The Democratic controlled Congress passed this legislation in 1965, twenty years after previous Democratic President Harry Truman had proposed such a program. The American Medical Association and many private health care providers turned the legislation "socialized medicine" and vigorously opposed it. Medicare consists of a Part "A" and a Part "B." Part "A" provides coverage for specified hospital services. Part "B" provides coverage for the services of individual health providers, such as doctors. Citizens over 65 years of age are eligible to participate in both programs and both parts "A" and "B" are health insurance programs, whereby those eligible pay premiums. Another form of "socialized medicine" in the U.S. was passed into law by Congress a year after Medicare and is now called Medicaid. This program is designed to provide health care to the poor and is supported by federal funds to assist state health programs. It provides medical and hospital assistance to those classified as living below the poverty level. Medicaid is fully sponsored by federal and state funds since it is designed to provide aid to those already receiving public assistance. Although Medicare and Medicaid are the law of the land in the U.S., the essential elements of the concept of socialized medicine do not exist here. Most health care practitioners and medical facilities are private. While many private health care providers participate in the government's programs, others adamantly refuse. Socialized medicine is the policy of some 50 countries, which have government sponsored compulsory health insurance programs.

Society of Heaven and Earth. See SECRET SOCIETIES.

Socrates Project. A comprehensive, covert investigation conducted during the 1980s by the U.S. Military Intelligence apparatus in collaboration with the intelligence community and foreign, non-hostile intelligence establishments, to protect American and Western technology from falling into "undesirable" hands.

Socratic Revolution. From approximately the fifth century on, the Greeks shifted their emphasis of research and education from the physical sciences to the social sciences and the humanities. The sophists, a group of professional educators, took the scientific method of Socrates, Plato, and Aristotle and began to concentrate on such disciplines as logic, psychology, ethics, politics, and religion—all of which were to allow man to better understand the political and legal aspects of politically organized society. Their teachings and research laid the foundation for the Industrial Revolution and the Age of Enlightenment when the struggle for the dignity of man and the notion of rule arising out of the consent of the ruled would take positive shape (particularly as expressed in the teachings and writings of Locke, Rousseau, Montesquieu, and Jefferson.

Soft Money. See LOCOFOCOS.

Soft State. A state that is characterized by poor planning of human and material resources; inconsistencies between policy formation and policy implementation and output allocation; lack of responsiveness on the part of its governmental components to the basic needs and aspirations of the people, on a daily, continuous basis. The opposite is a "hard state," one that is efficient and expedient in policy making and policy implementation, is responsive to the daily needs of its people, without being oppressive or totalitarian. The distinction here lies mainly in the cognitive abilities of the governing apparatus to expeditiously respond to the needs of the people according to some pragmatic and workable models, versus slow response to crisis situations alone, without workable models to follow, and without advanced planning. See CRISIS GOVERNMENT.

Soil Bank. A federally sponsored program in the United States under which the farmers may withhold a certain amount of arable land from production and be compensated for the loss of their income by the government. The two principal objectives of this program are: (1) soil conservation, and (2) control of overproduction of agricultural commodities (and thus control of prices on agricultural products). This program is also known as "land retirement."

Solar Coalition. See CONGRESSIONAL CAUCUS.

Soldiers for Democracy (Shield). A reform group of Russian soldiers (previously of the Soviet Red Army), organized in 1991 to help the leaders of the Commonwealth of Independent States (CIS) maintain control and order. The Air Force component and the Paratroops component of the Red Army were instrumental in defending the cause of President Boris N. Yeltsin and in helping him retain power and control. The Shield is particularly active within the Russian Armed Forces. It assisted in the transfer of nuclear warheads from other republics to the Russian Republic for safe storage and eventual destruction.

Solemn Referendum of 1920. U.S. President Woodrow Wilson (1913-1921), in his attempt to break the deadlock over America's ratification of the League of Nations Treaty, decided to take the matter directly to the American people during the 1920 presidential campaign, which was not successful. To Wilson's appeal, the socialist forces in New York City, for example, replied that the League of Nations was as "vital as a dead cat in a gutter." The conservative Republicans denounced the League as "superstate."

Solicitor General. An official within the United States Department of Justice who serves as the attorney (lawyer) for the United States Government. (Only the Solicitor General may grant permission to sue the Federal Government).

Solid South. Traditionally, the southern states have always stood together on matters of national policy (e.g., civil rights and economic issues) and their congressional delegations have often voted as a block. This solidarity eroded considerably under the administration of Lyndon B. Johnson (1963-1969), and regional differences were even less apparent under President Jimmy Carter (1977-1981), but unified again in 1992. There are many Republicans who moved from the East and North, and have weakened the solidarity.

Solidarity. The Solidarity movement in Poland can claim that it originated shortly after the 1968 invasion of Czechoslovakia by the Soviet Union and its satellites, which crushed the Prague Spring movement and its leader, Aleksander Dubcek. Like any political movement-to-be, Solidarity's ideology was cleverly hidden; its leaders knew that should it emerge as a political movement rather than as innocent demands by workers for better wages, more freedom at work, and better working conditions, it would encounter stiff opposition. Had the movement shown its real intention—to grab for power—it would have been crushed the first day. Lech Walesa was very knowledgeable in communist tactics, and with his labor union notions wrapped around with liberal Catholic ideology, he was fully cognizant of the fact that nothing worthwhile is ever easy. His leadership style was that of a Sunday School teacher rather than a political leader. The core of his ideology came from his religious, Catholic education, the mentorship by Karol Cardinal Wojtyla soon to Pope John Paul II (a grand tactician in his own right), and from the liberal democratic traditions of Poland that dated back ten centuries, when the nation was formed, adopted Christianity, and became a part of western culture. Lech Walesa, a master tactician and a great communicator and motivator, proceeded slowly while engaging the Polish communist regime in a political war of attrition. At the top, the communist regime, with a few exceptions like General Wojciech Jaruzelski, consisted of petty, uneducated, greedy, decadent, immoral, and incompetent bureaucrats. Moral support from the West, particularly from the United States and from the large groups of Poles in other parts of the world, was crucial in the final struggle. The demoralized communist leadership lacked the vision of Walesa and his followers and, therefore Walesa could outmaneuver in the end. After several months of protest, the Polish regime agreed on 30 August 1980 to 21 demands presented by Solidarity in the Lenin Shipyard in

Gdansk; one of the concessions was to allow the workers to form an independent trade union. Soon, when farmers and others joined in, the union grew to about ten million members (almost one-third of the entire population of Poland). On 12 December 1980, the union held a referendum to form a non-communist government. However, the communists deprived Solidarity of access to the media and the press. Fearful of Soviet intervention, the regime imposed martial law on 13 December 1981, and when demonstrations broke out, the leaders of the union, including Lech Walesa, were imprisoned, and Solidarity was declared illegal by the Sejm (Parliament) on 8 October 1982. In December 1982 martial law was lifted. During several years of terror, Solidarity maintained a conciliatory posture, waiting for the right moment to spring up again. Meanwhile, Soviet President Mikhail S. Gorbachev, who came to power in 1985, reassessed the situation and came to the conclusion that the satellite regimes were decadent, corrupt, incompetent, and that the best way to help them was to let them die. And that is what he did. On 5 April 1989, Solidarity reached an understanding with the decaying regime; parliamentary elections held on 4 June 1989 replaced most of the Sejm deputies with Solidarity followers. On 19 August 1989, Tadeusz Mazowiecki formed the first non-communist government in Eastern Europe, and in 1990 Lech Walesa was elected as president of the Republic of Poland; the communists dispersed only soon to reemerge as the most aggressive "free-market capitalists" ever, trading with the Polish people's money which they had stashed away while in power. According to a report of 15 March 1992, "Moscow would have sent the Red Army into Poland to crush Solidarity had martial law not been declared, a Russian general was quoted as saying. "Everything was ready," General Wiktor Dubynin said in an interview in the *Gazeta Wyborcza* newspaper. "Within one day or two, at most, Soviet troops would have been everywhere, in every town, every village." "Dubynin commands the army division that was stationed in Poland to lead the Warsaw Pact should it have gone into battle with NATO forces. He is now overseeing the withdrawal from Poland of his troops." See CRISIS STAFF, Appendix 91.

Solidarity Sunday Resolution. On April 30, 1976, the U.S. House of Representatives passed a resolution (Senate action is not required on such resolutions), calling upon the Soviet Union to stop oppression of the Jews and to let them emigrate freely. The sponsor of the resolution, Rep. Bella S. Abzug, (D-NY), stated, "We have notified the Soviet Union that we oppose its policy of restricting the emigration of Jews to Israel, and the harassment, punishment and imprisonment of Soviet Jews who seek to leave their country, or attempt to exercise their religious rights." A similar measure was passed in 1975 by the U.S. Senate when U.S. Senator Henry Jackson (D-WA) added an amendment of a similar nature to a trade bill with the Soviet Union. The so-called "Jackson-Vanik Amendment" to the foreign appropriation bill made trade concession with the Soviets depend on their elimination of restriction on the emigration of Jews from the USSR, but, in reality, it stifled the process when the Soviets frowned upon such linkage of trade for Jewish emigration. The Soviets compromised on Jewish emigration in the coming years. See JEWISH LOBBY.

Solon. Solon (638-559 BC.) was an active and prolific lawmaker in ancient Athens, Greece, and is considered as one of the wisest politicians and government officials of all time, particularly in the conception of legal norms. Also, one involved in lawmaking processes (e.g., U.S. Senator, Representative, or member of state legislature).

Solon Constitution. See COMPULSORY VOTING.

Son of Heaven. See V-J DAY.

Sonnenfeldt Doctrine. Helmut Sonnenfeldt, one-time special assistant to Dr. Henry A. Kissinger, U.S. Secretary of State (1969-1974), who was in charge of Russian and East European Affairs at the State Department, was of the opinion that the People's Democracies of Eastern Europe were an integral part of the Soviet socialist system, and that this should be viewed as an irreversible fact. Such pronouncements helped the Soviets hold on until it all collapsed in 1991.

Sons of Liberty. See STAMP ACT.

Sons of the Wild Jackass. In 1858, U.S. Senator from New Hampshire, George H. Moses, so named those U.S. Senators who favored the Populist movement and the interests of farmers and big business in the western territories of the United States.

Sophist. See SOCRATIC REVOLUTION.

Sounds of Little Hammers. In the politico-economic sense, a nation is at an advantage when many people in their spare time engage in all sorts of economic activities, primarily working with small tools (little hammers); such workers demonstrate ingenuity, add to the prosperity and sufficiency of the nation's economy, and, in the end, contribute to political stability. In America the term "Yankee ingenuity" is also used in a similar context, referring to people (more in the past, less now) who engage in basement, garage, or backyard discoveries and experimentations. Some of this activity has led to discoveries of popular products such as the automobile, the telephone, and Coca Cola. Similar ingenuity is common in Japan, Germany, France, England, Singapore, South Korea, Hong Kong, Taiwan, and a score of other nations. In these countries one of the important items of mass production is all sorts of tools, and mini-workshop systems including printed literature on how to use them, and how to produce small items, usually for domestic needs. One of the major faults of the failed economies of the communist/socialist states was not only lack of tools and initiative to use them, but the governments encouragement of people to attend a party, trade union, or sports events instead of engaging in pounding little hammers. Group activity was more susceptible to mass control by the regime and the police. In addition, these economies had mega-plans and ideas, but mini-resources and skills. Traveling through the countryside of the former Soviet Union and its former satellite states in Eastern Europe, one can see expensive equipment idling and rusting because of a minor defect which nobody could fix on the spot, due to lack of knowledge, tools, and incentive. Only major production plants were expected to do such repairs, but most of them also lacked tools, materials, and transport. See COMPARATIVE ADVANTAGE, CONSUMER ECONOMICS.

Sources of American Constitution. Some of the direct sources are the Articles of Confederation, state constitutions adopted after 1775, and the experiences of the Continental Congress, together with treaties and contractual agreements. The constitution-makers derived many of their ideas from antiquity (mainly the experiences of Roman lawyers), the British constitutional experiences (beginning with the *Magna Carta of 1215),* and the experiences of states in continental Europe, in addition to such published materials as William Blackstone's *Commentaries on the Laws of England,* John Locke's *Two Treatises on Government,* Baron de Montesquieu's *Spirit of Laws,* Jean Jacques Rousseau's *Social Contract,* Thomas Hobbes' *Leviathan,* and James Harrington's *The Government of Oceans,* to mention only a few.

Sources of International Law. According to Article 38 of the Statutes of the International Court of Justice, which was established in 1945, together with the United Nations Organization, there are four sources from which norms of international law may be derived: (1) international conventions, whether general or particular, establishing rules expressly recognized by consenting states; (2) international customs, as evidence of general practice accepted as law; (3) the general principles of law recognized by civilized nations; and (4) subject to provisions of Article 59 (". . . the decision of the Court has no binding force except between the parties and in respect of that particular case") judicial decisions and the teachings of the most highly qualified publicists of the various nations, as subsidiary means for the determination of rules of law.

Sources of Municipal (Domestic) Law. Traditionally, domestic laws are derived from constitutions, statutes (acts of the legislature), treaties with foreign nations, customs, judicial decisions and opinions (case law; particularly in the common law, or Anglo-Saxon legal systems), and teaching and writing by experts.

South Africa National Union (SWANU). A rival organization of the SWAPO in South West Africa struggling for the leadership of black Africans in that area. SWANU has no sanctions in the OAU (Organization for African Unity) for it advocates gradual accommodation with the white-controlled government in South Africa. See SWART GEVAAR, ZANU, ZAPU.

South Africa's Constitutional Settlement. See CONFERENCE FOR DEMOCRATIC SOUTH AFRICA (CODESA).

South Africa's Democratic Party. See CONFERENCE FOR DEMOCRATIC SOUTH AFRICA (CODESA).

South African Quadrangle Forces. See AFRICAN RESISTANCE MOVEMENT.

South-West Africa Peoples' Organization (SWAPO). A militant political and paramilitary liberation organization that was established during the late 1950s by Kenneth Kaunda of Zambia for the purpose of liberating Zambia and South West Africa (a territory called Namibia under the administration of the Republic of South Africa) from white rule. SWAPO was a branch of Kaunda's United National Independent Party, and when the party gained power in Zambia in 1964, SWAPO continued its struggle for the liberation of the entire territory of South West Africa (Namibia) from white rule by the South African regime. In 1971 SWAPO was recognized by many international organizations, including the United Nations and the Organization of African Unity, as the sole legitimate representative and spokesman for the people of Namibia. See SWANU, SWART GEVAAR, ZANU, ZAPU.

Southampton Insurrection. See TURNER'S REBELLION.

Southeast Asia Treaty Organization (SEATO). A regional defense organization that was set up by a mutual defense pact signed on September 3, 1954, in Manila, the Philippines, by the United States, England, Australia, Pakistan, France, Thailand, New Zealand, and the Philippines. The principal purpose of the alliance was to deter communist aggression in the area, particularly in Vietnam, but in reality only Thailand, New Zealand, and Australia lived up to their obligations during the Vietnamese conflict. When the Vietnamese conflict ended, the foreign ministers of the member states agreed, on September 24, 1975, to gradually phase SEATO out of existence. See Appendix 29.

Southern Christian Leadership Conference (SCLC). A libertarian and civil rights organization established in 1957 by Rev. Dr. Martin Luther King, Jr., in Atlanta, Georgia, after the successful bus boycott in Montgomery, Alabama; its purpose is to continue the struggle of blacks and other minorities as well as the poor for an equal place in American society.

Southern Confederacy. See CONFEDERATE STATES OF AMERICA (CSA).

Southern Manifesto. A group of ninety members of the U.S. Congress from the southern states of the United States, under the leadership of U.S. Senator Walter George, presented to Congress in March 1956 a manifesto (known as the "Declaration of Constitutional Principles"), in which they condemned the federal government for forcing the desegregation issue, and protested "against the encroachment of the central government upon the sovereignty of the several states and their people." (Three members of Congress from North Carolina refused to join the group and two of them, both Democrats, lost their bids for re-election in 1957.) In response to the Manifesto, only three states (Georgia, Mississippi, and Virginia) presented such declarations from states (known as "interpositions"). See BENIGN NEGLECT.

Southern Regional Council (SRC). A libertarian and civil rights organization established in 1918 in Atlanta, Georgia, for the purpose of assisting black Americans in registering and voting during elections, and of studying the trends and the developments of educational and employment gains of blacks.

Southern Strategy. See BENIGN NEGLECT.

Sovereign. One totally independent; one capable of making totally independent decisions; also, a monarch or absolute ruler.

Sovereign Capacity. The right of a free, sovereign, and independent state to act as a free agent on its own behalf. See POPULAR SOVEREIGNTY.

Sovereignty. Total and unreserved independence of a state; or a state able to make decisions without outside influence. Under democracy, sovereignty rests with the voters, the electorate. See POPULAR SOVEREIGNTY.

Sovereignty in an American Republic Belongs to a People, Never to a Government. A premise on which Jefferson Davis, who later became President of the Confederate States of America (1861-1865), justified the secession of the southern states from the Federal Union in 1861.

Soviet. In the Russian language, "council" (e.g., Council of Ministers of the USSR, or council of a ruling body on any level of government in the Soviet Union).

Soviet Coup. See STATE COMMITTEE ON THE STATE OF EMERGENCY.

Soviet Dissolution. See STATE COMMITTEE ON THE STATE OF THE EMERGENCY.

Soviet Hard-Liner Dictatorship. See NATIONAL SALVATION COMMITTEE.

Soviet Incursion in Afghanistan. See AFGHAN KHALG PARTY.

Soviet of Nationalities. One of two chambers of the national Soviet legislature, the Supreme Soviet of the former USSR (in the Russian language, "Vyerghovnoy Sovyet CCCP"), in which the various nationalities of the USSR were represented in the following ratio: twenty-five (25) deputies from each Union Republic; eleven (11) deputies from each Autonomous Republic; five (5) deputies from each Autonomous Region; and one (1) deputy from each National Area (Okrug). All deputies were elected for a term of four (4) years. There were approximately 750 deputies in the Soviet of Nationalities. The Soviet of Nationalities shared equal authority (legislative or otherwise) with the other chamber, the Soviet of the Union. It was dissolved in 1991. See Appendix 74.

Soviet of the Union. One of two chambers of the national Soviet legislature, the Supreme Soviet of the former USSR (in the Russian language, "Vyerghovnoy Sovyet CCCP"), to which the deputies were elected for a period of four (4) years from single member constituencies, each constituency having approximately three-hundred thousand (300,000) inhabitants. There were approximately 750 deputies in the Soviet of the Union. The Soviet of the Union shares equal authority (legislative or otherwise) with the other chamber, the Soviet of Nationalities. It was dissolved in 1991

Soviet Propaganda Alert. See PROJECT TRUTH.

Soviet Revisionism. See SINO-SOVIET SPLIT.

Soviet Socialism. The basic principles of Soviet socialism, according to Art. 12 of the Soviet Constitution, were: "He who does not work, neither shall he eat," and "From each according to his ability, to each according to his work." The second biblical principle is a modification of the theory of Karl Marx, who held that under communism there will be little demand and plenty of rewards to the individual according to the principle of: "From each according to his ability, to each according to his needs." See EURO-COMMUNISM, MARXISM, MATERIAL-TECHNICAL BASE OF COMMUNISM, SOCIALISM, SOCIALISM IN ONE COUNTRY.

Soviet Union. See UNION OF SOVIET SOCIALIST REPUBLICS (USSR).

Soviet Vietnam. See AFGHANISTAN WAR.

Sovietoid System. A political system that was either imposed on other states (e.g., in Poland, Czechoslovakia, Rumania, Hungary, East Germany, and Bulgaria) by the former Soviet Union (e.g., the so-called "people's democracies"), or one that was patterned after Soviet government and party structures (e.g., in Cuba and Angola).

Sovkhoz. In the Russian language, short for "Sovyetzghoye Hozyaystvo." A state-owned, state-operated agricultural farm in the Soviet Union. The sovkhoz differed from the "kolkhoz" in the following respects: all land, buildings, equipment, and whatever was produced belonged to the state while in a kolkhoz—though the land belonged to the state—the buildings, equipment, and whatever was produced belonged to the members of the cooperative; and while in the sovkhoz the worker received wages for his labor, in the kolkhoz all profit was shared among the members of the cooperative according to the individual contribution made in terms of working hours.) In 1991, the independent republics began experimenting with a decentralized, locally planned economy.

Sovnarkhoz. In the Russian language, short for, "Sovyet Narodnogho Hozyaystva," Council of National Economy. One of the economic regions into which the entire Soviet Union was divided for the purpose of greater autonomy and efficiency in production and distribution of goods and services. The

Councils were introduced during the late 1950s under the administration of Nikita S. Khrushchev, but were dissolved in 1991-1992.

Sovnarkom. In the Russian language, short for "Sovyet Narodgnygh Kommisarov," Council of People's Commissars in the Soviet Union: the cabinet ministers in council. Their titles were changed after World War II to "ministers."

Soyuz. See NATIONAL SALVATION COMMITTEE.

Spanish Civil War. See FALANGE, INTERNATIONAL BRIGADE.

Spanish Sahara Polisario Front. See POLISARIO FRONT.

Spartacus Uprising. The revolt that was staged against the oppressive government of Rome by a force of approximately 70,000 slaves led by a slave, Spartacus, in 73-71 BC. The revolt lasted for about a year and ended with the crucifixion of Spartacus and about 6,000 of his followers. This uprising has been a favorite source of inspiration for revolutionaries throughout the centuries. See SPARTAKUS MOVEMENT.

Spartakus Movement. A splinter group in Germany composed of pro-Soviet revolutionary elements of the German Communist party; it advocated the overthrow of the government by revolutionary means. The group (drawing its inspiration from the Spartacus uprising in ancient Rome) staged a revolution in the city of Berlin in 1919 which lasted several days. Its principal aim was to introduce a Soviet-type system of government in Germany. (The principal leaders of the movement were Rosa Luxemburg, a Polish revolutionary, and Karl Liebknecht, a German revolutionary, both of whom were soon killed by the German police.) The concerted effort of the German Communists (who were aided by Communists from Poland and the Soviet Union) was to bring Soviet-style rule to Germany. See SPARTACUS UPRISING.

Speaker. The presiding officer in a legislative body elected, as a rule, by the majority party for the duration of the tenure of the legislature. In the United States House of Representatives, the Speaker is elected at the beginning of a "new" Congress from the majority party (or re-elected as a rule if his party retains majority) for a period of two years. The Speaker exercises numerous functions and has considerable power. As the presiding officer, he may or may not recognize individual legislators during floor debates; at his discretion, he may rule individual legislators out of order (forbid them to speak further); he refers bills to committees for further action; he appoints members of joint (conference) and select committees; signs documents in the name of the House; and his ruling on the floor, particularly on the points of order, are final. In case of the death, disability, or resignation of the President and the Vice President of the United States, the Speaker is to assume the office of the Presidency until the next general election. The Speaker may take part in debates and vote on legislation. (Until the 1911 House Rules, the Speaker was also empowered to appoint the members of permanent or standing committees.) See CONGRESS OF THE UNITED STATES, HOUSE OF COMMONS, UNITED STATES HOUSE OF REPRESENTATIVES, Appendix 12.

Special Air Service Regiment (SAS). See DELTA FORCE.

Special Bill. See BILL.

Special Branch of the Scotland Yard. See SECRET INTELLIGENCE SERVICE. (SIS).

Special Charter. An instrument of incorporation that may be granted to a specific municipality (e.g., town, township, village, or city) thus making it a separate and distinct legal person.

Special Committee. A committee that may be designated by either house of the United States Congress (by their respective presiding officers, and subject to acceptance by the membership) for a single definite purpose, such as to study some particular aspects of a bill or to investigate a certain matter for the purpose of improving legislation. Such committees are also known as select or *ad hoc* committees.

Special Coordinating Committee of the National Security Council. See CENTRAL INTELLIGENCE AGENCY (CIA).

Special District. A limited-purpose governmental unit which exists as a separate corporate entity and which has considerable fiscal and administrative independence from general purpose governments. Virginia, for example, has 58 special Districts (e.g., civil defense, sanitation, water supply and purification, and air pollution). See POLITICAL INCREMENTALISM.

Special Drawing Rights (SDR). The supplementary reserves, often known as the "paper gold," against which a member-state of the International Monetary Fund (IMF) may draw money needed to offset deficits in its international balance of payments. Member-states may draw from the reserves in proportion to their contribution to the International Monetary Fund pool funds. In reality, the state may draw not on the amount of gold in its reserves, but on the basis of its economic strength, its "know-how." A state drawing money under the SDR device is obligated to repay only a part of it to the Fund. (This device is primarily designed to eventually eliminate the gold standard in the future.)

Special Economic Zone. In order to revive its stagnated economy, the leadership of the People's Republic of China allowed some economic activity based on capitalist market economy in special areas known as "Special Economic Zones," where the government maintained control sufficient enough to prevent the people from rebelling against their prevailing socialist economy, which provides little for the expanding population of China. Such zones were allowed during the late 1980s in areas of easy access to international shipping.

Special Grand Jury. See GRAND JURY.

Special Interest-Type Political Party. A political party that is interested mainly in capturing the control of government for the purpose of serving some specific lobby or interest group rather than the electorate at large (e.g., the Prohibition party in the United States, the German Block/Association of the Expelled and Disenfranchised [BG/BHE] in the Federal Republic of Germany, or a score of agrarian or consumer parties in Western Europe. To some extent the communist parties or other parties with narrowly-specified programs may fall into that category).

Special Missions Fleet. A unit of the United States Air Force (the 89th Military Airlift Wing, stationed at Andrews Air Force Base outside Washington, D.C.) consisting of approximately 23 aircraft and helicopters, including the Presidential "Air Force One," and the Vice Presidential "Air Force Two," which transport high government officials (and visiting foreign dignitaries) at government expense. The Pentagon maintains control over the operation.

Special Prosecutor. The office of the Special Prosecutor has been made permanent by the Watergate Reorganization and Reform Act of 1976, which gives the Prosecutor jurisdiction to investigate and to prosecute any possible violations of federal criminal laws by the President, the Vice President, senior government officials, members of Congress, and the judiciary. The law stipulates that the person holding the office must have at least five years of experience in a "high-level position of trust and responsibility," which includes political parties and the personal organizations of candidates for high federal offices (e.g., the President and Vice President). Since the Watergate scandal, the most recent Special Prosecutor was Lawrence Welsh for the Iran-Contra Affair of the 1980s. See SATURDAY NIGHT MASSACRE, WATERGATE.

Special Revenue Sharing. Formula distribution of money from the federal government to state and local governments without matching funds required; expenditures are limited to specified, though broad, purposes. Special revenue sharing programs may consolidate and supersede a series of categorical grants. Planning requirements and other conditions may be attached to special revenue sharing, unlike general revenue sharing. The Community Development Act of 1971 (H. R. 8853, S. 1618), is the Administration's proposal for special revenue sharing for community development. The four programs which would be combined to form a new common fund are urban renewal, model cities, water and sewer grants, and loans for the rehabilitation of existing structures. Eighty percent of this special revenue sharing fund would be assigned for use in Standard Metropolitan Statistical Areas. Funds would be allocated among and within such metropolitan areas according to a formula to be written into the law. Funding would be to general governments, i.e., cities and states rather than semi-autonomous urban renewal agencies. The President's Message on March 5, 1971, stated that cities could use their share of Urban and Community Development block grants for such purposes as acquiring, clearing, and renewing blighted areas, constructing public works; building streets and malls; enforcing housing codes in deteriorating areas; rehabilitating residential properties; funding demolition projects, and helping relocate those displaced from homes or business. Initial criticism centered on the allocation formula and the lack of planning application review or other performance requirements. Under the formula, substantial funds go to cities that were not previously active in HUD programs. "Hold harmless," i.e., insuring that no city get less funds than previously received, may not be sufficient for cities in trouble, especially since inflation and planned expansion in these cities create the need for more funds.

Special Services Staff. See COUNTERINSURGENCY IN AMERICA.

Special Sovereignty. See DEPENDENCY.

Specialized Agencies of the United Nations Organization. See UNITED NATIONS ORGANIZATION.

SPEDE. See SERVICE DE DOCUMENTATION EXTÉRIEURES ET DE CONTRE-ESPIONNAGE, SERVICE FOR FOREIGN INFORMATION AND COUNTERESPIONAGE.

Spirit of Addis Ababa. Applies to the Conference held in Addis Ababa, Ethiopia (May 1963) at which the Organization of African Unity (OAU) was agreed upon.

Spirit of Glassboro. A summit conference that was held between U.S. President Lyndon B. Johnson and Soviet Premier Alexei N. Kosygin on June 23, 1967, on the campus of Glassboro State College in Glassboro, New Jersey. President Johnson was interested, according to official press accounts, in getting Kosygin's support and cooperation in ending the conflict in Vietnam mainly by ending Soviet shipment of war materiel to North Vietnam. (The summit conference—which obviously accomplished little—was the only one held between the two leaders.)

Spirit of Jerusalem. See SADAT-BEGIN SUMMIT.

Spiritual Pollution. A series of measures that were undertaken by the communist regime in the Republic of China (1949-1976), to prevent teaching and literature that praised the so-called "decadent values of the decaying West." The measures included prohibition of the use of nude male and female models. The ban on using such models was lifted in 1984.

Splendid Isolation. British Prime Minister Lord Robert Cecil Salisbury (1895-1902), so characterized British foreign policy, because, while other European powers (e.g., Germany-Austria-Hungary and Italy when confronting France and Russia) had entered into several alliances by 1897, England was free from any entanglements. Being a sea power and "Queen of the Seas," England had no particular need for allies; it controlled vast colonies in Africa, Asia, and America, and was unchallenged. European powers like France, Germany, and Italy, and even Russia, had no powerful navies to challenge England's supremacy. After the "Foshida Incident," the French were restrained by England from future expansion in Egypt and other parts of Africa. Lord Salisbury even pronounced openly in 1867 that "France is, and always will remain, Britain's greatest danger. England was, however, apprehensive about the rapidly growing naval forces of Germany and Russia and decided to commence dialogue with the Japanese for an eventual alliance against Russia. In April 1901, the Japanese ambassador to England, Baron Tadasu Hayashi, and England's Lord Lansdowne held a conference on the issue of Russian expansion in Asia; and on 30 January 1902 signed an agreement on mutual protection of their interests in the Far East. This agreement freed the Japanese to attack and to defeat Russian naval forces in 1904 at Port Arthur. Peace between Japan and Russia was arranged by U.S. President Theodore Roosevelt (see TREATY OF PORTSMOUTH OF 1905). The treaty with Japan was the beginning of the end of the policy of "splendid isolation," as well as the beginning of the decline of the British Empire. England depended on alliances for its very survival during W.W.I, W.W.II, and the "Cold War" period, not only with its principal ally, the United States, but also with the Soviet Union against whom the treaty with Japan had been directed. The Soviet government, particularly Joseph Stalin, could never forget the past policies of the British, and Stalin remained suspicious of England, as well as of the United States and other western democracies, until the time he died, in March 1953. See AMERICAN-RUSSIAN ANTAGONISM.

Splendid Misery. Thomas Jefferson's opinion of the U.S. Presidency.

Splinter Group. A group of persons within an organization (e.g., within one political party) that breaks away, forms its own organization, and pursues its own objectives. See POLITICAL PARTY.

Splinter Party. See SPLINTER GROUP.

Split Ticket. The practice of marking ballots during elections for candidates of different political parties rather than of one party only. See VOTING.

Spoil System. See PENDLETON ACT OF 1883.

Spoiler. An unknown or unpopular politician who runs for a public office for one or a combination of the following reasons: (1) to split (spoil) the vote for another candidate and thus cause her or him to be defeated in an election (e.g., as a form of protest vote or simply political revenge); (2) to split the vote of the popular and favorite candidate so that a weaker and a less-known candidate running for the same office may become elected (e.g., as a form of political favor); and (3) to eventually become elected as a result of the split vote if the particular electoral system allows election by a plurality vote. As a matter of history, spoilers ordinarily represent third or fourth parties, or run as independents. See VOTING.

Spoils System. See MERIT SYSTEM.

Spreadsheet. An accounting document organized into a grid of horizontal rows and vertical columns, used organize or to manipulate data, usually of a financial nature, in order to present the status of a business operation; an accounting document showing the viability, or lack of it, of the financial aspects of an organization. Also a computer program used for that purpose.

Spring of Nations. Term referring to the major political and social upheavals against traditional monarchies in Europe, commencing particularly with the publication of the *Communist Manifesto* in 1848 ("The Year of Revolutions"), and serious weakening of the traditional monarchies, as well as the advancement of socialist and communist ideology versus capitalism and the traditional laissez faire economies. See COMMUNIST MANIFESTO, MARXISM.

Sputnik. In the Russian language, "fellow-traveler." Also, one of two first orbital satellites launched by the Soviet Union on October 4, 1957 ("Sputnik I"), and November 3, 1957 ("Sputnik II"), which created panic among many military planners in the West. (The United States, among other western powers, precipitated by the Sputnik panic, rapidly shifted to space and science technology, often to the detriment of other sciences.)

Sputnik Panic. See SPUTNIK.

Square Deal. A policy statement issued by U.S. President Theodore Roosevelt (1901-1909) promising to give each man an equal chance in getting benefits which his administration was to provide, mainly by trust-busting and stricter control of big business in general.

SR. Social Revolutionary, a political group in Tsarist, pre-Bolshevik Russia.

SRC. See SOUTHERN REGIONAL COUNCIL.

Sri Lanka Insurrections. See TAMIL SEPARATISM IN SRI LANKA.

SS-9. See MULTIPLE INDEPENDENTLY TARGETED RE-ENTRY VEHICLE (MIRV).

Staat. In the German language, "state."

Staff. See LINE MANAGEMENT.

Stages of Development of Society. See MARXISM.

Stagflation. An economic term for the combination of slow growth and rising prices that emphasizes the burden to consumers who have to pay more for goods and services but are not making more money to offset prices.

Staggered Term. A system of electing public officials for uneven tenures, or electing members to a legislative body in such a manner that their tenures do not end at the same time, thus providing for overlap and continuity (e.g., one-third of the United States senators are elected every two years for a tenure of six years; in the United States House of Representatives all members are elected every two years for a term of two years.) See U.S. SENATE, Appendix 11.

Stakhanovyetz. One who was achieving spectacular results in production in the former Soviet Union. The term was given for Alexei Stakhanov, a miner who, upon inspiration by a Communist party call for better productivity, mined single-handedly, on August 31, 1935, 102 tons of coal during one eight-hour shift, thus exceeding the quota expected of him by 1,300 percent. The Stakhanov movement was widely popularized thereafter by the Soviet leadership. Those who distinguished themselves were granted, in addition to monetary rewards, the title of either the *Hero of Socialist Labor* or the *Order of Lenin,* the highest order of the land.

Stalemate. A deadlock or lack of progress (e.g., in diplomatic negotiations) due to failure of the parties involved to compromise. See SUMMIT DIPLOMACY.

Stalwarts. See PLUMED KNIGHT.

Stamp Act. A Legislation passed by the British Parliament on March 22, 1765, aiming to acquire about 60,000 pounds per year in additional revenue. The act required payment for revenue stamps on items purchased by individuals such as playing cards, dice, newspapers, pamphlets, almanacs, and all legal documents. The opposition in the North American colonies was great, mainly in the New England area where opponents to the act formed "Sons of Liberty" clubs. From October 7-25, 1765, delegates from nine colonies met in New York City as the Stamp Act Congress, which launched the protest against taxation without representation and the agreement not to import to the colonies any articles which required the payment of such duties. The Stamp Act was repealed on March 18, 1766.

Stamp Act Congress. See STAMP ACT.

Stamp Tax. See STAMP ACT.

Stampede. A term used in practical politics to describe the practice of shifting support and loyalty from one who seems to be losing to one who seems to be winning. See VOTING.

Stand-by-President. See PRESIDENT-IN-WAITING.

Standard Bearer. See MISTER REPUBLICAN.

Standard Federal Regions and Federal Executive Boards. See Appendix 43.

Standard Metropolitan Statistical Area (SMSA). An SMSA is designated by the U.S. Office of Management and Budget as an area with a dominant central city having a combined population of at least 50,000 with a surrounding urbanized community that is economically and socially integrated with the central city. In all areas of the country except New England, SMSA's must be composed of at least a single county. In New England, SMSA's are composed of a series of urbanized and interconnected municipalities and townships.

Standing. A traditional doctrine, subscribed to by the United States Federal Courts, to the effect that courts refrain from adjudicating in general suits brought against the government or any of its agencies, unless there is sufficient evidence that some substantive right was violated. This doctrine stems from the general provision in the U.S. Constitution (Art. I, Sec. 2) that the federal judicial power is limited to *cases and controversies.*

Standing Congressional Committee. See CONGRESSIONAL COMMITTEES.

Standing to Sue. See STANDING.

Star Wars. See WINDOW OF VULNERABILITY.

Stare Decisis. In the Latin language, "to adhere to cases decided." Also, a principle in law that legal precedent is not necessarily binding. This doctrine does not apply to international law.

START. See STRATEGIC ARMS REDUCTION TALKS.

State. A concept, derived from either the German *Staat* or the French *état*, meaning a legal entity, a legal person or an organization of the highest order (e.g., as a corporation with the capacity to sue and to be sued) designed by man for the purpose of expediting his survival on earth through a set of prearranged institutions and processes. The necessary elements comprising a state in the classical sense are: (1) territory, regardless of size, but one that is not claimed by another legal entity (a state) and over which the state exercises absolute control (jurisdiction); (2) population, regardless of size or ethnicity (modern states are no longer ethnically and racially homogeneous) which consents to support the state (legitimacy) by paying taxes, obeying its laws, and, if need arises, fighting and dying for it or in its name (allegiance and loyalty). In return, the state protects its supporters and grants (or withholds) certain rewards or inflicts punishment for non-obedience and non-support, and usually reserves the right to take an individual's life under the doctrine of inherent right of the state for acts or activities harmful to the state (e.g., treason); (3) sovereignty, or the capability to make independent decisions binding the state and its people internally as well as externally (e.g., in diplomatic relations and treaty obligations). States lacking that attribute, sovereignty, are known as "satellite" states because their decisions are either influenced or dictated by another state (or states). In reality, no single modern state is entirely independent in its sovereign capacity due to interdependence—see INTERDEPENDENCE—with the probable exception of the former Soviet Union and the United States—see BIPOLARITY; (4) political institutions, or the government and the administrative apparatus which comprises the political system and sees to it that the state is sustained, preserved and perpetuated as a legal (or sovereign), political, and a national unit within the community of nations; (5) effective control, or a real and demonstrable capacity and capability to maintain control over the claimed population and territory through persuasion, motivation, or even the use of force if necessary (e.g., by the suppression of internal rebellions or revolutions which may undermine its internal structure and cause its dissolution); and (6) continuity, or continuous existence on a day-to-day basis, because an interruption of such existence is generally construed as dissolution or dismemberment of the legal entity, whether it be voluntary (e.g., as in the case of the Austro-Hungarian Empire which dissolved itself after World War I into Austria and Hungary) or as a result of absorption by another state or dismemberment (e.g., a partition) by two or more states (e.g., the partition of Poland by Austria, Prussia, and Russia during the nineteenth century). Internal changes within the state such as changes of government or a political system (e.g., the change from a monarchy to a republic in the Soviet Union in 1917), including political philosophy, do not necessarily cause the state to die. See DEMOCRACY, ORIGIN OF STATE THEORIES, POLITICS, UTOPIA.

State and Local Government Reorganization. A movement throughout the United States, intensified mainly during the 1970s aiming at state and local government reorganization with a view of the uniformity and simplification of systems and procedures. In the state of Virginia, for example, House Document No. 10 (formerly House Document No. 17), and additional recommendations from the Virginia Advisory Legislative Council and the Virginia Municipal League, call for the following uniform and/or money-saving measures: uniform budgetary procedures and reporting; government reorganization; the same powers for counties as for cities; and revised hiring practices, among others.

State Capitalism. See DEMOCRATIC CAPITALISM.

State Channeling. The process by which Federal funds for use by local or substate agencies are given first to the States and then reallocated by the States to the subunits, usually with some degree of control over the funds exercised by the States.

State Committee on the State of Emergency. On 19 August 1991, Soviet Radio broadcast a bulletin announcing that such a committee was established due to the "illness" of the President of the Soviet Union, Mikhail S. Gorbachev, then "vacationing" in the Crimea. Functions of the President were to be carried out by the Vice President, Gennady I. Yanayev, a man Gorbachev personally selected for that post. The emergency was to last six months and all powers were to be exercised by the Committee. Boris Yeltsin, President of the Russian Republic, appeared in public, despite the danger to his person, and climbed on an army tank to declare the coup illegal and invalid. The seven other co-conspirators involved in this coup were: Oleg D. Baklanov, first deputy chairman of the USSR Defense Council: Arrested after parliamentary immunity was lifted. Vladimir A. Kryuchkov, chairman of the KGB: Reported arrested, then fired from his job, and replaced temporarily by Leonid V. Shebarshin. Also fired was Lt. Gen. Yuri S. Plekhanov, head of the KGB guard service. Valentin S. Pavlov, prime minister of the USSR: Hospitalized with hypertension, under police guard, then dismissed, with no replacement named. Also dismissed was Gorbachev's chief of staff, Valery Boldin, who was replaced by Grigory Revenko. Boris K. Pugo, interior minister of the USSR: Committed suicide. Replaced by Lt. Gen. Vasily P. Trushin. Vasily A. Starodubtsev, chairman of the Farmers' Union of the USSR: Sought for arrest after parliamentary immunity lifted; Alexander I. Tizyakov, president of the Association of State Enterprises and Industrial, Construction, Transport and Communications Facilities of the USSR. Dmitri T. Yazov, defense minister of the USSR: Arrested and replaced by Gen. Mikhail Moiseyev, chief of the military's general staff. A deputy defense minister, and civil service head Gen. Vladimir L. Govorov, committed suicide. All the conspirators were subsequently detained when the coup failed on 21 August 1991 and Gorbachev returned to Moscow. He resigned as leader of the party on 24 August 1991 and the parliament suspended the party itself on 25 December 1991. Since this was not the only coup attempt, although others never materialized. When President Gorbachev was detained in house arrest by the coup conspirators, they claimed that he had the flu. Subsequently, when the coup failed, the conspirators themselves went into hiding under the pretex of having the flu, but subsequently were rounded up and arrested with the exception of those who committed suicide. This "flu plague" was termed "coup flu."

State, Development Theories of. See THEORIES OF THE DEVELOPMENT OF STATE.

State, Elements of. See STATE.

State Evidence. Factual evidence made in writing under oath, or orally in an open court of law, before a grand jury, or a prosecuting (state) attorney given by one who voluntarily submits it as amicus curia (for the benefit of the state and the society), or as a result of plea bargaining. Person making such material evidence available becomes known as a "state witness."

State Grand Jury. See GRAND JURY.

State Militia. The original name for what is known in the U.S. as the National Guard. A state militia remains under the jurisdiction and control of a particular state (the governor being its commander-in-chief) until it becomes incorporated into regular federal military forces. According to the U.S. Constitution (Art I, Sec. 8), a state militia may be nationalized by Congress (in reality by the U.S. President) for three distinct purposes: (1) *to execute the Laws of the Union,* (2) *to suppress insurrections,* and (3) *to repel invasions.*

State of the State Message. At the beginning of each year, the governors of the states in the American federation, deliver to joint sessions of the legislatures of their states and to the people at large, a "Message on the State of the State," similar to the "State of the Union Message" of the President of the United States.

State of the Union Message. The U.S. Constitution (Art. II, Sec. 3) requires that the U.S. President ". . . shall from time to time give to the Congress information on the state of the Union," which in practice is done once each year when the President meets both houses of Congress assembled (the House of Representatives and the Senate) and informs them about past problems and solutions as well as future legislation that may be required to implement certain desired policies and programs. During his 1977 State of the Union Message to Congress, U.S. President Jimmy Carter tagged his administration as "the New Spirit" and pleaded with Congress to approve his energy proposals. In his January 1992 message, President George Bush outlined many plans for economic reform, creation of jobs for the unemployed, and medical insurance for the needy. As usual, the Democratic Party responded to that message with its own plans, or at least some criticism of the President's plans, as a usual, traditional gesture. Democratic Senator from Iowa, Tom Harkin, responded while campaigning at the New Hampshire presidential primary in his own humorous way, calling President Bush's plan to stimulate the American economy, "As effective as giving more oats to a horse to feed the birds." See STATE OF THE STATE MESSAGE.

State of the World Report. A brief review of the political situation of the globe, and the role of the United States in world affairs that is given annually by the President of the United States. President Richard M. Nixon was the first to initiate this practice by delivering such a report (through all radio and television stations and overseas via communication satellites) for the first time on February 25, 1971. The principal objective of this report is to inform the general public, at home and abroad, and the leaders of nation-states, of the official policies of the administration-of-the-day.

State Planning. Zoning and land use control are inherent state powers which traditionally have been completely delegated in the name of home rule. In 1969, Oregon and Maine joined Hawaii in establishing state zoning controls. In 1970, Maine extended its statewide zoning power by giving the Environmental Improvement Commission veto power over commercial and industrial development anywhere in the State. Colorado created a State Land Use Commission to recommend a statewide land use map and classification system, and the Virginia General Assembly called for a study to lay the foundation for a state growth and development policy. Alabama, Georgia, North Carolina, and Ohio, among others, strengthened their state planning capabilities. Kentucky adopted legislation authorizing the State Program Development Office to designate sub-state regions and coordinate regional comprehensive development plans. Similar action has been taken by approximately forty states through executive order or legislation.

State Planning Committee. In the Russian language, "Gosudarstvyennaya Plannost" or, in short, Gosplan. An agency of the National Government of the former Soviet Union charged with the setting up of production plans and quotas for industry, manufacturing, farming, commerce and trade, for each five-year period. See FIVE-YEAR PLAN.

State Revenue Reform. While revenue sharing moved to the center stage for national political debate, a number of state revenue measures of special interest to urban residents were actually enacted in 1970. Ohio provided for the Civil Service Commission to make grants to state and local governments for planning and improving their systems of personnel administration; for developing and carrying out training plans; and for government service fellowships for employees selected for special graduate-level university training. Federal constraints are removed on the temporary exchanging of personnel between the Federal government and states and local governments. Thus, specific national recognition has finally been given to the need to strengthen core management at the state and local levels by upgrading personnel and personnel administration. At the end of 1971 there were essentially five major entrants in the legislative field aimed at the objectives of strengthening management capacity for planning and administration at the state and local level. These are Title II of the Administration's Urban Community Development Act of 1971 (S. 1618); the Administration's National Land Use Policy Act (S. 992); the National Land and Water Resource Planning Act of 1971 (S. 632); the Public Land Policy Act of 1971 (H.R. 7211); and the National Coastal Estuarine Zone Management Act of 1971 (S. 582, H.R. 2493).

State, Role of. See ROLE OF STATE.

State Unto Oneself. Throughout the political history of societies, numerous ideological trends have emerged such as that of the anarchists and the utopian socialists, advocating that a human being should not be restrained and subjected to any authority of a state and its government, but should remain an authority unto oneself, not subject to any rule of law; the notion that each individual should be considered as a sovereign entity. There are people who have renounced citizenship in their country of birth and have pronounced themselves to be citizens of the world instead. Under contemporary international law, such stateless persons remain under the protection of the United Nations, but the International Court of Justice refused in 1985, to grant the right to an individual to sue a sovereign state, because that Court has jurisdiction only over cases involving politically recognized states, and not individuals. One Gary Davis, an American bomber pilot during W.W.II, renounced his U.S. citizenship and declared himself a citizen of the world in 1985. Subsequently he petitioned the International Court of Justice that U.S. President Ronald Reagan and Soviet President Konstantin Chernenko be declared "war criminals," because, according to the Charter of the United Nations, preparation for war, which the two leaders were actively engaged in, was a criminal act under the Nuremberg Decisions. The Court rejected the petition on the grounds that it lacks jurisdiction in such matters. The European Court on Human Rights, however, allows such practices if, by a separate convention, states accept the jurisdiction of the Court in such matters; and many European citizens have brought their own governments before the Court and received satisfaction. See CITIZENSHIP.

State Visit. An official visit by a head of state and/or head of government upon the invitation of another. Official state visits are, as a rule, open rather than secret, and are rather ceremonial in substance and form. See SUMMIT DIPLOMACY.

State Witness. See STATE EVIDENCE.

Statecraft. The art of ruling or governing; or the art and the science that pertains to government or governing.

Statehood. According to the U.S. Constitution (Article I), admission of new states is reserved to the U.S. Congress upon application from the people of an area. U.S. President Gerald R. Ford recommended in November 1976 that the Commonwealth of Puerto Rico be granted statehood within the American Union. See Appendix 8.

Stateless Person. See CITIZENSHIP, STATE UNTO ONESELF.

Stateless Society. Traditionally, a society without the notion of and need for a structured political organization (government) or statehood (e.g., the Nambikuara Indians in the State of Mato Grosso in Brazil), or sanction. According to Karl Marx, a stateless society will be achieved at the highest stage of societal development, namely under communism, when the state, such as we know it today, will wither away. See CLASS CONSCIOUSNESS, CLASS STRUGGLE, MARXISM.

Staten Generaal. The bicameral legislative body, the States General, of the Netherlands. See EERSTE KAMER, TWEEDE KAMER.

State's Attorney. See PROSECUTING ATTORNEY.

States, Types of. See TYPES OF STATES.

States' Rights Doctrine. A notion that was held by the Anti-federalists who opposed strong central federal government in the United States as proposed under the new federal constitution, and demanded that the states remain as sovereign entities within the federal union. That notion was expressed in the Virginia Resolution of 1789 which, in the words of James Madison, emphasized that each state has a duty "to interpose its authority" in order to protect the liberty of the people as well as the sovereignty of the states. Furthermore, the doctrine was implemented in Amendment X to the U.S. Constitution as a part of the Bill of Rights, and it remains one of the principal points of discontent between the federal authority and the state authorities. See DIXIECRATS, KENTUCKY AND VIRGINIA RESOLUTION.

Statesman. One knowledgeable and experienced in government and politics; in diplomacy and policy making; in statecraft.

Static Region. See NATURAL REGION.

Statistically Uniform Region. See NATURAL REGION.

Statue of Liberty. A 305-foot high copper sculpture designed by Frederic Auguste Bartholdi which was donated by the French people to the American people in 1886, and accepted for the American people by President Grover Cleveland as symbol of French alliance with the colonies during their struggle for independence from England in 1776. The pedestal was financed by $300,000 donated in the U.S. The actual name of the statue is "Liberty Enlightening the World." The statue stands in New York harbor visible on approach from every direction. The words of Emma Lazarus inscribed on the base of the statue read: ". . . Give me your tired, your poor, your huddled masses yearning to breathe free, the wretched refuse of your teeming shore." As a symbol of freedom, it serves as an inspiration to Americans as well as people all over the world.

Status Offender. See JUVENILE DELINQUENCY.

Status Quo Ante Bellum. In the Latin language, "the situation prior to war." Also, a principle in international law whereby the prerequisite for any peace settlement between two or more belligerents is the return of any territory taken from one state by another as a result of war. The application of this is contingent upon cessation of all hostile military activity. Israel, for example, refuses to return Arab lands conquered during the 1967 war as a condition for peace settlement because acts of aggression against Israel have not been terminated. See ISRAELI SETTLEMENTS, SADAT-BEGIN SUMMIT.

Statute. A formal law or an order issued by proper authority (e.g., U.S. Congress, state legislature, or an organization). See LAW, STATUTE OF LIMITATION.

Statute of Limitation. A time limitation that may be fixed by law beyond which one guilty of a crime may no longer be convicted. In the United States both national and state laws stipulate such time limitations for certain categories of crimes. The statute of limitation does not apply, as a rule, to major felonious crimes such as murder, treason, or kidnapping.

Stay of Execution. An order that may be issued by an appropriate authority prohibiting the performance of a certain act or function (e.g., the governor of a state or a higher court in the United States may prevent the execution of a person convicted of a crime).

Steam Rolling. A term often used in practical politics to depict the practice of ruthlessly crushing opposition or disregarding customary rules of procedure (e.g., during a party convention, nominating a person for election to a public office with a total disregard of the rules of the convention). See POLITICAL MACHINE, PRESIDENTIAL ELECTOR.

Steel Belt. See SECTIONALISM.

Steel Caucus. See CONGRESSIONAL CAUCUS.

Steering Committee. See COMMITTEE ON COMMITTEES.

Stein Revolution. See REVOLUTION FROM ABOVE.

Step-by-Step Diplomacy. See ZIGS AND ZAGS DIPLOMACY.

Step-by-Step Mixing Plan. The U.S. Supreme Court ruled on 31 March 1992 that racial integration in public schools in America may be achieved in a more practical and an easier manner by step-by-step integration and that U.S. federal judges may cease to supervise intensive desegregation efforts as commanded by present statutes. See EDUCRATS.

Stern Gang. A guerrilla-terrorist organization in Israel, known also as the "Irgun Tzevai Leumi," which, under the leadership of Menachem Begin, conducted ruthless anti-British operations during the period of 1943-1947, and often joined forces with the Haganah (Defense) commandos under the leadership of David Ben-Gurion. The Irgun was reorganized into the Herut Party under Menachem Begin in the new Israeli Parliament in 1948.

Steward of the People. A concept of presidential leadership developed by U.S. President Theodore Roosevelt according to which the President, who holds the trust of all the people, not just those with vested interests, should feel free to take any action that is in the general interest of the people and which is not specifically forbidden by the laws or the Constitution.

Stewardship Theory of Leadership. See STEWARD OF THE PEOPLE.

Stimson Doctrine. After the invasion of Manchuria by Japan in 1931, United States President Herbert Hoover issued a policy statement to the effect that the United States would not recognize any territorial changes anywhere which were brought about by military means. The statement was prepared by Hoover's Secretary of State, Henry L. Stimson. (Secretary Stimson was the only high-level government official who openly opposed the use of the atomic bomb against Japan during World War II.)

Stock Exchange. A facility where persons registered by the government known as brokers, buy and sell securities for profit. The major exchanges in the United States are the American Stock Exchange and the New York Stock Exchange; in Europe known as Bourse or Börse, the major exchanges are those of London, Frankfurt, Rome, and more recently Warsaw, Prague, Budapest and Moscow; in Latin America the major exchanges are those of Mexico, Brazil, and Argentina; and in Asia the Tokyo, Hong Kong, and Singapore exchanges are most important.

Stockholm Appeal. The Soviet Union, in 1950, fearing America's nuclear might, inspired an appeal to all nations by fellow travelers and front organizations to oppose nuclear weapons, calling the United States a "war instigator" or "war monger," a favorite phrase repeated throughout the Cold War era. The Soviet propagandists disseminated information (and disinformation) about alleged preparations by the United States and "its Western puppet governments" for an attack on the Soviet Union and its satellite states. The Chinese communist propagandists called the United States and its allies "the running dogs of capitalism."

Stockholm Peace Appeal of 1950. See FRONT ORGANIZATION, WORLD PEACE MOVEMENT.

Stoicism. A political philosophy (introduced in ancient Greece by Zeno of Citium, [336-264 BC]) which holds that man and his environment are both rational and designed to sustain each other; that man's happiness arises from obeying the laws of man and those of the environment (the universe) no matter how harsh they may be at times. The name "stoic" is derived from the Greek word of *stoa*, meaning "porch" of a house from which Zeno delivered his lectures to informally gathered students. Stoicism became a dominant political philosophy in ancient Rome (e.g., of Marcus Aurelius, Cicero, and Seneca), and it has many followers among contemporary scholars.

Stolypin Reforms. A series of reforms, mostly related to agriculture, as proposed by the Premier of the Tsarist government between 1906-1911, Peter A. Stolypin. The purpose of the proposed reforms was twofold: (1) to eliminate the outdated commune system of land cultivation (by granting titles to land to individual peasants) as a hindrance to progress in agriculture, and (2) create a class of independent farmers who would have incentives and thus be willing to perpetuate the *status quo* of the Tsarist regime in Russia.

Stonewalling. The practice of preventing certain acts or activities which one considers harmful, or the practice among politicians and/or government officials of covert acts or activities aiming at preventing some undesirable act or action (e.g., U.S. President Gerald R. Ford [1974-1977], managed to stop a U.S. House of Representatives investigation into wiretapping by federal investigative agencies for national security reasons.) See PRESIDENTIAL ELECTOR.

Stopgap Law. A legislative act or an executive decision (a decree or an order) aiming to resolve or prevent a serious crisis situation (e.g., lowering taxes in a period of recession as a measure against tax revolt by the voters). See LAW, STATUTE.

Storting. Parliament of Norway. See LAGTING, ODELSTING.

Straight Ticket Vote. See PARTY COLUMN BALLOT.

Strange Alliance. A term used to describe the determination of England and the United States to aid the Soviet Union during World War II in repressing the Nazi invasion by extending material support under the Lend-Lease Program. The "strangeness" of the alliance resulted from the ideological differences between the Western nations and the Soviet Union as well as the fact that the Soviet Union became a partner to a pact with the Nazis (the Molotov-Ribbentrop Pact of 1939 dividing Poland between the two powers). See LEND-LEASE PROGRAM, HITLER-STALIN PACT.

Strategic Arms Limitation Talks (SALT). A series of bilateral conferences held between the representatives of the Soviet Union and the United States (in Helsinki, Finland; Vienna, Austria; Moscow, and Vladivostok, USSR; and Washington, D.C., USA), that were triggered by détente for the purpose of working out ways and means to effect an arms limitation and a parity of weapons systems between these two states. Two agreements on a parity of weapons systems were signed in Moscow during President Nixon's official state visit there in 1972. The second phase of the agreement, SALT II, was agreed upon as a test in 1979, but the Senate failed to ratify it. The Vladivostok gathering produced an Accord stating that the United States and the Soviet Union were to treat their nationals in accordance with international standards. Subsequently at the Belgrade Conference on Human Rights in 1978, the Soviets failed to accept the international standards as agreed in Vladivostok.

Strategic Arms Reduction Talks (START). A series of conferences held between Soviet and American disarmament officials for the purpose of mutual reduction of nuclear weapons in order to maintain the lesser evil, the "balance of terror." The superpowers possessed enough nuclear weapons to exterminate themselves and the entire world population several times over, a capability called Mutually Assured Destruction (MAD). Most of the discussions were conducted in 1983 and subsequent years. President Ronald Reagan insisted, however, that START talks would be held after the Soviets agreed to resolve the issue of nuclear forces in Europe, particularly as it pertained to the SS-20 Soviet rockets. The SALT II was sent by President Jimmy Carter to the Senate for ratification in 1979, but was not ratified. President Ronald Reagan opposed the SALT II agreement because it gave the Soviets an advantage in nuclear weapons, in the President's opinion. On his recommendation the Strategic Arms Reduction Talks (START) began in Geneva Switzerland in 1982, but there were no definite outcomes.

Strategic Defense Initiative (SDI). See WINDOW OF VULNERABILITY.

Strategic Planning. See PLANNING.

Strategic Raw Materials. See CRITICAL RAW MATERIALS.

Strategic Trust Territory. See TRUST TERRITORY.

Straw Vote. An unofficial, non-binding, pre-election vote that may be taken among a sample group of qualified voters for the purpose of forecasting the possible outcome of general elections. Also, used for commercial sampling of opinion. The survey is based on random sampling. See PRIMARY ELECTION.

Street Corner Conservative. A term often used in the language of politics to describe one who labels himself a conservative without really understanding the meaning of conservatism; a shallow-minded, nonintellectual. Also, a title of a book by William F. Gavin published in 1975.

Street-Level Populism. A term coined by the black political philosopher, Matthew Holden, denoting the unorganized, uninformed but overpoliticized masses whose political demands are rarely met by the government because of a lack of efficient organization or institutionalized action.

Strong Mayor Government. A type of local government in which the mayor is the real chief executive whose decisions may not be easily overridden by the council.

Structural Impediments Initiative (SII). A series of dialogues about mutual trade between Japan and the United States initiated in 1989, with emphasis on allowing more American-made products to enter Japan. As a result of such talks, the Japanese Government budgeted $1.6 billion for public work projects for the fiscal year 1992 (which ends in march 1993). During the January 1992 Summit Conference in Japan, U.S. President George Bush negotiated further reduction of Japanese trade barriers in order to reduce America's trade deficit with Japan. Japan's trade surplus in 1991 was about $104 billion and it is expected to jump to about $110 billion in 1992. Japan's trade surplus with the United States is expected to come to about $45 billion in 1992. For Japan to remove trade barriers, the so-called "structural impediments," would be like asking a goat to abandon his desire for fresh cabbage leaves. These impediments are deeply entrenched in Japan's industrial policy. See AMERICA BASHING, GUIDED FREE ENTERPRISE, JAPAN BASHING, KOKUTAI.

Structure. An institution or a pattern of activity which is an integral part of a political system, and which functions as one of its interacting variables. See POLITICAL SYSTEM, Appendices 1, 3.

Structuring the Vote. A concept coined by Leon D. Epstein (in his book *Political Parties in Western Democracies*), which he defines as "the imposition of an order or pattern enabling voters to choose candidates according to their labels" (whether or not the labels appear on the ballot). A vote by politicized voters; politicized methods used to influence voting behavior (the unknown and undetermined reasons for the voter to cast a ballot for or against an individual or an issue during an election) or the manipulation of voting behavior toward certain desired ends. See VOTING.

Struggle of Democratic Filipino Party. See PEOPLE POWER.

Students. See IRANIAN STUDENTS.

Student Nonviolent Coordinating Committee (SNCC). A biracial organization composed mainly of college and university students which emerged out of the sit-ins organized chiefly in the southern states of the United States during the late 1950s. Among the aims of the SNCC are: total racial integration, quality education, more student voice in policy-making and management of institutions of higher learning, and a government more responsive to the needs of the people.

Students for Democratic Society (SDS). An organization of students, founded in 1962 in the state of Michigan, advocating the total destruction of the American system of government and economy. The most militant faction of the SDS, the so-called "Weathermen," also advocated an immediate revolution in the United States as the only means of bringing about radical change in American society. The SDS had organized a series of violent demonstrations and riots during the 1960s and early 1970s (including the disruption of the Democratic National Convention in Chicago in 1968, when Hubert H. Humphrey was nominated for President). Its founder and leader, Mark Rudd, turned himself in to the FBI on September 14, 1977 (he had been in hiding since 1964); was tried on January 18, 1978; placed on two years' probation and fined $2,000, on only a single charge: "aggravated battery arising from demonstration" in Chicago, Illinois, in 1969. See NEW LEFT, WEATHER UNDERGROUND.

Students of the Leader. See THE GANG OF FOUR.

Sub Colore Juris. In the Latin language, "under the color of the law" or "according to the law." See SUB PRAETEXTO JURIS, SUB ROSA.

Sub Judice. In the Latin language, "an undecided case before a court of law."

Sub Praetexto Juris. In the Latin language, "under the rose," "in secrecy," or "under the pretext of the law." (In ancient times the rose symbolized silence or secrecy, hence the principle of not revealing the contents of any debate or decisions made in executive session to anyone.) See SUB ROSA.

Sub Rosa. In the Latin language, "under the rosebush." With the emergence of caucus politics in ancient times, executive sessions were often held outdoors (e.g., under the rosebush in a garden, and the rose was the symbol of virtue as well as the emblem of silence) in order to avoid interception. See SUB PRAETEXTO JURIS.

Subjects Mixtes. In the Latin language, "person with two citizenships" or "one with dual citizenship." See CITIZENSHIP.

Subjects of International Law. See INTERNATIONAL LEGAL PERSON.

Subornation of Perjury. The act of procurement of another person to make a false oath. Under most systems of jurisprudence it constitutes a felony. See PERJURY.

Subpoena. An order that may be issued by a proper authority (e.g., a court of law or a congressional committee in the United States) requiring an individual to appear in person and to give testimony (usually under oath or affirmation). Non-compliance with such an order usually carries some penalty (e.g., confinement or a fine) for contempt of either court or Congress, as the case may be. See LAW, STATUTE, WRITS.

Substandard Housing. A term used to describe a structure intended for human habitation which lacks certain delineated features, thus making it unsafe or unfit for living. Such structures may be a single family residence or a multi-family structure. Deficiencies are usually of a physical nature—structurally unsound; lack of indoor plumbing; lack of appropriate heating system; lack of or unsafe electrical system and other unacceptable conditions as specified in the building codes of the local government.

Substantive Question. See UNITED NATIONS ORGANIZATION: SECURITY COUNCIL.

Substate District. A geographic area into which a state may be subdivided for such purposes as facilitating state administration and achieving areawide program planning and policy development. Such districts are usually multi-county, or a combination of counties, cities, towns, and townships.

Substate Planning. See PLANNING, SUBSTATE DISTRICT.

Subsystem. See POLITICAL SYSTEM.

Suburban Caucus. See CONGRESSIONAL CAUCUS.

Suburban State. See URBAN STATE.

Suburbia. See BEDROOM COMMUNITY.

Subversion. The act of undermining the stability of a political system or any of its components (e.g., overthrow of the government by force). See MCCARTHYISM, RED MENACE, SUBVERSIVE ACTIVITIES CONTROL BOARD.

Subversive Activities Control Board. An agency of the federal government of the United States created in 1950 under the authority of the *Subversive Activities Control Act,* as amended by the *Communist Control Act of 1954*—for the purpose of conducting hearings and investigations to determine, upon petition by the Attorney General of the United States, whether an organization and its members are communist-oriented, a communist action group, a communist front organization, or actively advocate the forceful overthrow of the present political, social, and economic system in the United States. If an organization and its members are found by the Board to be falling into any of the categories, then the organization and its members are required to register with the Board. The Board is composed of five members appointed by the U.S. President and confirmed by the U.S. Senate for a tenure of five years. The decisions of the Board may be appealed to the U.S. Court of Appeals for the District of Columbia, or to the U.S. Supreme Court. Since there were no cases brought before the Board, the U.S. Senate voted in June 1972 to cut off its funds. See COMMUNIST CONTROL ACT OF 1954, LOYALTY LAWS, MCCARTHYISM, RED MENACE, SUBVERSION, SUBVERSIVE ORGANIZATIONS.

Subversive Organizations in the United States. See Appendix 24.

Suez Canal. The British withdrew from the Suez Canal Zone under the Anglo-Egyptian agreement of October 1954. In 1956, England and France (frustrated with the loss of its prestige after the defeat of its forces in Dien Bien Phu, Vietnam, which brought about the end of the French Empire), and Israel, interested in keeping the Egyptians out of Sinai, staged a war against Egypt. The U.S. opposed it as much as other nations did, and the failure of the French-British-Israel effort prompted Meggeridge to comment on the embarrassment of the Macmillan government in England: "There's nothing on earth less edifying or more ludicrous than the spectacle of the ruling class on the run."

Suez Crisis. The crisis that developed in the Middle East among the states of Israel, France, and England in 1956 following the nationalization of the Suez waterway by Egyptian President Gamal Abdel Nasser and the subsequent military invasion of the United Arab Republic by the forces of Israel, France, and England. The Canal remains under Egyptian control. It was temporarily closed to shipping during the so-called "Six Days War" in 1967. See Appendix 93.

Suffrage. The right to vote or be voted upon; the right to elect or be elected. See VOTING.

Summary Judgment. A pre-verdict judgment that may be rendered by a court of law in response to a motion by the plaintiff or the defendant who may claim that any one issue in the case or the entire substance of the case under dispute does not warrant the submission of the case to a jury. A device commonly used to dispose of cases with speed and avoid lengthy delays in rendering judgments. See JURY.

Summary Suspension Act. See LOYALTY LAW.

Summer Patriot. A term coined by Thomas Paine (1737-1809), American patriot, revolutionary, and author of *Common Sense* (the battle-cry of the American Revolutionary War in 1776), describing one who was willing to fight for America's independence during the warm summer days, but was less enthusiastic to fight during cold winter days. Also, one who professes to be a patriot when it is convenient, not necessarily out of conviction.

Summit Conference. A conference that may be held by two or more heads of state and/or heads of government; a conference held between persons with the highest authority (e.g., presidents or prime ministers of different states, or top executives of different organizations). Often known as "personal diplomacy." See DIPLOMACY, SHUTTLE DIPLOMACY.

Summit Diplomacy. See SUMMIT CONFERENCE.

Summit of Communist Parties. On June 29, 1976, communist parties of the world, led by the Communist Party of the Soviet Union (CPSU), with the Chinese, Albanian, and North Korean communist parties absent, met in East Berlin (German Democratic Republic). During the summit, the General Secretary of the CPSU attempted to bring unity among the western and the eastern parties, but instead a great disunity emerged. Josef Tito, leader of the League of Communists, the ruling communist party in Yugoslavia, stated that the parties of Yugoslavia, Italy, France, and Spain had adopted a new doctrine of "national socialism," meaning those parties would determine for themselves what was communist and what was not and what doctrine of communism they would follow, and that they rejected Soviet interference into their matters. The movement was also known as "Eurocommunism." Any attempts to reconcile the Soviet and the Chinese parties also failed. See SOCIALISM WITH A HUMAN FACE, WORKER'S COUNCILS.

Summons. An order issued by either a court of law or an arresting officer directing a defendant to appear in person and to answer to the charges placed against him. A summons may also be issued to a person who is to testify as a witness in a court of law. See LAW, STATUTE.

Sunday Law. See BLUE LAW.

Sunni Dissimulation. See SHIITE DISSIMULATION.

Sunshine Law. The U.S. House of Representatives passed on July 29, 1976, legislation (the U.S. Senate passed a similar measure in November 1975) to require all federal agencies to open their meetings to the public and to avoid private communication aimed at influencing decisions. Similarly, state legislatures and many local governments throughout the United States have adopted such "government in the sunshine" legislation or rules. The underlying philosophy is to open government to closer scrutiny by the people, to increase interaction between the governors and the governed, and to allow for greater input by citizens into policy formulation and decision making. The federal statute was signed by U.S. President Gerald R. Ford (1974-1977) on September 9, 1976, and opened to the public such once-secretive agencies as the Federal Power Commission, the Federal Communications Commission, the Federal Reserve Board, and the Securities and Exchange Commission. See FREEDOM OF INFORMATION ACT.

Suo Jure. In the Latin language, "in one's own right."

Suo Loco. In the Latin language, "in the proper place."

Super Delegate. A delegate to either the Republican or the Democratic convention, who was not elected by primary or caucus voting, is not committed, and who will cast her/his ballot for that party's presidential candidate during the party national convention. See BROKERED CONVENTION, PRIMARY ELECTION, SUPER TUESDAY, Appendix 19.

Super Tuesday. See PRIMARY ELECTION.

Superiority of Democracy Doctrine. U.S. President Jimmy Carter declared on January 6, 1978, in Paris, France, before his return to the United States from his multi-nation trip, that democracy, as a form of government, is superior to any other, not only in meeting basic material human needs, but spiritually as well. President Carter ridiculed those who claim that democracy is obsolete, referring probably to the French philosophers who claim that neither traditional democracy nor socialism (especially the Soviet style) is capable of satisfying human needs in modern times. See the NEW FRENCH PHILOSOPHERS.

Superstate. See SOLEMN REFERENDUM OF 1920.

Superstructure. See ECONOMIC BASE OF SOCIETY.

Supply-side Economics. See LAFFER CURVE.

Suppose They Had a War and Nobody Came? A popular slogan during the 1960s among Americans opposing the Vietnam War and U.S. participation in it.

Supranational Law. See VOLUNTAS CIVITATIS MAXIMAE EST SERVANDA.

Supranational State. One state made up of all nations; a world state; a world government embracing all nations; or one above any one nation or state.

Supraversion. See REVOLUTION FROM ABOVE.

Supremacy Clause. The provision in Article VI of the U.S. Constitution proclaiming that the Constitution and the provisions, and all treaties made under the authority of the United States, shall be the "supreme law of the land." See Appendix 8.

Supreme Court of Errors. The official name of the Supreme Court of the state of Connecticut in the United States.

Supreme Court of the United States. The highest and the only constitutional court of law in the United States and one of the three branches of the American national government. The Court is composed of eight Associate Justices and one Chief Justice (total nine), all nominated to their position by the President of the United States and confirmed by the United States Senate (upon recommendation by the Committee on the Judiciary) for a period of "good behavior," which may amount to a life-time. The Court has two types of jurisdiction: (1) original and (2) appellate. Under original jurisdiction, certain cases can be brought before the Court which involve (1) disputes between two or more states; (2) disputes between a state and the federal government; (3) disputes between a state and a citizen of another state; and (4) disputes between the United States and representatives of foreign nations (states). Under appellate jurisdiction cases are considered by an appeal or a writ of *certiorari* from lower courts of the land which involve cases pertaining to: (1) issues of federal law upon review by federal district courts and federal courts of appeal; (2) matters pertaining to the U.S. Constitution, laws and treaties with foreign nations which the Court is obliged to review upon appeal; (3) cases, which the Court selects for review upon its own discretion, which involve important principles of constitutional or statutory laws. When the Supreme Court refuses to review a case, the decision of the lower court stands. One of the most tangible powers that the U.S. Supreme Court has is that of judicial review, that is, to decide on the constitutionality of laws and acts of officers of the two remaining branches of the government: the President and the Congress (the Senate and the House of Representatives), as well as those of the states. The precedence of judicial review was established by the case of *William Marbury v. James Madison, Secretary of State of the United States*, 1 Cranch 137; 2 L. Ed. 60 (1803). The Court also serves as the balancer of the federal powers in the United States. See Appendices 44-51.

Supreme Court Reporter. See UNITED STATES REPORTS (U.S.).

Supreme Headquarters Allied Powers in Europe (SHAPE). See NATO.

Supreme Judicial Court. The official name of the Supreme Court in the states of Maine and Massachusetts in the United States.

Supreme Law of the Land. Depending on times and places, supreme law may constitute the will of the monarch (absolute ruler) or the dictator under a single-person dictatorship; the edict of the king, queen, emperor, tsar, or khnaz (in old Russia), or the monarch or the dictator working in concert (usually through a single political party); a written document which outlines the powers and limitations of the government; the basic political and governmental institutions and processes (e.g., electoral processes and judicial proceedings), and rights and obligations of citizens. In the United States, the U.S. Constitution, the treaties, and the statutes constitute the supreme law of the land. U.S. Supreme Court Justice John Marshall (1755-1835), (who wrote forty-four opinions in landmark cases during the formative years of the American States, see Appendix 8, 44-48) established in his opinion in *McCulloch v. Maryland* on March 6, 1819, the doctrine of the supremacy of federal laws over states' laws, and stated: "The government of the United States, though limited in its powers, is supreme; and its laws, when made in pursuance of the Constitution, form the supreme law of the land."

Supreme People's Council. The unicameral legislative body of Yemen.

Supreme Soviet. In the Russian language, "Vyerghovnoy Sovyet." The national bicameral legislative body of the Soviet Union composed of the House of the Union and the House of Nationalities, co-equal in authority. Since 25 December 1991, the legislative bodies in Russia, Belarus, Kazakhstan, and Ukraine, were renamed Congresses of People's Deputies. See SOVIET OF NATIONALITIES, SOVIET OF THE UNION.

Surprise Attack. Under the terms of the Hague Peace Conference and Convention of 1899, and ratified by all major powers, surprise attack is illegal, and a war-prone state must declare war prior to an attack. This prohibition was violated by Nazi Germany in its attack on Poland on 1 September 1939, which commenced W.W.II. Imperial Japan also violated it by attacking the United States at Pearl Harbor on 7 December 1941, marking the beginning of U.S. involvement in W.W.II. See PEARL HARBOR.

Sure District. See SAVE DISTRICT.

Sûreté. National security and intelligence gathering and evaluating agency of the Republic of France.

Sûreté Nationale. French security and intelligence force.

Surplus Value. According to Karl Marx, that part of the value of goods that the capitalist retains as his profit after selling the goods produced by the workers who are only partially rewarded for their labor. Marx claimed that the worker's wages represent only a part of the value that the worker produces. The real value of his labor is what he receives in wages plus what the capitalist receives upon selling the product of the worker. This is also known as the so-called "major discrepancy" or "contradiction" within the capitalistic system of economy. See GERMAN UNIFICATION.

Surrogate. A minor judicial officer under some jurisdictions in the United States (e.g., in the state of New York), one who is authorized and empowered to decide cases resulting from probate wills, the disposition of estates, and the guardianship of orphaned minors. See PROBATE COURT, SUPREME COURT OF THE UNITED STATES.

Surrogate Court. See PROBATE COURT, SURROGATE.

Survival Gap. See PARITY GAP.

Suspension of Rules. Upon a motion properly entertained and introduced, rules in a deliberating body (e.g., the United States Congress) may be suspended for the purpose of hearing a case of a unique nature. (In the U.S. House of Representatives a two-thirds vote is required before a rule in force can be suspended.) See UNITED STATES HOUSE OF REPRESENTATIVES.

Suspensive Veto. A veto that may only delay but not totally nullify a legislative act for a specified period of time. The House of Lords in England, for example, may delay legislative bills of the House of Commons by means of suspensive veto for several months; and if the Commons persist, the bills so suspended may become law upon the expiration of the time allowed for suspension. See HOUSE OF LORDS, PARLIAMENT.

Suspicion of Intent. See MINSK-PINSK TALE.

Suzerain. A protector state; a state which provides protection to another in return for some form of remuneration (e.g., a fee). See PROTECTORATE.

Suzerain State. In the anatomy of statehood, a sovereign state which exercises some binding and voluntarily accepted influence over another state.

Suzerainty. See SUZERAIN.

Swallow. See SEXPIONAGE.

SWANU. See SOUTH WEST AFRICAN NATIONAL UNION.

SWAPO. See SOUTH WEST AFRICAN PEOPLE'S ORGANIZATION.

Swart Gevaar. In the Afrikaans language, "black menace." Also, a common slogan of the anti-black groups in South Africa which comprise approximately 4.3 million, with 18 million blacks and 2.5 million of mixed blood, or "colored." There are also approximately 900,000 Asians, who, like the blacks and the colored, cannot vote or be voted upon.

Swing Vote. See SITTING ON THE FENCE.

Swiss Corridor. See AGONIZING REAPPRAISAL.

Switzerland of Asia. A plan designed by General Douglas MacArthur (1880-1964), when, as a military advisor to the Philippines (1935-1941), he presented a plan in 1936 to modernize the island in every respect. Plans ranged from modern schools to a modern air force, so the nation would be as clean and prosperous as Switzerland. From his position as marshal in the Philippine Army, he was recalled to the U.S. Army in 1941, and became commander of the U.S. Armed Forces in the Far East. When the Japanese invaded the Philippines on 10 December 1941, MacArthur's forces withdrew to the Bataan Peninsula, and MacArthur left for Australia. After months of heroic resistance with weapons consisting mainly of pistols and rifles, without logistic support of any kind, plagued with disease and fatigue, about 80,000 American soldiers surrendered to the Japanese on orders of U.S. Commander, General S. Wainwright. That was the largest ever surrender by Americans anywhere. About 20,000 of the American soldiers were subsequently killed by the Japanese. Upon his arrival in Australia the general stated, "I came through and I shall return." He did return, as promised, in January 1945. When General MacArthur left for Australia, most of the Allied troops, including the Americans, surrendered, but there was a small group which refused to surrender although, under the rules of engagement, soldiers who refuse to follow the order of surrender, can be shot instead of taken prisoner of war by the enemy. A large group of American soldiers stayed behind, fought as guerrillas with the Filipinos, and emerged as heroes when General MacArthur returned in glory. One of such heroes was U.S. Captain (later Colonel) Ed Ramsey, who survived the ordeal. See LEADERSHIP, NUTS!

Symbionese Liberation Army (SLA). An interracial terrorist organization established in California in 1971 aiming, through acts of terrorism (killings, assassinations, kidnappings), to disrupt and to undermine the political system of the United States. In 1974, Patricia Hearst, heiress to the Hearst newspaper publishing empire, was kidnapped by the SLA, but soon announced through the public media that she had decided to voluntarily join the organization in order to struggle against the "oppressive" American system. While with the SLA, Hearst took her *nom de guerre* of "Tania," the alias that was used by Tamara Bunke, the collaborator of Major Ernesto "Che" Guevara in Bolivia (but who in reality was an undercover agent of the East German Ministry of Security-intelligence, heavily involved in intelligence work against the West for East Germany and the USSR's KGB, intelligence). Patricia Hearst was captured by the FBI on September 18, 1975, and convicted of bank robbery on March 20, 1976.

Symbol of the Democratic Party of the United States. Cartoonist Thomas Nast so designated the donkey in 1874.

Symbol of the Republican Party of the United States. Cartoonist Thomas Nast so designated the elephant in 1874.

Symbol of the Unity of the Nation. See V-J DAY.

Symbolic Racism. A concept denoting the prevailing practices of racial discrimination in America which are no longer overt (open) because they are forbidden by law but which are covert (hidden, secretive), or institutionalized (practiced by persons who hide behind institutions in order not to be easily identified), so that legal remedies cannot be applied. Also, the acceptance of one race by another (blacks by whites) in a symbolic, artificial way, as demonstrated by tokenism and "window-dressing." See RACE WAR.

Sympathy Verdict. A verdict by a judge or a jury based on considerations other than the material facts at hand, or verdict bias often in favor of the accused.

Synacalism. The French brand of syndicalism which originated the concept of "workers' control" of the means of production and distribution in a socialist society. See MARXISM, SOCIALISM, SYNDICALISM.

Syndicalism. A kind of socialist philosophy that advocates, among other things: the ownership of the means of production and distribution by the workers rather than by the state, its government, or private persons; and the replacement of government with some kind of a cooperative enterprise supervised by the workers or by the producers of goods and services and not the investors or the managers of their investments. See MARXISM, SOCIALISM.

Synoptic Planning. See PLANNING.

Synthetic Political Theory. See POLITICAL THEORY.

System. A set of functionally related components which interact according to certain identifiable processes, and which produce desired (or nearly desired) outcomes. See POLITICAL SYSTEM in Appendix 3.

System Levels. A variety of hierarchical criteria applied to describe and to differentiate political systems in terms of geographical scope, composition of the system itself (membership), its range of functions, and the relationship of the authority within a certain system to those who have to obey that authority. See Appendices 3, 3-A.

Systematic Political Theory. See POLITICAL THEORY.

Systematic Theory in Political Science. See POLITICAL THEORY.

Systems Analysis. A technique used to coordinate the activities of governmental agencies for better efficiency by revealing irregularities and abuses of power and by trying to bring about accountability of public officials. See Appendix 3.

Sztab Kryzysowy. See CRISIS STAFF.

"You can fool all the people some of the time, and some of the people all the time, but you can not fool all the people all the time."
ABRAHAM LINCOLN, 1809-1865

Tabula Rasa. In the Latin language, "erased tablet" or "blind mind." A term often applied to persons who are ignorant of empirical realities of life and the utility of observation and experience in dealing with political and social phenomena. Also, persons who accept belief (or metaphysics) as the scientific method and who reject empirical research.

Taft-Hartley Act. A congressional law, also known as the "Labor-Management Act of 1947," named after its sponsors U.S. Senator Robert A. Taft, (R-Ohio) and Representative F. A. Hartley (R-New York). The law aims at restricting certain activities of organized labor (labor unions) particularly as they pertain to strikes. The law authorizes the U.S. President to invoke the Act against a striking union (as U.S. President Jimmy Carter did on March 6, 1978, against the striking United Mine Workers) requiring its members to return to work for a period of eighty days (known as "cooling-off" period) during which time negotiations between the union and the management may continue. Non-compliance with the invocation exposes the union leaders to a penalty of up to $10,000 for each day of continuous violation. If at the end of the "cooling-off" period no agreement has been reached between the union and the management, the President may nationalize the industry (if a subsequent walk-out would be considered detrimental to national interest), set the wages for the workers, and generally supervise and operate a given enterprise. (While invoking the Taft-Hartley Act on March 6, 1978, against the United Mine Workers, President Carter established a precedent under the law by allowing mine management to pay miners the wages that were agreed upon in a new contract. The miners had rejected that new contract by a nationwide vote on Sunday, March 5, 1978. Approximately 165,000 miners voted and the contract was rejected by a margin of almost two to one.) A provision in the Taft-Hartley Act requiring union leaders to file affidavits of loyalty to the United States (and a disclaimer of membership in the Communist Party) was removed from the law by the Landrum-Griffin Act of 1959. One of the most controversial provisions of the Taft-Hartley Act is its Section 14b which allows states to implement laws guaranteeing open shop economic activity (membership in a labor union is not required). This provision in the law is the main object of attack by organized labor (e.g., the AFL-CIO) in the United States, and the U.S. Congress is being constantly pressed to have that section of the law repealed.

Tailor President. A nickname of U.S. President Andrew Johnson (1861-1865), who in his youth was trained to be a tailor. See JOHNSON PROCLAMATION, RECONSTRUCTION.

Taiwan Issue. See SHANGHAI COMMUNIQUÉ.

Take a Walk. In practical politics the practice, by any delegate or the entire state delegation, of walking out of a national political party convention as a protest against the party's platform, one of its planks, or the nominees that the party selects for election to public offices.

Take Politics out of Government. See DEPOLITICIZING POLITICS.

Taking the Constitution Home. See BRITISH COMMONWEALTH OF NATIONS.

Tamil Separatism in Sri Lanka. The Tamils, descendants of Hindus who immigrated to Sri Lanka a long time ago, and who constitute about four million of the eighteen million population of Sri Lanka, rose up in sporadic attempts in 1970 demanding freedom to establish a separate state. The Tamil Separatists are also known as "Tamil Tigers." The Sinhalese majority, who are Buddhists, oppose

501

any division of the state. The struggle has intensified since the early 1980s and over 20,000 persons have perished.

Tamil Tiger. See TAMIL SEPARATISM IN SRI LANKA.

Tammany Hall. Once a term synonymous with the Democratic party machine in New York City which, until recent years, controlled politics in the city. The term is derived from the *Tammany Society, or Columbia Order Of New York*, which was a political society founded about 1786 for the purpose of organizing cultural and political activities particularly among the less affluent and less educated. The Democratic Party organization held its meetings during the last several decades in the hall of the *Tammany Society*, known as Tammany Hall, which is the seat of the Society. See POLITICAL MACHINE, TEAPOT DOME AFFAIR, WATERGATE AFFAIR.

Tanaka Plan. A plan devised by Imperial Japan's naval officer Raizo Tanaka (1892-1969) to conquer all of Asia, including Asian parts of the Soviet Union, and also the United States and Canada. The plan of conquest, to be implemented gradually, commenced with the invasion of Manchuria in 1931. Admiral Tanaka defeated the U.S. Naval force at the Battle of Tassafaronga on 30 November 1942, but he became critical of the Japanese High Command because of inadequate coordination of sea-air power in Guadalcanal, and for his criticism was removed from command.

Taqiyah. See SHIITE DISSIMULATION.

Tar Baby Policy. A term which may characterize the policy of U.S. President Richard M. Nixon (1969-1974) in regard to the dark continent, Africa. While the American government paid some lip service to the liberation movements (especially in Angola), it withdrew support from traditional colonial regimes in Africa (e.g., Portugal) and maintained at the same time good political and trade relations with the white ruling minorities in Rhodesia and South Africa. This policy brought about a considerable decline of American influence in Africa.

Tashkent Declaration. On January 10, 1966, India's Prime Minister, Lal Nahadur Shastri, and Pakistan's President, Ayub Khan, signed an agreement which officially ended a war (over Kashmir) between these two states. On January 11, 1966, Shastri died while on a visit to Moscow, USSR, and the Indian Parliament's majority party, the Congress People's Party, elected Mrs. Indira Gandhi as Prime Minister. On March 22, 1977, Mrs. Gandhi was forced to resign because of her dictatorial mode of ruling. Her authoritarian rule has created serious political and economic problems for India, setting back India's development several decades.

Tatemae. In the Japanese language, "the official story." See INTELLIGENCE.

Tax Court of the United States. A legislative court created by the U.S Congress in 1924 for the purpose of handling cases brought before it by the taxpayers against the Internal Revenue Service and other tax officers and agencies. The tribunal is composed of sixteen judges, and their decisions may be reviewed by the Federal Court of Appeals.

Tax Loophole. Tax legislation which may, by design or by coincidence, allow certain individuals or groups (such as corporations) to avoid payment of taxes or to pay reduced taxes. The term "tax shelter" is also often used. America is one among very few nations today where tax loopholes are very real due to constant lobbying by professionals, e.g., lawyers and accountants who represent rich interest groups, and the burden of taxation affects mainly the middle and the low-income 99 percent of the American taxpayers. As of April 1992, federal statistics indicate that one-percent of the population (about two million millionaires, paid little tax but retained about 40 percent of the national income, and the remaining 99 percent retained only about 60 percent of the income.

Tax on Sin. A tax on items such as alcohol and tobacco, which state or local governments collect in order to supplement their revenues, "with the theory that they are luxuries or on the grounds that people should not be buying these items in the first place" (though, given the revenue they produce, tax collectors might well be heartbroken if people stopped "sinning"). The term was coined by Professor Berman of Arizona State University.

Tax Revolt. A nation-wide grass-roots movement in the United States to keep taxation down or to lower taxes (e.g., real estate taxes). On June 7, 1978, for example, the voters of California voted on such a measure through the so-called "Proposition Thirteen." This movement for lower taxation is spreading to other states. The measure was challenged in court on 25 February 1992, by a group of younger home buyers in California, who claim that it favors older voters. According to 1992 statistics by the International Monetary Fund, by international standards, the American tax system is rather mild. Total tax revenue as a percentage of Gross National Product (GNP) in selected states is : Canada, 34%; France 42%; Germany 39%; Japan 27%; Holland 48%; Norway, 49%; Sweden, 51%; and the United States only 28%.

Tax Shelter. See TAX LOOPHOLE.

Tax Surcharge. An additional levy to a tax; or a tax on a tax.

Taxation without Representation. See STAMP ACT.

Tea Act. See TOWNSHEND REVENUE ACT.

Tea Party. See BOSTON TEA PARTY.

Teach-in. See ANTI-VIETNAM WAR SLOGANS.

Teapot Dome Affair. When President Warren G. Harding took office in 1921, a series of improprieties were discovered in his administration: such as the fact that his Director of the Veterans Bureau, "Colonel" Charles Forbes, was an Army deserter (never commissioned as an officer) who was taking bribes for government contracts (mainly building of Veterans hospitals) and was selling on the side building materials that belonged to the federal government; his Attorney General, Harry A. Daugherty, was a proprietor of an infamous "Little House" on H Street in Washington, D.C., where wild things were happening, and, above all, the incident which gave the name to the affair, was the fact that his Secretary of the Interior, Albert Fall, exchanged the right to exploitation of rich government oil reserves, the Teapot Dome Reserve in the state of Wyoming, and Elk Hill in the state of California, for the sum of $400,000 in bribery. This incident put Fall behind bars, discredited the Harding Administration, and led to some speculation concerning the nature of President Harding's death in 1923. See WATERGATE.

TECHINT. See INTELLIGENCE.

Techno-Globalism. See FEDERAL TECHNOLOGY AND TRANSFER ACT.

Techno-Nationalism. See FEDERAL TECHNOLOGY AND TRANSFER ACT.

Technocracy. A government and administration run by professionals rather than by amateur-politicians.

Technology Export. A standing policy of the United States and its Western allies, not to supply advanced technological know-how to states with hostile political systems (e.g., Soviet Union, Albania, People's Republic of China, North Korea, Vietnam, Cambodia, and the East European Socialist States), which they may deploy for purposes of conquest. This policy originated during the last days of the Harry S. Truman administration (Cold War era) and has been reinforced on September 3, 1977, by U.S. Secretary of Defense, Harold Brown. This policy aims particularly at strict control of the export of critical raw materials (e.g., uranium), advanced equipment (e.g., high-thrust aircraft engines and computers), and research findings, both theoretical and empirical.

Technostructure. The economic system of a society, composed of the personnel, the decision-makers in economic matters, and the facilities, or the means of production and distribution of goods and services. See TECHNOCRACY.

Technotronic. A term used to depict the impact that technology and electronics make upon contemporary societies, mainly on the mechanized day-to-day operations of the governmental machinery and military preparedness of states. See TECHNOCRACY.

Teflon President. See GREAT COMMUNICATOR.

Teheran Conference. A major summit conference held between U.S. President Franklin D. Roosevelt, British Prime Minister Winston Churchill, and Soviet Premier Josef Stalin from November 28 through December 1, 1943, in Teheran, Iran, during which the participants agreed upon, among other things, the spheres of influence in post-war Europe: the Western Allies were to retain their influence in Greece, Turkey, and Western Europe proper, while the Soviet Union was to retain influence in Eastern Europe and the Baltic area (Latvia, Lithuania, Estonia, and parts of East Prussia which formerly belonged to the German Reich; the three Baltic republics—Latvia, Lithuania, and Estonia—had already been incorporated into the Soviet Union in 1941). The Allies recognized the three Baltic republics as an integral part of the Soviet Union, the Polish-Soviet frontier as designated by the Curzon Line, and the partition of East Prussia between Poland and the Soviet Union. See MORGENTHAU PLAN.

Teleocracy. A term applied to the practice by a national leader or chief executive of a state who explores the medium of television for the purpose of conveying his views to the electorate and who seeks its support as a means of governance.

Teleology. A theory designed to explain that in human society phenomena do not occur automatically (according to purely mechanical laws), but are caused by the purpose which they are to serve. See POLITICAL TELEOLOGY.

Telephone Diplomacy. The practice of conducting diplomatic negotiations via the telephone or a similar means of transmission (e.g., the "hot line" that connects the White House and the Kremlin).

Television Diplomacy. The growing use and reliance on television broadcasting systems as a means for political-diplomatic communications on a global scale. See SADAT-BEGIN SUMMIT.

TELINT. See INTELLIGENCE.

Teller Amendment During the Cuban-Spanish-American War of 1898, when the United States aided Cuba in becoming independent from Spanish rule, U.S military aid was extended to Cuba on the premise that after Cuba gained independence, the United States would withdraw and renounce any and all territorial claims to Cuba. U.S. Senator J. Teller proposed this amendment as a rider to an appropriation bill and by 1902 American forces had pulled out. But the expansionist, imperialist forces in the United States saw a danger that Cuba on its own would become a part of the "Caribbean Black Belt" and, like Haiti, would not favor American business interests in Cuba; so U.S. interest turned to Cuba once more. See PLATT AMENDMENT.

Teller Vote. A manner of tabulating votes by counting those who raise hands or stand up when called upon. See VOTING.

Temple of Peace. The official seat of the International Court of Justice and the seat of the Permanent Court of Justice since 1899, in The Hague, the Netherlands. It was donated by an American "king of steel," Andrew Carnegie. See INTERNATIONAL COURT OF JUSTICE (ICJ).

Temporal Authority. Real or earthly authority. Authority that is not given by any supernatural being, but one that is derived from and exercised by man. See CAESAROPAPISM, ECCLESIASTICAL AUTHORITY, TWO SWORDS THEORY.

Temporary Bill. See BILL.

Temporary Commission on Employee Loyalty. See LOYALTY LAW.

Ten Million Americans Mobilizing for Justice. An extreme-right wing lobby of wealthy Americans who supported the "red witch hunt" conducted by Senator Joseph McCarthy during the 1950s.

Ten Percent Nation. Japan's Prime Minister Zenko Suzuku (1980-1982), so characterized Japan, because the nation commands ten-percent of the gross national product of the world. The Japanese use the term "ichiwari kokka."

Ten Rights. See TOWNSHEND REVENUE ACT.

Ten/Ten Agreement. See KUOMINTANG.

Ten Thousand-Days War. The Vietnam War. See VIETNAM WAR.

Tennessee Valley Authority (TVA). A federal corporation chartered by the United States Congress in 1933 for the purpose of constructing electric dams and other related structures on the Tennessee River and its tributaries and supplying electric energy, fertilizers, and nitrates for a fee. The TVA is one of few profit-making federal corporations in the United States. The Authority is composed of three directors appointed by the U.S. President and confirmed by the Senate. In 1933, President Franklin D. Roosevelt believed that the Tennessee River ought to be developed for the purpose of conservation of the forest and the soil in the Valley which extends into seven States (Tennessee—where most of the structures exist in 41,000 square miles—Alabama, Georgia, Kentucky, Mississippi, North Carolina, and Virginia). It supplies electric energy over a 91,000-mile network in several states. By law, TVA was assigned three principal water-related functions: flood control, navigation, and electric power. See SOCIALIZED ENTERPRISES IN THE UNITED STATES.

Tennis Cabinet. A facetious reference that adversaries of U.S. President Theodore Roosevelt (1901-1909) were making about his close advisers, many of whom were also the President's tennis partners. The regular cabinet members disliked those cronies (e.g., one Gilford Pinchot, a naturalist, who strongly influenced the President's interest in nature) as they always dislike any kitchen cabinet.

Tenure. The time-period, the condition, or the manner of holding office. The tenure of office for the U.S. President and Vice President is four years, for U.S. Senators, six years, and members of the U.S. House of Representatives, two years. The tenure for judges, unless otherwise stipulated by law, is ordinarily "the time of good behavior," or a life-time.

Tenure of Office Act. See IMPEACHMENT.

Tenure of Office of Members of the United States Congress. See BUSINESS OF CONGRESS IS RE-ELECTION BUSINESS.

Terra Communis. In the Latin language "communal property" or "international territory." Also, international waters, space, and lands unclaimed.

Terra Incognita. n the Latin language "unknown land," "unknown territory," or "mysterious land." Also, a term often used to describe some activity, the outcome of which cannot be foreseen.

Terra Nullius. In the Latin language, "no one's land" or "land unclaimed." Also, a principle of international law under which no-one's land can be claimed by its discoverer and/or occupant. The continent of Greenland, for example, was once claimed by England as well as by Denmark, but an international body of arbitrators to whom the case was submitted for adjudication ruled in favor of Denmark on the grounds that some time in the past (around the latter part of the eighteenth century) a group of Danish sailors established a settlement there, and some relics have been found (a letter in Danish) attesting to this effect.

Territorial Court. A federal court of the United States designed for any one of the American Territories (e.g., the Canal Zone, Guam, Puerto Rico, or the Virgin Islands).

Territorial Democracy. The U.S. Federal Constitution, a contractual agreement between the people and the states, provides for two systems of democracy—in which democratic ideas, ideals, and institutions and processes can be established and practiced—at the level of the several states as well as at the national, federal level. Also referred to as contractual democracy (e.g., the powers that are granted as well as those that are forbidden to states and to the federal government). See FEDERALISM.

Territorial Distribution of Power. See FRAGMENTATION OF POWER.

Territorial Imperative. The special privileges and rights that go with the territory (e.g., the land, the household—or the entire nation state in case of an absolute monarch—which one owns, possesses or controls); also rights arising from acquisition of a territory in case of war where the victor may claim sovereign rights. See POWER.

Territorial Imperialism. See COLONIALISM.

Territorial Waters. All bodies of water, such as lakes, bays, small rivers, and sea waters adjacent to the territory of a state, traditionally not extending beyond three miles from the shore. In recent years, however, many states, including the United States, have extended their territorial waters to two-hundred miles from the seacoast. The traditional three-mile limit originated in times when a cannon shot could only cover that distance. All waters not within territorial waters are considered international waters and, as such open to all nations for free use. See COD WAR, TUNA WAR.

Terrorism. Deliberate acts and activities aiming at the disruption and the destruction of political processes and political institutions in an organized society, including kidnapping, arson, and murder of private and public leaders. The success of terrorist tactic lies in (1) surprise and (2) excessive and savage use of violent force, both of which are designed not only to kill the target person (or persons) and to destroy property, but also to leave behind the picture of horror in order to instill fear. According to the American State Department (Ministry of Foreign Affairs), terrorism rose in 1991, particularly during the Persian Gulf War, to 557 as compared with 456 terrorist acts against Americans in 1990. States that were branded as state sponsors of terrorism were: Cuba, Iran, Iraq, Libya, North Korea, and Syria. See ANARCHISM.

Terrorist. One who resorts to violence in order to achieve desired objectives. See ANARCHIST.

Test Ban Treaty. See NUCLEAR TEST BAN TREATY.

Testament of Lenin. See LENIN'S TESTAMENT.

Tested and True. See MOSSADEGH.

That Government is Best Which Governs Not at All. A notion on the degree and scope of governmental powers and governance in general as developed by Henry Thoreau (1817-1862), which was similar to that of Thomas Jefferson (1743-1826) before him, and Ralph Waldo Emerson (1803-1882) after him.

That Man in the White House. See HUNDRED DAYS SESSION.

Thatcherism. See ELECTORALISM.

The Nail That Sticks Out Will be Pounded In. See FRAME SOCIETY.

The World Has Come Home to America. Statement made by former U.S. President Ronald W. Reagan (1981-1989) on 24 January 1992, when he was presented with a special humanitarian award for aiding famine-stricken nations in Africa. See AMERICAN CENTURY.

Theism. Acknowledgment of the existence of a God or gods. The opposite is "atheism" which denies the existence of God.

Theocracy. The rule by clergy or other persons controlled by an ecclesiastical authority.

Theoretical Truth. See POLITICAL ANALYSIS.

Theoretical Validity. See POLITICAL ANALYSIS.

Theories of the Development of State. Among the theories of the development of a state once it has been established are the following: (1) The Sea Power Theory—holds that states having access to the seas not only were able to survive and develop themselves but were capable of conquering others and of establishing empires (e.g., the early Phoenicians, the Vikings, the Dutch, the Spanish, the Portuguese, and the British); (2) The Land Power or Geopolitical Theory—holds that landmass is paramount to the development of a state in order to make it self-sufficient; therefore, sea powers, having limited land, seek conquests abroad in order to grow; (3) Revolutionary Theory—holds that in order to remain a viable political unit, the state must periodically overhaul its internal structure (e.g., change the form of government or mode of economic activity, such as in socialism and communism) and conquer other lands if necessary; and (4) Technological Progress Theory—holds that the growth and development of the state depends on the scope and degree of the explorations of its human and material resources; that the ultimate wealth of a nation is in the people and their skills (know-how); that innovative production of needed goods and services determines the growth of the state and the society (this theory is of modern origin and is commonly accepted today). See GEOPOLITICS.

Theory. An instrument, derived from a body of organized knowledge, which is capable of producing useful explanations of phenomena of life if properly utilized through mental processes.

Theory of Democratic Capitalism. See DEMOCRATIC CAPITALISM.

Theory of Evolution. See MONKEY TRIAL.

Theory of Value. See VALUE THEORY.

There is a Little Bit of Stalin in Each of Us. A slogan of the former Soviet Communist Party, popular after the Soviet victory over Nazi German invaders in 1945, justifying the creation of the greatest empire in modern history from thousands of unruly tribes of every existing race, religion, nationality, and personal habit on earth. Stalin and his associates were, in spite of the fact that between seventy and eighty million people were killed, viewed as men of genius and talent as well as cruelty and tyranny, the epitome of Soviet society. At a Kremlin reception, Russian Historian Melor Sturua related an episode in which Stalin was asked by Lady Astor of England when he would stop killing people. Stalin replied that he would stop "when it is no longer necessary."

There is No God but Allah. In the Arabic language, "La-ila-ha Il-lal-lah." See ISLAM.

There is No Substitute for Victory. See KOREAN WAR.

There is Only One China Doctrine. See SHANGHAI COMMUNIQUÉ.

They Can Have any Color They Want so Long as It's Black. See CONSUMER SOVEREIGNTY, MULTINATIONAL CORPORATION.

They Pretend to Pay Us, We Pretend to Work. See WE PRETEND TO WORK, THEY PRETEND TO PAY US.

They Shall Never Pass. See LA PASIONARIA.

Third Branch of Congress. The Rules Committee in the U.S. House of Representatives, which holds hearings and decides on the rules by which a certain piece of legislation will be considered. If the Committee (or its powerful chairman) decides to make no rules because it does not like or favor certain legislation, the bill will never reach the floor of the House.

Third House of Congress. A derogatory term for the ever present lobbyists that swarm upon Congress during each session, attempting to influence legislative behavior in favor of their clients.

Third International. See COMMUNIST INTERNATIONAL, THIRD, COMMUNIST ORGANIZATIONS.

Third Parties. Mostly confined to advocacy of some ideology or cause—interest groups whose cause is not sufficiently addressed by the two major parties.

Third Party Candidate. An aspirant for a public elective office in a traditionally two-party system (e.g., the United States, Great Britain, or Germany), who is running on a third-party ticket. See Appendix 19.

Third Reich. The Nazi state and its regime under the rule of Adolf Hitler from 1933 through 1945. (The other German Reichs were: the First Reich—the Holy Roman Empire of the German Nation [800-1806], and the Second Reich—under the leadership of Prince Otto von Bismarck [1871-1918]. The Third Reich followed the Weimar Republic [1919-1933]). See LEBENSRAUM, SCHWARZE KAPELLE, WEIMAR REPUBLIC.

Third World. In the language of international politics, those nation-states which do not consider themselves a part of either the Soviet or the American spheres of influence; blocs, led by the former Soviet Union and the United States respectively; or most of the Asian and the African nations which gained their independence after World War II. Most of the Third World nations are considered underdeveloped, that is, having limited capacity to satisfy the basic daily needs of their peoples; lacking capital, know-how, production capacity, and markets for their limited products. See BIPOLARITY.

Thirty-Six Thousand Governments. It is estimated that there are approximately 36,000 different sorts and levels of governmental units in the United States, beginning with the federal government down to regional, state, county, parish, borough, village, township, town, or city. Special authorities which deal with public matters, and several million persons are also involved, most of them without pay, or just token pay of a one dollar per year. Most of the commissions, boards, and authorities rely on volunteers. See NON-CANDIDATE CANDIDATE, VOLUNTARISM.

This is the Biggest Tax Bill We've Ever Passed! See SOCIAL SECURITY.

Thought. A process, which results from an intensive and concentrated mental activity, by which one designs (thinks up) and articulates (speaks or writes, using words) concepts and conceptual frameworks which can subsequently be converted into action (e.g., a policy). Also, as defined by Marcuse, "the labor which brings to life in us that which does not exist."

Thousand Points of Light. See AMERICAN CENTURY.

Threat of War. See WAR.

Three Bigs. Business, Government and Labor. See COUNTERVAILING POWER.

Three-Fifths Compromise. An agreement reached between the southern and the northern states during the Philadelphia Constitutional Convention in 1787, to the effect that three-fifths of the whole number of slaves would be counted when estimating a state's population for purposes of representation in Congress and appropriation of direct taxes. See PLANS OF THE AMERICAN UNION.

Three Fundamentals of the Israeli-Arab Settlement. See FUNDAMENTALS OF THE ISRAELI-ARAB SETTLEMENT.

Three-Mile Rule. See TERRITORIAL WATERS.

Three-Nos Doctrine. During the August 1967 Khartoum (Sudan) Arab Summit, held with Soviet backing, the representatives proclaimed the "Three Nos Doctrine": no peace, no recognition, no negotiations with the "Jewish Entity," as they called Israel.

Three People's Principles. A philosophical concept developed by the founding father of modern China, Dr. Sun Yat-sen (1867-1925), which is based on the combination of Confucian morality and Western European skills in statecraft. The document closely resembles Abraham Lincoln's "Gettysburg Address." These Principles, which were designed to serve as a basis for the unification of China, are: (1) Race-nationalism, which was to unite all Chinese peoples throughout the world under the leadership of the Kuomintang (Dr. Sun's political organization); (2) People's Livelihood, the experimentation in economic matters with non-imperialistic capitalism and non-revolutionary socialism (in order to weaken the economic power of the landlords); and (3) Democracy, which under the existing conditions could only be achieved through three stages: a) unification of the armed forces under the leadership of the Kuomintang; b) dictatorship by the Kuomintang; and c) self-government by the people upon free elections. Dr. Sun Yat-sen, once a citizen of the United States, became the president of the first republican government in China in 1912. These Principles were proclaimed to guide the state under the Kuomintang rule, but many of them, in varied scope and degree, were implemented by the Communists under Mao Tse-tung.

Three Worlds. A concept coined in 1970 by the leader of the People's Republic of China, Mao Tse-tung (1894-1976), envisioning the world as being politically divided into three worlds (tripolarity): the People's Republic of China leading the underdeveloped nations, the Soviet Union leading the developing nations (mainly those of the socialist bloc), and the United States, as a superpower, leading the developed (mainly capitalistic) nation-states. This strategic geopolitical concept was presented at the United Nations in 1974 by Chinese representatives, but it was not received with enthusiasm for the following reasons: (1) such division into spheres of influence obviously implies political hegemony, a form of domination which most nations find repugnant, particularly those which have just emerged from under such hegemony (e.g., the African states and other third-world countries); (2) considering the aspect of race, there is no tangible empirical evidence which would indicate a good rapport between black Africa and yellow Asia; (3) hegemony is not something that one proclaims or announces as a matter of public policy. It is something that one tries to accomplish subtly, covertly, without public pronouncements; and (4) the two major superpowers (the Soviet Union and the United States) were very comfortable with their bipolar arrangements and were not anxious to share their omnipotence with a third party because: (a) that would imply a status of equality; (b) it would require an eventual sharing of military and economic technologies and resources; and (c) it could lead to the minimization of inter-bloc conflict (e.g., reduce the need for armaments and war-tension which the infrastructures of both major superpowers need in order to please their elites, especially the military and the technostructure). Furthermore, the United States, whose currency (the dollar) is the "blood" which to a great extent determines the "health" of the economic systems of the world, will not voluntarily relinquish that position; and the Soviet Union, which struggled to be the repository of scientific Marxism-Leninism and Socialist know-how on governance, dissolved in 1991. See THREE PEOPLE'S PRINCIPLES.

Throw the Rascal Out! A slogan in response to officials in the United States elected to the U.S. Congress (House or Senate), state legislatures, county commissions, or city councils, whose services no longer satisfy voters. Voters in turn decide to remove them from office by not voting for them during the next election. This is the ultimate power voters have over elected officials, short of a difficult to obtain petition of recall. See REASONABLE CONTEMPORANEOUSNESS RULE.

Tiananmen Square Massacre. Inspired by China's attempt to revive economic activity by limiting central planning and an experimentation with private production and marketing, over 100,000 students from schools in the Beijing area gathered on the Tiananmen Square on 4 May 1989, demanding further reforms mainly in the areas of open expression and association. The students and their followers were emboldened by the first visit to China of Soviet president Mikhail S. Gorbachev, 15-18 May 1989. After Gorbachev's departure, the Chinese Army moved against the demonstrators of "China Spring" and picnickers on 3-4 June 1989, removing them by force. There were an estimated 10,000 killed and a larger number arrested and imprisoned, including the brave "yellow birds" who were stopping tanks with their bodies, as well as those who were risking their life and freedom by reciting western slogans for freedom and democracy. Included among them were readings from the American Declaration of Independence, President Lincoln's Gettysburg Address, and the display of miniature replicas of the Statue of Liberty.

Ticket. In the French language, "stick together." Also, an alliance among two or more politicians to run as partners during an election for public offices; a ballot on which the candidates for election to public offices are listed according to party affiliation; or a slate of candidates for election to public offices as presented by a political organization (e.g., a political party). See PRIMARY ELECTION.

Ticket Balancing. See BALANCED TICKET.

Ticket Punching. In the language of bureaucracy, everywhere, the prevailing attitude to do the things one is expected to do with effort and dedication sufficient for the next promotion or retirement with pension.

Tilden-Hayes Dispute. See HAYES-TILDEN DISPUTE.

Tinh. An administrative subdivision, a province, in Vietnam.

Tippecanoe and Tyler Too. A popular campaign slogan of William Henry Harrison, U.S. President for two months, March-April, 1841 (he died in office), and his running mate for Vice President, John Tyler, that was widely repeated during the 1840 campaign.

Toilers, Unite! See POPULIST.

Tokyo Rose. See TREASON.

Tolkatch. In the Russian language, "lobbyist," "pusher," or "arranger." Also, one who can expedite matters because of his knowledge of the bureaucratic procedures in the vast bureaucratic apparatus of the Soviet government. Such persons, as a rule, are concealed on the payroll of agencies under such titles as "researcher," or "special projects expediter." Their job is to see to it that the agency or enterprise acquires all the necessary materials or supplies that may be necessary under a production plan to earn a bonus or just simply to fulfill the quota imposed by the planning agency under the Five-Year-Plan arrangements.

Tomb of the Well-Known Warrior. See WHITE HOUSE.

Tonkin Gulf Resolution. See GULF OF TONKIN RESOLUTION.

Tontons Macoutes. Once a clandestine intelligence and security organization under the Haitian president François Duvalier "Papa Doc" (1957-1971) and his son, Jean Claude Duvalier or "Baby Doc" (In 1964, "Papa Doc" had been "elected" as "president-for-life." His son, who succeeded him, was deposed in 1986.) The Macoutes attempted to stage a coup in January 1991, but were unsuccessful. The group, about 5,000 strong, engages, by clandestine means, in gangsterism and terrorist activities aimed at material enrichment rather than as a grab for political power.

Too Dirty a Game for Anyone but a Gentleman to Play. See ALL NEWS IS BAD NEWS—IF IT IS ABOUT US!

Tools of Analysis of a Politically Organized Society. The factors of race, class and ethnicity—are the three major tools of analysis of a given society as a whole. See ETHNICITY.

Tools of Government. As common practice indicates, in order for a government to function and operate on a day-to-day basis, the following tools or instruments are necessary: (1) a constitution (or any basic, normative law), (2) an electorate (the voters who will elect public officials and thus review periodically the policies of the government), (3) a legislature (law-making body), (4) an executive (who will implement these laws), (5) a judiciary (which will interpret these laws), and (6) political parties (which will expedite the implementation of public policies and political processes by means of competition in bidding for power).

Tooth for a Tooth, an Eye for an Eye. See HAMMURABI CODE.

Torrijos-Carter Treaty. See PANAMA CANAL TREATIES.

Tort. Any wrongful act of a civil nature not involving a breach of contract.

Tory. Another name for the Conservative party of Great Britain. Also, the Royalists who opposed the American war for independence during the 1770s and remained loyal to King George III of England.

Total Liberty for Black People or Total Destruction for America. See BLACK PANTHER PARTY FOR SELF-DEFENSE.

Totalitarian Capitalism. See DEMOCRATIC CAPITALISM.

Totalitarian State. A state in which all executive, legislative, and judicial powers are centrally controlled by one person or by a collective; where there is usually only one political party, the ruling party; where personal and political rights and liberties of the individual are subjected to limitations as determined by the authority of the governing instrument (the government) within the state; where the maximum of efficiency and the minimum of waste is demanded and backed by laws; where the dignity and the worth of the individual is determined by the governing agent or agents (the party and the government); and where the interest of the state is paramount and the interest of the individual person is secondary. Totalitarianism is a characteristic mode of role under Communism, Fascism, Nazism, or Caesarism.

Totalitarian Theory. See ROLE OF STATE.

Totalitarianism. See TOTALITARIAN STATE.

Totis Belli. See TOTIS VIRIBUS.

Totis Viribus. In the Latin language, "with all the might" or "total war."

Totus Tuus. See AGGIORNAMENTO.

Tower Commission. See IRAN-CONTRA AFFAIR.

Town Meeting. A type of self-government in which the people (once restricted to adult males) gather together and make all decisions for a given community. (Common form of local government in New England settlements among the early immigrants from Europe to the North American continent.)

Townshend Revenue Act. In order to control revolutionary activity in North America and acquire additional revenue for covering the expenses of such controls, England's Chancellor of the Exchequer, Charles Townshend, issued an order requiring the colonists to pay import duties on such items as glass, tea, oil, paints, paper, and lead. The expected yearly revenue was about 40,000 pounds. The Massachusetts legislature (February 11, 1768) and the Virginia House of Burgesses (May 16, 1769) issued resolutions opposing England's right to tax the colonies. Virginia's Governor dissolved the House of Burgesses as a result of this protest, but the House met in secrecy until the Revolution. The colonies agreed to boycott all British goods imported. This led to several clashes between British troops and the colonies, one of which culminated in the "Boston Massacre" on March 5, 1770, in which British troops killed five colonists in Boston. Samuel Adams and Paul Revere denounced this as "massacre." The Townshend Act was repealed on April 12, 1770, on all goods except tea. England's King George III approved (May 10, 1773) the Tea Act passed by Parliament as a measure to save the East India company from bankruptcy and to undersell American tea merchants. In answer to this, the colonist revolutionaries staged the "Tea Party" in Boston when a group of men dressed as Indians boarded British ships in the harbor and dumped 342 chests containing tea into the water. As a reprisal to the "Boston Tea Party," the British monarch approved the "Intolerable Acts" aimed at making the colonists pay the sum of 18,000 pounds for the damaged tea; the Boston port was to be closed until the fine was paid in full; public meetings without the consent of the Governors of the colonies were banned; colonists were required to house British troops in private houses. These acts in turn led to the call, first by Rhode Island then by New York, for a meeting—the First Continental Congress—in Philadelphia on September 5, 1774, at which a declaration of ten rights was issued, among them the right to life, liberty and property, the right to peaceably assemble, and to petition the King. Patrick Henry of Virginia declared on March 23, 1775, "Give me liberty or give me death."

Toyota's Just-in-Time Production. See TOYOTA'S PRODUCTION SYSTEM.

Toyota's Production System. A modern successful production model that was developed by the Toyota Car Company in post-W.W.II Japan—widely copied around the world today—which consists of two principal components: (1) "just-in-time production"—keeping inventory of spare parts to the bare minimum so that no time and space will be wasted on storage and discarding of bad parts, saving space and overstock. Obviously, the spare part cannot be defective so that production will not be disrupted; and (2) a "total quality control," known as "autonomation," begins with having machines programmed to stop if a defect is found and continues as every employee is commanded to look for defects almost religiously. Once a defect is found, production stops and does not resume until and unless the error is eliminated and quality output is achieved. Quality control is total and adhered to by all employees in concert. A defective product is not a product, it is scrap and as such will not go to the consumer. The Japanese slogan for such total control is "muri, muda, mura," in the American language, "excess, waste, unevenness." These are the three obstacles to good production and a quality product. In contrast, according to Professor Robert Hogan of the University of Tulsa (as explained by Earl Ubell, *Parade Magazine*, 10 May 1992), 60 to 75 percent of American managers are incompetent, and he puts them in three categories: (1) the arrogant manager, one "who knows-it-all, and one who only makes sporadic, uneven, unsystematic impacts on employees; (2) the charmer, one who is rather lazy, popular and unthreatening and therefore survives; and (3) the passive aggressive, pleasant, with good social skills, but vicious and revengeful once criticized by employees. There are no poor employees, poor soldiers, or poor students (personal handicaps aside), but only poor managers, poor generals, and poor teachers—poor leaders unless the power and authority to lead is taken away from them. "Bad management is a principle cause of stress in the workplace," points out Dr. Hogan, and "It also is costly: Employees get ill, complain and don't perform." In the case of a classroom teacher the situation is somewhat more tragic in America. Most teachers are totally deprived of any degree of disciplinary control of their classroom clients, often to the degree of danger to their personal safety.

Teachers can teach but cannot require a student to learn, because they cannot impose disciplinary measures. At the pre-university level, ninety percent is discipline and ten percent is learning. Learning discipline is also an important knowledge. The old adage that one can bring the horse to water but, cannot make it drink is only half true. The whole truth is that if the horse is kept long enough, it will, with time, get thirsty and drink. Teachers must have the power to keep the horse by the water. However, the most dedicated teachers just as the workers on the assembly lines, are often stifled in their efforts to achieve quality because of the poor management system in which they are expected to produce quality. The world's most renowned authority on total quality control, the man who advised Japanese companies after W.W.II, among them Toyota, how to achieve quality, and who is now gaining popularity among American managers (e.g., Ford Motor Company, IBM, Xerox, AT&T, and hundreds of other successful enterprises in the U.S. and abroad), Dr. W. Edwards Deming, points out that dedication to total quality ought to begin at an early age, in school. Each year, the Japanese award the "Deming Prize," a most prestigious and coveted prize, to a company which can demonstrate its dedication and commitment to total quality control.

Toyota's Total Quality Control. See TOYOTA'S PRODUCTION SYSTEM.

Tractorcade. A nationwide motorcade (using tractors and other moving farm vehicles) organized by American farmers during the winter months of 1977-1978 to protest the low prices for their agricultural commodities (products) and to demand parity laws that would equalize the prices for their products with those produced by other industries. Several thousand farmers gathered in Washington D.C., where they were received by members of Congress and President Carter who listened to their grievances and promised legislative and executive action. One group of Virginia farmers carried a sign which read: "Born naked, wet, cold, and hungry. Whoever thought it would get worse?" See SHAY'S REBELLION.

Trade Deficit. See BALANCE OF PAYMENTS.

Trade-off. In decision making, the choices that one may make among several possible alternatives (e.g., choosing one course of action at the expense of another).

Trade Sanctions. A practice by a state to impose trade restrictions, or a blockade on imports and exports, against another state or group of states who are considered hostile or otherwise detrimental to the interest of the state. The United States, under various executive and legislative acts (e.g., the "Trading with the Enemy Act"), has the authority to impose such sanctions as well as lift them at will, by even granting a favorite trading status. Such trade sanctions are today in effect against Libya, Iraq, and Cuba. In February 1992, sanctions imposed against the Peoples Republic of China were lifted.

Trade Union Mentality. A term once used by Vladimir I. Lenin of Russia to describe those who preferred to bargain for social and political reforms rather than bring them about themselves by revolutionary means.

Trading with the Enemy Act of 1917, as Amended. This act outlawed trade with Germany and called for censorship of all publications exchanged between the United States and foreign countries. Subsequently, the Sedition Act of 1918, provided for penalties against persons who said anything derogatory about the U.S. government, the flag, the U.S. Constitution, or the uniforms of the U.S. Army and the Navy. Most recent updating of this legislation forbade trade with Cuba, Iraq, Libya, and North Korea. There were more restrictions on the American law books as to trade and travel restrictions with other countries, but they faded away with the advance of reason, education, advance in intelligence quotient (IQ), and political sophistication.

Tradition. A set of ideas, ideals, customs, practices, and institutions which are considered useful and appropriate over an extensive period of time (e.g., one or more generations).

Traditional Authority. See AUTHORITY.

Traditional Political Theory. See POLITICAL THEORY.

Traditional Power. See INFORMAL POWER.

Trail of Tears. With the expanding settlement of Southern, South-Western, and Western territories in the United States, many of the Indian tribes, unwilling to accommodate themselves with the invading Europeans, were forced to abandon their lands, in spite of numerous treaties that were signed with the U.S. Government and subsequently broken. Hundreds of thousands of American Indians perished in combat with the invading American military forces. The Cherokees, Seminoles, Chickasaws, Choctaws, and Creeks were forced to move, i.e., march, to reservations west of the Mississippi from the 1820s through the 1840s, and suffered greatly from disease, starvation, cold climate, and mistreatment. The route along which this migration took place is referred to as the "Trail of Tears." Following the War of Secession (Civil War) of 1860-1865, some of the Cherokee people returned to their land, particularly to North Carolina, because President Lincoln insisted that Indian tribes, like other people, including African-Americans, ought to be free and settle wherever they wished.

Train the Nation to Manage its Own Affairs. See REVOLUTION FROM ABOVE.

Train v. City of New York. See IMPOUNDED LEGISLATION.

Transactional Leadership. See LEADERSHIP BY PULLING.

Transafrica. An organization concerned with blacks in Africa. Loosely organized, and supported by American black leaders such as the Rev. Jesse Jackson and former U.S. Ambassador to the UN, and member of Congress, Andrew Young.

Transcendental Individualism. A philosophical-religious movement with strong implications on politics in America during the 1930s. It originated in the German universities and it rejected materialism of all forms and shapes; it considered the cotton mill as the most degrading to the human mind; it rejected empiricism (the methods of acquiring scientific evidence), and turned instead to intuition; it rejected rationalism which was so well nourished by Jefferson and Paine. The transcendentalists found in man three distinct attributes: (1) understanding—the faculty of dealing with sense and perception from which empirical knowledge of facts is derived, as the foundation of science; (2) reason—the intuitive faculty with which man could transcend sense experience and grasp immediately the ultimate truth; and (3) experience—which is man's consciousness of the conscience of God, through which man's action could be kept in line with divine and social justice. This movement delayed the rational approach to political thinking and political analysis for about three decades; blinding man's ability to better understand political phenomena.

Transcendentalism. A notion in philosophy pertaining to that which is unknown to the human mind, which is beyond the reach and the realm of the senses.

Transfer Payments. Payments in return for which no good or service is currently received—for example, welfare or Social Security payments or money sent to relatives abroad.

Transfer Technology. See INTERDEPENDENCE, TECHNOLOGY EXPORT.

Transform or Decline. Throughout the history of civilization, once great ideals and institutions (e.g., governments or even business and management organizations) declined, or even dissolved not because of change, but because of reluctance to change; the perpetual motion-like course of human events dictate systematic transformation, and any attempt to arrests history, whether under such totalitarian systems as fascism, nazism, or communism, is only a temporary expedient.

Transforming Leadership. See LEADERSHIP BY PULLING.

Transient Majority. A political force in a society which emerges suddenly, unexpectedly, often as a result of popularity of the issue which it presents (e.g., the prohibition forces in the United States, or the "red scare" forces), and which after a brief time recedes into a minority or ceases entirely to function as a political force (e.g., the black militant movement of the 1960s in the United States). Sophisticated political electorates, in order to avoid the problem of having them undone in the future, ordinarily do not allow such transient majorities to introduce major changes within the existing politico-economic-legal institutions. See TYRANNY OF THE MAJORITY.

Transition Act of 1973. See PRESIDENTIAL TRANSITION.

Transmission Belt. A term applied by Vladimir I. Lenin, leader of the Bolsheviks in Russia, to political parties, which, in his opinion, are nothing but a link connecting the masses with their government. This remark was made in reference to communist-type political parties only.

Transnational Corporation. A business enterprise operating in one or more nations devoid of any political, economic, or cultural loyalty or attachment; an entity once characterized by cartoonist and humorist Gerry Trudeau as that which ". . . swears allegiance to the country that gives it the best deal." See MULTINATIONAL CORPORATION.

Transnational Law. See VOLUNTAS CIVITATIS MAXIMAE EST SERVANDA.

Transnational State. See SUPRANATIONAL STATE.

Transplant Industry. With the growing number of multinational and transnational corporations, many foreign industries transplant their production to other countries where they deploy know-how capital and management, and the host country provides the facilities, infrastructure, and labor.

Treason. The highest felonious, heinous (hateful and atrocious) crimes that one can commit against the state or its government by joining in rebellion or insurrection against the authority of the state (the government) or by giving aid and comfort to the enemy. (See Article III, Sec. 3, of U.S. Constitution in Appendix 8 for a definition.) Aaron Burr, U.S. Vice President (1801-1805) was charged with treason in 1806 but was not tried due to lack of witnesses. In recent history, the most publicized case of treason was that of Iva Toguri D'Aquino, or "Tokyo Rose," a Japanese-American from California who went to Japan during World War II and broadcast anti-American programs to U.S. military forces in the Pacific. She was tried and convicted in 1949, receiving a ten-year sentence and a fine of $10,000. She was pardoned from the burden and the stigma of the crime by President Gerald R. Ford (1974-1977) on January 20, 1977, the President's last day in office—a midnight pardon! William Joyce, known as "Lord Haw Haw" (an American of British extraction, who collaborated with Nazi Germany, broadcasting pro-Nazi propaganda from Berlin, Germany), was tried and convicted of treason after World War II. See BURR CONSPIRACY.

Treaty. According to Article 2, of the *Vienna Convention on the Law of Treaties* of May 23, 1969, ". . . treaty means an international agreement concluded between states in written form and governed by international law, whether embodied in a single instrument or in two or more related instruments and whatever its particular designation." Treaties may be concluded between two states (bilateral treaty) or among many states (multilateral treaty); they require ratification by the sovereign authority of the concluding states (U.S. Senate in the case of the United States—see U.S. Constitution, Art. I.—where treaties constitute an integral part of the laws of the land); treaties establish new rights and obligations ordinarily to the parties involved; unlike customary rules of international law, treaties are the primary source of law; they must be observed and may be abrogated only upon mutual consent of the parties. As of the beginning of 1992, U.S. concluded 956 treaties and agreements. See EXECUTIVE AGREEMENT, PACTA SUNT SERVANDA, REBUS SIC STANTIBUS.

Treaty Concerning the Permanent Neutrality and Operation of the Panama Canal. See PANAMA CANAL TREATIES.

Treaty for the Renunciation of War. See KELLOG-BRIAND PACT.

Treaty of Berlin. See RAPALLO TREATY.

Treaty of Ghent. See WAR OF 1812.

Treaty of Paris of 1898. This treaty concluded the Spanish-Cuban-American War of 1898 and granted the United States, as the victor, the territories of Guam, the Philippine Islands, and Puerto Rico.

Treaty of Portsmouth of 1905. U.S. President Theodore Roosevelt (1901-1909) extended his good offices to warring Japan and Russia, and on September 5, 1905, a peace treaty was signed in Portsmouth, New Hampshire. Roosevelt was awarded the Nobel Peace Prize for his efforts (first prize ever to be awarded in this category).

Treaty of Rapallo. See RAPALLO TREATY.

Treaty of Reciprocal Assistance. See RIO TREATY.

Treaty of Washington of 1871. An agreement signed between England and the United States by which England agreed to pay $15,500,000 for damages caused to U.S. commerce on the high seas.

Triad. The three major and aggressive economies of United Europe, Japan, and the United States, characterized by what author Ohmae calls interlinkage. The triad is joined by the Mini-Tigers. Also, numerous organizations and societies, some less open than others, some political, economic, social, religious, charitable or criminal (popular in many Asian societies, mainly China.) See AMERICA BASHING, MINI DRAGONS.

Triad Society. See SECRET SOCIETIES.

Trial by Jury. See GRAND JURY.

Trial Lawyers Association. Professional association, pressure group to protect lawyers' economic interests.

Tribalism. An ideology and a way of life as well as governance among mainly primal societies, such as the Indians in both Americas, groups of tribal people in Asia, Africa, and in Oceania. Tribalism is either paternalistic or maternalistic—ruled by a male or a female. This principal leader often serves as the high priest and a physician at the same time.

Tribalistic Doctrine. See PAN-SOMALISM.

Tribunaux d'Instance. A court of "first instance" in France. (Local court of record with original jurisdiction.)

Tribunaux de Grande Instance. A higher court in France. (District court of record with original jurisdiction which also may, in some instances, hear cases on appeal from local courts.)

Tribune. A magistrate in ancient Rome elected for the purpose of overseeing and protecting the interests of the underprivileged masses of plebeians against the abuses by the privileged patricians. Also, one of the six military commanders of the Roman Legions holding the position of commander-in-chief of the armed forces for one year on a rotating basis.

Tricameral Parliament. Legislative branch of government of South Africa which consists of three chambers: the House of Assembly (white), House of Representatives (coloreds), and House of Delegates (Indians).

Trickle-down Theory. A theoretical assumption in a capitalist economy that if sufficient funds are made available to private business and if legislation is investor-friendly, then the economic life will be revived and benefits will flow down to the smallest enterprise as well as to the individual consumer. U.S. President John F. Kennedy (1961-1963) often cited the "two boats theory" according to which, once the waters are stabilized (with the inflow of capital and consumer confidence in the economy), the large boat as well as the little boat will derive expected outcomes. What President failed to mention (and nobody has done since) is what happens when the waters become very stormy (recession or inflation). What will happen to the little boat? Will the little boat, which is owned by one who borrowed money from a bank to purchase it, have the same chances of survival as the large boat which is owned by those who also own a bank? Will sketchy and sporadic tax incentives serve well the trickle-down economy? To paraphrase a statement made by Mortimer B. Zuckerman, editor-in-chief of *U.S. News & World Report* (16 March 1992), the effects of the current theory of trickle-down economy will be such that the jockey will receive all the benefits and nothing will go to the horse, and, at the end, the jockey will become too fat for the horse to take him to the desired destination. Many of the presidential contenders during the 1992 campaign have suddenly noted that the "middle class" is shrinking. During the Reagan years (1981-1989), five percent of the people in America controlled eighty percent of the income, and during the Bush administration (1989-), one percent controlled sixty percent of the income. The positive outcome of a sketchy tax incentive may not be sufficient to recover the economic equilibrium of the nation. Is there anything for the horse, that Mr. Zuckerman writes about?

Trilateral Commission. A policy-planning group of "private citizens of Western Europe, Japan, and North America" which was organized in 1973 by David Rockefeller of the Chase Manhattan Bank in New York City to generate information about the three geographic areas, their political systems and economies, and to render mutual assistance in problem solving. One of its co-founders, Dr. Zbigniew K. Brzezinski of Columbia University, who served as former President Carter's Adviser for National Security Affairs, described the philosophy of the Commission as "reformist and internationalist." Proceeding on the assumption that "demands on democratic government have grown" while at the same time "the capacity to meet them has shrunk," the Commission aimed, through its intellectual activities, to aid the less-developed countries by rendering the political structures in the advanced democracies more durable and effective. Some of its members who were connected with the Carter administration were: Cyrus Vance, Secretary of State; Walter Mondale, Vice President; W. Michael Blumenthal, Secretary of Treasury; Harold Brown, Secretary of Defense; and J. Paul Austin, Chairman of Coca-Cola Company.

Trim Down, America, Trim Down!. See PUT AMERICA ON DIET.

Tripartite. By, for, or of three parties; or among three parties.

Tripartite Agreement on Middle East. The United States, England, and France signed an agreement in 1950 not to provide the Arab and the Israeli states with heavy weapons and weapon systems, and to limit sales to small arms, such as those needed for internal police forces. Obviously, that did not hold for long.

Tripartite Pact of Berlin. On September 27, 1940, Nazi Germany, Fascist Italy, and Militarist Japan signed a Tripartite Pact in Berlin, Germany, by which they acknowledged their hegemonies over certain geographic areas of the world: Germany over Europe; Italy over Southern Europe and North Africa; and Japan over Asia. Japan was to conquer Asia and eliminate any western influence there (mainly the British) by closing the "Burma Road" that linked Asia with the outside world. They agreed to "assist one another with all political, economic and military means." See AXIS, LEBENSRAUM.

Triple Alliance. A military alliance formed among Austria-Hungary, Germany, and Italy in 1882 for the purpose of mutual protection against possible aggression by France, Russia, or England.

Triple Entente. A formal understanding between Great Britain, Russia, and France (in 1907) on mutual cooperation in counterbalancing the aims of the TRIPLE ALLIANCE formed by Austria, Hungary, Germany and Italy in 1882. Each of the Entente powers had definite reasons for entering into the alliance: England feared the rapidly growing industrial capacity of Germany; France was under constant fear of Germany and was seeking revenge; and Russia feared Austro-Hungarian influence in the Balkan area. All feared that the TRIPLE ALLIANCE would upset the international balance of power. See ENTENTE CORDIALE.

Tripolarity. See THREE WORLDS.

Tripoli War. The Tripoli ruler, the Pasha, declared war on all U.S. shipping in that area and demanded extortion payments for passage from ship captains. Such a payment was made once in 1798, but in 1801 U.S President Thomas Jefferson (1801-1809) refused to make such payments and instead sent U.S. Marines to confront the pirates. The war ended with the Treaty of 1805. See BARBARY PIRATES.

Triumphalism. A term used by liberal politicians in the United States to characterize those, mostly Republicans, who supported American involvement in the Persian Gulf War against Iraq's Saddam Hussein in 1991, and to characterize the way they boasted about the glory of the policies of President George Bush.

Triumvirate. See TROIKA.

Troika. In the Russian language, any combination of "three" things. As applied to international politics, the proposal once advanced by former Premier of the former Soviet Union, Nikita S. Khrushchev, to replace the office of the Secretary-General of the United Nations Organization with three persons having equal authority. Also, the top leadership in the Soviet Union, composed of the Secretary of the Communist Party of the Soviet Union (CPSU), the Chairman of the Council of Ministers of the USSR (the Premier of the Government-of-the-day), and the Chairman of the Supreme Soviet of the USSR (The Soviet Parliament). This triumvirate (rule by three persons or a coalition of three parties) lasted in the USSR until 1977, when the leader of the CPSU, Leonid Brezhneyev, adopted the title of President of the USSR while retaining the position of the General-Secretary of the CPSU.

Trojan Horse. A term often used in practical politics to describe deceitful practices (i.e., the infiltration of enemy troops or agents into the territory of another state for hostile purposes). The term is taken from Homer's *Iliad*, in which a huge, hollow, wooden horse filled with Greek soldiers was placed at the gates of the besieged city of Troy. The curious Trojans brought the horse inside the city and soon forgot about it. At night, the Greek soldiers came out of the wooden horse, opened the gates of Troy, and allowed the Greek army to come in and conquer the city.

Troppau Congress. See QUADRUPLE ALLIANCE.

Trotskyite. One who subscribes to the philosophy of Leon Trotsky and his brand of communism, mainly to the notion of "permanent revolution." See PERMANENT REVOLUTION.

Truancy. See JUVENILE DELINQUENCY.

Truce. An agreement on the temporary cessation of hostilities between belligerents for a certain purpose (e.g., to observe a holiday or to collect the bodies of the dead). See WAR.

True Bill. The indictment that may be sustained by a grand jury when sufficiently supported by evidence at hand. See INDICTMENT, JURY.

True Peace. Israel's concept of lasting peace which is possible only if it is based on full diplomatic, cultural, and commercial relations with the Arab neighbor-states, namely Jordan, Syria, and the Arab Republic of Egypt. See ISRAELI SETTLEMENTS, SADAT-BEGIN SUMMIT.

Truman Doctrine. In the main, the aid granted to Greece and Turkey after World War II in order to prevent the communist forces (supported by the Soviet Union) from taking control of their governments. On March 12, 1947, U.S. President Harry S. Truman received congressional authorization to extend 400 million dollars in aid to Greece and Turkey. This program was announced on June 5, 1947, and it aimed, in a broader scope, at aiding nations devastated by the war in rebuilding their economies. The Soviet Union and the East European states under Soviet domination denounced this aid as a plot by the United States to extend its domination.

Truman's Loyalty Order. See LOYALTY LAWS.

Trust. The newly established Soviet state, in 1917-1918, encountered considerable resistance from the former tsarist elements, called The "Whites," and their allies in the West. (The Bolsheviks led by Lenin, the communists, were called "Reds.") The Soviet Red Army engaged in terrorism during the "War Communism" period, but V. I. Lenin, the founder and the leader of the new Soviet state, was unable to cope with the opposition and decided to relax the situation by the New Economic Policy (NEP) program. Faithful to his unique strategy of "two steps forward, one step back," (the title of one of his books) and to the teaching of the ancient Chinese philosopher, war strategist and intelligence pioneer, Su Tzu, Lenin set up a deception scheme in order to weaken internal and external opposition to his new regime. This was done under the direction of Feliks Dzierzynski, the Polish nobleman who was a trusted collaborator of Lenin and founder of the Cheka—the secret police and intelligence organization (renamed several times, the latest as the KGB). Dzierzynski set up the fictitious counterrevolutionary, anti-Lenin organization known as "Trust," which was to let its members in Russia and abroad believe that they would overthrow the Bolshevik regime. Russian émigrés abroad received considerable monetary and logistical support, particularly in Britain, and the British top agent, Sidney Riley, was the principal leader of the Trust. The deceptive operation lasted from 1922 to 1927 during which time the Cheka of Dzierzynski depleted the Trust of large sums of money; rounded up all of its leaders, followers, and sympathizers; and not only disorganized them by confusing and disrupting their strategy and tactics, but also eliminated the intelligence assets of all western powers in Russia; gained influence abroad; and killed about 3,000 to 30,000 opponents of the Soviet system.

This was the largest and the most successful deception operation in modern times, and Western intelligence did not recover from it until the Soviet state dissolved in 1991. Su Tzu, sixth century BC, was the author of *The Art of War*, translated from the Chinese by Samuel B. Griffith, Oxford University Press. In this book, first published about 2,500 years ago, Su, like Niccolo Machiavelli, advises leaders on statesmanship and governance, and on the art of war and intelligence. This early founding father of intelligence advises leaders to gain foreknowledge of the adversary, the best means being covert action (espionage) and deception (counterespionage). The most important tactic is to disrupt the enemy's strategy, then disrupt his alliance, and then, if necessary, attack and kill him and his forces. However, killing is the last resort and not always advisable, because a good leader should win a war by deception short of killing. Su differs from modern strategist Karl von Clausewitz who advocates killing first and asking questions second (*On War*, edited and translated by Michael Howard and Peter Peret, Princeton University Press). Lenin used the tactics as suggested by Su, the American Rangers (See "Standing Orders, Rogers' Rangers," Appendix 30), and his own notion of guerrilla warfare. These proved to be the most successful and widely used methods employed by revolutionaries during this century. See DECEPTION, GUERRILLA WARFARE, INTELLIGENCE.

Trust Busting. A term associated with U.S. President Theodore Roosevelt who was instrumental in bringing about forty antimonopoly suits requiring large corporations to divest themselves of holdings that tended to stifle free competition. President Roosevelt utilized his powers under the *Sherman Antitrust Act* of 1890.

Trust Fund. A fund, designated as a trust fund by statute, that is credited with income from earmarked collections and charged with certain outlays. Collections may come from the public (for example, taxes or user charges) or from intra-budgetary transfers. More than 150 federal government trust funds exist, of which the largest and best known finance several major benefit programs (including Social Security and Medicare) and certain infrastructure spending (the Highway and the Airport and Airway trust funds). The term "federal funds" refers to all programs that are not trust funds.

Trust Territory. The act of placing a non-sovereign territory under the supervision of another state for the purpose of guidance and protection. Such a trust can be granted by some international authority (e.g., the United Nations or, prior to it, the League of Nations). Namibia, South-West Africa. Given to South Africa under League of Nations mandate after lost by Germany in W.W.I, South Africa refused to return to United Nations jurisdiction after World War II. Other trust territories are: The Pacific Islands (Micronesia) of Northern Mariana Caroline and Marshall Islands (which became Strategic Territories under U.S. administration, approved by the UN Security Council on April 2, 1947, approved by U.S. President and ratified by Congress on July 18, 1947. See AUTONOMY, COMMONWEALTH, SOUTH-WEST AFRICA PEOPLE'S ORGANIZATION (SWAPO), Appendix 75.

Trustee Electoral Board. A body of from three to five persons appointed by the local judge (e.g., Circuit Court Judge in a county or a city) for the purpose of selecting and appointing officials to specialized agencies of a local government (e.g., members of a school board).

Trusteeship Council. See UNITED NATIONS ORGANIZATION.

Truth-in-Landing Law. See CAVEAT EMPTOR.

Truth-in-Lending. Congressional legislation of 1968 that requires creditors to disclose the conditions of credit extended to consumers.

Truth Squads. In January 1978 a coalition of opponents to the Panama Canal Treaty organized a campaign by sending distinguished persons from the U.S. Congress, scholars, and business people (known as "Truth Squads") to speak in communities around the country and to urge people to appeal to the U.S. Senate to reject that treaty. Some of the leaders of the coalition were U.S. Senators Paul Laxalt (R-Nevada) and Jack Gam (R-Utah). The effect of the Squads on the Senate was limited, because an amendment to the treaty, proposing an extension of American military control over the Canal, was rejected by the Senate on February 27, 1978. See PANAMA CANAL TREATIES.

Tsar (or Czar). The official title of the ruler of Russia prior to 1917. A term often associated with a despotic or absolute ruler. (A female Tsar was referred to as "Tsaritza"; a son of the Tsar or Tsaritza, "Tsarevitch"; and the wife of a Tsar, "Tsarina.")

Tuna War. During the 1970s many nations began to challenge the traditional three-mile limit on territorial waters. Peru, for example, declared in 1972 a 200-mile limit and attempted to prevent all fishing for tuna within 200 miles from its shore. This led to several incidents with tuna fishing fleets, many of which have been detained by Peru and heavily fined. See COD WAR, TERRITORIAL WATERS.

Tupac Amaru. A Marxist revolutionary group pursuing traditional communist doctrines in gaining economic and political power in contemporary Peru in close collaboration with the pro-Mao revolutionary group of skillful guerrillas, the Shining Path. Both of these groups aim to replace a corrupt system, particularly the land-owning aristocracy and their latifundium system, and to distribute the land to peasants who live in poverty. The landed aristocracy together with corrupt politicians maintain the opposition system against the Shining Path and the Tupac Amaru mainly through death squad terror. In 1980 a new constitution was introduced, patterned on the American Constitution. (Its text was widely distributed throughout Peru for the masses to read—few of whom are literate—and the text was even published in telephone directories, but never became part of the academic curriculum in schools.) After centuries of military dictatorship, government was returned to civilians. However, the lack of reforms, particularly land reforms; led to rebellion by the masses. President Alberto Fujimori responded by suspending the constitution and disbanding the parliament, and thus returned the troubled land to dictatorship once more. Obviously, a garrison state will not be able to contain the rebellion of the guerrillas because they find strong support among the hungry and destitute, and land reform is the only rational way to defuse the conflict. See SHINING PATH.

Turkish Motherland Party. See MOTHERLAND PARTY.

Turkish Social Democratic Party. See MOTHERLAND PARTY.

Turn the Rascals Out. See LIBERAL REPUBLICAN PARTY.

Turner's Rebellion. Nat Turner, a black preacher and insurrectionist, rose in 1831 killing 57 white persons in Southampton County, Virginia. He was caught, tried, and executed.

Tutelary Democracy. A transitory political system allowing little freedom or liberty while building democratic institutions. See DEMOCRACY, GUIDED DEMOCRACY.

TVA. See TENNESSEE VALLEY AUTHORITY.

Tweede Kamer. Lower chamber of the legislature, the Second Chamber of States General of the Netherlands. See EERSTE KAMER, STATEN GENERAAL.

Tweed Machine. See POLITICAL MACHINE.

Twenty Committee. See SECRET INTELLIGENCE SERVICE (SIS).

Twenty Years of Treason. See MCCARTHYISM.

Two-Boats Theory. See TRICKLE-DOWN THEORY.

Two-China Policy. See SHANGHAI COMMUNIQUÉ.

Two Cows and One Bull Theory. See CAPITALISM.

Two-Cows Theory. See CAPITALISM.

Two-Pyramids Policy. See APARTHEID, PARALLEL DEVELOPMENT DOCTRINE.

Two Rivers of Blood. The first "river of blood" was caused by the Shah of Iran (1953-1979), when his secret police and intelligence, the SAVAK, arrested and killed thousands of Iranians opposing the Shah, and the second "river of blood" was a slogan by the leader of anti-shah forces, the Shiite Moslem Ayatollah Ruhollah Khomeini, calling for the abolition of the Shah. During and after the Revolution, thousands of pro-Shah or anti-Khomeini Iranians perished at home, and many other leaders were exterminated by means of assassinations abroad. See IRAN'S REVOLUTION.

Two Swords Theory. A concept applicable to the ancient rivalry between the church and the state for the supremacy of earthly powers. According to Pope Gesalius I, who developed this concept in 494, God handed down to his deputy two swords (powers)—one temporal and one ecclesiastical—both of which were to be the domain of and controlled by the Pope. Since the Pope, due to other more pressing duties, was unable to exercise them both at the same time, he had the authority to hand the temporal sword to a chosen prince or king, and by crowning him in the name of God, to grant him the authority to exercise the power of the temporal sword for good purposes. However, in case the prince or king utilized the temporal sword for purposes contrary to the good of the Church, the Pope had the power to withdraw that sword and give it to someone else. In case the prince or king refused to turn in his sword and his crown, he was subject to excommunication; and by virtue of that act, he ceased to be the rightful ruler of his subjects.

Types of Governments. A set of unique characteristics which identifies a particular type of government according to such criteria as: (1) The Locus of Sovereign Powers—which may be deposited with the electorate (as in a democratic republic), a certain small elite (as in an oligarchy), a single person (as in a dictatorship), or a single person of nobility whose power is hereditary (as in a monarchy); (2) The Nature of the Executive Organization—which may be self-appointive as in a dictatorship or oligarchy, appointive (e.g., by a legislature), hereditary nobility (e.g., monarchy), elective (e.g., president elected by the voters in a polyarchy); and (3) The Territorial Distribution of Sovereign Powers—which may be monopolized by a single person (e.g., in a monarchy or a dictatorship), a small elite (e.g., totalitarian dictatorship or an oligarchy) with little or no autonomy allotted to units by the central authority, territorially distributed on a contractual basis (of a constitution or other basic normative law) or it can be shared with other units of government (e.g., under confederation, federation, and some unitary systems with broad autonomy). See Appendices 80-82, 52-72.

Types of States. Throughout the political history of man several types of states have emerged, from the ancient city-state to feudal states, to national states, to multinational states, and some even suggest a supra-national state or a global state—one that would embrace all the nations of the world under a single authority. The notion of a supra-national or global state is being advocated by the communist doctrine and, to some extent, by the United Nations Organization. The global order under the UN auspices envisions strictly an administrative system with no particular political philosophy. States are basically constructed alike as legal entities, particularly as agents in international relations where their internal systems bear no relevance on their capacity to undertake and carry out obligations, unless the internal systems (e.g., ideology) make such interaction with other states impossible, unrewarding, or generally undesirable. (e.g., ideological differences between the United States and Cuba rendered diplomatic and trade relations undesirable as far as the United States is concerned.) See CITY-STATES, MULTINATIONAL STATE, NATIONAL STATE, STATE.

Tyranny. A dictatorial and oppressive form of government that ordinarily is exercised by a single tyrant or a group (collective) with total disregard for the laws, customs, and political and civil rights and liberties of the people.

Tyranny of the Majority. An ancient concept, dating back in recorded history to Aristotle (384-322 BC) who feared the tyranny of the majority and preferred a single noble ruler instead; Alexander Hamilton (1757-1804) who feared the masses and referred to them as the "beast"; and John C. Calhoun (1782-1850), U.S. Vice President under Andrew Jackson, who published an essay in 1828, entitled *The South Carolina Exposition*, in which he denounced federal tariffs imposed on imports (in 1816 and 1828) by the tyrannical majority of the northern states of the United States. In another work, *A Disquisition on Government*, published in 1850, Calhoun distinguished between "numerical" or "absolute majority," based on sheer numbers which can be oppressive, and "concurrent" or "constitutional majority," which is capable of placing a "negative power" or "restraining power" on the possible abuse of the numerical majority—which he also called the "single power." A single power in a state may act, but to a democratic government a restraining power is necessary, a power which prevents actions, unless concurrent consent is reached through peaceful political processes (bargaining, compromise, and reconciliation in the give and take process of politics). The existence of such powers makes for a constitutional government and allows it to maintain balances, and eliminates the use of force because democratic processes are allowed to take place. In most multiparty systems, the majority prevails, but the rights of the minority are protected and cherished as a balance, a critic, and something that keeps the party in power on guard. The minority always strives to become the majority through unseating the majority on election day. See ARISTOTLE'S CLASSIFICATION OF GOVERNMENTS in Appendix 1, FEDERALIST.

Tyranny Speech. See GIVE ME LIBERTY OR GIVE ME DEATH.

Tzar to Commissar. See RULERS OF THE SOVIET UNION.

U

"When a man assumes a public trust, he should consider himself a public property."
THOMAS JEFFERSON, 1743-1826

U2 Incident. On May 1, 1960, an American high-altitude (spy) aircraft was shot down over the Soviet Union while taking aerial photographs of Soviet military installations. The pilot, Francis Gary Powers, was taken prisoner and later exchanged for a Soviet spy in the United States, known as "Colonel Abel." The incident wrecked the planned Paris Conference to have been held between the Premier of the Soviet Union, Nikita S. Khrushchev, and the President of the United States, Dwight D. Eisenhower. The Soviets demonstrated then for the first time that they have the capacity and capability to deploy ground-to-air missiles. The "Cold War" took a turn from struggle in the sphere of ideology (without totally abandoning it) to struggle in weapon systems technology. The U-2 was used for the first time in 1956 when the French, British and the Israelis were preparing to attack Egypt after President Nasser nationalized the Suez Canal. The American pilot, Francis Gary Powers, died mysteriously in a helicopter crash in California several years after his release from Soviet prison. He was never forgiven by the American intelligence community for letting the Soviets gain some knowledge on sources and methods of U.S. Intelligence in exchange for his own life.

UAM. See UNION AFRICAINE ET MALAGACHE.

UAMCE. See UNION AFRICAINE ET MALAGACHE DE COOPÉRATION ECONOMIQUE.

UAS. See UNION OF AFRICAN STATES.

Ubi Societas, Ibi Jus. In the Latin language, "wherever there is society, there is law."

UCMJ. See UNIFORM CODE OF MILITARY JUSTICE.

UDE. See UNION DOUANIÈRE ÉQUATORIALE.

UDEAC. See L'UNION DOUANIÈRE ET ÉCONOMIQUE DE L'AFRIQUE CENTRALE.

UDI. See UNILATERAL DECLARATION OF INDEPENDENCE.

UDT. See UNION DÉMOCRATIQUE DES TRAVAILLEURS.

Ugodovshchik. In the Russian language, "an opportunist" or "materialist." Also, in official Soviet political parlance, an enemy of the working class and the Soviet state.

Ujaama. In the Kiswahili language, "familyhood," "communal life," or "communal development." A term often associated with the African concept of socialism.

Ukaz. In the Russian language, "decree" or "law."

Ultima Ratio Regum. In the Latin language, "the final words between adversaries before commencement of hostilities."

Ultimatum. The act of issuing certain definite demands and insisting on compliance within a specified period of time. In the relations between states, noncompliance with ultimatum demands may result in such retaliation as break-off of trade or diplomatic relations, abrogation of treaty obligations, or even war. See DIPLOMACY, WAR.

Ultra. The official designation for all intelligence information gathered through the enigma machine by deciphering German coded messages, which furnished the Allies with instant information on Nazi war plans, was "Ultra Secret," or "Most Secret Ultra." After the Polish intelligence passed the decoding system to the British, the British in turn did not share that information with the Americans whom they viewed as "green in intelligence matters." With time, that information was distributed to British and American leaders and military commanders in a highly controlled manner. Soviet spy, Kim Philby, had access to it and therefore so did the Soviets. It is estimated that the Ultra information allowed the Allies to win the war and shortened it by about two and half years. See ENIGMA, PURPLE.

Ultra Vires. In the Latin language, "to go beyond authority" or "to act outside the scope of authority." Also, one acting beyond the limits allowed by law.

Umbrella Agency. See UMBRELLA MULTI-JURISDICTIONAL ORGANIZATION (UMJO).

Umbrella Multi-Jurisdictional Organization (UMJO). A multi-jurisdictional organization which has area-wide comprehensive planning responsibility and policy control over one or more functional planning and policy development programs. U.S. President Gerald Ford, in his second biennial report to Congress on National Growth and Development, called for the establishment and strengthening of such multi-jurisdictional umbrella agencies for the purpose of promoting planning and coordinating by all units of government in the United States.

UMJO. See UMBRELLA MULTI-JURISDICTIONAL ORGANIZATION.

Umkhonto We Sizwe. See AFRICAN NATIONAL CONGRESS (ANC), CONFERENCE FOR DEMOCRATIC SOUTH AFRICA (CODESA).

Un-American Activities Committee. A standing (permanent) committee in the United States House of Representatives whose task was to investigate all activities which, in the Committee's opinion, tended to undermine the American system of government. In February 1969, the name of that committee was changed to Committee on National Security Affairs. See LOYALTY LAWS, MCCARTHYISM, RED MENACE.

Uncle Joe. A nickname for either Joseph G. Cannon, speaker of the U.S. House of Representatives (1903-1911), or of Josef Stalin, co-founder of the Soviet State, Secretary of the Communist Party of the Soviet Union, and Premier of the Soviet Government (1924-1953). See CANNON REVOLT, GREAT ECONOMIC DEBATE.

Uncle Sam. An affectionate nickname for the United States and its government, mainly the executive branch of the government (e.g., the President and the administrative apparatus).

Uncle Tom. A derogatory nickname for a black person who is humble, submissive, and considered a tool for the white society. The term is taken from a novel by the title of *Uncle Tom's Cabin* by Harriet B. Stowe. The term "Aunt Thomasina" denotes a female. See PEEPING THOMASINA.

Unconditional Surrender. See CASABLANCA CONFERENCE, SCHWARZE KAPELLE.

UNCTAD. See UNITED NATIONS CONFERENCE ON TRADE AND DEVELOPMENT.

Undeclared War. See ACT OF WAR.

Underclass. By U.S. federal standards, persons of employable age, without a completed high school education, without specific skills, and whose total yearly income, for a family of four persons, consists of less than $12,675. Federal and state spending on poverty reduced the ranks from 35.2 per cent of the labor force in 1959 to 11.4 per cent in 1989. See CAPITALIST MALADY OF CONTENTMENT, KERNER COMMISSION.

Underdeveloped Country. See THIRD WORLD.

Undersecretaries Committee of the National Security Council. An executive body composed of undersecretaries of the departments represented on the National Security Council, whose task is to supervise the implementation of decisions made by the Council.

Undersecretary. A federal officer ranking one step below the Secretary of a Department in the United States. See BUREAUCRACY.

UNESCO. See UNITED NATIONS EDUCATIONAL, SCIENTIFIC, AND CULTURAL ORGANIZATION, Appendices 74-79.

Unhealthy Tendencies. The Chinese Communist Party had approximately 48 million members in 1990, but almost 40,000 were expelled from the ranks for what the government termed "unhealthy tendencies" among party members and high government officials. These included among others, "ideological inadequacies" and "abuse of power." See CHISTKA, PURGE.

Unholy Alliance. See HITLER-STALIN PACT.

UNIA. See UNIVERSAL NEGRO IMPROVEMENT ASSOCIATION.

Unicameral. A legislative body composed of only one chamber. (Of the fifty states in the American Union only the state of Nebraska has a unicameral legislature).

UNICEF. See UNITED NATIONS INTERNATIONAL CHILDREN'S EMERGENCY FUND.

Unicentrism. See POLYCENTRISM.

Uniculture. See UNIPOLITICS.

Unification of Germany. The former German Democratic Republic (GDR) (the pro-Soviet eastern part of Germany) and the Federal Republic of Germany (FRG) (the western, democratic part) commenced a dialogue on reunification after Soviet President Mikhail S. Gorbachev announced he would no longer support the oppressive regimes in Eastern Europe; on 9 November 1989 the Berlin Wall was opened to the West, and on 23 August 1990 the East German Parliament agreed to reunify; this was concluded on 3 October 1990. The 11-month period of the reunification process of the two parts of Germany is also known as a "reunification express." See THE ONLY ARMY YOU CAN JOIN IS THE SALVATION ARMY.

Unification of Korea. See KOREAN WAR.

Unifier. Under the current constitution of Japan (which was introduced in 1947), the Emperor Hirohito, may not involve himself in either government or politics but may merely play the role of a "unifier." The Emperor performs no specific functions except that of serving as the titular head of the state and symbol of unity of his people. See V-J DAY.

Uniform Code of Military Justice (UCMJ). A body of laws and regulations pertaining to military personnel. See MARTIAL LAW.

Uniform Legislation. Also Uniform State Laws. Identical state laws and practices resulting from consultation and cooperation among the officials of two or more state governments. In 1892 the American Bar Association established a committee to look into the matter of developing uniform laws among the states in matters of commerce. As a result the National Commission for Uniform Laws was created. The Commission developed model laws such as a traffic code, consumer credit code and the Uniform Narcotics Drug Act. Such model laws have been adopted in many states. Some ninety year later (1982) the National Conference of Commissioners of Uniform State Laws has been established. Again the focus was on commercial transactions. Uniform laws accepted by all states deal with such matters as negotiable instruments, warehouse receipts, and stock transfers. Since its establishment the Conference has proposed hundreds of model laws to advance the cause of interstate relations. State legislatures, in adopting these proposed uniform laws may modify them to reflect local conditions. The Council of State Governments in Lexington, Kentucky continues the work of developing model laws for state legislatures. See MODEL ACT.

Uniform Statutes. See MODEL ACT.

Unilateral. By or of one party; by one side or one-sidedly.

Unilateral Declaration of Independence. The act of a formerly subservient group of people, a nation, or a portion of a state, announcing its intention to break away and form a separate, sovereign, and independent state. The American revolutionaries expressed their wish to break away from the mother country, England, and published a unilateral declaration to this effect. The British did not recognize this act and it took war to accomplish the separation. The Americans succeeded in their effort because they were able to defeat the British. However, when on 20 December 1860, the Southern Secessionists passed an ordinance of secession from the United States of America (USA) and formed the Confederate States of America (CSA), this unilateral act was not recognized by the federal government in Washington, D.C., and after a protracted and costly war, the South was brought back into the American Union. The act was first settled by the sword, then it was followed by law when in 1869, the U.S. Supreme Court ruled (in *Texas v. White*) that the act of secession was unconstitutional. Some disaffected groups in the South from time to time hint at separation again—that "the south shall rise again,"—but this is taken as in jest rather than as a real intention. In recent times, many groups with aspirations of independence took the unilateral route. For example, on 30 May 1967, the Eastern Region of Nigeria announced a break-away from Nigeria to form a new state, the Republic of Biafra. This act was made without prior consultations with the central government of Nigeria and triggered a revolution. Biafra capitulated on 12 January 1970. The Aswani League in East Pakistan, dissatisfied with the rigid control by West Pakistan, broke away unilaterally in 1971 and became Bangladesh; so did the former Soviet republics of Estonia, Latvia, and Lithuania which broke away from the Soviet Union in 1990 when the central Soviet government refused to recognize their desire for independence. A bilateral act is an agreement between the central government and the people who want to break away. When the British withdrew from India on 14 August 1947, for example, the Islamic majority in the west separated from the rest of India and became the state of Pakistan. The Republic of the Philippines which was sold to the United States by Spain following the Spanish-American War in 1898 for $20 million, was given independence on 4 July 1946 under an enabling act passed by the U.S. Congress in 1934. A multilateral arrangement for independence can be exemplified by an agreement of August 1991, between the major Soviet republics, Russia, Kazakhstan, and the Ukraine to become separate states, followed subsequently by Belarus and others, although they agreed to collaborate under an umbrella arrangement called the "Commonwealth of Independent States." In the case when one or more states wants to join in a union with another state or group of states, this is usually accomplished by a bilateral or multilateral arrangement. The Republic of Cuba—and some other states, mainly in Latin America in different times in history—twice announced unilaterally the intention to join the American union, the USA, but on both occasions the requests were denied. Quite often unilateral separatists, once defeated, move to another country that is friendly to their cause and establish a government in exile; the leaders reconcile their differences and integrate into the existing state, or are tried and executed for treason. See BANANA BUNCH, DECLARATION OF INDEPENDENCE, SEPARATISM.

Unilateral Global Keynesianism. According to author Walter Russell Mead (*The United States and the World Economy* and "From Bretton Woods to the Bush Team," *World Policy Journal*, Summer 1989), the major global powers, with the United States at the lead, came to understand that economic blocs lead, with time to military blocs which, with time, lead to war, and in order to avoid such calamities, the post-W.W.II arrangements are now becoming obsolete because Japan and Europe do not view America as the leader anymore. Global trading systems in the past, accepted the American dollar as the currency for global trade (even the Soviet bloc was using the dollar in world trade) and allowed the United States to unilaterally lead the nations in free and unrestricted global trade—operating on the principle of "global Keynesianism." (This meant that when inflation threatened the supply of money was restricted, and when recession threatened the economies, monetary policies and fiscal policies were loosened.) That arrangement served well, because America had a huge and dominant market and was not threatened with foreign competition; the other western partners (e.g., Japan, Germany, England, and France), were rebuilding their economies, and American products were selling well on their markets. The situation is changing now, however, and America is no longer the unilateral leader, because the Asian (Japanese) and the European (German) economic blocs are becoming potent forces in what could possibly become, with time, the next phase of W.W.III (in reality World War III commenced right after the end of W.W.II in 1945). After W.W.II, America shared over fifty percent of the world's GNP and today, 1992, it shares about twenty-one percent only.

See AMERICA BASHING, COMPARATIVE ADVANTAGE, JAPAN BASHING, KEYNESIAN ECONOMICS.

Union Africaine et Malagache (UAM). An informal union that was established between Africa and Malagasy during conferences held in Tananarive, Malagasy, in September 1961, with all of the Brazzaville States present. The purpose of the Union was to bring about closer cooperation and solidarity to maintain peace and security in Africa and to expedite trade among the signatories. The Union was dissolved and replaced with the UAMCE which serves a similar purpose. See ORGANIZATION OF AFRICAN UNITY (OAU).

Union Africaine et Malagache de Coopération Économique (UAMCE). African and Malagasy Union for Economic Cooperation. See UNION AFRICAINE ET MALAGACHE.

Union Calendar. A calendar that is maintained by the Committee of the Whole House (in the U.S. House of Representatives) which lists all bills pertaining to such measures as the raising of revenues or general appropriations. See CALENDAR OF BUSINESS, CALENDAR WEDNESDAY, CONSENT CALENDAR, HOUSE CALENDAR, PRIVATE CALENDAR.

Union Démocratique des Travailleurs (UDT). The Union of Democratic Workers. A political party in contemporary France.

Union des Démocrates Pour la République. In the French language, "democratic union for the republic." See ASSEMBLY FOR THE REPUBLIC, UNION DÉMOCRATIQUE DES TRAVAILLEURS.

Union des États d'Afrique Centrale (UEAC). An informal Union established in February 1968, between Zaire and the Central African Republic, upon the insistence of Joseph Mobutu resulting from a difference of opinion with the leaders of the UDEAC. This was merely a protest federation without any designated objectives. See L'UNION DOUANIÈRE ET ÉCONOMIQUE DE L'AFRIQUE CENTRALE (UDEAC).

Union Douanière Équatoriale (UDE). See UNION DOUANIÈRE ET ÉCONOMIQUE DE L'AFRIQUE CENTRALE (UDEAC).

Union Douanière et Économique de L'Afrique Centrale (UDEAC). An informal union formed in December 1964, as the outgrowth of the Union Douanière Équatoriale (UDE), which had existed since 1958 among Cameroon, Gabon, Central African Republic, Congo (Brazzaville), and Chad. The purpose of this union was to expedite trade through a common market system which was to be developed. Since a split developed within this union, Chad and the Central African Republic left the Union and joined the newly-formed UEAC.

Union for the New Republic (URN). In the French language, "Union Républicaine Nouvelle." A political party in contemporary France.

Union for the Total Liberation of Angola (UNITA). Political and guerrilla organization in Angola, under the leadership of Dr. Jonas Savimbi, professor of political science, opposing the communist government in power, through collaboration with anti-communist elements in South Africa and elsewhere. The UNITA controls about half of the territory of Angola and commenced peace process with the MPLA in May 1991 for possible merger of forces after elections. Also known as "National Union for Total Liberation of Angola." See POPULAR MOVEMENT FOR THE LIBERATION OF ANGOLA (MPLA).

Union Involved Racketeering (UNIRAC). The collaboration between organized labor (unions) and organized crime in such illegal activities as extortion, racketeering, kickbacks, loan-sharking, tax evasion, and other criminal activity.

Union Labor Party. A minor political party active in the United States during the 1880s. The party's principal aim was to improve the economic conditions of labor.

Union League. A secret political organization formed in the northern states of the United States in 1862 to combat sympathizers of the Southern Confederacy. See UNION LABOR PARTY.

Union of African States (UAS). This Union was formed in 1961, between Ghana and Guinea—later joined by Mali—and, according to its designer, Kwame Nkrumah of Ghana, was to serve as the nucleus of the "United States of Africa." The charter of the UAS came in force on July 1, 1961.

Union of Central African States (UEAC). A regional organization established in 1968 to foster economic and social cooperation among its three members, the Congo (Democratic Republic), the Central African Republic, and Chad. The UEAC charter provides for tariff reductions, travel between the three without visas, improved transport facilities, and the exchange of security information. The secretariat for UEAC is located at Bangui in the Central African Republic.

Union of Soviet Communist Youth of Lenin (Komsomol). In the Russian language, "Kommunistitcheskoy Soyuz Sovyetzkoy Molodyodjy Lenina." The only official communist youth organization in which membership was required of all young persons between the ages of 14 and 30 years of age. No one could become—under the statutes of the former Communist Party of the Soviet Union (CPSU)—a member or candidate-member of the CPSU without first being a member of the Komsomol. The organization was sponsored and directed by the CPSU, and all young people were required to participate in its scheduled activities. Dissolved 27 September, 1991.

Union of Soviet Socialist Republics (USSR). In the Russian language, "Soyuz Sovyetzkigh Sotzyalistitcheskigh Respubliks," CCCP. The official designation of the fomer Soviet Federation of fifteen Soviet Socialist Republics. The Republics were: (1) Armenia, (2) Azerbaijan, (3) Byelorussia (White Russia), (4) Estonia, (5) Georgia, (6) Kazakhstan, (7) Kirgkhizia, (8) Latvia, (9) Lithuania, (10) Moldavia, (11) Russia, (12) Tadzhikistan, (13) Turkmenistan, (14) Ukraine and (15) Uzbekistan. (Some of the Republics contained autonomous political subdivisions such as Autonomous Republics, Autonomous Regions and National Areas.) The USSR was dissolved in 1991 and the Commonwealth of Independent States was formed.

Union Party. A minor political party active in the United States during the 1930s. It advocated, among other things, that national wealth be shared by all the people rather than by the wealthy few.

Union Shop. A place of work where, after a given period of time (usually one month), membership in a labor union is required as a condition of employment. See CLOSED SHOP, TAFT-HARTLEY LAW.

Union Siciliano. See MAFIA.

Unipolarity. The world remaining under the influence of a single center of power, the United States, since the Soviet Union dissolved in 1991, as the second world power. The concept of bipolarity was once acclaimed as a positive global arrangement in the belief that the world would be safer if two opposing superpowers oversaw it without one attempting to eliminate the other. Bipolarity was viewed by some as the safest arrangement for global balance of power. U.S. Secretary of State James Baker III stated in 1992, that the dissolution of the bipolar arrangement was "a once-in-a-century opportunity to advance American interests and values throughout the world." The *New York Times* (7 March 1992) received and published information about a document prepared by the U.S. Defense Department which indicated that the United States military doctrine in the unipolar world would be that of "benevolent domination by one superpower," the United States, and that "collective internationalism" no longer applies. (This was the strategy that emerged after W.W.II when the five superpowers, the United States, France, Britain, the Soviet Union, and China, were managed via the United Nations.) It is expected that major international disputes will be handled unilaterally by the United States and its elite military force, called the "base force," of about two million troops. According to U.S. Secretary of Defense Dick Cheney, the major task of the United States now is to convince "potential competitors that they need not aspire to a greater role or pursue a more aggressive posture to protect their legitimate interests." Obviously, powerful Japan may combine forces with China, and in the equation the manpower-technology merger may create a challenge to American interests in the area. Germany will, under U.S. leadership, provide regional security and "the creation of a democratic zone of peace." See BIPOLARITY, MULTIPOLARITY, POLYCENTRISM.

Unipolitics. Concept that evolved during the World Habitat Conference in Canada in 1972, calling for the establishment of a unified, centralized global authority with enforcement powers, which would design and enforce cohesive policies for the survival of mankind. It would plan for better living conditions for all people, which could possibly lead to the emergence of a unified culture (uniculture) that all people, due to the growing global interdependence of people upon each other for survival, could accept. See GLOBAL VILLAGE, WORLD GOVERNMENT.

Unit Rule. A device used by some political parties or state party organizations in the United States requiring all state delegates to a national party convention to vote *en bloc*, as a unit, rather than to cast individual ballots for different candidates. (The practice has been common in the Democratic Party, and thus far, it has never been used by the Republican Party.) A primary election held under such system is referred to as "loophole primary." Unit rule was abolished in 1968, by the national organization of the Democratic Party, and an attempt is being made to abolish the loophole primaries as well. See DEMOCRATIC PARTY.

Unit System. See PLURALITY VOTE.

UNITA. See UNION FOR THE TOTAL LIBERATION OF ANGOLA.

Unitary Government. See UNITARY STATE.

Unitary School System. A single school district on an integrated basis (as opposed to a dual system, one for blacks and the other for whites); or the merging of small school districts into one larger one for the purpose of uniformity and economy. See *BROWN V. BOARD OF EDUCATION*, CIVIL RIGHTS ACTS.

Unitary State. A state in which the central government shares no powers with any other levels of government (as is the case under a federal system). All policy decisions are channeled through lower administrative echelons but all are finally subject to direction and control by the central government. In some unitary states (e.g., England and France), a degree of autonomy is granted to local government, but in the final analysis, they are the agents of the central government, without reserved powers. Unitary state is characterized by a highly centralized governmental apparatus. See Appendix 82.

United for Peace Resolution. See KOREAN WAR.

United Klans of America Knights of the Ku Klux Klan (KKK). See KU KLUX KLAN (KKK).

United Labor Party. A political party, active in the United States during the 1880s which advocated, among other things, a single tax as suggested by Henry George. See POLITICAL MACHINE, SINGLE TAX.

United Nations Assessment Formula. See ASSESSMENT FOR THE UNITED NATIONS.

United Nations Commission to Investigate Crimes of the Shah of Iran. Appointed by UN Secretary General Kurt Waldheim to investigate the crimes and atrocities committed by the former Shah of Iran and eventually to speed up the release of the American hostages held captive in Iran.

The Commission returned without accomplishing any business; without seeing the hostages on March 11, 1980. Its members were:

1. Louis-Edmond Pettiti of France, former president of the French Bar and a member of the European Court of Justice;

2. Andres Aguilar of Venezuela, former Ambassador to the U.S. and a strong critic of repressive government in Latin America; former head of the Inter-American Commission on Human Rights (1974-1979), and representative to the UN Conference on the Law of the Sea, law professor and law-school dean of the Central University of Venezuela; former Minister of Justice of Venezuela.

3. Hector Jaywardene of Sri Lanka.

United Nations Conference on Environment and Development. See RIO DE JANEIRO EARTH SUMMIT.

United Nations Conference on Trade and Development (UNCTAD). An informal organization of the United Nations which, since 1958, organizes conferences and meetings of experts in various parts of the world for the purpose of studying economic problems and possible solutions. UNCTAD closely collaborates, among other organizations, with the Economic Commission on Africa and African Governments. See Appendices 72-79.

United Nations Convention on the Privileges and Immunities of Specialized Agencies of the United States. See UNITED NATIONS-UNITED STATES AGREEMENT REGARDING THE HEADQUARTERS OF THE UNITED NATIONS.

United Nations Covenant of Civil and Political Rights. See INTERNATIONAL COVENANT ON CIVIL AND POLITICAL RIGHTS.

United Nations General Convention on the Privileges and Immunities of the United Nations. See UNITED NATION-UNITED STATES AGREEMENT REGARDING THE HEADQUARTERS OF THE UNITED NATIONS.

United Nations Organization (UNO). An international organization established upon the ratification of the United Nations Charter by the five permanent members of the Security Council (China, England, France, the former Soviet Union, and the United States) and by other member-states on October 25, 1945, for the purpose of maintaining international peace and security through the cooperation of its member-states. The principal organs of the UN are:

(1) **The General Assembly.** The Assembly is the law-making body of the United Nations, and it is composed of member-states who are admitted by the Assembly upon application. Each state may send not more than five delegates and may have only one vote. See Appendices 75-79.

(2) **The Security Council.** The Security Council consists of five permanent members (China, England, France, Russian Republic, and the United States) and ten other states elected to the Council by the General Assembly for two-year terms. The primary function of the Council is to deal with matters of international peace and security and, whenever or wherever peace is threatened, to make definite recommendations for action. The five permanent members of the Council exercise considerable influence upon the workings of that body because in voting on the so-called "substantive questions" the affirmative vote of nine members is required, including the unanimous vote of the five permanent members of the Council. In voting on so-called "procedural questions," the affirmative vote of any nine members will suffice. See Appendix 79.

(3) **The Secretariat.** The Secretariat consists of a staff, which serves with the approval of the General Assembly, and the Secretary-General, who is appointed to a five-year term by the General Assembly upon the recommendation of the Security Council. (All five permanent members of the Council must concur on the selection of the candidate for the office of the Secretary-General.) The Secretary-General is the principal spokesman for the United Nations and coordinates the activities of its agencies.

(4) **The Economic and Social Council.** A body of twenty-seven member-states elected by the General Assembly for three-year rotating terms to handle matters related to international economic cooperation, social services, health, and education.

(5) **The Trusteeship Council.** A body designated to supervise territories placed under the trust of individual states. The membership of the Council is composed of the five permanent members of the Security Council, the member-states which administer trust territories, and a number of other states equal to the five permanent members of the Security Council and the states having territories placed under their trust. (There are three major archipelagoes composed of about 2,400 small islands, with a total population of over 90,000, placed under the trusteeship of the United States. They are: the Carolines, the Marianas, and the Marshall Islands, all in the Pacific Ocean.)

(6) **The International Court of Justice (ICJ).** The Court is the judicial organ of the United Nations, and it is composed of fifteen justices appointed for nine-year terms by the General Assembly, one of the justices serving as the Court's President. Any nine justices present constitute a quorum, and a majority vote decides an issue.

In addition to the main organs of the United Nations a number of so-called "specialized agencies" are charged with specific tasks under the auspices of the United Nations. They are:

International Atomic Energy Agency (IAEA);
International Labor Organization (ILO);
Food and Agriculture Organization (FAO);
United Nations Education, Scientific and Cultural Organization (UNESCO);
World Health Organization (WHO);
International Bank for Reconstruction and Development (World Bank);
International Development Association (IDA);
International Finance Corporation (IFC);
International Monetary Fund (IMF, or FUND);
International Civil Aviation Organization (ICAO);
Universal Postal Union (UPU);
International Telecommunication Union (ITU);
International Maritime Consultative Organization (IMCO);
United Nation's Children's Emergency Fund (UNICEF);
World Meteorological Organization (WMO);

From time to time, as the need arises, the United Nations may establish additional agencies or discontinue those that no longer serve any purpose (e.g., the United Nations Relief and Rehabilitation Agency (UNRRA) which was established after World War II as a relief agency but has since been discontinued). See SAN FRANCISCO CONFERENCE, Appendices 75-79.

United Nations Resolution 242, 338. See SADAT-BEGIN SUMMIT.

United Nations Security Council Resolutions 242, 338. See SADAT-BEGIN SUMMIT.

United Nations-United States Agreement Regarding the Headquarters of the United Nations. Pursuant to UN Resolution of December 14, 1946, the United States designated a certain territory located on Manhattan Island in New York City as the sovereign area under the jurisdiction of the United Nations, with extraterritorial rights and privileges; granted the right to innocent passage to UN officials; secured the UN's communications; provided police protection to the headquarters district; and, de facto and de jure, ceded a part of U.S. territory for the creation of a sovereign state, the United Nations. The United States, however, refused to accept the UN's General Convention on the Privileges and Immunities of the United Nations of 1946 and the 1947 Convention on the Privileges and Immunities of Specialized Agencies of the United Nations. Separate municipal legislation by the United States, the U.S. International Organization Immunities Act of 1945 (59 Stat. 669, 22 U.S.C.A. secs. 228 ff.), is the guiding statutory law on immunities and privileges of international personnel in U.S. territory. See UNITED NATIONS ORGANIZATION (UNO).

United States-Canadian North American Air Defense System (NORAD). A mutual defense system of Canada and the United States, established after World War II.

United States Chamber of Commerce. A national organization of private business owners and operators established in 1912 for the purpose of lobbying for the private enterprise system in the United States.

United States Citizenship. See CITIZENSHIP.

United States Code (USC). A systematic compilation of congressional laws published under the title of *The Code of the Laws of the United States of a General and Permanent Character* and commonly referred to as the *United States Code*. See U.S. REPORTS.

United States Commissioner. A federal official, usually attached to a United States District Court, who holds preliminary hearings in cases involving violations of federal law and presents his findings to a grand jury for further action.

United States Conference of Mayors (USCM). Association of mayors—lobby for greater federal aid to cities.

United States Congress. See CONGRESS OF THE UNITED STATES.

United States Court of Appeal. See COURT OF APPEAL.

United States Court of Customs and Patent Appeals. A legislative court established in 1910, and reorganized in 1929, for the purpose of handling cases relating to customs, patents, and trademarks. The Court, composed of five judges, is restricted to cases brought before it on appeal. See SUPREME COURT OF THE UNITED STATES.

United States Customs Court. A legislative court established in 1890, and reorganized in 1929, for the purpose of interpreting tariff laws, classifying merchandise, and determining duties on goods imported. The Court consists of nine judges, and its permanent seat is in New York City. See SUPREME COURT OF THE UNITED STATES.

United States House of Representatives. One of the two chambers of the United States Congress, composed of 435 voting Representatives, each representing a congressional district constituency in states. (The membership of the House has been fixed at 435 since 1912.) The House also includes non-voting members, each elected for a term of four-years: a delegate from Washington, D.C., and the Resident Commissioner of the Commonwealth of Puerto Rico. Representatives are elected for two-year terms, and every two years the entire house membership is due for election. Congressional elections which do not coincide with the presidential elections are known as "by-year," "mid-term," or "off-year" elections. In the first Congress, in 1790, there were 65 members, one Representative for each 30,000 people; and in the 95th Congress in 1978, each of the 435 voting Congresspersons represented approximately 485,000 constituents each. According to the November 15, 1941, law, following each decennial (every ten years) national census, the number of electoral votes and congressional districts are determined for each state (but each state is entitled by the Constitution to at least one representative), so that the ratio of population in one district does not differ too much from that in another. All revenue legislation originates in the House under Section 7, Art. I, U.S. Constitution. Its sessions begin on January 3 of each year. The House, like the Senate, is organized into committees (see Appendix), and there have been as many attempts to reorganize that body as there have been Congresses since the first one in 1790. See CANNON REVOLT, CONGRESS OF THE UNITED STATES, CONGRESSIONAL REORGANIZATION ACTS, UNITED STATES HOUSE OF REPRESENTATIVES, Appendices 10, 12.

United States Information Agency (USIA). A federal agency established in 1954 and charged with the dissemination abroad of information about the United States. It acts mainly through its branch offices scattered throughout the world. (The USIA is forbidden to disseminate any information about the United States and its government within the United States or its territories.) The principal mediums of the USIA are the libraries it maintains abroad, radio broadcasts (the *Voice of America*) in numerous languages, exhibits and shows, and educational and cultural exchanges with other nations. The offices scattered abroad are known as United States Information Service. Its *Bulletin* and teletyped wire service renders useful information to the American press, the public and the academic communities. The USIA was reorganized and renamed on April 1, 1978, to "International Communication Agency (ICA) but in 1979 the new name was abandoned and the Agency returned to its original name. Overseas the USIA is known as "United States Information Service." See Appendix 34.

United States Information Service (USIS). See UNITED STATES INFORMATION AGENCY (USIA).

United States Intelligence Board (USIB). A consortium of intelligence services responsible for setting intelligence requirements and priorities for the United States. The consortium is composed of the following intelligence agencies: (1) the Central Intelligence Agency (CIA), which is responsible for the collection and evaluation of intelligence information and for espionage and counterespionage abroad (its Director serves as the Chairman of the Board); (2) the Atomic Energy Commission, which gathers information on nuclear tests by other states and estimates their nuclear capabilities; (3) the Defense Intelligence Agency (DIA), which coordinates intelligence activities of the Air Force, Army, and Navy; (4) the Federal Bureau of Investigation (FBI), which is charged with the responsibility of conducting counterespionage within the United States and of combating sabotage and subversion; (5) the Bureau of Intelligence and Research of the States Department, which collects political intelligence abroad; and (6) the National Security Agency (NSA), which provides coding and decoding services, monitors foreign communications, and conducts electronic surveillance. The over-all purpose of the Board is to provide the United States President and other authorized officers of the government with the most accurate and current information necessary for making day-to-day policy decisions. See CENTRAL INTELLIGENCE AGENCY (CIA), INTELLIGENCE, Appendices 32-34.

United States International Organization Immunities Act of 1945. See UNITED NATIONS-UNITED STATES AGREEMENT REGARDING THE HEADQUARTERS OF THE UNITED NATIONS.

United States Military Security Lobby. See CONGRESSIONAL CAUCUS.

United States of Africa. See UNION OF AFRICAN STATES (UAS).

United States of Europe (USE). A plan cultivated for decades by Europeans envisioning political and economic collaboration in order to prevent wars and human misery. The United States has been involved in providing the model and experience of the American union. The European Community of the present day is an offshoot of these efforts. See COAL AND STEEL COMMUNITY, COMMON MARKET, EUROPEAN ECONOMIC COMMUNITY, MAASTRICHT SUMMIT

United States Office of War Information. A federal agency charged with the responsibility for coordinating all overseas propaganda (except "black" or covert political warfare) for the United States as distinguished from intelligence operations which were delegated to the Office of Strategic Services (OSS) under the direction and supervision of the Joint Chiefs of Staff. Both, the Office of War Information and the Office of Strategic Services were established by an Executive Order on June 13, 1942, by President Franklin D. Roosevelt (1933-1945). These two agencies replaced the office of Coordinator of Information (CIO), which was established on June 18, 1941, under the direction of General William Danovan. After W.W.II, the function of the Office of War Information was taken over by the United States Information Agency (USIA) and the Office of Strategic Services by the Central Intelligence Agency (CIA) respectively. See PROPAGANDA.

United States Person. Under American law, the Foreign Intelligence Surveillance Act of 1978 [PL 95-511, October 25, 1978, 92 State 1783, Section 101 (i)], defines a United States Person ". . . a citizen of the United States, an alien lawfully admitted for permanent residence (as defined in section 101 (a) (20) of the Immigration and Nationality Act), an unincorporated association a substantial number of members of which are citizens of the United States or aliens legally admitted for permanent residence or a corporation which is incorporated in the United States, but does not include a corporation or an association which is a foreign power, as defined in subsection (a) (1), (2), or (3)." See COUNTERINSURGENCY IN AMERICA, IMMIGRATION.

United States Reports (US). One of the several publications in which decisions of the United States Supreme Court can be found. The *Reports*, which are published by the federal government, until 1882 carried the names of the reporters of the Supreme Court as follows:

1789-1800	Dallas (Dall.)	4 volumes
1801-1815	Cranch (Cr.)	9 volumes
1816-1827	Wheaton (Wheat.)	12 volumes
1828-1842	Peters (Pet.)	16 volumes
1843-1860	Howard (How.)	24 volumes
1861-1862	Black (Bl.)	2 volumes
1863-1864	Wallace (Wall.)	2 volumes
1875-1882	Otto	17 volumes

After 1882, beginning with Volume 108, the *Reports* were published by numbers rather than names of the reporters. The other publications in which Supreme Court decisions can be found are: the *United States Supreme Court Reports, Lawyers Edition* (cited as "*L. Ed.*"), published privately by the Lawyers Cooperative Publishing Company; and the *Supreme Court Reporter* (cited as "*Sup. Ct.*") published privately by the West Publishing Company. Decisions of lower federal courts are published in separate volumes by each state by private commercial publishing houses. See SUPREME COURT OF THE UNITED STATES, UNITED STATES CODE, Appendices, 44-51.

United States Senate. One of the two chambers of the United States Congress, composed of two Senators elected from each state *at large*, regardless of the size of the state's population, for a term of six years. Senators are elected on a staggered basis; that is, one-third of the 100-member legislature (or 33) is elected every two years so that there is continuity. One of the most important functions of the Senate (according to Section 2, Art. I of the U.S. Constitution) is to render its "advice and consent" to all presidential nominations for high government positions (e.g., members of the cabinet, ambassadors, commissioners, judges, and federal prosecutors) and to treaties. (It is not unusual for the procedure to be reversed on occasions when the Senators do the nominating and the President gives his advice and consent.) In practice, however, the U.S. President has an escape hatch for each of those eventualities. He may, for example, appoint officers, without Senate confirmation, as his personal assistants or envoys; and he can enter into executive or "gentleman's" agreements with other nations, without formalizing them as treaties. In case the President chooses to bypass the Senate, he may not, however, receive congressional appropriations for the implementation of his acts, except a small, (about 5 million dollars) non-accountable contingency fund of petty cash. The U.S. Vice President serves ex officio as the presiding officer of the Senate. See SENATORIAL COURTESY, UNITED STATES CONGRESS, UNITED STATES HOUSE OF REPRESENTATIVES, Appendices 9, 11, 17.

United States–Soviet Union Consular Convention. See VIENNA CONVENTION ON DIPLOMATIC RELATIONS.

United States Supreme Court. See SUPREME COURT OF THE UNITED STATES.

United States Supreme Court Reports, Lawyers Edition. See UNITED STATES REPORTS (US).

United World Federalists. See WORLD GOVERNMENT.

Uniting for Peace Resolution. The resolution that was passed by the General Assembly of the United Nations Organization on November 3, 1950, when the Security Council failed to act (first due to constant vetoing by the Soviet delegate, Jacob Malik) on the aggression of North Korea against South Korea. The resolution authorized the mobilization of military forces under the auspices of the United Nations (U.S. General Douglas MacArthur was designated as the Commander of the UN forces) and allowed for their dispatch to Korea to repel the aggressor. (This was the only time when the General Assembly was able to act in the interest of international peace and security by undertaking this collective security measure.) See KOREAN WAR, UNITED NATIONS ORGANIZATION (UNO).

Universal Declaration on Every Man's Right to Proper Nourishment. See HUNGER MIGRATION, HUNGER WARS.

Universal Negro Improvement Association (UNIA). An organization founded by Marcus Garvey in 1914 which was involved in many activities among black Americans. It urged them to stress their racial pride and history, and advocated self-development through self-help; the development of a distinctly Negro culture; the establishment of distinctly black business enterprises; and emigration to Africa.

Universal Postal Union. One of the oldest and least controversial international service organizations, established in 1875 and serving all nations. See INTERNATIONAL LEGAL PERSON, UN.

Universal Registration. U.S. Representative Morris Udall (D-Arizona) proposed legislation in 1976 suggesting that registration of voters for federal elections (for President, Vice President, U.S. Senators and U.S. Representatives) be universal and supervised by a federal agency instead of according to the present system whereby each individual state maintains records and supervises federal elections.

Unjust War. See BELLUM JUSTUM, WAR.

UNO. See UNITED NATIONS ORGANIZATION.

Unpledged Elector. A presidential elector in the United States who pledges before being elected to follow his or her conscience and the will of the popular vote, and is not committed to any partisan (party) candidate. During the 1960 presidential election, eight Mississippi and six Alabama electors ran as unpledged. The Mississippi electors voted for U.S. Senator Harry F. Byrd, Sr. (D-Va.), and the Alabama electors pledged not to vote for the Democratic Party nominee of 1960, U.S. Senator John F. Kennedy. See ELECTORAL COLLEGE, PRESIDENTIAL ELECTOR.

UNR. See UNION FOR THE NEW REPUBLIC.

Unrepentant Individualism. The notion, popularly discussed today and well articulated by Dr. William S. Dietrich (*In The Shadow of the Rising Sun: The Political Roots of American Economic Decline*, Pennsylvania State University Press), that Americans cherish their values, freedoms, liberties, and independence to the point that such attitudes often hinder the actions of the American government, particularly in external economic relations with other states in this highly competitive world; that Americans see the external image of their country, in terms of personal victories or failures, individually rather than as a whole. Americans cherish the ideals of Thomas Jefferson, who was very much concerned with protecting the individual from possible oppression by any group of persons or by the government. Alexander Hamilton, on the other hand, favored a strong government and fewer personal rights and liberties for individuals; he viewed the welfare of the nation superior to that of the individual and even suggested that George Washington declare himself "King George Washington I," in order to give more credence to the state and to government power over the individual. Because of the great range of personal freedoms and liberties that Americans enjoy, the American government is often handicapped and restricted in what it can do to strengthen the nation, particularly the economy, in external contact with other nations. Most of the major democracies today (e.g., France, Germany, and Japan) put the interest of the nation or state above that of the individual person and as a result do rather well in providing for their people in terms of stability, living standards, culture, health care, and education.

Unrestricted Partnership. See GENSCHER DOCTRINE.

UNRRA. See UNITED NATIONS ORGANIZATION, Appendices 75-79.

Unsocial Liberty. One among the several notions of the right to privacy, which has been one of man's most cherished yet most abused rights throughout the history of mankind (e.g., the government in a politically organized society is itself the result of an aggrandizement of certain rights of individual persons). Although a man is a social and a political animal and seeks association with others, man is also entitled to the right of being "let alone" (see *Griswold v. Connecticut* of 1965), to enjoy liberty through disassociation with others (unsocial liberty), and he may seek legal remedy to protect that right. See PRIVACY ACT OF 1974, RIGHT TO PRIVACY.

UNTAC. United Nations Transitional Authority for Cambodia. See CAMBODIAN RECONSTRUCTION.

Unwritten Constitution. A body of laws and/or customs used in lieu of a written constitution (e.g., the laws that comprise the constitution of England). See WRITTEN CONSTITUTION.

UPN. Unity Party of Nigeria.

Uptown Ku Klux Klan. See WHITE CITIZENS' COUNCIL.

Uranium Club. See CLUB.

Urban Agenda. The search for solutions to urban problems and the programs to deal with them. With the decline of agriculture and rural communities, more people seek a better life in the cities. However, urban infrastructure is not prepared to handle such influx due to inadequate housing, sanitation, health facilities, law and order setups, schools and jobs. See Appendices 85, 86.

Urban Coalition. A lobby-type, nonpartisan coalition of city government officials and sympathizers which attempts to influence the policies of government (at all levels) for the benefit of the cities and the urban communities in general. See URBAN GROWTH POLICY, URBANIZATION.

Urban Growth Policy. The Urban Development Act of 1970 and subsequent legislation had the following objectives: (1) to favor patterns of urbanization and economic development and stabilization which offer a range of alternative locations and encourage the wise and balanced use of physical and human resources in metropolitan and urban regions, as well as in smaller urban places which have a potential for accelerated growth; (2) to foster the continued economic strength of all parts of the United States, including the central cities, suburbs, smaller communities, local neighborhoods, and rural areas; (3) to help reverse trends of migration and physical growth which reinforce disparities among states, regions, and cities; (4) to treat comprehensively the problems of poverty and employment (including the erosion of tax bases and the need for better community services and job opportunities) which are associated with disorderly urbanization and rural decline; (5) to develop means to encourage good housing for all Americans without regard to race or creed; (6) to refine the role of the federal government in revitalizing existing communities and encouraging planned, large-scale urban and new community development; (7) to strengthen the capacity of general governmental institutions to contribute to balanced urban growth and stabilization; and (8) facilitate increased coordination in the administration of federal programs to encourage desirable patterns of urban growth and stabilization, the prudent use of natural resources, and the protection of the physical environment.

Urban Policy. See URBANIZATION.

Urban State. A term often applied to the United States, meaning that the U.S. is the global currency nation (i.e., the U.S. dollar remains the medium of international exchange), which controls global economic activity, including that of the former communist states, while the other nations remain suburban, although not necessarily dominated or controlled politically or economically. (The city has been traditionally considered the center of wealth and the suburbia only as the bedroom community.) Economist Winniski also observes that "New York City is the financial center of a financial storm" on which even the political capital of the United States, Washington, District of Columbia (which is "parochial, conducive only to hysteria in a crisis," and "imports ideas created elsewhere," e.g., in New York City's Wall Street financial empire), relies on for guidance in shaping its domestic and foreign policies.

Urbanization. Term associated with the origin, development, growth, and decline of cities and their surrounding suburban communities. In 1790, for example, there were only two cities in the United States with a population of 20,000 or more: New York City and Philadelphia, Pennsylvania. By 1860 there were forty-three cities of that size. The increase of population was due mainly to an influx of immigrants from foreign lands who were seeking a better life and were anxious to settle in the "New World," the "Promised Land," or the "Land of the Free" (as the new American state was then referred to). Growing industries required an ever larger labor supply (preferably cheap) which was lured with such slogans as "low taxes," "no compulsory military service," "plenty of cheap land," and "three meat meals a day." Immigrants were coming in larger numbers: over 150,000 by 1830; over 2,600,000 by 1860; and over 3,600,000 by 1900; and most of them settled in cities (some of which grew overnight). Cities also became centers of culture, education, arts, and places "where the action was . . . ." Chicago, Illinois, soon became a stockyard, a rail and water transportation center, and Cincinnati, Ohio, a meat packing (porkopolis) center. The city administrators limited themselves primarily to tax-collection and law enforcement, but neglected to plan for community development and orderly growth. Soon one side of a street was lined with palace-like structures of millionaires (many of whom enriched themselves at the expense of the immigrants), while the other was a slum. In modern times, many urban areas became centers of crime and human misery. The Black Revolution of the 1960s (e.g., the burning of Watts in California, with a chant: "Burn baby, Burn") called the government's attention to the problems of the urban communities. Soon two schools of thought evolved on how to approach the urban problems: (1) the "Cassandra" theory looks at America's urban problems as incurable, because the urban environment is not susceptible to growth but to decay; therefore, urban growth should be discouraged by building smaller communities and resettling people (and industries); (2) the "Pollyanna" theory is the opposite of the "Cassandra" theory. It sees a future in urban communities, and considers such experiences as the burning of Watts, Chicago, and Washington, D.C., as rational moves on the part of the dissatisfied and disenchanted which give the governments (at all levels) a sense of direction as to where the real problems of the nation lie. See BEDROOM COMMUNITY, PLANNING, URBAN GROWTH POLICY.

Urgency of the Situation Doctrine. See IMPEACHMENT.

Urgent Fury, Operation. The code name for the American incursion into Grenada in 1983, where the Cubans were building a military runway for possible use by Soviet forces.

U.S. Designating either the UNITED STATES or UNITED STATES REPORTS.

U.S.–British Plan on Rhodesia. On November 26, 1976, representatives of the governments of the United States and England met in Geneva, Switzerland, where a plan was presented to the Rhodesian government suggesting solutions for final peace in Rhodesia. Also present at the meeting were the black leaders of the Rhodesian African National Council (represented by Robert Mugabe), the Zimbabwe African National Union (ZANU), and the Zimbabwe African People's Union (ZAPU). The main proposal contained in the plan was that Rhodesia apply the principle of "one man, one vote," and turn the government over to the black leaders by March 1, 1978. That plan was accepted by the black groups but was rejected by Ian Smith, the Prime Minister of Rhodesia, who called it "mad," "crazy," and "insane," and asked, instead, that an International Police Force be provided by the United Nations. On September 24, 1977, representatives of the black groups from Rhodesia met with the representatives of neighboring states (Mozambique, Tanzania, Angola, Botswana, and Zambia) in Maputo, Mozambique, where the U.S.-British plan for settlement in Rhodesia was officially endorsed, subsequently, this plan was implemented and the state was renamed Zimbabwe in 1980. See ZANU, ZAPU.

U.S. Citizenship. See CITIZENSHIP.

U.S. Civil Service Commission. Created by Pendleton Act 1883 to implement a merit system for workers in federal bureaucracy.

U.S. Definition of Human Rights. See HUMAN RIGHTS: AMERICAN DEFINITION.

U.S. House of Representatives Manual. See BILL.

U.S. House of Representatives Select Committee on Intelligence. See CENTRAL INTELLIGENCE AGENCY (CIA).

U.S. Office of Federal Contract Compliance. See AFFIRMATIVE ACTION.

U.S. President: Quasi Legal Qualifications. See QUASI LEGAL QUALIFICATIONS FOR U.S. PRESIDENT.

U.S. Senate Select Committee on Intelligence. See CENTRAL INTELLIGENCE AGENCY (CIA).

U.S. Senate Select Committee to Study Government Operations with Respect to Intelligence Activities. See HT/LINGUAL.

Use Immunity. The practice of exempting a person who testifies as a witness before an investigative body (e.g., Congressional Committee in the United States) or a judicial body (e.g., court of law) from prosecution for anything he may say during testimony. The immunity does not extend to evidence gathered against the witness independently by other means. See JUSTICE, LAW, RIGHT.

USIA. See UNITED STATES INFORMATION AGENCY.

USIB. See UNITED STATES INTELLIGENCE BOARD.

USIS. See UNITED STATES INFORMATION SERVICE.

USSR. See UNION OF SOVIET SOCIALIST REPUBLICS.

Usury. The practice of lending money at excessive interest rates (beyond the limits allowed by law).

Utilitarianism. The notion that the worth or value of anything is determined solely by its usefulness. In the social sciences, a concept emphasizing that the purpose of any action should be to bring about the greatest happiness to the largest number of persons. Utilitarianism was named by Jeremy Bentham

(1748-1832) and given its widest application and acceptance through the writings of John Stuart Mill (1806-1873).

Utility Maximization. A complex of judgments based on tangible facts and rational thinking upon which a sophisticated voter or policy maker makes a decision on issues of public policy. The notion is derived from free market practices in a polyarchy (democratic) political system.

Utopia. An ancient dream of an ideal society to be characterized by lack of conflict (wars), mutual love among people and nations, and high prosperity with a minimum of physical exertion. The communists envision such a state of utopia as evolving once private property disappears, classes disappear, and exploitation of man by man disappears. Then, according to this theory, instead of compulsion by a state, people will manage themselves-motivated not by material incentives, but by self-consciousness about the communal well-being. In order to commence the creation of a utopian society, numerous experiments have been conducted by people everywhere. In the United States, for example, the movement toward a search for utopia was strong during the 1800s, as exemplified by the Oneida Colony founded in 1848 in New York, which practiced free love, common ownership of land and property, and advocated an eugenic selection of parents to produce superior offspring. When prosecuted by the authorities, the Oneida Colony introduced monogamy in 1879 and abandoned other communal practices. There also were: the New Harmony Settlement in Indiana, a communal colony, and Brook Farm in Massachusetts, an intellectual group which advocated "plain living and high thinking," and "working smarter not harder." Wealthy textile manufacturer, Robert Owen, was one of the supporters of such communes in the United States. He was the founder of New Harmony, which he called Preliminary Society, a community of equals, based on the Declaration of Mental Liberty as proclaimed by the Declaration of Independence. See MARXISM, UTOPIAN SOCIALISM.

Utopian Socialism. That body of social, economic, and political concepts which were developed before Karl Marx by such writers as François Babeuf (1760-1797), Henri Saint-Simon (1760-1825), Charles Fourier (1722-1837), Louis Blanc (1811-1882), and Robert Owen (1771-1837)—whom Marx appraised as "utopian" mainly because they rejected revolution as the vehicle for social change. Karl Marx referred to his brand of socialism as "scientific." See MARXISM, SOCIALISM, UTOPIA.

Uyezd. A small political subdivision within the gubernya (province) in pre-Bolshevik Russia. See Appendix 74.

"Peace, commerce, and honest friendship with all nations—entangling alliances with none."
THOMAS JEFFERSON, 1743-1826

V-E Day. The "Victory in Europe Day" when Nazi Germany accepted unconditional surrender on May 7, 1945; the official victory day proclaimed was May 8, 1945. See CASABLANCA CONFERENCE, SCHWARZE KAPELLE.

V-J Day. "Victory in Japan Day," September 2, 1945, when U.S. General Douglas MacArthur accepted unconditional surrender from Japan's Emperor Hirohito (the "Son of Heaven") aboard the U.S. Battleship *Missouri*, in Tokyo Bay. Japan accepted "unconditional surrender" only after an atomic bomb (the first ever used) had been dropped Hiroshima, August 6, 1945, killing 180,000 persons and on Nagasaki, August 9, 1945, killing 70,000 persons. The emperor was allowed to remain free as a "symbol of unity of the nation."

Valuation Tax. See CITY.

Value. Those tangible (material) and intangible (spiritual) things or thoughts which one holds supreme, priceless and uncompromising; anything that is useful and pragmatic in practical politics; or anything that is workable and applicable to problem-solving within the milieu of accepted political culture of the society. See POLITICAL CULTURE, POLITICAL ETHICS.

Value-Added Tax (VAT). A tax that may be added to or built into the price of merchandise sold on the market. It is computed by assessing a tax on each step of a product's preparation for market; that is, the "value added" to a product at each of these steps is taxed. See FLAT TAX.

Value Theory. In the development of public policy there is always the question of value. Values are the base for individual action (behavior). Values may also be attributed to groups in a society or to the whole of a society. As Professor R. C. Pratt states: "Primary values are first order values, the core belief of one's ethical and political value system for which we feel no justification is required and for which none can be offered. Secondary values are these for which reasons can be offered, reasons which refer back to the more fundamental primary values held by the individual." Primary values in a society may include: truth, justice, equality, one-man-one-vote, which are generally accepted in the abstract or theoretical level. Such values are often found in the basic documents of a society. In the United States, these basic values are found in the Declaration of Independence and the Constitution. However, in developing public policy to implement such values there may not be universal agreement in the society. To paraphrase from Orwell's *Animal Farm* "... all men are created equal, but some are more equal than others." In the late 1960s a new value dimension developed, one that went beyond the traditional concepts of efficiency and economy. It was EQUITY. The essence of this new value was that it was incumbent upon public policy administrators to seek out those for whom the policies had been developed to insure that they were aware of and received the benefits from those policies. The most in need to be served by this new value concept were those in the lower socio-economic status. In economic terms, Adam Smith's *Wealth of Nations* (1776) set forth a set of principles which were to become the basis for what was to be known as the classical tradition. A major theme for Smith was the explanation of value in use and value in exchange. Smith believed that labor—not land or money—was both the source and the final measure of value. Earlier in his classical work, Smith had delineated a distinction between "use value" and "exchange value." He then used water and diamonds to illustrate his point. Water, he observed, has great use value but little exchange value; whereas diamonds have great exchange value but relatively little value in use. Another writer on value was David Ricardo. Ricardo's major work, *Principles of Political Economy and Taxation*

538

(1817) was, in part, a re-evaluation of Adam Smith. Ricardo disagreed with Smith's labor theory of value, and provided further insight into Smith's distinction between value in use and value in exchange. He observed that for a commodity to have value in exchange, it must have utility. However, utility is not the measure of value. In brief, it can be stated that for Ricardo the differences in the volume of labor needed to produce commodities accounted for the differences in their value. Thus, for Ricardo, the value of a commodity is determined by the amount of labor needed in which its production. In 1848 John Stuart Mill wrote *Principles of Political Economy,* he sought to update the work of Adam Smith. In his discussion of exchange value, Smith is conditioned by his analysis of the interaction of the forces of supply and demand. While recognizing that value is set by the quantity of labor needed to produce commodities, the price of a good in the market is conditioned by factors by which the forces of supply and demand are significant determinants. Value theory is constantly evolving as time and conditions in society change. 1848 was one of those times of change in Europe. It was also the year that two thinkers of the political and social conditions in society published their observations. Friedrich Engels and Karl Marx outlined their reflections in a statement of principles ... *Communist Manifesto.* In dealing with the value question, Marx recognizes the traditional categories of use value and exchange value. He dismisses use value as not a matter of concern for the political economist. Instead, he focuses on exchange value because the value of labor is involved. Marx went on to discuss surplus value. He identified two parts to labor: necessary labor and surplus labor. The result of necessary labor is what the worker earns, the result of surplus labor is what the capitalist gets. He then stated that the value of surplus labor is equivalent to exploitation of labor. Thus he was able to develop the concept of class struggle between the working class and the ownership class in society. Value theory continues to be studied and additional theories develope as conditions in society change. See POLITICAL THEORY.

Value Theory in Political Science. See POLITICAL THEORY.

Vandenberg Resolution. See NORTH ATLANTIC TREATY ORGANIZATION (NATO).

Vanguard of the Proletariat. According to Vladimir I. Lenin, founder of the Soviet State and the Communist Party of the Soviet Union (CPSU), the Communist Party, which is the pathfinder and the leading force of the proletariat, is the vanguard of the proletariat everywhere. See MARXISM, SOCIALISM.

Vargas' Neutrality. One of the major coups of Anglo-American intelligence in political warfare during W.W.II was the turning about of pro-Nazi Brazil under the leadership of President Getulio Vargas into a neutral and, since the Rio Conference, anti-Axis nation in Latin America, thus depriving the Germans and the Italians of an important link with the Western Hemisphere and needed supplies of beef, war materiel, and intelligence. The intelligence service planted a letter on a German diplomatic courier traveling to Brazil, which was subsequently "stolen" and "leaked" to the press revealing German and Italian aggressive objectives toward Latin America and being very critical of Brazil, its President, and the Brazilian people (e.g., referring to the Brazilians as "monkeys"). When President Vargas learned about the "secret" communication, he decided: to declare neutrality; to close down the Italian airline, the LATI, which was the only remaining Axis link with the Western Hemisphere and a courier of war material and intelligence information needed by the Axis; and to join the United States and other Latin American nations (during the subsequent Rio Conference) in their common struggle against the Axis powers. Vargas was not aware that he was acting on the basis of fabricated information of Anglo-American intelligence; although in reality, Adolf Hitler did have a plan to establish a Nazi empire in Latin America in the future which was to be named "New Spain." See POLITICAL WARFARE, RIO CONFERENCE OF 1941-1942.

Variable. See DEPENDENT VARIABLES.

Vassal State. A state subservient to another; a satellite state. See SOVEREIGNTY.

VAT. See VALUE-ADDED TAX.

V.C. During the Vietnamese War, the letters stood for the radio calls of American soldiers, V for "Victor" and C for "Charlie." Also, used as a designation for "Vietnamese Communist."

Velcroid. One who worships and/or seeks personal contact or association with the head of state and/or the head of government (e.g., president, chancellor, prime minister, king or queen).

Velvet Revolution. As a result of well-organized anti-government demonstrations, the communist government in Czechoslovakia resigned in panic on 24 November 1989, and on 10 December a democratic government was formed with Vaclav Havel, a playwright and political dissident, who became President on 29 December 1989. President Havel was assisted in his efforts by a dedicated and knowledgeable nobleman, Prince Schwarzenberg, Langrf of Kleggau, Count of Sulz, Duke of Krumlof, who was broad and grew up in Czechoslovakia and dedicated his efforts to this fine country. Prince Scwarzenberg serves currently under President Havel as his Chancellor of the President. In May 1991 all Soviet troops stationed in Czechoslovakia pulled out and the state was renamed "Czech and Slovak Federated Republic." The American ambassador to Czechoslovakia was Shirley Temple Black, former child movie star and an institution in her own right. As an American diplomat as well as a private person, she rendered unprecedented and far-reaching aid and assistance to Vaclav Havel and his followers, thus making the revolution lady-like and soft as velvet. The term "Velvet Revolution" was coined by the President, Vaclav Havel. See CHARTER 77.

Veni, Vidi, Vici. In the Latin language, "I came, I saw, I conquered." A slogan of predatory imperialistic expansion first used by Roman Caesars; wherever they went and saw something of interest, they integrated it into the Roman Empire. Term often used in predatory management and politics, where winning is the ultimate goal.

Venture Capitalism. See WAR ON POVERTY.

Venue. The locality in which a case may be brought up before a court of law for trial. If a defendant justifiably suspects that he may not receive a fair trial in a given locality (e.g., due to hostile environment or too extensive pre-trial publicity), he may request that this case be tried in another locality by means of change of venue.

Verona Congress. See QUADRUPLE ALLIANCE.

Versailles Treaty. A peace settlement that was signed on June 28, 1919, in the Palace of Versailles, Paris, France, between defeated Germany and the Central Powers: England (ratified July 26, 1919), Germany (ratified July 10, 1919), Italy (ratified October 7, 1919), France (ratified October 13, 1919), Japan (ratified October 27, 1919), China (never signed), and the United States (submitted to the U.S. Senate on July 10, 1919, and rejected on November 19, 1919, on the ground that American sovereignty was not properly safeguarded in the League of Nations which was a part of the Treaty. Among the harsh measures that the Treaty (Articles 42-44) imposed on Germany (which subsequently helped Adolf Hitler to gain power) were: (1) prohibition of a standing army of over 100,000 men; (2) demilitarization of territories west of the Rhine River, where no fortifications of any kind could be constructed within fifty miles of the river bank. (This measure was reinforced by the Locarno Pact of 1925 by which the Germans agreed to guarantee the security of its western neighbors, mainly France); (3) prohibition of a standing navy and an air force. (The Nazi Luftwaffe was established and trained in the Soviet Union in secrecy from the western powers); and (4) a payment for war damages in the amount of $32,000,000,000, which was reduced to $714,000,000 in 1932 (or too little too late, because the German economy was destroyed before being allowed to recover, and the only rational and speedy means to recovery was sought by placing Adolf Hitler in charge). Between 1925 and 1939 Adolf Hitler not only repudiated the Versailles Treaty, but during the single month of March 1938, took possession of the Rhineland (that had been lost during World War I); annexed Austria; conquered Bohemia, Moravia, and a part of Lithuania (took the seaport of Memel); and abrogated a non-aggression pact with Poland. See LEAGUE OF NATIONS.

Verteilungskampf. See DISTRIBUTION BATTLE.

Vertical Distribution of Power. See FRAGMENTATION OF POWER.

Vertical Growth of Government. See POLITICAL DEVELOPMENT.

Vertical Imperialism. See COLONIALISM, IMPERIALISM.

Vertical Social Mobility. See SOCIAL MOBILITY.

Very Important Person (VIP). An informal designation of high government officials (e.g., politicians, administrators, diplomats, or persons who distinguish themselves in their professions or by service to the well-being of the society), particularly when they appear in public. See DIPLOMATIC PROTOCOL.

Vested Interest Lobby. A lobby that attempts continuously to influence legislation through individual legislators or their staffs to bring about the passage of laws that would give financial advantage to one group over another. Legislators susceptible to industry influence, for example, may be given such nicknames as "Pig Iron Kelly," "King Cotton Daddy," "Sugar Daddy," or "the Senator from Boeing." See ARAB LOBBY, JEWISH LOBBY, LOBBY.

Veto. In the Latin language, "I forbid." An executive device which nullifies legislative acts. Veto is the potent power of the U.S. President, which he may use when he disapproves of congressional legislation. U.S. President George Washington was the first U.S. President to exercise that right when he vetoed an apportionment bill in 1791. President Franklin D. Roosevelt (1933-1944) used his veto power 625 times in 12 years, with nine of his vetoes being overturned by Congress. President Gerald R. Ford (1974-1977) used the veto power 58 times during his short term in office and President George Bush, as of March 1992, 26 times. Seven U.S. Presidents never exercised the veto power: William Henry Harrison, 1841-1841; James K. Polk, 1845-1849; Millard Fillmore, 1850-1853; Franklin Pierce, 1853-1857; Rutherford B. Hayes, 1877-1881; James A. Garfield, 1881-1881; and Warren G. Harding, 1921-1923. See POCKET VETO.

Veto Proof Congress. See NON-VETOABLE LEGISLATION.

Veto Proof Legislation. See NON-VETOABLE LEGISLATION.

Vetting. A term associated with the investigation of the background of a person working for one political system (e.g., capitalistic) to find out if he has connections and sympathies with another system (e.g., socialistic) that may create a conflict of interests. See LOYALTY LAW.

Vice President of the United States. The second-ranking executive officer of the United States (second to the U.S. President) who is elected on the same ticket as the U.S. President (and as his running mate) in accordance with the provisions of Article II of the U.S. Constitution in Appendix 8). The only constitutional duties prescribed for the Vice President are those of presiding over the U.S. Senate (and vote in case of a tie), and succeeding to the presidency in case it becomes vacant (see Amendment XXV in Appendix 8). U.S. President D. D. Eisenhower (1943-1971), and other Presidents following him, have assigned additional duties to their Vice Presidents (e.g., presiding over the National Security Council or visiting foreign nations on good will tours). President John Adams, who served once as Vice President, described the office as "the most insignificant that ever the mind of man did conceive." Vice President Nelson Rockefeller, serving under President Gerald R. Ford (see Appendices 8, 16, 17), was the first to reside in an official residence designated for the U.S. Vice President (a large wooden structure, once used by the military, which hardly reflects the dignity of that high office). See PRESIDENT OF THE UNITED STATES, Appendix 16.

Vichy France. See VICHY GOVERNMENT.

Vichy Government. The government organized in France (upon its defeat by the forces of Nazi Germany during World War II which collaborated with the German occupational forces. The government was established by French Marshal Henri Philippe Pétain and lasted from 1940 to 1945. (The U.S. maintained its diplomatic relations with the Vichy regime until April, 1942.)

Victimless Crime. A harmful and illegal act under the "eyes of the law," which is self-inflicted (e.g., drug-taking, alcoholism, gambling, suicide, self-immolation—self-destruction by a flammable fluid, homosexuality) and does not directly harm other persons. This controversial concept is viewed differently under different judicial systems. Some (e.g., some segments of the Women Liberation Movement) claim that victimless crime is not the law's business. The prevailing view, however, is that there is no such thing as a "victimless crime" because no person lives in total isolation in a politically organized society; any crime always affects more than one individual, if not the whole society (e.g., the body of a suicide victim must be disposed of with some effort and expense, either to other persons or to the state).

Victoria et Impera. See DIVIDE ET IMPERA.

Vienna Convention on Consular Relations. See VIENNA CONVENTION ON DIPLOMATIC RELATIONS.

Vienna Convention on Diplomatic Relations. A UN-sponsored conference was held in Vienna, Austria, in 1961 for the purpose of codifying most of the existing customary laws of diplomatic immunities, which are binding even on nations which have not ratified the Convention. The Convention went into force on April 24, 1964, upon ratification by most European states, and by 1968 it had been ratified by sixty states. (Municipal law of the United States, for example, provides for penalties for assaulting foreign diplomats—18 U.S.C. sect. 112; for attempting to serve process on a diplomat—22 U.S.C. secs. 252—255; for picketing or protesting otherwise at foreign legations—22 U.S.C. secs. 255a, 255b.) A similar Convention was adopted in 1963, also in Vienna, Austria, pertaining to consular personnel (the Vienna Convention on Consular Relations), which went into force on July 15, 1968. The Soviet Union and the United States concluded a bilateral agreement regulating their diplomatic relations through the United States-Soviet Union Consular Convention of 1968.

Vienna Convention on the Law of Treaties. Concluded on May 23, 1969, in Vienna, Austria, the Convention codified a series of commonly recognized norms of international law pertaining to treaty-making and their observance by states. Its ultimate aim was to preserve international peace and security through rigid observance of existing and future treaty obligations among and between states. See PACTA SUNT SERVANDA, CLAUSULA REBUS SIC STANTIBUS.

Vienna Plan. A plan calling for the limitation of strategic missile launchers maintained by the Soviet Union and the United States. The plan, approved by the Soviet Union on July 24, 1970, was presented during one of the conferences on Strategic Arms Limitation Talks (SALT) held in Vienna, Austria. While it provides that each party (the Soviet Union and the United States) is to maintain not more than 2,000 missile launchers, it does not provide for any inspections in order to assure that the agreement is being complied with. See STRATEGIC ARMS LIMITATION TALKS (SALT).

Viet Cong (V.C.). Any member of the pro-communist forces in South Vietnam. See VIETNAMIZATION.

Viet-Minh. In the Vietnamese language, the "language of independence." Also, the political organization that was set up in 1941 by Vietnam's communist leader Ho Chi Minh for the purpose of combating the Japanese invaders and later, the French forces present in Indochina. In 1954 the forces of the Viet-Minh (under the leadership of General Giap) defeated the French at Dien Bien Phu (the cease-fire accord was signed in Geneva, Switzerland, on July 21, 1954) and established the so-called Democratic Republic of Vietnam (North Vietnam). In 1975, the Viet-Minh and the Viet-Cong (the southern faction of the Viet-Minh) took control of the entire country once the American forces pulled out, ending the Vietnamese War that had lasted from 1945-1974. Ho was 54 years old when he started his guerrilla group and in 1945 he was an agent of the American Office of Strategic Services (OSS), the predecessor of the CIA. The OSS allowed him to supervise a group of fifty other agents because he spoke some English, had been trained in France and had visited and studied in America (he always carried a copy of the American Declaration of Independence with him), and because of his diligent and reliable work. Ho was hopeful that in return for his collaboration the Americans would assist him in the establishment of a democratic regime in Vietnam after the expulsion of the Japanese. However, the Americans, instead, let the French restore their colonial domination and, disappointed, Ho sought help from anyone who would help him restore the Vietnamese government and remove the French. Only the Soviet Union and China were willing to help. He achieved his goal in 1954 by defeating the French in Dien Bien Phu, and when the Americans, in 1974, withdrew from Vietnam in frustration. When the United States had aided in the creation of the South Vietnamese government, Ho predicted very early, that, in case of war between the South and the North, the North would prevail, because the Southern leaders had no purpose or ideology of their own besides personal enrichment, and because, in case of a long-lasting, guerrilla-type protracted war, the American political temperament would not tolerate it, and, the United States, sooner or later, would abandon the Southern government. This prediction by Ho was made in 1961, shortly after President John F. Kennedy agreed to send an advisory team of some fifty U.S. soldiers to the South Vietnamese government. "Uncle Ho," as the Americans (at one time) and the Vietnamese called Ho, also decided that in retaliation for his betrayal by the Americans he would seek revenge by demoralizing any foreign soldier on his territory by means of free distribution of narcotics. This was a tactic similar to that used by the British during the Opium War when they wanted to demoralize the Chinese and gain political control over China's people and resources. Allegedly, about 95 percent of American servicemen engaged in combat in Vietnam experimented with narcotics—compliments of "Uncle Ho," and that is what he allegedly said when informed of the success: "Ho, Ho, Ho." Ho had also resented what he considered racial slurs when American soldiers referred to the Vietnamese as "gooks" and to the North Vietnamese or Viet Cong soldiers as "Charlies." See VIETNAM WAR, VIETNAMIZATION.

Vietnam-Cambodia War of 1977. See PROXY WAR.

Vietnam Era Proclamation. On May 7, 1975, President Ford signed the "Vietnam Era" Proclamation which ended wartime veterans' benefits for new military recruits.

Vietnam Moratorium Day. A nationwide campaign by anti-war groups in the United States calling upon the U.S. Government to terminate the war in Vietnam, or at least to withdraw its support of it. The Moratorium was held on October 15, 1969, without official sanction by the U.S. Government.

Vietnam Syndrome. The general dissatisfaction among Americans with their involvement and the outcome of the Vietnam War (1954-1974). The war divided the nation and depleted resources badly needed for domestic programs (e.g., the Great Society which was abandoned because of the war); and young Americans could not understand why they should go and eventually risk their life for some regime ten thousand miles away while there were problems to be taken care of at home (e.g., the civil rights movement by black Americans demanding a better life and larger share in the wealth of the nation). Also, the Vietnam War left Americans with a reluctance to intervene abroad militarily, and with doubts about the strength, resolve, and ability of their military forces. The Russians experienced a similar syndrome with their involvement in 1979 in Afghanistan, which they refer to as the "Afghanistan Syndrome."

Vietnamization. A series of steps, taken jointly by the United States (President Nixon wanted to withdraw "with honor") and South Vietnam, designed to render the South Vietnamese self-sufficient and capable of defending themselves against the North Vietnamese and the Vietcong once American forces departed. The first major step was the incursion into Cambodia (on April 30, 1974) to clean out the North Vietnamese sanctuaries there. President Nixon had not informed Congress about this move and, as a result, Congress voted not only to cut off funds for any further incursions outside Vietnam, but under the WAR POWERS ACT OF 1973 (introduced by U.S. Senator of New York, Jacob K. Javits) it forbade the President to deploy U.S. military forces anywhere without prior authorization from Congress. The bill was vetoed by President Richard M. Nixon (1969-1974) on the grounds that it would undermine this nation's ability to act decisively and convincingly in times of international crisis. Congress overrode Nixon's veto on November 7, 1973, by a vote of 284 to 135 in the House and 78 to 15 in the Senate (two-thirds majority required in each house to override a presidential veto). The second major step was the so-called "pacification program," a series of reforms and economic aid programs designed for the rural areas of Vietnam (the hamlets) to render them resistant to hostile influence.

Vietnik. One in opposition to the War in Vietnam and America's involvement in it. See ANTI-VIETNAM WAR SLOGANS.

Vigilante. In the Italian language, "look-out," "watch-out"; also, a volunteer police force in the American West during the 1800s that assisted sheriffs or marshals, or exercised its own brand of justice in the absence of law enforcement by the government; it also assisted in posse comitatus and often engaged in illegal exercise of judicial functions (Kangaroo courts) and in carrying out of sentences (vigilante justice). See POSSE COMITATUS.

Vigilante Justice. See VIGILANTE.

Vigorous Reaction to Cease-Fire Violation in Vietnam. See TRAGIC SITUATION.

Vik Democratic Cause Game. A political warfare game invented by a Polish professor during World War II for the purpose of subjecting Fascists, Nazis, and their sympathizers to ". . . continuous petty persecution with the object of wasting their time, confusing their affairs, fraying their nerves, and getting them in trouble with the local population," and to generally undermine their political system. The game was termed a "fascinating new pastime for all lovers of democracy," and the players were instructed to keep in mind that ". . . in playing Vik you are in your own small way acting as a fighting member of the forces of Democracy. Therefore, be silent, secret and discreet." The "game" was published in four languages (English, French, Spanish and Portuguese) with the aid of British intelligence. Some of such petty harassments of Nazis and Fascists and their sympathizers, particularly in third countries (e.g., outside the German Reich and Italy proper) were: "A Nazi could be telephoned at all hours of the night and when awakened could be apologetically assured that it was a wrong number; the air could be made to disappear mysteriously from his motor tyres; shops could be telephoned on his behalf and asked to deliver large quantities of useless and cumbersome goods— payment on delivery; masses of futile correspondence could reach him without stamps so that he was constantly having to pay out small sums of money; his girlfriend could receive anonymous letters saying that he was suffering from an unpleasant disease or that he was keeping a woman and six children in Detroit; a rat might die in his water-tank; his favourite dog might get lost; and street musicians might be hired to play *God Save the King* outside his house all night." In order to discredit a Nazi diplomat in Brazil, who was to be soon appointed as the new ambassador to that country, a letter was circulated attesting to the effect that he was lacking in skill as a diplomat as much as in virility. "Gentlemen," said the anonymous letter in part, "this man . . . is capable of robbing you of your money, your business and your country, but never of your wives." See POLITICAL WARFARE.

Vinculum Matrimonii. In the Latin language, "the bond of marriage" or "the act of marriage."

VIP. See VERY IMPORTANT PERSON.

Virginia Association of Counties (VACO). The Virginia Association of Counties (VACO) was established in 1935 as an independent, non-profit instrumentality of Virginia county governments. It provides professional support and legislative advocacy for Virginia's ninety-five (95) counties. The association also works cooperatively with its national counterpart in Washington, D.C., the National Association of Counties. Similar associations of county governments can be found in other states. While counties, as units of government, comprise the membership roster, elected officials from each county serve as officers of the association and members of its various committees.

Virginia Bill of Rights. One of the first bills of rights of a comprehensive nature that appeared in North America, which influenced similar activities in other states as well as in other nations the world over. It was drafted on May 15, 1776, during a State Convention which evolved from the House of Burgesses (which had been dissolved by Governor Dunmore in May 1774). The Convention, which acted as the legislature of the Virginia Colony for two years (1774-1776) also drafted a constitution for the Colony, and instructed its delegates to the Continental Congress to propose a declaration of independence from England, which was later prepared by Thomas Jefferson, a Virginian. Many of the provisions of the Virginia Bill of Rights were incorporated into the American Constitution and its amendments. The Bill reads in part: "SECTION 1. That all men are by nature equally free and independent, and have certain inherent rights, of which, when they enter into a free state of society, they cannot, by any compact, deprive or divest their posterity; namely, the enjoyment of life and liberty, with the means of acquiring and possessing property, and pursuing and obtaining happiness and safety"; "SECTION 2. That all power is vested in, and consequently derived from, the people; that magistrates and their trustees and servants are not all times amenable to them." The other provisions pertain to protection of freedoms (e.g., press, speech, assembly, worship), stating that ". . . religion . . . can be directed only by reason and conviction, not by force or violence"; and also stating that standing armies in peace should be avoided as dangerous to liberty; all armies and militia should be under civil control, and change of government should be made by peaceful means. The principal author of the Virginia Declaration of Rights was George Mason (1725-1792), a wealthy planter and statesman who in 1787 was a delegate to the Philadelphia Constitutional Convention. Once the Constitution was adopted, however, he refused to sign it (for fear of extensive federal powers) and when appointed the first U.S. Senator of Virginia under the new constitution he refused to serve.

Virginia Dynasty. See VIRGINIA: MOTHER OF PRESIDENTS.

Virginia: Mother of Presidents. The Commonwealth of Virginia is often referred to as the "Mother of Presidents," because the following chief executives of the American nation of states were born there: (1) George Washington, February 22, 1732-December 14, 1799; U.S President 1789-1797. In addition to being the first U.S. President, George Washington also served as Commander-in-Chief of the Revolutionary forces. (2) Thomas Jefferson, March 13, 1743-July 4, 1826; U.S. President 1801-1809. Jefferson also served as Vice President under John Adams, 1797-1801; U.S. Secretary of State under George Washington, 1789-1793; was chosen in June 1776 by the Second Continental Congress to draft the *Declaration of Independence*; served as Governor of Virginia, 1779-1781; served in the state legislature of Virginia, 1776-1779; and as U.S. Minister to France, 1785-1789. (3) James Madison, March 16, 1751-June 28, 1836; U.S President, 1809-1817; author of 54 of the 85 *Federalist Papers*; drafted the Constitution of Virginia in 1776; was a member of the executive council of Virginia which directed the Revolutionary War; member of the U.S. House of Representatives, 1789-1797; U.S. Secretary of State under Jefferson, 1801-1809; framed the Virginia Resolution of 1798 which condemned the Alien and Sedition Acts which the Federalists, particularly Alexander Hamilton, were instrumental in implementing. (4) James Monroe, April 28, 1758-July 4, 1831; U.S. President, 1817-1825, proclaimed the "Monroe Doctrine" in 1823; acquired Florida in 1819; was instrumental in the establishment of Liberia in Africa in 1817, as a colony of American Negroes. Its capital, Monrovia, was named in Monroe's honor; served as U.S. Secretary of State under Madison, 1811-1817; served as Governor of Virginia, 1799-1803; Minister to France, 1794-1796; served in the Continental Congress, 1791-1794; and in the Virginia legislature, 1782-1791. (5) William Henry Harrison, February 9, 1773-April 4, 1841; U.S. President, 1841-1841 (died in office); served as Governor of the Indian Territory, 1800-1812; became U.S. Representative, State Senator, and U.S. Senator from 1816 to 1841 combined. (6) John Tyler, March 29, 1790-January 18, 1862; U.S. President, 1841-1845; Vice President under Harrison, March 4, 1841-April 4, 1841; member of the state legislature, U.S. Congressman, and Governor of Virginia, between 1812 and 1841. (7) Zachary Taylor, November 24, 1784-July 9, 1850; U.S. President, 1849-1850 (died in office); favored admission of anti-slave California to the Union in 1850; Army general 1837-1845. (8) Woodrow Wilson, December 28, 1856-February 3, 1924; U.S President, 1913-1921; President of Princeton University, New Jersey 1902-1910; Governor of the state of New Jersey, 1910-1913; author of an important political treatise, *Congressional Government 1883*; creator after W.W.I of the League of Nations which the U.S. Senate rejected. Other famous Virginians in public affairs have included: John Marshall, Chief Justice of the U.S. Supreme Court, 1801-1831; instrumental in establishing the doctrine of judicial review in the landmark case of *Marbury v. Madison (1803)*; that individual states may not tax federal property located on their territory, was established as doctrine in *McCulloch v. Maryland (1819)*; that the scope and degree of application of federal statutes is subject to review by federal and not state courts and that federal courts have the power to review decisions by state courts was established in *Cohens v. Virginia (1821)*; that no state can abridge or invalidate a valid contract, was established in *Dartmouth College v. Woodward (1819)*; and that no state can by its own actions hinder interstate commerce which is subject to federal regulation, was established in *Gibbons v. Ogden (1824)*. John Blair, Associate Justice of the U.S. Supreme Court, 1789-1796; Philip P. Barbour, Associate Justice of the U.S. Supreme Court, 1836-1841; Peter V. Daniel, Associate Justice of the U.S. Supreme Court, 1841-1860; Lewis F. Powell, Jr., Associate Justice of the U.S. Supreme Court, 1971-. Philip B. Barbour, Speaker of the U.S. House of Representatives, 1821-1823. Andrew Stevenson, Speaker of the U.S House of Representatives, 1827-1834. Robert M. T. Hunter, Speaker of the U.S. House of Representatives, 1839-1841. John W. Jones, Speaker of the U.S. House of Representatives, 1843-1845. See Appendices 5-17.

Virginia Municipal League (VML). The League is a non-profit, non-partisan organization of cities, towns, and counties of Virginia. Counties that join the League are usually those which have increased in population, commercial, and industrial capacity so that they provide "urban" type services throughout their jurisdiction. Such counties are, in effect, no longer rural. The Virginia Municipal League was established in 1905 for the purpose of improving and assisting local government through legislative advocacy, education, research, and cooperative effort. Currently, all 41 Virginia cities, 156 towns and 16 counties are members of the League. While local governments, as corporate entities are members of the League, each is represented by elected and/or appointed officials. Such officials serve as officers of the organization and on the various committees established. Such organizations of local officials exist in every state, although the names may differ.

Virginia Nod. According to political legend, one desiring to enter politics in Virginia could do so only upon receiving an approving nod from the leadership of the Byrd Political Machine (named after Harry F. Byrd, Sr., a wealthy apple grower, once the Governor of Virginia and U.S. Senator.) See POLITICAL MACHINE.

Virginia Plan of the Union. A plan submitted to the Philadelphia Constitutional Convention in 1787 which called for the popular election of the members of the United States House of Representatives, who in turn would choose the members of the Senate, the President, and the judicial officers of the government. The plan was mainly the work of James Madison. See PLANS OF THE AMERICAN UNION.

Virginia Resources Authority (VRA). The Authority was created by the Virginia General Assembly in 1984. The Authority is authorized to provide financing for water, waste water treatment, drainage, drainfield management, and solid waste projects. The Authority has a "bond fund cap" of $400 million, and sells its bonds with a AAA credit rating with the moral backing of the Commonwealth of Virginia. The Authority is classified as a non-state agency and operates financially independent of the state government. The VRA manages two different loan programs: The Bond Loan Program and the Revolving Loan Funds. The governing Board of Directors includes private citizens as well as state government employees. In essence, the Authority seeks to provide financing for safe drinking water, waste water treatment, and solid waste management facilities to all Virginia communities in dealing with these environmental challenges.

Virtual Representation. See STAMP ACT.

Vital Interest. Ordinarily considered of vital interest are the existence and security of the people and the state; also territorial integrity and free exercise of sovereign powers; or a claim extended to other states (e.g., regarding oil in the Middle East, the Persian Gulf, and Latin America; free access to international waterways as in the Panama and Suez Canals; or other considerations). Presidential doctrines usually address issues and define them as vital to the interest of the United States. The term "vital" also applies to the several raw materials which the United States must import from other parts of the world because of insufficient supply at home. See CRITICAL RAW MATERIALS, NATIONAL INTEREST.

Vitalism. A philosophical doctrine which holds that the paramount reality is life, and everything else (e.g., thought, and matter) is only its manifestation.

Viva Voce Vote. In the Latin language, "live voice." Also, a voice vote indicating consent (or lack of it) and expressed by either "aye" (yes) or "nay" (no). See UNITED STATES CONGRESS, VOTING.

VKP (b). See COMMUNIST PARTY OF THE SOVIET UNION (CPSU).

Vladivostok Accord. See STRATEGIC ARMS LIMITATION TALKS, VLADIVOSTOK CONFERENCE.

Vladivostok Conference. See STRATEGIC ARMS LIMITATION TALKS (SALT).

Vladivostok Summit. U.S. President Gerald R. Ford and Soviet General-Secretary of the CPSU (and President of the USSR since 1977) Leonid I. Brezhneyev met on November 23-24, 1974, in this Siberian city in the USSR, where an agreement was reached on the limiting of the arms race. See STRATEGIC ARMS LIMITATION TALKS (SALT).

Vlasov Army. An army composed of two divisions (approximately 24,000 men) of deserters and prisoners of war of the Soviet Red Army. The army was organized in 1942 by Lieutenant General (Colonel General according to Soviet rank designation) Andrei A. Vlasov, a former commander of the Red Army who was captured by the Germans in 1942. Vlasov decided to collaborate with the enemy for the sake of destroying the Communist regime in the Soviet Union. For that purpose he also established the so-called "Free Russia Committee" which was to serve as the nucleus of the future government of Russia. Vlasov and his army were captured in 1944 in Czechoslovakia by the Third

Army of the United States commanded by General George Patton; they were subsequently returned to the Soviet authorities who executed them en masse in 1946.

VOA. Voice of America. See INTERNATIONAL COMMUNICATION AGENCY (ICA), UNITED STATES INFORMATION AGENCY (USIA).

Voice of America (VOA). See UNITED STATES INFORMATION AGENCY (USIA).

Voice Vote. See VIVA VOCE VOTE.

Volksgeist. In the German language, "people's spirit," or "spirit of the people;" a notion in German political culture to the effect that every nation has a special spirit from which the language, institutions, customs, and beliefs emerge and which holds the people together. The national community also has a Weltanschauung, or a view of the world, as well as a Weltgeist, a spirit of the world.

Volonté Générale. See GENERAL WILL, ORIGINS OF THE STATE THEORIES, SOCIAL WILL.

Volost. A political subdivision composed of several communes within an Uyezd in Tsarist Russia.

Volstead Act. See NATIONAL PROHIBITION ACT.

Voluntary Manslaughter. The killing of one person by another without premeditation or malice, e.g., under impulse, or as a result of provocation. See INVOLUNTARY MANSLAUGHTER.

Voluntary Segregation. See DOCTRINE OF INTERPOSITION.

Voluntaryism. The notion that one's personal will and perception of reality are the principal factors in human conduct as well as in coexistence with other human beings in a politically organized society. Society, therefore, to be governed justly and to meet society's stated desires, needs to draw on the talent not only of those who are elected or appointed to positions of trust but on the vast talent and skill, dedication, zeal, and intelligence of persons who volunteer their services without pay! No democratic society ever, anywhere, anytime, survived or prospered without input by volunteers. Such organizations as "Volunteers of America" perform a very useful, worthy service for society. See HAT IN THE RING, NO CANDIDATE CANDIDATE, THIRTY-SIX THOUSAND GOVERNMENTS.

Voluntas Civitatis Maximae est Servanda. In the Latin language, "the will of the international community must be obeyed." Also, a norm recognizing universal application of international law as the legal basis for regulating coexistence and cooperation among sovereign states. Sometimes international law is viewed as supra-national—one over all nations, or as transnational—one that transcends all nations at all times.

Volunteer Army. Compulsory military service in the United States ended on January 27, 1973, with the expiration of the draft law. The U.S. Armed Forces now consist of volunteers. See DRAFT.

Volunteers of America. See VOLUNTARISM.

Voschch. See CAESARISM.

Vote for Al Smith is a Vote for the Pope. A whispering campaign slogan during the mudslinging presidential campaign of 1928 aimed at the Democratic candidate, Al Smith (former Mayor of the city of New York) who was a Catholic. Smith was the first Catholic to run for the Presidency. In 1960 another Catholic, John F. Kennedy, campaigned for the Presidency and was successful, although an anti-Catholic campaign was conducted against him also.

Vote for Cold Water, Boys. See WOMEN'S CHRISTIAN TEMPERANCE UNION (WCTU).

Vote for Kennedy is a Vote for the Pope. See VOTE FOR AL SMITH IS A VOTE FOR THE POPE.

Vote Manipulation. See STRUCTURING THE VOTE.

Vote of Confidence. Under a parliamentary system of government, the formal approval of the policies of the government by the legislative body. See CABINET-PARLIAMENTARY GOVERNMENT.

Vote of Non-Confidence. Under a parliamentary system of government, the formal disapproval of the policies of the government by the legislative body. In case of a non-confidence vote, one of two events takes place: (1) either the government dissolves the parliament and orders new elections, or (2) the government resigns and the parliament elects a new one. See CABINET-PARLIAMENTARY GOVERNMENT.

Vote Structuring. See STRUCTURING THE VOTE.

Vote Your Pocket on the First Sunday and Your Heart on the Second. A term commonly applied to French parliamentary elections which are held on two consecutive Sundays: on the first Sunday the voters vote for the parties which will be represented on the run-off election on the next Sunday when the voters will decide which parties will have their candidates elected in order to form a coalition government. As a matter of practice, the French electorate traditionally votes for the leftist parties (e.g., the socialists and the communists) on the first Sunday, because these parties ordinarily promise better life, while the second Sunday they vote their heart, rejecting socialist and communist rule, and voting for candidates who represent the traditional democratic philosophy.

Voter Alienation. See DECADENCE, POLITICAL APATHY.

Voter Apathy. See POLITICAL SELF-ESTEEM.

Voting. An expedient for reaching a consensus in order to either avoid an extensive analysis of the issue of hand, lacking the ability or the willingness to undertake such analysis or cutting analysis short by shifting the responsibility for the outcome to the voters. Voting is most often used to legitimize (or to reject) public policy when a consensus cannot be easily reached through political interaction (or market interaction), particularly in a democracy where to achieve crystallized opinion is difficult. Through voting, the various publics express their preference on the basis of which a single public opinion is formed. The problem with extensive use of the voting device in a democracy is that the governors (e.g., the policy-makers and the policy-implementators) may spend too much of their valuable creative energies on finding ways to please the various publics rather than on finding, through extensive intellectual analysis, what is really good for those publics. (Continuous rejection by the electorate of the policies of a given government may result in personnel changes at the next election.) The prohibition issue, for example, was implemented (Amendment XVIII to the U.S. Constitution) upon the demand of certain elites, but it had to be subsequently repealed (Amendment XXI) because various publics withdrew their support. (It is not unusual for democratic constituencies when confronted with making important policy decisions, to appoint a committee and to take a vote, rather than to become involved in analysis and investigation. (A camel, someone said, is a horse designed by a committee.) Widespread voting practices in a democracy are meant to constantly enlarge and to reinforce the democratic base of a society by allowing more people to contribute toward public policy inputs. Ancient Athens's most distinguished law giver and political philosopher, Solon (638-589 BC), stated that "He shall be disfranchised who, in time of faction, takes neither side."

Voting Behavior. See STRUCTURING THE VOTE, VOTING.

Voting Certificate. A certificate by any federal district court in the United States (under the Civil Rights Act of 1960) to a voter who has experienced difficulties in registering to vote. Upon investigations by the so-called "overseers" or "voting referees" (federal officials who report their findings to the federal court), the court issues certificates which must be respected and honored by any official or authority in the United States. See CIVIL RIGHTS ACT OF 1965.

Voting Referee. See VOTING CERTIFICATE.

Voting Rights Act of 1965. A piece of legislation aimed at strengthening the previous Civil Rights Acts of 1957 and 1964. It was passed by Congress after a November 27, 1965 appeal by President Lyndon B. Johnson (1963-1969) and vigorous lobbying activity by the Southern Christian Leadership Conference (SCLC) led by Dr. Martin Luther King, Jr. The President told Congress: "I urge you to eliminate from this nation every trace of discrimination and oppression that is based upon race or color." In order to speed congressional consideration of the Act, the SCLC staged a major protest in Montgomery, Alabama, which was preceded by a march from Selma on March 21-25, 1965 involving about 3,300 persons when the march started and ending with more than 25,000 in Montgomery. President Johnson dispatched 4,000 troops to protect the marchers from attack by white segregationist groups. The Act was finally signed on August 6, 1965, and it gave the federal government the necessary powers to force local communities throughout the United States to allow blacks to register and to vote. Federal registrars were appointed to oversee registration practices; literacy tests were eliminated; voter registration was expedited by allowing it to be continued after November 1, 1965 (in all states voter registration for the November election—on the first Tuesday after the first Monday in November of every fourth year—ends one week prior to the election day); and the poll tax was forbidden. (Eliminated by Amendment XXIV to the U.S. Constitution of January 23, 1964, the tax had still been applied in some areas under various pretexts.) The constitutionality of the Act was tested in *South Carolina v. Katzenbach* in 1966, but the U.S. Supreme Court upheld the Act stating: "The constitutional propriety of the Voting Rights Act of 1965 must be judged with reference to the historical experience which it reflects. Before enacting the measure, Congress explored with great care the problem of racial discrimination in voting . . . ." The law was extended on August 6, 1975, by U.S. President Gerald R. Ford for seven more years. See POLL TAX, VOTING CERTIFICATE, WASHINGTON DEMONSTRATION.

Voting Tax. See POLL TAX.

Voting with One's Feet. See BRAIN DRAIN, CONFISCATORY POLICY.

Voting with Your Feet. See FREEDOM FLOAT.

Vouli. The unicameral legislative body, Parliament, of Greece.

Vox Populi. In the Latin language, "the voice of the people" or "people's voice." See VOX DEI EST, VOX POPULI.

Vox Populi, Vox Dei Est. In the Latin language, "The voice of the people is the voice of God." Also, an underlying philosophy of many of the Western European political systems based on Christian-Democracy (e.g., the Konrad Adenauer government in the German Federal Republic under the CDU/CSU). See CHRISTIAN DEMOCRACY.

Vulnus Immedicabile. In the Latin language, "an irreparable injury." Under traditional norms of international law, a state could resort to a war against another state in case of vulnus immedicabile. See INTERNATIONAL LAW, WAR.

WAC. See ORGANIZATION OF AFRICAN UNITY (OAU), WEST AFRICAN SUMMIT CONFERENCE (WASC).

Wafd Organization. See ARAB NATIONALISM.

Wagner Act. A public law sponsored in 1935 by U.S. Senator Robert F. Wagner, Sr. (D-New York), which gave labor the right to organize and to bargain with employers for better wages and working conditions. In order to regulate employer-employee relationships, the Act authorized a new federal agency, the National Labor Relations Board (NLRB). The Act was subsequently supplemented with additional legislation provided in the Taft-Hartley Act of 1947, which placed some restrictions on organized labor, allowing, among other things, the so-called "open shops," or "right-to-work" provisions, whereby employees do not have to recognize a labor union as a bargaining agent for all employees in a given industry. The right-to-work provisions, Section 14b of the Act, are left to the discretion of the states. Also restricting organized labor was the Landrum-Griffin Act of 1959 which holds, among other things, union officials accountable for union funds, restricts picketing and secondary boycotts, and requires that union elections be held according to accepted democratic principles.

Wake Forest Doctrine. During his March 17, 1978, speech at Wake Forest University in North Carolina, U.S. President Jimmy Carter stated in spite of some progress made between the Soviet Union and the United States in the Strategic Arms Limitation Talks, Part Two (SALT II), the United States was alarmed by the tremendous expansion of Soviet military capability (particularly conventional forces) and military involvement in Africa (Ethiopia). The President warned the USSR that "If they fail to demonstrate restraint in missile programs (referring to Cuban forces which aided Angola and the pro-Soviet forces of Ethiopia and other revolutionary movements in South Africa and Rhodesia) into other lands or continents, then popular support in the United States for . . . cooperation will erode." By way of response to the President's speech, the Soviet leadership (speaking through Georgi Arvatov, member of the Central Committee of the CPSU and director of the Institute on U.S.A. and Canada in the Soviet Union) pointed out (in an article printed in *Pravda* on March 28, 1978) that in order to achieve any degree of arms reduction (e.g., through the SALT talks) between the two states, all linkage should be avoided (e.g., linking the SALT agreements to the Soviet presence in the Horn of Africa where the USSR aided pro-Soviet Ethiopia or Soviet assistance to other revolutionary movements in Africa.) See DÉTENTE, LAGOS DOCTRINE, LINKAGE DIPLOMACY, STRATEGIC ARMS LIMITATIONS TALKS (SALT).

Walk for Freedom. Following the landmark decision by the U.S. Supreme Court in *Brown v. Board of Education* in 1954 (see Appendix 48) which outlawed school segregation in the United States, Dr. Martin Luther King, Jr., the founder and leader of the Southern Christian Leadership Conference (SCLC) exclaimed: "Free at last, free at last! Oh God Almighty, we are free at last!" (This speech was repeated by Dr. King at a Washington, D.C. civil rights rally in 1963.) But freedom did not necessarily guarantee equality. Segregation persisted and King organized a series of "walks" and "marches" for freedom particularly to Montgomery, Alabama and Little Rock, Arkansas, where schools were desegregated with the aid of federal troops. These "walks for freedom" and "freedom rides" resulted in legislation that outlawed all forms of racial discrimination in the United States. See CIVIL RIGHTS ACTS, LAGOS DOCTRINE, VOTING RIGHTS ACT OF 1965, WASHINGTON DEMONSTRATION.

Walk-in. A person who offers to spy for an intelligence service, usually a foreign one, whose services have not been solicited, and who may be motivated by profit, ideological reasons, or simply by desire for revenge against the target. Such persons usually walk into foreign embassies or seek contacts by other means (e.g., a telephone call or a letter). See INTELLIGENCE.

Walk in the Woods. While U.S. President Ronald Reagan was promoting in 1982 a "significant reduction" in the American-Soviet nuclear arsenal, a series of meetings were being held between representatives of the two powers under the so-called "Strategic Arms Reduction Talks (START)". The first series commenced on 29 June 1982 with Paul H. Nitze representing the United States and Yuly A. Kvitsinsky representing the Soviet Union. Both sides, suspicious of each other's motives, proceeded very slowly and without any tangible results. Then on 16 July 1982, the two representatives, without their negotiating staffs, met accidentally on a pathway in the woods of Switzerland; they sat on a log and from small talk moved to substantive issues of nuclear disarmament. That encounter contributed to better rapport among the negotiators; some cold war ice had been melted, and serious nuclear confrontation was averted. Inspired by this incident of diplomacy in the woods, Lee Blessing, internationally known playwright, wrote a stage production with the same title.

Walking Dead. See KHMER ROUGE, YEAR ZERO.

Walking on Both Sides of the Fence. In American political folklore, one who expresses conflicting views or opinions; usually a politician who expresses conflicting ideas to different groups in order to gain popularity and votes with each.

Want of Conclusive Evidence. Usually grounds for the dismissal of charges against the accused for lack of material proof, or corpus delicti.

War. Of the many definitions and conceptualizations of war, Karl von Clausevitz, a 19th-century German philosopher and war strategist, appears to have given the best operational definition (in his book *On War*): ". . . war is not merely a political act, but a real political instrument, a continuation of political intercourse, a carrying out of the same by other means . . . . War is no pastime, no mere passion for daring and winning, no work of a free enthusiasm; it is a serious means to a serious end. War always arises from a political condition and is called forth by a political motive." Another writer, Arnold Brecht (as quoted by Hans Speier and Alfred Kahler, eds., in *War in Our Time*) comments on causes of war: "There is a cause of wars between sovereign states, that stands above all others—the fact that there are sovereign states, and a very great many of them." War is a means, a violent one, of resolving conflicts among peoples with conflicting interests, whether they be material, ideological, cultural, or religious conflicts. Under modern norms of international laws (see United Nations Charter in Appendix 75), war is no longer legal; it is no longer an inherent right of a sovereign state to conduct a "just" war; war no longer can be utilized as an instrument of policy or as a conflict resolution. For war to be "just," it must be conducted only in self-defense and only through the machinery of the United Nations. Otherwise, the war is considered unjust (see Appendix 29, 31, 79). Looking beyond the behavioral-positivistic perspective of the inevitability of war, Professor Rummel observes that the only way to break this iron law of history is through the realization (1) that man, not physical nature, is the center of reality; (2) that man's behavior is not subject to the same cause-effect process we ascribe to physical reality, but rather is teleologically guided by his future goals; and (3) that man is mainly self-determined and morally responsible for his actions. Professor Quincy Wright, like Rummel, points out that war lies not in some causative features of the environment of man, but directly in his mind; and that it is within the power of man to avoid war. Wright points out that between the discovery of America in 1492 and the beginning of W.W.II, there were 278 major wars in the Western world alone, and projects that global (world) wars will become scarce, while regional (small) wars will be more common and the casualties will be larger. Many of them will be by proxy wars. See DETERRENT, PROXY WAR, SIVIC PACEM PARA BELLUM, Appendices 29, 31, 88.

War Against Slavery. See AMERICAN CIVIL WAR.

War, Articles of. See ARTICLES OF WAR, RULES OF LAND WARFARE.

War by Mistake. In a policy statement made during his visit to Warsaw, Poland on December 30, 1977, U.S. President Jimmy Carter said that the United States would never start a war except by mistake, and, referring to the Soviet Union, he added that he believed the USSR would begin a war only under "the most profound provocation or misunderstanding." The latter statement was construed to give the Poles encouragement to demand more from the Soviets, without fear of a war.

War by Proxy. See PROXY WAR.

War Cabinet. A group of top government officials, either members of the cabinet or not, who make the major decisions during wartime. See WAR.

War Communism. The state of martial law that was introduced in Russia during the civil war (1918-1921) between the Bolsheviks (Reds) and the anti-Bolsheviks (Whites). Under the War Communism Provisions, the Red Army was authorized to command absolute obedience, to requisition anything it needed without compensation, and to execute anyone on the spot (without trial) for any non-compliance or obstruction of the directives of the military commanders. While the Bolsheviks were fighting for their survival, the United States, England and France sent several thousand of their troops as an expeditionary force in order to aid the anti-Bolshevik White Armies, but they never became engaged in combat against the Red Army of the Bolsheviks. Some war materiel, however, was passed on to the White Armies. The expeditionary forces of the western allies were construed as an interventionist force by the Bolsheviks but they were too weak to engage in combat against them. After a two-year stay (1918-1920), the expeditionary forces withdrew from Russia and the Bolsheviks then consolidated their power and achieved a final victory over the White Armies. To this day, the Soviets consider this intervention by the allies as a hostile act against their state during its formative years. See WHITE ARMY.

War Crime. Any violation of the laws of war, as the international community of nations may determine. The basis for prosecuting war criminals is derived from many sources: among them, international treaties, international conventions (e.g., the Geneva Conventions and the Hague Conventions), the Charter of the United Nations, and general principles of international law. War crimes can be divided into the following general categories: (1) War crimes, generally—any violation of international law or customs such as invasion itself, mistreatment of civilian population, murder of innocent persons, enslavement or killing of hostages, confiscation of private property and the destruction of same, and the general devastation of the invaded state; (2) Crimes against peace—the act of waging war itself, conspiracy, and the violation of international treaties and agreements; (3) Crimes against humanity—the extermination of persons for religious, ethnic, or other reasons; enslavement; deportation or imprisonment of innocent persons; or the general mistreatment of human beings. On these general principles German war criminals were tried, convicted, and executed or imprisoned after the Nuremberg, Germany, trials, as well as in Japan after World War II. (The Treaty of Versailles of 1919, for example, also provided for the trial and punishment of the German Kaiser and his associates after World War I, but such action never materialized.) See NEUTRALITY.

War Debt. See ALLIED DEBT.

War Economic Theory. A notion, acknowledged more by practice than empirical research, that a nation engaged in war will experience full economic health, and that following war, the economy will decline. It is often said in the United States that U.S. presidents engage more actively in foreign affairs during times of poor economy than otherwise, and that directing attention to foreign problems may overshadow the severity of domestic problems. "If in trouble, travel," is allegedly a way to distract attention from domestic problems. There were problems, however, for some of those who took to travel in time of trouble, because once abroad, some group of opponents, usually the military, staged a coup d'état, and the traveling leader found himself deposed (e.g., President "for life" Kwame Nkrumah of Ghana, 1966). The best distracter from domestic problems is, of course, a veracious adversary, an enemy abroad, and, it has not been unusual, throughout the history of statesmanship, to seek external enemies and if none can be found to create them. Today this is not an easy task due to excellent mass communications with capability for instantaneous relay of information to the people.

War Hawk. One favoring war; a warrior who favors resolution of international conflicts through war as an instrument of policy. One opposing war is called a "dove." Those who claim to be "war hawks," but who avoid the draft, often by exploring the various loopholes in the draft law, desperately seeking deferment, are known as "chicken hawks." During the years of the Vietnam conflict, 1966 and 1973, of the twenty-six million men in America of draft age, fifteen-million never served; and of these, 570,000 evaded military service through various manipulations, including flight abroad, mainly to Canada as draft dodgers. Among some of the better known politicians who never served in the armed forces are: Richard Cheney, Secretary of Defense under President George Bush; Patrick Buchanan, the 1992 Republican challenger; Elliot Abrams, Assistant Secretary of State; U.S. Representatives Newt Gingrich of Georgia and Vin Weber of Minnesota, and the 1992 Democratic hopeful, Governor Bill Clinton of Arkansas.

War, Laws of. See ARTICLES OF WAR, RULES OF LAND WARFARE.

War of 1812. A war between the United States and England which was ended by the Treaty of Ghent (Belgium) in 1814. As a result of the Treaty, the United States gained fishing rights in Canadian waters, the British removed their forces from American ports, and the impressment of American citizens into the British military forces was stopped.

War of Annihilation. War with the purpose of complete eradication, destruction, or death of the enemy rather than just conquering or winning. Also, war aimed at complete destruction.

War of Attrition. An armed conflict, usually of long duration, which is characterized by the killing off of the armed forces and civilian population of the adversary rather than by a decisive victory or conquest. Also, a term often applied to the Arab-Israeli conflicts, and to the United States and the Soviet Union in the long run. Also, referred to as the "Peloponnesian Tactic," whereby the adversary's human and material resources are depleted through a prolonged war and harassment of all sorts, including psychological warfare and demoralization of the populace of the adversary. Such tactics were commonly employed by both Athens and Sparta in their protracted war between 431 and 404 BC. In modern times, the North Koreans, the North Vietnamese, the various guerrilla wars in Latin America, and the Arab and Palestinian struggle with Israel, are examples of such attrition strategy.

War of Austrian Succession. See WARS WITH GLOBAL IMPLICATIONS, Appendix 88.

War of Independence. See AMERICAN REVOLUTION.

War of Jenkins' Ear. A brief war between England and France in the Caribbean in 1739, which extended to Georgia, where James Oglethorpe took advantage of the situation and attacked the Spanish in neighboring Florida. This led to the War of Spanish Succession in 1740. See WARS WITH GLOBAL IMPLICATIONS, Appendix 88.

War of Laws. The conflict between Union and Republican laws in the former Soviet Union, mainly during the period between 1980 and 1991, due to political uncertainty and the rivalry for power between Union President Mikhail S. Gorbachev and Russian Republic President Boris N. Yeltsin. The conflict made it virtually impossible for domestic and foreign enterprises to function properly.

War of Secession. See SLAVOCRACY.

War of Second Revolution in America. See AMERICAN CIVIL WAR.

War of Spanish Succession. See WARS WITH GLOBAL IMPLICATIONS Appendix 88.

War on Poverty. A program aimed at eliminating poverty in the United States, which in 1963 affected 18 percent of Americans, as planned by President John F. Kennedy (1961-1963) and which subsequently was to commence with several legislative measures under President Lyndon Baines Johnson. Some of the measures were the Civil Rights Act of 1964 and the Economic Opportunity Act of 1964), designed to eliminate and to eradicate poverty in the United States through such measures as better preparation for work (through better educational opportunities), more access by more people to better paying employment, easier credit, and incentives to private and public economic sectors: the Job Corps, Volunteers in Service to America (VISTA), and on-the-job training programs. Over $1 billion were authorized for the introduction of the program. During the 1970s, groups which had not been satisfied with the federal programs launched a variety of "private," self-help programs. One of these is so-called "venture capitalism" in which private individuals combine their financial resources, without governmental assistance, to establish enterprises for profit and, in turn, to share the profit.

The program continues to this day in many lesser forms. See POVERTY WON!, VIETNAMIZATION.

War Powers Acts. A law of 1941 in which the U.S. Congress empowered the U.S. President to make changes deemed necessary within the executive branch of government for the conduct of war. This is generally known as the First War Powers Act. The Second War Powers Act was passed by Congress and signed by President Harry S. Truman on December 20, 1945. It gave the President additional powers to reorganize federal agencies as he deemed necessary and to appoint a Vice-President should the Vice Presidential Office become vacant because of death, disability, or resignation from office. (Such a vacancy had occurred when Harry S. Truman became President upon Roosevelt's death on April 12, 1945.) The appointed Vice President would serve until a new Vice President could be duly elected. The Presidential War Powers Act of 1973 was sponsored by U.S. Senator Jacob K. Javits of New York, in the heat of the Vietnam War and after the fiasco of the Gulf of Tonkin Resolution. It prevented the President from deploying military forces anywhere without prior authorization from Congress. The law very rigidly defines the situation where the President is authorized to use force abroad and report to Congress within thirty days. In the spirit of these restrictions, the President still may wage small wars silently through the Central Intelligence Agency (CIA), using its contingency funds, without prior congressional approval or even knowledge. During the 1975 Angolan crisis, for example, the CIA, which maintains its small army, including aircraft, conducted war against the MPLA (often referred to as the "MPLA-CIA WAR"), the revolutionary group in Angola which gained power with the aid of Cuba and the Soviet Union in that country. See GULF OF TONKIN RESOLUTION, PRESIDENTIAL SUCCESSION, VIETNAMIZATION.

War Risk Theory. A theoretical construct advanced in 1903 by Alfred von Tirpitz, the only Grand Admiral of the Imperial Navy in the Kaiser's Germany, pertaining to a tactical deployment of a small military force against a large one (that of Imperial England) in order to achieve victory in spite of the odds. The large Imperial Forces of Great Britain were spread out into many continents and, therefore, would not be able to concentrate sufficient forces in an area attacked by a small force and may even refrain from fighting. Ancient Chinese military philosopher Sun Tzu points out, the smartest strategy in war is to win without fighting! The crucial ingredients were the elements of swiftness, surprise, and decisiveness; similar to the American military doctrine from the Civil War era: "be fastest with the mostest." An early notion of guerrilla warfare tactics.

War Scenario. One of the main duties of any military establishment anywhere, is to constantly prepare and to revise plans—military strategies and tactics for an eventual war, and associated doctrines. War predictions, often resulting from gaming (game theory), are basically of two kinds: predictive—what is most likely to occur; and illustrative—how the war is envisioned. During the month of February 1992, the *New York Times* revealed information that the American Pentagon was working on illustrative scenarios for possible future wars in such areas as the Philippines, Japan, North and South Korea, Iraq Kuwait, and Middle East—where war between Arabs and Jews has never ended as yet; also being viewed were a possible Lithuania by Russia and wars between the former Soviet republics of Russia, Belorus, and Ukraine. Although most of the illustrative conflict areas are regional rather than global, the United States with its global concerns and interests would be physically involved in time of an actual conflict.

War to End Wars. See HOUSTON RIOT.

Wars with Global Implications. See APPENDIX 88.

Ward. One of the several subdivisions that a large city may be divided into for the purposes of expediency, better management, or elections. See POLITICAL MACHINE.

Ward Captain. See PRECINCT.

Ward Leader. See PRECINCT.

Warfare, Laws of. See ARTICLES OF WAR, RULES OF LAND WARFARE.

Warfare, Political. Those acts and activities which partisan agents undertake in order to cause despondency, alarm and mutual mistrust in adversary (enemy) circles, to weaken and/or to destroy the credibility and effectiveness of individuals, organizations, or systems; a series of highly sophisticated (usually covert) acts and activities in the realm of words (e.g., written and oral communications) based on merger facts or simply fabricated truths which one adversary state undertakes in order to undermine the political doctrine, governmental and political process, legal institutions, or the economy and the culture in general of another state for the purpose of weakening and/or destroying it. See PROPAGANDA ASSETS INVENTORY (PAI), VARGAS' NEUTRALITY, VIK DEMOCRATIC CAUSE GAME.

Warmonger. See WAR HAWK.

Warrant. A written order issued by proper authority, such as a judge, commissioner or any magistrate, authorizing an arrest, detention, or search and seizure. See WRITS OF COMMON USE.

Warren Commission. A commission of inquiry established by former United States President Lyndon B. Johnson's executive order in 1963 for the purpose of investigating the assassination of U.S. President John F. Kennedy in Dallas, Texas. The report of the Commission, submitted to President Johnson in September, 1964, stated that there is no evidence of conspiracy in the assassination; that the man who was held in connection with the assassination, one Lee Harvey Oswald, acted alone; and that the man who subsequently shot and killed Oswald, Jack Ruby, also acted alone.

Warren Court. See JUDICIAL ACTIVISM.

Warsaw Ghetto. An area in the western part of the city of Warsaw, Poland, designated in 1942 by the German Nazi occupants as a temporary detention ground for surviving Jews (mostly women and children) before their final shipment to the crematoria. Within several months, the Jews were able to establish an effective underground guerrilla organization and in 1944, virtually unarmed, they staged an uprising which lasted approximately 28 days. In retaliation for the death of approximately 400 SS-men (Nazi secret police) during the fight, the ghetto area was razed to the ground (through saturated bombing, house-to-house searches and killings, and burning of buildings with the help of gasoline). Of the approximately 495,000 persons living in the ghetto, only about 150 survived the Nazi ordeal. The Jewish uprising in the ghetto triggered a general uprising of the people of Warsaw under the leadership of the Polish Home Army, a guerrilla force supervised by the Polish government in exile in London, England. These forces were soon overpowered by the overwhelming German force and the entire city of Warsaw was virtually destroyed.

Warsaw Pact. See EAST EUROPEAN MUTUAL ASSISTANCE TREATY.

Warsaw Treaty Organization. See EAST EUROPEAN MUTUAL ASSISTANCE TREATY.

WASC. See WEST AFRICAN SUMMIT CONFERENCE.

Washington 2000 Plan. A plan for the development of the nation's capital, Washington, District of Columbia, worked out by the Washington Metropolitan Council of Governments during the 1960s and 1970s which provides, among other things, for the containment of physical growth of the city by establishing a series of satellite cities around the capital.

Washington Conference of 1889. The United States and sixteen Latin American republics gathered to discuss mutual problems and to lay the groundwork for future cooperation within the Pan-American framework. A clearinghouse was set up for expedition and dissemination of information among the states on matters of mutual interest. This was the first Pan-American Conference. See NINE-POWER TREATY.

Washington Demonstration. On August 27, 1963, over 200,000 persons gathered in Washington, D.C. in the area of the Washington Monument, as an expression of support for equal rights for black Americans, and particularly the principal leader of the civil rights movement in the United States, Dr. Martin Luther King, Jr., President of the Southern Christian Leadership Conference. On that day, Dr. King delivered his memorable "I have a dream . . . ." speech:

I say to you today, even though we face the difficulties of today and tomorrow, I still have a dream. It is a dream deeply rooted in the American Dream. I have a dream that one day this nation will rise up, live out the true meaning of its creed: "We hold these truths to be self-evident, that all men are created equal."

I have a dream that one day on the red hills of Georgia sons of former slaves and the sons of former slave owners will be able to sit down together at the table of brotherhood. I have a dream that one day even the state of Mississippi, a state sweltering with the heat of injustice, sweltering with the heat of oppression, will be transformed into an oasis of freedom and justice.

I have a dream that my four little children will one day live in a nation where they will not be judged by the color of their skin but by the content of their character.

I have a dream that one day every valley shall be exalted, every hill and mountain shall be made low. The rough places will be made plain, and the crooked places will be made straight. This is the faith that I go back to the South with. With this faith we will be able to hew out of the mountain of despair a stone of hope. With this faith we will be able to work together, to pray together, to struggle together, to go to jail together, to stand up for freedom together, knowing we will be free one day.

This will be the day when all of God's children will be able to sing with new meaning, "let freedom ring." So let freedom ring from the prodigious hilltops of New Hampshire. Let freedom ring from the mighty mountains of New York. But not only that. Let freedom ring from Stone Mountain of Georgia. Let freedom ring from every hill and molehill of Mississippi, from every mountain side.

When we allow freedom to ring—when we let it ring from every city and every hamlet, from every state and every city, we will be able to speed up that day when all of God's children, black men and white men, Jews and Gentiles, Protestants and Catholics, will be able to join hands and sing in the words of the old Negro spiritual, "Free at last, Free at last, Great God a-mighty, We are free at last."

See CIVIL RIGHTS ACTS, SOUTHERN CHRISTIAN LEADERSHIP CONFERENCE, WALK FOR FREEDOM.

Washington, District of Columbia. A federal city, without home rule, under the direct jurisdiction of the United States Congress. The mayor of the city is appointed for a term of four years by the president of the United States subject to confirmation by the U.S. Senate. The residents of the District of Columbia vote for president and vice president of the United States and, since 1968, may elect their own school board and one member to the U.S. House of Representatives. The District was designed as and remains the seat of the federal government.

Washington Fixers. See BEHIND-THE-SCENE POWER.

Washington Metropolitan Council of Governments (WMCOG). An informal governmental organization of Washington, D.C., and the surrounding communities in Maryland and Virginia, established in 1957 as the third metropolitan council of government in the U.S. for the purpose of cooperation and coordination of programs benefiting all member jurisdictions. In 1966 the WMCOG replaced a federal agency, the National Capital Regional Planning Council, and it prepared the famous "Washington 2000" plan for others to follow. See WASHINGTON 2000 PLAN.

Washington-Paris-Bonn-Moscow Axle. See GENSCHER DOCTRINE.

Washington's Farewell Address. A written statement issued by America's first president, George Washington, on September 17, 1796, in which he warned the nation about the dangers of political factions (parties) and involvement in world politics.

Watch-Out Policy. See COMMITTEE ON THE PRESENT DANGER.

Watchdog Committee. A legislative committee that is set up for the sole purpose of overseeing particular activities of the executive branch of the government (e.g., Committee in the United States

Congress overseeing the activities of the Central Intelligence Agency [CIA]). See CENTRAL INTELLIGENCE AGENCY (CIA).

Watergate Affair. The raiding and plundering of the headquarters of the Democratic National Committee (of the Democratic Party) at the Watergate apartment complex in Washington, D.C., on June 17, 1972, by persons allegedly connected with the Republican National Committee, the so-called Committee to Re-elect the President (CREEP), and Richard M. Nixon, the incumbent President (1969-1974), with some assistance from former agents of the CIA, the Internal Security Division of the U.S. Department of Justice, and the FBI. The Watergate Affair (or scandal) is generally recognized as the most publicized incident of political improprieties (including internal espionage against innocent citizens and groups) by the highest officials (including the U.S. President) of the U.S. government in modern times. The chronology of some of the Watergate-related incidents up to the time of the resignation of Richard M. Nixon as U.S. President is as follows: (1) March 23, 1973—James W. McCord, the key figure in the Watergate break-in, sent a letter to Federal Judge John Sirica in Washington, D.C., stating that political pressure was being applied against him, urging him to plead guilty and remain silent. McCord wondered in the letter why the other co-conspirators (he mentioned no names) were not indicted as they should have been; (2) April 30, 1973—President Richard M. Nixon addressed the nation via radio and TV, stating that, as the "top man in the organization," he accepted full responsibility for Watergate, although he himself was not in any way involved. Following the address, his Chief-of-Staff H. R. Haldeman; his Advisor for Domestic Affairs, John D. Ehrlichman; the U.S. Attorney General, Richard D. Kleindienst; and the Counsel to the President, John W. Dean, all resigned. (Dean would soon reveal that there existed an "enemies list" of names and addresses of opponents of the President's politics, and that the main purpose of the Watergate break-in was to find some evidence against the Democrats in order to "screw the opposition"); (3) May 14, 1973—E. Howard Hunt, Jr., co-defendant in the Watergate break-in, revealed in grand jury testimony that, on orders (and with pay) from the White House, he had participated in the break-in into Dr. Ellsberg's psychiatrist's office to obtain incriminating medical records of Dr. Ellsberg, who published the Pentagon Papers; (4) May 17, 1973—the United States Senate set up a Select Committee on Presidential Campaign Activities in the Watergate issue with U.S. Senator Sam J. Ervin (D-North Carolina) as its chairman; (5) May 5, 1973—President Nixon explained in a press conference that his reluctance to probe openly into the Watergate issue was motivated by matters of national security, and in order to stop leaks of security information he had organized in 1971 a unit in the White House (known as the "plumbers") which would monitor the sources of leaks and recommend plugs so that there would be no more such incidents as the leak of the Pentagon Papers. His domestic adviser, John D. Ehrlichman, was to supervise the "plumbers" through his subordinate, Egil Krogh, Jr.; (6) June 20, 1973—John W. Dean, III, former Counsel to the President, testified before the Senate Watergate Committee (in a broadcast testimony) that he had warned the President that "cancer spread over the office" when the White House decided to cover up its involvement (together with the Committee to Re-elect the President—CREEP—and the Justice Department) in the Watergate break-in and cover-up; (7) July 16, 1973—former Deputy Assistant to the President for Communications Alexander P. Butterfield revealed to the Watergate Committee that all conversations in the President's Office in the White House had been recorded since March 1971, and that they should contain the necessary evidence on the involvement of the White House in the Watergate cover-up; (8) July 16, 1973—Herbert Kalmbach, attorney and fund raiser for President Nixon, told the Senate Committee that he had been able to raise $220,000 for legal fees and for the support of families of the principal defendants in the Watergate break-in who were then in prison; (9) July 23, 1973—President Nixon refused to deliver the White House tapes (revealed by Butterfield on July 16, 1973) to the Senate Committee for examination, on the grounds of executive privilege and the separation of powers principle; (10) September 28, 1973—it was revealed by the Senate Watergate Committee that a record of $60.2 million in campaign funds were collected for the re-election of President Nixon; (11) October 10, 1973—U.S. Vice President Spiro T. Agnew resigned from office after pleading "no contest" before a court in Maryland to charges of taking bribes and evading income tax. This was the beginning of the loss of credibility in the Nixon Administration and in the President's honesty as well; (12) October 19-21, 1973—Arab oil-producing nations (and other members of OPEC) imposed an oil embargo upon all nations aiding the state of Israel (including the United States). President Nixon, unable to cope with the problem, lost considerable trust of constituents; (13) October 20, 1973—the famous "Saturday Night Massacre"— President Nixon relieved the Watergate Special Prosecutor, Archibald Cox (Professor of

Constitutional Law at Harvard University) from duties (fired him) when Cox insisted that the White House tapes be delivered to him for examination and threatened to go to court if his request was not granted. (The President had first asked the Attorney General, Elliot Richardson, to fire Cox. Richardson, instead, resigned, together with his deputy, William D. Ruckelshaus). President Nixon appointed a conservative Democrat from Texas, Leon Jaworski, on November 1, 1973, to serve as the new Watergate Special Prosecutor. Jaworski was promised "complete freedom" of action by the President; (14) November 9, 1973—Federal Judge John J. Sirica sentenced E. Howard Hunt, Jr. former CIA agent and a White House consultant, to 2 1/2 years to 8 years in prison, plus a $10,000 fine; James W. McCord, to 1 to 5 years in prison; Eugenio R. Martinez and Virgilio R. Gonzales, to 1 to 4 years in prison; Bernard L. Baker to 18 months to 6 years in prison; and G. Gordon Liddy (the young lawyer and the only one among the conspirators who never revealed anything, except reciting poetry by Schiller in the old German language) to 20 years in prison. (All the defendants, including Liddy, were released in 1977); (15) November 14, 1973—the federal court ruled that the firing of Cox by the President was illegal; (16) Egil Krogh, Jr., Ehrlichman's assistant in charge of the "plumbers" in the White House, was sentenced to serve 6 months in prison for violating the civil rights of Dr. Daniel Ellsberg's psychiatrist by burglarizing the physician's office. (U.S. representative Paul N. McCloskey, Republican from California, quickly hired Krogh as his assistant when Krogh left prison); (17) December 8, 1973—financial records of President Nixon revealed that he had taken a large deduction (almost $500,000) on his Vice Presidential papers, which he had donated to the National Archives; (18) February 25, 1974—Nixon's attorney, Herbert W. Kalmbach, pleaded guilty to promising a U.S. ambassadorship to a contributor of $100,000 to Nixon's campaign fund. (Kalmbach was fined $10,000 and was sentenced, June 17, 1974, to serve from 6 to 8 months; he was released on Judge Sirica's orders on January 8, 1975); (19) April 3, 1974—a joint congressional committee disallowed a tax deduction on Nixon's Vice-Presidential papers given to the National Archives, and the President was required to repay the government the sum of $432,787.13 in back taxes; (20) May 9, 1974—the Judiciary Committee of the U.S. House of Representatives opened impeachment hearings against President Nixon; (21) May 21, 1974—Jeb Stuart Magruder, former Deputy Director of CREEP, was sentenced to 10 months to 4 years in prison for his part in the cover-up of the Watergate scandal. (He was released by order of Judge Sirica on January 8, 1975); (22) July 12, 1974—John D. Ehrlichman, the President's assistant in charge of the "plumbers," was sentenced to 20 months to 5 years in prison. G. Gordon Liddy drew an additional 1-3 years sentence for the break-in into the office of Dr. Fiedling (the psychiatrist of Dr. Ellsberg). The other co-conspirators in the Dr. Fiedling break-in, Bernard L. Barker and Eugenio Martinez, drew one year each of suspended sentences; (23) July 24, 1974—the U.S. Supreme Court ruled that President Nixon must turn over his 64 tapes relating to the Watergate hearings to Special Prosecutor Leon Jaworski; (24) the U.S. House of Representatives Judiciary Committee recommended three articles of impeachment against President Nixon as follows: Article 1 (July 27, 1974, by a vote of 27 to 11) taking part in a criminal conspiracy to obstruct justice in the Watergate cover-up; Article 2 (July 29, 1974, by a vote of 28 to 10) failure to carry out his constitutional oath of office by abusing power; Article 3 (July 30, 1974, by a vote of 27 to 17) defiance of ten committee subpoenas to deliver the tapes as requested. This defiance was considered by many to be unconstitutional; (25) August 2, 1974—John W. Dean, III, former Counsel to the President, who pled guilty to conspiracy and cover-up, was sentenced to 1 to 3 years. (He was released by order of Judge Sirica on January 8, 1975); (26) August 5, 1974—in response to the Supreme Court order to release the White House Tapes to Special Watergate Prosecutor Leon Jaworski, the President delivered three tapes which revealed that not only had the President himself tried to cover up, but he had also tried to use the FBI to stop inquiries into the Watergate scandal, on grounds of national security; (27) August 9, 1974—President Richard M. Nixon resigned (first U.S. President to do so) and Vice President Gerald R. Ford was sworn in as President; (28) August 20, 1974—the U.S. House of Representatives (by of 413 to 3) accepted without debate the recommendations of the Judiciary Committee to impeach President Nixon for all possible federal crimes which he "committed or may have committed" as President; (29) January 1, 1975—after three months of trial by a jury, Nixon's collaborators were found guilty of obstruction of justice and abuse of power and were sentenced to prison terms as follows: H.R. Haldeman and John D. Ehrlichman, to 2 1/2 to 8 years in prison (reduced on October 4, 1977, by Judge Sirica to one to four years); John N. Mitchell, the former Attorney General and Nixon's campaign manager, to 10 months to 3 years (released for medical reasons on December 28, 1977); and an aide, Kenneth W. Parkinson, was acquitted; and (30) February 13, 1975—Ronald Ziegler, former

Press Secretary to President Nixon, stated "We conducted probably the worst public relations and press program in the history of the United States in the way we handled Watergate."

Watergate Prosecutor. See WATERGATE AFFAIR.

Watergate Reorganization and Reform Act of 1976. See SPECIAL PROSECUTOR.

Watergate Special Prosecution Force (WSPF). See SPECIAL PROSECUTOR.

WAU. See WEST AFRICAN SUMMIT CONFERENCE, WEST AFRICAN UNION.

WCTU. See WOMAN'S CHRISTIAN TEMPERANCE UNION.

We Are Not Animals. Statement made by Robert Gabriel Mugabe, Roman Catholic-Marxist, Prime Minister-elect of Rhodesia (renamed Zimbabwe on April 17, 1980) when the state was officially freed and became an independent republic, to British overseer of Rhodesia during the election period (February 26-28), Soames, asking Soames to "Stay with us. We are not animals." The stay was temporary until the situation in Zimbabwe was normalized. The statement was made on April 13, 1980. At the same time the former commander of Rhodesia's Armed Forces, General Peter Walls, remained in charge of the Zimbabwe Army and reorganized it. Walls and Mugabe were adversaries not long before and when Mugabe asked Walls following attempts on his life "Why are your men trying to kill me?" the white general replied: "If they were my men, you would be dead." (See *Newsweek*, March 17, 1980.) Mugabe joined Joshua Nkomo's ZAPU in 1960 as publicity secretary to Nkomo; he was imprisoned in 1964 and released in 1974 (by Rhodesia's Premier Ian Smith). In 1974 he formed his own organization ZANU, which was more pro-Marxist (based on the Chinese model). He did not allow collaboration with Nkomo and followed the socialist model of Mozambique's President Samora Machel. See ZANU, ZAPU.

We Are the Owners of this Country. The Guys in Washington Work for Us!. See GRASS-ROOTS PEROT.

We Believe in Two Things, the Jewish God and the Israel Defense Forces. See GOYIM.

We Don't Run For Public Office. We Own the Politicians. So boasted Benjamin (Bugsy) Siegel, reputed American underworld figure during the 1920s. See MAFIA.

We Don't Want Any More States Until We Can Civilize Kansas. See POPULIST.

We Have Your Bibles—You Have Our Land. See COLONIALISM.

We Pretend to Work, They Pretend to Pay Us. A popular saying among workers in the former Soviet Union and the East European socialist states where workers were receiving almost starvation wages for working very little. The communist rulers wanted the world to believe their nonsensical claim that there was no unemployment under their politico-economic system which has since dissolved in disgrace without a precedent in economic-political history.

We Shall Bury You. See I HAVE HAD ENOUGH OF WAR.

We Shall Continue. A statement made on November 22, 1963, in Dallas, Texas, when Vice President Lyndon B. Johnson was sworn in as President upon the assassination of President John F. Kennedy.

We Shall Surpass You. See I HAVE HAD ENOUGH OF WAR.

We the People, Take Back America! One of the main political campaign slogans of 1992 presidential hopeful Jerry Brown, former governor of California. He was nicknamed "Governor Moonbeam " because of his unorthodox political style and refusal to use an official car or sleep in the governor's mansion while in office. (Brown drove an old car, and slept on a plain mattress on the floor of a one-room apartment, for which he paid the rent out of his own pocket.) Having a small staff, limited campaign funds, and facing strong competition from the other presidential candidates, Jerry Brown tried to save money on advertising by citing his "One-Eight-Hundred" (toll-free call) telephone number whenever he was interviewed by television reporters. He ignored their instruction that this was not an appropriate practice as it constituted an advertisement for which the television station received no payment. Therefore, he was also often called the "One-Eight-Hundred-Candidate." Jerry Brown campaigned for the presidency for the first time in 1976 and, following the election of Jimmy Carter, went to Asia and joined a Bhuddist monastery for meditation purposes. Because of that experience (which he claimed was very helpful) and which he recommended to others, he was often referred to as the "Zen Yuppie." The 1992 campaign was his third in the quest for the presidency, the second being in 1980.

We're All Stuck Here for a While. Words by Rodney King, a black American, following the acquittal on 29 April 1992 of the four white policemen who had beaten and abused him in Los Angeles, California, on 3 March 1991. King made this appeal to those who rioted from 29 April to 2 May 1992 as a protest against the acquittal. About 3,200 businesses were damaged; property damage amounted to about $800 million, and 51 deaths resulted during the rioting. King did not seek revenge against the white policemen, in spite of the great personal suffering he sustained. See POLICE BRUTALITY.

Weak Mayor Government. A type of local government in which the position of the mayor is merely ceremonial and the important decisions are made by council or a manager. See Appendix 68.

Wealth as Authority. Many contemporary students of politics subscribe to the traditional intellectual notion that wealth, property, and authority all generate wealth and power.

Weather Underground. A revolutionary and militant faction of the Students For Democratic Society (SDS), which broke away from the SDS in 1970, in order to pursue active revolutionary activities in the United States, aimed mainly at disrupting and crippling political-governmental-legal-economic institutions and processes (e.g., by bombing buildings and raiding file cabinets which stored important information and by mass protests and the killing of public officials). According to media reports, the Weather Underground (the term "underground" was adopted in 1970 when the organization, after being sought by the FBI, resorted to clandestine, underground activity) closely collaborated with the Black Panthers and Cuban and North Vietnamese agents stationed at the United Nations in New York City and in Canada, providing funds and falsifying documents. (The North Vietnamese even suggested that the Weathermen "needed not just intellectual protesters but also physically rugged recruits." and had arranged for training in guerrilla warfare and the use of arms and explosives.) After the Vietnamese conflict came to an end, the organization's visibility faded and all of its members who were charged with violation of laws were paroled in 1979. See BLACK PANTHERS, NEW LEFT, STUDENTS FOR DEMOCRATIC SOCIETY (SDS).

Weatherman. See STUDENTS FOR DEMOCRATIC SOCIETY (SDS).

Wedge Issue. An issue or a problem, which divides voters in supporting a political candidate or a political party; an issue that divides a single constituency (e.g., the issue of abortion is a divisive issue around the world). The issue of slavery in the United States divided the political parties, the states, the union, and often families. In America, the two major political parties, the Democrats and the Republicans, often accuse each other of playing partisan politics with important national problems. Following the 1992 Los Angeles, California, riots, the Republicans accused the Democrats of neglecting poor people and race problems in America, particularly in urban areas, while the Democrats responded that it was the Republicans who, with the entry of Ronald Reagan, neglected these matters and did nothing to deal with the problems.

Wedge Politics. See WEDGE ISSUE.

Weed and Seed Program. By way of national policy assessment pertaining to poverty, justice, and race relations in America, following the April-May 1992 Los Angeles, California, riots, U.S. President George Bush outlined a program of action during his 8 May 1992 televised address, which he called a "weed and seed program," meaning that problems and those who create them will be weeded out and new policies and programs will be seeded in. Viewing "America as one people," the President decided to federalize local problems by more extensive assistance to local governments in coping with them; to initiate a "common sense agenda," meaning programs that are plain and simple, understood and appreciated by those they are designed to benefit, and that by the year 2000, America shall regain its status of a nation of hope and opportunity for all Americans.

Weighted Vote. A vote that is proportionate to each voter's financial contribution, or one that is based on some other criteria, such as vested interest of the voter (e.g., the number of shares of stock held in an enterprise, each share entitling the holder to one vote). See VOTE.

Weimar Constitution. See WEIMAR REPUBLIC.

Weimar Enabling Act. See WEIMAR REPUBLIC.

Weimar Republic. The democratic government (cabinet-parliamentary) that was set up in Germany after World War I, and which lasted from 1919 to 1933 (when Adolf Hitler came to power). The Weimar Constitution is considered to be the most democratic for that time, because it provided for proportional representation, universal suffrage when women in many democracies, (e.g., the United States and Switzerland, among others), were not allowed to vote or to be voted upon for elective offices, and recall of elected officials. Germany, however, burdened with heavy reparations imposed after W.W.I, experienced problems and during the fourteen years of existence, the Weimar republic had twenty-one governments until the Enabling Act of March 1933 allowed Adolf Hitler to step in.

Welfare. See WORKFARE.

Welfare Capitalism. During the late 1800s and early 1900s, large enterprises and corporations in the United States and other industrialized nations, characterized by an authoritarian system of management and fearful of organized labor and the spread of socialism and communism, provided certain benefits to labor (e.g., insurance, pensions, credit, housing, and social facilities), in order to retain its loyalty. They advocated and supported "open shop" laws (no union) and claimed this was legitimate, as the "American plan" and as such, should not be challenged by unions and strikes. As a result, many strikes by labor, organized by unions or not, were brutally suppressed, often with the aid of local police or the National Guard, as was the case when striking policemen in Boston were suppressed by the Massachusetts National Guard called by Governor Calvin Coolidge. See OPEN SHOPPISM, SILENT CAL.

Welfare Pension Socialism. A futuristic perception of the American system which rests on the assumptions that: (1) because federal spending vacillates between spending for defense or spending for welfare, which in either case removes capital from the productive sectors of the economy and transfers it (transfer payments) to the non-productive ones, such as welfare; and (2) because the government's capital "is becoming increasingly tied to social security and pension funds, which grant automatic cost-of-living increases with every turn of the inflationary spiral," Americans will become dependent upon welfare payments instead of relying on the profits from production. It is the productive sector of the economy that determines the Gross National Product (GNP), not welfare. The private productive sector itself aids in the shaping of this trend. Many producers of goods and/or services increase their profits, not by producing and selling more, but simply by increasing prices on their products or services. See WORKFARE.

Welfare State. A state in which the government assumes the responsibility for maintaining the minimum standards of living for all its nationals (citizens as well as aliens legally admitted for residence). See WORKFARE.

Weltanschauung. In the German language, "one's world outlook," or "one's personal philosophy." In politics, one's understanding and perception of the realities. See VOLKSGEIST.

Weltgeist. See VOLKSGEIST.

Weltmacht. See GERMAN UNIFICATION.

Wessi. See GERMAN UNIFICATION.

West African Conference of Berlin. A major gathering of representatives from Belgium, Britain, France, Germany, Italy, the Netherlands (Holland), Portugal, and Spain, held during December 1884-January 1885, in Berlin, Germany, where under the slogan: "Europeans, scramble for Africa," the participants partitioned the African continent among themselves. By mutual consent, Russia was not invited to the conference and received no part of Africa. The partition of Africa was justified, as one of the British delegates put it, on the grounds that "The practical man, the businessman, the man of affairs, the philanthropist, the missionary, all agreed that civilized folk have a perfect right to interfere with any native tribe too weak to resist their encroachment." Africa and particularly West Africa, had unlimited resources and was easy prey for the Europeans. The opening of the Suez Canal in 1869 and the news of large wealth of diamonds intensified the scramble. Cecil Rhodes, England's most aggressive imperialist, was already earning over ten thousand pounds a year from diamond exploration in Kimberley, which became the De Beers Diamond Company when he was only twenty-years old in 1873. But, in addition to gathering personal fortune, Rhodes also engaged in politics in order to expand and sustain British influence. "I would annex the planets if I could," he said. In 1886 large deposits of gold, 30 miles long and over 1,500 feet deep, were found in Witwatersrand, close to Johannesburg, and the news of that kind of wealth, like the California Gold Rush, intensified the scramble by the Europeans. With the arrival of the many different European groups, political friction intensified to a point that prompted Lord Salisbury, the Prime Minister of Britain to state that "Africa was created to be the plague of the foreign offices." See BOXER REBELLION.

West African Summit Conference (WASC). On April 23, 1968, nine West African States—Gambia, Ghana, Guinea, Dahomey, Liberia, Mali, Mauritania, Ivory Coast, and Upper Volta (Niger and Togo refused to take part)—met in Monrovia, Liberia, and adopted the "Articles of Association for the formation of a West African Community (WAC)." The principal purpose of the community is to strive for economic integration of the area as well as to bring closer cooperation among themselves and together—as a community—with French and French-speaking nations.

West African Union (WAU). See WEST AFRICAN SUMMIT CONFERENCE (WASC).

West Bank. See ISRAELI SETTLEMENT.

West Wall. See SIEGFRIED LINE.

Western European Union (WEU). An alliance among Belgium, Italy, Luxembourg, the Federal Republic of Germany (West Germany), the Netherlands (Holland), England, and France (France withdrew on February 17, 1969), established in 1954 for the purpose of coordinating plans for mutual security. All the member-states are pledged to support the North Atlantic Treaty Organization (NATO) on all defense matters.

Wet Affair. Term for the elimination "with extreme prejudice" (i.e., assassination by U.S. intelligence agents operating abroad), of a foreign leader who is damaging to a country's interests. Leaders considered by the U.S. as damaging have included Fidel Castro of Cuba during the 1960s Chou En-lai, premier of the Republic of China, when in 1955 he was attending the Third World Conference in Bandung and many others. The Soviet KGB maintained a special directorate in its apparatus exclusively for that purpose, called "mokrye dyela" or "wet affairs." This practice by American agents has been forbidden by presidential order since 1975. See RED SOX/ RED CAP.

Wetback. Term applied to illegal immigrants from Mexico and other Latin American countries, who cross the U.S. border illegally, usually swimming across the Rio Grande River from Mexico to the United States (hence, getting the back wet). Many illegal immigrants receive sanctuary in the United States, provided mainly by churches and religious-charitable organizations in defiance of U.S. Immigration laws. During the so-called "sanctuary movement" between 1984 and 1985, the U.S. courts dealt with the massive inflow of illegals, but sentences passed were limited to deportation. See BRAIN-DRAIN, CACTUS CURTAIN.

WEU. See WESTERN EUROPEAN UNION.

WFTU. See WORLD FEDERATION OF TRADE UNIONS.

Wheat Belt. See SECTIONALISM.

When in Doubt, Travel! See WHEN IN TROUBLE, TRAVEL.

When in Trouble, Travel. According to Joseph Kraft, one of America's leading syndicated journalists (*Field Enterprises*), whenever a United States President experiences problems at home, he takes a trip abroad. Kraft, who as a journalist has observed many presidents throughout the past three decades, claims that this maxim of presidential politics is particularly true when the President experiences problems with Congress (e.g., President Jimmy Carter's difficulty with the energy bill and the Panama Canal Treaties which he very much wanted to see passed). President George Bush had problems with balance of trade with Japan (about $50 billion minus), and unemployment at home, took a trip to Japan in January 1992 and to other countries, possibly as a means of searching for solutions. The term, "When in doubt, travel!" is also used to describe similar situations. See BARNSTORMING, SUMMIT DIPLOMACY.

When Things Go Wrong, First Look in the Mirror. A Chinese proverb, often repeated today in the Pacific realm—Japan, South Korea, Taiwan (Formosa), Hong Kong, and Singapore (the last four constituting the so-called "mini tigers" in the economic sense)—whenever any nation accuses another of unfair trade practices.

When You are President, the Only Future You Have is in the Memory of the People. U.S. President Harry S. Truman (1944-1953) so described the future and the rewards of the Presidency.

Where Once the Russian Flag Has Flown it Must Not be Lowered. See IMPERIALISM.

Where's the Beef? A statement that also became a popular slogan made by Walter Fritz Mondale (U.S. Vice-President 1977-1981) during his presidential campaign in 1980; he accused his Republican opponents, Ronald Reagan and George Bush, of making boastful promises to the American voters, while actually being able to deliver very little. This expression came from a popular Wendy's TV hamburger commercial which criticized competing hamburger sandwich makers for putting very little beef in their sandwiches.

Whig. A term taken from the Scottish word *whiggamoie* (meaning "one from western Scotland") to describe anyone who opposed British King Charles I and his interference in the life of the British colonies in North America. Whigs resented British control, favored independence of the American Colonies, and supported the American Revolutionary War against the Loyalists (Tories). See WHIG PARTY.

Whig Party. A political party founded in the United States in 1834 by National Republicans, Antimasons, and other splinter groups, with its southern wing controlled by slave-holding interests and the northern wing dominated by financial and manufacturing interests. The party advocated, among other things, strong protective tariffs, the chartering of the United States Bank, and the general expansion of the national economy. Four former United States Presidents were members of the Whig Party: William H. Harrison (1841-1841), John Tyler (1841-1845), Zachary Taylor (1849-1850), and Millard Fillmore (1850-1853). The Party became split on the issue of slavery and ceased to exist in 1854. Most of its northern ranks joined the newly emerging Republican Party.

Whiggamoie. See WHIG.

While Emergency Does Not Create Power, Emergency May Furnish the Occasion for the Exercise of Power. See IMPLIED POWER.

Whip. See PARTY WHIP.

Whip Inflation Now (WIN). A slogan of the G. R. Ford Administration (1974-1977) designed to engage the entire population of the United States in fighting inflation by saving fuel and restraining inflationary buying practices. At the same time, the Treasury Department returned to circulating $2 bills and encouraged the public to use them instead of the $1 bills, hoping to save from four to seven million dollars per year on the printing of one-dollar bills. (The purchasing power of a $2 bill in 1975 was approximately equal to that of a $1 bill in 1950.)

Whisky Rebellion. In the search for additional revenue, the federal government proposed (Alexander Hamilton was the author of the proposal), and received congressional authorization, to impose a license tax on distillers of whiskey and an additional tax per gallon on that product. Since the whisky-makers construed this measure as a heavy burden, they conspired to harass tax collectors. The climax was reached in 1794 when army units accompanying the tax collectors were attacked. President George Washington issued a proclamation (August 7, 1794) calling upon the rebels for restraint and for compliance with federal law by September 1, 1794. When the deadline expired without compliance, President Washington personally led 13,000 militiamen to western Pennsylvania (mainly the Pittsburgh area), where large numbers of the rebels were apprehended and subsequently tried and convicted.

Whistle-Blower. One who reports to the proper authority abuse of power, mismanagement, theft, incompetence, fraud, misappropriation of funds or embezzlement of funds, usually anonymously, either for reward or as a civic duty. Legislation in the United States, at all levels of government, protects such persons from repercussions from the powers-that-be, but many have found that it is not easy to fight the system. (On 1 January 1979, U.S. Congress established the U.S. Office of Special Counsel to investigate whistle-blowers allegations and in 1989 another law, the "Whistle-blower Protection Act of 1989" commands special protection to whistle-blowers from harassment by employers.)Prior to this law there were cases of whistle-blowers being punished by their employers. For example, U.S. General (3 stars) Hank Emerson was fired in 1977 for criticizing the shabby quality of some of the equipment the Army was purchasing; General Bruce Clark, a W.W.II tank commander and holder of many war decorations for heroism and leadership, was fired after criticizing the poor quality in armor and field performance of the M-2 Bradley fighting vehicle, stating openly that "most anything on the battlefield can blow a hole through it." The M-2 was produced by Ford Machine Corporation, at $1.5 million apiece. The champion of that vehicle, Chief of Staff General Edward Meyer, served on the board of directors of Ford Machinery Corporation upon his retirement from the service. Any officer who criticized the poor quality of the M-16 rifle, the M1-A1, the M60 tank, especially those who loudly claimed that the Soviet T-80 tank would crash the M60 American tank with ease and no harm to itself, was in great jeopardy. When whistle-blowers spread the factual field-test information that some of the military vehicles sold to the American armed forces required 8.6 gallons of fuel per-mile and after forty-eight miles of travel required major servicing, they were also in great danger of losing their jobs. The U.S. Congress insisted on getting "more bang for the buck," but intensive lobbying by the military-industrial complex was not easy to overcome in the realm of politics. U.S. President Dwight D. Eisenhower warned the nation against the military-industrial complex as much as President George Washington had warned about the dangers of foreign entanglements. War industries benefited from the know-how of retiring generals, many of whom served as lobbyists, advisers, members of boards, or top executive officers. General Alexander Haig, for example, joined United Technologies in 1980 as president upon his retirement from the service. His salary there was over $800,000 plus bonuses, and, together with his pension, lecturing, writing, and advising, the general's income for two years (1985-1987) came to over $3 million. See MILITARY-INDUSTRIAL COMPLEX.

Whistle Stopping. A phrase used in practical politics to describe a campaigning politician's practice of making frequent personal appearances and speeches to attract "grass-roots" support. (This phrase had particularly valid application in the past when the principal mode of transportation for a politician was the railroad and the platform of the railroad car, a podium from which to speak.) See BARNSTORMING, POLITICAL BEAUTY CONTEST, PRIMARY ELECTION.

White Army. Any of the several military groups in Russia that opposed the Bolsheviks and their Red Army between 1917-1921. Among the major groups were those led by former Tsarist generals Michael V. Alexeyev, Alexis M. Kaledin, Peter N. Krasnov, Anton I. Denikin, Admiral of the Black Sea Fleet Alexander V. Kolchak, and General Baron Peter N. Wrangel, to mention only a few. (By 1921 their armies were exterminated by the Red Army, and the Bolsheviks took complete control over Russia.)

White Book. See WHITE PAPER.

White Citizens' Council. A loose confederation of numerous groups and organizations that sprung up during the 1950s in opposition to federal desegregation policies and laws. The first such Council appeared in Mississippi in 1954 in protest to the *Brown v. Board of Education* decision by the U.S. Supreme Court. The NAACP organized a mass boycott of businesses owned and operated by persons known to be members of such councils, and they became labeled by blacks as the "Uptown Ku Klux Klan." See DOCTRINE OF INTERPOSITION, SOUTHERN MANIFESTO, Appendix 48.

White Cloud. See SECRET SOCIETIES.

White House. The official residence of the President of the United States, located at 1600 Pennsylvania Avenue, Northeast, Washington, D.C., designed by James Hoban. The location was selected by the planner of the city, a French architect, J. L'Enfant, in 1792. The first U.S. President to reside in the White House was John Adams, in 1800. The House contains 107 rooms, 40 corridors, 25 baths, a swimming pool, recreation facilities, library, map room, and other facilities. The Oval Office is the personal office of the U.S. President. Since brilliant political careers were ruined by serving in the office of the president, and since some presidents were not happy with that office, the House was called a "tomb of the well known warrior." See ROSE GARDEN.

White House Command Center. See INTELLIGENCE.

White House Tapes. See WATERGATE AFFAIR.

White Knights. See MISSISSIPPI WHITE KNIGHTS.

White Lily. See SECRET SOCIETIES.

White Man's Burden. The notion that the white man, being in possession of advanced technology and political power, is responsible for solving the ills of the world; for helping other nations by colonizing them in order to spread the benefits of modern (Christian) civilization—most often by the sword, as President T. Roosevelt (1901-1909) admitted openly in 1905: "I never take a step in foreign policy unless I am assured that I shall be able eventually to carry out my will by force." America's experience during the 1899-1909 period is well epitomized by this reply to Rudyard Kipling's poem: "We've taken up the white man's burden/Of ebony and brown;/Now will you kindly tell us, Rudyard,/How we may put it down?" See BIG STICK POLICY.

White Paper. A document containing broad and authoritative statements on some single important issue of public policy—either domestic or international—that may be issued by the government of a state. In reality such papers represent biased opinions and their primary objective is to influence the opinions of various publics. Such publications are so named after the color of the paper on which their texts are printed and the color of the binding. See INTER-AMERICAN CONFERENCE ON PROBLEMS OF WAR AND PEACE.

White Primary. Primary elections that were held in some Southern states of the United States from which black Americans were excluded on the grounds that political parties were private and not public organizations and as such were entitled to selective membership. This practice was declared unconstitutional by the Supreme Court of the United States in 1944. See PRIMARY ELECTION, WORLD APARTHEID MOVEMENT (WAM).

White Propaganda. See PROPAGANDA.

White Revolution. A program of intensive modernization of Iran undertaken by Shah Raza Pahlavi (1953-1979), which included measures, most of them very new to an Islamic society, such as profit sharing, woman suffrage, public health services and facilities, free education, (from kindergarten to post-doctoral studies), work projects and conservation measures with peace-corps like brigades housing projects, irrigation and forestation programs, specially good nutrition for pregnant women and children up to two years of age, social security insurance, land price control, disclosure of wealth by public officials, crackdown on profiteering (it is contrary to Islamic religion to charge interest on money lended), and price controls. His programs were viewed as a combination of capitalism and socialism and communism. The Mullahs (religious priests of Islam), were deprived of large land holdings. See IRANIAN REVOLUTION, MOSSADEGH.

WHO. See WORLD HEALTH ORGANIZATION, Appendices 75-79.

Who Gets What, When, How. See POLITICS.

Who Lost China? Following the takeover of the government in mainland China by the communist forces of Mao-Tse-tung following his "Long March," in 1949 there was bitter discussion in Washington, D.C., among politicians and the military establishment, blaming each other for neglecting to sufficiently aid the government and army of Chiang-kai Shek who was forced to settle in Taiwan (Formosa). The theme of the recrimination was, "Who Lost China?" Suspected were many liberal politicians and bureaucrats in Washington, D.C., particularly in the U.S. Department of State and in the military establishment. But there were many among American bureaucrats who honestly had no idea what China was all about, or where it was located, and some even suspected that there was no such thing as "China"—that it was something invented by greedy politicians and their soldier-friends so they could extract money from the American treasury and go to war against it. Some of the federal bureaucrats were even suspected of complicity. U.S. Senator Joseph McCarthy would explore that issue in years to come, looking for communists everywhere, beginning with the U.S. Army and the state department, and even regarding General Dwight D. Eisenhower (future U.S. President) as a possible Soviet agent of influence. The American government was spending billions on aid to Generalissimo Chiang Kai-shek and his Kuomintang forces, but these forces were corrupt and pocketed a great deal of the American money. Similarly, the South Vietnamese leaders, who surrendered to the North Vietnamese communists in 1974, were like the Nationalist Chinese, interested more in amassing personal fortunes than in saving their country from the communists. The Chinese were deserving of being lost, but recriminations prevailed. Similarly, former U.S. President Richard M. Nixon spoke publicly in March 1992 for more intensive aid to the former Soviet Union, particularly to Russia and its president, Boris N. Yeltsin. President Nixon called the attention of a somewhat annoyed President Bush to the fact that lack of active interest in the welfare of the Commonwealth of Independent States—meaning massive economic aid delivered at once—may allow the hard-liners to again combine their forces and cause Russia and the other states to be lost to democracy and to the West. Contrary to misleading opinions floating around the seats of power in the Western democracies, the three major states in the Commonwealth of Independent States, Russia, Ukraine, and Kazakhstan, are, in reality, nuclear superpowers with the capacity and capability to deliver a destructive blow anywhere on this planet. They have not destroyed, and they will not destroy, their nuclear weapons, and thinking otherwise is a futile exercise by the feeble-minded who have the tendency to confuse power politics with the Ten Commandments. See ATLANTIC PARTNERSHIP, DEFENSE PLANNING GUIDANCE, EUROPEAN ENERGY POLICY.

Who Lost Russia? See WHO LOST CHINA?

Who Will Own the 21st Century? See HOUSE OF EUROPE.

Wilayah. A governorate, an administrative subdivision, in Tunisia.

Will of All. See GENERAL WILL.

Will of Society. See INSTITUTIONALIZED WILL OF SOCIETY.

Willie Horton Syndrome. See DEFINING THE CANDIDATE.

Wilmot Proviso. See SLAVOCRACY.

Wilson's Fourteen Points. See FOURTEEN POINTS.

WIN. See WHIP INFLATION NOW.

Window of Vulnerability. A policy pronouncement by U.S. President Ronald Reagan (1981-1989), directed at the Soviet Union and its expansionist policies ("evil empire"), wherein every effort should be made to neutralize if not stop them completely. President Reagan kept the Soviet regime constantly accountable for every step in international diplomacy, ranging from violation of human rights, to Jewish emigration from the Soviet Union, to disarmament, and limitations on nuclear weapons. President Reagan's vigilance contributed to the dissolution of the "evil empire," due to the policy pronouncement, "peace through strength," where the U.S. maintained a strong military posture. The Strategic Defense Initiative, "Stars Wars," provided for formidable defense in space which the Soviets were not able to counter.

Winger. A term that was coined by Richard Scammon, one of America's more active political analysts, which denotes the political philosophy of a person (usually a politician) as being of the "right wing" (conservative or even reactionary), the "left wing" (extremely liberal, socialist, communist, or even radical), or "no wing." Such wingers commence their "wing-spreading" well in advance of an election in order to gather the support of those who favor that particular philosophy or the person who is its proponent. George McGovern, for example, built his support on the anti-Vietnam War elements in 1972; George Wallace, Governor of Alabama, gathered support from states' rights elements; Ronald Reagan took a strong stand against the Panama Canal Treaty in 1976; and Jimmy Carter was successful by capitalizing on promising a little bit of something to everybody—the safest, middle-road approach without going to extremes. See CONSERVATISM, LIBERALISM.

Wings-Spreader. See WINGER.

Winner-Driven Industrial Policy. See GUIDED FREE ENTERPRISE.

Winner Takes All. See PLURALITY VOTE.

Wirtschaftswunder. See GERMAN ECONOMIC MIRACLE.

Wisdom of the Masses. See JACKSONIAN DEMOCRACY.

Wisner's Wurlitzer. See PROPAGANDA ASSETS INVENTORY (PAI).

Wisper. See DECEPTION.

With All Deliberate Speed. See DELIBERATE SPEED.

Withering Away of the State. See MARXISM, STATELESS SOCIETY.

WNP. See WORLD NET PRODUCT.

Woman's Christian Temperance Union (WCTU). A militant organization established in 1874 by Frances E. Willard for the purpose of combating the consumption of alcohol and advocating planned parenthood. Soon, the WCTU joined forces with the Anti-Saloon League, formed in 1893, which added such slogans as "The Saloons Must Go" and "Vote for Cold Water, Boys." See PROHIBITION PARTY.

Woman's Civic Betterment League. Formed in 1907 in Roanoke, Virginia; it demanded a master plan for the development of the city, control of land speculation, and planned regulated growth. See NATIONAL ORGANIZATION FOR WOMEN (NOW), WOMEN'S POLITICAL RIGHTS.

Womb to the Tomb Law. See POST-INDUSTRIAL SOCIETY.

Women Equity Action League. See WOMEN POLITICAL ACTION GROUPS.

Women Political Action Groups. Among the most active and eloquent in presenting their views and agendas are the following: the League of Women Voters, the American Association of University Women, the National Organization of Women, the National Women's Political Caucus, and the Women's Equity Action League, just to name a few. Following W.W.II, women's groups were very active in promoting civil rights, better education and health services, protection of the environment, and the family. Although women are divided on the issue of abortion, they are better unified on the issue of equal rights for women. Although the 27th Amendment was never ratified, the issue still remains on the agenda of many women's organizations. During the past several years, women have taken up what is known as the "comparable worth" issue, addressing inequities in pay between the genders. Women claim they are often "stuck in women's work" earning less than men do for comparable work. The Supreme Court in the state of Washington agreed with women on the issue of "comparable worth," but the U.S. Supreme Court has taken no position on that issue as yet. In spite of some progress in politics, few women seek public elective offices and, as a result, the nation is deprived of the wisdom of the larger portion of the U.S. population.

Women Power. See NATIONAL ORGANIZATION FOR WOMEN.

Women Solidarity Movement. See WOMEN WALK HOME.

Women Walk Home. A mass protest of women of the island state of Cyprus against war between the Greeks and Turks competing for control of the island. The mass march of women commenced in 1974 when on 15 July the Cypriot National Guard led by Greek officers took control of the government. This provoked the removal of Archbishop Makarios and retaliation by the Turkish Army. On 8 June 1975 the Turkish Cypriots voted to establish their own state, and the island remains divided between the Greeks and the Turks. The women of Cyprus have since been joined by women from other parts of the world who on occasion come to Cyprus to join in protest against war and the misery war causes. The movement is growing to global proportion and it is often called "Women Solidarity Movement."

Women's Political Rights. A coalition of individuals and women's groups which in 1837 raised demands for the political and economic equality of women by virtue of their owning property and paying taxes, because women were not represented in the chambers of power (government and politics), and because all governments derive their just powers from the consent of the governed—a paraphrase of a passage in the Declaration of Independence. The coalition pointed out that women are politically non-existent—a legacy taken on by contemporary women's organizations such as the National Organization for Women (NOW). See NATIONAL ORGANIZATION FOR WOMEN (NOW), WOMEN'S POLITICAL RIGHTS.

Wonderful Nonsense. See ROARING TWENTIES.

Woothi Satha. See RATHA SATHA.

Wop. See MAFIA.

Work Ethic. A notion that labor, physical or mental, is the main source of all ultimate material wealth, and that man's survival depends on producing goods and services in order to satisfy personal needs and for the exchange of surplus for other goods and services. Some refer to the "Protestant work ethic" as the foundation on which modern capitalism was built and on which industrial societies have developed, producing enough for themselves as well as for others. There are indications that the work ethic is on the decline among the leading industrial nations, mainly in the United States, as an attractive human activity; that is "is being destroyed by liberal welfare programs"; that the goose that lays the golden egg (i.e., capitalism), is being slaughtered by votes of the unwashed masses. Economist Winniski observes "We are becoming more and more a nation of grasshoppers and less and less a nation of ants."

Work, Honesty, and Technology. See EMPEROR FUJIMORI.

Work of God. See OPUS DEI.

Work of the Satan. See EASTOXIFICATION.

Workers' Councils. In contemporary Yugoslavia, the management of all socialized industrial enterprises is exercised by so-called "workers' councils" (employees in the respective enterprises, about 95% of which are nationalized, that is, are owned and operated by the state). The Councils, together with the management, determine all production and marketing goals and, after paying taxes to the state, distribute the profits among themselves. This system is currently being tried in some Western European economies, particularly in France, Italy, and the Federal Republic of Germany, and is often referred to as "socialist capitalism," or "socialism with a human face." See SOCIALISM WITH A HUMAN FACE.

Workfare. A system under which welfare recipients are required to work on jobs assigned to them, or forfeit their welfare benefits.

Workie. See WORKINGMAN'S PARTY.

Working Smarter Not Harder. See UTOPIA.

Workingman's Party. During the 1930s, several splinter groups from the two major political parties in the United States attempted to form a genuine party of the workers which also advocated strong labor unions, to the great consternation of big business. The party was called the "workie," and the movement continued well into the 1960s, but American labor never succeeded, as did its counterparts in Europe, in forming a genuine party of workers.

Works Progress Administration (WPA). An agency of the federal government set up on May 6, 1935 (under the authority of the Emergency Relief Appropriations Act of April 1935) for the purpose of providing jobs for the unemployed. Between 1936 and 1941, over four billion dollars were spent on the building of such facilities as schools, highways, libraries, parks, airports, and playgrounds, and on other projects that would benefit the general public. Nearly three million persons were employed. Under a separate program, the so-called "National Youth Administration," young people in secondary and post-secondary schools were able to earn income to finance their education. These programs were part of the so-called "New Deal" era of the Franklin D. Roosevelt Administration.

World Apartheid Movement (WAM). A political organization, under the leadership of Koos Vermelen, of white opponents to the desegregation policies of South Africa's President F. W. de Klerk and his National Party. The Conservative Party of South Africa, under the leadership of Andries Treurnicht, receives considerable support from the WAM ranks, since both favor apartheid. Vermelen warns against the introduction of the American model of an electoral process based on the principle of "one man, one vote," and during a February 1992 rally in the town of Potcheftroom, shouted the slogan, "America is de Klerk's whore." The all-white primary in the spring of 1992 that President de Klerk proposed, in order to eventually gain the support of whites for the final abolition of apartheid, was opposed by the WAM, who consider it a sell-out, and by the black African National Congress, which viewed it as an attempt to delay the eradication of apartheid. The Inkatha Freedom Party, a powerful native Zulu force under the leadership of Chief Mangosuthu Buthelezi, showed no opposition to the primary.

World Congress of the Partisans of Peace of 1950. See WORLD PEACE MOVEMENT.

World Court. See INTERNATIONAL COURT OF JUSTICE (ICJ).

World Federal State. See ONE-WORLDER.

World Federalism. See ONE-WORLDER.

World Federalists. An international group that favors a single, federal world government.

World Federation of Trade Unions (WFTU). An informal international federation to which most of the communist-controlled and communist-dominated trade union organizations belong. The non-communist trade union organizations belong to the International Confederation of Free Trade Unions (ICFTU). See FRONT ORGANIZATION.

World Government. A dream as old as recorded history, of many internationalists and cosmopolites, to establish a single world government as the only means of guaranteeing tangible world peace and security. The likelihood of such a world government is probably best characterized by professors Norman D. Palmer and Howard C. Perkins who state: ". . . if a world government were established, it would be more likely to be established by force than by consent. It would, in other words, probably be a world imperium of a totalitarian nature rather than a revolutionary union of the free." See COSMOPOLITAN.

World Health Organization (WHO). See UNITED NATIONS ORGANIZATION.

World Net Product (WNP). The sum total of goods and services produced by the world's economies, minus depreciation. (Approximately 15 percent of WNP is produced by multinational corporations. In the United States, 60 percent of production is corporate; 80 percent of employment is in establishments of 20 or more employees; and the U.S. Department of Defense employs, excluding military personnel, over one million persons. It is the largest single employer, followed by American Telephone and Telegraph and General Motors, private enterprises. Capital-wise, the Exxon Corporation is larger than the financial resources of the state governments of New York, including New York City, and California. Cooperative production accounts for 1 percent of GNP in the United States, whereas it is 10 percent in Finland and 30 percent in Israel.)

World Peace Council. An informal organization established in 1975 in Havana, Cuba, for the purpose of aiding the Puerto Rican Socialist Party and its Army for Violent National Liberation (Fuerzas Armadas de Liberacion Nacional, FALN) in gaining independence for Puerto Rico from the United States, under whose jurisdiction it enjoys the status of a Commonwealth. In September 1975, the Council called a world-wide International Conference on Solidarity for Puerto Rican Independence, held in Havana, Cuba, with Cuban and Soviet assistance. Attending were 300 representatives of the Communist Party of the United States. (In 1967 a national referendum was held in Puerto Rico which gave the people a voice in determining the political future of the island. The choices were: remain a Commonwealth, request the U.S Congress for recognition as a separate state in the American Federal Union, or become a sovereign independent state. Of the approximately 700,000 votes cast, 98 percent favored the present status of a Commonwealth.) See FUERZAS ARMADAS DE LIBERACION NACIONAL.

World Peace Movement. During the late 1940s and early 1950s, the Soviet Union began an intensive campaign for the preservation of international peace through several offensives activated particularly in Western Europe. Thus, in 1950 the Stockholm Peace Appeal was originated—this at a time when the communists were preparing for an aggressive war in Korea—and a series of "peace congresses" were held in about fifty major cities of the world, including London, New York and Paris; a number of international organizations (such as the so-called "Partisans of Peace") were also established to carry out the Soviet-sponsored appeal for peace. The principal objectives of the so-called "peace movement" were: (1) to explore the anti-war sentiments still strong in the minds of many people and thus to establish the image of the Soviet Union as the "champion" of peace; (2) to incite strikes and anti-American sentiments in Europe, where the Soviet expansionist intentions were obvious; and (3) to mobilize world public opinion against the use of nuclear weapons (which at this time the Soviet Union did not yet possess) through the circulation of peace petitions sponsored by the Stockholm Peace Appeal. (Approximately 274 million persons from all over the world signed these petitions, including about one million Americans.)

World Policeman. Due to the bipolar division of the world politically, the former Soviet Union and the United States maintained their spheres of influence in the East and West respectively, and, in order to contain each other's expansion and influence, deployed force on occasion to police an area. (The U.S. sent troops to the Dominican Republic to preserve the status quo there, as it intervened in Korea and Vietnam; the USSR has intervened in Poland, Hungary, and Czechoslovakia for similar reasons.) Also, the peaceful competition (peaceful coexistence) between the Soviet Union and the United States was often construed as an attempt by one to eventually eliminate the other and maintain itself as a policeman not only of the power so conquered, but of the entire world. See BIPOLARITY, PEACEFUL COEXISTENCE, POLYCENTRISM.

World System. See WORLD GOVERNMENT, Appendices 75-79.

World Wars. See WARS WITH GLOBAL IMPLICATIONS, Appendix 88.

World Without the Bomb Conference. The international conference held in Accra, Ghana, in June, 1962, which most of the nations of the world attended, for purpose of petitioning the major powers, namely the Soviet Union and the United States, to abandon the development of nuclear weapons which may lead to nuclear war.

Wounded Knee Rebellion. In February 1973, Indian leader Russell Means and armed members of the American Indian Movement (AIM) seized the exchange post on the Sioux reservation at Wounded Knee, South Dakota, and declared Indian independence as a nation within the American nation. The rebellion was triggered by aggravated differences among the various tribes and between the poor and the well-to-do, the old and the young, the rural and the city Indians; but above all, the rebellion was triggered because of grievances against the government of the United States. The Sioux leaders presented the following demands to the federal government: (1) self-determination for all Indian tribes in the United States, including the power to educate, tax, and police their people and to utilize their financial resources without external controls; (2) return of once-Indian lands and compensation for property taken away from Indians in the past; (3) written assurances that their civil and political rights would in no way be abridged or violated; (4) more federal funds for the expansion of education and medical facilities; (5) the elimination of the Bureau of Indian Affairs (BIA) within the U.S. Department of Interior—which channels all federal funds to the Indians and supervises their activities—or the transfer of the BIA to Indian control; and (6) the overhaul of all federal policies pertaining to Indian affairs. The federal government agreed to consider AIM's grievances on the conditions that AIM cease its paramilitary activity, surrender all firearms, and present all members involved in the rebellion for legal action. By a confused and inconclusive agreement between AIM and the government, the siege of Wounded Knee ended on May 8, 1973. On September 2, 1977, the AIM renewed its demands for the return to the Indian Nations of all lands that presently constitute the states of Montana, Wyoming, and North and South Dakotas, or a payment in the lump sum of thirty billion dollars. The matter is currently being studied by the Bureau of Indian Affairs of the U.S. Department of the Interior (the official U.S. agency which oversees the welfare of American Indians).

WPA. See WORKS PROGRESS ADMINISTRATION.

Wriston Commission. In order to streamline and revitalize the American foreign service during the peak of the Cold War, U.S President Dwight D. Eisenhower (1953-1961) in 1954 authorized U.S. Secretary of State John Foster Dulles to set up a special commission for that purpose. The Commission, under the leadership of Dr. Henry Merritt Wriston, President of Brown University, completed its work by 1957 and recommended that the service be integrated into two groups: the Foreign Service Officers (the career diplomats) and the Foreign Service Staff Corps (the clerical personnel), both under the direction of the U.S. Department of State. The U.S. Foreign Service operates today on the basis of the Wriston reorganization plan. See FOREIGN SERVICE OFFICER (FSO).

Writ. An order issued by an appropriate authority: e.g., a court of law, a judicial officer, or a sovereign (king), commanding certain behavior, that is, to perform or not to perform a certain act.

Writ of Common Use. Any one of a number of writs listed below that are most commonly used, often referred to as "judicial writs:"

> **Writ of Appeal**—whenever a party to a suit sustains damages resulting from the decision of a lower court, the case can be brought to a higher court for review, in which case the higher court is obligated to act.

> **Writ of Certification**—this is an advisory writ. Whenever a lower court is not certain on a point of law, it may ask for advice from a higher court.

> **Writ of Certiorari**—In the Latin language, "To make more certain"—whenever a person, party to a suit, has been affected by the decision of a lower court, a higher court may be petitioned for review by means of certiorari. In this case, the higher court will summon the entire record of the case and decide whether to grant the writ or to reject it. (There is no appeal for denial of appeal.) A writ of review.

> **Writ of Ejectment**—takes away a position or property from one person and gives it to another.

> **Writ of Error**—allows for immediate appeal whenever the judge makes an error in reading the law or interpreting the facts.

> **Writ of Execution**—requires a defendant to satisfy a judgment in a civil suit.

> **Writ of Habeas Corpus**—In the Latin language, "to protect the body"—forbids detention agencies (police) to hold a person for any extensive period of time without specific charges being placed against him.

> **Writ of Injunction**—forbids the commission of certain acts that may bring damaging consequences, either on a temporary basis (preliminary injunction), or forever.

> **Writ of Mandamus**—In the Latin language, "to obey"—directs a public official to perform his duties as required by law.

> **Writ of Prohibition**—Prosecuting attorney appealing judge's sentence.

> **Writ of Quo Warranto**—In the Latin language, "to explain"—directs either a public official to explain by what right or law he ought to hold his office, or a public utility corporation to explain by what right or law it ought to pursue its line of business..

> **Writ of Subpoena**—requires one to appear as a witness or to produce evidence.

Writ of Summons—directs the plaintiff in a civil suit to appear and to answer to the complaint placed against him.

Writ of Warrant—grants the power to search, seize, or arrest and to command appearance.

Write-in Ballot. A ballot which allows voters to write-in the names of candidates of their choice on election day. Under some electoral systems, voters may enter additional candidates on the ballot in addition to those that are already printed on the ballot.

Written Constitution. An official document prepared by a competent authority of the state (e.g., the legislative body or a constitutional convention called for that particular purpose), which stipulates in writing the nature of the government, political and governmental institutions and officials and their powers and limitations, as well as the rights and obligations of citizens. All modern states today have written constitutions. See SUPREME LAW OF THE LAND, UNWRITTEN CONSTITUTION, Appendix 5.

WSPF. See SPECIAL PROSECUTOR, WATERGATE SPECIAL PROSECUTION FORCE.

WTO. See EAST EUROPEAN MUTUAL ASSISTANCE TREATY, WARSAW TREATY ORGANIZATION.

"The first requisite of a good citizen in this Republic of ours is that he shall be able and willing to pull his weight."

THEODORE ROOSEVELT, 1858-1919

X. See CONTAINMENT.

X-2. Common designation of counterintelligence, counterespionage, components of intelligence organizations. See COUNTERINTELLIGENCE.

XX. See COUNTERINTELLIGENCE, INTELLIGENCE, SECRET INTELLIGENCE SERVICE (SIS).

X, Y, Z Affair. Three French government officials (Bellamy, Hauteval, and Hottinguer) submitted their request to U.S. President John Adams (1797-1801) for a "loan" of 32,000,000 florina (approximately $250,000 today) as the price for their arranging an audience for the American envoy to France with the French Foreign Minister, Talleyrand. The French officials, identifying themselves only as X, Y, and Z had advance information on America's intentions to ask the French government to expedite a trade agreement between the two nations. (America's devastated economy was in great need of quick money, while the French economy was one of the most prosperous in the world). President Adams promptly revealed this international extortion information to the U.S. Congress, which condemned the French practices as the most inappropriate in relations between sovereign states, and the nation began to arm itself under the slogan "Millions for defense, but not one red cent for tribute." The French government construed the rebuke as an act of hostility and this led to the so-called "undeclared war" by France against the United States which lasted for two years, 1798-1800.

Y

"If I have seen further it is by standing on the shoulders of giants."

SIR ISAAC NEWTON, 1642-1727

YAF. See YOUNG AMERICANS FOR FREEDOM.

Yakuza. About 2,000 Mafia-type organizations which are active in Japan, clandestinely, within political groups and organized crime. The largest organization of Yakuza is the 11,000-member Yamaguchi-gumi. The Japanese Government declared in 1978 an all-out war, "Operation Bulldozer," against those organizations. See TERRORISM.

Yale School. See POSITIVIST VIEW OF LAW.

Yalta Conference. A major international summit conference held (February 4-11, 1945 at Yalta, the USSR (a resort city on the Crimean Peninsula), between President Franklin D. Roosevelt of the United States, Prime Minister Winston Churchill of Great Britain, and Premier of the Soviet Union and Secretary of the Communist Party of the Soviet Union (CPSU)—which then carried the name of "All-Soviet Communist Party" (Bolsheviks)—Josef Stalin. Major results of the conference were the following: (1) final plans for the defeat of Nazi Germany were worked out and the conference participants agreed that nothing but a total and unconditional surrender would be accepted from Germany; (2) they further agreed that the defeated German state would be divided into three zones of occupation, and the city of Berlin into three sectors, each sector under the separate jurisdiction and control of an allied power; (3) France was to be included as the fourth allied occupation power as soon as its government was formed, thus dividing Germany into four occupation zones and the city of Berlin into four sectors; (4) a new government was to be established in states liberated by the Red Army, namely, Poland, Czechoslovakia, Austria, Hungary, and Romania; and (5) a conference of the United Nations Organization was to be held in San Francisco, USA, with the Soviet Union represented by all of its fifteen Union Republics, thus having fifteen votes in the General Assembly of the United Nations. This agreement was amended so that the Soviet Union finally had three votes; namely, those of the Byelorussian (White Russian), the Ukrainian Soviet Socialist Republics, and the Soviet Union proper. (When the United States delegate to the Conference, John Foster Dulles, objected to the Soviet demand and asked in return for forty-eight votes for the United States, the Soviet delegate showed him a text of the United States Constitution and pointed out that there is no indication that the states in the American Union are in reality sovereign states. At this point the matter was dropped and the Soviet Union retained three votes while the United States settled for one vote). See SAN FRANCISCO CONFERENCE.

Yankee. Originally, anyone from the New England states in the United States; during the Civil War, anyone from the North; and generally, anyone considered to be an American. Also, as applied to any act or activity, private or public, that can in some way be associated with the United States, any of its officers (e.g., American emissaries abroad), corporations, or even individual persons. It may be referred to as "Yankee ingenuity" by friends and "Yankee imperialism" by adversaries (e.g., the socialist states and some third-world states in Africa, Asia and Latin America). A slogan such as "Yankee Go Home" can often be found on display in public places in many foreign countries (very often in those which benefit from American presence the most). Throughout Latin America, and particularly in Mexico, Americans are, pejoratively, referred to as "gringos," in the Spanish language, a "thief," or a "bandit," because of the many desperadoes who were invading Mexico from the Old West, and often mistreated the Mexicans. The term "Norte-Americano" is also used as a more friendly reference to Americans from the North.

Yankee go Home. See YANKEE.

574

Yankee Imperialism. See YANKEE.

Yankee Ingenuity. See SOUNDS OF LITTLE HAMMERS.

Yankeefication. A term used to describe the impact of northern Yankees who move to the southern states of the United States, affecting local and regional politics and culture, making changes in the traditional South.

Year-end Presidential Conference. U.S. President Jimmy Carter initiated the practice of holding a year-end press conference with mass media persons at the White House, at which past, present, and future problems and policies are discussed for public information. The first Year-End Conference was held by President Carter on Wednesday, December 28, 1977.

Year of Catastrophe. See ARAB NATIONALISM.

Year of Revolutions. See COMMUNIST MANIFESTO, SPRING OF NATIONS.

Year Zero. After the departure of American forces from Vietnam in 1975, the Vietnamese communist regime rounded up millions of people, mainly those who had collaborated with the Americans, and put them in so-called "reeducation" camps in order to convert them back to communism. Neighboring Cambodia, under the leadership of Pol Pot, decided to eradicate cities, schools, currency and other forms of societal infrastructure, by sending millions of people into the countryside to work on the land. It was a back-to-the-land movement on a massive scale. Millions perished in the march and many more were executed in what became known as the "killing fields." Pol Pot's policy was to rebuild Cambodian society from "year zero." The United States, under the "Reagan Doctrine," sent humanitarian aid to Cambodia and allowed almost a million persons from Cambodia and Vietnam, many of which were known as "boat people," to immigrate to the U.S.

Yea's and Nay's. See VIVA VOCE VOTE.

Yellow Bird Operation. See OPERATION YELLOW-BIRD, TIANANMEN SQUARE MASSACRE.

Yellow Dog Contract. An agreement between an employer and a potential employee stipulating that the latter will be employed only on condition that he will not seek membership in a labor union. Under the Norris-LaGuardia Act of 1932, such agreements are illegal and may not be forced in a court of law. See TAFT-HARTLEY LAW.

Yellow Dog Democrat. See PRIMARY ELECTION.

Yellow Peril. A term often used by some racist politicians to describe their fear that the peoples of the yellow race will multiply so rapidly that they will soon be in a position to gain substantial political power and eventually control the peoples of other races. See NUREMBERG LAWS, SWART GEVAAR.

Yellow Turbans. See SECRET SOCIETIES.

Yeltsin-Bush Summit. See PREVENTIVE DIPLOMACY.

Yeltsinovshchina. Term epitomizing the charismatic, resolute, and decisive leadership style of the President of Russia, Boris Nikolayevich Yeltsin (born 1 February 1931 in the small village of Butko, in the Tilitsky district of the province of Sverdlovsk in Russia). Yeltsin renounced communism and communist party membership at great personal risk; he stood up against the Soviet Party and the Soviet state, demanding restoration of freedom to citizens and a market-type economy, including the right of property ownership by individuals. He also called for closer collaboration with America and other democratic states. He stood up on top of an army tank (from which he could have been blown to pieces) while condemning the Moscow coup against President Mikhail S. Gorbachev, and emerged in 1991 as the leader of Russia as well as of the Commonwealth of Independent States.

Yes Party. See DA PARTY.

Yippies. See NEW LEFT, YOUTH INTERNATIONAL PARTY.

Yom Kippur War of 1973. On October 6, 1973, the Jewish Holy Day of Atonement, Egyptian forces with the aid of Jordanian and Iraqi formations attacked Israeli forces along the Suez Canal line and Syrian forces attacked in the Golan Heights area. On October 22, 1973, the U.S. Security Council passed a resolution calling for a cease fire, which went into effect on October 24, 1973, with supervision by UN forces. Egyptian forces for the first time used Soviet-made SAM-6 missiles (a deadly ground-to-air rocket weapon) which crippled the Israeli Air Force for several months. The Arab forces, however, failed to recover the lands which Israel acquired during the 1967 war. See SADAT-BEGIN SUMMIT.

You Can't Fight City Hall. An expression used when stifling, irresponsive, and aloof government bureaucracies (at all levels of government) are indifferent to the needs of the communities they serve. During the late 1800s and early 1900s many large cities in America were governed by strong mayors, often corrupt and partial to favored interests. Very often, the mayor was in collusion with the bureaucracy, the chief of police or the sheriff and the judge, so that individual persons, particularly immigrants and the poor, could not receive service or even justice.

You Can't Make Chicken Salad out of Chicken S..t. See POLITICAL SYSTEM, Appendix 3.

You Die, We Fly! A facetious remark about the frequent trips to funerals of foreign leaders and dignitaries made by U.S. Vice President George Bush (1981-1989).

You Do Your Damnedest. See PRESIDENTIAL DECISIVENESS, PRESIDENTIAL STYLE.

You Don't Need Evidence to Impeach a President, Only Votes. See IMPEACHMENT.

You Have No Time to Love, Because You are Too Busy Hating! See HATE CRIME.

You Meaner Beauties of the Night. See AMBASSADOR.

Young Americans for Freedom (YAF). A conservative organization composed mainly of college and university students dedicated to the preservation of what the YAF considers are real American values and ideals and to combating anything that it considers anti-American (e.g., socialist economy and an extensive involvement in global politics). The YAF opposes very strongly centralization of political and regulatory powers by the U.S. federal government and all measures which tend to weaken the private sector of the economy. The organization was founded in 1960 by William F. Buckley, Jr., noted writer and political commentator on the far-right of the American political spectrum.

Young Communist International. See COMMUNIST ORGANIZATIONS.

Young Socialists. See JUNGE SOZIALISTEN.

Young Turk. A member of an organization (e.g., a political party, a governmental agency, or a business enterprise) who is dissatisfied with the status quo and is seeking ways to bring about radical change. Also, an ambitious young man ascending an organization's power structure.

Young Urban Professional (YUPPIE). That portion of the Post W.W.II and Post-Korean War generation of Americans, highly educated, progressive, highly motivated, characterized by a competitive spirit and a desire to succeed in any chosen endeavor; entering important business and government decision and policy making position in America and shall determine its faith. Some black groups among them call themselves "buppies," or "black urban professionals." They influence product design, market needs and influence daily life. There are some voices to the effect that this particular group is also the best customer of drug pushers having the access to the funds required of supporting a drug habit.

Your Grandchildren Will Live in Freedom. Soviet Premier and Secretary of the Communist Party of the former Soviet Union (CPSU) Nikita Sergeyevich Khrushchev told U.S. Vice President Richard M. Nixon, "Your grandchildren will live under communism," when Nixon visited Moscow in 1959. In this famous "Kitchen Debate," held in the kitchen of a house on display at the Moscow State Fair, Nixon replied that "Soviet grandchildren will live sooner in freedom."

Your Grandchildren Will Live Under Communism. See YOUR GRANDCHILDREN WILL LIVE IN FREEDOM.

Your Right to Remain Silent. See MIRANDA CARD.

Youth International Party (Yippies). An unstructured political organization, with leftist orientation, consisting mostly of young people, college and university students, anti-Vietnam War activists, draft-dodgers, and anti-establishmentarians (the counterculture) which advocated disregard for the existing political-economic-social system in America. It was active during the late 1960s and early 1970s, and is considered to be a part of the so-called "new left."

Yug. Perjorative term for a "Yugoslav," especially one of the Broz Tito partisans in Yugoslavia who at the end of W.W.II decided to retain the City of Trieste because the Italians had been pro-Nazi participants in the war against the allies. The Yugoslav guerrillas were very hostile to American soldiers stationed there to protect the city from the Yugoslavs. In retribution, their favorite weapon against the Americans was piano wire stretched across a road to behead American GIs driving around in jeeps. The American soldiers allegedly had a song composed to this effect: "I lost my head in Yugoslavia."

Yugoslav-Soviet Split. President of independent Yugoslavia and W.W.II partisan leader, Josef Broz Tito, broke off with the Soviet brand of socialism in 1948, upon strong encouragement and support from the British and the American intelligence services, the MI-6 and the CIA respectively. Tito pronounced his to be the "Yugoslav way to socialism."

Yugoslavian Dissolution. See SEPARATISM.

Yugoslavization. A radical split of one confederate or federal state, e.g., Yugoslavia, into small states along nationalist lines, often accompanied by bitter and senseless killings of one national group by another.

Yuppie. See YOUNG URBAN PROFESSIONAL.

Z

"It is an economic axiom as old as the hills that goods and services can be paid for only with goods and services."
ALBERT J. NOCK, 1873-1945

Z. See CENTER.

Z Thesis. In 1989, an anonymous thesis, signed by "Z" was widely circulated in Europe and, clandestinely, in the Soviet Union, where it was intercepted by the Soviet secret police, the KGB, and delivered by hand to Mikhail S. Gorbachev. The thesis outlined the futile efforts of the Soviet system to democratize itself and project itself as more humanitarian, and stated that the Soviet system is and will remain totalitarian, oppressive, unable to satisfy the basic needs of its people, and that it would fall very soon, because such a system is beyond reform. The Soviet leadership was very much disturbed by the contents and wide circulation of this thesis which, one suspects, appeared with the knowledge of the Pope, as its reasoning was similar to that of the Pope in his decades of struggle with the communist system in Poland.

ZANLA. See ZIMBABWE AFRICAN NATIONAL UNION.

ZANU. See ZIMBABWE AFRICAN NATIONAL UNION.

Zapata Plan. See BAY OF PIGS.

ZAPU. See ZIMBABWE AFRICAN PEOPLE'S UNION.

Zarathustrianism. An Iranian religion, named after its founder, sixth century BC Iranian prophet, Zoroaster. The mixture of Zarathustrianism, Islamic religion transplanted by the Arabs (the Iranians are not Arabs), and the views and rituals of the Shiite Moslems, created a unique political culture which is not easily understood without closer study and lengthy observation. The prevailing notion common among Iranians, as well as Iran's neighbors, particularly Iraq, that "defeat makes us strong," and the sending of young boys to war with the full knowledge that they shall perish for the glory of Allah—as was the case during the Iran-Iraq ten-year war (1980-1990)—often leads leaders to simplistic conclusion that the sword is mightier than the Zarathustrian determination to endure and to survive. Zarathustrianism permeates the contemporary political Weltanschauung of some Iranian and Arab leaders. Modern Zarathustrians, whose symbol is the sun, often also worship the crescent, the symbol of Islam—a unique political-religious rapprochement.

Zemskiy Natchalnik. In the Russian language, "land commissioner" or "land administrator." Also, a land commissioner in Tsarist Russia who had administrative and judicial powers over the peasants.

Zemskiy Sobor. In the Russian language, "land council." Also, the rural government in Tsarist Russia from the 16th century to the time of the Bolshevik Revolution in 1917. See CHRISTIAN-DEMOCRATIC MOVEMENT OF RUSSIA.

Zemstvo. In the Russian language, "landed gentry" or "large landowners." Also the gentry class of landowners in Tsarist Russia; a unit of local government after the reorganization of 1864; an assembly of representatives from the UYEZD or the GUBERNYA representing all social strata.

Zen Yuppie. See WE, THE PEOPLE, TAKE BACK AMERICA.

Zengakuren. The so-called "All-Japan Federation of Student Self-Governing Organizations." A loose federation of socialist and communist organizations composed mainly of college and university students whose principal objective is to combat capitalism, particularly the American presence in any form, in Japan. Its paramilitary faction, the Japanese Red Army, was able to block President Dwight D. Eisenhower's visit to Japan in 1958. See ANARCHISM, TERRORISM.

Zentrumspartei. A minor political party in Germany. See CENTER.

Zero Budgeting. A system requiring an annual justification for all federal programs, both new and old, as a basis for determining their utility. President Jimmy Carter (1977-1981) advocates such a budgeting system.

Zero-Growth. See ROME CLUB.

Zero Year. See YEAR ZERO.

Zigs and Zags Diplomacy. During his October 1977 address to the United Nations General Assembly, U.S. President Jimmy Carter described zig-zag diplomacy as it pertains to the Middle East crisis (Israeli-Arab States): "A Geneva settlement is like a tall mountain, full of crevices and sharp rocks. Therefore, you don't go to it in a straight line. You go through zigs and zags. You even go down a little bit, then you keep moving. As long as you know where you're going, that's what's important. And we know where we're going. We know we've got to make zigs and zags." Also known as "step-by-step" diplomacy. See DIPLOMACY, SHUTTLE DIPLOMACY.

Zigzag Man. A pejorative term for U.S. President George Bush when seeking reelection in 1992, because of his changes on many issues of public policy, and especially for his deviation from his 1988 campaign statement, "Read my lips, no new taxes." President Bush himself admitted that the year 1992 was a difficult one for many Americans; he called it a "screwy year," and stated that he would seek the best solutions possible in spite of the fact that he expected little from the U.S. Congress in terms of legislation. He called on the legislators during the 1992 inaugural address to present a package, particularly as it pertains to taxes, by 20 March 1992. However, Warren Rudman, Republican senator from New Hampshire, challenged that optimism when he announced on 25 March 1992 that because of the wide-spread and deeply-rooted "conspiracy of silence" among legislators, the administration, and a large segment of the American electorate, positive reforms were not possible. Vested interests control the legislative process and the execution of policies by the administration. Senator Rudman announced that he would not seek reelection to the Senate, for these reasons, as a protest, when his term expires in 1993. Senator Rudman was co-author with Phil Gramm, Republican senator from Texas, of the so-called "Gramm-Rudman Hollings Deficit Reduction Act" of 1985, which called for a gradual balancing of the federal budget and control of deficit spending. The Balanced Budget and Emergency Deficit Control Act of 1985 aimed to achieve pay-as-you-go practices in federal spending. The law was abandoned in 1990. See GOVERNMENT BUDGET, PAY AS YOU GO POLICY.

Zimbabwe African National Liberation Army (ZANLA). See ZIMBABWE AFRICAN NATIONAL UNION (ZANU).

Zimbabwe African National Union (ZANU). A revolutionary, paramilitary organization formed during the 1960s in Southwest Africa and Rhodesia, which struggled for the liberation of Rhodesia from white rule. ZANU, under the leadership of Robert Mugabe, commanded a guerrilla army—the Zimbabwe African National Liberation Army (ZANLA)—of approximately 4,000 men (some of whom were trained in Cuba and the Soviet Union) and operated mainly from neighboring Mozambique. Mugabe and Joshua Nkomo, the leader of the second major liberation movement—the Zimbabwe African People's Union (ZAPU)—struggled for the total takeover of Rhodesia by blacks and without participation in a coalition government with the regime of Ian Smith. They both refused to join in the agreement for sharing power with Ian Smith which was signed on March 3, 1978, with black nationalist leaders (Bishop Abel Muzorewa, the Reverend Ndabaningi Sithole, and Chief Jeremiah Chirau). The agreement called for an equal share in the governance of Rhodesia by blacks and whites by the end of 1978. Mugabe and Nkomo hoped to break up this black-white coalition by deployment of their guerrillas and eventually to take over themselves. (The two groups, ZAPU and ZANU, were serious rivals for absolute power.) See ZIMBABWE AFRICAN PEOPLE'S UNION (ZAPU).

Zimbabwe African People's Union (ZAPU). A revolutionary, paramilitary organization formed in Rhodesia during the 1960s for the purpose of liberating Rhodesia (or "Zimbabwe" to the Africans) from white rule. ZAPU, under the leadership of Joshua Nkomo, maintained a guerrilla force of about 6,000 men (many of them trained in Cuba and/or the Soviet Union in military as well as political warfare), the Zimbabwe African People's Revolutionary Army (ZAPRA). The bulk of the war materiel was supplied by the Soviet Union either directly or through the Cubans as intermediaries. ZAPU was a rival of ZANU for political control of Zimbabwe.

Zimbabwe Peoples Revolutionary Army (ZIPRA). See ZIMBABWE AFRICAN PEOPLE'S UNION (ZAPU).

Zimmermann Affair. A note from Alfred Zimmermann (1864-1940) of the German Foreign Office to the German Minister in Mexico which directed him to inform the Mexican Government that Germany was willing to enter into alliance with Mexico in case the United States declared war on Germany, and that Germany would help Mexico regain California, New Mexico, Texas, and other territories once under Mexican jurisdiction. The message was intercepted by British intelligence and forwarded to the United States Government on January 19, 1917. On April 2, 1917, President Woodrow Wilson read the Zimmermann message to Congress, whereupon the Senate immediately adopted a war resolution (by vote of 82 to 6), and the House (by vote of 373 to 50) soon concurred in declaring war on Germany.

Zionism. A militant international movement of peoples of the Jewish faith mobilized to establish and maintain an independent Jewish State (Israel, which was established in 1948) and to protect the interest of Jews everywhere. Because of the superior ability of the Jews to adapt and to organize, the movement became very successful and thus the object of envy and, often, terrorist attacks. See ISRAELI SETTLEMENTS, SADAT-BEGIN SUMMIT.

Zionism Equals Racism. On October 17, 1975, the General Assembly of the United Nations adopted a resolution by a vote of 75 to 29, with the United States opposing it, equating Zionism (the Jewish religious and national movement) with racism and racial discrimination. On November 10, 1975, the General Assembly submitted this resolution for a general vote naming Zionism as "a form of racism and racial discrimination," and it was passed by a vote of seventy-two to thirty-five. The U.S. delegation called it "this infamous act," and, as a form of protest, on November 11, 1975, both houses of the U.S. Congress passed separate resolutions condemning the UN's anti-Zionist vote.

Zionist Federation. See HAGANAH, ZIONISM.

Zizhiqu. An administrative unit, an autonomous region, in China.

Zoku Giin. A strategy developed by the Liberal Democrat Party in the Japanese Diet for the purpose of influencing administrative policies of the bureaucracy of that sector of the economy over which they have legislative jurisdiction. This device allows for close collaboration between the legislators and the key government bureaucrats. See POLITICAL AFFAIRS RESEARCH COUNCIL (PARC).

Zollverein. The customs union that was organized in 1834 by Prussia; a model which other states copied. It enabled to solidify the German states into a single empire under the capable leadership of Prince Otto von Bismarck, Chancellor of the united Germany (1862-1890). Bismarck earned the reputation of "Iron Chancellor," and the nickname "Iron and Blood," because of his somewhat Machiavellian style demonstrated in the manipulation of politicians in Prussia as well as leaders of other states. Bismarck is credited with the introduction of a modern, well-trained civil service and the staffing of positions in government on the basis of merit rather than spoils.

Zoning. Legalized planning of land use for such purposes as building activity use, such as height, location, bulk, setback of structures, and structures for residential industrial, commercial, or public services. Zoning regulations (ordinances) as a rule are decided upon and determined by zoning boards or commissions and may be appealed to higher authority, either a zoning appeal board or the jurisdiction's highest executive body (e.g., mayor, city council, or governor of a state).

Zoning Law. See ZONING.

Zoning Ordinance. See ZONING.

Zoon Politikon. In the Greek language, "man is a political animal" or "man is a social animal." A conception of man by the ancient political philosopher, Aristotle (384-322 BC). See POLITICAL ECOLOGY, POLITICS, Appendix 1.

ZP. See ZENTRUMSPARTEI.

Zulu Nation. The ancient South African tribe of people organized in modern times into the Inkatha Freedom Party under the leadership of Chield Buthelezi. The Inkatha collaborates with the government of President F. W. de Klerk in a peaceful transition to sharing power with blacks on the principle of "one man, one vote," and it engages in sporadic clashes with the African National Congress (ANC) which advocates a more radical transition. See AFRICAN NATIONAL CONGRESS (ANC), AFRIKAANER RESISTANCE MOVEMENT (ARM), APARTHEID, CONFERENCE FOR DEMOCRATIC SOUTH AFRICA (CODESA).

"But it's the books, the reading, that can change one's life. I am the living evidence."
SEAN CONNERY — *JAMES BOND, 007*

"It takes two to speak the truth—one to speak, and another to listen."
HENRY DAVID THOREAU, 1817-1862

Appendices

"Where some people are very wealthy and others have nothing, the result will be either extreme democracy or absolute oligarchy, or despotism will come from either of those excesses."
ARISTOTLE, 384-322 B.C.

APPENDIX 1

Aristotle's Classification of Governments

Number of persons ruling or having direct influence upon the policies of the government	Government is classified according to whose interests it presents and whom its serves: public interest or the interest of the ruler and his followers	
Number of rulers	Represents public interest	Represents personal interest of the ruler or his followers
One virtuous person	Monarchy (the rule by one person who is virtuous)	Tyranny or autocracy
Rule by many who excel in virtues	Aristocracy	Oligarchy (the rich)
Considerable number of persons, or the majority of persons in the state	Polity	Democracy

Aristotle (384-322 B.C.), envisioned three good forms of government, or even the best, but not without pitfalls: 1. monarchy, by one virtuous person ruling in public interest, but this form may easily degenerate into tyranny; 2. aristocracy, by many persons who excel in virtues, but this form may easily change into oligarchy; and 3. constitutional (mixed) government, resting on the will of the majority, but this may turn into mob rule, the tyranny of the majority. Mixed government is the best, one that achieves a political equilibrium which is based on proper relationships of the executive, the legislative, and the judicial branches of the government (separation of powers principle).

APPENDIX 2

The Ten Commandments

I. "I am the Lord thy God; thou shalt have no other gods before me. II. Thou shalt not take the name of the Lord thy God in Vain. III. Remember the Sabbath day, to keep it holy. IV. Honor thy father and thy mother. V. Thou shalt not kill. VI. Thou shalt not commit Adultery. VII. Thou shalt not steal. VIII. Thou shalt not bear false witness against thy neighbor. IX. Thou shalt not covet thy neighbor's house. X. Thou shalt not covet thy neighbor's wife, nor his manservant, nor his maidservant, nor his ox, nor his ass, nor anything that is thy neighbors."

APPENDIX 3

The Anatomy of the Political System

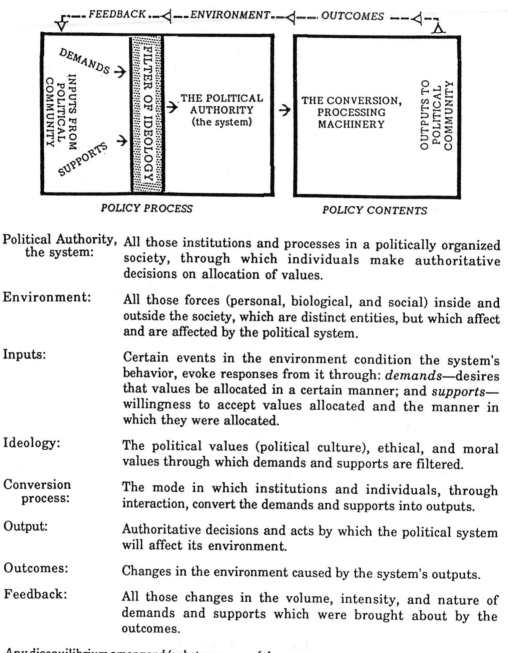

Political Authority,
the system:

All those institutions and processes in a politically organized society, through which individuals make authoritative decisions on allocation of values.

Environment:

All those forces (personal, biological, and social) inside and outside the society, which are distinct entities, but which affect and are affected by the political system.

Inputs:

Certain events in the environment condition the system's behavior, evoke responses from it through: *demands*—desires that values be allocated in a certain manner; and *supports*—willingness to accept values allocated and the manner in which they were allocated.

Ideology:

The political values (political culture), ethical, and moral values through which demands and supports are filtered.

Conversion
process:

The mode in which institutions and individuals, through interaction, convert the demands and supports into outputs.

Output:

Authoritative decisions and acts by which the political system will affect its environment.

Outcomes:

Changes in the environment caused by the system's outputs.

Feedback:

All those changes in the volume, intensity, and nature of demands and supports which were brought about by the outcomes.

Any disequilibrium among and/or between any of the components
may upset the functioning of the system.

APPENDIX 3-A

The Anatomy of Power

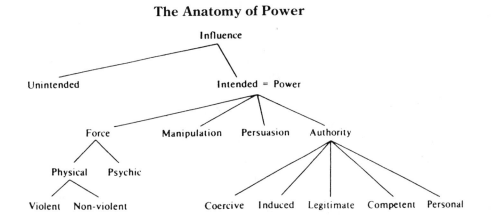

SOURCE: Dennis H. Wrong, *Power: Its Forms, Bases and Uses*, New York, Harper, 1979.

1. **INFLUENCE:**
    A. **Intended – Power:** a premeditated conveyance with the intention to have desired effect on others.
    B. **Unintended:** influence exerted without conscious intention; charismatic.

2. **INFLUENCE: INTENDED POWER:**
    A. **Force:** the creation of obstacles restricting the freedom of another.
    B. **Manipulation:** the effort to get a desired response or action from another, without revealing one's intent to do so.
    C. **Persuasion:** the effort to get a desired response or action from another by convincing one of its merits.
    D. **Authority:** successful ordering or forbidding, usually supported by custom, tradition, or law.

3. **INFLUENCE – INTENDED POWER: FORCE:**
    A. **Physical:** obstacles restricting freedom that are aimed at the body of another, e.g., imprisonment, denial of food or sleep, infliction of bodily harm.
    B. **Psychic:** infliction of mental or emotional harm to another.

4. **INFLUENCE, INTENDED POWER, FORCE, PHYSICAL:**
    A. **Violent:** assault upon the body of another to inflict pain, injury, or death.
    B. **Non-violent:** the use of one's body as a physical object to prevent or restrict actions by others.

5. **INFLUENCE, INTENDED POWER, AUTHORITY:**
    A. **Coercive:** using the threat of force to get a desired effect.
    B. **Induced:** the offering of rewards to get a desired effect.
    C. **Legitimate:** a power relation in which the power holder has an acknowledged right to command, and the power subject has an acknowledged obligation to obey.
    D. **Competent:** a power relation in which the subject obeys the order of another because of believe in competence or expertise of the power wielder.
    E. **Personal:** the subject obeys out of a desire to please or serve another person because of the latter's personal qualities. (Charismatic power).

Professor John Kenneth Galbraith (*The Anatomy of Power*, Houghton, Mifflin Company, 1983) points out that the actual sources of power are: personality, philosophy, property, and organization.

APPENDIX 4

Magna Carta of 15 June 1215

(Excerpts)

John, by the grace of God king of England, lord of Ireland, duke of Normandy and of Aquitaine, and count of Anjou, to his archbishops, bishops, abbots, earls, barons, justiciars, foresters, sheriffs, reeves, ministers, and all his bailiffs and faithful men, greeting. Know that . . . .

1. We have in the first place granted to God and by this our present charter have confirmed, for us and our heirs forever, that the English Church shall be free and shall have its rights entire and its liberties inviolate . . . We have also granted to all freemen of our kingdom, for us and our heirs forever, all the liberties hereinunder written, to be had and held by them and their heirs of us and our heirs.

9. Neither we nor our bailiffs will seize any land or revenue for any debt, so long as the chattels of the debtors are sufficient to repay the debt . . . .

13. And the city of London shall have all its ancient liberties and free customs, both by land and by water. Besides we will and grant that all other cities, boroughs, towns, and ports shall have all their liberties and free customs.

28. No constable or other bailiff of ours shall take grain or other chattels of any one without imediate payment therefor in money, unless by the will of the seller he may secure postponement of that (payment).

30. No sheriff or bailiff of ours, nor any other person, shall take the horses or carts of any freeman for carrying service, except by the will of that freeman.

38. No bailiff shall henceforth put any one to his law by merely bringing suit (against him) without trustworthy witnesses presented for this purpose.

39. No freeman shall be captured or imprisoned or disseised or outlawed or exiled or in any way destroyed, nor will we go against him or send against him, except by the lawful judgment of his peers or by the law of the land.

40. To no one will we sell, to no one will we delay or deny right of justice.

42. Every one shall henceforth be permitted, saving our fealty, to leave our kingdom and to return in safety and security, by land or by water, except in the common interest of the realm for a brief period during wartime, and excepting men imprisoned or outlawed according to the law of the kingdom . . . .

45. We will appoint as justiciars, constables, sheriffs, or bailiffs only such men as know the law of the kingdom and well desire to observe it.

52. If anyone, without the lawful judgment of his peers, has been disseised or deprived by us of his lands, castles, liberties, or rights, we will at once restore them to him . . . .

60. Now all these aforesaid customs and liberties, which we have granted, insofar as concerns us, to be observed in our kingdom toward our men, all men of our kingdom, both clergy and laity, shall, insofar as concerns them, observe toward their men.

63. . . . By the witness of the aforesaid men and of many others. Given by our hand in the meadow that is called Runnymede between Windsor and Staines, June 15, in the seventeenth year of our reign.

See MAGNA CARTA.

APPENDIX 5

The Declaration of Independence*

In Congress, July 4, 1776
The Unanimous Declaration Of The Thirteen United States Of America

When in the Course of human events, it becomes necessary for one people to dissolve the political bands which have connected them with another, and to assume among the powers of the earth, the separate and equal station to which the Laws of Nature and of Nature's God entitle them, a decent respect to the opinions of mankind requires that they should declare the causes which impel them to the separation.

We hold these truths to be self-evident, that all men are created equal, that they are endowed by their Creator with certain inalienable Rights, that among these are Life, Liberty and the Pursuit of Happiness. That to secure these rights, Governments are instituted among Men, deriving their just powers from the consent of the governed, That whenever any Form of Government becomes destructive to these ends, it is the Right of the People to alter or to abolish it, and to institute new Government, laying its foundation on such principles and organizing its powers in such form, as to them shall seem most likely to effect their Safety and Happiness. Prudence, indeed, will dictate that Governments long established should not be changed for light and transient causes; and accordingly all experience hath shown, that mankind are more disposed to suffer, while evils are sufferable, than to right themselves by abolishing the forms to which they are accustomed. But when a long train of abuses and usurpations, pursuing invariably the same Object evinces a design to reduce them under absolute Despotism, it is their right, it is their duty to throw off such Government, and to provide new Guards for their future security.——Such has been the patient sufferance of these Colonies; and such is now the necessity which constrains them to alter their former Systems of Government. The history of the present King of Great Britain is a history of repeated injuries and usurpations, all having in direct object the establishment of an absolute Tyranny over these States. To prove this, let Facts be submitted to a candid world.

He has refused his Assent, to Laws, the most wholesome and necessary for the public good.

He has forbidden his Governors to pass Laws of immediate and pressing importance, unless suspended in their operation till his Assent should be obtained; and when so suspended, he has utterly neglected to attend to them.

He has refused to pass other Laws for the accommodation of large districts of people, unless those people would relinquish the right of Representation in the Legislature, a right inestimable to them and formidable to tyrants only.

---

*On 7 June 1776 Richard Henry Lee of Virginia introduced three separate resolutions on the formation of a new union for the 13 colonies calling for : 1/independence, 2/ right to enter into alliances, and 3/ a plan for the union. In response to that, the Congress appointed a special committee which was to draft a declaration of independence. The committee consisted of John Adams, Benjamin Franklin, Thomas Jefferson, Robert Livingston, and Roger Sherman. The text was drafted and polished mainly by Thomas Jefferson (a work he supposedly completed within several hours), who was strongly influenced by writings of John Locke and W. Goslicki (1533-1607), a 16th century Polish bishop who wrote extensively on Christianity, love of freedom and patriotism, and against any form of foreign domination and oppression.

He has called together legislative bodies at places unusual, uncomfortable, and distant from the depository of their public Records, for the sole purpose of fatiguing them into compliance with his measures.

He has dissolved Representative Houses repeatedly, for opposing with manly firmness his invasions on the rights of the people.

He has refused for a long time, after such dissolutions, to cause others to be elected; whereby the Legislative powers, incapable of Annihilation, have returned to the People at large for their exercise; the State remaining in the mean time exposed to all the dangers of invasion from without, and convulsions within.

He has endeavoured to prevent the population of these States; for that purpose obstructing the Laws for Naturalization of Foreigners; refusing to pass others to encourage their migration hither, and raising the conditions of new Appropriations of Lands.

He has obstructed the Administration of Justice, by refusing his Assent to Laws for establishing Judiciary powers.

He has made Judges dependent on his Will alone, for the tenure of other offices, and the amount and payment of their salaries.

He has erected a multitude of New Offices, and sent hither swarms of Officers to harrass our people, and eat out their substance.

He has kept among us, in times of peace, Standing Armies, without the Consent of our legislatures.

He has affected to render the Military independent of and superior to the Civil power.

He has combined with others to subject us to a jurisdiction foreign to our constitution, and unacknowledged by our laws; giving his Assent to their Acts of pretended Legislation: For quartering large bodies of armed troops among us: For protecting them, by a mock Trial from punishment for any Murders which they should commit on the Inhabitants of these States: For cutting off our Trade with all parts of the world: For imposing Taxes on us without Consent: For depriving us in many cases, of the benefits of Trial by Jury: For transporting us beyond Seas to be tried for pretended offences: For abolishing the free System of English Laws in a neighbouring Provinces, establishing therein an Arbitrary government, and enlarging its Boundaries so as to render it at once an example and fit instrument for introducing the same absolute rule into these Colonies: For taking away our Charters, abolishing our most valuable Laws, and altering fundamentally the Forms of our Governments: For suspending our own Legislatures, and declaring themselves invested with power to legislate for us in all cases whatsoever.

He has abdicated Government here, by declaring us out of his Protection and waging War against us.

He has plundered our seas, ravaged our Coasts, burnt our towns, and destroyed the lives of our people.

He is at this time transporting large Armies of foreign Mercenaries to compleat the works of death, desolation and tyranny, already begun with circumstances of Cruelty & perfidy scarcely paralleled in the most barbarous ages, and totally unworthy the Head of a civilized nation.

He has constrained our fellow citizens taken Captive on the high Seas to bear Arms against their Country, to become the executioners of their friends and Brethren, or to fall themselves by their Hands.

He has excited domestic insurrections amongst us, and endeavoured to bring on the inhabitants of our frontiers, the merciless Indian Savages, whose known rule of warfare, is an undistinguished destruction of all ages, sexes and conditions. In every state of these Oppressions We have Petitioned for Redress in the most humble terms: Our repeated Petitions have been answered only by repeated injury. A Prince, whose character is thus marked by every act which may define a

Tyrant, is unfit to be the ruler of a free people. Nor have We been wanting in attentions to our British brethren. We have warned them from time to time, of attempts by their legislature to extend an unwarrantable jurisdiction over us. We have reminded them of the circumstances of our emigration and settlement here. We have appealed to their native justice and magnanimity, and we have conjured them by the ties of our common kindred to disavow these usurpations, which, would inevitably interrupt our connections and correspondence. They too have been deaf to the voice of justice and of consanguinity. We must, therefore, acquiesce in the necessity, which denounces our Separation, and hold them, as we hold the rest of mankind, Enemies in War, in Peace Friends.

WE, THEREFORE, THE REPRESENTATIVES OF THE UNITED STATES OF AMERICA, in General Congress, Assembled, appealing to the Supreme Judge of the world for the rectitude of our intentions, do, in the Name, and by Authority of the good People of these Colonies, solemnly publish and declare, That these United Colonies are, and of Right ought to be FREE AND INDEPENDENT STATES; that they are Absolved from all Allegiance to the British Crown, and that all political connection between them and the State of Great Britain, is and ought to be totally dissolved; and that as Free Independent States, they have full Power to levy War, conclude Peace, contract Alliances, establish Commerce, and to do all other Acts and Things which Independent States may of right do. And for the support of this Declaration, with a firm reliance on the protection of Divine Providence, we mutually pledge to each other our Lives, our Fortunes and our sacred Honor.

John Hancock

New Hampshire
Josiah Bartlett
Wm. Whipple
Matthew Thorton

Rhode Island
Step. Hopkins
William Ellery

Pennsylvania
Robt. Morris
Benjamin Rush
Benja. Franklin
John Morton
Geo. Clymer
Jas. Smith
Geo. Taylor
James Wilson
Geo. Ross

South Carolina
Edward Rutledge
Thos. Heyward, Junr.
Thomas Lynch, Junr.
Arthur Middleton

New York
Wm. Floyd
Phil. Livingston
Frans. Lewis
Lewis Morris

Connecticut
Roger Sherman
Sam'el Huntington
Wm. Williams
Oliver Wolcott

Virginia
George Wythe
Richard Henry Lee
Th. Jefferson
Benja. Harrison
Thos. Nelson, Jr.
Francis Lightfoot Lee
Carter Braxton

Massachusetts Bay
Saml. Adams
John Adams
Robt. Treat Paine
Elbridge Gerry

Delaware
Caesar Rodney
Geo. Read
Tho. M'Kean

Maryland
Samuel Chase
Wm. Paca
Thos. Stone
Charles Carroll of
Carrolton

New Jersey
Richd. Stockton
Jno. Witherspoon
Fras. Hopkinson
John Hart
Abra. Clark

Georgia
Button Gwinnett
Lyman Hall
Geo. Walton

North Carolina
Wm. Hooper
Joseph Hewes
John Penn

APPENDIX 6

Articles of Confederation of March 1, 1781

TO ALL TO WHOM THESE PRESENTS SHALL COME, WE THE UNDER SIGNED DELEGATES OF THE STATES AFFIXED TO OUR NAMES, SEND GREETINGS.

Whereas the Delegates of the United States of America, in Congress assembled, did, on the 15th day of November, in the Year of Our Lord One thousand Seven Hundred and Seventy seven, and in the Second Year of the Independence of America, agree to certain articles of Confederation and perpetual Union between the States of Newhampshire, Massachusetts-bay, Rhodeisland and Providence Plantations, Connecticut, New York, New Jersey, Pennsylvania, Delaware, Maryland, Virginia, North-Carolina, South-Carolina, and Georgia in the words following, viz. "Articles of Confederation and perpetual Union between the states of Newhampshire, Massachusetts-bay, Rhodeisland and Providence Plantations, Connecticut, New York, New Jersey, Pennsylvania, Delaware, Maryland, Virginia, North Carolina, South-Carolina and Georgia.

ARTICLE I. The Style of this Confederacy shall be "The United States of America."

ARTICLE II. Each state retains its sovereignty, freedom, and independence, and every Power, Jurisdiction and right, which is not by this confederation expressly delegated to the United States, in Congress assembled.

ARTICLE III. The said states hereby severally enter into a firm league of friendship with each other, for the common defence, the security of their Liberties, and their mutual and general welfare, binding themselves to assist each other, against all force offered to, or attacks made upon them, or any of them, on account of religion, sovereignty, trade, or any other pretence whatever.

ARTICLE IV. The better to secure and perpetuate mutual friendship and intercourse among the people of the different states in this union, the free inhabitants of each of these states, paupers, vagabonds and fugitive from justice expected, shall be entitled to all privileges and immunities of free citizens in the several states; and the people of each state shall have free ingress and regress to and from any other state, and shall enjoy therein all the privileges of trade and commerce, subject to the same duties, impositions and restrictions as the inhabitants thereof respectively, provided that such restriction shall not extend so far as to prevent the removal of property imported into any state, to any other state, of which the Owner is an inhabitant; provided also that no imposition, duties or restriction shall be laid by any state, on the property of the united states, or either of them.

If any Person guilty of, or charged with treason, felony, or other high misdemeanor in any state, shall flee from Justice, and be found in any of the united states, he shall, upon demand of the Governor or executive power, of the state from which he fled, be delivered up and removed to the state having jurisdiction of his offence.

Full faith and credit shall be given in each of these states to the records, acts and judicial proceedings of the courts and magistrates of every other state.

ARTICLE V. For the more convenient management of the general interests of the united states, delegates shall be annually appointed in such manner as the legislature of each state shall direct, to meet in Congress on the first Monday in November, in every year, with a power reserved to each state, to recall its delegates, or any of them, at any time within the year, and to send others in their stead, for the remainder of the Year.

No state shall be represented in Congress by less than two, nor by more than seven Members; and no person shall be capable of being a delegate for more than three years in any term of six years; nor shall any person, being a delegate, be capable of holding any office under the united states, for which he, or another for his benefit receives any salary, fees or emolument of any kind.

Each state shall maintain its own delegates in a meeting of the states, and while they act as members of the committee of the states.

In determining questions in the united states in Congress assembled, each state shall have one vote.

Freedom of speech and debate in Congress shall not be impeached or questioned in any Court, or place out of Congress, and the members of congress shall be protected in their persons from arrest and imprisonments, during the times of their going to and from, and attendance on congress, except for treason, felony, or breach of the peace.

ARTICLE VI. No state, without the consent of the united states in congress assembled, shall send any embassy to, or receive any embassy from, or enter into any conference, agreement, alliance or treaty with any King, prince or state; nor shall any person holding any office of profit or trust under the united states, or any of them, accept any present, emolument, office or title of any kind whatever from any king, prince or foreign state; nor shall the united states in congress assembled, or any of them, grant any title of nobility.

No two or more states shall enter into any treaty, confederation or alliance whatever between them without the consent of the united states in congress assembled, specifying accurately the purposes for which the same is to be entered into, and how long it shall continue.

No state shall lay any imposts or duties, which may interfere with any stipulations in treaties, entered into by the united states in congress assembled, with any king, prince or state, in pursuance of any treaties already proposed by congress, to the courts of France and Spain.

No vessels of war shall be kept up in time of peace by any state, except such number only, as shall be deemed necessary by the united states in congress assembled, for the defence of such state or its trade; nor shall any body of forces be kept up by any state, in time of peace, except such number only, as in the judgment of the united states, in congress assembled, shall be deemed requisite to garrison the forts necessary for the defence of such state; but every state shall always keep up a well regulated and disciplined militia, sufficiently armed and accoutered, and shall provide and constantly have ready for use, in public stores, a due number of field pieces and tents, and a proper quantity of arms, ammunition and camp equipage.

No state shall engage in any war without the consent of the united states in congress assembled, unless such state be actually invaded by enemies, or shall have received certain advice of a resolution being formed by some nation of Indians to invade such state, and the danger is so imminent as not to admit of a delay till the united states in congress assembled can be consulted: nor shall any state grant commission to any ships or vessels of war, nor letters of marque or reprisal, except it be after a declaration of war by the united states in congress assembled, and then only against the kingdom or state and the subjects thereof, against which war has been so declared, and under such regulations as shall be established by the united states in congress assembled, unless such state be infested by pirates, in which case vessels of war may be fitted out for that occasion, and kept so long as the danger shall continue, or until the united states in congress assembled, shall determine otherwise.

ARTICLE VII. When land forces are raised by any state for the common defence, all officers of or under the rank of colonel, shall be appointed by the legislature of each state respectively, by whom such forces shall be raised, or in such manner as such state shall direct, and all vacancies shall be filled up by the state which first made the appointment.

ARTICLE VIII. All charges of war, and all other expences that shall be incurred for the common defence or general welfare, and allowed by the united states in congress assembled, shall be defrayed out of a common treasury, which shall be supplied by the several states in proportion to the value of all land within each state, granted to or surveyed for any person, as such land and the buildings and improvements thereon shall be estimated according to such mode as the united states in congress assembled, shall from time to time direct and appoint.

The taxes for paying that proportion shall be laid and levied by the authority and direction of the legislatures of the several states within the time agreed upon by the united states in congress assembled.

ARTICLE IX. The united states in congress assembled, shall have the sole and exclusive right and power of determining on peace and war, except in the cases mentioned in the sixth article—of sending and receiving ambassadors—entering into treaties and alliances, provided that no treaty of commerce shall be made whereby the legislative power of the respective states shall be restrained from imposing such imposts and duties on foreigners as their own people are subjected to, or from prohibiting the exportation or importation of any species of goods or commodities, whatsoever—of establishing rules for deciding in all cases, what captures on land or water shall be legal, and in what manner prizes taken by land or naval forces in the service of the united states shall be divided or appropriated—of granting letters of marque and reprisal in times of peace—appointing courts for the trial of piracies and felonies committed on the high seas and establishing courts for receiving and determining finally appeals in all cases of captures, provided that no member of congress shall be appointed a judge of any of the said courts.

The united states in congress assembled shall also be the last resort on appeal in all disputes and differences now subsisting or that hereafter may arise between two or more states concerning boundary, jurisdiction or any other cause whatever; which authority shall always be exercised in the manner following. Whenever the legislative or executive authority or lawful agent of any state in controversy with another shall present a petition to congress stating the matter in question and praying for a hearing, notice thereof shall be given by order of congress to the legislative or executive authority of the other state in controversy, and a day assigned for the appearance of the parties by their lawful agents, who shall then be directed to appoint by joint consent, commissioners or judges to constitute a court for hearing and determining the matter in question: but if they cannot agree, congress shall name three persons out of each of the united states, and from the list of such persons each party shall alternately strike out one, the petitioners beginning, until the number shall be reduced to thirteen; and from that number not less than seven, nor more than nine names as congress shall direct, shall in the presence of congress be drawn out by lot, and the persons whose name shall be so drawn or any five of them, shall be commissioners or judges, to hear and finally determine the controversy, so always as a major part of the judges who shall hear the cause shall agree in the determination: and if either party shall neglect to attend at the day appointed, without showing reasons, which congress shall judge sufficient, or being present shall refuse to strike, the congress shall proceed to nominate three persons out of each state, and the secretary of congress shall strike in behalf of such party absent or refusing; and the judgment and sentence of the court to be appointed, in the manner before prescribed, shall be final and conclusive; and if any of the parties shall refuse to submit to the authority of such court, or to appear or defend their claim or cause, the court shall nevertheless proceed to pronounce sentence, or judgment, which shall in like manner be final and decisive, the judgment or sentence and other proceedings being in either case transmitted to congress, and lodged among the acts of congress for the security of the parties concerned: provided that every commissioner, before he sits in judgment shall take an oath to be administered by one of the judges of the supreme or superior court of the state, where the cause shall be tried, "well and truly to hear and determine the matter in question, according to the best of his judgment, without favour, affection or hope of reward:" provided also, that no state shall be deprived of territory for the benefit of the united states.

All controversies concerning the private right of soil claimed under different grants of two or more states, whose jurisdictions as they may respect such lands, and the states which passed such grants are adjusted, the said grants or either of them being at the same time claimed to have originated antecedent to such settlement of jurisdiction, shall on the petition of either party to the congress of the united states, be finally determined as near as may be in the same manner as is before prescribed for deciding disputes respecting territorial jurisdiction between different states.

The united states in congress assembled shall also have the sole and exclusive right and power of regulating the alloy and value of coin struck by their own authority, or by that of the respective state—fixing the standard of weights and measures throughout the united states—regulating the trade and managing all affairs with the Indians, not members of any of the states, provided that the legislative right of any state within its own limits be not infringed or violated—establishing or regulating post offices from one state to another, throughout all the united states, and exacting such postage on the papers passing through the same as may be requisite to defray the expences of the said office—appointing all officers of the land forces in the service of the united states, excepting regimental officers—appointing all the officers of the naval forces, and commissioning all officers whatever in the service of the united states—making rules for the government and regulation of the said land and naval forces, and directing their operations.

The united states in congress assembled shall have authority to appoint a committee, to sit in the recess of congress, to be denominated "A Committee of the States," and to consist of one delegate from each state; and to appoint such other committees and civil officers as may be necessary for managing the general affairs of the united states under their direction—to appoint one of their number to preside, provided that no person be allowed to serve in the office of president more than one year in any term of three years; to ascertain the necessary sums of money to be raised for the service of the united states, and to appropriate and apply the same for defraying the public expenses—to borrow money, or emit bills on the credit of the united states, transmitting every half year to the respective states an account of the sums of money so borrowed or emitted,—to build and equip a navy—to agree upon the number of land forces, and to make requisitions from each state for its quota, in proportion to the number of white inhabitants in such state; which requisition shall be binding, and thereupon the legislature of each state shall appoint the regimental officers, raise the men and cloath, arm and equip them in a soldier like manner, at the expence of the united states; and the officers and men so cloathed, armed and equipped shall march to the place appointed, and within the time agreed on by the united states in congress assembled: But if the united states in congress assembled shall, on consideration of circumstances judge proper that any state should not raise men, or should raise a smaller number than its quota, and that any other state should raise a greater number of men than the quota thereof, such extra number shall be raised, officered, cloathed, armed and equipped in the same manner as the quota of such state, unless the legislature of such state shall judge that such extra number cannot be safely spared out of the same, in which case they shall raise officer, cloath, arm and equip as many of such extra number as they judge can be safely spared. And the officers and men so cloathed, armed and equipped, shall march to the place appointed, and within the time agreed on by the united states in congress assembled.

The united states in congress assembled shall never engage in a war, nor grant letters of marque and reprisal in time of peace, nor enter into any treaties or alliances, nor coin money, nor regulate the value thereof, nor ascertain the sums and expences necessary for the defence and welfare of the united states, or any of them, nor emit bills, nor borrow money on credit of the united states, nor appropriate money, nor agree upon the number of vessels of war, to be built or purchased, or the number of land or sea forces to be raised, nor appoint a commander in chief of the army or navy, unless nine state assent to the same; nor shall a question on any other point, except by adjourning from day to day be determined, unless by the votes of a majority of the united states in congress assembled.

The congress of the united states shall have power to adjourn to any time within the year, and to any place within the united states, so that no period of adjournment be for a longer duration than the space of six Months, and shall publish the Journal of their proceedings monthly, except such parts thereof relating to treaties, alliances or military operations, as in their judgment require secrecy; and the yeas and nays of the delegates of each state on any question shall be entered on the Journal, when it is desired by any delegate; and the delegates of a state, or any of them, at his or their request shall be furnished with a transcript of the said Journal, except such parts as are above excepted, to lay before the legislatures of the several states.

ARTICLE X. The committee of the states, or any nine of them, shall be authorized to execute, in the recess of congress, such of the powers of congress as the united states in congress assembled, by the consent of nine states, shall from time to time think expedient to vest them with; provided that no power be delegated to the said committee, for the exercise of which, by the articles of confederation, the voice of nine states in the congress of the united states assembled is requisite.

ARTICLE XI. Canada acceding to this confederation, and joining in the measures of the united states, shall be admitted into, and entitled to all the advantages of this union: but no other colony shall be admitted into the same, unless such admission be agreed to by nine states.

ARTICLE XII. All bills of credit emitted, monies borrowed and debts contracted by, or under the authority of congress, before the assembling of the united states, in pursuance of the present confederation, shall be deemed and considered as a charge against the united states, for payment and satisfaction whereof the said united states, and the public faith are hereby solemnly pledged.

ARTICLE XIII. Every state shall abide by the determination of the united states in congress assembled, on all questions which by this confederation are submitted to them. And the Articles of this confederation shall be inviolably observed by every state, and the union shall be perpetual; nor shall any alteration at any time hereafter be made in any of them; unless such alteration be agreed to in a congress of the united states, and be afterwards confirmed by the legislatures of every state.

And Whereas it hath pleased the Great Governor of the World to incline the hearts of the legislatures we respectively represent in congress, to approve of, and to authorize us to ratify the said articles of confederation and perpetual union. Know Ye that we the undersigned delegates, by virtue of the power and authority to us given for that purpose, do by these presents, in the name and in behalf of our respective constituents, fully and entirely ratify and confirm each and every of the said articles of confederation and perpetual union, and all and singular the matters and things therein contained: And we do further solemnly plight and engage the faith of our respective constituents, that they shall abide by the determinations of the united states in congress assembled, on all questions, which by the said confederation are submitted to them. And that the articles thereof shall be inviolably observed by the states we respectively represent, and that the union shall be perpetual. In Witness whereof we have hereunto set our hands in Congress. Done at Philadelphia in the state of Pennsylvania the ninth day of July, in the Year of our Lord one Thousand seven Hundred and Seventy-eight, and in the third year of the independence of America.

Josiah Bartlett	John Wentworth Junr. August 8th, 1778	On the part and behalf of the State of New Hampshire.
John Hancock Samuel Adams Elbridge Gerry	Francis Dana James Lovell Samuel Holton	On the part and behalf of the State of Massachusetts Bay.
William Ellery Henry Marchant	John Collins	On the part and behalf of the State of Rhode Island and Providence Plantations.
Roger Sherman Samuel Huntington Oliver Wolcott	Titus Hosmer Andrew Adams	On the part and behalf of the State of Connecticut.
Jas. Duane Fra. Lewis	Wm. Duer Gouv. Morris	On the part and behalf of the State of New York.
Jno. Witherspoon	Nathl. Scudder	On the part and behalf of the State of New Jersey, Novr. 26, 1778.
Robt. Morris Daniel Roberdeau Jona. Bayard Smith	William Clingan Joseph Reed 22d July, 1778	On the part and behalf of the State of Pennsylvania.
Tho. M'Kean Feby. 12, 1779	John Dickinson May 5th, 1778 Nicholas Van Dyke	On the part and behalf of the State of Delaware.
John Hanson March 1, 1781	Daniel Carroll Mar. 1, 1781	On the part and behalf of the State of Maryland.
Richard Henry Lee John Banister Thomas Adams	Jno. Harvie Francis Lightfoot Lee	On the part and behalf of the State of Virginia.
John Penn July 21st, 1778	Corns. Harnett Jno. Williams	On the part and behalf of the State of North Carolina.
Henry Laurens William Henry Drayton Jno. Mathews	Richard Hutson Thos. Heyward Junr.	On the part and behalf of the State of South Carolina.

| Jno. Walton | Edwd. Telfair | On the part and behalf of the State of |
| 24th July, 1778 | Edwd. Langworthy | Georgia. |

Ratification by States was as follows:

South Carolina	February 5, 1778	Massachusetts	March 10, 1778
New York	February 6, 1778	North Carolina	April 5, 1778
Rhode Island	February 9, 1778	New Jersey	November 19, 1778
Connecticut	February 12, 1778	Virginia	December 15, 1778
Georgia	February 12, 1778	Delaware	February 1, 1779
New Hampshire	March 4, 1778	Maryland	January 30, 1781
Pennsylvania	March 5, 1778		

APPENDIX 7

Presidents of the Continental Congress Under the Articles of the Confederation

(The State of Maryland was the last one to ratify the Articles on 1 March 1781, and John Hanson is considered by many scholars to be the first President of the United States titled: "President of the United States in Congress Assembled." He served as head of the government, but a head of the state.)

Name	State	Elected
Peyton Randolph	Virginia	September 5, 1774
Henry Middleton	South Carolina	October 22, 1774
Peyton Randolph	Virginia	May 10, 1775
John Hancock	Massachusetts	May 24, 1775
Henry Laurens	South Carolina	November 1, 1777
John Jay	New York	December 10, 1778
Samuel Huntington	Connecticut	September 28, 1779
Thomas McKean	Delaware	July 10, 1781
John Hanson	Maryland	November 5, 1781
Elias Boudinot	New Jersey	November 4, 1782
Thomas Mifflin	Pennsylvania	November 3, 1783
Richard Henry Lee	Virginia	November 30, 1784
John Hancock	Massachusetts	November 23, 1785
Nathaniel Gorham	Massachusetts	June 6, 1786
Arthur St. Clair	Pennsylvania	February 2, 1787
Cyrus Griffin	Virginia	January 22, 1788

APPENDIX 8

Constitution of the United States of America of 1787*

PREAMBLE

We, the People of the United States, in Order to form a more perfect Union, establish Justice, insure domestic Tranquility, provide for the common defense, promote the general Welfare, and secure the Blessings of Liberty to ourselves and our Posterity, do ordain and establish this Constitution for the United States of America.

ARTICLE I

SECTION 1. All legislative Powers herein granted shall be vested in a Congress of the United States, which shall consist of a Senate and House of Representatives.

SECTION 2. The House of Representatives shall be composed of Members chosen every second Year by the People of the several States, and the Electors in each State shall have the Qualifications requisite for Electors of the most numerous Branch of the State Legislature.

---

*NOTE. The American Constitution is the only one in continuous existence in its original format (seven articles and ten first ten amendments, known as the "Bill of Rights," and the sixteen amendments subsequently added as times dictated. Since its adoption in America, the document was copied by other nations to one extent or another about 2,800 times, and some of its provisions can be found today in many contemporary constitutions around the world, but it never worked whenever and wherever it was adopted in its entirety. As a blueprint for governance, the constitution was a product of certain unique political cultures and political temperaments, and in order to succeed elsewhere, a good blueprint was not enough—the "plant" needed a certain kind of "soil" as well as a patient, diligent, and caring management to bring it to fruition. The document was not conceived in political or cultural vacuum, but is the product of rigorous study and examination of past constitutional experiences. It was Thomas Jefferson, while in Paris, who made an extensive study of the history of past models and human efforts in designing ways and means of establishing sound political institutions and harnessing political power. Jefferson never directly participated in the actual writing of the constitution, but he was widely sharing his ideas about it with those who were to be involved in that process. Jefferson was in Paris serving as a representative of the American Government but, in reality, he was in exile! There was a deep rivalry between Jefferson, an advocate of a decentralized democratic government and an agrarian/artisan society, and Alexander Hamilton, one with closer contact to George Washington than Jefferson, who advocated strong, centralized government, or even a form of a new type of monarchy. Despite of the distance, Jefferson's influence on the constitution-writers, all first rate political philosophers themselves, was great. Jefferson drew on some of the following past human experiences with government and political power and their moderate forms: 1/ *The Ten Commandments*, as engraved on stone tables and presented by God to Moses on Mount Sinai. This ancient document epitomized the noble aspirations of the Judeo-Christian tradition; 2/ the *Nihil Novi* provision of the 1505 constitutional law in Poland which established that the king could not legislate without the consent of the two-chamber parliament, the Seym and the Senate, considered a positive practice; 3/ the practice of *Liberum Veto* ("independent veto") in the Polish Commonwealth, demanding unanimity (used for the first time by a deputy, Wladyslaw Sicinski, in 1652) because a veto by one deputy rendered all legislation void, because the system called for an unanimous consent (as practiced today in the Security Council of the United Nations). Such practice obviously hampered political consensus. The prevailing contemporary practices in consensus seeking by voting are in the form of plurality vote, simple majority, absolute or qualified majority; and 4/ the experimentations and experiences by the Venetians, the British Parliament, the Castilian or Aragonese Cortes, and the Estates-General in France. Thomas Jefferson was in continuous correspondence with statesmen in these countries and, following the American Constitution, Poland passed a similar constitution on 3 May 1791, and France on 3 September 1791.

SECTION 2. The House of Representatives shall be composed of Members chosen every second Year by the People of the several States, and the Electors in each State shall have the Qualifications requisite for Electors of the most numerous Branch of the State Legislature.

No Person shall be a Representative who shall not have attained to the Age of twenty-five Years, and been seven Years a Citizen of the United States, and who shall not, when elected, be an Inhabitant of that State in which he shall be chosen.

Representatives and *direct Taxes shall be apportioned*[1] among the several States which may be included within this Union, according to their respective Numbers, *which shall be determined by adding to the whole Number of Free Persons, including those bound to Service for a Term of Years, and excluding Indians not taxed, three-fifths of all other Persons.*[2] The actual Enumeration shall be made within three Years after the first Meeting of the Congress of the United States, and within every subsequent Term of ten Years, in such Manner as they shall by Law direct. The Number of Representatives shall not exceed one for every thirty Thousand, but each State shall have at Least one Representative; *and until such enumeration shall be made, the State of New Hampshire shall be entitled to choose three, Massachusetts eight, Rhode-Island and Providence Plantation one, Connecticut five, New-York six, New Jersey four, Pennsylvania eight, Delaware one, Maryland six, Virginia ten, North Carolina five, South Carolina five, and Georgia three.*[3]

When vacancies happen in the Representation from any State, the Executive Authority thereof shall issue Writs of Election to fill such Vacancies.

The House of Representatives shall choose their Speaker and other Officers; and shall have the sole Power of Impeachment.

SECTION 3. The Senate of the United States shall be composed of two Senators from each State, *chosen by the Legislature thereof,*[4] for six Years; and each Senator shall have one Vote.

Immediately after they shall be assembled in Consequence of the first Election, they shall be divided as equally as may be into three classes. The Seats of the Senators of the first Class shall be vacated at the Expiration of the second Year, of the second Class at the Expiration of the fourth Year, and of the third Class at the Expiration of the sixth Year, so that one-third may be chosen every second Year; *and if vacancies happen by Resignation, or otherwise, during the Recess of the Legislature of any State, the Executive thereof may make temporary Appointments until the next Meeting of the Legislature, which shall then fill such Vacancies.*[5]

No Person shall be a Senator who shall not have attained to the Age of thirty Years, and been nine Years a Citizen of the United States, and who shall not, when elected, be an Inhabitant of that State for which he shall be chosen.

The Vice-President of the United States shall be President of the Senate, but shall have no Vote, unless they be equally divided.

The Senate shall choose their own Officers, and also a President pro tempore, in the Absence of the Vice-President, or when he shall exercise the Office of President of the United States.

The Senate shall have the sole Power to try all Impeachments. When sitting for that Purpose, they shall be on Oath or Affirmation. When the President of the United States is tried, the Chief

---

[1]Paid directly to the federal government. Modified by Amendment XVI in 1913.

[2]Modified by Amendment 14.

[3]Temporary provision.

[4]Modified by Amendment 17.

[5]*Ibid.*

Justice shall preside: And no Person shall be convicted without the Concurrence of two-thirds of the Members present.

Judgment in Cases of Impeachment shall not extend further than to removal from Office, and disqualification to hold and enjoy any Office of honor, Trust or Profit under the United States: but the Party convicted shall nevertheless be liable and subject to Indictment, Trial, Judgment and Punishment, according to Law.

SECTION 4. The Times, Places and Manner of holding Elections for Senators and Representatives, shall be prescribed in each State by the Legislature thereof; but the Congress may at any time by Law make or alter such Regulations, except as to the Places of choosing Senators.

The Congress shall assemble at least once in every Year, and such Meeting shall be on the first Monday of December, unless they shall by Law appoint a different Day.[6]

SECTION 5. Each House shall be the Judge of the Elections, Returns and Qualifications of its own Members, and a Majority of each shall constitute a Quorum to do Business; but a smaller Number may adjourn from day to day, and may be authorized to compel the Attendance of absent Members, in such Manner, and under such Penalties as each House may provide.

Each House may determine the Rules of its Proceedings, punish its Members for disorderly Behaviour, and, with the Concurrance of two-thirds, expell a Member.

Each House shall keep a Journal of its Proceedings, and from time to time publish the same, excepting such Parts as may in their Judgment require Secrecy; and the Yeas and Nays of the Members of either House on any question shall, at the Desire of one-fifth of those Present, be entered on the Journal.

Neither House, during the Session of Congress, shall, without the Consent of the other, adjourn for more than three days, nor to any other Place than that in which the two Houses shall be sitting.

SECTION 6. The Senators and Representatives shall receive a Compensation for their Services, to be ascertained by Law, and paid out of the Treasury of the United States. They shall in all Cases, except Treason, Felony and Breach of the Peace, be privileged from Arrest during their Attendance at the Session of their respective Houses, and in going to and returning from the same; and for any Speech or Debate in either House, they shall not be questioned in any other Place.

No Senator or Representative shall, during the Time for which he was elected, be appointed to any civil Office under the Authority of the United States, which shall have been created, or the Emoluments whereof shall have been increased during such time; and no Person holding any Office under the United States, shall be a Member of either House during his Continuance in Office.

SECTION 7. All Bills for raising Revenue shall originate in the House of Representatives; but the Senate may propose or concur with Amendments as on other Bills.

Every Bill which shall have passed the House of Representatives and the Senate shall, before it becomes a Law, be presented to the President of the United States; if he approves, he shall sign it, but if not, he shall return it, with his Objections, to that House in which it shall have originated, who shall enter the Objections at large on their Journal, and proceed to reconsider it. If after such Reconsideration two-thirds of the House shall agree to pass the Bill, it shall be sent, together with the Objections, to the other House, by which it shall likewise be reconsidered, and if approved by two-thirds of that House, it shall become a Law. But in all such Cases the Votes of both Houses shall be determined by Yeas and Nays, and the Names of the Persons voting for and against the Bill

---

[6]Modified by Amendment 20.

shall be entered on the Journal of each House respectively. If any Bill shall not be returned by the President within ten Days (Sundays excepted) after it shall have been presented to him, the Same shall be a Law, in like Manner as if he had signed it, unless the Congress by their Adjournment prevent its Return, in which Case it shall not be a Law.

Every Order, Resolution, or Vote to which the Concurrence of the Senate and the House of Representatives may be necessary (except on a question of Adjournment) shall be presented to the President of the United States; and before the Same shall take Effect, shall be approved by him, or being disapproved by him, shall be repassed by two-thirds of the Senate and the House of Representatives, according to the Rules and Limitations prescribed in the Case of a Bill.

SECTION 8. The Congress shall have Power: To lay and collect Taxes, Duties, Imposts, and Excises, to pay the Debts and provide for the common Defense and general Welfare of the United States; but all Duties, Imposts and Excises shall be uniform throughout the United States.

To borrow Money on the credit of the United States;

To regulate Commerce with foreign Nations, and among the several States, and with the Indian Tribes;

To establish an uniform Rule of Naturalization, and uniform Laws on the subject of Bankruptcies throughout the United States;

To coin Money, regulate the Value thereof, and of foreign Coin, and fix the Standard of Weights and Measures;

To provide for the Punishment of counterfeiting the Securities and current Coin of the United States;

To establish Post Offices and post Roads;

To promote the Progress of Science and useful Arts, by securing for limited Times to Authors and Inventors the exclusive Right to their respective Writings and Discoveries;

To constitute Tribunals inferior to the Supreme Court;

To define and punish Piracies and Felonies committed on high Seas, and Offences against the Law of Nations;

To declare War, grant Letters of Marque and Reprisal, and make Rules concerning captures on Land and Water;

To raise and support Armies, but no Appropriation of Money to the Use shall be for a longer Term than two Years;

To provide and maintain a Navy;

To make Rules for the Government and Regulation of the land and naval Forces;

To provide for calling forth the Militia to execute the Laws of the Union, suppress Insurrection and repel Invasions;

To provide for organizing, arming, and disciplining the Militia, and for governing such Part of them as may be employed in the Service of the United States, reserving to the States repectively, the Appointment of the Officers, and the Authority of training the Militia according to the discipline prescribed by Congress;

To exercise exclusive Legislation in all Cases whatsoever, over such District (not exceeding ten Miles square) as may, by Cession of particular States, and the Acceptance of Congress, become the Seat of Government of the United States, and to exercise like Authority over all Places purchased by the Consent of the Legislature of the State in which the Same shall be, for the Erection of Forts, Magazines, Arsenals, dock-Yards, and other needful Buildings;-And

To make all Laws which shall be necessary and proper for carrying into Execution the foregoing Powers, and all other Power vested by this Constitution in the Government of the United States, or in any Department or Officer thereof.

SECTION 9. *The Migration or Importation of such Persons as any of the States now existing shall think proper to admit, shall not be prohibited by the Congress prior to the Year one thousand eight hundred and eight, but a Tax or duty may be imposed on such Importation, not exceeding ten dollars for each Person.*[7]

The Privilege of the Writ of Habeas Corpus shall not be suspended, unless when in Cases of Rebellion or Invasion the public Safety may require it.

No Bill of Attainder or ex post facto Law shall be passed.

No Capitation, or other direct, Tax shall be laid, unless in Proportion to the Census or Enumeration herein before directed to be taken.[8]

No Tax on Duty shall be laid on Articles exported from any State.

No Preference shall be given by any Regulation of Commerce or Revenue to the Ports of one State over those of another; nor shall Vessels bound to, or from, one State, be obliged to enter, clear, or pay Duties in another.

No Money shall be drawn from the Treasury, but in Consequence of Appropriations made by Law; and a regular Statement and Account of the Receipts and Expenditures of all public Money shall be published from time to time.

No Title of Nobility shall be granted by the United States; And no Person holding any Office of Profit or Trust under them, shall, without the Consent of the Congress, accept of any present, Emolument, Office, or Title, of any kind whatever, from any King, Prince, or foreign State.

SECTION 10. No State shall enter into any Treaty, Alliance, or Confederation; grant Letters of Marque and Reprisal; coin Money; emit Bills of Credit; make any Thing but gold and silver Coin a Tender in Payment of Debts; pass any Bill of Attainder, ex post facto Law, or Law impairing the Obligation of Contracts, or Grant any Title of Nobility.

No State shall, without the Consent of the Congress, lay any Imposts or Duties on Imports or Exports, except what may be absolutely necessary for executing its inspection Laws; and the net Produce of all Duties and Imposts, laid by any State on Imports or Exports, shall be for the Use of the Treasury of the United States; and all such Laws shall be subject to the Revision and Control of the Congress.

No State shall, without the Consent of Congress, lay any Duty of Tonnage, keep Troops or Ships of War in time of Peace, enter into any Agreement or Compact with another State, or with a foreign Power, or engage in War, unless actually invaded, or in such imminent Danger as will no admit of delay.

---

[7]Temporary provision.

[8]Modified by Amendment 16.

ARTICLE II

SECTION 1. *The executive Power shall be vested in a President of the United States of America. He shall hold his Office during the Term of four Years, and, together with the Vice-President, chosen for the same Term, be elected, as follows:*[9]

Each State shall appoint, in such Manner as the Legislature thereof may direct, a Number of Electors, equal to the whole Number of Senators and Representatives to which the State may be entitled in the Congress: but no Senator or Representative, or Person holding an Office of Trust or Profit under the United States, shall be appointed an Elector.

The Electors shall meet in the respective States, and vote by Ballot for two Persons, of whom one at least shall not be an Inhabitant of the same State with themselves. And they shall make a List of all the Persons voted for, and of the Number of votes for each; which List they shall sign and certify, and transmit sealed to the Seat of the Government of the United States, directed to the President of the Senate. The President of the Senate shall, in the Presence of the Senate and the House of Representatives, open all the Certificates, and the Votes shall then be counted. The Person having the greatest Number of Votes shall be the President, if such Number be a Majority of the whole Number of Electors appointed; and if there be more than one who have such Majority, and have an equal Number of Votes, then the House of Representatives shall immediately choose by Ballot one of them for President; and if no Person have a majority, then from the five highest on the List the said House shall in like Manner choose the President. But in choosing the President, the Votes shall be taken by States, the Representation from each State having one Vote. A quorum for this Purpose shall consist of a Member or Members from two-thirds of the States, and a Majority of all the States shall be necessary to a Choice. In every Case, after the Choice of the President, the Person having the greatest Number of Votes of the Electors shall be the Vice-President. But if there should remain two or more who have equal votes, the Senate shall choose from them by Ballot the Vice-President.[10]

The Congress may determine the Time of choosing the Electors, and the Day on which they shall give their Votes; which Day shall be the same throughout the United States.

No Person except a natural born Citizen, or a Citizen of the United States, at the time of the Adoption of this Constitution, shall be eligible to the Office of President; neither shall any Person be eligible to that Office who shall not have attained to the Age of thirty-five Years, and been fourteen Years a Resident within the United States.

In Case of the Removal of the President from Office, or of his Death, Resignation, or Inability to discharge the Powers and Duties of the said Office, the Same shall devolve on the Vice-President, and the Congress may by Law provide for the Case of Removal, Death, Resignation or Inability, both of the President and Vice-President, declaring what Officer shall then act as President, and such Officer shall act accordingly, until the Disability be removed, or a President shall be elected.

The President shall, at stated Times, receive for his Services, a Compensation which shall neither be increased nor diminished during the Period for which he shall have been elected, and he shall not receive within that Period any other Emolument from the United States, or any of them.

Before he enters on the Execution of his Office, he shall take the following Oath or Affirmation:—"I do solemnly swear (or affirm) that I will faithfully execute the office of

---

[9]Amendment 20 limits the number of terms to two.

[10]Modified by Amendment 12 which in turn was modified by Amendment 20.

President of the United States, and will, to the best of my Ability, preserve, protect and defend the Constitution of the United States."

SECTION 2. The President shall be Commander in Chief of the Army and Navy of the United States, and of the Militia of the several States, when called into actual Service of the United States; he may require the Opinion, in writing, of the principal Officer in each of the executive Departments, upon any subject relating to the Duties of their respective Offices, and he shall have Power to grant Reprieves and Pardons for Offences against the United States, except in Cases of Impeachment.

He shall have Power, by and with the Advice and Consent of the Senate, to make Treaties, provided two-thirds of the Senators present concur; and he shall nominate, and by and with the Advice and Consent of the Senate, shall appoint Ambassadors, other public Ministers and Consuls, Judges of the Supreme Court, and all other Officers of the United States, whose Appointments are not herein otherwise provided for, and which shall be established by Law: but the Congress may by Law vest the Appointment of such inferior Officers, as they think proper, in the President alone, in the Courts of Law, or in the Heads of Departments.

The President shall have Power to fill up all Vacancies that may happen during the Recess of the Senate, by granting Commissions which shall expire at the End of their next Session.

SECTION 3. He shall from time to time give to the Congress Information of the State of the Union, and recommend to their Consideration such Measures as he shall judge necessary and expedient; he may, on extraordinary Occasions, convene both Houses, or either of them, and in Case of Disagreement between them, with Respect to the time of Adjournment, he may adjourn them to such Time as he shall think proper; he shall receive Ambassadors and other public Ministers; he shall take Care that the Laws be faithfully executed, and shall Commission all the Officers of the United States.

SECTION 4. The President, Vice-President and all civil Officers of the United States, shall be removed from Officer on Impeachment for, and Conviction of, Treason, Bribery, or other high Crimes and Misdemeanors.

ARTICLE III

SECTION 1. The judicial Power of the United States shall be vested in one Supreme Court, and in such inferior Courts as the Congress may from time to time ordain and establish. The Judges, both of the Supreme and inferior Courts, shall hold their Offices during good Behavior, and shall, at stated Times, receive for their Services, a Compensation, which shall not be diminished during their Continuance in Office.

SECTION 2. The judicial Power shall extend to all Cases, in Law and Equity, arising under this Constitution, the Laws of the United States, and Treaties made, or which shall be made, under their Authority;—to all Cases affecting Ambassadors, other public Ministers and Consuls;—to all Cases of admiralty and maritime Jurisdiction;—to Controversies to which the United States shall be a Party;—to Controversies between two or more States;—*between a State and Citizens of another State;*—between Citizens of different States;—between Citizens of the same State claiming Lands under Grants of different States, *and between a State, or the Citizens thereof, and foreign States, Citizens or Subjects.*[11]

In all Cases affecting Ambassadors, other public Ministers and Consuls, and those in which a State shall be Party, the Supreme Court shall have original Jurisdiction. In all the other Cases

---

[11]Limited by Amendment 11.

before mentioned, the Supreme Court shall have appellate Jurisdiction, both as to Law and Fact, with such Exceptions, and under such Regulations as the Congress shall make.

The Trial of all Crimes, except in Cases of Impeachment, shall be by Jury; and such Trial shall be held in the State where the said Crimes shall have been committed; but when not committed within any State, the Trial shall be as such Place or Places as the Congress may by Law have directed.

SECTION 3. Treason against the United States, shall consist only in levying War against them, or in adhering to their Enemies, giving them Aid and Comfort. No Person shall be convicted of Treason unless on the Testimony of two Witnesses to the same overt Act, or on Confession in open Court.

The Congress shall have Power to declare the Punishment of Treason, but no Attainder of Treason shall work Corruption of Blood, or Forfeiture except during the Life of the Person attained.

ARTICLE IV

SECTION 1. Full Faith and Credit shall be given in each State to the public Acts Records and judicial Proceedings of every other State. And the Congress may by general Laws prescribe the Manner in which such Acts, Records and Proceedings shall be proved, and the Effect thereof.

SECTION 2. The Citizens of each State shall be entitled to all Privileges and Immunities of Citizens in the several States.

A Person charged in any State with Treason, Felony, or other Crime, who shall flee from Justice, and be found in another State, shall on Demand of the executive Authority of the State from which he fled, be delivered up, to be removed to the State having Jurisdiction of the Crime.

No Person held to Service or Labour in one State, under the Laws thereof, escaping into another, shall, in Consequence of any Law or Regulation therein, be discharged from such Service of Labour, but shall be delivered up on Claim of the Party to whom such Service or Labour may be due.[12]

SECTION 3. New states may be admitted by the Congress into this Union; but no new States shall be formed or erected within the Jurisdiction of any other State; nor any State be formed by the Junction of two or more States, or Parts of States, without the Consent of the Legislatures of the States concerned as well as the Congress.

The Congress shall have Power to dispose of and make all needful Rules and Regulations respecting the Territory or other Property belonging to the United States; and nothing in this Constitution shall be so construed as to Prejudice any Claims of the United States, or of any particular State.

SECTION 4. The United States shall guarantee to every State in this Union a Republican Form of Government, and shall protect each of them against Invasion; and on Application of the Legislature, or of the Executive (when the Legislature cannot be convened) against domestic Violence.

ARTICLE V

The Congress, whenever two-thirds of both Houses shall deem it necessary, shall propose Amendments to this Constitution, or, on the Application of the Legislatures of two-thirds of the several States, shall call a Convention for proposing Amendments, which, in either Case, shall be

---

[12]Superseded by Amendment 13.

valid to all Intents and Purposes, as Part of this Constitution, when ratified by the Legislatures of three-fourths of the several States, or by Conventions in three-fourths thereof; as the one or the other Mode of Ratification may be proposed by the Congress; Provided *that no Amendment which may be made prior to the Year One thousand eight hundred and eight shall in any Manner affect the first and fourth Clauses in the Ninth Section of the first Article;*[13] and that no State, without its Consent, shall be deprived of its equal Suffrage in the Senate.

ARTICLE VI

All Debts contracted and Engagements entered into, before the Adoption of this Constitution, shall be as valid against the United States under this Constitution, as under the Confederation.

This Constitution, and the Laws of the United States which shall be made in Pursuance thereof and all Treaties made, or which shall be made, under the Authority of the United States, shall be the supreme law of the Land; and the Judges in every State shall be bound thereby, any Thing in the Constitution or Laws of any State to the Contrary notwithstanding.

The Senators and Representatives before mentioned, and the Members of the several State Legislatures, and all executive and judicial Officers, both of the United States and of the several States, shall be bound by Oath or Affirmation, to support this Constitution; but no religious Test shall ever be required as a Qualification to any Office or public Trust under the United States.

ARTICLE VII

The Ratification of the Conventions of nine States, shall be sufficient for the Establishment of this Constitution between the States so ratifying the Same.

DONE in Convention by the Unanimous Consent of the States present the Seventeenth Day of September in the Year of Our Lord one thousand seven hundred and Eighty-seven and of the Independence of the United States of America the Twelfth. In witness whereof We have hereunto subscribed our Names,

Go. Washington – Presidt.
and deputy from Virginia

		NOTES
New Hampshire	John Langdon Nicholas Gilman	Rhode Island refused to participate in the Convention and sent no delegation. It was also the last of the thirteenth and last state to ratify it on May 29, 1790.
Massachusetts	Nathaniel Gorham Rufus King	Convention delegates who refused to sign the new Constitution, mainly because it provided for a strong executive, were: Elbridge Gerry of Massachusetts, Robert Yates and John Lansing, Jr. of New York, Luther Martin—who was absent from the Convention for its entire period of deliberations, but who sent a note indicating his disapproval of it—and George Mason and Edmund Randolph of Virginia.

---

[13]Modified by Amendment 20.

Connecticut	Wm. Saml. Johnson Roger Sherman	James Madison of Virginia, who was the recording secretary during the sessions of the Convention spells the name of one of the delegates of Massachusetts, Nathaniel Gorham, "Nathaniel Ghorum."
New York	Alexander Hamilton	
New Jersey	Wil: Livingston David A. Brearley Wm. Paterson Jona: Dayton	
Pennsylvania	B. Franklin Thomas Mifflin Robt. Morris Geo. Clymer Thos. FitzSimons Jared Ingersoll James Wilson Gouv Morris	
Delaware	Geo: Read Gunning Bedfor Jun John Dickinson Richard Bassett Jaco: Broom	
Maryland	James McHenry Dan of St. Thos. Jenifer Danl. Carroll	
Virginia	John Blair James Madison Jr.	
North Carolina	Wm. Blount Richd. Dobbs Spaight. Hu Williamson	
South Carolina	J. Rutledge Charles Cotesworth Pinckney Charles Pinckney Pierce Butler	
Georgia	William Few Abr. Baldwin	

AMENDMENTS TO THE CONSTITUTION
ARTICLES IN ADDITION TO, AND AMENDMENTS TO THE CONSTITUTION OF THE UNITED STATES OF AMERICA, PROPOSED BY CONGRESS, AND RATIFIED BY THE LEGISLATURES OF THE SEVERAL STATES, PURSUANT TO THE FIFTH ARTICLE OF THE ORIGINAL CONSTITUTION

AMENDMENT I

Congress shall make no law respecting an establishment of religion, or prohibiting the free exercise thereof; or abridging the freedom of speech, or of the press; or the right of the people peaceably to assemble, and to petition the Government for a redress of grievances.

See CONGRESSIONAL PAY AMENDMENT.

AMENDMENT II

A well regulated Militia, being necessary to the security of a free State, the right of the people to keep and bear Arms, shall not be infringed.

AMENDMENT III

No Soldier shall, in time of peace be quartered in any house, without the consent of the Owner, nor in time of war, but in a manner to be prescribed by law.

AMENDMENT IV

The right of the people to be secure in their persons, houses, papers, and effects, against unreasonable search and seizures, shall not be violated, and no Warrants shall issue, but upon probable cause, supported by Oath or affirmation, and particularly describing the place to be searched, and the persons or things to be seized.

AMENDMENT V

No person shall be held to answer for a capital, or other infamous crime, unless on a presentment or indictment of a Grand Jury, except in cases arising in the land or naval forces, or in the Militia, when in actual service in time of War or public danger; nor shall any person be subject for the same offence to be twice put in jeopardy of life or limb; nor shall be compelled in any criminal case to be a witness against himself, nor be deprived of life, liberty, or property, without due process of law; nor shall private property be taken for public use, without just compensation.

AMENDMENT VI

In all criminal prosecutions, the accused shall enjoy the right to a speedy and public trial, by an impartial jury of the State and district wherein the crime shall have been committed, which district shall have been previously ascertained by law, and to be informed of the nature and cause of the accusation; to be confronted with the witnesses against him; to have compulsory process for obtaining witnesses in his favor, and to have the Assistance of Counsel for his defence.

AMENDMENT VII

In Suits at common law, where the value in controversy shall exceed twenty dollars, the right of trial by jury shall be preserved, and no fact tried by jury, shall be otherwise re-examined in any Court of the United States, than according to the rules of the common law.

AMENDMENT VIII

Excessive bail shall not be required, nor excessive fines imposed, nor cruel and unusual punishments inflicted.

AMENDMENT IX

The enumeration in the Constitution, of certain rights, shall not be construed to deny or disparage others retained by the people.

AMENDMENT X

The powers not delegated to the United States by the Constitution, nor prohibited by it to the States, are reserved to the States respectively, or to the people.

AMENDMENT XI
(Proposed March 4, 1794)
(Ratified January 8, 1798)

The Judicial power of the United States shall now be construed to extend to any suit in law or equity, commenced or prosecuted against one of the United States by Citizens of another State, or by Citizens or Subjects of any Foreign State.

AMENDMENT XII
(Proposed December 9, 1803)
(Ratified September 25, 1804)

The Electors shall meet in their respective states, and vote by ballot for President and Vice-President, one of whom, at least, shall not be an inhabitant of the same state with themselves; they shall name in their ballots the person voted for as President, and in distinct ballots the person voted for as Vice-President, and they shall make distinct lists of all persons voted for as President, and of all persons voted for as Vice-President, and of the number of votes for each, which lists they shall sign and certify, and transmit sealed to the seat of the government of the United States, directed to the President of the Senate;—The President of the Senate shall, in the presence of the Senate and House of Representatives, open all the certificates and the votes shall then be counted;— The person having the greatest number of votes for President, shall be the President, if such number be a majority of the whole number of Electors appointed; and if no person have such majority, then from the persons having the highest numbers not exceeding three on the list of those voted for as President, the House of Representatives shall choose immediately, by ballot, the President. But in choosing the President, the votes shall be taken by states, the representation from each state having one vote; a quorum for this purpose shall consist of a member or members from two-thirds of the states, and a majority of all states shall be necessary to a choice. *And if the House of Representatives shall not choose a President whenever the right of choice shall devolve upon them, before the fourth day of March next following,*[14] then the Vice-President shall act as President, as in the case of the death or other constitutional disability of the President.—The person having the greatest number of votes as Vice-President, shall be the Vice-President, if such number be a majority of the whole number of Electors appointed, and if no person have a majority, then from the two highest numbers on the list, the Senate shall choose the Vice-President; a quorum for the purpose shall consist of two-thirds of the whole number of Senators, and a majority of the whole number shall be necessary to a choice. But no person constitutionally ineligible to the office of the President shall be eligible to that of Vice-President of the United States.

AMENDMENT XIII
(Proposed January 31, 1865)
(Ratified December 18, 1865)

SECTION 1. Neither slavery nor involuntary servitude, except as a punishment for crime whereof the party shall have been duly convicted, shall exist within the United States, or any place subject to their jurisdiction.

SECTION 2. Congress shall have power to enforce this article by appropriate legislation.

AMENDMENT XIV
(Proposed June 13, 1866)
(Ratified July 28, 1868)

SECTION 1. All persons born or naturalized in the United States, and subject to the jurisdiction thereof, are citizens of the United States and of the State wherein they reside. No State shall make or enforce any law which shall abridge the privileges or immunities of citizens of the United States; nor shall any State deprive any person of life, liberty, or property, without due process of law; nor deny to any person within its jurisdiction the equal protection of the laws.

SECTION 2. Representatives shall be apportioned among the several States according to their respective numbers, counting the whole number of persons in each State, excluding Indians not

---

[14]Modifed by Amendment 20.

taxed. But when the right to vote at any election for the choice of electors for President and Vice-President of the United States, Representatives in Congress, the Executive and Judicial officers of a State, or the members of the Legislature thereof, is denied to any of the male members of such State, being twenty-one years of age, and citizens of the United States, or in any way abridged except for participation in rebellion, or other crime, the basis of representation therein shall be reduced in the proportion which the number of such male citizens shall bear to the whole number of male citizens twenty-one years of age in such State.

SECTION 3. No person shall be a Senator or Representative in Congress, or elector of President or Vice-President, or hold any office, civil or military, under the United States, or under any State, who, having previously taken an oath, as a member of Congress, or as an officer of the United States, or as a member of any State legislature, or as an executive or judicial officer of any State, to support the Constitution of the United States, shall have engaged in insurrection or rebellion against the same, or give aid or comfort to the enemies thereof. But Congress may by a vote of two-thirds of each House, remove such disability.

SECTION 4. The validity of the public debt of the United States, authorized by law, including debts incurred for payment of pensions and bounties for services in suppressing insurrection or rebellion, shall not be questioned. But neither the United States nor any State shall assume or pay any debt or obligation incurred in aid of insurrection or rebellion against the United States, or any claim for the loss or emancipation of any slave; but all such debts, obligations and claims shall be held illegal and void.

SECTION 5. The Congress shall have power to enforce, by appropriate legislation, the provisions of this article.

AMENDMENT XV
(Proposed February 26, 1869)
(Ratified March 30, 1870)

SECTION 1. The right of citizens of the United States to vote shall not be denied or abridged by the United States or by any State on account of race, color, or previous condition of servitude.

SECTION 2. The Congress shall have power to enforce this article by appropriate legislation.

AMENDMENT XVI
(Proposed July 12, 1909)
(Ratified February 25, 1913)

The Congress shall have power to lay and collect taxes on incomes, from whatever sources derived, without apportionment among the several States, and without regard to any census or enumeration.

AMENDMENT XVII
(Proposed March 13, 1912)
(Ratified May 31, 1913)

The Senate of the United States shall be composed of two Senators from each State, elected by the people thereof, for six years; and each Senator shall have one vote. The electors in each State shall have the qualification requisite for electors of [voters for] the most numerous branch of the State legislatures.

When vacancies happen in the representation of any State in the Senate, the executive authority of such State issue writs of election to fill such vacancies: *Provided*, That the legislature of any State may empower the executive thereof to make temporary appointments until the people fill the vacancies by election as the legislature may direct.

This amendment shall not be so construed as to affect the election or term of any Senator chosen before it becomes valid as part of the Constitution.

AMENDMENT XVIII
(Proposed December 18, 1917)
(Ratified January 29, 1919)

SECTION 1. *After one year from the ratification of this article the manufacture, sale, or transportation of intoxicating liquors within, the importation thereof into, or the exportation thereof from the United States and all territory subject to the jurisdiction thereof for beverage purposes is hereby prohibited.*

SECTION 2. *The Congress and the several States shall have concurrent power to enforce this article by appropriate legislation.*

SECTION 3. *This article shall be inoperative unless it shall have been ratified as an amendment to the Constitution by the legislatures of the several States, as provided in the Constitution, within seven years from the date of the submission hereof to the States by the Congress.*[15]

AMENDMENT XIX
(Proposed June 4, 1919)
(Ratified August 26, 1920)

The right of citizens of the United States to vote shall not be denied or abridged by the United States or by any State on account of sex.

Congress shall have power to enforce this article by appropriate legislation.

AMENDMENT XX
(Proposed March 2, 1932)
(Ratified February 6, 1933)

SECTION 1. The terms of the President and Vice-President shall end at noon on the 20th day of January, and the terms of Senators and Representatives at noon on the 3rd day of January, of the years in which such terms would have ended if this article had not been ratified; and the terms of their successors shall then begin.

SECTION 2. The Congress shall assemble at least once in every year, and such meeting shall begin at noon on the 3rd of January, unless they shall by law appoint a different day.

SECTION 3. If, at the time fixed for the beginning of the term of the President, the President elect shall have died, the Vice-President elect shall become President. If a President shall not have been chosen before the time fixed for the beginning of his term, or if the President elect shall have failed to qualify, then the Vice-President elect shall act as President until a President shall have qualified; and the Congress may by law provide for the case wherein neither a President elect nor a Vice-President elect shall have qualified, declaring who shall then act as President, or the manner in which one who is to act shall be selected, and such person shall act accordingly until a President or Vice-President shall have qualified.

---

[15]Repealed by Amendment 21.

SECTION 4. The Congress may by law provide for the case of the death of any of the persons from whom the House of Representatives may choose a President whenever the right of choice shall have devolved upon them, and for the case of the death of any of the persons from whom the Senate may choose a Vice-President whenever the right of choice shall have devolved upon them.

SECTION 5. Sections 1 and 2 shall take effect on the 15th day of October following the ratification of this article.

SECTION 6. This article shall be inoperative unless it shall have been ratified as an amendment to the Constitution by the legislatures of three-fourths of the several States within seven years from the date of its submission.

AMENDMENT XXI
(Proposed February 20, 1933)
(Ratified December 5, 1933)

SECTION 1. The eighteenth article of amendment to the Constitution of the United States is hereby repealed.

SECTION 2. The transportation or importation into any State, Territory, or Possession of the United States for delivery or use therein of intoxicating liquors, in violation of the laws thereof, is hereby prohibited.

SECTION 3. This article shall be inoperative unless it shall have been ratified as an amendment to the Constitution by conventions in the several States, as provided in the Constitution, within seven years from the date of the submission hereof to the States by the Congress.[16]

AMENDMENT XXII
(Proposed March 24, 1947)
(Ratified February 27, 1951)

SECTION 1. No person shall be elected to the office of the President more than twice, and no person who has held the office of President, or acted as President, for more than two years of a term to which some other person was elected President shall be elected to the office of President more than once. But this Article shall not apply to any person holding the office of President when this Article was proposed by the Congress, and shall not prevent any person who may be holding the office of President, or acting as President, during the term within which this Article becomes operative from holding the office of President or acting as President during the remainder of such term.

SECTION 2. This article shall be inoperative unless it shall have been ratified as an amendment of the Constitution by the legislatures of three-fourths of the several States within seven years from the date of its submission to the States by the Congress.

AMENDMENT XXIII
(Proposed June 16, 1960)
(Ratified March 29, 1961)

SECTION 1. The District constituting the seat of Government of the United States shall appoint in such manner as the Congress may direct:

---

[16]Thus far, the only amendment ratified by state conventions.

A number of electors of President and Vice-President equal to the whole number of Senators and Representatives in Congress to which the District would be entitled if it were a State, but in no event more than the least populous State; they shall be in addition to those appointed by the States, but they shall be considered, for the purposes of the election of President and Vice-President, to be electors appointed by a State; and they shall meet in the District and perform such duties as provided by the twelfth article of amendment.

SECTION 2. The Congress shall have power to enforce this article by appropriate legislation.

AMENDMENT XXIV
(Proposed August 27, 1962)
(Ratified January 23, 1964)

SECTION 1. The right of citizens of the United States to vote in any primary or other election for President and Vice-President, for electors for President or Vice-President, or for Senator or Representative in Congress shall not be denied or abridged by the United States or any State by reason of failure to pay any poll tax or other tax.

SECTION 1. The Congress shall have the power to enforce this article by appropriate legislation.

AMENDMENT XXV
(Proposed July 6, 1965)
(Ratified February 23, 1967)

SECTION 1. In case of the removal of the President from office or of his death or resignation, the Vice President shall become President.

SECTION 2. Whenever there is a vacancy in the office of the Vice President, the President shall nominate a Vice President who shall take office upon confirmation by a majority vote of both Houses of Congress.

SECTION 3. Whenever the President transmits to the President pro tempore of the Senate and the Speaker of the House of Representatives his written declaration that he is unable to discharge the powers and duties of his office, and until he transmits to them a written declaration to the contrary, such powers and duties shall be discharged by the Vice President as Acting President.

SECTION 4. Whenever the Vice President and a majority of either the principal officers of the executive departments or of such other body as Congress may by law provide, transmit to the President pro tempore of the Senate and the Speaker of the House of Representatives their written declaration that the President is unable to discharge the powers and duties of his office, the Vice President shall immediately assume the powers and duties of the office as Acting President.

Thereafter, when the President transmits to the President pro tempore of the Senate and the Speaker of the House of Representatives his written declaration that no inability exists, he shall resume the powers and duties of his office unless the Vice President and a majority of either the principal officers of the executive department(s) or of such other body as Congress may by law provide, transmit within four days to the President pro tempore of the Senate and the Speaker of the House of Representatives their written declaration that the President is unable to discharge the powers and duties of his office. Thereupon Congress shall decide the issue, assembling within forty-eight hours for that purpose if not in session. If the Congress, within twenty-one days after receipt of the latter written declaration, or, if Congress is not in session, within twenty-one days after Congress is required to assemble, determines by two-thirds vote of both Houses that the President is unable to discharge the powers and duties of his office, the Vice President shall continue to discharge the same as Acting President; otherwise, the President shall resume the powers and duties of his office.

AMENDMENT XXVI
(Proposed March 23, 1971)
(Ratified July 1, 1971)

SECTION 1. The right of citizens of the United States, who are 18 years of age or older, to vote shall not be denied or abridged by the United States or any other State on account of age.

SECTION 2. The Congress shall have the power to enforce this article by appropriate legislation.

AMENDMENT XXVII
(Proposed March 22, 1972)

SECTION 1. Equality of rights under the law shall not be denied or abridged by the United States or by any State on account of sex.

SECTION 2. The Congress shall have the power to enforce, by appropriate legislation, the provisions of this article.

SECTION 3. This amendment shall take effect two years after the date of ratification.

Sources: A. Hamilton, J. Jay and J. Madison. *The Federalist*, M. Farrand, ed. *The Records of the Federal Convention of 1787*, B. Long. *Genesis of the Constitution of the United States*, F. McDonald. *E Pluribus Unum: The Formation of the American Republic, 1776-1790*, W. P. Murphy. *The Triumph of Nationalism: State Sovereignty, the Founding Fathers, and the Making of the Constitution.*

APPENDIX 9

The Government of the United States

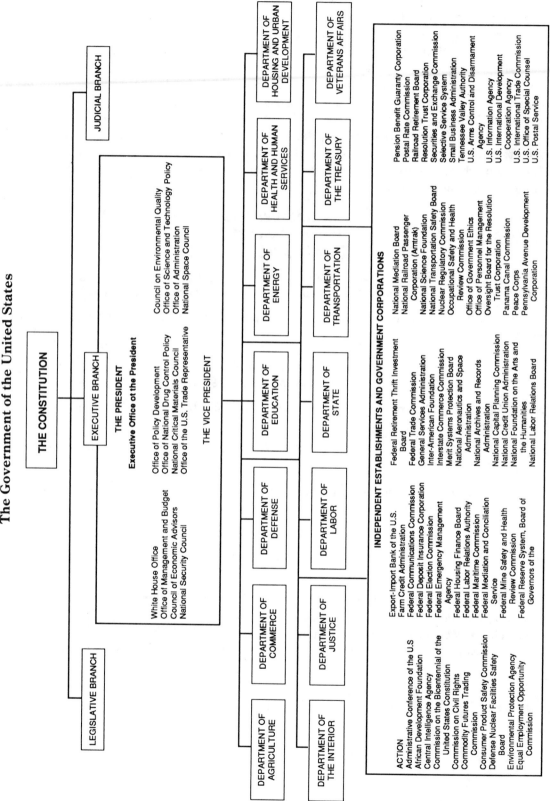

THE CONSTITUTION

LEGISLATIVE BRANCH

JUDICIAL BRANCH

EXECUTIVE BRANCH

THE PRESIDENT

Executive Office of the President

White House Office
Office of Management and Budget
Council of Economic Advisors
National Security Council

Office of Policy Development
Office of National Drug Control Policy
National Critical Materials Council
Office of the U.S. Trade Representative

Council on Environmental Quality
Office of Science and Technology Policy
Office of Administration
National Space Council

THE VICE PRESIDENT

DEPARTMENT OF AGRICULTURE

DEPARTMENT OF THE INTERIOR

DEPARTMENT OF COMMERCE

DEPARTMENT OF JUSTICE

DEPARTMENT OF DEFENSE

DEPARTMENT OF LABOR

DEPARTMENT OF EDUCATION

DEPARTMENT OF STATE

DEPARTMENT OF ENERGY

DEPARTMENT OF TRANSPORTATION

DEPARTMENT OF HEALTH AND HUMAN SERVICES

DEPARTMENT OF THE TREASURY

DEPARTMENT OF HOUSING AND URBAN DEVELOPMENT

DEPARTMENT OF VETERANS AFFAIRS

INDEPENDENT ESTABLISHMENTS AND GOVERNMENT CORPORATIONS

ACTION
Administrative Conference of the U.S
African Development Foundation
Central Intelligence Agency
Commission on the Bicentennial of the
   United States Constitution
Commission on Civil Rights
Commodity Futures Trading
   Commission
Consumer Product Safety Commission
Defense Nuclear Facilities Safety
   Board
Environmental Protection Agency
Equal Employment Opportunity
   Commission

Export-Import Bank of the U.S.
Farm Credit Administration
Federal Communications Commission
Federal Deposit Insurance Corporation
Federal Election Commission
Federal Emergency Management
   Agency
Federal Housing Finance Board
Federal Labor Relations Authority
Federal Maritime Commission
Federal Mediation and Conciliation
   Service
Federal Mine Safety and Health
   Review Commission
Federal Reserve System, Board of
   Governors of the

Federal Retirement Thrift Investment
   Board
Federal Trade Commission
General Services Administration
Inter-American Foundation
Interstate Commerce Commission
Merit Systems Protection Board
National Aeronautics and Space
   Administration
National Archives and Records
   Administration
National Capital Planning Commission
National Credit Union Administration
National Foundation on the Arts and
   the Humanities
National Labor Relations Board

National Mediation Board
National Railroad Passenger
   Corporation (Amtrak)
National Science Foundation
National Transportation Safety Board
Nuclear Regulatory Commission
Occupational Safety and Health
   Review Commission
Office of Government Ethics
Office of Personnel Management
Oversight Board for the Resolution
   Trust Corporation
Panama Canal Commission
Peace Corps
Pennsylvania Avenue Development
   Corporation

Pension Benefit Guaranty Corporation
Postal Rate Commission
Railroad Retirement Board
Resolution Trust Corporation
Securities and Exchange Commission
Selective Service System
Small Business Administration
Tennessee Valley Authority
U.S. Arms Control and Disarmament
   Agency
U.S. Information Agency
U.S. International Development
   Cooperation Agency
U.S. International Trade Commission
U.S. Office of Special Counsel
U.S. Postal Service

APPENDIX 10

U.S. House of Representatives

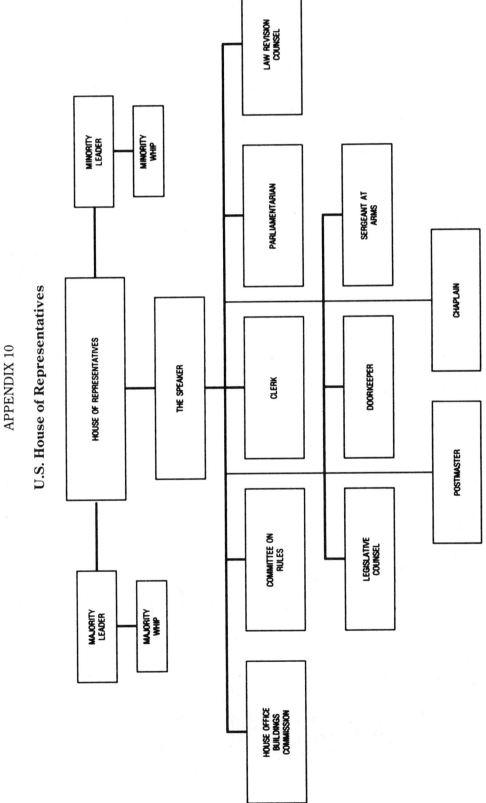

House Standing Committees

Agriculture; Appropriations; Armed Services; Banking, Finance and Urban Affairs; Budget; District of Columbia; Education and Labor; Energy and Commerce; Foreign Affairs; Government Operations; House Administration; Interior and Insular Affairs; Judiciary; Merchant Marine and Fisheries; Post Office and Civil Service; Public Works and Transportation; Rules; Science, Space, and Technology; Small Business; Standards of Official Conduct; Veterans' Affairs; Ways and Means.

APPENDIX 11

U.S. Senate

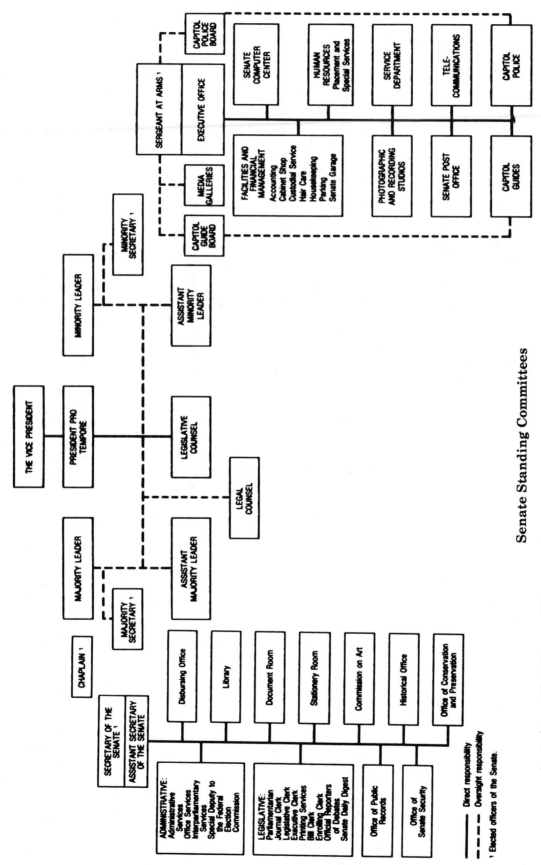

Senate Standing Committees

Agriculture, Nutrition, and Forestry; Appropriations; Armed Services; Banking, Housing, and Urban Affairs; Budget; Commerce, Science, and Transportation; Energy and Natural Resources; Environment and Public Works; Finance; Foreign Relations; Governmental Affairs; Judiciary; Labor and Human Resources; Rules and Administration; Small Business; Veterans' Affairs.

APPENDIX 12

Speakers of the U.S. House of Representatives

NO.	NAME	PARTY	STATE	TENURE	U.S. PRESIDENT IN OFFICE	PARTY
1.	Frederick A. C. Muhlenberg	F.	PA	1789-1791	George Washington	F.
2.	Jonathan Trumbull	F.	CT	1791-1793	George Washington	F.
3.	Frederick A. C. Muhlenberg	F.	PA	1793-1795	George Washington	F.
4.	Jonathan Dayton	F.	NJ	1795-1799	George Washington	F.
					John Adams	F.
5.	Theodre Sedgwick	F.	MA	1799-1801	John Adams	F.
6.	Nathaniel Macon	D.R.	NC	1801-1807	Thomas Jefferson	D.R.
7.	Joseph B. Varnum	D.R.	MA	1807-1811	Thomas Jefferson	D.R.
					James Madison	D.R.
8.	Henry Clay	D.R.	KY	1811-1814	James Madison	D.R.
9.	Langdon Cheves	D.R.	SC	1814-1815	James Madison	D.R.
10.	Henry Clay	D.R.	KY	1815-1820	James Madison	D.R.
					James Monroe	D.R.
11.	John W. Taylor	D.R.	NY	1820-1821	James Monroe	D.R.
12.	Philip B. Barbour	D.R.	VA	1821-1823	James Monroe	D.R.
13.	Henry Clay	D.R.	KY	1823-1825	James Monroe	D.R.
14.	John W. Taylor	D.	NY	1825-1827	John Quincy Adams	D.R.
15.	Andrew Stevenson	D.	VA	1827-1834	John Quincy Adams	D.R.
					Andrew Jackson	D.
16.	John Bell	D.	TN	1834-1835	Andrew Jackson	D.
17.	James K. Polk	D.	TN	1835-1839	Andrew Jackson	D.
					Martin Van Buren	D.
18.	Robert M. T. Hunter	D.	VA	1839-1841	Martin Van Buren	D.
					William Henry Harrison	W.
19.	John White	W.	KY	1841-1843	John Tyler	W.
20.	John W. Jones	D.	VA	1843-1845	John Tyler	W.
21.	John W. Davis	D.	IN	1845-1847	James Knox Polk	D.
22.	Robert C. Winthrop	W.	MA	1847-1849	James Knox Polk	D.
23.	Howell Cobb	D.	GA	1849-1851	Zachary Taylor	W.
					Millard Fillmore	W.
24.	Linn Boyd	D.	KY	1851-1855	Millard Fillmore	W.

Speakers of the U.S. House of Representatives, continued

NO.	NAME	PARTY	STATE	TENURE	U.S. PRESIDENT IN OFFICE	PARTY
25.	Nathaniel P. Banks*	A.	MA	1856-1857	Franklin Pierce	D.
26.	James L. Orr	D.	SC	1857-1859	Franklin Pierce	D.
27.	William Pennington	R.	NJ	1860-1861	James Buchanan	D.
28.	Galusha A. Grow	R.	PA	1861-1863	Abraham Lincoln	R.
29.	Schuyler Colfax	R.	IN	1863-1869	Abraham Lincoln	R.
					Andrew Johnson	R.**
30.	Theodore M. Pomeroy	R.	NY	1869-1869	Ulysses Simpson Grant	R.***
31.	James G. Blaine	R.	ME	1869-1875	Ulysses Simpson Grant	R.
32.	Michael C. Kerr	D.	IN	1875-1876	Ulysses Simpson Grant	R.
33.	Samuel J. Randall	D.	PA	1876-1881	Ulysses Simpson Grant	R.
					Rutherford Birchard Hayes	R.
34.	Joseph W. Keifer	R.	OH	1881-1883	James Abram Garfield	R.
					Chester Alan Arthur	R.
35.	John G. Carlisle	D.	KY	1883-1889	Chester Alan Arthur	R.
					Grover Cleveland	D.
36.	Thomas B. Reed	R.	ME	1889-1891	Benjamin Harrison	R.
37.	Charles F. Crisp	D.	GA	1891-1895	Benjamin Harrison	R.
					Grover Cleveland	D.
38.	Thomas B. Reed	R.	ME	1895-1899	Grover Cleveland	D.
39.	David B. Henderson	R.	IA	1899-1903	William McKinley	R.
					William McKinley	R.
40.	Joseph G. Cannon	R.	IL	1903-1911	Theodore Roosevelt	R.
					Theodore Roosevelt	R.
41.	James B. "Champ" Clark	D.	MO	1911-1919	William Howard Taft	R.
					William Howard Taft	R.
					Woodrow Wilson	D.
42.	Frederick H. Gillet	R.	MA	1919-1925	Woodrow Wilson	D.
					Warren Gamaliel Harding	R.
					Calvin Coolidge	R.

* Banks was originally elected on a Democratic ticket but later switched parties.

** Andrew Johnson was a Democrat, but was nominated by Republicans and elected with Abraham Lincoln.

*** Died in office after one day of service.

Speakers of the U.S. House of Representatives, continued

NO.	NAME	PARTY	STATE	TENURE	U.S. PRESIDENT IN OFFICE	PARTY
43.	Nicholas Longworth	R.	OH	1925-1931	Calvin Coolidge	R.
					Herbert Clark Hoover	R.
44.	John N. Garner	D.	TX	1931-1933	Herbert Clark Hoover	R.
45.	Henry T. Rainey	D.	IL	1933-1935	Franklin Delano Roosevelt	D.
46.	Joseph W. Byrns	D.	TN	1935-1936	Franklin Delano Roosevelt	D.
47.	William B. Bankhead	D.	AL	1936-1940	Franklin Delano Roosevelt	D.
48.	Samuel Reyburn	D.	TX	1940-1947	Franklin Delano Roosevelt	D.
					Harry S. Truman	D.
49.	Joseph W. Martin, Jr.	R.	MA	1947-1949	Harry S. Truman	D.
50.	Samuel Reyburn	D.	TX	1949-1953	Harry S. Truman	D.
51.	Joseph W. Martin, Jr.	R.	MA	1953-1955	Dwight D. Eisenhower	R.
52.	Samuel Reyburn	D.	TX	1955-1961	Dwight D. Eisenhower	R.
53.	John W. McCormack	D.	MA	1962-1970	John Fitzgerald Kennedy	D.
					Lyndon Baines Johnson	D.
					Richard Milhous Nixon	R.
54.	Carl Albert	D.	OK	1971-1977	Richard Milhous Nixon	R.
					Gerald R. Ford	R.
55.	Thomas ("Tip") P. O'Neill, Jr.	D.	MA	1977-1987	James ("Jimmy") E. Carter	D.
					Ronald Reagan	R.
56.	James Wright	D.	TX	1987-1989	Ronald Reagan	R.
					George Bush	R.
57.	Thomas S. Foley	D.	WA	1989-	George Bush	R.

PARTY DESIGNATIONS:

A. – American ("Know-Nothing")
D. – Democratic
D.R. – Democratic-Republican
F. – Federalist
R. – Republican
W – Whig

APPENDIX 13

Legislative Process in the United States: The Federal Level

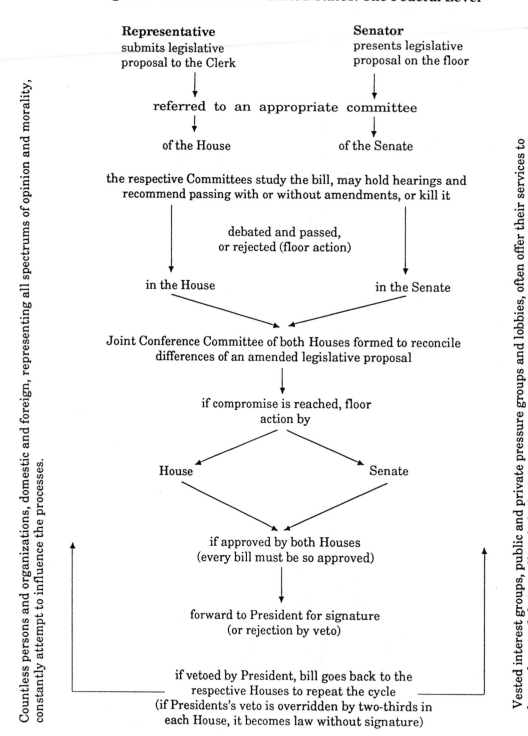

Representative
submits legislative
proposal to the Clerk

Senator
presents legislative
proposal on the floor

referred to an appropriate committee

of the House

of the Senate

the respective Committees study the bill, may hold hearings and
recommend passing with or without amendments, or kill it

debated and passed,
or rejected (floor action)

in the House

in the Senate

Joint Conference Committee of both Houses formed to reconcile
differences of an amended legislative proposal

if compromise is reached, floor
action by

House

Senate

if approved by both Houses
(every bill must be so approved)

forward to President for signature
(or rejection by veto)

if vetoed by President, bill goes back to the
respective Houses to repeat the cycle
(if Presidents's veto is overridden by two-thirds in
each House, it becomes law without signature)

Countless persons and organizations, domestic and foreign, representing all spectrums of opinion and morality, constantly attempt to influence the processes.

Vested interest groups, public and private pressure groups and lobbies, often offer their services to lawmakers and their staffs to help draft legislation.

APPENDIX 14

The Executive Office of the U.S. President

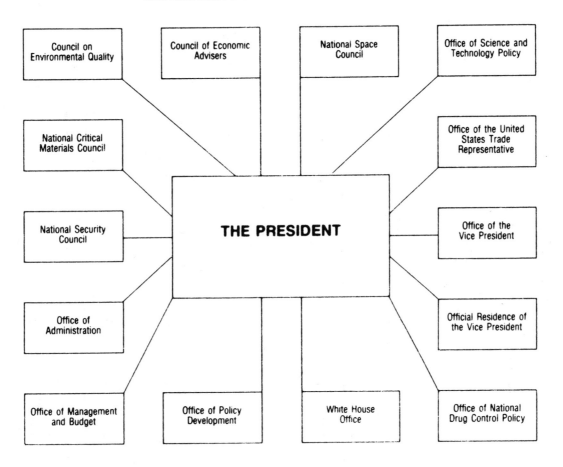

Source: *The United States Government Manual, 1991/92.*

APPENDIX 15

The Executive Departments of the U.S. Government

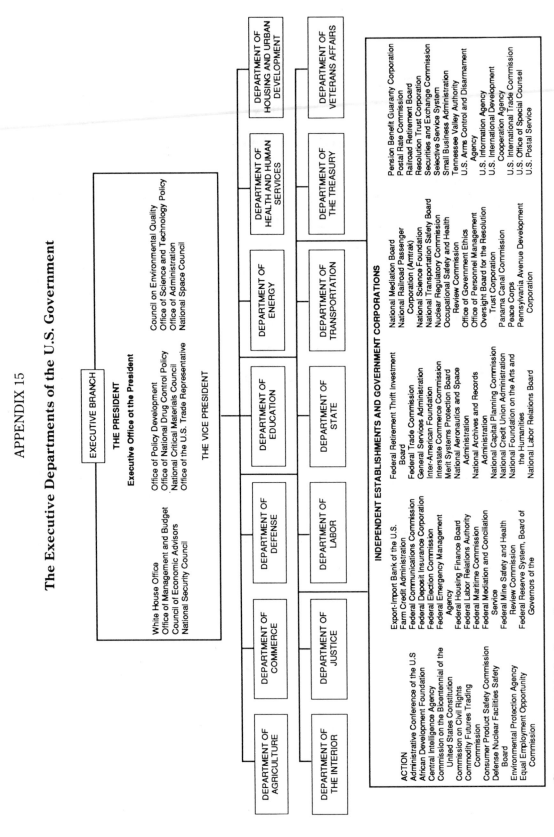

EXECUTIVE BRANCH

THE PRESIDENT

Executive Office of the President

White House Office
Office of Management and Budget
Council of Economic Advisors
National Security Council

Office of Policy Development
Office of National Drug Control Policy
National Critical Materials Council
Office of the U.S. Trade Representative

Council on Environmental Quality
Office of Science and Technology Policy
Office of Administration
National Space Council

THE VICE PRESIDENT

DEPARTMENT OF AGRICULTURE
DEPARTMENT OF COMMERCE
DEPARTMENT OF DEFENSE
DEPARTMENT OF EDUCATION
DEPARTMENT OF ENERGY
DEPARTMENT OF HEALTH AND HUMAN SERVICES
DEPARTMENT OF HOUSING AND URBAN DEVELOPMENT

DEPARTMENT OF THE INTERIOR
DEPARTMENT OF JUSTICE
DEPARTMENT OF LABOR
DEPARTMENT OF STATE
DEPARTMENT OF TRANSPORTATION
DEPARTMENT OF THE TREASURY
DEPARTMENT OF VETERANS AFFAIRS

INDEPENDENT ESTABLISHMENTS AND GOVERNMENT CORPORATIONS

ACTION
Administrative Conference of the U.S
African Development Foundation
Central Intelligence Agency
Commission on the Bicentennial of the
     United States Constitution
Commission on Civil Rights
Commodity Futures Trading
     Commission
Consumer Product Safety Commission
Defense Nuclear Facilities Safety
     Board
Environmental Protection Agency
Equal Employment Opportunity
     Commission

Export-Import Bank of the U.S.
Farm Credit Administration
Federal Communications Commission
Federal Deposit Insurance Corporation
Federal Election Commission
Federal Emergency Management
     Agency
Federal Housing Finance Board
Federal Labor Relations Authority
Federal Maritime Commission
Federal Mediation and Conciliation
     Service
Federal Mine Safety and Health
     Review Commission
Federal Reserve System, Board of
     Governors of the

Federal Retirement Thrift Investment
     Board
Federal Trade Commission
General Services Administration
Inter-American Foundation
Interstate Commerce Commission
Merit Systems Protection Board
National Aeronautics and Space
     Administration
National Archives and Records
     Administration
National Capital Planning Commission
National Credit Union Administration
National Foundation on the Arts and
     the Humanities
National Labor Relations Board

National Mediation Board
National Railroad Passenger
     Corporation (Amtrak)
National Science Foundation
National Transportation Safety Board
Nuclear Regulatory Commission
Occupational Safety and Health
     Review Commission
Office of Government Ethics
Office of Personnel Management
Oversight Board for the Resolution
     Trust Corporation
Panama Canal Commission
Peace Corps
Pennsylvania Avenue Development
     Corporation

Pension Benefit Guaranty Corporation
Postal Rate Commission
Railroad Retirement Board
Resolution Trust Corporation
Securities and Exchange Commission
Selective Service System
Small Business Administration
Tennessee Valley Authority
U.S. Arms Control and Disarmament
     Agency
U.S. Information Agency
U.S. International Development
     Cooperation Agency
U.S. International Trade Commission
U.S. Office of Special Counsel
U.S. Postal Service

APPENDIX 16

Presidents of the United States

NO.	Name	Born	Died	Tenure	State	Party	Age When Inaug.	Age When Died	Disp.
1.	George Washington	02-22-1732	12-14-1799	1789-1797	VA	Fed.	57	67	Retired*
2.	John Adams	10-30-1735	07-04-1826	1797-1801	MA	Fed.	61	90	Retired
3.	Thomas Jefferson	04-13-1743	07-04-1826	1801-1809	VA	Dem.-Rep.	57	83	Retired
4.	James Madison	03-16-1751	06-28-1836	1809-1817	VA	Dem.-Rep.	57	85	Retired
5.	James Monroe	04-28-1758	07-04-1831	1817-1825	VA	Dem.-Rep.	58	73	Retired
6.	John Quincy Adams	07-11-1767	02-23-1848	1825-1829	MA	Dem.-Rep.	57	80	Retired
7.	Andrew Jackson	05-15-1767	06-08-1845	1829-1837	SC	Dem.	61	78	Retired*
8.	Martin Van Buren	12-05-1782	07-24-1862	1837-1841	NY	Dem.	54	79	Retired
9.	William Henry Harrison	02-09-1773	04-04-1841	1841-1841	VA	Whig	68	68	Died*
10.	John Tyler	03-29-1790	01-18-1862	1841-1845	VA	Whig	51	71	Retired
11.	James Knox Polk	11-02-1795	06-15-1849	1845-1849	NC	Dem.	49	53	Retired
12.	Zachary Taylor	11-24-1784	07-09-1850	1849-1850	VA	Whig	64	65	Died*
13.	Millard Fillmore	01-07-1800	03-08-1874	1850-1853	NY	Whig	50	74	Retired
14.	Franklin Pierce	11-23-1804	10-08-1869	1853-1857	NH	Dem.	48	64	Retired*
15.	James Buchanan	04-23-1791	06-01-1868	1857-1861	PA	Dem.	65	77	Retired
16.	Abraham Lincoln	02-12-1809	04-15-1865	1861-1865	KY	Rep.	52	56	Assassinated

* U.S. Army General

Presidents of the United States, continued

NO.	Name	Born	Died	Tenure	State	Party	Age When Inaug.	Age When Died	Disp.
17.	Andrew Johnson	12-29-1808	07-31-1875	1865-1869	NC	1	56	66	Retired*
18.	Ulysses Simpson Grant	04-27-1822	07-23-1885	1869-1877	OH	Rep.	46	63	Retired*
19.	Rutherford Birchard Hayes	10-04-1822	01-17-1893	1877-1881	OH	Rep.	54	70	Retired*
20.	James Abram Garfield	11-19-1831	09-19-1881	1881-1881	OH	Rep.	49	49	Assassinated*
21.	Chester Alan Arthur	10-05-1830	11-18-1886	1881-1885	VT	Rep.	50	56	Retired
22.	Grover Cleveland	03-18-1837	06-24-1908	1885-1889	NJ	Dem.	47	71	Retired
23.	Benjamin Harrison	08-20-1833	03-13-1901	1889-1893	OH	Rep.	55	67	Retired*
24.	Grover Cleveland	03-18-1837	06-24-1908	1893-1897	NJ	Dem.	55	71	Retired
25.	William McKinley	01-29-1843	09-14-1901	1897-1901	OH	Rep.	54	58	Assassinated
26.	Theodore Roosevelt	10-27-1858	01-06-1919	1901-1909	NY	Rep.	42	60	Retired
27.	William Howard Taft	09-15-1857	03-08-1930	1909-1913	OH	Rep.	51	72	Retired
28.	Woodrow Wilson	12-28-1856	02-03-1924	1913-1921	VA	Dem.	56	67	Retired
29.	Warren Gamaliel Harding	11-02-1865	08-02-1923	1921-1923	OH	Rep.	55	57	Died
30.	Calvin Coolidge	07-04-1872	01-05-1933	1923-1929	VT	Rep.	51	60	Retired
31.	Herbert Clark Hoover	08-10-1874	10-20-1964	1929-1933	IA	Rep.	54	90	Retired
32.	Franklin Delano Roosevelt	01-30-1882	04-12-1945	1933-1945	NY	Dem.	51	63	Died
33.	Harry S. Truman	05-08-1884	12-26-1972	1945-1953	MO	Dem.	60	88	Retired
34.	Dwight David Eisenhower	10-14-1890	03-28-1969	1953-1961	TX	Rep.	62	78	Retired*
35.	John Fitzgerald Kennedy	05-29-1917	11-22-1963	1961-1963	MA	Dem	43	46	Assassinated
36.	Lyndon Baines Johnson	08-27-1908	01-22-1973	1963-1969	TX	Dem.	55	65	Retired
37.	Richard Milhous Nixon	01-09-1913		1969-1974	CA	Rep.	56		Resigned[2]

[1]Andrew Johnson was a democrat, but was nominated by Republicans and elected with Abraham Lincoln. He is the only U.S. President to be impeached by Congress on February 24, 1868, but was acquitted by the Senate on May 16, 1868 (by one vote cast by Sen. Edmund G. Ross, a radical freshman Republican from Kansas).

[2]A series of contributing events led to the resignation of Richard M. Nixon on August 9, 1974: (1) During the final stages of the impeachment

Presidents of the United States, continued

NO.	Name	Born	Died	Tenure	State	Party	Age When Inaug.	Age When Died	Disp.
38.	Gerald Rudolph Ford	07-14-1913		1974-1977	MI	Rep.	61		Retired[3]
39.	Jimmy Carter	10-01-1924		1977-1981	GA	Dem.	53		Retired
40.	Ronald Reagan	02-06-1911		1981-1989	IL	Rep.	69		Retired
41.	George Bush	06-12-1924		1989-	MA	Rep.	64		

proceeding by the U.S. House of Representatives, President Nixon told the press (on June 22, 1974) that "There is no involvement by the White House in the Watergate scandal," which commenced with the arrest of several burglars in the offices of the National Democratic Committee in Washington, D.C. (located in the Watergate Apartments) on June 17, 1972. (2) On October 10, 1973, Vice President Spiro Agnew resigned when charged with accepting some bribes and income tax evasion (without contest). (3) The Oil Producing Countries (OPEC0, and mainly the Arab States impose an oil embargo on October 17, 1973. (4) Nixon's escalation of the war in Vietnam causes Congress to limit the President's war powers (over Nixon's veto) on November 7, 1973. (5) Gerald R. Ford, House Republican Minority Leader, was sworn in as Vice President (on December 6, 1973) under the provisions of the 25th Amendment to the U.S. Constitution, (6) The House Judiciary Committee recommends three articles of impeachment of President Nixon (on July 27, 29, and 30, 1974). (7) The U.S. Supreme Court orders President Nixon to release Watergate-related tapes to the Special Prosecutor (which reveal his involvement in coverup). (8) On August 9, 1974, President Nixon informed the nation that he was resigning as President (first to do so in America's history). (9) On August 9, 1974, Vice President Ford was sworn in as President. (10) On September 8, 1974, President Ford granted an unconditional pardon to former President Richard M. Nixon.

[3]Born Leslie King, Jr., in Omaha, Nebraska, obtained the present name of Gerald Rudolph Ford after his stepfather. Ford, the Republican candidate for President, was defeated by Jimmy Carter during the 1976 general election. Carter was the nominee of the Democratic Party.

APPENDIX 17

Vice Presidents of the United States

No.	Name	Tenure	U.S. President	Disp.
1.	John Adams	1789-1797	George Washington	
2.	Thomas Jefferson	1797-1801	John Adams	
3.	Aaron Burr	1801-1805	Thomas Jefferson	
4.	George Clinton	1805-1809	Thomas Jefferson	
5.	George Clinton	1809-1812	James Madison	Clinton died April 20, 1812. Office vacant 318 days.
5.	Elbridge Gerry	1813-1814	James Madison	Gerry died November 23, 1814. Office vacant 2 years 101 days.
6.	Daniel D. Tompkins	1817-1825	James Monroe	
7.	John C. Calhoun	1825-1829	John Q. Adams	
7.	John C. Calhoun	1829-1832	Andrew Jackson	Calhoun resigned December 28, 1832. Office vacant 65 days.
8.	Martin Van Buren	1833-1837	Andrew Jackson	
9.	Richard M. Johnson	1837-1841	Martin Van Buren	
10.	John Tyler	1841-1841	William H. Harrison	Tyler succeeded to the Presidency upon Harrison's death on April 6, 1841. Office of Vice President vacant 3 years and 332 days.
11.	George M. Dallas	1845-1849	James K. Polk	
12.	Millard Fillmore	1849-1850	Zachary Taylor	Fillmore succeeded to the Presidency upon Taylor's death on July 10, 1850. Office vacant 2 years and 237 days.
13.	William R. D. King	1853-1853	Franklin Pierce	King died April 18, 1853. Office vacant 3 years and 320 days.

Vice Presidents of the United States, continued

No.	Name	Tenure	U.S. President	Disp.
14.	John C. Breckinridge	1857-1861	James Buchanan	
15.	Hannibal Hamlin	1861-1865	Abraham Lincoln	
16.	Andrew Johnson	1865-1865	Abraham Lincoln	Johnson succeeded to the Presidency upon Lincoln's assassination on April 15, 1865. Office vacant 3 years and 323 days.
17.	Schuyler Colfax	1869-1873	Ulysses S. Grant	
18.	Henry Wilson	1873-1875	Ulysses S. Grant	Wilson died on November 22, 1875. Office vacant 1 year and 102 days.
19.	William A. Wheeler	1877-1881	Rutherford B. Hayes	
20.	Chester A. Arthur	1881-1881	James A. Garfield	Arthur succeeded to the Presidency upon Garfield's assassination on September 20, 1881. Office vacant 3 years and 165 days.
21.	Thomas A. Hendricks	1885-1885	Grover Cleveland	Hendricks died on November 25, 1885. Office vacant 3 years and 99 days.
22.	Levi P. Morton	1889-1893	Benjamin Harrison	
23.	Adlai E. Stevenson	1893-1897	Grover Cleveland	
24.	Garret A. Hobart	1897-1899	William McKinley	Hobart died on November 21, 1899. Office vacant 1 year and 103 days.
25.	Theodore Roosevelt	1901-1901	William McKinley	Roosevelt succeeded to the Presidency upon McKinley's assassination on September 14, 1901. Office vacant 3 years and 171 days.
26.	Charles W. Fairbanks	1905-1909	Theodore Roosevelt	
27.	James S. Sherman	1909-1912	William H. Taft	Sherman died October 30, 1912. Office vacant 124 days.
28.	Thomas R. Marshall	1913-1921	Woodrow Wilson	
29.	Calvin Coolidge	1921-1923	Warren G. Harding	Coolidge succeeded to the Presidency upon Harding's death on August 3, 1923. Office vacant 1 year and 213 days.
30.	Charles G. Dawes	1925-1929	Calvin Coolidge	

Vice Presidents of the United States, continued

No.	Name	Tenure	U.S. President	Disp.
31.	Charles Curtis	1929-1933	Herbert C. Hoover	
32.	John N. Garner	1933-1941	F. D. Roosevelt	
33.	Henry A. Wallace	1941-1945	F. D. Roosevelt	
34.	Harry S. Truman	1945-1945	F. D. Roosevelt	Truman succeeded to the Presidency upon Roosevelt's death on April 12, 1945. Office vacant 3 years and 283 days.
35.	Alben W. Barkley	1949-1953	Harry S. Truman	
36.	Richard M. Nixon	1953-1961	D. D. Eisenhower	
37.	Lyndon B. Johnson	1961-1963	John F. Kennedy	Johnson succeeded to the Presidency upon Kennedy's assassination on November 22, 1963. Office vacant 1 year and 59 days.
38.	Hubert H. Humphrey	1865-1869	Lyndon B. Johnson	
39.	Spiro T. Agnew	1969-1973	Richard M. Nixon	Agnew resigned on October 10, 1973. Office vacant 56 days.
40.	Gerald R. Ford	1973-1974	Richard M. Nixon	Ford appointed by Nixon and confirmed on December 6, 1973. Ford succeeded to the Presidency upon Nixon's resignation on August 9, 1974. Ford appoints Nelson Rockefeller on August 20, 1974.
41.	Nelson Rockefeller	1974-1977	Gerald R. Ford	
42.	Walter F. Mondale	1977-1981	Jimmy Carter	
43.	George Bush	1981-1989	Ronald Reagan	
44.	Dan Quayle	1989-	George Bush	

APPENDIX 18

Democratic and Republican National Party Conventions and Their Candidates

YEAR	CONVENTION CITY	DATE	DEMOCRATIC CANDIDATE	NO. OF BALLOTS
1832	Baltimore, Maryland	May 21	Andrew Jackson* South Carolina	1
1825	Baltimore, Maryland	May 20	Martin Van Buren* New York	1
1840	Baltimore, Maryland	May 5	Martin Van Buren+ New York	1
1844	Baltimore, Maryland	May 27-29	James K. Polk* North Carolina	9
1848	Baltimore, Maryland	May 22-26	Lewis Cass+ Michigan	1
1852	Baltimore, Maryland	June 1-6	Franklin Pierce* New Hampshire	49

YEAR	CONVENTION CITY	DATE	DEMOCRATIC CANDIDATE	NO. OF BALLOTS	CONVENTION CITY	DATE	REPUBLICAN CANDIDATE	NO. OF BALLOTS
1856	Cincinnati, Ohio	June 2	James Buchanan* Pennsylvania	17	Philadelphia, Pennsylvania	June 17	John C. Fremont California	2
1860	Baltimore, Maryland	June 18	Stephen A. Douglass Illinois	2	Chicago, Illinois	May 16	Abraham Lincoln* Kentucky	3
1864	Chicago, Illinois	August 29	George B. McClellan Pennsylvania	1	Baltimore, Maryland	June 7	Abraham Lincoln* Kentucky	1
1868	New York, New York	July 4	Horatio Seymour New York	22	Chicago, Illinois	May 20	Ulysses S. Grant* Ohio	1

*Elected President.

+A Whig, William H. Harrison was elected President (Zachary Taylor, 1849-1850; John Tyler, 1841-1845; and Millard Filmore, 1850-1853, were the only Whig Presidents).

Democratic and Republican National Conventions and Their Candidates, continued

YEAR	CONVENTION CITY	DATE	DEMOCRATIC CANDIDATE	NO. OF BALLOTS	DATE	CONVENTION CITY	REPUBLICAN CANDIDATE	NO. OF BALLOTS
1872	Baltimore, Maryland	July 9	Horace Greeley, New York	1	June 5	Philadelphia, Pennsylvania	Ulysses S. Grant*, Ohio	1
1876	St. Louis, Missouri	June 27	Samuel J. Tilden, New York	2	June 14	Cincinnati, Ohio	Rutherford B. Hayes*, Ohio	7
1880	Cincinnati, Ohio	June 22	Winfield S. Hancock, Pennsylvania	2	June 2	Chicago, Illinois	James A. Garfield*, Ohio	36
1884	Chicago, Illinois	July 8	Grover Cleveland*, New Jersey	2	June 3	Chicago, Illinois	James G. Blaine, Maine	4
1888	St. Louis, Missouri	June 5	Grover Cleveland*, New Jersey	1	June 19	Chicago, Illinois	Benjamin Harrison*, Ohio	8
1892	Chicago, Illinois	June 21	Grover Cleveland*, New Jersey	1	June 7	Minneapolis, Minnesota	Benjamin Harrison, Ohio	1
1896	Chicago, Illinois	July 7	William J. Bryan, Nebraska	5	June 16	St. Louis, Missouri	William McKinley*, Ohio	1
1900	Kansas City, Kansas	July 4	William J. Bryan, Nebraska	1	June 19	Philadelphia, Pennsylvania	William McKinley*, Ohio	1
1904	St. Louis, Missouri	June 6	Alton B. Parker, New York	1	June 21	Chicago, Illinois	Theodore Roosevelt*, New York	1
1908	Denver, Colorado	July 7	William J. Bryan, Nebraska	1	June 16	Chicago, Illinois	William H. Taft*, Ohio	1
1912	Baltimore, Maryland	June 27	Woodrow Wilson*, Virginia	46	June 18	Chicago, Illinois	William H. Taft, Ohio	1
1916	St. Louis, Missouri	June 14	Woodrow Wilson*, Virginia	1	June 7	Chicago, Illinois	Charles E. Hughes, New York	3
1920	San Francisco, California	June 28	James M. Cox, Ohio	43	June 8	Chicago, Illinois	Warren G. Harding*, Ohio	10
1924	New York, New York	June 24	John W. Davis, West Virginia	103	June 10	Cleveland, Ohio	Calvin Coolidge*, Vermont	1
1928	Houston, Texas	June 26	Alfred E. Smith, New York	1	June 12	Kansas City, Kansas	Herbert Hoover*, Iowa	1

*Elected President

Democratic and Republican National Conventions and Their Candidates, continued

YEAR	CONVENTION CITY	DATE	DEMOCRATIC CANDIDATE	NO. OF BALLOTS	CONVENTION CITY	DATE	REPUBLICAN CANDIDATE	NO. OF BALLOTS
1932	Chicago, Illinois	June 27	Franklin D. Roosevelt* New York	4	Chicago, Illinois	June 14	Herbert Hoover Iowa	1
1936	Philadelphia, Pennsylvania	June 23	Franklin D. Roosevelt* New York	Accl.	Cleveland, Ohio	June 9	Alfred M. Landon Kansas	1
1940	Chicago, Illinois	July 15	Franklin D. Roosevelt* New York	1	Philadelphia, Pennsylvania	June 24	Wendell L. Wilkie New York	6
1944	Chicago, Illinois	July 19	Franklin D. Roosevelt* New York	1	Chicago, Illinois	June 24	Thomas E. Dewey New York	1
1948	Philadelphia, Pennsylvania	July 12	Harry S. Truman* Missouri	1	Philadelphia, Pennsylvania	June 21	Thomas E. Dewey New York	3
1952	Chicago, Illinois	July 21	Adlai E. Stevenson Illinois	3	Chicago, Illinois	July 7	Dwight D. Eisenhower* Texas	1
1956	Chicago, Illinois	August 13	Adlai E. Stevenson Illinois	1	San Francisco, California	August 20	Dwight D. Eisenhower* Texas	1
1960	Los Angeles, California	July 11	John F. Kennedy* Massachusetts	1	Chicago, Illinois	July 25	Richard M. Nixon California	1
1964	Atlantic City, New Jersey	August 24	Lyndon B. Johnson* Texas	Accl.	San Francisco, California	July 13	Barry M. Goldwater Arizona	1
1968	Chicago, Illinois	August 26	Hubert H. Humphrey Minnesota	1	Miami Beach, Florida	August 5	Richard M. Nixon* California	1
1972	Miami Beach, Florida	July 10	George McGovern South Dakota	1	Miami Beach, Florida	August 21	Richard M. Nixon* California	1
1976	New York, New York	July 12	Jimmy Carter* Georgia	1	Kansas City, Missouri	August 16	Gerald R. Ford Michigan	1
1980	New York, New York	August 11	Jimmy Carter Georgia	1	Detroit, Michigan	July 14	Ronald Reagan California	1
1984	San Francisco, California	July 16	Walter F. Mondale Minnesota	1	Dallas, Texas	August 20	Ronald Reagan California	1
1988	Atlanta, Georgia	July 18	Michael Dukakis Massachusetts	1	New Orleans, Louisiana	August 15	George Bush Texas	1
1992	New York, New York	July 13	Bill Clinton Arkansas		Houston, Texas	August 17	George Bush Texas	

*Elected President

*Elected President

APPENDIX 19

Evolution of the Two-Party System in the United States

Year	Hamiltonians (Federalists)	Jeffersonians (Anti-Federalists)
1792	Federalists	Democratic-Republicans
1816	Dissolution of the Federalist Ranks	
1820		Republicans (One party era; Era of Good Feelings)
1825	National Republicans	Democratic-Republicans (Jacksonian Democracy)
1831[1]		Anti-Masonic Party
1834	Whigs	Democrats
1854	Republicans	
1860[2]		Constitutional Union Party
		Secessionist Democrats
1892[3]		Populist
1912[4]		Progressive Bull Moose Party
1924[5]		Progressive
1948[6]		Progressive
1948[7]		States' Rights Dixiecrats
1968[8]		American Independent Party
1980[9]		Independent Party
		Neoconservatives[10]
1992		H. Ross Perot[11] (independent)

*Liberal   *Conservative
*Middle-of-the-Road

*Liberal   *Conservative
*Middle-of-the-Road

Evolution of the Two-Party System in the United States, continued

[1]Formed in the late 1920s in the western part of the state of New York as a splinter from Democratic and Republican ranks; during its 1931 convention it nominated William Wirt for president of the United States. The party opposed Masons, Catholics, Jews, foreigners, and all secret societies. The nominating convention system originated by the Anti-Masons was subsequently adopted by almost all political parties in America, and today the convention is a highly organized enterprise: a combination political rally, Octoberfest, county fair, turkey shoot, and church bazaar. The conventions are also called "political beauty contests."

[2]Also known as the National Constitutional Union, this party nominated U. S. Senator James Bell of Tennessee as its presidential candidate with a slogan: "No political principle other than the Constitution of the country, the union of the states, and the enforcement of the laws." It had no opinion on slavery, the important issue of the times. The majority of its members came from the Republican Whigs. The anti-Union Secessionist Democrats came from the secessionist states in the South following the election of Abraham Lincoln to the U. S. Presidency, and from the South Carolina convention where on 20 December 1860 the secessionists passed the secession ordinance. The states were: South Carolina, Florida, Mississippi, Alabama, Louisiana, Georgia, and Texas, followed by Virginia, North Carolina, and Tennessee after shots were fired on Fort Sumter in April 1861. These states formed the Confederate States of America (CSA). The U. S. Supreme Court ruled in "Texas v. White" in 1869 that secession was unconstitutional.

[3]Formed in 1891 by farmers, small businessmen and workers; it advocated silver, the abolition of national banks, and public ownership of public utilities (e.g., railroads, telegraph and telephone utilities, steamship lines); also a direct election of U. S. Senators. This was subsequently adopted as Amendment XVII to the U. S. Constitution in 1913. Its candidate for president was James W. Weaver. It switched to the Democratic party during the 1896 election.

[4]Organized under the leadership of former U.S. President Teddy Roosevelt, 1901-1909. It advocated direct primary, a short ballot, initiative, recall, referendum, women's suffrage, strong antitrust legislation, and prohibition of child labor. It called for the creation of a Department of Labor, a cabinet agency which was subsequently established. As a splinter of the Republican party, it enabled Democrat Woodrow Wilson to become president.

[5]Established by Robert La Follette, U.S. Senator from Wisconsin and its presidential candidate. It advocated strict control of monopolies, initiative, recall, referendum, and direct election of U.S. Senators; direct election of all judges for limited terms, public referenda on issues of war and peace, and public ownership of all utilities.

[6]Established by Henry A. Wallace, U.S. Vice President, 1941-1945; it advocated civil rights legislation, welfare, public housing, free education, public works, and repeal of the Taft-Hartley law. In foreign affairs, it opposed the Marshall Plan and the Truman Doctrine, and called for a peaceful reconciliation with the Soviet Union.

[7]Organized in 1948 by Southern Democrats; during its convention in Birmingham, Alabama, it nominated Governor J. Strom Thurmond of South Carolina for President. (Thurmond is currently U.S. Senator.) It opposed civil rights legislation and federal interference into the affairs of states through such measures as fair employment practices and the Taft-Hartley Law.

[8]Organized by Alabama's Governor, George Wallace, as an opposition to civil rights legislation, desegregation, and federal interference into the affairs of states. The party supported law and order, and American victory in Vietnam.

[9]Formed around John B. Anderson, Republican congressman from Illinois, who called for more social legislation and fiscal restraint, but mainly confined himself to criticizing the Republican candidate, Ronald Reagan, and his running mate, George Bush. Reagan called in his campaign for a "new beginning" in building America's strength against Soviet expansionism, and asked the American voters: "Are you better off now than you were four years ago?"

[10]A small but vocal, political-ideological lobby, rather than a splinter group, consisting mainly of doves who opposed America's involvement in Vietnam but turned hawks on support of Israel. They were fearful that American disenchantment with the Vietnam debacle would lead to America's refraining from involvements elsewhere in the world, mainly in supporting Israel in its quest in the Middle East. They voiced their views through their publication, the "American Spectator," and to some extent through the "New York Times." Patrick Buchanan, journalist, and on President Richard M. Nixon's staff, and 1992 Republican presidential hopeful, called them "ideological vagrants." Such political shadings as "liberal," "conservative," "leftist," "rightist," "middle-of-the-roader," often prefixed by "ultra" or "extreme," are usually meaningless since these concepts are never clearly defined as they are used in party jargon. These two parties are, in reality, large pressure groups with paid lobbyists striving for legitimacy as power brokers. They are holding the exclusive monopoly on national power (e.g., President, Congress, as well as high states offices, such as governorships). They often lack a clear-cut philosophy or ideology beyond the immediate pragmatic needs and their differences are rather in name and semantics used in articulating issues, mainly immediately proceeding and during major elections, and less thereafter. George Wallace, former Governor of Alabama, suggested once that "there is not a 'dime's worth of difference' between the Democrats and the Republicans"; and the former Soviet Premier and General Secretary of the CPSU, Nikita S. Khrushchev, observed during his official visit at Wall Street in 1959 that it makes no difference whether the Democrats or the Republicans win elections in America (e.g., under the "winner-takes-all" system of plurality); Wall Street (i.e., the financial center of the United States and of global capitalism, located on Wall Street in New York City) prevails anyway. One could possibly assert that most young liberals become conservatives with age and status.

[11]See GRASS-ROOTS PEROT, GRASS-ROOTS POLITICIAN.

APPENDIX 20

Federal Electoral Process
Positives (+)...Negatives (-)

Positive Features	Negative Features
(+) Primary elections are most commonly used to select candidates of a political party to run for public office.	(-) Candidates for the office of president and vice president are chosen in political party conventions, not by the general public.
(+) Voters directly elect their representatives to both houses of Congress.	(-) Political action committees (PAC) strongly influence elections by contributing funds to candidates.
(+) The electoral college is a safety valve against mob rule.	(-) Less than half of the eligible voters turn to vote on election day.
(+) Candidates for public office generally identify with one of the major political parties—Democrat, Republican.	(-)The president and the vice president are chosen by the electoral college, not by the voters.
(+) The major focus of elections is generally on the candidate rather than the party.	(-)Political parties have lost significant control over the selection of candidates for public office.
	(-) Generally voters favor their Congressmen but dislike the Congress.
	(-) Political party responsibility for government is virtually impossible today.
(+,-) Voters do not elect federal judges. They are appointed by the president with the advice and consent of the Senate.	

Electoral Process in the United States: The Federal Level

LEGISLATIVE BRANCH	JUDICIAL BRANCH	EXECUTIVE BRANCH

Federal Courts

Presidency

President → Vice President

four-year term

appoints

U.S. Supreme Court

U.S. District
Courts of Appeal
12 circuit, 3 judges each, and
one Temporary Emergency
Court

Electors in
Electoral College
(total number of
Representatives
and Senators in
the Congress

U.S. District Courts,
89 courts of general
jurisdiction,
one for District of Columbia
(District of Columbia, 7
judges)*

elect by states

U.S. Territorial
Courts (Canal Zone,
Guam, Puerto Rico,
Virgin Islands)

Courts of special
jurisdiction:
U.S. Court of
Customs and Patent
Appeals;
U.S. Customs Court;
U.S. Court of
Claims;
U.S. Tax Court

tenure for period of good
behavior (usually
for life)

confirms

Senate

elect by states at large for 6-year term ← 100 to

Congress

House of Representatives ← elect by district 435, for 2-year term

VOTERS

elect

* In addition the District of Columbia has two special courts: one Court of Appeals and one Superior Court.

© 1992 Brunswick Publishing Corporation

APPENDIX 21

Distribution of Electoral Votes by States
(Based on 1990 Census)

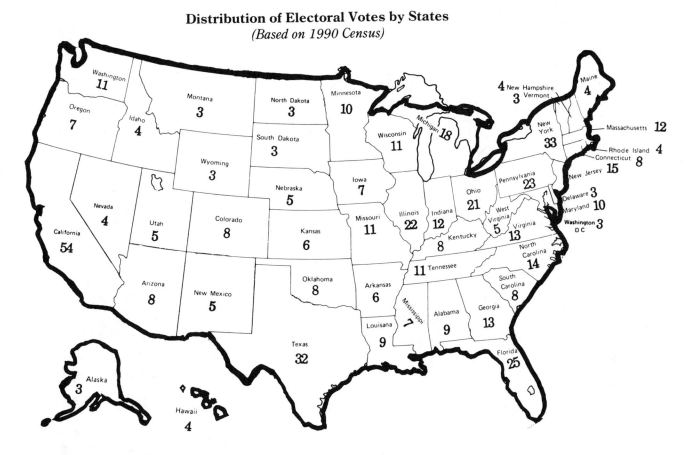

Alabama	9	Louisiana	9	Ohio	21
Alaska	3	Maine	4	Oklahoma	8
Arizona	8	Maryland	10	Oregon	7
Arkansas	6	Massachusetts	12	Pennsylvania	23
California	54	Michigan	18	Rhode Island	4
Colorado	8	Minnesota	10	South Carolina	8
Connecticut	8	Mississippi	7	South Dakota	3
Delaware	3	Missouri	11	Tennessee	11
Florida	25	Montana	3	Texas	32
Georgia	13	Nebraska	5	Utah	5
Hawaii	4	Nevada	4	Vermont	3
Idaho	4	New Hampshire	4	Virginia	13
Illinois	22	New Jersey	15	Washington	11
Indiana	12	New Mexico	5	Washington D.C.	3
Iowa	7	New York	33	West Virginia	5
Kansas	6	North Carolina	14	Wisconsin	11
Kentucky	8	North Dakota	3	Wyoming	3
					435

See ELECTORAL COLLEGE, PRESIDENTIAL ELECTOR and VOTING.

APPENDIX 22

Political Cultures Within the American States—The Belts

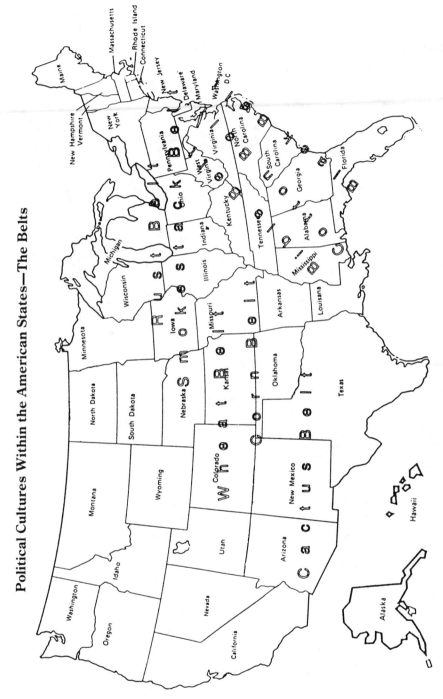

Political Belts. In the folklore of American politics, the country is divided into so-called "belts," with certain human, geographic, religious, or professional characteristics. Some of these "belts" may overlap. They are: the *"Bible Belt"*—the Southern states where the Baptist denominations are numerous; this belt also corresponds to the *"Black Belt"* and the *"Cotton Belt,"* because of the large black population and former agricultural practices there; the *"Rust Belt"* or *"Smokestack Belt,"*—the old industrial areas of Pennsylvania, Michigan, Ohio, Indiana, which also correspond more or less, with the prevalence of cold weather, thus referred to as the *"Ice Belt;"* the *"Cactus Belt"*— stretching from Texas to California where cacti grow, also corresponding with the *"Chicano Belt,"* because of the large Spanish-speaking population; the *"Wheat"* or *"Corn Belt"*—the agricultural plains states like Iowa, Nebraska, Kansas, and Missouri; the *"Germanic Belt"*— Pennsylvania, Minnesota, and the Northeast where the German-speaking population settled in large numbers; the *"Slavic Belt"*—basically the city of Chicago, and the states of Michigan, Pennsylvania, and New York where many Slavic peoples settled. Some political sociologists propose that persons within those "belts" share many political views in common and affect political policies and processes. See Appendix 19.

©1992 Brunswick Publishing Corporation

APPENDIX 23

Department of State

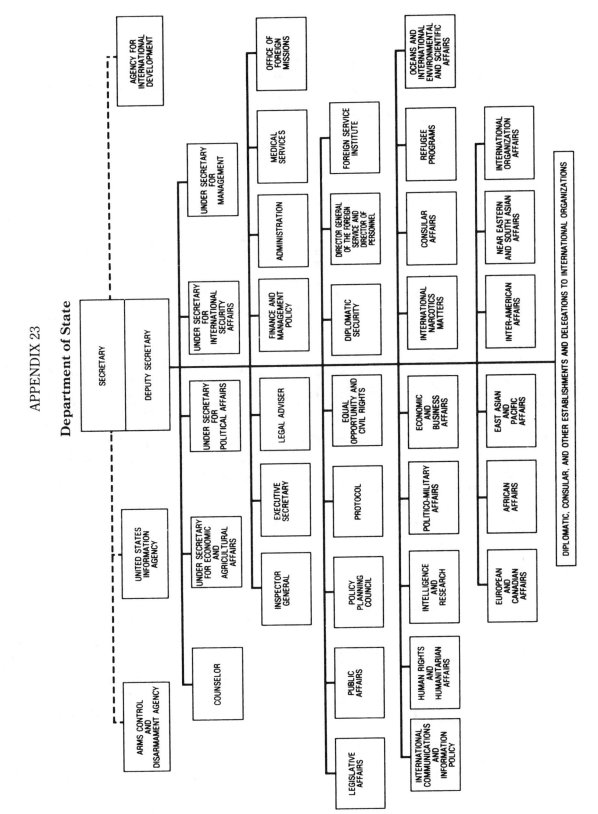

DIPLOMATIC, CONSULAR, AND OTHER ESTABLISHMENTS AND DELEGATIONS TO INTERNATIONAL ORGANIZATIONS

Source: The United States Government Manual, 1991/92.

APPENDIX 24

Secretaries of State of the United States

NO.	NAME	LIFE	YEARS IN SERVICE	SERVED UNDER PRESIDENT	POLITICAL PARTY
1.	John Jay	1745-1929	1784-1790	The Continental Congress	
2.	Thomas Jefferson*	1743-1826	1790-1793	George Washington	Fed.
3.	Edmund Randolph	1753-1813	1794-1795	George Washington	Fed.
4.	Timothy Pickering	1754-1829	1795-1800	George Washington	Fed.
				John Adams	Fed.
5.	John Marshall	1755-1835	1800-1801	John Adams	Fed.
6.	James Madison*	1751-1836	1801-1809	Thomas Jefferson	Dem.-Rep.
7.	Robert Smith	1757-1842	1809-1811	James Madison	Dem.-Rep.
8.	James Monroe*	1758-1831	1811-1817	James Madison	Dem.-Rep.
9.	John Quincy Adams*	1767-1848	1817-1825	James Monroe	Dem.-Rep.
10.	Henry Clay	1777-1852	1825-1829	John Quincy Adams	Dem.-Rep.
11.	Martin Van Buren*	1782-1862	1829-1831	Andrew Jackson	Dem.
12.	Edward Livingston	1764-1836	1831-1833	Andrew Jackson	Dem.
13.	Louis McLane	1786-1857	1833-1834	Andrew Jackson	Dem.
14.	John Forsyth	1780-1841	1834-1841	Andrew Jackson	Dem.
				Martin Van Buren	Dem.
15.	Daniel Webster	1782-1852	1841-1843	William Henry Harrison	Whig
16.	Abel Parker Upshur	1791-1844	1843-1844	John Tyler	Whig
17.	John Caldwell Calhoun	1782-1850	1844-1845	John Tyler	Whig
18.	James Buchanan*	1791-1868	1845-1849	James K. Polk	Dem.
19.	John Middleton Clayton	1796-1856	1849-1850	Zachary Taylor	Whig
20.	Daniel Webster (second service)	1782-1852	1850-1852	Zachary Taylor	Whig
21.	Edward Everett	1794-1865	1852-1853	Millard Fillmore	Whig

*Subsequently became U. S. President.

Secretaries of State of the United States, continued

NO.	NAME	LIFE	YEARS IN SERVICE	SERVED UNDER PRESIDENT	POLITICAL PARTY
22.	William Learned Marcy	1786-1857	1853-1857	Franklin Pierce	Dem.
23.	Lewis Cass	1782-1866	1857-1860	James Buchanan	Dem.
24.	Jeremiah Sullivan Black	1810-1883	1860-1861	James Buchanan	Dem.
25.	William Henry Seward	1801-1872	1861-1865	Abraham Lincoln	Rep.
			1865-1869	Andrew Johnson	*
26.	Elihu Benjamin Washburne	1816-1887	1869-1869	Ulysses Simpson Grant	Rep.
27.	Hamilton Fish	1808-1893	1869-1877	Ulysses Simpson Grant	Rep.
28.	William Maxwell Evarts	1818-1901	1877-1881	Rutherford Birchard Hayes	Rep.
29.	James Gillespie Blaine	1830-1893	1881-1881	James Abram Garfield	Rep.
			1881-1881	Chester Alan Arthur	Rep.
30.	Frederick Theodore Frelinghuysen	1817-1885	1881-1885	Chester Alan Arthur	Rep.
31.	Thomas Francis Bayard	1828-1898	1885-1889	Grover Cleveland	Dem.
32.	James Gillespie Blaine (second service)	1830-1893	1889-1892	Grover Cleveland	Dem.
33.	John Watson Foster	1836-1917	1892-1893	Benjamin Harrison	Rep.
34.	Walter Quintin Gresham	1832-1895	1893-1895	Grover Cleveland	Dem.
35.	Richard Olney	1835-1917	1895-1897	Grover Cleveland	Dem.
36.	John Sherman	1823-1900	1897-1898	William McKinley	Rep.
37.	William Rufus Day	1849-1923	1898-1898	William McKinley	Rep.
38.	John Hay	1838-1905	1898-1901	William McKinley	Rep.
			1901-1905	Theodore Roosevelt	Rep.
39.	Elihu Root	1845-1937	1905-1909	Theodore Roosevelt	Rep.
40.	Robert Bacon	1860-1919	1909-1909	Theodore Roosevelt	Rep.
41.	Philander Chase Knox	1853-1921	1909-1913	William Howard Taft	Rep.
42.	William Jennings Bryan	1860-1925	1913-1915	Woodrow Wilson	Dem.
43.	Robert Lansing	1864-1928	1915-1920	Woodrow Wilson	Dem.

* Andrew Johnson was a Democrat, but was nominated by Republicans and elected with Abraham Lincoln.

Secretaries of State of the United States, continued

NO.	NAME	LIFE	YEARS IN SERVICE	SERVED UNDER PRESIDENT	POLITICAL PARTY
44.	Bainbridge Colby	1869-1950	1920-1921	Woodrow Wilson	Dem.
	Charles Evans Hughes	1862-1948	1921-1923	Warren Gamaliel Harding	Rep.
45.			1923-1925	Calvin Coolidge	Rep.
46.	Frank Billings Kellog	1856-1937	1925-1929	Calvin Coolidge	Rep.
47.	Henry Lewis Stimson	1867-1950	1929-1933	Herbert Hoover	Rep.
48.	Cordell Hull	1871-1955	1933-1944	Franklin Delano Roosevelt	Dem.
49.	Edward Reilly Stettinius	1900-1949	1944-1945	Franklin Delano Roosevelt	Dem.
			1945-1945	Harry S. Truman	Dem.
50.	James Francis Byrnes	1879-1968	1945-1947	Harry S. Truman	Dem.
51.	George Catlett Marshall	1880-1959	1947-1949	Harry S. Truman	Dem.
52.	Dean Gooderham Acheson	1893-1976	1949-1953	Harry S. Truman	Dem.
53.	John Foster Dulles	1888-1959	1953-1959	Dwight David Eisenhower	Rep.
54.	Christian Archibald Herter	1919-1966	1959-1961	Dwight David Eisenhower	Rep.
55.	Dean Rusk	1909-	1961-1963	John Fitzgerald Kennedy	Dem.
			1963-1969	Lyndon Baines Johnson	Dem.
56.	William Pierce Rogers	1913-	1969-1973	Richard Milhous Nixon	Rep.
57.	Henry A. Kissinger	1924-	1973-1974	Richard Milhous Nixon	Rep.
			1974-1977	Gerald Rudolph Ford	Rep.
58.	Cyrus R. Vance	1921-	1977-1980	Jimmy Carter	Dem.
59.	Edmund S. Muskie		1980-1981	Jimmy Carter	Dem.
60.	Alexander M. Haig, Jr.		1981-1982	Ronald Reagan	Rep.
61.	George P. Shultz	1920-	1982-1989	Ronald Reagan	Rep.
62.	James A. Baker 3rd	1930-	1989-	George Bush	Rep.

APPENDIX 25

Department of the Treasury

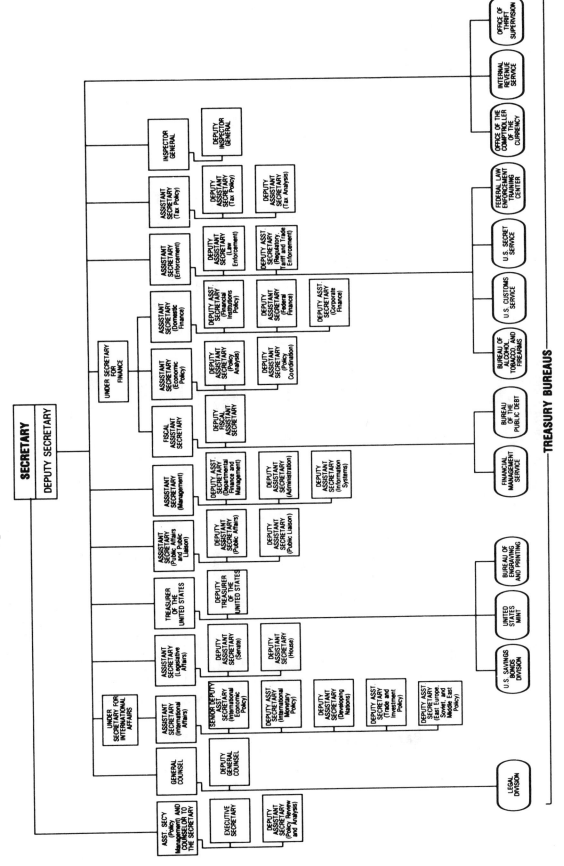

Source: *The United States Government Manual, 1991/92.*

APPENDIX 26

Department of Justice

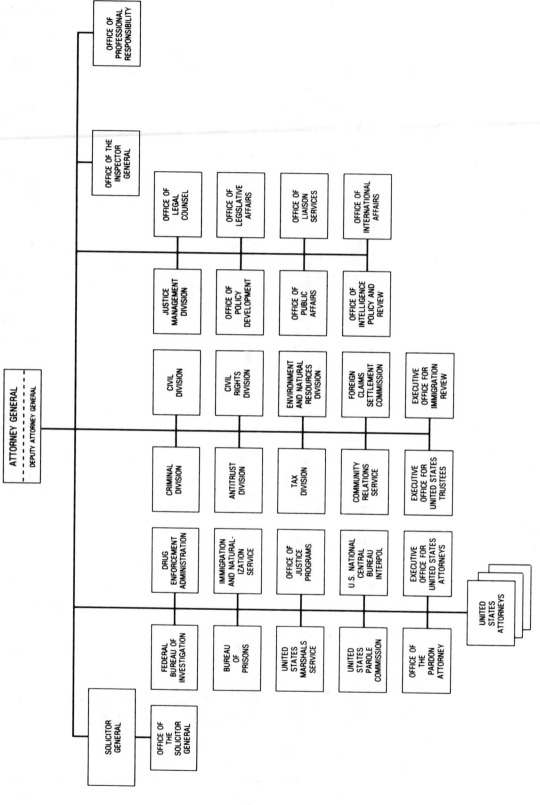

Source: *The United States Government Manual, 1991/92.*

APPENDIX 27

Subversive Organizations in the United States[1]

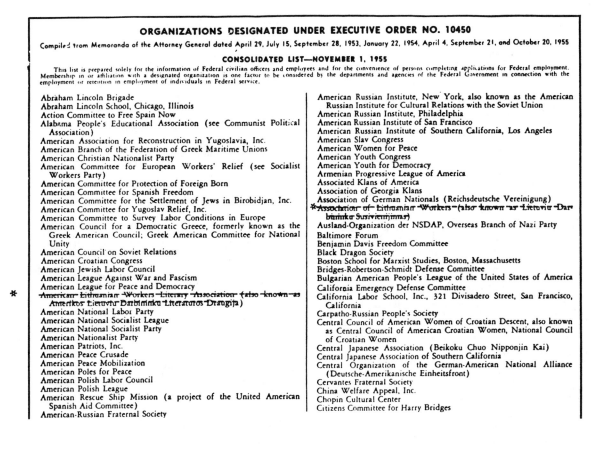

ORGANIZATIONS DESIGNATED UNDER EXECUTIVE ORDER NO. 10450

Compiled from Memoranda of the Attorney General dated April 29, July 15, September 28, 1953, January 22, 1954, April 4, September 21, and October 20, 1955

CONSOLIDATED LIST—NOVEMBER 1, 1955

This list is prepared solely for the information of Federal civilian officers and employees and for the convenience of persons completing applications for Federal employment. Membership in or affiliation with a designated organization is one factor to be considered by the departments and agencies of the Federal Government in connection with the employment or retention in employment of individuals in Federal service.

Abraham Lincoln Brigade
Abraham Lincoln School, Chicago, Illinois
Action Committee to Free Spain Now
Alabama People's Educational Association (see Communist Political Association)
American Association for Reconstruction in Yugoslavia, Inc.
American Branch of the Federation of Greek Maritime Unions
American Christian Nationalist Party
American Committee for European Workers' Relief (see Socialist Workers Party)
American Committee for Protection of Foreign Born
American Committee for Spanish Freedom
American Committee for the Settlement of Jews in Birobidjan, Inc.
American Committee for Yugoslav Relief, Inc.
American Committee to Survey Labor Conditions in Europe
American Council for a Democratic Greece, formerly known as the Greek American Council; Greek American Committee for National Unity
American Council on Soviet Relations
American Croatian Congress
American Jewish Labor Council
American League Against War and Fascism
American League for Peace and Democracy
* ~~American Lithuanian Workers Literary Association (also known as Amerikos Lietuvių Darbininkų Literatūros Draugija)~~
American National Labor Party
American National Socialist League
American National Socialist Party
American Nationalist Party
American Patriots, Inc.
American Peace Crusade
American Peace Mobilization
American Poles for Peace
American Polish Labor Council
American Polish League
American Rescue Ship Mission (a project of the United American Spanish Aid Committee)
American-Russian Fraternal Society

American Russian Institute, New York, also known as the American Russian Institute for Cultural Relations with the Soviet Union
American Russian Institute, Philadelphia
American Russian Institute of San Francisco
American Russian Institute of Southern California, Los Angeles
American Slav Congress
American Women for Peace
American Youth Congress
American Youth for Democracy
Armenian Progressive League of America
Associated Klans of America
Association of Georgia Klans
Association of German Nationals (Reichsdeutsche Vereinigung)
* ~~Association of Lithuanian Workers (also known as Lietuvių Darbininkų Susivienijimas)~~
Ausland-Organization der NSDAP, Overseas Branch of Nazi Party
Baltimore Forum
Benjamin Davis Freedom Committee
Black Dragon Society
Boston School for Marxist Studies, Boston, Massachusetts
Bridges-Robertson-Schmidt Defense Committee
Bulgarian American People's League of the United States of America
California Emergency Defense Committee
California Labor School, Inc., 321 Divisadero Street, San Francisco, California
Carpatho-Russian People's Society
Central Council of American Women of Croatian Descent, also known as Central Council of American Croatian Women, National Council of Croatian Women
Central Japanese Association (Beikoku Chuo Nipponjin Kai)
Central Japanese Association of Southern California
Central Organization of the German-American National Alliance (Deutsche-Amerikanische Einheitsfront)
Cervantes Fraternal Society
China Welfare Appeal, Inc.
Chopin Cultural Center
Citizens Committee for Harry Bridges

Source: U.S. Department of Justice

---

[1]In 1950, the U. S. Congress passed the *Subversive Activities Control Act*, also known as the *McCarran Act*, after U. S. Senator Pat McCarran, R-Nevada, its author, and over President Harry S. Truman's veto. This Act made it illegal to engage in the formation of a totalitarian form of government in the United States, aiming particularly at communist and communist-front organizations; it empowered the federal government to maintain strict control of hostile (ideologically) aliens and to depart undesirables; it required officers of all revolutionary, communist and communist-front organizations to register with the U.S. Attorney General and to report their financial means and sources of income. Subsequently, additional legislation was duly enacted, the *McCarren-Walter Act* (of June 1952), which more directly aimed at communist and communist-front organization activities and individuals. Under pressure by Congress and some segments of the population (see AMERICA FIRSTER and MCCARTHYISM), the President issued an order directing the U. S. Attorney General to compile a list of such organizations for public record and as a guide for federal employment, whereby ". . . past and present membership in them can be evaluated as part of the total pattern of a person's life." A consolidated list was compiled in 1955 and it has little changed throughout the years, until it was discontinued as of June 4, 1974.

Subversive Organizations in the United States, continued

Citizens Committee of the Upper West Side (New York City)
Citizens Committee to Free Earl Browder
Citizens Emergency Defense Conference
Citizens Protective League
Civil Liberties Sponsoring Committee of Pittsburgh
Civil Rights Congress and its affiliated organizations, including:
    Civil Rights Congress for Texas
    Veterans Against Discrimination of Civil Rights Congress of New
      York
Civil Rights Congress for Texas (see Civil Rights Congress)
Columbians
Comite Coordinador Pro Republica Espanola
Comite Pro Derechos Civiles
    (See Puerto Rican Comite Pro Libertades Civiles)
Committee for a Democratic Far Eastern Policy
Committee for Constitutional and Political Freedom
Committee for Nationalist Action
Committee for Peace and Brotherhood Festival in Philadelphia
Committee for the Defense of the Pittsburgh Six
Committee for the Negro in the Arts
Committee for the Protection of the Bill of Rights
Committee for World Youth Friendship and Cultural Exchange
Committee to Abolish Discrimination in Maryland
    (See Congress Against Discrimination; Maryland Congress Against
      Discrimination; Provisional Committee to Abolish Discrimination
      in the State of Maryland)
Committee to Aid the Fighting South
Committee to Defend Marie Richardson
Committee to Defend the Rights and Freedom of Pittsburgh's Political
    Prisoners
Committee to Uphold the Bill of Rights
Commonwealth College, Mena, Arkansas
Communist Party, U. S. A., its subdivisions, subsidiaries and affiliates
Communist Political Association, its subdivisions, subsidiaries and
    affiliates, including:
    Alabama People's Educational Association
    Florida Press and Educational League
    Oklahoma League for Political Education
    People's Educational and Press Association of Texas
    Virginia League for People's Education
Congress Against Discrimination
    (See Committee to Abolish Discrimination in Maryland)
Congress of American Revolutionary Writers
Congress of American Women
Congress of the Unemployed
Connecticut Committee to Aid Victims of the Smith Act
Connecticut State Youth Conference
Council for Jobs, Relief and Housing
Council for Pan-American Democracy
Council of Greek Americans
Council on African Affairs
Croatian Benevolent Fraternity
Dai Nippon Butoku Kai (Military Virtue Society of Japan or Military
    Art Society of Japan)
Daily Worker Press Club
Daniels Defense Committee
Dante Alighieri Society (between 1935 and 1940)
Dennis Defense Committee
Detroit Youth Assembly
East Bay Peace Committee
Elsinore Progressive League
Emergency Conference to Save Spanish Refugees (founding body of the
    North American Spanish Aid Committee)
Everybody's Committee to Outlaw War
Families of the Baltimore Smith Act Victims
Families of the Smith Act Victims
Federation of Italian War Veterans in the U. S. A., Inc. (Associazione
    Nazionale Combattenti Italiani, Federazione degli Stati Uniti
    d'America)
Finnish-American Mutual Aid Society
Florida Press and Educational League (see Communist Political Asso-
    ciation)
Frederick Douglass Educational Center
Freedom Stage, Inc.
Friends of the New Germany (Freunde des Neuen Deutschlands)
Friends of the Soviet Union
Garibaldi American Fraternal Society
George Washington Carver School, New York City
German-American Bund (Amerikadeutscher Volksbund)
German-American Republican League
German-American Vocational League (Deutsche-Amerikanische Berufs-
    gemeinschaft)
Guardian Club
Harlem Trade Union Council
Hawaii Civil Liberties Committee
Heimusha Kai, also known as Nokubei Heieki Gimusha Kai, Zaibel
    Nihonjin, Heiyaku Gimusha Kai, and Zaibei Heimusha Kai (Jap-
    anese Residing in America Military Conscripts Association)
Hellenic-American Brotherhood
Hinode Kai (Imperial Japanese Reservists)

Hinomaru Kai (Rising Sun Flag Society—a group of Japanese War
    Veterans)
Hokubei Zaigo Shoke Dan (North American Reserve Officers Associ-
    ation)
Hollywood Writers Mobilization for Defense
Hungarian-American Council for Democracy
Hungarian Brotherhood
Idaho Pension Union
Independent Party (Seattle, Washington)
    (See Independent People's Party)
Independent People's Party
    (See Independent Party)
Independent Socialist League
Industrial Workers of the World
International Labor Defense
International Workers Order, its subdivisions, subsidiaries and affiliates
Japanese Association of America
Japanese Overseas Central Society (Kaigai Dobo Chuo Kai)
Japanese Overseas Convention, Tokyo, Japan, 1940
Japanese Protective Association (Recruiting Organization)
Jefferson School of Social Science, New York City
Jewish Culture Society
Jewish People's Committee
Jewish People's Fraternal Order
Jikyoku Iinkai (The Committee for the Crisis)
Johnson-Forest Group
    (See Johnsonites)
Johnsonites
    (See Johnson-Forest Group)
Joint Anti-Fascist Refugee Committee
Joint Council of Progressive Italian-Americans, Inc.
Joseph Weydemeyer School of Social Science, St. Louis, Missouri
Kibei Seinen Kai (Association of U. S. Citizens of Japanese Ancestry
    who have returned to America after studying in Japan)
Knights of the White Camellia
Ku Klux Klan
Kyffhaeuser, also known as Kyffhaeuser League (Kyffhaeuser Bund),
    Kyffhaeuser Fellowship (Kyffhaeuser Kameradschaft)
Kyffhaeuser War Relief (Kyffhaeuser Kriegshilfswerk)
Labor Council for Negro Rights
Labor Research Association, Inc.
Labor Youth League
League for Common Sense
League of American Writers
Lictor Society (Italian Black Shirts)
Macedonian-American People's League
Mario Morgantini Circle
Maritime Labor Committee to Defend Al Lannon
Maryland Congress Against Discrimination
    (See Committee to Abolish Discrimination in Maryland)
Massachusetts Committee for the Bill of Rights
Massachusetts Minute Women for Peace (not connected with the
    Minute Women of the U. S. A., Inc.)
Maurice Braverman Defense Committee
Michigan Civil Rights Federation
Michigan Council for Peace
Michigan School of Social Science
Nanka Teikoku Gunyudan (Imperial Military Friends Group or South-
    ern California War Veterans)
National Association of Mexican Americans (also known as Asociacion
    Nacional Mexico-Americana)
National Blue Star Mothers of America (not to be confused with the
    Blue Star Mothers of America organized in February 1942)
National Committee for Freedom of the Press
National Committee for the Defense of Political Prisoners
National Committee to Win Amnesty for Smith Act Victims
National Committee to Win the Peace
National Conference on American Policy in China and the Far East (a
    Conference called by the Committee for a Democratic Far Eastern
    Policy)
National Council of Americans of Croatian Descent
National Council of American-Soviet Friendship
National Federation for Constitutional Liberties
National Labor Conference for Peace
National Negro Congress
National Negro Labor Council
Nationalist Action League
Nationalist Party of Puerto Rico
Nature Friends of America (since 1935)
Negro Labor Victory Committee
New Committee for Publications
Nichibei Kogyo Kaisha (The Great Fujii Theatre)
North American Committee to Aid Spanish Democracy
North American Spanish Aid Committee
North Philadelphia Forum
Northwest Japanese Association
Ohio School of Social Sciences
Oklahoma Committee to Defend Political Prisoners
Oklahoma League for Political Education (see Communist Political
    Association)

Subversive Organizations in the United States, continued

Original Southern Klans, Incorporated
Pacific Northwest Labor School, Seattle, Washington
Palo Alto Peace Club
Partido del Pueblo of Panama (operating in the Canal Zone)
Peace Information Center
Peace Movement of Ethiopia
People's Drama, Inc.
People's Educational and Press Association of Texas (see Communist Political Association)
People's Educational Association (incorporated under name Los Angeles Educational Association, Inc.), also known as People's Educational Center, People's University, People's School
People's Institute of Applied Religion
Peoples Programs (Seattle, Washington)
People's Radio Foundation, Inc.
People's Rights Party
Philadelphia Labor Committee for Negro Rights
Philadelphia School of Social Science and Art
Photo League (New York City)
Pittsburgh Arts Club
Political Prisoners' Welfare Committee
Polonia Society of the IWO
Progressive German-Americans, also known as Progressive German-Americans of Chicago
Proletarian Party of America
Protestant War Veterans of the United States, Inc.
Provisional Committee of Citizens for Peace, Southwest Area
Provisional Committee on Latin American Affairs
Provisional Committee to Abolish Discrimination in the State of Maryland
  (See Committee to Abolish Discrimination in Maryland)
Puerto Rican Comite Pro Libertades Civiles (CLC)
  (See Comite Pro Derechos Civiles)
Puertorriquenos Unidos (Puerto Ricans United)
Quad City Committee for Peace
Queensbridge Tenants League
Revolutionary Workers League
Romanian-American Fraternal Society
Russian American Society, Inc.
Sakura Kai (Patriotic Society, or Cherry Association—composed of veterans of Russo-Japanese War)
Samuel Adams School, Boston, Massachusetts
Santa Barbara Peace Forum
Schappes Defense Committee
Schneiderman-Darcy Defense Committee
School of Jewish Studies, New York City
Seattle Labor School, Seattle, Washington
Serbian-American Fraternal Society
Serbian Vidovdan Council

Shinto Temples (limited to State Shinto abolished in 1945)
Silver Shirt Legion of America
Slavic Council of Southern California
Slovak Workers Society
Slovenian-American National Council
Socialist Workers Party, including American Committee for European Workers' Relief
** ~~Socialist Youth League (see Workers P... e)~~
Sokoku Kai (Fatherland Society)
Southern Negro Youth Congress
Suiko Sha (Reserve Officers Association. Los Angeles)
Syracuse Women for Peace
Tom Paine School of Social Science, Philadelphia, Pennsylvania
Tom Paine School of Westchester, New York
Trade Union Committee for Peace
  (See Trade Unionists for Peace)
Trade Unionists for Peace
  (See Trade Union Committee for Peace)
Tri-State Negro Trade Union Council
Ukrainian-American Fraternal Union
Union of American Croatians
Union of New York Veterans
United American Spanish Aid Committee
United Committee of Jewish Societies and Landsmanschaft Federations, also known as Coordination Committee of Jewish Landsmanschaften and Fraternal Organizations
United Committee of South Slavic Americans
United Defense Council of Southern California
United Harlem Tenants and Consumers Organization
United May Day Committee
United Negro and Allied Veterans of America
Veterans Against Discrimination of Civil Rights Congress of New York (see Civil Rights Congress)
Veterans of the Abraham Lincoln Brigade
Virginia League for People's Education (see Communist Political Association)
Voice of Freedom Committee
Walt Whitman School of Social Science, Newark, New Jersey
Washington Bookshop Association
Washington Committee for Democratic Action
Washington Committee to Defend the Bill of Rights
Washington Commonwealth Federation
Washington Pension Union
Wisconsin Conference on Social Legislation
Workers Alliance (since April 1936)
** ~~Workers Party—including Socialist Youth League~~
Yiddisher Kultur Farband
Young Communist League
Yugoslav-American Cooperative Home, Inc.
Yugoslav Seamen's Club, Inc.

APPENDIX 28

Department of Defense

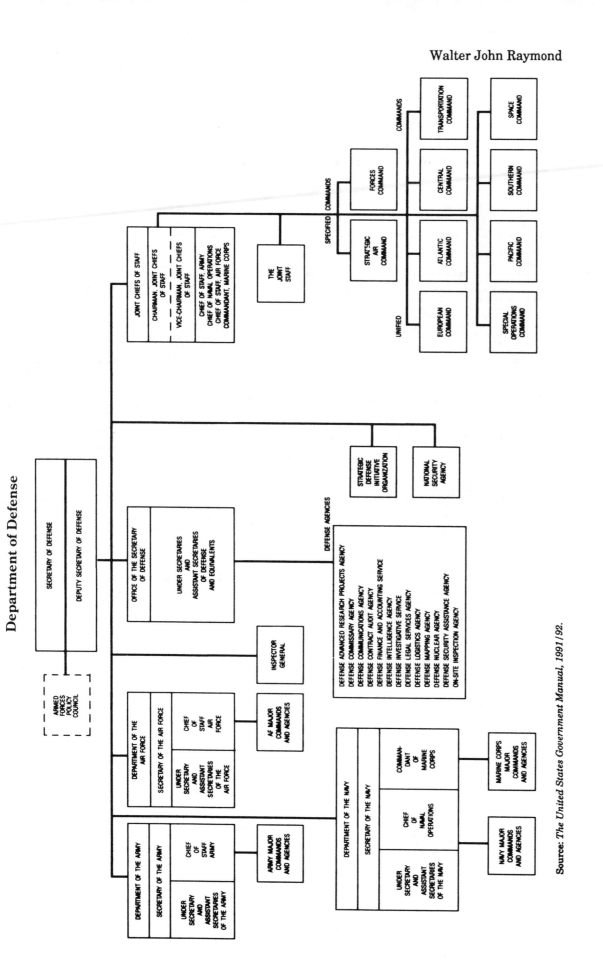

Source: *The United States Government Manual, 1991/92.*

APPENDIX 29

America's Collective Defense Arrangements: Global Alliances

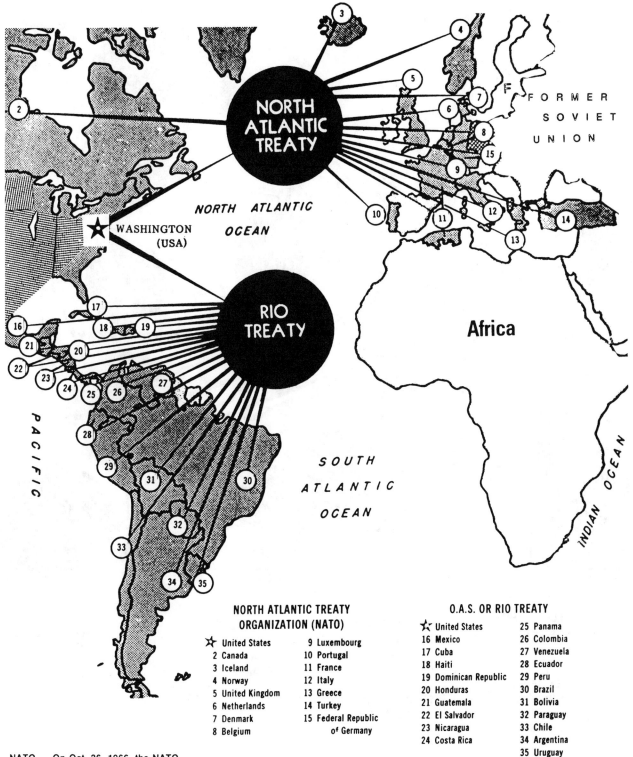

NORTH ATLANTIC TREATY ORGANIZATION (NATO)

☆ United States
2 Canada
3 Iceland
4 Norway
5 United Kingdom
6 Netherlands
7 Denmark
8 Belgium
9 Luxembourg
10 Portugal
11 France
12 Italy
13 Greece
14 Turkey
15 Federal Republic of Germany

O.A.S. OR RIO TREATY

☆ United States
16 Mexico
17 Cuba
18 Haiti
19 Dominican Republic
20 Honduras
21 Guatemala
22 El Salvador
23 Nicaragua
24 Costa Rica
25 Panama
26 Colombia
27 Venezuela
28 Ecuador
29 Peru
30 Brazil
31 Bolivia
32 Paraguay
33 Chile
34 Argentina
35 Uruguay

NATO — On Oct. 26, 1966, the NATO Council decided to transfer the seat of NATO from Paris to Brussels.

SOURCE: <u>Conflict and Cooperation Among Nations</u> by Ivo D. Duchacek with the collaboration of Kenneth W. Thompson. New York: Holt, Rinehart and Winston, Inc. Reproduced with permission.

America's Collective Defense Arrangements: Global Alliances, continued

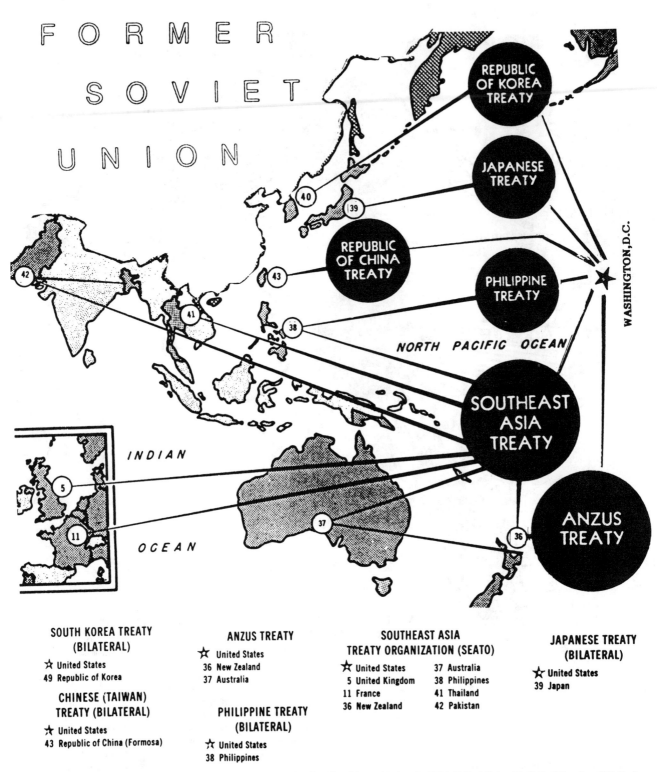

SOUTH KOREA TREATY (BILATERAL)

☆ United States
49 Republic of Korea

CHINESE (TAIWAN) TREATY (BILATERAL)

☆ United States
43 Republic of China (Formosa)

ANZUS TREATY

☆ United States
36 New Zealand
37 Australia

PHILIPPINE TREATY (BILATERAL)

☆ United States
38 Philippines

SOUTHEAST ASIA TREATY ORGANIZATION (SEATO)

☆ United States   37 Australia
5 United Kingdom   38 Philippines
11 France   41 Thailand
36 New Zealand   42 Pakistan

JAPANESE TREATY (BILATERAL)

☆ United States
39 Japan

CENTO — Central Treaty Organization of 1955 (known as "Baghdad Pact" until Iraq withdrew in 1959): United States (1), United Kingdom (25), Turkey (35), Pakistan (39), and Iran (41). Inactive since its inception. Dissolved *de facto* when Iran's Shah Mohammed Reza Pahlavi (installed in power in CIA's aid in 1953), abdicated and left Iran on January 16, 1979.

ANZUS — In 1972, Australia and New Zealand announced that they would reduce their armed forces and restrict their participation in ANZUS and in SEATO.

APPENDIX 30

Standing Orders, Rogers' Rangers*
(Major Robert Rogers, 1759)

1. Don't forget nothing.

2. Have your musket clean as a whistle, hatchet scoured, sixty rounds powder and ball, and be ready to march at a minute's warning.

3. When you're on the march, act the way you would if you were sneaking up on a deer. See the enemy first.

4. Tell the truth about what you see and what you do. There is an army depending on us for correct information. You can lie all you please when you tell other folks about the Rangers, but don't never lie to a Ranger or officer.

5. Don't ever take a chance you don't have to.

6. When we're on the march we march single file, far enough apart so one shot can't go through two men.

7. If we strike swamps, or soft ground, we spread out abreast, so it's hard to track us.

8. When we march, we keep moving till dark, so as to give the enemy the least possible chance at us.

9. When we camp, half the party stays awake while the other half sleeps.

10. If we take prisoners, we keep 'em separate till we have had time to examine them, so they can't cook up a story between 'em.

11. Don't ever march home the same way. Take a different route so you won't be ambushed.

12. No matter whether we travel in big parties or little ones, each party has to keep a scout 20 yards ahead, twenty yards on each flank and twenty yards in the rear, so the main body can't be surprised and wiped out.

13. Every night you'll be told where to meet if surrounded by a superior force.

14. Don't sit down to eat without posting sentries.

15. Don't sleep beyond dawn. Dawn's when the French and Indians attack.

16. Don't cross a river by a regular ford.

17. If somebody's trailing you, make a circle, come back onto your own tracks, and ambush the folks that aim to ambush you.

18. Don't stand up when the enemy's coming against you. Kneel down. Hide behind a tree.

19. Let the enemy come till he's almost close enough to touch. Then let him have it and jump out and finish him up with your hatchet.

---

* These guerrilla warfare rules were widely applied during the French, Indian, the Revolutionary War, and the War of Secession (Civil War) in America, and are considered a primary source in modern times together with the "mostest with the fastest" dictum. See ARMY RANGERS, GUERRILLA WARFARE, SIX "D's" OF GUERRILLA WARFARE.

APPENDIX 31

Global Collective Security:
An Approximation of the Present System of Collective Security

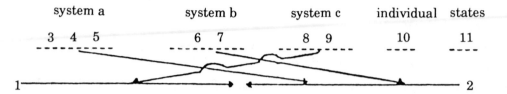

If state 1 threatens state 2, states in system *a* may honor their collective security (or treaty) obligations and come to the aid of state 2. States in system b may favor the actions by states in system *a* aiding state 2. States in system *c*, or any of the individual states, may favor state 1 against state 2, in spite of the fact that state 1 is an aggressor and state 2 is the victim of that aggression, particularly if states in system *c* consider states in system *a* as adversary, and will use that occasion to launch a major attack. Under this system collective security rests on a precise balance of power, or balance of terror.

An Approximation of a Desirable, Ideal System of Collective Security

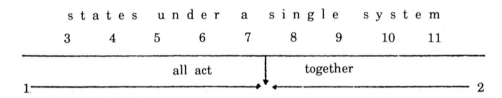

Neutrality forbidden, all states under this international system of collective security would come to the aid of state 2 for the purpose of restoring peace and security; would intervene with force to stop hostile activities, and settle disputes through conciliation and negotiation, subject to appeal to international judicial tribunal. This system is viewed as possible if: 1. states agree to considerably limit their sovereign rights (e.g., accept international adjudication as binding); 2. norms of international law are given universal recognition and application as the "law of nations," and not "law among nations;" 3. individual persons, like states, become subjects of international law; and 4. national armies accept, or become a part of, global command. The ultimate end of collective measures would be to eliminate conflict and not states, even though states originate conflict.

APPENDIX 32

U.S. Intelligence Community

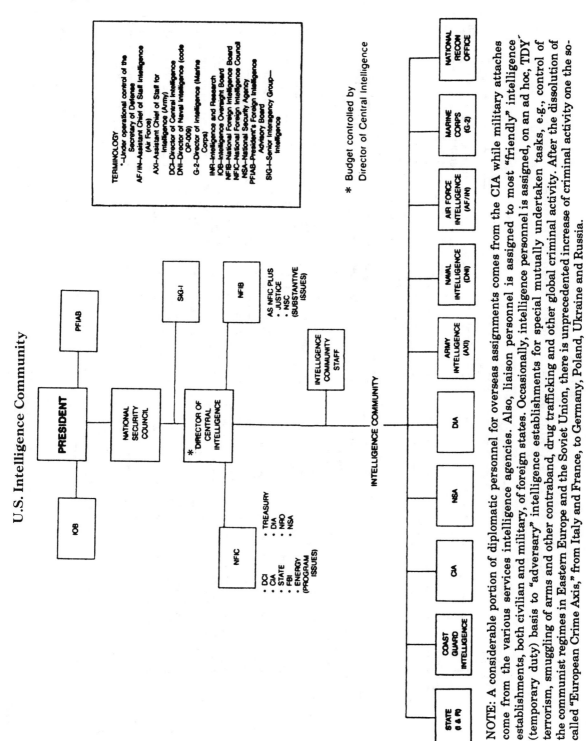

NOTE: A considerable portion of diplomatic personnel for overseas assignments comes from the CIA while military attaches come from the various services intelligence agencies. Also, liaison personnel is assigned to most "friendly" intelligence establishments, both civilian and military, of foreign states. Occasionally, intelligence personnel is assigned, on an ad hoc, TDY (temporary duty) basis to "adversary" intelligence establishments for special mutually undertaken tasks, e.g., control of terrorism, smuggling of arms and other contraband, drug trafficking and other global criminal activity. After the dissolution of the communist regimes in Eastern Europe and the Soviet Union, there is unprecedented increase of criminal activity one the so-called "European Crime Axis," from Italy and France, to Germany, Poland, Ukraine and Russia.

Source: The Central Intelligence Agency

APPENDIX 33

Director of Central Intelligence Command Responsibilities*

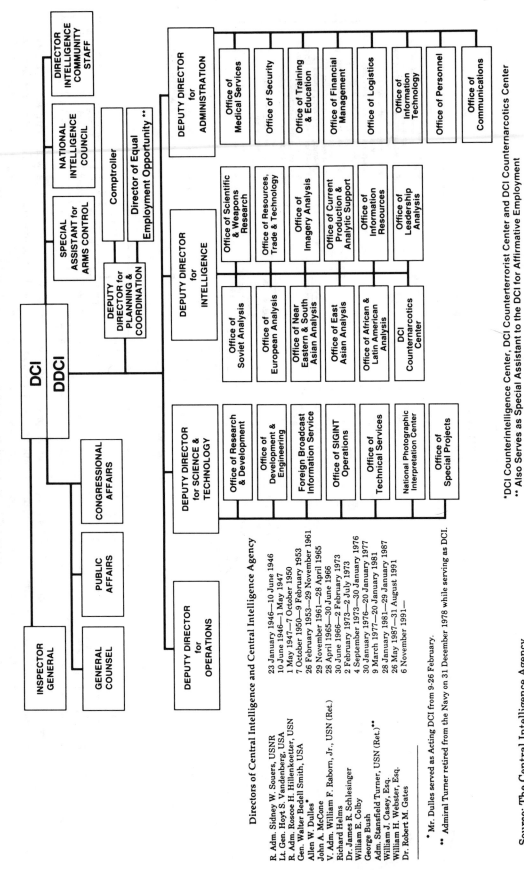

Directors of Central Intelligence and Central Intelligence Agency

R. Adm. Sidney W. Souers, USNR   23 January 1946—10 June 1946
Lt. Gen. Hoyt S. Vandenberg, USA   10 June 1946—1 May 1947
R. Adm. Roscoe H. Hillenkoetter, USN   1 May 1947—7 October 1950
Gen. Walter Bedell Smith, USA   7 October 1950—9 February 1953
Allen W. Dulles*   26 February 1953—29 November 1961
John A. McCone   29 November 1961—28 April 1965
V. Adm. William F. Raborn, Jr., USN (Ret.)   28 April 1965—30 June 1966
Richard Helms   30 June 1966—2 February 1973
Dr. James R. Schlesinger   2 February 1973—2 July 1973
William E. Colby   4 September 1973—30 January 1976
George Bush   30 January 1976—20 January 1977
Adm. Stansfield Turner, USN (Ret.)**   9 March 1977—20 January 1981
William J. Casey, Esq.   28 January 1981—29 January 1987
William H. Webster, Esq.   26 May 1987—31 August 1991
Dr. Robert M. Gates   6 November 1991—

* Mr. Dulles served as Acting DCI from 9-26 February.

** Admiral Turner retired from the Navy on 31 December 1978 while serving as DCI.

*DCI Counterintelligence Center, DCI Counterterrorist Center and DCI Counternarcotics Center
** Also Serves as Special Assistant to the DCI for Affirmative Employment

Source: The Central Intelligence Agency

APPENDIX 34

U.S. Information Agency

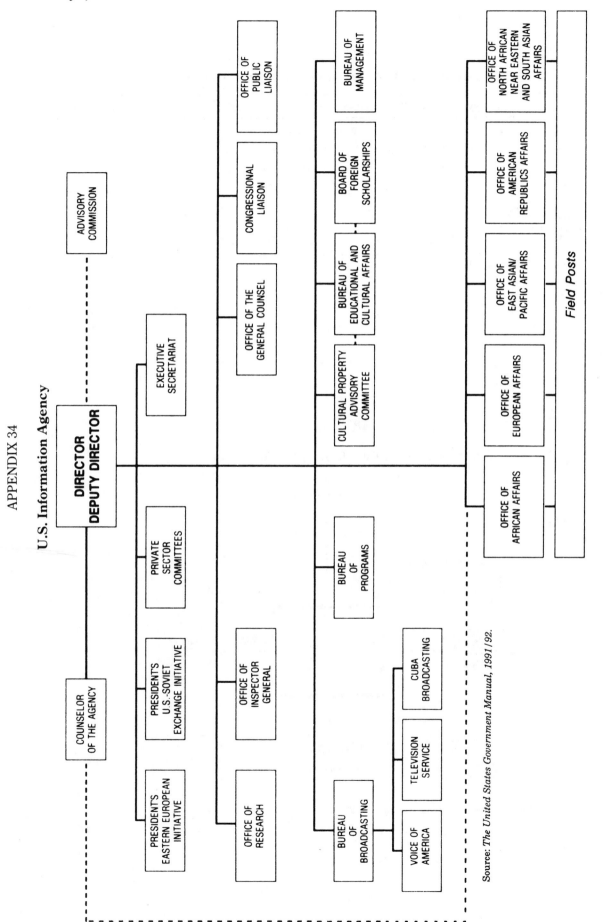

Source: *The United States Government Manual, 1991/92.*

APPENDIX 35

The Budget Outlook Through 2002 (By Fiscal Year)

	1992	1993	1994	1995	1996	1997	1998	1999	2000	2001	2002
In Billions of Dollars											
Revenues	1,102	1,179	1,263	1,342	1,415	1,492	1,580	1,667	1,758	1,854	1,955
Outlays	1,454	1,505	1,523	1,536	1,593	1,718	1,834	1,953	2,079	2,214	2.362
Deficit	352	327	260	194	178	226	254	286	322	360	407
Deficit Excluding Deposit Insurance and Desert Storm Contributions	290	258	227	210	222	254	272	298	332	369	414

SOURCE: Congressional Budget Office.

APPENDIX 36

U.S. International Development Cooperation Agency

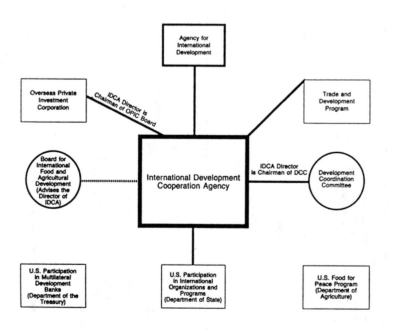

Source: *The United States Government Manual, 1991/92.*

APPENDIX 37

Major Categories of Federal Income and Outlays for Fiscal Year 1990

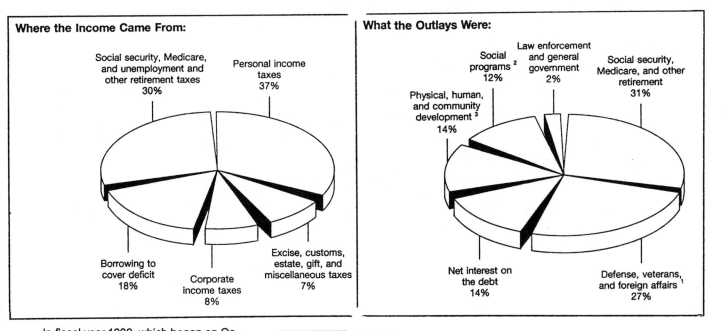

Where the Income Came From:

Social security, Medicare, and unemployment and other retirement taxes 30%

Personal income taxes 37%

Borrowing to cover deficit 18%

Corporate income taxes 8%

Excise, customs, estate, gift, and miscellaneous taxes 7%

What the Outlays Were:

Social programs [2] 12%

Law enforcement and general government 2%

Social security, Medicare, and other retirement 31%

Physical, human, and community development [3] 14%

Net interest on the debt 14%

Defense, veterans, and foreign affairs [1] 27%

In fiscal year 1990, which began on October 1, 1989, and ended on September 30, 1990, Federal income was $1,031.3 billion and outlays were $1,251.7 billion, leaving a deficit of $220.4 billion. The budget deficit is financed largely by government borrowing from the public. The government borrows from the public by selling bonds and other debt securities to private citizens, banks, businesses, and other governments.

The pie charts on this page show the relative sizes of the major categories of Federal income and outlays for fiscal year 1990.

Source: U.S. Internal Revenue Service, 1992

[1] About 23% was for defense; 2% was for veterans benefits and services; and 1% was for foreign affairs including military and economic assistance to foreign countries and the maintenance of U.S. embassies abroad.

[2] About 7% was spent to fund Medicaid, food stamps, aid to families with dependent children, supplemental security income, and related programs. About 5% was spent for health research and public health programs, unemployment compensation, assisted housing, and social services.

[3] This category consists of agricultural programs; natural resources and environmental programs; transportation programs; aid for elementary and secondary education and direct assistance to college students; job training programs; economic development programs including deposit insurance; and space, energy, and general science programs.

APPENDIX 38

Foreign Holdings of Federal Debt
(Dollar amounts in billions)

Debt held by the public				Borrowing from the public			Interest on debt held by the public		
Fiscal Year	Total	Foreign	Percentage foreign	Total	Foreign	Percentage Foreign	Total	Foreign	Percentage Foreign
1940.....43.3									
1965....260.8	12.3	4.7	3.9	0.3	6.4	9.6	0.5	4.9	
1970....283.2	14.0	5.0	3.5	3.8	107.2	15.4	0.8	5.5	
1975....394.7	66.0	16.7	51.0	9.2	18.0	25.0	4.5	18.2	
1980....994.3	121.7	17.2	69.5	1.4	2.0	62.8	11.0	17.5	
1985..1,499.4	222.9	14.9	199.4	47.4	n.a.	152.9	22.9	15.0	
1990..2,410.4	403.5	16.7	220.1	8.6	3.9	202.4	37.2	18.4	
1991..2,871.2	443.4	16.5	276.8	39.9	14.4	214.8	39.0	18.2	

Source: *Budget of the United States Government* FY 1993.

APPENDIX 39

National Debt of the United States
(Dollar amounts in billions)

Year	$	Year	$	Year	$	Year	$	Year	$	Year	$	Year	$	Year	$	Year	$
1900	1	1911	1	1922	23	1933	23	1944	201	1955	274	1966	329	1977	706	1988	2,600
1901	1	1912	1	1923	22	1934	27	1945	259	1956	273	1967	341	1978	787	1989	2,866
1902	1	1913	1	1924	21	1935	29	1946	269	1957	272	1968	370	1979	828	1990	3,113*
1903	1	1914	1	1925	21	1936	34	1947	256	1958	280	1969	367	1980	908		
1904	1	1915	1	1926	20	1937	36	1948	251	1959	288	1970	383	1981	994	*=Estimated	
1905	1	1916	1	1927	19	1938	37	1949	252	1960	291	1971	409	1982	1,136		
1906	1	1917	1	1928	18	1939	40	1950	256	1961	293	1972	437	1983	1,371		
1907	1	1918	12	1929	17	1940	43	1951	254	1962	303	1973	468	1984	1,564		
1908	1	1919	25	1930	16	1941	49	1952	258	1963	311	1974	486	1985	1,817		
1909	1	1920	24	1931	17	1942	72	1953	265	1964	317	1975	544	1986	2,120		
1910	1	1921	24	1932	20	1943	137	1954	271	1965	323	1976	632	1987	2,345		

Source: *Budget of the United States Government* FY 1993.

APPENDIX 40

Program/Regional Composition of U.S. Foreign Aid Program Request for FY1992

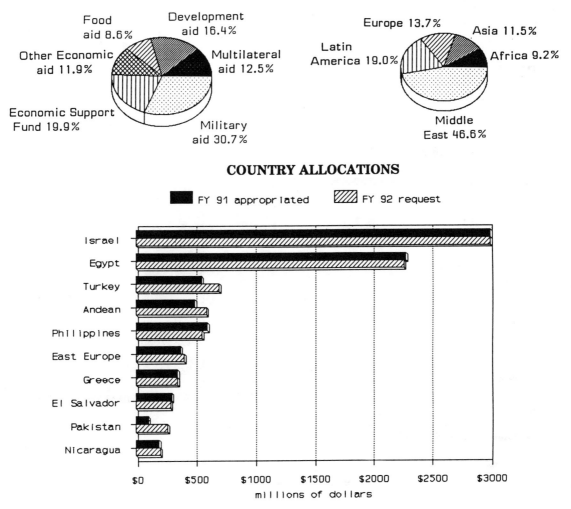

COUNTRY ALLOCATIONS

Source: Congressional Research Service-The Library of Congress

APPENDIX 41

Energy: Production, Import, Consumption

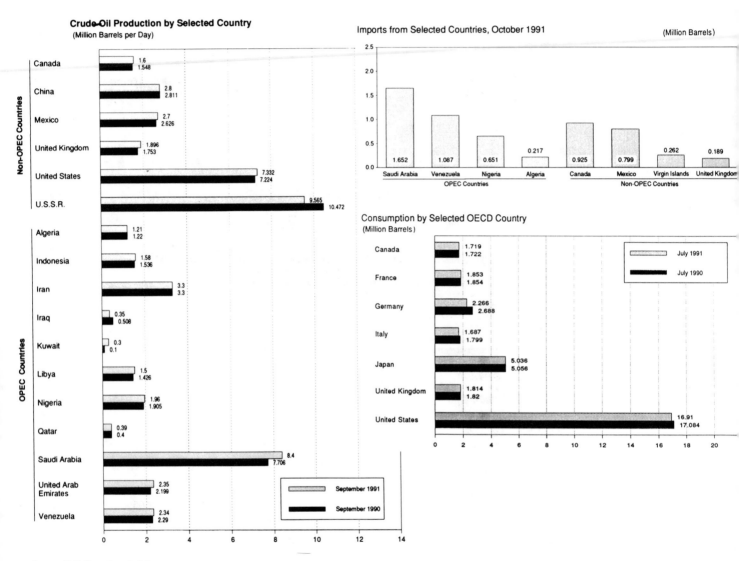

Source: U. S. Department of Energy

Energy: Production, Import, Consumption, continued

Energy Consumption Per Capita by State, 1989

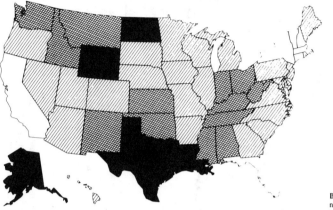

451 — 1,100 million Btu

351 — 450 million Btu

251 — 350 million Btu

151 — 250 million Btu

British Thermal Unit (Btu): The quantity of heat needed to raise the temperature of 1 pound of water by 1° F at or near 39.2° F.

Total Energy Consumption by State, 1989

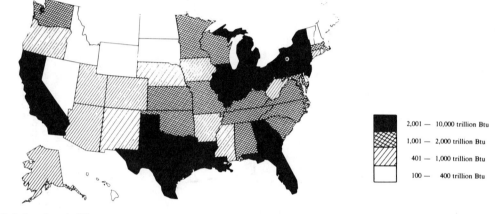

2,001 — 10,000 trillion Btu

1,001 — 2,000 trillion Btu

401 — 1,000 trillion Btu

100 — 400 trillion Btu

Source: U. S. Department of Energy

APPENDIX 42

Critical Raw Materials

	MATERIAL	U.S. IMPORTS (%)	U.S. PRODUCTION (%)
1.	Antimony	91%	9%
2.	Bauxite	84	16
3.	Beryllium	96	4
4.	Chrome	100	0
5.	Cobalt	90	10
6.	Industrial Diamonds	100	0
7.	Manganese	96	4
8.	Natural Rubber	100	0
9.	Nickel	91	9
10.	Oil	43	57
11.	Platinum	97	3
12.	Tin	100	0
13.	Tungsten (Wolfram)	42	58

APPENDIX 43

Standard Federal Regions

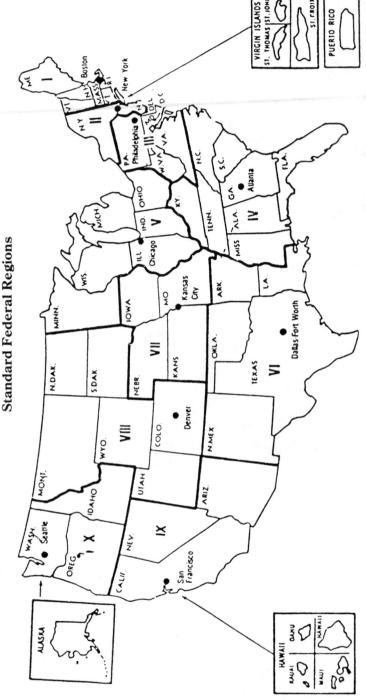

"Standard Federal administrative regions were established to achieve more uniformity in the location and geographic jurisdiction of Federal field offices. Standard regions are a basis for promoting more systematic coordination among agencies and Federal, State, and local governments and for securing management improvements and economies through greater interagency and intergovernmental cooperation. OMB Circular A-105, *Standard Federal Regions*, provides further guidance on the policies and requirements governing standard administrative regions. Boundaries were drawn and regional office locations designated for 10 regions, and agencies are required to adopt the uniform system when changes are made or new offices established Federal Executive Boards, (FEB's) were established by Presidential directive (a memorandum for heads of Federal departments and agencies dated November 13, 1961) to improve internal Federal management practices and to provide a central focus for Federal participation in civic affairs in major metropolitan centers of Federal activity. They carry out their functions under the supervision and control of the Office of Personnel Management (OPM). Federal Executive Boards are composed of heads of Federal field offices in the metropolitan area. A Chairman is elected annually from among the membership to provide overall leadership to the Board's operations. Committees and task forces carry out interagency projects consistent with the Board's missions. Federal Executive Boards serve as a means for disseminating information within the Federal Government and for promoting discussion of Federal policies and activities of importance to all Federal executives in the field. Currently, Federal Executive Boards are located in 27 metropolitan areas that are important centers of Federal activity. These areas, are: Albuquerque-Santa Fe, Atlanta, Baltimore, Boston, Buffalo, Chicago, Cincinnati, Cleveland, Dallas-Fort Worth, Denver, Detroit, Honolulu-Pacific, Houston, Kansas City, Los Angeles, Miami, New Orleans, New York, Newark, Philadelphia, Pittsburgh, Portland, St. Louis, San Antonio, San Francisco, Seattle, and the Twin Cities (Minneapolis-St. Paul)."

Source: *The United States Government Manual, 1991/92.*

APPENDIX 44

The Supreme Court of the United States

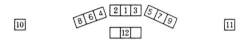

1. Chief Justice William H. Rehnquist

2. Justice Byron R. White
3. Justice Harry A. Blackmun

4. Justice John P. Stevens
5. Justice Sandra Day O'Connor

6. Justice Antonin Scalia
7. Justice Anthony M. Kennedy

8. Justice David H. Souter
9. Justice Clarence Thomas

10. Clerk of the Court
11. Marshal of the Court

12. Counsel

Silence is Requested

Source: The Supreme Court of the United States

APPENDIX 45

Administrative Office of the U.S. Courts

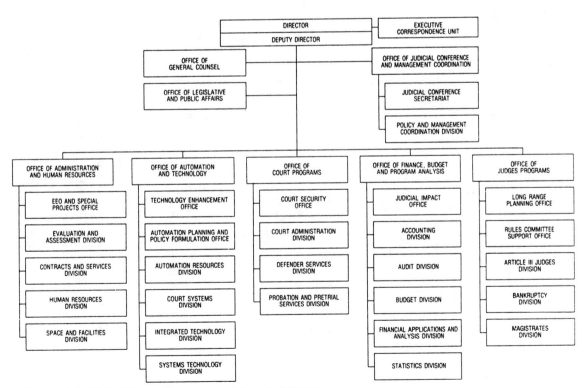

Source: *The United States Government Manual, 1991/92.*

APPENDIX 46

Chief Justices of the Supreme Court of the United States

NO.	NAME	LIFE	PARTY	STATE	YEARS OF SERVICE	APPOINTED BY	DISP.
1.	John Jay	1745-1829	Fed.	N Y	1789-1795	George Washington	Resigned[1]
2.	John Rutledge	1739-1800	Fed.	SC	1795-1795	George Washington	Unconfirmed[2]
3.	Oliver Ellsworth	1745-1807	Fed.	CT	1796-1800	George Washington	Resigned[3]
4.	John Marshall	1755-1835	Fed.	VA	1801-1835	John Adams	Died
5.	Roger B. Taney	1777-1864	Dem.	MD	1836-1864	Andrew Jackson	Died
6.	Salmon P. Chase	1808-1873	Rep.	OH	1864-1873	Abraham Lincoln	Died
7.	Morrison R. Waite	1816-1888	Rep.	OH	1874-1888	Ulysses S. Grant	Died
8.	Melville W. Fuller	1833-1910	Dem.	IL	1888-1910	Grover Cleveland	Died
9.	Edward D. White	1845-1921	Dem.	LA	1910-1921	William H. Taft	Died
10.	William H. Taft	1857-1930	Rep.	CT	1921-1930	Warren G. Harding	Resigned[4]
11.	Charles E. Hughes	1862-1948	Rep.	N Y	1930-1941	Herbert Hoover	Retired
12.	Harlan F. Stone	1872-1946	Rep.	N Y	1941-1946	Franklin D. Roosevelt	Died
13.	Fred M. Vinson	1890-1953	Dem.	KY	1946-1953	Harry S. Truman	Died
14.	Earl Warren	1891-1974	Rep	CA	1953-1969	Dwight D. Eisenhower	Retired
15.	Abe Fortas	1910-1982	Dem.	TN	1968-1968	Lyndon B. Johnson	Unconfirmed[5]
16.	Warren E. Burger	1907-	Rep.	MN	1969-1986	Richard M. Nixon	Resigned
17.	William H. Rehnquist	1924-	Rep.	AZ	1986-	Ronald Reagan	

[1]Resigned to serve as Governor of New York State.
[2]Rejected by the U.S. Senate and subsequently resigned.
[3]Resigned due to ill health.
[4]Resigned due to ill health. (The only man ever to serve both as U.S. President and later Chief Justice of the U.S. Supreme Court).
[5]Rejected by the U.S. Senate and subsequently resigned.

APPENDIX 47

Associate Justices of the Supreme Court of the United States

NAME	LIFE	PARTY	STATE	YEARS OF SERVICE	APPOINTED BY	DISP.
John Rutledge	1739-1800	Fed.	South Carolina	1789-1791	George Washington	Resigned*
William Cushing	1732-1810	Fed.	Massachusetts	1789-1810	George Washington	Died
James Wilson	1724-1798	Fed.	Pennsylvania	1789-1798	George Washington	Died
John Blair	1732-1800	Fed.	Virginia	1789-1796	George Washington	Resigned*
James Iredell	1750-1799	Fed.	Maryland	1790-1799	George Washington	Died
Thomas Johnson	1732-1819	Fed.	Maryland	1791-1793	George Washington	Resigned
William Paterson	1745-1806	Fed.	New Jersey	1793-1806	George Washington	Died
Samuel Chase	1741-1811	Fed.	Maryland	1796-1811	George Washington	Died[1]
Bushrod Washington	1762-1829	Fed.	Pennsylvania	1798-1829	John Adams	Died
Alfred Moore	1755-1810	Fed.	North Carolina	1799-1804	John Adams	Resigned*
William Johnson	1771-1834	Rep.	South Carolina	1804-1834	Thomas Jefferson	Died
Brockholst Henry Livingston	1757-1823	Rep.	New York	1806-1823	Thomas Jefferson	Died
Thomas Todd	1765-1826	Rep.	Kentucky	1807-1826	Thomas Jefferson	Died
Gabriel Duvall	1752-1844	Rep.	Maryland	1811-1835	James Madison	Resigned*
Joseph Story	1779-1845	Rep.	Massachusetts	1811-1845	James Madison	Died
Smith Thompson	1768-1843	Rep.	New York	1823-1843	James Monroe	Died
Robert Trimble	1777-1828	Rep.	Kentucky	1826-1828	John Quincy Adams	Died
John McLean	1785-1861	Dem.	Ohio	1829-1861	Andrew Jackson	Died
Henry Baldwin	1780-1844	Dem.	Pennsylvania	1830-1844	Andrew Jackson	Died
James M. Wayne	1790-1867	Dem.	Georgia	1835-1867	Andrew Jackson	Died

* The high number of resignations from the Court during the early days was due to the lack of its prestige. For the first three years there was not a single case brought before it and sessions were often held in such places as basements of apartment houses or committee rooms of Congress. Not until 1935 was the Supreme Court given its separate quarters.

[1] Justice Chase was impeached by the U.S. House of Representatives in 1804 for advising a grand jury, but the U.S. Senate failed to muster the necessary majority to remove him.

Associate Justices of the Supreme Court of the United States, continued

NAME	LIFE	PARTY	STATE	YEARS OF SERVICE	APPOINTED BY	DISP.
Philip P. Barbour	1783-1841	Dem.	Virginia	1836-1841	Andrew Jackson	Died
John Catron	1778-1865	Dem.	Tennessee	1837-1865	Martin Van Buren	Died
John McKinley	1780-1852	Dem.	Kentucky	1837-1852	Martin Van Buren	Died
Peter V. Daniel	1784-1860	Dem.	Virginia	1841-1860	Martin Van Buren	Died
Samuel Nelson	1792-1873	Dem.	New York	1845-1872	John Tyler	Resigned
Levi Woodbury	1789-1851	Dem.	New Hampshire	1845-1851	James K. Polk	Died
Robert C. Grier	1794-1870	Dem.	Pennsylvania	1846-1870	James K. Polk	Resigned
Benjamin R. Curtis	1809-1874	Whig	Massachusetts	1851-1857	Millard Fillmore	Resigned
John A. Campbell	1811-1889	Dem.	Alabama	1853-1861	Franklin Pierce	Resigned
Nathan Clifford	1803-1881	Dem.	Maine	1858-1881	James Buchanan	Died
Noah H. Swayne	1804-1884	Rep.	Ohio	1862-1881	Abraham Lincoln	Resigned
Samuel F. Miller	1816-1890	Rep.	Iowa	1862-1890	Abraham Lincoln	Died
David Davis	1815-1886	Rep.	Illinois	1862-1877	Abraham Lincoln	Resigned
Stephen J. Field	1816-1899	Dem.	California	1863-1897	Abraham Lincoln	Resigned
William Strong	1808-1895	Rep.	Pennsylvania	1870-1880	Ulysses S. Grant	Resigned
Joseph P. Bradley	1803-1892	Rep.	New Jersey	1870-1892	Ulysses S. Grant	Died
Ward Hunt	1810-1886	Rep.	New York	1872-1882	Ulysses S. Grant	Resigned
John Marshall Harlan	1833-1911	Rep.	Kentucky	1877-1911	Rutherford B. Hayes	Died
William B. Woods	1824-1887	Rep.	Georgia	1880-1887	Rutherford B. Hayes	Died
Stanley Matthews	1824-1889	Rep.	Ohio	1881-1889	James A. Garfield	Died
Horace Gray	1828-1902	Rep.	Massachusetts	1881-1902	Chester A. Arthur	Died
Samuel Blatchford	1820-1893	Rep.	New York	1882-1893	Chester A. Arthur	Died
Lucius Q. C. Lamar	1825-1893	Dem.	Mississippi	1888-1893	Grover Cleveland	Died
David J. Brewer	1837-1910	Rep.	Kansas	1889-1910	Benjamin Harrison	Died
Henry B. Brown	1836-1913	Rep.	Michigan	1890-1906	Benjamin Harrison	Resigned
George Shiras	1832-1924	Rep.	Pennsylvania	1892-1903	Benjamin Harrison	Resigned
Howell E. Jackson	1832-1895	Dem.	Tennessee	1893-1895	Benjamin Harrison	Died
Edward D. White	1845-1921	Dem.	Louisiana	1894-1910	Grover Cleveland	Died
Rufus W. Peckham	1838-1909	Dem.	New York	1895-1909	Grover Cleveland	Died

Associate Justices of the Supreme Court of the United States, continued

NAME	LIFE	PARTY	STATE	YEARS OF SERVICE	APPOINTED BY	DISP.
Joseph McKenna	1843-1926	Rep.	California	1898-1925	William McKinley	Resigned
Oliver Wendell Holmes	1841-1935	Rep.	Massachusetts	1902-1932	Theodore Roosevelt	Retired
William R. Day	1849-1923	Rep.	Ohio	1903-1922	Theodore Roosevelt	Resigned
William H. Moody	1853-1917	Rep.	Massachusetts	1906-1910	Theodore Roosevelt	Resigned
Horace H. Lurton	1844-1914	Dem.	Tennessee	1909-1914	William H. Taft	Died
Charles E. Hughes	1862-1948	Rep.	New York	1910-1916	William H. Taft	Resigned
Willis Van Devanter	1859-1941	Rep.	Wyoming	1910-1937	William H. Taft	Retired
Joseph R. Lamar	1857-1916	Dem.	Georgia	1910-1916	William H. Taft	Died
Mahlon Pitney	1858-1924	Rep.	New Jersey	1912-1922	William H. Taft	Retired
James C. McReynolds	1862-1946	Dem.	Tennessee	1914-1941	Woodrow Wilson	Retired
Louis D. Brandeis	1856-1941	Dem.	Massachusetts	1916-1939	Woodrow Wilson	Retired
John H. Clarke	1857-1945	Dem.	Ohio	1916-1922	Woodrow Wilson	Resigned
George Sutherland	1862-1942	Rep.	Utah	1922-1938	Warren G. Harding	Retired
Pierce Butler	1866-1939	Dem.	Minnesota	1922-1939	Warren G. Harding	Died
Edward T. Sanford	1865-1930	Rep.	Tennessee	1923-1930	Warren G. Harding	Died
Harlan F. Stone	1872-1946	Rep.	New York	1925-1941	Calvin Coolidge	Died
Owen J. Roberts	1875-1955	Rep.	Pennsylvania	1930-1945	Herbert Hoover	Resigned
Benjamin N. Cardozo	1870-1938	Dem.	New York	1932-1938	Herbert Hoover	Died
Hugo L. Black	1886-1971	Dem.	Alabama	1937-1971	Franklin D. Roosevelt	Resigned
Stanley F. Reed	1884-1980	Dem.	Kentucky	1938-1957	Franklin D. Roosevelt	Retired
Felix Frankfurter	1882-1965	Ind.	Massachusetts	1939-1962	Franklin D. Roosevelt	Retired
William O. Douglas	1898-1980	Dem.	Connecticut	1939-1975	Franklin D. Roosevelt	Retired[1]
Frank Murphy	1893-1949	Dem.	Michigan	1940-1949	Franklin D. Roosevelt	Died
James F. Byrnes	1879-1968	Dem.	South Carolina	1941-1942	Franklin D. Roosevelt	Resigned
Robert H. Jackson	1892-1954	Dem.	New York	1941-1954	Franklin D. Roosevelt	Died

[1]Serious efforts were made on three separate occasions to impeach this outspoken, liberal Justice. His strong stand on the extension of personal rights of Americans, particularly on civil rights and privacy, and at last his marriage to a young woman who could have been his great-grand-daughter, offended many conservative and traditional forces.

Associate Justices of the Supreme Court of the United States, continued

NAME	LIFE	PARTY	STATE	YEARS OF SERVICE	APPOINTED BY	DISP.
Wiley B. Rutledge	1894-1949	Dem.	Iowa	1943-1949	Franklin D. Roosevelt	Died
Harold H. Burton	1888-1964	Rep.	Ohio	1945-1958	Harry S. Truman	Retired
Tom C. Clark	1899-1977	Dem.	Texas	1949-1967	Harry S. Truman	Retired
Sherman Minton	1890-1965	Dem.	Indiana	1949-1956	Harry S. Truman	Retired
John Marshall Harlan	1899-1971	Rep.	New York	1955-1971	Dwight D. Eisenhower	Resigned
William J. Brennan, Jr.	1906-1990	Dem.	New Jersey	1956-1990	Dwight D. Eisenhower	Resigned
Charles E. Whittaker	1901-1973	Rep.	Missouri	1957-1962	Dwight D. Eisenhower	Retired
Potter Stewart	1915-1985	Rep.	Ohio	1958-1981	Dwight D. Eisenhower	Resigned
Byron R. White	1917-	Dem.	Colorado	1962-	John F. Kennedy	
Arthur J. Goldberg	1908-1990	Dem.	Illinois	1962-1965	John F. Kennedy	Resigned
Abe Fortas	1910-1982	Dem.	Tennessee	1965-1969	Lyndon B. Johnson	Resigned[1]
Thurgood Marshall	1908-	Dem.	New York	1967-1991	Lyndon B. Johnson	Resigned[2]
Harry A. Blackmun	1908-	Rep.	Minnesota	1970-	Richard M. Nixon	
Lewis F. Powell, Jr.	1907-	Dem.	Virginia	1971-1987	Richard M. Nixon	Resigned
William H. Rehnquist	1924-	Rep.	Arizona	1971-1986	Richard M. Nixon	[3]
John P. Stevens	1920-	Rep.	Illinois	1975-	Gerald R. Ford	
Sandra Day O'Connor	1930-	Rep.	Arizona	1981-	Ronald Reagan	[4]
Antonin Scalia	1936-	Rep.	Virginia	1986-	Ronald Reagan	

[1] In the place of rejected Abe Fortas, the President nominated Judge Clement F. Haynsworth, a Democrat from South Carolina, then Judge G. Harold Carswell, a Democrat from Florida, both of whom were rejected by the Senate. At last, Warren E. Burger was nominated and confirmed as Chief Justice.

[2] Due to growing litigation among Americans (many want to have a day in court), there is an acute shortage of law court judges at all levels, and, therefore, retiring judges, including the justices of the U. S. Supreme Court, may hear cases on a part-time basis. Retired Justice Thurgood Marshall, at age 83, decided to return to the bench at the U.S. Circuit Court of Appeals in New York City, because, as he put it, "...I enjoy working," although he states, "I am falling apart."

[3] Appointed Chief Justice.

[4] First woman Associate Justice.

Associate Justices of the Supreme Court of the United States, continued

NAME	LIFE	PARTY	STATE	YEARS OF SERVICE	APPOINTED BY	DISP.
Anthony M. Kennedy	1936-	Rep.	California	1988-	Ronald Reagan	1
David H. Souter	1939-	Rep.	Massachusetts	1990-	George Bush	
Clarence Thomas	1948-	Rep.	Georgia	1991-	George Bush	2

[1] Judge Robert H. Bork, the first nominee, was rejected as "too conservative," the next nominee, Douglas G. Ginsberg withdrew his nomination after revelation of his experimentation with drugs during his college days, which he acknowledged.

[2] Circuit Court of Appeals Judge Thomas was the second black ever nominated to serve as an Associate Justice of the Supreme Court and who was to replace retiring Justice Thurgood Marshall. Known for his conservative outlook, the liberal Democrats on the U. S. Senate Judiciary Committee were against his nomination especially after he refused to reveal his philosophy of law, natural law in particular, and, particularly his stand on abortion. The Liberal Democrats feared that Judge Thomas may vote to upset the landmark case of *Roe v. Wade*. Since this challenge produced little debate, suddenly a young black lawyer and now professor of Law at the University of Oklahoma, Anita Hill, submitted an affidavit to the Judiciary Committee stating that during her professional association with Judge Thomas, in the period of 1981-1983, he constantly asked her to date him and used in her presence sexually explicit language—all of which Professor Hill construed as sexual harassment. Judge Thomas denied her allegation and it all resulted in one person accusing another without material evidence to substantiate the charges. Extensive Senate hearing televised worldwide, revealed that Anita Hill considered Judge Thomas her mentor and career guide and followed him whenever he moved from one federal agency to another until recently when the association remained friendly but distant, and it turned cool when Thomas married again, but this time to a white woman. In spite of the gravity of the accusations leveled against the integrity of a person to serve on the highest court of the nation, the bulk of public opinion viewed Hill's accusations as her personal revenge and vendetta, and an act of a scorned pupil toward her mentor, and the Senate confirmed Judge Thomas in October 1991 by a vote of 52 to 48, with 46 Democrats and 2 Republicans voting against the confirmation.

NOTE: Four U.S. Presidents had no opportunity to make appointments to the U.S. Supreme Court. They were: William H. Harrison, March-April, 1841; Zachary Taylor, 1849-1850; Andrew Johnson (the only U.S. President without any formal education and a tailor by vocation), 1865-1869; and Jimmy Carter, 1977-1981.

APPENDIX 48

Selected Landmark Opinions by the United States Supreme Court

1. LEGISLATIVE POWER

Afroyim v. Rusk. [387 U.S. 253 (1967)]. Congress cannot deprive a U.S. citizen his citizenship for voting in a foreign election. The case upset the previous ruling in *Perez v. Brownell.*

Barenblatt v. United States. [360 U.S. 109 (1959)]. In the interest of the nation as a whole, the Congress has the right to investigate the association of individuals with the Communist Party.

McCulloch v. Maryland. [4 Wheat. 316 (1819)]. The Baltimore branch of the Second Bank of the United States ignored Maryland statute (which required all banks not chartered in the state to either pay an annual fee of $15,000 or pay a tax on each issuance of bank notes) and issued bank notes without paying any fees to the state of Maryland. The state took the case to its local court which upheld the state statute, but the cashier of the federal bank, McCulloch, carried the case in 1917, to the U.S. Supreme Court on a writ of error. The Court ruled in favor of the Bank, stating in parts that "The government of the United States, then, though limited in its powers, is supreme; and its laws, when made in pursuance of the Constitution, for the supreme law of the land, 'any thing in the Constitution or laws of any State to the contrary notwithstanding'." According to the supremacy of the federal government doctrine individual states may not tax federal property located on their territory.

Milligan, Ex Parte. [4 Wall. 2 (1866)]. Congress lacks the power to establish military commissions to try civilians for non-combat related matters in areas where civil courts are in operation.

Schlechter Poultry Corp. et al. v. United States. [295 U.S. 495 (1935)]. Legislative powers may not be delegated to the other branches (i.e., the executive and/or the judicial). The entire National Industrial Recovery Act was declared unconstitutional. (After that, President Franklin D. Roosevelt attempted to "pack" the Court. See COURT-PACKING).

Ullmann v. United States. [350 U.S. 422 (1955)]. Congressional committees have the right to grant immunity from criminal prosecution to witnesses who agree to testify in matters involving national security.

Watkins v. United States. [354 U.S. 178 (1957)]. Congress has the power to conduct investigations for legislative purposes, but the Court warned that this power should not be abused.

2. JUDICIAL POWER

Baker v. Carr. [369 U.S. 186 (1962)]. Federal courts have the right under the provisions of the 14th Amendment to scrutinize the reapportionment practices in states and to suggest means for the removal of inequities through such means as the one man, one vote principle. This provision has been reinforced by the ruling in *Reynolds v. Sims* [32 Law Week 4535 (1964)] where the Court ruled that popular approval of state apportionment in a referendum does not validate unequal or discriminatory voting districts. See ONE MAN, ONE VOTE.

Graves v. New York ex rel. O'Keefe. [306 U.S. 466 (1939)]. A federal employee may not be immune from paying states taxes because such immunity would ". . .impose to an inadmissible extent a restriction on the taxing power which the Constitution has reserved to the state governments." This ruling has modified the doctrine of intergovernmental tax immunity.

Luther v. Borden. [7 How. 1 (1849)]. The U.S. Constitution (Art. 4, Section 4) commands the federal government to guarantee to the states a republican form of government. The meaning of this provision is to be interpreted by the political branch of the government, the Congress, and not the courts.

Marbury v. Madison. [1 Cranch 137 (1803)]. The case established three distinct precedents: (1) the doctrine of judicial review—empowering the third branch of the U.S. Government, the U.S. Supreme Court, to review legislative acts as to their compliance with the letter and the spirit of the Constitution; (2) each incoming President has the right to appoint his own officers; and (3) declared the Judiciary Act of 1789 unconstitutional.

3. **EXECUTIVE POWER**

Arver v. United States. [245 U.S. 366 (1918)]. Service in the armed forces does not constitute involuntary servitude. It is a duty of a citizen.

Humphrey's Executor v. United States. (*Rathbun v. United States*). [295 U.S. 602 (1935)]. Presidential power of removal of federal officers, particularly those with semi-judicial and semi-legislative powers (as was the case of Humphrey, a Commissioner of the Federal Trade Commission), is limited, because these officers are installed with the advice and consent of the U.S. Senate.

Korematsu v. United States. [323 U.S. 214 (1945)]. World War II evacuation of over 100,000 Japanese-Americans from the West Coast (mainly California) to internment camps in the West (e.g., in Arizona), was constitutional and necessary.

Mississippi v. Johnson. [4 Wall. 475 (1867)]. The judiciary may not restrain the President from performing functions which were authorized by the Congress through specific legislation.

Missouri v. Holland, United States Game Warden. [252 U.S. 346 (1920)]. Upheld a 1918 treaty and a federal law aimed at the protection of migratory birds between the United States and Canada, without violation of states' rights under Amendment X to the Constitution.

Myers v. United States. [272 U.S. 52 (1926)]. The U.S. President was recognized in his right to remove any officer of the federal government, except judges. This power has been modified in *Humphrey's Executor v. United States.*

Snepp v. United States. [444 U.S. 507 (1980)]. An agent of the U.S. Central Intelligence Agency assigned to Saigon, South Vietnam CIA station during the Vietnam War, became disenchanted and wrote a book about the bungling of U.S. intelligence operation there. Because he broke all rules of ultimate secrecy, he was deprived of author's royalties for the book, "Decent Interval;" he took the CIA to the court, but lost. See SENSITIVE INFORMATION.

United States v. Curtiss-Wright Corp. et al. [299 U.S. 304 (1936)]. In matters pertaining to foreign affairs, the U.S. Congress may grant the U.S. President a degree of "discretion and freedom from statutory restriction which would not be admissible were domestic affairs alone involved."

United States v. Nixon. [385 U.S. 176 (1974)]. Limited the degree and the scope of the President's power to exercise his executive privilege in denying to turn over evidence to a court of law. Nixon was required to turn in the tapes as requested, and three days later, on August 9, 1974, he resigned as U.S. President.

Youngstown Sheet and Tube Co. et al. v. Sawyer. [343 U.S. 579 (1952)]. Denied the U.S. President the power to seize and to operate a private enterprise by force. (U.S. President Harry S. Truman ordered the company to be seized after a prolonged strike threatened defense production.)

4. **CONSTITUTIONAL AUTHORITY-CONTRACT CLAUSE**

Charles River Bridge Co. v. Warren Bridge Co. [11 Pet. 420 (1837)]. Contract is to be limited to the actual language contained in the document and nothing is to be implied.

Dartmouth College (The Trustees of Dartmouth College v. Woodward). [4 Wheat. 518 (1819)]. A corporate charter is a contract that is protected against infringement by a state legislature. Chief Justice John Marshall extended the contract clause in this case.

Home Building and Loan Association v. Blaisdell. [290 U.S. 398 (1934)]. The Court allowed states to use their power in upholding the rights of a contract—during the Great Depression-era Minnesota Mortgage Moratorium Act. Justice Hughes delivered the majority opinion which contains his famous statement: "While emergency does not create power, emergency may furnish the occasion for the exercise of power."

5. **FEDERAL AUTHORITY**

See EQUAL PROTECTION POWER, CIVIL RIGHTS CASES, **Cooper v. Aaron.**

See CONSTITUTIONAL AUTHORITY-CONTRACT CLAUSE, **Dartmouth College v. Woodward.**

See EQUAL PROTECTION POWER, **Dred Scott v. Sanford, Reynolds v. Sims, Shapiro v. Thompson.**

See BASIC FREEDOMS; SPEECH, PRESS, ASSOCIATION, CIVIL RIGHTS, **Freeman v. Maryland.**

Gibbons v. Ogden. [9 Wheat. 1 (1824)]. Federal authority to regulate interstate commerce is superior over that of states.

See DUE PROCESS-PROCEDURAL/SUBSTANTIVE, **Lochner v. New York, Malloy v. Hogan.**

See JUDICIAL POWER, **Luther v. Borden.**

Steward Machine Co. v. Davis. [301 U.S. 548 (1937)]. The Court upheld the constitutionality of the unemployment compensation provision of the Social Security Act of 1935.

6. **STATE AUTHORITY**

See JUDICIAL POWER, **Baker v. Carr, Graves v. New York ex. rel.**

See DUE PROCESS-PROCEDURAL/SUBSTANTIVE, **Adamson v. California, Home Building and Loan Association v. Blaisdell.**

See FREEDOM OF RELIGION, **Cantwell v. Connecticut, West Virginia State Board of Education v. Barnette.**

See EQUAL PROTECTION POWER, **Reitman v. Muckey, Sweatt v. Painter.**

See BASIC FREEDOMS-SPEECH, PRESS ASSOCIATION—CIVIL RIGHTS, SUNDAY CLOSING CASES.

See RIGHT TO PRIVACY, **Time, Inc. v. Hill.**

Adderley v. Florida. [385 U.S. 39 (1967)]. States may withhold public facilities to demonstrators in order to protect the facilities from damage.

Buck v. Bell. [274 U.S. 200 (1927)]. Compulsory sterilization under the statutes of the State of Virginia is constitutional. This was a first compulsory sterilization imposed ever in the U.S.

Edwards v. California. [314 U.S. 160 (1941)]. Voided California's so-called "Anti-Okie" law—bringing indigent persons into California—which interfered with interstate commerce.

Gibson v. Florida Legislative Investigating Committee. [372 U.S. 539 (1963)]. The Court imposed limitations on the scope and the degree of state legislatures to investigate persons for political activities.

Gitlow v. New York. [268 U.S. 652 (1925)]. New York criminal anarchy law was upheld.

National Association For The Advancement of Colored People v. Alabama. [357 U.S. 449 (1958)]. No state may require an organization to disclose its membership while that organization is planning or conducting a litigation, which in itself is a political right protected by the 1st Amendment.

NAACP v. Button. [371 U.S. 415 (1963)]. While voiding an anti-NAACP statute in Virginia, the Court stated that: "the activities of the NAACP, its affiliates and legal staff are modes of expression and association protected by the First and Fourteenth Amendments which Virginia may not prohibit."

Pennsylvania v. Nelson. [350 U.S. 497 (1955)]. No state may prosecute persons who advocate violent overthrow of the government "because the field of anti-subversive activities had been pre-empted by the federal government." The Court voided the Pennsylvania sedition law.

Smith v. Allwright. [321 U.S. 649 (1944)]. White primary to be held in Texas was declared unconstitutional.

7. **FEDERALISM**

See LEGISLATIVE POWER, **Mcculloch v. Maryland.**

Cohens v. Virginia. [6 Wheat. 264 (1821)]. The degree and scope of application of federal statutes is subject to review by state and federal courts. Federal courts have the power to review the decisions of state courts. Whenever federal issues (e.g., rights) are involved, federal courts prevail over state courts.

Cooley v. Board Of Wardens of the Port of Philadelphia. [12 How. 299 (1852)]. The commerce power of the federal government is exclusive with respect to some matters and concurrent with those of states with respect to others.

See FEDERAL AUTHORITY, **Gibbons v. Ogden.**

See STATE AUTHORITY, **Pennsylvania v. Nelson.**

See DUE PROCESS-PROCEDURAL/SUBSTANTIVE, **Slaughter House Cases.**

8. **CITIZENSHIP**

See LEGISLATIVE POWER, **Afroym v. Rusk.**

United States v. Schwimmer. [279 U.S. 644 (1929)]. Denied naturalization to a woman who indicated an unwillingness to take up arms in defense of the country.

9. **BASIC FREEDOMS—SPEECH, PRESS, ASSOCIATION,-CIVIL RIGHTS**

See EXECUTIVE POWER, **Arver v. United States.**

Alder v. Board of Education. [342 U.S. 485 (1952)]. A school board may dismiss an employee (a teacher) for advocating the overthrow of the U.S. Government by an unconstitutional means, including membership in organizations which advocate such causes.

A Book v. Attorney General. [383 U.S. 413 (1966)]. Obscene material is that which is utterly without redeeming social value. Since Cleveland's *Fanny Hill* does not lack such redeeming values, therefore it is not obscene as it was ruled by the Massachusetts Supreme Court.

See EQUAL PROTECTION POWER, **Crosson v. City Council, City of Richmond, Virginia.**

Dennis v. United States. [341 U.S. 494 (1951)]. Upheld the conviction of Dennis and ten other communists for violation of the Smith Act.

Freedman v. Maryland. [380 U.S. 51 (1965)]. Authorized prior restraint on showing a motion picture in public under the authority of a statute of the State of Maryland, pointing out that strict standards must be observed in order to avoid violation of freedom of speech.

Ginzburg v. United States. [390 U.S. 629 (1968)]. Ginzburg and Mishkin (in *Mishkin v. New York*) were charged with violation of the federal obscenity statute by using the mail for distribution of pornographic literature. Ginzburg's right to mail the literature was upheld.

New York Times Co. v. Sullivan. [376 U.S. 254 (1964)]. Criticism of the official conduct of a public official does not constitute a libelous speech.

Scales v. United States. [367 U.S. 203 (1961)]. The Court upheld a part of the Smith Act that considers a membership in an organization that advocates the overthrow of the American Government by force a criminal act, provided that one is an active member engaged for that particular purpose, with clear intent.

Schenk v. United States. [249 U.S. 47 (1919)]. The doctrine of "clear and present danger" was established while Justice Holmes was delineating between speech that can be protected by the freedom of speech provisions of the First Amendment and speech that is harmful and should be prohibited (e.g., such as screaming "fire" in a crowded theater, which can cause panic and be harmful to many).

Sunday Closing Cases. [366 U.S. 420 (1961)]. Four separate cases were considered at once pertaining to Sunday closing laws, or "blue laws" (from Maryland, Massachusetts and Pennsylvania). The Court ruled that blue laws violate no rights of citizens under the 1st Amendment.

10. DUE PROCESS-PROCEDURAL/SUBSTANTIVE

Adamson v. California. [332 U.S. 46 (1947)]. State courts are not required under the due process clause of the 14th Amendment to give protection to accused persons against self-incrimination under the 5th Amendment.

Adkins v. Children's Hospital. [261 U.S. 525 (1923)]. A minimum wage law for children and women in the District of Columbia was invalidated. The decision was based on the precedent established in the *Lochner* case, which construed legislative interference with the freedom of contract a violation of liberty without due process of law.

Amalgamated Food Employees Union Local 590 v. Logan Valley Plaza, Inc. [391 U.S. 308 (1968)]. Ownership of property does not constitute absolute dominion over it. The more the property is ued by the public, the more the rights of the owner are subjected to statutory limitations aimed at the protection of the rights of the users.

Bolling et al. v. Sharpe (Public School Segregation Cases). [347 U.S. 497 (1954)]. Racial segregation in public schools in the District of Columbia is a denial of due process of the 14th Amendment, as stated in *Brown v. Board of Education*.

Chimel v. California. [89 Sup. Ct. 2034 (1969)]. Limited the scope and degree of search by police without warrant.

Hoffa v. United States. 385 U.S. 293 (1966)]. Jimmy Hoffa, the former boss of the Teamsters, was charged with bribing a juror and had deprived the government of an informant. Hoffa's contention was that his rights had been violated by the government using informants against him. Hoffa lost.

Joint Anti-Fascist Refugee Committee v. McGrath. [341 U.S. 123 (1951)]. An act by the U.S. Attorney General of placing organizations on the subversive organizations list without prior notification of those organizations or without a hearing, is a capricious and an arbitrary act directed against individual freedoms.

Katz v. United States. [389 U.S. 347 (1967)]. Any electronic surveillance (mainly telephone wire-tapping) without specific authorization violates one's rights under the 1st Amendment.

Lochner v. New York. [198 U.S. 45 (1905)]. Defined liberty as including the freedom of contract, and state legislatures have limited power over free enterprise activity under their jurisdiction.

Malloy v. Hogan. [378 U.S. 1 (1964)]. The right to protection against self-incrimination is safeguarded against state action by the provisions of the 14th Amendment.

Munn v. Illinois. [94 U.S. 113 (1877)]. In a series of the so-called "Granger Cases," the Court ruled that maximum controls will be placed on railroads and grain storage facilities on the principle that "the more a business extends into society and that society becomes dependent on it and can be injured by it, the more the public has the right to control the practices of that business."

Olmstead v. United States. [277 U.S. 438 (1928)]. Wiretapping does not violate the unreasonable search and seizure clause of the 4th Amendment, but Justices Holmes and Brandeis dissented. They noted the close relationship between the self-incrimination provision and the unreasonable search and seizure.

Palko v. Connecticut. [302 U.S. 319 (1937)]. In the search to find a distinction between "essential" and "nonessential" rights of the defendant in criminal cases, the Court ruled that only the essential rights are protected in the Bill of Rights from abridgement by the state.

Slaughter House Cases. [16 Wall. 36 (1873)]. In its first test to interpret the provisions of the 14th Amendment, the Court held that (1) the 14th Amendment did not make the first eight Amendments to the Constitution incumbent upon states; (2) the majority opinion advanced the doctrine of dual citizenship whereby the federal government and the states each had its own category of immunities and privileges which they were obliged to respect. As a result, it was not incumbent upon the U.S. Government to take responsibility for the protection of the rights and privileges of the individual, but that function was to be shared with the states.

Trop v. Dulles. [356 U.S. 86 (1958)]. An American citizen may not be deprived citizenship (be denationalized) upon conviction of a felonious crime. The decision, delivered by Chief Justice Earl Warren, declared the Nationality Act of 1940 which authorized such measures unconstitutional. The Chief Justice stated that: "citizenship is not a license that expires." See CITIZENSHIP.

11. EQUAL PROTECTION POWER

Bakke Case. See **Regents of the University of California v. Bakke.**

Brown et al. v. Board of Education (Public School Segregation Cases). [347 U.S. 483 (1954)]. The doctrine of 'separate but equal' has no place in the field of public education, because it violates the equal protection of law provision of the 14th Amendment. Separate facilities are inherently unequal. It also indirectly overturned *Plessy v. Ferguson*.

Brown v. Board of Education (Second Case). [349 U.S. 294 (1955)]. Urged prompt compliance with desegregation of public schools in all districts where segregation prevailed.

Civil Rights Cases. [109 U.S. 3 (1883)]. The Civil Rights Acts of 1875 was held unconstitutional on the grounds that the 14th Amendment prohibits discrimination by states, but did not apply to private persons who might discriminate against Negroes.

Cooper v. Aaron. [358 U.S. 1 (1958)]. Refused to postpone the desegregation plan for the Little Rock, Arkansas school system. Desegregation was to proceed without exception in all states.

Crosson v. City of the City of Richmond, Virginia. [397 U.S. 168 (1989)]. When the City of Richmond—with a majority of black members on the Council—set aside 30% of all construction work to be awarded to minority (mainly black) business—subcontractors, the Supreme Court ruled in 1989 against it on the grounds that such program "was not tailored to remedy any specific acts of discrimination in the construction industry."

Dred Scott v. Sanford. [19 How. 393 (1857)]. The Taney Court gave recognition to the primacy of state over national citizenship (and an obvious support to the states' rights doctrine) when it ruled that Scott, a Negro, was a state and not a national citizen and, therefore, must be returned from freedom to slavery.

Gomillion v. Lightfoot. [364 U. S. 339 (1960)]. The legislature of the State of Alabama was restrained in redistricting the City of Tuskeegee in such a manner that it would deprive Negroes the right to vote and to equal representation in the town government. This practice was considered to be premeditated gerrymadering.

Keyishain v. Board of Regents. [385 U. S. 589 (1967)]. Voided all requirements for loyalty oaths and employment provisions as to membership in the Communist Party, which were directed against the entire membership rather than specific subversive acts or activities.

Murphy v. Waterfront Commission. [378 U. S. 52 (1964)]. A witness may exercise his privilege to refuse to answer questions in cases where immunity can be applied, unless that person in assured against prosecution by both state and federal authorities.

Plessy v. Ferguson. [163 U. S. 537 (1896).] The Court upheld a Louisiana statute which required separate but equal railroad and other facilities for blacks and whites. This ruling was upset by *Brown v. Board of Education.*

Regents of the University of California v. Bakke. (No. 76-881, *United States Report,* the United States Code). In the fall of 1972, Allen Bakke, a white Vietnam Veteran, applied for admission to the University of California Medical School at Davis. Despite his high academic standing, he was denied admission while minority students with less qualification were admitted. Title VI, Section 601 of the 1964 Civil Rights Act states that, "no person in the United States shall, on the ground of race, color, or national orgin, be excluded from participation in . . . any program or activity receiving Federal financial assistance." The school reserved 16 places in the beginning class of 100 students for minorities. Bakke sued the school because he felt that this quota policy was in violation of Title VI, Section 601 thus allowing him to be a victim of reverse discrimination. After 6 years of litigation, Bakke's case was finally decided on June 28, 1978, in his favor by a 5-4 decision of the United States Supreme Court. There was a broad spectrum of legal opinion amongst the Justices upon this decision. Justice Lewis F. Powell, Jr. wrote the controlling opinion: "The guarantee of equal protection cannot mean one thing when applied to one individual and something else when applied to a person of another color. If both are not accorded the same protection, then it is not equal . . . ." Justice John Paul Stevens's opinion upheld the legality of Title VI, Section 601; however, he stated that "the university , through its special-admissions policy, excluded Bakke from participation in its program . . . because of his race. The university also acknowledges that it was, and still is, receiving Federal financial assistance . . . (thus violating Title VI, Section 601). It is therefore our duty to affirm the judgement ordering Bakke admitted to the university." Justice William J. Brennan, Jr. led the minority opinion in the decision in approving the school's admissions policy and approving the denial of admission to Bakke. He said "a state government may adopt race-conscious programs if the purpose of such programs is to remove the disparate racial impact its actions might otherwise have . . . . There is no question that Davis's program (the school in question) is valid under this test." Associate Justice Thurgood Marshall, the only black member of the Supreme Court, wrote a separate minority opinion. He said that "while I applaud the judgement of the Court that a university may consider race in its admissions process, it is more than a little ironic that, after several hundred years of class-based discrimination against Negroes, the Court is unwilling to hold that a class-based remedy for that discrimination is permissible." The Court's decision thus decided for Bakke on the merits of his specific case while upholding Title VI, Section 601 of the 1964 Civil Rights Act implying that future cases of this nature will have to be decided individually based upon the facts of each case.

Reitman v. Mulkey. [387 U. S. 369 (1967)]. As pertains to open housing the states were not required to insert into their constitutions provisions barring antidiscrimination statutes in the future.

Reynolds v. Sims. See **Baker v. Carr.**

Shapiro v. Thompson. [89 Sup. Ct. 1322 (1969)]. Lengthy state residency requirements for welfare recipients were eliminated.

Shelley v. Kraemer. [334 U. S. 1 (1948)]. Past agreements on residential segregation were void under the 14th Amendment.

South Carolina v. Katzenbach. [383 U. S. 301 (1966)]. The Supreme Court upheld the constitutionality of the Voting Rights Act of 1965.

Sweatt v. Painter. [339 U. S. 629 (1950)]. In order to avoid collision with the law, the University of Texas established a separate law school for one black student, but the Court found that school to be inferior and considered the entire scheme to be unacceptable. The student was admitted to the regular school and the case of *Plessy v. Ferguson* was buried again.

United States v. Rabinovitz. [339 U. S. 56 (1950)]. Search without a warrant is legal if preceded by a lawful arrest.

Wesberry v. Sanders. [376 U. S. 1 (1964)]. The Court applied the one-man, one-vote principle not only to state legislatures, but also to congressional districts. The Court said: ". . . as nearly as practical, one person's vote in a Congressional election must be worth as much as another's."

12. FREEDOM OF RELIGION

Abington School District v. Schempp. [359 U. S. 187 (1959)]. Compulsory recitation of the Lord's Prayer and Bible reading are in violation of the provisions of Amendments I and XIV of the U. S. Constitution.

Cantwell v. Connecticut. [310 U. S. 296 (1940)]. Amendment 14th places restrictions on states in matters of freedom of religion which is guaranteed in Amendment I.

Employment Division (of the State of Oregon) v. Smith. [168 U. S. 672 (1990)]. The U. S. Supreme Court held that the state of Oregon was justified in denying unemployment benefits to two American Indians when they lost their employment with the state for using prohibited-by-law drugs. In this case, the Indians had participated in a ritual involving ingestion of peyote. The Indians claimed that the state action was violating their religious freedom, because the drug is an ancient traditional part of the religous ritual of the tribe. Justice Antonin Scalia argued that "the exercise of religion deserves no special protection, as long as the law or regulation impinging on it is 'neutral' and 'general applicable.'" The Court also added that "Although the First Amendment bans any law 'prohibiting the free exercise' of religion, all rights have some limitations."

Engel v. Vitale. [370 U. S. 421 (1962)]. A nondenominational prayer prepared by the New York Board of Regents for use in public schools violated the separation of church and state provisions of the U. S. Constitution.

Everson v. Board of Education. [330 U. S. 1 (1947)]. The establishment of the religion clause of the 1st Amendment applies to states as well as to the federal government.

Illinois ex rel. McCollum v. Board of Education. [333 U. S. 203 (1948)]. The use of school facilities, a public property, for released time religious education violates the doctrine of separation of church and state.

West Virginia State Board of Education v. Barnette. [319 U. S. 624 (1943)]. Students in public schools may not be required to salute the U. S. flag.

Yoder v. Wisconsin. [337 U. S. 414 (1972)]. The Old Amish group in Wisconsin demanded that their children not be required to attend school once they complete the eighth grade. The U. S. Supreme Court set a widely accepted standard: "Government should not restrict or burden religious practice unless it was necessary to serve a 'compelling' state interest and was the least restrictive way of doing so." The state of Wisconsin lost.

13. RIGHT TO PRIVACY

Roe v. Wade. [410 U. S. 113 (1973)]. The Court ruled that while the state (Texas) has an "important and legitimate interest in preserving and protecting the health of the pregnant woman" it may not "override the rights of the pregnant woman that are at stake." The woman sought to end her pregnancy by abortion.

Time, Inc. v. Hill. [385 U. S. 374 (1967)]. Upholding the New York statute on privacy, the Court declared that the news media may not violate basic human rights to privacy while seeking news.

SOURCES ON U. S. SUPREME COURT DECISIONS

P.B. Kurland, ed. *The Supreme Court Review, 1963* through *1977;* U. S. Government Printing Office. *United States Reports* (cited as "U. S."), *Preliminary Prints* (containing each decision before final binding); Bureau of National Affairs. *United States Law Week* (contains each opinion in a separate form); Commerce Clearing House. *Supreme Court Bulletin* (contains opinions announced by the Court before they appear in official binding); Cooperative Publishing Company. *Unites States Supreme Court Reports, Lawyers' Edition* (cited as "L. Ed. "); and West Publishing Company. *Supreme Court Reporter* (cited as "Sup. Ct."). The *Reporter* contains cases decided since 1882 (for earlier souces see UNITED STATES REPORTS).

SOURCES ON LOWER FEDERAL COURT DECISIONS

Decisions by Federal District Courts and Federal Courts of Appeal can be found in 300 volumes ending in 1924 in the *Federal Register* (cited as "Fed." or "F"), and after 1924, in the *Federal Reporter, second series* (cited as "Fed.(2d)" or "F 2d."). Since 1934, all decisions by the District Courts are published in *Federal Supplement* (cited as "F. Supp." or "F.S.")

SOURCES ON STATE COURT DECISIONS

Decisions by state supreme courts are published regionally. For example, the *Atlantic Reporter* carries decisions (since 1885) of Connecticut, Delaware, Maine, Maryland, New Hampshire, New Jersey, Pennsylvania, Rhode Island and Vermont; the *Southern Reporter* carries decisions of Alabama, Florida, Louisiana and Mississippi (since 1887); and similar *Reports* serve the Northeastern, Northwestern, Pacific, Southeastern and Southwestern regions.

APPENDIX 49

How to Read a United States Supreme Court Case

Title of Case			Citation
Willie	v. versus (against)	Johnny	205 U.S. 18; 30 Sup. Ct. 876; 53 L. Ed. 839 (1993)
Plaintiff or Petitioner (in *certiorari*) or Appellant (in Appeal)		Defendant or Respondent or Appellee	

The Citation means that the full text of the decision in this hypothetical case can be located in Volume 205 of the *United State Reports* at page 18, or in Volume 30 of the *Supreme Court Reporter* at page 876, or in Volume 53 of the *Lawyer's Edition* at page 839 for the year of 1993. Lower federal and state court cases read similarly.

APPENDIX 51

The Tree of Human Rights and Liberties

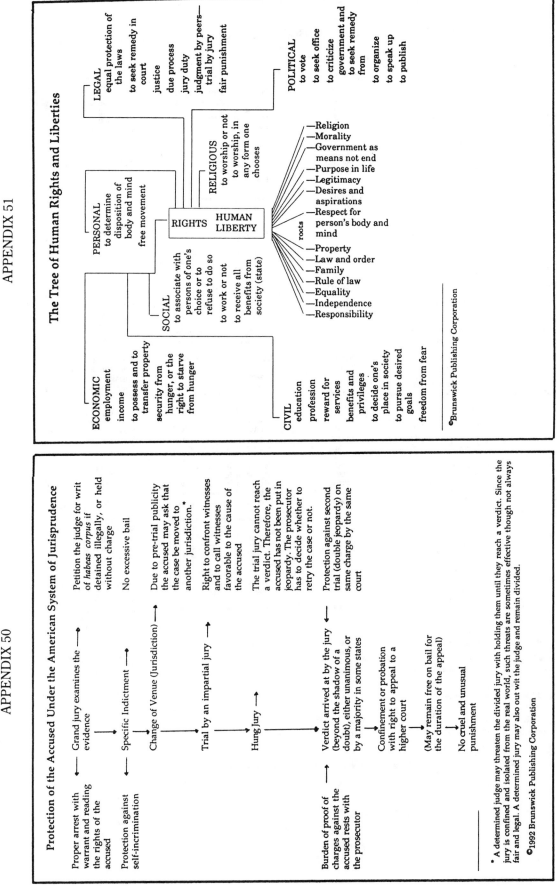

©Brunswick Publishing Corporation

APPENDIX 50

Protection of the Accused Under the American System of Jurisprudence

Proper arrest with warrant and reading the rights of the accused

Protection against self-incrimination

Grand jury examines the evidence → Petition the judge for writ of *habeas corpus* if detained illegally, or held without charge

No excessive bail

Specific Indictment →

Change of Venue (Jurisdiction) → Due to pre-trial publicity the accused may ask that the case be moved to another jurisdiction.*

Right to confront witnesses and to call witnesses favorable to the cause of the accused

Trial by an impartial jury →

Hung Jury → The trial jury cannot reach a verdict. Therefore, the accused has not been put in jeopardy. The prosecutor has to decide whether to retry the case or not.

Burden of proof of charges against the accused rests with the prosecutor

Verdict arrived at by the jury (beyond the shadow of a doubt), either unanimous, or by a majority in some states

Protection against second trial (double jeopardy) on same charge by the same court

Confinement or probation with right to appeal to a higher court

(May remain free on bail for the duration of the appeal)

No cruel and unusual punishment

* A determined judge may threaten the divided jury with holding them until they reach a verdict. Since the jury is confined and isolated from the real world, such threats are sometimes effective though not always fair and legal. A determined jury may also out wit the judge and remain divided.

©1992 Brunswick Publishing Corporation

APPENDIX 52

Names of State Legislative Bodies and Convening Places

State or other jurisdiction	Both bodies	Upper house	Lower house	Convening place
Alabama	Legislature	Senate	House of Representatives	State Capitol
Alaska	Legislature	Senate	House of Representatives	State Capitol
Arizona	Legislature	Senate	House of Representatives	State Capitol
Arkansas	General Assembly	Senate	House of Representatives	State Capitol
California	Legislature	Senate	Assembly	State Capitol
Colorado	General Assembly	Senate	House of Representatives	State Capitol
Connecticut	General Assembly	Senate	House of Representatives	State Capitol
Delaware	General Assembly	Senate	House of Representatives	Legislative Hall
Florida	Legislature	Senate	House of Representatives	The Capitol
Georgia	General Assembly	Senate	House of Representatives	State Capitol
Hawaii	Legislature	Senate	House of Representatives	State Capitol
Idaho	Legislature	Senate	House of Representatives	State Capitol
Illinois	General Assembly	Senate	House of Representatives	State House
Indiana	General Assembly	Senate	House of Representatives	State House
Iowa	General Assembly	Senate	House of Representatives	State Capitol
Kansas	Legislature	Senate	House of Representatives	State House
Kentucky	General Assembly	Senate	House of Representatives	State Capitol
Louisiana	Legislature	Senate	House of Representatives	State Capitol
Maine	Legislature	Senate	House of Representatives	State House
Maryland	General Assembly	Senate	House of Delegates	State House
Massachusetts	General Court	Senate	House of Representatives	State House
Michigan	Legislature	Senate	House of Representatives	State Capitol
Minnesota	Legislature	Senate	House of Representatives	State Capitol
Mississippi	Legislature	Senate	House of Representatives	New Capitol
Missouri	General Assembly	Senate	House of Representatives	State Capitol
Montana	Legislature	Senate	House of Representatives	State Capitol
Nebraska	Legislature	(a)		State Capitol
Nevada	Legislature	Senate	Assembly	Legislative Building
New Hampshire	General Court	Senate	House of Representatives	State House
New Jersey	Legislature	Senate	General Assembly	State House
New Mexico	Legislature	Senate	House of Representatives	State Capitol
New York	Legislature	Senate	Assembly	State Capitol
North Carolina	General Assembly	Senate	House of Representatives	State Legislative Building
North Dakota	Legislative Assembly	Senate	House of Representatives	State Capitol
Ohio	General Assembly	Senate	House of Representatives	State House
Oklahoma	Legislature	Senate	House of Representatives	State Capitol
Oregon	Legislative Assembly	Senate	House of Representatives	State Capitol
Pennsylvania	General Assembly	Senate	House of Representatives	Main Capitol Building
Rhode Island	General Assembly	Senate	House of Representatives	State House
South Carolina	General Assembly	Senate	House of Representatives	State House
South Dakota	Legislature	Senate	House of Representatives	State Capitol
Tennessee	General Assembly	Senate	House of Representatives	State Capitol
Texas	Legislature	Senate	House of Representatives	State Capitol
Utah	Legislature	Senate	House of Representatives	State Capitol
Vermont	General Assembly	Senate	House of Representatives	State House
Virginia	General Assembly	Senate	House of Delegates	State Capitol
Washington	Legislature	Senate	House of Representatives	Legislative Building
West Virginia	Legislature	Senate	House of Delegates	State Capitol
Wisconsin	Legislature	Senate	Assembly (b)	State Capitol
Wyoming	Legislature	Senate	House of Representatives	State Capitol
Dist. of Columbia	Council of the District of Columbia	(a)		District Building
American Samoa	Legislature	Senate	House of Representatives	Maota Fono
Guam	Legislature	(a)		Congress Building
No. Mariana Islands	Legislature	Senate	House of Representatives	Civic Center
Puerto Rico	Legislative Assembly	Senate	House of Representatives	The Capitol
Federated States of Micronesia	Congress	(a)		Congress Office Building
U.S. Virgin Islands	Legislature	(a)		Capitol Building

(a) Unicameral legislature. Except in Dist. of Columbia, members go by the title Senator.
(b) Members of the lower house go by the title Representative.

© 1992 The Council of State Governments. Reprinted with permission from *The Book of the States*.

APPENDIX 53

Legislative Process in the United States: The State Level*

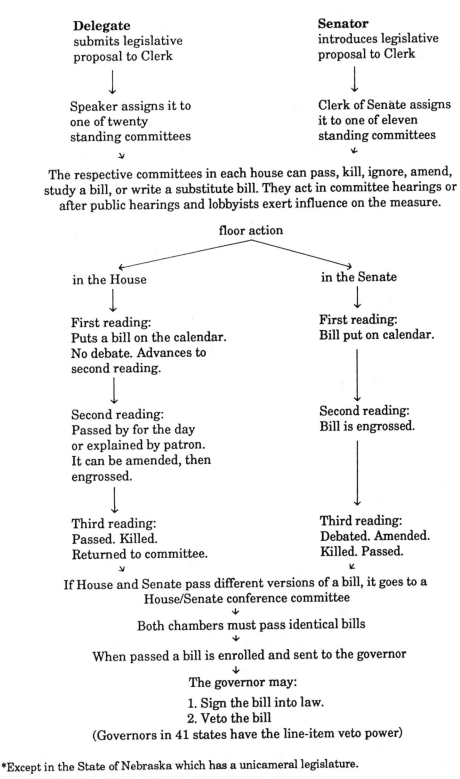

Delegate
submits legislative
proposal to Clerk

↓

Speaker assigns it to
one of twenty
standing committees

Senator
introduces legislative
proposal to Clerk

↓

Clerk of Senate assigns
it to one of eleven
standing committees

The respective committees in each house can pass, kill, ignore, amend, study a bill, or write a substitute bill. They act in committee hearings or after public hearings and lobbyists exert influence on the measure.

floor action

in the House

↓

First reading:
Puts a bill on the calendar.
No debate. Advances to
second reading.

↓

Second reading:
Passed by for the day
or explained by patron.
It can be amended, then
engrossed.

↓

Third reading:
Passed. Killed.
Returned to committee.

in the Senate

↓

First reading:
Bill put on calendar.

Second reading:
Bill is engrossed.

Third reading:
Debated. Amended.
Killed. Passed.

If House and Senate pass different versions of a bill, it goes to a
House/Senate conference committee

Both chambers must pass identical bills

When passed a bill is enrolled and sent to the governor

The governor may:

1. Sign the bill into law.
2. Veto the bill

(Governors in 41 states have the line-item veto power)

*Except in the State of Nebraska which has a unicameral legislature.

APPENDIX 54

Legislative Sessions: Legal Provisions

State or other jurisdiction	Regular sessions				Special sessions		
	Legislature convenes			Limitation on length of session (a)	Legislature may call	Legislature may determine subject	Limitation on length of session
	Year	Month	Day				
Alabama	Annual	Jan. Apr. Feb.	2nd Tues. (b) 3rd Tues. (c,d) 1st Tues. (e)	30 L in 105 C	No	Yes (f)	12 L in 30 C
Alaska	Annual	Jan. Jan.	3rd Mon. (c) 2nd Mon. (e)	120 C (g)	By 2/3 vote of members	Yes (h)	30 C
Arizona	Annual	Jan.	2nd Mon.	(i)	By petition, 2/3 members, each house	Yes (h)	None
Arkansas	Biennial-odd year	Jan.	2nd Mon.	60 C (g)	No	Yes (f,j)	(j)
California	(k)	Jan.	1st Mon. (d)	None	No	No	None
Colorado	Annual	Jan.	Wed. after 1st Tues.	(l)	By request, 2/3 members, each house	Yes (h)	None
Connecticut	Annual (m)	Jan. Feb.	Wed. after 1st Mon. (n) Wed. after 1st Mon. (o)	(p)	Yes (q)	(q)	None (r)
Delaware	Annual	Jan.	2nd Tues.	June 30	Joint call, presiding officers, both houses	Yes	None
Florida	Annual	Apr.	Tues. after 1st Mon. (d)	60 C (g)	Joint call, presiding officers, both houses	Yes	20 C (g)
Georgia	Annual	Jan.	2nd Mon. (d)	40 L	By petition, 3/5 members, each house	Yes (h)	(s)
Hawaii	Annual	Jan.	3rd Wed.	60 L (g)	By petition, 2/3 members, each house	Yes	30 L (g)
Idaho	Annual	Jan.	Mon. on or nearest 9th day	None	No	No	20 C
Illinois	Annual	Jan.	2nd Wed.	None	Joint call, presiding officers, both houses	Yes	None
Indiana	Annual	Jan.	2nd Mon. (d,t)	odd-61 L or Apr. 30; even-30 L or Mar. 15	No	Yes	30 L in 40 C
Iowa	Annual	Jan.	2nd Mon.	(u)	By petition, 2/3 members, both houses	Yes	None
Kansas	Annual	Jan.	2nd Mon.	odd-None; even-90 C (g)	Petition to governor of 2/3 members, each house	Yes	None
Kentucky	Biennial-even yr.	Jan.	Tues. after 1st Mon. (d)	60 L (v)	No	No	None
Louisiana	Annual	Apr.	3rd Mon.	60 L in 85 C	By petition, majority, each house	Yes (h)	30 C
Maine	(k,m)	Dec. Jan.	1st Wed. (b) Wed. after 1st Tues. (o)	100 L (g) 50 L (g)	Joint call, presiding officers, with consent of majority of members of each political party, each house	Yes (h)	None
Maryland	Annual	Jan.	2nd Wed.	90 C (g)	By petition, majority, each house	Yes	30 C
Massachusetts	Annual	Jan.	1st Wed.	None	By petition (w)	Yes	None
Michigan	Annual	Jan.	2nd Wed. (d)	None	No	No	None

© 1992 The Council of State Governments. Reprinted with permission from *The Book of the States*.

Legislative Sessions: Legal Provisions, continued

State or other jurisdiction	Regular sessions — Legislature convenes			Limitation on length of session (a)	Special sessions — Legislature may call	Legislature may determine subject	Limitation on length of session
	Year	Month	Day				
Minnesota	(x)	Jan.	Tues. after 1st Mon. (n)	120 L or 1st Mon. after 3rd Sat. in May (x)	No	Yes	None
Mississippi	Annual	Jan.	Tues. after 1st Mon.	125 C (g,y); 90 C (g,y)	No	No	None
Missouri	Annual	Jan.	Wed. after 1st Mon.	odd-June 30; even-May 15	No	No	60 C
Montana	Biennial-odd yr.	Jan.	1st Mon.	90 L (g)	By petition, majority, both houses	Yes	None
Nebraska	Annual	Jan.	Wed. after 1st Mon.	odd-90 L (g); even-60 L (g)	By petition, 2/3 members, each house	Yes	None
Nevada	Biennial-odd yr.	Jan.	3rd Mon.	60 C (u)	No	No	20 C(u)
New Hampshire	Annual	Jan.	Wed. after 1st Tues. (d)	45 L	By 2/3 vote of members	Yes	(u)
New Jersey	Annual	Jan.	2nd Tues.	None	By petition, majority, each house	Yes	None
New Mexico	Annual (m)	Jan.	3rd Tues.	odd-60 C; even-30 C	By petition, 3/5 members, each house	Yes (h)	30 C
New York	Annual	Jan.	Wed. after 1st Mon.	None	By petition, 2/3 members, each house	Yes (h)	None
North Carolina	(x)	Jan.	Wed. after 2nd Mon. (n)	None (x)	By petition, 3/5 members, each house	Yes	None
North Dakota	Biennial-odd yr.	Jan.	Tues. after Jan. 3, but not later than Jan. 11 (d)	80 L (z)	No	Yes	None
Ohio	Annual	Jan.	1st Mon.	None	Joint call, presiding officers, both houses	Yes	None
Oklahoma	Annual	Feb.	(ff)	90 L	By 2/3 vote of members	Yes	None
Oregon	Biennial-odd yr.	Jan.	2nd Mon.	None	By petition, majority, each house	Yes	None
Pennsylvania	Annual	Jan.	1st Tues.	None	By petition, majority, each house	No	None
Rhode Island	Annual	Jan.	1st Tues.	60 L (u)	No	No	None
South Carolina	Annual	Jan.	2nd Tues. (d)	1st Thurs. in June (g)	No	Yes	None
South Dakota	Annual	Jan.	Tues. after 1st Mon.	odd-40 L; even-35 L	No	No	None
Tennessee	(x)	Jan.	(aa)	90 L (u)	By petition, 2/3 members, each house	Yes	30 L (u)
Texas	Biennial-odd yr.	Jan.	2nd Tues.	140 C	By petition, 2/3 members, each house	No	30 C
Utah	Annual	Jan.	2nd Mon.	60 C	No	No	30 C
Vermont	(x)	Jan.	Wed. after 1st Mon. (n)	(u)	No	Yes	None
Virginia	Annual	Jan.	2nd Wed.	odd-30 C (g); even-60 C (g)	By petition, 2/3 members, each house	Yes	None
Washington	Annual	Jan.	2nd Mon.	odd-105 C; even-60 C	By petition, 2/3 members, each house	Yes	30 C

Legislative Sessions: Legal Provisions, continued

State or other jurisdiction	Regular sessions				Special sessions		
	Legislature convenes			Limitation on length of session (a)	Legislature may call	Legislature may determine subject	Limitation on length of session
	Year	Month	Day				
West Virginia	Annual	Feb. Jan.	2nd Wed. (c,d) 2nd Wed. (e)	60 C (g)	By petition, 3/5 members, each house	Yes (bb)	None
Wisconsin..........	Annual (cc)	Jan.	1st Tues. after Jan. 8 (d,n)	None	No	No	None
Wyoming	Annual (m)	Jan. Feb.	2nd Tues. (n) 2nd Tues. (o)	odd-40 L; even-20 L	No	Yes	None
Dist. of Columbia	(dd)	Jan.	2nd day	None			
American Samoa	Annual	Jan. July	2nd Mon. 2nd Mon.	45 L 45 L	No	No	None
Guam	Annual	Jan.	1st Mon. (ee)	None	No	No	None
Puerto Rico..........	Annual	Jan.	2nd Mon.	Apr. 30 (g)	No	No	20 C
U.S. Virgin Islands	Annual	Jan.	2nd Mon.	75 L	No	No	15 C

APPENDIX 55

Record of Passage of Uniform Acts*

(As of September 30, 1989)

State or other jurisdiction	Alcoholism and Intoxication Treatment (1971)	Anatomical Gift (1968) (1987)	Arbitration (1956)	Attendance of Out of State Witnesses (1931) (1936)	Audio-Visual Deposition (1978)	Certification of Questions of Law (1967)	Child Custody Jurisdiction (1968)	Class Actions (1976) (1987)	Commercial Code (1951) (1957) (1962) (1966)	Commercial Code-Article 2A (1987)	Commercial Code-Article 4A (1989)	Commercial Code-Article 6 (1989)	Commercial Code-Article 8 (1977)	Commercial Code-Article 9 (1972)	Common Interest Ownership (1982)
Alabama	...	★	...	•	...	...	★	...	•	...	...	...	...	★	★
Alaska	★	★	★	•	...	...	★	...	•	...	...	...	...	★	...
Arizona	...	★	★	•	...	...	★	...	•	...	...	...	★	★	...
Arkansas	...	•	☆	★	...	...	★	...	•	★	...	...	★	★	...
California	...	★	☆	•	...	...	★	...	•	...	...	...	★	★	...
Colorado	★	★	★	•	...	★	★	...	•	...	...	...	★	★	★
Connecticut	☆	•	☆	•	...	★	★	...	•	...	...	...	★	★	...
Delaware	★	★	★	•	...	...	★	...	•	...	...	...	★	★	...
Florida	☆	★	★	•	...	☆	★	...	•	...	...	...	...	★	...
Georgia	★	★	...	•	...	...	★	...	•	...	...	...	...	...	...
Hawaii	...	•	☆	•	...	...	★	...	•	...	...	...	★	★	...
Idaho	★	•	★	★	...	...	★	...	•	...	...	...	★	★	...
Illinois	★	★	★	★	...	...	★	...	•	...	...	...	★	★	...
Indiana	...	★	★	•	...	...	★	...	•	...	...	...	★	★	...
Iowa	★	★	★	☆	...	★	★	★	•	...	...	...	★	★	...
Kansas	★	★	★	•	...	★	★	...	•	...	...	...	★	★	...
Kentucky	...	★	★	•	...	...	★	...	•	...	...	...	★	★	...
Louisiana	...	☆	★	•	...	...	★	...	•	...	...	...	★	★	...
Maine	★	★	★	•	...	☆	★	...	•	...	...	...	★	★	...
Maryland	☆	★	★	•	...	...	★	★	•	...	...	...	★	★	...
Massachusetts	☆	★	★	•	...	★	☆	...	•	...	...	...	★	★	...
Michigan	☆	★	☆	☆	...	...	★	...	•	★	...	...	★	★	...
Minnesota	☆	★	★	•	...	★	★	...	•	...	...	...	...	★	...
Mississippi	...	★	...	•	...	...	★	...	•	...	...	...	...	★	...
Missouri	...	★	☆	•	...	...	★	...	•	...	...	...	...	...	...
Montana	★	•	★	•	★	...	★	...	•	...	...	...	★	★	...
Nebraska	...	★	★	•	...	...	★	...	•	★	...	...	★	★	...
Nevada	...	•	★	•	...	★	★	...	•	...	...	...	★	★	...
New Hampshire	...	★	☆	•	...	...	★	...	•	...	...	...	★	★	...
New Jersey	...	★	☆	•	...	...	★	...	•	...	...	...	★	★	...
New Mexico	...	★	★	•	...	...	★	...	•	...	...	...	★	★	...
New York	...	★	★	☆	...	...	★	...	•	...	...	...	★	★	...
North Carolina	...	★	★	•	...	...	★	★	•	...	...	...	★	★	...
North Dakota	...	•	★	★	★	★	★	★	•	...	...	...	★	★	...
Ohio	...	★	☆	•	...	...	★	...	•	...	...	...	★	★	...
Oklahoma	★	★	★	•	...	★	★	...	•	★	...	...	★	★	...
Oregon	...	★	☆	•	...	★	★	...	•	★	...	...	...	★	...
Pennsylvania	...	★	★	•	...	...	★	...	•	...	...	...	★	★	...
Rhode Island	☆	★	☆	★	...	★	★	...	•	...	...	...	...	★	...
South Carolina	...	★	★	•	...	...	★	...	...	...	...	...	...	...	...
South Dakota	★	★	★	•	...	...	★	...	•	★	...	...	★	★	...
Tennessee	...	★	★	•	...	...	★	...	•	...	...	...	★	★	...
Texas	...	★	☆	•	...	...	★	...	•	★	...	...	★	★	...
Utah	...	•	★	•	...	...	★	...	•	...	...	...	...	...	...
Vermont	...	★	...	•	...	...	★	...	•	...	...	...	...	...	...
Virginia	...	★	★	•	★	...	★	...	•	...	...	★	★	★	...
Washington	★	★	☆	•	...	☆	★	...	•	...	...	...	★	★	★
West Virginia	...	★	...	•	...	★	★	...	•	...	...	...	★	★	...
Wisconsin	★	★	☆	•	...	...	★	...	•	...	...	...	★	★	...
Wyoming	...	★	★	★	...	...	★	...	•	...	...	...	...	...	...
Dist. of Columbia	☆	★	★	•	...	★	★	...	•	...	...	...	...	★	...
Puerto Rico	...	...	☆	★	...	...	...	...	•	...	...	...	...	...	...
U.S. Virgin Islands	...	...	☆	•	...	...	★	...	•	...	...	...	...	...	...

Source: National Conference of Commissioners on Uniform State Laws.

Key:

★ — Enacted
• — Amended version enacted
☆ — Substantially similar version enacted
. . . — Not enacted

*Partial, exemplary listing.

APPENDIX 56

Record of Passage of Model Acts
(As of September 30, 1989)

State or other jurisdiction	Act to Provide for the Appointment of Commissioners (1944)	Anti-Discrimination (1966)	Class Actions (1976) (1987)	Eminent Domain Code (1974)	Insanity Defense and Post-Trial Disposition (1984)	Juvenile Court (1968)	Land Sales Practices (1966)	Minor Student Capacity to Borrow (1969)	Periodic Payment of Judgments (1980)	Post-Mortem Examinations (1954)	Public Defender (1970) (1974)	Real Estate Cooperative (1981)	Real Estate Time-Share (1980) (1982)	State Administrative Procedures (1981)	Statutory Construction (1965)	Water Use (1958)
Alabama	★	...	...	★	...	...	...	...	...	...	...	...	...	...	...	...
Alaska	...	...	...	...	...	...	★	...	...	...	...	...	...	...	...	...
Arizona	★	...	...	...	...	...	...	★	...	...	...	...	...	...	...	...
Arkansas	★	...	...	...	...	...	...	...	...	...	...	...	...	★	...	...
California	...	...	...	...	...	...	...	...	...	...	...	...	...	...	...	...
Colorado	...	...	...	...	...	...	...	...	...	...	...	...	...	...	★	...
Connecticut	...	...	...	...	...	...	★	★	...	...	...	...	...	...	...	...
Delaware	...	...	...	...	...	...	...	...	...	...	...	...	...	...	...	...
Florida	...	...	...	...	...	...	★	...	...	...	...	...	...	...	...	...
Georgia	...	...	...	...	...	☆	☆	...	...	...	...	...	...	...	...	...
Hawaii	...	★	...	...	...	...	★	...	...	...	...	...	...	...	...	...
Idaho	...	...	...	...	...	...	...	...	...	...	...	...	...	...	...	☆
Illinois	...	...	...	...	...	...	...	...	...	...	...	...	...	...	...	...
Indiana	...	...	...	...	...	...	...	...	...	...	...	...	...	...	...	...
Iowa	★	...	★	...	...	...	...	...	...	...	...	...	...	...	★	...
Kansas	...	...	...	...	...	...	★	...	...	...	...	...	...	...	...	...
Kentucky	★	...	...	...	...	...	...	...	...	...	...	...	...	...	...	...
Louisiana	...	...	...	...	...	...	...	...	...	...	...	...	...	...	...	...
Maine	★	...	...	...	...	...	...	...	...	...	...	...	☆	...	...	...
Maryland	...	...	...	...	...	...	...	...	...	...	☆	...	☆	...	...	...
Massachusetts	...	...	...	...	...	...	...	...	...	...	...	...	•	...	...	...
Michigan	...	...	...	...	...	...	...	...	...	...	...	...	...	...	...	...
Minnesota	...	...	...	...	...	...	...	...	...	...	...	...	...	...	...	...
Mississippi	★	...	...	...	...	...	...	...	...	...	...	...	...	...	...	...
Missouri	...	...	...	...	...	...	...	...	...	...	...	...	...	...	...	...
Montana	★	...	...	...	...	...	★	...	...	...	...	...	...	...	...	...
Nebraska	★	...	...	...	...	...	...	☆	...	...	...	...	...	...	...	...
Nevada	...	...	...	...	...	...	...	...	...	...	...	...	...	...	...	...
New Hampshire	★	...	...	...	...	...	...	...	...	...	...	...	...	...	...	...
New Jersey	...	...	...	...	...	...	...	...	...	...	...	...	...	...	...	...
New Mexico	...	...	...	...	...	...	...	...	...	...	...	...	...	...	...	...
New York	...	...	...	...	...	...	...	...	...	...	...	...	...	...	...	...
North Carolina	...	...	...	...	...	...	...	...	...	...	...	...	...	...	...	...
North Dakota	...	...	★	...	☆	★	★	...	...	...	...	...	...	...	...	...
Ohio	...	...	...	...	...	...	...	...	...	...	...	...	...	...	...	...
Oklahoma	...	★	...	...	...	...	...	★	...	...	...	★	...	...	...	...
Oregon	★	★	...	...	...	...	...	...	...	...	...	★	...	...	...	...
Pennsylvania	...	...	...	...	...	...	...	...	...	...	...	...	...	...	...	...
Rhode Island	...	...	...	...	...	...	...	...	...	...	...	...	★	...	...	...
South Carolina	...	...	...	...	...	...	...	...	...	...	...	...	...	...	...	...
South Dakota	...	...	...	...	...	...	...	...	...	★	...	...	...	...	...	...
Tennessee	...	...	...	...	...	...	...	...	...	...	...	...	...	...	...	...
Texas	...	...	...	...	...	...	...	...	...	★	...	...	...	...	...	...
Utah	...	...	...	...	...	...	...	...	...	...	...	...	...	...	...	...
Vermont	...	...	...	...	...	...	...	...	...	...	...	...	...	...	...	...
Virginia	...	...	...	...	...	...	...	...	...	...	...	★	...	...	...	...
Washington	...	...	...	...	...	...	...	★	...	...	...	...	...	...	...	...
West Virginia	...	...	...	...	...	...	...	...	...	...	☆	...	...	...	...	...
Wisconsin	...	...	...	...	...	...	...	...	...	...	...	...	•	...	★	...
Wyoming	...	...	...	...	...	...	...	...	...	...	...	...	...	...	...	...
Dist. of Columbia	...	...	...	...	...	...	...	...	...	...	...	...	...	...	...	...
Puerto Rico	...	...	...	...	...	...	...	...	...	...	...	...	...	...	...	...
U.S. Virgin Islands	★	...	...	...	...	...	...	...	...	...	...	...	...	...	...	...

Source: National Conference of Commissioners on Uniform State Laws.
Key:
★ — Enacted
• — Amended version enacted
☆ — Substantially similar version enacted
... — Not enacted

APPENDIX 57

Gubernatorial Executive Orders: Authorization, Provisions, Procedures

State or other jurisdiction	Authorization for executive orders	Provisions — Civil defense disasters, public emergencies	Energy emergencies and conservation	Other emergencies	Executive branch reorganization plans and agency creation	Create advisory, coordinating, study or investigative committees/commissions	Respond to federal programs and requirements	Procedures — State personnel administration	Other administration	Filing and publication procedures	Subject to administrative procedure act	Subject to legislative review
Alabama	S,I (a)			★ (b)	★					★ (c,d)		★
Alaska	C									★ (c)		★
Arizona	I	★	★ (a)	★ (a)	★	★	★	★	★	★		
Arkansas	S,I (e)	★	★	★		★	★			★		
California	S	★	★		★	★	★					
Colorado	S	★	★	★ (f)	★	★	★			★		
Connecticut	S					★				★		
Delaware	C	★	★	★ (qq)	★	★	★	★	★ (g,h)	★ (c)		
Florida	C,S	★	★	★	★	★	★	★	★ (g,h)	★		
Georgia	S,I (e)											
Hawaii	S		★									
Idaho	C		★		★	★						
Illinois	I		I	I	I	I	I	I		★ (c)		★ (k)
Indiana	S				★	★				★ (c)		
Iowa	S		★			★						
Kansas	S	★	★	★	★	★	★	★	★ (l)	★ (c,d,m)		
Kentucky	S	★	★	★ (n)	★	★	★	★	★ (k,o,p,q)	★ (c)	★	★ (s,t)
Louisiana	S (r)	★	★ (rr)	★	★	★	★		★ (j,s,t)	★ (m)	★	★ (x)
Maine	S	★	★	★ (u,v)	★	★	★			★ (d)		
Maryland	C,S	★	★	★ (f,u)	★	★	★	★	★ (w)	★	★	
Massachusetts	C,I	★	★			★			★ (q)	★ (m)		
Michigan	C,S	★	★		★	★	★	★	★ (z)	★ (c)		★ (y)
Minnesota	S	★	★		★	★	★		★ (aa,bb)	★ (c,m)		★ (x)
Missouri	C	★	★		★	★			★ (x)	★ (x)	★	★ (x,cc)
Montana	S,I	★	★	★ (u)	★	★	★	★	★ (q)	★ (c)		
Nebraska	S	★	★			★						
Nevada	I	★	★			★	★					
New Hampshire	S	★	★						★ (q)			
New Jersey	S	★	★ (a)	★ (dd)	★	★	★	★	★ (bb)	★	★	
New Mexico	S	★	★			★						★ (x)
New York	I	S	S	S	S,C	I	S	S	S	S		
North Carolina	S,I	★	★		★	★	★					
North Dakota	S,I	★	★						★ (bb)	★ (c)		
Ohio	C,S	★										
Oklahoma	S,I	★	★	★ (u)	★				★ (ee)	★ (c)		★ (x)
Oregon	S	★	★			★	★	★	★ (ff)	★ (c,m)		★ (x)
Pennsylvania	S (a)	★	★	★ (i,n,u,w)					★ (l)	★	★	
Rhode Island	S (a)	★ (bb)										
South Carolina	I (e)	★	★	★ (h,i)	★	★	★			★ (c,d,gg)		★

Gubernatorial Executive Orders, continued

State or other jurisdiction	Authorization for executive orders	Provisions								Procedures		
		Civil defense disasters, public emergencies	Energy emergencies and conservation	Other emergencies	Executive branch reorganization plans and agency creation	Create advisory, coordinating, study or investigative committees/commissions	Respond to federal programs and requirements	State personnel administration	Other administration	Filing and publication procedures	Subject to administrative procedure act	Subject to legislative review
South Dakota	C				★ (hh)				★ (s)			★
Tennessee	S,I	★	★	★		★	★	★		★ (c)	★	★
Texas	S	★	★	★		★	★	★		★ (c)	★	
Utah	S		★									
Vermont	S,I	★	★		★	★	★	★		★ (ii)		★ (jj)
Virginia	S,I	★	★	★ (r)	★ (kk)	★	★	★	★ (h,ff,ll,mm)	★ (c)	★	★
Washington	S	★		★			★	★		★ (c)	★	
West Virginia	S,I (e)	★		★		★		★	★ (nn)	★ (c,m)		
Wisconsin	S	★	★	★		★	★	★	★ (bb,oo,p)	★ (c)		
Wyoming	I											
American Samoa	C,S	★	★	★	★	★	★	★				
No. Mariana Islands	C											
Puerto Rico	I									★ (pp)	★ (pp)	

Sources: Massachusetts, Legislative Research Council, "Report Relative to Gubernatorial Executive Orders," House Document No. 6557, April 3, 1981, pp. 89-94; E. Lee Burnick, Department of Political Science, University of North Carolina at Greensboro; The Governors Center at Duke University (Survey, March 1984); The National Governors' Association 1985 survey; updated by The Council of State Governments' survey (1989).

Key:
C — Constitutional
S — Statutory
I — Implied
★ — Formal provision
∴ — No formal provision

(a) Broad interpretation of gubernatorial authority.
(b) To activate or veto environmental improvement authorities.
(c) Executive orders must be filed with secretary of state or other designated officer. In Idaho, must also be published in state general circulation newspaper.
(d) Governor required to keep record in office. In Maine, also sends copy to Legislative Counsel, State Law Library, and all county law libraries in state.
(e) Some or all provisions implied from constitution.
(f) To regulate distribution of necessities during shortages.
(g) To reassign state attorneys and public defenders.
(h) To suspend certain officials and/or other civil actions.
(i) To declare water, crop and refugee emergencies.
(j) To designate game and wildlife areas or other public areas.
(k) Only if involves a change in statute.
(l) To transfer allocated funds.
(m) Included in state register or code.
(n) To give immediate effect to state regulations in emergencies.
(o) To control administration of state contracts and procedures.
(p) To impound or freeze certain state matching funds.

(q) To reduce state expenditures in revenue shortfall.
(r) Broad grant of authority.
(s) Appointive powers.
(t) To suspend rules and regulations of the bureaucracy.
(u) For fire emergencies.
(v) For financial institution emergencies.
(w) To control procedures for dealing with public.
(x) Reorganization plans and agency creation.
(y) Legislative appropriations committees must approve orders issued to handle a revenue shortfall.
(z) To assign duties to lieutenant governor, issue writ of special election.
(aa) To control prison and pardon administration.
(bb) To administer and govern the armed forces of the state.
(cc) For meeting federal program requirements.
(dd) To declare air pollution emergencies.
(ee) Relating to local governments.
(ff) To transfer funds in an emergency.
(gg) Must be published in register if they have general applicability and legal effect.
(hh) Can reorganize, but not create.
(ii) Filed with legislature.
(jj) Only executive branch reorganization.
(kk) To shift agencies between secretarial offices; all other reorganizations require legislative approval.
(ll) To control state-owned motor vehicles.
(mm) Delegate powers to secretaries and other executive branch officials.
(nn) Regarding annual reports of state agencies.
(oo) To transfer functions between agencies.
(pp) If executive order fits definition of rule.
(qq) Local financial emergency, shore erosion, polluted discharge and energy shortage.
(rr) If an energy emergency is declared by the state's Executive Council or Legislature.

APPENDIX 58

The Governors: Powers

State or other jurisdiction	Budget-making power		Veto power (a)					Authorization for reorganization through executive order (b)	Other statewide elected officials (c)	
	Full responsibility	Shares responsibility	No item veto	Item veto—2/3 legislators present to override	Item veto—majority legislators elected to override	Item veto—3/5 legislators elected to override	Item veto—at least 2/3 legislators elected to override		Number of officials	Number of agencies
Alabama	★				★					17	8
Alaska	★						★	C	1	0 (d)
Arizona	★				★		★		8	6
Arkansas	★						★	S	6	6
California	★						★		7	7
Colorado		★					★		4	16
Connecticut	★					★	★	C	6	5
Delaware	★			★					5	5
Florida	★			★				S	6	6
Georgia							★		13	9
Hawaii	★						★	(e)	22	2
Idaho	★							C	6	0
Illinois	★					★			15	7
Indiana	★		★						6	6
Iowa	★			★			★		6	6
Kansas	★				★			C	15	6
Kentucky		★					★	S	7	7
Louisiana		★							21	10
Maine	★		★						0	0
Maryland							★	C	3	3

© 1992 The Council of State Governments. Reprinted with permission from *The Book of the States*.

The Governors: Powers, continued

State or other jurisdiction	Budget-making power — Full responsibility	Budget-making power — Shares responsibility	Veto power (a) — No item veto	Veto power (a) — Item veto—2/3 legislators present to override	Veto power (a) — Item veto—majority legislators elected to override	Veto power (a) — Item veto—3/5 legislators elected to override	Veto power (a) — Item veto—at least 2/3 legislators elected to override	Authorization for reorganization through executive order (b)	Other statewide elected officials (c) — Number of officials	Number of agencies
Massachusetts	★			★				C	5	6
Michigan	★ (f)							C	35	7
Minnesota		★					★	S	5	5
Mississippi		★					★	S	13	9
Missouri	★			★			★	C	5	15
Montana	★			★				S	11	15
Nebraska	★					★			26	8
Nevada	★		★						23	7
New Hampshire	★		★						5	1
New Jersey	★								0	0
New Mexico	★			★					19	8
New York	★			★			★ (k)		3	3
North Carolina		★	★ (g)					C	9	9
North Dakota	★						★		13	11
Ohio	★					★			6	29
Oklahoma	★ (f)			★			★	S	9	7
Oregon	★ (f)			★					5	5
Pennsylvania	★ (f)						★		4	4
Rhode Island			★						4	
South Carolina		★	★				★		8	10 (h)
South Dakota	★			★			★	C	9	7
Tennessee		★			★			S	3	1
Texas		★		★					9	7
Utah	★			★					4	30
Vermont	★							S	5	5
Virginia	★			★				S (i)	2	2
Washington		★		★					8	8
West Virginia	★			★				S	4	7
Wisconsin		★		★ (j)					5	5
Wyoming	★						★		4	4
American Samoa		★						S	1	1
Guam	★						★		36	3
No. Mariana Islands	★						★	C	1	1
Puerto Rico	★						★		0	0
U.S. Virgin Islands	★						★		1	0

Sources: The National Governors' Association 1985 survey of governors' offices; The Council of State Governments; and state constitutions and statutes.

Key:
C — Constitutional
S — Statutory

(a) In all states, except North Carolina, governor has the power to veto bills passed by the state legislature. The information presented here refers to the governor's power to *item* veto—veto items within a bill—and the votes needed in the state legislature to override the item veto. For additional information on vetoes and veto overrides, as well as the number of days the governor is allowed to consider bills, see Table 3.14, "Enacting Legislation: Veto, Veto Overrides and Effective Date."

(b) For additional information on executive orders, see Table 2.5, "Gubernatorial Executive Orders: Authorization, Provisions, Procedures."

(c) Includes only executive branch officials who are popularly elected either on a constitutional or statu- tory basis (elected members of state boards of education, public utilities commissions, university regents, or other state boards or commissions are also included); the number of agencies involving these officials is also listed.

(d) Lieutenant governor's office is part of governor's office.

(e) Implied through a broad interpretation of gubernatorial authority; no formal provision.

(f) Full to propose; legislature adopts or revises; and governor signs or vetoes.

(g) Governor has no veto power.

(h) Divisions within governor's office.

(i) For shifting agencies between secretarial offices; all other reorganizations require legislative approval.

(j) In Wisconsin, governor has "partial" veto over appropriation bills. The partial veto is broader than item veto.

(k) In New York, governor has item veto over appropriations.

APPENDIX 59

State Cabinet Systems

State or jurisdiction	Authorization for cabinet system				Criteria for membership			Number of members in cabinet (including governor)	Frequency of cabinet meetings	Open cabinet meetings
	Statute	Constitution	Governor	Tradition	Appointed to specified office	Elected to specified office	Gubernatorial appointment regardless of office			
Alabama	...	...	...	★	...	...	★	28	Twice monthly (a)	★
Alaska	...	...	★	...	★	...	...	17	Regularly	★ (b)
Arizona	...	...	★	...	★	...	...	19	Weekly	...
Arkansas	★	...	...	...	★	...	...	17	Regularly	...
California	...	...	★	...	★	...	★	11	Every two weeks	...
Colorado	...	★	...	...	★	...	...	21	Twice monthly	★
Connecticut	★	...	...	...	★	...	...	24	Gov.'s discretion	...
Delaware	★	...	...	...	...	...	★ (c)	19	Gov.'s discretion	★
Florida	...	★	...	...	...	★	...	7	Every two weeks	★
Georgia					(d)					
Hawaii	...	...	...	★	★	...	★	24	Gov.'s discretion	...
Idaho					(d)					
Illinois	★	...	...	...	★ (c)	...	...	42 (e)	Gov.'s discretion (f)	★
Indiana					(d)					
Iowa	★	...	...	...	...	...	★	5	Weekly	★
Kansas	...	...	★	...	...	...	★	14	Monthly (a)	...
Kentucky	★	...	...	...	★	...	...	13	Weekly	...
Louisiana	★	★	...	...	★	★	...	21	Monthly	...
Maine	...	...	...	★	...	...	★ (c)	20	Gov.'s discretion	...
Maryland	★	...	...	...	★ (c)	...	...	20	Weekly	...
Massachusetts	★	...	...	...	★	...	...	11	Twice monthly	...
Michigan	...	...	★	...	★	★	★	30	Gov.'s discretion	...
Minnesota	...	...	★	...	★	...	...	26 (h)	Regularly	...
Mississippi					(d)					
Missouri	...	★	...	★	★	...	...	16	Gov.'s discretion	...
Montana	...	...	★	...	★	...	...	24	Monthly	★
Nebraska	...	...	★	...	★	...	...	27	Monthly	...
Nevada					(d)					
New Hampshire					(d)					
New Jersey	★	★	...	...	★	...	...	21	Once or twice monthly	...
New Mexico	★	...	...	...	★	...	...	15	Weekly	...
New York	...	...	...	★	★	...	...	16	Gov.'s discretion	...
North Carolina (i)	...	...	★	...	...	...	★	10	Monthly	...
North Dakota					(d)					
Ohio	★	...	...	...	★	...	★	27	Gov.'s discretion	(g)
Oklahoma	★	...	...	...	...	...	★	11 (j)	Gov.'s discretion	...
Oregon	...	...	★	...	...	...	★	21	As needed	...
Pennsylvania	★	...	...	...	★	...	...	20	Gov.'s discretion	★
Rhode Island					(d)					
South Carolina					(d)					
South Dakota	...	...	★	...	★	...	★	22	Gov.'s discretion	...
Tennessee	★	...	...	★	★	...	...	29	Gov.'s discretion	★
Texas					(d)					
Utah	...	...	★	(k)	★	...	...	31	Monthly	★
Vermont	★	...	...	...	★	...	...	6	Gov.'s discretion	...
Virginia	★	...	...	...	★	...	...	9	Gov.'s discretion	...
Washington	...	...	★	...	★	...	...	26	Twice monthly	...
West Virginia	★	...	...	...	...	...	★	8	Weekly	...
Wisconsin	★	...	...	...	★	...	...	9	Monthly	★
Wyoming (l)	★	...	...	...	★	...	...	4	Gov.'s discretion	★
Puerto Rico	★	★	...	...	★	...	...	17	Weekly	...

Key:
★ — Yes
... — No

(a) More often during legislative sessions. Kansas—bi-weekly.
(b) Except when in executive session.
(c) With the consent of the Senate.
(d) No formal cabinet system. In Idaho, however, sub-cabinets have been formed, by executive order; the chairmen report to the governor when requested.
(e) Includes directors of three independent bonding agencies.
(f) Sub-cabinets meet monthly.
(g) In practice, the media and others do not attend, but cabinet meetings have not been formally designated closed.

(h) Five sub-cabinets have been formed.
(i) Constitution provides for a Council of State made up of elective state administrative officials, which makes policy decisions for the state while the cabinet acts more in an advisory capacity.
(j) Each cabinet member is chair of a sub-cabinet (each state agency). These sub-cabinets meet quarterly.
(k) State Planning Advisory Committee, composed of all department heads serves as an informal cabinet. Committee meets at discretion of state planning coordinator.
(l) A 4-year, phased-in executive reorganization currently being implemented. The first three cabinet-level agencies go on-line in July 1990.

APPENDIX 60

Government of the State of Kansas

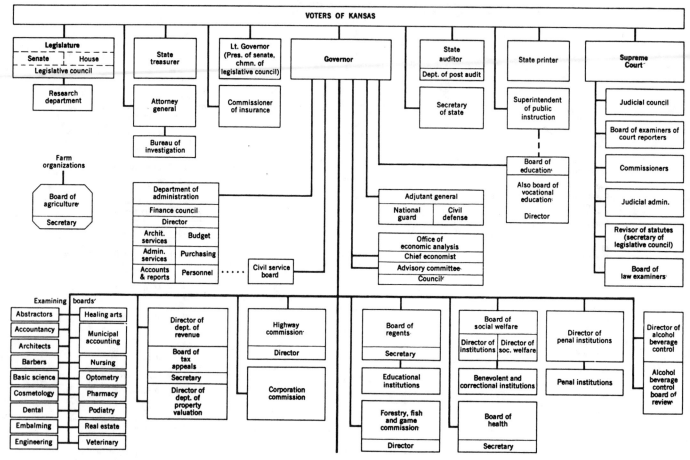

Source: The State of Kansas

APPENDIX 61

The Governors: Compensation

State or other jurisdiction	Salary	Governor's office staff (a)	Access to state transportation			Travel allowance	Official residence
			Automobile	Airplane	Helicopter		
Alabama..............	$ 70,223	22	★	★	★	(b)	★
Alaska...............	81,648	67	★	★	★	(b)	★
Arizona..............	75,000	50	★	★	★	(b)	...
Arkansas.............	35,000	48	★	...	...	(c)	★
California............	85,000	86	★	...	...	(c)	(d)
Colorado	70,000	41.5	★	★	...	(e)	★
Connecticut	78,000	38	★	...	(f)	(e)	★
Delaware	80,000	22	★	...	★	$ 21,900 (c)	★
Florida	100,883	129 (g)	★	★	...	(b)	★
Georgia..............	88,872	55	★	★	★	(e)	★
Hawaii	94,780	28 (g)	★	...	...	(e)	★
Idaho	55,000	16 (h)	★	★	...	(e)	...
Illinois..............	93,266	173	★	★	★	(b)	★
Indiana	77,194	34	★	★	★	0	★
Iowa	72,500	10	★	★	...	(b)	★
Kansas	73,137	22	★	★	...	(e)	★
Kentucky	69,731	78	★	★	★	(b)	★
Louisiana	66,096	46	★	...	★	(p)	★
Maine	70,000	21	★	★	...	(e)	★
Maryland	85,000	104 (j)	★	★	★	(e)	★
Massachusetts	75,000	81	★	★	★	(e)	...
Michigan	106,690	45	★	★	★	(e)	★
Minnesota	103,860	30	★	★	★	(e)	★
Mississippi	75,600	39 (k)	★	★	★	24,017 (c,e)	★
Missouri.............	88,541	34	★	★	...	(c)	★
Montana.............	51,713	24	★	★	★	(b)	★
Nebraska	58,000	16	★	★	★	(b)	★
Nevada	70,857 (l)	17	★	...	...	(c)	★
New Hampshire	75,753	27	★	★	...	(e)	★ (i)
New Jersey...........	85,000	60	★	...	★	(m)	★ (i)
New Mexico..........	90,000	38	★	★	★	(c)	★
New York	130,000 (m)	216	★	★	★	(b)	★
North Carolina	123,000	86	★	★	★	11,500	★
North Dakota	65,196	18.25	★	★	...	(e)	★
Ohio	65,000	60	★	★	★	(e)	★
Oklahoma	70,000	34	★	★	...	(e)	★
Oregon	77,500	44	★	...	...	0	★
Pennsylvania	85,000	60	★	★	...	(b)	★
Rhode Island	69,000	47	★	★	★	(e)	...
South Carolina	84,897	30	★	★	★	(e)	★
South Dakota	60,819	26	★	★	...	(e)	★
Tennessee	85,000	40	★	★	★	(e)	★
Texas................	93,432	178	...	★	★	(b)	★
Utah	69,992	18	★	★	...	26,000	★
Vermont	75,800	21	★	...	...	(e)	...
Virginia..............	85,000	36	★	★	★	(b)	★
Washington	96,700	37	★	★	...	N.A.	★
West Virginia	72,000	30	★	★	★	(n)	★
Wisconsin............	86,149	38	★	★	...	(e)	★
Wyoming	70,000	8 (o)	★	★	...	(c)	★
American Samoa	50,000	25	★	...	...	(c)	★
Guam	75,000	N.A.	★	...	...	N.A.	★
No. Mariana Islands ...	50,000	N.A.	N.A.	N.A.	N.A.	N.A.	N.A.
Puerto Rico	45,000	N.A.	★	★	★	(e)	★
U.S. Virgin Islands	$64,400	N.A.	★	...	...	N.A.	★

Key:
★ — Yes
... — No
N.A. — Not available

(a) Definitions of "governor's office staff" vary across the states—from general office support to staffing for various operations within the executive office.

(b) Reimbursed for travel expenses. Alabama—reimbursed up to $40/d in state; actual expenses out of state. Alaska—governor is reimbursed $80/d or if exceed for actual amount. Arizona—reimbursed for actual expenses to a maximum of $52.50/d in state and $55/d out of state. Florida—reimbursed at same rate as other state officials: in state, choice between $50 per diem or actual expenses; out of state, actual expenses. Idaho—standard per diem, $15/d in state; $20/d out of state. Illinois—No set allowance. Iowa—Limit set in annual office budget. Kentucky—mileage at same rate as other state employees. Montana—reimbursed for actual and necessary expenses in state up to $55/d, and actual lodging plus meal allowance up to $30/d out of state (no annual limit). Nebraska—reasonable and necessary expenses. New York—reimbursed for actual and necessary expenses. Pennsylvania—reimbursed for reasonable expenses. Texas—reimbursed for actual expenses.

(c) Amount includes travel allowance for entire staff. Arkansas, Michigan, Missouri—amount not available. California—$130,000 in state;

$27,000 out of state. Nevada—$19,411 in state, $9,389 out of state. New Mexico—$67,400 in state, $48,400 out of state. Wyoming—$45,536 in state; $46,158 out of state. American Samoa—$142,000.

(d) In California—provided by Governor's Residence Foundation, a nonprofit organization which provides a residence for the governor of California. No rent is charged; maintenance and operational costs are provided by California Department of General Services.

(e) Travel allowance included in office budget.

(f) Emergency authorization for use of National Guard's.

(g) In Florida, does not include Office of Planning and Budgeting and a number of state commissions located within executive office of governor for budget purposes. In Hawaii, does not include offices and commissions attached to governor's office.

(h) Number on staff varies from 12 to 20 during the year.

(i) Governor does not occupy residence.

(j) Includes positions added when Criminal Justice Coordinating Council moved into governor's office.

(k) Currently 18; budget request is for 39.

(l) On employee/employer paid retirement system.

(m) Accepts $100,000.

(n) Included in general expense account.

(o) Also has state planning coordinator.

(p) Provided as needed within budgetary constraints.

APPENDIX 62

Selected State Administrative Officials: Annual Salaries

State	Governor	Lieutenant governor	Secretary of state	Attorney general	Treasurer	Adjutant general	Administration	Agriculture	Banking	Budget
Alabama	70,223	43,860	36,234	77,420	49,500	56,812	...	49,156	56,812	88,504
Alaska	81,648	66,816 (d)	66,816 (d)	66,816 (d)	66,816 (d)	66,816 (d)	66,816 (d)	65,508 (d)	62,508 (d)	62,508 (d)
Arizona	75,000	...	50,000	70,000	50,000	46,606 (d)	61,362 (d)	46,606 (d)	46,606 (d)	46,606 (d)
Arkansas	35,000	14,000	22,500	46,785	22,500	50,864	71,905	48,405	64,061	49,199
California	85,000	72,500	72,500	77,500	72,500	79,399 (d)	...	101,343	95,052	(a-22)
Colorado	70,000	48,500	48,500	60,000	48,500	75,583	72,624	58,464	58,464	77,813
Connecticut	78,000	55,000	50,000	60,000	50,000	59,789 (d)	78,732 (d)	59,789 (d)	67,639 (d)	72,819 (d)
Delaware	80,000	35,100	69,900	81,400	63,000	60,400	65,600	60,400	68,300	76,100
Florida	100,883	91,301	52,762	91,301	91,301	78,192	84,925	91,301	(a-13)	73,547
Georgia	88,872	57,702	71,184	72,824	67,164	75,474	69,001	71,186	69,003	78,984
Hawaii	94,780	90,041	90,041	85,302	85,302	88,107	90,041	85,302	67,716	85,302
Idaho	55,000	15,000	45,000	48,000	45,000	65,000	58,947	58,947	58,947	58,947
Illinois	93,266	65,835	82,294	82,294	71,321	40,598	68,578	65,835	68,250	81,500
Indiana	77,194	63,986	45,994	59,202	45,994	57,018	67,990	41,834	61,204	65,000
Iowa	72,500	25,100	55,700	69,600	55,700	59,800	52,700 (d)	55,700	42,600 (d)	56,400 (d)
Kansas	73,137	20,688	56,400	65,345	56,816	58,850	73,323	60,000	49,307	66,908
Kentucky	69,731	59,263	59,263	59,263	59,263	64,260	69,594	59,263	52,500	64,260
Louisiana	66,096	63,367	60,169	66,566	60,169	78,749	66,492	60,164	73,000	48,732
Maine (c)	70,000	...	47,154	56,366	44,926	39,613	51,739	49,404	48,761	50,346
Maryland	85,000	72,500	45,000	72,500	72,500	70,092 (d)	81,756 (d)	81,756 (d)	60,093 (d)	95,360 (d)
Massachusetts	75,000	60,000	60,000	65,000	60,000	78,200	80,000	58,000	63,000	77,500
Michigan	106,690	80,300	89,000	89,000	80,300	72,500	80,300	80,300	65,000	80,300
Minnesota	103,860	57,125	57,125	81,138	54,042	66,607	67,500	67,500	64,039	78,500
Mississippi	75,600	40,800	54,000	61,200	54,000	50,400	...	54,000	49,200	56,791 (d)
Missouri	88,541	53,277	70,909	76,786	70,909	59,016	76,786	67,970	57,945	64,299
Montana	51,713	37,098	35,031	47,166	30,561	51,763	48,500	51,763	39,541	51,763
Nebraska	58,000	40,000	40,000	57,500	35,000	46,519	50,500	59,613	66,361	54,612
Nevada	70,857	12,500	50,500	62,500	49,000	54,794	62,009	48,584	48,310	(a-6)
New Hampshire	75,753	...	60,410	67,625	60,410	64,029	67,625	50,499	64,029	60,410
New Jersey	85,000	46,667	95,000	95,000	95,000	95,000	60,000 (d)	95,000	95,000	79,697 (d)
New Mexico	90,000	40,425	40,425	46,200	40,425	54,558	62,067	62,067	53,123	53,123
New York	130,000	110,000	87,338	110,000	(n)	87,338	91,957	87,338	87,338	96,662
North Carolina	123,000	70,992	70,992	70,992	70,992	64,548	70,992	70,992	68,304	38,549 (d)
North Dakota	65,196	53,496	49,300	55,704	49,300	76,920	(a-33)	49,296	49,800	(jj)
Ohio	65,000	46,883	66,997	66,997	66,997	65,416	58,843 (d)	53,331 (d)	53,331 (d)	53,331 (d)
Oklahoma	70,000	40,000	37,500	55,000	50,000	63,450	60,019	51,115	64,045	62,245
Oregon	77,500	(a-2)	59,500	64,000	59,500	69,180	84,072	69,180	56,904	76,224
Pennsylvania	85,000	67,500	58,000	84,000	84,000	58,000	65,000	58,000	58,000	65,000
Rhode Island	69,000	52,000	52,000	55,000	52,000	50,671 (d)	72,785 (d)	33,068 (d)	45,754 (d)	65,412 (d)
South Carolina	84,897	37,142	72,161	72,161	72,161	72,161	93,619 (d)	72,161	(a-4)	69,246 (d)
South Dakota	60,819	52,915	41,309	51,626	41,309	57,242	53,622	51,480	59,738	63,773
Tennessee	85,000	49,500	65,000	65,650	65,000	57,500	65,000	55,500	58,000	64,000
Texas	93,432	7,200	72,549	74,698	74,698	59,790	69,300	74,698	84,941	63,000
Utah	69,992	52,499	52,499	56,014	52,998	60,008	68,078	55,536	53,498	65,770
Vermont	75,800	31,600	47,700	57,300	47,700	49,254	65,229	55,744	54,205	57,013
Virginia	85,000	28,000	59.247	75,000	84,248	69,119	92,913	76,830	83,713	90,058
Washington	96,700	51,100	52,600	75,700	65,000	78,191	79,620	79,620	60,688	82,000
West Virginia	72,000	...	43,200	50,400	50,400	35,700	70,000	46,800	38,300	25,152 (d)
Wisconsin	86,149	46,360	42,098	73,903	42,098	50,461 (d)	62,964 (d)	54,323 (d)	46,871 (d)	50,461 (d)
Wyoming	70,000	52,500	52,500	63,147	52,500	58,525	66,329	63,013	55,008	60,000

Note: The chief administrative officials responsible for each function were determined from information given by the states for the same function as listed in *State Administrative Officials Classified by Function 1989-90*, published by The Council of State Governments.

Key:

N.A. — Not available

. . . — No specific chief administrative official or agency in charge of function

(a) Chief administrative official or agency in charge of function:
(a-1) Lieutenant governor
(a-2) Secretary of state
(a-3) Attorney general
(a-4) Treasurer
(a-5) Adjutant general
(a-6) Administration
(a-7) Agriculture
(a-8) Banking
(a-9) Budget
(a-10) Civil rights
(a-11) Commerce
(a-12) Community affairs
(a-13) Comptroller
(a-14) Computer services
(a-15) Consumer affairs
(a-16) Economic development
(a-17) Education (chief state school officer)

(a-18) Emergency management
(a-19) Employment services
(a-20) Energy resources
(a-21) Environmental protection
(a-22) Finance
(a-23) Fish and wildlife
(a-24) General services
(a-25) Health
(a-26) Highways
(a-27) Historic preservation
(a-28) Insurance
(a-29) Labor
(a-30) Mental health and retardation
(a-31) Natural resources
(a-32) Parks and recreation
(a-33) Personnel
(a-34) Planning
(a-35) Post audit
(a-36) Public utility regulation
(a-37) Public welfare
(a-38) Purchasing
(a-39) Revenue
(a-40) Social services
(a-41) Solid waste management
(a-42) Transportation

Selected Officials: Annual Salaries, continued

State	Civil rights	Commerce	Community affairs	Comptroller	Computer services	Consumer affairs	Corrections	Economic development	Education	Election administration
Alabama	...	86,764	56,812	61,022	56,654	34,554	68,576	(a-12)	103,856	29,796
Alaska	62,508 (d)	66,816 (d)	66,816 (d)	56,244 (d)	62,508 (d)	56,244 (d)	66,816 (d)	66,816 (d)	66,816 (d)	62,508 (d)
Arizona	51,074 (d)	51,074 (d)	...	...	46,606 (d)	55,989 (d)	67,225 (d)	51,074 (d)	50,000	(a-2)
Arkansas	N.A.	...	71,905	71,905	65,047	(a-3)	65,000	60,839	70,879	22,500
California	95,052	95,052	67,824	72,500	86,544	95,052	95,052	(a-11)	72,500	5,364 (d)
Colorado	...	....	58,464	58,464	58,464	59,056	70,000	77,813	79,742	41,556
Connecticut	63,246 (d)	67,639 (d)	50,009 (d)	50,000	63,246 (d)	67,639 (d)	72,681 (d)	77,681 (d)	78,732 (d)	55,415 (d)
Delaware	42,806	(a-2)	65,600	61,178	74,769	42,961	76,100	76,100	93,300	39,625
Florida	36,798	61,200 (d)	84,926	91,301	63,018	36,720 (d)	84,925	58,656	91,301	54,499
Georgia	55,194	77,850	77,838	71,172	67,200	61,098	69,000	77,850	72,824	61,500
Hawaii	...	85,302	...	85,302	63,348	65,000	85,302	85,302	90,041	90,041
Idaho	36,171	48,485	34,445	45,000	(a-6)	(a-3)	60,424	(a-11)	45,000	46,488
Illinois	57,057	65,835	(a-11)	71,321	(a-6)	(a-3)	65,835	(a-11)	108,696	63,000
Indiana	43,498	63,986	31,356	45,994	56,108	58,188	68,302	55,484	63,102	37,024
Iowa	38,500 (d)	52,700 (d)	49,046 (d)	56,400 (d)	49,064 (d)	47,257 (d)	56,400 (d)	63,000 (d)	63,000 (d)	(a-2)
Kansas	40,500	71,550	51,263	63,655	61,107	42,708	72,267	(a-11)	86,000	36,000
Kentucky	60,000	64,260	56,111	64,260	(a-13)	(a-3)	64,260	(a-11)	59,263	42,682
Louisiana	(a-3)	(a-16)	34,128	(a-6)	55,260	...	58,000	58,000	95,000	60,169
Maine (c)	39,527	59,821	39,056	48,033	67,464	40,248	47,026	(a-11)	59,816	(a-2)
Maryland	64,900 (d)	60,093 (d)	60,093 (d)	72,500	60,093 (d)	60,093 (d)	70,092 (d)	(a-11)	88,296 (d)	60,093 (d)
Massachusetts	58,100	(a-16)	67,000	75,000	63,200	64,500	77,500	70,700	77,500	49,300
Michigan	80,300	80,300	46,980 (d)	29,838 (d)	29,838 (d)	61,825 (d)	83,100	29,838 (d)	80,516	(a-2)
Minnesota	60,000	67,500	64,206	(a-9)	64,122	66,691	67,500	36,644	78,500	34,034
Mississippi	...	(a-16)	37,172 (d)	(a-9)	52,450 (d)	37,548 (d)	48,000	59,400 (d)	55,685 (d)	45,604 (d)
Missouri	50,340	(a-16)	(a-16)	57,973	57,973	...	67,970	67,970	75,252	29,532
Montana	32,868	51,763	41,425	(a-6)	47,393	33,731	51,763	37,195	40,643	23,061
Nebraska	66,036	(a-16)	37,800	53,568	57,324	26,928	66,612	68,783	(l)	(a-2)
Nevada	48,800	57,443	46,600	49,000	53,516	33,607	65,322	55,525	61,004	(a-2)
New Hampshire	37,947	50,499	(a-34)	53,209	60,410	(a-3)	60,410	50,499	67,625	(a-2)
New Jersey	59,471 (d)	95,000	95,000	(a-9)	85,000	62,445 (d)	95,000	73,150	95,000	(ff)
New Mexico	50,294	(a-16)	62,067	(a-4)	50,315	48,693	62,067	62,067	63,877	51,314
New York	79,437	87,338	(a-2)	(a-4)	(a-6)	73,482	98,399	(a-11)	131,250	79,437
North Carolina	38,549 (d)	70,992	40,377 (d)	110,772	61,474 (d)	46,411 (d)	70,992	42,229 (d)	70,992	46,411 (d)
North Dakota	(a-29)	(a-16)	41,736	(jj)	57,276	30,384	51,948	47,724	50,304	(a-2)
Ohio	43,867 (d)	(o)	39,832 (d)	(a-4)	39,832 (d)	43,867 (d)	58,843 (d)	39,832 (d)	97,677	40,394 (d)
Oklahoma	39,985	68,650	(a-11)	58,145	45,774	42,768	65,400	(a-11)	55,000	61,400
Oregon	56,904	(a-28)	62,700	59,500	62,700	...	76,224	56,904	59,500	51,576
Pennsylvania	64,998	61,500	58,000	54,000	64,626	60,401	61,500	(a-11)	65,000	41,500
Rhode Island	33,068 (d)	(a-16)	...	50,671 (d)	42,548 (d)	30,616 (d)	72,785 (d)	67,868 (d)	91,000	34,684
South Carolina	56,989 (d)	(a-16)	32,988	72,161	71,113 (d)	66,722 (d)	93,619 (d)	80,225 (d)	72,161	49,212 (d)
South Dakota	22,922	53,498	(a-16)	41,309	54,309	37,336	52,998	80,000	(pp)	(a-2)
Tennessee	52,000	64,500	(a-11)	65,000	63,000	38,000	62,000	(a-11)	90,000	41,500
Texas	52,133	74,970	58,800	74,698	75,600	75,283	84,000	(a-11)	114,474	52,730
Utah	45,157	62,150	(r)	65,936	56,389	37,294	62,150	50,814	69,742	52,499
Vermont	53,186	48,526	52,333	(a-9)	51,293	53,186	53,768	48,526	61,651	(rr)
Virginia	...	92,913	71,512	87,054	83,640	39,935	92,111	93,883	96,529	61,617
Washington	59,713	79,620	79,620	(a-4)	57,760	73,185	79,620	(a-11)	69,800	40,873
West Virginia	40,000	(y)	63,600	46,800	42,204 (d)	39,900 (d)	45,000	63,600	70,600	(a-2)
Wisconsin	40,442 (d)	54,324 (d)	43,389 (d)	43,389 (d)	40,442 (d)	(u)	54,324 (d)	37,567 (d)	72,337	40,442 (d)
Wyoming	54,149	62,500	(a-16)	52,500	57,486	35,486	62,121	58,658	52,500	(ww)

(b) Salary listed may be of military grade.

(c) Council of State Governments' survey (1988).

(d) Minimum figure in range; top of range follows:

Alaska: Lieutenant governor, $92,676; Attorney General, $92,676; Treasurer, $92,676; Adjutant general, $92,676; Administration, $92,676; Agriculture, $86,292; Banking, $86,292; Budget, $86,292; Civil rights, $86,292; Commerce, $92,676; Community affairs, $92,676; Comptroller, $77,424; Computer services, $86,292; Consumer affairs, $77,424; Corrections, $92,676; Economic development, $92,676; Education, $92,676; Elections administration, $86,292; Emergency management, $86,292; Employment services, $72,420; Environmental protection, $92,676; Finance, $77,424; Fish and wildlife, $92,676; General services, $86,292; Health, $92,676; Higher education, $89,580; Historic preservation, $63,084; Insurance, $86,292; Labor, $92,676; Licensing, $86,292; Mental health & retardation, $86,292; Natural resources, $92,676; Parks & recreation, $86,292; Personnel, $86,292; Post audit, $86,292; Pre-audit $86,292; Public library, $86,292; Public utility regulation, $86,292; Public welfare, $86,292; Revenue, $86,292; Social Services, $92,676; Solid waste management, $67,548; State police, $86,292; Tourism, $86,292; Transportation, $92,676

Arizona: Adjutant general, $70,532; Administration, $92,863; Agriculture, $70,532; Banking, $70,532; Budget, $70,532; Civil rights, $77,294; Commerce, $77,294; Computer services, $70,532; Consumer affairs, $84,734; Corrections, $101,738; Economic development, $77,294; Education, $50,000; Elections administration, $50,000; Emergency management, $53,553; Employment services, $53,553; Energy resources, $53,553; Environmental protection, $84,734; Finance, $77,294; Fish and wildlife, $70,532; General services, $58,699; Health, $101,738; Highways, $84,734; Historic preservation, $44,716; Insurance, $70,532; Labor, $77,294; Natural resources, $84,734; Parks & recreation, $64,320; Personnel, $77,294; Planning, $77,294; Post audit, $82,262; Public library, $40,215; Public utility regulation, $70,532; Purchasing, $64,320; Revenue, $92,863; Social Services, $77,294; Solid waste management, $64,320; State police, $85,000; Tourism, $70,532; Transportation, $101,738

California: Adjutant general, $92,111; Elections administration, $5,913; Public library, $5,005; Purchasing, $6,503

Connecticut: Adjutant general, $72,538; Administration, $99,913; Agriculture, $72,538; Banking, $81,686; Budget, $93,541; Civil rights, $76,424; Commerce, $81,686; Community affairs, $63,028; Computer services, $76,424; Consumer affairs, $81,686; Corrections, $88,024;; Economic development, $88,024; Education, $95,155; Elections administration, $71,083; Emergency management, $54,819; Employment services, $76,424; Energy resources, $72,538; Environmental protection, $88,024;; Finance, $99,913; Fish and wildlife, $76,882; Health, $88,024;; Highways, $76,424; Historic preservation, $49,933; Insurance, $81,686; Labor, $81,686; Licensing, $73,923; Parks & recreation, $76,802; Personnel, $76,424; Planning, $72,538; Post audit, $79,961; Public library, $72,538; Public utility regulation, $89,948; Public welfare, $88,024;; Purchasing, $76,424; Revenue, $81,686; Social Services, $81,686; Solid waste management, $76,882; State police, $88,024;; Tourism, $56,173; Transportation, $99,913; Delaware: Tourism, $60,040

Selected Officials: Annual Salaries, continued

State	Emergency management	Employment services	Energy resources	Environmental protection	Finance	Fish & wildlife	General services	Health	Higher education	Highways
Alabama	56,812	62,556	51,600	52,598	56,812	(a-31)	52,598	113,977	97,940	56,812
Alaska	62,508 (d)	52,548 (d)	. . .	66,816 (d)	56,244 (d)	66,816	62,508 (d)	66,816 (d)	64,620 (d)	(a-42)
Arizona	35,386 (d)	35,386 (d)	35,386 (d)	55,989 (d)	51,074 (d)	46,606	38,788 (d)	67,225 (d)	. . .	55,989 (d)
Arkansas	39,133	67,896	54,900	55,000	71,905	58,088	71,905	72,907	72,867	76,708
California	83,869	95,052	90,860	101,343	101,343	95,052	95,052	95,052	100,834	95,052
Colorado	48,108	72,624	43,992	55,680	(a-13)	58,464	72,624	83,830	88,000	80,925
Connecticut	45,311 (d)	63,246 (d)	59,789 (d)	72,681 (d)	82,669 (d)	59,935 (d)	(a-6)	78,732 (d)	101,800	63,246 (d)
Delaware	44,473	(a-29)	46,666	70,900	81,400	49,024	(a-6)	97,509	49,900	73,541
Florida	66,288	60,756	51,000	84,925	58,472	84,926	84,926	61,200 (d)	137,945	(a-42)
Georgia	75,474	59,688	61,098	78,349	67,164	67,234	(a-6)	95,962	133,300	(a-42)
Hawaii	88,107	(a-29)	60,912	74,880	(a-9)	33,000	(a-13)	85,302	90,041	68,784
Idaho	47,341	58,947	(a-31)	53,456	(a-9)	66,622	41,870	68,245	74,506	(a-42)
Illinois	40,598	71,321	(a-31)	65,835	(a-39)	65,835	(a-6)	71,321	124,200	(a-42)
Indiana	34,944	62,010	39,858	67,522	(a-9)	44,538	(a-6)	87,230	N.A.	69,992
Iowa	25,600 (d)	52,700 (d)	49,046 (d)	49,064 (d)	(a-13)	49,064 (d)	(a-6)	52,700 (d)	63,000 (d)	51,397 (d)
Kansas	41,107	(a-29)	38,880	60,878	(a-9)	(a-32)	(a-6)	100,225	91,500	(a-42)
Kentucky	43,291	51,511	(a-31)	(a-31)	(a-13)	58,000	(a-13)	94,570	82,344	56,700
Louisiana	32,360	45,228	53,164	58,000	(a-6)	58,000	(a-6)	110,000	78,479	58,455
Maine (c)	38,627	40,834	50,346	49,404	59,816	42,723	(a-22)	54,353	(x)	(a-26)
Maryland	51,520 (d)	64,900 (d)	39,383 (d)	81,756 (d)	(a-13)	42,534 (d)	81,756 (d)	95,360 (d)	88,296 (d)	89,903
Massachusetts	54,100	72,100	62,000	70,700	(a-6)	63,300	73,100	77,600	100,000	77,500
Michigan	44,370 (d)	29,838 (d)	. . .	29,838 (d)	(a-9)	(a-31)	29,838 (d)	80,300	50,863 (d)	(a-42)
Minnesota	51,553	64,248	54,643	(j)	(a-9)	57,190	(a-6)	67,500	83,875	73,351
Mississippi	33,600	51,600	(a-42)	42,119 (d)	. . .	38,696 (d)	(a-9)	67,290 (d)	98,000	54,000
Missouri	52,203	64,191	54,390	57,945	(k)	69,972	54,423	87,456	75,000	(a-42)
Montana	30,891	44,292	38,954	47,393	(a-9)	34,815	35,695	46,436	79,200	51,763
Nebraska	(a-5)	44,904	47,914	47,444	(m)	65,000	(a-6)	69,187	39,192	(a-42)
Nevada	38,447	53,516	46,600	51,689	(a-13)	48,676	52,968	50,320	107,100	(a-42)
New Hampshire	52,000	60,410	34,000	65,831	(a-6)	50,499	53,209	65,831	43,283	(a-42)
New Jersey	85,273 (d)	60,000 (d)	95,000	95,000	(a-4)	56,640 (d)	(a-6)	95,000	95,000	(a-42)
New Mexico	62,067	62,067	62,067	57,408	62,067	56,222	62,067	62,067	65,000	62,067
New York	98,399	91,957	87,338	91,957	(a-4)	(a-21)	(a-6)	(a-18)	(a-17)	98,399
North Carolina	36,823 (d)	68,304	38,549 (d)	(a-31)	(a-9)	58,884	35,143 (d)	78,057 (d)	134,450	56,000 (d)
North Dakota	39,744	55,596	41,736	60,144	(a-9)	48,180	(a-9)	78,012	93,528	58,100
Ohio	32,698 (d)	58,843 (d)	40,394 (d)	58,843 (d)	(a-9)	40,394 (d)	(a-6)	58,843 (d)	115,003	(a-42)
Oklahoma	(a-5)	(a-33)	51,115	39,985	(a-9)	60,949	(a-6)	87,288	120,000	(a-42)
Oregon	56,904	69,180	62,700	69,180	(a-9)	69,180	76,224	69,180	120,000	76,224
Pennsylvania	60,910	62,250	64,997	65,000	(a-39)	(nn)	61,500	65,000	64,500	64,500
Rhode Island	(a-5)	67,868 (d)	(a-36)	67,868 (d)	(a-9)	37,034 (d)	60,497 (d)	100,696	87,120	(a-42)
South Carolina	39,047	86,268	55,161	66,930 (d)	(a-6)	65,349 (d)	71,113 (d)	93,619 (d)	77,700	(a-42)
South Dakota	40,123	29,307	43,514	46,405	(a-9)	53,165	(a-6)	52,208	86,000	52,666
Tennessee	52,000	57,500	64,500	62,000	(a-6)	57,500	55,500	61,000	98,500	(a-42)
Texas	52,500	77,700	61,425	67,515	(a-13)	75,600	(a-6)	84,000	117,923	84,000
Utah	44,346	69,342	N.A.	58,760	(a-13)	48,422	(a-6)	80,517	N.A.	(a-42)
Vermont	39,042	53,061	58,157	49,005	(a-9)	47,008	50,003	63,003	39,624	61,714
Virginia	63,357	75,996	43,654	63,713	92,913	60,567	84,826	93,018	94,636	96,528
Washington	52,337	54,969	59,713	79,620	(a-9)	(ss)	(a-6)	79,620	85,000	(a-42)
West Virginia	32,000	45,000	(z)	(aa)	(a-6)	31,812 (d)	25,152 (d)	(vv)	70,000	60,000
Wisconsin	37,567 (d)	46,871 (d)	43,539 (d)	50,461 (d)	46,871 (d)	40,442 (d)	46,871 (d)	54,324	72,971 (d)	50,461 (d)
Wyoming	37,992	55,509	32,094	57,000	(a-13)	61,800	(a-6)	78,418	60,000	(a-42)

Florida: Commerce, $106,733; Consumer affairs, $63,371; Health, $106,733

Iowa: Administration, $64,700; Banking, $57,000; Budget, $75,100; Civil rights, $51,600; Commerce, $64,700; Community affairs, $61,984; Comptroller, $75,100; Computer services, $61,984; Consumer affairs, $64,958; Corrections, $75,100; Economic development, $89,300; Education, $89,300; Emergency management, $42,600; Employment services, $64,700; Energy resources, $61,984; Environmental protection, $61,984; Finance, $75,100; Fish and wildlife, $61,984; General services, $64,700; Health, $64,700; Higher education, $89,300; Highways, $64,958; Historic preservation, $64,700; Insurance, $64,100; Labor, $64,100; Licensing, $42,600; Mental health & retardation, $68,078; Natural resources, $75,100; Parks & recreation, $53,851; Personnel, $64,700; Planning, $89,300; Pre-audit $75,100; Public library, $49,700; Public utility regulation, $64,100; Public welfare, $64,100; Purchasing, $53,851; Revenue, $75,100; Social Services, $68,078; Solid waste management, $53,851; State police, $64,958; Tourism, $53,851; Transportation, $89,300

Maryland: Adjutant general, $86,205; Administration, $100,550; Agriculture, $100,550; Banking, $73,907; Budget, $117,281; Civil rights, $79,819; Commerce, $73,907; Community affairs, $73,907; Consumer affairs, $73,907; Corrections, $86,205; Economic development, 73,907; Education, $108,593; Elections administration, $73,907; Emergency management, $63,364; Employment services, $79,819; Energy resources, $51,730; Environmental protection, $100,550; Fish and wild-life, $55,869; General services, $100,550; Health, $117,281; Higher education, $108,593; Historic preservation, $73,907; Insurance, $73,907; Labor, $73,907; Licensing, $100,550; Mental health & retardation, $86,205; Natural resources, $108,593; Parks & recreation, $79,819; Personnel, $100,550; Planning, $79,819; Post audit, $93,102; Pre-audit $35,287; Public library, $73,907; Public utility regulation, $86,205; Public welfare, $79,819; Purchasing, $51,730; Social Services, $79,819; Solid waste management, $68,433; State police, $86,205; Tourism, $79,819; Transportation, $117,281

Michigan: Community affairs, $62,911; Comptroller, $77,987; Computer services, $77,987; Consumer affairs, $83,394; Economic development, $77,987; Emergency management, $59,299; Employment services, $77,987; Environmental protection, $83,478; General services, $72,140; Higher education, $68,027; Historic preservation, $77,987; Parks & recreation, $68,027; Purchasing, $77,987; Revenue, $72,140; Solid waste management, $83,478

Mississippi: Budget, $72,152; Commerce, $75,471; Community affairs, $47,232; Comptroller, $72,153; Computer services, $66,622; Consumer affairs, $56,228; Economic development, 75,471; Education, $70,733; Elections administration, $53,765; Environmental protection, $63,073; Fish and wildlife, $57,939; General services, $72,152; Health, $86,366; Natural resources, $67,623; Parks & recreation, $30,911; Personnel, $65,641; Planning, $47,232; Pre-audit $72,153; Public welfare, $75,471; Purchasing, $52,972; Solid waste management, $57,083; Tourism, $43,600

Selected Officials: Annual Salaries, continued

State	Historic preservation	Insurance	Labor	Licensing	Mental health & retardation	Natural resources	Parks & recreation	Personnel	Plannning	Post audit
Alabama	55,900	56,812	56,811	. . .	82,160	56,812	46,488	79,407	. . .	84,240
Alaska	45,972 (d)	62,508 (d)	66,816 (d)	62,508 (d)	62,508 (d)	66,816 (d)	62,508 (d)	62,508 (d)	. . .	62,508 (d)
Arizona	29,549 (d)	46,606 (d)	51,074 (d)	. . .	. . .	55,989 (d)	42,500 (d)	51,074	51,074 (d)	82,262 (d)
Arkansas	43,773	55,493	59,182	. . .	54,112	43,773	54,841	49,199	. . .	71,133
California	64,668	95,052	101,343	95,052	95,052	83,869	95,052	95,052	86,820	101,134
Colorado	. . .	52,932	58,464	72,624	58,464	75,219	58,464	63,246 (d)	(a-9)	72,908
Connecticut	38,929 (d)	67,639 (d)	67,639 (d)	57,632 (d)	(s)	(a-21)	59,935 (d)	63,246 (d)	59,789 (d)	62,336 (d)
Delaware	53,724	60,400	65,600	45,920	83,546	70,900	58,091	70,900	55,650	60,400
Florida	57,904	91,301	65,894	53,489	68,244	84,925	68,752	84,925	(a-9)	87,144
Georgia	51,492	71,172	71,184	61,218	95,962	78,349	61,676	77,862	78,984	70,640
Hawaii	85,302	67,716	85,302	85,302	42,132	85,302	48,504	85,302	85,302	64,356
Idaho	46,176	57,533	52,187	43,971	56,139	. . .	58,947	56,139	(a-11)	52,187
Illinois	67,792	60,349	60,349	61,488	71,321	57,057	65,835	57,504	56,710	68,250
Indiana	N.A.	50,024	50,024	39,260	63,024	65,702	54,938	66,820	47,684	57,980
Iowa	52,700 (d)	49,700 (d)	49,700 (d)	25,600 (d)	53,851 (d)	56,400 (d)	42,598 (d)	52,700 (d)	(a-16)	55,700
Kansas	39,708	56,816	58,575	N.A.	63,000	(a-21)	72,267	65,368	(a-9)	69,036
Kentucky	52,103	53,550	66,283	40,057	66,434	64,260	52,500	64,504	(a-9)	59,263
Louisiana	33,288	60,169	56,016	38,148	(g)	58,000	43,841	59,532	39,792	(f)
Maine (c)	35,114	48,825	49,404	32,656	54,272	(a-21)	42,794	45,781	52,874	37,085
Maryland	60,093 (d)	60,093 (d)	60,093 (d)	81,756 (d)	(h)	88,296 (d)	64,900 (d)	81,756 (d)	64,900 (d)	75,700 (d)
Massachusetts	44,100	63,300	52,100	52,100	(xx)	69,100	52,100	73,200	(a-16)	70,000
Michigan	29,838 (d)	72,015	65,020	80,300	80,300	83,100	50,863 (d)	80,300	. . .	69,500
Minnesota	N.A.	67,500	67,500	35,747	61,283	67,500	50,905	67,500	67,500	62,320
Mississippi	44,400	54,000	. . .	. . .	64,800	53,243 (d)	20,642 (d)	51,657 (d)	37,172 (d)	54,000
Missouri	30,072	57,945	67,970	54,396	75,930	67,970	57,945	54,423	(a-6)	70,909
Montana	28,819	36,048	51,763	44,292	(yy)	51,763	38,164	42,517	(a-9)	59,446
Nebraska	54,996	57,040	45,862	46,320	(ee)	51,492	65,000	51,500	47,914	35,000
Nevada	37,319	52,900	43,300	. . .	69,000	55,982	45,900	49,498	36,757	59,147
New Hampshire	39,684	67,625	50,499	(a-2)	65,831	67,625	50,499	55,001	52,000	61,000
New Jersey	38,336 (d)	95,000	95,000	(a-15)	(v)	78,500	59,471 (d)	95,000	95,000	80,000
New Mexico	45,573	50,232	46,592	(gg)	(hh)	62,067	53,872	53,123	. . .	40,425
New York	87,338	87,338	(a-19)	(a-2)	(ii)	(a-21)	(a-27)	87,338	87,338	(a-4)
North Carolina	32,023 (d)	70,992	70,992	. . .	53,383 (d)	70,992	38,549 (d)	70,992	38,549 (d)	70,992
North Dakota	28,620	49,300	45,996	(a-2)	50,652	. . .	44,532	49,116	(a-20)	(kk)
Ohio	. . .	48,360 (d)	48,360 (d)	. . .	(ll)	58,843 (d)	40,394 (d)	36,088 (d)	(a-9)	66,997
Oklahoma	48,400	75,400	42,140	. . .	(p)	55,000	(a-31)	55,400	. . .	50,000
Oregon	(mm)	76,224	59,500	(a-28)	(q)	59,700	62,700	69,180	62,700	59,700
Pennsylvania	51,462	58,000	65,000	50,600	57,487	(a-21)	60,988	64,000	51,000	84,000
Rhode Island	N.A.	67,868 (d)	60,497 (d)	37,034 (d)	75,240 (d)	(a-21)	38,388 (d)	53,128 (d)	53,218 (d)	(oo)
South Carolina	32,093	66,722 (d)	60,244 (d)	. . .	(s)	55,161	61,891 (d)	69,246 (d)	(a-33)	69,246 (d)
South Dakota	37,502	(a-11)	52,208	21,008	(t)	65,000	42,328	50,794	. . .	51,355
Tennessee	36,500	57,500	55,500	40,000	61,000	57,500	52,000	57,500	58,000	(a-13)
Texas	50,299	69,300	. . .	58,907	88,480	70,711	(a-23)	. . .	(a-9)	81,230
Utah	48,277	55,515	60,819	44,075	(zz)	65,770	50,315	62,150	(a-9)	(qq)
Vermont	37,045	54,205	51,646	26,416	63,107	62,026	50,835	52,562	45,989	47,700
Virginia	65,590	(a-8)	66,324	57,795	92,706	92,913	(a-27)	81,880	(a-9)	87,992
Washington	44,764	63,900	79,620	(a-6)	70,368	69,800	73,932	79,620	(a-9)	67,100
West Virginia	(bb)	36,700	35,700	. . .	47,250	(a-21)	49,980	38,300	(a-6)	N.A.
Wisconsin	37,567 (d)	50,461 (d)	54,324 (d)	46,871 (d)	34,809 (d)	58,483 (d)	(a-9)	54,324 (d)	32,253	37,567 (d)
Wyoming	51,425	44,160 (d)	45,556	31,563	44,437	41,272	30,566	54,149	48,880	(a-13)

New Jersey: Administration, $80,000; Budget, $111,519; Civil rights, $83,261; Comptroller, $111,519; Consumer affairs, $87,418; Elections administration, $59,178; Emergency management, $111,414; Employment services, $80,000; Fish and wildlife, $79,293; General services, $80,000; Historic preservation, $53,670; Licensing, $87,418; Mental health & retardation, $87,418; Parks & recreation, $83,261; Purchasing, $80,000; Revenue, $101,203; Solid waste management, $68,491; State police, $111,414

North Carolina: Budget, $63,072; Civil rights, $63,072; Community affairs, $66,096; Computer services, $101,688; Consumer affairs, $76,332; Economic development, 69,336; Elections administration, $76,332; Emergency management, $60,204; Energy resources, $63,072; Finance, $63,072; General services, $57,432; Health, $129,492; Highways, $92,400; Historic preservation, $52,284; Mental health & retardation, $88,104; Parks & recreation, $63,072; Planning, $63,072; Public library, $69,336; Purchasing, $72,768; Social Services, $80,052; Solid waste management, $66,096; State police, $76,332; Tourism, $66,096

Ohio: Administration, $82,680; Agriculture, $76,586; Banking, $76,586; Budget, $76,586; Civil rights, $64,251; Commerce, $70,138; Community affairs, $58,843; Computer services, $58,843; Consumer affairs, $64,251; Corrections, $82,680; Economic development, $58,843; Elections administration, $52,936; Emergency management, $49,317; Employment services, $82,680; Energy resources, $52,936; Environmental protection, $82,680;

Finance, $76,586; Fish and wildlife, $52,936; General services, $82,680; Health, $82,680; Highways, $82,680; Insurance, $70,138; Labor, $70,138; Mental health & retardation, $82,680; Natural resources, $82,680; Parks & recreation, $53,936; Personnel, $53,851; Planning, $76,586; Public library, $64,251; Public utility regulation, $82,680; Public welfare, $76,586; Purchasing, $53,851; Revenue, $76,586; Social Services, $76,586; Solid waste management, $52,936; State police, $64,251; Tourism, $64,251; Transportation, $82,680

Rhode Island: Adjutant general, $58,040; Administration, $80,156; Agriculture, $37,432; Banking, $53,128; Budget, $72,785; Civil rights, $37,432; Commerce, $75,240; Comptroller, $58,040; Computer services, $48,215; Consumer affairs, $34,624; Corrections, $80,156; Economic development, $75,240; Emergency management, $58,040; Employment services, $75,240; Energy resources, $70,326; Environmental protection, $75,240; Finance, $67,868; Fish and wildlife, $41,943; General services, $67,868; Highways, $80,156; Insurance, $75,240; Labor, $67,868; Licensing, $41,943; Mental health & retardation, $82,611; Natural resources, $75,240; Parks & recreation, $43,503; Personnel, $60,497; Planning, $60,497; Pre-audit $29,513; Public library, $62,956; Public utility regulation, $70,326; Public welfare, $58,040; Purchasing, $62,956; Revenue, $65,412; Social Services, $80,156; Transportation, $80,156

Selected Officials: Annual Salaries, continued

State	Pre-audit	Public library	Public utility regulation	Public welfare	Purchasing	Revenue	Social services	Solid waste management	State police	Tourism	Transportation
Alabama	(a-13)	55,000	47,891	56,812	61,022	56,812	(a-37)	47,658	50,102	56,812	33,134
Alaska	62,508 (d)	62,508 (d)	62,508 (d)	62,508 (d)	(a-24)	62,508 (d)	66,816 (d)	49,140 (d)	62,508 (d)	62,508 (d)	66,816 (d)
Arizona	. . .	40,215	46,606 (d)	. . .	42,500 (d)	61,362 (d)	51,074 (d)	42,500 (d)	85,000	46,606 (d)	67,225 (d)
Arkansas	31,136	50,136	58,183	. . .	49,199	53,210	58,022	55,000	49,174	38,327	76,708
California	72,500	4,540	90,860	95,052	5,898 (d)	95,052	95,052	79,676	101,343	67,824	95,052
Colorado	(a-13)	56,210	48,400	(a-40)	55,680	83,000	75,000	58,464	58,464	58,464	. . .
Connecticut	(a-13)	59,789 (d)	70,117 (d)	72,681 (d)	63,246 (d)	67,639 (d)	67,639 (d)	59,935 (d)	72,681 (d)	43,790 (d)	82,669 (d)
Delaware	60,400	42,012	46,301	66,641	48,589	70,469	81,400	. . .	67,841	36,054 (d)	76,100
Florida	74,460	62,194	84,925	67,989	61,556	85,292	70,686	65,468	70,386	58,624	86,700
Georgia	70,640	73,614	68,490	(a-40)	65,412	69,804	75,903	66,396	75,854	73,776	93,530
Hawaii	60,912	85,302	74,880	61,488	51,420	85,302	85,302	74,880	. . .	85,302	85,302
Idaho	(a-13)	34,445	50,003	60,424	40,872	39,749	54,787	46,176	48,485	(a-11)	73,445
Illinois	(a-13)	61,692	70,455	71,321	(a-6)	71,321	65,835	(a-31)	65,835	(a-11)	71,321
Indiana	(a-13)	57,096	53,014	65,000	(a-6)	65,000	(a-37)	38,844	59,956	45,916	55,016
Iowa	(a-39)	35,200 (d)	49,700 (d)	42,598 (d)	42,598 (d)	56,400 (d)	53,851 (d)	42,598 (d)	51,397 (d)	42,598 (d)	63,000 (d)
Kansas	(a-13)	53,295	74,347	53,500	56,286	72,267	72,795	(a-21)	55,710	49,400	72,267
Kentucky	(a-11)	53,028	60,900	65,098	44,404	64,260	59,322	50,431	64,260	64,260	64,260
Louisiana	(a-6)	48,713	61,536	53,500	(g)	58,000	58,000	51,000	52,000	43,842	58,455
Maine (c)	(a-13)	38,885	59,109	40,019	38,858	46,490	(a-37)	(a-21)	49,339	32,947 (d)	(a-26)
Maryland	26,867 (d)	60,093 (d)	70,092 (d)	64,900 (d)	39,383 (d)	(a-13)	64,900 (d)	55,642 (d)	70,092 (d)	64,900 (d)	95,360 (d)
Massachusetts	(a-13)	48,800	63,300	77,600	69,000	77,500	80,000	44,000	69,000	46,200	70,600
Michigan	(a-35)	. . .	65,000	80,300	29,838 (d)	(i)	80,300	29,838 (d)	80,300	72,119	80,300
Minnesota	68,361	59,299	45,790	51,052	63,141	78,500	55,228	62,181	58,005	63,600	78,500
Mississippi	(a-9)	44,400	33,600	59,713 (d)	35,356 (d)	60,000	N.A.	38,111 (d)	48,000	29,116 (d)	48,000
Missouri	(a-13)	60,462	67,970	61,521	54,423	76,787	70,909	41,508	63,700	54,396	79,788
Montana	. . .	42,517	38,295	51,763	39,763	51,763	51,763	39,763	44,579	39,541	33,731
Nebraska	(a-13)	48,144	37,992	(a-40)	44,736	66,612	63,370	(a-21)	51,565	38,388	65,522
Nevada	(a-6)	44,626	64,100	56,530	46,715	60,700	64,749	51,689	50,033	(w)	64,475
New Hampshire	53,209	50,499	67,625	53,209	(a-24)	67,625	67,625	39,685 (d)	60,410	33,248 (d)	67,625
New Jersey	(a-9)	76,990	95,000	76,000	60,000 (d)	72,286 (d)	95,000	48,929 (d)	(a-18)	75,625	95,000
New Mexico	46,592	40,789	56,077	41,621	49,317	62,067	53,123	54,558	58,760	52,884	62,067
New York	(a-4)	(a-17)	91,957	91,957	(a-6)	91,957	(a-37)	(a-21)	91,957	87,338	(a-26)
North Carolina	. . .	42,229 (d)	70,992	70,992	44,286 (d)	70,992	48,629 (d)	40,377 (d)	46,411 (d)	40,377 (d)	70,992
North Dakota	(a-9)	42,168	49,300	71,556	50,220	49,296	66,192	47,448	46,175	36,216	. . .
Ohio	(a-35)	43,867 (d)	58,843 (d)	53,331 (d)	36,088 (d)	53,331 (d)	(a-37)	40,394 (d)	43,867 (d)	43,867 (d)	58,843 (d)
Oklahoma	(a-9)	47,906	51,115	87,287	59,573	62,922	87,287	31,272	59,400	(a-31)	67,400
Oregon	. . .	62,700	69,180	76,224	51,576	76,224	84,072	(a-21)	76,224	56,904	76,224
Pennsylvania	(a-4)	. . .	57,519	65,000	49,135	(a-39)	57,750	53,790	61,500	(a-11)	65,000
Rhode Island	25,369 (d)	55,584 (d)	62,956 (d)	50,671 (d)	55,584 (d)	58,040 (d)	72,785 (d)	. . .	81,111	38,937	72,785 (d)
South Carolina	(a-13)	50,867 (d)	57,673	(a-40)	43,825 (d)	63,448	82,091 (d)	40,609 (d)	58,250 (d)	42,237 (d)	97,351 (d)
South Dakota	. . .	38,750	30,992	66,040	35,006	52,208	66,040	(a-21)	47,341	49,317	59,073
Tennesseee	54,000	64,500	65,000	61,000	40,000	61,000	45,500	52,000	55,500	57,500	61,000
Texas	(a-13)	54,600	(a-20)	84,000	(a-6)	(a-13)	(a-37)	58,244	79,800	64,260	(a-26)
Utah	(a-13)	51,334	51,542	55,515	47,008	65,166	68,078	51,834	54,142	49,816	68,058
Vermont	(a-9)	48,714	64,646	57,220	37,128	54,038	46,446	47,944	55,155	50,544	61,714
Virginia	(a-13)	76,830	(a-8)	84,131	74,499	90,055	84,131	60,407	81,880	68,157	96,528
Washington	. . .	(tt)	73,932	(uu)	53,629	79,620	(a-37)	42,226	79,620	56,346	98,459
West Virginia	(a-6)	47,500	50,000	47,800	27,636 (d)	(cc)	26,364 (d)	31,812	(dd)	47,250	70,000
Wisconsin	32,253 (d)	37,567 (d)	50,462 (d)	54,324 (d)	40,442 (d)	58,483 (d)	67,783 (d)	40,442 (d)	46,871 (d)	43,539 (d)	58,483 (d)
Wyoming	(a-13)	35,316 (d)	55,509	51,540	43,363	62,809	55,104	45,556	50,291	56,445	69,320

South Carolina: Administration, $126,661; Budget, $93,686; Civil rights, $77,103; Commerce, $108,539; Computer services, $96,211; Consumer affairs, $90,270; Corrections, $126,661; Economic development, $108,539; Elections administration, $66,580; Environmental protection, $100,394; Finance, $126,661; Fish and wildlife, $88,413; General services, $96,211; Health, $126,661; Higher education, $105,124; Highways, $131,711; Insurance, $90,270; Labor, $81,506; Mental health & retardation, $111,065; Parks & recreation, $83,735; Personnel, $93,686; Planning, $93,686; Post audit, $93,686; Public library, $66,819; Public welfare, $111,065; Purchasing, $65,737; Social Services, $111,065; Solid waste management, $60,913; State police, $87,376; Tourism, $63,355; Transportation, $131,711

West Virginia: Budget, $46,044; Computer services, $61,068; Consumer affairs, $47,250; Fish and wildlife, $58,248; General services, $46,044; Historic preservation, $38,220; Planning, $46,044; Purchasing, $50,568; Social Services, $48,264; Solid waste management, $58,248

Wisconsin: Adjutant general, $76,615; Administration, $86,149; Agriculture, $83,117; Banking, $70,629; Budget, $76,615; Civil rights, $60,047; Commerce, $83,117; Community affairs, $65,121; Comptroller, $65,121; Computer services, $60,047; Consumer affairs, $65,121; Corrections, $83,117; Economic development, $55,376; Elections administration, $60,047; Emergency management, $55,376; Employment services, $70,629; Energy resources, $65,121; Environmental protection, $76,615; Finance, $70,629; Fish and wildlife, $60,047; General services, $70,629; Health, $83,117; Higher education, $111,650; Highways, $76,615; Historic preser-

vation, $55,376; Insurance, $76,615; Labor, $83,117; Licensing, $70,629; Mental health & retardation, $50,591; Natural resources, $86,149; Parks & recreation, $60,047; Personnel, $86,149; Planning, $76,615; Post audit, $83,117; Pre-audit $46,882; Public library, $55,376; Public utility regulation, $76,615; Public welfare, $83,117; Purchasing, $60,047; Revenue, $86,149; Social Services, $86,149; Solid waste management, $60,047; State police, $70,629; Tourism, $65,121; Transportation, $86,149

Wyoming: Insurance, $69,900; Public library, $55,104.

(e) Responsibilities shared between Assistant Secretary, Office of Mental Retardation, Health & Human Resources Department, $63,327 and Assistant Secretary, Department of Health & Hospitals.

(f) Responsibilities shared between Commissioner, Division of Administration, $66,492 and Legislative Auditor, Office of Legislative Auditor.

(g) Responsibilities shared between Commissioner Division of Administration, $46,848 and State Director of Purchasing, same office.

(h) Responsibilities shared between Director, Developmental Disabilities Administration, Department of Health & Mental Hygiene, $70,092-$86,205 and Assistant Secretary, Mental Health-Addictions, Developmental Disabilities.

(i) Responsibilities shared between Commissioner of Revenue, Bureau of Revenue, Department of Treasury, $72,140 and Director, Local Finance Programs, same department $29,838-$72,140.

(j) Responsibilities shared between Commissioner, Pollution Control Agency, $67,500 and Executive Director, Environmental Quality Board.

APPENDIX 63

Selection of State and Local Judges in the United States

Alabama	Appellate, circuit, district, and probate judges elected on partisan ballots. Judges of municipal courts are appointed by the governing body of the municipality.
Alaska	Supreme court justices, superior, and district court judges appointed by governor from nominations by Judicial Council. Approved or rejected at first general election held more than 3 years after appointment. Reconfirmed every 10, 6, and 4 years, respectively. Magistrates appointed by and serve at pleasure of the presiding judges of each judicial district.
Arizona	Supreme court justices and court of appeals judges appointed by governor from a list of not less than 3 for each vacancy submitted by a 9-member Commission on Appellate Court Appointments. Maricopa and Pima County superior court judges appointed by governor from a list of not less than 3 for each vacancy submitted by a 9-member commission on trial court appointments for each county. Superior court judges of other 12 counties elected on nonpartisan ballot (partisan primary); justices of the peace elected on partisan ballot; city and town magistrates selected as provided by charter or ordinance, usually appointed by mayor and council.
Arkansas	All elected on partisan ballot.
California	Supreme court and courts of appeal judges appointed by governor with approval of Commission on Judicial Appointments. Run for reelection on record. All judges elected on nonpartisan ballot.
Colorado	Judges of all courts, except Denver County and municipal, appointed initially by governor from lists submitted by nonpartisan nominating commissions; run on record for retention. Municipal judges appointed by city councils or town boards. Denver County judges appointed by mayor from list submitted by nominating commission; judges run on record for retention.
Connecticut	All appointed by legislature from nominations submitted by governor, except that probate judges are elected on partisan ballot.
Delaware	All appointed by governor with consent of senate.
Florida	All trial judges are elected on a nonpartisan ballot. All appellate judges are appointed by the governor with recommendations by a Judicial Nominating Commission. The latter are retained by running on their records.
Georgia	All elected on partisan ballot, except that county and some city court judges are appointed by the governor with consent of the senate.
Hawaii	Supreme court justices and circuit court judges appointed by the governor with consent of the senate. District judges appointed by chief justice of the state.
Idaho	Supreme court and district court initially are nominated by Idaho Judicial Council and appointed by governor; thereafter, they are elected on nonpartisan ballot. Magistrates appointed by District Magistrate's Commission for initial 2-year term; thereafter, run on record for retention for 4-year term on nonpartisan ballot.

Illinois	All elected on partisan ballot and run on record for retention. Associate judges are appointed by circuit judges and serve 4-year terms.
Indiana	Judges of appellate courts appointed by governor from a list of 3 for each vacancy submitted by a 7-member Judicial Nomination Commission. Governor appoints members of municipal courts and several counties have judicial nominating commissions which submit a list of nominees to the governor for appointment. All other judges are elected.
Iowa	Judges of supreme, appeals, and district courts appointed initially by governor from lists submitted by nonpartisan nominating commissions. Appointee serves initial 1-year term and then runs on record for retention. District associate judges run on record for retention, if not retained or office becomes vacant, replaced by a full-time judicial magistrate. Full-time judicial magistrates appointed by district judges in the judicial election district from nominees submitted by county judicial magistrate appointing commission. Part-time judicial magistrates appointed by county judicial magistrate appointing commissions.
Kansas	Judges of appellate courts appointed by governor from list submitted by nominating commission. Run on record for retention. Nonpartisan selection method adopted for judges of courts of general jurisdiction in 23 of 29 districts.
Kentucky	All judges elected on nonpartisan ballot.
Louisiana	All elected on open (bipartisan) ballot.
Maine	All appointed by governor with confirmation of the senate, except that probate judges are elected on partisan ballot.
Maryland	Judges of court of appeals, court of special appeals, circuit courts, and Supreme Bench of Baltimore City appointed by governor, elected on nonpartisan ballot after at least one year's service. District court judges appointed by governor subject to confirmation by senate.
Massachusetts	All appointed by governor with consent of Executive Council. Judicial Nominating Commission, established by executive order, advises governor on appointment of judges.
Michigan	All elected on nonpartisan ballot, except municipal judges in accordance with local charters by local city councils.
Minnesota	All elected on nonpartisan ballot. Vacancy filled by gubernatorial appointment.
Mississippi	All elected on partisan ballot, except that city police court justices are appointed by governing authority of each municipality.
Missouri	Judges of supreme court, court of appeals, circuit and probate courts in St. Louis City and County, Jackson County, Platte County, Clay County, and St. Louis Court of Criminal Correction appointed initially by governor from nominations submitted by special commissions. Run on record for reelection. All other judges elected on partisan ballot.
Montana	All elected on nonpartisan ballot. Vacancies on supreme or district courts and Worker's Compensation Court filled by governor according to established appointment procedure (from 3 nominees submitted by Judicial Nominations Commission). Vacancies at end of term may be filled by election, except Worker's Compensation Court. Gubernatorial appointments face senate confirmation.
Nebraska	Judges of all courts appointed initially by governor from lists submitted by bipartisan nominating commissions. Run on record for retention in office in

	general election following initial term of 3 years; subsequent terms are 6 years.
Nevada	All elected on nonpartisan ballot.
New Hampshire	All appointed by governor with confirmation of Executive Council.
New Jersey	All appointed by governor with consent of senate except that judges of municipal courts serving one municipality only are appointed by governing bodies.
New Mexico	All elected on partisan ballot.
New York	All elected on partisan ballot except that governor appoints chief judge and associate judges of court of appeals, with advice and consent of senate, from a list of persons found to be well qualified and recommended by the bipartisan Judicial Nominating Commission, and also appoints judges of court of claims and designates members of appellate division of supreme court. Mayor of New York City appoints judges of the criminal and family courts in the city.
North Carolina	All elected on partisan ballot. By executive order, governor has established 1-year trial system for merit selection of superior court judges.
North Dakota	All elected on nonpartisan ballot.
Ohio	All elected on nonpartisan ballot, except court of claims judges who may be appointed by chief justice of supreme court from ranks of supreme court, court of appeals, court of common pleas, or retired judges.
Oklahoma	Supreme court justices and court of criminal appeals judges appointed by governor from lists of 3 submitted by Judicial Nominating Commission. If governor fails to make appointment within 60 days after occurrence of vacancy, appointment is made by chief justice from the same list. Run for election on their records at first general election following completion of 12 months' service for unexpired term. Judges of court of appeals, and district and associate district judges elected on nonpartisan ballot in adversary popular election. Special judges appointed by district judges. Municipal judges appointed by governing body of municipality.
Oregon	All judges except municipal judges are elected on nonpartisan ballot for 6-year terms. Municipal judges are mostly appointed by city councils except 1 Oregon city elects its judge.
Pennsylvania	All originally elected on partisan ballot; thereafter, on nonpartisan retention ballot, except police magistrates, city of Pittsburgh—appointed by mayor of Pittsburgh.
Rhode Island	Supreme court justices elected by legislature. Superior, family, and district court justices and justices of the peace appointed by governor, with consent of senate (except for justices of the peace); probate and municipal court judges appointed by city or town councils.
South Carolina	Supreme court and circuit court judges elected by legislature. City judges, magistrates, and some county judges and family court judges appointed by governor—the latter on recommendation of the legislative delegation in the area served by the court. Probate judges and some county judges elected on partisan ballot.
South Dakota	All elected on nonpartisan ballot, except magistrates (law trained and others), who are appointed by the presiding judge of the judicial circuit.
Tennessee	Judges of intermediate appellate courts appointed initially by governor from nominations submitted by special commission. Run on record for reelection. The supreme court judges and all other judges elected on partisan ballot,

except from some municipal judges who are appointed by the governing body of the city.

Texas	All elected on partisan ballot except municipal judges, most of whom are appointed by municipal governing body.
Utah	Supreme court, district court, and circuit court judges appointed by governor from lists of 3 nominees submitted by nominating commissions. If governor fails to make appointment within 30 days, chief justice appoints. Judges run for retention in office at next succeeding election; they may be opposed by others on nonpartisan judicial ballots. Juvenile court judges are initially appointed by the governor from a list of not less than 2 nominated by the Juvenile Court Commission, and retained in office by gubernatorial appointment. Town justices of the peace are appointed for 4-year terms by town trustees. County justices of the peace are elected for 4 years on nonpartisan ballot.
Vermont	Supreme court justices, superior court judges (presiding judges of county courts), and district court judges appointed by governor with consent of senate from list of persons designated as qualified by the Judicial Selection Board. Supreme, superior, and district court judges retained in office by vote of legislature. Assistant judges of county courts and probate judges elected on partisan ballot in the territorial area of their jurisdiction.
Virginia	Supreme court justices and all judges of circuit courts, general district, and juvenile and domestic relations district courts elected by legislature. Committee on district courts, in the case of part-time judges, certifies that a vacancy exists. Thereupon, all part-time judges of general district courts and juvenile and domestic relations courts are appointed by circuit court judges.
Washington	All elected on nonpartisan ballot except that municipal judges in second-, third- and fourth-class cities are appointed by mayor.
West Virginia	Judges of all courts of record and magistrate courts elected on partisan ballot.
Wisconsin	All elected on nonpartisan ballot.
Wyoming	Supreme court justices and district court judges appointed by governor from a list of 3 submitted by nominating committee and stand for retention at next election after 1 year in office. Justices of the peace elected on nonpartisan ballot. Municipal judges appointed by mayor.
Dist. of Col.	Nominated by the president of the United States from a list of persons recommended by the District of Columbia Judicial Nomination Commission; appointed upon the advice and consent of the U.S. Senate.
American Samoa	Chief justice and associate justice(s) appointed by the U.S. Secretary of Interior pursuant to presidential delegation of authority. Associate judges appointed by governor of American Samoa on recommendation of the chief justice, and subsequently confirmed by the senate of American Samoa.
Guam	All appointed by governor with consent of legislature from list of 3 nominees submitted by Judicial Council for term of 5 years; thereafter run on record for retention every 5 years.
Puerto Rico	All appointed by governor with consent of senate.

APPENDIX 64

State Courts of Last Resort

State or other jurisdiction	Name of court	Justices chosen (a)		No. of judges (b)	Term (in years) (c)	Chief justice	
		At large	By district			Method of selection	Term of service as chief justice
Alabama	S.C.	★		9	6	Popular election	6 years
Alaska	S.C.	★		5	10	By court	3 years (d)
Arizona	S.C.	★		5	6	By court	5 years
Arkansas	S.C.	★		7	8	Popular election	8 years
California	S.C.	★		7	12	Appointed by governor (e)	12 years
Colorado	S.C.	★		7	10	By court	At pleasure of court
Connecticut	S.C.	★		7	8	Nominated by governor, appointed by General Assembly	8 years
Delaware	S.C.	★		5	12	Appointed by governor with consent of Senate	12 years
Florida	S.C.	★		7	6	By court	2 years
Georgia	S.C.	★		7	6	By court	4 years
Hawaii	S.C.	★		5	10	Appointed by governor, with consent of Senate	10 years
Idaho	S.C.	★		5	6	By court	4 years
Illinois	S.C.		★	7	10	By court	3 years
Indiana	S.C.	★		5	10 (f)	Selected by judicial nominating commission from S.C. members	5 years
Iowa	S.C.	★		9	8	By court	Remainder of term
Kansas	S.C.	★		7	6	By seniority of service (g)	Remainder of term
Kentucky	S.C.	★	★	7	8	By court	4 years
Louisiana	S.C.	★	★	7	10	By seniority of service	Remainder pf term
Maine	S.J.C.		★	7	7	Appointed by governor, with consent of Senate	7 years
Maryland	C.A.	★		7	10	Designated by governor	Remainder of term
Massachusetts	S.J.C.	★		7	To age 70	Appointed by governor	To age 70
Michigan	S.C.	★		7	8	By court	2 years
Minnesota	S.C.	★		7	6	Popular election	6 years
Mississippi	S.C.		★	9	8	By seniority of service	Remainder of term
Missouri	S.C.	★		7	12	By court	2 years
Montana	S.C.		★ (h)	7	8	Popular election	8 years
Nebraska	S.C.	★		7	6	Appointed by governor	Life
Nevada	S.C.	★		5	6	By seniority of service (i)	1-2 years
New Hampshire	S.C.	★		5	To age 70	Appointed by governor and Council	To age 70
New Jersey	S.C.	★		7	7 (j)	Appointed by governor, with consent of Senate	7 years (j)
New Mexico	S.C.	★		5	8	By court	2 years
New York	C.A.	★		7	14 (j)	Appointed by governor, with consent of Senate	14 years (j)
North Carolina	S.C.	★		7	8	Popular election	8 years
North Dakota	S.C.	★		5	10	By Supremem and district court judges	5 years (k)
Ohio	S.C.	★		7	6	Popular election	6 years
Oklahoma	S.C.	★	★	9	6	By court	2 years
	C.C.A.			3	6	By court	2 years
Oregon	S.C.	★		7	6	By seniority of service	Remainder of term
Pennsylvania	S.C.	★		7	10	By seniority of service	Remainder of term
Rhode Island	S.C.	★		5	Life	By legislature	Life
South Carolina	S.C.	★		5	10	Joint public vote of General Assembly	10 years
South Dakota	S.C.		★ (l)	5	8	By court	4 years
Tennessee	S.C.	★		5	8	By court	18 months
Texas	S.C.	★		9	6	Popular election	6 years
	C.C.A.			9	6	Popular election (m)	6 years (m)
Utah	S.C.	★		5	10 (n)	By court	4 years
Vermont	S.C.	★		5	6	Appointed by governor, with consent of Senate	6 years

State Courts of Last Resort, continued

State or other jurisdiction	Name of court	Justices chosen (a) At large	Justices chosen (a) By district	No. of judges (b)	Term (in years) (c)	Chief justice Method of selection	Chief justice Term of service as chief justice
Virginia	S.C.	★		7	12	By seniority of service	Remainder of term
Washington	S.C.	★		9	6	By seniority of service	2 years
West Virginia	S.C.	★		5	12	By seniority of service	1 year
Wisconsin	S.C.	★		7	10	By seniority of service (o)	Remainder of term
Wyoming	S.C.	★		5	8	By court	2 years
Dist. of Columbia	C.A.	★		9	15	Designated by President (p)	4 years
American Samoa	H.C.	★		(q) 8	8 years	Appointed by Secretary of the Interior	(r)
Puerto Rico	S.C.	★		8	(r) To age 70	Appointed by President with consent of Senate	To age 70

Sources: National Center for State Courts, State Court Organization 1987; state constitutions and statutes.

Key:
S.C. — Supreme Court
S.C.A. — Supreme Court of Appeals
S.J.C. — Supreme Judicial Court
C.A. — Court of Appeals
C.C.A. — Court of Criminal Appeals
H.C. — High Court

(a) See Table 4.4, "Selection and Retention of Judges," for details.
(b) Number includes chief justice.
(c) The initial term may be shorter. See Table 4.4, "Selection and Retention of Judges," for details.
(d) A justice may serve more than one term as chief justice, but may not serve consecutive terms in that position.

(e) Subsequently, must run on record for retention.
(f) Initial two years; retention 10 years.
(g) If two or more qualify, then senior in age.
(h) Chief justice chosen statewide; associate judges chosen by district.
(i) If two or more qualify, then determined by lot.
(j) May be reappointed to age 70.
(k) Or expiration of term, whichever is first.
(l) Initially chosen by district; retention determined statewide.
(m) Presiding judge of Court of Criminal Appeals.
(n) Initial three years; retention 10 years.
(o) If two or more qualify, then justice with least number of years remaining in term.
(p) From list of nominees submitted by Judicial Nominating Commission.
(q) Chief judges and associate judges sit on appellate and trial divisions.
(r) For good behavior.

APPENDIX 65

State Intermediate Appellate Courts and General Trial Courts: Number of Judges and Terms

State or other jurisdiction	Intermediate appellate court			General trial court		
	Name of court	No. of judges	Term (years)	Name of court	No. of judges	Term (years)
Alabama	Court of Criminal Appeals	5	6	Circuit courts	124	6
	Court of Civil Appeals	3	6			
Alaska	Court of Appeals	3	8	Superior courts	30	6
Arizona	Court of Appeals	18	6	Superior courts	101	4
Arkansas	Court of Appeals	6	8	Chancery courts	34	4
				Circuit courts	33	6
California	Courts of Appeal	88	12	Superior courts	725	6
Colorado	Court of Appeals	13	8	District Court	110	6
Connecticut	Appellate Court	9	8	Superior courts	139	8
Delaware				Superior courts	15 (a)	12
Florida	District Court of Appeals	46	6	Circuit courts	372	6
Georgia	Court of Appeals	9	6	Superior courts	137	4 (b)
Hawaii	Intermediate Court of Appeals	3	10	Circuit courts	24	10
Idaho	Court of Appeals	3	6	District courts	33	4
Illinois	Appellate Court	34	10	Circuit courts	760 (c)	6
Indiana	Court of Appeals	12	10 (d)	Superior Court	129	6
				Circuit courts	90	6
Iowa	Court of Appeals	6	6	District courts	100 (e)	6
Kansas	Court of Appeals	10	4	District courts	146 (f)	6
Kentucky	Court of Appeals	14	8	Circuit courts	91	8
Louisiana	Court of Appeals	52	10	District courts	192	6
Maine				Superior Court	16	7
Maryland	Court of Special Appeals	13	10	Circuit courts	109 (g)	15
Massachusetts	Appeals Court	14	(i)	Trial Court	320	(i)
Michigan	Court of Appeals	18	6	Circuit courts	167	6
Minnesota	Court of Appeals	13	6	District courts	230	6
Mississippi				Chancery courts	39	4
				Circuit courts	40	4
Missouri	Court of Appeals	32	12	Circuit courts	133 (h)	6
Montana				District courts	36	6
Nebraska				District courts	48	6
Nevada				District courts	39	6
New Hampshire				Superior Court	25	(i)
New Jersey	Appellate Division of Superior Court	28	7	Superior Court	349	7
New Mexico	Court of Appeals	7	8	District courts	59	6
New York	Appellate Division of Supreme Court	47	5 (i)	Supreme Court	484	14 (i)
	Appellate Terms of Supreme Court	15	5 (i)			
North Carolina	Court of Appeals	12	8	Superior Court	74	8
North Dakota	Court of Appeals (temporary)	3		District courts	27	6
Ohio	Court of Appeals	59	6	Courts of common pleas	344	6
Oklahoma	Court of Appeals	12	6	District Court	71 (j)	4
Oregon	Court of Appeals	10	6	Circuit courts	87	6
	Tax Court	1	6			
Pennsylvania	Superior Court	15	10	Courts of common pleas	341	10
	Commonwealth Court	9	10			
Rhode Island				Superior Court	20	Life
South Carolina	Court of Appeals	6	6	Circuit Court	31	6

State Intermediate Appellate Courts and General Trial Courts, continued

State or other jurisdiction	Intermediate appellate court			General trial court		
	Name of court	No. of judges	Term (years)	Name of court	No. of judges	Term (years)
South Dakota	...	...	...	Circuit courts	35	8
Tennessee	Court of Appeals	12	6	Chancery courts	35	8
	Court of Criminal Appeals	9	8	Circuit courts	97 (k)	8
Texas	Courts of Appeals	80	6	District courts	385	4
Utah	Court of Appeals	7	10 (l)	District courts	29	6
Vermont	...	...	...	Superior courts	10	6
				District courts	15	6
Virginia	Court of Appeals	10	8	Circuit courts	122	8
Washington	Court of Appeals	16	6	Superior courts	136	4
West Virginia	...	...	...	Circuit courts	60	8
Wisconsin	Court of Appeals	13	6	Circuit courts	208	6
Wyoming	...	...	...	District courts	17	6
Dist. of Columbia	...	...	...	Superior Court	51	15
American Samoa	...	...	...	High Court: trial level	8 (m)	(n)
Guam	...	...	...	Superior Court	6	7
Puerto Rico	...	...	...	Superior Court	95	12

Sources: National Center for State Courts, *State Court Caseload Statistics: 1988 Annual Report;* state statutes and court administration offices.

Key:

... — Court does not exist in jurisdiction
(a) President judge, three resident judges and 11 associate judges.
(b) For judges of the Superior Court of the Atlanta Judicial Court, term of office is eight years.
(c) 389 authorized circuit, 371 associate circuit, plus 50 permissive associate judges.
(d) Two years initial; 10 years retention.
(e) Plus 42 district associate judges and 19 senior judges.

(f) Plus 69 district associate judges and 70 district magistrates.
(g) Includes judges of Circuit Court for Baltimore City.
(h) Plus 170 associate circuit judges.
(i) To age 70.
(j) Plus 77 associate judges and 60 special judges.
(k) With civil jurisdiction, 69 judges; with criminal jurisdiction, 28.
(l) Three years initial; 10 years retention.
(m) Chief justice and associate judges sit on appellate and trial divisions.
(n) For good behavior.

APPENDIX 66

The Virginia Judicial System

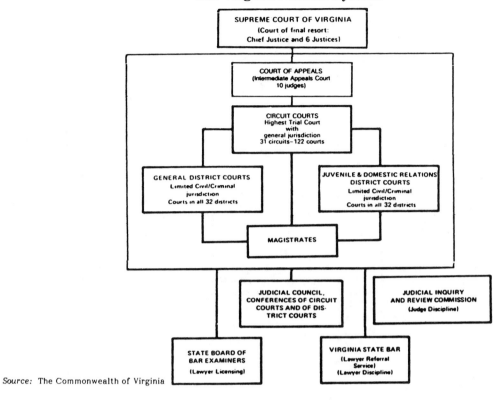

Source: The Commonwealth of Virginia

APPENDIX 67

County Government Not Centrally Controlled

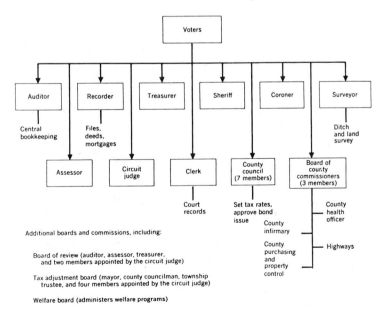

Source: Bureau of Government Research, Indiana University, Bloomington, Indiana.

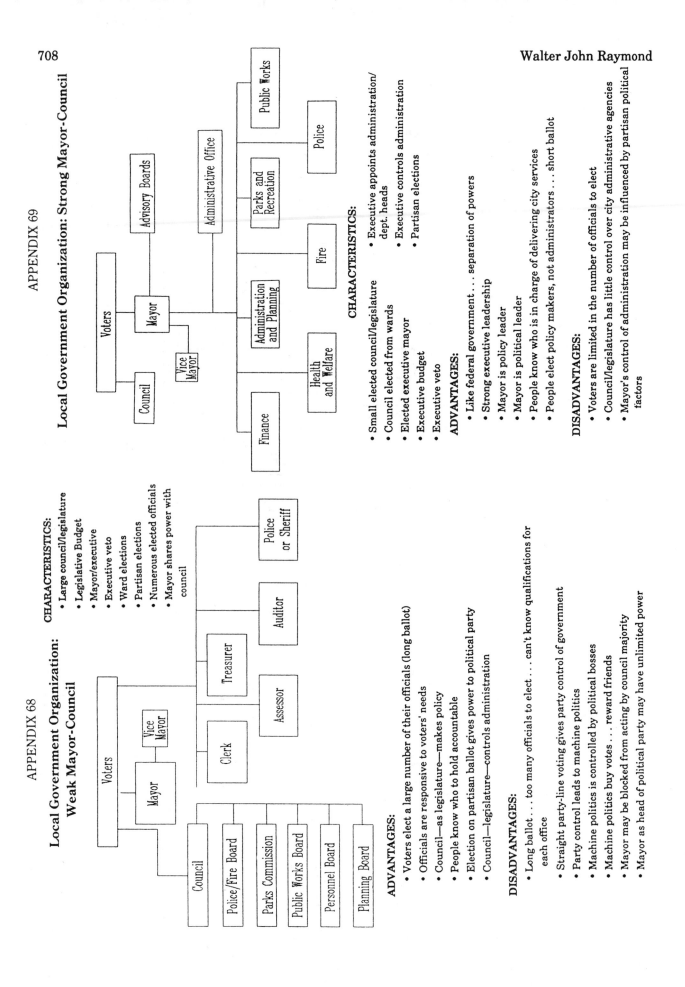

APPENDIX 69

Local Government Organization: Strong Mayor-Council

CHARACTERISTICS:
- Small elected council/legislature
- Council elected from wards
- Elected executive mayor
- Executive budget
- Executive veto
- Executive appoints administration/dept. heads
- Executive controls administration
- Partisan elections

ADVANTAGES:
- Like federal government . . . separation of powers
- Strong executive leadership
- Mayor is policy leader
- Mayor is political leader
- People know who is in charge of delivering city services
- People elect policy makers, not administrators . . . short ballot

DISADVANTAGES:
- Voters are limited in the number of officials to elect
- Council/legislature has little control over city administrative agencies
- Mayor's control of administration may be influenced by partisan political factors

APPENDIX 68

Local Government Organization: Weak Mayor-Council

CHARACTERISTICS:
- Large council/legislature
- Legislative Budget
- Mayor/executive
- Executive veto
- Ward elections
- Partisan elections
- Numerous elected officials
- Mayor shares power with council

ADVANTAGES:
- Voters elect a large number of their officials (long ballot)
- Officials are responsive to voters' needs
- Council—as legislature—makes policy
- People know who to hold accountable
- Election on partisan ballot gives power to political party
- Council—legislature—controls administration

DISADVANTAGES:
- Long ballot . . . too many officials to elect . . . can't know qualifications for each office
- Straight party-line voting gives party control of government
- Party control leads to machine politics
- Machine politics is controlled by political bosses
- Machine politics buy votes . . . reward friends
- Mayor may be blocked from acting by council majority
- Mayor as head of political party may have unlimited power

APPENDIX 71

Local Government Organization: Council-Manager

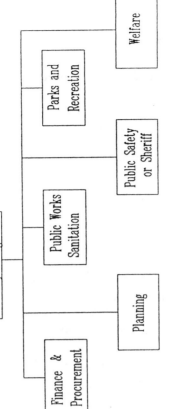

CHARACTERISTICS:

- Small council/legislature
- At-large elections
- Nonpartisan elections
- Council appoints manager
- Manager appoints department heads
- Manager appoints professionals
- Legislative Budget
- No Executive veto

ADVANTAGES:

- Separation of administration from political favoritism
- City services performed by professionals
- City hiring based on competence rather than political favors
- Council makes policy . . . manager carries it out

DISADVANTAGES:

- Voters do not elect manger
- Voters cannot remove manager from office
- Voters elect only a few city officials
- Mayor is one among equals
- Mayor has little or no political power

APPENDIX 70

Local Government Organization: Commission

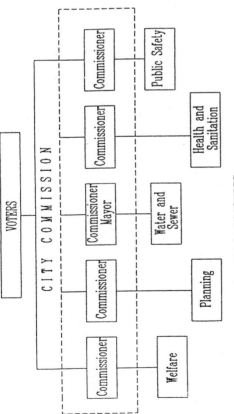
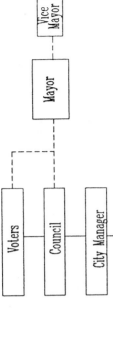

CHARACTERISTICS:

- Small council (Commissioners)/ legislature
- Commissioners elected to specific functions;
  - Public safety
  - Public works
  - Finance
  - Economic & community development
  - Health & welfare
- At-large elections
- Nonpartisan elections
- Executive budget
- No executive veto

ADVANTAGES:

- Voters elect qualified specialists
- Partisan politics generally not an issue
- Each office voted on separately by city-wide election

DISADVANTAGES:

- No separation of executive/legislative functions
- Commissioner's main concern is with own departments rather than total city needs
- No checks and balance system
- Mayor is one among equals
- Mayor has little or no political power

APPENDIX 72

Charter of the Town of Lawrenceville, Va.*
(Incorporated April 29, 1874.)

§ 1. Be it enacted by the General Assembly of Virginia, That the village known as the town of Lawrenceville, in the County of Brunswick, as the same may be laid off into lots, streets and alleys, shall be and is hereby made a town corporate, by the name of the town of Lawrenceville; and by that name and style shall have and exercise the power conferred upon towns by the fifty-fourth chapter of the Code of Virginia, eighteen hundred and seventy-three, so far as the same may be applicable to towns of less than five thousand inhabitants, and are not inconsistent with the provisions of this act.

§ 2. The boundaries of said town shall be as follows: the land extending one quarter of a mile north and east, and half a mile south and west, from the court house of the said county of Brunswick.

§ 3. Robert Kirkland is hereby appointed Mayor of said town, and D.S. Hicks, Benjamin Lewis, J. R. Thomas, William N. Watkins, T. C. Proctor and E. R. Turnbull, are hereby appointed councilmen thereof; and the said Mayor and councilmen shall have and exercise all the powers granted by the said fifty-fourth chapter of the Code, and by this act, to said officers, and remain in office until their successors shall be elected and qualified according to law, a majority of whom shall form a quorum for the transaction of business.

§ 4. The time for holding an election for mayor and councilmen, shall be the fourth Thursday in May, eighteen hundred and seventy-six, and once in every two years thereafter an election shall be held for said officers on the same day in May.

§ 5. The council shall have power and authority to improve the streets, walks and alleys of said town; to build a prison or jail house, and any other house necessary for said town; to arrest and punish, by reasonable fine and imprisonment, drunkenness, the firing of guns, running of horses, or other disorder; to license and regulate shows and other public exhibitions, and to tax the same, as they may deem expedient; to appoint all such officers as they may deem necessary for conducting the affairs of said town, not otherwise provided for in this act, and allow them such compensation as they may deem reasonable; and finally, to make all such by-laws, rules and regulations as they may deem necessary and proper for the good government of the town, provided, they be not contrary to the laws of this State or the United States; and the same to amend, repeal, or enforce, by reasonable fines and penalties, not exceeding for any one offense the sum of twenty dollars, to be recovered with costs, in the name of the Mayor of said town not exceeding one month's imprisonment in the town prison.

§ 6. A majority of said council shall have power to assess and collect an annual tax within the said town, for the purposes before mentioned, on all such property, real and personal, as is now or may be subject to taxation by the revenue laws of this Commonwealth; provided that the tax on said real and personal estate shall not exceed in any one year fifty cents on every hundred dollars value thereof, and a tax not exceeding fifty cents in any one year on all male inhabitants over twenty-one years of age within said town; and moreover it shall be competent for said council to conduct and distribute water into and through said town, upon a request to be made in such manner as the said council may deem best calculated to obtain a full expression of opinion upon the subject.

§ 7. The said council shall appoint annually a sergeant, who shall be a conservator of the peace, and who shall possess the like right of distress, and powers in collecting the said taxes, service and return of process, arising under the authority of this act, and the by-laws made in pursuance of it; and shall be entitled to like fees and commissions as are allowed by law to constables and collectors for similar duties and services. Said sergeant shall execute bond, with approved security, in such penalty as said council shall deem necessary, payable to them and their successors in office, conditional for the faithful discharge of his duties, and payment over of said taxes and moneys

---

*Source: The Town of Lawrenceville, Virginia

collected and received by him in virtue of his office; and he and his securities, his and their executors and administrators, shall be subject to such proceeding, by motion or otherwise, before the circuit or county courts of the County of Brunswick, for enforcing payment of such taxes and other moneys by him collected or received as aforesaid, at the suit or motion of the said mayor, or other person entitled, as collectors of county levies are by law subject to for enforcing payment of the levies by them collected.

§ 8. All fines, penalties and amercements, and other moneys received and raised by virtue of this act, and not otherwise directed to be applied, shall be at the disposal of council, for the use and benefit of the said town.

This act shall be in force from its passage.

CHARTER AMENDMENTS:

Amendment.

Chap. 141—An ACT to amend and re-enact, sections 2, 6, and 8 of an act entitled an act to incorporate the Town of Lawrenceville, Virginia, approved April 29, 1874, and to add two additional sections to said act.

Approved January 24, 1900.

1. Be it enacted by the general assembly of Virginia, That sections two, six, and eight of an act entitled an act to incorporate the Town of Lawrenceville, Brunswick county, Virginia, approved April twenty-nine, eighteen hundred and seventy-four, be amended and re-enacted so as to read as follows:

§ 2. The boundaries of said Town shall be as follows: The land extending one quarter of a mile north and east, half a mile south and three-quarters of a mile west, from the court-house of the said county of Brunswick.

§ 6. A majority of said council shall have power to assess and collect an annual tax within the said Town for the purposes before mentioned, on all such property, real and personal, as is now or may be subject to taxation by the revenue laws of this commonwealth, and upon dogs: provided, that the tax on said real and personal estate shall not exceed in any one year seventy-five cents on every hundred dollars value thereof: and moreover, it shall be competent for said council to conduct and distribute water into and through said Town, and to establish such water-works and other appliances as the council of the said Town may deem proper for that purpose.

§ 8. All fines and forfeitures provided for by this charter may be recovered as provided by law in cases of fines and forfeitures imposed by the laws of the State of Virginia, and shall be paid into the treasury of the corporation and used as a part of its revenue.

2. Be it further enacted that sections nine and ten be added to said act as follows:

§ 9. The property, real and personal, within the corporate limits of said Town, shall not be assessed with a road tax by the county authorities of Brunswick county so long as it keeps its streets in order.

§ 10. The boundaries of the said Town shall be deemed to constitute a lawful fence in all respects. The council shall have the power to make such ordinances, by-laws, orders, and regulations as they may deem necessary to prevent hogs, dogs, coks, horses, mules, and other animals from running at large in the limits of the Town, and may subject the owners thereof to such fines, regulations and taxes as the said council may deem proper, and may sell said animals at public auction, if said fines are not paid after five days' notice and out of the proceeds pay the expenses of keeping and selling said animals and said fines and costs, and the balance, if any, shall be paid to the owner of said animal or animals.

3. This act shall be in force from its passage.

APPENDIX 73

European Economic Community

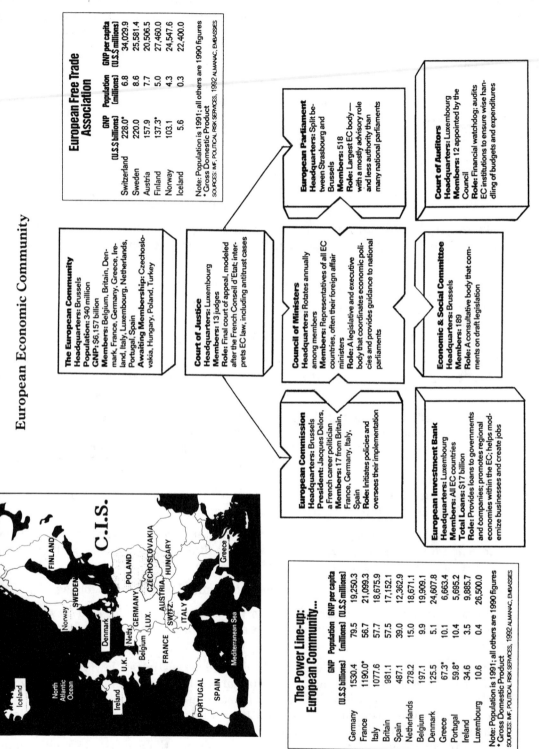

European Free Trade Association

	GNP (U.S.$ billions)	Population (millions)	GNP per capita (U.S.$ millions)
Switzerland	228.0*	6.8	34,029.9
Sweden	220.0	8.6	25,581.4
Austria	157.9	7.7	20,506.5
Finland	137.3*	5.0	27,460.0
Norway	103.1	4.3	24,547.6
Iceland	5.6	0.3	22,400.0

Note: Population is 1991; all others are 1990 figures
* Gross Domestic Product
SOURCES: IMF, POLITICAL RISK SERVICES, 1992 ALMANAC, EMBASSIES

The European Community
Headquarters: Brussels
Population: 340 million
GNP: $6,157 billion
Members: Belgium, Britain, Denmark, France, Germany, Greece, Ireland, Italy, Luxembourg, Netherlands, Portugal, Spain
Awaiting Membership: Czechoslovakia, Hungary, Poland, Turkey

Court of Justice
Headquarters: Luxembourg
Members: 13 judges
Role: Final court of appeal, modeled after the French Conseil d'Etat; interprets EC law, including antitrust cases

European Parliament
Headquarters: Split between Strasbourg and Brussels
Members: 518
Role: Largest EC body — with a mostly advisory role and less authority than many national parliaments

Court of Auditors
Headquarters: Luxembourg
Members: 12 appointed by the Council
Role: Financial watchdog; audits EC institutions to ensure wise handling of budgets and expenditures

Council of Ministers
Headquarters: Rotates annually among members
Members: Representatives of all EC countries, often their foreign affair ministers
Role: A legislative and executive body that coordinates economic policies and provides guidance to national parliaments

European Commission
Headquarters: Brussels
President: Jacques Delors, a French career politician
Members: 17 from Britain, France, Germany, Italy, Spain
Role: Initiates policies and oversees their implementation

Economic & Social Committee
Headquarters: Brussels
Members: 189
Role: A consultative body that comments on draft legislation

European Investment Bank
Headquarters: Luxembourg
Members: All EC countries
Total Loans: $17 billion
Role: Provides loans to governments and companies; promotes regional economies within the EC; helps modernize businesses and create jobs

The Expanding EC Club

- ☐ European Community members
- ☐ European Free Trade Association members
- ▨ Former Soviet bloc members that have trade agreements with the EC

The Power Line-up: European Community...

	GNP (U.S.$ billions)	Population (millions)	GNP per capita (U.S.$ millions)
Germany	1530.4	79.5	19,250.3
France	1190.0*	56.7	21,099.3
Italy	1077.6	57.7	18,675.9
Britain	981.1	57.5	17,152.1
Spain	487.1	39.0	12,362.9
Netherlands	278.2	15.0	18,671.1
Belgium	197.1	9.9	19,909.1
Denmark	125.5	5.1	24,607.8
Greece	67.3*	10.1	6,663.4
Portugal	59.8*	10.4	5,695.2
Ireland	34.6	3.5	9,885.7
Luxembourg	10.6	0.4	26,500.0

Note: Population is 1991; all others are 1990 figures
* Gross Domestic Product
SOURCES: IMF, POLITICAL RISK SERVICES, 1992 ALMANAC, EMBASSIES

Source: *International Business Magazine* (January 1992).

The Council of Europe: Organization and Purpose

The Council of Europe

Founded on 5 May 1949 to achieve greater unity between the European parliamentary democracies, the Council of Europe is the oldest of the European political institutions.

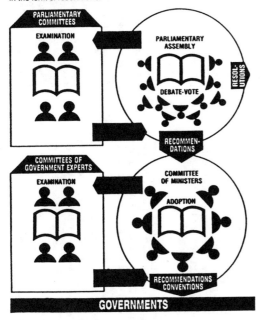

WHAT HAPPENS TO A PARLIAMENTARY PROPOSAL

The Assembly's recommendations go to the Committee of Ministers for action by governments; its opinion on important current issues is expressed in the form of resolutions.

Membership*

AUSTRIA	👤👤👤👤👤👤
BELGIUM	👤👤👤👤👤👤👤
CYPRUS	👤👤👤
DENMARK	👤👤👤👤👤
FINLAND	👤👤👤👤👤
FRANCE	👤👤👤👤👤👤👤👤👤👤👤👤👤👤👤👤👤👤
GERMANY (F.R.)	👤👤👤👤👤👤👤👤👤👤👤👤👤👤👤👤👤👤
GREECE	👤👤👤👤👤👤👤
ICELAND	👤👤👤
IRELAND	👤👤👤👤
ITALY	👤👤👤👤👤👤👤👤👤👤👤👤👤👤👤👤👤👤
LIECHTENSTEIN	👤👤
LUXEMBOURG	👤👤👤
MALTA	👤👤👤
NETHERLANDS	👤👤👤👤👤👤👤
NORWAY	👤👤👤👤👤
PORTUGAL	👤👤👤👤👤👤
SAN MARINO	👤👤
SPAIN	👤👤👤👤👤👤👤👤👤👤👤👤
SWEDEN	👤👤👤👤👤👤
SWITZERLAND	👤👤👤👤👤👤
TURKEY	👤👤👤👤👤👤👤👤👤👤👤👤
UNITED KINGDOM	👤👤👤👤👤👤👤👤👤👤👤👤👤👤👤👤👤👤

*The Parliaments of Hungary, Poland, the Commonwealth of Independent States (CIS), and Yugoslavia enjoy Special Guest Status. The State of Israel sends observers.

Source: Service de la communication, Conseil de l'Europe

The Council of Europe's two organs are the Committee of Ministers and the Parliamentary Assembly, assisted by an international secretariat of 850 officials. Through a flexible system of co-operation between governments, members of parliament and experts, the Council of Europe seeks to protect and develop human rights and democracy and to harmonise the policies of its 23 member states in a wide variety of fields including health, social welfare, education, culture, the environment, local government and justice but excluding defence.

Organisation

Every year the Assembly generally holds a session in three parts (spring, autumn and winter), each lasting about a week. Plenary sittings are held in the Assembly Chamber of the Palais de l'Europe in Strasbourg and are open to the public. To make itself better known in the member states, the Assembly holds a "summer session" in a different European city each year.

Speeches are normally made in one of the Assembly's six working languages—English, French, German, Italian, Spanish and Dutch—with simultaneous interpretation provided. Assembly documents are produced in the Council's two official languages, English and French.

From among its own members the Assembly elects its **President**, who traditionally stays in office for three years, and 14 **Vice-Presidents** of different nationalities elected for one year. Together they make up the **Bureau** of the Assembly whose job it is to draw up the agenda and the timetable of debates.

The Assembly's work is prepared by 13 **specialised committees** dealing with political, economic, social, cultural, legal affairs and so on.

The Parliamentary Assembly

Although the Council of Europe was designed mainly to promote co-operation between governments, the setting up of a Parliamentary Assembly bringing together members of the national parliaments added a new dimension to international relations.

The Parliamentary Assembly of the Council of Europe is a driving force in the organisation, influencing its intergovernmental activities in many ways.

Because the Assembly is essentially a consultative body it can be bold and original in its ideas. Being free to choose what subjects it will discuss, it can direct its attention towards longer-term issues—while not neglecting topical matters.

Through the national parliaments, where Assembly members can encourage action to follow up its work, the Assembly has a real influence on the member governments.

The Assembly is a genuine forum for democratic western Europe, keeping governments in constant touch with European public and parliamentary opinion, of which it expresses the views on the major problems of the day.

In the Assembly Chamber, representatives sit in alphabetical order, regardless of party or nationality. They express their own personal opinions and not those of their governments. As a rule, though, they vote as decided in the five **political groups** which have been formed: Socialist, European People's Party, European Democratic Group, Liberal, Democratic and Reformers Group and the Communist Group. A few members of the Assembly do not belong to any political group.

Representatives are assisted in their work by the Office of the Clerk of the Assembly, which is staffed by members of the permanent secretariat under the authority of the Clerk.

The Assembly elects the Secretary General of the Council of Europe and his deputy, as well as the Clerk of the Assembly and the judges of the European Court of Human Rights.

APPENDIX 73-B

The Council of Europe: Protection of Human Rights

AND The Protection Of Human Rights

Complaints of a violation of the Convention are made to the European Commission of Human Rights. Although one member state may bring proceedings against another – these are known as inter-state applications – the most frequent form of complaint is the individual application brought by a person, group of individuals or non-governmental organisation against a state within whose jurisdiction the alleged violation occurred. Before such cases can be lodged, the state concerned must have recognised by express declaration the right of individuals to lodge complaints against it.

The right of individual petition under Article 25 of the Convention was an important innovation in international law and is one of the most remarkable features of the enforcement machinery set up by the Convention.

PREPARATION OF THE COMMISSION'S REPORT

Once an application is declared admissible, the Commission's next task is to establish the facts. At this stage, the parties may be invited to submit further evidence, answer questions and give explanations. Hearings may be held or on-the-spot investigations conducted when witnesses and experts can be examined.

While seeking to establish the facts, the Commission is also under an obligation to put itself at the disposal of the parties with a view to securing a friendly settlement on the basis of respect for the human rights guaranteed in the Convention.

Where a settlement is reached, the Commission draws up a brief report on the case. This is sent to the state concerned, the Committee of Ministers and the Secretary General of the Council of Europe for publication.

AFTER THE COMMISSION'S REPORT

Within three months of the Commission's report being sent to the Committee of Ministers, the case may be referred to the European Court of Human Rights.

For a case to go to the Court, the defendant state must have accepted the compulsory jurisdiction of the Court or, failing that, agreed to accept the Court's jurisdiction in the particular case.

PROCEDURE OF THE COURT

The Court examines the case in the light of the report of the Commission together with any further written evidence or legal argument. There will also normally be a public hearing in Strasbourg when the delegate of the Commission and lawyers for the respondent government and the applicant will present or supplement their submissions and may be questioned about them by the judges.

Judgments are delivered in open court. Usually the President or Vice-President reads the part of the judgment containing the Court's legal findings, the full text being made available afterwards. The judgment of the Court is final and there is no appeal. It is binding on the state concerned but the Court has no enforcement powers of its own. The Committee of Ministers of the Council of Europe supervises the implementation of the Court's judgments.

After the hearing, the judges deliberate in private and vote on whether they consider there has been a breach of the Convention. The view of the majority forms the decision of the Court but separate and dissenting opinions are often annexed to the judgment.

In appropriate circumstances, the Court can afford the victim of a violation "just satisfaction" which may, for example, include an award of compensation and an order for the reimbursement of costs.

CASES NOT REFERRED TO THE COURT

Where a case is not referred to the Court, the Committee of Ministers of the Council of Europe decides, by a two-thirds majority, whether or not there was a breach of the Convention and whether to publish the Commission's report. In addition, the Committee of Ministers can recommend that a state afford the victim of a violation "just satisfaction", the modalities of which are fixed in consultation with the Commission. Like those of the Court, decisions of the Committee of Ministers are final and member states undertake to regard them as binding.

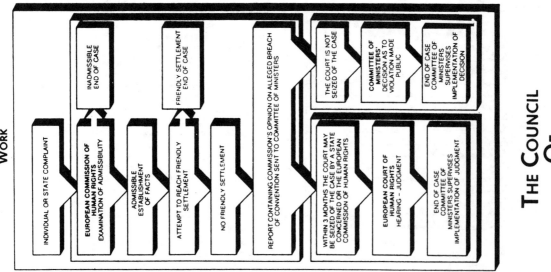

HOW THE HUMAN RIGHTS INSTITUTIONS WORK

INDIVIDUAL OR STATE COMPLAINT

EUROPEAN COMMISSION OF HUMAN RIGHTS EXAMINATION OF ADMISSIBILITY

INADMISSIBLE END OF CASE

ADMISSIBLE ESTABLISHMENT OF FACTS

ATTEMPT TO REACH FRIENDLY SETTLEMENT

FRIENDLY SETTLEMENT END OF CASE

NO FRIENDLY SETTLEMENT

REPORT CONTAINING COMMISSION'S OPINION ON ALLEGED BREACH OF CONVENTION SENT TO COMMITTEE OF MINISTERS

WITHIN 3 MONTHS THE COURT MAY BE SEIZED OF THE CASE BY A STATE CONCERNED OR THE EUROPEAN COMMISSION OF HUMAN RIGHTS

THE COURT IS NOT SEIZED OF THE CASE

COMMITTEE OF MINISTERS' DECISION AS TO VIOLATION MADE PUBLIC

END OF CASE COMMITTEE OF MINISTERS SUPERVISES IMPLEMENTATION OF DECISION

EUROPEAN COURT OF HUMAN RIGHTS HEARING – JUDGMENT

END OF CASE COMMITTEE OF MINISTERS SUPERVISES IMPLEMENTATION OF JUDGMENT

THE COUNCIL OF EUROPE

Source: Service de la communication, Conseil de l'Europe

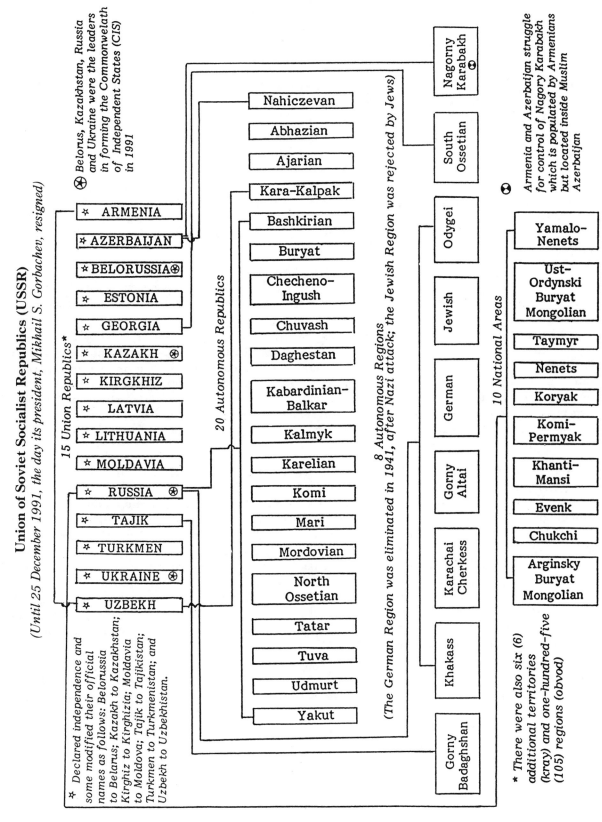

APPENDIX 74

Union of Soviet Socialist Republics (USSR)

(Until 25 December 1991, the day its president, Mikhail S. Gorbachev, resigned)

15 Union Republics*

☆ ARMENIA	
☆ AZERBAIJAN	
☆ BELORUSSIA ⊗	
☆ ESTONIA	
☆ GEORGIA	
☆ KAZAKH ⊗	
☆ KIRGKHIZ	
☆ LATVIA	
☆ LITHUANIA	
☆ MOLDAVIA	
☆ RUSSIA ⊗	
☆ TAJIK	
☆ TURKMEN	
☆ UKRAINE ⊗	
☆ UZBEKH	

⊗ *Belorus, Kazakhstan, Russia and Ukraine were the leaders in forming the Commonwelath of Independent States (CIS) in 1991*

☆ *Declared independence and some modified their official names as follows: Belorussia to Belarus; Kazakh to Kazakhstan; Kirghiz to Kirghizia; Moldavia to Moldova; Tajik to Tajikistan; Turkmen to Turkmenistan; and Uzbekh to Uzbekhistan.*

20 Autonomous Republics

Nahiczevan
Abhazian
Ajarian
Kara-Kalpak
Bashkirian
Buryat
Checheno-Ingush
Chuvash
Daghestan
Kabardinian-Balkar
Kalmyk
Karelian
Komi
Mari
Mordovian
North Ossetian
Tatar
Tuva
Udmurt
Yakut

8 Autonomous Regions

(The German Region was eliminated in 1941, after Nazi attack; the Jewish Region was rejected by Jews)

South Ossetian
Odygei
Jewish
German
Gorny Altai
Karachai Cherkess
Khakass
Gorny Badaghshan

Nagorny Karabakh ⊖

Ⓧ *Armenia and Azerbaijan struggle for control of Nagory Karabakh which is populated by Armenians but located inside Muslim Azerbaijan*

10 National Areas

Yamalo-Nenets
Ust-Ordynski Buryat Mongolian
Taymyr
Nenets
Koryak
Komi-Permyak
Khanti-Mansi
Evenk
Chukchi
Arginsky Buryat Mongolian

* *There were also six (6) additional territories (kray) and one-hundred-five (105) regions (obvod)*

©1992 Brunswick Publishing Corporation

Charter of the United Nations*

INTRODUCTORY NOTE

The Charter of the United Nations was signed on 26 June 1945, in San Francisco, at the conclusion of the United Nations Conference on International Organization, and came into force on 24 October 1945. The Statute of the International Court of Justice is an integral part of the Charter.

Amendments to Articles 23, 27 and 61 of the Charter were adopted by the General Assembly on 17 December 1963 and came into force on 31 August 1965. A further amendment to Article 61 was adopted by the General Assembly on 20 December 1971, and came into force on 24 September 1973. An amendment to Article 109, adopted by the General Assembly on 20 December 1965, came into force on 12 June 1968.

The amendment to Article 23 enlarges the membership of the Security Council from eleven to fifteen. The amended Article 27 provides that decisions of the Security Council on procedural matters shall be made by an affirmative vote of nine members (formerly seven) and on all other matters by an affirmative vote of nine members (formerly seven), including the concurring votes of the five permanent members of the Security Council.

The amendment to Article 61, which entered into force on 31 August 1965, enlarged the membership of the Economic and Social Council from eighteen to twenty-seven. The subsequent amendment to that Article, which entered into force on 24 September 1973, further increased the membership of the Council from twenty-seven to fifty-four.

The amendment to Article 109, which relates to the first paragraph of that Article, provides that a General Conference of Member States for the purpose of reviewing the Charter may be held at a date and place to be fixed by a two-thirds vote of the members of the General Assembly and by a vote of any nine members (formerly seven) of the Security Council. Paragraph 3 of Article 109, which deals with the consideration of a possible review conference during the tenth regular session of the General Assembly, has been retained in its original form in its reference to a "vote, of any seven members of the Security Council," the paragraph having been acted upon in 1955 by the General Assembly, at its tenth regular session, and by the Security Council.

WE THE PEOPLE OF THE UNITED NATIONS DETERMINED to save succeeding generations from the scourge of war, which twice in our lifetime has brought untold sorrow to mankind, and to reaffirm faith in fundamental human rights, in the dignity and worth of the human person, in the equal rights of men and women and of nations large and small, and to establish conditions under which justice and respect for the obligations arising from treaties and other sources of international law can be maintained, and to promote social progress and better standards of life in larger freedom, and for these ends to practice tolerance and live together in peace with one another as good neighbors, and to unite our strength to maintain international peace and security, and to ensure, by the acceptance of principles and the institution of methods, that armed force shall not be used, save in the common interest, and to employ international machinery for the promotion of the economic and social advancement of all peoples, have resolved to combine our efforts to accomplish these aims.

Accordingly, our respective governments, through representatives assembled in the city of San Francisco, who have exhibited their full powers found to be in good and due form, have agreed to the present Charter of the United Nations and do hereby establish an international organization to be known as the United Nations.

---

* Revisions and amendments are in italics

CHAPTER I

PURPOSE AND PRINCIPLES

ARTICLE 1

The Purposes of the United Nations are:

1. To maintain international peace and security, and to that end: to take effective collective measures for the prevention and removal of threats to the peace, and for the suppression of acts of aggression or other breaches of the peace, and to bring about by peaceful means, and in conformity with the principles of justice and international law, adjustment or settlement of international disputes or situations which might lead to a breach of the peace;

2. To develop friendly relations among nations based on respect for the principle of equal rights and self-determination of peoples, and to take other appropriate measures to strengthen universal peace;

3. To achieve international cooperation in solving international problems of an economic, social, cultural, or humanitarian character, and in promoting and encouraging respect for human rights and for fundamental freedoms for all without distinction as to race, sex, language, or religion; and

4. To be a center for harmonizing the actions of nations in the attainment of these common ends.

ARTICLE 2

The Organization and its Members, in pursuit of the Purposes stated in ARTICLE 1, shall act in accordance with the following Principles:

1. The Organization is based on the principle of the sovereign equality of all its Members.

2. All Members, in order to ensure to all of them the rights and benefits resulting from membership, shall fulfill in good faith the obligations assumed by them in accordance with the present Charter.

3. All Members shall settle their international disputes by peaceful means in such a manner that international peace and security, and justice, are not endangered.

4. All Members shall refrain in their international relations from the threat or use of force against the territorial integrity or political independence of any state, or in any any other manner inconsistent with the Purposes of the United Nations.

5. All Members shall give the United Nations every assistance in any action it takes in accordance with the present Charter, and shall refrain from giving assistance to any state against which the United Nations is taking preventive or enforcement action.

6. The Organization shall ensure that states which are not Members of the United Nations act in accordance with these Principles so far as may be necessary for the maintenance of international peace and security.

7. Nothing contained in the present Charter shall authorize the United Nations to intervene in matters which are essentially within the domestic jurisdiction of any state or shall require the Members to submit such matters to settlement under the present Charter; but this principle shall not prejudice the application of enforcement measures under CHAPTER VII.

CHAPTER II

MEMBERSHIP

ARTICLE 3

The original Members of the United Nations shall be the states which, having participated in the United Nations Conference on International Organization at San Francisco, or having previously signed the Declaration by United Nations of January 1, 1942, sign the present Charter and ratify it in accordance with ARTICLE 110.

ARTICLE 4

1. Membership in the United Nations is open to all other peace-loving states which accept the obligations contained in the present Charter and, in the judgment of the Organization, are able and willing to carry out these obligations.

2. The admission of any such state to membership in the United Nations will be effected by a decision of the General Assembly upon recommendation of the Security Council.

ARTICLE 5

A Member of the United Nations against which preventive or enforcement action has been taken by the Security Council may be suspended from exercise of the rights and privileges of membership by the General Assembly upon the recommendation of the Security Council. The exercise of these rights and privileges may be restored by the Security Council.

ARTICLE 6

A member of the United Nations which has persistently violated Principles contained in the present Charter may be expelled from the Organization by the General Assembly upon the recommendation of the Security Council.

CHAPTER III

ORGANS

ARTICLE 7

1. There are established as the principal organs of the United Nations: a General Assembly, a Security Council, an Economic and Social Council, a Trusteeship Council, an International Court of Justice, and a Secretariat.

2. Such subsidiary organs as may be found necessary may be established in accordance with the present Charter.

ARTICLE 8

The United Nations shall place no restrictions on the eligibility of men and women to participate in any capacity and under conditions of equality in its principal and subsidiary organs.

CHAPTER IV

THE GENERAL ASSEMBLY COMPOSITION

ARTICLE 9

1. The General Assembly shall consist of all the Members of the United Nations.

2. Each Member shall have not more than five representatives in the General Assembly.

FUNCTIONS AND POWERS

ARTICLE 10

The General Assembly may discuss any questions or any matters within the scope of the present Charter or relating to the powers and functions of any organs provided for in the present Charter, and except as provided in ARTICLE 12, may make recommendations to the Members of the United Nations or to the Security Council or to both on any such questions or matters.

ARTICLE 11

1. The General Assembly may consider the general principles of cooperation in the maintenance of international peace and security, including the principles governing disarmament and the regulation of armaments, and may make recommendations with regard to such principles to the Members or to the Security Council or to both.

2. The General Assembly may discuss any questions relating to the maintenance of international peace and security brought before it by any Member of the United Nations, or by the Security Council, or by a state which is not a Member of the United Nations in accordance with ARTICLE 35, paragraph 2, and, except as provided in ARTICLE 12, may make recommendations with regard to any such questions to the state or states concerned or to the Security Council or to both. Any such question on which action is necessary shall be referred to the Security Council by the General Assembly either before or after discussion.

3. The General Assembly may call the attention of the Security Council to situations which are likely to endanger international peace and security.

4. The powers of the General Assembly set forth in this Article shall not limit the general scope of ARTICLE 10.

ARTICLE 12

1. While the Security Council is exercising in respect of any dispute or situation the functions assigned to it in the present Charter, the General Assembly shall not make any recommendation with regard to that dispute or situation unless the Security Council so requests.

2. The Secretary-General, with the consent of the Security Council, shall notify the General Assembly at each session of any matters relative to the maintenance of international peace and security which are being dealt with by the Security Council and shall similarly notify the General Assembly, or the Members of the United Nations if the General Assembly is not in session, immediately the Security Council ceases to deal with such matters.

ARTICLE 13

1. The General Assembly shall initiate studies and make recommendations for the purpose of:

a. promoting international cooperation in the political field and encouraging the progressive development of international law and its codification;

b. promoting international cooperation in the economic, social, cultural, educational, and health fields, and assisting in the realization of human rights and fundamental freedoms for all without distinction as to race, sex, language, or religion.

2. The further responsibilities, functions, and powers of the General Assembly with respect to matters mentioned in paragraph 1 (b) above are set forth in Chapters IX and X.

ARTICLE 14

Subject to the provisions of ARTICLE 12, the General Assembly may recommend measures for the peaceful adjustment of any situation, regardless of origin, which it deems likely to impair the general welfare or friendly relations among nations, including situations resulting from a violation of the provisions of the present Charter setting forth the Purposes and Principles of the United Nations.

ARTICLE 15

1. The General Assembly shall receive and consider annual and special reports from the Security Council; these reports shall include an account of the measures that the Security Council has decided upon or taken to maintain international peace and security.

2. The General Assembly shall receive and consider reports from other organs of the United Nations.

ARTICLE 16

The General Assembly shall perform such functions with respect to the international trusteeship system as are assigned to it under Chapters XII and XIII, including the approval of the trusteeship agreements for areas not designated as strategic.

ARTICLE 17

1. The General Assembly shall consider and approve the budget of the Organization.

2. The expenses of the Organization shall be borne by the Members as apportioned by the General Assembly.

3. The General Assembly shall consider and approve any financial and budgetary arrangements with specialized agencies referred to in ARTICLE 57 and shall examine the administrative budgets of such specialized agencies with a view to making recommendations to the agencies concerned.

VOTING

ARTICLE 18

1. Each member of the General Assembly shall have one vote.

2. Decisions by the General Assembly on important questions shall be made by a two-thirds majority of the members present and voting. These questions shall include: recommendations with respect to the maintenance of international peace and security, the election of the non-permanent members of the Security Council, the election of the members of the Economic and Social Council, the election of members of the Trusteeship Council in accordance with paragraph 1 (c) of ARTICLE 86, the admission of new Members to the United Nations, the suspension of the rights and privileges of membership, the expulsion of Members, questions relating to the operation of the trusteeship system, and budgetary questions.

3. Decisions on other questions, including the determination of additional categories of questions to be decided by a two-thirds majority, shall be made by a majority of the members present and voting.

ARTICLE 19

A Member of the United Nations which is in arrears in the payment of its financial contributions to the Organization shall have no vote in the General Assembly if the amount in arrears equals or exceeds the amount of the contributions due from it for the preceding two full years. The General Assembly may, nevertheless, permit such a Member to vote if it is satisfied that the failure to pay is due to conditions beyond the control of the Member.

PROCEDURE

ARTICLE 20

The General Assembly shall meet in regular annual sessions and in such special sessions as occasion may require. Special sessions shall be convoked by the Secretary-General at the request of the Security Council or of a majority of the Members of the United Nations.

ARTICLE 21

The General Assembly shall adopt its own rules of procedure. It shall elect its President for each session.

ARTICLE 22

The General Assembly may establish such subsidiary organs as it deems necessary for the performance of its functions.

CHAPTER V

THE SECURITY COUNCIL COMPOSITION

ARTICLE 23

1. The Security Council shall consist of *fifteen* Members of the United Nations. The Republic of China, France, the Union of Soviet Socialist Republics, the United Kingdom of Great Britain and

Northern Ireland, and the United States of America shall be permanent members of the Security Council. The General Assembly shall elect *ten* other Members of the United Nations to be non-permanent members of the Security Council, due regard being specially paid, in the first instance to the contribution of Members of the United Nations to the maintenance of international peace and security and to the other purposes of the Organization, and also to equitable geographical distribution.

2. The non-permanent members of the Security Council shall be elected for a term of two years. *In the first election of the non-permanent members after the increase of the membership of the Security Council from eleven to fifteen, two of the four additional members shall be chosen for a term of one year.* A retiring member shall not be eligible for immediate re-election.

3. Each member of the Security Council shall have one representative.

FUNCTIONS AND POWERS

ARTICLE 24

1. In order to ensure prompt and effective action by the United Nations, its Members confer on the Security Council primary responsibility for the maintenance of international peace and security, and agree that in carrying out its duties under this responsibility the Security Council acts on their behalf.

2. In discharging these duties the Security Council shall act in accordance with the Purposes and Principles of the United Nations. The specific powers granted to the Security Council for the discharge of these duties are laid down in Chapters VI, VII, VIII, and XII.

3. The Security Council shall submit annual and, when necessary, special reports to the General Assembly for its consideration.

ARTICLE 25

The Members of the United Nations agree to accept and carry out the decisions of the Security Council in accordance with the present Charter.

ARTICLE 26

In order to promote the establishment and maintenance of international peace and security with the least diversion for armaments of the world's human and economic resources, the Security Council shall be responsible for formulating, with the assistance of the Military Staff Committee referred to in ARTICLE 47, plans to be submitted to the Members of the United Nations for the establishment of a system for the regulation of armaments.

VOTING

ARTICLE 27

1. Each member of the Security Council shall have one vote.

2. Decisions of the Security Council on procedural matters shall be made by an affirmative vote of *nine* members.

3. Decisions of the Security Council on all other matters shall be made by an affirmative vote of *nine* members including the concurring votes of the permanent members; provided that, in decisions under Chapter VI, and under paragraph 3 of ARTICLE 52, a party to a dispute shall abstain from voting.

PROCEDURE

ARTICLE 28

1. The Security Council shall be so organized as to be able to function continuously. Each member of the Security Council shall for this purpose be represented at all times at the seat of the Organization.

2. The Security Council shall hold periodic meetings at which each of its members may, if it so desires, be represented by a member of the government or by some other specially designated representative.

3. The Security Council may hold meetings at such places other than the seat of the Organization as in its judgment will best facilitate its work.

ARTICLE 29

The Security Council may establish such subsidiary organs as it deems necessary for the performance of its functions.

ARTICLE 30

The Security Council shall adopt its own rules of procedure, including the method of selecting its President.

ARTICLE 31

Any Member of the United Nations which is not a member of the Security Council may participate, without vote, in the discussion of any question brought before the Security Council whenever the latter considers that the interests of that Member are specially affected.

ARTICLE 32

Any Member of the United Nations which is not a member of the Security Council or any state which is not a Member of the United Nations, if it is a party to a dispute under consideration by the Security Council, shall be invited to participate, without vote, in the discussion relating to the dispute. The Security Council shall lay down such conditions as it deems just for the participation of a state which is not a Member of the United Nations.

CHAPTER VI

PACIFIC SETTLEMENT OF DISPUTES

ARTICLE 33

1. The parties to any dispute, the continuance of which is likely to endanger the maintenance of international peace and security, shall, first of all, seek a solution by negotiations, inquiry, mediation, conciliation, arbitration, judicial settlement, resort to regional agencies or arrangements, or other peaceful means of their own choice.

2. The Security Council shall, when it deems necessary, call upon the parties to settle their dispute by such means.

ARTICLE 34

The Security Council may investigate any dispute, or any situation which might lead to international friction or give rise to a dispute, in order to determine whether the continuance of the dispute or situation is likely to endanger the maintenance of international peace and security.

ARTICLE 35

1. Any Member of the United Nations may bring any dispute, or any situation of the nature referred to in ARTICLE 34, to the attention of the Security Council or of the General Assembly.

2. A state which is not a Member of the United Nations may bring to the attention of the Security Council or of the General Assembly any dispute to which it is a party if it accepts in advance, for the purposes of the dispute, the obligations of pacific settlement provided in the present Charter.

3. The proceedings of the General Assembly in respect to matters brought to its attention under this ARTICLE will be subject to the provisions of ARTICLES 11 and 12.

ARTICLE 36

1. The Security Council may, at any stage of a dispute of the nature referred to in ARTICLE 33 or of a situation of like nature, recommend appropriate procedures or methods of adjustment.

2. The Security Council should take into consideration any procedures for the settlement of the dispute which have already been adopted by the parties.

3. In making recommendations under this ARTICLE the Security Council should also take into consideration that legal disputes should as a general rule be referred by the parties to the International Court of Justice in accordance with the provisions of the Statute of the Court.

ARTICLE 37

1. Should the parties to a dispute of the nature referred to in ARTICLE 33 fail to settle it by the means indicated in that ARTICLE, they shall refer it to the Security Council.

2. If the Security Council deems that the continuance of the dispute is in fact likely to endanger the maintenance of international peace and security, it shall decide whether to take action under ARTICLE 36 or to recommend such terms of settlement as it may consider appropriate.

ARTICLE 38

Without prejudice to the provisions of ARTICLES 33 to 37, the Security Council may, if all the parties to any dispute so request, make recommendations to the parties with a view to a pacific settlement of the dispute.

CHAPTER VII

ACTION WITH RESPECT TO THREATS TO THE PEACE, BREACHES OF THE PEACE, AND ACTS OF AGGRESSION

ARTICLE 39

The Security Council shall determine the existence of any threat to the peace, breach of the peace, or act of aggression and shall make recommendations, or decide what measures shall be taken in accordance with ARTICLES 41 and 42, to maintain or restore international peace and security.

ARTICLE 40

In order to prevent an aggravation of the situation, the Security Council may, before making the recommendations or deciding upon the measures provided for in ARTICLE 39, call upon the parties concerned to comply with such provisional measures as it deems necessary or desirable. Such provisional measures shall be without prejudice to the rights, claims, or position of the parties concerned. The Security Council shall duly take account of failure to comply with such provisional measures.

ARTICLE 41

The Security Council may decide what measures not involving the use of armed force are to be employed to give effect to its decisions, and it may call upon the Members of the United Nations to apply such measures. These may include complete or partial interruption of economic relations and of rail, sea, air, postal, telegraphic, radio, and other means of communication, and the severance of diplomatic relations.

ARTICLE 42

Should the Security Council consider that measures provided for in ARTICLE 41 would be inadequate or have proved to be inadequate, it may take such action by air, sea, or land forces as may be necessary to maintain or restore international peace and security. Such action may include demonstrations, blockade, and other operations by air, sea, or land forces of Members of the United Nations.

ARTICLE 43

1. All Members of the United Nations, in order to contribute to the maintenance of international peace and security, undertake to make available to the Security Council, on its call and in accordance with a special agreement or agreements, armed forces, assistance, and facilities, including rights of passage, necessary for the purpose of maintaining international peace and security.

2. Such agreement or agreements shall govern the numbers and types of forces, their degree of readiness and general location, and the nature of the facilities and assistance to be provided.

3. The agreement or agreements shall be negotiated as soon as possible on the initiative of the Security Council. They shall be concluded between the Security Council and Members or between the Security Council and groups of Members and shall be subject to ratification by the signatory states in accordance with their respective constitutional processes.

ARTICLE 44

When the Security Council has decided to use force it shall, before calling upon a Member not represented on it to provide armed forces in fulfillment of the obligations assumed under ARTICLE 43, invite that Member, if the Member so desires, to participate in the decisions of the Security Council concerning the employment of contingents of that Member's armed forces.

ARTICLE 45

In order to enable the United Nations to take urgent military measures, Members shall hold immediately available national air-force contingents for combined international enforcement action. The strength and degree of readiness of these contingents and plans for their combined action shall be determined, within the limits laid down in the special agreement or agreements referred to in ARTICLE 43, by the Security Council with the assistance of the Military Staff Committee.

ARTICLE 46

Plans for the application of armed force shall be made by the Security Council with the assistance of the Military Staff Committee.

ARTICLE 47

1. There shall be established a Military Staff Committee to advise and assist the Security Council on all questions relating to the Security Council's military requirements for the maintenance of international peace and security, the employment and command of forces placed at its disposal, the regulation of armaments, and possible disarmament.

2. The Military Staff Committee shall consist of the Chiefs of Staff of the Permanent members of the Security Council or their representatives. Any Member of the United Nations not permanently represented on the Committee shall be invited by the Committee to be associated with it when the efficient discharge of the Committee's responsibilities requires the participation of that Member in its work.

3. The Military Staff Committee shall be responsible under the Security Council for the strategic direction of any armed forces placed at the disposal of the Security Council. Questions relating to the command of such forces shall be worked out subsequently.

4. The Military Staff Committee, with the authorization of the Security Council and after consultation with appropriate regional agencies, may establish regional subcommittees.

ARTICLE 48

1. The action required to carry out the decisions of the Security Council for the maintenance of international peace and security shall be taken by all the Members of the United Nations or by some of them, as the Security Council may determine.

2. Such decisions shall be carried out by the Members of the United Nations directly and through their action in the appropriate international agencies of which they are members.

ARTICLE 49

The Members of the United Nations shall join in affording mutual assistance in carrying out the measures decided upon by the Security Council.

ARTICLE 50

If preventive or enforcement measures against any state are taken by the Security Council, any other state, whether a Member of the United Nations or not, which finds itself confronted with special economic problems arising from the carrying out of those measures shall have the right to consult the Security Council with regard to a solution to those problems.

ARTICLE 51

Nothing in the present Charter shall impair the inherent right of individual or collective self-defense if an armed attack occurs against a Member of the United Nations, until the Security Council has taken the measures necessary to maintain international peace and security. Measures taken by Members in the exercise of this right of self-defense shall be immediately reported to the Security Council and shall not in any way affect the authority and responsibility of the Security Council under the present Charter to take at any time such action as it deems necessary in order to maintain or restore international peace and security.

CHAPTER VIII

REGIONAL ARRANGEMENTS

ARTICLE 52

1. Nothing in the present Charter precludes the existence of regional arrangements or agencies for dealing with such matters relating to the maintenance of international peace and security as are appropriate for regional action, provided that such arrangements or agencies and their activities are consistent with the Purposes and Principles of the United Nations.

2. The Members of the United Nations entering into such arrangements or constituting such agencies shall make every effort to achieve pacific settlement of local disputes through such regional arrangements or by such regional agencies before referring them to the Security Council.

3. The Security Council shall encourage the development of pacific settlement of local disputes through such regional arrangements or by such regional agencies either on the initiative of the states concerned or by reference from the Security Council.

4. This ARTICLE in no way impairs the application of ARTICLES 34 and 35.

ARTICLE 53

1. The Security Council shall, where appropriate, utilize such regional arrangements or agencies for enforcement action under its authority. But no enforcement action shall be taken under regional arrangements or by regional agencies without the authorization of the Security Council, with the exception of measures against any enemy state, as defined in paragraph 2 of this ARTICLE, provided for pursuant to ARTICLE 107 or in regional arrangements directed against renewal of aggressive policy on the part of any such state, until such time as the Organization may, on request of the Governments concerned, be charged with the responsibility for preventing further aggression by such a state.

2. The term enemy state as used in paragraph 1 of this ARTICLE applies to any state which during the Second World War has been an enemy of any signatory of the present Charter.

ARTICLE 54

The Security Council shall at all times be kept fully informed of activities undertaken or in contemplation under regional arrangements or by regional agencies for the maintenance of international peace and security.

CHAPTER IX

INTERNATIONAL ECONOMIC AND SOCIAL COOPERATION

ARTICLE 55

With a view to the creation of conditions of stability and well-being which are necessary for peaceful and friendly relations among nations based on respect for the principle of equal rights and self-determination of peoples, the United Nations shall promote:

a. higher standards of living, full employment, and conditions of economic and social progress and development;

b. solutions to international economic, social, health, and related problems, and international cultural and educational cooperation; and

c. universal respect for, and observance of, human rights and fundamental freedoms for all without distinction as to race, sex, language, or religion.

ARTICLE 56

All Members pledge themselves to take joint and separate action in cooperation with the Organization for the achievement of the purposes set forth in ARTICLE 55.

ARTICLE 57

1. The various specialized agencies, established by intergovernmental agreement and having wide international responsibilities, as defined in their basic instruments, in economic, social, cultural, educational, health, and related fields, shall be brought into relationship with the United Nations in accordance with the provisions of ARTICLE 63.

2. Such agencies thus brought into relationship with the United Nations are hereinafter referred to as specialized agencies.

ARTICLE 58

The Organization shall make recommendations for the coordination of the policies and activities of the specialized agencies.

ARTICLE 59

The Organization shall, where appropriate, initiate negotiations among the states concerned for the creation of any new specialized agencies required for the accomplishment of the purposes set forth in ARTICLE 55.

ARTICLE 60

Responsibility for the discharge of the functions of the Organization set forth in this Chapter shall be vested in the General Assembly and, under the authority of the General Assembly, in the Economic and Social Council, which shall have for this purpose the powers set forth in Chapter X.

CHAPTER X

THE ECONOMIC AND SOCIAL COUNCIL COMPOSITION

ARTICLE 61

1. The Economic and Social Council shall consist of *twenty-seven* Members of the United Nations elected by the General Assembly.

2. Subject to the provisions of paragraph 3, *nine* members of the Economic and Social Council shall be elected each year for a term of three years. A retiring member shall be eligible for immediate re-election.

3. At the first election *after the increase in the membership of the Economic and Social Council from eighteen to twenty-seven members, in addition to the members elected in place of the six members whose term of office expires at the end of that year, nine additional members shall be elected. Of these nine additional members, the term of office of three members so elected shall expire at the end of one year, and of the three other members at the end of two years,* in accordance with arrangements made by the General Assembly.

4. Each member of the Economic and Social Council shall have one representative.

FUNCTIONS AND POWERS

ARTICLE 62

1. The Economic and Social Council may make or initiate studies and reports with respect to the international economic, social, cultural, educational, health, and related matters and may make recommendations with respect to any such matters to the General Assembly, to the Members of the United Nations, and to the specialized agencies concerned.

2. It may make recommendations for the purpose of promoting respect for, and observance of, human rights and fundamental freedoms for all.

3. It may prepare draft conventions for submissions to the General Assembly, with the respect to matters falling within its competence.

4. It may call, in accordance with the rules prescribed by the United Nations, international conferences on matters falling within its competence.

ARTICLE 63

1. The Economic and Social Council may enter into agreements with any of the agencies referred to in ARTICLE 57, defining the terms on which the agency concerned shall be brought into relationship with the United Nations. Such agreements shall be subject to approval by the General Assembly.

2. It may coordinate the activities of the specialized agencies through consultation with and recommendations to such agencies and through recommendations to the General Assembly and to the Members of the United Nations.

ARTICLE 64

1. The Economic and Social Council may take appropriate steps to obtain regular reports from the specialized agencies. It may make arrangements with the Members of the United Nations and with the specialized agencies to obtain reports on the steps taken to give effect to its own recommendations and to recommendations on matters falling within its competence made by the General Assembly.

2. It may communicate its observations on these reports to the General Assembly.

ARTICLE 65

The Economic and Social Council may furnish information to the Security Council and shall assist the Security Council upon its request.

ARTICLE 66

1. The Economic and Social Council shall perform such functions as fall within its competence in connection with the carrying out of the recommendations of the General Assembly.

2. It may, with the approval of the General Assembly, perform services at the request of Members of the United Nations and at the request of specialized agencies.

3. It shall perform such other functions as are specified elsewhere in the present Charter or as may be assigned to it by the General Assembly.

VOTING

ARTICLE 67

1. Each member of the Economic and Social Council shall have one vote.

2. Decisions of the Economic and Social Council shall be made by a majority of the members present and voting.

PROCEDURE

ARTICLE 68

The Economic and Social Council shall set up commissions in economic and social fields and for the promotion of human rights, and such other commissions as may be required for the performance of its functions.

ARTICLE 69

The Economic and Social Council shall invite any Member of the United Nations to participate, without vote, in its deliberations on any matter of particular concern to that Member.

ARTICLE 70

The Economic and Social Council may make arrangements for representatives of the specialized agencies to participate, without vote, in its deliberations and in those of the commissions established by it, and for its representatives to participate in the deliberations of the specialized agencies.

ARTICLE 71

The Economic and Social Council may make suitable arrangements for consultation with non-governmental organizations which are concerned with the matters within its competence. Such arrangements may be made with international organizations and, where appropriate, with national organizations after consultation with the Member of the United Nations concerned.

ARTICLE 72

1. The Economic and Social Council shall adopt its own rules of procedure, including the method of selecting its President.

2. The Economic and Social Council shall meet as required in accordance with its rules, which shall include provision for the convening of meetings on the request of a majority of its members.

CHAPTER XI

DECLARATION REGARDING NON-SELF-GOVERNING TERRITORIES

ARTICLE 73

Members of the United Nations which have or assumed responsibilities for the administration of territories whose peoples have not yet attained a full measure of self-government recognize the principle that the interests of the inhabitants of these territories are paramount, and accept as a sacred trust the obligation to promote the utmost, within the system of international peace and security established by the present Charter, the well-being of the inhabitants of these territories, and, to this end:

a. to ensure, with due respect for the culture of the peoples concerned, their political, economic, social, and educational advancement, their just treatment, and their protection against abuses;

b. to develop self-government, to take due account of the political aspirations of the peoples, and to assist them in the progressive development of their free political institutions, according to the particular circumstances of each territory and its peoples and their varying stages of advancement;

c. to further international peace and security.

d. to promote constructive measures of development, to encourage research, and to cooperate with one another and, when and where appropriate, with specialized international bodies with a view to the practical achievement of the social, economic, and scientific purposes set forth in this ARTICLE; and

e. to transmit regularly to the Secretary-General for information purposes, subject to such limitations as security and constitutional considerations may require, statistical and other information of a technical nature relating to economic, social, and educational conditions in the territories for which they are respectively responsible other than those territories to which Chapters XII and XIII apply.

ARTICLE 74

Members of the United Nations also agree that their policy in respect of the territories to which this Chapter applies, no less than in respect of their metropolitan areas, must be based on the general principle of good-neighborliness, due account being taken of the interests and well-being of the rest of the world, in social, economic, and commercial matters.

CHAPTER XII

INTERNATIONAL TRUSTEESHIP SYSTEM

ARTICLE 75

The United Nations shall establish under its authority an international trusteeship system for the administration and supervision of such territories as may be placed thereunder by subsequent individual agreements. These territories are hereinafter referred to as trust territories.

ARTICLE 76

The basic objectives of the trusteeship system in accordance with the Purposes of the United Nations laid down in ARTICLE 1 of the present Charter, shall be:

a. to further international peace and security;

b. to promote the political, economic, social, and educational advancement of the inhabitants of the trust territories, and their progressive development towards self-government or independence as may be appropriate to the particular circumstances of each territory and its peoples and the freely expressed wishes of the peoples concerned, and as may be provided by the terms of each trusteeship agreement;

c. to encourage respect for human rights and for fundamental freedoms for all without distinction as to race, sex, language, or religion, and to encourage recognition of the interdependence of the peoples of the world; and

d. to ensure equal treatment in social, economic, and commercial matters for all Members of the United Nations and their nationals, and also equal treatment for the latter in the administration of justice, without prejudice to the attainment of the foregoing objectives and subject to the provisions of ARTICLE 80.

ARTICLE 77

1. The trusteeship system shall apply to such territories in the following categories as may be placed thereunder by means of trusteeship agreements:

a. territories now held under mandate;

b. territories which may be detached from enemy states as a result of the Second World War; and

c. territories voluntarily placed under the system by states responsible for their administration.

2. It will be a matter for subsequent agreement as to which territories in the foregoing categories will be brought under the trusteeship system and upon what terms.

ARTICLE 78

The trusteeship system shall not apply to territories which have become Members of the United Nations, relationship among which shall be based on respect for the principle of sovereign equality.

ARTICLE 79

The terms of trusteeship for each territory to be placed under the trusteeship system, including any alterations or amendment, shall be agreed upon by the states directly concerned, including the mandatory power in the case of territories held under mandate by a Member of the United Nations, and shall be approved as provided for in ARTICLES 83 and 85.

ARTICLE 80

1. Except as may be agreed upon in individual trusteeship agreements, made under ARTICLES 77, 79, and 81, placing each territory under the trusteeship system, and until such agreements have been concluded, nothing in this Charter shall be construed in or of itself to alter in any manner the right whatsoever of any states or any peoples or the terms of existing international instruments to which Members of the United Nations may respectively be parties.

2. Paragraph 1 of this ARTICLE shall not be interpreted as giving grounds for delay or postponement of the negotiation and conclusion of agreements for placing mandated and other territories under the trusteeship system as provided for in ARTICLE 77.

ARTICLE 81

The trusteeship agreement shall in each case include the terms under which the trust territory will be administered and designate the authority which will exercise the administration of the trust territory. Such authority, hereinafter called the administering authority, may be one or more states or the Organization itself.

ARTICLE 82

There may be designated, in any trusteeship agreement, a strategic area or areas which may include part or all the trust territory to which the agreement applies, without prejudice to any special agreement or agreements made under ARTICLE 43.

ARTICLE 83

1. All functions of the United Nations relating to strategic areas, including approval of the terms of the trusteeship agreements and of their alteration or amendment, shall be exercised by the Security Council.

2. The basic objectives set forth in ARTICLE 76 shall be applicable to the people of each strategic area.

3. The Security Council shall, subject to the provisions of the trusteeship agreements and without prejudice to security considerations, avail itself of the assistance of the Trusteeship Council to perform those functions of the United Nations under the trusteeship system relating to political, economic, social, and educational matters in the strategic areas.

ARTICLE 84

It shall be the duty of the administering authority to ensure that the trust territory shall play its part in the maintenance of international peace and security. To this end the administering authority may make use of volunteer forces, facilities, and assistance from the trust territory in carrying out the obligations towards the Security Council undertaken in this regard by the administering authority, as well as for local defense and the maintenance of law and order within the trust territory.

ARTICLE 85

1. The functions of the United Nations with regard to trusteeship agreements for all areas not designated as strategic, including the approval of the terms of the trusteeship agreements and of their alteration or amendment, shall be exercised by the General Assembly.

2. The Trusteeship Council, operating under the authority of the General Assembly, shall assist the General Assembly in carrying out these functions.

CHAPTER XIII

THE TRUSTEESHIP COUNCIL COMPOSITION

ARTICLE 86

1. The Trusteeship Council shall consist of the following Members of the United Nations:

a. those Members administering trust territories;

b. such of those Members mentioned by name in ARTICLE 23 as are not administering trust territories; and

c. as many other Members elected for three-year terms by the General Assembly as may be necessary to ensure that the total number of members of the Trusteeship Council is equally divided between those Members of the United Nations which administer trust territories and those which do not.

2. Each member of the Trusteeship Council shall designate one specially qualified person to represent it therein.

FUNCTIONS AND POWERS

ARTICLE 87

The General Assembly and, under its authority, the Trusteeship Council, in carrying out their functions, may:

a. consider reports submitted by the administering authority;

b. accept petitions and examine them in consultation with the administering authority;

c. provide for periodic visits to the respective trust territories at times agreed upon with the administering authority; and

d. take these and other actions in conformity with the terms of the trusteeship agreements.

ARTICLE 88

The Trusteeship Council shall formulate a questionnaire on the political, economic, social, and educational advancement of the inhabitants of each trust territory, and the administering authority for each trust territory within the competence of the General Assembly shall make an annual report to the General Assembly upon the basis of such questionnaire.

VOTING

ARTICLE 89

1. Each member of the Trusteeship Council shall have one vote.

2. Decisions of the Trusteeship Council shall be made by a majority of the members present and voting.

PROCEDURE

ARTICLE 90

1. The Trusteeship Council shall adopt its own rules of procedure, including the method of selecting its President.

2. The Trusteeship Council shall meet as required in accordance with it rules, which shall include provision for the convening of meetings on the request of a majority of its members.

ARTICLE 91

The Trusteeship Council shall, when appropriate, avail itself of the assistance of the Economic and Social Council and of the specialized agencies in regard to matters with which they are respectively concerned.

CHAPTER XIV

THE INTERNATIONAL COURT OF JUSTICE

ARTICLE 92

The International Court of Justice shall be the principal judicial organ of the United Nations. It shall function in accordance with the annexed Statute, which is based upon the Statute of the Permanent Court of International Justice and forms an integral part of the present Charter.

ARTICLE 93

1. All Members of the United Nations are *ipso facto* parties to the Statute of the International Court of Justice.

2. A state which is not a Member of the United Nations may become a party to the Statute of the International Court of Justice on conditions to be determined in each case by the General Assembly upon the recommendation of the Security Council.

ARTICLE 94

1. Each Member of the United Nations undertakes to comply with the decisions of the International Court of Justice in any case to which it is a party.

2. If any party to a case fails to perform the obligations incumbent upon it under the judgment rendered by the Court, the other party may have recourse to the Security Council, which may, if it deems necessary, make recommendations or decide upon measures to be taken to give effect to the judgment.

ARTICLE 95

Nothing in the present Charter shall prevent Members of the United Nations from entrusting the solution of their differences to other tribunals by virtue of agreements already in existence or which may be concluded in the future.

ARTICLE 96

1. The General Assembly or the Security Council may request the International Court of Justice to give an advisory opinion on any legal question.

2. Other organs of the United Nations and specialized agencies, which may at any time be authorized by the General Assembly, may also request advisory opinions of the Court on legal questions arising within the scope of their activities.

CHAPTER XV

THE SECRETARIAT

ARTICLE 97

The Secretariat shall comprise a Secretary-General and such staff as the Organization may require. The Secretary-General shall be appointed by the General Assembly upon the recommendation of the Security Council. He shall be the chief administrative officer of the Organization.

ARTICLE 98

The Secretary-General shall act in that capacity in all meetings of the General Assembly, of the Security Council, of the Economic and Social Council, and of the Trusteeship Council, and shall perform such other functions as are entrusted to him by these organs. The Secretary-General shall make an annual report to the General Assembly on the work of the Organization.

ARTICLE 99

The Secretary-General may bring to the attention of the Security Council any matter which in his opinion may threaten the maintenance of international peace and security.

ARTICLE 100

1. In the performance of their duties the Secretary-General and the staff shall not seek or receive instructions from any government or from any other authority external to the Organization. They shall refrain from any action which might reflect on their position as international officials responsible only to the Organization.

2. Each Member of the United Nations undertakes to respect the exclusively international character of the responsibilities of the Secretary-General and the staff and not to seek to influence them in the discharge of their responsibilities.

ARTICLE 101

1. The staff shall be appointed by the Secretary-General under regulations established by the General Assembly.

2. Appropriate staffs shall be permanently assigned to the Economic and Social Council, the Trusteeship Council, and, as required, to other organs of the United Nations. These staffs shall form a part of the Secretariat.

3. The paramount consideration in the employment of the staff and in the determination of the conditions of service shall be the necessity of securing the highest standards of efficiency, competence, and integrity. Due regard shall be paid to the importance of recruiting the staff on as wide a geographical basis as possible.

CHAPTER XVI

MISCELLANEOUS PROVISIONS

ARTICLE 102

1. Every treaty and every international agreement entered into by any Member of the United Nations after the present Charter comes into force shall as soon as possible be registered with the Secretariat and published by it.

2. No party to any such treaty or international agreement which has not been registered in accordance with the provisions of paragraph 1 of this ARTICLE may invoke that treaty or agreement before any organ of the United Nations.

ARTICLE 103

In the event of a conflict between the obligations of the Members of the United Nations under the present Charter and their obligations under any other international agreement, their obligations under the present Charter shall prevail.

ARTICLE 104

The Organization shall enjoy in the territory of each of its Members such legal capacity as may be necessary for the exercise of its functions and the fulfillment of its purposes.

ARTICLE 105

1. The Organization shall enjoy in the territory of each of its Members such privileges and immunities as are necessary for the fulfillment of its purposes.

2. Representatives of the Members of the United Nations and officials of the Organization shall similarly enjoy such privileges and immunities as are necessary for the independent exercise of their functions in connection with the Organization.

3. The General Assembly may make recommendations with a view to determining the details of the application of paragraph 1 and 2 of this ARTICLE or may propose conventions to the Members of the United Nations for this purpose.

CHAPTER XVII

TRANSITIONAL SECURITY ARRANGEMENTS

ARTICLE 106

Pending the coming into force of such special agreements referred to in ARTICLE 43 as in the opinion of the Security Council enable it to begin the exercise of its responsibilities under ARTICLE 42, the parties to the Four-Nation Declaration, signed at Moscow, October 30, 1943, and France, shall, in accordance with the provisions of paragraph 5 of that Declaration, consult with one another and as occasion requires with other Members of the United Nations with a view to such joint action on behalf of the Organization as may be necessary for the purpose of maintaining international peace and security.

ARTICLE 107

Nothing in the present Charter shall invalidate or preclude action, in relation to any state which during the Second World War has been an enemy of any signatory of the present Charter, taken or authorized as a result of that war by the Governments having responsibility for such action.

CHAPTER XVIII

AMENDMENTS

ARTICLE 108

Amendments to the present Charter shall come into force for all Members of the United Nations when they have been adopted by a vote of two-thirds of the members of the General Assembly and ratified in accordance with their respective constitutional processes by two-thirds of the Members of the United Nations, including all the permanent members of the Security Council.

ARTICLE 109

1. A General Conference of the Members of the United Nations for the purpose of reviewing the present Charter may be held at a date and place to be fixed by a two-thirds vote of the members of the General Assembly and by a vote of any seven members of the Security Council. Each Member of the United Nations shall have one vote in the conference.

2. Any alteration of the present Charter recommended by a two-thirds vote of the conference shall take effect when ratified in accordance with their respective constitutional processes by two-

thirds of the Members of the United Nations including all the permanent members of the Security Council.

3. If such a conference has not been held before the tenth annual session of the General Assembly following the coming into force of the present Charter, the proposal to call such a conference shall be placed on the agenda of that session of the General Assembly, and the conference shall be held if so decided by a majority vote of the members of the General Assembly and by a vote of any seven members of the Security Council.

CHAPTER XIX

RATIFICATION AND SIGNATURE

ARTICLE 110

1. The present Charter shall be ratified by the signatory states in accordance with their respective constitutional processes.

2. The ratifications shall be deposited with the Government of the United States of America, which shall notify all the signatory states of each deposit as well as the Secretary-General of the Organization when he has been appointed.

3. The present Charter shall come into force upon the deposit of ratifications by the Republic of China, France, the Union of Soviet Socialist Republics, the United Kingdom of Great Britain and Northern Ireland, and the United States of America, and by a majority of the other signatory states. A protocol of the ratifications deposited shall thereupon be drawn up by the Government of the United States of America which shall communicate copies thereof to all the signatory states.

4. The states signatory to the present Charter which ratify it after it has come into force will become original Members of the United Nations on the date of the deposit of their respective ratifications.

ARTICLE 111

The present Charter, of which the Chinese, French, Russian, English, and Spanish texts are equally authentic, shall remain deposited in the archives of the Government of the United States of America. Duly certified copies thereof shall be transmitted by that Government to the Governments of the other signatory states.

In faith whereof the representatives of the Governments of the United Nations have signed the present Charter.

Done at the city of San Francisco the twenty-sixth day of June, one thousand nine hundred and forty-five.

APPENDIX 76

Statute of the International Court of Justice

Article 1

The International Court of Justice established by the Charter of the United Nations as the principal judicial organ of the United Nations shall be constituted and shall function in accordance with the provisions of the present Statute.

CHAPTER I

ORGANIZATION OF THE COURT

Article 2

The Court shall be composed of a body of independent judges, elected regardless of their nationality from among persons of high moral character, who possess the qualifications required in their respective countries for appointment to the highest judicial offices, or are jurisconsults of recognized competence in international law.

Article 3

1. The Court shall consist of fifteen members, no two of whom may be nationals of the same state.

2. A person who for the purposes of membership in the Court could be regarded as a national of more than one state shall be deemed to be a national of the one in which he ordinarily exercises civil and political rights.

Article 4

1. The members of the Court shall be elected by the General Assembly and by the Security Council from a list of persons nominated by the national groups in the Permanent Court of Arbitration, in accordance with the following provisions.

2. In the case of Members of the United Nations not represented in the Permanent Court of Arbitration, candidates shall be nominated by national groups appointed for this purpose by their governments under the same conditions as those prescribed for members of the Permanent Court of Arbitration by Article 44 of the Convention of The Hague of 1907 for the pacific settlement of international disputes.

3. The conditions under which a state which is a party to the present Statute but is not a Member of the United Nations may participate in electing the members of the Court shall, in the absence of a special agreement, be laid down by the General Assembly upon recommendation of the Security Council.

Article 5

1. At least three months before the date of the election, the Secretary-General of the United Nations shall address a written request to the members of the Permanent Court of Arbitration belonging to the states which are parties to the present Statute, and to the members of the national groups appointed under Article 4, paragraph 2, inviting them to undertake, within a given time, by national groups, the nomination of persons in a position to accept the duties of a member of the Court.

2. No group may nominate more than four persons, not more than two of whom shall be of their own nationality. In no case may the number of candidates nominated by a group be more than double the number of seats to be filled.

Article 6

Before making these nominations, each national group is recommended to consult its highest court of justice, its legal faculties and schools of law, and its national academies and national sections of international academies devoted to the study of law.

Article 7

1. The Secretary-General shall prepare a list in alphabetical order of all the persons thus nominated. Save as provided in Article 12, paragraph 2, these shall be the only persons eligible.

2. The Secretary-General shall submit this list to the General Assembly and to the Security Council.

Article 8

The General Assembly and the Security Council shall proceed independently of one another to elect the members of the Court.

Article 9

At every election, the electors shall bear in mind not only that the persons to be elected should individually possess the qualifications required, but also that in the body as a whole the representation of the main forms of civilization and of the principal legal systems of the world should be assured.

Article 10

1. Those candidates who obtain an absolute majority of votes in the General Assembly and in the Security Council shall be considered as elected.

2. Any vote of the Security Council, whether for the election of judges or for the appointment of members of the conference envisaged in Article 12, shall be taken without any distinction between permanent and non-permanent members of the Security Council.

3. In the event of more than one national of the same state obtaining an absolute majority of the votes both of the General Assembly and of the Security Council, the eldest of these only shall be considered as elected.

Article 11

If, after the first meeting held for the purpose of the election, one or more seats remain to be filled, a second and, if necessary, a third meeting shall take place.

Article 12

1. If, after the third meeting, one or more seats still remain unfilled, a joint conference consisting of six members, three appointed by the General Assembly and three by the Security Council, may be formed at any time at the request of either the General Assembly or the Security Council, for the purpose of choosing by the vote of an absolute majority one name for each seat still vacant, to submit to the General Assembly and the Security Council for their respective acceptance.

2. If the joint conference is unanimously agreed upon any person who fulfils the required conditions, he may be included in its list, even though he was not included in the list of nominations referred to in Article 7.

3. If the joint conference is satisfied that it will not be successful in procuring an election, those members of the Court who have already been elected shall, within a period to be fixed by the Security Council, proceed to fill the vacant seats by selection from among those candidates who have obtained votes either in the General Assembly or in the Security Council.

4. In the event of an equality of votes among the judges, the eldest judge shall have a casting vote.

Article 13

1. The members of the Court shall be elected for nine years and may be re-elected; provided, however, that of the judges elected at the first election, the terms of five judges shall expire at the end of three years and the terms of five more judges shall expire at the end of six years.

2. The judges whose terms are to expire at the end of the above-mentioned initial periods of three and six years shall be chosen by lot to be drawn by the Secretary-General immediately after the first election has been completed.

3. The members of the Court shall continue to discharge their duties until their places have been filled. Though replaced, they shall finish any cases which they may have begun.

4. In the case of the resignation of a member of the Court, the resignation shall be addressed to the President of the Court for transmission to the Secretary-General. This last notification makes the place vacant.

Article 14

Vacancies shall be filled by the same method as that laid down for the first election, subject to the following provision: the Secretary-General shall, within one month of the occurrence of the vacancy, proceed to issue the invitations provided for in Article 5, and the date of the election shall be fixed by the Security Council.

Article 15

A member of the Court elected to replace a member whose term of office has not expired shall hold office for the remainder of his predecessor's term.

Article 16

1. No member of the Court may exercise any political or administrative function, or engage in any other occupation of a professional nature.

2. Any doubt on this point shall be settled by the decision of the Court.

Article 17

1. No member of the Court may act as agent, counsel, or advocate in any case.

2. No member may participate in the decision of any case in which he has previously taken part as agent, counsel, or advocate for one of the parties, or as a member of a national or international court, or of a commission of enquiry, or in any other capacity.

3. Any doubt on this point shall be settled by the decision of the Court.

Article 18

1. No member of the Court can be dismissed unless, in the unanimous opinion of the other members, he has ceased to fulfil the required conditions.

2. Formal notification thereof shall be made to the Secretary-General by the Registrar.

3. This notification makes the place vacant.

Article 19

The members of the Court, when engaged on the business of the Court, shall enjoy diplomatic privileges and immunities.

Article 20

Every member of the Court shall, before taking up his duties, make a solemn declaration in open court that he will exercise his powers impartially and conscientiously.

Article 21

1. The Court shall elect its President and Vice-President for three years; they may be re-elected.

2. The Court shall appoint its Registrar and may provide for the appointment of such other officers as may be necessary.

Article 22

1. The seat of the Court shall be established at The Hague. This, however, shall not prevent the Court from sitting and exercising its functions elsewhere whenever the Court considers it desirable.

2. The President and the Registrar shall reside at the seat of the Court.

Article 23

1. The Court shall remain permanently in session, except during the judicial vacations, the dates and duration of which shall be fixed by the Court.

2. Members of the Court are entitled to periodic leave, the dates and duration of which shall be fixed by the Court, having in mind the distance between The Hague and the home of each judge.

3. Members of the Court shall be bound, unless they are on leave or prevented from attending by illness or other serious reasons duly explained to the President, to hold themselves permanently at the disposal of the Court.

Article 24

1. If, for some special reason, a member of the Court considers that he should not take part in the decision of a particular case, he shall so inform the President.

2. If the President considers that for some special reason one of the members of the Court should not sit in a particular case, he shall give him notice accordingly.

3. If in any such case the member of the Court and the President disagree, the matter shall be settled by the decision of the Court.

Article 25

1. The full Court shall sit except when it is expressly provided otherwise in the present Statute.

2. Subject to the condition that the number of judges available to constitute the Court is not thereby reduced below eleven, the Rules of the Court may provide for allowing one or more judges, according to circumstances and in rotation, to be dispensed from sitting.

3. A quorum of nine judges shall suffice to constitute the Court.

Article 26

1. The Court may from time to time form one or more chambers, composed of three or more judges as the Court may determine, for dealing with particular categories of cases; for example, labour cases and cases relating to transit and communications.

2. The Court may at any time form a chamber for dealing with a particular case. The number of judges to constitute such a chamber shall be determined by the Court with the approval of the parties.

3. Cases shall be heard and determined by the chambers provided for in this article if the parties so request.

Article 27

A judgment given by any of the chambers provided for in Articles 26 and 29 shall be considered as rendered by the Court.

Article 28

The chambers provided for in Articles 26 and 29 may, with the consent of the parties, sit and exercise their functions elsewhere than at The Hague.

Article 29

With a view to the speedy dispatch of business, the Court shall form annually a chamber composed of five judges which, at the request of the parties, may hear and determine cases by summary procedure. In addition, two judges shall be selected for the purpose of replacing judges who find it impossible to sit.

Article 30

1. The Court shall frame rules for carrying out its functions. In particular, it shall lay down rules of procedure.

2. The Rules of the Court may provide for assessors to sit with the Court or with any of its chambers, without the right to vote.

Article 31

1. Judges of the nationality of each of the parties shall retain their right to sit in the case before the Court.

2. If the Court includes upon the Bench a judge of the nationality of one of the parties, any other party may choose a person to sit as judge. Such person shall be chosen preferably from among those persons who have been nominated as candidates as provided in Articles 4 and 5.

3. If the Court includes upon the Bench no judge of the nationality of the parties, each of these parties may proceed to choose a judge as provided in paragraph 2 of this Article.

4. The provisions of this Article shall apply to the case of Articles 26 and 29. In such cases, the President shall request one or, if necessary, two of the members of the Court forming the chamber to give place to the members of the Court of the nationality of the parties concerned, and, failing such, or if they are unable to be present, to the judges specially chosen by the parties.

5. Should there be several parties in the same interest, they shall, for the purpose of the preceding provisions, be reckoned as one party only. Any doubt upon this point shall be settled by the decision of the Court.

6. Judges chosen as laid down in paragraphs 2, 3, and 4 of this Article shall fulfil the conditions required by Articles 2, 17 (paragraph 2), 20, and 24 of the present Statute. They shall take part in the decision on terms of complete equality with their colleagues.

Article 32

1. Each member of the Court shall receive an annual salary.

2. The President shall receive a special annual allowance.

3. The Vice-President shall receive a special allowance for every day on which he acts as President.

4. The judges chosen under Article 31, other than members of the Court, shall receive compensation for each day on which they exercise their functions.

5. These salaries, allowances, and compensation shall be fixed by the General Assembly. They may not be decreased during the term of office.

6. The salary of the Registrar shall be fixed by the General Assembly on the proposal of the Court.

7. Regulations made by the General Assembly shall fix the conditions under which retirement pensions may be given to members of the Court and to the Registrar, and the conditions under which members of the Court and the Registrar shall have their travelling expenses refunded.

8. The above salaries, allowances, and compensation shall be free of all taxation.

Article 33

The expenses of the Court shall be borne by the United Nations in such a manner as shall be decided by the General Assembly.

CHAPTER II

COMPETENCE OF THE COURT

Article 34

1. Only states may be parties in cases before the Court.

2. The Court, subject to and in conformity with its Rules, may request of public international organizations information relevant to cases before it, and shall receive such information presented by such organizations on their own initiative.

3. Whenever the construction of the constituent instrument of a public international organization or of an international convention adopted thereunder is in question in a case before the Court, the Registrar shall so notify the public international organization concerned and shall communicate to it copies of all the written proceedings.

Article 35

1. The Court shall be open to the states parties to the present Statute.

2. The conditions under which the Court shall be open to other states shall, subject to the special provisions contained in treaties in force, be laid down by the Security Council,

but in no case shall such conditions place the parties in a position of inequality before the Court.

3. When a state which is not a Member of the United Nations is a party to a case, the Court shall fix the amount which that party is to contribute towards the expenses of the Court. This provision shall not apply if such state is bearing a share of the expenses of the Court.

Article 36

1. The jurisdiction of the Court comprises all cases which the parties refer to it and all matters specially provided for in the Charter of the United Nations or in treaties and conventions in force.

2. The states parties to the present Statute may at any time declare that they recognize as compulsory *ipso facto* and without special agreement, in relation to any other state accepting the same obligation, the jurisdiction of the Court in all legal disputes concerning:

    a. the interpretation of a treaty;

    b. any question of international law;

    c. the existence of any fact which, if established, would constitute a breach of an international obligation;

    d. the nature or extent of the reparation to be made for the breach of an international obligation.

3. The declarations referred to above may be made unconditionally or on condition of reciprocity on the part of several or certain states, or for a certain time.

4. Such declarations shall be deposited with the Secretary-General of the United Nations, who shall transmit copies thereof to the parties to the Statute and to the Registrar of the Court.

5. Declarations made under Article 36 of the Statute of the Permanent Court of International Justice and which are still in force shall be deemed, as between the parties to the present Statute, to be acceptances of the compulsory jurisdiction of the International Court of Justice for the period which they still have to run and in accordance with their terms.

6. In the event of a dispute as to whether the Court has jurisdiction, the matter shall be settled by the decision of the Court.

Article 37

Whenever a treaty or convention in force provides for reference of a matter to a tribunal to have been instituted by the League of Nations, or to the Permanent Court of International Justice, the matter shall, as between the parties to the present Statute, be referred to the International Court of Justice.

Article 38

1. The Court, whose function is to decide in accordance with international law such disputes as are submitted to it, shall apply:

    a. international conventions, whether general or particular, establishing rules expressly recognized by the contesting states;

    b. international custom, as evidence of a general practice accepted as law;

    c. the general principles of law recognized by civilized nations;

    d. subject to the provisions of Article 59, judicial decisions and the teachings of the most highly qualified publicists of the various nations, as subsidiary means for the determination of rules of law.

2. This provision shall not prejudice the power of the Court to decide a case *ex aequo et bono*, if the parties agree thereto.

CHAPTER III
PROCEDURE

Article 39

1. The official languages of the Court shall be French and English. If the parties agree that the case shall be conducted in French, the judgment shall be delivered in French. If the parties agree that the case shall be conducted in English, the judgment shall be delivered in English.

2. In the absence of an agreement as to which language shall be employed, each party may, in the pleadings, use the language which it prefers; the decison of the Court shall be given in French and English. In this case the Court shall at the same time determine which of the two texts shall be considered as authoritative.

3. The Court shall, at the request of any party, authorize a language other than French or English to be used by that party.

Article 40

1. Cases are brought before the Court, as the case may be, either by the notification of the special agreement or by a written application addressed to the Registrar. In either case the subject of the dispute and the parties shall be indicated.

2. The Registrar shall forthwith communicate the application to all concerned.

3. He shall also notify the Members of the United Nations through the Secretary-General, and also any other states entitled to appear before the Court.

Article 41

1. The Court shall have the power to indicate, if it considers that circumstances so require, any provisional measures which ought to be taken to preserve the respective rights of either party.

2. Pending the final decision, notice of the measures suggested shall forthwith be given to the parties and to the Security Council.

Article 42

1. The parties shall be represented by agents.

2. They may have the assistance of counsel or advocates before the Court.

3. The agents, counsel, and advocates of parties before the Court shall enjoy the privileges and immunities necessary to the independent exercise of their duties.

Article 43

1. The procedure shall consist of two parts: written and oral.

2. The written proceedings shall consist of the communication to the Court and to the parties of memorials, counter-memorials and, if necessary, replies; also all papers and documents in support.

3. These communications shall be made through the Registrar, in the order and within the time fixed by the Court.

4. A certified copy of every document produced by one party shall be communicated to the other party.

5. The oral proceedings shall consist of the hearing by the Court of witnesses, experts, agents, counsel, and advocates.

Article 44

1. For the service of all notices upon persons other than the agents, counsel, and advocates, the Court shall apply direct to the government of the state upon whose territory the notice has to be served.

2. The same provision shall apply whenever steps are to be taken to procure evidence on the spot.

Article 45

The hearing shall be under the control of the President or, if he is unable to preside, of the Vice-President; if neither is able to preside, the senior judge present shall preside.

Article 46

The hearing in Court shall be public, unless the Court shall decide otherwise, or unless the parties demand that the public be not admitted.

Article 47

1. Minutes shall be made at each hearing and signed by the Registrar and the President.

2. These minutes alone shall be authentic.

Article 48

The Court shall make orders for the conduct of the case, shall decide the form and time in which each party must conclude its arguments, and make all arrangements connected with the taking of evidence.

Article 49

The Court may, even before the hearing begins, call upon the agents to produce any document or to supply any explanations. Formal note shall be taken of any refusal.

Article 50

The Court may, at any time, entrust any individual, body, bureau, commission, or other organization that it may select, with the task of carrying out an enquiry or giving an expert opinion.

Article 51

During the hearing any relevant questions are to be put to the witnesses and experts under the conditions laid down by the Court in the rules of procedure referred to in Article 30.

Article 52

After the Court has received the proofs and evidence within the time specified for the purpose, it may refuse to accept any further oral or written evidence that one party may desire to present unless the other side consents.

Article 53

1. Whenever one of the parties does not appear before the Court, or fails to defend its case, the other party may call upon the Court to decide in favour of its claim.

2. The Court must, before doing so, satisfy itself, not only that it has jurisdiction in accordance with Articles 36 and 37, but also that the claim is well founded in fact and law.

Article 54

1. When, subject to the control of the Court, the agents, counsel, and advocates have completed their presentation of the case, the President shall declare the hearing closed.

2. The Court shall withdraw to consider the judgment.

3. The deliberations of the Court shall take place in private and remain secret.

Article 55

1. All questions shall be decided by a majority of the judges present.

2. In the event of an equality of votes, the President or the judge who acts in his place shall have a casting vote.

Article 56

1. The judgment shall state the reasons on which it is based.

2. It shall contain the names of the judges who have taken part in the decision.

Article 57

If the judgment does not represent in whole or in part the unanimous opinion of the judges, any judge shall be entitled to deliver a separate opinion.

Article 58

The judgment shall be signed by the President and by the Registrar. It shall be read in open court, due notice having been given to the agents.

Article 59

The decision of the Court has no binding force except between the parties and in respect of that particular case.

Article 60

The judgment is final and without appeal. In the event of dispute as to the meaning or scope of the judgment, the Court shall construe it upon the request of any party.

Article 61

1. An application for revision of a judgment may be made only when it is based upon the discovery of some fact of such a nature as to be a decisive factor, which fact was, when the judgment was given, unknown to the Court and also to the party claiming revision, always provided that such ignorance was not due to negligence.

2. The proceedings for revision shall be opened by a judgment of the Court expressly recording the existence of the new fact, recognizing that it has such a character as to lay the case open to revision, and declaring the application admissible on this ground.

3. The Court may require previous compliance with the terms of the judgment before it admits proceedings in revision.

4. The application for revision must be made at latest within six months of the discovery of the new fact.

5. No application for revision may be made after the lapse of ten years from the date of the judgment.

Article 62

1. Should a state consider that it has an interest of a legal nature which may be affected by the decision in the case, it may submit a request to the Court to be permitted to intervene.

2. It shall be for the Court to decide upon this request.

Article 63

1. Whenever the construction of a convention to which states other than those concerned in the case are parties is in question, the Registrar shall notify all such states forthwith.

2. Every state so notified has the right to intervene in the proceedings; but if it uses this right, the construction given by the judgment will be equally binding upon it.

Article 64

Unless otherwise decided by the Court, each party shall bear its own costs.

CHAPTER IV

ADVISORY OPINIONS

Article 65

1. The Court may give an advisory opinion on any legal question at the request of whatever body may be authorized by or in accordance with the Charter of the United Nations to make such a request.

2. Questions upon which the advisory opinion of the Court is asked shall be laid before the Court by means of a written request containing an exact statement of the question upon which an opinion is required, and accompanied by all documents likely to throw light upon the question.

Article 66

1. The Registrar shall forthwith give notice of the request for an advisory opinion to all states entitled to appear before the Court.

2. The Registrar shall also, by means of a special and direct communication, notify any state entitled to appear before the Court or international organization considered by the Court, or, should it not be sitting, by the President, as likely to be able to furnish information on the question, that the Court will be prepared to receive, within a time

limit to be fixed by the President, written statements, or to hear, at a public sitting to be held for the purpose, oral statements relating to the question.

3. Should any such state entitled to appear before the Court have failed to receive the special communication referred to in paragraph 2 of this Article, such state may express a desire to submit a written statement or to be heard; and the Court will decide.

4. States and organizations having presented written or oral statements or both shall be permitted to comment on the statements made by other states or organizations in the form, to the extent, and within the time limits which the Court, or, should it not be sitting, the President, shall decide in each particular case. Accordingly, the Registrar shall in due time communicate any such written statements to states and organizations having submitted similar statements.

Article 67

The Court shall deliver its advisory opinions in open court, notice having been given to the Secretary-General and to the representatives of Members of the United Nations, of other states and of international organizations immediately concerned.

Article 68

In the exercise of its advisory functions the Court shall further be guided by the provisions of the present Statute which apply in contentious cases to the extent to which it recognizes them to be applicable.

CHAPTER V

AMENDMENT

Article 69

Amendments to the present Statute shall be effected by the same procedure as is provided by the Charter of the United Nations for amendments to that Charter, subject however to any provisions which the General Assembly upon recommendation of the Security Council may adopt concerning the participation of states which are parties to the present Statute but are not Members of the United Nations.

Article 70

The Court shall have power to propose such amendments to the present Statute as it may deem necessary, through written communications to the Secretary-General, for consideration in conformity with the provisions of Article 69.

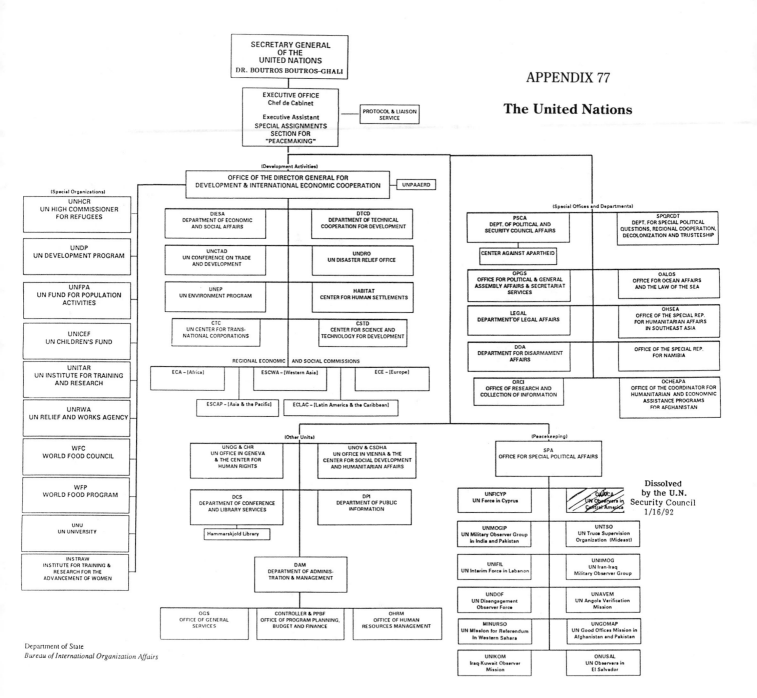

APPENDIX 77

The United Nations

Department of State
Bureau of International Organization Affairs

APPENDIX 78

United Nations Membership by States and Year of Admission

With the dissolution of the Soviet Union and the creation of the Commonwealth of Independent States by 11 of the former constituent republics, the number of Member States of the United Nations remains at 166. The Soviet Union's membership in the Security Council and all other United Nations organs has been continued by the Russian Federation; Belarus (formerly Byelorussia) and Ukraine, with the support of the members of the Commonwealth, remain United Nations Members. The current United Nations Members and the dates on which they joined the Organization as of 3 March 1992 are:

NATION STATE	YEAR	NATION STATE	YEAR	NATION STATE	YEAR
Afghanistan	1946	Congo	1960	Indonesia[6]	1950
Albania	1955	Costa Rica	1945	Iran	1945
Algeria	1962	Côte d'Ivoire	1960	Iraq	1945
Angola	1976	Cuba	1945	Ireland	1955
Antigua and Barbuda	1981	Cyprus	1960	Israel	1949
Argentina	1945	Czechoslovakia	1945	Italy	1955
Armenia	1992	Denmark	1945	Jamaica	1962
Australia	1945	Djibouti	1977	Japan	1956
Azerbaijan	1992	Dominica	1978	Jordan	1955
Austria	1955	Dominican Rep.	1945	Kazakhstan	1992
Bahamas	1973	Ecuador	1945	Kenya	1963
Bahrain	1971	Egypt[3]	1945	Kirgkhizia	1992
Bangladesh	1974	El Salvador	1945	Korea, North	1991
Barbados	1966	Equatorial Guinea	1968	Korea, South	1991
Belarus[1]	1945	Estonia[4]	1991	Kuwait	1963
Belgium	1945	Ethiopia	1945	Lao People's Dem.	
Belize	1981	Federated States		Republic	1955
Benin	1960	of Micronesia	1991	Latvia[7]	1991
Bhutan	1971	Fiji	1970	Lebanon	1945
Bolivia	1945	Finland	1955	Lesotho	1966
Botswana	1966	France	1945	Liberia	1945
Brazil	1945	Gabon	1960	Libya	1955
Brunei Darussalam	1984	Gambia	1965	Liechtenstein	1990
Bulgaria	1955	Germany[5]	1973	Lithuania[8]	1991
Burkina Faso	1960	Ghana	1957	Luxembourg	1945
Burundi	1962	Greece	1945	Madagascar	
Cambodia	1955	Grenada	1974	(Malagasy)	1960
Cameroon	1960	Guatemala	1945	Malawi	1964
Canada	1945	Guinea	1958	Malaysia[9]	1957
Cape Verde	1975	Guinea-Bissau	1974	Maldives	1965
Central Afr. Republic	1960	Guyana	1966	Mali	1960
Chad	1960	Haiti	1945	Malta	1964
Chile	1945	Honduras	1945	Marshall Islands	1991
China[2]	1945	Hungary	1955	Mauritania	1961
Colombia	1945	Iceland	1946	Mauritius	1968
Comoros	1975	India	1945	Mexico	1945

Moldova	1992	Rwanda	1962	Thailand	1946
Mongolia	1961	Saint Kitts		Togo	1960
Morocco	1956	and Nevis	1983	Trinidad & Tob.	1962
Mozambique	1975	Saint Lucia	1979	Tunisia	1956
Myanmar (Burma)	1948	Saint Vincent		Turkey	1945
Namibia	1990	and Grenadines	1980	Turkmenistan	1992
Nepal	1955	Samoa	1976	Uganda	1962
Netherlands	1945	San Marino[11]	1992	Ukraine	1945
New Zealand	1945	Sao Tomee Principe	1975	United Arab Emirates	1971
Nicaragua	1945	Saudi Arabia	1945	United Kingdom	1945
Niger	1960	Senegal	1960	United Republic	
Nigeria	1960	Seychelles	1976	of Tanzania[13]	1961
Norway	1945	Sierra Leone	1961	United States	1945
Oman	1971	Singapore	1965	Uruguay	1945
Pakistan	1947	Solomon Islands	1978	Uzbekistan	1992
Panama	1945	Somalia	1960	Vanuatu	1981
Papua New Guinea	1975	South Africa	1945	Venezuela	1945
Paraguay	1945	Spain	1955	Vietnam	1977
Peru	1945	Sri Lanka (Ceylon)	1955	Yemen[14]	1947
Philippines	1945	Sudan	1956	Yugoslavia	1945
Poland	1945	Suriname	1975	Zaire	1960
Portugal	1955	Swaziland	1968	Zambia	1964
Qatar	1971	Sweden	1946	Zimbabwe	1980
Romania	1955	Syria[12]	1945		
Russian Federation[10]	1945	Tadjikistan	1992		

---

[1] On 19 September 1991, Byelorussia informed the United Nations that it had changed its name to Belarus.

[2] China was an original Member of the United Nations from 24 October 1945, represented by the Republic of China, which was based in Taiwan since 1949 following the establishment of the People's Republic of China. On 25 October 1971, the General Assembly decided to "restore all its rights to the People's Republic of China and to recognize the representatives of its Government as the only legitimate representatives of China to the United Nations." By that resolution, the Assembly also acted to "expel forthwith the representatives of Chiang Kai-shek from the place which they unlawfully occupy at the United Nations and in all the organizations related to it."

[3] Egypt and Syria were original Members of the United Nations from 24 October 1945. Following a plebiscite on 21 February 1958, the United Arab Republic was established by a union of Egypt and Syria and continued as a single Member. On 13 October 1961, Syria, having resumed its status as an independent State, resumed its separate membership in the United Nations. On 2 September 1971, the United Arab Republic changed its name to the Arab Republic of Egypt.

[4] Estonia was a constituent republic of the Soviet Union, which was an original United Nations Member from 24 October 1945. On 17 September 1991, Estonia was admitted to United Nations membership as an independent State.

[5] The German Democratic Republic was admitted to membership in the United Nations on 18 September 1973. Through its accession to the Federal Republic of Germany with effect from 3 October 1990, the two German States have united to form one sovereign State.

[6] By letter of 20 January 1965, Indonesia announced its decision to withdraw from the United Nations "at this stage and under the present circumstances." By telegram of 19 September 1966, it announced its decision "to resume full cooperation with the United Nations and to resume participation in its activities." On 28 September 1966, the General Assembly took note of this decision and the President invited representatives of Indonesia to take seats in the Assembly.

[7] Latvia and Lithuania were constituent republics of the Soviet Union, which was an original United Nations Member from 24 October 1945. On 17 September 1991, Latvia and Lithuania were admitted to United Nations membership as independent States.

[8] Latvia and Lithuania were constituent republics of the Soviet Union, which was an original United Nations Member from 24 October 1945. On 17 September 1991, Latvia and Lithuania were admitted to United Nations membership as independent States.

[9] The Federation of Malaya joined the United Nations on 17 September 1957. On 16 September 1963, its name was changed to Malaysia, following the admission to the new federation of Singapore, Sabah (North Borneo) and Sarawak. Singapore became an independent State on 9 August 1965 and a Member of the United Nations on 21 September 1965.

[10] The Union of Soviet Socialist Republics was an original Member of the United Nations from 24 October 1945. In a letter dated 24 December 1991, Boris Yeltsin, the President of the Russian Federation, informed Secretary-General Javier Pérez de Cuéllar that the membership of the Soviet Union in the Security Council and all other United Nations organs was being continued by the Russian Federation with the support of the countries of the Commonwealth of Independent States. According to President Yeltsin, the Russian Federation remains responsible in full for all the rights and obligations of the former Soviet Union under the United Nations Charter.

[11] Official name: Most Serene Republic of San Marino, in the Italian language, "Serenissima Republica de San Marino." One of the oldest states in Europe, dating to the 4th Century A.D.

[12] Egypt and Syria were original Members of the United Nations from 24 October 1945. Following a plebiscite on 21 February 1958, the United Arab Republic was established by a union of Egypt and Syria and continued as a single Member. On 13 October 1961, Syria, having resumed its status as an independent State, resumed its separate membership in the United Nations.

[13] Tanganyika was a Member of the United Nations from 14 December 1961 and Zanzibar was a Member from 16 December 1963. Following the ratification on 26 April 1964 of Articles of Union between Tanganyika and Zanzibar, the United Republic of Tanganyika and Zanzibar continued as a single Member, changing its name to the United Republic of Tanzania on 1 November 1964.

[14] Yemen was admitted to membership in the United Nations on 30 September 1947 and Democratic Yemen on 14 December 1967. On 22 May 1990, the two countries merged and have since been represented as one Member with the name "Yemen."

APPENDIX 79

The United Nations System

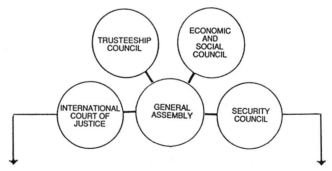

INTERNATIONAL COURT OF JUSTICE

As of 8 January 1992, the International Court of Justice has 15 members, elected by both the General Assembly and the Security Council. Judges hold nine-year terms

SECURITY COUNCIL

As of 7 January 1992, the Security Council has 15 members. The Charter designates five States as permanent members, and the General Assembly elects 10 other members for two-year terms.

APPENDIX 80

Confederate Political System

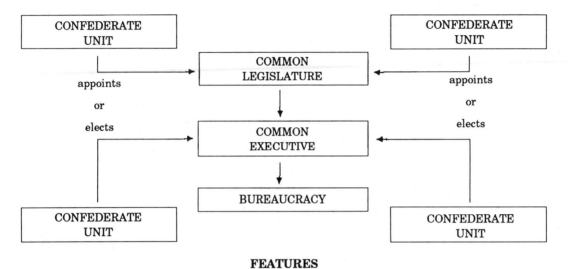

FEATURES

POSITIVE

- This system of government is created by the unanimous vote of the sovereign member states.

- The units (states) of the confederation retain all attributes of sovereignty as states.

- The central government obtains those powers which are delegated to it by the member states.

- The central government (legislature) is elected and/or appointed by the member states.

- Each member state has one vote in the national legislature.

- On certain legislative matters (e.g., declaration of war) consent of all members is required.

- All judicial powers, as a rule, are retained by the member states of the confederation.

- This form of government displays many of the characteristics commonly found in international organizations.

- Member states were in complete control of governmental responsibilities within their respective borders.

- Member states are, in effect, NATION STATES.

NEGATIVE

- The member states may withdraw powers delegated to the central government at any time.

- This system is a union of states and not a government of the people.

- All acts of the central legislative body are subject to approval (a for of ratification) by the member states of the confederation.

- Confederations are known to be inefficient.

- Confederations are slow in policy formation and in the implementation of public policy.

- There is no executive in this form of government. Rather, a committee may be created to carry out responsibilities at the direction of the member states.

- There is no separate judicial branch in the central government.

- Member states do not have to abide by the decisions of the central legislature.

- Member states did not have to cooperate with each other, or recognize the laws of members.

- The central government was, in effect, powerless to enforce any of its actions within the member states.

After its independence from Great Britain, the United States adopted the Articles of Confederation which established this form of government. Experiencing much turmoil with this system, the member states met to amend the Articles to make a more effective governmental system. Instead, the delegates created a new document ... The Constitution ... which established the new FEDERAL POLITICAL SYSTEM.

It is worthy of note that in the late 20th century the member units of the former Soviet Union are going through the same process for establishing a new governmental system (confederation) that the United States did back in the 18th century. It remains to be seen whether they will end up with a federal system.

APPENDIX 81

Federal Political System

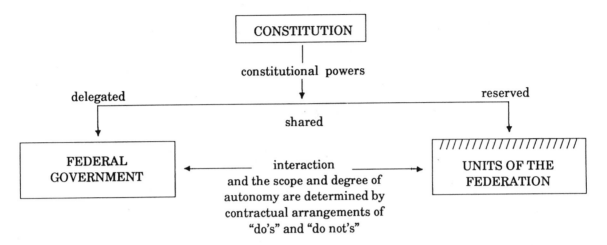

| CONSTITUTION |

constitutional powers

delegated   reserved

shared

| FEDERAL GOVERNMENT | ← interaction → | UNITS OF THE FEDERATION |

interaction
and the scope and degree of
autonomy are determined by
contractual arrangements of
"do's" and "do not's"

FEATURES

POSITIVE

• The federal system is composed of a sovereign central (federal) government, sovereign member governments (states) and local governments created by the states. Both the federal government and the state governments exercise exclusive power within their constitutional authority.

• Power is distributed territorially: the federal government retains certain exclusive powers (e.g. declare war and coin money); the federal government shares powers with states and local governments (e.g. taxation).

• The federal government exercises certain implied powers under the "necessary and proper" clause (Art. I).

• The states hold and exercise powers which are not otherwise clearly enumerated and identified (e.g. matters of education and interstate commerce. (See Amendment X in Appendix 3).

• At the federal level and at the state level power is balanced between the executive branch, the legislative branch, and the judicial branch.

• All legislators at all levels of government are directly elected by the people.

• The implementation of most policy decisions must be shared with the lower units of government.

• In the U.S. Senate each state is equally represented.

• The Federal government is responsible to the voters and not to the units of the federation.

• All levels of government (e.g., federal, state, local) maintain some degree of separation of powers between the executive, the legislative, and the judicial functions.

• The federal government has no direct power over local units of government, but may exercise some control through a system of grants.

• As members comprising the federation, states may not unilaterally, or collectively withdraw from the union.

• In general, relationships between the federal government and the governments of the units of the federation (the states) rests on federalism (contractual division of authority).

NEGATIVE

• The federal executive (President) is not directly elected by the people, but by a special body ... the Electoral College.

• All federal judges and some state judges are appointed rather than elected by the people.

• The federal system is less efficient and slower in the policy making process since inputs from the lower units of government and from the people must be considered.

• Local government units within each state have only those powers which the state government wishes to grant.

• All local governments are created by the state government.

• At the federal and state levels policy making may become stymied when the executive and the legislative majority represent different political parties.

• It is not uncommon for voters to elect an executive from one political party and a legislative majority from another political party with the expectation that each will control the exercise of power by the other.

APPENDIX 82

Unitary Political System

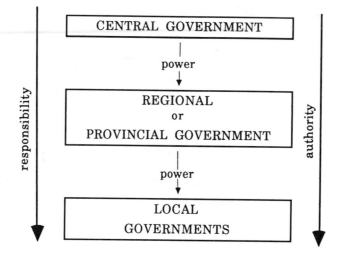

	CENTRAL GOVERNMENT	

power

REGIONAL
or
PROVINCIAL GOVERNMENT

power

LOCAL
GOVERNMENTS

responsibility → authority

POSITIVE   **FEATURES**   NEGATIVE

• Top officers of the central government may be elected by the voters.

• Shared powers ... officers of the regional or provincial governments appointed by central government and elected by voters.

• Shared powers ... local officials appointed by regional officers subject to central government confirmation.

• Regional and local governments have input on national policies. Final decision is made by central government. Regional and local governments then implement with a minimum of discretion.

• Decision making and policy implementation are considered most expedient, especially so in dictatorships.

• Citizens may have choice among political party candidates.

• Opposition parties allowed to exist.

• To form government, power may be shared among several political parties.

• All powers, with some minor exceptions, are vested in the central government.

• Powers are channeled down through the regional or provincial sub-governments to the local units for implementation.

• Top officers may be appointed by a ruling party (e.g., under totalitarian dictatorships).

• All officers of the regional or provincial governments appointed by the central government.

• All local government officials appointed by central government.

• National policies are conceived and coordinated by central government. Other levels of government have only to implement.

• Decision making and policy implementation can be arbitrary and capricious, especially so in dictatorships.

• Citizens are powerless.

• Elections, if allowed, are for show and results are predetermined.

• Only one political party's candidates allowed on ballot.

The terms "positive" and "negative" convey values which are conditioned by use. As used here the terms are meant to reflect the relationship between a form of government and its people. Thus, the frame of reference is "government as the servant of the people (democracy)." In the frame of reference of "government rules the people (dictatorship)" the listing of "positive" and "negative" would be reversed.

APPENDIX 83

Types of Politico-Economic Systems*

Systems which are	Democratic	Socio-Democratic (mixed)	Command-Authoritarian Totalitarian
Market/Consumer Oriented	Britain, North America		
Market/Consumer Oriented with Centralized Authority (mixed)	Western European Democracies Japan, South Korea, Taiwan and other Asian Democracies		
Centralized State Authority	The Former Socialist States of Eastern Europe Africa		Angola, Cuba, North Korea; war materiel of all states **

APPENDIX 84

Types of Market Systems*

Systems which are	Consumer oriented (responds to the needs and wishes of consumers)	Consumer and Planner Oriented (mixed)	Planner Oriented (responds to commands of central planner
Private/Consumer Oriented	Britain, North America		
Private/Public Shared authority (mixed)	Western European Democracies Japan, and other Asian Democracies		
Public (state authority)	Former Socialist States of Eastern Europe, China, Africa		Angola, Cuba, North Korea; war materiel of all states **

* Because of the dynamics of every politico-economic system and every type of market system, there are constant vacillations, horizontally and vertically, as domestic political or economic consideration may demand, and as changes in the external environment occur. Due to speedy communications and rapid exchange of information globally, changes within any single system are affected by global changes. Thus, in the case of Poland, for example, where the economy is undergoing an economic "shock therapy"—restructuring through privatization of production and marketing in a very rapid pace (on commands of a central planner from the International Monetary Fund who has replaced the former state planner) rapid political changes necessitated production and market changes, and the nation moved from a Command-Authoritarian-Totalitarian system—with centralized authority—to a somewhat socio-democratic (mixed) system, with a market more consumer oriented. Furthermore, no politico-economic system or market system today will perfectly fit into any arbitrary category, because even the Western democratic systems where private means of production and distribution remain in the private sector and most production is consumer-oriented, there are remnants of public-planned enterprises, such as the military, the Tennessee Valley Authority, the U.S. Postal Service and the Social Security in the United States to mention just a few for example. There is, therefore, an overlap in the equation of public and private enterprises and markets. In addition, there is considerable change because, according to Professor Isao Kubota (of the Overseas Economic Cooperation Fund of Japan), "In the past, the competition was between command economies (e.g., of the former Soviet Union and the East European states) and market economies, but now it is within capitalism itself." Professor Lester Thurow (*Head to Head: The Coming Economic Battle Among Japan, Europe, and America*) points out additional distinctions between the "individualist Anglo-Saxon British-American capitalism" and the "communitarian German and Japanese variant of capitalism," which further add to the dynamics.

** With the dissolution of the Bretton Woods monetary system and the GATT arrangements, as well as the emergence of the three major trading blocs: the European, the American, and the Japanese, future interbloc trade, according to Professor Thurow, "will be managed by governments." See COMPARATIVE ADVANTAGE, LEVEL PLAYING FIELD, UNILATERAL GLOBAL KEYNESIANISM.

APPENDIX 85

World's Population, 1980, 2000
(in millions)

Year	Africa	Asia	China	Europe	India	Latin America	North America	Oceana	Former Soviet Union
1980	498	826	1,000	488	845	378	256	24	270
2000	847	1,482	1,200	511	937	549	286	30	302

APPENDIX 86

Population in Selected Cities, 1980, 2000
(in millions)

City	1980	2000
Beijing	8.9	20.9
Bombay	12.9	16.8
Cairo	7.3	12.1
Calcutta	11.2	16.4
Hong Kong	5.9	6.1
Jakarta	9.4	15.7
Mexico City	21.2	31.0
Moscow	8.6	9.8
New York-New Jersey	13.6	22.4
Rio de Janeiro	12.6	19.0
São Paulo	16.9	25.8
Shanghai	12.4	23.7
Tokyo-Yokohama	13.6	23.7

APPENDIX 87

The United States of America (USA) and the Confederate States of America (CSA)

THE CONFEDERACY

States which seceded from the Union on 20 December 1860: Alabama (Montgomery capitol of the CSA until 1863), Florida, Georgia, Louisiana, Mississippi, South Carolina, Texas

on 11 April 1860, following the firing on Fort Sumter: Kentucky, Tennessee, Virginia (Richmond capitol of CSA from 1863 until the end of the war in 1865).

©1992 Brunswick Publishing Corporation

APPENDIX 88

Wars with Global Implications

Years		Years	
1688-1697	War of the League of Augsburg	1689-1697	King William's War (Anglo-French War)
1701-1713	War of Spanish Succession	1702-1713	Queen Anne's War
1740-1748	War of Austrian Succession	1744-1748	King George's War
1756-1763	Seven Years' War	1754-1763	French and Indian War
1778-1783	War of the American Revolution	1775-1783	The American Revolution
1793-1802	Wars of the French Revolution	1798-1800	Undeclared War with France
1803-1815	Napoleonic Wars	1812-1814	War with England
1914-1918	World War I	1917-1918	World War I *
1939-1945	World War II	1941-1946	World War II *
1948-present	Arab States-Israel	1948-present	Arab States-Israel *
1950-1954	Korean War	1950-1954	Korean War *
		1954-1974	Vietnam War *
1990-1991	Persian Gulf War	1990-1991	Iraq-U.S. and Coalition Forces*

*U.S. Involvement

APPENDIX 90

Global Population by Class (Wealth) and Race (Color)

(Illustrative Approximation)
(In Round Figures, Based on Materials Available as of May 1992)

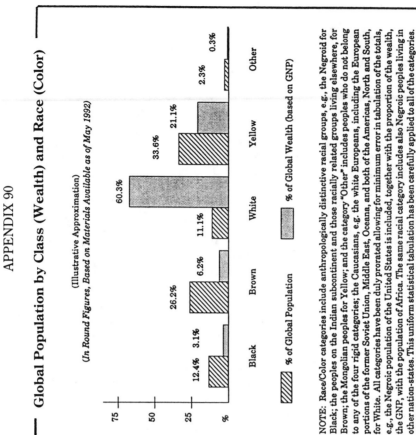

Black   Brown   White   Yellow   Other

12.4%   3.1%   26.2%   6.2%   11.1%   60.3%   33.6%   21.1%   2.3%   0.3%

▨ % of Global Population

▥ % of Global Wealth (based on GNP)

NOTE: Race/Color categories include anthropologically distinctive racial groups, e.g., the Negroid for Black; the peoples on the Indian subcontinent and those racially related groups living elsewhere, for Brown; the Mongolian peoples for Yellow; and the category "Other" includes peoples who do not belong to any of the four rigid categories; the Caucasians, e.g. the white Europeans, including the European portions of the former Soviet Union, Middle East, Oceana, and both of the Americas, North and South, for White. All categories have been duly prorated allowing for minimum error in tabulation of the totals, e.g., the Negroic population of the United States is included, together with the proportion of the wealth, the GNP, with the population of Africa. The same racial category includes also Negroic peoples living in other nation-states. This uniform statistical tabulation has been carefully applied to all of the categories.

©1992 Brunswick Publishing Corporation

APPENDIX 89

Drugs and the Andean Nations

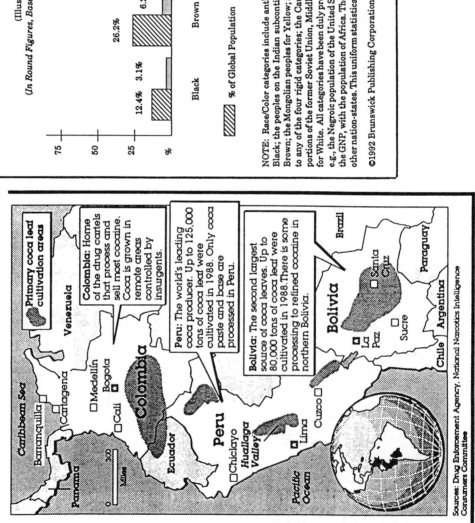

■ Primary coca leaf cultivation areas

Colombia: Home of the drug cartels that process and sell most cocaine. Coca is grown in remote areas controlled by insurgents.

Peru: The world's leading coca producer. Up to 125,000 tons of coca leaf were cultivated in 1988. Only coca paste and base are processed in Peru.

Bolivia: The second largest source of coca leaves. Up to 80,000 tons of coca leaf were cultivated in 1988. There is some processing to refined cocaine in northern Bolivia.

Caribbean Sea — Panama — Barranquilla — Cartagena — Venezuela — Medellín — Bogota — Cali — Colombia — Ecuador — Chiclayo — Huallaga Valley — Peru — Lima — Cuzco — Pacific Ocean — La Paz — Sucre — Santa Cruz — Bolivia — Brazil — Chile — Argentina — Paraguay

0   300   Miles

Sources: Drug Enforcement Agency. National Narcotics Intelligence Consumers Committee

Source: Knight-Ridder Tribune/Staff Graphic. Reproduced with permission.

APPENDIX 91

Partitions of Poland

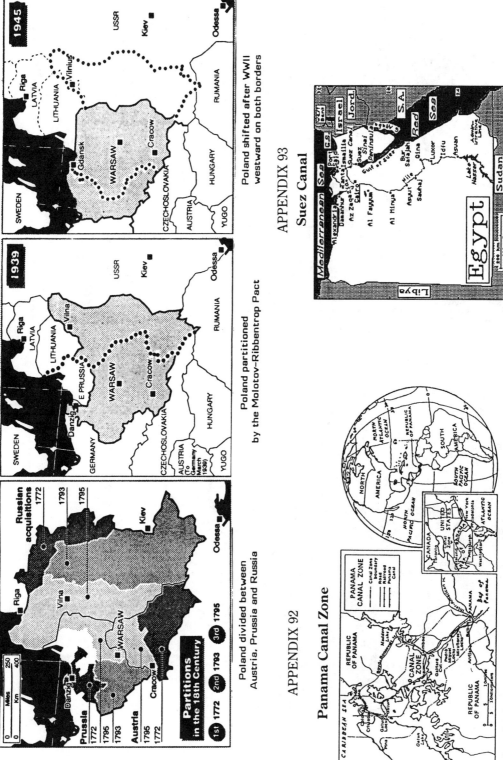

Poland divided between
Austria, Prussia and Russia

Poland partitioned
by the Molotov-Ribbentrop Pact

Poland shifted after WWII
westward on both borders

APPENDIX 93

Suez Canal

APPENDIX 92

Panama Canal Zone

Source: U. S. Department of State.

APPENDIX 94

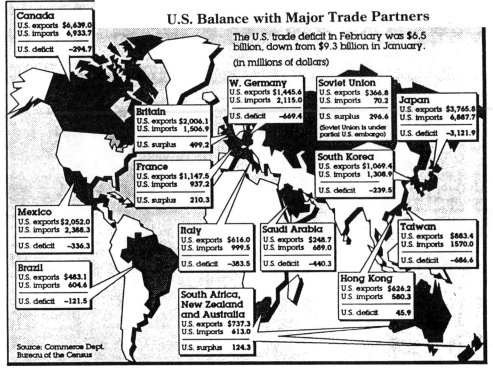

U.S. Balance with Major Trade Partners

The U.S. trade deficit in February was $6.5 billion, down from $9.3 billion in January.

(in millions of dollars)

Canada
U.S. exports $6,639.0
U.S. imports 6,933.7
U.S. deficit −294.7

W. Germany
U.S. exports $1,445.6
U.S. imports 2,115.0
U.S. deficit −669.4

Soviet Union
U.S. exports $366.8
U.S. imports 70.2
U.S. surplus 296.6
(Soviet Union is under partial U.S. embargo)

Japan
U.S. exports $3,765.8
U.S. imports 6,887.7
U.S. deficit −3,121.9

Britain
U.S. exports $2,006.1
U.S. imports 1,506.9
U.S. surplus 499.2

France
U.S. exports $1,147.5
U.S. imports 937.2
U.S. surplus 210.3

South Korea
U.S. exports $1,069.4
U.S. imports 1,308.9
U.S. deficit −239.5

Mexico
U.S. exports $2,052.0
U.S. imports 2,388.3
U.S. deficit −336.3

Italy
U.S. exports $616.0
U.S. imports 999.5
U.S. deficit −383.5

Saudi Arabia
U.S. exports $248.7
U.S. imports 689.0
U.S. deficit −440.3

Taiwan
U.S. exports $883.4
U.S. imports 1570.0
U.S. deficit −686.6

Brazil
U.S. exports $483.1
U.S. imports 604.6
U.S. deficit −121.5

South Africa, New Zealand and Australia
U.S. exports $737.3
U.S. imports 613.0
U.S. surplus 124.3

Hong Kong
U.S. exports $626.2
U.S. imports 580.3
U.S. deficit 45.9

Source: Commerce Dept. Bureau of the Census

Source: Knight–Ridder Tribune/Staff Graphic. Reproduced with permission.

APPENDIX 95

Middle East: The Cradle of WWIII

////, Territories occupied by Israel since 1967
(Gaza Strip, Golan Heights, West Bank)

APPENDIX 96

Black Sea Pact

APPENDIX 97

Territorial Expansion of the United States

©Brunswick Publishing Corporation

APPENDIX 98

The United States of America: Regions and Geographic Divisions

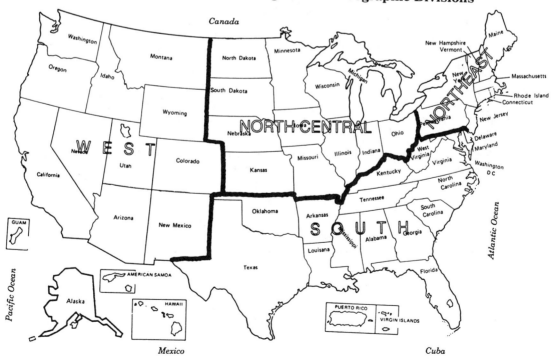

Source: U.S. Department of Commerce, Bureau of the Census

754 Walter John Raymond

APPENDIX 99

World

APPENDIX 100

Africa

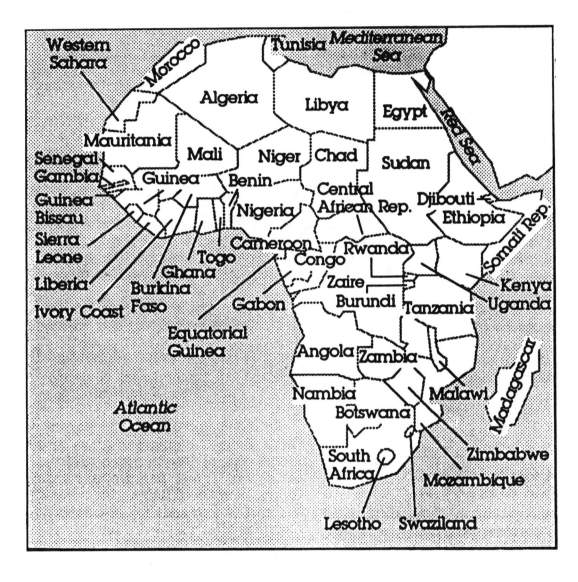

APPENDIX 101

Asia

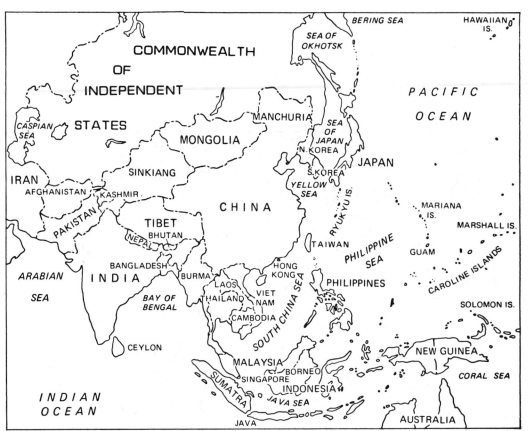

APPENDIX 102

The Middle East

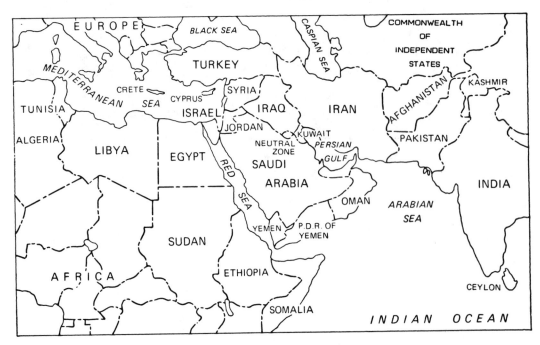

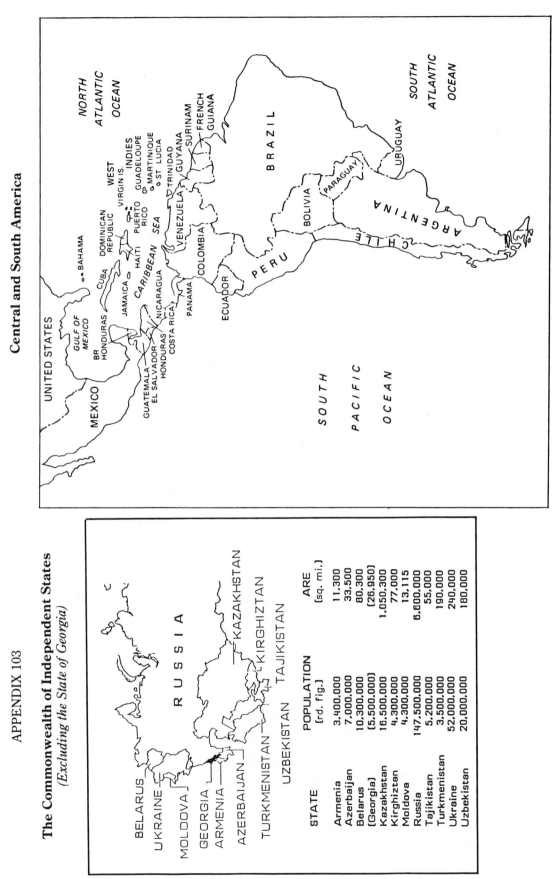

APPENDIX 104

Central and South America

APPENDIX 103

The Commonwealth of Independent States
(Excluding the State of Georgia)

STATE	POPULATION [rd. fig.]	AREA [sq. mi.]
Armenia	3,400,000	11,300
Azerbaijan	7,000,000	33,500
Belarus	10,300,000	80,300
[Georgia]	[5,500,000]	[26,950]
Kazakhstan	16,500,000	1,050,300
Kirghiztan	4,300,000	77,000
Moldova	4,300,000	13,115
Russia	147,500,000	6,600,000
Tajikistan	5,200,000	55,000
Turkmenistan	3,500,000	190,000
Ukraine	52,000,000	240,000
Uzbekistan	20,000,000	180,000

Europe

APPENDIX 106

Swiss Federation

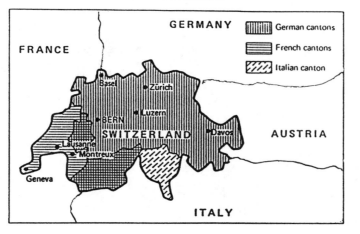

North America: Canada

APPENDIX 107-A

North America: United Mexican States
(Estados Unidos Mexicanos)

APPENDIX 107-B

North America: The United States of America

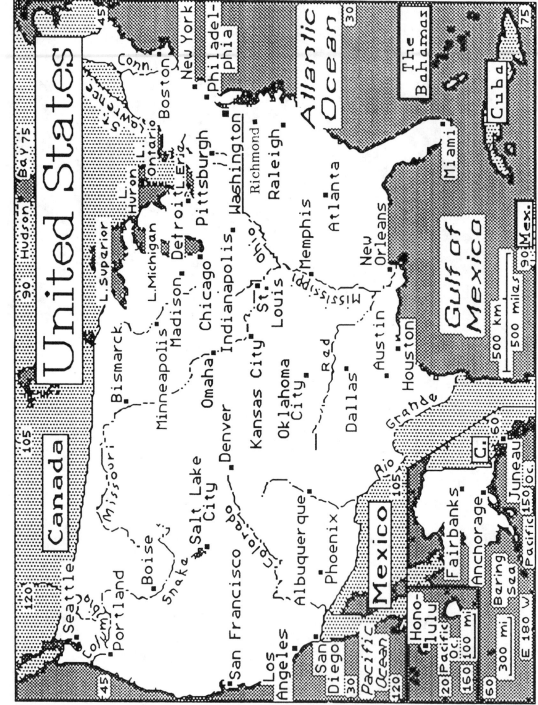

ABOUT THE AUTHOR. **Attended universities in Poland, Germany, England, Canada, and the United States, and holds the Baccalaureate in Social Science; Masters Degree in Political Science; Masters Degree in Law and Jurisprudence; Doctor of Philosophy in Political Science and Doctor of Juridical Science. In his professional career, the author was engaged in farming, transportation, elementary and university education and administration, journalism, foreign intelligence, and publishing.**

The author devotes his time now to research and writing on the effects of political culture on domestic productivity and international trade.

To order additional copies of this book, please use coupon below.

Mail to:

Brunswick Publishing Corporation
P.O. BOX 555
LAWRENCEVILLE, VIRGINIA 23868

Order Form

Please send me _____ copy(s) of *Dictionary of Politics* by Walter John Raymond, ISBN 1-55618-008-X, at $60.00 per copy plus $5.00 mailing and handling. Overseas clients will be charged overseas shipping rates. Virginia residents add 4.5% ($2.70) sales tax.

☐ Check enclosed.   Charge Orders — 804-848-3865
☐ Charge to my credit card: ☐ VISA   ☐ MasterCard

Card #_____ Exp. Date _____

Signature: _____

Name _____

Address _____

City _____ State _____ Zip_____

Phone # _____